An Index to English Periodical Literature on the Old Testament and Ancient Near Eastern Studies

Volume IX

Part 2: Subject Index J–Z, Foreign Word Index, and Citation Index

Compiled and Edited by William G. Hupper

ATLA Bibliography Series, No. 21

A book should serve as an axe for the frozen sea within us.—Franz Kafka

The Scarecrow Press, Inc., and
American Theological Library Association
Lanham • Toronto • Plymouth, UK
2011

Published by Scarecrow Press, Inc.
A wholly owned subsidiary of The Rowman & Littlefield Publishing Group, Inc.
4501 Forbes Boulevard, Suite 200, Lanham, Maryland 20706
http://www.scarecrowpress.com

Estover Road, Plymouth PL6 7PY, United Kingdom

Cover illustration is a "Coin of Sardis" (public domain)

British Library Cataloguing in Publication Information Available

Library of Congress Cataloging-in-Publication Data

The Library of Congress has cataloged the combined volume as follows:

Hupper, William G.
An index to English periodical literature on the Old Testament and ancient Near Eastern studies.
(ATLA bibliography series; no. 21)
Includes bibliographies.
1. Bible. O.T.—Periodicals—Indexes.
2. Near East—Periodicals—Indexes.
I. Americal Theological Library Association.
II. Title. III. Series
Z7772.A1H86 1987 [BS1171.2] 016.221 86-31448

ISBN 0-8108-1984-8 (v. 1)
ISBN 0-8108-2126-5 (v. 2)
ISBN 0-8108-2319-5 (v. 3)
ISBN 0-8108-2393-4 (v. 4)
ISBN 0-8108-2618-6 (v. 5)
ISBN 0-8108-2822-7 (v. 6)
ISBN 0-8108-3493-6 (v. 7)
ISBN 0-8108-3645-9 (v. 8)
ISBN 978-0-8108-7805-1 (v. 9)

∞™ The paper used in this publication meets the minimum requirements of American National Standard for Information Sciences—Permanence of Paper for Printed Library Materials, ANSI/NISO Z39.48-1992.

Printed in the United States of America

Table of Contents

Volume IX - Part 1

Preface v

Key to Index x

Periodical Abbreviation List xi

Errata xl

Additions lxxxi

Author Index 1

Subject Index - A-I 201

Volume IX - Part 2

Key to Index iv

Periodical Abbreviation List v

Subject Index - J-Z 571

Foreign Words and Phrases Index 983

Greek Index 1009

Hebrew Index 1019

Aramaic Index 1049

Cuneiform Sign List 1051

Egyptian Hieroglyphic Index[1] 1055

Hebrew Bible Text Index 1109

New Testament Text Index 1205

Apocrypha Text Index 1207

Pseudepigrapha Text Index 1210

Qumran Text Citations 1212

Museum Registration Number Index 1213

1. Hieroglyphs are correct as shown in the index. Where rectification has been made from the text, a "†" (dagger) has been added to the page number.

Key to Index

EXAMPLE	MEANING
I:	Bold Roman Numerals indicates Volume number.
§100	Section numbers are indicated by section sign § in bold.
(**§36**)	Section numbers in parentheses indicates *no entries* for this section.
220	Pages numbers in bold indicate major references to subject matter.
249*(4)*	Numbers in parentheses*(#)* following specific page indicates author or subject is mentioned more than once on a particular page.
216	Page numbers in *italics* indicates passing reference to a subject.
499‡	Page number followed by double-cross (‡) indicates an article on indicated page has a bibliography, or is a bibliographical article.
508(?)	Page number in Author Index indicates author uncertain but assumed based on other criteria such as time frame or subject matter.

NOTATION	AUTHOR INDEX
A	Appendix
C	Author has written a comment/communication, forward or note on a particular article.
D	Author has written in discussion of a particular article.
E	Editorial
j	Joint authorship of an article and is shown after the page number (453j *or* cxiij)
R	Rejoinder / reply—author is responder to another article.
t	Translator of an article.

EXAMPLE	SUBJECT INDEX
Foreign Words	Foreign Words in the Subject Index are in *italics* (E.g. *Gattungsforschung*)
PROPER NAMES	Proper names of authors in the Subject Index are in SMALL CAPS (E.g. ALBIRGHT, WILLIAM FOXWELL)
Subheadings	in ***bold italics*** and may be followed by a section sign (§) indicates a major division in the index.

Periodical Abbreviations*

A

A&A	*Art and Archaeology; the arts throughout the ages* (Washington, DC, Baltimore, MD, 1914-1934)
A/R	*Action/Reaction* (San Anselmo, CA, 1967ff.)
A&S	*Antiquity and Survival* (The Hague, 1955-1962)
A(A)	*Anadolu (Anatolia)* (Ankara, 1956ff.) [Subtitle varies; Volume 1-7 as: *Anatolia: Revue Annuelle d'Archeologie*]
AA	*Acta Archaeologica* (Copenhagen, 1930ff.)
AAA	*Annals of Archaeology and Anthropology* (Liverpool, 1908-1948; Suspended, 1916-1920)
AAAS	*Annales archéologiques arabes Syriennes. Revue d'Archéologie et d'Histoire* (Damascus, 1951ff.) [Volumes 1-15 as: *Les Annales archéologiques de Syrie* - Title Varies]
AAASH	*Acta Antiqua Academiae Scientiarum Hungaricae* (Budapest, 1951ff.)
AAB	*Acta Archaeologica* (Budapest, 1951ff.)
AAI	*Anadolu Araştirmalari Istanbul Üniversitesi Edebiyat Fakültesi eski Önasya Dilleri ve Kültürleri Kürsüsü Tarafindan Čikarilir* (Istanbul, 1955ff.) [Supersedes: *Jahrbuch für Kleinasiatische Forschungen*]
AAOJ	*American Antiquarian and Oriental Journal* (Cleveland, Chicago 1878-1914)
AASCS	*Antichthon. The Australian Society for Classical Studies* (Sydney, 1967ff.)
ABBTS	*The Alumni Bulletin [of] Bangor Theological Seminary* (Bangor, ME; 1926ff.)
ABenR	*The American Benedictine Review* (St. Paul, 1950ff.)
ABR	*Australian Biblical Review* (Melbourne, 1951ff.)
Abr-N	*Abr-Nahrain, An Annual Published by the Department of Middle Eastern Studies, University of Melbourne* (Melbourne, 1959ff.)
ACM	*The American Church Monthly* (New York, 1917-1939) [Volumes 43-45 as: *The New American Church Monthly*]

*This is a complete, corrected, and updated listing. All the journals indexed are listed in the Periodical Abbreviations even though no specific citation may appear in the present volume. Although the titles of many foreign language journals have been listed, only English Language articles are included in this index (except as noted). Articles from Modern Hebrew Language Journals are referred to by their English summary page.

Periodical Abbreviations

ACQ	*American Church Quarterly* (New York, 1961ff.) [Volume 7 on as: *Church Theological Review*]
ACQR	*The American Catholic Quarterly Review* (Philadelphia, 1876-1929)
ACR	*The Australasian Catholic Record* (Sydney, 1924ff.)
ACSR	*American Catholic Sociological Review* (Chicago, 1940ff.) [From Volume 25 on as: *Sociological Analysis*]
ADAJ	*Annual of the Department of Antiquities of Jordan* (Amman, 1957ff.) [Volume 14 not published—destroyed by fire at the publishers]
AE	*Annales d'Ethiopie* (Paris, 1955ff.)
AEE	*Ancient Egypt and the East* (New York, London, Chicago, 1914-1935; Suspended, 1918-1919)
Aeg	*Aegyptus: Rivista Italiana di Egittologia e di Papirologia* (Milan,1920ff.)
AER	*American Ecclesiastical Review* (Philadelphia, New York, Cincinnati, Baltimore, 1889ff.) [Volumes 11-19 as: *Ecclesiastical Review*]
AfER	*African Ecclesiastical Review: A Quarterly for Priests in Africa* (Masaka, Uganda, 1959ff.)
Aff	*Affirmation* (Richmond, VA, 1966ff.) [Volume 1 runs from 1966 to 1980 inclusive]
AfO	*Archiv für Orientforschung; Internationale Zeitschrift für Wissenschaft vom Vorderen Orient* (Berlin, 1923ff.)
AfRW	*Archiv für Religionswissenschaft* (Leipzig, 1898-1941)
AHDO	*Archives d'histoire du droit oriental et Revue internationale des droits de l'antiquité* (Brussels, 1937-38, 1947-1951, *N.S.*, 1952-53)
AHR	See *AmHR*
AIPHOS	*Annuaire de l'institut de philologie et d'histoire orientales et slaves* (Brussels, 1932ff.)
AJ	*The Antiquaries Journal. Being the Journal of the Society of Antiquaries of London* (London, 1921ff.)
AJA	*The American Journal of Archaeology* (Baltimore, 1885ff.) [Original Series, 1885-1896 shown with *O. S;* Second Series shown without notation]
AJBA	*The Australian Journal of Biblical Archaeology* (Sydney, 1968ff.) [Volume 1 runs from 1968 to 1971 inclusive]
AJP	*The American Journal of Philology* (Baltimore, 1880ff.)
AJRPE	*The American Journal of Religious Psychology and Education* (Worcester, MA, 1904-1915)
AJSL	*The American Journal of Semitic Languages and Literatures* (Chicago, 1884-1941) [Volumes 1-11 as: *Hebraica*]
AJT	*American Journal of Theology* (Chicago, 1897-1920)

Periodical Abbreviations

AL	*Archivum Linguisticum: A Review of Comparative Philology and General Linguistics* (Glasgow, 1949-1962)
ALUOS	*The Annual of the Leeds University Oriental Society* (Leiden,1958ff.)
Amb	*The Ambassador* (Wartburg Theological Seminary, Dubuque, IA, 1952ff.)
AmHR	*American Historical Review* (New York, Lancaster, PA, 1895ff.)
AmSR	*American Sociological Review* (Washington, DC, 1936ff.)
Anat	*Anatolica: Annuaire International pour les Civilisations de l'Asie Anterieure* (Leiden, 1967ff.)
ANQ	*Newton Theological Institute Bulletin* (Newton, MA, 1906ff.) [Title varies as: *Andover-Newton Theological Bulletin; Andover-Newton Quarterly, New Series,* beginning 1960ff.]
Anthro	*Anthropos; ephemeris internationalis ethnologica et linguistica* (Salzburg, Vienna, 1906ff.)
Antiq	*Antiquity: A Quarterly Review of Archaeology* (Gloucester, England, 1927ff.)
Anton	*Antonianum. Periodicum Philosophico-Theologicum Trimestre* (Rome, 1926ff.)
AO	*Acta Orientalia ediderunt Societates Orientales Bœtava Donica, Norvegica* (Lugundi Batavorum, Havniæ, 1922ff.)
AOASH	*Acta Orientalia Academiae Scientiarum Hungaricae* (Budapest, 1950ff.)
AOL	*Annals of Oriental Literature* (London, 1820-21)
APST	*Aberdeen Philosophical Society, Transactions* (Aberdeen, Scotland, 1840-1931)
AQ	*Augustana Quarterly* (Rock Island, IL, 1922-1948)
AQW	*Anthropological Quarterly* (Washington, DC, 1928ff.) [Volumes1-25 as: *Primitive Man*]
AR	*The Andover Review* (Boston, 1884-1893)
Arch	*Archaeology* (Cambridge, MA, 1948ff.)
Archm	*Archaeometry. Bulletin of the Research Laboratory for Archaeology and the History of Art, Oxford University* (Oxford,1958ff.)
ARL	*The Archæological Review* (London, 1888-1890)
ArOr	*Archiv Orientální. Journal of the Czechoslovak Oriental Institute, Prague* (Vlašska, Czechoslovakia, 1929ff.)
AS	*Anatolian Studies: Journal of the British Institute of Archaeology at Ankara* (London, 1951ff.)
ASAE	*Annales du service des antiquités de l'Égypte* (Cairo, 1899ff.)

ASBFE	*Austin Seminary Bulletin. Faculty Edition* (Austin, TX; begins with volume 71*[sic]*, 1955ff.)
ASR	*Augustana Seminary Review* (Rock Island, IL, 1949-1967) [From volume 12 on as: *The Seminary Review*]
ASRB	*Advent Shield and Review* (Boston, 1844-45)
ASRec	*Auburn Seminary Record* (Auburn, NY, 1905-1932)
ASSF	*Acta Societatis Scientiarum Fennicae* (Helsinki, 1842-1926) [Suomen tideseura]
ASTI	*Annual of the Swedish Theological Institute (in Jerusalem)* (Jerusalem, 1962ff.)
ASW	*The Asbury Seminarian* (Wilmore, KY, 1946ff.)
AT	*Ancient Times: A Quarterly Review of Biblical Archaeology* (Melbourne, 1956-1961)
ATB	*Ashland Theological Bulletin* (Ashland, OH, 1968ff.)
ATG	*Advocate for the Testimony of God* (Richmond, VA, 1834-1839)
AThR	*The American Theological Review* (New York, 1859-1868) [*New Series* as: *American Presbyterian and Theological Review*, 1863-1868]
'Atiqot	*'Atiqot: Journal of the Israel Department of Antiquities* (Jerusalem, 1955ff.)
ATJ	*Africa Theological Journal* (Usa River, Tanzania, 1968ff.)
ATR	*Anglican Theological Review* (New York, Lancaster, PA; 1918ff.)
AubSRev	*Auburn Seminary Review* (Auburn, NY, 1897-1904)
Aug	*Augustinianum* (Rome, 1961ff.)
AULLUÅ	*Acta Universitatis Lundensis. Lunds Universitets Årsskrift. Första Avdelningen. Teologi, Juridik och Humanistika Åmnen* (Lund, 1864-1904; *N. S.*, 1905-1964)
AUSS	*Andrews University Seminary Studies* (Berrien Springs, MI, 1963ff.)
AusTR	*The Australasian Theological Review* (Highgate, South Australia, 1930-1966)

B

B	*Biblica* (Rome, 1920ff.)
BA	*The Biblical Archaeologist* (New Haven; Cambridge, MA; 1938ff.)
Baby	*Babyloniaca Etudes de Philologie Assyro-Babylonienne* (Paris, 1906-1937)

Periodical Abbreviations

BASOR	*Bulletin of the American Schools of Oriental Research* (So. Hadley, MA; Baltimore, New Haven, Philadelphia, Cambridge, MA;1919ff.)
BASP	*Bulletin of the American Society of Papyrologists* (New Haven, 1963ff.)
BAVSS	*Beiträge zur Assyriologie und vergleichenden semitischen Sprachwissenschaft* (Leipzig, 1889-1927)
BBC	*Bulletin of the Bezan Club* (Oxford, 1925-1936)
BC	*Bellamine Commentary* (Oxon., England; 1956-1968)
BCQTR	*British Critic, Quarterly Theological Review and Ecclesiastical Record* (London, 1793-1843) [Superseded by: *English Review*] *(Title varies)*
BCTS	*Bulletin of the Crozer Theological Seminary* (Upland, PA, 1908-1934)
Bery	*Berytus. Archaeological Studies* (Copenhagen, 1934ff.)
BETS	*Bulletin of the Evangelical Theological Society* (Wheaton, IL, 1958ff.)
BFER	*British and Foreign Evangelical Review, and Quarterly Record of Christian Literature* (Edinburgh, London, 1852-1888)
BH	*Buried History. Quarterly Journal of the Australian Institute of Archaeology* (Melbourne, 1964-65; 1967ff.)
BibR	*Biblical Repertory* (Princeton, NJ; New York, 1825-1828)
BibT	*The Bible Today* (Collegeville, MN, 1962ff.)
BIES	*Bulletin of the Israel Exploration Society* (Jerusalem, 1937-1967) [*Yediot-* ידיעות בחקידת ארץ־ישראל ועתיקותיה-Begun as: *Bulletin of the Jewish Palestine Exploration Society* through volume 15. English summaries discontinued from volume 27 on as translations published in: *Israel Exploration Journal*]
BIFAO	*Bulletin de l'institut français d'archéologie orientale au Caire* (Cairo, 1901ff.)
BJ	*Biblical Journal* (Boston, 1842-1843)
BJRL	*Bulletin of the John Rylands Library* (Manchester, 1903ff.)
BM	*Bible Magazine* (New York, 1913-1915)
BMB	*Bulletin du Musée de Byrouth* (Paris, 1937ff.)
BN	*Bible Numerics: a Periodical Devoted to the Numerical Study of the Scriptures* (Grafton, MA; 1904)
BO	*Bibliotheca Orientalis* (Leiden, 1944ff.)
BofT	*Banner of Truth* (London, 1955ff.)
BOR	*The Babylonian and Oriental Record: A Monthly Magazine of the Antiquities of the East* (London, 1886-1901)
BQ	*Baptist Quarterly* (Philadelphia, 1867-1877)
BQL	*Baptist Quarterly* (London, 1922ff.)

BQR — *Baptist Quarterly Review* (Cincinnati, New York, Philadelphia, 1879-1892)
BQRL — *The British Quarterly Review* (London, 1845-1886)
BR — *Biblical Review* (New York, 1916-1932)
BRCM — *The Biblical Review and Congregational Magazine* (London, 1846-1850)
BRCR — *The Biblical Repository and Classical Review* (Andover, MA, 1831-1850) [Title varies as: *Biblical Repository; The Biblical Repository and Quarterly Observer; The American Biblical Repository*]
BRec — *Bible Record* (New York, 1903-1912) [Volume 1, #1-4 as: *Bible Teachers Training School, New York City,Bulletin*]
BRes — *Biblical Research: Papers of the Chicago Society of Biblical Research* (Amsterdam, Chicago, 1956ff.)
BS — *Bibliotheca Sacra* (New York, Andover, Oberlin, OH; St. Louis, Dallas, 1843, 1844ff.)
BSAJB — *British School of Archaeology in Jerusalem, Bulletin* (Jerusalem, 1922-1925)
BSOAS — *Bulletin of the School of Oriental and African Studies. University of London* (London, 1917ff.)
BSQ — *Bethel Seminary Quarterly* (St. Paul, MN; 1952ff.) [From Volume 13 on as: *Bethel Seminary Journal*]
BT — *Biblical Theology* (Belfast, 1950ff.)
BTF — *Bangalore Theological Forum* (Bangalore, India, 1967ff.)
BTPT — *Bijdragen Tijdschrift voor philosophie en theologie* (Maastricht,1938ff.) [Title varies as: *Bijdragen. Tijdschrift voor filosofie en theologie*]
BTr — *Bible Translator* (London, 1950ff.)
BUS — *Bucknell University Studies* (Lewisburg, PA; 1941ff.) [From Volume 5 on as: *Bucknell Review*]
BVp — *Biblical Viewpoint* (Greenville, SC, 1967ff.)
BW — *Biblical World* (Chicago, 1893-1920)
BWR — *Bible Witness and Review* (London, 1877-1881)
BWTS — *The Bulletin of the Western Theological Seminary* (Pittsburgh, 1908-1931)
BZ — *Biblische Zeitschrift* (Paderborn, 1903-1939; *New Series,* 1957ff.) [*N.S.* shown without notation]

C

C&C — *Cross and Crown. A Thomistic Quarterly of Spiritual Theology* (St. Louis, 1949ff.)
CAAMA — *Cahiers archéologiques fin de l'antiquité et moyen age* (Paris, 1961ff.)

Periodical Abbreviations

CAAST	*Connecticut Academy of Arts and Sciences, Transactions* (New Haven, 1866ff.)
Carm	*Carmelus. Commentarii ab instituto carmelitano editi* (Rome, 1954ff.)
CBQ	*Catholic Biblical Quarterly* (Washington, DC; 1939ff.)
CC	*Cross Currents* (West Nyack, NY; 1950ff.)
CCARJ	*Central Conference of American Rabbis Journal* (New York,1953ff.)
CCBQ	*Central Conservative Baptist Quarterly* (Minneapolis, 1958ff.) [From volume 9, #2 on as: *Central Bible Quarterly*]
CCQ	*Crisis Christology Quarterly* (Dubuque, IA; 1943-1949) [Volume 6 as: *Trinitarian Theology*]
CD	*Christian Disciple* (Boston, 1813-1823) [Superseded by: *Christian Examiner*]
CdÉ	*Chronique d'Égypte* (Brussels, 1925ff.)
CE	*Christian Examiner* (Boston, New York, 1824-1869)
Cent	*Centaurus. International Magazine of the History of Science and Medicine* (Copenhagen, 1950ff.)
Center	*The Center* (Atlanta, 1960-1965)
CFL	*Christian Faith and Life* (Columbia, SC, 1897-1939) [Title varies: Original Series as: *The Bible Student and Religious Outlook,* volumes 1 & 2 as: *The Religious Outlook;* New Series as: *The Bible Student;* Third Series as: *The Bible Student and Teacher;* several volumes as: *Bible Champion*]
ChgoS	*Chicago Studies* (Mundelein, IL; 1962ff.)
CJ	*Conservative Judaism* (New York, 1945ff.)
CJL	*Canadian Journal of Linguistics* (Montreal, 1954ff.)
CJRT	*The Canadian Journal of Religious Thought* (Toronto, 1924-1932)
CJT	*Canadian Journal of Theology* (Toronto, 1955ff.)
ClR	*Clergy Review* (London, 1931ff.)
CM	*The Clergyman's Magazine* (London, 1875-1897)
CMR	*Canadian Methodist Review* (Toronto, 1889-1895) [Volumes 1-5 as: *Canadian Methodist Quarterly*]
CNI	*Christian News from Israel* (Jerusalem, 1949ff.)
CO	*Christian Opinion* (New York, 1943-1948)
Coll	*Colloquium. The Australian and New Zealand Theological Review* (Auckland, 1964ff.) [Volume 1 through Volume 2, #1 as: *The New Zealand Theological Review*]
CollBQ	*The College of the Bible Quarterly* (Lexington, KY, 1909-1965) [Break in sequence between 1927 and 1937, resumes in 1938 with volume 15 duplicated in number]
ColTM	*Columbus Theological Magazine* (Columbus, OH; 1881-1910)
CongL	*The Congregationalist* (London, 1872-1886)

Periodical Abbreviations

CongML	*The Congregational Magazine* (London, 1818-1845)
CongQB	*The Congregational Quarterly* (Boston, 1859-1878)
CongQL	*The Congregational Quarterly* (London, 1923-1958)
CongR	*The Congregational Review* (Boston, Chicago, 1861-1871) [Volumes 1-6 as: *The Boston Review*]
CongRL	*The Congregational Review* (London, 1887-1891)
ConstrQ	*The Constructive Quarterly. A Journal of the Faith, Work, and Thought of Christendom* (New York, London, 1913-1922)
Cont	*Continuum* (St. Paul, 1963-1970)
ContextC	*Context (Journal of the Lutheran School of Theology at Chicago)* (Chicago, 1967-1968)
ContR	*Contemporary Review* (London, New York, 1866ff.)
CovQ	*The Covenant Quarterly* (Chicago, 1941ff.) [Volume 1, #1 as: *Covenant Minister's Quarterly*]
CQ	*Crozer Quarterly* (Chester, PA; 1924-1952)
CQR	*Church Quarterly Review* (London, 1875-1968)
CR	*The Church Review* (New Haven, 1848-1891) [Title varies; Volume 62 not published]
CraneR	*The Crane Review* (Medford, MA; 1958-1968)
CRB	*The Christian Review* (Boston, Rochester; 1836-1863)
CRDSB	*Colgate-Rochester Divinity School Bulletin* (Rochester, NY; 1928-1967)
Crit	*Criterion* (Chicago, 1962ff.)
CRP	*The Christian Review: A Quarterly Magazine* (Philadelphia, 1932-1941)
CS	*The Cumberland Seminarian* (McKenzie, TN; Memphis; 1953-1970)
CSQ	*Chicago Seminary Quarterly* (Chicago, 1901-1907)
CSQC	*The Culver-Stockton Quarterly* (Canton, MO; 1925-1931)
CSSH	*Comparative Studies in Society and History: An International Quarterly* (The Hague, 1958ff.)
CT	*Christian Thought* (New York, 1883-1894)
CTJ	*Calvin Theological Journal* (Grand Rapids, 1966ff.)
CTM	*Concordia Theological Monthly* (St. Louis, 1930ff.)
CTPR	*The Christian Teacher [and Chronicle]* (London, 1835-1838; *N.S.*, 1838-1844 as: *A Theological and Literary Journal*) [Continues as: *The Prospective Review; A Quarterly Journal of Theology and Literature*]
CTSB	*Columbia Theological Seminary Bulletin* (Columbia, SC; Decatur, GA; 1907ff.) [Title varies]
CTSP	*Catholic Theological Society, Proceedings* (Washingon, DC; Yonkers, NY; 1948ff.)
CTSQ	*Central Theological Seminary Quarterly* (Dayton, OH; 1923-1931)

CUB — *Catholic University Bulletin* (Washington, DC; 1895-1914) [Volumes 1-20 only]

D

DDSR — *Duke Divinity School Review* (Durham, NC; 1936ff.) [Volumes 1-20 as: *The Duke School of Religion Bulletin;* Volumes 21-29 as: *Duke Divinity School Bulletin*]

DG — *The Drew Gateway* (Madison, NJ; 1930ff.)

DI — *Diné Israel. An Annual of Jewish Law and Israeli Family Law* דיני ישראל, שנתון למשפט עברי ולדיני משפחה בישראל (Jerusalem, 1969ff.)

DJT — *Dialogue: A Journal of Theology* (Minneapolis, 1962ff.)

DownsR — *Downside Review* (Bath, 1880ff.)

DQR — *Danville Quarterly Review* (Danville, KY; Cincinnati; 1861-1864)

DR — *Dublin Review* (London, 1836-1968) [Between 1961 and 1964 as: *Wiseman Review*]

DS — *Dominican Studies. A Quarterly Review of Theology and Philosophy* (Oxford, 1948-1954)

DSJ — *The Dubuque Seminary Journal* (Dubuque, IA; 1966-1967)

DSQ — *Dubuque Seminary Quarterly* (Dubuque, IA; 1947-1949) [Volume 3, #3 not published]

DTCW — *Dimension: Theology in Church and World* (Princeton, NJ; 1964-1969) [Volumes 1 & 2 as: *Dimension* ; New format beginning in 1966 with full title, beginning again with Volume 1]

DTQ — *Dickinson's Theological Quarterly* (London, 1875-1883) [Superseded by *John Lobb's Theological Quarterly*]

DUJ — *The Durham University Journal* (Durham, 1876ff.; *N.S.*, 1940ff.) [Volume 32 of *O.S.* = Volume 1 of *N.S.*]

DUM — *Dublin University Magazine* (Dublin, London, 1833-1880)

DunR — *The Dunwoodie Review* (Yonkers, NY; 1961ff.)

E

EB — *Economic Botany* (Lancaster, PA; Kutzman, PA; Baltimore, MD; Lawrence, KS, 1947ff.)

EgR — *Egyptian Religion* (New York, 1933-1936)

EI — *Eretz-Israel. Archaeological, Historical and Geographical Studies* (Jerusalem, 1951ff.) ארץ־ישראל, מחקרים בידיעת הארץ ועתיקותיה [English Summaries from Volume 3 on]

EJS	*Archives européennes de Sociologie / European Journal of Sociology / Europäisches Archiv für Soziologie* (Paris, 1960ff.)
EN	*The Everlasting Nation* (London, 1889-1892)
EQ	*Evangelical Quarterly* (London, 1929ff.)
ER	*Evangelical Review* (Gettysburg, PA; 1849-1870) [From Volume 14 on as: *Evangelical Quarterly Review*]
ERCJ	*Edinburgh Review, or Critical Journal* (Edinburgh, London, 1802-1929)
ERG	*The Evangelical Repository: A Quarterly Magazine of Theological Literature* (Glasgow, 1854-1888)
ERL	*The English Review, or Quarterly Journal of Ecclesiastical and General Literature* (London, 1844-1853) [Continues *British Critic*]
ESS	*Ecumenical Study Series* (Indianapolis, 1955-1960)
ET	*The Expository Times* (Aberdeen, Edinburgh, 1889ff.)
ETL	*Ephemerides Theologicae Lovanienses* (Notre Dame, 1924ff.)
Eud	*Eudemus. An International Journal Devoted to the History of Mathematics and Astronomy* (Copenhagen, 1941)
Exp	*The Expositor* (London, 1875-1925)
Exped	*Expedition* (Philadelphia, 1958ff.) [Continues: *The University Museum Bulletin*]

F

F&T	*Faith and Thought* (London, 1958ff.) [Supersedes: *Journal of the Transactions of the Victoria Institute, or Philosophical Society of Great Britain*]
FBQ	*The Freewill Baptist Quarterly* (Providence, London, Dover, 1853-1869)
FDWL	*Friends of Dr.Williams's Library (Lectures)* (Cambridge, Oxford, 1948ff.)
FLB	*Fuller Library Bulletin* (Pasadena, CA; 1949ff.)
FO	*Folia Orientalia* (Kraków, 1960ff.)
Focus	*Focus. A Theological Journal* (Willowdale, Ontario, 1964-1968)
Folk	*Folk-Lore: A Quarterly Review of Myth, Tradition, Institution & Custom being The Transactions of the Folk-Lore Society And Incorporating the Archæological Review and the Folk-Lore Journal* (London, 1890ff.)
Found	*Foundations (A Baptist Journal of History and Theology)* (Rochester, NY; 1958ff.)
FUQ	*Free University Quarterly* (Amsterdam-Centrum, 1950-1965)

G

GBT	*Ghana Bulletin of Theology* (Legon, Ghana; 1957ff.)
GJ	*Grace Journal* (Winona Lake, IN; 1960ff.)
GOTR	*Greek Orthodox Theological Review* (Brookline, MA; 1954ff.)
GR	*Gordon Review* (Boston; Beverly Farms, MA; Wenham, MA; 1955ff.)
GRBS	*Greek, Roman and Byzantine Studies* (San Antonio; Cambridge, MA; University, MS; Durham, NC; 1958ff.) [Volume1 as: *Greek and Byzantine Studies*]
Greg	*Gregorianum; Commentarii de re theologica et philosophica* (Rome, 1920ff.) [Volume 1 as: *Gregorianum; rivista trimestrale di studi teologici e filosofici*]
GUOST	*Glasgow University Oriental Society, Transactions* (Glasgow, 1901ff.)

H

H&T	*History and Theory: Studies in the Philosophy of History* (The Hague, 1960ff.)
HA	*Hebrew Abstracts* (New York, 1954ff.)
HDSB	*Harvard Divinity School Bulletin* (Cambridge, MA; 1935-1969)
Herm	*Hermathena; a Series of Papers on Literature, Science and Philosophy by Members of Trinity College, Dublin* (Dublin, 1873ff.) [Volumes 1-20; changes to issue number from #46 on]
HeyJ	*The Heythrop Journal* (New York, 1960ff.)
HJ	*Hibbert Journal* (London, Boston, 1902-1968)
HJAH	*Historia. Zeitschrift für alte Geschichte / Revue d'Histoire Ancienne / Journal of Ancient History / Rivista di Storia Antica* (Baden, 1950ff.)
HJud	*Historia Judaica. A Journal of Studies in Jewish History Especially in the Legal and Economic History of the Jews* (New York, 1938-1961)
HQ	*The Hartford Quarterly* (Hartford, CT; 1960-1968)
HR	*Homiletic Review* (New York, 1876-1934)
HRel	*History of Religions* (Chicago, 1961ff.)
HS	*Ha Sifrut. Quarterly for the Study of Literature* הספרות, רבעון למדע הספרות (Tel-Aviv, 1968ff.)
HSR	*Hartford Seminary Record* (Hartford, CT; 1890-1913)
HT	*History Today* (London, 1951ff.)

HTR *Harvard Theological Review* (Cambridge, MA; 1908ff.)
HTS *Hervormde Teologiese Studien* (Pretoria, 1943ff.)
HUCA *Hebrew Union College Annual* (Cincinnati, 1904, 1924ff.)

I

IA *Iranica Antiqua* (Leiden, 1961ff.)
IALR *International Anthropological and Linguistic Review* (Miami, 1953-1957)
IAQR *Asiatic Quarterly Review* (London, 1886-1966) [1st Series as: *Asiatic Quarterly Review,* (1886-1890); 2nd Series as: *The Imperial and Asiatic Quarterly and Oriental and Colonial Record,* (1891-1895); 3rd Series, (1896-1912); New Series, Volumes 1 & 2 as: *The Asiatic Quarterly Review* (1913); Volumes 3-48 (1914-1952) as: *Asiatic Review, New Series;* Volumes 49-59 (1953-1964) as: *Asian Review, New Series;* continued as: *Asian Review, Incorporating Art and Letters [and] the Asiatic Review, New Series,* Volumes 1-3 (1964-1966)]
ICHR *Indian Church History Review* (Serampore, West Bengal, 1967ff.)
ICMM *The Interpreter. A Church Monthly Magazine* (London, 1905-1924)
ICQ *Irish Church Quarterly* (Dublin, 1908-1917)
IEJ *Israel Exploration Journal* (Jerusalem, 1950ff.)
IER *Irish Ecclesiastical Record (A Monthly Journal under Episcopal Sanction)* (Dublin, 1864-1968)
IES *Indian Ecclesiastical Studies* (Bangalore, India, 1962ff.)
IJA *International Journal of Apocrypha* (London, 1905-1917) [Issues #1-7 as: *Deutero-Canonica,* pages unnumbered]
IJT *Indian Journal of Theology* (Serampore, West Bengal, 1952ff.)
ILR *Israel Law Review* (Jerusalem, 1966ff.)
Inter *Interchange: Papers on Biblical and Current Questions* (Sydney, 1967ff.)
Interp *Interpretation; a Journal of Bible and Theology* (Richmond, 1947ff.)
IPQ *International Philosophical Quarterly* (New York, 1961ff.)
IR *The Iliff Review* (Denver, 1944ff.)
Iran *Iran: Journal of the British Institute of Persian Studies* (London, 1963ff.)
Iraq *Iraq. British School of Archaeology in Iraq* (London, 1934ff.)
IRB *International Reformed Bulletin* (London, 1958ff.)

IRM — *International Review of Missions* (Edinburgh, London, Geneva, 1912ff.)
Isis — *Isis. An International Review devoted to the History of Science and Civilization* (Brussels; Cambridge, MA; 1913ff.)
ITQ — *Irish Theological Quarterly* (Dublin, Maynooth, 1906ff.)

J

JAAR — *Journal of the American Academy of Religion* (Wolcott, NY; Somerville, NJ; Baltimore; Brattleboro, VT; 1938ff.) [Volumes 1-4 as: *Journal of the National Association of Biblical Instructors;* Volumes 5-34 as: *Journal of Bible and Religion*]
JANES — *Journal of the Ancient Near Eastern Society of Columbia University* (New York, 1968ff.)
Janus — *Janus; Archives internationales pour l'Histoire de la Médecine et pour la Géographie Médicale* (Amsterdam; Haarlem; Leiden; 1896ff.)
JAOS — *Journal of the American Oriental Society* (Baltimore, New Haven, 1843ff.)
JAOSS — *Journal of the American Oriental Society, Supplements* (Baltimore, New Haven, 1935-1954)
JARCE — *Journal of the American Research Center in Egypt* (Gluckstadt, Germany; Cambridge, MA; 1962ff.)
JASA — *Journal of the American Scientific Affiliation* (Wheaton, IL, 1949ff.)
JBL — *Journal of Biblical Literature* (Middletown, CT; New Haven; Boston; Philadelphia; Missoula, MT; 1881ff.)
JC&S — *The Journal of Church and State* (Fresno, CA; 1965ff.)
JCE — *Journal of Christian Education* (Sydney, 1958ff.)
JCP — *Christian Philosophy Quarterly* (New York, 1881-1884) [From Volume 2 on as: *The Journal of Christian Philosophy*]
JCS — *Journal of Cuneiform Studies* (New Haven; Cambridge, MA;1947ff.)
JCSP — *Journal of Classical and Sacred Philology* (Cambridge, England, 1854-1857)
JEA — *Journal of Egyptian Archaeology* (London, 1914ff.)
JEBH — *Journal of Economic and Business History* (Cambridge, MA;1928-1932)
JEOL — *Jaarbericht van het Vooraziatisch-Egyptisch Gezelschap Ex Oriente Lux* (Leiden, 1933ff.)
JES — *Journal of Ethiopian Studies* (Addis Ababa, 1963ff.)

JESHO	*Journal of the Economic and Social History of the Orient* (Leiden, 1958ff.)
JHI	*Journal of the History of Ideas. A Quarterly Devoted to Intellectual History* (Lancaster, PA; New York;1940ff.
JHS	*The Journal of Hebraic Studies* (New York; 1969ff.)
JIQ	*Jewish Institute Quarterly* (New York, 1924-1930)
JJLP	*Journal of Jewish Lore and Philosophy* (Cincinnati, 1919)
JJP	*Rocznik Papirologii Prawniczej-Journal of Juristic Papyrology* (New York, Warsaw, 1946ff.) [Suspended 1947 & 1959-60]
JJS	*Journal of Jewish Studies* (London, 1948ff.)
JKF	*Jahrbuch für Kleinasiatische Forschungen* (Heidelberg, 1950-1953) [Superseded by *Anadolu Araştirmalari Istanbul Üniversitesi Edebiyat Fakültesi eski Önasya Dilleri ve Kültürleri Kürsüsü Tarafindan Čikarilir*]
JLTQ	*John Lobb's Theological Quarterly* (London, 1884)
JMTSO	*Journal of the Methodist Theological School in Ohio* (Delaware, OH; 1962ff.)
JMUEOS	*Journal of the Manchester Univeristy Egyptian and Oriental Society* (Manchester, 1911-1953) [Issue #1 as: *Journal of the Manchester Oriental Society*]
JNES	*Journal of Near Eastern Studies* (Chicago, 1942ff.)
JP	*The Journal of Philology* (Cambridge, England; 1868-1920)
JPOS	*Journal of the Palestine Oriental Society* (Jerusalem, 1920-1948) [Volume 20 consists of only one fascicle]
JQR	*Jewish Quarterly Review* (London, 1888-1908; *N.S.*, Philadelphia, 1908ff.) [Includes 75th Anniversary Volume as: *JQR, 75th*]
JR	*Journal of Religion* (Chicago, 1921ff.)
JRAI	*Journal of the Royal Anthropological Institute of Great Britain and Ireland* (London, 1872-1965) [Volumes 1-69 as: *Journal of the Anthropological Institute* Continued as: *Man, N.S.*]
JRAS	*Journal of the Royal Asiatic Society of Great Britain and Ireland* (London, 1827ff.) [*Transactions,* 1827-1835 as *TRAS; Journal* from 1834 on: (Shown without volume numbers)]
JRASCS	*Centenary Supplement of the Journal of the Royal Asiatic Society, being a Selection of papers read to the society' during the celebrations of July, 1923* (London, 1924)
JRelH	*Journal of Religious History* (Sydney, 1960ff.)
JRH	*Journal of Religion and Health* (Richmond, 1961ff.)
JRT	*Journal of Religious Thought* (Washington, DC; 1943ff.)

JSAH	*Journal of the Society of Architechtural Historians* (Troy, NY; New York; Philadelphia, 1941ff.) [Volumes 1-4 as: *Journal of the American Society of Architectural Historians*]
JSL	*Journal of Sacred Literature and Biblical Record* (London,1848-1868)
JSOR	*Journal of the Society of Oriental Research* (Chicago, 1917-1932)
JSP	*The Journal of Speculative Philosophy* (St. Louis, 1868-1893)
JSS	*Journal of Semitic Studies* (Manchester, 1956ff.)
JTALC	*Journal of Theology of the American Lutheran Conference* (Minneapolis, 1936-1943) [Volumes 1-5 as: *American Lutheran Conference Journal;* continued from volume 8, #3 as: *Lutheran Outlook* (not included)]
JTC	*Journal for Theology and the Church* (New York, 1965ff.)
JTLC	*Journal of Theology: Church of the Lutheran Confession* (Eau Claire, WI; 1961ff.)
JTS	*Journal of Theological Studies* (Oxford, 1899-1949; *N.S.*, 1950ff.)
JTVI	*Journal of the Transactions of the Victoria Institute, or Philosophical Society of Great Britain* (London, 1866-1957) [Superseded by *Faith & Thought*]
Jud	*Judaism. A Quarterly Journal of Jewish Life and Thought* (New York, 1952ff.)
JWCI	*Journal of the Warburg and Courtauld Institutes* (London,1937ff.)
JWH	*Journal of World History-Cahiers d'Histoire Mondiale -Cuadernos de Historia Mundial* (Paris, 1953ff.)

K

Kêmi	*Kêmi. Revue de philologie et d'archéologie égyptiennes et coptes* (Paris, 1928ff.)
Klio	*Klio. Beiträge zur alten Geschichte* (Leipzig, 1901ff.)
Kobez	*Kobez (Qobeṣ);* קובץ החברה העברית לחקירת ארץ־ישראל ועתיקתיה (Jerusalem, 1921-1945)
KSJA	*Kedem; Studies in Jewish Archaeology* (Jerusalem, 1942, 1945)
Kuml	*Kuml. Årbog for Jysk Arkæologisk Selskab* (Århus, 1951ff.)
Kush	*Kush. Journal of the Sudan Antiquities Service* (Khartoum, Sudan, 1953-1968)
KZ	*Kirchliche Zeitschrift* (St. Louis; Waverly, IA; Chicago; Columbus; 1876-1943)

KZFE — *Kadmos. Zeitschrift für vor-und frühgriechische Epigraphik* (Berlin, 1962ff.)

L

L — *Levant (Journal of the British School of Archaeology in Jerusalem)* (London, 1969ff.)
Lang — *Language. Journal of the Linguistic Society of America* (Baltimore, 1925ff.)
LCQ — *Lutheran Church Quarterly* (Gettysburg, PA; 1928-1949)
LCR — *Lutheran Church Review* (Philadelphia, 1882-1927)
Lěš — *Lěšonénu. Quarterly for the Study of the Hebrew Language and Cognate Subjects* לשוננו (Jerusalem, 1925ff.) [English Summaries from Volume 30 onward]
LIST — *Lown Institute. Studies and Texts* (Brandeis University. Lown School of Near Eastern and Judaic Studies. Cambridge, MA; 1963ff.)
Listen — *Listening* (Dubuque, IA; 1965ff.) [Volume numbers start with "zero"]
LofS — *Life of the Spirit* (London, 1946-1964)
LQ — *The Quarterly Review of the Evangelical Lutheran Church* (Gettysburg, PA; 1871-1927; revived in1949ff.) [From 1878 on as: *The Lutheran Quarterly*]
LQHR — *London Quarterly and Holborn Review* (London, 1853-1968)
LS — *Louvain Studies* (Louvain, 1966ff.)
LSQ — *Lutheran Synod Quarterly* (Mankato, MN, 1960ff.) [Formerly *Clergy Bulletin* (Volume 1 of *LSQ* as *Clergy Bulletin,* Volume 20, #1 & #2)]
LTJ — *Lutheran Theological Journal* (North Adelaide, South Australia, 1967ff.)
LTP — *Laval Theologique et Philosophique* (Quebec, 1945ff.)
LTQ — *Lexington Theological Quarterly* (Lexington, KY; 1966ff.)
LTR — *Literary and Theological Review* (New York; Boston, 1834-1839)
LTSB — *Lutheran Theological Seminary Bulletin* (Gettysburg, PA; 1921ff.)
LTSR — *Luther Theological Seminary Review* (St. Paul, MN; 1962ff.)

LWR — *The Lutheran World Review* (Philadelphia, 1948-1950)

M

Man — *Man. A Monthly Record of Anthropological Science* (London,1901-1965; *N. S.*, 1966ff.) [Articles in original series referred to by *article* number not by *page* number - New Series subtitled: *The Journal of the Royal Anthropological Institute*]

ManSL — *Manuscripta* (St. Louis, 1957ff.)

MB — *Medelhavsmuseet Bulletin* (Stockholm, 1961ff.)

MC — *The Modern Churchman* (Ludlow, England; 1911ff.)

McQ — *McCormick Quarterly* (Chicago, 1947ff.) [Volumes 1-13 as: *McCormick Speaking*]

MCS — *Manchester Cuneiform Studies* (Manchester, 1951-1964)

MDIÄA — *Mitteilungen des deutsches Instituts für ägyptische Altertumskunde in Kairo* (Cairo, 1930ff.)

Mesop — *Mesopotamia* (Torino, Italy, 1966ff.)

MH — *The Modern Humanist* (Weston, MA; 1944-1962)

MHSB — *The Mission House Seminary Bulletin* (Plymouth, WI; 1954-1962)

MI — *Monthly Interpreter* (Edinburgh, 1884-1886)

MidS — *Midstream (Council on Christian Unity)* (Indianapolis, 1961ff.)

Min — *Ministry. A Quarterly Theological Review for South Africa* (Morija, Basutolan, 1960ff.)

Minos — *Minos. Investigaciones y Materiales Para el Estudio de los Textos Paleocretenses Publicados Bajo la Dirección de Antonio Tovar y Emilio Peruzzi* (Salamanca, 1951ff.) [From Volume 4 on as: *Minos Revista de Filología Egea*]

MIO — *Mitteilungen des Instituts für Orientforschung [Deutsche Akademie der Wissenschaften zu Berlin Institut für Orientforschung]* (Berlin, 1953ff.)

Miz — *Mizraim. Journal of Papyrology, Egyptology, History of Ancient Laws, and their Relations to the Civilizations of Bible Lands* (New York, 1933-1938)

MJ — *The Museum Journal. Pennsylvania University* (Philadelphia,1910-1935)

MMBR — *The Monthly Magazine and British Register* (London, 1796-1843) [*1st Ser.*, 1796-1826, Volumes 1-60; *N.S.*, 1826-1838, Volumes 1-26; *3rd Ser.*, 1839-1843, Volumes 1-9, however, Volumes 7-9 are marked 95-97*[sic]*]

ModR — *The Modern Review* (London, 1880-1884)
Monist — *The Monist. An International Quarterly Journal of General Philosophical Inquiry* (Chicago; La Salle, IL; 1891ff.)
Mosaic — *Mosaic* (Cambridge, MA; 1960ff.)
MQ — *The Minister's Quarterly* (New York, 1945-1966)
MQR — *Methodist Quarterly Review (South)* (Louisville, Nashville, 1847-1861; 1879-1886; 1886-1930) [*3rd Ser.* as: *Southern Methodist Review;* Volume 52 (1926) misnumbered as 53; Volume 53 (1927) misnumbered as 54; and the volume for 1928 is also marked as 54]
MR — *Methodist Review* (New York, 1818-1931) [Volume 100 not published]
MTSB — *Moravian Theological Seminary Bulletin* (Bethlehem, PA; 1959-1970) [Volume for 1969 apparently not published]
MTSQB — *Meadville Theological School Quarterly Bulletin* (Meadville, PA;1906-1933) [From Volume 25 on as: *Meadville Journal*]
Muséon — *Le Muséon. Revue d'Études Orientales* (Louvain, 1882-1915;1930/32ff.)
MUSJ — *Mélanges de l'Université Saint-Joseph. Faculté orientale* (Beirut, 1906ff.) [Title varies]
Mwa-M — *Milla wa-Milla. The Australian Bulletin of Comparative Religion* (Parkville, Victoria, 1961ff.)

N

NB — *Blackfriars. A Monthly Magazine* (Oxford, 1920ff.) [From Volume 46 on as: *New Blackfriars*]
NBR — *North British Review* (Edinburgh, 1844-1871)
NCB — *New College Bulletin* (Edinburgh, 1964ff.)
NEAJT — *Northeast Asia Journal of Theology* (Kyoto, Japan, 1968ff.)
NEST — *The Near East School of Theology Quarterly* (Beirut, 1952ff.)
Nexus — *Nexus* (Boston, 1957ff.)
NGTT — *Nederduitse gereformeerde teologiese tydskrif* (Kaapstad, N.G., Kerk-Uitgewers, 1959ff.)
NOGG — *Nihon Orient Gakkai geppo* (Tokyo, 1955-1959) [Being the *Bulletin of the Society for Near Eastern Studies in Japan*-Continued as: *Oriento*]
NOP — *New Orient* (Prague, 1960-1968)

NPR	*The New Princeton Review* (New York, 1886-1888)
NQR	*Nashotah Quarterly Review* (Nashotah, WI; 1960ff.)
NT	*Novum Testamentum* (Leiden, 1955ff.)
NTS	*New Testament Studies* (Cambridge, England; 1954ff.)
NTT	*Nederlandsch Theologisch Tijdschrift* (Wageningen, 1946ff.)
NTTO	*Norsk Teologisk Tidsskrift* (Oslo, 1900ff.)
Numen	*Numen; International Review for the History of Religions* (Leiden, 1954ff.)
NW	*The New World. A Quarterly Review of Religion, Ethics and Theology* (Boston, 1892-1900)
NYR	*The New York Review. A Journal of The Ancient Faith and Modern Thought (St. John's Seminary)* (New York, 1905-1908)
NZJT	*New Zealand Journal of Theology* (Christchurch, 1931-1935)

O

OA	*Oriens Antiquus* (Rome, 1962ff.)
OBJ	*The Oriental and Biblical Journal* (Chicago, 1880-1881)
OC	*Open Court* (Chicago, 1887-1936)
ONTS	*The Hebrew Student* (Morgan Park, IL; New Haven; Hartford; 1881-1892) [Volumes 3-8 as: *The Old Testament Student;* Volume 9 onwards as: *The Old and New Testament Student*]
OOR	*Oriens: The Oriental Review* (Paris, 1926)
OQR	*The Oberlin Quarterly Review* (Oberlin, OH; 1845-1849)
Or	*Orientalia commentarii de rebus Assyri-Babylonicis, Arabicis, and Aegyptiacis, etc.* (Rome 1920-1930)
Or, N.S.	*Orientalia: commentarii, periodici de rebus orientis antiqui* (Rome, 1932ff.)
Oriens	*Oriens. Journal of the International Society of Oriental Research* (Leiden, 1948ff.)
Orient	*Orient. The Reports of the Society for Near Eastern Studies in Japan* (Tokyo, 1960ff.)
Orita	*Orita. Ibadan Journal of Religious Studies* (Ibadan, Nigeria, 1967ff.)
OrS	*Orientalia Suecana* (Uppsala, 1952ff.)
OSHTP	*Oxford Society of Historical Theology, Abstract of Proceedings* (Oxford, 1891-1968) [Through 1919 as: *Society of Historical Theology, Proceedings*]
Osiris	*Osiris* (Bruges, Belgium; 1936-1968) *[Subtitle varies]*

OSOCP *Oriental Studies. A Selection of the Papers read before The Oriental Club of Philadelphia, 1888-1894.* (Boston: 1894)
OTS *Oudtestamentische Studiën* (Leiden, 1942ff.)
OTW *Ou-Testamentiese Werkgemeenskap in Suid-Afrika, Proceedings of die* (Pretoria, 1958ff.) [Volume 1 in Volume 14 of: *Hervormde Teologiese Studies*]

P

P *Preaching: A Journal of Homiletics* (Dubuque, IA; 1965ff.)
P&P *Past and Present* (London, 1952ff.) *[Subtitle varies]*
PA *Practical Anthropology* (Wheaton, IL; Eugene, OR; Tarrytown, NY; 1954ff.)
PAAJR *Proceedings of the American Academy for Jewish Research* (Philadelphia, 1928ff.)
PAOS *Proceedings of the American Oriental Society* (Baltimore, New Haven; 1842, 1846-50, 1852-1860) [After 1860 all proceedings are bound with *Journal*]
PAPA *American Philological Association, Proceedings* (Hartford, Boston, 1896ff.) [*Transactions* as: *TAPA. Transactions* and *Proceedings* combine page numbers from volume 77 on]
PAPS *Proceedings of the American Philosophical Society* (Philadelphia, 1838ff.)
PBA *Proceedings of the British Academy* (London, 1903ff.)
PEFQS *Palestine Exploration Fund Quarterly Statement* (London, 1869ff.) [From Volume 69 (1937) on as: *Palestine Exploration Quarterly*]
PEQ *Palestine Exploration Quarterly* [See: *PEFQS*]
PER *The Protestant Episcopal Review* (Fairfax, Co., VA; 1886-1900) [Volumes 1-5 as: *The Virginian Seminary Magazine*]
Person *Personalist. An International Review of Philosophy, Religion and Literature* (Los Angeles, 1920ff.)
PF *Philosophical Forum* (Boston, 1943-1957; *N.S.*, 1968ff.)
PHDS *Perspectives. Harvard Divinity School* (Cambridge, MA; 1965-1967)
PIASH *Proceedings of the Israel Academy of Sciences and Humanities* (Jerusalem, 1967ff.)
PICSS *Proceedings of the International Conference on Semitic Studies held in Jerusalem, 19-23 July 1965* (Jerusalem, 1969)

PIJSL — *Papers of the Institute of Jewish Studies, London* (Jerusalem,1964)
PJT — *Pacific Journal of Theology* (Western Samoa, 1961ff.)
PJTSA — *Jewish Theological Seminary Association, Proceedings* (New York, 1888-1902)
PP — *Perspective* (Pittsburgh, 1960ff.) [Volumes 1-8 as: *Pittsburgh Perspective*]
PQ — *The Presbyterian Quarterly* (New York, 1887-1904)
PQL — *The Preacher's Quarterly* (London, 1954-1969)
PQPR — *The Presbyterian Quarterly and Princeton Review* (New York, 1872-1877)
PQR — *Presbyterian Quarterly Review* (Philadelphia, 1852-1862)
PR — *Presbyterian Review* (New York, 1880-1889)
PRev — *The Biblical Repertory and Princeton Review* (Princeton, Philadelphia, New York, 1829-1884) [Volume 1 as: *The Biblical Repertory, New Series;* Volumes 2-8 as: *The Biblical Repertory and Theological Review* (1878-1884) as: *Princeton Review*]
PRR — *Presbyterian and Reformed Review* (New York, Philadelphia, 1890-1902)
PSB — *The Princeton Seminary Bulletin* (Princeton, 1907ff.)
PSTJ — *Perkins School of Theology Journal* (Dallas, 1947ff.)
PTR — *Princeton Theological Review* (Princeton, 1903-1929)
PUNTPS — *Proceedings of the University of Newcastle upon Tyne Philosophical Society* (Newcastle upon Tyne, 1964-70)

Q

QCS — *Quarterly Christian Spectator* (New Haven, 1819-1838) *[1st Series* and *New Series* as: *Christian Spectator]*
QDAP — *The Quarterly of the Department of Antiquities in Palestine* (Jerusalem, 1931-1950)
QRL — *Quarterly Review* (London, 1809-1967)
QTMRP — *The Quarterly Theological Magazine, and Religious Repository* (Philadelphia, 1813-1814)

R

R&E — *[Baptist] Review and Expositor* (Louisville, 1904ff.)
R&S — *Religion and Society* (Bangalore, India, 1953ff.)

RAAO	*Revue d'Assyriologie et d'Archéologie Orientale* (Paris, 1886ff.)
RChR	*The Reformed Church Review* (Mercersburg, PA; Chambersburg, PA; Philadelphia; 1849-1926) [Volumes 1-25 as: *Mercersburg Review;* Volumes 26-40 as: *Reformed Quarterly Review; 4th Series* on as: *Reformed Church Review*]
RCM	*Reformed Church Magazine* (Reading, PA; 1893-1896) [Volume 3 as: *Reformed Church Historical Magazine*]
RdQ	*Revue de Qumran* (Paris, 1958ff.)
RDSO	*Rivista degli Studi Orientali* (Rome, 1907ff.)
RÉ	*Revue Égyptologique* (Paris, 1880-1896; *N.S.*, 1919-1924)
RefmR	*The Reformation Review* (Amsterdam, 1953ff.)
RefR	*The Reformed Review. A Quarterly Journal of the Seminaries of the Reformed Church in America* (Holland, MI; New Brunswick, NJ; 1947ff.) [Volumes 1-9 as: *Western Seminary Bulletin*]
RÉg	*Revue d'Égyptologie* (Paris, 1933ff.)
RelM	*Religion in the Making* (Lakeland, FL; 1940-1943)
Resp	*Response—in worship—Music—The arts* (St. Paul, 1959ff.)
RestQ	*Restoration Quarterly* (Austin, TX; Abilene, TX; 1957ff.)
RFEASB	*The Hebrew University / Jerusalem: Department of Archaeology. Louis M. Rabinowitz Fund for the Exploration of Ancient Synagogues, Bulletin* (Jerusalem, 1949-1960)
RHA	*Revue Hittite et Asianique* (Paris, 1930ff.)
RIDA	*Revue internationale des droits de l'antiquité* (Brussels, 1948ff.)
RJ	*Res Judicatae. The Journal of the Law Students' Society of Victoria* (Melbourne, 1935-1957)
RL	*Religion in Life* (New York, 1932ff.)
RO	*Rocznik Orjentalistyczny. (Wydaje Polskie towarzystwo orjentalisyczne)* (Kraków, Warsaw, 1914ff.)
RP	*Records of the Past* (Washington, DC; 1902-1914)
RR	*Review of Religion* (New York, 1936-1958)
RS	*Religious Studies* (London, 1965ff.)
RTP	*Review of Theology and Philosophy* (Edinburgh, 1905-1915)
RTR	*Recueil de travaux relatifs à la philologie et à l'archéologie egyptiennes et assyriennes* (Paris, 1870-1923)
RTRM	*The Reformed Theological Review* (Melbourne, 1941ff.)

S

SAENJ	*Seminar. An Annual Extraordinary Number of the Jurist* (Washington, DC; 1943-1956)
SBAP	*Society of Biblical Archæology, Proceedings* (London, 1878-1918)
SBAT	*Society of Biblical Archæology, Transactions* (London, 1872-1893)
SBE	*Studia Biblica et Ecclesiastica* (Oxford, 1885-1903) [Volume 1 as: *Studia Biblica*]
SBFLA	*Studii (Studium) Biblici Franciscani. Liber Annuus* (Jerusalem, 1950ff.)
SBLP	*Society of Biblical Literature & Exegesis, Proceedings* (Baltimore, 1880)
SBO	*Studia Biblica et Orientalia* (Rome 1959) [Being Volumes 10-12 respectively of *Analecta Biblica. Investigationes Scientificae in Res Biblicas*]
SBSB	*Society for Biblical Studies Bulletin* (Madras, India, 1964ff.)
SCO	*Studi Classici e Orientali* (Pisa, 1951ff.)
Scotist	*The Scotist* (Teutopolis, IL; 1939-1967)
SCR	*Studies in Comparative Religion* (Bedfont, Middlesex, England, 1967ff.)
Scrip	*Scripture. The Quarterly of the Catholic Biblical Association* (London, 1944-1968)
SE	*Study Encounter* (Geneva, 1965ff.)
SEÅ	*Svensk Exegetisk Årsbok* (Uppsala-Lund, 1936ff.)
SEAJT	*South East Journal of Theology* (Singapore, 1959ff.)
Sefunim	*Sefunim (Bulletin)* [היפה] ספונים (Haifa, 1966-1968)
SGEI	*Studies in the Geography of Eretz-Israel* מחקרים בגיאוגרפיה של ארץ־ישראל (Jerusalem, 1959ff.) [English summaries in Volumes 1-3 only; continuing the *Bulletin of the Israel Exploration Society (Yediot)*]
SH	*Scripta Hierosolymitana* (Jerusalem, 1954ff.)
Shekel	*The Shekel* (New York, 1968ff.)
SIR	*Smithsonian Institute Annual Report of the Board of Regents* (Washington, DC; 1846-1964; becomes: *Smithsonian Year* from 1965 on]
SJH	*Seminary Journal* (Hamilton, NY; 1892)
SJT	*Scottish Journal of Theology* (Edinburgh, 1947ff.)
SL	*Studia Liturgica. An International Ecumenical Quarterly for Liturgical Research and Renewal* (Rotterdam, 1962ff.)

Periodical Abbreviations

SLBR	*Sierra Leone Bulletin of Religion* (Freetown, Sierra Leone; 1959-1966)
SMR	*Studia Montes Regii* (Montreal, 1958-1967)
SMSDR	*Studi e Materiali di Storia Delle Religioni* (Rome, Bologna, 1925ff.
SO	*Studia Orientalia* (Helsinki, 1925ff.)
SOOG	*Studi Orientalistici in Onore di Giorgio Levi Della Vida* (Rome, 1956)
Sophia	*Sophia. A Journal for Discussion in Philosophical Theology* (Parkville, N.S.W., Australia, 1962ff.)
SP	*Spirit of the Pilgrims* (Boston, 1828-1833)
SPR	*Southern Presbyterian Review* (Columbia, SC; 1847-1885)
SQ/E	*The Shane Quarterly* (Indianapolis, 1940ff.) [From Volume 17 on as: *Encounter*]
SR	*The Seminary Review* (Cincinnati, 1954ff.)
SRL	*The Scottish Review* (London, Edinburgh, 1882-1900; 1914-1920)
SS	*Seminary Studies of the Athenaeum of Ohio* (Cincinnati, 1926-1968) [Volumes 1-15 as: *Seminary Studies*]
SSO	*Studia Semitica et Orientalia* (Glasgow, 1920, 1945)
SSR	*Studi Semitici* (Rome, 1958ff.)
ST	*Studia Theologica* (Lund, 1947ff.)
StEv	*Studia Evangelica* (Berlin, 1959ff.) [Being miscellaneous volumes of: *Text und Untersuchungen zur Geschichte der altchristlichen Literatur,* beginning with Volume 73]
StLJ	*The Saint Luke's Journal* (Sewanee, TN; 1957ff.) [Volume 1, #1 as: *St. Luke's Journal of Theology*]
StMR	*St. Marks Review: An Anglican Quarterly* (Canberra, A.C.T., Australia, 1955ff.)
StP	*Studia Patristica* (Berlin, 1957ff.) [Being miscellaneous volumes of: *Text und Untersuchungen zur Geschichte der altchristlichen Literatur,* beginning with Volume 63]
StVTQ	*St. Vladimir's Theological Quarterly* (Crestwood, NY; 1952ff.) [Volumes 1-4 as: *St. Vladimir's Seminary Quarterly*]
Sumer	*Sumer. A Journal of Archaeology in Iraq* (Bagdad, 1945ff.)
SWJT	*Southwestern Journal of Theology* (Fort Worth, 1917-1924; *N.S.,* 1950ff.)
Syria	*Syria, revue d'art oriental et d'archéologie* (Paris, 1920ff.)

T

T&C	*Theology and the Church / SÎN-HÁK kap kàu-Hōe (Tainan Theological College)* (Tainan, Formosa, 1957ff.)
T&L	*Theology and Life* (Lancaster, PA; 1958-1966)
TAD	*Türk tarih, arkeologya ve etnoğrafya dergisi* (Istanbul, 1933-1949; continued as: *Türk arkeoloji Dergisi,* Ankara, 1956ff.)
TAPA	*American Philological Society, Transactions* (See: *PAPA*)
TAPS	*Transactions of the American Philosophical Society* (Philadelphia, 1789-1804; *N.S.,* 1818ff.)
Tarbiẕ	*Tarbiẕ. A quarterly review of the humanities;* ,תרביץ רבעון למדעי היהדות (Jerusalem, 1929ff.) [English Summaries from Volume 24 on only]
TB	*Tyndale Bulletin* (London, 1956ff.) [Numbers 1-16 as: *Tyndale House Bulletin*]
TBMDC	*Theological Bulletin: McMaster Divinity College* (Hamilton, Ontario, 1967ff.)
TD	*Theology Digest* (St. Mary, KS, 1953ff.)
TE	*Theological Education* (Dayton, 1964ff.)
Tem	*Temenos. Studies in Comparative Religion* (Helsinki, 1965ff.)
TEP	*Theologica Evangelica. Journal of the Faculty of Theology, University of South Africa* (Pretoria, 1968ff.)
Text	*Textus. Annual of the Hebrew University Bible Project* (Jerusalem, 1960ff.)
TF	*Theological Forum* (Minneapolis, 1929-1935)
TFUQ	*Thought. A Quarterly of the Sciences and Letters* (New York, 1926ff.) [From Volume 15 on as: *Thought. Fordham University Quarterly*]
ThE	*Theological Eclectic* (Cincinnati; New York, 1864-1871)
Them	*Themelios, International Fellowship of Evangelical Students* (Fresno, CA; 1962ff.)
Theo	*Theology; A Journal of Historic Christianity* (London, 1920ff.)
ThSt	*Theological Studies* (New York; Woodstock, MD; 1940ff.)
TLJ	*Theological and Literary Journal* (New York, 1848-1861)
TM	*Theological Monthly* (St. Louis, 1921-1929)
TML	*The Theological Monthly* (London, 1889-1891)
TPS	*Transactions of the Philological Society* (London, 1842ff.) [Volumes 1-6 as: *Proceedings*]
TQ	*Theological Quarterly* (St. Louis, 1897-1920)

Tr	*Traditio. Studies in Ancient and Medieval History, Thought and Religion* (New York, 1943ff.)
Trad	*Tradition, A Journal of Orthodox Jewish Thought* (New York, 1958ff.)
TRAS	*see: JRAS*
TRep	*Theological Repository* (London, 1769-1788)
TRFCCQ	*Theological Review and Free Church College Quarterly* (Edinburgh, 1886-1890)
TRGR	*The Theological Review and General Repository of Religious and Moral Information, Published Quarterly* (Baltimore, 1822)
TRL	*Theological Review: A Quarterly Journal of Religious Thought and Life* (London, 1864-1879)
TT	*Theology Today* (Lansdowne, PA; Princeton, NJ; 1944ff.)
TTCA	*Trinity Theological College Annual* (Singapore, 1964-1969) [Volume 5 apparently never published]
TTD	*Teologisk Tidsskrift* (Decorah, IA; 1899-1907)
TTKB	*Türk Tarih Kurumu Belleten* (Ankara, 1937ff.)
TTKF	*Tidskrift för teologi och kyrkiga frågor (The Augustana Theological Quarterly)* (Rock Island, IL; 1899-1917)
TTL	*Theologisch Tijdschrift* (Leiden, 1867-1919) [English articles from Volume 45 on only]
TTM	*Teologisk Tidsskrift* (Minneapolis, 1917-1928)
TUSR	*Trinity University Studies in Religion* (San Antonio, 1950ff.)
TZ	*Theologische Zeitschrift* (Basel, 1945ff.)
TZDES	*Theologische Zeitschrift (Deutsche Evangelische Synode des Westens, North America)* (St. Louis, 1873-1934) [Continued from Volumes 22 through 26 as: *Magazin für Evangel. Theologie und Kirche;* and from Volume 27 on as: *Theological Magazine*]
TZTM	*Theologische Zeitblätter, Theological Magazine* (Columbus,1911-1919)

U

UC	*The Unitarian Christian* (Boston, 1947ff.) [Volumes 1-4 as: *Our Faith*]
UCPSP	*University of California Publications in Semitic Philology* (Berkeley, 1907ff.)
UF	*Ugarit-Forschungen. Internationales Jahrbuch für die Altertumskunde Syrien-Palästinas* (Neukirchen, West Germany; 1969ff.)

ULBIA	*University of London. Bulletin of the Institute of Archaeology* (London, 1958ff.)
UMB	*The University Museum Bulletin (University of Pennsylvania)* (Philadelphia, 1930-1958)
UMMAAP	*University of Michigan. Museum of Anthropology. Anthropological Papers* (Ann Arbor, 1949ff.)
UnionR	*The Union Review* (New York, 1939-1945)
UPQR	*The United Presbyterian Quarterly Review* (Pittsburgh, 1860-1861)
UQGR	*Universalist Quarterly and General Review* (Boston, 1844-1891)
URRM	*The Unitarian Review and Religious Magazine* (Boston, 1874-1891)
USQR	*Union Seminary Quarterly Review* (New York, 1945ff.)
USR	*Union Seminary Review* (Hampden-Sydney, VA; Richmond; 1890-1946) [Volumes 1-23 as: *Union Seminary Magazine*]
UTSB	*United Theological Seminary Bulletin* (Dayton, 1905ff.) [Including: *The Bulletin of the Evangelical School of Theology; Bulletin of the Union Biblical Seminary,* later, *Bonebrake Theological Bulletin*]
UUÅ	*Uppsala Universitets Årsskrift* (Uppsala, 1861-1960)

V

VC	*Virgiliae Christianae: A Review of Early Christian Life and Language* (Amsterdam, 1947ff.)
VDETF	*Deutsche Vierteljahrsschrift für englisch-theologische Forschung und Kritik / herausgegeben von M. Heidenheim* (Leipzig, Zurich, 1861-1865) [Continued as: *Vierteljahrsschrift für deutsch – englisch- theologische Forschung und Kritik...* 1866-1873]
VDI	*Vestnik Drevnei Istoriĭ. Journal of Ancient History* (Moscow, 1946ff.) [English summaries from 1967 on only]
VDR	*Koinonia* (Nashville, 1957-1968) [Continued as: *Vanderbilt Divinity Review,* 1969-1971]
VE	*Vox Evangelica. Biblical and Historical Essays by the Members of the Faculty of the London Bible College* (London, 1962ff.)
Voice	*The Voice* (St. Paul, 1958-1960) [Subtitle varies]
VR	*Vox Reformata* (Geelong, Victoria, Australia, 1962ff.)
VT	*Vetus Testamentum* (Leiden, 1951ff.)

VTS *Vetus Testamentum, Supplements* (Leiden, 1953ff.)

W

Way *The Way. A Quarterly Review of Christian Spirituality* (London, 1961ff.)
WBHDN *The Wittenberg Bulletin (Hamma Digest Number)* (Springfield, OH; 1903ff.) [Volumes 40-60 (1943-1963) only contain *Hamma Digest Numbers*]
WesTJ *Wesleyan Theological Journal. Bulletin of the Wesleyan Theological Society* (Lakeville, IN; 1966ff.)
WLQ *Wisconsin Lutheran Quarterly* (Wauwatosa, WI; Milwaukee;1904ff.) [Also entitled: *Theologische Quartalschrift*]
WO *Die Welt des Orients . Wissenschaftliche Beiträge zur Kunde des Morgenlandes* (Göttingen, 1947ff.)
Word *Word: Journal of the Linguistic Circle of New York* (New York, 1945ff.)
WR *The Westminster Review* (London, New York, 1824-1914)
WSQ *Wartburg Seminary Quarterly* (Dubuque, IA; 1937-1960) [Volumes 1-9, #1 as: *Quarterly of the Wartburg Seminary Association*]
WSR *Wesleyan Studies in Religion* (Buckhannon,WV; 1960-1970) [Volumes 53-62 only*[sic]*]
WTJ *Westminster Theological Journal* (Philadelphia, 1938ff.)
WW *Western Watch* (Pittsburgh, 1950-1959) [Superseded by: *Pittsburgh Perspective*]
WZKM *Wiener Zeitschrift für die Kunde des Morgenlandes* (Vienna, 1886ff.)

Y

YCCAR *Yearbook of the Central Conference of American Rabbis* (Cincinnati, 1890ff.)
YCS *Yale Classical Studies* (New Haven, 1928ff.)
YDQ *Yale Divinity Quarterly* (New Haven, 1904ff.) [Volumes 30-62 as: *Yale Divinity News,* continued as: *Reflections*]
YR *The Yavneh Review. A Religious Jewish Collegiate Magazine* (New York, 1961ff.) [Volume 2 never published]

Z

Z	*Zygon. Journal of Religion and Science* (Chicago, 1966ff.)
ZA	*Zeitschrift für Assyriologie und verwandte Gebiete* [Volumes 45 on as: *Zeitschrift für Assyriologie und vorderasiatische Archäologie]* (Leipzig, Strassburg, Berlin, 1886ff.)
ZÄS	*Zeitschrift für ägyptische Sprache und Altertumskunde* (Leipzig, Berlin, 1863ff.)
ZAW	*Zeitschrift für die alttestamentliche Wissenschaft* (Giessen, Berlin, 1881ff.)
ZDMG	*Zeitschrift der Deutschen Morgenländischen Gesellschaft* (Leipzig, Wiesbaden, 1847ff.)
ZDPV	*Zeitschrift des Deutschen Palästina-Vereins* (Leipzig, Wiesbaden, 1878ff.) [English articles from Volume 82 on only]
ZfRG	*Zeitschrift für Religions und Geistesgeschichte* (Marburg, Köln, Leiden-Heideberg, 1948ff.)
Zion	*Zion. A Quarterly for Research in Jewish History, New Series* ציון, רבעין לחורתולדוה ישראל (Jerusalem, 1935ff.) [English summaries from Volume 3 on only]
ZK	*Zeitschrift für Keilschriftforschung* (Leipzig, 1884-1885)
ZNW	*Zeitschrift für die neutestamentliche Wissenschaft und die Kunde des Urchristentums (…Kunde der älteren Kirche,* 1921—*)* (Giessen, Berlin, 1900ff.)
ZS	*Zeitschrift für Semitistik und verwandte Gebiete* (Leipzig, 1922-1935)

J

J.B. (the play) **VIII**: 173.
Jaazaniah:
Seal of **III**: 650.
Jaazer: **II**: 290.
Jabal El-Jofeh Al Sharqi:
Iron Age Tomb from, Amman **III**: 559.
Jabal el-Qusur: **II**: 391.
Jabal Nuzah:
Tomb, at Amman **III**: 559.
Jabbok: **I**: *359;* **VI**: 81.
Jabbul, Plain of: **II**: 391.
Jabel ed-Druse: **III**: 412.
Jabesh-Gilead: **II**: *312,* **391**, *498*.
Jabez: **I**: **50**; **VI**: 587.
Jabnea, Jabneh (Jamnia): **II**: 392.
Jabneel: **II**: 283, 284.
Jabneh, *see:* **Great Synagogue**
"Jachin and Boaz": **V**: *71(3), 72(5), 73(3).*
Jackal-God: **V**: 207.
Anubis **III**: 752.
JACKSON, A. V. WILLIAMS: ***Bibliography of*** **I**: 20.
JACKSON, GEORGE: **IV**: 267.
JACOB, EDWARD: **VIII**: 13.
Jacob (Israel): **I**: **50-51**, *58, 223;* **II**: *458, 485;* **III**: 117, 318; **IV**: 369; **VI**: 16, 76*(3),* 77, 415; **VIII**: 222.
Angel and **VI**: 727.
Bahr-Jūsuf and the Prophecy of **VI**: 91.
Blessed by Isaac **IV**: 313.
Blessing of **VIII**: 388.
Blessings of, and Targums of Jonathan ben Uziel and Jerusalem **VI**: 91, 710.
Blessings of, in Syriac and Rabbinic Exegesis **IV**: 321; **VI**: 716, 724.
Career of **IV**: 315.
Cattle of, and Genetics **IV**: 320.
Death of, and Relic Worship **VI**: 91.
Deception of his Father **IV**: 317.
Embalming of, Illustrated from Herodotus **VI**: 94.
Esau and **IV**: 317.
Flight, Journey of **IV**: 313*(2),* 317.
"God of Jacob" in the Psalms **IV**: 317.
Historicity of **I**: 50, 475.
Hosea and **IV**: 430; **VI**: 371, 372*(3).*
Jabbok, Wrestling of, at **VI**: 81, 82*(2).*
Laban and, in Light of the Nuzi Tablets **VI**: 79.
Laban, Complaint Against, by **VI**: 80.
Laban's Reception of **IV**: 319.
Last Words of **VI**: 91.
Mandrakes and **VI**: 79.
Marriages of and Ancient Near Eastern Customs **I**: 51.
Masi and **V**: 143.
Messianic Prophecy of **VI**: 92, 93.
Name **IV**: 219; **V**: 299, 507*(2),* 508*(2);* **VII**: 176.
Name, Original, of **V**: 302.
Peniel / Penuel at **IV**: 317, 318; **VI**: 81, 82.
Prophecy of **VI**: 91, 92, 93.
Prophecy of, and the Bahr-Jūsuf **VI**: 91.
Route from Haran to Shechem **II**: 288.
Testament of (Gen. 49) **VI**: 91.
"Wrestling Jacob", Poem by Charles Wesley **VIII**: 365.
Jacob's Well: **I**: 357, 359*(4),* 361, 362; **II**: 308, **392**.
JACOTIN, PIERRE: **II**: 258.

Jael:	**I**: *38, 47,* **51**; **IV**: 367*(3)*, 368; **VI**: 179*(2)*, 182*(3)*, 616.
Ethics and	**VIII**: 223*(2)*.
Jaffa:	**I**: *176, 313, 352, 451;* **II**: 301, 302, 441; **III**: *723;* **VI**: *132*.
Canaanite Tombs near	**III**: 545.
Meoteorological Observations at	**II**: 242.
Rainfall at	**II**: 241, 242*(3)*.
Jah, *see also:* **Jehovah, Yahweh**	**VIII**: 107, **§987, 112-120**.
Jahu:	**VIII**: 118, 123.
Jahwist, *see:* **JEDP**	
Jahzah, Jahaz:	**II**: 290.
Jair:	**II**: 383; **IV**: 228.
Jambres:	**IV**: 324.
Jamdat Nasr:	**III**: *635, 636, 638, 639*.
Jami'a Abu Nejeim:	**II**: 284.
Jamnia, *see also:* **Jabneh:**	**II**: 392, 393.
Jamnia, Council of:	**I**: 175; **IV**: **§293, 208**.
Rise of Normative Judaism and	**V**: 18*(2)*.
Jamnia Period:	**I**: 175.
Janiah, Janieh (Jânîyeh):	**III**: 445.
Greek Inscription at	**VII**: 316, 317.
Jannes:	**IV**: 324.
Janoah:	**II**: 284; **VI**: 398.
Janoah at Hunin:	**II**: 287.
Janua:	**II**: 284.
Janus:	
Shrine of, at the Forum	**III**: 513; **V**: 254.
Janus Geminus:	
Shrine of, in Rome	**V**: 270.
Japan:	
Assyriology in	**III**: 775.
Bible as Material for Religious Education in	**VIII**: 401.
Near Eastern Studies in	**III**: 451.
Tenno-Sama, or Mikoshi; Ark-Shrines of	**V**: 139.
Japhet(h):	**I**: **51**, *80(2)*, 326; **IV**: 310.
Name	**V**: 292.
Jar(s):	**III**: 605.
Alabaster, with name of Nebuchadnezzer	**III**: 604.
Burial, *see:* ***Burial Jars***	
Canaanite	**III**: 637, 773.
Canopic	**I**: 371.
Corinthian	**III**: 619.
Egyptian, Predynastic	**III**: 610.
Ghassul, Jar-Incision	**III**: 631.
Hittite, with animal figures	**III**: 589.
Inscribed, from Azor	**III**: 590.
Inscribed, from Bat-Yam	**III**: 633.
Jar-Incision from Ghassul	**III**: 631.
Megiddo, Inscribed, from	**III**: 613.
Moabite	**VII**: 111.
Moabite, with Translation	**III**: 601.
Montet	**I**: 336.
Oil, of Sicily	**III**: 571.
Predynastic, Funerary Designs on	**III**: 710.
Provision, of the Time of Asosis	**III**: 590.
Rhodian	**III**: 601.
Stirrup, Aegean, Coarse Ware	**III**: 630.
Stirrup, Inscribed, from Thebes	**III**: 591*(2)*.
Syro-Palestinian, from Vounous, Cyprus	**III**: 618.
Wine, First Dynasty	**III**: 590.
Jar Handles, *see also specific locations,* i.e., Gibeon	**III**: **§215, 661-666**.
El-Jib, Inscribed, from	**III**: 666.
Gezer, Inscribed, from	**III**: 604, 663*(4)*.
Gibeon, Inscribed, from	**III**: 665; **VII**: 95, 96; **IX**: cxxvi.
Hebrew Inscribed	**VII**: 90.
Hyksos Scarab, from Bethel	**III**: 665.

Inscribed, of Hebron, found at Tell Zakariya	**III**: 662, 663; **VII**: 90.
Jaffa, from	**III**: 665.
Khirbet Yarmuk, Stamped, from	**III**: 666.
Palestine, Inscribed, from	**III**: 662*(2)*.
Phoenician Inscription on	**VII**: 114.
Ptolemaic, from Judah	**III**: 666.
Rhodian, from Tell Sandahannah	**III**: 663*(3)*.
Royal Israelite	**III**: 662.
Spectrographic Investigation	**II**: 219; **III**: 666.
Tell Judeida, Stamped, from	**III**: 665.
Winged figures on	**III**: 662, 663, 664.
Jar Stamps:	**III**: **§215**, **661-666**; **IX**: **§215**, **cxxv-cxxvi**.
Eliakim, Steward of Joiachin	**III**: 664.
Hebrew, from Ramat Raḥel	**III**: 666.
Impressions on Vase Handles from the Foot of the Temple Wall	**III**: 661.
Lachish, from	**III**: *652*, 665.
"Le-Melekh" Inscriptions	**III**: 665.
'Royal', of Judah	**II**: 219.
Tell Ed-Duweir, from	**III**: 665.
JARCHI, SOLOMON:	
Commentary on Isaiah 52:13-Chapter 53	**VI**: 306.
Jareb:	**II**: **54**,*78*, *79(3)*, *84*, *102 (4)*, *183(3)*, *184*, *191(4)*; **IV**: 181; **VI**: 213; **VII**: 159.
Great King	**IV**: 220.
Hosea, in	**IV**: 427; **VI**: 367, 369.
Jarmo:	**I**: *255*, *286*; **III**: **129**, *159*.
Jasher, Book of:	**IV**: 177, **§284**, **178**.
First Kings 8 (LXX) and	**VI**: 223.
Jason:	**III**: *704;* **V**: 254.
Lysippean, Date of	**III**: 570.
Tomb of	**III**: 560.
Jason of Pherae:	**VII**: 327.
Jasper:	**I**: 285.
JASTROW, JR., MORRIS:	**V**: 293.
Bibliography of	**I**: 20.
Life and Contributions of	**I**: 23, 24*(2)*.
Talmudic Dictionary	**VI**: 699.
Jauf:	
Aramaic Inscription from	**VII**: 125.
Jauhari, al-:	**IX**: *cxliii*.
The Jaulân:	**II**: 393; **III**: 130.
Jâ'uni:	**II**: 367.
Javan:	**I**: 51; **III**: **130**; **VI**: 54*(2)*.
Javelin:	**I**: 313; **V**: 567.
Goliath's	**I**: 317; **IV**: 377.
"Sigynna", or Cypriot	**I**: 312; **III**: *540*, 681.
Jazer, Jaazer:	**II**: 290*(2)*, **393**.
Jearim, Mount:	**II**: 284.
Jebail:	
Marble Fragment from	**III**: 563*(2)*.
Jebeil:	
Pottery, Early, from	**III**: 608.
Jebel Ahmar:	**I**: *280*, *290*; **III**: *460*, *562*.
Jebel Fureidis:	**II**: 284.
Jebel Ḫallet eṭ-Ṭûri:	
Aramaic Qobān Inscripition from	**VII**: 129.
Jebel Musa:	**III**: 130.
Jebel 'Osha:	**II**: 393.
Jebel Tor'an:	**II**: 393.
Jebel Usdum (Mount Sodom)	**II**: 249; **III**: 445.
Jeble el-Aala:	**III**: 439.
Jebusites:	**IV**: 373.
"JEDP", *see also:* **Documentary Hypothesis**	
Chronology of the Flood in P	**I**: 394.
Date of J and E, Driver on	**IV**: 255.
E and Dream-Theophany	**IV**: 262; **VIII**: 104.

E and J Sources in the Books of Samuel — IV: 250, 373.
Elohist, Date of — IV: 260; VI: 85.
Elohist, lingistic affinities — IV: 246.
Elohist Narrative in Exodus 3:1-15 — IV: 258; VI: 99.
Elohistic Theories — IV: 246.
Feast of Unleveaned Bread in — I: 250; IV: 260.
Genesis and — IV: 322.
J Code, Final Redaction — IV: 261.
J Decalogue, So-called — IV: 255.
J Narrative in the Former Prophets — IV: 358.
J of Gen-Num, Nationalist and Humanist Sections — IV: 261.
Jahwist (Yahwist) — I: *151, 152;* IV: 257, 251, 261, 262.
Jahwist, (Yahwist) Kerygma of — IV: 262.
JE in the Middle Books of the Pentateuch — VI: 97, 103, 105, 109.
JE, Origin of — IV: 261, 329.
Jehovistic Theories — IV: 246.
Kerygma of the Yahwist — IV: 262.
Laws of J, E, and D — I: 250; IV: 260.
Passover in — I: 250; IV: 260.
Primeval History in JE — IV: 260*(2)*.
Prophetic Narratives, J and E — VIII: 241.
בְּרִית in JE — I: 516.
Yahwist Corpus — VI: 212.

Jef Ajla: — III: 130.
Jehanah: — II: 394; VI: 591.
Jehoahaz: — VI: 230, 231.
Jehoezer: — I: 51.
Jehoiachin (Jeoiakin) — I: **92**, 167; III: *651;* IV: *219*.
Jehoiakim: — I: 91; II: 186.
Beginning of the Reign of — IV: 414.
Enigma in the Chronology of the reign of — VI: 568.
Fourth Year of — IV: 414.
Jeremiah's Labor Under — IV: 410*(2)*.
Reign of — VIII: 390.
Third Year of, and Daniel — IV: 528.

Jehoram: — I: 92; VI: 592.
Jehoshaphat: — I: *86*, **92**, *312*.
Jehovah, *see also:* **Yahweh** — VI: 26, 292; VIII: 55, **§987, 112-120**.
Abrahamic Age, in — VIII: 115.
Advent of — VIII: 237.
Ark of the Covenant as Throne of(?) — V: 54.
China, Supreme Object of Worship in, Was it(?) — V: 18.
Christ is — VIII: 137*(2)*.
Christ, Scriptural Identification with — VIII: 116, 125, 127.
"Day of," *see:* ***"Day of the Lord"***
Descriptive of the Divine Character — VIII: 115.
Esther, Name of, in — IV: 519; VIII: 114.
Exodus, Book of, as Proof of Existence and Character of — IV: 326; VIII: 116.
Feasts of — V: 84, 85, 88, 89*(2)*.
Fetish Stone(?) — VIII: 114.
Genesis, in — IV: 264*(2);* VIII: 111, 113*(2)*.
God of Israel, in Amos — IV: 433.
God of Redemption — VIII: 57.
Jesus Christ is — VIII: 118*(2)*.
Kingship of — VIII: 114.
Meaning of — VIII: 115, 117, 118.
Memorial Name, as — VIII: 113*(3)*.
Name of, on Seals — III: 644; VIII: 115.
National Deity in Preprophetic Times(?) — VIII: 115.
Origin, Hypothesis of the Egyptian or Indian — VIII: 113.
Origin of the Name/Word — VIII: 113*(2)*, 114.
Patriarchs, Name Known to(?) — VIII: 116, 117.

Pentateuch in **IV**: 229; **VIII**: 111, 116.
Pronunciation of the Sacred Name **VIII**: 115.
Septuagint Translation of **VIII**: 113.
Translating, in the OT **VIII**: 118.
Universal God, or Only a National God **VIII**: 59.
Jehovah Jireh: **VIII**: 124.
"Jehovah of Hosts": **VIII**: 107*(2)*, 114*(2)*.
Jehovah (YHWH) *Tsidhkēnu*: **VIII**: 125.
Jehovah-Jesus: **VI**: 267.
Jehu: **I**: **92**, *94*.
Israel and Judah during the Dynasty of **VIII**: 389.
Jehud: **II**: 305.
"Jehweh":
Canaanite(?) **V**: 190.
Jelemie (Jelemiye): **II**: 303, 342, 394, 428.
JELLINEK, ADOLPH: **VIII**: 374.
Jemdet Nasar:
Human Remains from **III**: 357.
Painted Pottery from **III**: 614.
Sumerian Texts from **VII**: 270.
Jemmeh, Tell: **II**: 299, 394, **496**.
Jemrurah: **II**: 284.
JENSEN, P.:
Kosamologie **VII**: 224, 265.
Jephthah: **I**: 52; **VI**: 2, 188.
Adoption of **VI**: 187.
Daughter of **VI**: 186*(2)*, 187; **VIII**: 359.
Daughter of, in Honolulu **IV**: 372.
Disinheritance of, in the Light of the Lipit-Ishtar Code **IV**: 372; **VII**: 268.
Iphigenia, Sacrifice of, and **IV**: 372.
Jephthah's Vow **IV**: **§333**, **371-372**; **VI**: 186, 187*(6)*.
Jerome's Interpretation of **IV**: 372.
Vow (a poem) **VIII**: 359.
Jerābees: **III**: 5.
Jerabis:
Inscribed Stones from in Hittite **VII**: 300, 309, 311.
Jerāblus: **III**: 5, *721*.
Monuments from **VII**: 56.
Jerahmeel Theory: **I**: **§60**, **157-158**; **II**: 451.
Jerahmeelites: **I**: 157; **II**: 129.
Jerash: **II**: 309, 310, 370, **394**, 422; **III**: 423.
Forum at **III**: 484.
Greek Inscripions from **V**: 256; **VII**: 313, 343.
Jewish Architecture at **III**: 470.
Synagogue at **III**: 523.
Theatre at **II**: 394*(2)*.
Jereb, *see:* **Jareb**
Jeremiah Apocryphon: **VI**: 643.
Jeremiah, Book of: **I**: *117, 199, 234, 479;* **II**: *337, 337, 493;* **III**: *651;* **VI**: 6, 243; **VII**: *245;* **VIII**: 239.
Act of 621, and, a Protesting Witness of **IV**: 383, 411.
Almond Rod in **VI**: 321.
Astral-Mythology **II**: 229; **V**: 135.
Authenticity and Authorship of **IV**: **§351**, **416-417**; **V**: 704.
Baruch's Roll **IV**: 412.
Bibliography of **I**: **§18**, **12**.
Charchemish and **IV**: 416.
Consolation **IV**: 416.
Covenant and **IV**: 414, 415; **VI**: 336, 338*(3)*.
Date of **IV**: **§351**, **416-417**; **VI**: 321.
"Day of the Lord" **IV**: 414.
Deuteronomistic Book of **VI**: 322.
Deuteronomy and **I**: 117; **IV**: 349, 350*(2)*, 352, 384*(2)*, 411, 412*(2)*, 415.

Deuteronomy, composition of, and Forms of Address in	**IV**: 348, 355.
Deuteronomy, Language of, compared with	**IV**: 347, 410.
Diplomatic Term (עֶבֶד) in	**IV**: 416.
Double Reading in	**VI**: 345.
Double Text of (LXX and MT Compared)	**IV**: 410.
Exegetical Studies on	**VI: §611, 320-344.**
Face of the Pot	**VI**: 321.
Faith, Stamina of	**IV**: 412.
Form Criticism of Chapter 36	**V**: 694.
Georgian Fragments of	**IV**: 45.
Grace and Judgment	**IV**: 413.
Greek Translators or	**IV**: 105, 411.
Growth of the Book	**IV**: 413.
Historical Difficulties in	**IV**: 195.
Ibn Qutaiba, "Citation" in	**VIII**: 369.
Individualism in	**IV**: 390; **VIII**: 191.
Irony in	**IV**: 417; **V**: 704; **VI**: 336.
Judgment, Grace and	**IV**: 413.
Justin Martyr and	**VI**: 328.
Law-Gospel Tension in	**IV**: 415.
Literary Considerations of the Theology of	**VIII**: 17.
Literary Criticism of	**IV: §350, 410-416; IX: §350, cxxxii.**
Mary in	**VI**: 337.
Matthew's References to	**VI**: 320; **VIII**; 285.
Messianic Hope of	**IV**: 413; **V**: 130.
Metaphor in	**VI**: 331, 339.
Nebuchadnezzar and	**II**: *69(2)*; **IV**: 410, 415, 416.
New Testament, Influence on	**VIII**: 276.
North, Doom / Enemy / Peril, from	**IV**: 412, 413*(2)*.
Oarcles Against Nations	**IV**: 415.
Oarcles, Earliest	**IV**: 413.
Peake, Arthur S., on	**IV**: 411.
Poetry of	**IV**: 411, 413, 415; **V**: 687, 703.
Poetry-Pose Problem	**IV**: 414.
Political Context, in	**IV**: 414.
Politics and Prophecy in	**IV**: 415.
Politics in	**I**: 470; **IX**: c.
Polychrome Edition	**IV**: 58.
Preacher's Use of	**VIII**: 374.
Preaching Values in	**VIII**: 377.
Problems of, Structure of, and Their Significance for the Interpreter	**IV**: 413.
Prophecies, Arrangement	**IV**: 414.
Prophecy and Politics in	**IV**: 415.
Prophecy and the Sabbath	**IV**: 412.
Prophecy, Beginning of	**IV**: 415.
Prophecy in	**I**: 470; **IV**: 411.
Prototype and Copies	**IV**: 414.
Pseudo-Jeremiah	**VI**: 326.
Pun in	**VI**: 332*(3)*.
Reform, Failure of	**IV**: 413.
Relevance of	**IV**: 413.
Religion, Essence of, and	**IV**: 411.
Religious Reform and	**IV**: 411.
Sabbath and Prophecy	**IV**: 412.
Second	**IV**: 410.
Seething Cauldron	**VI**: 321.
Sin, Concept of	**VIII**: 17, 184.
Sources of	**IV: §351, 416-417.**
Structure of	**V**: 703.
Structure of, its Problems and Their Significance for the Interpreter	**IV**: 413.
Study Program	**VIII**: 394*(2)*.
Style of	**IV**: 417; **V**: 704.
Suffering, Nature of, in	**IV**: 416; **VIII**: 187.
"Suffering Servant" in Deutero-Isaiah, and	**IV**: 412; **VIII**: 145.
Symbolism of	**VIII**: 309.
Targum to	**IV**: 410; **VI**: 711.
Text of	**VI**: 320*(2)*.
Textual Problems	**VI**: 320*(2)*.
Theology of	**VIII**: 17.

Torah in **IV**: 412*(2)*.
Visions, Opening **IV**: 410.
Vulgate, Gleanings from **VI**: 320.
Wit of **V**: 703.

Jeremiah, Book of, Manuscripts of: **VI**: **§612, 345.**
Gairo Genīzah Parchment **VI**: 345.
Georgian Fragments of **VI**: 345*(2)*.
Khanmeti Palimpsest of **VI**: 345.
Lucian Version **VI**: 345.
Pethion Ibn Ayyûb Al-Sahhâr edition of **VI**: 345.
Polychrome Edition of **VI**: 345.
Workman on the Variations between Hebrew and Greek of **VI**: 345.

Jeremiah, Chapter 2:
Authorship of **IV**: 417.

Jeremiah, Chapter 8:
Deuteronomic Gloss in **VI**: 326.
Ugaritic Parallel to **VI**: 327.
Date of **VI**: 321.

Jeremiah Chapter 31:
Authorship of **IV**: 416.

Jeremiah, Person: **I**: *43*, **52-55**, *94, 117, 165, 166(2), 474;* **VIII**: 240.
Absurdity of the Prophet **I**: 55.
Aramaic Saqqârah Papyrus from Time of **VII**: 127.
Biographer of **IV**: 416*(2)*.
Call of **I**: 52, 54, 55*(2)*, 115; **IV**: 410, 411, 413, 417; **V**: 699; **VI**: 147; **IX**: lxxxii.
Character of **IV**: 416.
Confession of **VI**: 330*(2)*.
Confessions of **IV**: 413.
Confessions of, and the Meaning of Prayer **IV**: 412.
Contemporaries, and **IV**: 411.
Cult and **IV**: 414*(2)*; **V**: 108.
Decalogue in the Preaching of **IV**: 412; **VI**: 159.
Despair of **IV**: 414.
Development of Thought **I**: 52.
Dichotomy of **IV**: 415.
Egypt, Flight into **IV**: 410.
Egypt, in **IV**: 415.
Ethical Ideas **VIII**: 231.
Girdle of **VIII**: 358.
God and the World in the Religious Faith of **I**: 53.
God, Nature of, According to **IV**: 416; **VIII**: 73.
Human Affliction and **I**: 55.
Individual Religion, Concept of **IV**: 414; **VIII**: 192.
Individualism Developed by **I**: *43*, 52.
Inner Life of **I**: 52.
Jehoiakim, Labors under **IV**: 410*(2)*.
Jerusalem and **II**: 411.
Jerusalem, Fall of, and **I**: 55; **II**: 421; **IV**: 410, 411, 416.
Jesus, and **I**: 53*(2)*.
Josiah and **I**: 53, 54; **IV**: 384, 413.
Judah, Fall of, and **I**: 52; **IV**: 410.
Kierkegaard and **I**: 54; **IV**: 413.
Kings of Judah, Last Two, and **IV**: 413.
Linen Girdle of **IV**: 410.
Message and Character of **IV**: 416.
Message of **I**: 52*(2)*, 53.
Mind of the Prophet **IV**: 420*[citation misplaced]*
Ministry of **I**: 53.
Morality and **IV**: 414; **V**: 38.
Moses and **IV**: 415*(2)*.
Mysticism of **I**: 54.
Nation, State of, on **IV**: 412.
Orator, as **IV**: 413.
Passion of **IV**: 414.
Pathos of the Life of **I**: 53.
Patriot as **I**: 53.
Paul and **I**: 54.
Personal Goodness **I**: 52; **V**: 8.
Personality of **I**: 54, 55.
Pessimist(?) **IV**: 411.

Political Context, in **I**: 55.
Politics of **I**: *48*, 52, 460.
Prayer in the Life of **I**: 54; **VIII**: 203.
Prayer, Meaning of, and the Confessions of **IV**: 412; **VIII**: 203.
Prayer of **I**: 55.
Priest, as(?) **I**: 53.
Prophecies, Early, of, in Their Setting **IV**: 414.
Prophecy, Beginning of **IV**: 415.
Prophetic Activity, Setting of **IV**: 415.
Prophets and **IV**: 415.
Reappeance of **IV**: 414.
Religion of **I**: 54.
Religion of Israel, Evolution of, and **V**: 14.
Religious Consciousness of **IV**: 412.
Roll, Burning of **IV**: 410.
Samuel and **IV**: 415.
Sanctified in the Womb(?) **I**: 53.
Self-Understanding of, Background of **IV**: 415.
Sermons, Prose, of Date of **IV**: 413, 416.
Siege, in the **VI**: 336, 339, 340.
Social Reform, and **IV**: 414; **VIII**: 228; **IX**: lxxxv.
Solidarity Developed by **I**: *43*, 52.
Statesman, as **I**: 53.
Suffering as Divine Discipline in **VIII**: 186.
Symbolism of **IV**: 416.
Temperment of **I**: 52.
Temple Address (Sermons) of **IV**: 412; **VI**: 325*(2)*, 335.
Trial of **VI**: 335.
Vision of Cosmic Destruction **IV**: 415.
War and **IV**: 412; **VIII**: 234.
"Weeping Prophet" a Pessimist? **IV**: 411.
"Word of the Lord" and **I**: 53; **VIII**: 50; **IX**: cxxxii.
World of **IV**: 414.

Jeremy, Epistle of / Letter of Jeremiah
Exegetical Studies on **VI**: **§719, 639**.
Literary Criticism of **VI**: **§701, 625**.
Palestinian Syriac Texts of **VI**: 608.
Textual Criticism of **VI**: **§683, 608**.

Jericho: **I**: *151, 256,* 341, *376;* **II**: 284, 292, 310, *316, 362,* **395-400**, 422, 485; **III**: 163, 423*(2), 431,* 447, *772;* **IV**: 217, 363; **VI**: 167; **VII**: *149, 176;* **IX**: cxv, cxlvii.
Aqhat and **IX**: cxlix.
Bones, Radioactivity of, from **II**: 221.
Capture / Fall of **I**: 145; **IV**: 362*(3)*, 363*(4)*.
Capture / Fall of, Archaeology and **IV**: 363.
Curse by Joshua on **VI**: 168, 227*(2)*, 232; **VIII**: 248; **IX**: cxlvii.
Elisha's Miracle at **VI**: 168, 227*(2)*, 232; **VIII**: 248.
Exodus, Date of, and **IV**: 338, 339*(6)*.
Fall of, Imaginary Story **VIII**: 367.
Goats from early **III**: 375.
Hiel, Punishment of the Rebuilder of **VI**: 227.
Moabite Occupation of **II**: 396; **IV**: 220.
Neolitic Portait Skulls from **III**: 351.
New (Tulul Abu el-'Alayiq) **III**: *431*.
Plains of **II**: 306.
Pottery from in the Hunterian Museum **III**: 610.
Radiocarbon Date from **II**: 217.
Rebuilding of, Qumran Reference **VIII**: 471.
Rose of **VI**: 635.

Scrolls in the Neighborhood of **VIII**: 429.
Seal Impression from and Treasurers of the Second Temple **III**: 655; **V**: 78.
Siege of, and the Strategy of the Exodus **IV**: 335.
Tomb, Excavated, from **III**: 555.
Tombs, Bronze Age, of **III**: 555.
Topographical List, in, of Ramesses II **II**: 270.
Walls of **II**: 395.
Waters at, Radioactivity of **II**: 222; **IX**: cxlvii.

Jericho Pentateuch: **IV**: 10.

Jerishe, Tell: **II**: 298.
Bronze Age Tomb at **III**: 551.

Jeroboam: **I**: *99;* **II**: *332, 336;* **III**: *656;* **IV**: 330; **VI**: 225, 237.
Biographical Studies **I**: 93.
Feast / Festival of **I**: 93, 397; **IV**: 436, *439;* **VI**: 225.
Golden Calves of **V**: 108.
Home of **II**: 292; **III**: 419.
Israel and Judah during the Dynasty of **VIII**: 389.
Rabbinic Interpretations of **VI**: 716.
Rise and Decline of **VI**: 376.
Samaritan Calendar and **I**: 93, 397.
Schism, of, Biblical Authors on **IV**: 382.
Septuagint's Rival Version of **IV**: 383.

Jeroboam II:
Israel and Judah during the Dynasty of **VIII**: 389.

JEROHAM, SALOMON BEN:
Commentary on Psalms **VI**: 483.
Commentary on Ruth, Did he compose a **IV**: 510; **VI**: 726.

Jerome (Hieronymus) Sophronius Eusebius: **III**: *366;* **IV**: *33,* 40, 42, *115.*
Hebrew in the Time of **V**: 468.
Hebrew, Pronunciation, of, by **V**: 475.
Hebrew Text of **IV**: 12*(3).*
Inerrancy of Scripture, on **VIII**: 50.
Inspiration of the OT, on **VIII**: 46, 50, 299.
Jephthah's Vow Interpreted **IV**: 372.
Jeremiah, on **VI**: 322.
Jews and **VI**: 686.
Life and Contributions of **I**: 24.
Old Testament Student, as **IV**: 40.
Psalms, on **IV**: 475, 477, 480, 482, 488.
Psalter and **IV**: 41*(2),* 42.
Vulgate and **IV**: 40, 41, 42.
Moslem Traditions of **II**: 418.

Jerualem Literary Society: **III**: 415.

Jerubbaal: **IX**: lxxxi*(2).*

Jerusalem: **I**: *119, 146, 154, 162, 165(2), 176, 207, 264, 284, 290 (2), 320, 357, 358, 359, 360(4), 361(5), 362(2), 363, 386, 440, 452, 454, 462;* **II**: *255, 273, 276, 277, 292,* 297, 298, 300, 302, 303*(2),* 304, 305*(2),* 306, 308*(4),* 309, *328,* 350, *351(2), 397,* **400-421**, *500, 501(3);* **III**: *157,* 409, *412, 420(2), 421(2),* 438*(3),* 441, 442, 444, 446, 447*(2), 501, 532, 549, 558, 665;* **IV**: 217, 220, *261(2);* **V**: *12, 26, 30, 49, 45;* **VI**: 2, 91, *209,* 590; **VII**: *291;* **VIII**: *342(2);* **IX**: cxv.

Alexander the Great's conquest of, Influence on Jewish life	**II**: 9.
Alexander the Great's visit to in Josephus	**II**: 9.
Amorite Name	**V**: 508.
Assyrian Tablet from	**VII**: 174.
Athens and / or	**VIII**: 335, 337.
Atmospheric Pressure at	**II**: 240.
Babylonian Capture of, in 597 B.C.	**II**: 418.
Babylonian Chronicle and Capture of in 597 B.C.	**II**: 418.
Bibliography of Excavations	**II**: 416‡.
Birds of	**III**: 369.
Captives of, in the Time of David	**IX**: cxv.
Catastrophe of 485 B.C., Light from Isaiah, on	**II**: 420.
Citadel	**II**: 416*(2)*, 417; **VI**: 209.
Climate of	**II**: 236*(2)*, 237.
Dante, and	**VIII**: 367.
David's Capture of	**VI**: 209*(3)*, 590.
Desolation, Second, of	**II**: *24*.
Destruction of under Titus	**I**: 175*(3)*.
Deuteronomy and the, Cult-Tradition	**IV**: 352.
Deuteronomy and the Priest-Preachers of	**IV**: 355.
Drunken Parent, as	**VI**: 306.
Eastern Hill	**II**: 414*(2)*, 415*(4)*.
EDWARD ROBINSON in	**III**: 427.
Ezekiel's Knowledge of	**IV**: 423.
Ezekiel's Visions of	**IV**: 419.
Ezra's Arrival at, Date of	**I**: 45*(2)*.
Fall of	**IX**: cxv.
Fall of, and Jeremiah	**I**: 55; **II**: 421; **IV**: 415, 416.
Fall of, and Last Kings of Judah	**II**: 421.
Fall of, Guilt and Rites of Purification related to	**II** 421; **III**: 30; **VIII**: 184.
Fortifications in First Century A.D.	**II**: 417.
Gates of, *see:* ***Gates***	
Geological Conditions Influencing the Development of	**II**: 251, 420.
Greek Inscription from Northern Necropolis of	**VII**: 317.
Hall of Reckonings in	**I**: 464; **II**: 416.
Hebrew Ostracon from	**VII**: 124.
Isaiah and the Siege of	**IV**: 395.
Isaiah, on	**IV**: 394.
Israel, in Historic Conscienceness of	**II**: 418.
Jeremiah and	**II**: 411.
Jeremiah and the fall of	**I**: 55; **II**: 421; **IV**: 410, 415, 416.
Jewish Hypogeum near	**III**: 546; **VII**: 92*(2)*.
Joab's Taking of, and Israel's Military History	**IV**: 378.
Latin (Roman) Inscription at	**VII**: 366.
Meteorological Observations at	**II**: 239*(10)*, 240*(5)*, 241*(6)*, 242*(4)*, 243.
Name	**V**: 293, 508.
Nebuchadnezzar and	**II**: 69, 418; **VII**: 240.
New	**VIII**: 254.
Paronomasias on the Name	**V**: 508*(2)*.
Pentateuch, Absence of the Name of, in	**IV**: 259.
Politics in, and B.M. 21,901	**I**: 462; **IV**: 360.
Population of, During Siege of Titus	**II**: 259.
Priest-Preachers of, and Deuteronomy	**IV**: 355.
Quarries, Royal	**II**: 276, 402.
Qumran and	**V**: 26; **VIII**: 416.
Rainfall in	**II**: 239, 244.
Rock Indications at	**II**: 305.
Sennacherib's Siege of	**II**: 89*(6)*, 90, 410*(2)*, 411.
Siege of, and Isaiah	**IV**: 395.
Sieges of	**II**: 414.
Sin of	**IV**: 414.
Solomon's Buildings in	**II**: 412.
"Solomon's Stables"	**III**: 480.

Stone hat T'aim at **II**: 403.
Stones of **II**: 247.
Synagogue of Theodotos at **III**: 523.
Tannaitic Law, in **VI**: 695.
Temperature, Air, at **II**: 240.
Temple, Location of, in **II**: 412.
Temple-Mount at **VI**: 72.
Tomb Chamber in the Syrian Orphanage **III**: 548.
Tomb-Cave, Cypriote Pottery from, near **III**: 612.
Tombs from Period of the Kings of Judah, at **III**: 555.
Topography of **II**: 281, 400, 401*(5)*, 402*(2)*, 403, 406, 410, 412, 413, 420.
Tumuli, Finds in **VI**: 209.
Tumuli, West of, Survey and Excavations **II**: 311.
Valleys of **II**: 412.
Walls of, *see:* ***Walls***
Yahweh and **II**: 413; **VIII**: 116.
Yavneh or **VIII**: 336.
Zion, not Jerusalem **II**: 349*(2)*.

Jerusalem Bible: **IV**: *64(7)*.
Biblical Translation and the Church **IV**: 110.
Pentateuchal Criticism in **IV**: 329.
Jeshanah: **II**: 284, 421.
Jeshimon: **II**: 409.
Jeshua: **II**: 284.
Jeshua ben Galgolah:
Letters to **VIII**: 472, 473.
Jeshurun: **III**: 595.
Jesse:
Nahash and **IV**: 373.
Shoot of **VI**: 272.
Jesus (Christ): **I**: *53(2), 64, 72, 475;* **II**: *187;* **IV**: 84; **VI**: 26; **VIII**: 140.
Angel of the Lord, and **VIII**: 143.
Apocalyptic Hope and the Teaching of **VIII**: 280; **IX**: cxlix.
Baptism of, in Mark, and Isaiah 63 **VI**: 315.
Bible, Attitude Toward **VIII**: 281, 292.
Bible of **VIII**: 279, 282.
"Brick, Putting up a", and **IX**: cxli, cl*(2)*.
Christian (Early) Interpretation of, as Messiah **VIII**: 140.
Cleansing of the Temple and Zechariah 14:21 **VIII**: 286.
Culture, Relation to **VIII**: 280.
Deutero-Isaiah and **VIII**: 279.
Deutero-Isaiah and the Forcefullness of **IV**: 400; **VIII**: 279.
Err, Could He(?) **VI**: 516.
Ethical Teachings of, in Relation the Old Testament **VIII**: 220, 281.
Ethical Teachings of, in Relation to the Pharisees and the Old Testament **V**: 98; **VIII**: 220.
Exodus and, in Jude **VIII**: 295.
Extra-Canonical Literature, Relation to **VIII**: 280.
Ezekiel and **I**: 43; **VIII**: 282.
Forcefullness of, and Deutero-Isaiah **IV**: 400; **VIII**: 279.
God of the OT and **VIII**: 281.
Habakkuk Pesher, in **VIII**: 456.
Hillel and **VI**: 685*(2)*.
History, Conception of, by the Prophets and **IV**: 357.
Hosea, Use of, by **IV**: 428; **VIII**: 279.
Isaiah 53, Referred to, in **VI**: 309.
Jewish Apocalypse in the Time of **V**: 123, 124.
Jewish Eschatology and the Teaching of **VIII**: 250.
Jewish Thought about **VIII**: 332.
Job, in **IV**: 459.
Jonah, Reference / Testimony of, to **IV**: 440; **VIII**: 279*(2)*.

Josephus' Testimony of **VI**: *679(2)*.
Joshua and **V**: 293.
Judaism, Types of, in Time of **V**: 11.
Law and **VIII**: 280, 282*(2)*.
Messiah and the Christ of History **V**: 125.
Messiahship of **V**: 127; **VIII**: 138.
Messianic Conciousness **VIII**: 140, 141.
Messianic Hope, Transformation of, by **V**: 127.
Messianic Views of Christ's Contemporaries **V**: 126.
Mosaic Age, Attitude towards **VIII**: 278.
Old Testament and/in **IV**: 162, 169; **VIII**: 126, 282.
Old Testament Citations of **VIII**: 271.
OT Prophecy, Subject of(?) **VIII**: 125, 238.
Parables of, and Jubilees **VIII**: 280.
Parables of, Sources and Parallels **VIII**: 280.
Priesthood of, and OT Preisthood, and the Book of Hebrews **V**: 42.
Proverbs, Use of, by **IV**: 499; **VIII**: 278.
Psalm 22 as used by **VI**: 468.
Psalms, as Used by **VIII**: 281.
Qumran and **VIII**: 427.
Reclaiming, by the Jews, **VIII**: 127.
Reclaiming, Wolfson, on **VIII**: 127.
Religion of Israel, Evolution of, to **V**: 14.
Resurrection of, OT Passages used by NT as Prophetic of **VIII**: 298.
Sacrifice of Christ, and Jewish Sacrifices **V**: 56, 57.
Sadducees and **V**: 100.
Sayings of, in the DSS **VIII**: 424.
Second Coming of, and the Servant of Isaiah **IV**: 400.
"Suffering Servant" and **VIII**: 147.
Tacitus on **VI**: 680.
Talmud, in **VI**: 700.
Teacher of Righteousness and **VIII**: 421*(2)*, 479, 480.
Teachings of, Old Testament in the **VIII: §1041, 278-283**.
Temptation of, in the Light of Deuteronomy **VIII**: 286.
Testament of Solomon and **VIII**: 281.
Time-Consciousness of **I**: 415.
"Tomb of Jesus" **III**: 354.
Trial of, and Psalm 110 **VI**: 517; **VIII**: 286.
Unity of the Bible and **IX**: cxxx.
Vocabulary of, and Daniel 7 **VI**: 574.
Wisdom and, in NT **V**: 118.
Zealots, and Program of **V**: 102.

Jethlah: **II**: 284.
Jethro: **IV**: 261, 329; **VI**: 110.
Jett: **II**: *215*, 308; **III**: *621*.
JEUNE, CHAMPOLLION LE: **V**: 362.
Jew: **V**: 508*(3)*.
First Greeek **VII**: 327.
God's Witness to the World **VIII**: 213.
Isolation of the **VIII**: 210.
Palestine and the **VIII**: 210.
Jewelry, *see also:* **Gems and Minerals** **I: §95, 280-284**; **III**: **§209, 591-594**, 755; **IV**: 219; **IX: §95, xci; §209: cxxv**.
Etruscan **III**: 593.
Eye-stone of Esarhaddon's Queen **VII**: 178; **IX**: cxxv.
Jewels:
Borrowing of, by the Israelites from the Egyptians **IV**: 324; **VIII**: 230.
Jewess: **V**: 508.
Jewish: **V**: 508.
Jewish Arabic Studies: **V**: 144.

Raja Doctrine V: 144.
Shittic Elements in Jewish Sectarianism V: 144*(2)*, 145.
Jewish-Christian Dialogue: IV: 158.
"Jewish Church": V: 6.
History of V: 7.
Old Testament in IV: 119*(3)*.
Jewish Encyclopedia: VIII: 397.
Jewish Exegesis:
Baptism and I: 369.
Christian and IV: 94.
English Bible and IV: 110.
Medieval IV: 97, 98.
Nestorian, and, on Genesis, compared IV: 97; VI: 16, 723.
"Plain" Meaning in IV: 98.
Jewish Exiles:
Babylon in Time of III: 41*(2)*.
Judah and Israel in VIII: 390.
Nabonidus, and II: 65.
Return of, in Ezra VI: 579.
Return of, in Nehemiah VI: 585.
Return under Cyrus II IV: 543.
Seals of the III: 658, 659.
Jewish History:
Geniza, Importance for VII: 107.
Jewish Inscriptions: III: *645*.
Jewish Museum (London):
Catalogue of Coins in I: 458.
Jewish Philosophy, *see:* **"Hebrew" Philosophy**
Jewish Religion, *see also:* **Israelite Religion** III: *594*.
Coins, in Light of Their I: 451; V: 24.
Establishment of, and the Political Condition of Egypt I: 488; VII: 81.
Jewish Chruch V: 6.
Jonah and IV: 441.
Modern Palestine, in I: 387.
Orthodoxy V: 6*(2)*.
Jewish-Christian Dialogue: VIII: **§1057, 328-**331‡-338‡-**339**.
Messianic Prophecy and VIII: 329.
Philosemitism in the Baroque Period VIII: 336.
Jewry: V: 508*(2)*.
Jews: I: *120,* 143, 145, 146‡, 322, *372,* 384; II: *115, 166;* VIII: 212, 333*(2)*, 334*(3)*.
Alexander the Great's Conquest of Jerusalem, Influence on Jewish Life II: 9.
Ancient World, Jewish Problem in the VIII: 333.
Antiquity of I: 139.
Antrhopology of III: 344.
Archaeology and the III: 428.
Archaeology, Contribution to the Knowledge of IV: 151.
Art, Fine, Among III: 694.
Astrology and II: 230.
Bible and VIII: 329.
Bokhara, Colony of at Jerusalem II: 407.
China, in I: 137, 174.
Christian, Early Attitudes Toward V: 23.
Christian Faith and VIII: 334.
Church, and VIII: 332, 334.
Church Fathers, in I: 140*(3)*; VI: 719.
Controvresy with, Old Testament in VIII: 336.
Conversion of VIII: 340.
Creed of a Believing V: 6.
Cromwell, Oliver, and VIII: 326.
Damian, Peter, Attitude Toward VIII: 338.
Damian, St. Peter, Attitude Toward IV: 158.
Economic Conditions of I: 143.
Egypt, in, Greek Inscription Conerning VII: 335.
Egypt, Roman and I: 175, 177*(2)*.

Eschatology and / of	**VIII**: 249*(2)*.
Fasts, among Modern	**I**: 385.
Feasts, among Modern	**I**: 385.
Future Condition of, and the Spirit of Prophecy	**VIII**: 236.
Future of	**VIII**: 340.
Gentiles, Attitude of, Towards Non-Jews	**I**: 174, *186;* **VIII**: 233.
Gods of the, at Elephantine	**V**: 23.
Greek Names among	**V**: 302.
Halachic-Historic Study	**VIII**: 337.
History of	**I**: 137*(6),* 138, 139, 141, 142*(2),* 143*(3),* 144*(3),* 145, 146, 147*(3)*.
History of, in connection with the Laws of Moses	**I**: 472.
Influence on the History of Mankind	**VIII**: 328.
Inventory of, at the Beginning of the Christian Era	**V**: 21.
Jerome and	**VI**: 686.
K'ai-Feng	**IV**: *236*.
Karl Barth and	**VIII**: 335.
Languages, Non-Hebrew, Used by the	**V**: 278.
Mind Realtive to the Scriptures	**VIII**: 328*(2)*.
Mirror of Our Sins	**VIII**: 181.
Modern Customs of	**I**: 384.
Mourning rites of	**I**: 375.
Names of	**V**: 302.
Names of, in Rome	**V**: 299.
Old Testament and	**IV**: 175; **VIII**: 332*(2)*.
Oriental	**I**: 139.
OT in Thought and Life	**I**: 392.
Palestine, Modern, in	**I**: 385.
Persian, Books and Rituals	**I**: 384.
Political Status of	**I**: 143.
Proverbs of Spanish	**I**: 383.
Race, as	**VIII**: 333.
Race, Nation, or Religion(?)	**V**: 21; **VIII**: 332.
Raical Characteristics of	**III**: 339*(2)*.
Religion of	**V**: 6.
Religion of the, at Elephantine	**V**: 30.
Restoration of	**VIII**: 340*(2),* 341, 343, 347.
Return of, to Palestine	**VIII**: 340*(2),* 342.
Revolt of at Cyrene	**I**: 356.
Roman Empire and	**I**: 178*(2)*.
Roman Law and	**I**: 506.
Samaritans and, in the Persion Period	**I**: 336.
Songs of Modern Oriental	**I**: 385.
Spartans and	**I**: 332.
Survival of, and the World Crisis	**VIII**: 333.
Toynbee, Arnold, and	**VIII**: 336.
Jezebel:	**I**: 93; **IV**: 180; **VI**: 231.
'Anat and	**V**: 197.
Elijah and	**IV**: 381.
Seal of	**III**: 658.
Table of	**III**: 462, 499.
Jezer, Tell:	**II**: 306.
Jezireh:	**III**: 130.
Jezreel:	**I**: *85, 95;* **II**: 284, **421**.
Jezreel, Plain of:	**II**: 360.
Jihād:	**V**: 145.
Jiphtah-el at W. el Melek	**II**: 287.
Jirbās:	**III**: 5.
Jisr Banāt Ya'qūb:	**II**: 296.
Joab:	**II**: *499;* **IV**: *377;* **VI**: 214.
Jerusalem Taken by, Israel's Military History an Unwritten Chapter in	**IV**: 378.
Joash:	**I**: **93-94**; **II**: 472; **VI**: *376,* 592; **VII**: 204.
Job, Book of:	**I**:*73, 120;* **IV**: 456; **V**: 116; **VI**: 9, 596.
Abraham as Author of	**IV**: 472*(2)*.

Abraham's Trial and	**I**: 31; **IV**: 469; **VIII**: 187.
Accent Systems of	**V**: 691.
Additions to, Date of	**IV**: 472.
Alienation, Sense of, in	**IV**: 469.
Allegory(?)	**IV**: 466.
Alphabetic Psalms and	**IV**: 456.
Arabic Original(?)	**IV**: 472.
Argument of	**IV**: 458.
Art-Composition, as	**IV**: 458.
Astronomy in	**II**: 226, 233*(2)*; **IV**: 458; **VI**: 426*(3)*, 439*(2)*.
Authenticity, Authorship, of	**IV**: **§382, 471-472**; **VI**: 435, 436.
Babylonian Dialogue on Theodicy and	**IV**: 466; **VII**: 263.
Babylonian Literary Fragment and	**VII**: 261.
Babylonian Parallel to (Tabi-utul-Bel)	**IV**: 461, 462, 471.
Bibliography	**I**: **§23, 13**.
"Book of the Dead" and	**VII**: 53.
Broadway, on	**VIII**: 353.
Budde, Karl, on	**IV**: 460.
Canon of Ecclesiasticus, Reference to	**IV**: 460; **VI**: 638.
Canon of OT, and	**IV**: 201.
Carteret P. Carey's, Translation of	**IV**: 457.
Christ in	**IV**: 459.
Christian Element in	**IX**: cxxxiii.
Commentary, Old, on	**VI**: 726.
Composition of	**IV**: 465.
Conculsion, Original, to	**IV**: 464.
Cosmology, Muslim, and	**IV**: 460.
Criticism of	**IV**: 461.
Cultic שגגה, Influence on	**V**: 455.
Curse, Misdirected, in	**VI**: 422.
Date of	**IV**: 457, 465, **§382, 471-472**.
David in	**I**: 89; **IV**: 462.
Dialgoue of, Poetic Structure in the	**V**: 706.
Dialogue of, Progress of Thought in	**VIII**: 63.
Difficulties of	**IV**: 465.
Divine Names in	**IV**: 458; **VIII**: 19, 107.
Doctrinal Suggestions on	**IV**: 459.
Doctrine of	**IV**: 457, 471.
Drama of	**IV**: 461, 465*(2)*.
Dramatic Character of	**IV**: 460.
Driver, S. R., and Gray, G. B., Marginal Notes	**IV**: 465.
Early Persian Period and	**IV**: 464.
Egyptological Interpreation of	**IV**: 463.
Elihu Speeches in	**IV**: 462, 465.
Eliphaz, Double Entendre in the First Speech of	**IV**: 464.
Eliphaz, Vision of, in	**VI**: 423.
Emendation in the Text of	**VI**: 420.
Epic Substratum in the Prose of	**IV**: 468.
Epilogue to	**VI**: 440*(2)*.
Eschatology of	**VIII**: 249.
Ethical Teaching of, Concerning Conduct of God Toward Man	**IV**: 459; **VIII**: 220.
Evil, Problem of, and	**IV**: 468; **VIII**: 182.
Exegetical Studies on	**VI**: **§643, 419-441**.
Faust and	**IV**: 460*(2)*; **VIII**: 361.
Fiction, as	**IV**: 460.
Figurative Element in	**IV**: 459.
Future Life According to the Greek Translator of	**VIII**: 19.
Future Life in	**VIII**: 19.
Future State and	**IV**: 462; **VIII**: 261, 262.
Garden, Charles, on	**V**: 456.
Grammar of	**IV**: 460.
Greek Text of, Corruptions in	**VI**: 420.
Greek Translator of, Theological Approach	**IV**: 113.

Greek Version, Additions in **IV**: 463.
Gregory of Nyssa, Commentary on **VI**: 723, 726.
Hebrew (עזב) Root II, in **IV**: 468.
Hebrew סֵפֶר, Inscription **IV**: 466.
Hebrew Theology, Contribution to, as **VIII**: 19.
Historical Background of **IV**: 466.
History of Religion, Significance for **V**: 5.
Hobbes, Thomas, and **IV**: 467.
Homiletic Suggestions on **IV**: 459.
Illustrations of, (Language, Civilization, and Natural History) **IV**: 460.
Immortality and **VI**: 431, 435.
Inorgainc Nature in the Poem of **IV**: 459.
Integrity of **IV**: 459, 460.
Interpretation of **IV**: 459, 461, 465.
Interpreters of **IV**: 464.
Isagogical Study of **IV**: 468.
Israel, Nation of, and **IV**: 465, 466*(2)*; **VIII**: 210*(3)*.
"J.B." and **IV**: 468; **VIII**: 369.
Job in Other Literatures **IV**: 459.
Jung on **IV**: 467.
Kautzsch, Emil, on **VI**: 420.
Lessons of **IV**: 458, 463.
Life, Idea of, in **IV**: 468; **V**: 113.
Life, on **IV**: 458.
Life's Mystery and **IV**: 461.
Literary Criticism of **IV**: **§381, 456-470; IX: §381, cxxxiii.**
Literary Interest in **IV**: 462.
Literary Structure of **V**: 705.
Literature of **IV**: 457.
Maccabees, I and II, and **IV**: 464.
Man, Doctrine of, in **IV**: 468; **VIII**: 173.
Masoretic and Septuagint of, compared **IV**: 14, 31.
Meaning of **IV**: 468*(2)*.
Message of **IV**: 464, 469.
Messiah, Revelation of, and **IV**: 461; **VIII**: 140.
Messianic Element in **IV**: 459.
Messianic Prophecy in **IV**: 459; **VIII**: 133.
Metaphor in **VI**: 432.
Misinterpretations of **IV**: 113.
Misunderstood, Why(?) **IV**: 465.
Muslim Cosmology and **IV**: 460; **VIII**: 85.
Mythological Background **VI**: 429.
Mythological Element in **IV**: 459.
Nahor, Genealogy of the Sons of, and Historical Background of **IV**: 466.
New Reading of **IV**: 459.
Northwest-Semitic Words in **IV**: 468.
Object of **IV**: 457.
Paraphrase of **VI**: 422.
Patriarchal Religion Developed as in **IV**: 457; **V**: 6.
Pico, Giovanni, Version **IV**: 54.
Poem of **IV**: 466.
Poem, Original **IV**: 471*(2)*.
Poem, Problem of the **IV**: 461.
Poetic Structure in the Dialgoue of **V**: 706.
Poetic Structure of, and Ugaritic Literature **IV**: 466.
Poetry of / in **IV**: 459, 461, 465; **V**: 688.
Problem of, in the Twentieth Century **IV**: 462.
Problem(s) of **IV**: 458, 460, 461, 469.
Prologue of **VI**: 421.
Psychoanalytic Comment on 3:25 **VI**: 422.
Read, How to **VIII**: 392.
Redeemer in **IV**: 465.
Rénan, E., on **IV**: 457, *503*.
Resurrection, on **IV**: 458, 462, 467; **VI**: 430, 431*(2)*; **VIII**: 260, 269*(2)*, 270.
Revised English Version of **IV**: 457, 458.

Salvation by Grace, in Job's Theology **VIII**: 19, 189.
Science, Modern, and **IV**: 464.
Semitic Field of "Folly" in **VI**: 419.
Septuagint, *'Αποβαίνω* and *ἐπιβαίνω* in **IV**: 465.
Septuagint, *'Εα δέ let alone* **IV**: 466.
Septuagint of, Studies **IV**: 467, 468; **VI**: 421.
Soliloquy of **VI**: 434*(3)*, 435.
Sources of **IV**: **§382, 471-472**.
Spirituality of **VI**: 428*(2)*.
Stock, Joseph, on **IV**: 456.
Strophic Patterns in **IV**: 469.
Structure of **IV**: 460.
Subject of **IV**: 457.
Suffering, Human, Mystic Value of **IV**: 466.
Suffering in Jewish Theology, and **IV**: 461.
Suffering in the Plan of God Debated in **IV**: 465.
Suffering, Problem of, and **IV**: 463*(2)*, 464*(2)*, 466*(2)*, 467, 469; **VIII**: 186*(4)*.
Sumerian Variation on the "Job" Motif **VII**: 275.
Teaching of **IV**: 461.
Text of **IV**: 462.
Theme of **IV**: 467.
Theological Approach of the Greek Translator of **VIII**: 19.
Theology of **IV**: 466; **VIII**: 19.
Theophany, in **VI**: 438*(2)*, 440.
Theophany, Religious Significance of **IV**: 468.
Therapy in **IV**: 467.
Time of **IV**: 458.
"Torah", in **IV**: 456.
Ugaritic Literature and **IV**: 466.
Unity of **IV**: 457, 469.
Vulgate Translation of **IV**: 95*(2)*, 115.
War-Horse in **VI**: 439.
wayyomar (וַיֹּאמַר), Accentuation of, in **IV**: 462.
Whirlwind, Voice out of **IV**: 464.
Yahweh Speeches in **IV**: 468*(2)*.

Job, Book of, Manuscripts of: **VI**: **§644, 441**.
Arabic Version of **VI**: 441.
Leipsic MS No. 102 of, Commentary on Job **VI**: 441.
Massoretic Text and LXX compared **VI**: 441.
Sahidic Translation of **VI**: 441*(2)*.
Septuagint of **VI**: 441*(2)*.

Job, Chapters 24-30:
Composition of **IV**: 471.

Job, Chapters 32-37:
Authenticity of **IV**: 471; **VI**: 435, 436.

Job, Person: **I**: *31*, *39*, **56-57**, *119*; **V**: *115*; **VI**: 441; **VIII**: 403.
Affliction of **III**: 397.
Affliction, Philosophy of **IV**: 461.
Agnostic, as(?) **I**: 56, 57.
Answers by Job to God **IV**: 465.
Babylonian **V**: 176; **VII**: 259*(2)*.
Budda and **IV**: 462; **V**: 145.
Character of **I**: 56, 57.
Character of, According to the Greek Translator **I**: 56; **IV**: 467.
"Comforters" of **IV**: 465.
Cuneiform Inscriptions, of **V**: 176.
Dannaba and **IV**: 461.
Dostoievsky as a Modern **IV**: 469; **VIII**: 370.
Enigma of **IV**: 469.
Epic of **IV**: 460.
Existentialism, Fore-Runner of(?) **IV**: 46.
Friends of, Integrity of **IV**: 464.
God and **IV**: 467.
God, Conception of **IV**: 467; **VIII**: 60.
God Unjust in(?) **IV**: 465.
God's Witness, as **IV**: 467.
Gospel of **IV**: 466.

Hobbs vs. Job, Power and Justice **IV**: 467.
Home, Original, of **IV**: 462.
Impatience of **I**: 56, 57.
Kafka as a Modern **IV**: 469; **VIII**: 370.
Legend of **IV**: 471*(2)*; **V**: 689.
Maimonides and **IV**: 469.
Melville as a Modern **IV**: 469; **VIII**: 370.
Messianic Hope of **IV**: 464*(2)*.
Murmurings of **IV**: 466.
Old Testament Skeptic **IV**: 460, *513*; **VI**: *548*.
Patience of **I**: 56, 57; **IV**: 462, 467*(2)*.
Paul and **I**: 56; **VIII**: 292, 293.
Pharisee, as **IV**: 465.
Philosophy of Affliction **IV**: 461.
Power and Justice, *Hobbs vs. Job* **IV**: 467.
Prince of the East **IV**: 460.
Prometheus and **I**: 56; **IV**: 461, 467; **VIII**: 100.
Prophet Attacks Profit **IV**: 465.
Redeemer of **IV**: 469.
Repentance of **IV**: 467, 468.
Righteousness of **I**: 57.
Sermon on the Mount and **I**: 56.
Story of **IV**: 469.
Suffering of **I**: 57.
Temptation of **I**: 56; **VIII**: 191.
Vindication of **I**: 56.
West African Religion, in **V**: 151.
Wisdom of God and **IV**: 467; **VIII**: 98.

Job Stone: **VII**: 26, 73.

Job, Testament of:
Cod. Vatican. Graecus 1238, of **VI**: 646, 647.
Exegetical Studies on **VI**: **§800, 670**.
Literary Criticism of **VI**: **(§774), 660**.
Textual Criticism on **VI**: **§748, 647**.

Job's Wife: **I**: 57.

Joel, Book of: **IV**: *434, 439*.
Authenticity, Authorship, Date, and Sources of **IV**: **§358, 432-433**.
Call to Repentance in **VI**: 373.
Chronological position among the Prophets **IV**: 432.
"Day of the Lord" in **IV**: 431, 432.
Dionysius Bar Ṣalîbi, Commentary on **VI**: 726.
Documents in **IV**: 432.
Exegetical Studies on **VI**: **§619, 373-375**.
Historical Situation in **IV**: 431, *439*.
Inductive Study of **VIII**: 390.
Literary Criticism of **IV**: **§357, 431-432**.
Locust in **IV**: 432*(2)*.
Messianic Prophecy in **IV**: 431; **VIII**: 132.
Parallel Passages in, and the Question of Date **IV**: 432.
Post-Exilic Community and **IV**: 432.
Teacher of Righteousness and **IV**: 432; **VI**: 370, 374.
Unity of **IV**: 432*(2)*.
Valley of the Gorge in **IV**: 432.

Joel, Book of, Manuscripts of: **VI**: 362, (**§620**), **375**.

John Carter Brown Library: **IV**: *10*.

John, Gospel of:
Abraham in **VIII**: 288*(2)*.
Baruch, and John 1:9 **VI**: 666; **VIII**: 288.
Cosmological Similes in, in Light of Rabbinics and Pseudepigrapha **VIII**: 288.
Dead Sea Scrolls and the Background for **VIII**: 479.
Deutero (Second) Isaiah and **IV**: 401, 403; **VIII**: 288, 289.
Deutero-Isaiah and **IV**: 403.

Dualism in the Manual of Discipline, and in **VIII**: 463, 482.
Exodus a Literary Type for **VIII**: 289.
Ezekiel and **IV**: 423; **VIII**: 289.
Fulfillment of OT in **VIII**: 289.
Genesis 1-3 and **VI**: 18; **VIII**: 288.
God, Old Testament Description of, and **VIII**: 71, 289.
Irenaeus and **VI**: 658, 718.
Light as Figure and Symbol in **V**: 510; **VIII**: 307.
Logos and the Memra of, and the Palestinian Targum **VI**: 105, 714; **VIII**: 131.
Logos in, and Proverbs **IV**: 501; **VIII**: 131, 289.
Logos, in, *see also:* ***Logos***
Manual of Discipline and **VIII**: 461, 479.
Missionary Tract to Israel(?) **VIII**: 288.
Odes of Solomon and **VIII**: 288.
Old Testament Description of God, and its Use in **VIII**: 71.
Old Testament, Use of, in **VIII**: **§1043**, **287-290**.
Origin of, and Qumran **VIII**: 481.
Polycarp and **VI**: 658, 718.
Proverbs, *Logos* in, and **IV**: 501; **VIII**: 131, 289.
Psalm 82, Citation of, in **VI**: 502*(2)*; **VIII**: 289.
Psalm 82, Rabbinic Interpretation of and **VI**: 502, 716; **VIII**: 289.
Qoheleth and **IV**: 517; **VIII**: 289.
Qumran Scrolls and **VIII**: 479, 481.
Testament of the Twelve Patriarchs in Relation to **VI**: 658, 718; **VIII**: 287.
Theology of, and the OT **VIII**: 289.

John Hopkins University: **III**: *606*.

Coptic inscriptions in the Collections (and Abbott) of **VI**: 451.
Greek, at Yale University, Stoddard Collection **III**: 605.

John Rylands Library: **II**: *258;* **IV**: *23*.

John, Saint:
Crypt of **II**: 300.

John the Baptist: **I**: 39; **IV**: 455.
Messiah, Monks of Qumran, and **VIII**: 142, 482.
Qumran (DSS) and **VIII**: 142, 419, 422, 431, 479. 481*(2)*.

Joiachin, *see also:* **Jokim** **III**: *664*.

Jokdeam: **II**: 291.

Jokim, *see also:* **Joiachin** **I**: *38*.

Jonah, Book of:
Aramaic, Originally Written in(?) **IV**: 446.
Assyrian Archaeology and **IV**: 444.
Authenticity, Authorship, Date, and Sources of **IV**: 165, **§364**, **446**.
Benjoin, George, on **IV**: 440.
Buddhist Parallel to **IV**: *378*, 444; **V**: 147, 148.
Exegetical Studies on **VI**: **§625**, **388-390**.
Gattung and Intention in **V**: 705.
Great Fish in Ancient and Medieval Story **IV**: 444; **VII**: 1.
Great Fish (Whale) of **IV**: 440*(2)*, 441, 442, 443*(3)*, 444, 445; **VII**: 1
Higher Criticism and **IV**: 443*(2)*.
Historical Value of **IV**: 444.
Historicity of **IV**: 440, 441*(2)*, 442*(3)*.
Inductive Study of **VIII**: 389.
Intention and Gattung in **V**: 705.
Isaiah 51-53, Connection to **IV**: 445, *448*, *551;* **VI**: *305*.
Jesus' Reference / Testimony to **IV**: 440; **VIII**: 279*(2)*.

Jonah's Gourd **VI**: 389, 390.
Jonah's Gourd, Translation Problems **IV**: 115.
Kerygma of **IV**: 445.
Kindred Legends, and **IV**: 442.
Lamentations, Connection to **IV**: 445, *448, 551;* **VI**: *305.*
Literary Criticism of **IV**: **§363, 440-445**.
Meditation on **IV**: 445.
Message of **IV**: 443, 444*(2)*, 445.
Motif of "Three Days and Three Nights" **VI**: 389.
Mythological Aspects of **IV**: 444.
Nahum, Connection to **IV**: 445*(2)*, *448(2), 551;* **VI**: *305.*
Oannas and Dagon and **IV**: 441.
OT Hermeneutics and **IV**: 88, 445.
OT Interpretation and **IV**: 87.
Parable, a(?) **IV**: 442.
Ships, Monsters and **IV**: 445.
Spiritual Horizon of Judaism, Enlarged in **IV**: 444, *509.*
Spiritual Side of **IV**: 442.
Teaching Values of **IV**: 445.
Theology of **VIII**: 18.
Twentieth Century Message of **IV**: 443.
Whale, a Barge(?) **IV**: 442.

Jonah, Book of, Manuscripts of: **VI**: 362; **§626, 390**.
Berl. Sept. 18 Codex **VI**: 390.

Jonah, Person: **I**: 57.
Art, In **III**: 704.
Deliverance a Miracle(?) **IV**: 442.
Easter Study from **IV**: 444.
Fugitive Prophet **I**: 57.
God, Will of, and **IV**: 444; **VIII**: 98.
History of **I**: 57.
Legend of, in India **V**: 143.
Libel of **IV**: 443.
Message of, Timeless **IV**: 444.
Mission to Nineveh **IV**: 440, 441, 442.
Missionary Prophet **IV**: 444.
Modern, a(?) **IV**: 442*(2)*.
Nineveh, and / in **IV**: 440*(2)*, 443.
Pre-Christian Apostle to the Gentiles **IV**: 443.
Preaching of **IV**: 440.
Prophetic Experience and **I**: 57.
Sign of **IV**: 444, 445.
Twentieth Century Message of **IV**: 443.

Jonathan: **I**: **58**, *90;* **II**: *377;* **VI**: 192, 200.
David's Lament over **VI**: 207*(6)*.
Elegy on the Death of **VI**: 191.
Hachish Use by(?) **I**: 58; **III**: 404; **VI**: 200.
Tomb of **II**: *377;* **III**: 541.

JONES, GEORGE: **III**: 438.

JONES, HAROLD:
Collection (of Egytian Artifacts) **III**: 569.

JONES, JOHN: **VIII**: 28.

JONES, WILLIAM:
Persian Linguistics **V**: 677.

Joppa: **II**: **422**; **III**: 130.
Harbor of **III**: 414.
Legend of the Capture of **VII**: 77.

Jordan, Country of - General Studies: **I**: *392;* **II**: *319, 419,* **422-423**; **III**: *19,* 431‡, 444*(3)*, 445, *532;* **VIII**: 348.

Jordan:
Archaeological Bibliography of **III**: 430.
Dolmen Sites in **III**: 558.
Exploration of **III**: 409*(2)*.
Name **V**: 508.
Positions East of **II**: 282*(2)*.
Topography of **II**: 422, 423.

Jordan River:	**I**: *154, 325, 343;* **II**: *122, 292, 325,* 351*(5),* **423-426**, 462, 482, 489; **III**: *419,* 445.
Bridges over	**II**: 285.
Cossing / Passage of, by Israelites	**VI**: 107, 108, 166*(2).*
Division of in 1546	**VI**: 166.
Exploration of with U.S. Navy	**II**: 310, 353.
Late Quaternary Observations of	**II**: 251.
Manasseh, Settlement, East of	**II**: 439.
Stoppage, in A.D. 1267	**VI**: 166.
Jordan Valley:	**II**: 286*(2),* 312, *326,* 350, **423-426**, *460(2), 469, 485, 495(2);* **III**: 208, *635.*
Band-Slip Ware from	**III**: 621.
Biblical Sites in	**II**: 425.
Bronze Age Mounds of	**II**: 293, 309; **III**: 420.
Fluviomorphology of, Lower	**II**: 251, 426.
Hasa formation, alluvial depostion in	**II**: 252*(2).*
Quaternary in Northern	**II**: 252.
Sulphur of	**II**: 211.
JORDAN, W. G.:	**IV**: 138.
Joseph (Story):	**I**: *50,* **58-61**, *104, 373, 488;* **III**: 191; **IV**: 318*(3),* 320, 321*(2);* **VI**: 84*(2),* 88, 89*(2),* 90.
Amenhetep IV as Pharaoh of the Famine	**I**: 58; **IV**: 313.
Asenath, as Wife of	**I**: **35**, *59;* **VI**: 696.
Blessing of, Possible Mesoptamian Background to	**VI**: 94.
Blessings of	**VI**: 91.
Bones of, and Exodus	**IV**: 328.
Bones of, and Shechem	**II**: 475.
Canal of	**VI**: 91.
Cares for His Kindred	**IV**: 317.
Coat of Many Colors	**IV**: 316; **VI**: 84.
Egyptian Name of	**I**: 59*(3),* 60*(2);* **V**: 292, 295*(2),* 296*(2),* 298*(2);* **VI**: 88*(3).*
Egyptian Papyrus bearing on	**IV**: 319.
Egyptolotical Remarks on the Story in Genesis	**IV**: 319.
Esther, Book of, in the Light of	**IV**: 320, *521.*
Evolution of the, Story	**IV**: 318.
Forgives His Brothers	**IV**: 317.
Hindu Fiction, in	**I**: 59, *76;* **VIII**: 367.
Historical Elements in the Story of	**IV**: 317.
Miracle in the Story of	**IV**: 316.
Mythical Elements in the Story of	**IV**: 317.
Offical Despatches of	**V**: 684; **VI**: 89.
Patristic Teaching, in	**I**: 60; **VI**: 722.
Pentateuchal Criticism and	**IV**: 236, 321.
Rule Over Egypt, as	**IV**: 317.
Septuagint, in	**IV**: 317.
Sociology of Joseph's Day	**I**: 59, 180*(3),* 373, 488; **V**: 11; **VIII**: 221.
Sold by His Brothers	**IV**: 317; **VI**: 85*(2).*
Story of, on a Coptic Tapestry	**VIII**: 356.
Temptation of	**VI**: 86.
Textual Criticism of, in answer to Higher Criticism of the Story	**IV**: 316.
Tomb of, in Sechem	**III**: 531.
Joseph, Testament of:	**VI**: 646.
Armenian Text of	**VI**: 646.
JOSEPHUS, FLAVIUS, **Life and Works**	**I**: *136, 175(2), 465;* **II**: *58, 172(2), 417, 499;* **III**: *531;* **V**: *647;* **VI**: 16, §**807**, **679-684**.

Abraham as Greek Philosopher in	**I**: 32.
Akra, Leveling of, in	**VI**: 680.
Alabarches of	**III**: 483.
Alexander Jannaeus in	**II**: 53.
Alexander the Great's visit to Jerusalem in, and Daniel's Prophecies	**II**: 9, 406; **IV**: 525; **VI**: 679.
Alexander Yannai, with Surname of Trachides, in	**VI**: 684.
Antiochus III Letter to Zeuxius on Establishing Jewish Military Colonies	**I**: 172; **VI**: 683.
Antiquites 13	**II**: 439.
Antiquites 15:136	**VI**: 683.
Antiquites XVIII, 18-22	**V**: 97.
Antiquities 11	**VI**: 684.
Antiquities 11 and First Esdras	**II**: 179; **VI**: 629, 679.
Antiquties VII, 6, 3	**IV**: 361.
Aramaic Source for *Antiquities of the Jews*	**VI**: 684.
Aramaism in	**VI**: 681.
Armenian Verision of	**VI**: 680.
Bible (Scriptures) and	**VI**: 679, 684.
Biblical Geography of	**II**: 256; **VI**: 684.
Biblical Studies, Imporatance of, in	**VI**: 684.
Brass Gate, metion of, by	**II**: 409.
Censorship in the Transmission of	**VI**: 682.
Christ, Testimony of, by *(Testimonium)*	**VI**: 679*(2)*, 680*(4)*, 681*(2)*, 683.
Christian Interpolations	**VI**: 681.
Christian Origins, and	**VI**: 681.
Christianity, on	**VI**: 681.
Chronology of	**VI**: 679*(2)*.
Cumanus' Term in Office	**VI**: 682.
Daniel and	**IV**: 532; **VI**: 684.
ΔΕΣΠΟΤΗΣ in	**V**: 674; **VI**: 683.
Eisler, Robert, on	**VI**: 681.
Essenes and (Anitquities XVIII, 18-22)	**V**: 97*(2)*; **VI**: 683*(2)*.
Essenes in	**V**: 97*(2)*; **VI**: 683*(3)*, 723.
Essenes in Slavonic	**VI**: 683.
Fate and Free Will in Jewish Philosophies in	**V**: 111; **VI**: 681.
Felix' Term in Office	**VI**: 682.
Fortress of, Missing	**III**: 489.
Herod's Temple in	**V**: 75.
Historian, as a	**VI**: 679, 680.
Historical Source, as	**VI**: 682.
Illustrations of OT and NT in	**VI**: 679.
Jewish War, Slavonic Version of the	**VI**: 681.
Judah's Speech to His Father in	**VI**: 679.
Language of	**VI**: 681.
Language Spoken in Palestine in the Days of Christ and	**VI**: 679.
Laws, Anti-Traditional, of	**I**: 463; **VI**: 680.
Literary Projects of	**VI**: 683.
Maccabees and	**II**: 58; **VI**: 683.
Marissa of *Antiquities* XIII, 275.	**II**: 439, 472.
Nehemiah in	**IV**: 540; **VI**: 680.
Old Testament and	**VI**: 679.
Passover Texts in	**V**: 87; **VI**: 676, 682.
Pharisees' Doctrine of Fate and (Anitquities XVIII, 1, 3)	**V**: 99; **VI**: 681.
Photius, Bibliothecea of, References to, in	**VI**: 682.
πνεῦμα in	**V**: 655; **VI**: 683.
Pollio, Identified as a Pharisee, in	**V**: 99; **VI**: 683.
Presentation , Method of, in Jewish Antiquties	**VI**: 682.
Propaganda in the Transmission of	**VI**: 682.
Pseduo-Josephus, fragments of *de Universo*	**VI**: 684.
Religion of	**VI**: 680.
Renegade or Patriot(?)	**VI**: 683.
Riddles of	**VI**: 683.
Russian Version	**VI**: 680, 683.

Samaria and the "Marissa" in Antiquties XIII, 275 **VI**: 682.
Samuel, Second, in **IV**: 377.
Samuel, Text of, in **IV**: 6.
Sanballat in **I**: 79.
Slavonic **VI**: 680, 681, 682*(3)*.
Slavonic, and the DSS **VI**: 684; **VIII**: 438.
Slavonic, in Relation to Joisppon **VI**: 681.
Slavonic Version of the Jewish War **VI**: 681.
Synedrion in **VI**: 682.
Syria, Source of History for, in **VI**: 679; **IX**: cxx.
Yaḥad (יחד) in DSS and **VI**: 677, 683; **VIII**: 423.
Zealots and **V**: 102*(2)*; **VI**: 683, 684.

Joshua, Book of: **I**: *153, 472;* **II**: *142*.
Altar at Ebal **II**: 284.
Arabic Book of, Samaritan Hebrew Sources of **IV**: 366.
Authorship and Authenticity of **IV**: **§330, 336**.
Bibliography of **I**: **§11, 11**.
Cambridge LXX, Apparatus, Corrections **IV**: 31.
Colenso, John, on **IV**: 225, 362.
Conflate Readings in, and Judges **VI**: 166, 176, *177*.
Conquest and El-Amarna Letters **IV**: 363.
Date of **IV**: **§330, 336**.
Deuteronomist in(?) **IV**: 366.
Deuteronomistic, Priestly, or Prophetic Writing **IV**: 358.
Deuteronomy and, 1-11 as one book **IV**: 356, 366.
Doublets in **IV**: 362; **V**: 692.
Exegetical Studies on **VI**: **§593, 166-175**.
History, Ideal *vs.* Real, in **IV**: 364.
Jericho, Siege of **II**: 395.
Jerusalemite Confederation Joshua's defeat of **IV**: 363; **V**: 390.
Joshua's "Long Day" **IV**: **§329, 364-365**; **VI**: 168, 169*(6)*, 170*(6)*.
Keil, Karl F., on **IV**: 362.
Literary Criticism of **IV**: **§328, 361-364**.
Parable in **IV**: 176.
Pentateuch, and **IV**: 227, 251, 362*(2)*.
Ruiling Ideas of **IV**: 362.
Samaritan Book of, Heterodox Theology in **VIII**: 16.
Sources of **IV**: **§330, 336**.
Territorial Allotments in **IV**: 366.
Topography of **II**: 253, 283; **IV**: 358, 366.
Town Lists in **II**: 269; **IV**: 363.

Joshua, Book of, Manuscripts of: **VI**: **§594, 175**.

Joshua, Chapter 10
Judges 1 and, Literary and Historical Problem of **IV**: 358.

Joshua, Manuscripts of: **VI**: **§594, 175**.
Greek Codices, Grouping **VI**: 176.
Hebrew*Vorlage* of the LXX of **VI**: 176.
K Text of **VI**: 176.
Lyons Codes of Old Latin **VI**: 176.
Samaritan Book of **IV**: 30, 363, 366*(2)*; **VI**: 175*(5)*, 176.
Septuagint, Corrections in the Apparatus of **VI**: 176.
Washington Manuscript of **VI**: 175.

Joshua, Person **I**: **61**, *137(2), 152;* **II**: *131(2), 353, 384;* **VI**: 173, 175, *184*.
Assyria in the Days of **II**: 287; **III**: 26.
Coronation of, in Zechariah **VI**: 407, 408.
Covenant of, and Shechem **II**: 478; **V**: 70; **IX**: ciii.

Curse of, on Jericho **VI**: 168, 227*(2)*, 232; **VIII**: 248; **IX**: cxlvii.
El-Amarna Letters and Conquest by **IV**: 363.
Genealogy **I**: 61, 119.
Home of **II**: 292; **III**: 419.
Name, and Jesus **V**: 293.
Palestine in the Days of **II**: 287; **III**: 26.
Procopius's Monument to Conquest of Canaan **III**: 255.
Sepulcher, Mohammedan Traditions Respecting **III**: 531.
Tomb of **II**: 284; **III**: 531.

"Joshua the Robber":
Inscription regarding **I**: 61; **VII**: 116.

Josiah: **I**: *91*, **94**, *162, 165, 166, 184, 316;* **II**: *163;* **V**: 10*(2);* **VI**: 593.
Battle of Megiddo and **I**: 94; **IV**: 382; **VI**: 243.
"Book of the Law", discovery of **IV**: 384.
Central Sanctuary, Idea of, New in Time of(?) **V**: 13.
Closing Years of **IV**: 414.
Contemporaneous History with **II**: 1.
Deuteronomy and, Reformation **IV**: 384.
Deuteronomy from the Reign of(?) **IV**: 355.
Eighteenth Year of **IV**: 413.
Gadd's Babylonian Tablet and **I**: 94; **VII**: 268.
Jeremiah and **I**: 53, 54; **IV**: 384, 413.
Law Book of, and Theodoret **IV**: 94, 383; **VI**: 719.
Reform(ation) of **I**: *94, 162, 166;* **III**: *665;* **IV**: 383, 384; **V**: 10; **VI**: 228, 242.
Reign of **VIII**: 390.
Restoration of True Religion and Covenant **VI**: 6.

Josippon:
Apocrypha and **VI**: 611.
Slavonic Josephus and **VI**: 680.

Jotapata: **II**: *366, 367*, 426, 488.

Jotham: **I**: *86, 87, 90*, **95**; **II**: *83, 88, 92, 102, 180, 189, 191;* **III**: *656.*

Jotham's Fable: **I**: 486; **VI**: 185*(2)*.

Journey:
Day's, caluclation of **I**: 414.

JOWETT, LEWIS CAMPBELL:
Philo, on **VI**: 672.

JOWETT, WILLIAM: **VI**: 204, 307, 528.

Juba II: **II**: 54.

Jubal:
Eliot, George, Legend of **VIII**: 364.

Jubeiah: **II**: 426.

Jubilee:
Aten's **II**: 205.
Egyptian, Illuminating the Thrones at **V**: 214.
Second, Amenophis II's **II**: 16.

Jubilee (Year): **I**: 189, 260, *304*, 399, **§119**, **413**, 463.
Babylonian **I**: 413.
Social Reform and the Biblical **I**: 413; **VIII**: 234.

Jubilees, Book of / The Laws of Moses **VI**: 597.
Calendar in **I**: 394, 404, 405*(2)*, 406*(2);* **VI**: 649, 654, 655*(3)*.
Dating of **VI**: 655*(2)*.
Ethiopic MSS, Translation from Uncollated **VI**: 645.
Exegetical Studies on **VI**: **§790**, **667**; **IX**: **§790**, **cl.**
Genesis, as Commentary on **IV**: 267; **VI**: 654.
Hebrew Fragment of **VI**: 645.
Jesus' Parables and **VIII**: 286.

Kingdom of God in	**VI**: 655; **VIII**: 255.
Literary Criticism of	**VI: §764, 654-655.**
Manual of Discipline and	**VI**: 655; **VIII**: 461.
New Edition, Project for a	**VI**: 645.
Pentateuch and	**IV**: 236; **VI**: 655.
Pentecost, Day of, in	**V**: 89; **VI**: 655; **VIII**: 415.
Qumran Texts of	**VIII: §1113, 452.**
Rabbinic Halakah and	**VI**: 654, 692.
Textual Criticism on	**VI: §738, 644-645.**
Judadiah, Tell:	**III**: 130.
Judah, *see also:* **Judea**	**I**: 327, 329, *349;* **II**: 325, **426-427**; **IV**: 181; **VI**: 640; **VII**: 159.
Administrative Divisions of	**I**: 463; **II**: 275*(2)*.
Antiochus Epiphanes and	**II**: *18(2)*.
Army, Reorganization of, under Josiah	**I**: 316.
Assyria, Tribute to, by	**IV**: 382; **VII**: 204.
Babylonian Captivity	**I: §66, 166-168.**
Boundary Lists of the Kingdom of	**II**: 270, 275.
Boundary of	**II**: 274, 275, 276, 291
Calendar Reckoning, Divergences in	**I**: 405.
Casemate Walls in, Purpose of	**III**: 489.
Chronology of	**I**: 161*(3)*; 162*(5)*; **II**: 177, 178, 181*(2)*, 182, 184*(2)*, 188*(3)*, *194*.
Conquest of, Chaldean	**IV**: 421.
Division of, Fourfold	**II**: 276.
Edomites in Southern	**II**: 123.
Egypt, Relations with, in the Age of Isaiah	**IV**: 395.
Fall of, and Jeremiah	**I**: 52, 54; **IV**: 410.
Hill Country of	**II**: 306.
Jeremiah and the Fall of	**I**: 52; **IV**: 410.
"Judah on Jordan"	**VI**: 173.
Kingdom of	**I**: 137*(2)*, **§65, 165-166.**
"Men of", in the El-Amarna tablets	**VII**: 169.
Name of, Supposedly in List of Sheshonq	**V**: 292; **VII**: 81.
Plain of	**II**: 306.
Preëxilic History	**III**: *649;* **IV**: 421.
Province Lists of the Kingdom of	**II**: 270, 271.
Sectional Rivalry in the Kingdom of	**IV**: 380.
Sennacherib's Invasion	**II**: 90*(2)*.
Shame of	**IV**: 414.
JUDAH BEN BARZILAI:	**IV**: 101*(2)*.
Judah Ben Ishmael:	
Inscription of	**VII**: 92.
Judah, Person:	**I**: **61**; **VI**: 85, 88.
Blessing of	**VI**: 93.
Family of, and Chronology	**I**: 61; **II**: 179.
Gradson's of	**IV**: 313.
Name	**V**: 299, 508*(2)*.
Pentateuch, in	**IV**: 236.
Prophecy Concering	**VI**: 93.
Speech to His Father in Josephus	**VI**: 679.
Tamar and	**VI**; 727.
Judah, Testament of:	
Armenian Text of	**VI**: 646.
Judah, Tribe of:	**I**: 151, 155, 157, *269(2)*.
Town Lists of	**II**: 271*(2)*.
Judahites:	
Pseudo-Philo and	**VI**: 678.
Judaism, *see also:* **Jewish-Christian Dialogue**	**V**: 19; **VI**: 124; **VIII**: 334*(4)*, 336.
Adaptation in	**V**: 28.
Adiabene, Conversion of	**VI**: 684.

Ancients, Attitude toward	**VIII**: 327*(2)*.
Anthropological View of the Cultural Setting of	**V**: 37.
Atonement, in, and the Missionary Approach	**VIII**: 195, 336.
Authority in	**V**: 9*(2)*, 21, 32; **VIII**: 335.
Babylon, in, 3rd Century	**I**: 135; **VI**: 691.
Babylon Religion and	**V**: 141, 172.
Bible and	**V**: 6.
Biblical Science and	**I**: 143.
Buddhism, Similarities	**I**: 183; **V**: 151.
Burber's, Martin, Biblical	**V**: 29.
Burning Bush and the Origin of	**V**: 13.
Captivity, After the	**V**: 6.
Catholic, of the First Century and Philo	**IV**: 13.
Change in	**V**: 28.
Christian, Early Attitudes Toward	**V**: 23.
Christian Origins and	**V**: 14, 19.
Christian Piety of Pre-Destruction Hebraic	**V**: 27.
Christian Writers on	**V**: 18.
Christianity and	**V**: 9, 28*(2)*, 141, 149; **VIII**: 215, 275, 299, 328, 332*(2)*, 333*(2)*, 338; **IX**: cxxxvii.
Christianity, Dependence of Early, on	**VIII**: 298.
Christianity, Primitive, Relation to Jewish Thought and Teaching	**V**: 147.
Christianity, Separation of, from	**VIII**: 333.
Church, a(?)	**V**: 12.
Cultural Setting, An Anthropological View	**V**: 37.
Dissident Laity in Early	**V**: 23.
Distortion and Reality	**V**: 25; **VIII**: 336.
Dogma in	**V**: 9*(2)*.
Dogmas of	**V**: 110.
Dura-Europos, at	**V**: 26, 28.
Epistle of Barnabas, Confutation of, in	**VI**: 717; **VIII**: 337.
Errors of, in Christ's Day	**V**: 9.
Eschatology and	**VIII**: 250.
Ethics in, and Monotheism	**V**: 35.
Evolution of, in the Post-Exilic Period	**V**: 20; **VI**: 601.
Expansion of	**V**: 9.
Fail, Did it(?)	**V**: 18.
Feminine Element and	**I**: 199; **V**: 30.
Fiction, in	**VIII**: 360.
Fossil Religion(?)	**VIII**: 336.
Fundamentals of	**V**: 27.
Future of	**VIII**: 331, 332.
Genius of	**V**: 7.
Greek Culture and	**IV**: 34.
Greeks, Outlook on	**I**: 123.
Hadrian and	**VIII**: 423.
Hellenism and	**V**: 37; **IX**: cxxxiv.
Hellenistic	**V**: 21.
Hellenization of	**V**: 25.
Hermas and	**V**: 29; **VI**: 718.
Ides of March and	**IX**: cxxxiv.
Image in, and the Second Commandment	**VI**: 163.
Images and	**V**: 107
Interculture Contacts, Effects upon	**V**: 20.
Inventory of, at the Beginning of the Christian Era	**V**: 21.
Israel and	**VIII**: 338.
Jewish Supernaturalism, Defense of, and Modern Humanism	**VIII**: 335.
Justification of	**VIII**: 329.
Justin Martyr, in	**VI**: 724.
Kant's Interpretation of	**VIII**: 336.
Latin Pagan Side-Lights on	**V**: 10.
Liberal, and Liberal Christianity	**VIII**: 332.
Mazdayasna and, Dissimilarities	**V**: 147.
Menorah as a Symbol of	**V**: 53; **VIII**: 308.
Misconceptions of, by Christianity	**VIII**: 329.
Mission of	**VIII**: 330.

Monotheism and Ethics in	**V**: 35; **VIII**: 227.
Monuments and	**VI**: 687.
Mystery Religions and	**V**: **§476, 240**.
New Testament and	**VIII**: 272.
New Testament, and Its Genesis	**V**: 9.
New Testament Era, in	**V**: 16.
Newer Estimate of	**V**: 19.
Normative, Rise of, to the Close of the Mishnah	**V**: 18.
Normative, Rise of, to the Reoganization at Jamnia	**V**: 18.
Origin of, and the Burning Bush	**V**: 13.
Originality of	**V**: 12.
Pagan Symbols, Use of, after 70 C.E.	**V**: 38; **VIII**: 308.
Palestine, in, 1st Century	**I**: 135; **VI**: 691.
Paul and	**VIII**: 294.
Persain Beliefs, Influence on	**V**: 36, 230.
Persian Dualism in	**V**: 37.
Philo's Place in	**VI**: 677.
Philosophical Elements in Early and Zunz's Concept of History	**IX**: lxxxvii.
Philosophy of, How It Should Be Taught	**V**: 111.
Philosophy of Religion and	**V**: 110.
Post-Exilic	**V**: 11.
Post-Exilic, Unrealistic Attitude of	**V**: 23.
Priest and Prophet in	**V**: 41.
Principles of, in Historical Outline	**V**: 17.
Professors of Religion and	**VIII**: 408.
Prophet and Priest in	**V**: 41.
Proselyte Movement, First to	**VI**: 410.
Psychology of	**V**: 20.
Psychonanalitic Study of	**V**: 20; **IX**: lxxxvii.
Qumran and Its Relation to	**VIII**: **§1086, 426**.
Rabbinic	**V**: 18.
Rabbinic, Analysis of	**V**: 8.
Rabbinic, and Hasidism	**V**: 25.
Rabbinic, and Paul	**VIII**: 293.
Rabbinic, and Rebuilding of the Temple and Sacrifice	**V**: 62.
Rabbinic, and the Epistles of St. Paul	**VI**: 686; **VIII**: 291.
Rabbinic, Foundations of	**V**: 24; **VI**: 689.
Rabbinic, From Hellenism to Christianity, and Problem of Continuity	**V**: 22.
Rabbinic, the Wise Man in	**V**: 267; **VI**: 691.
Reality and Distortion	**V**: 25.
Religion, as	**V**: 22.
Religion, Fundamentals of, as Interpreted by Rabbinic	**V**: 18.
Religious Idea of, from Ezra to Maccabees	**V**: 11.
Rome, in	**V**: 7.
Sects of, *see:* ***Judaism, Sects of***	
Secular State and	**I**: 470; **V**: 29.
Spirit and Letter in, and Christianity	**VIII**: 329.
Spirit of Early, Contrast of Post and Pre-Exilic Age	**V**: 17*(3)*.
Spirit of Early. Dominant Motive of the Pre-Exilic Activiy	**V**: 17.
Spiritual Horizon, Enlarging from Jonah and Ruth	**IV**: 444.
Symbolism in	**VIII**: 306.
Task of	**VIII**: 332.
Theist's Impression of	**VIII**: 330.
Tradition and Literature in Early	**IV**: 177.
Tradition, Notion of, in	**V**: 23.
Tribal Religion(?)	**V**: 7.
Types of, in the Time of Jesus	**V**: 11.
Unitarianism and, in Their Relation to Each Other	BV; **141.**
Universality of	**V**: 28.
War, Attitude Towards	**VIII**: 232.

Weber's, Max, "Ancient Judaism" a Reevalutation of **V**: 30.
Woman's Position in Ancient and Modern **V**: 14.
Womanhood and **I**: 197.
Zoroastrian Critique of **V**: 27.
Zoroastrian Influence on **V**: 36, 231.
Zoroastrian Influence on Doctrines, in the Inter-Testamental Period **V**: 16, 36.
Zunz's, Leopold, Philosophical Elements in Early **IX**: lxxxvii.

Judaism, Modern: **V**: **§419**, **31-32**; **VIII**: 330, 331*(2)*; **IX**: **§419**, **cxxxiv**.
Bible in the Light of Modern Criticism for Reform **IV**: 138; **VIII**: 330.
Bible, Significance of, for Reform **V**: 31.
Existentialist Approach to **V**: 32.
Humanist Approach to **V**: 32.
Liberal **V**: 31*(2)*.
Messianic Hope and **VIII**: 331*(2)*.
Orthodox, Religious Life of in Palestine **V**: 31.
Principles of **V**: 31.
Progressive **V**: 31.
Rabbinic Tradition, the Bible, and **VIII**: 339.
Reformed **V**: 31*(2)*; **VIII**: 329*(2)*.
Reformed, and the Halacha **VIII**: 334, 335.
Reformed and Conservative **VIII**: 334, 335*(3)*.
Reformed, and Unitarianism **VIII**: 331.
Reformed, God and **VIII**: 63.
Religious Education and **V**: 31.
Sacrifice Before Shrines in **V**: 31.
Science of **V**: 32.
Science of, Zunz, on **V**: 31.
Traditional Approach to **V**: 32.
Woman's Position in **V**: 31.

Judaism, Sects of - General Studies: **V**: **§448**, **95-96**.
Al-Qirqisānī's Account of, and Christianity **V**: 95.
Doctrines of **V**: 95.
History of **V**: 95.
Origin of **V**: 95.
Qumran and **VIII**: **§1087**, **426-427**.
Second Jewish Commonwelath, During **V**: 129.

Judas, Jesus' Disciple:
Dichotomized Servant (Qumran) and **VIII**: 482.
Hand in the Bowl and **VIII**: 482.

Judas (of Galilee): **II**: 54.

Judea, *see also*: **Judah** **I**: 177*(2)*; **II**: *247*, 286, 303, *387*; **III**: 23, 420; **IX**: cxvi.
Adminstrative Divisions of, at End of Second Temple Period **II**: 304.
Antiochus Epiphanes and the Rebirth of **I**: 18.
Borders of **II**: 286.
Buqêʿah, Exploration in **II**: 310, 344.
Central Range **II**: 286.
Deserts in, *see:* ***Deserts, Judean***
el Mird in Wilderness of **II**: 445.
Future of **VIII**: 340.
Herod made king of **II**: 47.
Karnak Lists, in **II**: 264.
Land, Cultivated in **II**: 298.
Nebuchadnezzar and History of **II**: 69.
Palaeolithic Cave in Western **II**: 278.
Partition of by Gabinius **II**: 427.
Roman Province of **I**: 177*(2)*
Seleucid, Tribute and Land-tax in **I**: 482.
Status after Destruction of Second Temple **I**: 492, **II**: 427.
Void (Buqêʿah), Exploration in **II**: 310.

Judeida, Tell (Judeideh, Tell el): II: 427; III: *665*.
Judex: I: 500.
Judge:
Term V: 508*(2)*.
Judge-Affixer: I: 505*(2)*.
Judges, Book of: I: *153, 466;* II: *344*.
Authorized Version of IV: 366.
Authorship and Authenticity of IV: **§334, 372-373**; VI: 177.
Bibliography of I: (**§12**), 11.
Canannites, Israelite Tribes, and their Relation to the, in IV: 369.
Chronology of II: 180, 181, 182, 184; IV: 366, 367*(3)*.
Chronology of, and the Date of the Exodus IV: 336, 368.
Conflate Readings in, and Joshua VI: 166, *176*, 177.
Conquest, Period, and IV: 359.
Date of IV: **§334, 372-373**.
Deborah's Song IV: **§332, 370-371**.
Deuteronomic Redactor of IV: 373.
Exegetical Studies on VIII: **§595, 176-191**.
Exodus, Date of, and I: 186; IV: 336*(2)*, 368.
Geographical Terms in IV: 369.
Hexaplaric Element in Septuagint of IV: 33, 369.
Introduction, Composition of VI: 178.
Israelite Tribes, in, and their Relation to the Indigenous Canannites IV: 369.
Jephthah's Vow IV: **§333, 371-372**.
Judges i-ii, 5, on the Authorship of IV: 373.
Kingdom, Preparation for IV: 368.
Leading Ideas in IV: 367, 368.
Literary Appreication of V: 702.
Literary Aspects of V: 701.
Literary Criticism of IV: **§331, 366-370**.
Literary Form of Biblical HIstory of V: 701.
Message Formula in IV: 370; V: 702.
Mishpat (מִשְׁפָּט) in IV: 370.
Monarchy, Apology for(?) IV: 370.
New Version of IV: 367, *476*.
Old Latin Version of IV: 40.
Parable in IV: 176.
Peshṭtia Palimpsest of IV: 46.
Ruth and IV: 367, 368, *508, 509*.
Ruth, Samuel and, Form one Book IV: 367, *374, 509*.
Shophet (שָׁפַט) in IV: 370.
Sources of IV: **§334, 372-373**.
Structure of IV: 369.
Judges, Book of, Manuscripts of: VII: **§596, 191**.
Old Latin Versions of VI: 191.
Sixth Century Palimpsest VI: 191.
Theodotion's Influence on the Alexandrian Text of VI: 191*(2)*.
Judges, Chapter 1:
Joshua 10 and, Literary and Historical Problem of IV: 358.
Judges Chapter 13-16:
Stucture and Style in V: 702.
Judges, Legal: I: 495.
Judges, Period of the: I: **§58, 153-154**; IV: 367; IX: **§58, lxxxiv**.
Archaeological Observations on IV: 358.
Art in III: 699.
Earlier and Later Sources for IV: 370.
Israelite Law in I: 466.
Javelin-Heads from III: 683.
Jurispurdence, Ancient Israelite in I: 468; IV: 369.

Judges, Persons: IV: 370; V: 78, 379.
- Biographical Studies I: 25.
- Ruler, and V: 454*(2)*, 457, 458.
- Tombs of II: 407; III: 414, 535.

Judgment:
- Agag and VIII: 224.
- Anxiety to Secure Just VI: 146.
- Assize, Doctrine of VI: 596.
- Dead, of, Osirian V: 220.
- Egyptian, Significance of the Cone on the Head of the Defunct in III: 696.
- Foreign People, in Amos VI: 377.
- Forgiveness in the Prophecy of IV: 357; VIII: 193.
- ***God, of*** VIII: **§1033, 256**.
- God's Kingdom and VIII: 255.
- Isarel, against, in Amos VI: 375.
- Nations, upon, in Amos VI: 375.
- Oded, and Mercy VIII: 224.

Judicial Integrity:
- Code of Hammurabi on I: 478, 496.

Judicial Procedure:
- Athens, and the Judge-Affixer I: 505.
- Town Gate, at I: 469, 492.

Judith: I: 51; VI: 179, 616.
- Character of Susanna and VI: 616, 625.
- Du Batras, of VIII: 363, 366.
- Genealogy of VI: 616.
- Moore, Sturge, Poem of VIII: 365.
- Play by John Fitzgerald Pennie on VIII: 363.
- Schutze, Martin, on VIII: 364.
- Seventeenth Century Histories of VIII: 364.

Judith, Book of: IV: 168; VI: 597, 615, 616; **§696, 616**.
- ***Exegetical Studies on*** VI: **§714, 631**.
- Geography of VI: 616.
- Hebrew Political Romance VI: 616.
- Hebrew Version of VI: 603*(2)*.
- Liturgy, in VIII: 384.
- Message of VI: 616.
- Northumbrianized Version of the Old Metrical VIII: 360.
- Old English Poem of VIII: 362.
- Pauline Epistles, Quote in 1 Corinthians from VI: 631; VIII: 292.
- ***Textual Criticism of*** VI: **§678, 603**.

Jufna: II: 308.
- Fountains at VI: 2.

Jug(s), *see also:* **Drinking Vessels**
- Bronze, Long-Beaked in Greek Lands III: 590.
- Ewer, painted, from Lachish III: 614.
- Festival III: 589.
- Silver III: 589.

Juglet:
- Jericho, Unique, from III: 591, 635.

Jujube Tree: III: 391.

Julian, Emperor: I: 174.
- Jews and the Proposed Rebuilding of the Temple V: 68*(2)*.
- Old Testament, Aquaintance with VIII: 361.

JULIUS AFRICANUS:
- Letter to Origen on the Story of Susanna VI: 626, 721.

JUNG, CARL GUSTAV:
- Job, on IV: 467.

Jungle:
- Semachontis as II: 292; V: 567.

Junior-Right: I: 226.

JUNKER, HERMANN:
- ***Bibliography of*** I: 20.

Jupiter, (god):
- Dolichenus V: 267.
- The Gaza Jupiter III: 720.

Jupiter, Planet:
- Star Hêlēl(?) II: 230; VI: 274.

Jurisprudence:
- Halaka, Tannaitic VI: 692.

Hebrew Secular Law in Light of Comparative **I**: 461.
Influence of the Bible on Modern **VIII**: 220, 350.
Jewish Law, influence of, in Christian Orient **I**: 474.
Judges, and Ancient Israelite **I**: 468; **IV**: 369; **V**: 379.

Jurisprudence (in Israel): **I**: **§127**, **460-471**, 499.
Roman **I**: 465, 499.
Talmudic **I**: 471; **VI**: 695.
Tannaitic **VI**: 688.
Tannaitic, on Intention **I**: 463.

Jurists:
Roman **I**: 500.

Jurn, Tell el-, *see also*: **Engedi** **II**: 427.

Justice: **I**: 465, 466; **V**: 508, 509*(3)*; **VIII**: 216, 225, 228.
Administration of, in Early Jewish Era from Talmudic Records **I**: 461.
Administration of, in Israel **I**: 461.
Adoni-Bezek and **VIII**: 224.
Babylonia, Relation of Certain Gods to Equity and **I**: 498; **V**: 184.
Deuteronomy, in **I**: 477; **IV**: 352.
Egypt, in **I**: 489.
Goren at the City Gate. Justice and the Royal Office **VII**: 144.
Greek Courts, and **I**: 495*(2)*.
Greek, Indo-European origins of **I**: 501.
Immortality and **VIII**: 265.
Industry, Relevance of Biblical, to **VIII**: 234.
Israel, Ancient **I**: 461.
Israel, in and Covenant **VIII**: 217.
Jewish Conception of **VIII**: 232.
Jewish, Early **I**: 461.
King's, in Pre-exilic Israel **I**: 486; **V**: 437, 457; **VIII**: 142.
Lipit-Ishtar's Hall of **V**: 186.
Nuzi, at **I**: 490.
Oriental, and the Law **I**: 388.
Proverbs, in **IV**: 502.
Retributive, Jewish and Pagan Conceptions of **VI**: 596.
Social, in the OT Prophets **I**: 189; **IV**: 389.
Symbols of **I**: 468.

Justification: **VIII**: **§1019**, **197**.
Covenant and **VIII**: 217.
Faith, by in the OT **VIII**: 197*(2)*.
Rabbinic Anticipation of **VIII**: 197.

JUSTIN MARTYR:
Jeremiah and **VI**: 328, 721.
Jewish Messianic Belief in *Dialogue with Trypho* **V**: 130; **VI**: 725.
Old Testament and Judism in **VI**: 724.
Old Testament Quotations in, and the Greek Dodekapropheton **VI**: 722.
παῖς θεοῦ in, and his *Dialogue with Trypho* **VI**: 724.

Juxta Examplar (Vulgate) **IV**: 40.

K

K'ai-Feng Jews: **IV**: *236*.

Ka(𓂓): **V**: 208, 211, 215, 327, 328.
Egyptian, and *Ba* in Africa **V**: 150.
King of Abydos **II**: 4, 207.
Modern Egypt and Old Arabia, Traces of **V**: 209.
Scarabs, on **III**: 668; **V**: 207.
Statues, abnormal men on **III**: 349.

***Ka*-House:** **III**: 490.

Ka-Nefer:
Remains of family of **III**: 359.

Ka-mes:
Fan-bearer, Body-guard of Amenhetep III **II**: 55; **III**: *724*.

Kabara Cave: **II**: 280.

Kabbalah: VI: 687.
Genizah Fragments on VII: 107.
Matronit, Goddess of the V: 167.
Kabr Hebrun: II: 284.
Kabri: II: 428.
Kadarenes:
Wateh-ben-Hazel, Prince of II: 107; VII: 183.
Kaddīsh VIII: 205*(2)*.
Lord's Prayer and V: 143.
Kadesh: II: 268*(3)*, 308; IV: 331; VI: 476.
Genizah Fragments on VII: 107.
Kadesh-Barnea: I: *152;* III: **132-133**; IV: 328*(2)*.
Kadesh-Naphtali: II: *368,* **428**; VI: 167, 171, 179.
Kadesh on Orontes: I: 313, 319; II: *80(2), 157,* 293; III: **131-132**, 421.
Battle of I: 313, 319; II: *80(2);* III: 131*(2)*, 132*(5)*.
Battle of, Texts of VII: 16.
Kadmos: III: 776; V: 253.
Kâdy, Tell el-: II: 390, 423.
KAFKA, FRANZ:
Job and IV: 469; VIII: 370.
Kafr Kama: II: 302.
Kafr Kenna: II: 428.
Kafr Yasif: II: 342, 394, 428.
Kaftor: V: 400.
Kagemni:
Instructions addressed to VII: 11*(3)*.
Kah-ankh-ra Sebekhetep: III: *493*.
KAHLE, PAUL E.: IV: 47; VI: 96, 713*(2)*.
Kahriye Cami: III: 263.
Kahun Papyrus: I: *402;* II: 209.
Kai(?): II: *6,* **54**.
Stela of II: 205.
Kai-Khosru: I: *34*.
K3ỉ-ʿpr:
Scribe of the Early Fifth Egyptian Dynasty II: 54.
K'aifeng:
Jewish Inscriptions of VII: 96.
Kakai: V: 299.
Kala't esh Shukif: II: *287*.
Kalabsha, Kalâbsheh:
Divinities in the Area of V: 224.
Greek Inscription from VII: 318.
Kalamis:
Possible Signature of II: 54.
Kalamu Inscriptions: VI: 529; VII: 87, 92, 123.
Kalandia:
Hyksos Tomb at III: 553.
Kalat el Hosn: II: 308.
Kalenderhane Camisi: III: 267.
Kalḫu *see:* **Nimrud**
Kalil, Tel: II: 303.
Ḳalilag Wᵉdamnag: V: 530.
KALISH, MARCUS:
Leviticus, on IV: 342.
Kalkiliash: II: 290.
Kaller, *see also:* **Zenjirli**
Hittite Monuments at III: 492.
Kallimachos:
Crime and Punishment in *Hymn to Delos* V: 266.
Kalpis, *see:* **Hydria**
Kaluraz: III: 125.
Kamarbi, *see:* **Hittite Epic and Mythology**
Kamōse:
Defeat of the Hyksos by VII: 16.
KAMPHAUSEN, ADOLPH:
Daniel on IV: 535.
Kamu'a el Hirmil: II: 308.
Kânâ: III: *722(2)*.
Kanah, River: II: 274.
Kanakht: VII: *10*.
Kanarese: VII: 353.
Kanawat:
Altar of Baal and Ashtoreth at V: 189*(2)*, 190.

Kandalanu: II: *22,* **55**, *192.*
Dating by IX: xcviii.
Kandaules: II: 55.
Kaneš, *see also:* **Kaniš, Kültepe** II: 271; III: 263.
Kangavar: III: 125.
Kaniš (Kaniş), *see also:* **Kanesh, Kültepe** II: 272; III: 133, *176, 264, 265(2).*
Art and Architecture of III: 476, 693.
Assyrian Merchants of (Idiom) V: 570.
Eponyms, Rotation of, at V: 303.
Kanro:
Contemporary of Moses II: 4.
KANT, IMMANUEL:
Judaism, Interpretation of VIII: 336.
Old Testament Ethics and VIII: 225.
Kapporoth: VI: 688.
Kara Dagh: VII: 303.
Kara-höyök: III: 93, **133**.
Kara-Viran-Göl: III: 258.
Kara-Eyuk:
Cappadocian Tablets from VII: 162.
Karabel:
Hittite Monument of VII: 306.
Karahöyük: III: 264.
Skulls from III: 359.
Ḳaraites: I: *250;* VIII: 410.
Bible Commentaries of IX: cli*(2).*
Doctrinal Aspects of the Damascus Covenant in Light of VIII: 416.
Qumran and VIII: 426.
Two Messiahs, Doctrine of, among VIII: 418.
Karaman: III: *53(3), 54.*
Karamania: III: 133, 138.
Karanis: I: *255;* III: **133**, *485.*
Karasu: III: *746.*
Karataş-Semayük: III: **134**, 265, 266*(2)*, 267.
Human Skeletal Remains at III: 362, 363.
Karatepe: I: 347; III: 262*(3)*, 263*(3), 479;* V: *400, 522;* VII: *118.*
Amarna, Bearing on V: 549*(2)*, 613*(2).*
Hittite Hieroglphics, Key to III: 135; V: 612.
Near Eastern Textual Criiticism and IV: 5.
Religious Problems of V: 226.
Karatepe Inscriptions: V: 462; VII: 304*(2)*
Yearly Sacrifice in V: 64.
Karbala Liwa: II: *250;* III: 208.
Karbi: II: 301.
Kardaki Temple: III: 514*(2).*
Kareth, *see:* **Death, Premature**
Karian Inscriptions: V: 678; VII: *15(2), 20,* 373, 374*(2)*, 376.
Graffiti, from Hesha VII: *122, 318,* 374.
S-ankh-ka-Ra, of VII: 374.
Sudan, from VII: *15, 318,* 374.
Karian Language: V: 678, 680.
Ḳarīn: IX: xcvii.
Ḳarīneh: IX: xcvii.
Karīr: V: 235*(2).*
Karkheh: III: *60,* 136.
KARLSTADT, ANDREAS BODENSTEIN VON:
Canon and IV: 202.
Karm al-Shaikh: II: 428; IX: cxvi.
Karnak: II: *7,* 70; III: *96,* **136**, *177,* 415, *754;* V: *341.*
Altars for Offerings from VII: 73.
Hypostyle Hall at III: 512.
Inscribed blocks from VII: 24.
Libation Bowl from VII: 73.
Obelisks of Pylon VII at VII: 20.
Pylon at, Restoration of III: 481.

Ramesses II and the Princes, in the Relief of Seti I at **II**: 80.
Reliefs at, and the Ritual of Amenophis I **VII**: 69.
Salt, Damage caused by, at **II**: 214; **III**: 455.
Temple of Amenophis III at **III**: 136.
Temple of Amora at **III**: 512.
Theban Necropolis at **III**: 136.
Karnak List(s): **II**: *263(3), 264(3);* **III**: *242(3);* **V**: 351.
Karneia: **V**: 255.
Karomama: **III**: *769.*
Kartal: **III**: 13.
Karum of Kanish: **III**: *4, 147.*
Karystos: **I**: *293.*
Kas: **III**: 136, *148.*
Kasdim: **II**: 147.
Kuššara (Kuşşara): **III**: **148**.
Kassite Language, *see:* **Elamite**
Kassite Period:
Synopsis of Royal Sources of **VII**: 239.
Kassites (Kashshites): **I**: 326, 329; **II**: 3, **147**,*175, 211*
Atanah-Samas, King of **II**: 23.
Kasu: **III**: 136.
Katna: **III**: 137, *168.*
Kato Zakro: **III**: **137**, 502.
Kattath at Khashash: **II**: 287.
KAUFMANN, YEHEZKEL:
Israelite Religion, on **V**: 26.
Life and Contributions of **I**: 24.
Kaunakes: **I**: 280.
Kaunos: **III**: 266.
KAUTZSCH, EMIL:
Job, on **VI**: 420.
Psalter, New Edition of **VI**: 443*(3)*, 462, 463.
Kavousi: **III**: 137.
Kavusi: **III**: *68, 540.*
Kay Kâûs Legend: **II**: *232;* **V**: 181; **VII**: 372.
Kayalidere: **III**: **137**.
Kayay:
Round Topped Stele of **VII**: 20.
Kayseri:
Seals allgedly from **III**: 658.
Kazallu: **VII**: 279; **IX**: civ.
Kazaphani: **III**: 137.
Kazel, Tell: **III**: *367.*
Kea,*see also:* **Ceos, Keos** **III**: **137**, *634.*
KEATE, W.:
Psalm 109 on **VI**: 515.
Keb:
Egyptian Earth-God in Cuneiform **V**: 209.
Keban (Region): **III**: 266*(2).*
Keban:
Bronze Age Development **IX**: cxix.
Salvage Araeology at **III**: 458.
Kebaran: **III**: 353.
Kebeleh: **III**: 138.
Kedar: **VI**: 2.
Kedarenes: **II**: *107.*
Kedesh of Naphtali: **II**: 281, 368, 487*(2).*
Kedesh-Barnea: **II**: 281.
Kedeshah: **III**: 132.
Kedron Valley: **I**: *359;* **II**: 409.
Hebrew Ossuaries from **III**: 545.
Jewish Tombs in **III**: 549, 551.
Peculiar Rock-Cutting in **III**: 537.
Kef Kalesi: **III**: **138**, 266.
Kefar Ḥebron: **II**: 428, *430.*
Kefar Shemaryahu: **II**: 298.
Kefer Gil'adi: **II**: 428.
Kefr Aziz: **II**: 283, 307.
Kefr esh Shems:
Greek Inscriptions from **III**: *642;* **VII**: *103.*
Kefr Kama: **II**: 284.
Kefr Kenna: **II**: *287.*
Kefr Lam: **II**: 284.
Kefr Likitia: **II**: 284.
Kefr Shiyan: **III**: 445.
Keftiu: **II**: *154(2)*, 267; **III**: 69, 133, **138**.
Spell **V**: 212.

Keftiu-People: **II**: 147.
KEIL, KARL F.:
Joshua, on **IV**: 362.
KEITH, ARTHUR, SIR: **III**: 315, 342*(2)*.
KEITH, JOHN ALEXANDER:
Prophecy, on **VIII**: 236.
Kelishin:
Uratian-Assyrian Inscriptions from **VII**: 288.
Kenath: **II**: *329, 391,* 428.
Ḳenbetu **V**: 292, 586.
Kenchreai: **I**: *459;* **III**: **138**.
Shipwreck at **III**: 454*(2)*.
KENEALY, EDWARD VAUGHAN HYDE:
Enoch, on **VIII**: 364.
Ḳenḫikopshef:
Prophylactic Charm of **VII**: 41, 74.
Kenites: **II**: **147**, 157, *158*.
Budde's Hypothesis of Kenite Origin of Mosiac Religion **V**: 11.
Hobab the **V**: 49.
Treaty with Israel **I**: 514.
Kenizzites: **II**: *147,* **148**.
KENNEDY, A. R. S.: **IV**: 123.
Samuel, on **IV**: 376.
KENNEDY-HEBERT, A.:
Chronology proposed by **II**: 203; **VII**: 135.
KENNETT, ROBERT HATCH:
Isaiah, on **IV**: 393.
KENT, CHARLES FOSTER: **I**: 69; **VI**: 71.
Kenties: **I**: 514.
Keos, *see also:* **Ceos, Kea** **III**: **138-139**, *719, 751*.
Kephala: **III**: 138, 139.
Cemetery at **III**: 59.
Kerak, *see also:* **Beth Yerah** **I**: *344;* **II**: 265, 291, **429**,*459;* **III**: 416.
Kerameikos:
Corinthian **III**: 611.
Lacedaemonians Buried in **III**: 357.
Kerâzeh: **II**: 429.
Domen Field at **II**: 310; **III**: 423, 548.
Synagogue Inscription of **VII**: 91.
Keres: **V**: 270.
Keret Epic (Legend): **II**: 268; **V**: 195, 199, 533; **VII**: 146.
Banquet Motif in **VI**: 541; **VII**: 145.
Dwarf-Craftsmen in, and North-West Semitic Mythology **V**: 134; **VII**: 144.
Glosses on **VII**: 145.
House of **V**: 199; **VII**: 145.
King Keret **VII**: 144.
Mathematical Conundrum in **VII**: 144.
Seven Wives of King **VII**: 143.
Vow to Asherah in **VII**: 142.
Keriat: **VI**: 167.
Kerkenes Dagh: **III**: 139.
Kerma: **III**: **139**, *683, 773*.
Kertch:
Egyptian Objects from **III**: *686, 762;* **VII**: 37, 65.
Keruthim: **II**: 284.
Kerygma:
Chonicler, of **IV**: 543.
Jonah, of **IV**: 445.
Proverbs, of **IV**: 502.
KESSLER, W.:
Decalogue on **VI**: 160.
Kesweh: **III**: 440.
Kethib-Qere, Problems of: **IV**: **§240, 19-20**; **V**: 447; **IX**: **§240, cxxviii**.
Isaiah DSS and **IV**: 19.
Judges 19:13, on **VI**: 191.
Septuagint and origin of **IV**: 19, 32.
Vocalization of, in A **IV**: 19.
Kethubim: **IV**: 204.
Ketubah: **I**: 216, 218.
Kezzuwatna: **VII**: 308.
Kfar Bar'am: **III**: *745*.
Kfar Baruch: **II**: 300.

Kfar Gil'adi:
Neolithic Site near II: 302.
Mausoleum at II: 302.
Kfar Monash: II: 429; III: *677, 684*.
Trace-Element Content in Artifacts of, Hoard II: 219; III: 569.
ʿKhaʿkwre, *see:* **Semnah**
Kha-em-maat:
Official of the Royal Barge of Amenhetep III II: 55.
Kha-nefer-Ra: II: 55, *86*.
Khabiri, *see:* **The Habiru / Hebrew Question**
Khafâjeh: III: **139**, *250*.
Archive of the Sin Temple in (Tutub) VII: 239.
Hurrian Material from III: 567.
Khalasa: II: 297.
Khalbi: II: *148;* III: 139.
Khalit el-Ful: II: 304.
Khaliut:
Stela of Prince VII: 22.
Khamuas Stories: V: 361; VII: 32.
Khan(?): III: 483.
Khan Minyeh: IX: cxv, cxvi.
Capernaum, possible site of II: 346.
Khan-Sheikhoun: III: 140.
Khana: III: **140**.
Contract from VII: 249.
Khana, Mounds of: II: 255; III: 421.
Khanmeti Palimpsest:
Old Georgian of Jeremiah VI: 345.
Khapiru, *see also:* **The Habiru / Hebrew Question** II: 148; III: 139.
Khapu: III: *741*.
Kharacen: I: 394; II: *50*.
Kharag Oasis: VII: *327*.
Demotic Rock Inscriptions of Gabal el-Teir at VII: 69. 82.
Kharakein: VII: 20.
Kharazieu: VII: 20.
Kharga:
Roman Temple near III: 516.
Khartoum: III: *228*.
Khartoum Museum: I: *45;* III: *683, 746*.
Kharu: II: *143;* VII: *64*.
Khasekhmui: II: **55**, *60*.
Khashash: II: *287*.
Khatâʿna Qantîr: III: 140.
Khatti: II: 3.
Khattusaš, *see:* **Boğazköy**
Khaʿẏ (Khaʿ): II: **55**.
Tomb of III: 560.
Khazars: II: *122(2)*, **148**.
Khazza Lawizza: I: 239.
"Khefren":
Royal Name, Pronunciation of V: 309.
Kheleifeh, Tell el-, *see also:* **Elath** and **Ezion-Geber** II: 297, 298, 359, 364*(4)*; III: *651;* IV: *219*.
Edomite Pottery from III: 635.
Khentybau: II: 56.
Kheops, *see:* **Cheops**
Kheper-ka-RA: II: 56.
Kheruef:
Tomb of III: 136, 551, 556, 559.
Khety: I: *273*.
Khiana, *see:* **Khana**
Khirbet ʿAdaseh: II: *377(2)*, 403, **430**.
Khirbet BelʿAmeh: I: *361*.
Khirbet Delhamiyah: II: 430.
Khirbet ed Deir: II: 298; III: 430.
Khirbet el Mefjer: II: 431.
Khirbet el Muqannaʿ: II: 359*(2)*, **431**.
Khirbet El-Kôm:
Iron Age Epigraphic Material from II: 252.
Khirbet er-Ruweisa, Tell: II: 368.
Khirbet esh-Sheikh Ibrahim: II: *389*, 431.

Khirbet et-Tannūr: I: *408;* II: 296, 297
Nabataean Temple at III: 515*(3)*.
Khirbet et-Tananir: II: 304.
Zodiac of I: 408.
Khirbet Futies: II: 299.
Khirbet Ḥabra: II: *428,* 430.
Khirbet Ḥaiyân: II: 430.
Khirbet Iskander: II: **430**.
Khirbet Judeiyideh: II: 430.
Khirbet Karak: II: 298; III: 430.
Khirbet (el-)Kerak: II: 343; III: *772*.
Khirbet Kerak Ware, *see:* **Pottery**
Khirbet Ḳumrân, *see:* **Qumran**
Khirbet Māsi: II: *308,* 431.
Khirbet Mazin: II: 431.
Khirbet Minya: II: 296, 297.
Khirbet Minyeh: III: 423.
Khirbet 'Omra: II: 431.
Khirbet Sheikh 'Ali: II: 300.
Khirbet Wadi Ez-Zaraniq: II: 431.
Khirbet Yahuda: II: 432.
Khirbet Yarmuk: III: *666*.
Khita: III: 116; VII: 301.
Khnememḥab:
Papyrus of VII: 78.
Khnems:
Vizier of Sekhem-ka-RA II: 56, *86*.
Khnum: II: *19,* 56.
Khnumḥotep: II: 56.
Khnumḥotpe II: IX: cv.
Khons: V: 207, 208.
Khonserdaisu:
Bronze Statuette of III: 762; IX: cv.
Khonsu:
Statuette of II: 56.
Khôr Hardân: III: 89.
Khor Rori (Dhofar): III: 140, *628*.
Sacred Stone Circle of V: 49.
Khorsabad: II: *209(2),* 210; III: 140, 468, *698*.
Temple of Sibitti at III: 518.
Khoun-Aten: IX: cv.
Khuenaten:
Inscription of VII: 59.
Portrait of, with inscribed slab II: 56.
Khufu: VII: 62.
Khurab Makran:
Khurāb Mahurāb: III: *677*.
Khurbert Umm el' Amud: II: 308.
Synagogue of III: 523.
Khurbet Beit Sawir:
Megalithic Building at III: 482.
Ruin at III: 481.
Khurbet Harrawi:
Greek Inscriptions from VII: 318, 343.
Khurbet Husheh:
Greek Inscription from VII: 314.
Khyan:
Sealing of III: 658.
Kia:
Stela of II: 205.
Kibbutz Kabri: III: *676*.
Kibbutz Shamir: II: 303.
Kibêgi: V: 574, 580.
Kiblah: I: 366.
Kichyros: III: 97, 141.
Kid:
Seething in Mother's Milk Prohibited I: 249*(3),* 250*(3);* **VI**: 114*(4),* 115, 119*(3),* 145*(4)*.
Kiddush Hashem: VIII: 111.
Kidnapping: VI: 113.
Code of Hammurabi on I: 478, 496.
Kidneys:
Assyrian Prescriptions for Stones in III: 405.
Kidron (Valley): II: *389,* **432**; V: 509.
Inscribed Ossuaries in III: 557.

KIERKEGAARD, SØREN:
Abraham and I: 31.
Ethical, Telelogical Suspention of, Jewish(?) **VIII**: 228.
Jeremiah and **I**: 54; **IV**: 413.
Man, Dignity of, on **V**: 266; **VIII**: 175.
Kiev: **II**: *71.*
Kikaion: **III**: 391.
Killara: **III**: 141.
Kiln: **I**: 288, 289.
Pre-dynastic, at Mahâsna **III**: 603.
Kilwa: **II**: 432.
Kîmân-Fâris: **I**: *241;* **II**: *86;* **III**: *764;* **VII**: *66.*
KIMCHI, DAVID
Commentary on Isaiah 52:13-Chapter 53 **VI**: 306.
ḲIMḤI, DAVID:
Psalms, Commentary on Fifth Book of **VI**: 726.
Psalms, Commentary on the Book of **VI**: 483.
Kimmerians, *see:* **Cimmerians**
Kin: **I**: 208.
Next of, Rights and Duties of **I**: 209.
"Kind": **III**: 307, 324, 326*(2),* 327.
King:
Akkadian Word for **V**: 542*(2).*
Fertility and **VI**: 215.
Term in Post-exilic Writings **V**: 509.
KING, EDWARD: **VI**: 388, 389.
King-God:
Western Semintes, among **V**: 196, 505; **VI**: 228.
King James Verion, *see:* **Authorized Version of 1611**
KING, L. W.:
Babylonian Chronicles **VII**: 238.
"King of Kings": **V**: 519*(2), 520.*
"King of Persia": **IV**: 197, 522, 528; **V**: 519*(2).*
"King's Friend": **V**: 519.
King's Highway: **I**: 349.
"King's Son":
Ugarit, at and among the Hittites **V**: 519.
Kingdom, Studies concerning **V**: 509. **VI**: 333.
Apcalyptists, among **VI**: 596.
Apocryphal Literature, in **VI**: 611.
Christ, of, in Psalm 2 **VI**: 451.
Enoch, First Book, in **VI**: 651.
Greatness of **VIII**: 255.
Jubilees, in **VI**: 655.
Messianic **VI**: 410, 596; **VIII**: 254, 255
Kingdom of God: **VI**: 333; **VIII**: 278.
Apocyprhal Literature, in **VI**: 611; **VIII**: 255.
Daniel, in **VI**: 574.
Enoch, First, in **VI**: 651; **VIII**: 255.
Jewish Conception / Expectation of **VIII**: 254*(2).*
Jubilees, in **VI**: 655; **VIII**: 255.
Millennial **VIII**: 254.
Old Testament, in **VIII**: 254*(4),* 255*(2).*
Prophets, among **VI**: 596.
III: *328.*
Eschatology and **VIII**: 250, 268.
Kingdom of Judah, *see:* **Judah**
Kingi: **V**: 574, 580.
Kings - General Studies: **I**: *114.*
Achaemenian, Affecting Israelite Politics **I**: 322.
Anointing of **VII**: 138
Assyrian, Affecting Israelite Politics **I**: 322.
Babylonian, Affecting Israelite Politics **I**: 322.
Babylonian, Deification of and Ancestor-Worship **V**: 178, 179.

Babylonian, *see also:* ***Babylonian King Lists*** **I**: *120;* **II**: 181, 206, 211; **VII**: 153.

Divine (Sacral), *see:* ***Kingship***

Egyptian **II**: 4, 211.

Egyptian, Killing of, Custom **V**: 206.

Greek, Decline of Early **II**: 134.

Hittite, Priestly Dress of **V**: 226.

Intef, Parentage of **II**: 209.

Magic of **I**: 482.

Napatan, and Apis Worship **V**: 220; **VII**: 38.

Oath of, at Nuzi **I**: 511.

Persian **II**: 202, 208.

Shepherd, of Palestine **III**: 46.

Kings, Books of:

Archival Data in **IV**: 380*(2)*.

Armeanian Version of **VI**: 219.

Authorship and Authenticity of **IV**: 379, **§340**, **381**.

Axiology of **IV**: 380.

Bibliography of **I**: **§14**, **11**.

Chronology of **II**: 181, 184; **IV**: 379.

Date, Sources, Authorship, Authenticity of **IV**: **§340**, **381**.

David, So-Called Biography of, in **IV**: 358.

Death and Burial Formulas in **V**: 702, 707.

Double Readings in **IV**: 380; **VI**: 219.

Earliest **IV**: 380.

Edification from **IV**: 379.

Exegetical Studies on **VI**: **§601**, **219**.

Greek Translators of the Four Books of Kings **IV**: 379; **VI**: 219.

Hebrew Concept of History as seen in **I**: 132; **IV**: 380*(2)*.

Hebrew Variants in **VI**: 219.

Historical Difficulties in **IV**: 195.

History as **IV**: 381.

History, Uniqueness of **I**: 132; **IV**: 380*(2)*.

Israel, Use of the Name in **IV**: 357.

Literary Criticism of **IV**: **§339**, **379-380**.

Old Recension of **IV**: 361*(2)*, 380, 544*(2)*.

Parallels to Chronicles and Samuel **IV**: **§327**, **359-361**, 380*(2)*.

Purpose of **IV**: 379*(2)*.

Solomonic Apologetics in **IV**: 358.

Sources of **IV**: 379, **§340**, **381**.

Structure of **IV**: 379.

Synchronisms in **IV**: 380.

Theme of **IV**: 379.

Translator of, Princples of Interpretation for (3 K. 22:1- 4 K. 25:30) **IV**: 107; **VI**: 219*(2)*.

Two, in English Bibles **IV**: 101.

1 Kings: **VI**: 591.

Exegetical Studies on **VI**: **§602**, **219-232**; **IX**: **§602**, **cxlvi-cxlvii**.

Gregory the Great, Commentary on **VI**: 727.

Literary Criticism of **IV**: **§341**, **381-382**; **IX**: **§341**, **cxxxi**.

Midrash and Text Problems in **IV**: 382.

1 Kings 1 and 2:

Probable Displacement in, Historical and Literary Consequences of **VI**: 219.

2 Kings:

Exegetical Studies on **VI**: **§603**, **232-244**; **IX**: **§603**, **cxlvii**.

Literary Criticism of **IV**: **§342**, **382-383**.

Metrical Structure of **V**: 691.

Moabite Stone and **IV**: 382*(2)*.

Old Testament, History and a New Tablet [BM 21901] **IV**: 382.
Samaria, Fall of, in **II**: 472; **IV**: 383.
Shimei Duplicate and 3 Reigns II **VI**: 220, 221.

2 Kings 19:
Metrical Structure of **V**: 691, 702.

Kings, Books of, Manuscripts of: **VI**: **§604, 244**.
Armenian Version of 1 and 2 Kings **VI**: 244.
Ethiopic Version of 1 Kings **VI**: 244.
Peshitta Version of 2 Kings **VI**: 244.
Textual History of Codex Vaticanus in Kings **VI**: 244.

Kings of Abydos:
Aha **II**: 4, 207.
Azab **II**: 4, 207.
Den **II**: 4, 207.
Ka **II**: 4, 207.
Merneit **II**: 4, 207.
Mersekha **II**: 4, 207.
Narmer **II**: 4, 207.
Qa **II**: 4, 207.
Ro **II**: 4, 207.
Sma **II**: 4, 207.
Zer **II**: 4, 207.
Zeser **II**: 4, 207.
Zet **II**: 4, 207.

Kings of Israel and Judah - General Studies : **I**: **§46, 83-85**.
Chronology of **II**: 177, 178, 181*(2)*, 182, 183, 184, 187*(4)*, 188*(5)*.
Deuteronomic Judgments of the Kings of Judah **IV**: 379.
Egyptian Element in the Names of Hebrew, Bearing on the Exodus **IV**: 332; **V**: 291.
God's Standards for the **VIII**: 199.
Israel's Demand for a **IV**: 374, 377.
Jeremiah and the Last Two Kings of Judah **IV**: 413.
Last of, and the Fall of Jerusalem **II**: 421.
Last Two Kings of Judah, and Jeremiah **IV**: 413.
Names of the First Three **V**: 292.
Royal Records, Formulas from the **IV**: 381.

Kings of Israel and Judah - Alphabetical Listing **I**: **§47, 85-100**; **IX**: **§47, lxxxii**.
Ahab **I**: **85-86**.
Ahaz **I**: 86.
Amon **I**: 86.
Asa **I**: 86.
Athaliah **I**: 87.
Azariah *see also:* ***Uzziah*** **I**: 87.
David **I**: **87-90**.
Hezekiah **I**: **90-91**.
Hoshea **I**: 91.
Jehoiachin **I**: 92.
Jehoiakim **I**: 91.
Jehoram **I**: 92.
Jehoshaphat **I**: 92.
Jehu **I**: 92.
Jeroboam **I**: 93.
Joash **I**: **93-94**.
Josiah **I**: 94.
Jotham **I**: 95.
Omri **I**: 95.
Pekah **I**: 95.
Rehoboam **I**: 96.
Saul **I**: *79, 89,* **96-97**; **IV**: 222, 374.
Solomon **I**: **98-99**.
Uzziah, *see also:* ***Azariah*** **I**: 100.

Kingship, *see also:* **Monarchy** **I**: 485*(2)*, 486*(5)*, 487*(4)*; **V**: 26, 78.
Ancient Near East, in **I**: 483.
Assyrian Art and **III**: 706.
Authority of **I**: 487.
Canaanite, in Theory and Practice **IV**: 188; **IX**: ci.

Covenant and — **I**: 485, 512; **V**: 25.
Cult and — **I**: 486; **V**: 26.
Cult of, Third Dynasty Ur — **V**: 184.
Deification of Kings in Babylon and Ancestor Worship — **V**: 178, 179.
Divine Kings and Dying Gods — **V**: 24, 25*(2)*.
Divine (Sacral) — **I**: 482, 483*(3)*, 485*(5)*, *486(3)*; **V**: 24, 25*(2)*, 30, 158*(2)*, 161, 166; **VI**: 48.
Edfu, Temple of, Inscriptions on, at — **I**: 484.
Effect on Israelite Religion — **I**: 486; **V**: 26.
Foundation of, Biblical Narrative on Israelite — **I**: 484.
Gideon and — **I**: 45, 483.
God, of, Hebrew Conception — **VIII**: 68.
Greek — **I**: 483.
Hebrew, Limitations of — **I**: 485, 486.
Hellenistic Political Philosophy of — **I**: 482.
Homeric — **I**: 483.
Ideal King of Judah — **I**: 486.
Institution of — **I**: **§133**, **482-484**; **IX**: **§133**, **ci**.
Iran, charisma of, in — **I**: 483.
Israel, in — **I**: 469, 471, 492, 493.
Israelite King as Son of God — **I**: 486; **V**: 26.
Jewish, and Sacred Combat — **I**: 482, 485; **V**: 21, 107.
King-God Among Western-Semites — **V**: 196.
Macedonian — **I**: 483.
Messiah-King — **V**: 128.
Post-exilian Writings, in — **IX**: ci.
Psalms, References to "King" in, and Messianic Belief — **IV**: 475*(2)*, 490*(2)*; **V**: 126.
Ptolemaic, and Aristeas — **VI**: 661.
Religious Aspects of Hebrew — **V**: 20; **IX**: ci.
Royal Ritual Formula, Traces of, in OT & NT — **V**: 108.
Sacral, Ashanti Footnote — **V**: 151.
Samuel's Denuciation of, and Ugarit — **VI**: 196.
Sumer, in — **I**: 469, 483, 492, 493.
Tree of Life and the King in Ancient Near Eastern Religion — **I**: 483.
Tyrian King-God — **V**: 196.
Ur, in — **I**: 483.
Western Semitic — **I**: 483, 487; **IV**: 321.

Kinnereth:
EB Tomb found at — **III**: 550, 551, 619.

KINNIER, JOHN MACDONALD: — **III**: 435.

Kinship: — **I**: 208, 209.
Hebrew — **I**: 212, 220.
Iranian — **I**: 213.
Israelite, Termininology and Social Structure — **I**: 195.
Semitic — **I**: 210*(2)*.
West-Semitic, in the Patriarchal Period — **I**: 487; **IV**: 321; **V**: 130.

Kinyras: — **V**: 536.
Kir: — **II**: 265; **III**: 271.
Kirişkal Hüyük: — **III**: 266.
Kirjath-Jearim: — **II**: 275, 291*(2)*, 308, **432**, *455;* **VI**: 198.
Ark and — **VI**: 196, 211.
Kirjath-Sepher, *see also:* **Tell Beit Mirsim** — **II**: 333, **433**.
Kirjath-arba: — **VI**: 177.
Kirkuk: — **I**: *202;* **II**: 143, *267;* **III**: **141**, 188, 189, *280*.
Kirkuk Documents, *see:* **Nuzi Texts**
Kirman Area (Iran): — **III**: 125.
Kirrha: — **III**: 141.
Kirsehir: — **III**: *52,* 141.
Kirsha: — **I**: 301.

Kĭs: II: *194,* 209.
  Assyrian Texts from VII: 175.
Kish: III: *44, 123,* **141-142**.
  Akkadian Grammatical Text from VII: 148.
  Assyrian Tablets from Mound Z of VII: 193; IX: lxxxvi.
  Conquest of, under Agga, Cuneiform Tablet on VII: 278.
  Goats from III: 375.
  Inscriptions from VII: 210.
  Kings of II: 5, *84, 93,* 208, 210; III: 142, 164; IX: cxii.
  Mananâ-Iapium Dynasty II: 208*(2)*.
  "Plano-Convex Building" at III: 502.
  Pottery from III: 613, 638.
  Sumerian Grammatical Text from VII: 270.
  Tablets from VII: 149, 211.
Kiškanu:
  Legend of the V: 184; VII: 157, 201, 282, 286.
Kishon: II: 433.
Kishyôn: II: 433.
Kitāb Al-Anwār of Ya'qūb Al Qirqisānī: I: 464; VIII: 233.
Kitāb al-Khilaf:
  Mishael ben Uzziel's Treatise on Hebrew MSS IV: 7.
Kitâb Masâlik an-Naẓar VI: 725.
Kitchen(s): I: 210; III: 588.
KITCHENER, HORATIO \ HERBERT, LORD: III: 417.
  Palestine, Work in III: 417.
Kites: I: 317, *332;* III: 484, *654*.
Kition: I: *312;* III: *540, 681*.
  Early Iron Age Tomb at I: *312;* III: 540.
  Phoenician Inscription, Fifth-Century, from VII 88.
Kittim:
  Daniel Chapter 11 and VI: 577.
  Dead Sea Scrolls and VIII: 423.
KITTO, JOHN:
  Bible Dictionary of VIII: 397.
Kizilbel:
  Lycian Painted Tomb near Elmali III: 561.
Ḳizzuwadna, *see also:* **Cilicia and Mersin** II: 140, 266*(2)*, 267*(2);* III: 61-62, **142**.
KLEIN, S.: II: 297, 456; VI: 640.
Kleon: I: 400; II: **56**; III: 112.
  Assessment List, and IX: c, civ.
  Letter from Philonides to VII: 331.
KLOSTERMANN, AUGUST: IV: 264.
  Pentateuch on IV: 228, 239, 242.
Knankeh: II: 404.
Knee:
  Egyptian Word for V: 339.
Knidos: III: **142-143**, 266, 267.
KNIGHT. G. A. F.:
  Christian Theology of OT VIII: 12.
Knights:
  Spartan I: 195.
Knives, *see also:* **Daggers**; **Weapons**
  Blade, Bronze, from the Dictæan Cave, Crete III: 674.
  Egyptian, Ancient, in Modern Egypt III: 674.
  Flint I: 280, 290; III: 460, 562, 673, 676.
  Handles, *see:* ***Handles, Knife***
  Mycenaean III: 677.
  Sea of, Mythical, Egyptian V: 223.
  Sino-Scythian III: 674.
Knossos: I: 120; II: *64;* III: **143**, *198, 475, 711*.

Palace at — **III**: *499(2), 503(2)*, 633, *634*.
"Unity of the Archives" at — **VII**: 363.
Knossos Tablets: — **I**: 236; **V**: 619, 622; **VII**: 362*(4)*, 363, 364.
Sets and Files within the — **VII**: 364.
Knots: — **I**: 265.
Know:
"To Know" = Sexual Commerce — **V**: 509.
Knowledge: — **V**: 509, *512;* **VIII**: 199.
Dead Sea Scrolls, in, and Matthew 11:25-30 — **VIII**: 479*(2)*.
KÖBNER, JULIUS:
The Song of God: A Didactic Poem by — **VIII**: 360.
Ḳode: — **II**: 266; **III**: *142*.
Kokhav Hayarden: — **II**: 303*(2)*.
Kokkinovrisi: — **III**: 143.
Kolenieh:
Tomb, Rock-hewn, at — **III**: 533.
Kom Abou Billo(u): — **II**: 261; **III**: *518*.
Kom Barnougi: — **VII**: *62*.
Kom El-Dikka: — **III**: 144.
Kôm el-Ḫisn: — **III**: **144**.
Kom el-Kharaz:
Cemetery, Graeco-Roman — **III**: 144.
Kom el-Wist: — **III**: 144.
Kom Frin: — **VII**: *62*.
Kôm Ganâdy: — **I**: *241*.
Kom Washim: — **III**: *465, 588*.
Kom-Ombo: — **VII**: *15*.
Komistratos: — **III**: 144.
KÖNIG, EDUARD: — **IV**: 232*(2)*.
Ezekiel, on — **VI**: 347.
Genesis, on — **IV**: 269.
Isaiah, on — **IV**: 395.
Konya Plain: — **II**: 3; **III**: 264, *477, 626*.
Koppa: — **I**: 433.
Koptos: — **III**: 145.
New Empire Stela from — **VII**: 20.
Kor: — **III**: 145.
Korah (Qorah): — **I**: 62; **VI**: 130*(5)*.
Psalms of (and Sons of) — **IV**: 484; **VIII**: 390.
Koran:
Bible, Influence of, on — **VIII**: 367.
Charity or Almsgiving in — **V**: 65.
"God", Use of, in — **IV**: 233; **VIII**: 109.
Higher Criticism and — **IV**: 136; **V**: 143.
Intercession in — **VIII**: 204.
Ishtar Cult, Reference to — **V**: 169.
Israelite Tradition in — **VIII**: 367.
"Lord", Use of, in — **IV**: 233; **VIII**: 109.
Pentateuch and — **IV**: 230.
Sinai, Events at, and — **IV**: 328.
Talmudic Saying in the — **VI**: 700.
Korban, *see:* **Corban**
Koroneia:
Funeral Monument for — **III**: 558.
Korucutepe: — **III**: **145**.
Kos, Island of:
Pre-Hellenic Signs from — **VII**: 358.
KOSCHAKER, P.: — **I**: *497*.
Theory on Assyrian Law: — **I**: 502.
KOSTERMANN, AUGUST: — **IV**: 228*(2)*.
Koszylowce: — **III**: 145.
Kothar: — **V**: 536.
Kottabos: — **I**: 240.
KOTZEBUE, MORITZ VON: — **III**: 436.
Kouft: — **III**: 84, 85.
Kouklia: — **III**: 145.
Kourion: — **II**: 111; **III**: **145-146**, *574(2), 628*.
Late Cypriote II Tombs at — **III**: 549, 555*(2)*.
Kourion-Bamboula: — **II**: 433; **III**: 146, 472, *628, 629*.
Tomb, Early Classical, at — **III**: 555.
Koutzopodi: — **III**: 20.
Kouyunjik:
Akkadian Letters from — **VII**: 155.
Door Lintel found at — **III**: 461.
Letters of the Sargon Period, Textual Notes — **VII**: 155.

KRAETZSCHMAR, RICHARD: **I**: *516*.
KRAPF, JOHANN LUDWIG:
Translation of Genesis into Sooahele Language **IV**: 72.
Kraters:
Aegistus Citharista, Calyx-Crater **III**: 705.
Anacreon, Greek Inscriptions on **VII**: 329.
Attic Calyx **III**: 617, 618
Bell **III**: 618.
Bell, by Christie Painter **III**: 711.
Bichrome Ware, from Tel Nagila **III**: 632.
Boston Oresteia **III**: 633.
Bouzyges, and First Plough on **III**: 611.
Four-Spouted, from Karataş **III**: 636.
Italiote **III**: 619.
Men in Women's Attire, depicted on **I**: 279.
Phoenican, from Akhziv **III**: 634, 635.
Syrian, from Bamboula **III**: 628.
White-Ground, Sherds **III**: 622.
KRAUSS, SAMUEL: **II**: 69.
Talmud, Addenda to **VI**: 702.
Kremaste: **III**: *650*.
Krishna:
Messiah, as **V**: 151.
Kronion, Mount:
Caves at **II**: 279.
Kronos: **V**: 246*(2)*.
Kroton, *see:* **Croton**
Krt: **II**: 268.
Ksār 'Ākil ('Ākil): **II**: **434**; **III**: **146**, *677*.
Rock Shelter of **II**: 277, 434.
Kubaba: **V**: 226.
Küçük Höyük: **III**: 106.
Kudādi, Tell el: **II**: 297.
Kudur-Lagmar: **VI**: 62.
***Kudurr* Inscriptions:** **I**: 513; **IV**: 404, 437.
Kudurrus: **II**: 276*(2)*; **VII**: 241.
Ḳuë: **III**: 146; **IV**: 220; **VI**: 224, 590.
KUENEN, ABRAHAM: **IV**: 118, 119*(2)*, 120, *139*, 248, 261; **V**: 7, 8.
Bibliography of **I**: 20.
Kufä: **III**: *75*, 146.
Kufic, *see:* **Arabic**
KUHN, GOTTFRIED:
Qoheleth and **IV**: 515.
Kültepe(-Kanish): **III**: **146-147**, 262*(2)*, 263*(4)*, 264*(4)*, 265*(3)*, 266.
Alabaster Idols from **III**: 578; **V**: 227.
Marble Idols from **III**: 579.
Statuettes from **III**: 579.
Kululu: **III**: *636*.
Kūm-el-aḫmar:
Inscription at **VII**: 57, 58.
Kumma: **III**: 147, 177.
Epigraphic Mission to **VII**: 72.
Kummanni:
Muwatallis' Prayer to **V**: 227; **VII**: 309.
Kummukh: **III**: *63*, 147.
Kumran, *see:* **Qumran**
Kundi: **II**: *83*.
Kurba'il: **II**: *93*.
Kurd:
Name, and its Philological Connexions **V**: 298.
Kurdish Mountains: **III**: *180*.
Kurdistan: **I**: *257*, 391; **III**: **147**, *179*, *440*; **V**: *529*.
Tomb in **III**: 548.
Travels, Modern, in **III**: 438.
Kurigalzu:
Diorite Statue of **VII**: 238.
Kürigin Kaleh: **III**: 147.
Kurium: **III**: *640*.
Kurnub, *see:* **Mamshit**
KURTZ, JOHANN HEINRICH: **IV**: 117; **VIII**: 2.
Kusa: **III**: *136*, 148.
Kusae:
Temple of Ḥatḥōr, at **III**: 518.

Kush, *see also:* **Cush** — **II**: *107;* **III**: 100, **148**, 175.
- Graffiti and Work of the Viceroys of, in the region of Aswan — **VII**: 13.
- Hindu, Alexander the Great, and — **II**: 10.
- Viceroys, First two, of — **II**: 5.

Kushites, *see:* **Cushites**

Kussar: — **II**: 140; **III**: 148.

Kussîs, Tell el: — **II**: 434.

Kustul: — **II**: 284.

Kutha: — **III**: 148.

Kutluca (Bithynia): — **III**: 267.

Kuwait: — **III**: 148, 197.

Kyathos: — **III**: 588, 619.

Kybele, *see:* **Cybele**

Kyky:
- Theban Tomb of — **III**: 559.

KYLE, MELVIN GROVE: — **III**: 422.
- Pentateuch and — **IV**: 233*(2)*.

Kylichnis, *see:* **Pyx**

Kylix, *see:* **Cylix**

Kyniska: — I: 237; **II**: **57**.

Kyrenia:
- Shipwreck off the Coast of — **III**: 454*(2)*, 455*(2)*.

Kythera:
- Greek Inscription in — **VII**: 330.

Kythereia: — **V**: 536.

L

Lab'ayu: — **VII**: 172.

Laban:
- Hammurabi, Code of, and — **IV**: 317.
- Jacob and, in Light of the Nuzi Tablets — **VI**: 79.
- Jacob's Complaint Against — **VI**: 80.
- Jacob's Reception by — **IV**: 319.

Laban's Daughters: — **VI**: 79.

Label:
- Tags and, from Nippur — **VII**: 219.
- Wooden and Ivory, Ist Dynasty — **III**: 686*(2)*, 770. 773.

Labor: — **I**: 186, 189, 302, 303, 308.
- Agriculture, Seasonal — **I**: 255.
- Babylonian Pay-List, Diverse Names in — **VII**: 252.
- Corvée — **I**: 191, 192*(2)*, 257, 261, 271*(3)*, 308, 309*(2)*, *364*.
- Manual, Greek Attitude Toward — **I**: 189, 271, 307.
- Seasonal, according to GURUŠ Texts from Umma — **VII**: 252.
- Sorrow, and Life — **VI**: 506.
- Ur-Dynasty Tablets dealing with — **VII**: 253.
- Work Week, Length of — **I**: 305.

Laborers: — **I**: 189.
- Status of in Jewish Law, Tannaitic Period — **I**: 467.

Labranda: — **III**: 149, 262*(2)*.

Labyrinth:
- Cretan — **III**: 69.
- Egyptian, and Herodotus — **III**: 462.
- Enigma, Archaeological Suggestions — **III**: 478.
- Meander Door as Symbol of — **III**: 478.
- Pylos, from (?) — **III**: 485.

Lacedaemonians: — **III**: 357.

LACHEMAN, ERNEST R.: — **VIII**: 440.

Lachish: — **I**: *152, 424, 443;* **II**: 284, 296, 297, 303, 304, 357, *358, 369, 385,* **434-436**, *442, 472;* **III**: *651;* **IV**: 167, 218, 219; **VI**: *340*.
- Cuneiform Inscriptions found at — **VII**: 147.
- Exodus, Date of, and — **IV**: 338.
- Men of — **III**: 358; **IX**: cxvi.
- Old Testament and Excavations of — **IV**: 193.
- Proto-Canaanite Inscription fom — **VII**: 87.

Sennacherib's Attack (Siege of) on **II**: 90, 435; **IV**: 214; **VI**: 239*(2)*.
'Solar Shrine' at **II**: 436.
Trephined Skulls from **III**: 357, 401, 408.

Lachish (Letters) Ostraca: **I**: *73;* **II**: 357; **III**: 411; **VII**: **§859, 99-102**.
Aramaic Text Contemporary with **VII**: 127.
III, 11. 14-18 **VI**: 335.
Jerusalem in **II**: 417; **VII**: 101.
Letter IV **VII**: 100, 102*(2)*.
Letter IV: 7-10 **VII**: 101.
North Semitic Alphabet in **V**: 286; **VII**: 100.
Ostraca I **VII**: 101.
Ostraca II **VII**: 101.
Ostraca III: 13-18 **VII**: 101.

LACHS, JOHN:
God, Concepts of, on **VIII**: 100.

Laconia:
Hittites in **II**: 140*(2)*.

Lacuna: **IV**: 18.

Ladel:
Silver, from Greece **III**: 588*(2)*.

Ladle:
Urartian **III**: 573.

Lady Lever Art Gallery:
Canpic Jars in **III**: 580.

Lag Ba 'Omer: **I**: 367.

LAGARDE, PAUL DE: **IV**: 26.

Lagash: **I**: *271;* **II**: *106(2), 168,* 268, 270, 273; **III**: *106,* **149**, *465, 763*.
Divine Service in *(Sumerian Religion)* **V**: 182.
Kings of **III**: 164; **IX**: cxii.
Nam-maḫ-ni, Govenor of **VII**: 237.
Rulers of **VII**: 276.
Ur III Tablets from **VII**: 211.
URÚ.ki, Quarter of **II**: 270.

LAGRANGE, R. P.: **VIII**: 51.

Lahm, Tel el: **III**: *2,* **149**, *170, 227*.

Lahun: **I**: *281;* **III**: 149.

Laish: **II**: 284, 436.
Danite Migration to **I**: 156; **II**: *436;* **IV**: 369; **VI**: 190.

Lake(s):
Holy Land, of, in the Talmud **VI**: 699.
Sacred, at Karnak **III**: 136.

Lake Moeris: **III**: 103, **169**.
Name of **III**: 169; **V**: 300.

Lakhmu: **V**: 171.

Lama: **V**: 187.
Goddess, at Ur, Statue of **III**: 747.

LAMARCK, JEAN BAPTISTE PIERRE ANTONE DE: **III**: 302.

Lamashtu:
Amulets of **III**: 581.

Lamb:
Christian, with Cross **III**: 699.
Images of, and Assyrian Religious Texts **V**: 170.
Misuse of the Tern in EV **V**: 509.
Paschal **V**: 85.
Paschal, Bones of **VI**: 106; **IX**: cxxxv.
Paschal, Date of the Slaughter of **V**: 87.
Sumerian Art and **III**: 699.
Symbolism of **III**: 377; **VIII**: 303.

Lambaesis: **III**: 149.

Lamech: **IV**: 297; **VI**: 45*(2)*.

Lamech Scroll, *see:* **Genesis Apocryphon**

Lament:
Divine Funeral **VI**: 276, 343, 355.
Erechite's, Over the Desolation of His Fatherland (Sumerian) **VII**: 274.
"Lament of the Daughter of Sin" **VII**: 242, 254.
Rachel's **II**: 465.

Lamentations:
Aruru, to **VII**: 261.
Babylonian, to Tammuz **V**: 178.
Harper's Lament **V**: 211.
Meopotamian Background **VI**: 559.
Nippur, Over the Destruction of **VII**: 276.
Ur, Over the Desolation of **VII**: 274.

Lamentations, Book of:
Authenticity, Authorship, Date, and Origin of **IV**: **§399, 511**; **VI**: 560.
Bibliography of **I**: (**§29**), 14.
Exegetical Studies on **VI**: **§654, 558-560**.
Isaiah, Connection to **IV**: *445, 448,* 511; **VI**: *305*.
Jonah, Connection to **IV**: *445, 448,* 511; **VI**: *305*.
Literary Criticism of **IV**: **§398, 511**.
Metrical Structure of Qinoth **IV**: 511.
Nahum, Connection to **IV**: *445, 448,* 511; **VI**: *305*.
Parallelism in **V**: 690.
Philological Studies in **IV**: 511.
Rhythm in **V**: 690.
Sumerian Influence upon, Alleged **IV**: 511.
Symmetrical Repetitions in 1 and 2 **V**: 706.
Syriac Text of **IV**: 46.

Lamentatons 5:
Date of **VI**: 560.

Lamentations 1 and 2:
Symmetrical Repetitions **V**: 706.

Lamentations, Book of, Manuscripts of: **VI**: (**§655**), **560**.

Lampāka:
Aramaic Inscriptions found at **VII**: 128.

Lamponia: **III**: *104*, 149, *200*.

Lamps, Lighting Fixtures, and Related Articles: **III**: **§210, 594-596**.
Antique, in Harvard Semitic Musuem **III**: 449.
Corith, Wheel-made, from **III**: 594.
Egyptian **III**: 595*(2)*.
Graeco-Roman **III**: 595.
Greek **III**: 594*(2)*.
"Herodian" **III**: 595.
Jewish, from Cyrene **III**: 569.
Nabataean, from Petra **III**: 595.
Roman Terra-cotta **III**: 594.
Samaritan **III**: 594, 595; **VII**: 137.

Lampstand(s):
Greek **III**: 594.

Lance:
Butt **III**: 682.
Head **III**: 682.

Land: **I**: 387.
Administrative Divisions of, in Israel and Judah **I**: 463.
Attic Public Land-ownership **I**: 261.
Babylonian Land Grant **VII**: 248.
Conveyance of, from the Reign of Ellil-bani **VII**: 250.
Cost of, in Egypt **I**: 308.
Crown, Given by Ptolemies **I**: 226.
Deeds of Sale and lease **VII**: 253; **IX**: lxxxix, cxli, cxlii, cxliii.
Distribution of, in Ancient Greece **I**: 505.
Distribution of, on Earth's Surface According to Hebrew Sources **II**: 256.
Division, Mycenaean **I**: 255.
Fertility of, in Messianic Prophecies **VIII**: 136.
Land Records on a Stelae of the XIIth Dynasty **VII**: 31.
Landholders of Pylos **VII**: 360*(2)*.
Legislation under Caesar **I**: 497.

Not to be Sold — **VI**: 126.
Sale of a Field — **I**: 467.
Sale of Land in the reign of Philopator — **VII**: 28.
Temple and, in Israelite Worship — **IV**: 484; **V**: 27, 45, 70.
Use, Royal policies at Mari — **I**: 309.
"Land Beyond the River": — **III**: 40.
Land Bridge:
Eurafrican — **III**: 156, 356.
"Land of the Living":
Gilgamesh and — **V**: 185.
Land Tenure: — **I**: **§89, 260-262**, *383(2)*.
Aristotle on — **V**: 245; **IX**: xciii.
Landmarks: — **VI**: 147.
"Lands Beyond the Sea": — **VII**: 371.
LANDSBERGER, BENNO: — **III**: 366.
Landscapes:
Numismatic — **I**: 456.
Pictorial — **I**: 456.
LANE, E. W.:
Arabic Lexicon of — **V**: 594.
LANG, R. HAMILTON: — **V**: 190.
LANGLAND, WILLIAM: — **VIII**: 369.
Language, *see also:* **Philological Studies** — **I**: *122*.
Afroasiatic — **V**: **§489, 305**.
Ancient and Modern, Compared — **V**: 275.
Ancient, pronunciation of — **V**: 279.
Babylonian Number idioms — **I**: 432.
Biblical — **IV**: 92*(2)*.
Biblical, Advantage in Knowing — **V**: 279.
Biblical, in the Theological Curriculum — **V**: 280.
Biblical, Study of — **V**: 279.
Biblical Teaching about the Origin of — **V**: 279.
Bilingualism in Italy, and Shift of, from Sixth to third Century B.C. — **V**: 280.
Buried, Resurrecton of — **VII**: 1.
Classification of — **V**: 276.
Classification of, in conformity with Ethnology — **V**: 277.
Confusion of, at "Babel" — **IV**: 311*(3)*, 312*(3)*; **VI**: 57.
Creatan, Linguistic Influence — **I**: 325.
Decipherment of Unknown Writing and — **VII**: 2.
Development of — **V**: 276, 279*(2)*.
Divine Origin of — **V**: 281.
Figures of Speech in — **V**: 280.
Gowth of — **V**: 276*(2)*.
Growth of, taken from Semitic — **V**: 279.
Hamitic, Noun Classes and Polarity in — **II**: *166*.
History of — **V**: 276.
Le Pasteur Fesquet's Theory of the Origin of — **V**: 386.
Mediterranean, Ancient, Reciprocal Influence amid — **V**: 276.
Old Testament, Knowledge of Languages in — **V**: 280.
Origin of — **III**: 350; **V**: 1, 275*(2)*, 276*(5)*, 277*(3)*, 279*(3)*, 280, 281.
Origin of, Le Paseur Fesquet's Theory — **V**: 278.
Origin of, with special reference to the Paleolithic Age — **V**: 279.
Palestine, in the Days of Christ, and Josephus — **VI**: 679.
Primeval — **V**: 275.
Primitive Man, of — **IV**: 289; **V**: 277.
Primitive Thought, Effects on — **V**: 278, 279.
Prohibition on Study of Greek — **I**: 182.
Provincial, in the Roman Empire — **V**: 280.

Race and	**III**: 336, 338; **V**: 277; **IX**: ciii.
Relations of	**V**: 276.
Religious, of the Bible	**V**: 512.
Roman Tolerance toward Greek	**I**: 122.
Science of	**V**: 276*(2)*.
Science of, and Chronology	**II** 180.
Speech, Parts of, and the Development of	**V**: 279.
Structure of, of the Ancient Orient	**V**: 279.
Symbolic, and Literary Forms Used in OT	**IV**: 215.
Theology and	**VIII**: 9.
Theory of	**V**: 279.
Theory of (Noire's)	**V**: 277.
Theory of, Plato and	**V**: 279.
Thoth, as Creator of	**V**: 217.
Thought and, Relation Between, and the Doctrine of Inspiration	**V**: 278.
Translation of, Capturing	**IV**: 112.
Transliteration of Non-Roman	**V**: **§487**, **290-291**.
Variation of, and Species	**V**: 276.
Variations of	**III**: 335.
Languages, Other unspecified Bearing on the ANE:	**V**: **§555**, **678-680**; **IX**: **§555**, **cxliv**.
Laocrites:	**I**: 495.
Laodiceans:	
Epistle to	**VI**: 533, 536.
Lapethos:	**VII**: *121*.
Lapidary:	**I**: **§98**, **290-293**.
Lapis-lazuli:	**I**: 285, 287, 342; **II**: 267.
Cylinders of, from Thebes	**III**: 593.
Disc of, with cuneiform inscription	**VII**: 206.
Trade, Early Phases of its	**III**: 660; **IX**: xcii.
Larasa:	**I**: *364, 506*.
Lares:	**III**: 696; **V**: 268.
Mother of the	**V**: 269.
Larisa:	**III**: *123*.
Greek Inscription from	**VII**: 313.
Larissa:	**II**: *172;* **III**: 150, *650*.
Lark:	
Hittite *(Korud)*	**III**: 377.
Larnaca:	
Digraphic (Cypriote) Text	**VII**: 356.
Larnax, Lapethos:	
Bilingual Phoenicial / Greek Inscription from	**VII**: 331.
Larsa:	**I**: *307;* **II**: *19;* **III**: 150.
Contracts from	**VII**: 279.
Lasso:	**III**: 610.
Last Things, *see:* **Eschatology**	
"Last Times":	**V**: 9, 520; **VIII**: 251.
Latamne:	**III**: **150**.
Geological Observations near	**II**: 251.
Mammals, Middle Pleistocene, from	**III**: 367.
Latex, *see:* **Rubber**	
Latin, Bible Versions, *see:* **Old Latin VSS, Latin Vulgate**	
Protestant, Reformation	**IV**: 48.
Quotations, of: Somnium Neronis	**VIII**: 365.
Latin Grammar and Etymology - General Studies:	**V**: **§552**, **663-670**.
Ablative of Association	**V**: 667.
Accent	**V**: *633*, 666*(2)*, 667, 669.
Accent, Relation to Elision	**V**: 667.
Accusative, Greek, Origin of, in	**V**: *635*, 669.
Acute	**V**: 667.
Adjectives, Compound, in Early Poetry	**V**: 668.
Affix, Peculiarities of, in	**V**: *630*, 665.
Allophonies of /i/	**V**: 669.
Cases	**V**: 664.

Conditional Sentences in **V**: *626,* 664, 667.
Conjuctions, Subordinating **V**: 669.
Dative Singular of Pronominal Declension **V**: 667.
Diphthong -ui in **V**: 667.
-eis in Accusative Plural of the Third Declension **V**: 668.
Elision and Hiatus in Prose and Poetry **V**: 668.
Elision, Relation to Accent **V**: 667.
Enclitics, Effect on Word Accent **V**: 667.
Fifth Declension in **V**: 669.
Genitive Singular of Pronominal Declension **V**: 667.
Gerund, and Hittite Verbal Nouns in *-tar* **V**: 611.
Gerund in, and Hittite Verbal Nouns **V**: *611,* 669.
Gerundive and other *-nd-* Formations **V**: 669.
Grave **V**: 667.
Hiatus and Elision in Prose and Poetry **V**: 668.
Imperative **V**: 666.
Indefinties and Hittite **V**: *609,* 668.
Indirect Discourse, Moods in **V**: 669.
Indirect Object **V**: 667.
Infinitive, Imperfect **V**: 275.
Infinitive with Subj. Acc. **V**: 669.
Metric **V**: 666.
Moods in Indirect Discourse **V**: 669.
Neuter Substantives **V**: 665.
Passive, Nature of **V**: 668.
Passive Periphrastic in **V**: 667.
Perfect Tense in, and the Hebrew Piʿel, Analogy **V**: *468,* 663.
Peronsal Ending, 2 Pl. Med-Passive in **V**: 669.
Potential (?) **V**: 666.
Prepositions **V**: *634, 635,* 669*(2).*
Prepositions, Suffixes of **V**: *625,* 664.
Present Participle **V**: 667.
Prohibitions **V**: 666.
Pronoun, Reflexive **V**: 669.
Pronouns **V**: 663.
Purpose Clause in, Origin **V**: *631,* 666.
Re-acute **V**: 667.
Rhythm **V**: 667.
Semitic Words in **V**: 374, *637,* 667.
Sentence Connection, Anticipatory Element in **V**: 667.
Subjunctive **V**: 664.
Subjunctive "Comparative" Clause in **V**: 665.
Subjunctive, Stipulative **V**: 666.
Syntax **V**: 664, 665, 666.
Syntax, Combinatory of Greek and **V**: *634,* 668.
Tenses, Sequences of, in **V**: 665*(3).*
Terminations *tia, tio-* **V**: 663.
Unreal Condition in **V**: 666.
Verbs, Comparison with Greek Verbs **V**: 624, 663.
Verbs, Perfect Tense **V**: 663*(2).*
Verbs, Tenses, Formation of Completed Action in Finite **V**: 664*(2).*
Voice of Non-Finite Verb **V**: 669.
Vowel, Short, with Final *s* **V**: 669.
Vowels, Prothetic, in **V**: *633,* 668.
Zero Stress **V**: 667.

Latin Inscriptions, Texts: **VII: §951, 365-368.**

Amphitruo of Plautus, Composition of **VII**: 365.
Apamea, Great Inscription from **II**: 281; **VII**: 312.
Arabia, from **VII**: 367.
Assuan, at **VII**: 366.
Autobiographical Elements in **VII**: 367*(2).*
Baalbek, from **VII**: 366.
Bath, Records of a Roman, in Upper Egypt **VII**: 368.
Beirut Museum, in **VII**: 366.
Bowdoin College, in **VII**: *328,* 368.
Bronze Medal from Jaulan **VII**: 366.
Duenos Inscription **VII**: 366, 367*(2).*

Elegiacs from Corinth **VII**: 368.
Elogia of Julius Cesar's Father **VII**: 368.
Epigraphy **VII**: 368.
Graffito **VII**: 368.
History of Roman Literature **VII**: 365.
Horace, Life and Writings **VII**: 365.
Horace, Satires of **VII**: 366.
Horace, Translators of **VII**: 365, 366.
Ḫurrian Sala(s) **VII**: 368.
Iguvine **V**: 664.
Index Verorum for **V**: *634*, 669.
Inscriptions, Contributions of, to the Study of Latin Language **V**: 666; **VII**: 366.
Inscriptions relating to Hadrian's Jewish War **VII**: 366.
Jersualem, at **VII**: 366.
Laudatio Turiae, fragment **VII**: 368.
Lebanon, in **VII**: 367*(2)*.
Livy XXXVI, 40 **VII**: 368.
Pisidian Antioch, from **VII**: 368.
Qui Terminum Exarasset **VII**: 368.
Roman Campaigns in Palestine, Relating to **VII**: 367*(2)*.
Rome, from **VII**: 367.
Rylands Collection of Greek and Latin Papyri **VII**: *354*, 368.
Sardis, from **VII**: *318*, 367.
Sinope, from **VII**: *317(2)*, 366*(3)*.
Stele in the Roman Forum **VII**: 367.
Titus, on **VII**: 366*(2)*.
University of Pennsylvania, in **VII**: 367.
Vespasaian on **VII**: 366*(2)*.
Virgil, English Translators **VII**: 365.
Wax Tablet **VII**: 368.

Latin Language:
Assimilation of *ti* and *di* before a vowel in Vulgar **V**: 668.
Canting Puns **V**: 668.
Clipped Words in **V**: 668.
Etymology **V**: *638*, 663*(2)*, 665.
Etymology, Change of *L* to *D* **V**: *629*, 665.
Etymology, Peile's **V**: *626*, *627*, 664*(2)*.
G, Origin of Letter in **V**: 666.
Greek and **V**: 623, 624, 663.
Greek Influence on Vulgar **V**: 633, 668.
Greek Inscriptions, Latin Words in, of Asia Minor **V**: 668.
Greek Writers, Knowledge of, among **V**: 665.
Inscriptions as Contributions to the Study of **V**: 666; **VII**: 366.
Loan-Words in **V**: 665.
Monphthongization of *æ* **V**: 668.
ν, Letter , Transliteration and Pronunciation of, in **V**: 667.
Philological Study **V**: 663.
Pronunciation, Differences Among Ancient Romans **V**: 664.
Pronunciation, History of **V**: 664.
Pronunciation, presented in Grammars **V**: 664*(2)*.
Sanskrit, compared **V**: 275*(2)*.
Sentence Structure in Prose Writers **V**: 667.
Talmud on Pronunciation of certain Letters in **V**: 665.
Uncial, Origin of **V**: 667.
Vocalic Laws of **V**: 665.
Vowel Length, Devices for Indicating **V**: 668.
Vulgar, Importance of Special Languaes in the Study of **V**: 668.
Word Order in **V**: 666.
Z, Letter in (?) **V**: 666.
Z, Origin of Letter in **V**: 666.

Latin Lexicography: **V**: 663, 665.
Derivations and Affinities of Greek and Latin Words **V**: *624*, 663.
Dictionaries **V**: 663, 666.
Word Studies **V**: 667.

Latin Literature, *see:* **Latin Inscriptions**

Latin Manuscripts, Texts:
- Ambrosian — **VII**: 365.
- Codex Sangallensis 912, Hebrew Words in the Latin Glossary — **V**: 392.
- Corpus of, Ritschl and Mommsen's New — **VII**: 365.
- Latin Uncial, Parentage of — **V**: 667.
- Old Latin Palimpsest Fragments of Numbers — **VI**: 139.
- Paris B.N. 16558, Talmudic Terms and Idioms in — **VI**: 705.
- Transliteration of Hebrew in a 13th Century MS — **V**: 291.

Latin Superscriptio MSS: — **IV**: 12.

Latin Word Studies - Alphabetical Listing — **V**: **§553, 670-674**.

Latium: — **III**: 150.
- Cists from — **III**: 550.

Lató pros Kamara:
- Greek Inscriptions from — **VII**: 315.

Latter Prophets, Books of:
- ***Bibliography of*** — **I**: **§15, 12**.
- Character of — **IV**: 388.
- Composite Character of — **IV**: 126.
- Contrast, Prophet's Use of — **V**: 703.
- Covenant Lawsuit in — **IV**: 389*(2)*; **V**: 692, 693.
- Covenant Message of — **IV**: 389; **VIII**: 216.
- Divine Names, Occurrence in — **IV**: 385; **VIII**: 107.
- Ethics and — **IV**: 388, 389; **VIII**: 226, 228, 231.
- "Execration Texts", Patterns of, in — **V**: 703.
- ***Exegetical Studies on*** — **VI**: **§605, 245**.
- Future in — **IV**: 387; **VIII**: 251.
- Hebrew Tradition, Witness to — **IV**: 388.
- Higher Criticism and — **IV**: 388.
- Historical Setting of — **IV**: 389.
- ***Literary Criticism of*** — **IV**: **§344, 385-389**; **IX**: **§344, cxxxii**.
- ***Literary Style of*** — **V**: **§568, 703**.
- Message of — **IV**: 388.
- Messianic Idea in — **IV**: 386.
- Messianic Passages in — **IV**: 389.
- Modern Interpretation of — **IV**: 387.
- Moral Message of — **IV**: 388, 389.
- Patriarchal "Benediction" and Prophetic Book — **V**: 703.
- Pertinence of — **IV**: 388.
- Relevance of — **IV**: 389*(2)*.
- Revelation, as a Medium of — **IV**: 388.
- Rhetroical Form in — **V**: 703.
- Social Justice of — **IV**: 389.
- Socialism, Alleged, of — **IV**: 385.
- Targum of, Critique of the Text of — **VI**: 711.
- Transpositions in — **VI**: 270.
- Wisdom in — **IV**: 389; **V**: 117.
- Woe-Oracles of — **IV**: 389.

LAURENT, PETER EDMUND: — **III**: 463.

Laurentian Bible:
- Marco Polo's Bible — **IV**: 42.

Laver:
- Molten Sea before Solomon's Temple — **V**: 50, 72*(2)*.
- Symbol on Ancient Jewish Coins — **I**: 451; **V**: 53.

Law, General Studies, *see also:* **Legislation** — **IX**: cxx.

"The Law" in Israel - Specifically, *see also:* **Decalogue** — **I**: **§129, 472-477**, 514; **VIII**: 349; **IX**: **§129, c**.
- Accident and Error in the Bible — **I**: 466.
- Administration of, in Early Jewish Era from Talmudic Records — **I**: 461.
- Administration of, in Israel — **I**: 461.

Animals, Medical Treatment of, in Jewish	**III**: 366.
Anti-Traditional of Josephus	**I**: 463; **VI**: 680.
Arbitration in Jewish	**I**: 468, 503.
Archaeology and ANE	**I**: 463.
Art in	**IX**: c.
Art in Jewish	**III**: 701.
Asylum	**II**: 311.
Authority and,	**I**: 491.
Babylon in Jewish	**I**: 479.
Bible Illustrating, in the Ancient World	**V**: 22.
Biblical	**I**: 466*(2)*, 471*(2)*, *496*, 507.
Birds in	**III**: 369.
"Book of the Law" discovered in the Temple	**IV**: 359, 383*(2)*, 384*(4)*; **VI**: 232.
Case Law, Precedent, and 'Fazanias'	**I**: 461.
Causations, direct and indirect in Biblical	**I**: 469.
Ceremonial	**I**: 472; **V**: 38.
Change, of	**VI**: 693.
Christ and	**VIII**: 279.
Classification of, in Mishneh Torah	**I**: 475.
Commentaries on Hebrew	**I**: 472.
Common Life, Israelite, on	**I**: 466.
Conscience and	**I**: 471; **VIII**: 175.
'Corporate Personality' in	**I**: 470, 508.
Covenant and	**I**: 477, 514, 515; **VIII**: 217.
Covenant Code and	**I**: 477, 505.
Criminal, Jewish	**I**: 463.
Deposit, of, in Old Testament	**I**: 304.
Deuteronomic, *see:* ***Deuteronomic Code / Law***	
Dietary	**I**: **§87**, **249-250**; **VI**: 114, 119, 693.
Divorce in Jewish	**I**: 218.
Dodging the	**I**: 502.
Error and Accident in the Bible	**I**: 466.
Esdras, Fourth, in	**I**: *479;* **VI**: 614; **VIII**: 181.
Ethics of Mosaic	**I**: 474; **VI**: 156; **VIII**: 220, 222.
Ezra's Recension of the	**I**: 44.
Faith and	**VIII**: 200.
Family	**I**: 460, 471, 516.
'Fazanias' in Bible History	**I**: 461.
Fiction, Legal, in Jewish	**I**: 465.
Genesis as a source of	**I**: 469; **IV**: 271.
Giving of the	**VI**: 96.
God's, and Precepts of Men	**I**: 365.
God's, Conception of, in the Prophets and Jesus	**I**: 475.
Goring Ox, and	**I**: 466, 500.
Gospel and (Decalogue)	**VI**: 160.
Gospel or	**VI**: 111.
Grace and, in Judaism and Luteranism	**I**: 477; **VIII**: 197.
Health, and their influence on Life-Conditions	**III**: 396.
Hebrew, Bibliography of	**I**: 471‡.
Hebrew, Development of	**I**: 473.
Hebrew Legal Terms	**V**: 401, 404, 405.
Hebrew, Origin of	**I**: 464, 468, 513.
Hebrew Secular in Light of Comparative Jurisprudence	**I**: 461.
Hebrew, Theological Presuppositions of	**I**: 476.
Hebrew, Unwritten	**I**: 464.
Hebrew, Western Semitic Curses and Origin of	**I**: 513.
Homicide, in Hebrew	**I**: 462.
Humaneness of	**I**: 472*(2)*, 473.
Hypothec in Talmudic	**I**: 471.
Information, Sharing of	**VI**: 121.
Interest, in Old Testament	**I**: 306.
Israel, in - General Studies	**I**: **§127**, **460-471**; **IX**: **§127**, **c**.
Israelite, Concept of	**I**: 505.

Israelite, in Period of the Judges	**I**: 466.
Israelite, Origin of	**I**: 462.
Ius redemptionis in Hebrew	**I**: 468.
Jesus and	**VIII**: 280, 282*(2)*.
Jewish, and Other Ancient Legal Systems	**I**: 468, 503.
Jewish, Art in	**III**: 701.
Jewish compared with Roman	**I**: 479, 499.
Jewish, Contrectatio in	**I**: 466, 500.
Jewish, of Agency	**I**: 462.
Jewish, relation to Babylonian	**I**: 462, 480, 489, 504.
Jewish, Specificato in	**I**: 468, 503.
Josephus, Anti-Traditional, of	**I**: 463; **VI**: 680.
Judicial Petition from Meẕad Ḫashavyahu	**VII**: 95.
Laborers, Status of in Jewish	**I**: 467.
Land	**I**: **§89**, **260-262**, 462, 472; **VI**: 126.
Late, in Early Narratives	**I**: 466.
Legal Certificate from Bar Kochba's Days	**VII**: 94.
Legal Document from Murabbaʿat	**VII**: 94.
Legal Precedents	**I**: 461, 474.
Levitical	**I**: 472, 473*(2)*; **IV**: *377*.
Levitical, as a Tuition to Theism	**V**: 8.
Levitical, Ezekiel and	**IV**: 417*(3)*, 419*(2)*.
Life under Jewish	**I**: 473*(2)*; **IX**: lxxxv*(2)*.
Love and, in the OT	**VIII**: 230.
Medical Treatment of Animals in Jewish	**III**: 366.
Mercy, Provision of in Israelitish	**I**: 473.
Minor, Status of in Jewish	**I**: 475.
Mosaic, Abolished(?)	**I**: 476.
Mosaic, and with other Law Codes and Hammurbi	**I**: *69(3)*, **§130**, **478-480**, 496*(6)*; **IX**: **§130, c**.
Mosaic Codes and Popular Hebrew Religion	**V**: 16.
Mosaic, Economic Principles of	**I**: 475.
Mosaic, in connection with the History and Character of the Jews	**I**: 472.
Mosaic, Origin and Scope of	**I**: 475.
Mosaic, *see also:* ***"The Law" in Israel - Specifically***	**I**: *304*, 365, **§129**, **472-477**, 514; **IV**: 361; **IX**: **§129, c**.
Motive Clauses in OT	**I**: 476.
Natural	**I**: 463, 465, 466, 469; **III**: 303; **V**: 113.
"Nazir" Legislation	**VI**: 128.
New Testament, Relation of Mosaic, to	**I**: 473; **VIII**: 230.
Noachic	**VI**: 654.
Offender of, Halachic Status of Non-Halachic Jews	**I**: 471.
Paradise, of	**IV**: 286.
Peculium in Jewish	**I**: 466.
Pentateuch, in	**I**: 472, 475, 476; **IV**: 143.
Pentateuch, Order of, in	**IV**: 239.
Persons, Law of, in Jewish Jurisprudence	**I**: 465.
Philo's Exposition of	**VI**: 675.
Pignus in Talmudic	**I**: 471.
Pledge, Clause on Seizure of, Aramaic Papyri	**VII**: 130.
Pledges in Biblical	**I**: 513.
Poor Laws, Hebrew	**I**: 460*(3)*.
Possession in Talmudic	**I**: 471.
Post-Exilic Legalism	**V**: 9.
Priestly Element in	**IV**: 251.

Priests, Concerning **IV**: 252; **V**: 40.
Progressivness of, Old Testament **I**: 462.
Prophets to the **V**: 8.
Punishment, Public, in Mosaic **I**: 462, 475.
Rabbinic, of Sale **I**: 463; **VI**: 693.
Races, Ancient, Survival of, in **I**: 326; **II**: 260; **IX**: cxxi.
Reading of, and the Samaritan Liturgy **V**: 228, 229.
Reign of, as Incentive to Prayer **VIII**: 201.
Ruth, Legal Problems in **I**: 470; **IV**: 510.
Sacrifice, Sin and, in OT **V**: 60; **VIII**: 179.
Sale, Rabbinic, of **I**: 463; **VI**: 693.
Sanitary, Mosaic **I**: 472; **III**: 396.
Scroll of, Writing a **I**: 384.
Self-help in Hebrew **I**: 468.
Self-Help in Jewish **I**: 467, 502.
Septuagint, Legal Interpretations in **I**: 467; **VI**: 83, 113, 114.
Septuagint Renderings of **V**: 509.
Septuagint Renderings of OT Terms **I**: 463; **V**: 637.
Shemitta **V** 425.
Sin, Concept of, in **VIII**: 183.
Sin, Sacrifice, and in OT **V**: 60; **VIII**: 179.
Sinfulness in, Concessions to **VIII**: 183.
Slavery, Laws on **I**: 201, 463, 469.
Social (Development) and **I**: 190, 467, 472, 474; **III**: *396*.
Social Teaching of **VIII**: 231.
Tannaitic, Jerusalem and **II**: 421.
Tannaitic Jurisprudence **VI**: 692.
Tannaitic, Sources of **VI**: 692.
Teaching of, in Lifetime of Apostles **I**: 473; **VIII**: 271.
Testate Succession in Jewish **I**: 468.
Theological Implications **VIII**: 5.
Tithe, of **V**: 65*(2)*.
Usufructus in Jewish **I**: 467, 502.
Worship, Place of, on **V**: 39.

Law (outside Israel): *see also specific Texts e.g. Greek Legal Texts* **I: §135, 488-494; IX: §135, ci-cii.**
Administrative **I**: 501.
Affidavit of a Legionary **VII**: 354.
Agrarian, First, Roman **I**: 506.
Ancient, Bibliography on **I**: 499*(2)*.
Ancient World, in **I**: 464, 465, 491, 495, 505.
Arbitration in Roman **I**: 468, 503.
Arbitration, Private in Greco-Roman Egypt **I**: 502.
Associations, of, in Greco-Roman Egypt **I**: 501.
Assyrian **I**: 498, 502.
Assyrian, Koschaker's theory regarding **I**: 498.
Assyro-Babylonian, Scope and Methods of a History of **I**: 497.
Athens, Marriage Law and Family Organization in **I**: 188, 211, 499.
Babylonian **I**: 461, 466, 496*(4)*, 497, 498, 502, 509*(2)*; **IV**: 182; **V**: 174.
Babylonian, relation to Jewish **I**: 462, 480, 489, 504.
Babylonian, Social **I**: 497.
Babylonian, Sword Obligations in **VII**: 28.
Babylonian, Temple and Suretyship **I**: 498.
Canaan **I**: 467, 491.
Codification of, causes **I**: 503.
Corn, Roman and Greek **I**: 495.
Creatan **I**: 495*(3)*.
Cuneiform **I**: 125, 492, 505.
Customary **I**: 499.
Debtor, Ephesian **I**: 499.
Deposit, of, in Babylon **I**: 304.
Domicle, Inviolability of, in Graeco-Roman Egypt **I**: 227.
"DonatioMortisCausa" **I**: 503.

Egyptian	**I**: 491, 498, 499‡*(2)*, 501, 502, 503, 509; **VII**: 30.
Egyptian, Codification of, by Darius	**VII**: 29.
Egyptian. Judicial Papyrus of Turin	**VII**: 30.
Egyptian, Sword Oblications in	**VII**: 28.
Egyptian Word for (Demotic)	**V**: 352.
English Law comparied with Hebrew	**I**: 473.
Ephesian Debtor	**I**: 499.
Eshnunna, of	**I**: 501, 504.
Goring Ox, and Babylonian	**I**: 466, 500.
Goring Ox, and Near Eastern Law	**I**: 470, 505.
Greek	**I**: 499‡*(2)*, 500, 501, 502*(2)*, 504.
Greek, Amendments to Athenian Decrees	**I**: 498; **VII**: 340.
Greek, in Athens, Relation between Private and Public	**I**: 188, 499.
Greek, Legal History	**VIII**: 341.
Greek Revenue Laws	**VII**: 342.
Hellenistic	**I**: 500.
Hittite	**I**: 205, 491, 497, 498, 500, 501, 504, 505, 506, 507; **III**: 776; **IV**: 193; **VII**: **§933, 307**.
Hittite, and Abraham's purchase of Machpelah	**IV**: 319.
House, Inviolability of, in Graeco-Roman Egypt	**I**: 227.
International and Ancient	**I**: 495; **VIII**: 350.
International, Biblical Roots of	**I**: 464, 499.
Jews and Roman	**I**: 506.
Land, other than Israel	**I**: 464, 497, 499.
Laws of Specific Foreign Countries	**I**: **§136, 495-507**.
Legal Formula in Aramaic, Egyptian and Murabba'at Documents	**I**: 503; **VII**: 31, 128.
Legal Formula in Aramaic Papyri and Daniel 4:14	**VI**: 571; **VII**: 30, 128.
Legal Formula in the Susa Tablets and Daniel 4:14	**VI**: 571; **VII**: 30, 128.
Legal Formula in Twelfth Dynasty Egyptian Document and Daniel	**VI**: 571; **VII**: 30, 128.
"Letters of Agreement"	**V**: 345.
Lex Vatinia de imperio Caesaris	**I**: 506.
Licinio-Sextian	**I**: 490.
Maledictions, Babylonian	**V**: 576.
Maritime	**I**: 355, 506; **VII**: 342.
Marriage Law and Family Organization in Athens	**I**: 188, 211, 499.
Median	**I**: 495.
Mesopotamian	**I**: 471, 491, 500, 503, 507.
Oldest (Sumerian)	**I**: 497.
Oriental Justice, and	**I**: 388.
patria potestas in pre-Hammurabian Sources	**I**: 211.
Peculium in Roman	**I**: 466.
Penal	**I**: 501.
Persian	**I**: 495.
Persons, Law of, in Roman Jurisprudence	**I**: 465.
Political	**I**: 501.
Pre-Hammurabian	**I**: 500.
Pre-Israelite	**I**: 462.
Private	**I**: 501.
Private, in Greco-Roman Law of Egypt	**I**: 502.
Private Legal Acts in Greco-Roman Egypt	**I**: 502.
Ptolemaic Egypt, Plurality of, in	**I**: 504.
Roman	**I**: 491, 495*(2)*, 498, 499‡*(2)*, 500, 501, 502*(2)*, 505.

Roman, 'acceptilatio' in	**I**: 504.
Roman, and Magic	**I**: 498.
Roman, compared with Jewish	**I**: 479, 499.
Roman, Contrectatio in	**I**: 466, 500.
Roman, Dictionary of	**I**: 501.
Roman, Divorce in	**I**: 218.
Roman Legal Institutions in Acta Martyrum	**I**: 490; **VI**: 688.
Roman Legal Institutions in Early Rabbincs	**I**: 490; **VI**: 688.
Roman, reorganization of (Licinio-Sextian)	**I**: 490.
Roman, Specificato in	**I**: 468, 503.
Sabaean Penal	**I**: 501.
Salic	**I**: 497.
Samaritan, in Funeral Rites	**I**: 377, 477; **VIII**: 9, 254, 386.
Self-Help in Roman	**I**: 467, 502.
Semitic	**I**: 497.
Solon, Code of	**I**: 500.
South Arabic, Word in	**V**: 595.
Sumaritan Funeral Rites, in	**VIII**: 9.
Sumerian	**VII**: 272.
Sumerian, compared with Code of Hammurabi	**I**: 497; **VII**: 245.
Sumerian, Sex Offences	**I**: 505.
Surveyorship in Greco-Roman	**I**: 437.
Ugaritic Legal Formula, and Biblical Parallel	**VI**: 126.
Unwritten, affecting Arab Women	**I**: 391.
Ususfructus in Roman	**I**: 467, 502.
Water Rights	**I**: 364.
Law and the Gospel:	**VIII**: **§1028, 230**.
"Law and the Prophets":	**IV**: 235, 242, 359; **V**: 16, 17.
Gospel and	**V**: 27.
Law Codes, *see also:* **Codes:**	
Ancient Near Eastern	**I**: 506.
Assyrian	**VII**: 192*(2)*, 193.
Assyrian, Old Empire, Institutions (Family Law)	**I**: 498.
Babylonian	**I**: 479, 496, 504.
Cretan Gortyna	**I**: 226, 495*(3)*; **VII**: 338.
Eshnunna, of, from Tell Harmel	**VII**: 154, 155*(3)*, 252.
Hammurabi, *see:* ***Hammurabi, Code of***	
Harmel, Tell, from	**VII**: 193, 252.
Hittite	**I**: 497, 505.
Hittite §10, and Exodus	**VI**: 113.
Israelite	**I**: 479, 496.
Lipit-Ishtar	**IV**: *372*.
Oldest Written	**I**: 497.
Pre-Hammurabi	**I**: 501.
Saxon, Influence of the Bible on	**VIII**: 352.
Sumerian	**I**: 497.
Ur-Nammu	**I**: 502, 506.
Law of Moses, *see:* **"The Law" in Israel**	
LAW, WILLIAM JOHN:	
Hannibal, on	**IX**: civ.
Lawgiver:	
Divine, and Sin	**VIII**: 177, 193.
Hebrew	**I**: 460, 461, *474*.
Laws of Foreign Countries *(i.e. other than Israel)*	**I**: **§136, 495-507**.
Demetrius of Phalerum, of	**I**: 497.
Samuel, Legal Practices in compared with ANE	**IX**: c.
Laws of Moses, *see:* **Jubilees, Book of**	
Lawsuit:	
Covenant, in the Latter Prophets	**IV**: 389.
Egyptian	**VII**: 28.
Egyptian, regarding the Purchase of Two Slaves	**VII**: 29.
Prophetic, Speeches	**IV**: 357, 389.
Sacreligious Theft, regarding, at Erech	**I**: 501.

Tried before the Laocrites — **I**: 495.

Lawyer:

Ethics of a Hebrew — **VIII**: 223.

LAYARD, HENRY: — **III**: 36*(5)*, 179, 180*(5)*,443*(2)*.

Lazarus:

Lukan Deuteronomy and — **VIII**: 287.

Parable of, Dives and, and Enoch 22 — **VI**: 664; **VIII**: 284.

Lead: — **I**: 296, 300; **V**: 551; **IX**: xciii.

Glass, in — **II**: 218.

Isotope Studies of Ancient — **I**: 301; **II**: 220, 221.

Mines — **I**: 291.

Writing with — **I**: 233; **VI**: 430.

Learning:

Hebrew, Greek and Roman compared — **V**: 138.

Leather:

Drehem Tablet dealing with — **VII**: 150.

Leaven: — **I**: 247.

Casting Out of — **VI**: 106, 146.

Gentiles, Belonging to, or to the Sanctuary — **VI**: 105, 694.

Lebanon: — **II**: *111, 142, 313*, **436**; **III**: *52*, 409, *430*, 431‡, *677, 725*.

Cedars of — **III**: 388*(6)*.

Heights in, determined by Barometrical means — **II**: 286, 287, 436.

Plants from — **III**: 384.

Symbolic Interpretation of in the Church Fathers — **II**: 436; **VI**: 723.

Symbolic Interpretation of in the Targums — **II**: 436; **IV**: 97; **VI**: 712.

Travels, Modern, in — **III**: 436, 442, 444.

Lebanon Baqʽa: — **III**: *683*.

Lebanon, Mount: — **I**: *263, 289, 293*; **II**: *123*, **437**; **III**: *76, 146*, **150-151**, 151‡, 245‡, 436, 439, 440.

Glacial Action on, Traces — **II**: 247, 437

Route from, to Báalbek — **II**: 281.

Temple, on — **III**: 507.

Watershed (Boundaries) — **II**: 276.

Lebensmüder, 86-88: — **V**: 343.

Lebensmüde, 131-2 — **V**: 351.

Lebensmüde, 83 — **VII** 73.

Lebo Hamath, *see:* **Hamath**

Lechaeum: — **III**: 151.

Lectern:

Design of in Ancient Synagogues (ἀνλογεῖον) — **III**: 524.

Lectionary / Lectionaries: — **IV**: **§242, 20**.

Apocrypha in the — **VIII**: 378.

Irish, Apocrypha in the — **VIII**: 381.

Oxford, for College Use — **VIII**: 382.

Palestinian Syriac — **IV**: 20.

Principles governing the making of a — **VIII**: 385.

Psalter and, in Public Worship — **VIII**: 382; **IX**: cxxxiii.

Pseudepigrapha, from, a Plea for — **VIII**: 382.

Revised Revision of — **VIII**: 382.

Scottish, Apocrypha in the — **VIII**: 381.

Weakness of — **VIII**: 380.

Lecythus: — **III**: *538*.

Diphilos-Dromippos — **III**: 603, 607.

White, on Grave Stelae — **III**: 603.

LEE, WILLIAM: — **VIII**: 38.

Leech: — **VI**: 549*(2)*.

LEEMANS, W. F.: — **I**: 307.

LEER, E. FLESSEMAN-VAN: — **VIII**: 336*(2)*.

LEES, G. R.: — **III**: 594; **VII**: 58.

LEFÈVRE, JACQUES D'ETAPLES:

Canon and — **IV**: 202.

Lefkandi: — **I**: *350*; **III**: **151**, *635(2)*.

Left:
Roman Art, Right and, in **III**: 697.
Legal Documents, *see:* **Documents, Legal**
Legal Institutions:
Legal Transactions of a Family - Demotic **VII**: 29.
Roman, in Rabbinics **I**: 490.
Legal Precedent: **I**: 461*(2)*, 498.
Legal Privilege:
Roman Empire, in **I**: 506.
Legal Status:
Servile, in Ancient Greece **I**: 504.
Legal Systems:
Antiquity, in **I**: 468.
Nuzi Legal Procedure **I**: 499.
Procedure and Execution **I**: 501.
Legal Terms: *see also specific terms*
Hebrew **I**: 468, 470, 471.
Legalism:
Pharisees, of **V**: 99.
Legend(s), *see also:* **Haggadah**
Adam's Bridge, of **V**: 142.
Alexander the Great, Syriac, concerning **II**: 11.
Ashmedai, and the Babylonian Talmud **V**: 133.
Babylonian **VII: §898, 222-223.**
Babylonian Gods of War and their **V**: 176.
Babylonian Kutha **VII**: 223.
Babylonian, of the Serpent-Temper **VII**: 265
Bel-Merodach and the Dragon **V**: 164.
Bilingual, Assyrian and Phoenician **VII**: 113.
Chinese, concerning Babylonian Fishermen **I**: 269.
Coin types, and Biblical Studies **I**: 452.
Cuthaean, of Naram-sin **VII**: 202.
Cyrus the Great and **II**: 33.
Genesis, of **IV**: 265.
Grecian, and Early History **V**: 244.
Hittite **V**: 226.
Hittite, of Great Serpent **V**: 225.
Jonah and Kindred **IV**: 442.
Kay Kâûs **II**: *232;* **V**: 181, 237; **VII**: 222.
Kiškanu, of the **V**: 184; **VII**: 157, 201, 282, 286.
Kuthaean, of Creation **VII**: 266.
Lot, Daughters of, in **IV**: 321; **V**: 137.
Man, First, Parsic and Jewish **IV**: 290; **VI**: 696, 715.
Memphite, Ever-Blooming Wreaths of Tindium as feature of **V**: 212.
Osiris, of **V**: 206.
Pheidian **V**: 261.
Plague, of Chaldea **VII**: 198.
Poetical, of the Talmud **VI**: 695.
Pre-Homeric of the Voage of the Argonauts **VII**: 346.
Pygmy, in Jewish Literature **V**: 133.
Rabbinic, Gnostic Background of **V**: 240.
Sarpedon of, and the Saga of the Archer **V**: 264.
Sea, of, of and the Astarte Papyrus **V**: 148, 212, 226; **VII**: 39, 308.
Sumerian, on the Infancy of Man **V**: 185.
Sumero-Babylonian Origin of Adam **I**: 33; **V**: 184.
Talmud, Poetical, of the **VI**: 695.
Talmudic, as the Source for the Josephus Passage **VI**: 682.
Water Miracles of Moses in Jewish **VIII**: 357.
Legendary Works:
Exegetical Studies on **VI: (§789), 667.**
Literary Criticism of **VI: (§763), 654.**
Textual Criticism on **VI: (§737), 644.**

LEGH, THOMAS:	**III**: 435, 436*(2)*.
Legio:	**II**: 280; **IX**: cxvi*(3)*.
Legislation:	
Babylonian	**I**: 497*(2)*.
Deuteronomy, Sacrificial, in	**IV**: 350.
Hebrew	**I**: 460, 496.
Humanitarian Element in Old Testament	**I**: 461.
Israelite	**I**: 479, 496.
Old Testament	**I**: 464, 497.
OT, in relation to that of Babylon	**I**: 479.
Pentateuch, and	**I**: 472, 475; **IV**: 225, 240.
Pentateuch, Mosaic Authenticity of	**IV**: 257.
Roman, under Caesar	**I**: 506.
Legislations:	
Babylonia, of	**I**: 461, 488.
Israel, of	**I**: 461, 488.
LEIBNIZ, GOTTFRIED:	**VIII**: 84.
Leicester City Museum:	
Four Stelae in	**VII**: 25.
Lejjûn:	
Greek Inscription from	**VII**: 314.
Lekythos, Lekythoi:	
Attic Black-Figured	**III**: 619.
Red-Figured	**III**: 629, 715.
Skopelos, from	**III**: 621.
White, from Attika	**III**: 601.
Lelantine War:	**II**: 74.
Lemon(s):	**I**: 247; **III**: 391.
LENORMANT, FRANÇOIS L.:	**IV**: 298; **VII**: 294.
Leon the Toparch:	**II**: 57.
Leontes:	
Natural Bridge of	**II**: 281.
Leontopolis:	
Qumran Sect, Relation to	**VIII**: 423.
Temple of Onias in	**I**: 141; **V**: 69.
Lepcis Magna:	**II**: *156;* **III**: 168.
M'. Aemilius Lepidus	
Denarius of	**I**: 448.
Leprosy:	**III**: **§179, 406-407**; **V**: 509; **VI**: 123; **IX**: **§179, cxxii**.
Azariah's	**VI**: 237.
Babylonian Medicine and	**III**: 406.
Cosmic	**III**: 399, 407; **V**: 156.
House of	**VI**: 123.
Laws, So-Called	**VI**: 122.
Mesopotamia, in	**III**: 407.
Nubia, Early case of, in	**III**: 404.
Translation problems of	**III**: 407.
LEPSIUS, KARL RICHARD:	**III**: 81.
Sinai Peninsula, on	**III**: 231.
Leptis Magna:	**III**: **151**, *258*.
Lerna:	**I**: *333;* **III**: **151-152**, *627*,
Palace, Bronze Age, at	**III**: 501.
People of	**III**: 361.
Royal Shaft Graves at	**III**: 557.
Lesbos:	**III**: 152.
Sactuary of Zeus, Hera, and Dionysus at(?)	**V**: 263.
LESCOW, THEODOR:	**VI**: 394.
Letoon:	**III**: 266, 267.
Letopolis:	**V**: 212.
Letters, *see:* **Correspondence**	
Lettuce:	
Aphrodisiac, as	**III**: 400.
Northwest-Semitic Covenant making, and	**I**: 511
Levant:	**III**: 152, *573*.
Early Settlement and Holocene Enviroment	**II**: 245.
Levantine Texts, *see:* **Northwest Semitic Texts**	
LEVI, DAVID:	
Prophecy, on	**VIII**: 235.
Levi, Person:	
Genaeology of:	**I**: 118.
Levi, Testament of:	
Aramaic Text of	**VI**: 646.
Messiah in	**VI**: 669, 670*(2);* **VIII**: 141*(3)*.

Qumran Texts of	**VIII**: **§1114, 452**.
Levi, Tribe of:	**I**: 155*(2)*, 156*(3)*; **IV**: 261, 373; **V**: 43.
Genealogies of, in 1 Chronicles 23-26	**I**: 118; **V**: 42; **VI**: 589.
Leviathan:	**VI**: 2, 31, 513; **VIII**: 84.
Battle Between, and Behemoth in *Piyyut*	**V**: 137; **VIII**: 83, 371.
Lotan and	**V**: 196, 509.
Symbol of Evil	**III**: 377; **VIII**: 183.
Levirate Marriage:	**I**: 214, **§78, 224**; **VI**: 695.
G^{e}'ullāh	**IV**: 508.
Levites:	**I**: *71;* **IV**: 367; **V**: 42, 43*(3)*.
Cities of, *see:* ***Levitical Cities***	**II**: 312.
Deuteronomy, in	**IV**: 351; **V**: 43.
Exodus and Early Levite History	**V**: 43.
Ezekiel's	**IV**: 418*(2);* **V**: 42*(2)*, 43; **VI**: 360.
Hymns of, for Days of the Weeks	**VI**: 447.
Levitical Genealogical Accretions in P	**I**: 120.
Masorah and	**IV**: 19, 97; **V**: 43.
Moses and	**V**: 43
Origin of	**V**: 42.
Priests, and, in Wellhausen	**IV**: 255.
Psalms as Evidence of a Levitical System	**IV**: 475; **V**: 9.
Subsitute for First-Born	**I**: 366; **VI**: 127.
Levitic Code, *see:* **Priestly Code**	
Levitical Cities and Cities of Refuge	**II**: **§166, 311-312**, 353; **VI**: 139; **IX**: **§166, cxiv**.
Ceremony of Admission to	**II**: 312.
Gezer, Excavations at	**II**: 311, 373; **IV**: 362.
Release of Homicides from	**VI**: 139.
Utopia and Historical Reality of	**II**: 312*(2)*.
Levitical Priesthood:	**V**: **§424, 42-43**.
Babylonian Elements in Levitic ritual	**V**: 42.
Exodus and Early Levite History	**V**: 43.
History of	**V**: 43.
Social Development	**V**: 42.
Leviticus, Book of:	**IV**: 101, 230, 231.
Bibliography	**I**: **(§6)**, 10.
Date, Authorship, Sources and Authenticity	**IV**: **§319, 344**; **VI**: 121.
Driver, S. R., on	**IV**: 342.
Exegetical Studies on	**VI**: **§583, 121-126**.
Gospel in	**IV**: 343.
Homiletic Value of	**VIII**: 372.
Judeo-Persian	**IV**: 49.
Kalisch, Marcus, on	**IV**: 342.
Literary Criticism of	**IV**: **§317, 324-343**.
Qumran Texts (4QLXXLev)	**VIII**: **§1098, 443**.
Sa'adyah's Commentary on, in Arabic	**VII**: 290; **IX**: cli.
Samaritan Pentateuch, in	**IV**: 21.
Scapegoat	**IV**: **§318, 343-344**.
Septuagint of	**IV**: 24, 30*(3)*, 343.
Study Program	**VIII**: 394.
Leviticus, Book of, Manuscripts of:	**VI**: **§584, 127**.
Samaritan Pentateuch and	**VI**: 127.
Septuagint Version of	**VI**: 127.
LEWIS, C. G.:	**II**: *225*.
LEWIS, GEORGE CORNEWALL, SIR:	**II**: 159, 160.

LEWIS, TAYLER:
Bible Study, on **VIII**: 387.
Cosmology, on **VIII**: 85.
Creation, on **IV**: 274*(3)*.
Lex Aquilla: **I**: 503.
Lex talionis, see: **Retribution**
Lex Vatinia de imperio Caesaris: **I**: 506.
LEXA, FRANTIŠEK:
Bibliography of **I**: 20.
Lexicographical Studies:
Meteorological Terminology in the OT **II**: 244.
Semitic, Comparative **V**: 379, 381.
Lexicon, Greek:
Comparative, from Rabbinic Sources **V**: 640.
Liddell and Scott **V**: 638*(2)*, 639*(2)*, 640*(2)*.
Pickering's **V**: 637.
Septuagint, Towards a **V**: 638*(2)*.
Stephano's **V**: 623.
Lexicon, Hebrew: **V**: **§507**, **466-467**, 472, 473; **VI**: 6, 7, 378, 379*(2)*, 380, 381, 384, 385, 433, 436.
Lexicon to Josephus:
Thackeray's **VI**: 681.
Lexigram: **V**: 569.
Lezoux: **III**: *666*.
Liability: **I**: 503.
Aedilician **I**: 501.
Sea Carriage, and **I**: 504.
Warehousing, and **I**: 308.
Liâṯneh: **II**: 461.
Libations:
Imhotep, and the Scribe's **VII**: 60.
Minoan Libation Formula **VII**: 364.
Nubia, to the Dead **I**: 374.
Religious Washings in the Graeco-Roman World **V**: 243.
Significance of, and Incense in Funerary and Temple Rituals **V**: 206.
Spondee **V**: 691.
Water, in the OT **V**: 61.
LIBBY, WILLIAM: **II**: 424.
Libertines:
Synagogue of the **III**: 523.
Liberty:
Civil **I**: 460, 472.
Greek **I**: 508.
Libit-Ishtar: **VII**: 234.
Inscription of **VII**: 238.
Libnah: **II**: 306, *369*, **437**.
Libraries: **I**: **§83**, **235-236**.
Akhenaten's **I**: 237.
Alexandrian **I**: 235, 236.
Assyrian **I**: 235; **VII**: 173, *205*.
Babylonian **VII**: *173;* 205.
Hexateuch and **IV**: 174*(4)*, 253*(3)*.
Nippur **I**: 237*(3)*; **III**: 481.
Oldest **II**: *117*.
Oral Tradition and **IV**: 174*(4)*, 253*(3)*, 254.
Library of Congress: **IV**: *9*, *35*.
Libya: **III**: **152**, *204*, *257*, *514*.
Greek Texts from **VII**: 325.
Place Names in Eastern **II**: 266.
Rock-pictures in, Desert **III**: 710.
Libyans, *see also:* **"Sea-Peoples"** **II**: *126*, *129*, **148**.
Minoan Crete, Relations with **IX**: xcv.
Licinio-Sextian Laws: **I**: 490, *502*.
Life:
Common Basis for Jews and Gentiles **VIII**: 333.
Creation, in **IV**: 284.
Ecclesiastes (Qoheleth), Problem of, and **IV**: 512.
Greek Conception of **V**: 250, 254.

Greek Fear of V: 254.
Hebrew and Greek Ideas of V: 110, 251.
Hebrew Conception of V: 110.
Homeric Concept of V: 246.
Job, Book of, in / on IV: 458, 468; V: 113.
Meaning of *(Ḥayyim)* in Proverbs, Job, and Ecclesiastes V: 112, 117, 509, 510.
Mystery of, and the Book of Job IV: 461.
Old Testament Outlook / View on V: 110*(2)*.
Public, in Philo VI: 675.
Talmud in VI: 698.
Term in the OT V: 504, 509.

Life, Origin of, *see:* **Creation and Evolution**

Life, Private, *see also:* **Homes and Domestic Life**
Athenian, as reflected in Parthenon Sculptures I: 209; III: 727.
Babylonian I: 208, 209*(3)*.
Egyptian I: 208, 210.
Greek I: 208.
Private Activities in Athens, and Public Service I: 188, 210, 507.
Roman I: 208.

Lifespans: II: 261.
Anatolia, in Chalcolithic and Copper Age II: 261.
Antediluvians II: 259*(2)*, 260*(3)*.
Egypt, Graeco-Roman II: 261.
Greek, from Inscriptions II: 260.
Patriarchs II: 259, 260*(3)*.
Roman Empire, in II: 261.
Ususfructus and I: 504.

Light:
Chaos and the Origin of VI: 23.
Creation of IV: 276.
Figure and Symbol in OT V: 510; VIII: 307.
Figure and Symbol in St. John V: 510; VIII: 307.
Genesis Creation and IV: 280.
Origin and Propagation of, According to Moses VI: 25.
OT Idea of VIII: 83.
Palestinian Folklore, and I: 390.
Sabbath IV: 277.
Shechem Inscription, in VII: 85; VIII: 86.

"Light and Darkness":
Biblical Understanding of VIII: 84, 289.
Qumran and the Conflict of VIII: **§1081**, **422**.
War Scroll, in VIII: 464*(2)*.
Zoroastrian View V: 236.

Lighthouse:
Alexandria, at III: 482.

Ligure stones: I: 285.

Lihyanic:
Article V: 377, 679.
b "son" V: 377.
Prepositions V: 377, 679.

Liḫyānite Inscriptions: VII: 292.
South Arabian coins, on I: 453; VII: 293, 375.

LIKHACHEFF, N. P.: III: *664*.

Lilith: I: xvii (n15); III: 736; V: **§462**, **137**; VI: 287.

Lilul-dannum: II: 57.

Lily:
Egyptian III: 710.
Water, in Egypt III: 391.

Lilybaeum: III: 152.

Limes:
Herodian II: 391; III: 490.
Idumean II: 391; III: 490.
Iron Age Fortresses in the Negev II: 454; III: 490; IX: xciv.
Masada and II: 440.
Palestinian, Intitial Date of III: 489.
Pontic III: 490.

Limestone:	I: 280, 290*(2);* III: 460, 562.
Coatings,Ferrous, from Plain of Sharon	II: 216.
LINDBLOM, JOHANNES: Life and Contributions of	I: 24.
Lineage:	
Hebrew, System and Enslavement	I: *203(2), 211,* 228*(2);* VI: 90.
Levitical Code and Kindred Affinity	VI: 124.
Linear A, B Texts, *see also:* **Myceanæan / Minoan Texts**	V: 614, 622; VII: **§650, 358-365**.
Declension	V: 619.
Hieroglyphic Sign 12	V: 622.
Hieroglyphic Sign 18, Origin of	V: 622.
Hieroglyphic Sign 36	V: 622.
Inflection in	V: 619.
Language of Linear A	V: 620.
Ligatured Signs in Creatan Linear Scripts	V: 621.
Linear B Arms and Armour Tablets	VII: 364.
Linear B, Decipherment of	VII: 361.
Linear B Decipherment, Problem of Verifying	V: 620.
Linear B, Horse-head Ideogram	V: 621.
Linear B Ideogram for Woman	V: 621.
Linear B-abel. Transcription of	V: 621.
Luvian and Linear A	V: 620.
Names for Linear B Writing and for its signs	V: 621.
non-Greek Names on Linear B	V: 622.
Phonetic Values	V: 619.
Syllabary, Linear B	V: 622.
"Total" in Linear B	V: 619.
Vocabulary of Linear A	V: 622.
Linen:	I: 273, 278.
Cyril of Alexander on	VI: 721.
Egyptian Word for	V: 340*(2).*
Textiles from the Cave of Ain Feshkha	VIII: 412.
Linguistics:	
Areal and Hittite	V: 612.
Areal and "Indo-Hittite"	V: 611.
Babylonian and Israel, Evidence for contact	I: 324.
Bible Translation and	IV: 108; V: 280.
Biblical Chronology and	II: 180.
Biblical Study, Contribution of, to	V: 280.
Creatan influence	I: 325.
Hypostatization of Phenomena Theological Interpretation	V: 280.
Orientalist and	V: 278.
Philology and, Conflict between in Semitic	V: 380.
Philology and Practical	V: 277.
Tiberian Vocalization and the Principles of	V: 481.
Transposition, Assimilation, Conformation	V: 278.
Lintel:	
Arcuated, Symbolic Interpretation in Art	III: 470.
Kouyunjik, found at	III: 461.
Limestone	III: 481.
Lion(s)	III: **377-378**, *382(2),* 689, *743.*
Amphipolis, at	III: 736.
Anatolian Architecture, in	III: 378, 478, 754.
Art, in Ancient	III: 695, 696.
Babylonian, at Yale	III: 733.
Babylonian, in Toledo	III: 378, 749.
Bones of at Petra	II: 277, 460; III: *731.*
Conquering, as Symbol	VIII: 308.
Etruscan	III: 569.
Figurine of	III: 769.
Hunting	I: 239, 240*(2), 318;* III: *590, 742.*
Mesopotamian Figure of	III: 742.
Oriental Art, in	III: 701.

Polychrome, from Babylon III: 377, 724.
Prudoe VII: 67.
Psalms, in VI: 479.
Shoulder Ornament (Hair Whirl) of III: 700*(5)*.
Lion-cult: V: 219.
Lion-Griffith:
Development of, in Art III: 703.
Lion-Bull Combat Motif: II: 234; V: 188; IX: cxxvi.
Lipit-Ishtar:
Cone of VII: 252.
Hall of Justice V: 186.
Lipit-Ishtar Code: VII: 280*(4)*.
Jephthah, Disinheritance of, in the light of IV: 372; VII: 268.
Lips:
Egyptian word for V: 325.
Liptobiolite: II: 250.
Liquid:
Sample of, Report on, from small jar II: 213.
Sarchophagus of Ptȝḥ-špss, found in II: 215.
Liquor, *see also:* **Alcoholic Beverages; Temperance** I: 237, 249; VIII: 219.
Lishanum: III: 153; VII: 210.
Lisht: III: 153, *505*.
Scarabs found at III: 668.
Lîtâny:
Natural Bridge of II: 281.
Literacy, *see:* **Writing**
Literary Criticism of the Old Testament - General Studies: IV: **§278, 116-159**; IX: **§278, cxxix**.
American Church, in IV: 120.
Apologetic Value of Modern Criticism IV: 132.
Archaeology and IV: 126, 148, 149, 152, 210*(2)*, 217, 220.
Biblical Studies, present condition of IV: 138.
Common Sense and IV: 152.
Faith and IV: 139.
German Rationalism in IV: 116.
God, Work of, and IV: 136.
Hexateuch, of, Parallels in other OT Books IV: 123.
Jewish Home Teaching and IV: 134; VIII: 400.
Liturgical Factor or IV: 148.
Modern, and the Preaching the OT VIII: 372, 373.
Old Testament Literature, Practical Value of IV: 141.
Oral Tradition and IV: 155, 176.
OT, of, in the Light of NT Quotations IV: 121; VIII: 272.
Patristic Writings, Value for VI: 718*(2)*.
Revelation and VIII: 31.
Scriptural Sense and IV: 90.
Spinozism and IV: 118.
Strange Fruit of IV: 152.
Teaching, OT, Problems IV: 151; VIII: 399.
Theology and IV: 137.
Traditional and Analytical Views contrasted IV: 133.
Literary Style of the Old Testament - General Studies: V: **§564, 695-700**; IX: **§564, cxlv**.
Literary Style - General Studies, *see also:* **Writing**
Anthropocentic Aspects V: 700.
Apocalyptic Style in the OT, Development V: 120, 696.
Aristotelan Syllogism and the Qal Wa-Ḥọmer V: 698.
Art Form and the Genius of the Bible V: 698.
Chiasmus in the OT V: 697.
Convention in Hebrew Literature: Reaction to Bad News V: 699.

Conventional Formulations, Form and Structure **V**: 699.
Figurative Language **V**: 695*(2)*.
Genres in the Bible **V**: 699.
Graphic Element in OT **V**: 695.
Humor, *see:* ***Humor***
Imagery, Structure of OT **V**: 698.
Imagination, Biblical Authors and **V**: 697.
Metrical Lists **V**: 698.
Narrator's Devices in **V**: 702.
Parable, Juridical (The Poor Man's Ewe-Lamb) **IV**: 378; **V**: 702.
Parables **V**: 695.
Parallelism **V**: 697.
Pattern Theory in Old Testament Studies **I**: 337; **IV**: 159; **V**: 700.
Rhetorical Figures in OT **V**: 695*(2)*.
Riddle in the Bible **V**: 697.
Semitic Inscriptions and Biblical Literature, Affinities of **V**: 698.
Semitic Thought-Pattern in Sacred Scripture **V**: 699.
Sequence x/x + 1 in the Old Testament **VIII**: 312; **IX**: cxlv.
Similies, Similitudes **V**: 695, 696, 704.
Stylistic Patterns in Biblical and Ugaritic Literature **V**: 537, 700; **VII**: 145.
Sublimity in OT **V**: 696.
Symbolic Language in OT **V**: 696.
Themes in OT Stories **V**: 698.
Vividness of OT Representation **V**: 695.

Literature - General Studies (and Other Inscriptions)*see also:* **VII**: **§953, 373-376**.
Specific Kind, eg. Amonite, Chinese, *etc*.
Ancient Near Eastern, *see:* ***ANE Literature***
Art of Authorship Among the Ancients **VII**: 3.
Coincidences between, and Hebrew Literature **IV**: 180.
Development of - General Studies **VII**: **§821, 3**.
Drama in Ancient **VII**: 2.
East Mediterranean, Origin and Character of **IV**: 193; **VII**: 3.
History of, Cuneiform Studies and **VII**: 2.
Mulsim, Bible in Early **VIII**: 368.
Myth in Ancient **VII**: 2.
Old Testament, Practical Value of **IV**: 141.
Old Testament, Wisdom Doctrines in **V**: 117.
Persian Contributions to **VII**: 371.
Phases of, Old Testament and the Ancient Orient **IV**: 179.
Psalms in Universal **IV**: 476.
Ritual in Ancient **VII**: 2.
Theory of, Simpler (Psalms) **IV**: 481.
Unwritten **I**: *464;* **V**: *99*, 697; **VII**: 2.

Literature, Modern:
American Novel, Biblical Adventures in **VIII**: 369.
Apocrypha in **VIII**: 364.
Bible and English **VIII**: 366*(3)*, 370.
Bible and / in **VIII**: 366, 368.
Bible, Authorized Version, Influence on English Literature **VIII**: 364*(2)*, 370.
Bible in American Fiction **VIII**: 369.
Biblical Motifs in *All the King's Men* **VIII**: 370.
Hebraism and Hellenism in **VIII**: 361.
Lord Byron's Hebrew Melodies **VIII**: 359.
Moses in the Literary Tradition of Ireland **VIII**: 369.
New Apocrypha **VIII**: 360*(2)*.
Old English, on the Apocryphal Passage in Daniel, Chapter Three **VIII**: 363.

Old Testament, and (Influence on) **VIII**: **§1062, 359-371**.
Quartet from Genesis **VIII**: 371*(4)*.
Litigants: **I**: 495.
Litigation:
Greek, Judicial, Origin of **I**: 490, 500.
Lipit-Ishtar's Hall of Justice **V**: 186.
LITTLEDALE, RICHARD FREDERICK:
Psalms, on **IV**: 474.
Liturgy:
Atonement and Sacrifice in Contemporary Jewish **V**: 32.
Babylonian **VII**: 260.
Babylonian and Genizah-Studies **VIII**: 386.
Babylonian, Calendars of **VII**: 262.
Christian and Synagogue **V**: 93.
Decalogue and **VIII**: 206.
Decalogue and Christian **VI**: 160.
Egyptian, Daily Temple **V**: 208.
Egyptian, Daily Temple, Horus-Seth Motif in **V**: 219.
Egyptian, Funerary **VII**: 70.
Genesis, First Chapter, in **VI**: 24; **VIII**: 383.
Genizah Studies in the Babylonian **VII**: 109.
(Greek) Bilingual Sale of **VII**: 343.
Hallel and the Canonization of the Hebrew **VIII**: 207, 385.
Hanukkah of, and Books of Maccabees **VI**: 627.
Hebrew, Canonization of **VIII**: 206, 385.
Hebrew, Historical Study **VIII**: 207.
Hexameron **VIII**: 383.
Jerusalem, Acrostic of Nahum in **VI**: 396.
Jewish **V**: 92; **VIII**: 205*(2)*, 381, 384, 385.
Jewish, Modern. Atonement and Sacrifice in **V**: 32.
Jewish, St. Peter in **VIII**: 205.
Judith, Book of, in **VIII**: 384.
Liturgical Elements in Babylonian and Assyrian Cylinder Seals **III**: 648.
Liturgical Formula. The God of Abraham, Isaac, and Jacob, as **V**: 107.
melekh ha-ʿolam as Zealot influence on(?) **VIII**: 207.
Miqra'qodesh in the Synagogue **VIII**: 386
Monetary, in Hellenistic Athens **I**: 454.
New Year **I**: 394; **V**: 85; **VIII**: 207.
Ninib (Ninurashā), to **VII**: 261.
Nippurian, fragment of **V**: 177; **VII**: 260.
Old Testament in **VIII**: **§1064, 378-386**.
OT Criticism and **IV**: 148.
Piyyutim **V**: 85.
Prayers of the Apocrypha and Jewish **VI**: 600; **VIII**: 202, 382.
Psalmody **VIII**: 378*(2)*.
Psalms and **VIII**: 385.
Psalms in Jewish **IV**: 493; **VIII**: 206.
Psalms, Liturgies of Depature in **IV**: 480.
Psalter and the **VIII**: 385.
Psalter, Liturgical **VIII**: 384.
Rosh Hashana, Origins of **VIII**: 386.
Samaritan **I**: *377, 477;* **V**: 228, 229.
Sidrahs, Seven Pairs of **VI**: 716.
Spring Festival at Jerusalem in the Age of Abaraham **VII**: 139.
Synagogue and Christian **V**: 93.
Synagogue, and the Term Miqra'qodesh **VI**: 124.
Tobit, Book of, in **VIII**: 384.
Wisdom of Solomon, in **VIII**: 384.
Zechariah in **VIII**: 383.
Lituus:
Hittite **I**: 283; **III**: 575, *643*.
Live-stock, *see also:* **Animals, Domesticated** **I**: 255.

Liver:
Babylonian Signs and Names for V: 573.
Liver Models: III: 579; V: 197.
Liverpool Museum of Archaeology:
Cappadocian Tablets in VII: 162.
Liverpool Public (City) Museum: III: *733;* VII: *213*.
Ægean Material in III: 567, 577.
Akkadian Tablets in VII: 151.
Hittite Material in III: 567, 577.
Liverpool Royal Institution, Museum:
Greek Inscriptions in VII: 319.
Lives of the Prophets:
Exegetical Studies on **VI: (§791), 668**.
Literary Criticism of **VI: §765, 655**.
Textual Criticism on **VI: (§739), 645**.
Livestock: I: 255.
Livia: II: 57.
"Living Water": V: 520, *521*.
LIVY:
Psalm 126 and VI: 526.
Scripture, as V: 148.
XXXVI, 40 VII: 368.
Loans:
Babylonian Temple I: 308.
Guarantor, at Elephantine-Syene I: 311.
Interest on, Pohibitions against in Hebrew Law I: 307.
Sea, Risk of, in Ancient Athens I: 304.
Seed, Terms for Repayment of (Egyptian) VII: 30.
Loanwords:
Egyptian, in the OT IV: 190; V: 309.
Lobnah: II: 284.
Locks: III: 469; IV: 419.
LOCKYER, J. NORMAN: II: 125.
Locri: III: *69,* **153**.
Doric Temple at III: 509.
Locris: III: **153**.
Greek Inscription from VII: 320.
Rock Altar near Thronion in III: 516.
Locust(s): III: *375,* **378**, 387*(3),* 388
Joel, in IV: 432*(2)*.
Palestine, Invasions of Rare III: 378.
LOFTHOUSE, W. F.:
Pentateuchal Criticism and IV: 232*(3),* 257.
Log, Ship's: I: 346, 353; VII: 65.
Logic: VIII: 29.
Syllogistic, Arabic Technical Terms of, and Their Greek Originals V: 592, 635, 638.
Logistics:
Supplies and Defence I: 313.
Logogram: V: 569.
Logos: VIII: *52,* **§994, 129-131**, 290.
"Ahuna-Vairya" and V: 232; VIII: 130.
Alxandrian VIII: 130.
Athena, Sophia and the V: 253; VIII: 131, 150.
Babylonian Conception of V: 180; VIII: 130.
Babylonian Derivation of VIII: 130.
Chaldean Story of Creation, in V: 174; VIII: 130.
Divine, in Jewish Apocalyptic V: 122; VIII: 131.
False Philoian VIII: 130.
Fourth Gospel, of, and the Memra of the Palestinian Targum VI: 105, 714; VIII: 131, 290.
Japanese Buddhism and VIII: 130.
John in, (and Philo) VI: 672*(2),* 673, 674; VIII: 129*(2),* 130*(3)*.
Philo, in VI: 673, 675, 676; VIII: 130*(2),* 131*(3)*.
Philo of VI: 672*(2),* 673, 674; VIII: 129*(2),* 130*(2)*.

Philosophy, Meaning and History of, in	V: 248.
Proverbs and the Gospel of John, in	**IV**: 501; **VIII**: 131, 289.
Vohu Manah as Philo's	**VI**: 673; **VIII**: 130.
Logos Ebraikes:	
Book of Encoh, and, in the Magic Papyri of Paris	**VI**: 649; **VII**: 342; **VIII**: 130.
Loin-cloth:	**I**: 278; **IV**: 219.
Lokroi:	**III**: 762.
LONGFELLOW, HENRY WADSWORTH:	
Bel and the Dragon, on	**VIII**: 362.
"Judas Maccabaeus"	**VIII**: 363.
Old Testament in Poems of	**VIII**: 366.
Longsuffering:	**V**: 510.
Loom Weights:	**III**: 572.
Looms:	**I**: 273, 274*(2);* **III**: 572.
Lord, *see:* **God**	
"Lord of Heaven":	
Ezekiel, in	**IV**: 419; **VIII**: 58.
"Lord of Hosts":	**IV**: *254;* **VIII**: 108*(2),* 109, 110, 124, 125.
"Jehovah of Hosts"	**V**: 8.
Pentateuch, Absence of the Divine Title, in	**IV**: 259.
"Lord of Lords":	**V**: *519,* 520.
Lord's Supper:	
Jewish Passover and	**V**: 87.
OT Covenant and	**VIII**: 215.
Lore:	
Egyptian	**I**: 266, *332;* **II**: 224.
Mis-Translations as source of Jewish and Christian	**IV**: 113.
Loryma:	
Greek Inscriptions from	**VII**: 319.
"Lost Books" of the OT	**IV**: **§283**, **177**.
"Book of the Wars of the Lord"	**VI**: 132.
Jashar, Books of	**VI**: 223.
Lot:	
Abraham's Help	**IV**: 316.
Biographical Studies	**I**: 62.
Daughters of	**IV**: 321; **V**: 137.
Lot's Wife:	
Biographical Studies	**I**: 62.
Lotan:	
Leviathan and	**V**: 196, 509.
Lotapes:	**VIII**: 123.
Lots, Casting:	**I**: 183.
Qurman at, and in the Book of Acts	**VIII**: 290, 414.
Lotus:	
Evolution of, Ornament	**III**: 695.
Loutrophoros, *see:* **Vases**	
Louvre Museum:	**III**: *574, 601, 614, 730, 761;* **VII**: *41, 44.*
Ancient Monuments in, Illustrative of Biblical History	**III**: 494; **IV**: 174.
Palestinian Antiquities, in, Catalog of	**III**: 690.
Phoenician Inscription, Royal, Forged, in	**VII**: 118.
Stele C 14 in	**VII**: 18, 21.
Love:	**I**: *388, 477;* **V**: 510*(2);* **VIII**: 199.
Deuteronomy, in	**I**: 477; **IV**: 352.
Divine, in the OT	**VIII**: 95.
Divine Love Lyrics from Babylon	**VII**: 221.
Faithful Lover in an Old Babylonian Dialogue	**VII**: 221*(2).*
Hosea, in	**VI**: 369.
Human and Divine in Post-Biblical Literature	**VIII**: 223.
Incarnate, in Proverbs	**IV**: 499.
Law and, in the OT	**VIII**: 230.
Manual of Discipline, in	**VIII**: 294, 463, 481.
Philo's Homilies on, and Their Relation to Palestinian Midrashim	**VI**: 678.
Plato's Discourse on, in Phaedrus	**V**: 265.

Sumerian Culture, in I: 125; VIII: 227.
Love Letter:
Oldest VII: 9.
LOWE, HELEN:
Prophecy of Balaam and Other Poems VIII: 359.
Lower Critcism: *see:* **Textual Criticism**
Loyalty:
Filial, as a Testimony of Legitimacy VI: 204.
Lú-dingir-ra:
Message of, to his Mother VII: 305.
LUBBOCK, JOHN: III: 336*(2)*.
Lucania: III: **153>**
Lucian: III: 399.
Septuagint, Recension of IV: 38, 39, 40.
Lucifer: VI: 274; VIII: 163.
Fall of VIII: 163*(2)*.
Name V: 292, 510; VIII: 163.
LUCKENBILL, D. D.:
Bibliography of I: 20.
Lucretius: V: 247.
Religion of V: 242.
Student of Roman Religion V: 268.
Lucus Feroniae:
Roman Painted Tomb near III: 557.
Lugal-ki-GUB-ni-dú-dú: II: *38*, **57**.
Lugalanda: I: *397;* II: **57**.
Luke-Acts:
Univeralism in, and Deutero-Isaiah IV: 405; V: 29.
Luke, Apostle:
Historian, as a VI: 680.
Knowledge of OT(?) VIII: 284.
Luke, Gospel of:
Apocalypse of Zacharias and VI: 663; VIII: 283.
Deuteronomy and VIII: 287.
Enoch, Use of, in VI: 650, 651; VIII: 284, 287.
Genealogy of Christ in, and OT Laws of Inheritance VIII: 285.
Letter of Aristeas and VI: 660.
"Times of the Gentiles" in Tobit 14:5 and VIII: 284.
Wisdom of Solomon, Influence on (?) VI: 618; VIII: 284.
Lulab Coins: I: 365, 440.
Lulianus: I: 176.
Lullabies:
Arabian I: 391.
Lunacy:
Palestinian Folklore and I: 390.
Lunar Mansions:
Egypt, in II: 231.
Lungs:
Assyrian Prescriptions for III: 405.
Egyptian Word for V: 313 (#21).
Lūristān: I: *301;* III: 35, **153**, *251*.
Lushtamar:
Babylonian Letter to VII: 217.
Lustration, *see:* **Purification, Rites of**
LUTHER, MARTIN: IV: 72, 95, 106, 201, 202*(2);* VI: 374.
Apocrypha, Prefaces to VI: 600.
Baptism in "Lectures on Genesis" IV: 98.
Bible Translator, as IV: 105, 106*(2)*.
Christmas Prophecy, on, Isaiah 9 VI: 268.
Decalogue and VI: 157, 158.
Genesis 1-3, Interpretation of VI: 19.
Psalm 46, on VI: 486.
Sabbath and VI: 164.
Text-Critical Study of 2 Samuel 23:8 by VI: 217.
Translation of 2 Samuel 22:36 and Psalm 18:36 IV: 108; VI: 216, 464.
Translation of Almah in Isaiah 7:14 VI: 262.

Lutheran Theological Seminary: **VI**: *330*.

Lutheranism:
- Law and Grace in, and Judaism — **I**: 477; **VIII**: 197.

Luvian (Luwian): **V**: 614, 680.
- Linear A and — **V**: 620.
- Personal Name in Aramaic — **V**: 303.
- Vowel *a* — **V**: 614.

Luwain: **VII**: 304.

Luwian: **V**: 612.

Luxor: **III**: 154.
- Great Pylon of the Temple — **VII**: 73.
- Temple of — **II**: 70, *265;* **III**: 253, 510, 522; **VII**: *22*.

Luz: **IV**: 320.

LUZZATO, SAMUEL DAVID:
- Life and Contributions of — **I**: 24.

LXX, *see:* **Septuagint**

Lycaonia: **I**: *348*.
- Speech of — **V**: 678.

Lycia: **III**: *262, 263,* 263, *264, 362*.
- Travels, Modern, in — **III**: 439, 441.

Lycian Inscriptions: **VII**: 373*(3)*, 374, 375.

Lycian (Lukian): **III**: **154**, **V**: 612, 678*(2)*, 679, 680*(2)*.
- Grammar — **V**: 680.
- Greek Transcription of — **V**: 680.
- Nouns of Relationship in — **V**: *606,* 679.
- Suffixes — **V**: 679.
- Systems of Relationship in — **I**: 211; **V**: 680.
- Vocalic Harmony in — **V**: 678.

Lydia: **I**: *191, 196;* **II**: *55, 173, 201, 202*.
- Ashurbanipal, Annals of, and Chronology of — **VII**: 182.
- Greek Inscriptions from — **VII**: 318.
- Herakleid Dynasty of — **II**: 139.
- Jewish Military Colonies — **I**: 172; **VI**: 683.

Lydia (City of Arabia Petraea) **II**: 290.

Lydian (Inscriptions) Texts **VII**: 374*(3),* 375*(2)*.
- Bilingual Inscription from Sardis — **VII**: *124,* 374.

Lydian Language:
- New Evidence Bearing on a Lydian Sign ["↑" "[̈"] — **V**: 680.

Lydians: **II**: *130;* **III**: *181, 221*.

LYELL, CHARLES, SIR: **III**: 334.

Lyre: **I**: 244, 246.

Lysander: **II**: 57.

LYSIAS:
- Speech of — **VII**: 4, 336.

Lysimachos: **I**: *445*.

Lystra:
- "Priest" of Zeus at — **V**: 251.
- Zeus and Hermes at — **V**: 251.

LYTTON, EDWARD BULWER, BARON: **III**: 28.

Lyttos:
- Greek Inscriptions from — **VII**: 315.

M

m h n w t f:
- Tomb of — **III**: 543.

Ma'et:
- Statuette of — **III**: 769; **VII**: 74.

Ma'abarot:
- Fenestrated Axe found at — **III**: 561.

Maacah: **I**: 62; **II**: *372,* 437; **VI**: 215.

Maachah: **I**: *26, 27, 86;* **IV**: 361.
- Biographical Studies — **I**: 62.

Maa'di: **III**: **154**.

Maala: **III**: 708.

Maaleh-Aqrabbim: **I**: *348*.

Maassara:
- Egyptian II Dynasty Tomb — **III**: 550.
- Shaft Tombs at — **III**: 550.

Ma'ayan Barukh:
- Bronze Age Tombs at — **III**: 557.

MACAULAY, THOMAS BABINGTON (LORD):
Scripture, Use of **VIII**: 360.
Maccabaeus, Judah (Judas): **I**: *174*, 312; **II**: **58**.
Acrostic Poem in Praise of **VI**: 640
Embassy to Rome **I**: 337.
Military Strategist, as **II**: 58.
Prayers for the Dead and **VI**: 641*(2)*; **VIII**: 202.
Maccabaeus, Simon: **II**: 58.
Maccabean Period: **I**: **§69, 173-174**.
Apocalyptic Hope in **V**: 120.
Genties, Attitudes and Policies Toward, in the **I**: 174; **VIII**: 235.
Sabbath Years **II**: 188.
Maccabees (Maccabeans): **I**: *169, 316, 461(2)*; **II**: *18*, **58**; **V**: 11.
Antiochus Epiphanes and **VIII**: 364.
Josephus and **II**: 58; **VI**: 683.
Menorah of, Fate and Form of **V**: 53.
Name Maccabee, Origin of **V**: 299.
Name Maccabees **VI**: 640*(2)*.
Sepulchre of **III**: 547.
Tombs of the **III**: 531.
Warfare of **VIII**: 422.
Zealots and **V**: 102.
Maccabees, Books of
Armenian Text of **VI**: 609.
Elegies **VI**: 627.
Esther Revised by **IV**: 521; **V**: 91.
Exegetical Studies on **VI**: **(§724), 640**.
Jewish Sermon on **VIII**: 382.
Job and **IV**: 464, 627.
Literary Criticism of **VI**: **§706, 627**.
Liturgy of Hanukkah in **IV**: 627; **VIII**: 384.
Niese, Benedikt (Benedictus) on **VI**: 627.
Preacher and **VI**: 627.
Syriac MS of **VI**: 609*(2)*.
Textual Criticism of **VI**: **§688, 609**.
I Maccabees:
Acrostic Poem in **VI**: 640.
Akra, Leveling of, in **VI**: 640, 641.
Emendation of the Text of 1 Macc 3:48 **VI**: 609.
Exegetical Stuides on **VI**: **§725, 640-641**.
Hebrew Text of **VI**: 609.
Integrity of **VI**: 628.
Original Name of **VI**: 628.
Pardoxes in **VI**: 628.
Pauline Epistles, Traces of, in **VI**: 628; **VIII**: 293.
Proper Names in **VI**: 640, 641.
Sarbeth Sabanaiel **VI**: 628.
Textual Criticism of **VI**: **§689, 609**; **IX**: **§609, cxlix**.
Topographic Notes **VI**: 640.
Written by a Sadducee(?) **VI**: 628.
II Maccabees:
Antiochus IV Epiphanes Death, and **VI**: 628.
Aristeas and **VI**: 628.
Eleazar's Martyrdom in; Latin Evidence for **VI**: 628.
Exegetical Studies on **VI**: **§726, 641**.
Literary Criticism of **VI**: **§708, 628**.
Prayers for the Dead and **VI**: 641*(2)*; **VIII**: 202.
Purgatory and **VI**: 641.
Textual Criticism of **VI**: **§690, 609**.
III Maccabees:
Aristeas and **VI**: 656.
Dositheos, Son of Drimylos, in **VI**: 656.
Exegetical Studies on **VI**: **(§792), 668**.
Greek Romance and **VI**: 656; **VII**: 347.
Historical Source, as **VI**: 656.
Literary Criticism of **VI**: **§766, 656**.
Metrical Fragments in **VI**: 645.
Patriotic Romance and **VI**: 656.
Pseudo-Aristeas and **VI**: 656, 660.
Textual Criticism on **VI**: **§740, 645**.

IV Maccabees: **VI**: 597.
- Eusebes Logismos in **VI**: 668.
- ***Exegetical Studies on*** **VI**: **(§793), 668.**
- Hebrews, Parallels to, in **VIII**: 296.
- ***Literary Criticism of*** **VI**: **§767, 656.**
- Origen's Exortation to Maryrdom and **VI**: 656, 668, 720.
- ***Textual Criticism on*** **VI**: **§741, 645.**

Mace (heads): **I**: 312; **III**: 681*(2)*, 684*(2)*.
- Assyrian Word for **I**: 312; **V**: 563.
- Lagash, with Inscription **VII**: 273.

Macedonia: **I**: *483;* **III**: **154-155**, *227, 258,* 260.
- C. Cosconius C. f., Proconsul of **II**: 5.
- Greek Inscriptions from **VII**: 323, 325.
- Woman-Power in **I**: 198; **II**: *39*.

Macedonian Regency: **II**: 134.

Macedonians: **II**: 149.

MACGREGOR, W.:
- Head of Amenemmēs in the collection of **II**: 15.

Machaerus: **II**: *326, 327, 345(2),* **437-438.**

Machines:
- Harvesting, Gallo-Roman **I**: 258.

Machnadebai:
- Nebo as a element in the Hebrew Proper Name **V**: 294.

Machpelah: **II**: 276, 438.
- Abrham's Purchase of, and Hittite Law **I**: 501; **VI**: 73.
- Cave of **II**: 277*(3)*, 278, 292; **III**: *541;* **VI**: 73.

MACKAY, ROBERT WILLIAM: **V**: 6.

Macron:
- Askos by **III**: 607.

Madaba: **II**: 302, 422.

Madder: **III**: *389,* 392.
- Rose **II**: 216; **III**: 713.

Madeba: **II**: 291, *345, 438(2);* **III**: 416.
- Mosaic Map at **II**: 257*(2)*.

Madient Habu: **V**: 363; **VII**: 65.

Madmenah: **II**: 268, *368,* 438; **VI**: 271.

Maecenas:
- Auditorium **III**: 482.

Maenads: **I**: 238.

Magan: **I**: 296, *327, 341;* **II**: *60, 66, 174, 197,* 266, 273; **III**: **155**, *160(4)*.

Magasthenes: **II**: *11*.

Magdiel: **II**: 284.

Mághára 'Isá: **III**: 354.

Maghâret et-Wâd: **II**: 309, 310; **III**: 422, 423.

Magharians: **V**: 95; **VIII**: *158*.

Magi:
- Murder of **V**: 235; **VII**: 372.

Magic: **V**: 103*(3)*, 104; **VI**: 147*(2);* **VIII**: 160; **IX**: cxxxvi.
- Amulets, with Magic Inscriptions **V**: 105.
- Aramaean Text in Hebrew **VII**: 93; **VIII**: 351.
- Arslan Tash, Inscription **VII**: 94.
- Assyrian **V**: 562.
- Astrology and **II**: 229.
- Babylonian, Sympathetic, by Buning Images **VII**: 263.
- Bowls, with Magic Inscriptions **V**: 105.
- Brick, Egyptain Magical **VII**: 41.
- Canaanite Magical Text **V**: 193.
- Chaldeans, of **V**: 170.
- Coptic Magical Text **VII**: 83.
- Demons and **VIII**: 161.
- Egyptian **III**: 438; **V**: 199; **VII**: 40.
- Formula, Numerical Value **VIII**: 311.
- Formula. The God of Abraham, Isaac, and Jacob, as **V**: 107.

Greek Magical Notes **VII**: 333.
Kings, of **I**: 482.
Lead Figures from Tell Sandahannah **VII**: 342.
Mano Cornuta, (apotropaic gesture) **V**: 159.
Ostracon, Magical **VII**: 35, 40.
Pig in **III**: 380, *399*.
Primitive Religion and **V**: 3.
Religion and, in Early Hellenic Society **V**: 252.
Roman Law, Interdiction of, in **I**: 498.
Symbols for Masculinity and Femininity in ANE Sympathetic, Rituals **V**: 160.
Tabellae Defixionum, Old Testament Parallels **V**: 105*(3)*, 144, 145*(2)*, 268*(2)*.
Terms in the OT **V**: 399*(2)*.
Used in Harem Conspiracy against Ramesses III(?) **II**: 81; **VII**: 31.
Written Word, and **VIII**: 24.

Magicians: **I**: 186, 270*(2)*.
Egyptian, contrasted with the Miracles of Moses and the Apostles **VIII**: 89.
Pharaoh's **V**: 214; **VI**: 103*(2)*.

Magistrates:
Alabarches of Josephus **III**: 482.
Egyptian Word for **V**: 339.
Roman **II**: 5.

Magma:
Phenomema of, in the Makhtesh Ramon **II**: 249.

Magna Græcia: **I**: *443;* **V**: *258*.

Magnesia:
Hieroglyphics on the Niobe of Cybele at **VII**: 56.

Magnesium:
Egyptian Copper-bronze Objects, found in **II**: 215.

Magnificant:
Prototype of, in the Song of Hannah **VI**: 193; **VIII**: 283.

Magyar: **III**: 332.

Mahanaim: **II**: 290, 438; **VI**: 81.
Angels of God at **VI**: 81.

Mahanaim at es Salt: **II**: 287

Mahâsna: **III**: *603*.

Mahri: **V**: 595.

"Mail", *see:* **"Postal Service"**

Maimonides: **IV**: 83.
God, Problem of the Existence of, in **V**: 111; **VIII**: 61.
Jewish View of Natural Law and **V**: 113.
Job and **IV**: 469.
Logic, Treatise on **V**: 114.
Man's Position in the Universe, and Saadia Gaon **VIII**: 174.
Prophecy, on **VIII**: 244*(2)*.
Tannaitic Midrashim and **VI**: 707.

Ma'in: **II**: 297.

Maiorum:
Images of on Roman Coins **I**: *456*.

"Maison Carrée": **III**: 460.

MAITLAND, S. R.: **VIII**: 291.

Major Prophets, Books of: **I**: *474*.
Bibliography of **I**: **§16, 12**.
Exegetical Studies on **VI**: (**§606**), **245**.
Literary Criticism of **IV**: **§345, 390**.
Literary Style of **V**: **§569, 703-704**.
Theological Studies **VIII**: **§963, 17**.

Makan: **III**: 155, *167*.

M'kaur: **II**: *345*, 438*(2)*

Makhmur Plain: **III**: 155.

Makhtesh Ramon:
Magmatic Phoenomena in **II**: 249.

Makkabaios: **V**: 301.

Makkedah: **II**: 438, 482.

Makkeph: **V**: 476.

Makmish: **II**: 301, **438**.

Malachi, Book of: **VI**: **§639**, **414-417**.
Authenticity, Authorship, Date, and Sources of **IV**: **§378**, **455**.
Elijah in **I**: 39; **IV**: 455*(6)*; **VI**: 416, 417*(2)*.
Exegetical Studies on **VII**: **§638**, **414-417**.
Historical Background of **IV**: 455.
Jewish Exposition of **VI**: 414.
John the Baptist and **IV**: 455.
Literary Criticism of **IV**: **§377**, **455**.
Rebukes in **VI**: 414.
Spiritual Message of **IV**: 455.
Tammuz Worship in **IV**: 455; **V**: 184; **VI**: 415.
Theology of **VIII**: 18.
Malachi, Book of, Manuscripts of: **VI**: **§640**, **418**.
Codex Syro-Hexaplaris Ambrosianus on **VI**: 418.
Peshitta of **VI**: 418.
Malachi, Person:
Prophecy of **IV**: 455*(2)*
Malagasy:
African and Arabian Influences Upon Religious Beliefs of **V**: 147.
Malak:
Arabic Word(?) **V**: 590.
Malalas:
Seleucid Chronology in **II**: 164, 203.
Malatya (District) **III**: 22*(5)*, 155, 267.
Seals allgedly from **III**: 658.
MALCOLM, JOHN, SIR: **III**: 196.
MALCOLM, NEILL, SIR: **VII**: 292.
Malediction:
Amos, Book of, in **I**: 513.
Isaiah, Book of, in **I**: 513.
Old Testament, in **I**: 513.
Sytled **V**: 185
Vassal-Treaties, in **I**: 513.
Males:
Status of minor, in Talmud **I**: 466; **VI**: 692.
Malḫat, Tel: **II**: 303, 439.
Malignano: **I**: *458*.
Mallia: **III**: *475*.
MALLON, PERE: **II**: 376*(2)*.
Mallorca: **III**: 155, 203.
Malophoros:
Cult of, at Selinus **III**: 486; **V**: 266.
Malta: **I**: *345, 346, 347;* **II**: *218;* **III**: **156**, *480, 592, 742, 762*.
Egyptian Objects Found at **III**: 546; **VII**: 21.
Egyptian Statuette in **VII**: 69.
"Neolithic" Temples at **III**: 512.
Personal and Place Names in **V**: 297; **IX**: cxiii.
Pottery, Prehistoric in **III**: 602, 604.
Sacred Stones in **V**: 241; **VII**: 333.
Semitic Inscriptions from **VII**: 95, 120.
Maltese:
Etymological Notes **V**: 680.
Hebraico-, notes **V**: 390.
Superlative in **V**: *495*, 680.
Mammals:
Assyrian Sculptures, on **III**: 364, 694, 720.
Middle Pleistocene, from Latamne, Orontes **III**: 367*(2)*.
Mammoth: **III**: 297; **IV**: 301.
Mampsis, *see also:* **Mamshit** **II**: 439, *456;* **III**: *18*.
Mamshath: **II**: 439.
Mamshit (Kurnub): **II**: 303*(3)*, 434, 439; **III**: *661*.
Mamzeruth: **VI**: 694.
Man, *see also:* **Mankind, Doctrine of**; **Homo Sapiens; Human Race**
Abnormal, in Egypt (Old Kingdom) **III**: 349.
Africa, Near-Man, from **III**: 361.
Age of **I**: 120; **III**: 293,

Age of *(cont.)*	296, 327, 338, 339, 341, 342*(2)*, 343*(2)*, 344, 347, 348, 349*(2)*.
Anglo-Saxon Bible, in	**IV**: 107.
Antiquity of	**II**: 173; **III**: 176, 291, 292, 334*(7)*, 335*(4)*, 336, 337*(3)*, 338*(3)*, 340*(3)*, 341*(2)*, 342, 343, 344*(6)*, 347, 348, 349, 350, 352, 353, *696;* **IV**: 282; **VIII**: 29, 168; **IX**: cxiii.
Apes and	**III**: 336.
Carmel Man and Middle Palaeolithic in ANE	**III**: 362.
Civlized, Antiquity of	**IX**: lxxxiii.
Cosmic, and Homo Signorum	**V**: 156.
Creation and / of	**III**: 331, 335*(3)*, 340, 345, 346; **IV**: 275, 276*(2)*, 279*(4)*, 280*(2)*, 281*(4)*, 285, 296; **VII**: 267.
Creation of, and the Jericho Statues	**V**: 151; **VIII**: 80; **IX**: cxxvii.
Creation, the Fossil Record and	**VIII**: 83.
Cro-Magnon	**III**: 347*(2)*, 363.
Date of Apperance on Earth	**III**: 352.
Dawn Man, Real or Imaginary	**III**: 346.
Decent of	**III**: 289, 335, 343.
Development of	**III**: 341, 349.
Development of in Greek and Latin Literature	**V**: 242.
Dignity of, in light of the Bible	**VIII**: 174.
Dignity of, Kieregaard and Socrates on	**V**: 266; **VIII**: 175.
Duties of, in Proverbs	**IV**: 499.
Early	**III**: 353.
Edenic Period of	**III**: 337.
Enviroment, Influence on	**III**: 343.
Evolution and	**III**: 315, 323, 337, 340, 342, 344, 346, 347, 351, 352, 353; **VIII**: 171; **IX**: cxx, cxxi.
First, in Jewish Literature	**IV**: 290; **VI**: 696, 715.
First, in Parsic Literature	**IV**: 290; **VI**: 696, 715.
Four-Footed, in Greek Anthropology	**V**: 251.
Free Will in Jewish Philosophies According to Josephus	**V**: 111; **VI**: 681.
Free Will of, in Talmudic Literature	**VIII**: 169.
Free Will of, Philo on	**VI**: 676.
Genesis of	**IV**: 274*(4)*.
God, Yearning of, in Philo	**VI**: 674.
God's Approach to, Philo's Conception of	**VI**: 674.
Hebrew Words for	**V**: 399, 510; **VIII**: 170; **IX**: cxli.
High German Bible, in	**IV**: 107.
Image of God in, Alexandrian Orientations	**VI**: 723.
Infancy of, in a Sumerian Legend	**V**: 185.
Inheritance of Characters, Mental and Moral compared with Physical	**III**: 341.
Intellectual Adventure of Ancient	**V**: 149.
Iran, 9th Century, in	**III**: 353.
Jewish Reflection upon the Beginnings of	**VIII**: 170.
Jewish Reflection upon the Beginnings of	**VIII**: 170.
Language of Prmitive	**IV**: 289.
Longevity of	**III**: 364; **IX**: cxiii.
Love of	**VI**: 161.
Mental Function, Origin and Development of	**III**: 336.
Moral Relations and	**VIII**: 176.
Neanderthal	**II**: 302; **III**: 327, 347, 352*(2)*.

Near-Man from Africa	**III**: 361.
Oriental(?), Represented in Old Kingdom	**III**: 352.
Origin of	**III**: 290, 293, 321, 335, 336, 337, 338*(2)*, 340*(3)*, 341, 343, 344*(2)*, 345*(4)*, 346, 347*(3)*, 348*(2)*, 349, 350, 351*(3)*, 352*(3)*, 353; **VI**: 32; **VIII**: 168*(2)*, 169*(2)*, 170, 173, 174, 175.
Origin of, and Fall	**VIII**: 180.
Original State of	**IV**: 289.
Palaeolithic, Evidence for Religious Beliefs	**V**: 4.
Palaeolitic, at Gibraltar	**III**: 346.
Palaeolitic, in Egypt	**II**: 248; **III**: 88, 177, 347, 348, 353.
Palaeolitic, in Greece	**III**: 351.
Palaeolitic, of Palestine	**III**: 350.
Philology and Origin of	**III**: 334.
Pre-Adamite	**III**: 334.
Prehistoric	**III**: 343*(2)*, 346, 348, 350*(2)*, 354, 357.
Prehistoric, Civilization of	**V**: 2.
Prehistoric, Religion of	**V**: 2.
Primeval	**III**: 296, 332, 333, 335*(2)*, 339*(2)*, 340*(3)*, 340; **IV**: 287, 323; **VIII**: 168.
Primeval, High Intellect of	**III**: 343.
Primitive	**III**: 336*(3)*, 338, 340, 342, 344, 350, 352; **IV**: 287.
Primitive State of	**IV**: 274.
Primitve State of, Civilized not savage	**III**: 332, 341.
Psychology, Comparative of	**III**: 336.
Sabbatical Year, and	**I**: 367, *413*.
Spiritual Nature / Status of	**IV**: 272; **VIII**: 168, 174.
Yellow-skinned, Representation of, in Old Kingdom	**III**: 352.
Man, Doctrine of:	**VIII**: 59, **§1011**, **166-175**, 407.
Amsterdam Philosopy, in	**VIII**: 173.
Biblical, and some Formulae of Christian Teaching	**VIII**: 173.
Brute in	**VIII**: 168, 173.
Christian View of	**VIII**: 174*(2)*.
Corruption of	**VI**: 460.
Darwin and	**VIII**: 173.
Destiny of	**VIII**: 174.
Free Will of	**III**: 284; **VIII**: 170, 174.
God, Can He Create, and Address Man(?)	**VIII**: 72.
God's Search for, in OT	**VIII**: 191.
Gordon, A. D., on	**VIII**: 174.
Hebrew Concept of	**VIII**: 174.
Human Freedom and Divine Power	**VIII**: 100.
Image of God, as	**VIII**: 166, 167*(2)*, 170, 171, 172*(4)*, 173*(2)*, 174, 175*(2)*.
Immortality of	**VIII**: 264.
Job, in	**IV**: 468; **VIII**: 173, 369.
Mechanism, as	**VIII**: 173.
Nature of	**VIII**: 172, 175*(2)*.
Pre-eminence of, in Ecclesiastes	**IV**: 514.
Qumran "Hodayot", in	**VIII**: 466.
Spirit of	**VI**: 543; **VIII**: 152, 167, 170.
Spirits, Two, of (Qumran)	**VIII**: 417.
Triparite Nature; Trichotomy	**VIII**: 166, 167*(2)*, 168.
Unity of	**VIII**: 172.
Universe, Place in,	**VIII**: 170.
Will of	**VIII**: 167.
Wrath of	**VIII**: 97.
Man, Fall of, *see:* **"Fall of Man"; Eden and the Fall**	

"Man of God": V: 461, 520
Man-Stealing, *see:* **Kidnapping**
Mana:
Greece and Rome, in V: 243*(2)*.
Manahat:
Tombs near III: 558.
Manamaltel:
Babylonian King of the First Dynasty II: 59; VII: 234.
Mananâ-Iapium Dynasty: II: 208*(2)*.
Manassas, Prayer of:
Esther, and IV: 520.
Manasseh:
Ephraim and VI: 91; IX: cxxxi.
Manasseh, King: VI: 594.
Jerusalem under II: 411, 412.
Reign of VIII: 390.
Wall of, at Jerusalem II: 417.
Wickedness and Penitence VI: 6.
Manasseh, Prayer of *see:* **Prayer of Mannasseh**
Esther, Book of, and IV: 520; VI: 627.
Hebrew Text of VI: 627.
Manasseh, Tribe of: I: 155, 156*(2)*.
Boundaries II: 273, 274*(2)*, 275, 276*(3)*.
Territory of II: **439**.
Topography of Western II: 439, 490.
Manchester Museum: III: *576*.
Babylonian Tablets in VII: 210.
Manchester New College: V: *384*.
Mandaic:
האאתה V: 377.
Mandali: III: *42*, **156**.
Mandane:
Daughter of Astyages II: *31, 33*.
Mandanis: II: *11*.
Mandrake(s): III: **392**.
Cuneiform Word for III: 392, *395*.
Jacob and VI: 79.
Mandulis:
Dream of VII: 325.
Maneh-Obolos: I: 447.
Manetho: II: **59**, *80*, 196*(2)*, 198, *206(2)*; III: *339*.
Chronology of II: 196*(2)*.
Manethome Aelian: V: 219.
Manhood: I: 189, 191; VIII: 219.
Manisa: III: 13.
Manisa Museum: III: 746.
Maništušu:
Cruciform Monument of III: 497.
Manitou:
Yahveh and V: 142; VIII: 114.
Mankind, *see also:* **Human Race, Man:**
Ages of, in Genesis IV: 270; V: 257.
Ages of, in Hesiod IV: 270; V: 257.
Alexander the Great, and the Unity of II: 10, 11; III: 348, 352; V: 256, 262.
Babel, Dispersal of, at IV: 311, 312*(2)*.
Destinies, Early, of IV: 276; V: 413.
Early History of III: 335, 346, 355.
Egyptian Inscription on the Destruction of, in the Tomb of Rameses III VII: 40.
Ethnology and Revelation IV: 160.
Religious History of V: 1.
Talmud, in VI: 698.
Unity of IX: cxxi.
Unity of, and Linear History I: 135; III: 347*(2)*, 348, 353.
Manna: I: 422; IV: 324*(2)*, 325, 326*(3)*, 327*(3)*, 328, 336; V: 510; VI: 108*(2)*, 109*(2)*, 128; IX: cxxxi, cxl.
"Manner for Manner":
Dante, in VIII: 370.
Manners:
Morals and, in Israel and the Time of Isaiah VIII: 221.

Mannu-ki-Inurta:
Seal of III: 658.
Mano Cornuta: V: 159.
Manshîyet eṣ-Ṣadr:
Stela from VII: 22.
MANSOUR, M. A.: III: 484.
Manual of Discipline (DSD; 1QS): VIII: 435, 436*(2)*, **§1125**, *456*, 459, 460, **460-463**.
Baptism in VIII: 461.
"Discipline" in VIII: 461.
Dittography in VIII: 461.
God, Idea of, in VIII: 463.
Gospel of John and VIII: 461, 479.
Gospels and VIII: 461, 479.
Impersonal Subject, Expression of, in VIII: 477.
Interchange of ע and ח in VIII: 461, 477.
Jerusalem Church of Acts and the Community of VIII: 461*(2)*, 479*(2)*.
Jubilees and VI: 655; VIII: 461.
Paul and VIII: 461, 479.
Syntax of VIII: 462.
Textual Notes on VIII: 461.
Verbal Statement Clause of, Order VIII: 462.
waw and *yod* in VIII: 462.
Zadokite Document, Parallels in VI: 670.
Manuel Biblique: IV: 166*(2)*.
Manufacturing: I: 265*(2)*, 302, *322*.
Babyonian, illustrative of Prophetic Scriptures VIII: 236.
Manumission, *see:* **Slavery, Manumission**
Alexander's gold-lettered IV: 13; VI: 695.
Archaeology and IV: 12.
Babylonian-Yemenite IV: 16.
Barberini IV: 202.
Ben Asher IV: 7, 13, 14, 15.
Ben Naphtali Manuscript IV: 7, 10.
Codex of, w/Massora of IV: 14.
Biblical, in America, U.S. IV: 11, 12.
Freer Manuscripts IV: 29, 30*(3)*; VI: 155.
Freisingen IV: 202.
Hamburg Stadtbibiothek Codex No. I IV: 11.
Hebrew Bible in Abbreviations IV: 11.
Hebrew Illuminated MSS IV: 10.
Hebrew, in England IV: 12.
Hebrew, in University of Bologna IV: 12.
History of Biblical IV: 11.
Jerome's Hebrew Text IV: 12*(2)*.
Latin Superscriptio MSS on Hebrew Bible IV: 12.
Michicagn Codex IV: 12.
Miniatures, Rockefeller McCormick, Lost IV: 11.
Origen's Greek IV: 38.
Manuscripts, Scrolls, Codices, General Studies, O/T Qumran *see also:* ***Codex (Biblical)*** IV: **§236, 10-12**.
Syriac, Torah IV: 14.
Theodulfian (Vulgate) IV: 41.
Mânûskîhar:
Epistles of VII: 374.
Ma'on:
Aramaic Text in the Synagogue of III: 527; VII: 129.
Synagogue at I: *454(2)*; III: 526*(9)*.
MAP, WALTER:
Bible Quotations in the *de Nugis Curialim* of VIII: 368.
Maps: I: *315, 344(2)*; II: **§159, 257-258**.
Aid to Preaching the Old Testament II: 257; VIII: 373.
Babylonian, Ancient II: 257, 258.
Babylonian, Orientation of II: 258.

Babylonian Tourist of the Abrahamic Age, and his Map of the World **I**: 344*(2)*; **II**: 257*(2)*.
Bible, Biblical **II**: 258*(3)*.
Cartography of Palestine **II**: 258.
Geomorphological, of Judean Desert **II**: 251, 258.
Jacotin's of Palestine, Surveyed during Napoleon's Campaign **II**: 258.
Meredis Lacus on Ptolemaic **III**: 83.
Mosaic, at Madeba **II**: 257*(2)*, 288.
Nuzi, Found at **II**: 257; **III**: 687.
Ophel, Palestine Exploration Fund, of **II**: 257, *457*(2).
Palestine Exploration Fund **II**: 257.
Palestinian, Ancient Sites **II**: 257.
Ptolemaic **III**: 207.
Roman Empire, of **II**: 258.
Sumerian Plan in the John Rylands Library **II**: 258.
Symbols, Proposed International Code of **III**: 410.
Syriac geographical chart **II**: 257.
Theban 1/1000 scale **II**: 257*(2)*; **III**: 76.

Maqizi: **II**: 5.
MAR-Moeris: **III**: *45*, 157.
Mar Samuel: **VI**: 694; **IX**: lxxxvi.
Marad:
Human and Animal Remains from **III**: 354.
Patesi of **III**: *153*.; **VII**: 210.
Maranatha: **VIII**: 138.
Mar'ash, Syria:
Hittite Communion Table from **V**: 225.
Inscribed Lion from **VII**: 301*(2)*.
Royal Hittite Monument from **III**: 494.
Marashu Sons: **VII**: 175, 249.
Marathon: **I**: 314, 321; **III**: 120, **157**, *625*.
Epigram on the Fallen at **VII**: 346.
Marathon Boy, and Eros **V**: 265.
Monuments Erected after the Victory of **VII**: 336.
Marble:
Ancient, in Great Britain **III**: 624, 625, 626, 627.
Attic Epigraphy, in **II**: 216.
Eglin, Color on **III**: 480, 695, 707, 724.
Fragment, from Aptera **III**: 728.
Jebail, Fragment from **III**: 563*(2)*.
Painted, from Thessaly **III**: 727.
Parian **I**: *456*.
Quarry at Karystos **I**: 293.
Roman Trade of **I**: 341.
Marbles, *see:* **Sculpture**
Marcellinus, Gnaeus Cornelius Lentulus: **II**: 59.
MARCELLUS OF ANCYRA: **VI**: 510, 721.
MARCION:
Diatessaron and the Armenian Marcionites **VI**: 721.
Marcionites:
Diatessaron and **IV**: 48, 270.
Marco Polo: **IV**: *42*.
Marcus Antonius, *see also:* **Mark Anthony** **I**: 5.
Marcus Aurelius:
Talmud and **VI**: 697.
Marcus Primus: **I**: 503.
Marcus Vipsanius Agrippa:
Bronze Head of **III**: 755.
Mards: **III**: 157.
Marduk: **II**: *43*, 59; **V**: 175, 184.
Address of, to the Demons **VII**: 158, 202.
Ashur and Osiris, Relation to **V**: 146, 182, 209.
Babylon, Return to, of, with Shamashahumukin **VII**: 201.
Golden Boats of **VII**: 261.
Mars Dux and **V**: 177, 267.
Ὁ ΜΟΡΔΟΚα, a corruption of **V**: 173.

Osiris and V: 148, 185, 213.
Tiamat, Battle between V: 188; **VII**: 265.
Ningišzida Temple built by **III**: 518.
Marduk-apla-iddina II:
Barrel Cylinder of **VII**: 188.
Ningišzida Temple of **III**: 518.
Marduk-bel-zeri:
Babylonian King **II**: 59.
Marduktabikzirim:
Cylinder of **VII**: 233.
Mareshah, *see also:* **Marisa** **II**: *499;* **VI**: *592.*
MARGOLIOUTH, D. S.:
Ecclesiastes, Date of, on **IV**: 518; **IX**: cxxxiv.
Mari: **I**: *157, 181, 190, 192, 261, 309, 364;* **II**: 3, 176, *199,* 255, 256; **III**: 23, **157-158**, 421, 427; **IV**: 187.
Abraham Lived in **IV**: 319.
"Anatolian" Personal Names from V: 303.
Archives, Royal, of **III**: 158*(2)*, 427.
Ban in **I**: 183.
Hazor in, Documents **II**: *273, 385.*
Hosea and Prophecy at **IV**: 431.
Old Testament Studies and **IV**: 193.
Patriarchs and **III**: 158; **IV**: 318, 320.
Prophecy at, and Biblical **VIII**: 35, 247, 248; **IX**: cxxxviii*(2)*.
Prophecy, History of, and **VIII**: 248.
"Prophecy" in Documents at V: 273, 274.
Prophetism at, and OT Parallels **VIII**: 248*(2)*.
Ras Shamra and **III**: 157, 268.
Samsi-Adad's Journey to **IX**: xcv.
Mari Texts: **VII**: **§881, 163-164**.
Baḫdi-Lim, Correspondence of **VII**: 164.
Economic Texts **VII**: 164.
Execration Texts **VII**: 164*(2)*.
Gudea of Lagash in **VII**: 166.
History and Prophetic Vision in Mari Letter V: 274; **VII**: 164.
Letters **VII**: 164.
NÌG·DU V: 551.
Palace Archives, Mari II **VII**: 164.
Palace Archives of **VII**: 163.
"Prophecy" in **VII**: 164*(6)*.
Prophetic Revelations in, and the Bible **VIII**: 35, 247.
Šamši-Adad's Military Texts from **VII**: 163.
Mârib:
Temple of the Moon at **III**: 517*(2)*.
Marina: **II**: 308.
Marisa, Marissa, *see also:* **Mareshah** V:*72.*
Samaria and in Josephus' *Antiquities* XIII, 275 **VI**: 682.
Tombs, at **III**: 539*(2)*.
Tombs, from the Necropolis of **III**: 538.
Maritime Laws **I**: 355, 506.
Maritime Nation
Assyria as **I**: 322.
Babylonia as **I**: 322.
Israel, of **I**: 333.
Marius: **I**: 5.
Mark Antony (Marcus Antonius): **I**: 5; **II**: **19**.
Mark, Gospel of:
Baptism of Jesus in, and Isaiah 63 **VI**: 315.
Greek Old Testament and Chapter 13 of **VIII**: 285.
OT Quotations in **VIII**: 283.
Targum to Psalms, and 14:24 **VI**: 713; **VIII**: 286.
Transfiguration in, and Isaiah 63:9 **VI**: 316; **VIII**: 287.
Market-place:
Greek **IX**: cxxiii.
Roman **I**: 415; **III**: 488.

Markets:
Athens, of **IX**: xciii.
Babylonian **I**: 307.
Nundines **IX**: xcvii.
Marlik Tepe: **III**: 158, *199*.
Objects from **III**: 570, 599.
Marmarica: **III**: 158.
Marmaris:
Greek Inscriptions from **VII**: 328.
Maronites: **I**: 382, 383.
Marriage: **I**: 188, *209, 211, 213(2);* **§77, 214-223**, 365, *373,* 502; **IV**: 219; **IX**: **§77, lxxxvii**.
Abstinence in **VI**: 69; **IX**: cxlv.
Adam and Eve, of **IV**: 296.
Agnate **I**: 224; **VI**: 695.
Apocrypha, in **I**: 215; **VI**: 610.
Aramaic, Contracts **VII**: 129.
Babylonian Contract **I**: 223; **VII**: 220, 249, 253.
Babylonian Wedding **VII**: 173*(2);* **IX**: lxxxvi*(2)*.
Benna **I**: 216*(2)*.
Bridegroom, Rejected **VII**: 195.
Brother / Sister **I**: 218, 220.
David and Michal's **VI**: 210.
Demotic Marriage Contract, Ptolemaic **VII**: 28, 31.
Divorce and, in Egypt **VII**: 28.
Egyptiam Marriage Settlements, Clause in **V**: 355, 363.
Egyptiam Marriage Settlements, XXth Dynasty, at Turin **VII**: 29.
Egyptian, Earliest Contracts **VII**: 28.
Egyptian Marriage Documents **VII**: **§832, 28-31**.
Elephantine Contracts at **VII**: 135.
Elephantine Contracts, Heredity Rights in **VII**: 136.
Eshnunna, in **VII**: 155.
Ethics of, Ezra on Intermarriage and Divorce **I**: 222; **IV**: 539.
Father / Daugther in Egypt **I**: 220.
Fidelity of, and Monotheism **V**: 35.
Gods, of, in Canaaite Mythology **V**: 192.
Homeric World, in **I**: 281*(2),* 502.
Intermarriage **VI**: 654.
Intermarriage, Offspring of **I**: 212.
Israel, in, according to the Book of Hosea **IV**: 430.
Jacob's, and Ancient Near Eastern Customs **I**: 51.
Kephar Bebhayu Marriage Document **VII**: 95*(2)*.
Laws of **VI**: 654.
Laws regarding in Athens **I**: 188, 211, 499.
Levirate **I**: 214, **§78, 224**; **IX**: v, n.3.
Mamzeruth, Medieval Problems in **VI**: 694.
Mesopotaima, Ancient in **I**: 221.
Monarchy and **I**: 219, 483, 486.
Nuzi Contract **VII**: 167.
Nuzi, Customs **I**: 217; **VII**: 166.;
Rabbinical Sayings on **VI**: 686.
Relatives by, Egyptian Term for **V**: 325.
Royal, and Martilineal Descent **IX**: lxxxiii, lxxxvii.
Royal, in Psalm 45 **VI**: 485.
Sacred, in Mesopotamia **I**: 217.
Sumerian Marriage Songs and the "Song of Songs" **IV**: 506; **VII**: 276.
Sumerian Marriage Texts **VII**: 2, 281.
Symbol of God's Relationship with His People **VIII**: 306.
Tobit and the Hindu-Christian Ideal **VI**: 615.
Tribal Intermarriage, Hebrew **I**: 217.
Wedding Song from Ras Shamra **VII**: 141.
Zadokite Doument and **I**: *215,* 397; **V**: *82;* **VI**: 662.

Mars:
Signs and Names of Planet — **II**: 229; **V**: 562, 573.
Mars Dux:
Mar(u)duk and — **V**: 177, 267.
Mars (Roman God): **V**: 269.
Marsa Maṭrûḫ
Archaic Burials at — **III**: 542.
Marsala: **III**: *169*.
Marseilles: **III**: 158.
Marselles Inscription:
Sacrifices in — **V**: 58.
Marsh:
Terrestrial, and Solar Mat — **V**: 220.
Zubediyah, Stratagraphy of — **II**: 250; **III**: 281.
MARSH, HERBERT: **V**: 623.
MARSH, JAMES: **V**: 683.
Marsovan: **II**: *138*.
MARSTON, CHARLES: **II**: *395*.
Archaeological Expedition — **II**: 357, 395.
Marsyas: **III**: *728*.
Marten: **III**: *371*, 378, *743*.
MARTIN, JOHN: **VIII**: 354.
MARTIN, THEODORE: **VII**: 366.
Martyr(s), Martyrdom: **I**: *112*.
English Bible, for — **IV**: 53.
Festival of Lives Given for Jewish Nation and Christian Faith — **I**: 365.
Maccabean, Sepulchre of — **I**: 173.
Martytrological Tradition in the Prophets — **VIII**: 386.
Origen's Exortation to, and IV Maccacbees — **VI**: 656, 668, 720.
Unknown, in Zechariah — **VI**: 411.
Martyrology:
Apocalpyse to — **V**: 122.
Maru-Aten:
Pleasure Resort or Temple — **I**: 240; **III**: 518.
Masada: **II**: 281, 290, 303, **439-440**; **III**: 420, 423, 445; **VIII**: 434.
Ben Sira Scroll from — **VI**: 608*(2)*; **VIII**: **§1148, 474**.
Exodus Fragment from — **V**: 120.
Qumran and — **VIII**: 411.
Talmud and — **II**: 440; **VI**: 705.
Masai:
Higher Criticism and — **IV**: 243; **V**: 143.
Traditions of — **V**: 143*(2)*.
Masai-Nandi Group: **I**: 327; **III**: 346; **V**: 322.
Mashita: **II**: 440.
Masks: **I**: 237; **II**: 234.
Greek Drama and — **I**: 237.
Medusa, and Astronomy — **II**: 234.
MASON, P. T.:
Hebrew Grammar, on — **V**: 486.
Masonry: **I**: 290, 293; **III**: 458, 470.
Cubit used by Herod's Masons — **V** 76.
Drafted — **III**: 460.
Drafted, Marginally, Pecked — **III**: 474.
Early Bronze — **III**: 468.
Egyptian — **III**: 471.
Haram Wall, of — **II**: 402*(2)*, 403*(2)*; **III**: 487*(3)*.
Mason's Marks — **III**: 458.
Mason's Pick — **III**: 674.
Maṣor:
Rivers of — **VI**: 289.
Masora(h), Studies concerning: **IV**: **§239, 17-19**.
Babylonian — **IV**: 19*(2)*.
Breaks in the Midst of Verses — **IV**: 18.
Dead Sea Scrolls and — **IV**: 18; **VIII**: 437.
Diḳdûḳê ha-ṭeʿamîm — **IV**: 163.
High Priest and Tannaitic — **V**: 45.
Hosea, in — **VI**: 363, 371, 372*(2)*.
Lacuna — **IV**: 18.
Levites and — **IV**: 19, 97; **V**: 43.
Masora Magna in Leningrad B19a — **IV**: 19.

Minor Prophets, Massoretical Note at end of IV: 163.
Piska IV: 17.
Problems of IV: 103.
פסקא באמצע פסוק IV: 18*(2)*.
Stichometry IV: 18.
Syriac IV: 17*(2)*, 18, 47.
Tikkun Sopherim IV: 17
Treatise, Fragment of IV: 18.
Vowel Points IV: 18.
Masoretes: IV: 98.
Masoretic Texts: IV: 11; **§238, 13-17**, 22, 30; V: *683;* IX: **§238, cxxviii**, cxxix.
Abbreivations in IV: 16.
Abbreviated System IV: 16, 17.
Babylonian Yemenite MS IV: 17
Criticism of, from Psalm 1 IV: 14.
Division into Verses IV: 101.
Double Readings in IV: 6.
Editorial Alteration and Adaption in IV: 97; IX: cxxviii*(2)*.
Exaggeration of Errors in VI: 7.
Hebrew, Pronunciation of, and IV: 15; V: 475.
Inferior Readings in IV: 232.
Nahum, of IV: 448.
Origin of, in the Light of Rabbinic Literature and the Dead Sea Scrolls IV: 16; VI: 689.
Orthography of the Pentateuch IV: 5.
Pre-Masoretic Texts IV: **§237, 13**.
Alexander's IV: 13.
Codex Reuchlinianus IV: 13.
Pronouns and Suffixes in, and the Scrolls V: 484.
Qumran and IV: 16*(3);* VIII: **§1094, 441-443**.
Qumran Literature in Relation to VIII: **§1094, 441-443**.
Qumran Thanksgiving Hymns and VIII: 467.
Revision of, Plea for IX: cxxviii.
Septuagint and, compared IV: 1; 5, 13*(2)*, 14*(2)*, 25, 31*(2)*, 259; VI: 206.
Targum Onkelos, and IV: 15; VI: 712.
Uncertainty of IV: 14.
Variants, Perpetuation of IV: 15, 100.
MASPERO, G.: II: 16, 125.
Massalia: I: *301, 342;* III: 159.
Massorites, *see:* **Masoretes**
Maṣṣoth: I: 365.
Mastaba: III: *85*.
Egyptian "Palimpsest" on III: 691.
Sakkara, IIIrd Dynasty Chapels, at III: 512.
Saqqara, False, of *Hwi-b ȝ.w* at Saqqara III: 554.
Saqqara, Reparation of, at III: 456.
Mat(s):
Impressions of Pot Bases III: 572, 616.
Solar V: 220.
Umma Texts Concerning Reed Mats VII: 280.
Weaver of from the Tomb of Khety I: 273.
Matâni: II: 264.
Mater Magna: I: 5.
Materialism:
Evolution and III: 292, 293.
Mathematics and Numbering Systems: I: **§122, 428-436**; IX: **§122, xcix**.
Arabic Numerals on Babylonian Tablet (?) I: 431*(2);* VII: 255, 256.
Arithmetical proportion VI: 222.
Assyrian List of Key Numbers for VII: 195.
Assyro-Babylonian I: *424,* 433; V: 564; VII: 156.

Babylonian **I**: 431*(3)*, 432*(4)*, 433*(5)*, 434, 435; **II**: *223;* **VII**: 255, 256*(2)*, 257*(6)*.
Cipher, Cuneiform Prototype of **I**: 430; **VII**: 156.
Conundrum in the Ugaritic Keret Poem **VII**: 144.
Cube Root, Babylonian Problem of Finding **I**: 434; **VII**: 257.
Cuneiform Prototype of Cipher **I**: 430; **VII**: 156.
Cuneiform Prototype of Zero **I**: 430; **VII**: 156.
Cuneiform Sign for Zero, Astronomical Texts [≮] **I**: 432; **II**: 231.
Cuneiform Texts on **I**: 432, 433; **VII**: 256*(2)*.
Egyptian **I**: 430*(6)*.
Egyptian Mathematical Texts **VII**: **§834, 33-35**.
Egyptian, Truncated Pyramid in **III**: 505.
Factional Expression in Babylonian **VII**: 256.
Fractions, Addition of Egyptian Unit **I**: 435.
Fractions in Biblical and Mishnaic Hebrew **I**: 435.
Geometrical Figures, Transcription of Arabic Letters in **V**: 592.
Greek **I**: 431, 435.
Hebrew **I**: 432*(2);* **II**: 231.
Minoan **I**: 431, 434; **VII**: 361.
Multiplication, Atypical from Uruk **I**: 435; **VII**: 257.
Multiplication Tablets, Babylonian, in Ontario **I**: 430; **VII**: 255.
Nuzi, Old Akkadian Texts from, Metrological Pecularities **VII**: 166.
Pyramid, Truncated, in Egyptian **III**: 505.
Quadratic Equations, Origin and Development **I**: 432*(2)*.
Reciprocals, Babylonian Tables of **I**: 431.
Reciprocals of Irregular Numbers in Babylonian **I**: 434; **VII**: 257.
Reciprocals of Sexagesimal Numerals in Babylonian **I**: 433; **VII**: 256.
Reciprocals, Table of, with Sumerian Spellings **IX**: xcix.
Scheil-Esagil Tablet, in **IX**: xcix.
Selucid **I**: 435.
Sexagesimal system **I**: 432, 433.
X = 10 **I**: 435.
Zero, Cuneiform Prototype of **I**: 430; **VII**: 156.
Zero, Cuneiform Sign for Astronomical Texts [≮] **I**: 432; **II**: 231.

MATHEWS, I. G.: **IV**: 140.

Mati'el:
Aramaic Treaty of, and Mati'el **I**: 511, 513; **V**: *527;* **VII**: 125.

Matriarchy: **I**: *199*.
Royal Marrages and Matrilineal Descent **IX**: lxxxiii, lxxxvii.

Matronit: **V**: 167.

Matronymic Family:
Hebrew Social Organization and **I**: 185, 197, 209.

Mattanah: **II**: 290.

Mattarah, Tell: **III**: 129, **159**.

Matter:
Ancient Meanings of **II**: 224.
Arabic and Hebrew Terms for, with Reference to Saadia **V**: 112, 399, 590.
Creation of **VIII**: 78.
Intellectual Element in **VIII**: 75.

Matthew, Gospel of:
Apocalyptic Editor **VIII**: 286.
Fulfillment Texts in **VIII**: 286.
Genealogy of, and the LXX of Chronicles **IV**: 541; **VIII**: 283.
Habakkuk Commentary (1QpHab) and **VIII**: 457, 479.

Isaiah 42:3, 4, and **VIII**: 283.
Isaiah 7:14, and **VI**: 264.
Isaiah 9: 1, 2, and **VIII**: 283.
Jeremiah, References to **VI**: 320; **VIII**; 285.
Literary Genus of Chapters 1-2 **VIII**: 286.
Micah 5:1, and **VIII**: 283.
Old Testament, Use of in **VIII**: 286*(3)*.
OT Quotations in **VIII**: 283, 285.
Wilderness and Testing in, and in Qumran **VIII**: 482.
Zechariah 9:13 and **VIII**: 283.
Matthew's Bible: **IV**: 52, 53.
Maul: **III**: 681.
Mauramai Batita:
Libyan (Rabu) King **II**: 59.
Mausoleums:
Halicarnassus, at **III**: 543.
Kfar Gil'adi, at **II**: 302.
Rosh Ha-Ayin, of **II**: 302.
Yif'at, of **II**: 302.
Maximianopolis: **II**: 280; **IX**: cxvi*(3)*.
May:
High-priest of Amun **II**: 59.
Mayer: **II**: 60.
MAYER, L. A.:
Bibliography of **I**: 20*(2)*.
MAZAR (MAISLER), BENJAMIN: **II**: *340*.
Bibliography of **I**: 20.
Mazâr, Tell el- **III**: 159, 206; **IX**: cxvi, cxvii.
Mazdaism: **V**: 231.
Mazdayasna:
Judaism and, Dissimilarities **V**: 147.
Mazzaroth: **VI**: 439*(2)*.
Mazzeboth: **V**: 50.
MCCLELLAND, ALEXANDER:
Prophecy, on **IV**: 78; **VIII**: 236.
McCormick Theological Seminary:
Rehnborg Collection of the Dead Sea Scrolls **VIII**: 431.
MCCOSH, JAMES: **III**: 313.
MCFADYEN, JOHN E.:
Pentateuch, on **IV**: 231.
McGill University:
Dead Sea Scrolls at **VIII**: 430.
MCKIM, RANDOPH H.:
Pentateuch on **IV**: 230.
MCNEILE, A. H.:
Exodus, Book of, on **IV**: 326.
MCWHORTER, ALEXANDER: **VIII**: 120.
Me-Silim:
Text Referring to a Stele of **VII**: 276.
MEAD, CHARLES M.: **IV**: *69*.
Meals:
Birkath Ha-Zimmum **I**: 367.
Covenant, in OT **V**: 87.
Havurah **I**: 367.
Jewish Sacramental **I**: 365.
MEANDER: **I**:*198;* **V**: *606*.
Bust of **III**: 738.
Dyskolos **VII**: 348*(2)*.
Genius of **VII**: 346.
Meannesi:
Son of Enannatum I Statue of **II**: 60.
Me'arat Qedumim: **II**: 303.
"Measure for Measure" *see:* **"Manner for Manner"**
Measurement (includes length andcapacity) *see also:* **Weights:** **I**: **§121, 417-427**; **IX**: **§121, xcix.**
Akkadian, from Nuzi **I**: 424, *433*.
Assload **I**: 426*(2)*.
Assyrian **I**: 422, 424, 425.
Assyrian, *piḫû* (liquid) **IX**: xcix.
Assyrian, Shorter Units of Length **I**: 426.
Assyrian, *tikpu,* (length) **I**: 421.
Babylonian **I**: 419*(4)*, 420, 422*(2)*, 424*(3)*, *432*.
Doric Foot Standard **I**: 426; **VI**: 141.

- Egyptian **I**: 417, 418*(2)*, 419, 423*(2)*, 424*(3)*, 425; **III**: 777.
- Egyptian **I**: 419*(2)*.
- Egyptian Kat **I**: 420.
- Ethiopian **I**: 427*(2)*.
- Geophysical, Application of to Archaeology **II**: 215; **III**: 427.
- Hebrew **I**: 417, 420, 422, 423; **III**: 777.
- Indus Valley **I**: 426.
- Jewish, Capacity **I**: 419.
- Land, *see:* ***Surveying*** **I**: **§124, 437.**
- [cuneiform] as designation of measure **I**: 422.
- Minoan **I**: 425, 426*(2);* **III**: 474.
- Moabites, of, by David **VI**: 212.
- Mycenaean **I**: 426.
- Nuzi, Capacity **I**: 425.
- Omer **I**: 422.
- Palestinian, Ancient **I**: 424.
- Parthenon Foot Standard **I**: 426; **VI**: 141.
- Parthian Standard **I**: 423.
- Persian **I**: 424.
- Rabbinical Ordinances, as **I**: 427; **VI**: 691.
- Royal **I**: 426.
- Sack **I**: 426.
- Shiʿurim **I**: 427.
- Stadium Foot **I**: 427.
- Sumerian **I**: 421, 426.

Meat: **I**: 249.
- Masi and the Permission to Eat Flesh **V**: 143.
- Prohibition of **V**: 145.

Mecca: **II**: 281; **III**: 231, 437.

Mechanism:
- Man as **VIII**: 173.

Mechanum: **II**: 283.

Mechu:
- Tomb of **III**: 533.

Mecyberna: **III**: **159**.

Medallion:
- Dahshûr, of **III**: 592.
- Petra, from **III**: 754.
- Terracotta **III**: 593.

Medals: **I**: 282, 440.
- Broze, from Jaulan **VII**: 366.
- Shekel **I**: 447.
- Wappenmünzen **I**: 457.

Medea (Medeia): **III**: 625; **V**: 254.

Medeba: **I**: *344;* **II**: 441; **VI**: 212, 588.

Medes: **II**: *31, 33,* **149**,*153(2);* **IV**: 543
- Chronology of **II**: 202.
- Daniel, in **IV**: 532.
- Law of **I**: 495; **II**: *172, 179.*

Media: **II**: *173, 201, 267;* **III**: 92, 159, *197, 394.*

Median Texts: **VII**: 373*(2)*
- Tri-lingual Text from Hamadan **VII**: 153.

Medians: **II**: 1; **III**: 125, *181.*

Mediator:
- ***Christ as*** **VIII**: **§1003, 149.**
- High God and (Greek) **V**: 264.

Medical Equipment:
- Hippocratean Physicians **III**: 401.

Medical Practices, *see:* **Disease, Hygiene** *and* **Physicians**

Medicine, *see also:* **Disease §177; Drug Use and Abuse §178**
- Animals in Egyptian **III**: 366, 368.
- Animals, Treatment of in Jewish Law **III**: 366, 402.
- Aphorism, Philological Commentaries on **I**: 403.
- *Ascalabotes fasicularis,* in Babylonian **III**: 399.
- Assyrian **III**: 398, 399.
- Assyrian Medical Text **VII**: 195.
- Assyrian, Physiology **III**: 396.
- Babylonian **III**: 396, 399, 403; **VII**: 255.
- Babylonian, *Ascalabotes fasicularis,* in **III**: 399.

Babylonian Medical Textbooks, Title of **III**: 398.
Beetle in **III**: 369.
Bible and **III**: 403.
Bottles **III**: 406, 588.
Cairo Genizah, Fragment of Medical Vocabulary **VII**: 107.
Ebers Medical Papyrus **I**: *418;* **III**: 396*(2);* **VII**: 34*(2)*.
Egyptian **III**: 397, 402.
Egyptian and Mice **III**: 379.
Egyptian Medical Texts **III**: *366, 374, 385(3)*, 400*(2)*, 401*(2)*, 405; **VII**: **§834, 33-35**.
Epidaurus and Greek and Roman **III**: *97*, 398.
Genizah Fragments on **VII**: 107.
Greek **III**: 398*(3)*, 402.
Health Laws in Israel **III**: 396.
Hebrew **III**: 396, 401.
Hebrew Medical Expressions **III**: 402; **V**: 401.
Henbane as Healing Herb **IX**: cxxii*(2)*.
Herbs, Healing, of Bible **III**: 386, 403.
Hermetic in Qumran Literature **III**: 404; **VIII**: 415.
Iraq Medical Journals **III**: 404.
KÙ.GI in medical texts **III**: 403.
"Measuring" the patient in Egyptian Medical Texts **III**: 404.
Medical Profession in in light of Cairo Geniza **III**: 403.
Mouse and Egyptian **III**: 379.
Nimrud, Two Medical Texts from **III**: 402; **VII**: 156.
Old Testament and Modern Medical Knowledge **III**: 401.
Omina, Nimrud Catalog of Medical and Physiognomical **VII**: 156.
Origin of **III**: 406.
Pig in **III**: *380*, 399.
Plants in Egyptian **III**: 385*(3)*.
Prehistoric **III**: 399, *408*.
Psychological Development of **III**: 396.
Pulse, Observation of, in Mesopotamian Medicine **III**: 403.
Reeds, Use in (?) **III**: 398.
Roman **III**: 398.
Talmud, in **III**: 396; **VI**: 699.
Medina: **III**: 437.
Medinat Habu: **II**: 6, 81.
Ancient Graffiti at **VII**: 13.
Medīnet Hab(o)u: **III**: 85.
Geographical List from **II**: 270.
Greek Text from **VII**: 316.
Naval Battle Pictured at **VII**: 17.
Palace of **III**: 84, 85.
Reliefs at **VII**: 69.
Sarcophagus of Prince Ramessu from **III**: 551.
Temple of **III**: 516.
Medinet Habu Lists: **II**: 273.
Medinet-Qûta: **III**: 104.
Medio-Passive:
Origin of **V**: 608.
Mediterranean: **I**: *333(2), 334(3), 338, 340, 350;* **II**: *218*.
Eastern, 1600-1400 B.C. **I**: 124.
Human Race, name as applied to part of **III**: 336.
Phoenicians in West **II**: 156.
Soils of the Eastern **II**: 250*(2)*.
Mediterranean Sea: **I**: *252, 362;* **III**: *156(2)*, **160**.
Dunes around Coast of **II**: 254.
Piracy in the Eastern **I**: 326.
Power Source, as, for Palestine **I**: 362; **VI**: 360, 413.
Tidal Waves in Eastern **II**: 250.
Mēdūm:
Chapel of Atet at **III**: 711.
Hieratic Inscriptions in a Pyramid at **VII**: 61.
Medusa: **V**: 265.
Artemis, as, in the Temple at Corfu **V**: 253.

Myth of, and Greek Art **III**: 691; **V**: 253.

Medusa Mask:

Interpretation of, and Astronomy **II**: 234.

Megadim, (Megaddim), Tel: **II**: 303, 304, **441**.

Megalography: **III**: 716*(2)*, 717*(3)*.

Megasthenes: **II**: *11*.

Megiddo: **II**: *189*, 280, 284*(2)*, 296*(2)*, 297*(3)*, 303*(2)*, 309, 310, *339*, *344*, *346*, *373*, *385*, *435*, **441-444**, *472*, *486;* **III**: 422, 423*(2);* **IV**: 218, 219, 220; **VI**: 412; **IX**: cxvi*(3)*.

Battle of **I**: 442.

Deborah's Song and **IV**: 371.

Geology and Morphology of, Area **II**: 249, 442.

Inscribed Jar from **III**: 613.

Ivories **III**: 771, 772.

Joash and the Battle of **I**: 94; **IV**: 382.

Location of, and the Annals of Thuthmose III **VII**: 15.

Plain of **II**: 289.

Solomon's Palace at **III**: 503.

Solomonic Gateway at, and Ezekiel's Temple **VI**: 360.

Sumerian Seal Impression from **III**: 650.

Megilla: **VIII**: 207.

Yemenite MS of **VI**: 701.

Megillat Setarim: **VI**: 689.

Megillat Taanit: **I**: *172(2)*.

Megilloth:

Bibliography **I**: **(§26)**, 14.

Exegetical Studies on Several Books of **VI**: **(§649)**, **551**.

Hand-Painted, 17th and 18th Century **VIII**: 358.

Italian Engraved, Earliest **VIII**: 358.

Literary Criticism of **IV**: **§393**, **503**.

Megilloth Genuzoth: **VIII**: 428, 458.

Meʿarat Shovakh: **II**: 440.

Mehendi: **VII**: 20.

Mehri: **V**: 361.

Meie, Queen:

Tomb of, at Thebes **III**: 539.

MEIER, ERNST: **V**: 473.

Meiron:

Synagogue, Ancient , at **III**: 523.

Mejarkon: **VI**: 173.

Mekaz: **II**: 284.

Mekilta: **VI**: 692, 708.

Arrangement and Division of **VI**: 707.

De-Rabbi Ishmael, Date of **VI**: 710.

Deuteronomy, to **IV**: 348.

Genizah Fragments of **VII**: 109.

Name of the **VI**: 707.

Pentateuch, on **IV**: 234; **VI**: 708.

Two **VI**: 707.

Mekkedah: **II**: 306.

Melcarth: **III**: 496.

Melchizedek: **I**: *26*, *32*, *82*, *90;* **V**: 64; **VI**: 63, 65*(4)*, 66, 112, 144, 517, 529; **VII**: 139.

Aaron and **V**: 41.

Biographical Studies **I**: **63-65**.

Christ and **VIII**: 296.

Patristic Interpretation of **VI**: 721.

Sacrifice of **VI**: 65.

Melchizedek, Midrash on (11QMelch) **VI**: 315; **VIII**: **§1130**, **467-468**.

Isaiah 61 and **VIII**: 468.

New Testament and **VIII**: 467, 482.

Son of Man, and **VIII**: 468.

Meleager:

Statue of **II**: 60; **III**: 724.

melekh ha-ʿolam: **VIII**: 207*(3)*, 208, 386.

Anti-Gnostic Protest, as **VIII**: 207.

Zealot influence on liturgy(?) **VIII**: 207.

Meli-Sikhu:
Inscription of **VII**: 249.
Melite:
Herakleion Shire in **III**: 518
"Melitensis Quinta" **VII**: 114*(3)*.
Melito:
Pascal Homily of, and Barnabas' Text of Isaiah **VI**: 319, 717, 724.
Melkath:
Temple of **II**: 308.
Melloth: **II**: 284.
Melon(s): **I**: 247; **III**: 387, 392, *395*.
Melothesia: **I**: 408; **VII**: *350*.
Melqart: **III**: 656.
Meluḫa (Meluḫḫa): **I**: *327, 341;* **II**: *60, 66, 174, 197,* 266, 273; **III**: *155(4)*, **160**.
MELVILLE, HERMAN:
Job and **IV**: 469; **VIII**: 370.
Memnon:
Statue (Colossus) of **II**: 60; **III**: 741, 748.
Memorial(s):
Cairn of Hani **III**: 485.
Rome, of, in Italian Colonies **III**: 482.
Memorizer:
Official, of the Palestinian Schools (רוֹבֶה) **IV**: 175; **VI**: 688.
Memory, Historical:
Greece, in **IX**: lxxxiv.
Primordial **IX**: lxxxiv.
Memphis: **II**: *92;* **III**: **160-161**, *166, 241, 246, 252, 381, 602, 614, 645, 737, 748, 766.*
Pharaonic Tablets of **VII**: 55.
Ptah's, at **III**: *359*.
Ramesses III, Cult of, at **V**: 222.
Reliefs from the Memphite Necropolis **VII**: 74.
Sarcophagus from Mit-Rahîna **III**: 549.
Temple at **III**: 512.
Memra: **VI**: 105, 714; **VIII**: 101*(2)*, 103, 109, 131, 137, 149*(3)*, 290.
Palestinian Targum in, and the Logos of the Fourth Gospel **VI**: 105, 714; **VIII**: 131.
Mena: **II**: *55,* **60**.
Tablet of **VII**: 60.
Menahem: **IV**: 181; **VII**: 159.
Israel and Judah during the Dynasty of **VIII**: 389.
Mende: **III**: 161, *223, 257*.
Mendel's Law:
Evolution and **III**: 314, 321.
MENDELSSOHN, FELIX:
"Elijah" **VIII**: 358.
MENDELSSOHN, MOSES:
Jewish Viewpoint on Natural Law and **V**: 113.
Life and Contributions of **I**: 24.
Mendes, *see also:* **Tell el Rub'a:** **III**: **161**.
Fish of **III**: 374; **V**: 333.
Stela from **VII**: 26.
Mending:
Ancient Methods of **I**: 268.
Pottery and Stone Vessels **I**: 289.
Mene Mene Tekal Upharsin: **I**: *431;* **VI**: 572*(3)*, 574.
Menekles: **VII**: 330.
Μενελιατου:
Egypt, in **III**: 84.
Egypt, in **III**: 84.
Meneptaḥ *see:* **Merenptah**
Menes: **I**: 326, 327; **II**: **60-61**,*66(3)*, *174(2)*, 196, 197*(2)*, *225;* **III**: *155, 160, 777.*

Tablet of	**VII**: 61.
Tomb of	**III**: 535.
Menkaura:	
Bust of	**II**: 61.
Menkheperreʿsenb:	
Statue of	**II**: **61**, *90;* **VII**: 65.
Menna:	
Tomb of	**III**: 542.
Menology:	**I**: 400, 403, 404.
Menophres:	**II**: **61**, *195.*
Menorah:	
Arch of Titus, on	**V**: 52.
Door-Panel from 'Ibellin in Galilee with	**III**: 472.
Fate and Form of the, of the Maccabees	**V**: 53.
Foot of, Shape of	**V**: 53.
History of	**V**: 53.
Symbol of After-Life	**V**: 53; **VIII**: 265.
Symbol of Judaism	**V**: 53; **VIII**: 308.
Menorah Conference;	**VIII**: 326.
Menshah:	**III**: *596.*
Menteḥetef:	
Egyptian Vizier	**II**: 61.
Mentḥotpe:	
King in the Eleventh Egyptian Dynasty	**II**: 61.
Menthuhotep (Menthuhetep):	**II**: *4, 83;* **V**: 292; **IX**: cxxvi.
Ebony Statue of	**III**: 729.
post- Twelfth Dynasty Egyptian King	**II**: 61*(2).*
Stela of	**VII**: 19.
Stele of	**VII**: 18*(2).*
Tomb of, at Deir el-Bahari	**III**: 537*(2).*
Mentu:	
Nes-a-ched, Priest of, Ushabti-box of	**III**: 574.
Mentuemhat:	
Tomb of at Thebes	**III**: 748.
Mentusa:	
Tablet of (XII Dynasty)	**VII**: 58.
Mephaʿath:	**II**: 444.
Mer-n-Neith-it-s:	**VII**: *64.*
Mera:	**II**: *99.*
Seal of Tarqumuwa, from	**III**: 650.
Merab:	**IV**: 373; **VI**: 215.
Mercenaries:	**I**: 321*(2).*
Cretan, (Cherethites)	**II**: 121, 122.
Nubian	**I**: 318.
Philistine	**I**: 318; **III**: *556.*
MERCER, SAMUEL A. B.	
Egyptrian Gammar of	**V**: 362.
Merchants:	**I**: 269, 271, 302, 307, 308, 309, 341; **VII**: 308.
Assyrian, of Kanish (Idiom)	**V**: 570.
Foreign, at Ugarit	**I**: 342, 506.
Jewish, called Radanites	**I**: 306.
Seafaring, of Ur	**I**: 340.
Ugarit, at, and Patriarchal Narratives	**IV**: 320.
Ura, of, and Abraham	**I**: 31; **VI**: 73.
Mercury:	
Roman Medicine, Use in	**III**: 405.
Mercury, Planet:	
Babylonian Method of Computation for Visibilities of	**II**: 233.
Mercy:	**V**: 510.
Oded, Judgment and	**VIII**: 224.
Unearned, and Merit	**VIII**: 196.
Mercy Death, *see:* **Euthanasia**	
Meredis Lacus:	**III**: 83.
Merenptah:	**I**: 333,*369;* **II**: **61-62**, *163, 164.*
Aid to Hittites	**I**: 513.
Building of, Mit Rahineh	**III**: 511.
Death of	**II**: 62.
Etruscan Inscriptions and	**II**: 61; **VII**: 373.
Exodus and	**II**: 62*(2);* **IV**: 335*(2).*
Invasion of Syria by(?)	**II**: 62.
Lintel of, at Mitrahineh	**VII**: 61.
Monument of Prince	**VII**: 65.
Mummy of	**I**: 378, 379, 380; **II**: 62; **III**: 355.

Pharaoh of the Exodus(?) **II**: 62; **IV**: 336.
Sea Peoples of **VII**: 14*(2)*.
Statue of, found at Athar en-Nabi **VII**: 66.
Stela of **I**: 62, 265.
Text of, Fourth year at Amada **VII**: 18.
Throne Room of **III**: 500*(2)*.
Tomb of **III**: 538.
Merenptah Inscription: **III**: *667*, **VII**: **§831, 27-28.**
Exodus, Mentioned on **IV**: 336.
Merenra: **II**: 62.
Merer:
Stela of, in Cracow **VII**: 25.
Meribath-Kadesh: **III**: 161.
Merimda: **I**: 377; **III**: 162.
Μερισμος Ανακεχωρηκοτων: **III**: 89, 90.
Merismus: **V**: 460.
Merit:
Unearned Mercy and **VIII**: 196.
MERIVALE, CHARLES:
Roman Empire, on **II**: 159*(2)*, 160.36
Rome, on **III**: 211.
Merkabah: **VIII**: 61.
Mermnadæ: **II**: 206.
Merneit:
King of Abydos **II**: 4, 207.
Merodach: **V**: 175, 177.
Merodach Baladan: **II**: **62**, *251(2), 320, 322*.
Dial of Ahaz and **II**: 62; **IV**: 390.
Meroë: **III**: 148, **162**, *511, 751, 756;* **IX**: civ.
Culture of **III**: 90.
Ethiopian Sovereigns at **II**: *129*.
Stela found on the Site of **VII**: 20, 289.
Sun Temple of **III**: 511.
Temple of Basa **III**: 511.
Meroitic (Studies): **VII**: 63*(3)*.
Decipherment of **VII**: 61.
Four Inscriptions **VII**: 24.
Inscriptions **VII**: 61.
King's Name in **V**: 301.
Merom: **II**: **444**; **VI**: 171.
Meronoth: **II**: 284*(2)*, 291.
Merotic:
King's Name in **V**: 301; **VII**: 69.
Merptaḥ
Memphite Stela of **VII**: 24.
MERRILL, SELAH: **II**: 413.
Mersekha:
King of Abydos **II**: 4, 207.
Mersin, *see also:* **Cilcia and Kizzuwadna** **III**: 61-62, **163**, 263.
Culture, Earlier, at **III**: 62.
Meru:
Tomb of **VII**: 42.
Mery:
Stela of **VII**: 22.
Merynar: **II**: **63**, *66*.
Meryt:
Tomb of **III**: 560.
Meryt-Amon: **II**: 63.
Mes:
Inscription of **VII**: 28.
Mes-kalam-dug: **III**: *682*.
Mesa, Moabite King: **II**: 354.
Meşad Gozal, *see:* **Gozal**
Meşad Ḥashavyahu: **II**: 444.
Hebrew Inscription from **VII**: 96.
Judicial Petition from **VII**: 102.
Letter, from, 7th Century **VII**: 96*(3)*.
Meşad Yeruḥam: **II**: 444.
Mesada: **II**: 290.
Mesannepadda: **II**: 63*(2)*.
Meselieh: **II** 308.
Meşer: **II**: **445.**
Mesha: **I**: 321; **II**: **63**; **III**: 163; **IV**: 214; **V**: *475*. **VII**: 110*(2)*, 111; **IX**: cxvi.
Meša Inscription, *see:* **Moabite Stone**
Mešek: **III**: 163, *261*.

Mêshitug:
King of Adab II: 63.
Meshwesh: II: *95*, 149.
Mesilim: II: 63*(2)*; VII: 235.
Meskene: III: *170*.
Mesolithic Period:
Palestine in III: 427.
Mesopotamia: I: 126, *259*, 326*(2)*, 327, 328*(2)*, 330*(2)*, 331*(2)*, 332, 333, 335*(2)*, 336,*338*, *341*, *347*, *382*, *491(2)*; II: *143*, *166*, *195*; III: *17*, *44*, *48(2)*, *115*, *138(2)*, *147*, **163-165**, *184*, *196*, *244*, *274(2)*, *278*, *357*, 424, *589*, *598*, *637*.
Antiquities, Prehistoric, of III: 566.
Assembiles, Ancient, in I: 491*(2)*.
"Chalice" Ware of, and its Historical Significance III: 612.
Chronology, Stratigraphic Confirmation II: 174.
Civilization I: 124*(2)*, 126; III: 142, 164, 165*(4)*.
Constitutional Development in Early I: 493.
Democracy, Primitive, in IX: cii.
Distillation, Sublimation and Extraction, Evidences of, in II: 224.
Early Inhabitants of III: 340*(2)*.
Ethnic Problems in III: 48, 348.
Family Life in I: 213, *221*.
Food, Chemical Processes in Ancient I: 248.
Irrigation, Ecological Effects of in Ancient I: 364; II: 245.
Literary Style in First Millennium VII: 3.
Living Conditions in I: 211.
Marriage in I: *213*, 217, 221.
Nomadism, Economic Basis of, in I: 182, 310.
Partian Remains found in III: 142.
Poltical Development in I: 491.
Population of II: 259.
Religion in, *see also*: ***Mesopotamian Religion*** V: 165, 187; VIII: 233.
Rural Production, Administration of IX: cii.
Sassanian Remains found in III: 142.
Settlement Patterns and Urban Origins in I: 208.
Small State in Poltical and Cultural History of I: 490.
Topography of III: 164.
Travels, Modern, in III: 438, 446.
War in V: 165; VIII: 233.
Women in Ancient I: 198.
Mesopotamian Religion: I: 341; V: 158, 164, 167.
Gods, Symbols of, in the Cylinder Seals III: 655; VIII: 306.
Religious Year. Great Battle of, in Akītu House V: 167.
Scorpion in III: 380, 699; V: 165.
Mesopotamians: II: 149.
Historiography of I: 134.
Relations, Susa at III: 240.
Unity of, and Royal Hymns I: 508; IX: cix.
Mesore:
Egyptian Month of I: 396.
Mesozoic Period: IV: 305.
Messabahs:
Palestine, of V: 106.
Messalla, Potitius Valerius: II: 63.
Meṣṣebah: I: 373.
Messen: VII: 56.
Messenia: III: **165-166**.

Messenian Peninsula:
Mycenaean Coastal Settlements, Possible Disapperance of **III**: 173.
Messiah, *see also:* **Christ** **VIII**: 137, **§997, 138-142**.
Apocalyptic Literature, Doctrine of, in **V**: 121, 127; **VI**: 611; **VIII**: 140.
Apocrypha, Doctrine of, in **V**: 121, 127; **VI**: 611; **VIII**: 140.
Apocrypha, Teaching in **V**: 127; **VI**: 596.
Archaeology, Symbols of, in Palestine **VIII**: 306.
"Begotten", in the Qumran Scrolls **VIII**: 419.
ben Ephraim, Rabbis' and Pseudo-Philo's Saul **V**: 129; **VI**: 678; **VIII**: 142; **IX**: cli.
ben Joseph **V**: 128*(2)*; **VIII**: 141.
Birth Traditions **VIII**: 139.
Christ of History and **V**: 125.
Christ of NT, and **VIII**: 140.
Christian (Early) Interpretation of Jesus as **VIII**: 141.
Christian, in th Light of Judaism Ancient and Modern **VIII**: 140, 330.
Christianity, in **V**: 128.
Coins, and Traditions Concerning **I**: 442*(2)*; **V**: 127*(2)*.
Coming of. A Jewish Exposition **V**: 125.
Damascus Document, of **VI**: 663; **VIII**: 421.
Damascus, Land of, and Messianic Redemption **V**: 131; **VIII**: 420.
Daniel, in **IV**: 524.
David's Family in Relation to the **I**: 87; **VIII**: 138.
Deity of **VIII**: 138, 139, 143*(2)*.
Demons and Pre-Christian **VIII**: 161.
Divine **VIII**: 140, 142.
Economistic Reign of, over Israel and the World **VI**: 496.
Ephraim, Son of **VIII**: 141.
Esdras, IV, Teaching of **V**: 127.
God's Begetting the, in 1QSa **VIII**: 142, 464.
Godhead of, in the OT **VIII**: 138.
Heathen **V**: 155.
Historical Development of the Word **V**: 510.
History and Development of the Messianic Idea **V**: 126.
Human and Superhuman **V**: 127.
Isaiah 1-39, in **VI**: 247.
Isaiah Passages as Predicting the **VI**: 254, 261, 262*(2)*.
Isaiah Prediction of the Mother of the **VI**: 263.
Isaiah's, and Virgil's **IV**: 394; **V**: 268; **VIII**: 140.
Jacob's Prophecy of **VI**: 92, 93; **VIII**: 132.
Jesus and the OT **VIII**: 142.
Jesus as the True **VIII**: 138.
Jesus not the OT **VIII**: 138.
Jewish and Persian **V**: 125, 139.
Jewish Conceptions of **V**: 125.
Jewish Expectation, What Kind(?) **V**: 129.
Jewish Philosopher (Modern) and the Doctrine of **VIII**: 141.
Job and the Revelation of **IV**: 461; **VIII**: 140.
John the Baptist and **VIII**: 142, 419, 482.
Judaism, in **V**: 182.
King **V**: 128; **VI**: 484*(2)*.
Kingdom of **VI**: 410, 596.
Messianic Fox **III**: 374.
Michael the **V**: 126; **VIII**: 140, 156.
Mishpaṭ and **VIII**: 142.
Moreh haṣṢedeq **VIII**: 142.
New Testament, Relation to His Jewish Prototype **VIII**: 139*(2)*.

Patriot Songs and	**I**: 243.
Persian and Jewish	**V**: 125, 139.
Pre-existence of	**VIII**: 128*(2)*.
Priest and	**VIII**: 142.
Priest-King of Psalm 109	**VI**: 517; **VIII**: 141.
Priestly	**VIII**: 142.
Psalms, in	
Purifying	**VI**: 308.
Qādiān, of	**V**: 143.
Qumran, Monks of, and	**VIII**: 142, 482.
Qurmran, Testimonia from	**VIII**: 471*(2)*.
Reign of, Temporary, in Literature of Early Judausm	**VIII**: 255.
Religion and	**VIII**: 139.
Royal Messiahs	**V**: 129.
Samaritan Doctrine of	**VIII**: 139, 140; **IX**: cxxxvii*(2)*.
Search for	**V**: 130.
Song of Solomon and	**IV**: 507.
Suffering and Atoning taught in the OT	**VIII**: 144.
Suffering, and Judaism	**VIII**: 145.
Suffering Servant and Davidic	**VIII**: 142, 147.
Suffering, Song of	**VI**: 491.
Superhuman and Human	**V**: 127.
Symbols of, in Palestine Archaeology	**VIII**: 306.
Talmud Concerning	**V**: 126; **VI**: 699; **VIII**: 139.
Temporary Reign of, in Literature of Early Judaism	**V**: 123; **VIII**: 136.
Testament of Levi, in	**VI**: 669, 670*(2)*; **VIII**: 141*(3)*.
Title, בר נשא, as	**V**: 462; **VIII**: 139.
Title, Rise of the	**V**: 510; **VIII**: 141.
Two	**VIII**: 141.
Two, Doctrine of, among the Jews	**V**: 125; **VIII**: 419.
Two, in the Testament of the Twelve Patriarchs	**V**: 129; **VI**: 659; **VIII**: 141.
Virgil's, and Isaiah's	**IV**: 394; **V**: 268; **VIII**: 140.
Virgil's Messianic Expectation	**V**: 269.
Virigin Birth of	**VIII**: 141.
Wisdom of Jesus the	**VIII**: 140.
Zadokite, Two Messiahs	**VI**: 662; **VIII**: 140.
Zoroastrian	**V**: 232*(3)*.
Messianic *(Term)*:	**V**: 510.
Messianic Aramaic Text (4QMess ar / 4QNoah ar)	**VIII**: **§1137, 469**.
Messianic Conspiritors:	
Zechariah, in	**VI**: 410.
Messianic Expectation in Israel, *(see also:* **Messianic Prophecy**	**V**: **§459, 125-131**; **IX**: cxxx*(2)*, **§459, cxxxvi**.
Archangels and Spirits, and Associations of	**V**: 128.
Assumption of Moses in	**V**: 129; **VI**: 653.
Christ of Jewish, and the Christ who came	**V**: 128.
Christian Eschatology and	**V**: 130*(2)*.
Development of	**V**: 126*(3)*; **VIII**: 127.
Elijah, Expectation of	**V**: 128.
Enoch, Book of, Doctrine in, and its Influence on the New Testament	**V**: 126; **VI**: 649; **VIII**: 298.
Essenes and	**V**: 97, 129.
Ezekiel, Messianic Concepts of	**IV**: 421; **V**: 129.
Genesis, in	**IX**: cxxx, cxxxvi.
Growth of	**V**: 128.
Haggai, Element in	**IV**: 451.
Hasidism, Messianic Idea and Messianic Trends in the Growth of	**V**: 130.
Hasidism, Neutralisation of the Messianic Element in Early	**V**: 131.
Isaiah, Messianic Ideal of	**V**: 128.
Isaiah, Messianic Teaching of	**IV**: 394; **V**: 128; **VIII**: 140.

Israel, Messianic Concept in — **V**: 130.
Jeremiah, Messianic Hope of — **IV**: 413; **V**: 130.
Jewish Expectation at Time of Jesus — **V**: 126.
Jewish Theories of — **V**: 126.
Jews, Modern, Views of — **V**: 125, 127*(2)*, 130.
Job, Messianic Element in — **IV**: 459; **V**: 126.
Job, Messianic Hope in — **IV**: 464*(2)*; **V**: 128*(2)*.
Justin Martyr's *Dialogue with Trypho*, in — **V**: 130; **VI**: 725.
Latter Prophets, Messianic Ideas in — **IV**: 386; **V**: 126.
Messianic Prophecy Illustrated by Joel — **IV**: 431.
Messianic Secret — **V**: 131.
Messianic Views of Christ's Contemporaries — **V**: 126.
Micah, Messianic Scope of — **IV**: 447; **VIII**: 18.
Modern Judaism and — **VIII**: 331*(2)*.
New Testament Messianic Interpretation — **V**: 130.
Old Testament Idea of — **V**: 125.
Old Testament Saints, Knowledge and Faith of — **V**: 125.
Origin and Character of — **V**: 125.
Origin of — **V**: 127.
Pattern of — **V**: 129.
Pledge of Blessing (Paraphrase of Pss. 114) — **V**: 705.
Pre-Christian Apocalyptic Literature, in — **V**: 120, 125.
Psalms, Reference to "King" in, and — **IV**: 475*(2)*, 490*(2)*; **V**: 126.
Psalter, in — **IV**: 390; **V**: 128.
Qumran Literature, in (4Q252) — **VIII**: 468.
Qumran Literature, in (4QFlor / 4QEschMid) — **VIII**: **§1131**, **468**.
Rabbinic Messianic Interpretation — **V**: 130.
Religions, Ancient, Messianic Idea in — **V**: 127.
Revelation, Organic Development of — **V**: 129.
Rise and Development of — **V**: 126.
Rise and Fall of, in the Sixth Century — **V**: 17, 128.
Saadia Gaon's Messianic Computation in his Commentary on Daniel — **VI**: 726.
Samaritans, Hope of — **V**: 127; **VIII**: 140.
Second Esdras, Teachiing — **VI**: 613*(2)*.
Transformation of by Jesus and His Apostles — **V**: 127.
Transformation of, in NT — **VIII**: 298*(2)*
Two Messiahs, Doctrine of in Sectarian Literature, Second Commonwealth — **VIII**: 419.

Messianic Prophecy, *see also:* **Messianic Expectation in Israel** — **VI**: 261, 306, 308*(2)* **VIII**: **§995**,**132**-133‡-**137**, 245; **VIII**: 138, 295, 297, 298, 329; **IX**: cxlix.
Apologetics and — **VIII**: 137.
Brigg's, C. A. on, Criticised — **VI**: 29.
Christian Interpretation of — **VIII**: 134, 273.
"Court Style" Phraseology — **VIII**: 134.
Davidson, A. B., on — **VIII**: 240.
Eschatology, Popular, and — **VIII**: 134, 251.
Extra-Israelite Beliefs, and — **VIII**: 136.
Fulfillment in St. Paul — **VIII**: 137.
Fulfillment of — **VIII**: 134*(2)*, 250.
Gospels and — **VIII**: 298.
Hengstengerg, E. W., on — **VIII**: 126.
Higher Criticism and — **VIII**: 134.
Huehn, Eugen, on — **VIII**: 134.
Interpretation of — **VIII**: 298*(2)*.
Isaiah, in — **IV**: 394; **VIII**: 135.
Jewish Problem and — **VIII**: 331.
Job, in — **IV**: 459; **VIII**: 133.
Joel, Illustrated by — **IV**: 431; **VIII**: 132.
Micah, in — **VI**: 392.

Nathan's Prophecy to David	**VIII**: 132.
Rectilinear Interpretation	**VIII**: 137.
Suffering as an Element of	**VIII**: 134.
Typological Interpretation	**VIII**: 137.
Woes	**VIII**: 242.
Messianic Psalms:	**IV**: 477, **§385, 489-490**; **VI**: 450, 451.
Calvin, John and Interpretation of	**IV**: 490.
Christ and Christianity, Witness of, to	**IV**: 489.
Hodayot (1QH6 = 1QHiii)	**VIII**: 466.
Psalm 22 as	**VI**: 468*(2)*.
Psalm 8 as(?)	**VI**: 456.
Tholuck, A., on	**IV**: 489.
Messianism:	
Aeschylus and the Messianic Idea	**V**: 149.
Amos, of	**VIII**: 18, 136.
Ancient Religions, Messianic Idea in	**V**: 145.
Apologetics and	**VIII**: 136.
Babylonian Ideas, Influence of, on Jewish	**V**: 128.
Crises of	**V**: 130.
Deuteronomy, in	**VIII**: 16, 136.
Economic Significance of	**V**: 128.
Genesis, in	**VIII**: 16, 136.
Gospel, and Qumran Use of Prophecy	**VIII**: 420, 422.
Haggai, of	**VIII**: 136.
Herod's	**II**: 47; **VIII**: 142.
Historical Origin and Morphology	**V**: 130.
History of a Messianic Movement, Jerusalem 201 to 199 B.C.E.	**V**: 129.
Hosea, in	**VIII**: 18, 136.
Javanese Messianic Expectations	**V**: 150.
Jewish and Christian	**V**: 129.
Jewish History, in	**V**: 130.
Krishna and Mithra as Messiahs	**V**: 151.
Messianic Symbolism in Palestine Archaeology	**V**: 129; **VIII**: 142.
Proto-Zacharias, of	**VIII**: 136.
Qumran of	**V**: 129; **VIII**: 419, **§1078, 418-420**.
Virgil, Messianic Idea in	**V**: 267.
Wisdom Concept in Relation to Biblical	**V**: 118.
Metal Articles (Metalware):	**III**: **§211, 596-600**, 627.
Metallurgy:	**I**: **§99, 294-302**, **II**: 214, 223; **III**: 456; **V**: 337; **IX**: **§99, xcii-xciii**.
Alloys, Ancient, Diffusion in	**II**: 220.
Ancient Metals from Tel-el-Hesy	**II**: 212.
Ancient Techniques and a 'Luristan' Dagger	**II**: 219; **III**: 684.
Archaeology, Metallugrical	**III**: 124.
Arsenical Bronzes, Early	**II**: 221.
"Caster, Founder"	**V**: 433.
"Casting On", Technique as Applied to Daggers	**I**: 301; **III**: 684.
Copper and Bronze Tools in Cyprus	**V**: 673.
Corrosion Products of Metal Antiquities	**II**: 219.
Cycladic, and Aegean Early Bronze Age	**I**: 301; **II**: 221.
Egyptian Metal Objects, Analyses of	**II**: 214.
Foundary of the Second Temple at Jersualem	**V**: 74.
Hebrew Terminology regarding	**I**: 299; **V**: 401.
Metal Vessel Industry at Gordion, 8th Cent. BC	**I**: 289, 300*(2)*; **III**: 599.
Mirrors, Greek Caryatid, Analyses of	**II**: 221.
Neo-Sumeran, Lexical Notes on	**I**: 300; **V**: 584.
Phrygian Metal-Working Techniques	**I**: 289, 300; **III**: 599
Science, Early, and	**II**: 223.

Metals, *see also:* **Metallurgy**
Diffusion of, in Early Bonze Age Anatolia — **I**: 299.
Influence on Social and Religious History — **I**: 295.
Names of, in Ancient Oriental and Caucasian — **I**: 301; **V**: 600.
Metapa: **III**: 166.
Metaphor: **V**: 695, 703.
Cataloge of Bibical — **V**: 695.
Hebrew Daily Life Surviving only in — **V**: 399; **VI**: 9.
Jeremiah, in — **VI**: 331, 339.
Job, in — **VI**: 432.
Zephaniah, in — **VI**: 403.
Metaphysics: **VIII**: 79.
Biblical — **VIII**: 86, 87.
Genesis, of — **IV**: 272*(3)*.
Impact on Religious Thought — **VIII**: 66.
Prayer and — **VIII**: 203.
Scripture, of — **VIII**: 85.
Metaponto: **III**: *755*.
Metatechnology: **VIII**: 161.
Metatron: **VIII**: 101, 103, 109, 137, 149*(4)*, 157.
Meteorites, *see also:* **Baetylus**
Amūn's and Omphaloi — **V**: 214.
Amūn's Relation to Zeus, and Connection to — **II**: 230; **V**: 147, 211, 255.
Joshua's "Long Day" and — **IV**: 365.
Meteorological Studies: **II: §156, 236-246**.
Phenomena and Terminology in the OT — **II**: 244.
Metheg: **V**: 477.
Metheg-ammah: **VI**: 211.
Methodist Church:
Higher Criticism and — **IV**: 142*(3)*, 143, 268*(2)*, 443.
Ministerial Training and the OT — **IV**: 143.
Methone: **I**: 481.
Methuselah: **II**: *181(2);* **IV**: 297; **VI**: 46, 47.
Metonic Cycle: **II**: 199*(2)*.
Athens, in — **I**: 406.
Metonymy:
2 Samuel in — **VI**: 207.
Metope:
Pausanias and — **V**: 254.
Metopes: **III**: 465*(2)*, 730*(2)*.
Metrics:
Metrical Lists — **V**: 698.
Metrology: **I: §121, 417-427; IX: §121, xcix**.
Akkadian, from Nuzi — **I**: *433*.
Assyro-Babylonian — **VII**: 156.
Biblical — **I**: 417.
Chinese — **I**: *425*.
Ebers Papyrus, in — **III**: 396.
Historical, and Temple of Zeus at Athens — **III**: 474.
Neo-Babylonian Tabelts from Nippur — **VII**: 256.
Metropolitan Museum of Art **I**: *282, 298;* **II**: *104, 207;* **III**: *525, 577, 589, 593, 597(4), 599, 602, 606, 608, 609, 616, 618, 642, 661, 668, 712, 722, 730, 736(2), 739, 748, 757, 762, 764, 771(2), 773;* **VII**: *336, 357*.
Ancient Glass Collection — **III**: 583.
Egyptian Acquisitions of — **III**: 687.
Greek Footbath in — **III**: 588.
Recent Acquisitions of — **III**: 567.
Metsad: **II**: 303.
Meunim: **VI**: 592.
MEUX, HENRY B.: **VII**: 47.
Mevasseret Yerushalayim: **II**: 445.
Mevo-Beitar Highway: **I**: *348, 349*.

Meydûm: I: *270;* III: **166**.
Sculpture from III: 734.
Mezad Hashavyahu:
Judical Petition from VII: 95.
Mezad Yaroham: II: 303.
Mezer: II: 300.
Mezuzah: I: 365, 366*(2)*, 392.
Micah, Book of: IV: 386.
Authenticity of **IV: §366, 447**; VI: 394.
Authorship, Date, and Sources of **IV: §366, 447**.
Bibliography I: *§15, 12*.
Capucinade in IV: 446.
Divine Subject of the Verb in IV: 447.
'ènān (אֶתֵּנָן) in IV: 447.
Eschatology in VIII: 253.
Exegetical Stuides on **VI: §627, 390-395**.
Form Criticism of 6:1-8 V: 694.
Geography in VI: 390.
Inductive Study of VIII: 390.
Israel, Use of the Name in IV: 386.
Literary Criticism of **IV: §365, 446-447; IX: §365, cxxxiii**.
Messianic scope of IV: 447; VIII: 18.
Northern Prophecy in VI: 394.
Pre-exilic Prophetism, Possible Parallels to VI: 391.
Strophic Structure of V: 704.
Structure of IV: 446, 447; VI: 252.
Text of VI: 395.
Topography of Palestine in II: 296; IV: 446.
Universal Peace, Picture of VI: 6.
Micah, Book of, Manuscripts of: **VI: §628, 395**.
Micah, Person: I: *110;* IV: 446.
Biographical Studies I: 66.
Isaiah 9:2-7 & 11:1-9, Did Amos Know IV: *437*, 446; VI: 268*(2)*, 272*(2)*; IX: cxxxii.
Message of I: 66.
Message of, for Today IV: 446.
Prophet as Orator as Illustrated from IV: 387.
Prophet in Crisis IV: *431, 438*, 447.
Pseudo-prophets, dispute with IV: 447.
Tomb of II: 284.
Michael (Angel): II:*173;* VIII: 154, 156.
Alexander Jannaeus and VIII: 158.
MICHAELIDES, G:
Demotic Plea to Thoth in the Library of VII: 38.
MICHAELIS, J. D.: V: 405; VI: 329.
Michal: I: *90;* IV: 373; VI: 215.
Biographical Studies I: 66.
David and VI: 210.
Michaux:
Assyrian Inscription of VII: 182.
Michigan Codex: IV: 12.
Microbes:
Pathogenic from the Mud of the Dead Sea II: 212.
Midas, King: V: 604.
Midbar:
Cities of the II: 284.
Middle Ages: I: *465*.
Biblical Study in IV: 94.
Middoth: V: 67, 74*(3)*, 75; VI: 686.
Midea:
Mycenaean Age Tombs at III: 548.
Midian: III: 166, *337, 672;* IV: 229.
Gideon's War with, A Military Approach I: 317; IV: 369.
Mines in I: 290, 294.

Midianites:
Hebrew Religion, Midianite Elements in V: 37.

Midrash, Midrashim: I: *112;* IV: *101;* VI: 45, 687, 692*(3);* **§813, 706-710**.
Agadath Shir Hashirim IV: 504.
Allegorists in VI: 701, 706, 715.
Alphabetic in Syriac VI: 706.
Authorship of V: 691, 709.
Babylonian Creation Stories and, Parallels V: 142; VI: 626, 687; VII: 266; VIII: 83.
Ben Zebul of Eliezer Crescas and Bible References in the VI: 715.
Biblical, and Homeric Exegesis IV: 97; VI: 709.
βία—βίος in V: 645; VI: 710.
Chronciles, Element in IV: 541.
Date of VI: 707.
Deuteronomy 14:2, to VI: 145.
Deuteronomy, of VI: 706, 707.
Exegesis, Patristic Scholastic and Jewish Midrashim VI: 1.
Genesis Apocryphon and VI: 690; VIII: 451.
Genesis, David ha-Nagid's Manuscript VI: 708.
Genesis Rabbah on Death VI: 708; VIII: 187.
Genizah Fragments of VI: 708; VII: 106.
Haggadol, Authorship of VI: 709.
Haggadol, Rhyming Techiniques of VI: 709.
Historical Study VI: 708.
History and VI: 709.
Hosea's Marriage Story a IV: 429.
Interpretation, Thirty-two Rules of, in VI: 707.
Lekah Tob's Dependence upon Targum to Song of Songs VI: 555.
Leviticus Rabba, Doubtful Authenticity in VI: 710.
Literary Genre of VI: 710.
Maimonides and VI: 707.
Mechilta to Detueronomy VI: 706.
Mezuqqar and the *Pi'el Ziqqer* in VI: 709.
Numbers, on VI: 706.
Paronomasia in V: 696; VI: 701, 706.
Pesikta, Prolegomenon to VI: 708.
Philo's Homilies on Fear and Love and Their Relation to Palestinian VI: 678.
Philosophy Implicit in V: 113; VI: 708.
Pi'el Ziqqer in VI: 709.
Political Views of VI: 707.
Proems of Canticles Rabba VI: 709.
Propagandist Nature of VI: 707.
Prophets and Prophecy in I: 112; IV: 235; VI: 372, 708; VIII: 245.
Prophets (Isaiah), in VI: 285.
Qumran Literature and VIII: 438.
Qumran Texts, Parallels VI: 709.
Rabbinic Literature, Relation to VI: 707.
Reading the VI: 707.
Rhyming Techniques in the Poems of V: 691.
Sabbath, Allusions to in the Ugaritic Texts in the Light of V: 83; VI: 708; VII: 143.
Samuel, Books of, in IV: 374.
Song of Solomon, on IV: 504; VI: 706*(4)*.
Source of the Tannaitic VI: 708.
Ten Kings, of V: 124.
Theological Views of VI: 707.
Triennial Cycle of the Psalms, Midrash Tillim VI: 707.
Turkish Tale in VI: 706.
Verses, Division into IV: 18.
Woman in the I: 196; VI: 706.
Yannay's *Qerova* to Lev 15:1 III: 403; VI: 709.
Zeus in the VI: 699.

Midrash of Ephrem:
Shamone **VIII**: 362.
Midrash Rabboth: **VI**: 25.
Migdol (Place) **III**: *160*, 166, *241, 252*.
Migdol, *see:* **Towers**
Migration: **I**: *122, 155;* **III**: 342; **IX**: xcv.
Art History as Key to Racial **II**: 261; **III**: 698.
Climate and **II**: 243, 246, 260, 262.
Danite, to Laish **I**: 156; **II**: 436.
Ecology and **II**: 246, 262.
Hittite **II**: 140.
Ionian **II**: 146.
Iranian, into Zagros **II**: 146.
Man, of, after the Flood **III**: 332.
Minyan **II**: 150.
Nomadic **II**: 259.
Philo Concerning **VI**: 674.
Ships as Evidence of **I**: 351; **II**: 260.
Shishak **II**: 94.
Miket: **V**: 224.
Mikhmoret: **II**: 445.
Mikon: **III**: 625, 702.
Milath Gerim (Guerim): **I**: 369*(2)*.
Milcah: **I**: **66**, *80*.
Milestones: **I**: 344, 347.
Miletus: **III**: **167**, *203*, 263*(2)*, 265, 266, 267.
Temple of Didymaean Apollo near **III**: 509.
Milia:
Late Cypriote Tombs at **III**: 550.
Milindapañha: **VII**: 377; **IX**: cxxxvii.
Military:
Draft **I**: 316*(2)*, 317.
Draft, Exemption from **I**: 317.
Egyptian Titles **V**: 347.
Elamite, Aid to Merodach Baladan **I**: 320.
Instruction of the Hittite King Tuthaliya IV(?) **VII**: 306.
Philistine, Base found **II**: 292; **III**: 419.
Standards **I**: 315.
Strategy, *see:* ***Strategy, Military***
Milkah, *see:* **Milcah**
Milky Way:
Babylonian Name of **II**: 230; **V**: 565.
MILLARD, DAVID: **III**: 439.
Millennialism: **VIII**: 254*(2)*, 255*(2)*.
Daniel, Book of, and Misconceptions of Millenialists **IV**: 531.
Misleading Conceptions **VIII**: 313.
MILLER, HUGH:
Geology, on **III**: 284, 285*(3)*.
Millo: **II**: 284, 349, 350*(2)*, *379*, **445**, *480, 500(2);* **VI**: 185.
MILLS, WILLIAM: **VIII**: 258.
Millstone: **I**: 267, 288; **III**: 571*(3)*.
MILMAN, HENRY HART: **I**: 137, 138*(2)*.
Milraʿ: **V**: 480.
MILTON, JOHN:
Apocrypha and **VIII**: 363.
Enoch and **VI**: 651.
First Esdras, on **VIII**: 365.
Hebrew, Knowledge and Use of **VIII**: 370.
Samson Agonistes, of **VIII**: 366, 367.
Scriptures and **VIII**: 368.
Miluχ: **III**: *155*, 167.
Milya:
An Anatolian language **V**: 680.
Milyas:
Travels, Modern, in **III**: 439, 441.
Min: **V**: 216, 220.
Celestial Associations of **V**: 213.
Emblem of ( ) **V**: 212.
Herodotus on **V**: 216.
Royal Decrees from the Temple at **VII**: 17.
Min-khar:
Coffin of **III**: 548; **VII**: 44.

Min-Mes:	
Statuette of	**III**: 760; **IX**: cv.
Min-nekht:	
Statue of, Superintendent of Granaries under Thothmes III	**II**: *63(2)*; **VII**: 60.
Mina:	
Maneh	**I**: 447.
Solon's Change of Weight of	**I**: 426, 456.
Minaean Kings:	
Chronology of	**II**: *114*, 174, 204; **III**: 18.
Minaean Texts:	**VII**: **§923, 295**.
Minaeans:	**II**: 149.
Asherah among	**V**: 190, 237.
Minatures:	
Rockefeller McCormick, Reconstruction of Lost	**IV**: 11.
Mind:	**V**: *507*, 510, *516*.
Human vs. Brute	**III**: 337; **IX**: cxx.
Mental Evolution, Provelm of	**VIII**: 169.
Mineralogy:	
Contribution of in the Study of Terracottas	**II**: 219.
Cylinder Seal and	**III**: 661.
Greek Pottery	**II**: 219; **III**: 631.
Minerals:	**I**: **§96, 285-287**; **IX**: **§96, xci**.
Assyrian	**V**: 568.
Diorite	**I**: 286; **II**: 214.
Influence on Social and Religious History	**I**: 295.
Murrhine (Fluorspar)	**III**: 622.
Mines, Mining Industry:	**I**: **§98, 290-293**, 299; **IX**: **§98, xci-xcii**, cxii*(4)*.
Athenian	**I**: 291.
Copper	**I**: 290, 291, 292*(2)*, 294; **II**: 277.
Flint, Prehistoric Egyptian	**I**: 290; **III**: *538*; **IX**: xci.
Gold	**I**: 291, 295.
Iron	**I**: 292.
King Solomon's	**I**: 291, **292**; **III**: *277(3)*.
Lead	**I**: 291*(2)*.
Midian, in	**I**: 290, 294; **III**: 166.
Stone vessel from ancient	**III**: 608.
Mînet el Beiḍa:	**III**: 423.
Mingana 535:	**VI**: 96.
Miniéh:	
Antiquities found in	**III**: 564.
Minim:	
Imprecation Against, in the Synagogue	**VI**: 566, 686.
Minni:	**VI**: 344.
Minnith:	**II**: 291.
Minoan Language, *see also:* **Myceanæan / Minoan Language**	**V**: **§546, 618-623**.
Cypro-Minoan Script	**V**: 619.
Decipherment of	**V**: 620.
Grammar of	**V**: 621.
"Libation Formua"	**V**: 622.
Mediterranean "Substrate Studies"	**V**: 622.
Syllabary	**V**: 619.
Texual Note: KN SD0450 + 0483	**V**: 620.
Texual Note: PY An607	**V**: 620.
Words, Statitical Data on	**V**: 620.
Minoan Religion:	**V**: **§478, 241-242**.
Minoan Texts, *see:* **Myceanæan / Minoan Texts**	
Minoans:	**I**: *181, 332, 354*; **II**: **150**, *151*; **III**: *68*, 342.
Chronology	**II**: 195, 204*(3)*.
Minor Prophets, Books of - General Studies:	
Babylonian Codex of	**IV**: 17.

Bibliography of I: **§20, 13.**
"Day of Yahweh"
Editor in IV: 427.
Editing of the IV: 427.
Exegeitical Studies on Serveral Books of VI: **§615, 362.**
Henderson, E., on IV: 426*(2)*.
Linguistic and Textual Problems VI: 362*(2)*.
Literary Criticism of IV: **§354, 426-427.**
Literary Style of V: **§570, 704-705.**
Masoretic Note at end of IV: 163.
Modern Anguish and IV: 427.
Neglect of IV: 427.
Old Latin Texts of IV: 39*(6)*.
OT Quotations of Justin and the Greek Dodekapropheton VI: 363, 722.
Qumran Texts (4QXII?) VIII: **§1106, 448.**
Sketch of IV: 427.
Text of IV: 427.
Text Rearrangements in VI: 362.
Type, Considered as a IV: 427.
Wellhausen's IV: 427.
Minor Prophets, Books of, Manuscripts of VI: **§616, 362-363.**
Babylonian Codex of, Compared with Masoretic Texts VI: 362.
Freer Papyrus on VI: 363*(4)*.
Greek Dodekapropheton VI: 363.
Old Latin Texts of VI: 362*(5)*, 363.
Minorities: I: 508.
Minors:
Place in Society I: 184, 185, 227.
Talmud, status of male, in I: 466.
Minos: I: *310, 325*, 328, *339, 349;* II: **64**; III: 69, 143, **167**, 173.
Gold Treasure from III: 567.
Palace of III: 499*(2)*, 500*(2)*, 633, *634*.
Minotaur: III: 734.
Mint (Plant): III: 392.
Mints: I: 458.
Bar-Kokhaba(?), of I: 448.
Camarina, of I: 451.
Greek Coinage, Issue of I: 439, 452.
Herod the Great, of(?) I: 458.
Ionian Revolt, of I: 458.
Julio-Claudian Emperors, of I: 448.
Roman at Alexandria I: 447, 448, 450, 452.
Roman, Issue of I: 452.
Seleucid, at Dura-Europos I: 446.
Tyre, Major Source of Silver Coins I: 457.
Minturnæ (Minturno) I: *206;* III: **167-168**; III: *616, 619, 756*.
Minya: III: 168.
Minyans: II: 150.
Miracles: VIII: **§979, 89-94**; IX: cxx.
Anthropomorphism and VIII: 93, 103.
Apostles, of, contrasted with the Egyptian Magicians VIII: 89.
Bible, of VIII: 91, 92*(2)*, 93.
Christian Religion and VIII: 92.
Classification and Evolution of VIII: 92.
Contranatural View of VIII: 94.
Creation and / of VIII: 75, 78, 93.
Credibility of Biblical VIII: 92.
Definition of VIII: 89.
Dionysiac, at Corinth III: 466.
Ecclesiastical VIII: 89.
Evidence of Divine Revelation VIII: 30, 90.
Evolution, and III: 330.
Evolution, Law, and III: 303; VIII: 91, 304.
Exegesis and VI: 2; VIII: 94.

Historical Student, Attitude of, toward **VIII**: 92.
Joseph Story, in **IV**: 316.
Moses, of, contrasted with the Egyptian Magicians **VIII**: 89.
Mount Carmel, on **VI**: 229.
Myth and **V**: 135; **VIII**: 93; **IX**: cxxxvii.
Natural Causes / Law and **VIII**: 91, 92, 93*(2)*.
Nature of **VIII**: 91.
Nature, Relation to, and **VIII**: 91.
NT Miracle Stories and OT Prophecy **VI**: 288; **VIII**: 275, 298.
Old Testament **VIII**: 90*(2)*, 91*(2)*, 92*(2)*, 93*(3)*.
Origins, Study of, and **VIII**: 94.
Prayer and **VIII**: 90.
Prophecy and/of **VIII**: 92.
Prophecy, Fulfilled, and **VIII**: 90, 238.
Prophecy, Value of, and **VIII**: 92, 242.
Pseudo-Scientific View of **VIII**: 90.
Revelation, Adjunct to **VIII**: 93.
Reversable **VIII**: 94.
Science and **VIII**: 91, 93.
Sennacherib's Army, Destruction of, a(?) **VI**: 289.
Shakespeare and **VIII**: 367.
Spiritual Idea of **VIII**: 91.
Sun, in the Old Testament **IV**: 365, **VI**: 169, 242, 290, 291, 638; **VIII**: 93, 94*(2)*.
Supernatural, signs of **VIII**: 93.
Testimony to God **VIII**: 91.
Thaumaturgy in the Bible **VIII**: 92*(2)*.

Mirgissa (Mirgisse): **III**: **168**.
Temple at **III**: 512.

Miriam: **I**: *26*, **66**.
"Song of Miriam" **IV**: 329.

Mirrors, *see also:* **Glass, Glassware** **III**: **§205, 583-585**
Anatolian Bronze **III**: 585.
Caryatid, Greek, Metallic Analyses **II**: 221.
Etruscan **III**: 583, 584*(4)*.
Gazing Ceremonies, Modern Egyptian **I**: 388.
Graeco-Scythian **III**: 585.
Greek **III**: 584*(3)*.
Handle, Egyptian, in fossil bone **III**: 584.
Handle, from Barhar temple, Bahrain **III**: 585.
Michigan 'Rosetta' **III**: 584.
Urartean **III**: 585.

Misfortune:
Talmud, in **VI**: 698.

Mishael at Rushmia: **II**: 287.

MISHAEL BEN UZZIEL: **IV** 7.

Mishnah, *see also:* **Talmudic Literature** **I**: *185, 204, 209, 219, 469;* **VI**: 687, 692*(2)*, 694, **§812, 697-706**; **IX**: **§812, cl.**
Apikoros *Epikoros)* in **VI**: 690.
Brass Gate, metion of, in **II**: 409.
Divine Name, Writing of, in the **VIII**: 123.
Law, Classification of, in **I**: 475; **IX**: cli.
Lexicon and Grammar **V**: 404.
Mishnayot in B. Kama **VI**: 703.
Quotations, Formulas for Introducing Scripture in **VIII**: 275.
Rosh Hashana, on **V**: 85.
Sanhedrin 17a **V**: 464.
Sanhedrin 93a and Daniel Chapter 3 **VI**: 570.
Temple, on the **V**: 69.
Tractate Me'ila, of **VI**: 705.
Zeus in the **VI**: 699.

'Mišneh' of Jerusalem: **II**: 417.

Mishneh Torah:
Classification of Law in **I**: 475.

Mishpaṭ: **I**: *486*.
Messiah and **I**: 486; **VIII**: 142.

Mishrifeh: **II**: 293; **III**: 421.

Miši: **II**: 150.

Misis: **III**: 263.
Missing Link: **III**: 346.
Mission: **VIII**: 189*(2)*.
Missionaries:
Translation Problems, among Protestant, for Chinese Words **IV**: 111.
Missionary Activity, *see:* **Proselytizing**
Missione Archaeologica Italiana a Cesarea: **II**: 302.
Missions:
Atonement in Judaism and **VIII**: 195, 336.
Church, Biblical Foundation of, in OT **VIII**: 209.
Foreign, Old Testament Foundations of **VIII**: 208.
Israel and **VIII**: 208.
Old Testament Attitude **VIII**: 208.
OT Theology and **VIII**: 8.
Mist:
Clouds and, in Egyptian Mythology **V**: 200*(2)*.
Primal Fire **III**: 316.
Misthia: **III**: 168.
Mistletoe: **V**: 393.
Mit-Rahîna (Mit Rahineh, *see also:* **Memphis** **III**: *381*, *766*.
Building of Merenptah at **III**: 511.
Sarcophaus from **III**: 549; **VII**: 66.
Mita: **II**: *157*, 272.
Paḫḫuwa, of **VII**: 306.
Mita, King *see:* **Midas**
Mitanni: **I**: 329; **II**: *140*, **150**; **III**: 41, 137, **168**; **V**: *159*.
Amarna Tablets, in **II**: *140;* **III**: *41*, *168;* **VII**: 170.
Indo-Aryan Names from **V**: 301.
Language of **V**: 679.
Tushratta, King of **VII**: 167.
MITCHELL, HINCKLEY G.: **IV**: 140.
MITFORD, WILLIAM:
Greece, History of, on **III**: 109, 110*(2)*.
Mithra(s):
Messiah, as **V**: 151.
Roman World and **V**: 238.
Tarsus, Religion of, and Origin of **V**: 237.
Zoroastrianism, Part in **V**: 236.
Mithradates I: **II**: 64.
Mitrahineh:
Lintel of Merenptah at **VII**: 61.
Mitzvah of Kashrut: **I**: *250*.
Mizpah, Mizpeh: **II**: 283, 284, 291, **446**; **VI**: 81*(3)*, 197, 584.
Mizpah Galeed at Suf: **II**: 287.
Mizpeh: **II**: *369;* **VI**: 584.
Mizraim: **II**: **150**, *158;* **III**: *71*, **169**, 171.
Mnemonics: **V**: 116; **VI**: 623; **IX**: cxxxiii.
Mnesimachus Inscription: **VII**: 318.
Mnṯyw: **II**: 150.
Moab: **I**: *161*, *321*, 328, 331, 337; **II**: *63*, *217*, *292*, 309, *315*, *354(3)*, *358(2)*, *360*, **446-447**, 484; **III**: *241*, *255*, *419*, 442, 444; **IV**: 229, 353; **IX**: cxvii.
Arels of **VI**: 217.
Cubical Stones at (Asheroth(?)) **V**: 46.
Greek Inscriptions in **VII**: 315.
Isaiah against **VI**: 276.
Sojourn of Ruth in **VI**: 556.
Topography of **II**: 447.
Towers, Round of **III**: 488.
Moab, Steppes of: **II**: 289, 447.
Moabite Inscriptions: **VII**: **§864, 110-113**.
Dibon, from **VII**: 113.
Jars, with Translation **VII**: 111.
Kerak, from **VII**: 113.
Moabite (Language): **V**: **§526, 522**.
Syntax **V**: 522.

Moabite Stone: **II**: 282, *354;* **IV**: 211; **VII**: 110, **111-112**.
Black Obelisk and **VII**: 112, 191.
Hebrew Records and **IV**: 382*(2)*.
Israelite Divine Name and **VII**: 112; **VIII**: 122.
Mokhrath of **II**: 290.
Moabites: **II**: 150.
Capital City of **II**: 292, 309; **III**: 419.
Idols of **V**: 237.
Jericho, Occupation of, by **II**: 396; **IV**: 220.
Measurement of, by David **VI**: 212.
Monolith (Pillar) **V**: 48.
Mob, Roman: **I**: 193; **II**: 161.
Mochlos, Island of: **III**: 68.
Model(s):
Egytian "sculptors" **III**: 725.
Liver **III**: 579.
Nile Boat **III**: 686.
Silversmith **III**: 596.
Modern Beliefs and Customs Illustrating ANE and OT: **I**: **§115**, **382-392**; **IX**: **§115**, **xcvii**.
Modin: **II**: 306.
Moeris Bais: **III**: 83.
Moesia: **I**: 335.
MOFFATT, JAMES: **IV**: 59; **VI**: 204.
Mohammedans:
Anthropometric Comparison with Copts and "Mixed" Group **III**: 342.
Commentary on the Bible **IV**: 117, 118.
Criticism of the Bible **IV**: 128.
Mohenjo-Daro: **III**: 169.
Mōḥōn: **VII**: 20.
Mokhrath: **II**: 290.
Mold, Mould:
Arrowheads, for, found near Mossul **III**: 672, 680.
Bronze 'Trinket' **I**: 284, 301.
Clay, in Iraq Museum **III**: 687.
Goldsmith's **III**: 672.
Jewelry, from Mycenae **III**: 593.
Molech (Moloch) **V**: 157, 189, 190.
Cult of **V**: 198; **VI**: 243.
MOLLOY, GERALD: **III**: 288.
Mollusk:
Fossil, at Gibraltar **III**: 106, 366.
Moly: **III**: 392.
MOMERIE, ALFRED WILLIAMS: **VIII**: 42.
MOMMSEN, THEODOR: **II**: 160.
Monarchies:
Ancient **II**: 1*(3)*.
Monarchy, *see also:* **Kingship**
Amos, Attitude Toward Israelite **I**: 484; **IV**: 428, 435.
Archaeological Observations on Early **IV**: 358.
Assyrian **II**: 208.
Egyptian **II**: 207*(3)*.
Hittite **I**: 483; **V**: 227.
Hosea, Attitude Toward Israelite **I**: 484; **IV**: 428, 435.
Israel, in **I**: *466,* **§134**, **484-487**; **IV**: 220; **IX**: **§134**, **ci**.
Israelite Religion and **I**: *114,* 486; **V**: 21, 27.
Israelite, Setting up of the **IV**: 374.
Judges, an Apology for(?) **IV**: 370.
Organs of Statecraft in the Israelite **VI**: 225.
Samuel and the Israelite **I**: 484; **IV**: 374, 376; **IX**: ci.
Shilonite Priesthood in the United, of Israel **V**: 42.
Succession, Problems of, in the Israelite **I**: *96,* 470, 484, 487, 493.
Theocracy, Transition from **IV**: 374.
Monastery:
Christian, Early, Four in Central Lycia **III**: 264.
Monastic Research **II**: 309; **III**: 422.

Monasticism:
St. Benedict's Rule and the Monks of Qumran **VIII**: 410.
MOND, ROBERT [M.]: **III**: *252*.
Monetary Systems, Ancient: **I**: **§125, 438-439**.
Greek Monetary Standards **I**: 438.
Pre-Exilic Palestine, Development of **I**: 439.
Roman Gold Standard **I**: 439.
Roman Money, Value of **I**: 438.
Silver Standard in Sumer and Accad **I**: 438.
Money, *see also:* **Monetary Systems** **I**: 302, 303, 308, *415, 425*.
Atonement **V**: 63.
Earliest Biblical Allusion to Coined **I**: 452.
Roman, Value of **I**: 438.
Money Changers: **I**: 439.
Jewish Iconography, in **III**: 703.
Mongoose (Ichneumon): **III**: 765; **V**: 217.
Monisim:
Brahmanism and **V**: 230.
Zoroastrianism and **V**: 230.
Monkey: **III**: *339*.
Monks:
Jewish, in the Days of Christ **V**: 95.
Mono-Jahwehism, *see:* **Monotheism**
Monogamy: **I**: *211*, 217, 221.
Monolatry, *see:* **Monotheism**
Monopolies: **I**: 303, 305, 336, 338.
Ptolemaic Perfume **I**: 336.
Monotheism: **V**: **§420, 32-36**; **VIII**: 121, *202;* **IX**: **§420, cxxxiv**.
Akhenaten (Ikhnaton) and **II**: 8; **V**: 34, 208, 211.
Amenemope, Wisdom of, and **V**: 35; **VII**: 11.
Amos, Before(?) **V**: 34; **VIII**: 62.
Anitquity of Israelite **IX**: cxxxiv.
Antiochus Epiphanes Persecution of **V**: 36.
Argument of **V**: 35.
Babylonian **V**: 33, 175.
Deuteronomy and Mono-Jahwism **IV**: 349.
Early **V**: 33.
Egyptian **V**: 33.
Ethics of Judaism and **V**: 35; **VIII**: 227.
Freud on Moses and **I**: 71; **V**: 35.
Greeks, Development of **V**: 32, 33*(2)*, 245, 246*(2)*, 247.
Hebrew **IV**: 254; **V**: 34*(2)*.
Hebrew, Beginnings of **V**: 33.
Hebrew, Dual Origin of **V**: 34; **VI**: 294.
Hebrew, Origin of **V**: 34.
Historical Process and **V**: 35.
India, in, and the Modern Hindu Doctrine of Faith **V**: 34, 144.
Israel, Advent of, in **V**: 35.
Israel, Babylonian Influence(?) **V**: 34.
Israel, Development of, in **V**: 32, 33.
Israel, Early, in **V**: 33.
Israel, Nature of, in **V**: 32.
Israel, Religion of, and **V**: 35.
Israelite, Antiquity of **V**: 23; **VIII**: 65.
Israelite, Problem of **V**: 35.
Jewish, Persian Influence on **V**: 33, 36.
Logical Consequences of **VI**: 596.
Marital Fidelity and **I**: 220; **V**: 35.
Mono-Jahwism in Deuteronomy **IV**: 349; **V**: 34.
Moses and **I**: 71, *220;* **V**: 34, 35*(3)*.
Myth, not a **V**: 33.
Mythology and **V**: 33.
Origin of **V**: 34, 35.
Pagan **V**: 32, 34.
Persecution of, by Antiochus Ephphanes **II**: *18*.
Persecution of, by Antiochus Epiphanes **V**: 36.

Persian Influence
  on Jewish   **V**: 33, 36.
Pre-Islamic, in Arabia   **V**: 35.
Prehistoric   **V**: 32.
Prevalence of, Before
  Polytheism   **V**: 33.
Primeval   **V**: 34(2)
Primeval and Shechem   **II**: 475; **V**: 34.
Primitive   **V**: 33, 35(2).
Psalms and   **VI**: 445.
Psychodynamic
  Aspects of   **V**: 35.
Repression and   **V**: 35.
Revelation, not a Myth   **V**: 33.
Semitic   **V**: 33, 34.
Shechem and Primeval   **II**: 475; **V**: 34.
Sumerian Religion,
  Predecessor of
  Polytheism   **V**: 35, 185.
Zoraster and Archaic   **V**: 33, 229.
MONRO, VERE: **III**: 438.
Mons Janiculum: **III**: 212.
Monsters:
  Art, in   **III**: 704.
  Biblical Earth, in the
    Cosmogonic Combat
    Myth   **V**: 137; **VIII**: 83.
  Lîlîth, *night monster*   **V**: 137.
  Mythological in the OT   **V**: 136.
Montefiore:
  Roman Tomb of   **III**: 558.
Montefioreh: **II**: 407.
Montet Jar: **I**: 336.
MONTGOMERY, EDMUND: **III**: 296.
MONTGOMERY, JAMES ALAN:
  Bibliography of   **I**: 21.
Months, *see also:*
  Calendar Studies;
  Menology   **I**: 397.
  Adar, Cuneiform Name of   **I**: 397.
  Arab Folklore and   **I**: 391, 400.
  Assyrian   **I**: 394.
  Assyro-Babylonian   **I**: 394; **II**: 207; **V**: 164.
  Avesta, Names of in the   **I**: 395.
  Babylonian   **I**: 396, 397(2).

  Cappadocian, month
    Ḫubur   **IX**: xcvii.
  Coptic   **I**: 405.
  Daylight, Length
    of in each   **I**: 400.
  Dorian Calendar, in   **I**: 402.
  Egyptian   **I**: 393, 395, 396, 403(2), 404(3).
  Elamite   **I**: 400.
  Etruscan   **I**: 401.
  Grain Growing   **I**: 397.
  Greek Honorific   **I**: 399.
  Hebrew   **I**: 394, 414.
  Ḫubur   **IX**: cxxxvii.
  Latin   **I**: 401.
  Lunar Month, 6th Day of   **I**: 405.
  Names, Problem of   **I**: 404(2).
  Nuzi   **I**: 400.
  Palestinian, Names of   **I**: 398.
  Persian   **I**: 397, 400.
  Phoenician, Names of   **I**: 398.
  rkḫ wr, date of the month   **I**: 404.
  Roman Honorific   **I**: 399.
  Sign 𒉺 in Name of
    the Fourth Month
    at Umma   **I**: 398; **V**: 581.
  Star Barsag, Month
    when it Sets   **II**: 229.
  Sumerian   **I**: 397.
Mont(u)hotp, Vizier: **III**: *671.*
Monuments and
  Obelisks, Fountains
  and Sphinxes: **III**: §190, 491-498.
  Akkadian, Cruciform   **III**: 494(2).
  Aniconic   **III**: 496.
  Assyrian, and the Bible   **IV**: 181, 244.
  Assyrian, Birds on   **III**: 689(2).
  Assyrian, in America   **III**: 492.
  Assyrian, Winged Figures   **III**: 689.
  Athenian, Interpretations
    of, by Early Travelers   **III**: 497.
  Axum, from   **III**: 498.
  Babylonian, in America   **III**: 492.
  Biyahmû, of   **III**: 496.

British Museum, Ancient in, as Illustrative of Biblical History	**III**: 493.
Carchemish, from	**III**: 498.
Cleopatra's Needles	**II**: 492.
Crocodilopolis, at, from the Ptolemaic Period	**III**: 497.
Darius, of, at Bisitun	**III**: 498.
Destruction and Protection of	**III**: **455**.
Egyptian	**III**: 493, 494*(4)*, 495*(4)*; **VII**: 57.
Egyptian, as seen by V. R. Prutky in the 18th Century	**III**: 498.
Egyptian, at Venice	**VII**: 57.
Egyptian, Dated in the Museum Meermanno-Westreenianum, Haag	**VII**: 56.
Egyptian, in the British Museum	**III**: 493.
Egyptian, in the Museum at Karlsruhe	**VII**: 57.
Egyptian of El-Amarna	**III**: 491.
Egyptian, Old Kingdom, in Cairo Museum	**III**: 498.
Egyptian, Paran on	**III**: 493.
Egyptian, Photographic Collection of	**III**: 493.
First Dynasty	**VII**: 57.
Higher Criticism and	**IV**: 125.
Hittite	**III**: 492*(3)*, 493, 494*(4)*, 497, *720*, *721(2)*.
Hittite, and Phrygian Rock Façades	**III**: 472, 497.
Hyksos	**III**: 496.
Iraqi-Persian Boundary, Ancient on	**III**: 498.
Isaiah, Light from, on the Times of	**IV**: 392.
Judaism and	**VI**: 687.
Koroneia, Funeral, for	**III**: 558.
Lessons from (Background to OT)	**IV**: 179*(4)*.
Louvre Museum, Ancient in, as Illustrative of Biblical History	**III**: 494; **IV**: 174.
Maništušu, Cruciform, of	**III**: 497.
Marathon, for Victory at	**III**: 496.
Megalithic	**II**: 483; **III**: 495, *674*.
Mesopotamian, and the Reliability of Scripture	**IV**: 195.
Method in Bible Study of	**III**: 412.
Nereide, Restoration	**III**: 473*(2)*.
Niobe, Lydo-Assyrian, of Mt. Sipylus	**III**: 491*(2)*; **V**: 245.
Partho-Roman, at Susa	**III**: 240.
Phoenician	**III**: 495.
Primitive Pharaohs, of	**III**: 493.
Ptolemaic, Inscribed	**VII**: 26.
Rude Stone (Pillars)	**V**: 46*(2)*, 47.
Saite, Fragments of	**III**: 498.
Sandon, of Tarsus	**III**: 496.
Scripture, Truth of, and	**IV**: 194, 195*(3)*.
Sesostris I, Single Dated	**III**: 497.
Seti I, from Abydos, Protection of	**III**: 456.
Sneferu's, at Dahshur	**III**: 497.
Sudanese Nubia, Removal of Endangered	**III**: 457*(2)*.
Syriac, in Vilayet of Urfa	**III**: 497.
Trilithon at Baalbek	**III**: 479, 509.
Tshok-Göz-Köprüköe, of	**III**: 494.
Moon:	**VI**: 169*(2)*, 170*(2)*.
Diameter of, and Eclipse Tables in Babylonian	**II**: 231.
Great New-, Day	**V**: 85.
Lunar Longitudes, Table of	**VII**: 195.
Lunar Texts, Two, of the Achaemenid Period	**II**: 235.
Lunar Visibilities in Ancient Babylon	**II**: 234.
Paschal Full, Dates of Occcurance	**I**: 395.
Pasht, the Cat, and, Relations between, in Egypt	**V**: 200.
Roman Farmer and	**I**: 252.
Table of Lunar Longitudes	**II**: 226.
Travel, Restriction of, on New Moon Holidays	**I**: 346; **V**: 85.

Moon Cult:
Assyro-Babylonian **V**: 165.
Sinai, in, on Egyptian Monuments **V**: 155.
Moon-God: **V**: 183.
Babylonian **V**: 182.
Begetting of, by Earth God and Goddess **V**: 182.
Hymn to **V**: 180.
Terah as(?) **I**: 81.
Worship of at Ur and Tel al-Obeid **III**: 272.
MOORE, DUNLOP:
Pentateuch on **IV**: 229*(2)*.
MOORE, GEORGE FOOT: **I**: 176*(2)*.
MOORE, STURGE:
Judith, Poem of, on **VIII**: 365.
MOORE, THOMAS V.:
Zechariah, on **IV**: 454.
Mor, Tell: **II**: **447**>
Morality:
Bible Oriental in Its Standards of **VIII**: 225.
Chrstian, and the Idea of a Cosmic Fall **IV**: 296.
Divine in the OT **VIII**: 222.
Egypt, Ancient, in **VIII**: 222.
God and the Moral Law **VIII**: 63, 226.
Greek Religion and, in Pindar **V**: 251.
Greek View of Relation Between Poetry and **VIII**: 222.
Greeks and Romans, Relations Between Religion and **V**: 243; **VIII**: 225.
Greeks, Religion and **V**: 246.
Immorality of OT Heroes **VIII**: 220.
Israelite Religion and **V**: 15.
Jeremiah and **IV**: 414; **V**: 38.
Old Testament **VIII**: 219, 221*(2)*, 227.
Religion, of **VIII**: 224.
Sacrifices and **V**: 63*(2)*; **VIII**: 22792*)*.
Semites, Relation Between Religion and **V**: 161; **VIII**: 225.
Morals, *see also:* **Ethics**
Assyrian **VIII**: 224.
Babylonian **VIII**: 224*(2)*.
Before Moses **VIII**: 220.
Bible and **VIII**: 219, 223*(2)*.
Difficulties in OT **VIII**: 219, 220, 223.
Early Prophetic, in Israel **VIII**: 224.
Egyptian **VIII**: 218, 224*(2)*.
Evolution of OT **VIII**: 220.
Fellahin and **I**: 384.
Genesis a Miracle in **IV**: 268; **VIII**: 223.
Hebrew Bondage and Its Influence on Hebrew **VIII**: 224.
Inheritance of, in Man **III**: 314.
Late Prophetic, in Israel **VIII**: 224.
Man's Moral Nature **III**: 338.
Mesopotamia, in **VIII**: 227.
Old Testament **VIII**: 220, 221, 222.
Pre-prophetic, in Israel **VIII**: 224.
Priestly, in Israel **VIII**: 224.
Primitive Jews and **I**: 460.
Prophets as a Moral Code **VIII**: 225.
Science of **VIII**: 1.
Sumerians, of **VIII**: 223.
Theology **VIII**: 229.
Mordecai: **I**: 66.
Tomb of **III**: 536*(2)*.
Moreh: **VI**: 60, 72.
MORELL, JOHN DANIEL:
Inspiration, Theory of **VIII**: 38.
MORGA, DE: **III**: 690
MORGAN, HOMER B.: **VII**: 312.
MORGAN, J. DE: **II**: 174; **III**: 23, 234, 239.
Morgantina: **I**:*452, 455;* **III**: 169, **226**, *571(2), 685*.
Lead *Tabellae* from **VII**: 334*(2)*.
Portrait Head from **III**: 748.
Tomb Group, Fourth Century B.C. from **III**: 557.

Moriah, Mount: **II**: 412, 417, **447-448**, 499, *500;* **VI**: 60, 72, 228; **VIII**: *302*.
Holiness of, compared with Mount Zion **V**: 7.
MORIER, JAMES JUSTINIAN: **III**: 19, 435*(2)*, 436.
Morning:
House of, in Egyptian Religion **V**: 208.
Morocco:
Arabic spoken of **V**: 587*(2)*.
Biblical Parallels from **IV**: 191.
Travels, Modern, in **III**: 435.
Morphology:
Carmel Coast **II**: 251.
Hymns of the Judean Scrolls **VIII**: 458.
Isaiah Scroll from Qumran **VIII**: 445.
Megiddo Area **II**: 249.
Razzaza (Karbala Liwa), Abu Dibbis, Geological History and **II**: 250.
MORRITT, ROBERT D.:
Troy, on **III**: 259.
Mortar:
Desert, from Rhomboïdal Pyramid at Dahshûr **II**: 216.
Egyptian **II**: 213.
Pestle and **VI**: 459, 547*(2)*.
Mortuary:
Amenhotep I, Temple Reliefs, Restoration of **III**: 728.
Osiris, God of Royal **V**: 220.
Suites, Egyptian New Kingdom **III**: 486, 561.
Mosaic(s): **I**: 273; **III**: 689.
'Ain Duk, from **VII**: 91.
Beth Alpha, Sacrifice of Isaac in **VIII**: 356.
Daphne, of **V**: *656*.
Early Dynastic Period, in **III**: 718.
Gordion, in **III**: 693.
Incribed, near Mt. Nebo **II**: 292.
Jersualem, at Damscus Gate **II**: 407.
Jews, Legally Permitted to, as Art(?) **III**: 698.
Ma'on Synagogue Pavment **III**: 526*(2)*.
Olynthos, from **III**: 691.
Origin of **III**: 699.
Rainbow, at Pergamon **III**: 718, 719.
Roman Floor, Stratum in **III**: 477.
Mosaic Law, *see:* **"The Law" in Israel**
Moscho-Hittite: **II**: 141.
Inscriptions **VII**: 303*(2)*.
Moscow Mathematical Papyrus: **I**: 430*(2)*, 431, 434; **VII**: 34*(2)*.
Moses: **I**: *28(2), 40,* **66-73**, *119, 153, 460, 472 (2), 473, 496, 507;* **II**: *4(2), 8;* **III**: *339;* **IV**: 165, 175, 215, *238, 239, 240(4), 241(3);* **IV**: *313*, 321, *415;* **VI**: 99, 100, 118, 129, 151, 441; **VII**: *81;* **VIII**: 392.
Apocalypses of **VI**: 100, 102, 103.
Archaeology and the Mosaic Period **IV**: 213.
Ascetical and Mystical Traits of **VIII** 305.
Atomism and **VIII** 81.
Ayun Musa, Wells of **III**: 34.
Birth of **VI**: 97; **IX**: lxxxii.
Blessing of, in Deuteronmy **IV**: 348, 350, 351; **VI**: 152*(3)*, 153*(2)*.
"Bloody Husband", as **I**: 370; **VI**: 101*(5)*, 102.
"Books of Moses" **IV**: 230, 235, 237, 244.
Brazen Serpent and **IV**: 345.

Burial of	**I**: 67; **VI**: 417*(2)*; **VIII**: 297*(2)*.	Last Days of	**VI**: 129, 131, 142, 154.
Call of	**I**: 115; **V**: 699; **VI**: 99; **IX**: lxxxii.	Last Words of	**VI**: 152, 153.
Cathedra of, in Ancient Synagogues	**III**: 523.	Legends on the Youth of	**VI**: 97, 98.
Central African Folk-Lore and	**V**: 144.	Levites and	**V**: 43.
Colenso, John, on	**IV**: 225*(2)*.	Literary Tradition of, in Ireland	**VIII**: 369.
Contemporaries of	**II**: 4.	Michael Angelo's	**VIII**: 354.
Covenant with Yahweh, and	**V**: 14.	Miracles of, contrasted with the Egyptian Magicians	**VIII**: 89.
Date of	**I**: *28(2)*.	Monuments and	**IV**: 241.
Davwin *vs.*	**VIII**: 77.	Muhammad and	**IV**: 233.
Death of, in the Literature of the Falashas	**I**: 72; **VII**: 289*(2)*; **VIII**: 369.	Name of the God of	**VIII**: 111, 114, 124.
Death of, Midrash	**I**: 72; **VI**: 709.	Name, Use of in Deuteronomy	**IV**: 347.
Decalogue and	**VI**: 160, 161.	Nephews of	**VI**: 122.
Deuteronomy, Use of the Name, in	**IV**: 347.	Nestorian Legend on	**I**: 67.
Divine Providence from the Life of	**VIII**: 88.	Oration of (from Qumran)	**VIII**: 471.
Egyptian Derivation of the Name	**I**: 67.	Pentateuch, Written in Cuneiform by(?)	**IV**: 240.
Face of, Shining	**VI**: 120.	Perplexity of	**VI**: 102.
Face of, Veil on the	**VI**: 120.	Pharaoh, Dealings of, with	**VI**: 103.
Faith in the Divine Mission of, the Prophets and Christ	**VIII** 277.	Pharaohs of	**I**: 68; **II**: 182, 196.
Freud and	**I**: 71; **V**: 35.	Political Economist, as	**I**: 68, 460.
Gergory of Nyssa on	**VI**: 722.	Prayer of	**VI**: 117, 507.
God of, a Revelation	**VIII**: 59.	Princess who rescued	**IV**: 328.
Greek Etymology of the name of	**V**: 300.	Prophet, as	**IV**: 328.
Gregory of Nyssa, Commentary on Exod. 33:11-23	**VI**: 726.	Pseudo-Levite, as	**I**: 71*(2)*.
Hammurabi and	**I**: 69*(3)*, 496; **II**: 42*(3)*.	Religion of	**V**: 10, 11, 16.
"Horns of"	**I**: 72; **VI**: 115; **VIII**: 355.	Religion of, Barton, G. A., on	**V**: 17.
Irenaeus and the Song of	**IV**: 350; **VI**: 721.	Rephidim, Battle of, at	**VI**: 109.
Islamic Tradition on	**I**: 72.	Samaritan Doctrine of	**I**: 72.
Jannes and Jambres withstanding	**IV**: 324.	Science and	**III**: 314; **IV**: 278; **VI**: 719.
		Second Coming of	**I**: 71.
		Sepulcher of	**III**: 533.
		Sin of	**VI**: 131.
		Sinai Inscriptions and	**I**: 70; **VII**: 82.
		Song of	**IV**: 350, 351; **VI**: 107, 108, 150*(5)*.
		Song of, and Irenaeus	**IV**: 350.

Song of, Wisdom Influence on V: 119.
Theology of V: 10.
Typology of St. Paul, in VIII: 293.
Virgin Birth of(?) I: 71.
Water Miracles in Jewish Legend and Byzantine Art VIII 357.
Wells of III: 34.
Wife, Scolding(?) VI: 101.
Will of God and VIII: 88.
Words / Sayings of (1QDM) VIII: *416, 418,* **§1129, 467**.

Moses, Assumption of, *see:* **Assumption of Moses**

Moses bar Kepha: I: *368.*

Moslems, *see;* **Muslim**

Mosul (Mossoul, Mossul): III: *180, 440, 672, 680.*
Folklore of I: 386*(3).*

Môt: V: 196.
'Al'êyân Ba'al and V: 191*(2),* 193; VII: 87, 139*(3),* 140.
Ba'al and V: 196, 197; VII: 142, 145*(2).*
Vine and. Ugaritic Fertility Rite V: 197.

Mother(s):
Hebrew (Exod. 1:19) VI: 98.
Sons of Gods, and IV: 278; V: 141.
Worship of, in Egypt V: 210.

Mother-Right: I: 197*(2),* 198*(2).*

Motifs:
Aḥiqar Romance, in VI: 204.
Apologetic, in Targum to the Song of Solomon IV: 507; VI: 714.
Courtroom, in Amos V: 692, 705.
Covenant, in OT V: 699; VIII: 216.
Cow and Calf as III: 701.
"Creation" in Ancient Hebrew Poetry V: 689.
Cultic, in Hebrew Thought V: 697; VI: 202.
Decorative, Raliscan III: 704.
Desert, in Bible and Qumran Literature V: 700; VIII: 443.
Exposed Child, Literary V: 701.
Haggadic, in Jewish Iconography III: 703.
Heroic, on Attic Vases III: 719.
Lion-Bull Combat II: 234; V: 188; IX: cxxvi.
Mesopotamian, Animals in III: 706.
Mosaic, Glossary of III: 703.
Oriental Solar III: 704.
Pattern in Mesopotamian Stuccowork III: 700.
Raliscan Red-Figure, Decorative, Exclusive to III: 715.
Sarcophagus, King or God III: 703.
Servant-Ruler, in Early Israelite Religion V: 22.
Snuff-Shovel as Jewish III: 698; V: 52.
Sucession History, in VI: 212.
Terra-Cotta Whorls III: 700.
Wife Sister Motif IV: 320, 321.

Motion Pictures:
Archaeology and III: 419*(3),* 421, 691.
Art and III: 421, 691.

Motya: III: *152,* **169-170**.

Moukhtar: III: 697.

MOULTON, JAMES HOPE:
Bibliography of I: 21.

Mounds:
Stone, on the Rephaim Plains III: 480.

Mount Holyoke College: III: *635, 637.*

Mountain(s):
Holy VI: 505.
Holy (Gebel Baral in Ethiopia) V: 237.
Sacred, in Old Asiatic Religion V: 166.

"Mountain of God": VIII: 72.

Mourning: I: **§113, 371-377**.
Bewailing the King in the Pyramid Texts VII: 46.
Color of I: 373.
Jewish Customs I: 372*(5),* 375.
Mycenaean Custom I: 377.
Old Testament, in I: 377.
Samaritan Custom I: 375.
Symbols of I: 372; VIII: 303.
Mouse: III: **378-379**.
Coffins for I: 373.
Egyptian Medicine and III: 379.
Emerods and Mice III: 378*(2),* 397*(4);* VI: 195, 196.
Jumping, from Babylon III: 379.
Metal, at Jaffa III: 378, 580, 596; VI: 196.
Mouth:
Cosmic V: 156.
Rite of Opening of, in Egypt and Babylonia V: 183, 209, 211, 223*(2)*.
Contribution to Biblical Studies (Psalms) IV: 486.
MOWINKEL, SIGMUND: IV: 485.
Life and Contributions of I: 24.
Old Testament Study and IV: 158.
Mozia: III: 170.
MOZLEY, J. R.: V: 7.
Mu'lula: V: 586*(2)*.
Mu-tem-ua: VII: 76.
Mud Showers:
Palestine, in II: 238, 239.
Mud-Bricks:
Preservations II: 220.
Mudiriah: III: *596*.
MUELLER, J. G.: II: 119.
Mufla:
Office of VI: 702.
MUGELN, HEINRICH VON:
Psalm Translation of IV: 108.
Mughâhat al-Waṭat: II: 277, 297.
Mugharat el-Bezez: III: 170.
Mughâret Abū Uṣba': II: 277, 278, 297, **448**.
Chronology and II: 203, 448.
Pottery-Bearing Strata from, Date of III: 638.
Mughâret an-Nuqṭah: II: 277, 297.
Mugharet el-Emireh: III: 676; IX: cxv, cxvii.
Mugharet el-Kebarah: III: 170.
Mughâret el-Wâd: II: 309; IX: cxvii*(2)*.
Extended Burials at IX: cxvii.
Mugharet esh-Subbabiq: II: 440, 448.
Mugharet Umm El-'Amad:
Jewish Tomb at III: 551.
Mughâret Wadī Fallâh: II: 277, 297.
Mugheir, *see:* **Ur**
Muğla Vilayet: III: 265.
Muhammad:
Moses and IV: 233.
Old Testament, Knowledge of VIII: 368.
MUIR, EDWIN:
Eden's Gate: Later Poetry of VIII: 370.
Mukams: V: 46.
Mukiš-Nuḫaššše-Nii: I: *494;* II: 3, **64**.
Mulberry Tree: III: 392.
Mule:
Aramaic for III: 379; V: 523, *555*.
Cappadocian, *Kutin* III: 379; V: 523, 555.
Psalms, in VI: 478.
MÜLLER, J. G.:
Semtic Theory of V: 373; IX: cx.
MÜLLER, MAX: V: 1*(2)*.
Coptic Inscriptions, Translation of, by VI: 451; VII: 82.
Multiplications:
Cosmic V: 156.
"Mixed Multitude": IV: 229.
Mumar: VI: 690.

Mummies, Mummification I: **§114, 378-381**; IX: **§114, xcvii**.
Dried Flowers in Wrappings I: 372.
Fatty Matter in, Composition of II: 213.
"Heart and Reins" in I: 379; V: 519.
Herodotus on I: 380.
Stuffing Materials, used in I: 381.
Torres Straits, from III: 356.
Mummu: V: 566.
Mummy Case:
Fish, for a I: 378.
Inscription on a XIXth Dynasty VII: 56.
Symbolism of I: 377.
Mummy Cloth: I: 274, 380.
Mummy Labels, Tickets: VII: 83, 332*(3)*, 333.
Mummies, Egyptian: I: *274*.
Akhenaton, of III: 356.
Amenophis I, among the ones at Daïr el-Baharî II: 16.
Amenophis I, X-ray exam III: 357.
Amentefnekht, method of I: 380.
Apis I: 378; III: 777.
Dahshur, small, from Pyramid of III: 358.
Duke of Sutherland, Two belonging to III: 356.
Egyptian, of Graeco-Roman Period III: 362.
Greek Mummy Ticket VII: 20.
Manuscripts Found with a VII: 61.
Merenptah I: 378, 379, 380; II: 62; III: 355.
Nes-Ames I: 378; II: **71**; III: 354, 532.
Persian Period, of the III: 356.
Pettigrew, T. J., on I: 380.
Priestess of Amen Ra III: 355.
Psusennes II II: 76, 81.
Ra-Nafer, of II: 81; III: 355.
Ramesses the Great I: 378.
Sit-Amûn, of III: 358*(2)*.
Skeleton of an Egyptian III: 354.
Ta-usert-em-suten-pa II: 99; III: 355.
Two, in Hancock Museum III: 362.
Mummy Wrappings:
Ta-usert-em-suten-pa, of II: 99; III: 355.
Thuthmosis III, of VII: 44.
Munhata, *see:* **Horvat Minha**
Munich:
First Zionist Congress and VIII: 345.
Munich Palimpsest:
Exodus 40:17-19 in VI: 120.
Muqayyar, Tell el-, *see:* **Ur**
Muqeyer: III: **170**.
(Wadi) Murabba'at: II: **494**.
Bar Kokhba Letter from VIII: 473.
Documents from I: 503; VII: 31, 94, 128; VIII: 429, 472*(2)*, 473.
Legal Document from VII: 94.
Legal Formula in Documents from I: 503; VII: 31, 94, 128.
Papyrus VII: 96.
Mural(s):
Akhetaten, in III: 709.
Beginnings of III: 716.
Boscoreale, from III: 714*(2)*.
Jews, Legally Permitted to, as Art (?) III: 698.
Murashu:
Business House of I: 303; VII: 121.
Murder: VI: 161.
Atonement for Unsolved; Breaking of the Heifer's Neck VI: 147.
First IV: 298.
MURE, WILLIAM: III: 439; V: 624.
Murex, Murices:
Ugaritic Mythology, in V: 199.
(Tell) Mureybiṭ: III: **170-171**.
Architecture of III: 478.
Muristan: I: *360;* II: 306, 308, 407*(3)*.
Tomb at II: 408.

Muristan Inscription: **II**: 407.
Murmuring: **VI**: 129.
MURPHY, JAMES G.:
Documentary Hypothesis **IV**: 249, 265.
Genesis, on **IV**: 249, 265.
MURRAY, MARGARET ALICE:
Bibliography of **I**: 21.
Murrhine: **III**: 622.
Murrians: **V**: 226.
Murshid District, Sudan: **II**: *252*.
Mursili II: **VII**: *241*, 307.
Prayers of **VII**: 308.
Mursilis: **I**: 334; **II**: **64**.
Annals of **VII**: 241.
Sins of (KubXXI 33) **VII**: 145.
Muṣaṣ(ṣ)ir: **III**: 171.
Musawwarat es Sufra, (Masawwarat es Sufra): **III**: 159, **171**, *174*.
Musée Fol: **III**: *640*.
Musée Guimet:
Egyptian Inscriptions in **VII**: 58.
Musei Civici: **III**: *622*.
Museo Poldi-Pezzoli: **III**: *619*.
Muses:
Solon's Prayer to **V**: 260.
Museum, *see also under specific name:*
Anthropological, Exhibits Classification and Arrangement of, in **III**: 341.
Anthropology, Relationship to **III**: 342.
Museum in Alexandria: **III**: *778*.
Museum of Art, Cleveland, Ohio:
Egyptian Collection in **III**: 566.
Ptolemaic *Στρατηγος* of hte Mendesian Nome **VII**: 70.
Museum of Bath:
Egyptian Stele in **VII**: 19.
Museum of Beirut: **VII**: *147*.
Babylonian Tablet in **VII**: 207.
Sefire Treaty in **VII**: 129.
Museum of Bombay:
Ḥimyaritic Inscriptions in **VII**: 294.
Museum of Constantinople: **III**: *495, 546, 720, 759;* **VII**: *302*.
Museum of New York:
Ostracon in **VII**: *35*.
Museum of the Academy of Science, Leningrad: **III**: *664*.
Museum of the Société Jersiaise **III**: 563.
Museum of Turin: **VII**: *29*.
Cylinderial Monument of Nechtharhebes in **VII**: 18.
Demotic Papyri in **VII**: 81.
Museum of Villa Giulia: **III**: *631*.
Museum Vleeshuis: **III**: *750*.
Mushki: **II**: *157*, 272.
Music: **I**: **§85, 242-246**; **IX**: **§85, lxxxviii**.
Egyptian, Intervals in **I**: 244.
Fellahin and **I**: 384.
Hebrew **IX**: lxxxviii.
Hebrew Language, Influence on Contemporary Israeli **VIII**: 357.
Hebrew, with reference to Musical Intonations in Recital of the Pentateuch **VIII**: 382.
Jasher, Book of, in **IV**: 178.
Monody, Oxyrhynchus Musical **I**: 220; **VII**: 354.
Old Testament, and (Influence on) **VIII**: **§1061, 358-359**.
Oriental and Western Singing (Psalms) **IV**: 481.
Phaestos Disk as Oldest Written **I**: 244; **VII**: 358.
Psalms, in **I**: 245*(2);* **IV**: 482, 483.
Sacrament of **VIII**: 359.
Synagog **I**: 243, 244, 246.
Synagogue Worship, in **V**: 94.

Temple I: 242*(2)*.
Worship in Ancient Israel V: 29, 30, 40*(2)*.
Musical Instruments, *see also specific names:* **I: §85, 242-246; III: §219, 678-679; IX: §85, lxxxviii.**
Psanterin VI: 570.
Revised Version of 1881, in IV: 111.
String-Instruments in Egyptian Statuary III: 767.
Sūmpōnyāh VI: 570.
Musical Terms:
Babylonian I: 244.
Greek I: 242.
Hebrew I: 244.
Musicians:
Temple V: 78
Muskebi-Dirmil: III: 264.
Mulsim:
Apocrypha, Use of, by Muslim Writers VIII: 366.
Bible and IV: 96, 154.
Interpretation of the Bible IV: 96.
Muṣri: I: *46;* II: 265; V: 570; VI: 221, 225.
Mussaf-Kedushah: VIII: 199.
Mustard:
Assyrian Word for(?) III: 392; V: 563.
Mût: V: 202, 102.
Sekhemet Presents a Sistrum to VII: 71.
Sekhemet Statues of the Temple of, at Karnak VII: 60.
Temple of, at Karnak III: *760*.
Mutesellim, Tell el-, *see:* **Megiddo**
Queen Mutnedjemet:
Tomb of(?) II: 64; III: 560.
Mutninu: V: 556.
Muwatallis:
Prayer of, to be Spoken in an Emergency V: 227; VII: 309.
Prayer of, to Storm-God Kummanni V: 227; VII: 309.
Muzri: III: 169, 171.
"My God": V: 520.
Myceanæan Language:
Cretan Hieroglyphic / Linear Scripts VII: 363*(2)*.
Dipinto III: *634*.
Final ν, Abscence of V: 620.
i/e Alternation in V: 620.
Monophonemic Dipthongs V: 621.
Sibilants V: 622.
Signs on the Base of Vases V: 622.
Verb, Voice in V: 623.
Verbal Ending -TOL V: 622.
Myceanæan / Minoan Texts:
"Adze" Tablets from Knossos VII: 359.
Akkadian Tablets in Minoan Dress VII: 360.
Amulet, Inscribed VII: 363.
Bibliograpy VII: 360*(3)* ‡, 361*(2)* ‡.
"Cattle" Tablets from Knossos VII: 359.
Cup, Inscribed, at Knossos VII: 363.
Decipherment, *see* ***Interpretation of***
Enkomi, Tablets VII: 357*(2)*, 358*(2)*, 359*(2)*.
Eteocreatan Inscriptions, Interpreting VII: 365.
Graffito, from Knossos VII: 364.
Hagia Triada Tablets VII: *299*, 362, 363.
Hieroglyphic Script VII: 365.
"House of Frescoes", Linear Signs from VII: 364.
ILA II 7a VII: 363.
Interpretation of VII: 359, 360.
Iraklion Musuem, in VII: 360.
Knossos Tablets VII: 362*(4)*, 363.
Kos, from VII: 358.
Ligatured Signs in the Creatan Linear Scripts VII: 363.

Linear A	**VII**: 360, 361*(3)*, 362*(2)*, 363, 364*(3)*, 365*(3)*.
Linear B and Hesiod's "Bread-winners'	**VII**: 361.
Linear Script B, Seals and	**III**: 658, 659; **VII**: 363, 364.
Linear Script B (Tablets)	**VII**: 359*(2)*, 361, 362*(2)*, 365.
LM III B, from Knossos	**VII**: 365.
Minoan half-cylinder, (Oxford) AM 1938. 790, Authenticity of	**VII**: 364*(2)*.
Minoan Script According to Bedřich Hronzý	**VII**: 359.
Nestor Excavaions and	**VII**: 361.
Onomastica, Cypriot and Creatan	**VII**: *358*, 363.
Phaestos (Phaistos) Disk	**I**: 244; **VII**: 358, 359, 360*(3)*, 363.
PY Ad 684	**VII**: 360.
Pylian Ta tablets	**VII**: 364.
Pylos Texts	**VII**: 359, 360*(2)*, 361*(2)*.
Religious Texts from Pylos	**VII**: 361.
Sherd, Inscribed	**VII**: 362, 363.
Tomb Inventory	**VII**: 360.
Tsepis Stele	**VII**: 361.
Mycenae:	**I**: *212, 257, 261, 264, 325, 339, 349;* **II**: *49;* **III**: *95, 96, 167,* **171-173**, 205, *593(2), 653.*
Capture by the Argives	**II**: 114.
Chronology of	**II**: 151, 203.
Grave Circle A at	**III**: 173, 560.
Grave Circle, New, at	**III**: 554, 555.
Mycenae Homer and	**IX**: lxxxv.
Inscribed Sherd from	**VII**: 362.
Palace at	**III**: 502.
Sanctuary, Classical, near	**III**: 520.
Shaft Graves at	**III**: 553.
Mycenaean Religion:	**V**: **§478, 241-242**.
Mycenaean Tablets:	**II**: *49*.
Fr- Tablets	**V**: 621.
Homer and	**VII**: 350*(2)*, 360*(2)*.
Mycenaeans:	**I**: *181, 327, 332, 340, 350;* **II**: *150,* **151**, 313; **III**: 4, 342.
Burial Customs	**I**: 376.
Chronology, Palaeogrpahical Evidences and	**V**: 620.
Mourning Customs	**I**: 377.
MYERS, W. J.:	**III**: *588*.
Mykenai:	**III**: 174.
Shaft Graves and Tholos Tombs at	**III**: 547.
Mykonos:	**III**: 174.
Mylasa:	
Hellenistic Tomb in	**III**: 553.
Myos Hormos:	**III**: 89.
Myrelaion:	**III**: 265, 266.
Myrina:	**III**: *759*.
Myrlaca:	**III**: 263.
Myron:	**III**: 728*(2)*.
Myrrh:	**I**: *308, 340, 468, 492;* **III**: *390(3),* **392**, *394;* **IX**: xcv.
Myrtilus:	
Wheel of Life in Story of	**V**: 268.
Mystery, Mysteries:	
Egyptian, Zoolatry of	**V**: 217, 260.
Eleusian and Orphic	**V**: 253.
Eleusinian	**V**: 246, 251; **VII**: 333.
Eleusinian, Rules on Celebration of	**V**: 263.
Greek, Preparation for Christianity	**V**: 248.
Imperial, Aspect of Emperor Cult	**V**: 273.
Jewish Apocalyptic and	**V**: 121.
Orphic	**V**: 254.
Pre-Christian Semitic Concept of	**V**: 510.
Semitic Background of NT *Mysterion*	**VIII**: 276.

Mystery Play:
Serpent with Human Head in **VIII**: 355, 366.
Mystery Religions:
Hellenistic and the OT **V**: 254.
Judaism and **V: §476, 240.**
Mystic:
Prophets as a **I**: 109.

Mysticism:
Founding of the Halacha, in **VIII**: 80.
Greece, of **V**: 252.
Greek Scientifiic thought and **II**: 233.
Halakah, in the Founding of **VIII**; 252.
Jewish **V**: 107, 240*(2)*.
Jewish, and Philosophy **V**: 112.
Old Testament **V**: 136.
Plato, of **V**: 253.
Pyramids at **III**: 505.
Rabbinical Literature and **V**: 240.
Religion and **V**: 3.
Rome, of **V**: 268.
Ultimate and the Mystery. A Critique of Some Neo-Mystical Tenents **V**: 113.
Myth(s):
Abraham as a **I**: 28, 29.
Ages, of the **V**: 260.
Alexander **I**: 9.
Ancient Literature, in **VII**: 2.
Archaeology and **IV**: 213.
Babylonian **I**: *461, 496;* **IV**: 182; **V**: 174, 189.
Babylonian **VII: §898, 222-223.**
Babylonian, and Hebrew Tradition **V**: 146.
Bible, and **I**: 135, *461, 496.*
Biblical Interpretation, in **I**: 135; **IV**: 87, 92; **V**: 136, 137.
Bilulu **V**: 187.
Canaanite Seasonal **V**: 194.
Classic, in Art **III**: 695.
Cosmogonic Combat, Biblical Earth Monster in **V**: 137; **VIII**: 83.
Cosmogony-Science, Genesis, and **VIII**: 82.
Development and **V**: 133, 137.
Dione, and Aphrodite **V**: 250.
Documentary Hypothesis and Origin of **IV**: 259.
Dragon, of the East **V**: 153.
Eden as **IV**: 292.
Egypt, Royal, in Ancient **V**: 219.
Egyptian **VII: §838, 38-40.**
Egyptian, and Hebrew Tradition **V**: 146.
Elkunirsa, reconsidered **V**: 227; **VII**: 308.
Eschatology and **V**: 133; **VIII**: 252.
Eurydice and Orpheus **V**: 266.
Evolution as Cultural **III**: 327.
Fall of Man as **IV**: 293.
Folklore, in Canaanite Myth **V**: 193.
Functions of, and Scripture **V**: 136.
Genesis **IV**: 266, 267*(2)*, 271, 279.
Genesis 14 as(?) **IV**: 214.
"Gracious Gods", of **V**: 191.
Helena, Variant of **V**: 265.
History and **VIII**: 28.
Horus, Eyes of **V**: 220.
Horus, of Edru **V**: 213, 215*(2)*, 216, 219; **VII**: 39*(5)*
Hurrian, in Semitic Dress **V**: 192; **VII**: 141.
Hurro-Hittite, Intrusvie **V**: 226.
Hypothesis **V**: 135.
Inanna **V**: 187.
Indian, of "Churning the Ocean" and Babylonian Creation-Myth **V**: 155, 179.
Kumarbi, Hittite Version **VII**: 300, 308.
Kumarbi, Semitic Elements in **V**: 162.
Medusa, and Greek Art **III**: 691.
Metaphor and, (Chinese) **V**: 145.

Miracle and V: 135; **VIII**: 93; **IX**: cxxxvii.
Mycenaean Vase Painting and **III**: 626, 715.
Mythic Phrases Used by OT Writers **IX**: cxxxvi.
Mythos and Ethos **V**: 262.
Nature and Function of **V**: 134.
Origin of **V**: 132, 134.
Orpheus and Eurydice **V**: 266.
Osiris Unnefer **V**: 201*(2)*.
Pattern and, in the OT **V**: 135, 136.
Plato, of **V**: 249.
Pre-Classical Art, in **III**: 701; **V**: 133, 241.
Sacred History and Cosmic **I**: 135; **V**: 136; **VIII**: 87.
Saitic in Arabic Tradition **II**: 127.
Samson as a Sun **I**: 78.
Sargonid Seals and **III**: *650*.
Sea of Knives (Egyptian) **V**: 223.
Semitic Nature **IV**: 450; **VI**: 509.
Serpent in **IV**: 294.
Serpent, of Ancient Egypt **V**: 199.
"Solar Myth", Origin of, and the History of Ancient Thought **V**: 131.
Sparta and Argos in **II**: 135.
Springs, Myth of, Ugarit **VII**: 140.
Story and **V**: 136.
Sumerian, of Beginnings **V**: 179.
Sumerian, "Paradise" **V**: 186.
Sun, in Babylonian Deluge Story **V**: 183.
Transference and Development **V**: 133, 144, 145. 178*(2)*.
Ugaritic Fertility **IV**: 188; **V**: 197*(2)*.
Ugaritic, of the Sea and its Biblical Counterparts **IV**: 188; **V**: 137.
Word and **V**: 132.
Yahweh-Tehom **VIII**: 76.

Mythology - includes Folklore, Legends and Supersitiions: **V**: **§460, 131-134**, 167; **IX**: **§460, cxxxvi-cxxxvii.**
Aeschylus, in **V**: 259.
American, as related to Asiatic and Hebrew Tradition **IV**: 192.
Aryan **V**: 131, 152, 235.
Aryan, Sources of **V**: 153.
Ass in Semitic **V**: 161.
Assyrian **V**: 167*(2)*, 168; **VII**: 197.
Astral **V**: 178.
Astral, in Old Testament **II**: 229; **V**: 135.
Babylonian and Astral **V**: 178.
Bible and Mythological Polytheism **V**: 108, 133.
Biblical, Analytical Approach to **V**: 137.
Birds, Ethnologically Considered **III**: 364; **V**: 131, 152.
Birds, Wise, of **III**: 365; **V**: 132, 154.
Burning Bush in Comparative **IV**: 290; **V**: 132.
Canaanite, and Hebrew Traditions **IV**: 187; **V**: 194.
Canaanite, *see:* ***Ugaritic Mythology***
Comparative **V**: 144.
Comparative, Hebrew Terms Explained by Sanskrit **V**: 132, 143, 387.
Comparative, with the Origin of Culture in America **III**: 410; **V**: 162; **IX**: xciv.
Dwarf-Craftsmen in the Keret Epic and NW Semitic **V**: 134; **VII**: 144.
Egyptian, *see:* ***Egyptian Mythology***
Ezekiel, Allusions of, in **VI**: 356.

Feather and Wing in Early	**IX**: cxxxvi.
Fire in, Canaan and Israel	**V**: 134, 136, 197.
Garden of Eden in Comparative	**IV**: 290; **V**: 132.
God of the OT, None About	**V**: 22.
Greek, and the Bible	**IV**: 191.
Greek, and Vase-Painting	**III**: 623, 714.
Greek, *see:* ***Greek Mythology***	
Habakkuk, Background	**VI**: 401.
Hattian	**I**: *483;* **V**: 227.
Hebrew Attitude towards Mythological Polytheism	**V**: 133.
Hebrew, Goldziher on	**V**: 131*(2)*.
Hebrew Mythological Terms	**V**: 132, 143, 387, 393*(2)*.
Hittite and the OT	**IV**: 193.
Hittite, *see:* ***Hittite Mythology***	
India, Interpretation of	**V**: 247.
Job, Mythological Element in	**IV**: 459.
Memory and Forgetting in Ancient Greece	**IX**: lxxxiv.
Mesopotamian	**V**: 165, 166*(2)*.
Monotheism and	**V**: 33.
Monsters, mythical, in OT	**V**: 136.
Old Testament and	**IV**: 219; **V**: **§461**, **134-137**.
Patriarchs and	**IV**: 315, 316; **V**: 132.
Pig in	**III**: 380, *399*.
Polytheism, Mythological, and the Bible	**V**: 108, 133.
Prehistoric / Protohistoric	**III**: 410; **V**: 162, *277*.
Primitive Religion and	**V**: 3.
Psalm 82, Background to	**VI**: 502.
Psychoanalysis and	**V**: 133.
Remythologizing, Key to Scripture	**V**: 136.
Revelation and	**V**: 134; **VIII**: 29.
Roman, *see:* ***Roman Mythology***	
Scientific System of	**V**: 131.
Seleucid	**II**: *49;* **V**: 160.
Semitic, and Zodiacal Light	**II**: 231.
Semitic, Ass in	**V**: 161.
Semitic Nature-, Battle of the Rain and the Sea	**VII**: 141.
Semitic Religion and	**V**: 140.
Semitic, Serpents in, and the Gilgamesh Epic	**III**: 381; **V**: 133; **VII**: 266.
Serpent Tempter in Oriental	**IV**: 288; **V**: 153.
Sumerian	**V**: 186.
Sumerian, Blood-Plague Motif in	**V**: 186.
Sumero-Akkadian, Plaga Septenrionalis in	**V**: 186.
Triad, Divine, in Biblical	**VIII**: 105.
Ugaritic, *see:* ***Ugaritic Mythology***	
Value and Methods of, Study	**V**: 133.
Vanetic, *see:* ***Vanetic Mythology***	
Myus:	**III**: 266.

N

Na'aneh:	**III**: *723*.
Na-Amen-Rē':	**II**: 269.
Naamah:	**I**: **73**, *81*.
Naaman:	**VI**: 234*(2)*.
Baptism of	**IV**: 382.
Na'ame, Tell:	**II**: 368.
Naarath:	**II**: 284, 449.
Nabataean Period:	**II**: 176.
Nabataean Texts:	**VII**: 121, 294, **§924**, **295-296**.
'Avadat (Oboda), from	**VII**: 296*(3)*.
Contract from the Dead Sea Region	**VII**: 296.
Egypt, from	**VII**: 296*(2)*.
Etabi District, in	**VII**: 295.
Glaser Collection	**VII**: 295.
Graffiti from Egypt	**VII**: 295, 296.
Palestine, Alleged, from	**VII**: 114, 295.
Petra, from	**VII**: 295*(2)*.

Philip, Tetrach of Aurantis, concerning **VII**: 295.
Sinaitic **VII**: 295.
Nabataeans: **II**: **151-152**, 462, 490; **III**: 19.
Nabatene: **II**: 461.
Nabhrakhta: **VI**: 616.
Nablus: **I**: *344;* **II**: 299. 308, *365;* **III**: *585, 586.*
Bronze Objects from **VI**: 347.
Greek Inscription from **VII**: 316.
Pentateuch from **IV**: 21.
Samaritan Tablet from, at Leeds **VII**: 136.
Nabonassar: **II**: 64.
Nabonidus: **I**: 167, 327; **II**: *26, 52,* **64-65**; **III**: 488; **VII**: *247.*
Arabia, in **II**: 64, 65.
Art, and **II**: 65.
Chronicle of **VII**: 186.
Coronation Decree of **VII**: 233.
Cylinder of, referring to Belshazzar **VII**: 241.
Daniel, in **IV**: 530.
E-MAŠ-DA-RA, Restoration of **VII**: 237, 262.
Harran Inscription of **VII**: 240.
Ina Bit Saggil tuklat, Daughter of **II**: 52, 64.
Inscription of **VII**: 182, 232.
Jewish Exiles, and **II**: 65.
Moon Cult, in Time of **V**: 165.
Prayer of (4QPrNab ar) **VIII**: **§1115, 452.**
Royal Tithe of **VII**: 258.
Sickness of **II**: 65.
Stele of **VII**: 233.
Nabopolassar: **II**: 65.
Chronicle of **VII**: 186, 237.
Inscriptions of **VII**: 234.
Naboth: **V**: 197; **VI**: 231*(2).*
Nabu:
Eye of **III**: 574.
Golden Boats of **VII**: 261.
Jews of Elephantine and **V**: 30.
Nabu, Nimrud **III**: 178, 501.
Nabu Temple: **III**: 178, 501, 518*(2), 518.*
Nabu-pal-iddina: **VII**: 234.
Nabû-shum-libur: **I**: *421;* **II**: **65**.
Nabuna'id:
Inscriptions of **VII**: 236.
Nadan:
Haikar's Sister's son **II**: *42,* **65**; **VII**: 289.
Naddah **III**: 403.
NADIR SHAH: **IV**: *75.*
Naga: **III**: *159,* 174.
Naga ed-Deir (el Deir): **III**: 89, **174**; **VII**: *42.*
Cemetery, Predynastic, at **III**: 174.
Three stelae from **VII**: 21.
Nagadah Period: **III**: 779.
Nagila, Tell: **II**: **449**, **450**; **III**: *632.*
Fortress, Iron Age II, on **III**: 489.
Nahal Amud: **II**: 449.
Nahal B'sor: **II**: 302.
Naḥal Hardor: **I**:*455.*
Naḥal Ḥever: **I**: *279;* **II**: *152,* 279.
Documents from **VIII**: 472.
Naḥal Mishmar, *see also:* **Cave of Treasure** *under:* **Caves** **II**: 279.
Greek Documents from **VII**: 328.
Nahal Mizraim, *see:* **Egypt, River of**
Naḥal Oren: **II**: 449.
Naḥal Ṣeelim: **I**:*455.*
Greek Documents from **VII**: 328.
Naharin: **II**: 269.
Nahariya: **II**: 304.
Bronze Age Temple at **III**: 517.
Flints from **III**: 676.
Geological History of **II**: 249.
Nahash:
Jesse and **IV**: 373.

Nahor:
Biographical Studies **I**: 73.
Genealogy of, the Sons of **I**: 120.
Genealogy of the Sons of, and the Book of Job **IV**: 466.
God of **VI**: 81.
Nahor (Place): **III**: 175.
Nahr ez Zerka:
Crocodiles in **III**: 372.
Nahr Malka: **III**: 175; **VII**: 279.
Nahr Ruben: **II**: 450.
Nahr-el-Kelb:
Assyrian Inscriptions at **VII**: 183.
Cuneiform Inscription on **VII**: 205, 231.
Egyptian Inscriptions at **VII**: 56.
Nahum, Book of:
Acrostic in **VI**: 396*(2)*, 397.
Alphabetic Hymn in **VI**: 396.
Alphabetic Poem in **IV**: 447*(2)*, 448.
Archaeological Light on **IV**: 448.
Assyrian, Influence of, in **VI**: 397.
Assyriology and **IV**: 447.
Authenticity, Authorship, Date, and Sources of **IV**: **§368**, **448**; **IX**: **§368**, **cxxxiii**.
Bibliography **I**: *12*.
Day, concept of, in **IV**: 448.
Elkosh and **IV**: 448.
Exegetical Studies on **VI**: **§629**, **396-399**.
God, Concept of, in **IV**: 448.
Hebrew Text of **VI**: 396, 399.
Inductive Study of **VIII**: 390.
Isagogical Introduction to **IV**: 447.
Isaiah 51-53, connections **IV**: *445*, 448, *511*; **VI**: *305*.
Ishtar Epithet in **VI**: 398.
Jonah, Connection to **IV**: *445(2)*, 448*(2)*, *511*; **VI**: 305.
Lamentations, connections to **IV**: *445*, 448, *511*; **VI**: *305*.
Legal Activities of the Lord according to **IV**: 448.
Literal and Free Translation of **IV**: *440*, 448, *452*.
Literary Criticism of **IV**: **§367**, **447-448**.
Nineveh and **IV**: 448; **VI**: 396.
Nineveh and Assyrian Empire in **VI**: 396.
Nineveh, Fall of, and **III**: 181, 183; **IV**: 447, 448.
Origins of **IV**: 448.
Paronamasia in **IV**: 448; **VI**: 398.
Pesher of (4QpNah) **VI**: 398.
Style and Manner of **V**: 704; **VI**: 396.
Time of Prophecy **VI**: 396.
Nahum, Book of, Manuscripts of: **VI**: **§630**, **399**.
Hebrew Text of **VI**: 396, 399.
Massoretic and Qumran Texts of, compared **VI**: 399.
Septuagint Translation of **VI**: 399.
Targum and Collated Text **VI**: 399, 711.
Targum (Jonathan) of **VI**: 399, 711.
Vulgate Translation of **VI**: 399.
Nahum, Commentary - Pesher (4QpNah): **VI**: 398; **VIII**: 411; **§1120**, **454- 455**, *457*.
Oral Exegesis, Attack on(?) **VIII**: 455.
Teacher of Righteousness and **VIII**: 421.
Nahum, Person: **I**: 73.
Birthplace of **I**: 73.
Date of his Prophecy **IV**: 448.
Native Place of **VI**: 396.
Oracle of **VI**: 397.
Nail(s):
Clay, of Hammurabi **III**: 687.
Nain: **II**: 284.
Naioth(?); **VI**: 202.
Najile, Tel en: **II**: 299.
NAKARAI, TOYOZO W.:
Bibliography of **I**: 21.
Nakht:
Sheikh el-Beled **II**: 65.
Nakhtmin: **II**: 66*(2)*.

Nakurah: II: 308.

Nam-maḫ-ni (Govenor of Lagash):

Clay Cone of   VII: 237.

Namburbi:

Texts of, in the British Museum   VII: 153(2), 154.

"Name":

Christ, Relation to   VIII: 118, 125.

Egypt and Israel, in   V: 223; VIII: 111.

Manifestation of the Divine   VIII: 128.

Power of the   VII: 40.

Name(s), *see also:* **Onomatology, Divine Names**

"A New Name" in Isaiah 65:15   VI: 317.

Abraham, of   I: 28, 30, 32; V: 291.

Abram, of   I: 30(2).

Adam, Translation of   I: 33.

Amorite Personal , in Genesis 14   V: 296; VI: 62, 63.

Amurrite in Ur III and Early Isin Texts   V: 383.

Anatolia, Linguistic Continuity of,Shown by its Proper Names   V: 302.

Anatolian   V: 302.

Anatolian Proper, Theophorous Element in   V: 302.

Aphal Name Form in OT   V: 304.

Arabian Personal borne by the Israelites in the Mosaic Period   V: 297; VI: 139.

Aramaic, in Accadian   V: 302; VII: 151.

Araunah, a Hittite   VI: 217.

Ashurbanipal, Proper, in the Annals of   V: 295.

Assyrian Eponyms   VII: 197.

Assyrian, Personal   V: 296.

Assyrian, Proper   V: 294.

Assyrian Proper, in 'Ia'   V: 293.

Babylonian Theophoric   V: 269.

Biblical Concept of   V: 303.

Biblical, Folk etymology   V: 303.

Biblical, Illustrated from the Monuments   V: 296.

Biblical Proper, Religion of   V: 295.

Canaanite, ending in *an*   V: 300.

Compound, and Western Semitic Deities   V: 160.

Coptic Proper   V: 298.

Divine, in Classical Greece   V: 263.

Divine, in Genesis   IV: 3(2), 11, 22, 30, 256, 264(2), 265.

Divine, *see also:* **Divine Names**

Egyptian   IV: 229.

Egyptian, Historical Value of   V: 298.

Egyptian, Late, in   V: 302, 379.

Egyptian ⌐◡🗚⌐◻   V: 292.

Egyptian, Royal nomen and prenomen   V: 303.

Elohistic and Jehovistic Proper   V: 292, 293.

Etruscan   V: 293.

Etrusco-Roman, Phonology of   V: 301.

Execration Texts, in   V: 302.

God *Ym* in proper   V: 301, 389.

Gods (*ḪW* and *MWT*) in Proper   V: 300.

Greek, among the Jews   V: 302.

Greek, in Semitic World   V: 303.

Hebrew   V: 292.

Hebrew, 9th Century B.C.   V: 296.

Hebrew, ending in *an*   V: 300.

Hebrew, in Inscriptions from Babylon   V: 294.

Hebrew, Interpretation of, in Origen   V: 302; VI: 722.

Hebrew Personal, on Intaglios   IX: cxxv.

Hebrew (Proper)   V: 294(4), 299.

Hebrew Proper, with compounded יָהּ and יְהוֹ   V: 293.

Hebrew Proper, with the element בשת **V**: 293.
Hebrew Theophoric **V**: 296.
Hebrew, with nominal prefix *n* **V**: 298.
Hidden, in 1 Enoch 59 **VI**: 665.
Hittite, Egyptian Transliteration of **V**: 298.
Hittite, Name-giving, in **V**: 304.
Hittite Personal **V**: 295.
Hittite Proper **V**: 298.
Iranian בגדאנא **V**: 296, 457; **VI**: 664; **VIII**: 156.
Iranian, in Elamite **V**: 304.
Iterative, in Old Akkadian Texts from Nuzi **VII**: 165.
Jews, Names of **V**: 302.
"Kanishite" Proper, Suffixes in **V**: 302.
"Khefren", Pronunciation of **V**: 309.
Libyan **V**: 293.
Lihyanite **V**: 304.
Malta, Personal, in **V**: 297.
Men of a *(Use of Seals)* **III**: 648.
Mitannian Personal **V**: 295.
National, as indicating Bible Pedigree of Nations **II**: 1, 2.
New-born Child, Naming the **V**: 304.
Nin-Šubur, name element in **IX**: cxxxvii; cxxxviii.
Northwest Semitic, in a List of Egyptian Slaves **V**: 302.
Nuzi Personal **V**: 301.
Old Testament **V**: 293, 294, 295.
Old Testament, Giving of Proper, in **V**: 303.
Old Testament, Semitic Analogies for **V**: 295.
Origin of Ancient, of Countries, Cities, Individuals, and Gods **IX**: cxiii.
Pay-List, Diverse Names in an Old Babylonian **VII**: 252.
Persian, in Babyloian Contracts **VII**: 248.
Proper, Giving of, in OT **V**: 303.
Proper, in Deut. 3:16 **VI**: 141.
Proper, Translation of **IV**: 105.
Royal, Cerastes in **V**: 299.
Royal, on objects in the 'King Fouad I' collection **III**: 568.
Sabaean Eponymate **V**: 304.
Semitic **V**: 297.
Semitic, Early **V**: 292*(2)*.
Semitic, in Greek World **V**: 303.
Semitic, in the Fara Period **V**: 303.
Semitic Personal **II**: *17;* **IX**: cxxv, cxxxviii.
Shaddai, of **I**: 30.
Siginificance of **V**: 297.
South Arabian Eponyms **V**: 303.
South Arabian Proper **V**: 297.
Sumerian Proper **V**: 296.
Syrian, at Tel El-Amarna **V**: 293.
Thebes, Derivation of **III**: 252.
Translation of Proper **IV**: 105.
Yahweh, Modification of in Proper **VIII**: 118.

Nanna(r): **III**: 273; **V**: 184.

Nanshe(k): **VII**: 271.
Invocation to the Reed **VII**: 271.

Naophorous:
Inscriptons on a Statue of **VII**: 63*(2)*.

Naos:
Bast, of **III**: 574.
Decades, with the **VII**: 38.
El-'Arîsh **V**: *341.*

Naoum Beg Shuquair: **IV**: 336.

Napata: **III**: 148, *577, 593, 732;* **V**: *207.*

Napata-Meroë: **III**: 175.

Napatan:
King's Name in **V**: 301; **VII**: 69.
Kings and Apis Worship **V**: 220; **VII**: 38.

Naphath-Dor:
Hill Sanctuary(?) **V**: 49.

Naphtali:
Blessings of **VI**: 91.
Testament of, Hebrew Text of **VI**: 646*(2)*.

Naphtali, Tribe of:
Borders of — **II**: *273(2)*.
Naphtha: — **I**: 286.
Naples: — **III**: *120*.
Bay of, Underwater Archaeology in — **III**: 454.
NAPOLEON: — **II**: *258;* **III**: *86, 742;* **VII**: 69.
Naqada: — **III**: **393**.
Naqadeh:
Small Objects from — **III**: 566.
Nâr-Ba-Thai: — **II**: **66**, *67;* **VII**: 35, 78.
Nâr-Mertha: — **II**: *66*, **67**; **VII**: 35.
Narâm-Šin: — **I**: 326, 327; **II**: *60(3)*, **66**, *84*, 174*(2)*, 197*(2);* **III**: *155, 160, 663*.
Cuthaean Legend of — **VII**: 202.
Foundation Stone of — **VII**: 236.
Inscriptions of — **VII**: 154, 186, 235, 250.
Nard, *see:* **Spikenard**
NARKISS, MORDECAI:
Bibliography of — **I**: 21.
Narmer: — **II**: *63*, **66**.
King of Abydos — **II**: 4, 207.
Pallete of — **I**: *332;* **III**: *654*.
Narrative Repetition - "Doublets" — **IV**: 33*(2)*, 168; **V**: **§559, 692**.
Doublets and Contamination — **V**: 692.
Joshua, Book of, in — **V**: 692.
Kings, Books of, in — **IV**: 380
Narratives:
Biblical Event, and Historical Truth — **IV**: 199.
Biblical, Interpretation of, and Poetics — **IV**: 378; **V**: 702.
Dechronologized in OT — **II**: 190; **V**: 700.
Early, and "Late" Law in — **I**: 466.
OT, Historical Character — **IV**: 195.
Veracity of Old Testament — **V**: 692.
Narthex: — **III**: 671.
Narû: — **III**: 575.
Naṣbeh, Tell en-: — **II**: 309, 327, **450**; **III**: 422, 423.
Four-Room Buildings of — **III**: 521.
Hebrew Inscription from — **VII**: 94.
Long-Room House of — **III**: 470.
Tomb from the time of Herod Archelaus — **III**: 547.
Nasben, Tell en-: — **III**: *664*.
Nash Papyrus: — **IV**: **§235, 9-10**; **VIII**: 436, 439.
Decalogue — **VI**: 142.
Naṣḫana: — **III**: 175, *214*.
Nasi: — **V**: 45, 101.
Nastosenen:
Inscription of King — **VII**: 55.
Natal, South Africa: — **I**: *441*.
Nathan: — **VI**: 210.
David and — **VIII**: 179.
Messianic Interpretation of Prophecy to David by — **VIII**: 132.
Prophecy of — **VI**: 210.
National Museum (Washington): — **III**: *562(2)*, 563.
Nationalism: — **VI**: 294.
Egyptian, under Greek and Roman Rule — **II**: 126.
Prophets and — **I**: 109, 507.
Prophets Revolt Against, in Religion — **V**: 21.
Psalms, in — **IV**: 480; **IX**: cii.
Nationalmuseet Kobenhavn: — **III**: *649*.
Nations, Peoples and Their History (Alphabetical Listing): — **II**: 3, **§142, 111-171**; **IX**: **§142, cvi-cxi**.
Abraham and the — **I**: 32.
Chronology of, Various, Unclassified — **II**: **§151, 202-206**.
Pedigree of — **II**: 1, 2.
Prophets of the, Rabbinic Homilies on — **IV**: 346; **VI**: 696.
Table of, in Genesis — **IV**: 311.

Natron: I: 286.
- Egyptian use in Mummification I: 379, 380*(2)*, 381.

Natufians: II: 152; III: 353; IX: cix.

Natural History: I: 389*(2)*; III: **§172, 364**.

Natural Law: I: 463, 465, 466, 469; III: 303.
- Ethics, in, Objections to VIII: 228.
- Jewish View of V: 113.
- Miracles, Evolution, and III: 303; VIII: 91, 304.

Natural Religion: V: 13.

Natural Theology: VIII: **§957, 13-15**, 69*(2)*.
- Biblical Basis of VIII: 15.
- Brougham, Henry (Lord), on VIII: 13.
- Chambers, Robert, on VIII: 13.
- Christianity, Testimony to VIII: 84.
- Crombie, Alexander, on VIII: 13.
- Faith, Basis of Science and Religion VIII: 14.
- Geology and VIII: 13.
- Ministry of the Word and VIII: 15.
- Natural Religion Prophetic of Revelation VIII: 14.
- Ontological Arugument and VIII: 15*(2)*.
- Paley, William, on VIII: 13.
- Persistence of Force in the Argument of VIII: 14.
- Spirit of VIII: 14.
- Testimony of, to Christianity VIII: 13.
- Values and Limitations of VIII: 15.

Nature: VIII: 82.
- Biblical View of VIII: 84.
- Craftsman, as, in Greek Thought V: 264.
- Divine Interpositions in VIII: 89.
- God and/in VII: 30; VIII: 66, 78, 84, 93.
- Goddess of, in Funeral Art (Greek) V: 258.
- Greek Art as Expression of the Love of III: 697.
- Hebrew View of V: 112; VIII: 78.
- Law of Consistancy Subordinate to Higher Law of Change VIII: 90.
- Man's Place in VIII: 167.
- Mesopotamia Art, Interpretation of, in III: 705.
- Plato on V: 244.
- Psalms, in IV: 478, 480, 485; VI: 444, 465.
- Revelation and III: 288.
- Sabbatical Year, and I: 367, *413*.
- Supernatural in VIII: 85.

Nature Worship: V: 153.
- Genesis 1, as a Manifesto Against(?) V: 106; VI: 23.

Naucratis (Naukratis): II: 71, *82;* III: 83, 88, 111, **175**, *763*.
- Inscriptions from VII: 63, 318.
- Stela from VII: 23.

Naunakhte:
- Will of VII: 30.

Nauri Decree: VII: 30, 70.

Naveh Yam: II: 451.

Navigation: I: *340*, **§105, 351-356**; IX: **§105, xcvi**.
- Birds and Early I: 354; III: 369.
- Jewish Seafaring I: 354.

NAVILLE, EDOUARD: III: 201*(2)*; IV: 165*(2)*.
- "Book of the Dead", Edition of VII: 48.
- Exodus, Geography, on IV: 337.
- Genesis, Composition and Sources of, on IV: 323.
- Pentateuchal Hypothesis IV: 243.

Navy:
- Athenian, Arsenal of Philon III: 458; VII: 335.
- Athenian Naval Catalogue VII: 335, 336.
- Egyptian I: 316*(2)*.
- Exploration of Dead Sea and Jordan with U.S. II: 310.
- Forests and I: 313; II: 243; III: 384.

Jewish, Destruction of, at Jaffa in 68 **I**: 175, 313, 352.
Naval Battle Pictured at Medinet Habu **VII**: 17.
Salamis, Battle of, Position and Tactics of Contending Fleets **III**: 215.
Solomon's **I**: 316.
Solomon's Naval Base at Ezion-Geber **I**: 315; **II**: 364.
Tarshish **I**: *92*, 311, 312.
Naxos: **I**: *453*.
Greek Tower in **III**: 488.
Nazarenes: **V**: 95.
Nazareth: **II**: 302*(2)*, 367, **451**; **III**: 444*(2)*, *525*.
Greek Inscription from **III**: *642*; **VII**: *103*, 315*(2)*.
Meteorological Observations at **II**: 236.
Prophecy, in **VIII**: 134.
Virgin's Fountain at **I**: 362.
Nazarite: **I**: 367.
Guilt-Offering of a Defiled **V**: 64.
"Nazir" Legislation **VI**: 128.
Nb(ꞌı͗)kꜣ-(ꞌı͗): **II**: 67.
Nby:
Inscription of **IX**: cxxxviii.
Inspector of the *Śẖ* of Horus **IX**: cxxxviii.
NEALE, JOHN MASON:
Psalms, on **IV**: 474.
Neanderthal: **II**: 302; **III**: 327, 347, 352*(2)*, 360*(2)*.
Sex of Certain Fossil Humanoids from Spy, Problem of **III**: 360.
Skeletons, Three Adult, from Shanidar Cave **III**: 361, 362.
Skeletons, Two, from Shanidar Cave **III**: 361.
Dalam Cave, Malta, and **III**: 356.
Neapolis: **III**: 441.
Near East, Cities and Places outside Israel (Palestine) **III**: **§168, 1-282**; **IX**: **§168, cxviii-cxx.**
Nearchos:
Aryballos by **III**: 612.
Neb-Ḥepet-Rē Mentu-Ḥotpe: **II**: 67; **III**: *228*; **IX**: cv.
Neb-kau-re:
King of the Eloquent Peasant **VII**: *10*.
Neb-Neteru:
Mummy Case of **I**: 379.
Nebaloth: **II**: 290.
Nebḫepetre Mentuḥotpe: **II**: *46*.
Nebi Rubin: **I**: *425*; **III**: *656*.
Nebipusenwosret:
Stela of (B.M. No. 101) **VII**: 22.
Nebo:
Element in Hebrew Proper Names, Machnadebai and Barnabas **V**: 294.
Iron Age Tombs at **III**: 559.
Nebo Elam: **II**: 283.
Nebo, Mount: **II**: 308, **451**.
Hellenistic to Arabic Remains at **II**: 451.
Mosaic, Inscribed, near **II**: 292.
Nebo, Region of: **II**: 302.
Stone Age Culture in **II**: 451.
Nebopolassar: **II**: 67; **V**: 173.
Nebpeḥtire: **III** *136*.
Nebt:
Edjo, Mistress of **V**: 222.
Nebt-ant:
Queen of Sebekhetep III **II**: **67**, *86*.
Nebt-nenat: **II**: 67.
Nebtu:
Priest of the Goddess **V**: 207.
Nebuchadnezzar: **I**: *317*, *357*; **II**: **67-69**, *353*; **VI**: 335, 336*(2)*, 339, 341, 344.
Abasement of **II**: 68; **IV**: 527.

Accession of, and Eclipse of 585 BC **II**: 68, 225.
Babylon in days of **III**: 41*(2)*.
Borsippa Inscription of **VII**: 232.
Chronicles of **VII**: 240.
Cylinder(s) of **VII**: 231, 232*(3)*, 235, 236*(2)*, 238*(2)*, 240.
Daniel, in **II**: 68; **IV**: 526.
Dream of **VI**: 569.
Egypt, in **II**: 68; **III**: 82.
Egyptian Hieroglyphic Inscription concerning Conquest of **II**: 68; **VII**: 14.
Folly of **II**: 68.
Hymn to **VII**: 259.
Inscriptions of **VII**: 154, 186, 230, 231*(5)*, 232*(5)*, 233*(4)*, 235, 237, 240, 241, 250.
Jar, Alabaster, with name of inscribed on **III**: 604.
Jeremiah and **II**: 69*(2)*; **IV**: 410, 415, 416.
Jerusalem and **II**: 69, 418; **VII**: 240.
Judean History and **II**: 69.
Palace of **III**: 501*(2)*.
Palace of, Belshazzar's Hall **III**: 499.
Palestinian Campaigns of **II**: 69.
Reconquest of Phoenicia and Palestine in Ezekiel **IV**: 422.
Shrine of **III**: 514.
Tabi-utul-Bel and **V**: 177.
Throne-Room of, Unearthed **III**: 499.
Tree, Vision of, in Daniel **VI**: 569.
Tyre captured by **II**: 68*(4)*, 491*(4)*.

Nebuchadnezzar II:
Cylinder Inscription of **VII**: 239.
Inscriptions of **VII**: 232*(3)*.
Nebuchadnezzar III: **II**: 69, *96*.
Nebuchadnezzar IV: **II**: 69, *96*.
Nebular Hypothesis:
Gregory of Nyssa and **IV**: 278.
Neby Lawih: **II**: 284.
Necho: **II**: **69**, 70.
Bronze Statuette of Necho I **III**: 759.
Necho II:
Relic of (Text) from Phoenicia **VII**: 59.
Syrian Campaign of **II**: 70; **VI**: 243.
Nechtharhebes:
Altar of, Inscription upon **VII**: 55.
Cylindrical Monument of, in Musem of Turin **VII**: 18.
Necklaces: **I**: 281, 282.
Necla: **II**: 290.
Necromancy: **V**: 106.
Sin of **VI**: 146.
Necropolis:
Cretan, Three **III**: 536.
Esquiline **III**: 212, 549.
Giza **III**: 506.
Mycenaean, under Agora **III**: 484.
Saida, Royal at **III**: 533.
Theban **III**: 482, *711*.
Nectanebus: **II**: 70.
Egypitan Legend of **II**: 70.
Nector: **IX**: cxxxi, cxl.
Nedabiah: **I**: 73; **VII**: 100.
Nefer-heteph:
Tomb of **V**: 211.
Nefer-ronpet:
Stela of **VII**: 22.
Nefer-Seshem-Ra:
Inscribed Offering-Table, of **VII**: 72.
Nefer-Sma-Āa:
Statue of **II**: 70.
Neferkerēʻ: **II**: **70**, *81*.
Statue of **II**: 70.
Nefert-ari:
Tomb of **III**: 538*(2)*.
Neferurēʻ:
Portrait of **II**: 70.
Negadah: **III**: *2*, 175.
Tablet of Menes **VII**: 61.
Tablet(s) of **VII**: 61*(2)*.
Negadeh: **III**: 85.

Negev (Negeb): I: *151, 155, 255(3), 256(3), 257, 258;* **II**: *121, 122,* 292, 295, 301, 310, *327,* **451-454**, *489(2);* **III**: 424, 440; **VIII**: 347; **IX**: cxvii.
- Abraham, Age of, in the **IV**: 319.
- Agriculture in **II**: 452, 453, 454, 466.
- Bedouins of **II**: 118.
- Bronze Age, Middle I, in **I**: 341; **IV**: 320.
- Cities in, and Tribal Boundaries **II**: 274, 451.
- Cities of the **II**: 284*(2)*, 301.
- Climate of **II**: 244, 452.
- Conquest of, and the Exodus **IV**: 337.
- Demography of Ancient **II**: 262.
- Dendrochronological Studies of **II**: 245.
- Egypt and Early History of **III**: 88.
- Exodus, Book of, in **IV**: 327.
- Fortresses in, Forerunners of Limes **II**: 454; **III**: 490.
- Geography of **II**: 275, 453.
- Geomorphology of Central Highlands **II**: 299, 452.
- Land Use in Ancient **II**: 262.
- Rain and water conditions in **I**: 363; **II**: 243, 246, 452.

Negligence:
- Criminal, in Code of Hammurabi **I**: 478, 496.
- Talmud, in **VI**: 693.

Negotiable Instruments: **I**: 304.

Negroes: **III**: 338.
- Bronze Statue(tte) of **III**: 351, 756, 766.
- Egyptian Ebony Statuette of a Negress **III**: 760.
- Greece, Ancient, in **I**: 188.
- History, Appearance in **III**: 345, 346.

Nehavand: **I**: *282;* **III**: *614.*

Neḫebkau: **V**: 213.

Nehelamite: **I**: *117.*

Nehemiah, Book of: **VIII**: 395.
- ***Authenticity, Authorship, Date, and Sources of*** **IV**: **§414**, **540-541**, 585.
- Authorship, Common, with Ezra and Chronicles **IV**: 522, 540, 541.
- ***Bibliography of*** **I**: (**§35**), 14.
- Dates Relative with Ezra **IV**: 539, 540.
- Egyptian Papyri and **IV**: 540.
- Elephantine and **III**: 93.
- ***Exegetical Studies on*** **VI**: **§665**, **582-586**.
- Genealogies in **IV**: 540; **IX**: lxxxii.
- Greek Versions of **IV**: 522.
- Josephus' Account of **IV**: 540; **VI**: 680.
- ***Literary Criticism of*** **IV**: **§413**, **540**.
- Outline of **IV**: *451, 453, 520,* 537.
- Topography in **VI**: 585.
- Walls, Rebuilding of **IV**: 540*(2)*.

Nehemiah, Chapter 7:
- "Gōlā list" in **VI**: 579, 585.

Nehemiah, Chapter 9:
- Source of **VI**: 585.

Nehemiah, Book of, Manuscripts of: **VI**: **§666**, **586**.
- Septuagint Text of **VI**: 586*(2)*.
- Syro-Hexaplar Version of **IV**: 45; **VI**: 586, 601.

Nehemiah, Person: **I**: *44, 166, 399, 461.*
- Biographical Studies **I**: **73-74**.
- Devotion of **IV**: 540.
- Ezra and **I**: 44.
- Ezra, and, Contemporaries or Successors **IV**: 537.
- Ezra, was, **I**: *45,* 74.
- Inspection Tour of **VI**: 583.
- Jerusalem and **I**: 74; **II**: 411, 416.

Night Ride of IV: 540; VI: 582, 583*(2)*.
Religion of Israel, Evolution of, and V: 14*(2)*.
Sanballat and VII: 136.
Nehhalin Bethulia: II: 284.
Nehushtan: I: *82;* V: 225; VI: 132.
Neiel: II: 283.
Neith of Sais: V: 202.
Neitocross, Princess: III: *646*.
Nekhbet: V: 206.
Nekhebu:
Biographical Inscriptions of VII: 17.
Nekhen: I: *347;* III: *739;* VII: 69.
Nekht:
Barge Official of Amenhetep III II: 70.
Nekhti:
Inscriptions of VII: 15.
Nemea: III: **176**.
Nemesis:
Temple of, at Rhamnous III: 522.
Nemi:
Sculpture from III: 726.
Votive Chamber at III: 516.
Nemrud Dagh: III: 121, 263.
Tomb of Antiochus I, at III: 553.
Neo-Orthodoxy:
Anthropology and III: 351.
Archaeology and IV: 154, 199, 221.
Neo-Othodoxy:
Neo-Babylonian Tablets IV: 219.
Neofiti Codex 1: VI: 713.
Palaeographical Character VI: 713.
Neolithic Period: III: 13*(2)*.
Anatolia, in
Chronology of Greek II: 200*(2)*.
Genesis, and the Antiquity of Adam IV: 296.
Greece I: *333*.
Macedonia, of III: 155.
Palestine, Cultures of I: 124.
Palestine in III: 427.
Rub' al Khali, Neolithic Site in II: 218.
Western Asia II: 174; III: 23.
Neoliths: III: 565.
Neotera: II: 71.
Nephthys:
Isis and, as Wailing Women V: 220.
Songs of VII: 78.
Nephtoah: II: 455.
Nepiriuriu: V: 351.
Cornelius Nepos: II: 153.
Nĕrab II:
Northwest Semitic Text VII: 85.
Nerfer-Sma-Āa: II: 70.
Nergal: III: *653;* V: 186.
Egypto-Libyan Background V: 187.
Myth of VII: 203.
šu-il-la Prayer to VII: 201.
Nergal-ereš:
Stela of VII: 190.
Nergalsharezer Shamgar: VI: 340.
Neriglissar: VII: *251*.
Chronicles of VII: 240.
Inscription of VII: 233.
Nero:
Talmudic Legend, in VI: 705.
Neronian Sacra Via: III: 212.
Nes-Ames:
Mummy and Coffin of I: 378; II: **71**; III: 354, 532.
Nes-pa-ched:
Ushabti-box of III: 574.
Neša: II: 271; III: 176.
Neskhons:
Decree of Amonrasonthēr for VII: 70.
Nesnebneteru:
Statue of II: 71.
Nespeḥerʻan:
Funerary Papyrus of VII: 44.

Nestor:	**III**: *114, 173,* 204; **VII**: 361.
Palace of	**I**: *426;* **III**: 173, 204, 501*(6),* 502*(7);* **V**: 621.
Nestor, King	
Four-Handled Cups of	**V**: 620.
Nestorian Church:	
Apocrypha in East Syrian Daily Offices	**VIII**: 381.
Exegesis of, on Genesis	**IV**: 97; **VI**: 16, 723.
Nestorians:	
Exegesis of, and Jewish compared	**IV**: 97; **VI**: 16.
Moses, Legend of among	**I**: 67.
Study of Syraic among	**V**: 530.
Neter (𓊹) **Pole:**	
Ashera and	**V**: 49, 161, 217.
Cult of	**V**: 216.
Nether World, *see also:* **Future State, Underworld**	
Entrance to, at Thebes	**V**: 206.
Isthar's Decent into	**V**: 185*(3).*
Sumerian Literary Texts on	**V**: 187.
Nethinim:	**I**: 191, *204;* **II**: *131;* **IV**: 536; **V**: 77*(2),* 78*(3).*
Netopha:	**II**: 283, 307.
Nets:	
String, XVII Dynasty	**III**: 673.
NEUBAUER, ADOLF:	**V**: 474.
"New Heaven and New Earth":	**VIII**: 250.
New Jerusalem, *see:* **Jerusalem**	
New Kingdom:	
Egyptian, Chronology	**II**: 128*(2),* 199*(2).*
Egyptian, History of	**II**: 128*(2), 199.*
New Testament:	
11Q Melchizedek and	**VIII**: 467, 482.
"4Q Testamonia" and	**VIII**: 471, 480.
Abrahamic Covenant and	**VIII**: 214.
Apocrypha and	**VI**: 600; **VIII**: 273, 274, 276.
Apocrypha and Pseudepigrpaha	**VIII**: 272, 274.
Aramaic Intermediate Version	**VIII**: 274.
Assyriology and	**II**: 222.
Authorship of Old Testament and	**IV**: 161*(2).*
"Bible" of	**VIII**: 275.
Canon, Formation of	**IV**: 207.
Christ in	**VIII**: 125.
Christ in the OT, Validity of NT Discernment of	**VIII**: 273.
Correct Knowledge of, Value of OT for a	**VIII**: 271.
Covenant, Concept of, in	**VIII**: 215.
Covenant, Divine, in the Bible	**VIII**: 215.
Criticism	**IV**: 129.
Damascus Document / Covenant, compared with	**VIII**: 217.
Decalogue and	**VI**: 160.
Divorce in the	**VI**: 36, 694; **VIII**: 276.
Dualism of "Flesh and Spirit" in, and the DSS	**VIII**: 417.
Elijah, Role of, in	**VIII**: 277.
Enoch, Book of, and	**VI**: 649; **VIII**: 272.
Enoch, Book of, Messianic Doctrine of, and its Influence on the	**V**: 126; **VI**: 649; **VIII**: 298.
Eschatological Interpretation of the Sinai-Tradition in	**VIII**: 420, 482.
Exodus in	**VIII**: 274, 276.
Extra-Canonical Jewish Literature and	**VIII**: 272.
Ezekiel in	**I**: 44.
Fufillment in, Idea of	**VIII**: 277.
Haggai and	**VIII**: 275.
Hebrew Thought and	**VIII**: 276.
History of	**III**: 777; **IV**: 217.
History of Religion and	**II**: *222.*
Interpretation of OT, in	**VIII**: 277*(2).*
Isaiah and / in	**VIII**: 277, 278.
Israel and	**I**: 177.
Jeremiah, Influece on the	**VIII**: 276.

Jewish Alexandrian Thought and NT Theology **VIII**: 273.
Jewish Literature and **VIII**: 273.
Jewish Wisdom Literature in **V**: 117; **VIII**: 275.
Judaism and **VIII**: 272.
Language of **IV**: 217.
Messianic Interpretation **V**: 130.
Messianic Motifs of Qumran and **VIII**: 419.
Midrash in **VIII**: 275, 276, 296.
Miracle Stories - OT Prophecy Preparation for **VI**: 288; **VIII**: 275.
Old Testament and **V**: 7.
Old Testament Criticism in light of NT Quotations **IV**: 121; **VIII**: 272.
Old Testament Heroes of Jewish Legend in **VIII**: 276.
Old Testament Prophecies quoted in **VIII**: 270.
Old Testament Quotations and Inspiration **VIII**: 20, 45, 271, 272.
Old Testament Quotations in **VIII**: 270*(2)*, 271*(9)*, 272*(2)*, 273*(2)*, 274*(3)*, 275, 276*(4)*, 277*(4)*, 442.
Old Testament Quotations, Sources of **VIII**: 274.
Old Testament, Theological Interpretaion in, Deliberative **VIII**: 277.
Old Testament, Use of, in **VIII**: 45, **§1040, 270-278**.
Palestinian Targum and **VI**: 713; **VIII**: 277.
Philo's Influence on **VI**: 675; **VIII**: 274.
Priesthood, Old Testament, Fulfilled in **V**: 40.
Prophecy, Old **VIII: §1050, 297-298**.
Psalter and **IV**: 477*(2)*; **VIII**: 273*(2)*.
Qumran 4QTestimonia and **VIII**: 471.
Qumran Literature and Its Relation to **VIII: §1155, 479-483**.
Quotations, Formulas for Introducing Scripture in **VIII**: 275.
Quotations of OT in NT Speeches, Text Presupposed(?) **IV**: 3; **VIII**: 272.
Quotations, Old Testament in, and the Septuagint **IV**: 25, 27, 31, 33; **VIII**: 271, 272, 274.
Quotations, Old Testament Respect for Context in **VIII**: 277.
Rabbinic Parallels to **VI**: 686; **VIII**: 272.
Rockefeller McCormick Manuscripts of **VI**: 95.
Septuagint and **IV**: 32, 33, 34, 35, 36; **VIII**: 23, 277.
Septuagint, Greek of, and **V**: 640.
"Spirit" and "Flesh" in, and the DSS **VIII**: 482.
Symbols, Use of OT **V**: 58; **VIII**: 273.
Talmud and **VI**: 698.
Targum and **VI**: 712; **VIII**: 275.
Teaching Undergraduates, to, and the Dead Sea Scrolls **VIII**: 408.
Terminology of, and Qumran (Three Nets of Belial) **VIII**: 482.
Testament of the Twelve Patriarchs and **VI**: 658; **VIII**: 273*(2)*.
Testament of the Twelve Patriarchs, Influence on **VI**: 659; **VIII**: 276.
Textual Background of the OT used by the **VIII**: 275.
Tobit and **VI**: 615; **VIII**: 274.
Wilderness, Preparation in and in Qumran **VIII**: 416.
Women, OT in **VIII**: 273.

New Year:
Babylonian Festival **V**: 184.
Day **I**: 365.
Gifts to the Pharaoh **V**: 224.
Liturgy and **I**: 394; **V**: 85.
Semitic, and the Origin of Eschatology **I**: 398; **VIII**: 251.
New Year's Day: **I**: 365; **V**: 84.
Hittite word for **V**: 612.
Psalms for Jewish **IV**: 376, 478; **V**: 85; **VI**: 502.
Song of Hannah and **IV**: 376, 478; **V**: 85.
Third Benediction of **VIII**: 207.
New York Univeristy Archaeological Museum: **III**: *577, 615, 616*.
New Zealand:
Religious Instruction in Schools **VIII**: 405.
Newĕmisah: **III**: 152.
NEWMAN, FRANCIS WILLIAM: **I**: 484.
NEWMAN, JOHN HENRY: **VIII**: 41.
Newness: **V**: 511.
News:
Bad, Reaction to, in OT **V**: 699.
NEWTON, ISAAC:
Ezra-Nehemiah, on **IV**: 536*(2)*.
Nfr-mȝ'.t:
Tomb of **III**: 554.
Nfr-Šḫrw:
Stela of, Artisan of Ptaḥ, at Saqqarah **VII**: 25.
'nḫ-n.ś-Ppy: **II**: 71.
'nḫ-Snwsrt: **II**: 269.
Nḫj: **V**: 222.
Ni-kau-Ptah:
False Door of **VII**: 20, 63.
Nicanor: **II**: 418.
Nicholson Museum: **III**: *599;* **VII**: *20, 374*.
Nickel: **I**: 299, 300*(2)*, 334, *452*.
Ancient Bronzes, in **I**: 299; **II**: 217.
Nicopolis: **II**: *23;* **III**: *4*.
Nicosthenes: **II**: 71; **III**: 691; **IX**: cv.
NIEBUHR, BARTHOLD GEORG: **II**: 253.
Eusebius and **II**: 172.
Roman History, on **II**: 159;
Rome, History of, on **III**: 210*(2)*.
NIESE, BENEDIKT (BENEDICTUS):
Maccabees, Books of, on **VI**: 627
Niffer, *see:* **Nippur**
Nigeria: **I**: *374*.
Night:
Egyptian Word for **V**: 325.
Hittite Word for **I**: 403.
Night-jar **V**: 137; **VI**: 287.
Nikarawas:
Dogs of **V**: 610.
Nike: **III**: *466(2), 467, 731, 732*.
Athena, Greek Inscriptions of **VII**: 320.
Head of, from Athenian Angora **III**: 741.
Νικετου:
Egypt, in **III**: 84.
Nikkal-Wïb: **V**: 195.
Nikosthenes (Nicosthenes): **III**: 608, 609.
Nile River: **I**: *345, 351(2), 352;* **II**: *254*, 266; **III**: *86*, **176-177**.
Alluvium of, Antiquity of **III**: 334.
Babylon on the **III**: 42.
Blue Nile **III**: 90.
Colors of **III**: 177.
Cow's Belly as name of apex of Delta **II**: 268.
Delta, Petrie's Work in **III**: 85.
Egyptian Name of **V**: 352.
Levels at Karnak and History of Libyan Period **III**: 177.
Levels at Kumma **III**: 147, 177, 225.
Sedimentation above Wadi Halfa during last 20,000 years **II**: 251; **III**: 177.
Source of **III**: 176*(5)*.

Nile Valley:	**III**: 83, 88, **176-177**, *228*, 437, *672(2)*.
Geological History of	**II**: 284; **III**: 88, 177, 347.
History and Geology of and Palaeolithic Man	**II**: 248; **III**: 82, 177, 347.
Nilometer:	
Philoe, of	**II**: 222.
University of California, in Egyptian Collection	**II**: 223.
Nimbus:	
Rainbow and	**IV**: 309.
Nimes:	**III**: *460*.
Nimrod:	**I**: **74-75**; **III**: 78; **IV**: 180, 181; **V**: 172*(2)*; **VI**: 55; **VII**: 159.
Alphabetic Inscriptions on Ivories from	**VII**: 96, 130.
Assyrian Inscriptions and	**VII**: 182.
Babylonian Epic	**VII**: 222, 224, 225.
Baylonian Gish-du-bara indentified with(?)	**V**: 171, 172.
Language of	**V**: 601.
Sumerian original of the name(?)	**I**: 75; **V**: 297.
Nimrud:	**I**:*405, 453;* **III**: **178-179**, 599, *771(2);* **VII**: *188, 203(2)*.
Aramaic Ostracon from	**VII**: 129.
Building Inscriptions from from Fort Shamlaneser	**VII**: 189.
Burnt Palace at	**III**: 178, 501, 518.
Inscribed Statue fragments	**VII**: 177.
Medical Texts from	**III**: 402; **VII**: 156.
Nabu Temple at	**III**: 501.
Pottery from	**III**: 624*(2)*.
Shalmaneser III, Statue from	**VII**: 189; **IX**: cxxvii.
Nimrud "Letters" / Tablets, *see also:* **Assyrian Correspondence**	**VII**: 180*(4)*, 181*(4)*, 188*(2)*, 190*(3)*, 191, 195.
Nimrûd Obelisk, *see:* **Black Obelisk**	
Nin-Uraš:	**III**: *184;* **V**: 182.
Nin-eb-nadin-šum:	**VII**: *233*.
Nin-IB (Nin-urta, Nin-urash):	**V**: 183.
Nin-Magʿ:	
Cylinder	**VII**: 233.
Inscription	**VII**: 233*(2)*.
Nin-Šubur:	**IX**: cxxxvii; cxxxviii.
Nina:	**III**: 181; **V**: 175*(2)*.
Nine:	
Hebrew word for	**I**: 428.
Nineveh:	**II**: *88, 140, 172;* **III**: 25*(2)*,*36(6)*, 41, *147*, **179-183**, 440, *592, 689, 756;* **IV**: 181; **V**: 175*(2);* **VII**: 185*(3)*.
Aramaic Inscription from	**VII**: 125.
Artist's Visit to, in 1850	**III**: 426.
Assyrian Inscriptions from	**VII**: 172*(2)*, 173, 176, 185.
Buildings on Quyunjiq at	**III**: 467.
Chronology of Sieges of	**III**: 179.
Cuneiform Characters and	**VII**: 146.
Evolution and	**II**: *140;* **III**: *41*, 182, 345.
Fall of, (and Date of)	**II**: *68, 172,* 201; **III**: 40, 180, 181*(5)*, 182*(4)*, 183*(2);* **VII**: 237*(2)*.
Fall of, and Nahum	**IV**: 447, 448.
Jonah's Mission to	**IV**: 440.
Monuments of, in Cuneiform	**V**: 553.
Nahum and	**VI**: 396.
Name, Continuance of the, After 607-6 B.C.	**V**: 293.
Palace at	**III**: 499, 500.
Sennacherib at	**II**: 89; **III**: 181.
Temple at	**III**: 499.
Temple of Ishtar at	**III**: 183, 514.
Tobit, in	**VI**: 615.
Topography of	**III**: 180.
Vocabulary of	**V**: 577.

Ningal: V: 205.
Egyptian Text, in VII: 36.
Eyes of VII: 286.
Ningišzida (Ningizzida) V: 185.
Temple of III: 518.
Ninib, Ninip (Ninurashā): V: 175*(2)*, 176*(2)*, 566.
Liturgy to VII: 261.
Ninkasi:
Hymn to V: 180.
Ninlil: V: 178, 181, 222*(2)*.
Nintinugga:
Dedication of a Dog to VII: 287.
Ninurta:
Prayer to VII: 287.
Ninus, *see also:* **Carchemish** III: 183.
Niobe: III: 491*(2);* V: 245; VII: 56.
Niobid: III: 726*(2)*.
Nippur: I: *303, 364;* III: 23, **183-185**, *460, 487, 771;* V: *182;* VII: *121*.
Aramaic Incanation Texts from VII: 124.
Architecture of III: 462.
Babylonian Inscriptions from VII: 206, 207*(2)*.
Coins from I: 443.
Ellil, the God of V: 169.
Incantation Bowls from III: 605.
Lamentation Over the Destruction of VII: 276.
Marashu Sons of VII: 175.
Numerical Fragment from IX: clii.
Raman (Bin) and Bel of V: 171.
"Seige Documents" from VII: 213.
Sumerian Hymn from V: 182.
Tablets from VII: 147; IX: lxxxi.
Temple Archives of VII: 235.
Temple of Inanna at III: 519*(2)*.
Texts from the Library of VII: 187, 202.
Niqum: VII: *149*.
Nirâm-Sin: II: *174(2)*.
Nirim: I:*454;* II: 300.
Synagogue at, *see:* ***Ma'on***
Nisa: III: 185, *214*.
Aramaic Ostracon from VII: 131.
Nisroch: V: 163, 169, 394; VI: 6.
Niṣṣanah-Beerothaim: I: *256*.
Nitocris: II: 71, *82*.
Nitokris-Naqî'a: II: 71.
Noachism:
Judaism and Christianity in the Light of V: 28.
Noah: I: 75; IV: 299; VI: 47.
Blessing of VI: 53.
Curse of I: 200; IV: 310; VI: 53.
Drunkeness of IV: 310.
Inheritance of IV: 303.
Log-Book of IV: 303.
Prophecy of, regarding Population of Palestine II: 260.
Races, Origin of, and III: 352.
Righteousness of VI: 50.
Sacrifice of IV: 303.
Sacrifice of, Michael Angelo's VIII: 356.
Vine-Dresser, as VI: 53.
Nob: I: *360;* II: *344, 378,* **455**; IV: 373; V: 46; VI: 271*(2)*.
Nobility:
Philo Concerning VI: 674.
Roman, and Economics I: 191, 308.
NOCK, ARTHUR D.: V: 149.
Nod: III: **185**.
Noematics: VIII: 6.
Nomadism: I: 182, 186.
Hebrew Origins and I: 145.
Herd Composition and social structure, models of I: 392.
Mesopotamia, Economic Basis of, in I: 194, 310.

Migration and II: 259.
Nomadic Ideal in the OT V: 110, 111.

Nomads:
Hebrews as I: 141*(3)*.

Nomarch:
Hepzefa, of Siûṭ III: 543.
Thinite nome, of III: 554.

Nomes:
Egyptian, Ensigns II: 126.
Egyptian XXIInd, Name of II: 269.
Helioplitan V: 321.
Herakleopolite, Tree of V: 209.
Thinite, Nomarchs and officials of III: 554.

Nominatio: I: 506.

Non-Canonical Writings:
Bibliography of I: **§37, 14**.
Righteousness Between the Testaments VIII: 199.

Non-Pauline Epistles:
First John, Psalm 119 a Clue to VIII: 296.
First Peter and the Book of Enoch VI: 649; VIII: 295.
James, Midrashic Terms and Techniques in VIII: 296.
James, Rabbinical Illustrations of VIII: 295.
Jude and the Assumption of Moses VI: 653; VIII: 295.
Jude, Jesus and the Exodus in VIII: 295.
Old Testament, Use of, in VIII: **§1047, 295-296**.

Non-Violence:
Passover and V: 88; VIII: 229.
Talmud, in VIII: 229.

Nonexistence:
Egyptian Expressions for V: 344.
Saadia's Second Doctrine of Creation and the Problem of, (Kalam) V: 112; VIII: 78.

Norbanus: II: 161.

NORDHEIMER, ISAAC: V: 468.

Norse:
Second Singular for Third Singular in V: 613.

North:
Hole in the VI: 433.

North Arabia: III: 18*(3)*, 19, *278;* VI: *221, 225*.
Bedouins in II: 118.
Bible and IV: 191.
Sealand and III: 18.

North Arabian Theory, *see:* **Jerahmeel Theory**

North Sea:
Shipping Problems on I: 355.

Northwest Semitic (Levantine): V: **§499, 381-382**.
BRDL, B(A)RZ(E)L "Iron", Cuneiform Background of V: 382.
Consonants, Shared, in V: 382.
Enclitic *Mem* in V: 381.
Job, in IV: 468.
"Lettuce" in V: 381.
Proverbs and IV: 501.
"Puppy" in V: 381.
Qoheleth, and, Philology IV: 517; V: 381.
Syllabic Character of West Semitic Writing V: 381.
Totality, Figurative Equivalent of, in V: 381.

Northwest Semitic (Levantine) Texts: VII: **§852, 84-85**.
Texts in Latin and Greek Letters VII: 85.

Norwegians:
Old Testament and IV: 131.

Nose:
Cosmic V: 156.

Notary:
Thebes, in VII: 29.

NOTH, MARTIN: Life and Contributions of I: 24.

NOURSE, JAMES:
English Translation of the Bible **IV**: 51.
NOYES, GEORGE RAPALL:
Latter Prophets, on **IV**: 385*(2)*.
Poetical Books, on **IV**: 51, 456.
Psalms, on **VI**: 442, 473.
Nub-χās:
Relative of Queen **II**: 71.
Nubia: **I**: *264, 291, 292, 346, 374, 457;* **II**: *265;* **III**: *25, 45,* 88, *92, 99, 121, 176,* **186-188**; **VII**: *24*.
Border of **II**: 275.
Deluge in Lower **III**: 188.
Egyptian Activity in **III**: 188.
Epigraphic Expedition to **VII**: 72*(2)*.
Faunal Assemblages from **III**: 367.
Fortresses of, Ancient List **VII**: 16.
Leprosy, Early case of, in **III**: 404.
Monuments, Removal of Endangered **III**: 457*(2)*.
Neolithic Site in **III**: 188*(2)*.
Palaeolithic **III**: 187, 188.
Post-Pharaonic **III**: 187*(2)*.
Racial Relationship with Egypt **IX**: cviii*(2)'*
Salvage Archaeology **III**: 457*(2)*.
Travels, Modern, in **III**: 435, 436*(3)*, 437*(2)*, 444, 447.
Nubian Inscriptions: **VII**: 15, *374*.
Nubians (Nubas): **II**: 152; **III**: 338, 711; **IX**: cix*(2)*.
Anthropology Section, University of Colorado, Report **III**: 362.
Kingdom of the Intermediate Period **III**: 186.
Nubkhaes: **VII**: *65*.
NUGENT, LORD: **III**: 566; **VII**: 63.
Numbering Systems, *see also;* **Numerology**
Babylonian **I**: *398*.
Babylonian, and Origin of the Calendar **I**: 430.
Egyptian **I**: 428.
"Finger-Numbering" in the Pyramid Texts **V**: 209.
Hebrew **I**: 428.
Numerical Catagories in Ancient Rabbinic Literature, *10, 7, & 4* **VI**: 690.
Numerical Fragment from Nippur **IX**: clii.
Numbers:
12,900,000 **I**: 429.
"80", Sportive Writing of, in Egyptian **V**: 351.
Æonic Number in Babyon **I**: 429.
Artificial or Illustrative, Use of, in the OT **VIII**: 310.
Authenticity of in OT Historical Books **IV**: 198.
Babylonian idoms of **I**: 432.
Egyptian, Gender of Tens and Hundreds in **I**: 431; **V**: 363.
Egyptian Numerals **V**: 359.
Enneads of Gods **V**: 220.
Exaggeration in **IV**: 196.
Forty, Peculiar Use of **VIII**: 309.
Forty-three, Basal Biblical Number(?) **VIII**: 309.
Four as a Divine Title **VIII**: 310.
Four, in Hittite and Luwian **V**: 614.
Greek Numerals **VII**: 350.
Hebrew, Gender of **I**: 433.
Hebrew Use of / in **VIII**: 309, 310.
Heptad, Element in Biblical and Rabbinic Style **VIII**: 311.
Large, in OT **IV**: 199, 339; **VIII**: 312; **IX**: cxxx.
Mnemonic Use of, in Proverbs and Ben Sira **V**: 116; **VI**: 623; **IX**: cxxxiii.
Nineteen **VIII**: 311.
Numerical Errors in OT **VIII**: 310.
Pentateuch, High, in **IV**: 225; **VIII**: 309.
Plato's Nuptial Number **I**: 429.

Rhetorical Use of, in OT	**VIII**: 312.
Seven, Among Chinese	**V**: 145.
Seven as a Divine Title	**VIII**: 310.
Seven, in Egyptian Texts	**VIII**: 311.
Seven, in Ugaritic Texts	**V**: 538.
Seventy in Semitic	**VIII**: 311.
Sexagesimal System	**I**: 432, 433.
Three as a Magic Number in Latin Literature	**I**: 430.
Twenty-three, and other Numerical Expressions	**VIII**: 310.
Universal Type and Pyramid Casing Stones	**III**: 503.
Numbers, Book of:	**IV**: 230, 231.
Bibliography	**I**: (**§7**), 10.
Chronology of	**IV**: 344.
Date, Authorship, Sources, and Authenticity	**IV**: **§321**, **347**.
Exegetical Studies on	**VI**: **§585**, **127-139**.
Judeo-Persian	**IV**: 49.
Literary Criticism of	**§320**, **344-346**; **IX**: **§320**, **cxxxi**.
Literary Illustrations of	**VIII**: 365.
Midrash on	**VI**: 706.
Quails, Story of, in	**IV**: 346.
Qumran Texts (4QLXXNu)	**VIII**: **§1099**, **444**.
Samaritan Pentateuch, in	**IV**: 21.
Scholia to, Samaritan-Arabic Pentateuch	**IV**: 23.
Theology of	**VIII**: 16.
"Waters of Bitterness"	**VI**: 128.
Numbers, Book of, Manuscripts of:	**VI**: **§586**, **139**.
Numbers, Chapter 1	
Census Lists in	**VI**: 137.
Numbers, Chapter 26	
Census Lists in	**VI**: 137.
Numbers, Manuscripts of:	**VI**: **§586**, **139**.
Old Latin Palimpsest of	**VI**: 139.
Samaritan Pentateuch on	**VI**: 139.
Numerals:	
Akkadian	**I**: 428*(3)*, 433; **V**: 541*(3)*, 548.
Arabic	**I**: 430*(2)*.
Arabic, Kabbalistic Theory of the Origin of	**VIII**: 310.
Arabic, on Babylonian Tablet (?)	**I**: 431*(2)*; **VII**: 255, 256.
Assyrian	**I**: 428*(3)*; **V**: 555*(3)*, 556; **IX**: xcix.
Egyptian	**I**: 428.
Etruscan	**I**: 428, 435.
Greek	**I**: 417, 433, 434.
Hebrew	**I**: 431.
Hieratic, in Hebrew Ostraca	**I**: 426, 435.
Hieratic, on Hebrew Weights	**I**: 427, 435; **VII**: 96.
Hittite "Four"	**IX**: xcix.
Hittite "One" *(šanna)*	**IX**: xcix.
Luwain "Four"	**IX**: xcix.
Lycian	**I**: 433.
Nine *(Tisâ)*	**I**: 429.
Nuzi Tablets, in	**I**: 431; **V**: 546.
One, Origin of	**I**: 434.
Origin of	**IX**: xcix.
π and Elohim	**I**: 429.
Roman	**I**: 436.
Semitic "Two"	**I**: 429.
Ugaritic	**IX**: xcix.
Ugro-Altaic: 1-5	**I**: 428; **V**: 542.
Numerics, *see:* **Numerology**	
Numerology:	**VIII**: **§1053**, **309-312**.
Bible Numerics	**VIII**: 311.
Cosmic Five, Seven and Twelve	**VIII**: 310.
Forty, Peculiar Use of	**VIII**: 309.
Number in Nature and Bible, indicating a Supreme Intellegence	**VIII**: 311.
Number-symbolism in the Goseples, Rabbinics and Qumran (DSS)	**VIII**: 311.

Numerical Codes in Bible Prophecy **VIII**: 246.
Plato's Number **VIII**: 309.
Prophecy, Numerical Codes in Bible **VIII**: 246, 311.
Rabbinic Literature, Numerical Categories, *ten, seven* and *four* in **VIII**: 311.
Sequence x/x + 1 in the Old Testament **VIII**: 312; **IX**: cxlv.
Symbolic and Sacred Numbers in Scripture **VIII**: 311.
Symbolism of Numbers in the Ancient Religions, Bible, and Philosophies **VIII**: 309.

Numidia: **III**: *712*.

Numismatics, *see also:* **Coins, and Coinage** **I**: **§126, 440-459**; **IX**: **§126,c.**
A.I.N.A. Convention in Tel-Aviv **I**: 459.
Architecture, Oriental, and **I**: 459.
Bibliography of Jewish **I**: 458.
Dead Sea Scrolls and **I**: 453.
Greek **I**: 440, 451, 453.
Hapax-Legomena in **I**: 457; **V**: 404.
Investigation, Method of, and Historical Significance **I**: 454.
Jewish **I**: 454.
Landscapes and **I**: 456.
Roman **I**: 440, 451, 452, 454.
Yale Numismatic Collection **I**: 449*(3)*.

Nundinae: **I**: 404.

Nundines: **IX**: xcvii.

Nuri Language:
Grammatical Structure of **V**: 600.

Nursery Rhymes:
Palestinian **I**: 391.

Nusku: **V**: 163, 169, 170, 394; **VI**: 6, 287.

Nut (Goddess): **V**: 208.
Night Journey of the Sun and **V**: 213.

Nutrition: **I**: **§86, 247-249**.

Nuzi (Nuzu), *see also:* **Yargon Teppe** **I**: *202, 213, 227(3), 270, 433, 490, 499, 511(2), 512;* **II**: 143; **V**: 550, 551*(2)*.
Akkadian Texts from **VII**: 163, 165.
Cappadocian Texts from **VII**: 163, 165.
Geographical Names **II**: 268*(2)*.
Glyptic Art of **III**: 700.
Horite Language, Evidence of, at **V**: 679.
Indo-Aryan Names from **V**: 301.
Legal Procedure in **I**: 499.
Map Found at **II**: 257.
Marriage Customs at **I**: 217; **VII**: 166.
Sistership Contract at **I**: 199, 516; **VII**: 167.
Text, Historical Geography of **II**: 273.
Woman, Status of **I**: 198.

Nuzi Texts (Tablets): **I**: *181, 424* ; **II**: *143,* 214, *217;* **IV**: 219; **VII**: **§882, 165-167.**
aḫḫûttû Documents from **VII**: 166.
Biblical Customs and **IV**: 318; **VII**: 166.
Dialect of **V**: 547.
esrêti-Women in **V**: 546.
Iterative Names in **VII**: 165.
Jacob and Laban in the Light of the **VI**: 79.
Kirkuk Docments Relating to Security Transactions **VII**: 165.
"Kirkuk" Documents **VII**: 165.
"Kirkuk" Documents, Date of **VII**: 165.
Legal Document from **VII**: 165*(2)*.
Nouns in **V**: 546.
Numerals in **I**: 431; **V**: 546.
Pre-Ḫurrian Texts **VII**: 166.
Pronoun in **V**: 546.
Slaves, Kirkuk documents relating to **VII**: 165.
Theft, Tablets Relating to **VII**: 165; **VIII**: 233.
Titennûttu Texts from **VII**: 166, 168.

Ny Carlsberg Glyptothek: **II**: *104*.
Ny-Swtḫ: **II**: 72.
Nymph(s):
Cult of, as Water-Deities among the Romans **V**: 267.
Nyneter: **II**: 72.
Statuette of **II**: 72.
Nysa Scythopolis: **II**: 455.

O

Oak Tree:
Abraham's, at Hebron **III**: 393; **VI**: 83.
Oannas:
Jonah and **IV**: 441.
Oannes:
Dagon and **V**: 173, 190.
Oasis: **II**: *264;* **III**: 43.
Baḥrēn, Libya **III**: 152.
Baḥria **III**: **43**, 102*(3), 515, 540, 550.*
El-A'reg, Libya **III**: 152.
Farafra **III**: 43*(3)*, **102**, *540, 550.*
Kadesh-Barnea **III**: 132, 133.
Kharga **III**: **140**, *569*
Nuwēmisah, Libya **III**: 152.
Siva **III**: 235.
Oaths: **I**: **§138, 509-516**; **IX**: **§138**, **ciii**.
Amen as an Oath Formula **I**: 515.
Aposiopesis in Hebrew Conditional **I**: 514; **V**: 498.
Babylonian Court, in **I**: 510.
Babylonian Inscriptions, in **I**: 510*(2)*.
Babylonian word *ni š*, for **I**: 510; **V**: 574; **VI**: 109; **VIII**: 117; **IX**: cxxxix.
Biblical **I**: 515.
By the gods **V**: 550, 618.
Concerning credit and debt **I**: 311, 515.
Cuneiform Inscriptions, in **I**: 510; **VII**: 251.
Egypt, in **I**: 511.
False **I**: 512.
Halakah and **I**: 515; **VI**: 695.
Hebrew Conditional **I**: 514.
Hebrew Particles
חַי and חֵי in **V**: 482.
Jewish and Muslim Laws, Relation between **I**: 511.
Neo-Assyrian Vassal, and Ezekiel **I**: 512.
Neo-Babylonian Vassal, and Ezekiel **I**: 512.
Nuzi, by Ordeal **I**: 499, 511.
Nuzi, of King at, in Legal Prodedure **I**: 511.
Nuzi, terminology of, by the gods **I**: 512.
Old Testament, in **I**: 510, 513.
Ordeal Signs, and **I**: 514*(2)*
Sumerian **VII**: 279.
Use of ראש in **IX**: ciii.
Obadiah, Book of: **IV**: *432, 434*.
Authenticity, Authorship, Date, and Sources of **IV**: **§362, 440**.
Exegetical Studies on **VI**: **§623, 388**.
Historical Situation in **IV**: *431*, 439.
Israel and Edom in **IV**: 439.
Literal and Free Translation of **IV**: 440, *448, 452*.
Literary Criticism of **IV**: **§361, 439-440**.
Structure of **IV**: 439; **V**: 704.
Unity of **IV**: 439.
Obadiah, Book of, Manuscripts of: **VI**: **(§624), 388**.
Obadiah, Person:
Message of **IV**: 440.
Seal of **III**: 640.
Obedience:
First test of, in Eden **IV**: 286*(2)*.
Sacrifice and **V**: 30; **VI**: 250.
'Obeid, Tell el: **I**: 327; **III**: 41, **189**, *272, 681, 730, 756;* **V**: 183; **VII**: *276;* **IX**: cxviii, cxix, cxx.

Pottery, from, compared with Egyptian **III**: 608.
Statuettes, from, compared with Egyptian **III**: 761.
Obeisance: **V**: 511.
Obelisks: **III**: **§190, 491-498**.
Assyrian, "Broken" Problem of the **III**: 497.
"Black", and the Moabite Stone **VII**: 112, 191.
Black, *see also:* ***Black Obelisk***
Broken, of Ashurakhbal **VII**: 182.
Constantinople, Part of Hatshapsôwet(?) **III**: 495.
Egyptian (with Texts) **VII**: **§830, 18-27**.
Hatshapsôwet, Part in Constantinople(?) **III**: 495.
Inscriptions on **V**: 362.
New York, Bronze Crab Inscription of **VII**: 313.
Problem of **III**: 495.
Rameses the Great, Removal of, to Cairo **III**: 494.
Oblation, *see:* **Offerings**
Obligations:
Babylonian Sworn **I**: 509.
Egyptian Sworn **I**: 509*(2)*.
Legal, in Israel **I**: 466.
Religious, in Israel **I**: 466.
Service, in Palestine **I**: 482, 487.
Supererogation and, in the Halakah **VI**: 695.
Oboda: **II**: *439*, 456; **III**: *18*.
Oboe: **I**: 244.
Obolos:
Aramaic Ostrakon from Nippur and the Greek **VII**: 123.
Mina and **I**: 447.
Obols: **I**: 439.
Oboth: **II**: 290.
Obsequies, *see:* **Funerals**
Obsidian: **I**: 285, 286, 287*(2)*, 293*(2)*, 342*(2)*.
Analysis of **I**: 287, 342; **II**: 222.
Core, (Tool?) **III**: 676.
Head of Ammenemes III **III**: 728.
Occult:
Science in the Temples of Ancient Egypt **V**: 201.
Occupations: **I**: 265, **§92, 269-272**, 387; **IX**: **§92, xc**.
Oceanic Islands:
Flood, Testimony of, to **IV**: 305..
Oceanic Languages:
Names for "God" in **IV**: 115.
Oded: **I**: 75; **VI**: 593*(2)*; **VIII**: 224.
Odeinon: **III**: 472.
Odes of Solomon: **I**: *368*; **VI**: 657*(2)*; **IX**: cl.
Apocalypse of Peter and **VI**: 717.
Biblical Targums and **VI**: 711.
Eprem's Hymns on Epiphany and **VI**: 720.
Jewish or Christian(?) **VI**: 671.
John, Gospel of, and **VIII**: 288.
Philo and **VI**: 674.
Pseudepigrapha and **VI**: 648.
Odysseus: **I**: *356*; **III**: *613*, 680,*743*; **V**: 250.
Etymology of the name **V**: 298.
Palace of **III**: 500*(3)*.
Sculpture of **III**: 743.
Odyssey:
Etruscan Grave Stele, Scenes from, on **III**: 728.
Homer's Writing of **V**: 258, 259.
Structural Unity of *Odyssey* Eight **VII**: 350.
Œdipus:
West African Religion, in **V**: 151.
Oenanthe: **II**: **72**, *101*.
Husbands of **II**: 7.
Oenochoë, *see:* **Pitcher**

Offerings, *see also:*
Altars, Sacrifices V: **§430, 56-64**.
Abraham's, of Isaac IV: 314*(2)*, 315*(3)*, 316*(3)*, 317*(2)*.
Babylonian Ritual V: 181.
Byblos, "Offering Deposits" V: 198.
Cakes, Sacrificial VI: 325*(2)*, 341*(2)*.
Ceremonial Payment V: 550.
Egypt, in V: 204.
Egyptian Doctrine of the Transformation of Funeral V: 204.
Egyptian, of Truth, in the Temple of Edfu VII: 38.
First Fruits, of V: 57; VI: 42.
Fish, in Mesopotamia V: 186.
Greek, Public Appropriations for Individual V: 249.
Guilt V: 64.
Guilt, of the Defiled Nazarite V: 64.
Hair V: 61.
Half-Shekel, in the DSS V: 63*(2)*.
Ka receiving V: 206.
Leaven in Mosaic V: 57.
Levitical V: 61.
Meal V: 434.
Ningal-Temple, Accounts conerning Allocation of Provisions for, at Ur V: 187.
Ningal-Temple at Ur, Accounts of Allocations VII: 263.
Oblation and Sacrifice V: 60.
Organization, Problems of V: 63.
Peace V: 59.
Phallic, to Hathor V: 210.
Poor, Ex-Votos of, Egypt V: 223.
Shekhar in Mosaic V: 57.
Sin V: 56, 58, 62, 64.
Tell Edrû, Tables of VII: 20.
Temple Gates, to, at Ur V: 198; IX: cxxxvii.
Thank, among the Greeks V: 251, 252.
Trespass V: 62.
Votive, to Venetic Goddess Rehtia V: 268.
Wave V: 63, 84, 89*(2)*; VI: 124.
World-Wide Pure VI: 415.

Officers: V: 511.

Officials:
Ay, of II: 6.
Egyptian, of the IV and V Dyanasties II: 4.
Royal, Egyptian II: 5.
Tut'ankhamūn, of II: 6, *24, 44, 60, 66*.

OFFORD, JOSEPH: III: *644;* VII: *207*.

Offspring:
Intermarriage, of I: 212.

Og: I: **76**, 337; IV: 353.
Bedstead (or Couch) of VI: 141.

OHNEFALSH-RICHTER, MAX:
Cypriote Texts discovered by VII: 356.

Oil: I: 267.
Anointing VI: 116*(3)*.
Castor, for Medical Purposes III: 405.
Essene Avoidance of VIII: 415.
Fish, Akkadian for (*ikuku*) V: 547.
Gazing Ceremonies, Modern Egyptian I: 388.
Olive, *see:* ***Olive Oil***
Palestine, in II: 381.
Sample of Liquid from a small jar V: 213.

Oinochoe, *see:* **Pitchers**

Okoumené: III: 350.

Öküzini:
Human Skeleton fround in III: 361.

Olbia:
Cyclic Poetry in VII: 348.
Egyptian Objects from III: *686, 762;* VII: 37, 65.

Old Age: I: 188.
Egyptian Word for "Old" V: 343.

Old Latin Versions *(of the Bible):* **IV**: **§252, 39-40**.
- Hieronymian Version **IV**: 39*(2)*.
- Lyons Codex of Joshua **V**: 176.
- Minor Prophets, of **VI**: 362*(5)*, 363.
- Somnium Neronis **IV**: 39.

Old Testament, *see also:* **Bible; Hebrew Bible, Hebrew Literature:** **I**: *387*.
- African Church, Message of, and **VIII**: 353*(2)*.
- Amen-em-ope' and **VII**: 11.
- American Albright School **IV**: 158.
- Animal Worship in **I**: 382.
- Animism in(?) **V**: 15.
- Anthropological Approach **IV**: 148.
- Antiquity of **IV**: 160, 162.
- Arabia and **III**: 18.
- Arabic Parallels to **VI**: 134.
- "Arabisms" in **IV**: 191, 192; **V**: 386.
- Aramaic, Written in(?) **IV**: 165.
- Aramaims in **V**: 525.
- Arrangement of **IV**: 101.
- Aryan Words in **V**: 387*(3)*.
- Assyrian Archaeology and **III**: 775; **IV**: 212.
- Assyriology and **II**: *222;* **III**: 775*(3);* **IV**: 182*(4)*, 183*(2);* **VI**: 89, 128.
- Astral-Mythology in **II**: 229.
- Astronomy, Primitive, and **II**: 228.
- ***Authenticity*** **IV**: **§279, 160-169**, 194*(2);* **VIII**: 23; **IX**: **§279, cxxix**.
- Authority of, *see also : **Historical Reliability*** **VIII**: 25‡, 28‡, **§971, 25-28**, 44*(2)*, 47, 278.
- ***Authorship*** **IV**: **§279, 160-169**; **V**: 695; **VIII**: 23, 45.
- Baba Bathra of the Talmud and **IV**: 119; **VI**: 698.
- Babylonian Archaeology and **III**: 775; **IV**: 212.
- Babylonian Palæography **IV**: 111, 182.
- Balance in **V**: 27.
- ***Bibliography*** **I**: **§2, 5-9**.
- Birds in **III**: 369, 370*(2)*.
- British Criticism of **IV**: 123.
- Bultmann's View of **IV**: 158.
- Canon, in, *see: **"Canon, Biblical"***
- Catanæ, Greek, on **VI**: 719.
- Character of, Distinctive **VIII**: 2.
- Character of, Inferred from Its Versions **IV**: 165.
- Christ's Authority and **IV**: 162.
- Christian and Islamic Approaches to, Comparison of **V**: 151.
- Christian Attitude toward **IV**: 120.
- Christian Church and / in **IV**: 122, 130, 149, 152, 157; **VIII**: 25, 351.
- Christian Criticism of **IV**: 96, 157; **VIII**: 300.
- Christian Faith, Place in **IV**: 155.
- Christian Scripture, as **VIII**: 25.
- Christian Theology of **VIII**: 6.
- Christian Use of **IV**: 144, 167.
- Christianity and **IV**: 29, 33, 162; **VIII**: 299.
- Chronology of **II**: 178*(2)*, 180, 182, 183, 185, 186, 188*(2)*.
- Church and **IV**: 103, 130, 141, 156, 157, 168, 233; **VIII**: 191, 192.
- Church and State, according to the **IX**: c.
- Church, Early, in **IV**: 151; **VIII**: **§1051, 299-301**.
- Church in **V**: 28.
- Civic Value of **VIII**: 351.
- Civilization, Attitude toward **I**: 124.

College, Teaching the, in **VIII**: 399*(2)*, 401, 402*(2)*, 403.
Commentaries, Medieval, on **VI**: 726.
Compilation in Structure of Books **IV**: 161.
Composite Writings of **IV**: 164.
Computers and **IV**: 159.
Conflict Over **IV**: 145.
Constructive Value of **IV**: 144.
Contraditions, Alleged, in **IV**: 160.
Coptic Terms and **IV**: 192; **V**: 368.
Credibility **IV**: 161.
Critical Studies **IV**: **(§232), 1**.
Critical Study, and "Historical" Traditions in **I**: 133; **V**: 26.
Criticism, Present State of **IV**: 144, 145.
Cultural Value of **IV**: 149; **VIII**: 351.
Cuneiform, Early OT Books written in(?) **IV**: 164, 165.
Cuneiform Parallels to **VII**: 134.
Current Studies on **IV**: 158.
Damian, Peter, Attitude Toward **IV**: 158; **VIII**: 338.
Date **IV**: **§279, 160-169**.
Diction, Hebrew, as Evidence of Dates of **IV**: 166.
Divine-Human Conflicts in **IV**: 137, 510; **VI**: 82, 101.
Driver's *Introduction to* **IV**: 122, 123*(4)*, 127.
Egyptian Ideas and OT Thought **V**: 217; **IX**: cxxx.
Egyptian Loanwords in **IV**: 190; **V**: 309.
Elephantine Papyri and **IV**: 190, 191, 192*(2)*; **VII**: 133, 134, 135.
Emperor-Worship in **V**: 272.
Errors in **IV**: 161*(2)*, 162, 164, 168, 169.
Ethics, Hebrew, as Evidence of Dates of **IV**: 161; **VIII**: 219.
Evaluations **IV**: 151.
Evangelist of **V**: 8.
Exegetical Studies - General Studies **VI**: **§575, 1-2**.
Faith in **VIII**: 9.
Feminine Element in **IV**: 168.
Folk-Lore / Tales in **IV**: 174, 175.
Foreign Words in, Text **V**: 392.
France, Recent work **IV**: 152.
God, Author of **IV**: 167.
Greek Criticism of **IV**: 96; **VIII**: 300.
Greek Versions of, *see:* ***Septuagint***
Haper, William Rainey and **IV**: 133.
Hebrew Diction, as Evidence of Dates of **IV**: 166.
Hebrew Ethics as Evidence of Dates of **IV**: 161; **VIII**: 219.
Hebrew Literature, as **IV**: 148.
Hebrew, Written in(?) **IV**: 165*(2)*
Hellenistic Mystery Religion and **V**: 254.
Historical Method in the Study of **IV**: 145; **VIII**: 395.
Historical Narratives and Pre-Islamic Arabic Traditions **IV**: 193.
Historical Reliability of, *see also:* ***Authority of*** **IV**: 160, **§291, 194-199**; **V**:*79;* **VI**: 2; **VIII**: 23; **IX**: **§291, cxxx**.
"Historical" Traditions in, and Critical Study **I**: 133; **V**: 26.
Historical Trustworthiness **IV**: 190.
Historical Writings **IV**: 174.
Historicity of **II**: *112, 253, 282;* **IV**: 166, 167, 169, 195, 196, 197.
History **I**: 128*(3)*, 129, 131, 132, 135; **IV**: 167, 169; **VIII**: 9.
History and Word of God in **IV**: 153.
History, Secular, Emphasis of OT on **VI**: 240.

History Writing in	**IV**: 166*(2)*, 176; **IX**: lxxxiii.
Hittite Law and	**I**: 506.
Hittite Mythology and	**V**: 227.
Homer and	**V**: 138.
Human Element in	**IV**: 162, 163, 168*(2)*; **VIII**: 39.
Indian Theological Education, Place in	**VIII**: 405, 407.
Inerrancy, *see: **Scripture, Inerrancy of***	
Infallibility of	**IV**: 160, 161; **VIII**: 38*(2)*.
Inspiration of	**IV**: 162.
Introductions, Trends in	**IV**: 152.
Islamic and Christian Approaches to, Comparison of	**V**: 151.
Jesus and / in	**IV**: 162, 169; **VIII**: 126, 282.
Jewish Thought and Life, in	**I**: 392.
Jews and	**IV**: 175; **VIII**: 332*(2)*.
Jews, Controversy with, in	**VIII**: 336.
Language and Script of Earlier OT Books	**IV**: 164.
Language of	**IV: §279, 160-169.**
Languages, Knowedge, of, in the	**V**: 280.
Liberal View of	**IV**: 123.
Literary Criticism of	**V**: 471.
Literary Evolution of	**IV**: 174.
Literary Forms Used in	**IV**: 215.
"Lost Books" Quoted in	**IV**: 177*(2)*
Mari and	**III**: 158.
Mediterranean Factor in	**I**: 334.
Messianic Element in	**V**: 125.
Metallurgy in	**I**: 291, 300.
Modern Criticism, before	**IV**: 138.
Mowinkel, and	**IV**: 158.
Muhammad's Knowldge of	**VIII**: 368.
Mythology and	**V: §461, 134-137.**
Names applied to	**IV**: 160.
Negative Criticism of	**IV**: 124.
Negative Internal Evidence	**IV**: 160.
Netherlands, Twenty-five Years of Study on	**IV**: 157.
New Testament and	**V**: 7.
New Testament and the authorship of OT	**IV**: 161*(2)*.
New Testament use of	**VIII**: 45, **§1040, 270- 278.**
Norwegians and	**IV**: 131.
Numerical System of	**VIII**: 309.
Origin of	**IV: §282, 173-177.**
Other Oriental Wisdom and	**V**: 116, 147.
Pattern theory in	**I**: 337; **IV**: 159.
Permanent Value of	**IV**: 150.
Philology and	**IV**: 165; **V**: 278, 387.
Philosophy in(?)	**V**: 112.
Philosophy of	**V**: 112.
Pottery, and	**III**: 630, 639.
Pottery Vessels of	**III**: 617, 619.
Practical Value of, Literature	**IV**: 141.
Pre-Eminence of	**VI**: 596.
Priestly Element in	**IV**: 252*(10)*, 253*(3)*.
Problems, in Light of Recent Archaeological Discoveries	**IV**: 216.
Problems, Living, of, Interview with Scholars	**IV**: 132.
Prose Fiction Relating to	**VIII**: 365.
Pseudonymity	**IV**: 168.
Pulpit and	**IV**: 132.
Rabbinic Approach to	**IV**: 153; **VI**: 716.
Ras Shamra and	**IV**: 84, 188, 193; **VII**: 140, 145.
Reality in	**V**: 28.
Redactors of the	**IV**: 254.
Reformation Perspective, Modern Problem	**IV**: 159.
Relevence for Today	**VIII**: 352.

Religion of, *see:* ***Israelite Religion***
Religion of the Near East and **I**: 392; **V**: 37.
Religious Controversy in **V**: 15.
Religious Ideas of **V**: 7.
Religious Philosophers in **V**: 112.
Religious Value of **IV**: 132, 149.
Research, Fifty Years of **IV**: 139, 158.
Research in, 1914-1925 **I**: 144.
Restoration Movement, in **IV**: 158, 159*(3)*.
Scandinavian Contributions **IV**: 154.
Scientific enquiry of **IV**: 129, 145.
Scientific study of **IV**: 140.
Semantics and **V**: 279.
Sources, "Lost Books" Quoted in **IV**: 177*(2)*.
Sources, non-Inspired and **IV**: 176.
Sources of **IV**: **§282, 173-177**, 251*(2)*; **V**: 697.
Spinoza and **IV**: 124.
Spirit of **V**: 6.
"Story" in the **V**: 701.
Structure of **IV**: 161.
Study, Methodology of **IV**: 156.
Study, Proportion and Method in **VIII**: 391.
Study, Tendencies of **IV**: 133.
Studying, Methods of **VIII**: **§1065, 387-397**.
Style as factor in Authorship of **IV**: 163.
Stylistic Patterns in, and Ugaritic Literature **V**: 537, 700; **VII**: 145.
Symbolic Language in **IV**: 215.
Tannaitic Literature and **VI**: 702.
Theological Seminaries, in **IV**: 124.
Theological Univeralism, in **V**: 23.
Theological Use of **VIII**: 2.
Translating, Impossibility **IV**: 112.
Translatinon Problems, *see:* ***Translation Problems***
Transmission of **IV**: **§282, 173-177**.
Trends and Issues **IV**: 156.
Twentieth Century View **IV**: 123.
Ugaritic Literary Parallels **IV**: 188.
Ugaritic Poetic Style and **V**: 533, 688.
Unity of **IV**: **§280, 169**, 177.
Value of, for Our Day **IV**: 150.
Versions - General Studies **IV**: **§244, 24**, 165.
Vision and Wisdom in **V**: 116.
Vitality of **IV**: 158, 176.
Wisdom, Concept in Canonical **V**: 118.
Wisdom, Other Oriental and **V**: 116.
Word of God in **IV**: 153.

Old Testament Backgrounds, General Studies: **IV**: **§285, 178-180**.
Aramaic Inscription of Biblical Interest **VII**: 123.
Assyrian and Babylonian **IV**: **§286, 181-184**, 194; **VI**: 480; **VII**: 159*(2)*.
Canaanite, including Ugaritic **IV**: **§288, 186-188**; **V**: 535; **VI**: 490; **VII**: 142, 143.
Egyptian **IV**: **§289, 189-190**, 194; **VI**: 513; **IX**: **§289, cxxx**.
Egyptian, Egyptology as Ancient Commentary **III**: 779.
Other Backgounds - Unclassified **IV**: **§290, 191-193**.
Ramesside Parallel to 1 Kings 2:33, 44-45 **VI**: 220.

Old Testament Chronology, *see:* **Biblical Chronology**

OT Criticism, *see also:* **Higher Criticism; Literary Criticism**
Alleged Reaction **IV**: 145.
Divine Elemens in **VIII**: 39.
Elephantine Papyri and **IV**: 191; **VII**: 133.

Old Testament Persons - Aphabetical Listing: I: **§45, 26-82**; **IX**: **§45, lxxxi-lxxxii**.

Old Testament Society in Berlin: **III**: 448.

Old Testament - Teaching the: **VIII**: **§1067, 398-407**.
Adult Bible Class and Modern Biblical Scholarship **VIII**: 399.
Blackboard, Use of, in **VIII**: 400.
Costumes, Objects and Models in **VIII**: 403.
Dead Sea Scrolls and, to Undergraduates **VIII**: 406.
Genesis 1-11, Seminary Scripture Course **VI**: 17.
Haggadah in Jewish Bible Study **VI**: 697.
Mime, Use of, in **VIII**: 405.
Minsterial, and the Hebrew Scriptures **VIII**: 400.
Oral Method of **VIII**: 401.
Temple Model as Visual Aid in **VIII**: 406.
Undergraduates, to, and the Dead Sea Scrolls **VIII**: 408.
Visual Aids in **VIII**: 404.
Wartburg Seminary, OT Dept., Responsibilities **VIII**: 404.
Archaeology, Contribution of, to **IV**: 223; **VIII**: 8.
Biblical Criticism and **VIII**: 6.
Death and Rebirth of **VIII**: 4.
Eichrodt, Walther, on **VIII**: 12.

Old Testament Theology *see also:* **Theology - General Studies** **VIII**: 1, 2*(3)*, 3*(4)*, 4, 5*(2)*, 6‡, 7*(6)*, 8*(4)*, 9*(4)*.
Hebrew Religion, History of, and **V**: 23; **VIII**: 5.
Heilsgeschichte, as **VIII**: 8.
History of **VIII**: 4, 6.
History of Relgion and **VIII**: 6.
Israel, History of, and **VIII**: 6.
Jacob, Edwmond, on **VIII**: 12.
Knight, G. A. F., Christian Theology of the Old Testament **VIII**: 12.
Kurtz, Johann Heinrich, on the History of the Old Covemant **VIII**: 2.
Minsterial Training, in **VIII**: 407.
Missons and **VIII**: 8.
Nature and Function of **VIII**: 5.
Present Ills of, and Their Remedy **VIII**: 4.
Prolegomena to **VIII**: 6.
Reviving **VIII**: 5.
Rowley, H. H., on **VIII**: 5.
Schultz, Helmann, on **VIII**: 2.
Semantics and **VIII**: 5.
Trends in **VIII**: 6.
Von Rad, Gerhard, on **VIII**: 7, 12.
Vriezen, V. Th. C., of **VIII**: 12.
Wisdom Literature and **V**: 117; **VIII**: 6.
Wisdom, Place and Limit of, in **V**: 119; **VIII**: 8.

Oligarchy: **IX**: cii.

Olive(s): **IX**: cxxii.

"Olive Land": **II**: 266; **V**: 335.

Olive Oil: **I**: 254, 266.

Olives, Mount of: **II**: 297, 405, 407, **456**; **VI**: 413.
GreekInscription at **VII**: 314.
Josephus' Jewish Wars, V, 12, 2, in **VI**: 682.
Phoenician Inscription at **VII**: 116.
Temple and **V**: 68.
Topography of **II**: 456.

OLIVIER, GUILLAUME ANTOINE: **III**: 435.

Olivine: **I**: 280, 290; **III**: 460, 562.

Oltos: **II**: 72; **III**: 711.

Olympia: **I**: 237*(2)*, 238; **III**: 113, **189-190**, *741*.
Olympiads: **II**: 200.
Olympus:
Gods of, How Many(?) **V**: 248.
Olynthos (Olynthus): **I**: *206(2)*; **III**: *159*, **190**, *225*, 691.
Cemeteries at **III**: 190.
Deed of Sale at **VII**: 339.
Greek Inscriptions from **VII**: 322, 323.
Houses, Block of, at **I**: *444*; **III**: 190.
Villa of Good Fortune at **III**: 490.
Om Harb, Tell: **III**: 191.
Oman: **I**: *285*, 338; **III**: 190.
Gulf Coast of **III**: 197.
Omar, Caliph: **I**: 235.
Omar Khayyám:
Qoheleth and **IV**: 513.
Omar, Tell, *see also:* **Opis; Tell 'Umar** **III**: 191.
Omen Texts *(See also Specific Languages)*
Akkadian, Anatomical Nomencalture in **III**: 402; **VII**: 156.
Assyrian (K.45) **V**: 563.
Babylonian, Expressed in Numbers **VII**: 264.
Hittite Parallel to an Old Babylonian Omen Text **VII**: 264, 309.
Nuzi, from **VII**: 165.
Omens: **V**: 134.
Astronomy and **II**: 223, 231.
Babylonian Dog, and Talmudic and Later Jewish Parallels **V**: 146; **VI**: 701.
Omer: **I**: 422.
Omnipotence, Omniscience, Omnipresence, *see:* **Studies on the Nature of God**
Omoroka: **V**: 180.
Omphalos: **III**: 577; **V**: 214.
Napata, from **V**: 207.
Omri: **I**: 95.
Chronological Data on the Dynasty of **VI**: 231.
Dynasty of, Conditions under the **IV**: 379.
House of, Deuteronimic Presentation of **IV**: 381.
Israel and Judah during the Dynasty of **VIII**: 389.
Omride Wars:
Elisha Cycle and **IV**: 380.
Omrides: **VI**: 231*(2)*.
On, *see also:* **Heliopolis:** **III**: 119, **191**; **V**: 106; **VII**: *84*.
"On Every High Hill and Under Every Green Tree" **V**: 520.
"On the Head of": **V**: 520.
Onager: **III**: 367.
Onan: **VI**: 86.
Onchsheshonqy:
Hesiod and the Instructions of **VII**: 12, 347.
Instructions of **VII**: 11.
Instructions of, and Biblical Wisdom **VII**: 12.
One:
Numeral, origin of **I**: 434.
Oneiros: **VIII**: 360.
Onesimos: **III**: *633*.
Onias, *see also:* **Honi** **III**: **191**; **VI**: 411.
Temple of **I**: 141.
Onias III: **VI**: 641.
Death of **II**: 72.
Onion:
Hittite word for **III**: *393*.
Onkhef:
Stele of **VII**: 21.
Onkhsheshonqy:
Instructions of and Biblical Wisdom **V**: 118.
Instructions of, Cairo text **VII**: 11.
Onomasticon: **II**: 264, 268.
Onomatology and Tekonymy, *see also:* **Names** **IV**: 373; **V**: **§488, 291-304**; **IX**: **§488, cxxxviii**.
Akkadian **V**: 548.

Amorite Names **IX**: cxxxviii.
Amurrite Names in Ur III and Early Isin Texts **VII**: 215.
Anatolia, Proper Names at showing Lingustic Continuity **III**: 12.
Antediluvian Patriarchs, Names Translated **IV**: 298.
Assyria, Origin of Name **III**: 26.
Babylon **III**: 36.
Biblical Proper Names from External Sources **II**: 263.
Cerates in Royal Names **V**: 299.
Coan Inscriptions, Names found on **V**: 249.
Coptic Names **V**: 291.
Damascus, Origin of **III**: 74.
Egyptian Names in Genesis **II**: 264; **IV**: 265.
Egyptian, royal nomen and prenomen, meaning **V**: 366.
Giving of Proper Names in the OT **I**: 212.
Graeco-Egyptian Names **V**: 291.
Hebrew Kings, Egyptian Element in, and bearing on the Exodus **IV**: 332; **V**: 291.
Hittite, Egyptian Transliteration of **V**: 308, 605.
Hittite Personal Names **V**: 604.
"Hittite" Proper Names **V**: 566, 605.
Indo-Iranian Names in Cuneiform Inscriptions **VII**: 148.
Jersualem, Name **II**: 410.
"Kanishite", Suffixes in Proper Names **V**: 551.
Malta, Personal Names in **V**: 297; **IX**: cxiii.
Mitannian Personal Names **V**: 604.
Name-Giving in Hittite **I**: 213.
Orthography of Royal Names of Assyrian and Babylonian History **V**: 553.
Personal Names among Modern Palestinians **I**: 385.
Prophetic Names **V**: 291.
Roman, Origin and Meaning of **V**: 291.
Royal Names and Families (Egyptian) **II**: *4*.
Sabaean Onomastic Lists **VII**: 297.
Scripture Names, Transmission of **V**: 291; **VI**: 2.
Scripture Proper Names, Signification **V**: 291.
Sumerian Proper Names, Religious Conceptions Underlying **V**: 179.
Temple-Overseers, Names **VII**: 219.

Onqelos Manuscript:
Pentateuch, of, with Babylonian Vocalization **VI**: 14.

Ontology: *see also:* **God, Ontological Argument** **VIII**: 87*(2)*.

Onyx: **I**: 285; **VI**: 33.

Ophel: **I**: *417, 426, 444;* **II**: 292, 350, 412, *448,* **456-457**, *500*.
Cult-Objects from **V**: 106; **IX**: cxxiv.
Inscribed Hebrew Objects from **VII**: 91.
Ostracon **VII**: 93.
Seal found on **III**: 642*(2)*.
Sepulcher of David at **III**: 535, 541.

Ophir: **I**: 338*(2);* **II**: 457; **III**: **191- 192**.

Ophrah:
Gideon's Wine-press at **IV**: 366.

Ophthalmias: **III**: 402.

Opis, *see also:* **Tell Omar, Tell 'Umar** **III**: **192**, *235*.

Opisthodomos: **III**: 483*(2)*.

Opous: **III**: 192.

OPPERT, JULIUS: **VI**: 699; **VII**: 205.
Bibliography of **I**: 21.

Optical Illusion:
Khorsabad, at **III**: 698.

Oracle(s): **VI**: 286.
Alas-Oracles of the Eighth Century Prophets **IV**: 389.
Can God "Speak" **VIII**: 96.
David, of **VI**: 191.

Delphic — V: 253, 255, 261, 265, 273.
Dumah, of — VI: 280.
Egyptian Texts — **VII: §839, 40-41.**
Foreign Nations, Against — V: 700; VIII: 248.
Kôm el-Wist, at — III: 578.
Old Testament, in — V: 698; VIII: 243.
Patriarchal Traditions and "Oracle of Salvation" — IV: 177; V: 700.
Woe-Oracles of the Prophets — IV: 389.
"Oracle of Yahweh": V: 520.
Oral Tradition: **IV: §282, 173-177.**
Dialects and, Methology for Evaluating — V: 280.
Exegesis, Influence on — IV: 88, 176.
Hexateuch and — IV: 174*(4)*, 253*(3)*.
Libraries and — IV: 174*(4)*, 253*(3)*.
Literary Criticism and — IV: 155, 176.
Scandinavian School — IV: 158.
Uppsala School and — IV: 153, 176.
Written Language among the Hebrews and, in the Light of Arabic — IV: 176; V: 699.
Written Transmission and — IV: 176, 177.
Orators:
Attic — I: *465*.
Poetry Used to Train Ancient — VII: 2.
Prophets as — I: 102, 110.
Oratory:
Greek, Legal — I: 495.
Orbo, *see:* **Oreb**
Orchards: I: 253.
Taxation of, in the Zenon Papyri — I: 481; VII: 339.
Orchestra:
Greek, Form and Evolution — III: 476.
"Ordain a Lamp": V: 520.
Ordeal(s):
Incense in the Ancient Orient — V: 106.
Oath by, at Nuzi — I: 499, 511.
Poison in the Ancient Orient — V: 106; IX: lxxxvi.
Signs, and Oath — I: 514*(2)*.
Trial by — I: *181(2)*, 463, 466; VI: 127*(2)*, 128.
Ordinances (4QOrd): **VIII: §1135, 469.**
Ordination:
Christian — I: 366, 367.
Jewish — I: 366, 367; V: 42.
Ore:
Palestine, found in Eastern — II: 248*(2)*.
Oreb, Orbo, Rock: II: 290.
'Oreimeh, Tell el-: III: 423.
ORELLI, CONRAD:
Prophecy, on — VIII: 237.
Oresteia: I: 481.
Organ: I: 243, 245.
Orgeones: V: 259.
Orichalch: I: 299.
Orient: I: 330, *338*.
Language, Structure of, of the Ancient — V: 279.
Roman — I: 329.
Oriental: V: 511.
Word Study — V: 511.
Oriental Exploration Fund: III: 449.
Oriental Institute (Chicago) Museum: I: *283;* III: 418, 449*(3)*, 450*(2)*, *741;* IV: *218;* VII: *40*.
Oriental Resreach: III: 411.
Orientalia:
Bibliography — I: 3*(2)*.
Orientalism:
Plato, of — V: 246.
Orientation:
Babylonian — II: 229.
Origen: IV: 33*(2)*, **§250, 38**, 95; VI: 721; **IX: §250, cxxix.**

Adultery, Punishment of, in Jewish Law, and **I**: 219; **VI**: 723.
Esdras A and B, and the Hexapla and Tetrapla of **VI**: 601, 719.
Evaluation of Textual Variants in the Greek Bible by **IX**: cxxix*(2)*.
Hebrew Names, Interpretation of, in **V**: 302; **VI**: 722.
Hermeneutics of **IV**: 94.
Letter of Julius Africanus on the Story of Susanna to **VI**: 626, 721.
Martyrdom, Exortation to, and IV Maccabees **VI**: 656, 668, 720.
Scripture, Interpretation of, from his *Philocalia* **VI**: 721.
Second Column of **IV**: 38*(2)*.
Secunda, and Samaritan Hebrew **V**: 390, 529; **VI**: 725.

Origin of Species: **III**: 286*(8)*, 290, 292, 303, 318*(2)*, 328*(2)*, 337; **IX**: cxxi.

Origines Biblicæ: **I**: 127.

Origins:
Concept of **V**: 151.
Great Problem of **VIII**: 77.
Miracles and the Study of **VIII**: 94.
Stories of **VI**: 16.

Orion: **VI**: 439.
Great Star and **II**: 230.
Myth of, and the Canaanite Story of Aqhart **V**: 149.

ORLINSKY, HARRY: **VIII**: 477.

Ormidhia: **III**: *623*.

Ornament(s): **I**: 276, 281, 287; **III**: 703.
Assyrian Throne **III**: 743.
Egyptian **III**: 701.
Lotus, Evolution of **III**: 695.
Lotus, on Cypriote Vases **III**: 707.
Modern Palestinian **I**: 387.
Mount Horeb, from **VI**: 117.
Shoulder, (Hair Whirl) of Lions **III**: 700*(5)*.

Oroanda: **III**: 258.

Orontes River: **III**: 192.

Orontes Valley:
Middle Pleistocene mammals from **III**: 367*(2)*.

Orontids: **II**: 72.

Oroomiah: **III**: *180, 440;* **V**: *529*.

Oropus: **III**: 55*(2)*, **192-193**.

Orotalt / Obotalt / Obdat and Alilat: **V**: 154.

Orpah: **I**: 76.

Orphans: **I**: 199, 504.
Wisdom Literature and ANE Legal Literature, in **I**: 192; **VII**: 2.

Orpheus:
Eurydice and, Myth of **V**: 266.
Synagogue of Dura-Europos, in **III**: 526*(2)*.

Orphism: **V**: 256, 258.
Origins of **V**: 253.

ORR, JAMES: **IV**: 134, 135, 136, 137.

Orthodox Church:
Psalter in **VIII**: 386.

Orthodoxy:
Jewish **V**: 6*(2)*.

Orthogenesis: **III**: 330, 331.

Orthography:
Dead Sea Scrolls **VIII**: 429.
Egyptian Syllabic **V**: 309.
Hebrew, Quiescents (Vowel- Letters) in Ancient **V**: 476.
Isaiah Scroll from Qumran **VIII**: 445.
Masoretic Text and the Qumran Scrolls **IV**: 16.
Masoretic Text of the Pentateuch **IV**: 5.
Royal Names of Assyrian and Babylonian History **V**: 291.
Syriac Ittafal **V**: 377.

Orthography - Hebrew: **V**: **§511, 479-481**.
Arad Ostraca, of **VII**: 97.

Orvieto:
- Black-Figured Amphoræ from — **III**: 606, 707.
- Bowls, Covered, from — **III**: 606.
- Sarcophagus of Torre San Savero in — **III**: 543.
- Vase, Attic, from — **III**: 605, 607.

OSBORN, HENRY FAIRFIELD: **III**: 311.

OSBORN, HENRY STAFFORD: **II**: 282.

Osheh: **II**: 284.

Osimandya:
- Sarcophagus of — **III**: 530.

Osiris: **V**: 146, 202*(2)*, 210, 216, 220, 321.
- Arsenuphis (Nubian God) as — **V**: 205, 237.
- Cult of — **V**: 216.
- D̲D-Emblem of — **V**: 208.
- Fertility-Rite and — **V**: 215.
- "Flail" of — **I**: 482.
- Hymn to — **VII**: 43, 46.
- Idols of, in the Bible — **V**: 216.
- *'Iti* Stela of, at Saqqara — **VII**: 25.
- King, Ancient, Deified(?) — **V**: 220.
- Legend of — **V**: 206.
- Marduk and — **V**: 148, 185, 213.
- Marduk's Relation to, and Ashur — **V**: 146, 182, 209.
- Name — **V**: 293, 296.
- Origin of — **V**: 212.
- Osirids — **V**: 200.
- Pillar and Tree, in — **V**: 211.
- Prayer to — **VII**: 42.
- Rites of — **V**: 214*(2)*.
- "Scourge" of — **I**: 482.
- Statue of, made for Ankhefenamun — **III**: 741; **VII**: 69.
- Tammuz and — **V**: 146, 179, 207.
- Temple of, at Abydos — **III**: 522.
- Tomb of — **III**: 535, 542.
- Tree and Pillar, in — **V**: 211.
- Unnefer, Myth of — **V**: 201*(2)*.

Osor-ur:
- Libation Vase of — **III**: 574.

Osorkon I: **I**: *412*.
- Bronze Statuette of — **III**: 759

Osorkon II:
- Inscriptions on the Statue of — **VII**: 71.
- Sed-Festival, of, Date of — **V**: 223.
- Statue of — **III**: 747; **IX**: cv.

Ossuaries, Ossuary: **III**: *556*.
- Chalcolithic — **III**: 558.
- Hebrew, from Kedron Valley with Graffiti — **III**: 545.
- Hebrew, Inscribed — **VII**: 92.
- Jerusalem, from — **VII**: 90.
- Jewish, Inscribed — **III**: 576; **VII**: 89, 91*(3)*.
- Jewish, Jerusalem's Tomb Monuments — **III**: 560.
- Kidron Valley, Inscribed — **III**: 557.
- Leaden — **III**: 545.

Ostia: **III**: **193**, *476*.
- *Domus* of Cupid and Psyche in — **III**: 521.
- Monument of the *Lares Augusti* in the Forum of — **III**: 498.

Ostraca, *see also:* **Papyri and, (as Materials of Textual Criticsm)**
- A1/382 from Hazor — **I**: 342.
- Aramaic — **II**: *2, 87, 85, 185, 197*.
- Astrological — **II**: 234‡.
- Astronomical — **II**: 234‡.
- Domestic cock, Earliest Drawing of, on — **III**: *372*, 709.
- Egyptian, Semitic Loan Words in — **V**: 366.
- Greek, in America — **VII**: 316.
- Greek Mathematical — **I**: 435.
- Greek, Sambathis — **VII**: 325.
- Greek, *see also:* ***Greek Inscriptions,Texts***
- Hebrew with Hieratic Numerals — **I**: 426, 435.
- Ophel — **VII**: 93, *98, 104*.
- Preservation of — **III**: 456, 457.
- Samaria — **I**: *308, 426, 492;* **II**: *272*.

Ostracism: **I**: 508*(3)*.
Ostracon:
Coptic, metioning Iēb **VII**: 83.
Coptic, Metron 1 **VII**: 83.
Samaria, C-1101 **VII**: 93.
Ostrich: **III**: 379, 589; **V**: 511.
Assyrian, "Horsebird" **III**: 379; **V**: 561.
Egg with Decoration **III**: 379, 589.
Egg-Shell Cups from Mesopotamia **III**: 379, 589.
Egyptian Word for *(nau* or *nenau)* **V**: 320, 360.
Hebrew Names for **III**: 379.
Job, in **VI**: 439.
Otago Museum: **III**: *676*.
Othniel: **VI**: 177.
Ottoman Empire:
Travels, Modern, in **III**: 435.
OUSELEY, WILLIAM, SIR: **III**: 436.
Outward: **VIII**: 173.
Ovens: **I**: 266, 270.
Grain Preparation, for **I**: 252; **III**: 571.
Image of in Hosea **VI**: 368.
Ovens, The:
Xerxes' Fleet at **II**: 108.
Overflow:
Egyptian Word for **V**: 325.
Semitc Word for **V**: 325.
Overseer:
Egyptian word for **V**: 348*(2)*, 358.
Ovid:
Genesis 18-19 and **VI**: 69.
Metamorphoses and Genesis, Coincidendes **IV**: 273.
Owl: **III**: 379*(2)*.
Coins, on **I**: 449, 457.
Dance of, Significiance in Greek Religion and Drama **V**: 258.
Ox, Oxen:
Goring **I**: xvii, n15; 466, 470, 500, 505.
Graves of, in Egypt **III**: 379, 545.
Hittite Use of Ox Head to Scare Away Evil **V**: 225.
Hunchbacked, in Syrian Art **III**: 379, 696.
Oxford Sterotype Bible: **IV**: 50*(3)*.
Oxus: **III**: 6.
Oxyrhynchus: **III**: *45, 157*.
Library of a Greek at **I**: 236.
Oxyrhynchus Papyri: **I**: *220, 236;* **VII**: 351*(5)*
Apocalypse of Baruch in **VI**: 643.
Hebrew **VII**: 94.
Hebrew, in the British Museum **VII**: 105.
Homer in **VII**: 349, 351.
Kanarese Speeches in **VII**: 353.
Pentateuchal Criticism and **IV**: 231.
Philo's Exegesis and **VI**: 678.
Public Office, Avoidance of, in, and Talmudic Sources **VI**: 704; **VII**: 342.

P

Pa-shedu:
Tomb of **III**: 537.
pꜣ-ꜥhꜣty:
Stela of **VII**: 25.
Pa-Ramessu:
Sarcophagus of **II**: **72**, *92;* **III**: 544.
Pa-suten-se:
Shrine of the Scribe **VII**: 59.
Pabēsi: **III**: *769;* **V**: 224.
Pachomius:
Name **V**: 294.
Pacifism: **VIII**: 233.
Passover and Non-Violence **V**: 88.
Pre-Exilic Prophets and **IV**: 388; **VIII**: 233.
Paestrum: **III**: **193**.
Temple of Poseidon at **III**: 517.
Paestum:
Painted Tomb at **III**: 556.
Paganism: **V**: 237.
Books of and Bible compared **V**: 681.

Evil, Idea of the Nature of, in **V**: 140.
Evil, Idea of the Origin of, in **V**: 140.
Faith of **III**: 410; **V**: 140; **VII**: *1*.
Literature of **III**: 410*(2)*; **V**: 140*(2)*; **VII**: 1, 8.
Literature of, in Relation to Faith **III**: 410; **V**: 140; **VII**: 1.
Monotheism of **V**: 32.
Popular Relgion, Graeco-Roman Egypt - Pagan Period **V**: 27.
Psychological Background of Late Greek **V**: 260.
Redemption, Idea of, in **V**: 140.
Roman, Transformation of **V**: 268.

Pagans:
Anti-Semitism and **I**: *187*; **VIII**: 327.

Pagasæ: **III**: 193.

Paheri:
Banquet of **V**: 203.

Pahlavi Texts: **VII**: 374*(4)*.
Biblical Influence in Turfan Pahlavi Fragment M. 173. **VIII**: 368.

Pain, *see:* **Suffering**

Paint:
Reattachment of Flaking **III**: 457.

Paint-Grinder:
Superintendent of King Bener-mert **II**: 26.

Painter(s):
Agros, and Dancing Pan **III**: 715.
Ampersand **III**: 715.
Band-Cup **III**: 715.
Bonn **III**: 712.
Christie **III**: 711.
Comar **III**: 712.
Corinthian Chimaera **III**: 715.
Dionysios **III**: 717.
Geras **III**: 710, 712.
Kleitias **III**: 716.
Lekythoi, Red-Figured **III**: 629, 715.
Medallion **III**: 628, 715.
Menon as, Psiax **III**: 711.
Nikoxenos **III**: 716.
Niobid **III**: 716.
Panaitios **III**: 716.
Panaitios, Love Scene by **III**: 634, 718.
Pisticci **III**: 621.
Polyphemos **III**: 714.
Populonia **III**: 717.
Protome Vase **III**: 714.
Psiax as Menon **III**: 711.
Sphinx **III**: 717.
Stamnoi **I**: 188; **IX**: lxxxv.
Woman Eros **III**: 715.

Painting(s), *see also:* **Mural(s)** **III: §225, 707-719; IX: §225, cxxvi-cxxvii.**
Alexandria, Tomb Paintings from the Necropolis of **III**: 717.
Chapel of Atet at Mēdūm **III**: 711.
Color Samples Scraped from Monuments **III**: 707.
Dirâʿ Abu'l Negâ, Unusual Tomb Scene from **III**: 709.
Dura-Europos Synagogue **III**: 524*(4)*, 525*(2)*, 715, 718; **VIII**: 356, 357.
Egyptian, Middle Kingdom at Bersheh **III**: 714.
(Egyptian) Wall Ornament **III**: 713.
Etruscan, in the Tomb of Hunting and Fishing at Tarquinii **III**: 717.
Etruscan Tomb, Chronology of, Campana Tomb at Veii **III**: 718.
Etruscan Wall **III**: 712.
Hellenistic in a Thracian Tomb **III**: 551.
Hepzefa, in the Assiut Tomb of **III**: 714.
Hierakonpolis **III**: 712.
Isthmia, Wall Painting at **III**: 719.

Jerusalem, Warship from Wall Painting at **III**: 718.
Keos, Wall Painting at **III**: 719.
Multiple Brush **III**: 715.
Nabataean **III**: 714.
Polygnotan **III**: 716.
Prehistoric Towns, of **III**: 708.
Rock, *see also:* ***Drawings; Pictorgraphs*** **III**: 718, 719*(2)*.
Roman Style Wall **III**: 712.
Roman Wall, Style in **III**: 700.
Sculpture, Reationship between in Greece **III**: 714, 746.
Temples, Egyptian, of **III**: 714.
Tomb, Egyptian, Occurrences of Corn-*'arūseh* in **V**: 209.
Wall in Tomb 35 at Dra Abu el-Naga, Restoration of **III**: 458.

Paionios:
Master of Olympia(?) **III**: 738.

Pakhuwa: **III**: 193.

Palaces: **III: §191, 499-503; IX: §191, cxxiii.**
Ahab's **III**: 462, 499, *582*.
Ahab's at Samaria **I**: 85.
Ahasuerus, and the Book of Esther **IV**: 519; **IX**: cxxiii.
Alexander's at Rhacotis **III**: 489, 501, 517.
Arslan Tash, at **III**: 503.
Assurnasirpul **III**: 502.
Darius I, of **III**: 499, 500*(2)*.
Darius, of, at Persepolis **III**: 500.
Hittite, at Sakçegözü **III**: 502*(2)*.
Istanbul, Emperors at **III**: 263.
Kato Zakro **III**: 502.
Knossos, at **III**: 143*(3)*, 499*(2)*, 502.
Knossos, at, Style of **III**: 475.
Knossos, at, Throne Room **III**: 475.
Mesopotamian, and the "Plano-Convex Building" and Kish **III**: 502.
Minoan, New **III**: 502.
Minoan, Planning **I**: 425; **III**: 474, 477.
Minoan, Residential Quarter of **III**: 501.
Minos, at **III**: 499*(2)*, 500*(2)*.
Mycenae, of **III**: 502.
Nestor, of **I**: *426;* **III**: 173, 204, 501*(6)*, 502*(7)*.
Nimrud, Burnt, at **III**: 178, 501, 518.
Nineveh, at **III**: 499.
Oriental, Ancient **III**: 499.
Persian of Ukheithar **III**: 499.
Phaistos, 'Piano Nobile' **III**: 473.
Rhacotis, Alexander's at **III**: 489, 501, 517.
Sety I, at Abydos **III**: 502, 520; **VII**: 18.
Shushan, at **III**: 230.
Solomon's, and Pharaoh's Daugther **V**: 72.
Solomon's, at Megiddo **III**: 503.
Solomon's, Building of **IV**: 379.
Tell es-Sa'idiyeh, at **II**: 469.
Thetis, of, on a François Vase **III**: 499, 707.
Tiglath-pileser III's **III**: 503.
Umaiyad **II**: 297; **III**: 500.
Windows, Recesses and Piano Nobile in Mionan **III**: 474.

Palae Tyrus: **II**: 308.

Palaeography:
Dot in Semitic **V**: 375, 480.
Hebrew Script, Distribution of **V**: 390.
Mcyenaean Chronology and **V**: 620.
Old Testament and Babylonian **IV**: 111, 182.
Qumran Scrolls, of **VIII**: 429; **§1093, 439-441.**

Palaeolithic Period:
Palestine in **III**: 427.
Palaeontology:
Contribution of in the Study of Terracottas **II**: 219
Palaikastro: **III**: 68.
Cemeteries at **III**: 193.
Dancing Figures from **V**: 241; **IX**: cxxvii.
Palatine: **III**: 211.
Paleography, *see also:* **Textual Criticism** **IV: §272, 98-100.**
Dead Sea Scrolls, *see:* ***Qumran Literature*** **VIII: §1093, 439-441.**
Hebrew **I**: *440;* **IV**: 5, 98, 99.
Hebrew Coin Script, and **I**: 454.
Inverted Nuns (׆) **IV**: 98.
Jewish Coins and **IV**: 98.
Mycenaean Chronology and **II**: 206.
Square Characters, in Biblical MSS **IV**: 98.
Paleontology: **II**: 248, 297.
Palermo Stone: **II**: *105;* **VII**: 62.
Palestine: **I**: *131, 323(2), 325(2), 328(2), 329(2), 330,* 331*(2)*, 332, 333*(3)*, 335, *358(3), 363, 364, 375, 376, 382, 383(7), 385, 386(2), 387(11), 388, 389(2), 390(5), 391, 398, 418(2), 421(2), 422 (2), 439, 440, 443, 445, 447, 448, 482;* **II**: *94, 112, 113(2), 116, 117, 143, 155, 158, 187, 215, 223, 237,* 300, *459;* **III**: *13, 231(3), 241, 242, 243(2), 244(4), 413(2), 423(2),* 430*(2)*, *430,* 439, 440, *513, 532, 624, 653, 672, 673, 674, 675(2), 676, 679, 680, 683, 693, 700, 711(2), 723;* **IV**: *179(2), 209, 215;* **VIII**: 341.
Palestine *(cont..)*
2000 B.C. in **II**: 293.
Abraham, in the Time of **II**: 288; **IV**: 315.
Aegean Civilization, Influence on South **I**: 323.
Aman-ḥatpe, Egyptian Governor of **II**: 12.
Arab Geographers and Travellers on **II**: 286.
Arabs in **VIII**: 344*(3)*.
Archaeological Excavations, Bibliography **III**: 423, 425*(3)*, 426, 427, 428*(2)*, 429*(2)*, 430.
Archaeological Research **III: 449.**
Archaeology and the History of **II**: 285, 289, 292*(2)*, 294*(2)*, 295*(3)*, 296, 297, 303, 304*(2)*, 309, 310*(2)*, *490(2), 491;* **III**: 27, 418, 421, 422*(2)*, 423*(3)*, 424*(3)*, 426, 428*(2)*, 431, 432*(2);* **IV**: 179*(2)*, 180, 213, 216.
Artifacts from, in the Haverford Collection **III**: 567.
Atomospheric Pressure in, Compared with England for Ten Years **II**: 238.
Babylonian Civilization, and Influence on **III**: 41, 88.
Babylonian Name of **II**: 266.
Babylonians in **II**: 117.
Biblical Background in **II**: 294.
Boundary, Northern, of **II**: 273.
Bronze Age in **II**: 175, 189, 300, 303, 304.

Bronze Age Sites in Eastern **III**: 422.
Cartography of **II**: 258.
Ceramics and History in **III**: 637.
Chalcolithic Period in **I**: 333*(3)*; **II**: 187, 204, 295.
Chronology of **II**: 180, 186, 188*(2)*, 191, 196; **III**: 418.
Cities, Locating and Excavating in **II**: 295.
Cities of **II**: 287, 309.
Climate and Religion in **II**: 243; **V**: 19.
Climate of **II**: 236, 238, 242, 254.
Coastal Plain, Geology of **II**: 248, 249.
Condition of, Present **II**: 285.
Conquest of, by Israelites **I**: 147, **§57, 150-153**; **IV**: 260, 338, 359.
Crete, and the History of **II**: 291; **III**: 68, 86.
Crocodiles in **III**: 372*(3)*.
Cultivation (Modern) and Electrification of, using Mediterranean Sea **I**: 362; **VI**: 360, 413.
Cultural History of, to Roman Times **I**: 124.
Cuneiform Inscriptions, in **II**: 262.
Dew, Importance of, in **II**: 243.
Disease in Modern, and in Biblical Times **III**: 398.
Division of Year in **I**: 398.
Dolmens of **III**: 550, 559.
Earliest Historical Period **II**: 295.
Early **II**: 287.
Eastern **II**: 285, 288, 289, 307; **III**: 424*(3)*, 428.
Egyptian Civilization, and Influence on **III**: 41, 88.
Egyptian Conquest in, Before Joshua **II**: 283.
Excavated Sites, Map of **II**: 258, 294.
Excavation Methods in **III**: 427, 434*(2)*.
Excavation of Bibilical Sites in **II**: 289; **III**: 414.
Excavations, Findlers Petrie's in **III**: 421.
Excavations in **II**: 288, 289*(2)*, 290*(2)*, 291*(3)*, 292*(2)*, 293*(2)*, 294‡, 295, 295‡*(3)*, 296‡*(2)*, 296*(3)*, 297, 297‡, 298*(4)*, 298‡*(4)*, *490*, 490‡; **III**: 412, 414, 415*(3)*, 416, 417, 419*(2)*, 420, 421*(3)*, 422, 425*(3)*, 427, 428*(3)*, 429*(3)*, 430*(2)*, 432.
Exodus, Before the **II**: 288.
Expedition, Bonaparte's, in 1799 **III**: 417.
Exploration, American, in **III**: 409, 410, 411.
Exploration of, *see also:* ***Israel, Exploration of*** **II**: 282, 283*(2)*, 284, 285*(4)*, 286*(2)*, 288*(2)*, 289*(2)*, 295, 296*(2)*, 308*(2)*, 309, 310; **III**: 409, 410, 411*(2)*, 415, 418*(2)*, 419, 424*(4)*, 426*(2)*, 427, 428.
Ezra's, and Periclean Athens **IX**: lxxxiv.
Fertility of **I**: 251, 258; **II**: 236, 237, 246, 283; **VI**: 2; **IX**: cxiv.
Fertility of, compared with Egypt **I**: 251; **II**: 236.
Flora of **III**: 384.
Folk-Memory of **VI**: 229.
Forests, Ancient, in Archaeological Indications **II**: 244, 256, 299.
Geographical Studies **II**: **§164, 280-304.**

Geography of, 17th Century	**II**: 283.
Geography of, and the Historical Truth of the Bible	**II**: 253, 282; **IV**: 194.
Geography of, compared with Sinaitic Peninsula	**II**: 282; **III**: 232.
Geology of	**II**: 247*(2)*, 248*(2)*, *482*.
Geomorphology of	**II**: 250.
Gerzean Period, in	**I**: 330.
Giants in	**III**: 349*(2)*.
Gods, Primitive, of	**V**: 163.
Greek Culture in, during the Talmudic Period	**VI**: 691.
Greek Influences in	**I**: 327.
Greek Inscription from	**VII**: 316.
Greek Language, in	**V**: 636.
Ground-Water in	**I**: 363.
Health of	**II**: 254.
High Places in	**V**: 49*(2)*.
Hills of	**II**: 287.
History of, Egyptian Source for	**II**: 2, 266, 295; **III**: *244*; **VII**: 16, 17, 77, 82; **IX**: cxiii.
Hittites in	**II**: 138*(2)*, 141*(2)*.
Identifications, made by Lieut. Conder, Index of	**II**: 307.
Inhabitants of, Modern	**I**: 385, 386.
Iron Age Sites in Eastern	**III**: 422.
Jew and	**VIII**: 210.
Jewish Claim to	**VIII**: 341.
Jewish Life and Literature, in	**VIII**: 333.
Jewish Rights in	**VIII**: 210.
Jewish Theology, in	**II**: 293; **VIII**: 3.
Jews in Modern	**I**: 385*(2)*; **VIII**: 344*(3)*.
Jews, Modern, and	**VIII**: 341.
Jews, Return of, to	**VIII**: 342, 346, 347.
Joshua, Before	**II**: 288.
Joshua, in the Days of	**II**: 287; **III**: 26.
Karnak Lists of	**II**: 264.
Locusts, Invasion of Rare, in	**III**: 378.
Lord Balfour and	**VIII**: 343.
Map, Jacotin's Surveyed during Napoleon's Campaign, 1799	**II**: 258.
Meteorological Observations in	**II**: 237*(2)*.
Mud Showers in	**II**: 238, 239.
Natural History of	**II**: 254.
Nebuchadnezzar's Reconquest of Phoenicia and, in Ezekiel	**IV**: 422.
Neolithic Cultures in	**I**: 124.
Oil in	**II**: 381, 484.
Organization of by Gabinius	**I**: 177.
Pagan Survivals in	**I**: 388.
Palaeolithic People of	**III**: 350.
Patriarchal	**II**: 297; **IV**: 220, 318.
Pepi I, Military Campaign of, in Southern	**II**: 74.
Phoenician Cemetery in	**III**: 554.
Physical Features of	**II**: 289.
Physical Preparation of, for Israel	**II**: 288, 483; **VIII**: 91.
Place Names in	**II**: 266, 269, 271.
Pliny the Elder, description of, by	**II**: 304.
Population of	**II**: 259, 261.
Population of, as Prophesied by Noah	**II**: 260; **IV**: 310.
Population, Pre-Israelite	**II**: 259.
Position of	**II**: 285.
Post-Exilic, Archaeolgical Report	**II**: 304.
Pre-Gerzean Period, in	**I**: 330.
Pre-Israel	**II**: 289.
Pre-Mosaic	**II**: 288.
Pre-Philistine Inhabitants of	**II**: 2, 326.
Prehistoric Man in	**III**: 350, 357.
Prehistory of	**II**: 294.
Primitive Religion, Survival of, in Modern	**I**: 387.
Ptolemies, under (Zenon Papyri)	**VII**: 353.

Rainfall in, *see:* ***Rainfall***
Reconnaissances, Limits of Error in Latitudes and Longitudes during **II**: 285, 307.
Religion and Climate in **II**: 243; **V**: 19.
Religion, Early, of **V**: 190.
Religion in Ancient, and the Excavations at Gezer **II**: 374; **V**: 13, 160.
Religion of at the time of the Israelite Conquest **V**: 190.
Religious Life in, during the Hyksos Rule **V**: 158.
Restoration of Israel and **VIII**: 210*(2)*.
Restoration / Regineration of **VIII**: 340*(2)*, 342.
Revelation and **V**: 11; **VIII**: 31.
Riviera and **II**: 285.
Roebuck in **III**: 380.
Roman Campaigns in, Latin Texts Relating to **VII**: 367*(2)*.
Roman Culture in **I**: 334.
Scenery of **II**: 285.
Self-government in **I**: 494.
Semainean Period, in **I**: 330.
Serpent-cult in **V**: 156.
Soil of **II**: 254.
South, Survey and Researches in **II**: 309; **III**: 411.
Southern, and the Tel-el-Amarna Tablets **VII**: 168.
Southern, Dawn of History in **II**: 300.
Springs, Hot Sulphur, in **II**: 237, 247.
Stanley, Arthur Penrhyn, on **III**: 231.
Stone Age in **II**: 294, 295.
Temperature in, Compared with England for Ten Years **II**: 238*(3)*.
Topography, Medieval **II**: 287, 306.
Topography of **II**: 288, 290; **III**: 419, 424.
Topography of, in Book of Micah **II**: 296.
Trans-Jordanic **II**: 285.
Transformation of **II**: 291.
Travels by E. ROBINSON, E. SMITH and others, 1852 **III**: 440*(2)*.
Travels, Modern, in **III**: 435, 437, 438, 439, 440*(3)*, 441*(3)*, 444*(2)*, 445*(2)*, 446, 447*(6)*.
Troglodytes in **III**: 349*(2)*.
Water Supply of **II**: 254.
West of the Jordan **II**: 285.
Western **II**: 288, 307, 308*(2)*, 310; **III**: 411.

Palestine Archaeological Museum **I**: *330;* **III**: *675.*
Coins in **I**: 444*(2)*, 446.

Palestine Exploration Fund: **III**: 412, 413, 417, 448.
Centenary of **III**: 433.

Palestine Exploration Fund Museum:
Weights in **I**: 422.

Palestine Mandate: **VIII**: 343*(2)*.

Palestine Oriental Society: **III**: 449.

Palestinian Targum: **VI**: 713, 714.
Antiquity of **VI**: 713.
Codex Neofiti 1 **VI**: 713*(2)*, 714.
Habakkuk Commentary (1QpHab) and **VI**: 712; **VIII**: 456.
Logos of the Fourth Gospel and the Memra **VI**: 105, 714; **VIII**: 131, 290.
Manuscript, recently discovered **VI**: 713.
Manuscript, recently discovered, early dating **VI**: 713.
New Testament and **VI**: 713; **VIII**: 277.
Pentateuch of, and Early Rabbinic Citations **VI**: 691, 714.
Peshiṭta Version of Genesis and **IV**: 47; **VI**: 96, 713*(2)*.
Relation to other Tragums **VI**: 713.
Sixth Century Fragment of(?) **VI**: 712.

Palestinians: **IX**: cx.
Folklore among, Modern I: 383, 385, 386, 390*(4)*, 391*(2)*.
Palette(s): **III**: 685*(9)*, 771; **VII**: **§836, 36**.
Narmer I: *332;* **VII**: 36.
PALEY, WILLIAM: **VIII**: 13.
PALFREY, JOHN GORHAM: **IV**: *224*.
PALGRAVE, WILLIAM GIFFORD: **III**: 442*(2)*.
"Palibothra": V: 234.
Palimpsest:
Septuagint **IV**: 27, 34.
Three Old Kingdom, in the Louvre **VII**: 72.
Twelfth Century Bronze **VII**: 88.
Palladas: **VIII**: 170.
Palliati: I: 279; **IX**: xc.
Palm-Tree *see also:* **Date Palm**
Pith of (Apocrypha of Jeremiah) and **VI**: 717.
Saints compared to **VI**: 509.
Sign of **VIII**: 304.
Palmaḥim: **II**: 457.
PALMER, A. SMYTH: **IV**: 364.
PALMER, WILLIAM: **III**: 82.
Palmyra: I: *144;* **III**: *74*, **194**, 443*(2)*.
Barometrical Observations in **II**: 239.
Human Remains from **III**: 354.
Plants from **III**: 384.
Tessera (coin) from I: 452.
Palmyrene Inscriptions: **VII**: 121, 122*(2)*, 127, 128; **IX**: cliii.
Herodotus and V: 154; **VII**: 121, 335.
Pamir: **VII**: 147.
Pamphylia: **III**: *104*, 194, *267;* **IX**: cii.
Fortifications on Side of **III**: 489.
Pan *(Greek Mythology)*: **III**: 715; V: 133, 144, 145, 178*(2)*, 251*(2)*, 252.
Arcadian God V: 251.
Pan-Babylonian Theory, *see:* **Babel-Bible Controversy**
Pan-Orientalism: **IV**: 136.
Panaghai: **III**: *536*.
Panakton: **III**: 194.
Panammu I:
Inscription of, on the Immortality of the Soul V: 190; **VIII**: 260; **IX**: cli.
"Panathenaic Ship": **III**: 29.
Panbabylonianism, *see also:* **Babel-Bible Controversey** V: 177.
Pandora: V: 260.
Pandore: I: 244.
Pandrosus:
Priestess of **VII**: 333.
Panepi: V: 210.
Panhellenism: **III**: 477, *753*.
Pannonia: I: 177.
Panoply, *see also:* **Armor**
Ethiopian I: 314*(2);* **III**: 597*(2)*.
Panta: V: 234.
Pantano Longarini:
Shipwreck at **III**: 454.
Pantheism:
Brahmanism and V: 230.
Zoroastrianism and V: 230.
Pantheon:
Ashurbanipal, of V: 168.
Gudean Cylinders, of V: 174.
Pap. B.M. 10298 **VII**: 79.
Pap-due-garra:
Hymn to (K. 128) **VII**: 262.
Paper:
Manufacture of (Papyrus) I: 235; **III**: 393.
Paphos: **III**: 145.
Solomon's Temple and Temple Paphos V: 72.
Pappus: I: 176.
Papremis: **III**: 194.
Papua New Guinea:
Religious Education in State Schools of **VIII**: 405.

Papyri and Ostraca (as Materials of Textual Criticism): **IV**: **§234, 8-9.**
Papyrologist: **VII**: 8.
Papyrology: **VII**: **§822, 4-8.**
Approach to, through Egyptian Hieratic **VII**: 7.
Bibliography **VII**: 6‡.
Bibliography, Greco-Roman Egypt **VII**: 4‡*(11)*, 5‡*(8)*, 6‡*(4)*.
British, during the War **VII**: 6.
Egypt, in **VII**: 5.
England, in **VII**: 5.
Finland, Work in **VII**: 6.
Jewish History in the Light of **I**: 146.
Methods of Publication **VII**: 5.
Science of, Progress of **VII**: 6.
Survey of Literature and **VII**: 6*(4)*, 7*(13)*, 8*(2)*.
Survey of Soviet Juristic **VII**: 7, 8.
Sweden, Work in **VII**: 6.
Transcribing, Text and Context in **VII**: 8.
Transliteration of **VII**: 5.
Twenty-five Years of **VII**: 4.
United States, Studies in **VII**: 5, 6.
Univeristy of Michigan, Work at **VII**: 5.
Papyron: **II**: 268, 425.
Papyrus: **III**: **393**; **IV**: **8-10**.
Astrological **II**: 234‡.
Astronomical **II**: 234‡.
Astronomical, and Related Problems in Ancient Geograpy **II**: 231, 255.
Baraize **VII**: 431.
Coptic - Cop Pap. LV (I) = [Crum 46] *Sahidic* **IV**: 8.
Coptic - Cop Pap. XI (I) = [Crum 52] *Sahidic* **IV**: 8.
Coptic, Topographical Notes from **II**: 253.
Demotic **I**: *217, 439, 512;* **II**: *78, 201.*
Demotic, Astronomical in the Carlsberg Collection **II**: 233.
Demotic Mathematical **I**: 436.
Demotic, University of Michigan, in **II**:*78;* **V**: 345, 349, 355.
Egyptian, Miscellaneous **V**: 318.
Elephantine *see also:* ***Elephantine Papyri*** **I**: *79*, 489; **II**: 203; **III**: 94.
Geometric **I**: 428.
Greek, and Textual Criticism **IV**: 3.
Heidelburg, at **IV**: 8.
Herald in the law of **I**: 189.
John Rylands Library, Uncatalogued **IV**: 9.
Legal **I**: 501.
Magical (Greek) **VII**: 343.
Magical, Leid V (Y. 384) (Greek) **VII**: 343.
Magical, of Paris (Greek) **VI**: 649; **VII**: 342.
Manufacture of **I**: 235.
Medical, Egyptian **III**: *366, 374, 385(3)*, 396*(2)*, 397, 398.
Phoenician **VII**: 119.
Ptolemaic **I**: *398, 465;* **II**: 201.
Romans, MSS of, in Harvard Semitic Museum **III**: 449.
Sahidic, of the OT **IV**: 8.
Samaria **VII**: 96.
Septuagint **IV**: 8*(3)*, 9*(5)*.
University of Michigan, Enoch, at **VI**: 642.
Writing Material, as **I**: 233, 234.
Papyrus (Named): **VII**: 76.
Abbott **VII**: 76.
Amenneb c. 125 l. 6 **V**: 315.
Amenneb c.3 1.1 **V**: 315.
Anastasi I **I**: *265, 317;* **VII**: 34, 71, 79, 82.
Antinoë, from **III**: 16.
Assuan **I**: *403;* **VII**: 77.
Astarte **V**: 148; **VII**: 76.

Ayer **I**: 429.
Baraize **I**: 500.
Barcinonenis **VI**: 593*(2)*, 594.
Berlin (2nd) **V**: 319.
Bremner-Rhind **VII**: 78*(4)*.
Burgh **VII**: 76.
Chester Beatty **IV**: 8*(6)*, 9.
d'Orbiney **VII**: 76*(2)*.
d'Orbiney, Hero of, and relation to *nʿr*- fish **VII**: 35, 76, 78.
d'Orbiney, Historical and Mythological Features of **VII**: 13, 38.
Dodgson **VII**: 77.
Ebers **I**: *393(2), 418;* **III**: *368, 396(2)*.
Elkan Adler **VII**: 80.
Harris **I**: *26, 488;* **VII**: 6, 75*(3)*, 77.
Harris 500 **VII**: 77.
Harris, and the establishment of the Jewish Religion **I**: 488; **VII**: 7. 81.
Harsiesis (*variant*) **V**: 316.
Hay **V**: 317.
Hood **VII**: 77, 78, 79.
Kahun **I**: *402;* **II**: 209; **VII**: 78; **IX**: cxii.
Kerasher **VII**: 78.
Kraeling **V**: 528.
Lansing **V**: 356; **VII**: 78.
Lee 1, 1 **V**: 354.
Libby **VII**: 77.
Lythgoe **II**: 107.
Mayer **VII**: 75, 77*(2)*.
Meris **VII**: 76.
Millingen **VII**: 10.
Mississippi Collection **IV**: 9.
Moscow Mathematical **I**: 430*(2)*, 431, 434.
Nevill **VII**: 41.
Oxyrhynchus **I**: *220, 236*.
Papyrus Lansing 3,9-3,10 **VII**: 79.
Peteesi **VII**: 77.
Petharpaχrat c. 148, of **V**: 319.
Prisse (Oldest Book) **VII**: 9, 76, 77.
Rainer **I**: *187*.
Rhind Mathematical **I**: *419,* 429*(4)*, 432; **VII**: 76.
Rollin **VII**: 76.
Rylands **VII**: 6.
Rylands IX **V**: 365.
Sachau's Elephantine **I**: 489.
Sallier, First, Fragment of **VII**: 75.
Sallier, Third **VII**: 14.
Scheide, on Ezekiel **VI**: 361*(5)*.
Turin **II**: *105,* 209.
Westcar **VII**: 76.
Westcar 7.17ff. **V**: 362.
Westcar XI, 6ff. **V**: 362.
Wilb(o)ur **I**: *262(2);* **VII**: 137.
Zenon **I**: *172, 253, 304, 481;* **III**: *467*.

Parable: **V**: 695.
Assyrian **VII**: 181.
Dives and Lazarus, and Enoch 22 **VI**: 664.
Hebrew, and Poetic Style **V**: 685.
Isaiah's, on the Vineyard **IV**: 392.
Jesus', Sources and Parallels **VIII**: 280.
Juridical Example of. The Poor Man's Ewe-Lamb **IV**: 378.
Old Testament, in **V**: 699; **VI**: 690, 691.
Ploughman and Thresher **VI**: 284*(4)*.
Rabbinic Literature, in **V**: 699; **VI**: 690, 691.
Unjust Steward in the Light of Qumran **VIII**: 481.
Vineyard, of, in Isaiah **VI**: 255.

Paradise, *see also:* **Eden; Future State, Heaven** **IV**: 289, 290*(3);* **V**: 184, 188*(2)*, 511; **VI**: 31, 36, 721.
Apocrpha and Pseudepigrapha, in **VI**: 595.
Babylonian, and Rivers of **V**: 180.
Chinese, Among **V**: 145.
Fall, after the **VIII**: 359.

Guardian Angels of **IV**: 295.
Law of **IV**: 286.
Myth of, Significance of **IV**: 294.
Northern **IV**: 293.
Rivers of **IV**: 290, 291*(2)*.
Significance of the Story **IV**: 294.
Site of **IV**: 289*(3)*.
Sources of the, Story **IV**: 293.
Sumerian Epic of, **V**: 180; **VII**: 222, 227, 282*(5)*.
Sumerian Epic of, Gardener in the **V**: 180.
Sumerian, Myth **V**: 186; **VII**: 281*(3)*, 283.
Sumerian, of the Gods **V**: 181.
Vineyard **V**: 181.
Whole Earth as **IV**: 286.

Paradise Lost:
Enoch and **VI**: 651.

Parahhotep:
Man Who Was Tired of Life **VII**: 11, 12.

Parahyba:
Phoenician Text from **VII**: 120.

Paralipomenon, *see:* **Chronicles**

Parallel Transmission, *see also:* **Narrative Repetition**
Biblical Passages, Hebrew Based Upon **V**: 388.

Parallelism:
Isaiah 1-35 and 37:22-35 **VI**: 289.
Isaiah 11-35, in **VI**: 272.
Sequence x/x + 1 in the Old Testament **VIII**: 312; **IX**: cxlv.

Parallelomania: **IV**: 90; **VIII**: 276.

Paran: **III**: 194; **VI**: 402.

Parapet:
Sculptured, of Athena Nike **III**: 466*(2)*, 467, 731, 732.

Parchment:
Writing Material, as **I**: 234.

Pardon:
Punishment and **VIII**: 195.

di Parentes: **V**: 243.

Parents:
Attacks on, in Code of Hammurabi **I**: 478, 496.

Parisos: **III**: *712*.
Siren from **V**: 259.

PARKER, THEODORE: **IV**: 116.

Parks: **I**: 239.

Parlipomenon of Jeremiah, *see:* **1 Baruch**

Parmenio: **II**: *10*, **72**.

Parnach: **V**: 297; **VI**: 138.

Parnapištim **VII**: 225.

Paronomasia: **V**: 695, 697, 699, 705.
Jerusalem, on the Name **V**: 508*(2)*, 697*(2)*.
Nahum, in **IV**: 448.
Talmud and Midrash, in **V**: 696; **VI**: 701, 706.

Parrasios: **III**: 713.

Parrhasios: **IX**: cv.

Parsees: **V**: 230.
Zoroaster and **V**: 232.

Parshiyyot: **VIII**: 206.

Parthenogenesis:
Cosmic **V**: 156.

Parthenon: **III**: 458, 459, 482*(2)*, 483*(2)*, 485, 518, *720*, *721*, *727*.
Attic Building Accounts **VII**: 338.
Color, on **III**: 480, 695. 707, 724.
Curvature, Aesthetics of **III**: 476, 486.
Destruction of **III**: 529.
Dimensions of **III**: 461, 480.
Pediment of **III**: 457, 465, 472, 751*(2)*, 752*(2)*.
Sculpture Fragments from **III**: 726.
Steps, Curvature of **III**: 467.

Parthia: **III**: 194.
Egyptian Vase from **III**: 611.

Parthian Language:
Epigraphy **V**: 680.

Parthian Texts *see:* **Iranian Texts**

Parthians: **I**: 335, 336*(2), 489;* **II**: *146.* **152**,*164;* **III**: *44.*

Parthian Remains found in Central Mesopotamia **III**: 142.

Political Ideology of **I**: 492.

Particularism:

Exile and the Restoration, in **V**: 27.

Partnerships: **I**: 304.

Parva Ne Pereant: **I**: 450.

Pasargadae: **I**: *456;* **III**: **194-195**, *677;* **V**: 199.

Inscripttions at **VII**: 373.

Paser:

Tomb of, at Thebes **III**: 551.

Ushabti Figure of **III**: 574.

Vizier, Mayor of Thebes **II**: 73.

PASHLEY, ROBERT: **III**: 438.

Pasht:

Relations between the Moon, the Cat, and, in Egypt **V**: 200.

Sed Festival and **V**: 203.

Passage(s):

Souterrians **V**: 67.

Passhur: **VI**: 332.

Passion Narrative:

Zechariah and **IV**: 454.

Passion Play:

Hebrew, from Ras Shamra **V**: 192; **VI**: 314; **VII**: 141.

Passover: **IV**: 324; **V**: 84, **§441, 86-88**; **VI**: 105*(2);* **IX**: **§441**, **cxxxv**.

Aramaic Name of **V**: 86.

Christian Church, in **V**: 86.

Date of **I**: 399.

Elephantine Ostracon and **V**: 86*(2);* **VII**: 127, 134.

Elephantine Papyrus **VII**: 134*(3)*.

Full Moon, Dates of Occurences **I**: 395; **V**: 86.

Hezekiah's Great **VI**: 6.

Initiation and **V**: 87.

Israelite, Problems **V**: 88.

Jewish Paschal Mystery **V**: 88.

Josephus, Important Texts on **V**: 87; **VI**: 676, 682.

Lamb of **V**: 86.

Lamb of, Date of the Slaughter of **V**: 87.

Lord's Supper and **V**: 87.

Meal, Time of **V**: 87.

Method Celebrating **V**: 87.

Non-Violence and **V**: 88; **VIII**: 229.

Old Testament, in **V**: 88.

Origin of **V**: 87.

Pesaḥim **VI**: 694.

Philo, Important Texts on **V**: 87; **VI**: 676, 682.

Priestly Code and **IV**: 258.

Rabbinic Literature, in **V**: 88; **VI**: 689.

Reflections on *(Sefath Emeth)* **V**: 88.

Samaritan

Samaritan Manuscript **VII**: 136.

Samaritan, Modern, of 1861 **I**: 385.

Seder-Table **V**: 86.

Unleavened Bread and **I**: 250; **IV**: 260; **V**: 85, 86*(3)*, 87*(2)*, 88.

Pastor: **V**: 511.

Pastoral Epistles:

Philo and **VI**: 675.

Patera:

Kourion, from **III**: 574*(2)*.

Pathology:

El Amarna, at **III**: *11,* 400, *697.*

Ezekiel and **I**: *43, 44, 113;* **VI**: 349.

Prophets and **I**: *113*.

Psychopathology, Ancient **III**: 402.

Saul and **I**: *96, 97(2)*.

Pathos:
Divine **VIII**: 67.
Pathros:
Psalms and **IV**: 475.
Patience: **V**: 511.
PATON, LEWIS B.:
Esther, on **IV**: 520.
patria potestas: **I**: 211, 500.
Patriarchal (Age) Period: **I**: 147;*153, 181, 305(2);* **II**: *158;* **IV**: 217, 220, **§311, 313-312**; **IX**: **§311, cxxxi**.
Camels in **III**: 370, 371.
Canaan during **II**: 299; **IV**: 319.
Egyptian Data on Palestine in **IV**: 318.
Exodus, The, Interrelation of Dates with **IV**: 319, 339.
Literary Analysis of **IV**: 319.
Social Analysis of **IV**: 319.
West-Semitic Kinship in **I**: 487; **IV**: 321; **V**: 130.
Patriarchal Blessings (4Q252): **VIII**: **§1132, 468**.
Patriarchal Narratives: **I**: *309;* **IV**: 272, 318, 319.
Camel in **III**: 371; **IV**: 321.
Historical Character of **IV**: 314, 316.
Merchants at Ugarit, and **IV**: 320.
"Oracle of Salvation", and **IV**: 177; **V**: 700.
Oral Sources of **IV**: 322.
Political Motives in the **IV**: 319.
Wife-Sister Motif in **IV**: 320.
Patriarchs: **IV**: 316; **VIII**: 226.
Antediluvian, Longevity of **II**: 259*(2)*, 260; **IV**: 298, 299*(3)*.
Antediluvian, Names Translated **IV**: 298.
Antediluvians **IV**: 297*(2)*, 298*(2)*; **VI**: 8.
Arameans, as Wandering **IV**: 320.
"Benediction" and prophetic book **VI**: 91.
Berosus, Ten of **II**: 173; **IV**: 299.
Bodies of **IV**: 314*(5)*.
Chronology of **II**: 189; **IV**: 320.
Chronology of the LXX and Antediluvian **II**: 181; **IV**: 297.
Genealogical Table of **II**: 181.
Habiru (Hapiru) and **I**: 160; **IV**: 320.
Hebrew Patriarch Names in Babylonia **V**: 297.
Historicity of **IV**: 315.
History and **I**: 133, 146, 147; **IV**: 319, 320*(2)*.
History, Contemporary **IV**: 319.
History of Religion and **IV**: 316; **V**: 13.
Immoralities of, as per Late Middle Age and Reformation Exegesis **IV**: 318.
Longevity of **II**: 189, 259, 260*(2)*, 262; **IV**: *237*, 310, 317.
Mari and **III**: 158; **IV**: 318, 320.
Mythology and **IV**: 315, 316.
Political Motives in Stories of **I**: 467.
Post-Diluvian in Hebrew History **IV**: 317.
Practical Principles from **IV**: 321.
Promise and **V**: 30.
Religion of, as Developed in the Book of Job **IV**: 457; **V**: 6.
Religion of, Attempt at Synthesis **V**: 28.
Religion of, Historicity, Modern Attack on **V**: 10.
Revealed Religion, Evidence of **III**: 17.
Sins of **IV**: 313.
Tombs of **II**: 284.
Western Semitic Kinship and **I**: 487; **IV**: 321; **V**: 130.
Patriarchs, Post-Deluvian: **IV**: 317.
Biographical Studies **I**: 25.
Name of Yahweh unknown to (?) **VI**: 103*(2)*.
Patriarch's Wives:
Biographical Studies **I**: 25.

Patriciate: I: 321.
Patriotism: I: §137, 507-509.
Babylonian Patriotic Sayings VII: 236.
Israelite View of I: 507.
Patriotic Tendencies in Targum Onkelos VI: 714.
Prophets and I: 111, 507.
Patris: II: 284.
Patristic Exegesis:
Interpretation of Gen. 1:1 VI: 724.
Jewish Midrashim and VI: 708.
Patristic Tradition, *see also:* **Church Fathers**
Biblical Chronology and II: 183; VI: 719.
Dietary Laws in I: 250; VI: 723.
Ḥasidism, and Hellenistic Literature, Link between V: 95; VI: 722.
Jewish Sectarianism, Accounts of, in VI: 723.
Joseph in I: 60.
Joseph the Patriarch in I: 60; VI: 722.
Scholastic Exegssis and Jewish Midrashim VI: 1.
Wisdom in the Light of Biblical and Rabbinic Research, in VI: 690, 724.
Patro:
Tomb of III: 553.
Pattern Theory: I: 337; IV: 159; V: 700.
PATTERSON, JAMES LAIRD: III: 440.
Paul, the Apostle: I: 56, 63*(2)*, 477, 479.
Abraham, Justification of, in VIII: 294.
Adam, in Paul's Thought VIII: 294*(2)*.
Bible, Attitude Toward VIII: 281, 292.
Creation, Doctrine of VIII: 7, 294; IX: cxxxvii.
Creation in Genesis and VIII: 292.
Daniel and IV: 531; VIII: 293.
Dead Sea Scrolls and Pauline Studies VIII: 482.
Deutero-Isaiah and the Forcefulness of IV: 400; VIII: 279.
Exegesis and Rabbinic Exegesis VI: 715.
Faith, Doctrine of, from the Old Testament VIII: 292.
Fall of Man, of VIII: 7, 294; IX: cxxxvii.
God, Experience of, in, and in Qumran VIII: 482.
Habakkuk and IV: 450; VIII: 457, 480.
Jeremiah and I: 54.
Job and I: 56; VIII: 292, 293.
Judaism and VIII: 294.
Law and Sin in, and in Second (Fourth) Esdras I: *479;* VI: 614; VIII: 181, 293.
Manual of Discipline and VIII: 461, 479.
Moses in the Typology of VIII: 293.
Original Sin, in VIII: 7, 185, 294.
Pharisee, as V: 100.
Philo and VI: 674, 675; VIII: 292*(2)*.
Psalms, as Used by VIII: 281, 292, 293, 294.
Qumran, Did he go to(?) VIII: 481.
Qumran Parallel to VIII: 463.
Rabbinic Judaism and VIII: 293.
Righteousness, in VIII: 96.
Second (Fourth) Esdras and VI: 614*(2);* VIII: 292.
Self-Understanding of, compared with Qumran Sectarian VIII: 294, 417.
Sin and Sacrifice as OT Background of Thought VIII: 294.
Wisdom Figure in the Wisdom of Solomon Christ, relation between VI: 618; VIII: 292.
Wisdom of Solomon and VI: 618; VIII: 292*(2)*.
Pauline Epistles:
Allegorical Use of the Mosaic Narrative VIII: 291.
Deutero-Isaiah and VIII: 291.
Enoch and 2 Corinthians VIII: 292.

Exodus as used in 1 Corinthians **VIII**: 293.
Exodus in 1 Corinthians **VIII**: 293.
First Maccabees, Traces of, in **VI**: 628; **VIII**: 293.
Genesis, Use of in Romans **VIII**: 294.
Israelites and Jews in **VIII**: 294.
Jeremiah in **VIII**: 291.
Judith, Quotation in 1 Corinthians **VI**: 631; **VIII**: 292.
Messianic Fulfillment in **VIII**: 137, 294.
Old Testament, Use of, in **VIII, §1046, 291-295.**
Pentateuch, Christian Midrash on **VIII**: 292.
Philo and 1 Corinthians **VI**: 672; **VIII**: 291.
Psalm 22 in **VI**: 468.
Quotations, Method of **VIII**: 291.
Rabbinic Background of ὑπέρακμος in 1 Corinthians 7:36 **VIII**: 294.
Rabbinic Judaism and **VI**: 686; **VIII**: 291.
Righteousness of God in **VIII**: 291.
Romans and 1QS x, 17-20 **VIII**: 294.
Secrets of Enoch in Ephesians 5:14 **VI**: 652; **VIII**: 291.
Sources of **VIII**: 291.
PAULOS, DAWIDH BAR:
Syriac grammarian **V**: 530.
Pausanias: **V**: 254.
Pawen-Ḥatef:
Tomb of at al-Fosṭâṭ **III**: 549.
Pawn, *see:* **Pignus**
Payrus 91061: **VII**: 79.
Paytanim: **I**: 243.
Pazarlik: **III**: **195**.
Pazuzu: **III**: 581; **VII**: 215.
Bronze Statuette **III**: 758, 768.
Pe: **III**: *739*.
Peace:
Appeal for, in Ugarit V AB **VII**: 143.
Biblical View of **VIII**: 229.
Doctrine in the OT **VIII**: 231.
Eternal, in Isaiah and Micah **VI**: 252.
God's Mandate for **VIII**: 227.
Jewish Tradition, in **VIII**: 233.
OT Ideas of **VIII**: 232.
Policy of Perikles **I**: 335, 493.
Prophetic Doctrine of **I**: 464; **IV**: 357.
Peacocks: **I**: *338, 341;* **III**: *192,* 379.
Hittite, Name imported into **V**: 606.
PEAKE, ARTHUR S.: **IV**: 136.
Jeremiah, on **IV**: 411.
Wellhausen and **IV**: 250.
Pearl(s): **I**: 267, 283; **V**: 445, 511.
Pectorals: **I**: 372; **III**: 593.
Peculium: **I**: 466.
Pedeamūn-nebnesuttaiu:
Statue of **II**: 73; **VII**: 75.
Pedeēset:
Statuette of **II**: 73.
Pediments:
Perthenon **III**: 465.
Pedineit: **III**: *646.*
Pedubast: **II**: 73.
PEEK, HENRY: **III**: *642(2).*
PEEL, EDMUND: **VIII**: 364.
PEET, T. E.:
Bibliography of **I**: 21.
Pegasus:
Aera Signata, on **I**: 443; **VIII**: 304.
Incuse Stater of Croton, overstruck on **I**: 459.
Pehlevi: **III**: *649;* **V**: 373.
PEILE, JOHN:
Greek and Latin Etymology by **V**: *626, 627, 664(2).*
Peisistratus: **II**: 73.

Pekah: I: **76**, *86, 91,* **95**; VI: 238, 259, 267*(2),* 593.
- Israel and Judah during the Riegn of VIII: 390.

Pekahiah:
- Israel and Judah during the Reign of VIII: 390.

Pekersala: II: 73.
Pekiin: III: 195, 524, *733.*
Peking: III: *358.*
Pekun, *see:* **Bekun**
Peleg: VI: 57.
Pelethites: II: *121,* **153**.
Pelican: III: *370,* 379.
Pelike, *see:* **Amphora**
Pella: I: *343;* II: **457-458**, III: **195**.
Peloponnesian Wars: I: 315, 321.
Peloponnesus: II: *151;* III: *116, 454, 597.*
Pelops: II: **73**, *77.*
Pelusium: II: *56.*
Pendant(s):
- Babylonian Bronze III: 591.
- Egyptian, Inscribed VII: 60.
- Inscribed III: 591.
- Usertsen III, on statues of III: 592, 726.

Pendeli, Mount: III: *478(2).*
Pendulum:
- Egyptian I: 423.

Peniel: I: 50; VI: 82.
- Elephantine, Hebrew Name at, and VII: 135.

Penmanship:
- Chirography of the Hammurabi Code VII: 243.

PENNIE, JOHN FITZGERALD:
- Judith-Play, of VIII: 363.

Penre:
- Stele of, Builder of Ramesseum VII: 24.

PENROSE, JOHN: VIII: 28, 89.
Pens: I: 234.
Pentacomia: II: 290.
Pentapolis: I: 176, 356; II: *315, 380, 381,* **458**, 484, 485, *501;* VI: 56.
- Ashdod, a city of the Philistine II: 324.

Pentateuch, *see also:* **Torah** I: *346;* II: *146, 383;* III: 336; IV: 126.
- Aboomanzur al-Damari's Commentary on VI: 725.
- Age of, *see:* ***Date of***
- Amos, Theology of, and IV: 240.
- Anachronisms, Alleged in IV: 228.
- Anti-Anthropomorphisms in the Septuagint IV: 234; VIII: 16, 103.
- Anti-Homeric Theory as applied to IV: 237.
- Antiquity of IV: 217.
- Apostolic Teaching on IV: 240; VIII: 299.
- Arabia and III: 18.
- Aramaean Synagogue IV: 20.
- Archaeologist on IV: 243.
- Archaeology of IV: 243.
- Aristeas, Letter of, and Greek Translation of the VI: 660.
- Ashburnham VIII: 358.
- ***Assyrian and Babylonian Backgrounds to*** IV: **§299**, **244**, 260*(2).*
- ***Authenticity of*** IV: 217, **§296**, **237-242**, 245*(2).*
- ***Authorship*** IV: **§296**, **237-242**, 333.
- Authorship, Law and History of Exodus, and IV: 333.
- Authorship, Mosaic, Origin of IV: 238*(2),* 239*(4),* 240*(7),* 241*(4),* 242*(4).*
- Authorship, Mosaic, Origin of, Ante-Nicene Fathers and IV: 238; VI: 718, 719.
- ***Backgrounds of*** IV: **§298**, **243**.

Bibliography	I: **§3, 10**.
Canon, and Fixation in Writing of the	IV: 205.
Catholic Church and	IV: 229, 230*(4)*.
Chariot and	IV: 241.
Christ and / in	IV: 238*(3)*, 239; VIII: 15, 127, 281, 283.
Christian Midrash on	VIII: 292.
Chronology of	II: 186; IV: 233.
Codex B and A on	IV: 33.
Colenso, John, on	IV: 224*(4)*, 225*(4)*, 246*(2)*.
Colophons, Judaeo-Persian to	IV: 236.
Composition of	IV: 232, 233*(3)*, 242, 251.
Covenant Making in	I: 516; IV: 236.
Criticism, Conservative	IV: 231*(2)*.
Criticism, Dogmatic Aspects of, on	IV: 226*(2)*.
Criticism, Method of	IV: 228.
Criticism, Negative	IV: 232.
Criticism, Present State of	IV: 226.
Criticism, Recensional	IV: 231.
Cuneiform Originals of	IV: 242.
Dancing in	IV: 227.
Date of	IV: **§296, 237-242**, 248.
Davidson, Peter, on	IV: 224, 225, 246.
Delitzsch, Franz, on	IV: 226, 227, 242.
Deuteronomy and	IV: 351.
Diatessaron and Analysis	IV: 48*(2)*, 227, 228.
Dignity under	VIII: 228.
Divine Names in	IV: 230, 231, 235; VIII: 108, 109*(2)*.
Elohim / Jehovah	IV: 229, 259.
Documentary Hypothesis	IV: **§302, 246-262**.
Driver, S. R. and	IV: 233.
Ecclesiastes, discrepancies between, explained	IV: 224.
Egyptian Backgrounds to	I: **§300, 244-245**.
Egyptian Terms in	IV: 245.
Egypticity and	IV: 227, 239.
Eiselen, F. C. and	IV: 232.
Ethnic Terms in	I: *147;* II: *113, 114, 120, 141, 143;* IV: 236; V: 402.
Ethnic Testamonies to	IV: 225.
European Study in	IV: 235.
Exegetical Studies on Multiple Books	VI: **§577, 13**.
Ezekiel and Dating of	IV: 240, 419.
Ezekiel, Did he Write, Edit, or Remodel the	I: 43; IV: 238.
Ezra, Did he Write or Amend the	I: 44*(2);* IV: 238.
Fixation in Writing of	IV: 205.
Future Life, Ideas of, in	VIII: 260.
Genuineness of	IV: 237*(5)*, 238, 245, 246*(2)*.
Glosses in	IV: 232.
Gospels and	IV: 227; VIII: 272.
Green, William H. on	IV: 249.
Hamburg Stadtbibiothek Codex No. I	IV: 11.
Hebrew MS of, in China	IV: 10.
Hebrew Music with reference to Musical Intonations in Recital of	VIII: 382.
Hebrew, Written in(?)	IV: 241.
Hengstenberg on	IV: 246.
Higher Criticism, and	IV: 5, 99, 226, 227*(2)*, 230, 233, 234.
Higher Criticism, Fallacies of, in	IV: 228.
Historical Character of	IV: 229, 245.
Historical Evidence for	IV: 230.
Historical Reliability of	IV: **§301, 245-246**.
Historical Value of	IV: 245.
Historicity of	IV: 240.

History of Criticism on	**IV**: 226*(3)*, 228, 229.
History, Truth of	**IV**: 226.
Hosea, Theology of, and	**IV**: 240.
Hosea's Testimony to	**IV**: 238.
"House of God / Lord" in LXX of	**IV**: 235.
Human Rights under	**VIII**: 228.
Indus Civilization and	**IV**: 323.
Inspiration and	**IV**: 228.
Introduction to	**VIII**: 393.
Israel, History of, and	**IV**: 229.
Jahu, Temple of, in Syene, and	**IV**: 231; **V**: 77.
Jericho MS	**IV**: 10.
"Jerusalem", Absence of the Name in	**IV**: 259.
Joseph Story and	**IV**: 236, 321.
Joshua, Book of, and	**IV**: 227, 251, 362*(2)*.
Jubilees, Book of, and	**IV**: 236; **VI**: 655.
Judeo-Persian	**IV**: 49.
Klostermann, August, on	**IV**: 228*(2)*, 239, 242.
König, Edward and	**IV**: 232*(2)*.
Koran and	**IV**: 230.
Kyle, M. G. and	**IV**: 233*(2)*.
Language of	**IV**: **§296, 237-242**.
Language of, and Egyptian	**IV**: 241.
Law(s) in	**I**: 472, 475, 476; **IV**: 143.
Legal Sections, Forms of Address in	**IV**: 234.
Legal Study of	**IV**: 231.
Legislation, Mosaic Authenticity of	**IV**: 257.
Legislation of	**I**: 472, 475; **IV**: 225, 240.
Letters, Number of, in	**IV**: 233.
Literary Criticism of	**IV**: **§295, 224-236**.
Literary Style of	**V**: **§565, 700-701**.
Lofthouse, W. F. and	**IV**: 232*(3)*.
"Lord of Hosts", Absence of, in	**IV**: 259.
Masai and Higher Criticism	**IV**: 243.
McFadyen, John E. on	**IV**: 231.
McKim, Randolph, on	**IV**: 230.
Mekilta on	**IV**: 234; **VI**: 708.
Mosaic Origin, Denial of	**IV**: 237.
Mosaic Origin of, and Ante-Nicene Fathers	**IV**: 227, 238.
Mosaic Words in	**IV**: 226.
Moses, Wrote in Cuneiform(?)	**IV**: 240.
Naville, Eduard on	**IV**: 243.
Numbers, High, in	**IV**: 225; **VIII**: 309.
Origin and Sources of	**IV**: 227, **§297, 242-243**, 259.
Orthography of the Masoretic Text	**IV**: 5.
Oxyrhynchus Papyri and	**IV**: 231.
Papal Commission and	**IV**: 230*(2)*, 241*(2)*.
Parable in	**IV**: 176.
People of God in	**IV**: 235; **V**: 25; **VIII**: 211.
Pharaohs, Indentification of, in	**II**: 5; **IV**: 245.
Poetry of	**IV**: 224.
Prayer in the	**VIII**: 203.
Prideaux	**IV**: 13.
Priestly Dues, on	**IV**: 228.
Prophetic Testamony to	**IV**: 228, 385.
Rabbinic Exegesis of	**IV**: 96, 235; **VI**: 13, 716, 722.
Rashi's Commentary on	**IV**: 234, 236; **VI**: 727.
Reconstruction of	**IV**: 247*(2)*
Religion of	**IV**: 233; **V**: 17.
Resurrection in	**VIII**: 269.
Retaliation, Law of, in	**IV**: 234; **IX**: c.
Sacred Song, Absence in Rituals of	**IV**: 259.
Samaritan Exegesis of	**IV**: 96, 235.
Samaritan, *see:* ***Samaritan Pentateuch***	**IV**: **§243, 20-23**.

Sayce, A. H., on **IV**: 251.
Science in **IV**: 225.
Septuagint and **IV**: 30, 232.
Septuagint, Anti-Anthropomorphisms **IV**: 234; **VIII**: 16, 103.
Septuagint Version of **IV**: 24, 35, 224.
Sermon on the Mount, Themes of, in **VIII**: 283.
Sinaicity of **IV**: 326.
Smith, W. Robertson, on **IV**: 225, 226*(2)*, 238.
Sources in **IV**: 176.
Strack, Hermann, on **IV**: 226.
Structure of **IV**: 227.
Syriac Exegesis of **VI**: 13, 716, 722.
Syriac Verion of **IV**: 45, 47.
Targums on **VI**: 711.
Teaching, to the Young **VIII**: 399.
Technical Terms in **IV**: 235*(2)*.
Textual History of **IV**: 99.
Theological Currents in **VIII**: 16.
Theological Studies in **VIII**: **§959, 15-16.**
Three Scrolls, Found in the Temple **IV**: 11, 12.
Time Measures in **II**: 186*(2)*; **IV**: 233, 234.
Time-Measures in **IV**: 233.
Tyndale's Translation of **IV**: 52.
Unity of **IV**: 226, 232, 235.
Uppsala School on **IV**: 235.
Vatican and **IV**: 230.
Wellhausen on, *see:* ***Documentary Hypothesis***
Wiener, Harold M. on **IV**: 231, 232, 255.
Wine in **IV**: 231.
Yahweh Translation of, by *(ho) Theos* in **VIII**: 118.

Pentateuch, Manuscripts of: **VI**: **§578, 14**.
Hebrew of, from the Jewish Congretation at Kai-fung-fu, China **VI**: 14.
Onqelos MSS of, with Babyloinan Vocalization **VI**: 14.
Prideaux Pentateuch **IV**: 13; **VI**: 14.

Pentateuchal Criticism, *see also*: **Documentary Hypothesis** **I**: *237.*
Jerusalem Bible, in **IV**: 329.

Pentathlon: **I**: 240*(2)*.

Pentecontaetia: **I**: 321.

Pentecost, Day of: **V**: **§443, 89**.
Jubilees, Qumran and Acts, in **V**: 89; **VI**: 655; **VIII**: 415.

Penteskouphia: **III**: *579.*

Penuel: **II**: **458**, *485(4)*; **IV**: 317, 318, 369; **VI**: 82.

Peoloponnese: **III**: **195**.

"People of God" *see also:* **Chosen People** **VIII**: 213*(3)*, 349*(2)*.
Church and, in the OT **VIII**: 191.
Individual and the **VIII**: 193.
Study in the Doctrine in the Pentateuch **IV**: 235; **V**: 25; **VIII**: 211.

People of Israel: **V**: 511*(2)*.

Peoples, *see:* **Nations, Peoples and Their History**
Hebrew World, Early, in **III**: 349.
Prehistoric, and Theory of Evolution **II**: 2; **III**: 345*(3)*.

Peor (Baal Peor): **II**: 308; **VI**: 137.

Pepi I (Pepy): **II**: **73-74**, 198.
Abydene Marriage of **II**: 74.
Harem Investigation, date of, under **II**: 73.
Military Campaign of, in Southern Palestine(?) **II**: 74.
Pyramid of **III**: 504*(2)*.
Sarcophagus of **III**: 504, 531.
Seal of **III**: 643.
Statuette of **II**: 73.
Tomb of **III**: 536*(2)*.

Peplos: **III**: 582.

Perachora: **II**: 108; **III**: 195.

Peraea:
Herod Antipas, Tetrach of — **II**: 48.
Peran-ankalaia: **II**: 271.
Perch, resting place:
Egyptian word for — **V**: 325.
Perdikkas II:
Alliance of Athens with — **VII**: 339.
Pere:
Graffito from the Tomb of — **VII**: 13.
Perea: **II**: 424; **III**: 196.
Perez: **VI**: 86.
Perez-uzzah: **VI**: 210.
Perfection: **V**: 511.
Perfume: **I**: 282, 283, 284, 336; **II**: 224.
Incense or — **V**: 61.
Ptolemaic monopoly on — **II**: 284; **VII**: 342.
Pergamene Ware: **III**: 616, 669.
Pergamon (Pergamum): **I**: *494;* **III**: 196, 264, *740, 748, 750*.
Great Altar at — **VIII**: 200; **IX**: cxxxv.
Rainbow Mosaic at — **III**: 718, 719.
Perge: **III**: 263*(2)*, 267.
Pericles (Perikles): **I**: 335, 493; **II**: **74**; **III**: *461*.
Odeum of, and the Periclean Reconstruction of the Theater — **III**: 529.
Peace Policy of — **I**: 514; **II**: 74.
Perikles: **I**: 335, 493.
Periodic Theory: **VIII**: 91.
Periplus: **VII**: 121.
Pernesbastet:
Stela of, from Hassaïa — **VII**: 20.
PEROWNE, J. J. STEWART:
Genesis, on — **IV**: 277.
Psalms, on — **IV**: 474, 492.
PERROT, GEORGES: **II**: 427; **III**: 23, 219.
Persea Tree: **III**: 393.
Persecution:
Hadrianic — **I**: 463.
Political, in 90 B.C. — **II**: 161.
Persephone:
Crown of — **III**: 593.
Grief of — **V**: 259.
Persepolis, *see also:* **Behistun Inscription** **III**: **196**, *197(2), 256;* **VII**: *299*.
Achæmenian Tomb-Inscription from — **VII**: 370.
Darius' Palace at — **III**: 500; **VII**: 298.
Inscriptions from — **II**: *178*.
Persepolis Tablets: **II**: *21(2)*, 35; **VII**: 298.
Perservation:
Mud-Brick — **II**: 220.
Perseus: **III**: 713, *718*.
Assyrian Elements in the Perseus-Gorgon Story — **V**: 256.
Chaldean — **VII**: 224.
Persia, *see also:* **Iran** **I**: *282*, 324, 331, *340, 481;* **II**: *193, 202;* **III**: *19, 36*, 91, *208, 209, 239, 240, 251(2)*, 444; **III**: *548, 671, 700, 722;* **V**: *529;* **IX**: cxii.
Anthropological Notes on — **III**: 342; **V**: 587; **IX**: cxliii.
Artifacts from Northwest — **III**: 569.
Climate of — **III**: 196, *235*.
Hellenic League against — **II**: 134.
Kings of — **II**: 202, 208.
Literature, Contribution to — **VII**: 371.
Peoples of the Empire — **III**: 343.
Prince of — **I**: 495; **II**: *172, 173, 179*.
Shah of — **III**: 442.
Travels, Modern, in — **III**: 435*(3)*, 436*(4)*, 437, 439, 441, 445, 446*(2), 530*.
Persian:
Biblical Religion, Influence on — **V**: 36.
Messiah, and Jewish — **V**: 125.
Monarchy — **II**: 153.
Studies, Present Status — **VII**: 371.

Persian Bible: **IV**: 48, 49*(8)*.
Tafsir **IV**: 49.
Persian Captivity:
Egyptian History up to **II**: 125.
Persian Chronology: **II**: 186, *198*, 203, 204.
Aramaic Papyri and **I**: 396; **VII**: 133.
Persian Gulf: **III**: **197-198**.
Persian Language (Grammar and Lexicography): **V**: **§554**, **675-678**; **IX**: **§554**, **cxliv**.
Accusative in *mām kāma* **V**: 676.
Article **V**: 676.
Cuneiform Script **VII**: 372.
Dialect Variation in **V**: 677.
Etymology **V**: 676.
Finals Vowels in **V**: 677.
Hesychius, Pesian Words in the Glosses of **V**: 640.
Interpretation of Words **V**: 676.
Jones, William, Lingustics of **V**: 677.
/L/ Phoneme **V**: 677.
Monosyllables, Phonological Analysis **V**: 676.
Nominal Compounds of **V**: 677.
"Passive" Constructions in Aramaic in Light of **V**: 528.
Perfect, Pre-Aryan Origins of **V**: 675.
Phonetic Laws in **V**: 675.
Phonology of Modern **V**: 676.
Relationship to Sanskrit, Khan-i- Arzu on **V**: 678.
Relationship to Sanskrit, Khan-i- Arzu on **V**: 678.
Relative **V**: 676.
Signs of Persian Cueniform Alphabet **V**: 675.
Subordinate Imperative in **V**: 676.
Syntax of Old-Persian Cuneiform Inscriptions **V**: 675.
Transliteration of **V**: *588*, 675.
Vocalic *r* Before *n* in Old Persian **V**: 676.
Vowel Phonemes **V**: 677.
Vowel Phonemes in Modern **V**: 677.
Persian Period, *see also:* **Post-Exilic Period, Israel in**
Chronology of **II**: 186, 204.
Israel in **I**: **§67**, **169-171**; **II**: *186;* **III**: 427.
Jewish History and **II**: 186.
Jews and Samaritans, Relations of, in **I**: 336; **II**: 163.
Job and **IV**: 464.
Post-Exilic Legalism and Post-Exilic Literature **V**: 9.
Persian Religions, especially Zoroastrianism **V**: **§473**, **229-236**.
Jewish Influence on Persian Beliefs **V**: 36, 230.
Persian Inscriptions and Texts: **VII**: **§952**, **369-373**; **IX**: cxliv, **§904**, **cliii**.
Achæmenian Tomb-Inscription at Persepolis **VII**: 370.
Amardian or "Ptromedic" Tablets **VII**: 369.
Artaxeres I, of **VII**: 372.
Artaxeres II (Mnemon), Trilingual Insciprtion of **VII**: 233, 369.
Artaxeres II, of **VII**: 370.
Artaxeres III, of **VII**: 370.
Assyro-Babylonian, Stylistic Paralells Between **VII**: 147.
Avesta, Fragment of **VII**: 370.
Behistun Inscription, *see:* ***Behistun Inscription***
Behistun, Old Persian Inscriptions at **VII**: 369.
Catalgoue of MSS in the Library of the University of Glasgow **VII**: 2.
Cuneiform Inscriptions **VII**: 369.
Cuneiform Inscriptions, Key to Assyrian **VII**: 369.
Cyrus Vase Inscription and Behistun **VII**: 369.

Cyrus Vase Inscription: Ezra and Isaiah **VII**: 369.
Daiva- Inscription of Xerxes **VII**: 371.
Darius Hystaspes, Monuments of **VII**: 182, 369.
Darius, of **VII**: 370, 372.
Darius, of, from Pasargadae **VII**: 372.
Darius, on a Gold Tablet **VII**: 370*(2)*.
Dubious Tablet in Philadelphia **VII**: 371.
Eugubine Tablets **VII**: 369.
Hamadan, from **VII**: 369.
Inscription Analogous to Behistun **VII**: 369.
Kay Kâûs Legend **II**: *232;* **V**: 181; **VII**: 372.
Kerman inscription of Darius **VII**: 235, 298, 370.
Legal Documents **VII**: *192,* 370.
Naqš-i Rustam, of Darius **VII**: 371, 372*(3)*.
Oldest **VII**: 372.
Oscan Inscription **VII**: 369.
Pahlavi Inscription **VII**: 371*(2)*.
Parsī-Persian Omen Calendar **VII**: 370.
Pelasig Inscription **VII**: 369.
Provinces, List of **VII**: 371.
Saqqara, from **VII**: 370.
Stone-Sculptured Texts and Manuscripts, Harmony and Authority **VII**: 370.
Textual Notes on **VII**: 370.
Thucydides, Persian Letter in **VII**: 370.
Tri-lingual, from Hamadan **VII**: 153.
Weight with trilingual inscription **VII**: 369.
Xerxes, of **VII**: 371*(2)*.
Zendan Inscription **VII**: 372.

Persians: **I**: *163, 301, 307, 331, 453;* **II**: *31, 33,* 101, *115, 149(2),* **153**, *172;* **III**: *159, 163, 196(2),* **196-197**, *508;* **IV**: 543.
Deutero-Isaiah, and **IV**: 404.
Law of **I**: 495; **II**: *172, 179*.
Magyar, Descent of, from **III**: 332.
Military Colony at Elephantine under **III**: 93.
Non-Aryan, in the Bible (Ezra 4:9) **VI**: 580.
Pre-Christian Religion of **V**: 233.
Two Officers named Bagoas **II**: 24.
World-Year of **V**: 236.

Persis: **III**: 199.

Person:
Education and the Biblical Concept of a **VIII**: 407.

Personalities:
Greek, Real and Conventinal, in History **II**: 5.
Historic, Value of, in Archaeology **II**: 5.

Personality:
Corporate, in Israel **I**: 470, 508; **VIII**: 175.
God, Knowledge of, in Relation to Hebrew Concept of **VIII**: 66, 171, 191.
Hebrew Psychology, in **VIII**: 173.
Surrender to Deity, among Syrians and Arabs **V**: 154.

Personification:
Greek Mode of Thought, as **V**: 261.

Persons, Ancient Near Eastern - Alphabetical Listing, *see also specific individual names* **II**: **§141, 6-110**; **IX**: **§141, ciii-cvi**.

Persopolis Plain: **III**: 125.

Perspective (in Art): **III**: **§225, 707-719**.

Perugia: **III**: *467*.

Pesher, Pesharim from Qumran - General Studes *see also:* Specific Pesher, *(e.g. Habakkuk Commentary)*	**VIII**: **§1117**, **453**.
Pesaḥim:	
Perek Arvei	**VI**: 694.
Peshiṭta, *see also:* **Syriac Versions**	**IV**: 7, **§259**, **45-48**.
Authorship of	**IV**: 46.
Concordance to	**IV**: 46.
Genesis (B.M. Add. 14425)	**IV**: 7; **V**: 531; **VI**: 96.
Isaiah in	**VI**: 319*(2)*.
Origins of	**IV**: 46*(3)*.
Palestinian Targum; Targum Onkelos and Book of Genesis in	**IV**: 47; **VI**: 713*(2)*.
Printed Texts of	**IV**: 46.
Septuagint, influence of, on	**IV**: 27, 31, 45, 47.
Song of Songs in	**VI**: 555.
Translation of *Ṭabbur Ha'ares* in	**VI**: 186.
Urumia Concordance to, Loss of	**IV**: 46.
Peshiṭṭo:	**IV**: 24.
Persian:	
Pesikta:	
Prolegomenon to	**VI**: 708.
Pesikta Rabbati:	**VI**: 709.
Editorial Terms in	**VI**: 709.
God's Replenishment of Israel from	**VI**: 690.
Pesiktta de Rav Kahana:	
Bible Quotations in	**VIII**: 371.
Pessimism:	
Babylonian Dialogue of	**VII**: 221*(2)*.
Israel, in	**V**: 114.
Pestle:	**VI**: 459, 547*(2)*.
Thumb and Finger	**III**: 675.
Pesuke De-Zimra Benedictions:	**VIII**: 206.
Peter, St.:	
Jewish Liturgy, in	**VIII**: 205.
PETERS, JOHN PIMMET:	**III**: 445; **IV**: 216; **V**: 181, 470.
Bibliography of	**I**: 21.
Pethion Ibn Ayyûb Al-Sahhâr:	**VI**: 345.
Pethor:	**I**: *117*.
Petra:	**I**: *346, 350, 377, 400;* **II**: *151(2), 152,* 254, 291, 296, 310, 424*(2), 429,* **459-462**; **III**: *247,* 423, 437, 438, *595, 753*.
Altar at	**V**: 47.
Arched Gate at	**III**: 489.
Folklore of	**II**: *267*.
Giant Races in Arabia	**III**: 342.
High Place at	**II**: 459*(4)*, 460*(4)*, 461; **V**: 47*(7)*, 48*(2)*, 49.
Nabataean Sactuary near	**III**: 519.
Qasr Bint Far'un	**III**: 485, 486, 521.
Seal from	**III**: 652.
Semitic Cult Complex at	**V**: 162.
Topgraphy of	**II**: 267, 461*(2)*.
PETRE, WILLIAM MATTHEW FLINDERS:	**II**: 197, 293; **III**: *145, 166, 355,* 443.
Egyptian Inscriptions in the Collection of	**VII**: 61.
Exodus, on	**IV**: 334.
Petrie-Hirshfeld Papyri:	**IV**: 8.
PETRIE, WILLIAM MATTHEW FLINDERS:	**III**: 22, 85, 119, 160, 166, 191, 233, 245, 339.
Petroglyphs:	
Umm el-Biyara, found at	**III**: 270.
Petrology:	
Cylinder Seal and	**III**: 661.
Petronius:	
Talmudic Proverb in	**VI**: 699.

PETTIGREW, THOMAS JOSEPH:
Mummies, on **I**: 380.
PFEIFFER, ROBERT HENRY: **IV**: 151.
Phædon, *see:* **Soul**
Phaedrus:
Plato's Discourse on Love in **V**: 265.
Phaestos (Phaistos) Disk: **I**: 244; **VII**: 358, 359, 361*(3)*, 363.
Sign 24 on **V**: 621.
Phaëthon: **V**: 259.
Phaistos: **III**: *143*, **198**, *475*.
Phaleron: **III**: *723*.
Phalerum: **I**: *497;* **III**: **198**.
Phaleric Wall **III**: 488.
Phallic Figure: **III**: 576.
Phallism:
Egypt, in **V**: 210.
Phallic Offerings to Hathor **V**: 210.
Pharaoh(s): **II**: 124*(2)*, 125.
Arrogance of **IV**: 324.
Baptism of **V**: 217*(2)*.
Birth of **V**: 223.
Butler of, and the Cup **IV**: 315.
Dream of Lean Years **IV**: 316.
Ethiopian, Names in Genesis 10 **VI**: 54.
Maqrizi's Names of **II**: 5.
Moses dealings with **VI**: 103.
Moses, during time **I**: 68; **II**: 4, 182, 196.
Name of **V**: 511.
New Year Gifts to **V**: 224.
Pentateuch, Identification of, in **II**: 5.
Stella Destiny of, and Air Shafts, So Called, of Cheops' Pyramid **III**: 476.
Pharaoh of the Exodus: **II**: 182, 196; **IV**: 324, 325*(2)*, 326, 327*(2)*, 333*(2)*.
Destruction of **IV**: 323.
Hardening of, Heart **IV**: 324, 325, 326, 327, 329.
Merenptah, as **II**: 62; **IV**: 336.
Opression of Israel under **VI**: 97.
Ramesses II as Pharaoh of the Opression and **II**: *80*.
Pharisees: **I**: *177*, 477; **V**: 97, **§450**, **98-100**, 240; **VI**: 690.
Alexander Jannaeus, and **II**: 53; **V**: 98, 99.
Controversey with the Sadducees over the High Priest **V**: 44, 98, 100.
Defining, Tannaitic Sources **V**: 100.
Doctrine of Fate, Josephus' Statement (Antiq. XVIII, 1, 3) **V**: 99; **VI**: 681.
Eschatology of **VIII**: 250.
Ethical Teachings of, in Relation to Jesus, and the Old Testament **V**: 98; **VIII**: 220.
Ethics of Anonymity Among **V**: 99.
Garments of, White(?) **V**: 98.
Herodian Dynasty, Attitude of, on **V**: 99*(2)*.
History of **V**: 100.
Jewish Revolution of 66-73, and **V**: 99.
Law, Attitude Toward at the Time of Christ **V**: 100.
Legalism of **V**: 99.
Origin of **I**: 166; **V**: 98, 99, 100*(2)*.
Origin of the Name **V**: 98, 99.
Orthodox Party, as **V**: 98.
Philosophy of **V**: 99.
Politics and **V**: 100.
Pollio Identified as a, in Josephus **V**: 99.
Righteousness of **V**: 98, 102; **VI**: 668*(2)*.
Roman Rule, Attitude of, on **V**: 99*(2)*.
Sadducees and **V**: 98*(3)*, 99*(2)*, 100*(5)*.
Social Milieu of **V**: 100.
Teachings of **V**: 99.
Pharmacology: **I**: xvii (n.15).
Psalms, in **VI**: 492.

Pharmacy, *see:* **Drug Use and Abuse**
Pharpar River: **III**: 198.
Pheidias: **III**: *741.*
Pheidon: **I**: *454;* **II**: **74**.
Phenomena:
Spiritual as Natural Convulsions **VIII**: 238.
Phiala, Lake: **II**: 390, 423, 424, 462.
Phiale:
Greek **III**: 618.
Greek Fifth-Century Silverware **III**: 598.
Greek Gold **III**: 599.
Panagyurishte Gold **III**: 590.
Silver, Greek, in the Metropolitan Museum **I**: 298; **III**: 597.
Phibis: **VII**: *31.*
Phidias: **III**: *461.*
Philadelphia University Museum: **III**:*751;* **VII**: *29, 31.*
Assyrian Texts in **VII**: 178.
Family Stela in **VII**: 22.
Philadelphos, Arsinoe:
Portrait of **II**: 74.
Philae: **III**: **198**.
Doomed Island of **VII**: 62; **IX**: cxx.
Four Granite Stands at **III**: 483.
Temples at **III**: 508, 513.
Phileh Qal'eh: **III**: *158,* 199.
Philetairos:
Portrait of **II**: 74; **III**: 765.
Philgaleia: **III**: *507.*
Philhellenism: **II**: *152.*
Philip II:
Hypaspists and **I**: 321.
Philip, Tetrach of Aurantis:
Nabataean Inscription concerning **VII**: 295.
Philippi: **III**: 441.
Philippus: **II**: 134.
Philistia: **I**: 352; **II**: **463**.
Egyptian Name for **II**: 265.
Plain of **II**: 283, 463.
Philistines: **I**: *100, 147, 295, 313,* 337*(2), 343;* **II**: **154-155**, *326, 492;* **III**: *54, 69,* 138.
Corps of the Scimitar from Gath **VI**: 216.
David's War Against **IV**: 378.
Graves Found at Gezer **III**: 539.
Military Base of **II**: 292.
Society, Structure of **II**: 369.
Uzziah and **IV**: 541.
Phillippus: **II**: 134.
PHILLIPS, GEORGE:
Psalms, on **IV**: 473.
Philo (of Alexandria), Life and Works of: **I**: *230, 415, 465, 507;* **V**: 36, 110, 232; **VI**: *143;* **§805**, **672-678**, 677‡; **IX**: *cxlv.*
Abraham, Writings on **I**: 30, 31, 32; **VI**: 677*(2).*
Αἰώνιος as used by **VI**: 672.
Akenside's *Pleasures of Imagination* and **VI**: 672.
Alexandrian Version quoted by **IV**: 201.
Allegorical Interpretation of the Scriptures in **VI**: 678.
Aquila's Text in **IV**: 37; **VI**: 676.
Armenian Text of "Quaestiones in Genesim" Books I-III **VI**: 676.
Armenian Translation of Questiones in Genesim et Exodum **VI**: 675.
Bible and **VI**: 673.
Bible of, Textual-Exegetical Note on **VI**: 677.
Bible, of, Textual-Exegetical Note on Genesis 27:41 **VI**: 77.
Bryant, Lewis C., on **VI**: 672; **VIII**: 129.
Christian Theology and **VI**: 676.
Conscience in **VI**: 675.
Contemplative Life **VI**: 673.
Curses, Concerning **VI**: 674.

Day of Atonement in	**V**: 89; **VI**: 674.
De Somniis I	**VI**: 674.
De Vita Mosis of	**VI**: 675.
Didache and	**VI**: 673, 717, 719.
Divine Comedy	**VI**: 99, 675.
Drummond, James, on	**VI**: 673.
δυνάμεις and the Amesha Spenta	**V**: 232; **VI**: 673.
Ecclesiasticus and	**VI**: 621, 673.
Education, on	**VI**: 674.
Environment of	**VI**: 677.
Epic Poet, as	**VI**: 677.
Ethics, Confrontation of Greek and Jewish in De Decalogo and	**VI**: 678; **VIII**: 229.
Etymologies of	**V**: 404, 475; **VI**: 678.
Exegesis of	**VI**: 677, 678.
False Philoian Logos	**VIII**: 130.
Florilegium	**VI**: 673.
Free Will, on	**VI**: 676.
God, Names of, and	**VI**: 675.
God of Revelation in	**VI**: 677; **VIII**: 68.
God's Approach to Man, Concept of	**VI**: 674.
Ḥasidim in	**V**: 95; **VI**: 677.
Hebrew, Did He Know?	**V**: 390; **VI**: 677, 678.
Homilies on Fear and Love, Relation to Palestinian Midrashim	**VI**: 678.
Immortality, on	**VI**: 676.
Inspiration, on	**VI**: 675; **VIII**: 48.
Intellectuals and	**VI**: 675.
Irenaeus, Quotation of, in	**VI**: 677, 723.
Jewish Citizenship in Alexandria, on	**VI**: 676.
Jowett, Lewis Campbell on	**VI**: 672.
Judaism of the First Century and	**V**: 13; **VI**: 674.
Judaism, Place in	**VI**: 677.
Law, Exposition of, and De Vita Mosis	**VI**: 675.
Leviticus 18:30 and	**VI**: 124, 674.
Logos in	**VI**: 673, 675, 676.
Logos of, and in John	**VI**: 672*(2)*, 673, 674; **VIII**: 129*(2)*, 130*(2)*.
Logos of, Personal or Impersonal(?)	**VI**: 677.
Man's Yearning for, in	**VI**: 674.
Method in Studying, Problems of	**VI**: 675.
Migration, Concerning	**VI**: 674.
Neo-Pythogorean Source	**VI**: 675.
New Testament, Influence of, on	**VI**: 675; **VIII**: 274.
Nobility, Concerning	**VI**: 674.
Obscure Tradition in Rabbinic Literature and, Mutually Clarified	**VI**: 678.
Odes (of Solomon) and	**VI**: 674.
Old Testament Quotations	**VI**: 676.
Old Testament, Relation to	**VI**: 674.
Old Testament, Use of, by	**VI**: 675.
Opinions of	**VI**: 672.
OT Canon, and his mode of quoting the Alexandrian Version	**IV**: 201; **VI**: 673.
Passover Texts in	**V**: 87; **VI**: 676, 682.
Pastoral Epistles and	**VI**: 675.
Paul and	**VI**: 674, 675; **VIII**: 292*(2)*.
Philo-semitism among Ancient Intellectuals	**V**: 113.
Philosophy of	**V**: 109; **VI**: 672, 676.
Plato and	**VI**: 677.
Platoism of	**VI**: 672.
Prayer of Petition in	**VI**: 676.
Public Life, and	**VI**: 675.
Pupils of, An Imaginary Dialogue	**VI**: 677.
Rabbinic Literature, Mentioned in(?)	**VI**: 675, 688.
Repentence, Concerning	**VI**: 674.
Rossi, Azariah de, on	**VI**: 676.
Sanhedrin (Synedrion) in	**I**: 465; **VI**: 676.

Septuagint Text of IV: 26, 27; VI: 673*(3)*.
Septuagint *Vorlage* and IV: 35; VI: 660, 677.
St. John and VI: 673.
St. Paul (1 Cor.) and VI: 672.
Therapeutae and VI: 672*(2)*.
Time, Concept of VI: 677.
Virgin-Birth in VI: 99, 675.
Vohu Manah, as Logos of VI: 673; VIII: 130.
Yaḥad (יַחַד) in DSS and VI: 677, 683; VIII: 423.
Zarathustra and V: 36, 232; VI: 674.
Zohar and V: 240*(2)*; VI: 677.

Philo of Byzantion: III: *488*.
Philocalia: VI: 721.
Philoe: II: *222*.
Philological and Epigraphical Studies III: 285; IV: 216; V: **§484, 275-280**; VIII: 1.
Ablative Case, Origin of V: 278.
Akkadian and Sumerian in Comparative V: 542, 578.
Babylonian V: 577.
Biblical V: 278.
Biblical, and the Concordance V: 280.
Biblical Archaeology and, Contributions of V: 278.
Cognates, Study of V: 277.
Comparative V: 275, 280.
Comparative, with the Origin of Culture in America III: 410; V: 162; IX: xciv.
Future of V: 277.
Genitive Case, Origin of V: 275.
Geology and V: 275.
Georgian and Sumerian, in Comparative V: 580*(2)*.
Hebrew / Sanskrit, Comparative V: 132, 143.
Linguistics and, Conflict bewteen in Semitic V: 380.
Man's Origin and III: 334.
Old Testament and IV: 165; V: 278.
Oriental V: 275, 279.
Practical Lingusitics and V: 277.
Prehistoric / Protohistoric III: *410;* V: *162*, 277.
Semitic, Comparative V: 276, 305*(2)*.
Sumerian and Akkadian in Comparative V: 542, 578.
Sumerian and Georgian, in Comparative V: 580*(2)*.
Textual Criticism and IV: 6, 70; V: 280.
Theology and V: 275.
Transposition, Assimilation, Conformation V: 278.
Ugaritic V: 390, 533, 537.
Witness of, to Truth of the OT IV: 165.

Philon: I: *311*.
Athenian Naval Arsenal of III: 458; VII: 335.

Philonides:
Letter of, to Kleon VII: 331.

Philopator: VII: *28*.
Philosemitism: VIII: 336.
Philosophers:
Greek, and Hebrew Prophets, Symbolic Acts of I: 110; V: 256, 273.
Mutual Duties Between, and Theologian VIII: 1.

Philosophumena:
Essenes in V: 97*(2)*; VI: 683*(2)*, 723.

Philosophy: III: 288, 291; IV: 150; VIII: 8, 247.
Ancient, History of V: 109.
Arabic Terms of V: 677.
Babylonian Philosopher of History V: 186.
Bible and IV: 157.
Biblical Theology and VIII: 11, 13.
Coinage and I: 444.
Creation, Philosopher's View of VIII: 79.

Darwin's Impact on	**III**: 327.
Egyptian, of a Memphite Priest	**V**: 204; **VII**: 10, 39.
Exegesis and	**IV**: 98.
God, Belief in, and	**VIII**: 66.
Greek and Hebrew Thought Compared	**I**: 126, *331(2)*,
Greek, Early Philosophers	**V**: 249.
Greek, in Septuagint(?)	**IV**: 26.
Greek, Logic of Early	**V**: 249.
Greek, Relation to Religion in	**V**: 244.
Greek, *see also:* ***Greek Mythology***	
Greek, Synopsis of, by Bar 'Ebhrâyâ	**V**: 110.
Handmaiden of Theology	**VI**: 725.
Hebrew, *see:* ***Hebrew Philosophy***	
Internal Senses in Latin, Arabic, and Hebrew Philosophicla Texts	**V**: 112, 148.
Jewish, is there a(?)	**V**: 113.
Jewish Mysticism and	**V**: 112.
Jewish Philosopher on the Doctrine of the Messiah	**VIII**: 141.
Logos, Meaning and History of, in	**V**: 248.
Midrash, Implicit in	**V**: 113.
Old Testament, in(?)	**V**: 113.
Old Testament, of	**V**: 112.
Omnipotence and	**VIII**: 100.
Orphism, or Popular(?)	**V**: 258.
Persian Terms of	**V**: 677.
Pharisees of	**V**: 99.
Plato's Conception of	**V**: 264.
Revelation, and	**VIII**: 32.
Septuagint, Greek, in(?)	**IV**: 26.
Stoic, the Wise Man in	**V**: 267.
Theology and	**VIII**: 5.
Philoteria, *see also:* **Beth Yerah**	**II**: 343, 463; **IX**: cxvii, clii*(2)*.
Philus:	**III**: **199**.
Phinehas:	**I**: 76.
Phistyon:	
Greek Inscription from	**VII**: 326.
Phlius:	
Pottery Sherds from	**III**: 634.
Votive Deposit from	**III**: 579.
Phocaean Gold (Coins)	**I**: 445.
Phocis (Phokis):	**I**: 301; **III**: *141*, 199.
Phoenicia:	**I**: *323(2)*, *340(2)*, *362*; **II**: 304; **III**: 56, **199**, *247(2)*, 442, *759*.
Archaeolgical Remains in Southern	**II**: 293; **III**: 421.
Bronze Age in	**II**: 175, 189.
Coast Road of	**I**: 347.
Egyptian Inscription from	**VII**: 59.
Gods of	**V**: 191.
Hawk in	**III**: 375, 699.
Irrigation Culture of Northern	**II**: 293; **III**: 421.
Isarel and	**II**: 156.
Polynesia, Intercourse with	**IX**: xcv.
Ralwinson, George, on the History of	**II**: 156.
Relic of Pharaoh Necho (II) from (Text)	**VII**: 59.
Phoenician, including Carthaginian	**V**: *503*, 512*(2)*, **§527**, **522-523**, *528*.
Dialect of Larnax Tes Lapethou	**V**: 523.
Enclitic *men* in	**V**: 522.
Etymologies of North African Toponyms	**II**: 272; **V**: 523.
Grammar of	**V**: 522.
Hieroglyphics and Pre-Phœnician Script	**V**: 307, 522.
Infinitive Absolute in	**V**: 522.
Infinitive Absolute in the Inscription of Azitawadd	**V**: 522.
Particle אש	**V**: 522.
Particles of the Yqtl Pattern	**V**: 522.
Possesive Pronouns in	**V**: 523.

Pronominal Suffixes in **V**: 522.
Script, Ezekiel and **VI**: 355.
Phoenician Chronology: **II**: 203.
Phoenician Inscriptions and Texts: **VII**: **§865, 113-121**.
Aḫîrâm, of **VII**: 117*(4)*.
Arrow-head, with **III**: 683; **VII**: 120.
Azitawad's Inscription from Karatepe **V**: 400, 522; **VII**: 119*(2)*, 306.
Bilingual, Assyrian and **VII**: 113, 197.
Bilingual, Cypriote and **VII**: 115, *357*.
Bilingual, Greek and, at Larnax, Lapethos **VII**: 331.
Bod ʿAšhtart, of **VII**: 116*(2)*, 117.
Brazil, Pseudo-Phœnican **VII**: 86, 114, 120*(3)*.
Byblus, 10th Cent. B.C. **VII**: 118.
Cilicia, from **VII**: 118*(3)*, 119*(2)*.
Cilician Bilinguals, Contribution to the Decipherment of Hittite **V**: 612; **VII**: 119.
Cylinder with **VII**: 115.
Cyprus, at **VII**: 115.
Cyprus Collection of Di Cesnola, in **VII**: 114*(2)*, 115*(3)*.
Cyprus Museum, in **VII**: 117.
Elibaʿal, of **VII**: 117.
Esmun Temple, of **VII**: 116*(2)*.
Ex-voto from Temple of Baal at Carthage **VII**: 115.
Forged, in the Louvre **VII**: 118.
Funeral Tablet **V**: 189; **VII**: 115.
Gems with **VII**: 114.
Geography of **VII**: 116.
Gesenius, on **VII**: 113, 118.
Greenock, at **VII**: 116*(2)*.
Hanno's Periplus, Background of **VII**: 121.
Hebrew, in Phoenician Characters **III**: 409*(2)*.
Hispania 14 **VII**: 120.
Jar, from Shiqmona **VII**: 120.
Karatepe, from **VII**: 118*(3)*, 119*(4)*, 120.
Larnaca, at, discovered by Cobham **VII**: 114*(2)*, 115*(2)*.
Larnax Tēs Lapēthou **VII**: 117, `10.
Malta, from **VII**: 120.
"Melitensis Quinta" **VII**: 114*(3)*.
Melrose, at **VII**: 115.
Neopunic, in England **VII**: 118.
Nimrud Bronze Bowls, with **VII**: 120*(2)*.
Palestine, Alleged, from **VII**: 114, 295.
Papyrus from Saqqara **VII**: 119.
Phoenician-Hittite (Laīnuha) **VII**: 304.
Pœnulus of Platus, in **VII**: 114*(2)*.
Political Document **VII**: 118.
Ptolemaic Date, of **VII**: 118.
Punic, from Amtas **VII**: 121.
Punic, from Pyrgi **VII**: 120*(2)*.
Punic, in the British Museum **VII**: 115.
Rhodes, Fragment from **VII**: 118.
Royal Inscription from Cilicia **III**: 135.
Sanchuniaton **V**: 569; **VII**: 119.
Saqqara, Papyrus from **VII**: 119.
Seals with **III**: 640, 641*(2)*.
Semitic, from Malta **VII**: 120.
Sidon, at **VII**: 117.
Sidonian Sarcophagus **III**: *530;* **VII**: 113*(3)*.
Spindle Whorl with **VII**: 120; **IX**: cxxiv.
Tabnit, from **VII**: 115.
Tell el Hesy, of **VII**: 116.
Temple of Esmun at Sidon, from **II**: 203.
Ur, from **VII**: 117.
Vase Ḥandles on, from Jerusalem **VII**: 116.
Votive Statue with **III**: 761; **VII**: 117.

Phoenician Language: V: 280, 383, *473*.
Conjugation, ת in V: 372, 486, 522, 523. 554, 558, 585.
Infinitive Absolute in V: 539.
Pre-Phœnician Script and Hieroglyphics V: 307.
Phoenician Religion: V: **§469, 189-199**.
Worship of heptad called κάβειροι = כַּבִּירִים V: 195.
Phoenicians: I: *332*, 338, 340, *462, 489;* II: **155-157**; III: *151*.
Anthropology of II: 157; III: 353.
Assembly of a Phoenician City V: 433.
Hebrews and IV: 246; V: 1, 6.
Nebuchadnezzar's Reconquest of, and Palestine, in Ezekiel IV: 422.
Old Testament and IV: 186.
Scandiavia, Colonization in IX: xcvi, cx.
Spain, in III: 210, 237, 247.
Sumerians, as IX: cvii, cx, cxi.
Tripoli, in (?) III: 258.
Word Study V: 503.
Phoenix: III: 777; V: 199.
Job, in VI: 435.
Phoinikaios:
Greek Month of I: 401; V: 258.
Phokaia: III: 263.
Phokas, Cape: III: *152;* V: *263*.
Phonetics:
Hebrew V: 474.
Phonology:
Hebrew V: 475, 479.
Indo-European V: *429*.
"Sabra"-Hebrew, of V: 475.
Photius: V: *606*.
Josephus, References to, in the Bibliotheca of VI: 682.
Photogrammetry:
Archaeological Use of II: 220; III: 222; IX: cxii.
Phrases Keyed to English: **V: §525, 518-521; IX: §525, cxli.**
Phreatto: I: 500.
Phrygia: I: *175(2);* III: *262*.
Jewish Military Colonies I: 172; VI: 683.
Phrygian Language:
Medial Verbal *-r* Termination in V: 679.
Phrygian Texts: VII: 374, 375.
Phrygians: II: 157, *272;* III: *71*.
Phylacteries: I: 365, **§112, 371**; VIII: 436.
Qumran from (4QPhyl) **VIII: §1142, 471.**
Samariatan V: 228.
Physicians: III: 396.
Asclepiad, of Cnidus and Cos III: 403, 518.
Assyrian, Letter of VII: 178.
Hippocratean Patient and III: 401.
History of, and Sun-God as Great Physician III: 397.
Israel, Social Position of III: 403.
Liturgy (Greek), Exception of, from VII: 344.
Medical Equipment of Hippocratean III: 401.
Ur-ᵈLugal-edin-na III: 399, *647*.
Physics: III: 325, 329.
Application to coins by x-ray analysis I: 457.
Coins, analysis of by charged particles and fast neutrons I: 459.
Man, Origin of, and III: 290.
Posidian, Cosmogony and Stereometry in II: 223.
Physiognomics: III: 354; VII: 156.
Physiology:
Assyrians, among Ancient III: 396.
Sabbath and V: 79.

Phytios: III: 708.

Pi (π):
- Elohim and I: 429; **IV**: 254.

Pi-Ra'messe-mi-Amūn: **III**: **200**, *246*.

Piankhi: **II**: **74**, *82*.
- Instructions to His Army **VII**: 66.

Piankhy:
- Sandstone Stela of **VII**: 21.

Piatane: **II**: 463, *464*.

Picenum: **III**: *100*, 199, *213*.

Pick, *see also:* **Axes**
- Khurab, Camel on **III**: 370, *676*.
- Mason's **III**: 674.

PICO, GIOVANNI:
- Job, on **IV**: 54.

Pictorgraphs: **III**: 718*(2)*.

PIELE, JOHN:
- Etymology, Latin and Greek, of **V**: 626, 627.

PIERIDES, ZENO: **III**: *661*.

Piety: **VIII**: 199.
- Biblical Criticism and **IV**: 116; **VIII**: 314.
- Christian, of Pre-Destruction Hebraic Judaism **V**: 27.
- Dead, Disposal of, and Origins of **I**: 375.
- Death, Problem of, in Popular Judaeo-Hellenistic **VIII**: 263.
- Greek and Hebrew, Contrasting Attitudes **V**: 151; **VIII**: 199; **IX**: cxxxviii.
- Individual, in the OT **VIII**: 198.
- Sumerian Kings, of **V**: 185.

Pig(s), *see also*: **Pork**: **I**: 182, 247.
- Cult-Animal of Set **III**: 380; **V**: 211.
- Egypt, in **III**: 380, 399.
- Pohibition of Breeding **I**: 182.

Pignus: **I**: 471.

Pilate, Pontius: **I**: *449;* **II**: **74-75**.
- Dismissal from Judea **II**: 75.
- Syrian Coinage, and **II**: 74.

Pileh Qal 'eh: **III**: *158*.

Pilgrimages:
- Jerusalem, to, in time of Second Temple **I**: 366.

"Pillar of Salt": **II**: 380, 484; **VI**: 70*(2)*.

Pillars, Cultic *see also:* **Columns** **V**: **§426, 46-50**.
- Druidical Stone, Supposed **V**: 46.
- Epistlye from Nereid Monument, Resotration **III**: 473*(2)*.
- Lachish **III**: 480.
- Moabite Monolith **V**: 46.
- Osirids **V**: 200.
- Porch of, Solomon's Temple **V**: 72.
- Reliefs on *κιονίσκοι* **III**: 724.
- Stone, partly quarried **III**: 461.
- Tell el Hesy, at **V**: 46.

Pinax, Pinakes: **III**: 579, 614.

Pindar: **III**: *597*.
- Greek Religion and Morality in **V**: 251.
- Odes of Victory **VII**: 346.

PINKHAM, F. J.:
- Psalter, on **IV**: 494.

Pins, Linch: **III**: 677.

Pins, Toggle: **III**: 600, 675*(2)*.

Pionia: **III**: *104, 149*, 200.

Piqquaḥ Hefesh **VI**: 690.

Pir-idri *see also:* **Ben-Hadad** **II**: 27; **VI**: 235; **VII**: 186.

Piracy: **I**: 326, 352.

Piraeus: **I**: *313;* **III**: 200, *466*.

Pirathon: **II**: 284.

Pirke Aboth: **VI**: **§814, 710**.
- Analysis of **VI**: 710.
- Polemic of Second Century Gnosticism **VI**: 710.
- Textual Criticism of **VI**: 710.

Pirkê de Rabbi Eliezer: **VI**: 707.

Pisgah (Mount): **II**: *389*, **463**; **VI**: 154; **IX**: cxvii.

Pīsh-i-Kūn: **III**: 35, 153, 200.

Pisidia: **III**: **200**, 263.
Greek Inscripions from **VII**: 328*(2)*, 331.
Pisistratus: **II**: 75.
Piska: **IV**: 17, 18*(2)*.
Piso: **III**: 104, 194; **IX**: cii.
Pit, *see also:* **Sheol** **VIII**: 267.
"Going down to the" **IV**: 220.
Job, in **VI**: 436.
Pitane:
Painted Sarcophagi from **III**: 559.
Pitch:
Glance, from Tel Beit Mirsim **II**: 249.
Pitcher:
Oenochoë, Arapides **III**: 623.
Oenochoë, from Athenian Agora **III**: 618.
Oenochoë, Geometric, with Ship Scene **III**: 634, 718.
Oenochoë, Red-figured **III**: 634.
Pithecanthropian Remains **III**: 363.
Pithecanthropus Erectus: **III**: 355, 358.
Pithekoussai: **I**: 356; **III**: 200.
Pithom: **III**: 83, *121*, **201-202**, 207*(4)*, *238*, *281;* **IV**: 332, 333; **VI**: 98.
Semitic Name of **III**: 202; **V**: 297.
Pithos:
Attic, Development of **III**: 634.
Fragments of Cretan **III**: 461.
Two, from Beth-Shean Region and Jordan Valley **III**: 635.
Pity:
Self-Pity **VIII**: 67, 172.
Piyyuṭ (Piyyuṭim): **IV**: 5; **V**: 85, 689.
Battle Between Behemoth and Leviathan in **V**: 137; **VIII**: 83, 371.
Cairo Genizah from **VII**: 108*(4);* **VIII**: 206.
Hasha'not—Remnants of Ancient **VIII**: 207.
Roots of the Language of **V**: 689.
Place Names and Town Lists: **II**: **§161, 262-273**; **IX**: **§161, cxiii-cxiv**.
A-bi/pí-ak **II**: 271.
A-pi$_4$-sal.ki **II**: 270.
Aegean, in a List of Amenophis III **II**: 272.
Aegean, in an Egyptian Inscription **II**: 272.
Anatolian **II**: 267, 270, 271.
Asia Minor. Pre-Greek **II**: 271.
Assyrian **II**: 264, 265*(2)*.
Assyrian, of Egyptian Locations **II**: 262*(2)*.
Babylonian **II**: 265*(2)*.
Babylonian NIN-IP **V**: 297.
Bašam lú Simanum.ki **II**: 271.
Biblical Cities in Cuneiform Records **II**: 268.
Canaanite Toponymy **VI**: 172, 173*(2)*.
Definite Article in Palestinian **II**: 268.
Egyptian, *see also:* Karnak Lists, and Shishak Lists **II**: 262, 265, 266, 268, 271*(2)*.
Geniza Fragments with **II**: 268.
Greek **II**: 268.
Greek, Pre- **II**: 267, 271.
Hebrew Toponyms **II**: 273.
Hittite Geographical **II**: 267.
Hurrian **II**: 270.
Ka-ma-ri.ki **II**: 271.
Khâna **V**: 544.
KIŠ.ki **II**: 271.
KS.ZAL.LU.ki **II**: 271.
lú Ka-zal-lu.ki **II**: 271.
Ma-hi-li.ki **II**: 271.
Malta, in **V**: 297.
Malta, in **V**: 297; **IX**: cxiii.
MAR AD.ki **II**: 271.
Palestinian **II**: 268.
Palestinian, Hellenistic **II**: 269.

Palestinian, Israelite **II**: 271.
Palestinian, Pre-Israelite **II**: 271.
Palestinian, Southern **II**: 266.
Phoenician **II**: 272.
Phoenician Etymologies of North African Toponyms **II**: 272; **V**: 523.
Pre-Greek, Geographical Distribution of **IX**: cxiv.
Samaria Ostraca, in **VII**: 95.
Samaria*SPR* **V**: 529; **VII**: 137.
Sinuhe's Flight, Route of **II**: 270.
Syrian **II**: 266.
Talmudic, Identification of **II**: 270.
Transtrigridian **II**: 273.

Placenta:
Pharaoh's, and the Moon-god Khons **V**: 207, 208.

Plaga Septentrionalis:
Sumero-Akkadian Mythology, in **V**: 186.

Plague(s): **IV**: *146*.
Assyrian Plague-tablets **VII**: 199.
Blood-, Motif in Sumeran Mythology **V**: 186; **VII**: 283.
Bubonic(?) (and Mice) **III**: 378*(2)*, 397*(4)*; **VI**: 195*(2)*.
Chaldea, Legends **VII**: 198.
Egyptain Word for (?) **V**: 344.
Insects, caused by **III**: 365, 398; **VI**: 195.
Philistines of **VI**: 195*(2)*.
Rodents, caused by **III**: 365, 398; **VI**: 195.

Plagues of Egypt: **IV**: 325, 329, 330; **VI**: 102, 105*(2)*.
Biological Sequence of **IV**: 328.
Death of the Firstborn **IV**: 329.
Miraculous Element in **IV**: 325.
Science and **IV**: 328.
Sixth **IV**: 327.
Tradition in Ps 105 **VI**: 514.

Plaid: **IV**: 219.

Plain:
"Cities of the Plain" **II**: 284.

Plamochoe:
Cosmic Significance of **V**: 267.

Planetary Tables (Texts):
Babylonian **II**: 234.
Defects in **II**: 225; **III**: 777.
Egyptian **II**: 231; **VII**: 35.

Planetary Week:
Origin of, in Hebrew Literature **II**: 232; **IX**: xcvii.

Planets:
Babylonian Astronomy **II**: 227.
Babylonian Planetary Theory **II**: 233, 235.
Babylonian Sign and Name for **II**: 228; **V**: 573.
Egyptian Planetary Texts **II**: 231.
Jupiter = Star Hêlēl(?) **II**: 230.
Lists of Longitudes of, in Late Babylonian **II**: 234.
Mars **II**: 229.
Mercury, Babylonian Method of Computation for Visibilities of **II**: 233.
Saturn **II**: 229.
Venus Tablets of Ammiṣaduqa **II**: 232.

Plants: Botanical Studies - General: **III**: 364*(2)*, **§175, 383-386**.
Alliaceous **III**: 385.
Alphabetical Listing of Plants **III**: **§176, 386-396**.
Assyrian Monuments, Unnoticed, on **III**: 383.
Babylonia, Names of, and Things made from **III**: 384, 563, 572.
Bak(h)a **II**: 266; **III**: 387.
Broom **III**: 387.
Calendar **III**: 387, 389.
Caper-plant **VI**: 565.
Cultivated from 'Afula **III**: 385.
Cultivated, Remains of, from Ḥorvat Beter **III**: 386.
Cultivation, Origin of **I**: 253; **III**: 384.
Cyperus esculentus, L. **V**: 336.
Distribution of **III**: 314, 364.

Economic, of the Bible **IX**: cxxii.
Egypt, in **III**: 384.
Egypt, Medical Uses of, in Modern **IX**: xcvii.
Evolution of **III**: 314.
Fertilization, Assyrian and Fossil Pollen **III**: 386.
Flora of Syria, Palestine, and Sinai **III**: 384.
Flora of the Bible and Biblical Scholarship **III**: 386.
"Hairs of the Earth" **III**: 391.
Hebrew names for some **III**: 386.
Medea's and Mandrake **III**: 392.
Medical Use in Egypt **III**: 385*(3)*; **IX**: cxxii.
Moly **III**: 392.
Names, Ancient **III**: 384*(3)*.
Oil, from Anatolia **III**: 386.
Palestinian Superstition, and **I**: 390.
Plant-Lore in Olden Times **III**: 384.
Pollen, Fossil **III**: 386.
Soda Plant **III**: *394*.

Plaque:
Bossed Bone **III**: 772.
Bronze, from Cyrene **III**: 753, *769*.
Engraved, in the collection of the Earl of Carnarvon **IX**: cxxvi.
Engraved Stone, Nippur **III**: 771.
Hyksos **III**: 668.
Inscribed with name of Bak-en-Khensu **III**: 680.
Marble, Decorated **III**: 749.

Plaster Casts:
Ancient, of Greek Metalware **I**: 299.

Plataea: **III**: *590*.

Plataia: **III**: **202**, *487*.
Temple, Archaic, at **III**: 508.

Platanos: **II**: *463*, 464.

Plate(s):
Allotment, *see; **Allotment***
Black Figured, with Illustration of Hesiod by the Strife Painter **III**: 610.

Platform:
Copper, Before Solomon's Temple **IV**: 220; **VI**: 591.
Temple, Herod's, Position of **V**: 76.

Platinum: **I**: 294.

Plato: **I**: 193, *429*; **II**: **75**, *135*, *224*; **III**: *31*; **VII**: 345*(2)*, 346.
Anthropology and **III**: 351.
Articular Infinitive in **V**: 629.
Christianity, Foreshadowings of, in **V** 245.
Death, Conception of **V**: 249.
Etymology of Greek Mythological Terms According to **V**: 250, 637.
"Forms" of **V**: 255*(3)*.
Geology and **II**: 222.
God of **V**: 255*(4)*.
Humor of **V**: 258.
Immortality and **V** 244, 246.
Language, Theory of, and **V**: 279.
Laws of compared with Mosaic **I**: 479.
Logic and Literary Form in **V**: 266; **VII**: 348.
Mysticism of **V**: 253.
Myths of **V**: 249.
Nature, System of, on **V** 244.
Number of **VIII**: 309.
Ontological Argument of **VIII**: 70; **IX**: cxxxviii.
Orientalism of **V**: 246.
Philo and **VI**: 677.
Philo, Platoism of **VI**: 672.
Portrait of **III**: 721.
Republic, and Ezekiel's Holy State **IV**: 419.
Republic, Evolution of **VII**: 347.
Theology of, Background **V**: 256.
Transmigration in **V**: 262.
War and **VIII**: 233.
Wisdom of Solomon and **VI**: 619.

Plautus: **I**: *344*.
Parallels (Comparative Religions) from **V**: 143.

Roman Religion, as Source Book for V: 270.
Playthings:
Greek I: 238.
Plebeian State:
Rise of Patrician— II: 134.
Plebiscite:
Licinio-Sextian I: 502.
Pledge:
Clothes VI: 379.
Code of Hammurabi on I: 478, 496.
Inalienablity of Mobile and Immmobile, in Bible I: 513.
Pleiades: VI: 439.
Plesheth: II: *154, 155.*
Pliny the Elder: II: 75, *304.*
Damophon and III: 699.
Death of, and Amphora III: 610.
Emperor Worship, on V: 272.
Relics of, Located III: 566, 687.
Pliny the Younger: II: 75; VIII: 369.
Emperor Worship, on V: 272.
Plotinus: V: 110.
PLOTINUS: VIII: 98.
Anthropology and III: 351.
Plow: I: 252, 253; III: 571; IX: lxxxix*(2)*, xcv.
Abraham as Inventor of the Improved I: 29*(2)*, 252*(2)*.
First, on a Krater by the Painter of the Naples Hephaistos III: 611.
Ploughing in Talmudic Literature VI: 694.
Plumes: I: 278.
Plunder: VI: 145.
Pluralism:
Religious, A Jewish View VIII: 337.
Plutarch:
Isis, Name of, in V: 215, 258.
Zoraster and Avesta, in *Artaxerxes,* Ch. iii, 1-10 V: 230.
Plutonion: V: 255; VII: 322.
Pneumatology *see:* **Holy Spirit**
Pneumonia:
Assyrian Prescriptions for III: 405.
Pnubs: III: 20, 202, 522.
"Pocket": III: 686.
POE, EDGAR ALLAN:
Bible and VIII: 367.
Pœnulus of Plautus:
Phœnician passage in VII: 114*(2)*.
Poesidon:
Temple of, at Isthmia III: 501.
Poetical Books:
Bibliography I: **(§22)**, 13.
Exegetical Studies on Several Books of the VI: **§642, 419.**
Literary Criticism of IV: **§380, 456.**
Literary Style of V: **§572, 705-706.**
Noyes, George R., on IV: 456.
Poetics:
Interpretation of the Biblical Narrative and IV: 378; V: 702.
Poetry:
Akkadian V: 541; VII: 146; IX: cxliv.
Alans, Epic Poetry of the VII: 137.
Arabian, and Hebrew Literature of the OT IV: 192.
Arabic in Isaiah 27(?) VI: 283.
Aramaic Liturgical, of the Jews V: 688.
Aramaic Verse VII: 124.
Aristotle's Theory of III: 694; VII: 346.
Assyrian Royal VII: 181.
Babylonian V: 544.
Babylonian and Hebrew V: 685*(2)*; VII: 254*(3)*, 268.
Babylonian Religious VII: 258.
Bible and the Poets VIII: 361.
Bible in Contemporary VIII: 369.
Bible in Non-Hebaric VIII: 361.
Cairo Genizah Fragments VII: 106*(6)*, 107.
Canaanite IV: 187.
Deborah's Song as Earliest Form of Hebrew Verse IV: 371; V: 686.

Divine Nature of, in Antiquity **V**: 260.
Egyptian, *see:* ***Egyptian Secular Songs and Poems***
Epos **II**: 163*(2)*.
Epos, Ugaritic **V**: 196.
Greek, Cyclic, in Olbia **VII**: 348.
Greek, Relation Between Morality and **VIII**: 222.
Hebrew Poetic Structure as a Translation Guide **IV**: 106, 107; **V**: 687, 688.
Hebrew, *see:* ***Hebrew (OT) Poetry***
Hittite Epic, Metre in **V**: 614.
North-Canaanite **VII**: 117, 138.
Orators, as training for **I**: 182.
Patriotic, in Amarna Letters(?) **VII**: 171.
Phoenician Poem, at Ras Shamra **VII**: 117, 138.
Plato's Conception of **V**: 264.
Prophecy and **VIII**: 398.
Proverbs, Book of, Greek, in **IV**: 500.
Righteous Sufferer, of **VII**: 181.
Roman, Observations on the Gods, in **V**: 270.
Sacred **VIII**: 360.
Sumerian Love **VII**: 274.
Transmission of Poetic Text **IV**: 5.
Ugaritic **VII**: 139, 141*(2)*.
Ugaritic and Biblical **V**: 688.
Ugaritic, on the Conquest of Death **VII**: 138.
Use of, in Training of the Ancient Orator **VII**: 2.

Poets:
Greek, and Hebrew Prophets **I**: 113; **V**: 150.
Prophets and **I**: 105*(2)*, *110, 113;* **VIII**: 368.

Poggio Civitate: **III**: 202.

Poison: **III**: 405.
Assyrian Prescriptions for **III**: 405.
Egypt, in **III**: 406.
Ordeals by, in the Ancient Orient **V**: 106.

Polarity:
Hamitic Languages, in **V**: 305*(2)*.

Polatli: **III**: 203.

Poleg, Tel: **II**: 464.

Polemics:
Jewish, Against Gnosticism **V**: 240.
Jewish-Christian and Origenes' Commentaries on Song of Songs **VI**: 716, 727.
Jewish-Persian Argument **VI**: 727.
melekh ha-ʿolam as anti-Gnostic protests **V**: 240.

Police:
Roman Times, and **I**: 493, 509.

Polis:
Was Jerusalem a(?) **II**: 419.

Political Crime:
Egypt, in **I**: 497.

Political Gratitude: **I**: 489.

Political Institutions:
Israel, in **I**: 470.
Sumer, in **I**: 470.

Political Motives:
Patriarchal Stories, and **I**: 467.

Political Parties:
Israel, in **I**: 460.
Roman **I**: 489.

Political Theory:
Biblical **I**: 466; **VIII**: 216.

Politics: **I**: *160, 181, 322, 338;* **III**: *594*.
104 B.C., (in Rome) **I**: 493.
Alexander Jannaeus and **II**: 53.
Amarna Age **I**: *494;* **II**: 3.
Greece, Constitutions, Inheritance, and Land Distribution **I**: 228, 261.
Herod of **I**: 178, 469, 470; **II**: 47.
Hezekiah and Imperial **I**: 469.
High Priests and, in Roman Palestine **I**: 469; **V**: 45.

Isaiah and — **I**: 460, 469.
Israel, as Affected by Assyrian, Babylonian, and Achaemenian Kings — **I**: 322.
Israel, Characteristics of Political Life in — **I**: 460.
Israel - General Studies — **I**: *96*, **§127, 460-471**; **IX: §127, c.**
Jeremiah and — **I**: 460.
Jeremiah, Book of, in — **I**: 470.
Jerusalem, in and Tablet BM 21,901 — **I**: 462; **IV**: 360; **VII**: 236.
Lamps and — **III**: 594.
Patriarchs, Political Motives in Stories of — **I**: 467.
Pharisees and — **V**: 100.
Phoenician Political Document — **VII**: 118.
Prophets and — **I**: *102, 460(2), 469.*

Politics (outside Israel): — **I**: **§135, 488-494**; **IX**: **§135, ci-cii.**
Alexander and 'Homonoia' — **II**: 11.
Aristotle and — **I**: 494; **IX**: cii.
Assyrian — **I**: 461; **VI**: 237.
Athenian — **I**: 488.
Babylonian, Development of — **I**: 489.
Demeter's Sicilian Cult as Political Instrument — **I**: 493; **V**: 238.
Egyptian (Stela of <u>D</u>*MY*) — **VII**: 16.
Hittite, Geography — **III**: 104.
'Homonoia' and Alexander — **II**: 11.
Incense Trade, Effects on — **I**: 340, 468, 492; **IX**: xcv.
Mesopotamian — **I**: *490*, 491.
Parthian — **I**: 492.
Roman, Stoicism and — **I**: 492; **V**: 270; **IX**: cii.
Senatorial, 168-146 B.C. — **I**: 494.
Shamash, Political Hymn to — **VII**: 260.
Syrian, with reference to Israelite kingdoms — **I**: 470; **III**: 245.

Polity:
Hebrew, Ancient — **I**: 461, 462*(2)*.
Poll-tax: — **I**: 482.
Pollen:
Fossil, and Assyrian Plant Fertilization — **III**: 386.
Pollentia: — **III**: 203.
Pollio:
Pharisee, in Josephus — **V**: 99; **VI**: 683.
Jewish Interests of — **II**: 75.
Pollio, Vedius: — **I**: *504*.
Pollion: — **VI**: 680.
Pollux: — **I**: *276*.
Polos: — **I**: 280.
Polyandry, *see also:* **Polygamy** — **IX**: v, n.3.
Polybius: — **II**: 75.
POLYCARP:
Fourth Gospel and — **VI**: 658, 718.
Testament of the Twelve Patriarchs and — **VI**: 658, 718; **VIII**: 287.
Polychrome Bible:
Assyrian Flood Tablet and — **IV**: 252.
Polychromy, *see:* **Color**
Polygamy: — **I**: *211*, 214, 217, 219, 221, 222*(2)*; **VI**: 213.
Polyglot Bibles: — **IV**: 10, 49, 72, 102.
Complutensian — **IV**: 103*(2)*.
Polygnotos II: — **III**: 615.
Polygons:
Babylonian Mathematics and — **I**: 435.
Greek Mathematics and — **I**: 435.
Polykates: — **II**: 76.
Polynesia:
Phoenician Intercourse with — **IX**: xcv.
Polyperchon: — **II**: 134.
Polytheism: — **I**: 183; **V**: 153; **VIII**: 105.
Bible and Mythological — **V**: 108, 133.
Egyptian Mythologies — **V**: 200.

Genesis I, in **VI**: 23.
Hebrew Attitude towards Mythological **V**: 133, 158.
High Culture and **V**: 160.
Israel, in **V**: 103.
Israelites, Were they Ever Polytheists(?) **V**: 11.
Jewish, Prayer in **VIII**: 202.
Monotheism Before, **V**: 33.
Monotheism Predecessor to, in Sumerian Religion **V**: 35, 185.
Tolerance of, in Classical Antiquity and its Limits **V**: 159.

Pomegranate(s): **III**: **393**, *593*.

The Pomegranate, *see:* **Rock Rimmon**

Pompeius:
Distirubition of forces in Campaign of 67 B.C. **II**: 76.

Pompey: **I**: 176,*490;* **II**: **76**; **III**: *203*.
Capture of Jerusalem and the Habakkuk Scrolls **VIII**: 456.

Pont du Gard: **I**: 362.

Ponte di Nona:
Votive Deposit at **III**: 576.

Pontus: **III**: 203; **VII**: *312*.

Pools: **I**: 358*(2)*, 359*(2)*, 363*(2)*; **IV**: 220.
Abydos, Great Pool at **III**: 542.
Bethesda, Pool of **I**: 357*(3)*, 358*(4)*, *360*, 362*(2)*; **III**: 411.
Conduit to Upper **I**: 363; **VI**: 240, 259.
Gibeon, Pool at **I**: 363.
Jerusalem, of **I**: 361; **II**: 412.
Jerusalem, Old, west of **II**: 407.
Rock, in Central Sudan **I**: 364.
Siloam, Pool of **I**: 357*(4)*.
Solomon's Pool **I**: 357.
Strouthion, of **III**: 409.

Poor, *see:* **Poverty**

Poppy:
Egyptian Art, in **III**: 393, 695, 707.

Population Studies, *see also:* **Demography** **I**: *258, 334;* **II**: 1, 245, **§160**, **259-262**.
Age of Man determined by **III**: 341.
Antediluvian World **II**: 259.
Antioch **II**: 261*(2)*; **III**: 15*(2)*.
Babylonian, nomadic contribution to **II**: 261.
Bible Confirmed by **II**: 259.
Canaan, Indigenous of, and Israel, in the Book of Judges **IV**: 369.
Canaan, Indigenous of, and Israel, in the Books of Samuel **IV**: 375.
Craniology, the Copper Age and Hittite Populations in Anatolia **II**: 261.
Exodus, Israelite, at **IV**: 331.
Israelite at the Exodus **IV**: 331.
Jerusalem, of, during Siege of Titus **II**: 259.
Levant, Early Settlement in and Holocene Enviroment **II**: 245.
Nomads, contribution to Babylonian Population **II**: 261.
Palestine, Population of **II**: 259.
Palestine, Population of and Prophecy of Noah **II**: 260.
Palestine, Pre-Israelite **II**: 259.
Pre-Semitic in Semitic Lands **II**: 1.
Syria, Pre-Israelite **II**: 259.
Total, World **II**: 262.

Pork, *see also:* **Swine** **I**: 247.

Porphyry:
Daniel, on **IV**: 523.

Porridge Stirrer:
Egyptian Word for **V**: 341.

Porsuk: **III**: 267.
Hittite Inscription from **VII**: 304.

Portal:
Cemetery **III**: 542.

Portal Coins: **I**: 365, 440.

PORTER, J. L.: **III**: 74, 194.

PORTER, SIR R. KER: **III**: 36, 436, 437, 530.

Portico, *see;* **Stoa**

Porto Cheli, *see also:* **Halieis:** **III**: 116*(3)*, 203, 363.

Portrait(s), *see also:* **Heads**

Alexander the Great, terracotta head of **II**: 9*(2)*; **III**: 720, 721.

"Alexandrian" **III**: 747.

Amenemhat III **III**: 727

Bust, Egyptian **III**: 720.

Cheops **II**: 29.

Daedalid **III**: 730*(2)*.

Egyptian **III**: 690, 736, 744.

Egyptian, Old Man **III**: 713.

Egyptian Sculptor, Studio **III**: 728.

First Century B.C., of **III**: 713, 742.

Glass Bust, in the Cairo Museum **III**: 750.

Greek **III**: 751, 758.

Greek, in British Museum **III**: 729.

Heads by Athenian Artists **III**: 713.

Hellenistic **III**: 730.

Hellenistic, Late **III**: 704.

Iris, from the Frieze of the Parthenon **III**: 721.

Khuenaten, of **II**: 56.

Morgantia, from **III**: 748.

Neferure, of **II**: 70.

Neolitic, Skulls **III**: 692.

Official, XVIIIth Dynasty **III**: 727.

Palmyrene Funerary Bust **III**: 733;**VII**: 124.

Philadelphos, of **II**: 74.

Philetairos, of **II**: 74; **III**: 765.

Plato, of **III**: 721.

Ptolemaic Coin **I**: 449.

Ptolemies, of **II**: 77*(2)*.

Ra-Nafer **II**: 81.

Republican, from Sabina **III**: 749.

Roman **III**: 708*(2)*, 717, 726, 727, 728, 743, 744, 751, 758.

Roman, Early Poet, of **III**: 738.

Semitic, Traces of **III**: 695, 726.

Terracotta, Laughing Girl **III**: 721.

Tuthmosis III, Head of **II**: *45*, 104.

Ports:

Cenchreae at Corinth **III**: 58.

Cosa, at **III**: 67.

Egypt's Earliest Mediterranean **I**: 324.

Ezion-Geber **II**: 364, 365.

Gaza **II**: 369, 463.

Mikhmoret **II**: 445.

Wadi Arabah, Solomon's Industrial **I**: *292;* **III**: 277.

Poseidon: **V**: 304.

Isthmian Sactuary of **III**: 66, 517, 518; **V**: 262.

Parthenon, West Pediment **III**: 752.

Temple of, at Isthmia **III**: 501.

Temple of, at Paestum **III**: 517.

Wind or Sea God(?) **V**: 264.

POSENER, G.: **II**: 44.

Posidonius: **II**: *255*.

Post Diluvian Period to "Babel" **IV**: **§309, 310-311**.

POST, GEORGE E.: **VII**: 121.

Post-Exilic Period, *see: also:* **Persian Period, Israel in**

"Postal Service" **I**: 343, 344, 346.

Postal Register of the Ramesside Age **VII**: 67.

Postexilic Period, *see also:* **Persian Period** **I**: 147.

Pot(s): **III**: 612.

Ancient, from Sea near Israel **III**: 635.

"Beaker", in Stockholm Egyptian Museum **III**: 611.

Cyprus, Imported, from **III**: 617.

Egyptian, for milk **V**: 325.

Egyptian, Predynastic, Modern painting on **III**: 613.

Gordion, from **III**: 631.

Hebrew Word for **V**: 440.

Pot Support **III**: 588*(2)*.

Prehistoric, from Edfu **III**: 587.

Pot-Fabrics:
Asia Minor, Early, of **III**: 603.
Potasimto:
Objects belonging to, in the Egyptian Museum **III**: 567.
Potina: **V**: 241.
Potiphar:
Biographical Studies **I**: **76**.
Hindu Fiction, in **I**: *59*, 76; **VIII**: 367.
Potnia Taurōn: **III**: 737; **V**: 257.
Potsherds: **VII**: 1.
Eleventh Century B.C. **VII**: 88.
Etruscan, Guilloche Pattern on **III**: 602.
Hebrew and Aramaic, from Samaria **VII**: 125.
Hebrew, Inscribed **III**: 615; **VII**: 92, 93; **IX**: cli.
Isaiah 45:9, in **VI**: 301.
Kululu, from **III**: 636.
Mediterranean, Neutron Activation Study of **II**: 217.
Palestinian, at Athens **III**: 614.
Petrographic Examination of, from Troy **II**: 215.
Samaria, Inscribed with the Divine Name **III**: 615; **VIII**: 110, 123.
Transjordan Desert, from **III**: 611.
Troy, Petrographic Examination of **III**: 619.
Potter(s): **III**: 614.
Agathobulus, Rhodian **II**: **7**.
Amarousion **III**: 626.
Jeremiah's Use of the Figure of **VI**: 331*(3)*.
Lekythoi, Red-Figured **III**: 629, 715.
Menaidas **III**: 632.
Royal **VI**: 587.
Potter's Marks: **III**: **§215**, **661-666**.
Pottery Finds, *see also:* **Glaze**; **Vessels** **III**: **§212**, **601-637**.
Aegisthus Citharista **III**: 634; **V**: *266*.
Alaca Höyük, of **III**: 621.
'Amman Tombs, of **III**: 620.
Anatolia, Iron age, from **III**: 624.
Anatolian, Agean Area **III**: 265, 266.
Anatolian, Western, sites **III**: 13, 632.
Antikythera, from **III**: 452.
Archaeologists and Modern School of **III**: 417.
Aryballos, Boston Siren **III**: 622.
Aryballos by Nearchos **III**: 612.
Aryballos, Protocorinthian **III**: 613.
Asine, Mycenaean, from and Aegean Connections **III**: 634.
Assyrian, from Fort Shalmaneser **III**: 627.
Assyrian, from Nimrud **III**: 624.
Athens, Periclean **III**: 625.
Attic Geometric **III**: 625, 629.
Band-Slip Ware in Jordan Valley and Gilead **III**: 621.
Baradost, from Caves of **III**: 622.
Barghuthiat, from **III**: 613.
Base-ring Ware in Palestine **III**: 624.
Basketry, Influence on Attic Geometric **III**: 572, 622.
Bell-krater, Boeotian **III**: 622.
Beth Shan, Mycenaean, at **III**: 633.
Beth-Shan, Earliest, from **III**: 614.
Beth-Shan, from, (Roman Date) **III**: 615.
Beth-Zur, Hellenistic, from **III**: 626.
Bethany, of, Stamped impressions on **III**: 665.
Beycesultan, from **III**: 626.
Bichrome Ware from Egypt **III**: 646.
Biscuit or Egg-shell Ware **III**: 605.
Black **III**: 612.
"Black Incised" from Sudan **III**: 623.
Black topped **III**: 612.
Black topped Red, Origin of **III**: 628.
Black-Figure **III**: 619.
Bowls, Painted Greek **III**: 713.
Bronze Age **III**: 627, 628, 630.
Bronze Age, from Ceos **III**: 633.

Byblos, from **III**: 637.
Byzantine, from Athenian Agora **III**: 612.
Caeretan Figured Group, Greek **III**: 633.
Calenian **III**: 599, 627.
Campanian Black **III**: 630.
Cappadocian **III**: 610.
Censer Types from Palestine **III**: 618.
Chalcholithic, from ʿAffûleh **III**: 615.
Chalcidian in the University Museum **III**: 609.
Chalcolithic, from Beersheba **III**: 624.
Chalcolithic, from Palestine **III**: 623, 628
Chalcolithic, Late, from North-West Turkey and Aegean **III**: 629, 631.
"Chalice" Ware of Northern Mesopotamia **III**: 612, 637.
Chimaera Group, Greek **III**: 629.
Chronology and **II**: 187, 189; **III**: 620.
Chronology of **III**: **§231, 637-640**.
Cilician **III**: 621.
Color of, Especially that of Ancient Egypt **III**: 610.
Combed Ware **III**: 624.
Coptic, Painted **III**: 614.
Corinth, Deposit near Temple E **III**: 616.
Corinthian, Geometric **III**: 625.
Corinthian, Geometric Workshops **III**: 635.
Corinthian, Protogeometric **III**: 617.
Corinthian Relief Ware **III**: 623.
"Cream Ware" of Gezer **III**: 624.
Cypriot, from Al-Mina **III**: 627.
Cypriote Connections with Greek Geometric **III**: 638.
Cypriote, from Palestine **III**: 638.
Dalma Painted Ware **III**: 630.
Deir ʿAlla, from **III**: 632.
Design, Cretan Birds in **III**: 704.
(Dhofar) Khor Rori , Imported, from **III**: 628.
Djerabis, from **III**: 622.
Edfu, from **III**: 726.
Edomite, from Tel el-Kheleifeh **III**: 635.
Egyptian **III**: 601.
Egyptian, Black-Topped **III**: 633.
Egyptian, Classification **III**: 601, 638.
Egyptian, Geometrical Ornamentation on **III**: 614.
Egyptian, Red and Black **III**: 630.
Egyptian, XVIII Dynasty Spectrographic Analysis **II**: 220; **III**: 633.
Etruscan, Black Wares, Manufacture of **III**: 607.
Etruscan Bucchero **III**: 633.
eẓ-Ẓâherîyeh and **II**: 496.
Ez-Zahiriyye and Ancient **III**: 625.
Ezion-Geber, Iron Age II **III**: 637.
Faïence: **I**: 289; **III**: 617, 635, 636.
Fifth Century **III**: 623.
Firing, Draw Pieces as Aids to Correct **III**: 627.
Fractional Stamped Containers **III**: 621.
Geometric **III**: 625.
Geometric, Greek **III**: 602, 617.
Geometric, in Sardis **III**: 620.
Geometric, Inscriptions on, from Hymettos **III**: 613.
Giseh, from **III**: 562, 601.
Glazed Ware in Egypt, India and Mesopotamia **III**: 615.
Gordion, Manufacture of **I**: 289; **III**: 599, 629
Gournia, at **III**: 603*(2)*.
Gözlü Kule, Tarsus, Roman and Hellenistic from **III**: 617.
Greek **III**: 611, 615, 619.
Greek, Acropolis Fragment **III**: 631.
Greek, Caeretan Figured Group **III**: 633.

Greek, Chimaera Group	**III**: 629.
Greek, from the Agora	**III**: 613.
Greek, from the Near East	**III**: 624, 625.
Greek, Geometric	**III**: 602, 617.
Greek Geometric, Cypriote Connections	**III**: 638.
Greek Metal Vases, Bearing on Vase Forms in	**I**: 298; **III**: 598, 621.
Greek, Onesimos Fragment	**III**: 633.
Greek, Pre-Hellenistic, in Palestine	**III**: 613.
Grey Wares	**III**: 637.
Halaf, Halafian Ware	**III**: 628, 634.
Hassuna	**III**: 632.
Hazer Merd, from cave of	**III**: 622.
Helladic, Late, from Lefkandi in Euboea	**III**: 635.
Hellenistic, from Beth-Zur	**III**: 626.
Hellenistic from Gözlü Kule, Tarsus	**III**: 617.
Hellenistic, from Samaria	**III**: 632.
Hellenistic, from the Antikythera Wreck	**III**: 627.
Herodian, Alphabet and	**V**: 289.
Herodian, Stamps on	**III**: 662.
History of Ancient	**III**: 601.
Hydria	**III**: *372*.
Indian	**III**: 612.
Iran, Figurative, Prehistoric, in	**III**: 628.
Iran, from	**III**: 628*(2)*, 639.
Iranian, East	**III**: 612.
Iraq,	**III**: 632, 639*(2)*.
Iraq, Painted, from Jemdet Nasr	**III**: 614.
Iron Age, from Macedonia	**III**: 609.
Israel, Recovered from Sea off the Coast of	**III**: 630.
Israelite, in Galilee	**II**: 368, 625.
Italian	**III**: 630.
Italian "China" in Palestinian Homes	**III**: 617.
Jamdat Nasr, from	**III**: 635, 636.
Jericho, in the Hunterian Museum	**III**: 610.
Jewish Ossuary-Tombs, Types of, from	**III**: 623*(2)*.
Kantharos(?)	**III**: 631.
Karchesion(?)	**III**: 631.
Kea, Made at(?)	**III**: 137, 138, 634.
Khirbet Kerak Ware	**II**: 176, 215, 322; **III**: 229, 280, *551*, 619, 621, 635, 639.
Khor Rori (Dhofar), Imported, from	**III**: 628.
Kish, from	**III**: 613.
Kleophrades Painter	**III**: 614.
Knossos, Palace of, and	**III**: 633, 634.
Konya Plain, Second Millennium, from	**III**: 626.
Lewis Painter = Polygnotos II	**III**: 615.
Lydian Imitation of Phrygian Metal Bowl	**III**: 632.
Maccabaean	**III**: 608, 609*(2)*.
Manufacturing of	**I**: **§97, 288-289**; **III**: 599, 614, 627, 629, *665;* **IX**: **§97, xci**.
Medallion Painter	**III**: 628.
Megiddo, Early, from	**III**: 617.
Mending, Functions of, in Excavations	**III**: 639.
Metallic Gloss	**III**: 630, 716.
Mineralogical Study of Greek	**II**: 219; **III**: 631.
Moabite (Shapira)	**VII**: 109*(2)*.
Murrhine	**III**: 622.
Mycenaean	**III**: 628, 636.
Mycenaean, at Beth Shan	**III**: 633.
Mycenaean Bull-Craters	**III**: 625.
Mycenaean, from Asine, and Aegean Connections	**III**: 634.
Mycenaean from Thebes, Greece	**III**: 253.
Mycenaean, Late, with Pictorial Representations	**III**: 618, 619, 699.

Mycenaean, Pictroal Fragments, from Kourion **III**: 628
Mycenaean, Potmark **III**: 634.
Mycenaean, relation to "Philistine" **III**: 615.
Nabataean, from the Negeb, Distribution in Palestine **III**: 614.
Nabataean, in the British Museum **III**: 631.
Nabataean, Pattern Familes, Painted Ware **III**: 638.
Nabataean, Physical Nature **III**: 631.
Neolithic Burnished Ware in the Mainland Greece **III**: 631, 632.
Neolithic Burnished Ware in the Near East **III**: 621.
Neolithic, Northern Fayum Desert **III**: 609, *674*.
Neolithic Painted Ware in the Adriatic **III**: 633.
Nimrud, Assyrian, from **III**: 624.
Nimrud, Palace Wares from, Techinical Observations on **III**: 624.
Ninevite V **III**: 636, 639*(2)*.
Old Testament, and **III**: 630, 639.
Orange Gloss **III**: 630, 716
Painted, 2nd Millennium, Chronological Background **III**: 638.
Painted, from Syria and Turkey, 2nd Millennium **III**: 623.
Painted, in Northern Mesopotamia, continuance of **III**: 609.
Painted Ware, Proto-Mesopotamian from Balîkh Valley **III**: 609.
Painting **III**: 712.
Palestine, Bronze Age **II**: 220; **III**: 628, 630.
Palestine, Chalcolithic from **III**: 623, 628
Palestine, Story of, in **III**: 625.
Palestinian, in Bible Times **III**: 620, 621.
Palestinian, Triangular Impressed Design **III**: 618.
Panaitios Painter, Love Scene by **III**: 634.
Persian **I**: 282; **III**: 614.
Petrographical Examination of **II**: 215; **III**: 621.
"Philistine", relation to Mycenaean **III**: 615.
Phlius, Sherds from **III**: 634.
Phlyax Types **III**: 616.
Pisticci Painter **III**: 621.
Pithoi, Fragments of Cretan **III**: 461.
Prehistoric **III**: 613.
Prehistoric, from Antitaurus **III**: 635.
Prehistoric in the Valletta Museum **III**: 602.
Prehistoric, of Carchemish **III**: 613.
Prehistoric Ware from Baluchistan **III**: 622.
Protocorinthian **III**: 632.
Protocorintian Geometric **III**: 618.
Rās el ʿAin, from **III**: 615.
Red-Figured **III**: 616.
Red-Figured, Wings in **III**: 711.
Roman (Arretine) **III**: 604.
Roman, from Athenian Agora **III**: 612, 618.
Roman, from Castel Campanile **III**: 617.
Roman from Gözlü Kule, Tarsus **III**: 617.
Roman, Late Republican, Early Imperial **III**: 634.
Roman, Provinicial, Standardized(?) **III**: 633, 634.
"Roman", Red-glazed **III**: 613.
Salammbo, Precint of Tanit, from **III**: 616.
Samaria, Hellenistic, from **III**: 632.
Samarran, Painted from Baghouz **III**: 568.
Science and **II**: 221.
Shapira (Moabite) **VII**: 109*(2)*.
Shechem, from **III**: 637.

Sigillata Red **III**: 630.
Spectrographic Analysis of, from Royal Tombs, Abydos, and Palestine **II**: 220; **III**: 630.
Sudan, "Black Incised" from **III**: 623.
Sumerian, Typological Examination **III**: 638.
Syrian, from Al-Mina **III**: 627.
Syrian Glazed, Hellenisitic Influences in **III**: 612.
Technological Methods in Study of, from Greece and Italy **II**: 215; **III**: 638.
Tell Billa, of **III**: 612.
Tell el-Yahudiyeh Ware, in Syria **III**: 625.
Terra Sigillata, Technological Analysis of **II**: 215.
Thessaly, Pottery Types **III**: *349,* 638.
Trade, Evidence for in the Aegean **I**: 339, 356; **III**: 617.
Troy VI, from **III**: 616.
Troy VIII, from **III**: 616.
Turkey, Distribution and Varieties in South-East **III**: 638.
Umm el-Biyara, at **III**: 270.
Ur, from **III**: 610.
Uruk, from **III**: 614, 621, 632, 636, 639*(3)*.
Vrysoula Classical **III**: 633.
White Slip Sequence at Bamboula, Kourion **III**: 629.
Xenokles **III**: 629.
Yortan, from **III**: 614.

Pottery Chronology, History and Scientific Study **III: §213, 637-640.**
Attic Hellenistic **III**: 639.
Bâb ed-Drâ', Bronze Age **III**: 638.
"Chalice" Ware of Northern Mesopotamia **III**: 612, 637.
Diyala Sequence, Relevance to Mesopotamian Sites **III**: 639.
Iran, Western, Comparative **III**: 639.
Khirbet Kerak Ware, Chronological Problems **III**: 639.
Mycenaean, Distribution **III**: 639.
Nabataean, Fine Ware, Classification of **III**: 639.
Painted, 2nd Millennium **III**: 638.
Palestinian **III**: 638.
Pottery- Mending, Functions of, in Excavations **III**: 639.
Protoattic Style **III**: 639.
Sequences, Prehistoric Remains **III**: 637.

Poverty: **I**: 184, 186, 192*(3)*, 193*(3)*, 303, 304, 309*(3)*, 310*(2)*, 504; **VIII**: 235.
Pauper, Biblical Teaching **VIII**: 231.
Poor, Ex-votos of, Egypt **V**: 223.
Poor in Wisdom Literature and ANE Legal Literature **I**: 192; **VII**: 2.
Poor in Wisdom Literature of Hebrew and Accadian **V**: 118; **VII**: 3, 96, 152.
Poor, Religion of, in Egypt **V**: 207.

Power: **V**: 512.
Caesar and Corruption of **I**: 491; **II**: 27.
Divine, and Human Freedom **VIII**: 174.
Political, Concept of, in Ancient Israel **I**: 471.

Praefects:
Egyptian **II**: 4*(2)*, 6.
Egyptian, Powers of **I**: 491.
Roman **I**: 500.

Praesapians: **III**: 360.
Praesens II: **V**: 366.
Praesos: **III**: **203**.
Praetorium:
Lambaesis, at **III**: 149.
Praetorship:
Peregrine **I**: 490.

Praha:
- Egyptian Texts, bearing on Prehistoric Burials, Oriental Institute in — **VII**: 66.
- Hittite Text in the Oriental Institute in — **VII**: 304.

Praise:
- God, of — **VIII**: 203.
- Verbs of in the LXX — **V**: 641.

Praisos: — **III**: 68.

PRATT, JOSIAH: — **IV**: 49.

Praxiteles: — **III**: 733*(4)*, 746.

Prayer(s) *see also:*
- **Piyyuṭ** — **VIII**: **§1022, 201-204**.
- Answers to — **VIII**: 200, 201, 202.
- Apocrypha of, and Jewish Liturgy — **VI**: 600; **VIII**: 202, 382.
- "Appearing Ghosts", Against — **V**: 158, **VII**: 158.
- Ashurnasirbal, of — **VII**: 198.
- Assyrian — **VII**: 198.
- Assyrian, in the Annals of Assurbanipal — **VII**: 198.
- Assyrian Prayer Cycle in the *bît rimki* Ritual — **VII**: 202.
- Assyrian, Royal — **V**: 163.
- Babylonian — **V**: 163; **VII**: 259*(2)*.
- Babylonian, Calendars of — **VII**: 262.
- Babylonian, from Nippur — **V**: 260.
- Babylonian, Ritualistic to astral deities in ceremonies of divination — **V**: 261.
- Babylonian, Royal — **V**: 163.
- Balaam, of — **VI**: 135.
- Ben Abdas, of — **VII**: 116.
- Bible, of — **VIII**: 203.
- Biblical Conception of — **VIII**: 201.
- Biblical, History of — **VIII**: 201.
- Christian, and Jewish Psalms — **IV**: 482.
- Daily — **I**: 365; **VIII**: 201.
- Daily, of Priest — **VI**: 521.
- Daniel as Man of — **I**: 37.
- Dead, for, in 2 Maccabees — **VI**: 641*(2)*; **VIII**: 202.
- Demanding Prayer. Honi the Circle-Maker — **V**: 108.
- ***Egyptian Prayers Hymns*** — **V**: 217; **VII**: **§840, 41-43**.
- Elijah as Illustration of — **I**: 39; **VIII**: 202.
- Epicureans, among — **V**: 250.
- First Recorded in the Bible — **VI**: 69, 82; **VIII**: 202.
- Gesture in Sumerian and Babylonian — **V**: 164, 181; **VII**: 285.
- "Gods of the Night", to — **VII**: 264.
- Grace, as a Means of — **VIII**: 201.
- Grace before Meat (Egyptian) — **VII**: 42.
- Greek — **V**: 259.
- Greek, for Charaxus — **VII**: 343.
- Habakkuk, of — **V**: 684, 704; **VI**: 401.
- Hasidism, Kavvanoth of, in Early — **VIII**: 204.
- Hellenistic Jewish — **VIII**: 204.
- History of — **VIII**: 201, 202.
- Hittite, of Mursili II — **VII**: 308.
- Hittite, Royal — **V**: 227; **VII**: 309.
- Hittite, to the Sun — **V**: 227; **VII**: 309
- Human Freedom and — **VIII**: 202.
- Individual, in Sumerian — **V**: 188; **VII**: 287.
- Intercession / Intercessory — **VIII**: 202, 203, 204*(2)*.
- Isthar, to, and Its Two Versions from Boğasköy — **VII**: 202, 309.
- Jeremiah, Confessions of, and the Meaning of — **IV**: 412; **VIII**: 203.
- Jeremiah, in the Life of — **I**: 54; **VIII**: 203.
- Jewish, and Synagogue Architecture — **III**: 526; **VIII**: 204.
- Jewish, in a Greek Papyrus — **VII**: 333.
- Kaddish, and the Lord's — **V**: 143.
- Law, Reign of, as Incentive to — **VIII**: 201.
- Limits of — **VIII**: 201, 204.

Lord's, and the Book of Daniel	**VIII**: 20.
Metaphysical Gleanings	**VIII**: 203.
Miracles and	**VIII**: 90.
Morgantina, Lead *Tabellae* from	**VII**: 334.
Moses, of	**VI**: 117.
Nature of	**VIII**: 202.
Old Testament, of / in	**VIII**: 201, 203, 204.
Pattern in Judaism	**VIII**: 204.
Pattern of Biblical	**VIII**: 204.
Pentateuch, in	**VIII**: 203.
Petition	**VIII**: 203.
Petition of, in Philo	**VI**: 676.
Physical Value of	**VIII**: 201.
Praying on the House-Tops	**VI**: 2.
Promethian Element in	**VIII**: 203.
Psalms and	**IV**: 483; **VI**: 474.
Psychology of	**VIII**: 202.
Rabbinic Ideas on	**VIII**: 202.
Reasonableness of	**VIII**: 201.
Root פלל and Its Connotation with	**VI**: 152.
Sappho's, to Aphrodite	**V**: 257.
Science and	**VIII**: 201.
Science and the Christian Idea of	**VIII**: 201.
Science of	**VIII**: 202, 203.
Scripture, in	**VIII**: 202.
Shamash-sum-ukîn, of	**III**: *647;* **V**: 181; **VII**: 261.
Social Implication of	**VIII**: 203.
Suffering as Source of(?)	**VIII**: 203.
Sumerian	**VII**: 274, 280.
Theological Disciple and	**VIII**: 204.
War-Time, in	**VIII**: 202.
Weather, a Ligitimate Subject for(?)	**VIII**: 202.
Prayer Books:	
Archbishop of Canterbury and Revision of the	**IV**: 493.
Psalms and	**IV**: 474, 493.
Prayer of Azariah / Song of the Three Young Men:	
Aramaic Original of Theodotion's Additions to Daniel	**VI**: 625, 639.
Blackie's "Benedictie"	**VIII**: 362.
Daniel, Chapter 3 and	**VI**: 625.
Exegetical Studies on	**VI**: **§720, 639**.
Greek Bibles, in	**VI**: 625.
Literary Criticism of	**VI**: **§702, 625**.
Textual Criticism of	**VI**: **§684, 608**; **IX**: **§684, cxlix**.
Wilton's "Benedictie"	**VIII**: 364.
Prayer of Manasseh:	
Exegetical Studies on	**VI**: **(§723), 640**.
Literary Criticism of	**VI**: **§705, 627**.
Syrian MSS of	**VI**: 609.
Textual Criticism of	**VI**: **§687, 609**.
Prayers (1QPrayers, 4QPrayers)	**VIII**: **§1139, 469-470**.
Prayers, Specific, *see also:* **Benediction**	**VIII**: **§1023, 205-208**.
"Apotropaic", Jewish	**VIII**: 208, 452.
"Apotropaic", Qumran	**VIII**: 208, 452.
Beth Midrash Origin, of	**VIII**: 207.
Civic, of Jerusalem	**VIII**: 207.
Eighteen Benedictions	**VIII**: 205.
Essene	**VIII**: 205.
Haftaras of the Triennial Cycle	**VIII**: 205.
Havdalah-Shiv'atot in Palestinian Ritual	**VIII**: 208.
Hebrew Prayer Book, Spiritual Elements in	**VIII**: 205.
Jewish in a Greek Papyrus	**VIII**: 206.
Jewish Morning, and Early Christian Anaphoras	**VIII**: 207.
Jewish Prayer Book	**VIII**: 205.
Kaddish	**VIII**: 205*(2)*.
Order of, at Qumran	**VIII**: 416.
Qiddush Hashem in	**VIII**: 207.

Rain, for — **VI**: 521; **VIII**: 205.
Taḥanun, Origin of — **VIII**: 205.
Tefilah — **VIII**: 206.

Praying Mantis:
Babylonian word for — **III**: 380.

Pre-Adamites: — **III**: 337*(2)*; **IV**: 264.
Deluge, Ruin or — **IV**: 282, 306.

Pre-Masoretic Texts, *see:* **Masoretic Texts**

Preaching, *see also:* **Homiletics** — **I**: *113*, 114.
Bible Study for — **VIII**: 397.
Christian and Jewish, Reflections on — **VIII**: 377.
Deuteronomy, of, and from — **IV**: 351; **VIII**: 377.
Expository — **VIII**: 371.
Graphic, and the Bible — **VIII**: 374.
Historical Method and — **IV**: 147.
Isaiah's Technique of — **I**: 49; **VIII**: 377.
Jewish — **VIII**: 374.
Jewish and Christian, Reflections on — **VIII**: 377.
Jewish Pulpits and Biblical Criticism — **VIII**: 373.
Map as aid to, of the Old Testament — **II**: 257.
Modern OT Criticism and — **IV**: 129.
Old Testament, Use of, in — **VIII**: **§1063, 371-378**.
Prophecy, is it(?) — **VIII**: 376.
Prophetic Teaching on Righteousness and Our — **VIII**: 199.
Rabbinic Sources for — **VIII**: 377.
Theology, Relation to — **VIII**: 4, 374.

Precedent:
Legal — **I**: 461*(2)*, 498.

Precious Stones, *see:* **Stones, Gem**

PRÉCIS: — **III**: 323.

Predestination: — **VI**: 143.

Prefects:
Egyptian, (30 BC to 299 AD) — **II**: 6; **VII**: 337.

Pregnancy:
Egyptian Superstitions on — **I**: 210.

Prehistoric Times: — **III**: 349‡.
Near East, Research in — **III**: 348.

Prehistory:
Genesis 1-11 and — **VI**: 17*(3)*.

Premillennialism:
Abrahamic Covenant and — **VIII**: 216.

Prepis: — **VII**: 330.

Preservation and Restoration, *see:* **Antiquities, Preservation of**

PRESTWICH, J.:
Flood, Biblical, on — **IV**: 302.

Prices, *see* **Cost of Living**

Prideaux Pentateuch: — **IV**: 13; **VI**: 14.

Priene: — **III**: **203**.

Priestess(es):
Armed, in Hittite Religion — **V**: 225.
Pandrosus, of — **VII**: 333.

Priesthood, Israelite - General Studies — **I**: *79;* **IV**: *156, 324;* **V**: **§423, 40-42**.
Aaronite, Origin of — **V**: 40*(2)*.
Bible of — **IV**: 257.
Caesarea, List of Priestly Courses from — **VII**: 96.
Christ, Priesthood of and, NT Book of Hebrews — **V**: 42; **VIII**: 297.
Christian Ministry Viewed in the Light of — **V**: 40.
Christianity and Judaism, in — **V**: 41.
Contemporary Thought, in — **VIII**: 9.
Course of, Twenty-Six — **V**: 41.
David's Sons, of — **V**: 40.
Development of, and Egypt, compared — **V**: 40, 202.
Idea of — **V**: 40.
Idea of, Fulfilled in NT — **V**: 40.
Judaism and Christianity, in — **V**: 41.
Levitical Priesthood — **V**: **§424, 42-43**.
Prophecy, Wisdom, and the Knowledge of God — **V**: 41.

Sacrifice and, in Judaism and Christianity **V**: 62.

Samuel, the Ark and **V**: 41, *55*.

"Second Priest" **VI**: 244.

Shilonite **I**: *157;* **V**: 42.

Southern, and the Conflict with Northern Prophecy **IV**: 376; **V**: 20.

Zadokite, and Ezekiel **IV**: 423; **V**: 41.

Priestly (Levitic) Code: **IV**: *251,* 252*(10)*, 253*(3)*, 260, 261, 262.

Anti-Temple(?) **IV**: 262.

Atonement in **VIII**: 194.

Apocrypha and Pseudepigrapha, in **IV**: 257; **VI**: 596.

Date of **IV**: 261, 262*(2);* **V**: *458*.

Elephantine and **III**: 94; **IV**: 256; **V**: 60; **VII**: 133.

Ezekiel and **IV**: 250, 254*(4)*, 418, 419*(2)*.

Ezra and **IV**: 255.

Flood, Chronology of, in **I**: 394; **II**: 183; **IV**: 249, 303.

Hebronite Tradition in, Genesis **IV**: 260, 270.

Historical Status of **V**: 52.

Historical Writings in **IV**: 253*(2)*, 257; **VI**: 596.

Levitical Genealogical Accretions in and the Chronicler **I**: 120; **IV**: 260, 543.

Origin of **IV**: 262; **V**: 56.

Origin of, Not Post-Exilic **IV**: 354.

Passover and **IV**: 258; **V**: 87.

Post-Exilic(?) **IV**: 255, 256.

Proper Names in **IV**: 251.

Sacrifice, Laws of **V**: 60.

Secret Document(?) **IV**: 262.

Tablernacle, Construction of, and **V**: 51.

Priests, Israelite, *see also:* **High Priest** **I**: *51,* **§48, 100-101**, 106*(4)*, 107, 109, 110, 112, 113, 114*(2)*, 115; **V**: 43*(2)*, 78.

Aaronite **V**: 42.

Administrative Body of, and a Consecrated People **V**: 28, 42.

Anathoth, at **IV**: 413.

Appointment of **V**: 42.

Cities of, *see:* ***Levitical Cities*** **II**: 312.

Deuteronomy, in **V**: 43.

Exodus, in **VI**: 110*(3)*.

Ezekiel as **I**: 43.

Ezekiel's **IV**: 418*(2);* **V**: 42*(2)*, 43; **VI**: 360.

Hair Dressing of Ezekiel's **VI**: 360.

Israelite Religion, Effect on **I**: 486; **V**: 26.

Laws Concerning **IV**: 252; **V**: 40.

Levites, and, in Wellhausen **IV**: 255.

Modern World, Debt of, to **VIII**: 381.

Office of **V**: 40.

Oridnation of **V**: 42.

Pentateuch Respecting Priestly Dues **IV**: 228.

Prayer, Daily of **VI**: 521.

Priest-Preachers of Jerusalem and Deuteronomy **IV**: 355.

Prophets and **V**: 40, 41*(2)*, 42.

Prophets and, in Contemporary Thought **V**: 28.

Prophets and, in Hebrew Ethics **V**: 41; **VIII**: 221.

Prophets and, in Judaism **V**: 41.

Prophets, Relation to, Before the Exile **V**: 13.

Prophets *vs.*, a False Antithesis **V**: 22.

Qumran, at **VIII**: 414.

Role of, in the Bible V: 42.
Sacrifice, Relation to, Before the Exile V: 41.
Scraping out of the Hands VI: 324.
Social Ideals of I: 187.
Synagogue, of III: 525; V: 93.
Terms Descriptive of, in Post Restoration Period V: 41.
Wicked (Qumran) VIII: 416.
Zadokite V: 42.

Priests, Priesthood (Non-Israelite) I: 106*(4)*, 107, 109, 110, 112, 113; V: 11.
Assyrian. *ramku* V: 430, 563.
Athens, of, Historical Development in V: 262.
Attys-, among the Hittites V: 225.
Babylonian, King-Priests III: 36.
Babylonian, Sale of a VII: 251, 252.
Development of Israelite and Egypt, compared V: 40, 202.
Egyptian II: 107.
Egyptian, Ptaḥmase as Memphie High III: 567.
Endowments to, by Sargon VII: 187.
Hittite Text on Duties of, and Temple Servants V: 226; VII: 308.
Memphite, Philosopy of V: 204.
Roman Nobility and the Three Major V: 271.
Samaritan, Chain of High Priests V: 228.
Semitic *kalû* V: 544, 578.
Sumerian *sur-ru* V: 544, 578.

Primeval History: I: 121; III: 288; IV: 260*(2)*, 261, 285.
Animal Series in IV: 286.
Genesis and IV: 263, 272, 295, 323*(2)*; VI: 17*(2)*.

Primogeniture: I: 226, 228; VI: 148.

Prince of Grecia: II: *173*.

"Prince of Peace": VI: 268; VIII: 135.

Prince of Persia: I: 495; II: *172, 173, 179*.

Princes:
Byblos, of, 18th Century II 6.
Forgotten VII: 14.
Hellenistic, and Athens III: 113.
Karnak Relief, in II: 4, *80*.
Procession of, at Medinant Habu II: 6.

Princeton Art Museum: III: 692.

Principate:
Evolution of Augustus' I: 491.
Imperial and Senatorial Juristiction in Early I: 491.
Maladministration under I: 492.
Origin of I: 489.

Prinià: III: 68.

Prinias:
Greek Temple at III: 510.

Printing: V: 281.

Prisoners:
Amnesty for I: 194.

Prisons:
Excavated, and Origin of Mankind III: 334.

PRITCHARD, ANDREW: III: 332.

Privacy: VI: 121.j

Probability:
God's Providence and VIII: 89.

Problems:
Egyptian, Mechanical I: 265.

Processional:
Jerusalem (Songs of Ascent) IV: 489*(2)*; VI: 504*(2)*, 506*(2)*.

Processions: I: 389.

Procopius: I: *151*.

Procurators:
Coins of, with dates I: 452, 453.

Production:
Administration of Rural, in an Early Mesopotamian Town IX: cii.
Mode of, in Western Asia, Second Millenium I: 195.

Productivity:
Administration of Rural in Mesopotamia **I**: 311.
Roman Agricutural Labor **I**: 257.
Proesilemmene: **III**: 446.
Profanity: **I**: 179.
Professions: **I: §92, 269-272**; **IX**: **§92, xc.**
Profit:
Job, "Prophet attacks..." **IV**: 465; **VIII**: 225.
Qoheleth, "Prophet attacks..." **IV**: 515; **VIII**: 225.
Rights of Private **I**: 227, 305.
Progeniture: **I**: 228.
Progress:
Archaeology and the Concept of **III**: 432.
Prohedria:
Marble, in the Theater of Dionysus **III**: 529, 583.
Proletarian:
Canaanite term for "Free Proletarian" **I**: 188.
Prometheus: **III**: *617;* **V**: 247, 260.
Cain and **VI**: 42.
Job and **I**: 56; **IV**: 461, 467; **VIII**: 100.
"Prometheus Bound", Theology of **V**: 251.
Rereading of "Prometheus Bound" **V**: 149.
Pronoun(s):
Personal, "I" (West Semitic Inscriptons) **V**: 377.
Pronouns, Hebrew, *see:* **Hebrew Grammar**
Proof Texts: **VIII**: 1.
Use of **IV**: 80.
Propaganda: **I**: 490, **§137, 507-509**; **VI**: 596*(2);* **IX**: **§137, cii-ciii.**
Ancient Jewish **IX**: cii*(2).*
In the Transmission of Josephus **VI**: 682.
Political, in Greek Chronology **I**: 508; **II**: 200.
Roman Republican, on coins **I**: 493, 509.
Property, *see also:* **Land**
Acquisition of, Biblical Teaching on **I**: 461*(2).*
Babylonian Deeds **VII**: 248*(2).*
Babylonian Legal Documents on House **VII**: 247.
Descent of, in Egypt **I**: 496.
Near Eastern Society, Structure of, and **I**: 194.
Personal, Gods of Thebes as Guarantors of **V**: 221.
Private **I**: 305.
Prohibition to Sell Hereditary Property **VI**: 146.
Proverbs, Teaching on **IV**: 499.
Sale of a Field in Talmudic Law **I**: 467.
Sale of, in Egyptian, Egyptian-Aramaic and Murabba'at Documents **I**: 503; **VII**: 31.
Sale of Inherited, First Century B.C. **VII**: 31.
Seizure of, for Debt **I**: 307.
Seizure of, for Debt, Sumerian Law **VII**: 280.
Settlement, Demotic **I**: 309.
Stolen, Penalties for, in Ramesside Times **I**: 498; **VII**: 30.
Property Rights: **I**: **§80, 226-229**, 305, 495; **IX**: **§80, lxxxviii.**
Eighth Commandment and **VI**: 165.
Prophecy: **I**: *102, 103(2), 104(2), 106, 107, 108(2), 109(2), 113(2), 243;* **IV**: *156;* **V**: *41, 103;* **VIII**: 8, 126, **§1030, 235-248**, 348; **IX**: cxxxvi.
Amos, Book, Features of, OT, Illustrated by **IV**: 433; **VIII**: 238.
Apocalypse of John and **V**: 120.

Apocalyptic, Biblical, and	**V**: 124; **VIII**: 246, 247, 252, 253.
Apocalypticism and	**V**: 123.
Asceticism and	**V**: 113; **VIII**: 243.
Babylonian	**VII**: 264.
Babylonian, and Old Testament compared	**V**: 177; **VIII**: 241.
Babyonian, Commerce and Manuracturig illustrative of	**VIII**: 236.
Background of	**VIII**: 248.
Balaam as Symbolic of the Origins of	**IV**: 345.
Balaam, Symbolic of the Origins of	**I**: 36; **VIII**: 242.
Bible, Place in the	**VIII**: 242
Botanical Figures in	**VIII**: 243.
Character of OT	**VIII**: 245.
Characteristics	**VIII**: 246.
Christ as Interpreter of	**VIII**: 280*(2)*.
Classification of Prophetic Material	**VIII**: 239.
Compenetration of	**VIII**: 243.
Conditional Element in	**VI**: 318; **VIII**: 238*(2)*.
Critical Schools, in	**VIII**: 237.
Davidson, A. B., on	**VIII**: 240, 241.
Decalogue, Relation to	**VI**: 158; **VIII**: 242.
Development of	**VIII**: 245, 246.
Development of, and the Holy Man in Israel	**VIII**: 245.
Distinguishing Features of OT	**VIII**: 240.
Divine Passibility and Prophetic Theology	**VIII**: 245.
Divine Pathos. Basic Category of Prophetic Theology	**VIII**: 67.
Divine Revelation, as Evidence of	**VIII**: 32, 243.
Dreams and	**I**: 102; **VIII**: 237.
Early, Conservatism of	**VIII**: 242.
Ecstatic Element in	**I**: 102, 106, 108, 109,**VIII**: 237, 244, 248.
Eschatology and	**VIII**: 245, 246, 252.
Eschatology and, Interprophetic Re-interpretation	**VIII**: 248, 253, 287.
Essance of	**VIII**: 241.
Ethical Insights of	**VIII**: 225, 243.
Exegesis of OT, with reference to the Future of Israel	**VIII**: 212, 246.
Faber, George S., on	**VIII**: 236.
Fairbairn, Patrick, on	**VIII**: 236, 237.
False	**VI**: 336.
False and True	**VI**: 333, 336; **VIII**: 246.
Fasting and, in Pagan and Christian Antiquity	**V**: 149, 273.
Fulfilled	**VIII**: 238, 242.
Fulfilled, Apologetic Argument from	**VIII**: 244.
Fulfillment, and, Hermeneutics	**IV**: 88, 89.
Fulfillment of	**VIII**: 236, 246*(2)*, 272, 298.
Fulfillment of, and Christianity	**VIII**: 274.
God and the World in Jewish	**VIII**: 65, 245.
Greek, Religious Prophetism Among	**V**: 249, 273.
Greek, Unconscious	**V**: 246, 273.
Halevi, on	**VIII**: 244*(2)*.
Hebrew, a Unique Divine Bestowal	**VIII**: 243.
Hebrew, Foreign Influences in	**VIII**: 243.
Hebrew, Metrical Basis of	**VIII**: 242.
Hebrew, Southern Influences on	**VIII**: 242.
Hermenenutics and	**IV**: 88, 93; **VIII**: 248.
Historical Element in	**VIII**: 238.
History and	**I**: 104, 128, 130; **VIII**: 238, 246.
History of, and Mari	**VIII**: 248.

History of OT **VIII**: 239*(8)*, 240.
Ideal Element in **VIII**: 239.
Inspiration and **I**: 107; **VIII**: 49, 244.
Interpretation of **IV**: 78, 79; **VIII**: 237, 240, 242*(2)*, 244*(2)*, 245, 246, 251.
Interpretation of, Reformation Principle of Exegesis **IV**: 81; **VIII**: 241.
Invisible Church in Hebrew **VI**: 415.
Isaiah and Prophetic Truth **IV**: 395.
Isaiah and the Spirit of **IV**: 391.
Israel, in **IV**: 385; **VIII**: 237*(3)*, 245, 246*(2)*, 248.
Israel, in, after the Captivity **VIII**: 237.
Israelitish **VIII**: 239.
J and E, Messages of the Prophetic Narratives **VIII**: 241.
Jeremiah, Book of, and **I**: 470; **IV**: 411.
Jesus the Subject of OT(?) **VIII**: 125, 238.
Jewish Interpretation of **VIII**: 237.
Jews, Future Condition of and the Spirit of **VIII**: 236.
Keith, John A., on **VIII**: 236.
Levi, David, on **VIII**: 235.
Literal Interpretation of **IV**: 390.
Maimonides, on **VIII**: 244*(2)*.
Mari Texts and Biblical **IV**: 431; **V**: 273, 274*(3)*; **VII**: 164*(2)*; **VIII**: 35, 247, 248.
McClelland, Alexander, on the Interpretation of **VIII**: 236.
Messianic, *see:* ***Messianic Prophecy***
Midrash, in **I**: 112; **IV**: 235; **VI**: 689, 708; **VIII**: 245.
Millennial **VIII**: 255.
Miracle and Fulfilled **VIII**: 90, 238.
Miracle of / and **VIII**: 241, 243.
Miracles, Value of, and **VIII**: 92, 242.
Modern Ciriticsm and Hebrew **VIII**: 238, 239*(2)*.
Nathan's **VI**: 210, 211.
Nations in Hebrew **VIII**: 247.
Nations, of, Historical Setting of **VI**: 410.
Nature of **VIII**: 238, 240, 243*(2)*, 244*(2)*, 245.
New Testament Revision of **VIII**: 298.
New Testament, Use of OT, in **VIII: §1050, 297-298.**
Noah, of, and Population of Palestine **II**: 260.
NT Mircale Stories - Old Testament, and **VI**: 288; **VIII**: 275.
Numerical Codes in Bible **VIII**: 246, 311.
Obscurity, Alleged, of **VIII**: 236.
Old Testament, and NT Miracle Stories **VI**: 288; **VIII**: 275, 298.
Orelli, Conrad, on **VIII**: 237.
Origin(s) of **VIII**: 240, 245.
Origins of, Balaam Symbolic of **IV**: 345.
Pagan and Christian Antiquity, in **V**: 149.
Patriarchal "benediction" and prophetic book **VI**: 91.
Peace, Prophetic Doctrine of **I**: 464.
Perspective of OT **VIII**: 247.
Poetry and **VIII**: 398.
Predictive Element in **VIII**: 238, 240, 243.
Predition and **VIII**: 245.
"Prenouncement" and **VIII**: 244.
Priesthood, Southern, and Conflict with Northern **IV**: 376.
Principles of **IV**: 386.
Probability of Biblical **VIII**: 245.
Prophetic Symbolism and Sacrifice **V**: 61*(2)*; **VIII**: 244*(2)*.

Prophetic Theology and Divine Passibility	**VIII**: 245.
Psalms, Seasonal, and	**IV**: 487; **VIII**: 247.
Psychical Research and	**VIII**: 165, 251.
Psychology of / and	**I**: 107; **VIII**: 241, 242, 243, 244*(2)*, 245.
Qumran Use of, and Gospel Messianism	**VIII**: 420, 422.
Reformation Principle of Exegesis and the Interpretation of	**IV**: 95.
Restoration of Israel, Palestine and	**VIII**: 210*(2)*, 242*(2)*.
Sabbath and	**IV**: 412.
Sacrifice and	**V**: 61; **VIII**: 243.
Sacrifice and Prophetic Symbolism	**V**: 61*(2)*; **VIII**: 244*(2)*.
Semitic	**VIII**: 242.
Smith, George, on	**VIII**: 39.
Social Location of Israelite	**VIII**: 247, 248.
Spirit of	**VIII**: 238, 247.
Spirit of, and Isaiah	**IV**: 391.
Spirit of, in Relation to the Future State of Israel	**VIII**: 209.
Supernatural in	**VIII**: 243.
Swedish Study of Hebrew	**VIII**: 244.
Symbols, Prophetic	**IV**: 78.
Talmud, in	**I**: 112; **IV**: 235; **VI**: 689, 708; **VIII**: 245.
Talmudic Interpretation of	**VIII**: 245.
Tholuck, Aguustus, on	**VIII**: 236.
Turth, Prophetic and Isaiah	**IV**: 395.
Two, from 520-516 B.C.	**VI**: 312, 314*(2)*.
Unfulfilled	**VIII**: 242.
Unfulfilled, Reasons for	**VIII**: 238*(2)*.
War and	**VIII**: 233, 244.
Wisdom and	**V**: 118; **VIII**: 247.
Written Word and	**VIII**: 24.
Yom Kippur and	**V**: 89; **VI**: 312, 313.
Zadokite Document in	**VIII**: 421, 460.
Zionism and	**VIII**: 344.
Zouch, Thomas, on	**VIII**: 235.
Prophecy, Non-Hebrew, *see also:* **Prophecy**	**V: §483, 273-274; IX, §483, cxxxviii.**
Akkadian	**VII**: 158.
Egyptian Texts	**VII: §839, 40-41.**
Mari, at	**IV**: 431; **V**: 273, 274*(3)*; **VII**: 164*(6)*; **VIII**: 35, 247, 248; **IX**: cxxxviii*(2)*.
Ram Gods (Egyptian), Prophecies of	**V**: 223, 274.
Prophesying:	
Liberty of in Israel	**I**: 109.
"Prophetic Father":	**II**: v; **V**: 520.
Prophetic Succession:	**I**:*40, 41;* **IX**: lxxxii.
Prophetism:	**VIII**: 244, 247.
Amos and	**IV**: 438.
Mari at, and OT Parallels	**VIII**: 248*(2)*.
Micah and possible parallels to pre-exilic	**VI**: 391.
Prophets, Books of [Former and Latter] - General Studies:	**IV**: *168*, 235.
Atonement in	**VIII**: 194.
Bibliography of	**I: §9, 11.**
'Church and State', according to the	**I**: 508.
Covenant and	**IV**: 385*(2)*.
Ethics to Religion, Relation of, in Prophetic Literature	**V**: 23; **VIII**: 199, 226.
Exegetical Studies	**VI: (§591), 166.**
Forgivness in Judgment, in	**IV**: 357.
Foundation of, and OT Authenticity	**IV**: 167.
God, Kingship of, in	**VIII**: 69.
God of the Prophets	**VIII**: 54.
Grace of God in	**IV**: 357*(3)*.
Greek Translators of	**IV**: 106, 357.

Hebrew Tradition, as Witness to	**IV**: 260.
History, Conception of, in	**IV**: 357.
Holiness in	**VIII**: 199.
Interpretation, Modern, of	**IV**: 357.
Interpretation of, Rules on	**IV**: 80.
Interpretation, Principles of	**IV**: 97.
Law in	**I**: 474, 475.
Literary Criticism of	**IV: §324, 357-358.**
Literary Style of	**IV: (§566), 701.**
Martyrological Tradition in	**VIII**: 386.
Message to Man Through	**VIII**: 212.
Missonary Spirit of	**VIII**: 208.
Paronomasia in	**IV**: 448.
Peace, Doctrine of, Beginnings of	**IV**: 357.
Preaching from the	**VIII**: 375.
Prophetic Lawsuit Speeches in	**IV**: 358.
Relevance of, for Today	**IV**: 357.
Religion to Ethics, Relation of, in Prophetic Literature	**V**: 23.
Teaching the, Syllabus	**VIII**: 404.
Theological Studies	**VIII: (§960) 16.**
Transpositions in	**VI**: 413.
Verses, Number of, in	**IV**: 18.
Prophets, Eighth Century:	**I**: *486*.
Aeschylus and	**V**: 703.
Prophets, Persons - General Studies:	**I**: *83*, 100*(5)*, 101*(4)*, **§49, 102-116**; **V**: 8, 11, 78, *103;* **V**: 512*(2);* **VIII**: 237, 238, 243, 389; **IX: §49, lxxxii.**
Absurdity of the Prophet, Jeremiah and	**I**: 55.
Apocalypticism and	**V**: 122; **VIII**: 243.
Assyrian Period, of	**IV**: 386.
Assyrian word for *(Asipu)*	**V**: 168.
Babylonian Period, of	**IV**: 386.
Contemporary Thought, in	**VIII**: 9.
Council of Yahweh and	**I**: 114; **VIII**: 71.
Covenant and	**I**: 114; **IV**: 385; **VIII**: 217.
Cretan	**V**: 241.
Cultus and	**IV**: 387; **V**: 17, 107.
Cultus and Prophetic Words	**V**: 23, 107.
Dilemma of	**VIII**: 245.
Disobedient	**VI**: 225.
Distinguishing Features of OT	**VIII**: 240.
Domestic Relations and	**I**: 211.
Early	**IV**: 381, 385, 386.
Ecstasy and	**I**: 102, 106, 107, 115*(2)*, 116; **VIII**: 237, 244.
Egyptian and Hebrew	**IV**: 500.
Eighth Century	**I**: 103**IV**: 387; **V**: 14.
Eighth Century, Archaeological Background	**IV**: 387.
Exile and	**V**: 8.
Exilic	**IV**: 390.
Exilic Period, of	**IV**: 386.
Faith in the Divine Mission of, and Moses, and Christ	**VIII**: 278.
Folk-Song in Mouth of	**IV**: 173.
Hebrew and Egyptian	**IV**: 500.
Hebrew, and Greek Poets	**I**: 113; **V**: 150; **VI**: 255.
Historians and	**I**: 115, *136;* **VI**: 238, 243, 258.
Intercessor, as	**I**: 112.
Israel, in	**VIII**: 237*(3)*.
Israelite Religion, Effect on	**I**: 486; **V**: 26.
Jeremiah and	**IV**: 415.
Jeremiah and Absurdity of the Prophet	**I**: 55.

Jonah and the Prophetic Experience	**I**: 57.
Law and	**I**: 112.
Life of	**I**: 102; **VIII**: 237.
Literary Aspects of Hebrew	**I**: 112; **IV**: 176.
Mishpaṭ and	**I**: 486.
Moral Code as	**VIII**: 225.
Moses, Prophet Like	**VI**: 146, 147.
National Crises and	**IV**: 357.
Nationalism and	**I**: 109, 507.
Nationalism, Revolt Against, in Religion	**V**: 21.
Nations, of, Rabbinic Homilies on	**IV**: 346; **VI**: 696, 708.
Old, in 1 Kings 13	**VI**: 225.
Omri Dynasty and	**I**: 111.
One True, in Arabic Stuides	**V**: 145.
Orator, as	**IV**: 387.
Outside Israel(?) Zoroastrianism	**V**: 236.
Pathological Experiences, Evaluating	**I**: 113.
Patriotism and	**I**: 111, 507.
Poets and	**I**: 105*(2)*, 110; **VIII**: 368.
Politics and	**I**: 114, 186, 460*(2)*, 463, 464, 469.
Pre-Exilic Period, in	**V**: 15.
Priests and	**V**: 40, 41*(2)*, 42.
Priests and, in Contemporary Thought	**V**: 28.
Priests and, in Hebrew Ethics	**V**: 41; **VIII**: 221.
Priests and, in Judaism	**V**: 41.
Priests, Relation to, Before the Exile	**V**: 13.
Priests, *vs.*, A False Antithesis	**V**: 22.
Prophet-Scribes, Historic Aim of	**VI**: 256.
Prophets of the Nations in Rabbinic Writings	**IV**: 346; **VI**: 696, 708.
Psychological Aspects of Hebrew	**I**: 112; **IV**: 176.
Psychology of	**I**: 107.
Rabbinic Homilies on the Prophets of the Nations	**IV**: 346; **VI**: 696, 708.
Reaction against	**I**: 184.
Restoration, of the	**IV**: 386, 387, 427.
Revelation, as Instrument of	**VIII**: 33.
Ritual and the Hebrew	**V**: 25.
Sacrifice and	**II**: 105, 111*(4)*, 112; **IV**: 351; **V**: 58, 61, 62*(2)*; **VIII**: 196.
Sacrifice, Attitude to, and Deuteronomy	**V**: 63.
Samaria, Old Prophet who Dwelt in	**VI**: 225.
"Schools of the Prophets"	**I**: **§50**, **116-117**.
Seventh Century	**IV**: 387.
Social Ideas and Problems	**I**: 110, 111, 113, 114, 115, 184, 186, 187*(2)*, 188, 463, 464; **IV**: 386, 387; **IX**: lxxxii, lxxxv.
Social Justice of	**I**: 189; **IV**: 387.
Society and	**IX**: lxxxii.
"Sons of the Prophets"	**I**: 116*(3)*, 117*(2)*; **II**: v.
Specific Prophets, *see:* ***Alphabetical Listing of OT Persons***	**I**: **§45**, **26-82**; **IX**: **§45**: **lxxxi-lxxxii**.
Suffering in the Pre-Exilic	**IV**: 387; **VIII**: 186.
Symbolic Acts of	**I**: 110, 111, 116*(2)*.
Symbolic Acts of Greek Philosophers and	**I**: 110; **V**: 256, 273.
Talmud and Midrash, in	**I**: 112; **IV**: 235; **VI**: 372, 689, 708.
Task of	**IV**: 387; **VI**: 257*(2)*.
Time-Consciousness of	**I**: 415.

Unnamed, of Judges 6 **VI**: 182.
War and **I**: 109; **IV**: 387, 394; **VIII**: 232, 233.
West Africa, and **I**: 391
Will of God, and **VIII**: 88.
World-Order, and **I**: 108; **VIII**: 86.

Prophets, Post-Exilic:
History, Use of by **IV**: 357.
Religion of **V**: 11.

Prophets, Pre-Exilic: **IV**: 385; **V**: 15.
History, Use of by **IV**: 357.
Pacifism and **IV**: 388; **VIII**: 233.
"Spirit" in **IV**: 387*(2)*; **VIII**: 18, 152.
Suffering in **IV**: 387.
"Word" in **IV**: 387*(2)*; **VIII**: 18, 152.

PROPHYRY:
Daniel, on **VI**: 718.

Propontis: **III**: 263.

Propylaea: **III**: 29.
Attic Building Accounts **VII**: 338.

Propylaia: **III**: 480.

Propylon, *see:* **Gates**

Proselytes, Proselytizing: **V**: 25.
Admission of **VI**: 520.
Baptism of **I**: 368*(6)*.
Gerim Gerurim **VI**: 691.
Halakah, in **VI**: 693.
Zechariah, in **VI**: 410.

Proselytizing and Missionary Activities: **VIII**: **§1024, 208-209**.
Evangelism in the OT **VIII**: 209.
Missionary Spirit of the Psalms and Prophets **VIII**: 208.

Prosopography:
Cuneiform Material for Egyptian **V**: 301.
Dositheos, Son of Drimylos and **VI**: 656.
Treaty between Athens and Haliai, notes on **I**: 511.

Prospecting:
Archaeological **II**: 221.

Prostanna: **III**: 203.

Prostitution: **I**: 215.
Babylonian Laws on rights of Prostitutes **I**: 497.
Qedesh **V**: 78.
Zonah **V**: 78.

Prostration:
From Afar in Ugaritic, Accadian and Hebrew **V**: 167, 198.
Selah as "Reverential" **IV**: 492.

Prosymna: **I**: *401;* **III**: 204.

Protection:
Divine **VIII**: 88.
Legal, in Papyri **I**: 501.

Proto-Semitic:
Perfect and Jussive, in **V**: 491, *594, 599*.

Proto-Byblian Inscriptions: **VII**: 87.

Proto-Sinaitic Inscriptions, *see also:* **Sinaitic Inscriptions** **VII**: **§853, 85-86**, *100*.
Egyptian Hieroglyphs and the Proto-Sinaitic Semitic Alphabet **V**: 309.

Protoevangelium: **VI**: 455.

Proton Magnometer:
Use in Underwater Archaeology **III**: 453.

Provenience:
Sumerian, and Greek Defensive Sanctity **V**: 257.

Proverbs:
Arabic **I**: 382, 383*(2)*, 389, 391.
Babylonian **VII**: 221*(2)*.
Book of, and other **IV**: 499.
Egyptian Book of **VII**: 10*(2)*.
Hebrew, in Amarna Letters **VII**: 171.
Hittite **VII**: 305.
Jewish, Spanish **I**: 383.
Modern, Oriental **I**: 388*(2)*.
Neo-Aramaic of the Jews of Zakho **I**: 392.
Ptah-Hotep, of **VII**: 10.
Syrian **I**: 385, 392.

Proverbs, Book of: **I**: *231, 288;* **IV**: *456;* **V**: 115, *116;* **VI**: 9, *479,* 701.

Accent Systems of **V**: 691.

Adversity in **IV**: 501.

Amen-em-ope, Teaching of, and **IV**: 500*(2);* **V**: 213; **VII**: 11*(2).*

Authenticity and Authorship of **IV**: **§392, 502.**

Avesta and Wisdom in **IV**: 499.

Baer, S., Errata in the Edition of **IV**: 499.

Bibliography **I**: **§25, 13.**

Christ's Use of **IV**: 499; **VIII**: 278.

Confucius, and **IV**: 500, 501; **V**: 148, 151.

Date of **IV**: **§392, 502.**

Davidson, Samuel, on **IV**: 550.

Delitzsch, Franz, Errata in Edition of **IV**: 499.

Diligent Husbandman in. Paraphrase of 27:23-27 **V**: 705.

Doublets in **IV**: 501.

Editor, Single, for **IV**: 502.

Egyptian Contribution to **IV**: 502.

Egyptian Ethics and **IV**: 500.

Egyptian Texts and **IV**: 500*(2).*

Emendations in **VI**: 545*(2).*

Ethics of **IV**: 500; **VIII**: 221.

Exegetical Studies on **VI**: **§647, 537-550; IX**: **§647, cxlix.**

God and Man, Relationship in **IV**: 501.

Gospel in **IV**: 501; **VIII**: 275.

Healing in **IV**: 501.

Hebrew gbîrâ (גְּבוּרָה) in **IV**: 502.

Hexaplaric Signs in the Syro-Hexaplar of **IV**: 501.

Humour of **IV**: 500.

Justice in **IV**: 502.

Literary Criticism of **IV**: **§391, 499-502; IX**: **§391, cxxxiii.**

Logos in, and the Gospel of John **IV**: 501; **VIII**: 131, 289.

Love Incarnates in **IV**: 499.

Man and God, Relationship in **IV**: 501.

Man, Duties of, in **IV**: 499.

Mnemonic Use of Numbers in **V**: 116; **VI**: 623; **IX**: cxxxiii.

Northwestern Semitic Literature and **IV**: 501.

Other Proverbs and **IV**: 499.

Pedagogical Hints from **VI**: 538.

Pedagogical Value of **IV**: 499.

Philological Notes on **VI**: 537.

Poem on **VIII**: 365.

Poetry in the Greek **IV**: 500.

Poverty in **IV**: 501.

Preacher and the Maxims of **VIII**: 375.

Preaching from **VIII**: 376.

Property, Teachings on **IV**: 499.

Proverb Custers in **IV**: 501.

Psychological Terms in **IV**: 500

Rabbinic Exegesis in the Vulgate of **IV**: 500; **VI**: 715.

Religion, Aspects of, in **IV**: 500, 502; **V**: 116.

Religious Value of **IV**: 502.

Riches in **IV**: 501.

Righteousness in **IV**: 502.

Saadia's Commentary on **VI**: 726.

Self-Control in **IV**: 500.

Semitic Field of "Folly" in **VI**: 419.

Septuagint of, as a Hellenistic Document **IV**: 501.

Septuagint, Studies in **IV**: 501.

Seven Columns of Wisdom's House in **VI**: 538.

Solomonic, Classification **IV**: 499.

Sources of **IV**: **§392, 502; IX**: **§392, cxxxiii.**

Structure of IV: 499.
Textual Notes on VI: 537*(2)*.
"Torah", in IV: 456.
Tree of Life in IV: 294, 501.
Utilitarian(?) IV: 500.
Vulgate of, Rabbinic Exegesis in IV: 500.
Wisdom, Concept of, in VI: 540.
Wisdom, Deuteronomic in IV: 501.
Wisdom in, and the Avesta IV: 499; V: 142.
Wisdom Personified in IV: 499*(3)*.
Wisdom, Secular in IV: 501.

Proverbs 1-9:
Literary Problems in V: 706.

Proverbs 9:
Banquet Motif in, and Keret VI: 541.

Proverbs, Book of, Manuscripts of: VI: (**§648**), **550**.

Providence:
Creation and III: 292.
God, of *see:* ***God, Doctrine of***
Hebrew and Greek Ideas IX: cxxxvii.
Physical Laws and Divine VIII: 88.
Promise and VIII: 213.
Sin and its Relation to Divine VIII: 88, 176.

Provincia Arabia: II: *439, 456*.

Prussia:
Historical Parallel with Assyria II: 116.

Prutah: I: 457.

PRUTKY, V. R. III: 498.

Prytaneion: III: 471.

Psaix: III: 602.

Psalmic Literature:
Apocryphal Psalms in Syraic VI: 656.
Exegetical Studies on VI: (**§794**), **668**.
Literary Criticism of VI: **§768, 656-657**.
Textual Criticism on VI: **§742, 645**.

Psalmody: I: *243;* IV: 478, 484.493, 494; VIII: 378*(2)*.
Church Fathers, on VI: 721.

Psalms, Apocryphal: VI: 645.
Syriac VI: 645, 656.

Psalms, Books of the *see also* : **Psalter** I: xviii (n18); *192, 510;* IV: 126, *267, 456;* VI: 9; VIII: 396.
Abiding Religious Value of IV: 478.
Accent Systems of V: 691.
Acrostic VI: 451*(2)*, 457*(4)*, 517, 521.
Alphabetic, and Job IV: 456.
Alphabetical IV: 474; V: 116.
Alternate Versions of IV: 474.
American Bapitist Publication of IV: 59.
ANE Literature, Parallels to IV: 498.
Anthropomophisms / Anthropopathisms in the LXX of IV: 483; VIII: 103.
Anthropomorphisms, Avoidance of in the Targum of IV: 486; VI: 714; VIII: 105.
Apocrypha, from Qumran VIII: 449*(2)*.
Apologetic, Modern, in IV: 474; VIII: 315.
Archaeology and Higher Criticism of IV: 215*(2)*, 478, 479.
Asaph of IV: 484; VIII: 390.
Authenticity and Authorship of IV: 490, **§390, 496-498**; VI: 449.
Autobiographic Element of IV: 478.
Babylonian and, Compared IV: 477; VII: 254, 268.
Babylonian, Rythmn in VII: 259.
Background of IV: 481.

Barnes', Version of	**IV**: 484.
Baxter, Richard, Paraphrase of, by	**IV**: 479.
Bible Revision and	**IV**: 474.
Bibliography	**I**: **§24, 13**.
Briggs on	**IV**: 139; **VI**: 449.
Bush, George, on	**IV**: 473.
Calvin, John, Influence of, on Life and Thought	**VIII**: 370.
Canaanite Literature and	**IV**: 498*(2)*; **VII**: 144.
Canaanite Vestiges in	**IV**: 497.
Catacombs, in	**VIII**: 378.
Cheyne, T. K., on	**IV**: 475, 496; **V**: 9.
Chiasmus in	**V**: 706.
Christ and Christianity, Witness of, to	**IV**: 489.
Christ, at the time of	**IV**: 485.
Christ in	**IV**: 483.
Christian Interpretation of	**IV**: 484.
Christian Prayers and Jewish Psalms	**IV**: 482.
Christian Use of	**IV**: 473.
Church's Use of	**VIII**: 382.
City of Adam in (?)	**II**: 315.
Classes of	**IV**: 481.
Collection of	**IV**: 481.
Collocation of	**IV**: 476.
Covenant of Creation in	**I**: 510; **IV**: 478; **VIII**: 77.
Covenants in	**IV**: 478.
Criticism, Aid in the Interpretation of	**IV**: 476.
Criticism of	**IV**: 474, 476*(2)*.
Criticism of, between 1900 and 1935	**IV**: 483.
Criticism, Radical, of	**IV**: 480.
Cult and	**IV**: 482, 486; **V**: 24.
Cultic שגגה, Influence on	**V**: 455.
Curses in	**IV**: 473, 487.
Cursing	**IV**: 488*(2)*; **VIII**: 386.
Date of	**IV**: 475*(2)*, 479, 481, 489*(2)*, **§390, 496-498**; **VI**: 471.
David and	**I**: 88, 89; **IV**: 473, 476, 477, 496*(4)*; **VIII**: 389*(3)*, 391, 449*(2)*.
De Burgh, William, on	**IV**: 474.
Delitzsch, Franz, on	**IV**: 475.
Development of	**IV**: 496.
Diction of	**V**: 705*(3)*, 706.
Diction of, as a Clue to Its Development	**IV**: 497.
Divine Forgiveness in	**IV**: 485; **VIII**: 196.
Divine name 'Ēlî, in	**IV**: 483; **VIII**: 110.
Divine Personal Pronoun in	**IV**: 481; **VIII**: 110.
Divisons into Sections of	**IV**: 491.
Douay Version	**IV**: 474.
Duplicates in	**IV**: 475.
Early Church, Interpretation of, by	**IV**: 484; **VI**: 724.
East and West, of	**VIII**: 361.
Ecclesiasticus Testimony as to	**VI**: 623.
Elohim-Psalms and Psalm 14, 53	**IV**: 481; **VI**: 460, 491.
Emendations on	**VI**: 442, 444, 447, 482, 489, 503, 505, 513, 517.
Enemies and Evildoers in	**IV**: 485.
Enemies of	**IV**: 481.
English, More Rhythmical Version of	**VI**: 446.
Enthronement, Cutic Setting of	**IV**: 485.
Enthronement, Liturgical Aspects in	**IV**: 483.
Eschatology of the	**VIII**: 249, 250.
Ethical Concepts of	**IV**: 481; **VIII**: 226.
Ethiopic MSS of	**IV**: 44.

Festival, Doxology of **VIII**: 206.
Future Life in **IV**: 481; **VIII**: 263.
Geddes's Translation of **IV**: 473.
Genres, Literary, of **IV**: 487; **V**: 706.
God, Idea of, in **IV**: 479, 480; **VIII**: 61*(2)*.
God, in **VI**: 465, 475.
God, Kinship of, in **VIII**: 69.
God, Names of, in **IV**: 480, 491; **VIII**: 109.
"God of Jacob" (אלהי יעקב) in **IV**: 481.
God, Works of, in **VI**: 465.
God's Kindness Emphasied in **IV**: 483.
Grosseteste, Robert, on **IV**: 479.
Gunkel, Hermann, on **IV**: 480.
Hebrew (שׁפט) in **IV**: 485.
Hebrew (רִנָּה) in **IV**: 484.
Hebrew, in the Liturgy **VIII**: 385.
Hebrew (כל), Constructive Use of in **IV**: 481.
Hebrew (מַשְׂכִּיל) in **IV**: 490, 491.
Hebrew Metre and the Text of **IV**: 480.
Hebrew (אנשי דמים) in **IV**: 486.
Heinrich von Mugeln, Translation of, by **IV**: 108.
Heman, Sons of, by **IV**: 498.
Hengstenberg, E. W., on **IV**: 473.
Heraldry, in **VIII**: 352.
Herbert of Bosham's Commentary on Jerome's Hebrew **IV**: 482.
Higher Criticism of, and Archaeology **IV**: 215*(2)*, 478, 479.
Hippolytus on **VI**: 718.
History, and / in **IV**: 476, 485; **VIII**: 350.
Hupfeld, Hermann, on **IV**: 473.
Immortality, Hope of, in **VI**: 444; **VIII**: 263.
Inspiration of, and Imprecatory Psalms **IV**: 487; **VI**: 454.
Interpretation of **IV**: 487.
Interpretation, Reflections on the **IV**: 486.
Introductory Notes of **IV**: 485.
Israel's Songs and **V**: 686, 705.
Jerome on **IV**: 475, 477, 480, 482, 488.
Jewish, and Christian Prayers **IV**: 482.
Jewish New Year's Day for **IV**: 376, 478.
Jewish Psalmody, Late, for Understanding of OT Psalmodic Tradition **IV**: 484.
Kimhi, David, Commentary on Psalms **VI**: 483.
Kimhi, David, Commentary on the Fifth Book of Psalms **VI**: 726.
King, References to, in and Messianic Belief **IV**: 475*(2)*, 490*(2)*.
Korah, Date of **IV**: 496.
Korah of **IV**: 484.
Lament, of **VIII**: 72.
Latin Translation of, New **IV**: 61.
Latin Verse Translation of **IV**: 75.
Levitical System, as Evidence of **IV**: 475; **V**: 9.
Limitations of **IV**: 480.
Literary Criticism of **IV**: **§383, 473-486**; **IX**: **§383, cxxxiii.**
Literary Forms in, New Classification of **IV**: 484.
Littledale, Richard F., on **IV**: 474.
Liturgic, from Qumran **VIII**: 449.
Liturgies of Depature in **IV**: 480.
Liturgy and **VIII**: 385.
Liturgy, Jewish, in **IV**: 493; **VIII**: 206.
Locality, Notes of **IV**: 479.
Maccabean **IV**: 474, 477, 478, 496*(3)*, 497, 498.

Mansucript of	**IV**: 11.
Martin Luther's Preface to	**IV**: 484.
Masoretic MS from 1300	**IV**: 13.
Masoretic Text, Criticism of, from First Psalm	**IV**: 14.
Mather, Cotton, on	**IV**: 473.
Meaning of	**IV**: 485.
Messianic, *see:* ***Messianic Psalms***	**IV**: 477, **§385, 489-490**.
Metric System in	**IV**: 481.
Middrash to	**VI**: 708.
Minatory	**IV**: 487.
Minister / Preacher and	**VIII**: 376, 388, 406.
Minstier and	**VIII**: 385.
Missionary Spirit of	**VIII**: 208.
Modern Life and	**IV**: 479.
Mowinckel's Contribution to Biblical Studies	**IV**: 486.
Music in	**I**: 245*(2)*; **IV**: 482, 483.
Mystic Passages in	**IV**: 475.
Mystical Interpretation of	**IV**: 479.
Nationalism in	**IV**: 480; **IX**: cii.
Natural Strength of	**IV**: 478.
Nature in	**IV**: 478, 480, 485; **VI**: 444, 465, 475.
Nature-Poetry of	**IV**: 477*(3)*; **V**: 685, 686*(3)*.
Neale, John Mason, on	**IV**: 474.
Negro Spirituals and	**VIII**: 359.
New Version of	**IV**: *367*, 476.
Noyes, George R., on	**IV**: 473.
Noyes's Translation of	**VI**: 442.
Ostraca fragments, LXX	**IV**: 9.
Out of Door World in	**IV**: 479.
Parallelism, "Synonymous" in	**IV**: 484.
Paseq, Use of in	**IV**: 474, 475.
Pastoral Study of	**VIII**: 372.
Pastoral Theology and	**VIII**: 386.
Pathos in	**IV**: 475.
Pathros and	**IV**: 475, 495*(2)*.
Penitential	**IV**: 478.
Perowne, J. J. S., on	**IV**: 474, 492.
Personal Element in	**IV**: 478.
Personal Experience, in	**VI**: 448.
Personality in	**IV**: 482.
Peshiṭta Text of	**IV**: 46.
Phillips, George, on	**IV**: 473.
Philological Notes on	**VI**: 491, 528*(2)*.
Philology in	**VI**: 502.
Piety, Personal, of	**IV**: 478.
Poetry of	**IV**: 476, 479; **V**: 685.
"Polyglot" Arabic	**IV**: 482.
Position of in the OT	**IV**: 474.
Prayer and	**IV**: 483.
Prayer-Book and	**IV**: 474.
Preaching From / Value of	**VIII**: 374, 375, 377.
Preposition ב in, = *from*	**VI**: 448.
Pronominal Suffixes in	**IV**: 484; **V**: 484.
Qumran and	**IV**: 158.
Quotations of	**IV**: 475*(2)*.
Reeves, John, on	**IV**: 473.
Religion of	**IV**: 480.
Research in Since 1955	**IV**: 486*(2)*.
Revised Standard Version of	**IV**: 482, 486.
Revised Version (1881)	**VI**: 442, 443*(2)*.
Rhythmical Rendering of	**IV**: 482.
Rhythmical Restoration of	**IV**: 483.
Ritual in	**IV**: 478.
Ritual Use of	**IV**: 478.
Root GMR (גמר) in	**IV**: 483.
Samuel, Second, Dating of, from	**IV**: 377.
Scandinavian Research in, after Mowinckel	**IV**: 485.
Seasonal, and Prophecy	**IV**: 487; **VIII**: 247.
"Selah", Studies concerning	**IV**: **§388, 492**.
Self-Pity in	**IV**: 481.
Semitic Field of "Folly" in	**VI**: 419.
Sickness, in Times of	**VI**: 444.
Sin, Experience of, in	**IV**: 484.
Sin, Rememberance of, in	**VI**: 481.

Social Concepts in, and Relation to Canaanite Residental Area **IV**: 485.
Solomon, of **II**: *45;* **IV**: 496.
"Songs of Zion" as a Literary Category of **IV**: 485.
Sources of **IV**: 475, 481, 482, 485, **§390, 496-498**.
Study Between 1955 and 1969, in **IV**: 486.
Style, Hebrew (Two Hidden Comparatives) **V**: 706.
Suffering in **IV**: 483; **VI**: 454, 475; **VIII**: 187.
Superscriptions of, 'Al (עַל) in **IV**: 491.
Swedish, Sources of **IV**: 74.
Symbolism and Theology of **VIII**: 19, 307.
Symbolism of **VIII**: 19.
Syriac, Inner, Corruptions in **IV**: 481.
Targum to, and Mark 14:24 **VI**: 713; **VIII**: 286.
Technical Terms in **IV**: 481.
Temple in
Tenses, Importance of, for Interpretation of **IV**: 479.
Theodicies, Psalms 37; 49; 83 as **VI**: 480, 488, 498.
Theodicy in, Problem of **IV**: 486; **VIII**: 185.
Theology and Symbolism of **VIII**: 19, 307.
Theology of **VIII**: 19.
Title, Psalm 16 **VI**: 442.
Titles and Divisons of **I**: *88;* **IV**: 481, **§387, 490-491**; **VIII**: 310.
Torah and **IV**: 236, 486.
Traditionalism in **IV**: 482.
Traditions, Early Israelite, in **IV**: 486.
Translating **IV**: 109, 110, 486; **VIII**: 378.
Translation of, New **IV**: 485.
Travell, F. T., on **IV**: 473; **VI**: 458.
Understanding, Present, of **IV**: 485.
Universal Literature, in **IV**: 476.
Use of, Today **IV**: 494.
Vengeance, of **IV**: 488.
"Vengeful" **VI**: 447.
Verses in **VIII**: 310.
Vespers, for **IV**: 494, 495.
Vindictive **IV**: 487*(4)*.
Vulgate, Influence on English Translation of **IV**: 42.
Watts, Isaac, on **IV**: 474.
West-Saxon **IV**: 48.
Wisdom and **IV**: 483; **V**: 117.
Wisdom of Solomon, Borrowing from the **VI**: 619.
"Wisdom Psalms" Classification of **V**: 118.
"Wisdom Psalms", Consideration of the Classification **IV**: 485.
Worship, in **VI**: 448; **VIII**: 378, 382.
Yahweh and, Lament **V**: 29.
Yahweh Ṣeḇa'oṯ in **VIII**: 125.
Yiddish Translation of **IV**: 486.
Zionism in **IV**: 480; **VIII**: 344; **IX**: cii.

Psalms 1-150: **IV**: 481.

Psalm 1:
Authorship of **IV**: 496; **VI**: 449.
Masoretic Text of **VI**: 449.
Metre in **V**: 691.
Metre of **VI**: 450.
Poetic Form of **V**: 705.
Tenses of **VI**: 449.

Psalm 2:
Christ, Kingdom of, in **VI**: 451.
Divine Sonship of Christ in **VI**: 451.
Messianic Application of **VI**: 450.
Prophecy and **VI**: 450.
Tenses of **VI**: 450.

Psalm 8:
Messianic(?) **IV**: 490.
Psalm 10:
Egyptian Light on **VI**: 458.
Psalm 14: **IV**: 481.
Psalm 16:
Christian Faith, Historical Origin of, and **VI**: 461.
Psalm 18:
Theophany Celebrated in **VI**: 464.
Psalm 19:
Christopher Columbus and **VI**: 465.
Psalm 21:
Covenant-Song(?) **VI**: 467.
Psalm 22: **IV**: 484.
Christological Revelation, Illustrating Prophetic **VI**: 468.
Psalm 23:
Beatitudes in **VI**: 470; **VIII**: 279.
Christian Worship, in **VIII**: 383.
Date and Interpretation of **IV**: 497.
Date of **VI**: 471.
Metrical Structure of **VI**: 471.
Poetic Form of **V**: 705.
Psalm 24:
Ancient Form of Recital of **VI**: 473, 526.
Date of **IV**: 498.
Eschatological Interpretation of **VI**: 473.
Psalm 25: **IV**: 484.
Psalm 27:
Metre of **VI**: 474.
Psalm 29:
Canaanite Psalm, as **VI**: 475.
Canaanite Vestigates in **VI**: 475.
Strophe in Hebrew Poetry and **V**: 691, 706.
Ugarit and **VI**: 475.
Psalm 33:
St. Augustine, Sermon on the Title of, by **IV**: 491*(2)*.
Psalm 44:
Authorship of **IV**: 497.
Psalm 45: **IV**: 484.
Psalm 46:
Martin Luther and **VI**: 486.
Psalm 49:
Sheep of Death in **VI**: 487.
Psalm 50:
Polemic Against Animal Sacrifice **VI**: 489.
Psalm 51:
Authorship of **IV**: 496.
Realized Eschatology in **VIII**: 253.
Psalm 53: **IV**: 481.
Psalm 68:
Ugaritic Tablets and **VI**: 495.
Psalm 72:
Hymn to Jehovah **VI**: 496.
Psalm 74:
Cultic Situation of **IV**: 498.
Psalm 75:
Selah, a Lost, and **IV**: 493.
Psalm 77:
Date of **IV**: 498.
Psalm 80:
Date of **IV**: 498.
Psalm 81:
Exodus, and **IV**: 339; **VI**: 502.
Psalm 82:
Canannite Background to **VI**: 502.
God and the Gods in Assembly and **VI**: 503.
Mythological Background **VI**: 502.
Rabbinic Interpretation of, and the Gospel of John **VI**: 502, 716.
Psalm 83:
Historical Background to **VI**: 503.
Psalm 89:
Literary Form and Liturugical Background **V**: 706.
Psalm 91:
Demonology of the OT and **VI**: 508; **VIII**: 160.
Psalm 104:
Akhnaton and **VI**: 513.
Egyptian Prototype of **VI**: 513.
Feeling for Form in **V**: 706.

Psalm 105:
Plagues Tradition in **VI**: 514.
Psalm 106:
Classical Parallels to **VI**: 514.
Stichometry and the Hallel **VI**: 514.
Psalm 107:
Unknown Interpretation in among the DSS **VI**: 515.
Psalm 109:
Hebrew Tenses in **VI**: 515*(3)*.
Keate, W., on **VI**: 515.
"Vindictive" Psalm **VI**: 515.
Psalm 110: **VIII**: 132.
Authorship of **IV**: 497*(3)*, 498; **VI**: 517.
Canaanite(?) **VI**: 517.
Christ Enthroned in **VI**: 516*(2)*.
Medieval Hebrew Interpretations of **VI**: 517.
Rabbinic Interpretation of, Refutation of by Jesus **VI**: 517.
Trial of Jesus and the Interpretation of **VI**: 517.
Psalm 115:
Setting of **VI**: 519.
Psalm 116:
Liturgy, in **VIII**: 384.
Psalm 118:
Authorship of **VI**: 522.
Psalm 124:
Ancient Form of Recital of **VI**: 473, 526.
Psalm 126:
Livy, Illustrated from **VI**: 526.
Psalm 127:
Metrical Version of **VI**: 527.
Psalm 132:
Form Criticism of **V**: 694; **VI**: 529.
Psalm 139:
Atharva-Veda and **VI**: 531.
Background of **VI**: 531.
Psalm 145
Theology of **VI**: 532; **VIII**: 19.
Psalm 146:
Theology of **VI**: 532; **VIII**: 19.
Psalms, Books of the, Manuscripts of: **VI**: **§646, 534-536.**
Baber's Psalter, from the Alexandrian Manuscript **VI**: 534.
Bodl. Baroccianus 15, Prologue **VI**: 535.
Coptic inscriptions / Fragments of **VI**: 451, 534*(2)*.
Coptic MSS in the Freer Collection **VI**: 535*(2)*.
Coptic Psalter **VI**: 534.
Ethiopian Manuscript in the Astor Library **VI**: 534.
Fragments of, with Palestinian Punctuation **V**: 473.
Freer Psalter **VI**: 535*(3)*.
Hebrew Manuscript of, Fourteenth Century C.E. **VI**: 534.
Latin Text of the Paris Psalter **VI**: 535.
Latin Verse Translations **VI**: 536.
Mandaic Version of 114 **VI**: 519.
Monte Cassino Psalter **VI**: 535.
Peshitta Text **VI**: 535.
Sahidic Text of **VI**: 534.
Septuagint Fragment of **VI**: 532, 534*(2)*, 536*(2)*.
Septuagint Version of **VI**: 448.
Syriac Liturgy on, found in Peking *ca.* 1925 **VI**: 536.
Syriac Psalter **VI**: 534.
Syriac Psalter, "Nicene" Creed in the **VI**: 534.
Theodulfian MSS of the Vulgate **VI**: 535.
Uncial Codex of **VI**: 534, 535.
Vulgate **VI**: 534.
Psalms Commentary Pesher (4QpPs37): **VIII**: **§1122, 457-458.**
Psalms, Exegetical Studies on: **VI**: **§645, 442-533**; **IX**: **§645, cxlviii.**
Recent Trends in **IV**: 485.
Psalms from Qumran: **VIII**: **§1107, 448-450.**

11Q Counterpart to Psalm 151, 1-5 — **VI**: 533.
11QPs[a]Plea — **V**: 537; **VIII**: 449.
11QPss — **VI**: 533.
OT Canon and — **IV**: 207*(2)*.

Psalms, Imprecatory: — **IV**: **§384, 487-488**.
Authorship of — **IV**: 496.
Ethical Problems of — **IV**: 488.
Hebrew Tenses in Ps 109 — **VI**: 515.
Hun and — **IV**: 487.
Inspiration of the Psalms, and — **IV**: 487.
Reconcilation with the Spirit of the Gospel — **IV**: 488.
Southern Rebellion and — **IV**: 487.
"Vindictive" Psalm (109) — **VI**: 515.

Psalms of Solomon: — **II**: *45*.
Christianity and — **VI**: 657.
Exegetical Studies on — **VI**: **§795, 668-669**.
Greek Fragment of — **VI**: 646.
Hasmonean Decline and — **VI**: 657.
Historical Allusions in — **VI**: 668, 669*(2)*.
Literary Criticism of — **VI**: **§769, 657**(*‡2*)*;* **IX**: **§769, cl**.
Religious Background of, and Qumran Literature — **VIII**: 483.
Syriac Version of — **VI**: 645.
Textual Criticism on — **VI**: **§743, 645-646**.
Theological Contents of — **VI**: 657.

Psalms, Qumran Commentaries on: — **VIII**: **§1122, 457-458**.
11QPs[a] — **VI**: 520.
11QPsaPlea 3-4 — **VI**: 427.
Psalm 107, Unknown Interpretation among DSS — **VI**: 515; **VIII**: 457.

Psalms, Songs of Ascent: — **IV**: **§385, 489**; **VI**: 473, 524*(4)*, 526*(2)*.
Authorship of — **IV**: 497.
Egyptian Hallel — **IV**: 489.
Gradual Psalms — **IV**: 489.
Hallel Psalms, Last of — **IV**: 489.
Jerusalem Processional — **IV**: 489*(2)*; **VI**: 504*(2)*, 506*(2)*.
Metrical Form of — **VI**: 524.
Moods of Worship in — **IV**: 489.
Pilgrim Psalms / Psalter — **IV**: 489*(2)*.
Priestly Blessing and — **VI**: 128.

Psalter, *see also:* **Psalms, Book of** — **I**: *510;* **IV**: 477, **§389, 492-495**; **IX**: **§389, cxxxiii**.
Bay Psalm Book and Harvard Hymnody — **IV**: 493.
Breviary — **IV**: 494.
Catholicity of — **IV**: 482.
Cheyne's Bampton Lectures on — **V**: 9; **IX**: cxxxiii.
Church of England, in Parish Worship of — **VIII**: 384*(2)*.
Church of England, Servies of, in — **VIII**: 381.
Coptic Versions — **IV**: 43.
Coverdale and — **IV**: 53.
Date of — **IV**: 479.
English — **IV**: 493, 494.
English, 13th Century — **IV**: 495.
Ethiopic — **IV**: 44.
Evesham — **IV**: 495.
Irish — **IV**: 48.
Jerome's "Hebrew Psalter" — **IV**: 494.
Jerome's Work on the — **IV**: 41*(2)*, 42.
Jewish — **IV**: 493.
Kautzsch, Emil, on — **VI**: 443*(3)*, 462, 463.
Latin, New Version of — **IV**: 75, 107, 493, 494*(5)*, 495, 446, 447, 449, 453, 454*(2)*, 457, 458, 460, 461, 463, 470, 474, 475, 476, 477, 490.
Latin, Obscurities in — **VI**: 445*(2)*.

Lectionary and, in Public Worship	**VIII**: 382; **IX**: cxxxiii.
Liturgical	**VIII**: 384.
Liturgy and	**VIII**: 385.
Metrical Version	**IV**: 493.
New	**IV**: 107.
New Testament and	**IV**: 477*(2)*; **VIII**: 273*(2)*.
New Version of	**IV**: 107, *367*.
Orthodox Church, in	**VIII**: 386.
Oxford, in English Verse	**IV**: 492.
Pinkman, F. J., on	**IV**: 494.
Preaching, Use of, in	**VIII**: 376.
Reading the	**VIII**: 396*(2)*.
Revised of 1881, of	**IV**: 65.
Revision of	**IV**: 493*(2)*; **IX**: cxxxiii.
Scottish, First	**IV**: 493.
Scottish Metrical Version	**IV**: 493.
Septuagint, Ostraca of	**IV**: 34.
Triennial Cycle of, Midrash Tillim and	**VI**: 707.
Triennial Cycle on	**IV**: 476.
Utrecht and the Athanasian Creed	**IV**: 493.
Worship, Aid to	**VIII**: 381.
Psametik I:	
Inscription of, in the Museum at Palermo	**VII**: 56.
Psammetic-Neith:	
Statue of	**II**: 76.
Psammetichus II (Psammetikh II):	
Ezekiel and	**VI**: 351.
Stela of from Shellal	**II**: 76; **III**: 493; **VII**: 19, 26.
Pseudepigrapha:	**V**: 123; **VI**: **§671, 595-597**.
Bibliography of	**I**: **§39, 15**.
Christian, Eastern origin of	**VI**: 717.
Christian Ethics and	**VIII**: 222.
Deane, William John, on	**VI**: 642.
Deuteronomy and	**IV**: 351.
Garshūni, Christian Documents in, Tranlastions	**VI**: 642, 657.
Greek	**VI**: 642.
Lections on, a Plea for	**VIII**: 382.
Literary Criticism of - General Studies	**VI**: **§753, 648**.
Moral Character of	**VI**: 642.
New Testament, of, and Qurman Literature	**VIII**: **§1156, 483**.
Odes of Solomon and	**VI**: 648.
Pardise in	**VI**: 595; **VIII**: 268.
Syriac, Christian Documents in, Tranlastions	**VI**: 642.
Textual Criticism on	**VI**: **§727, 642**.
Pseudepigraphal Books (Miscellaneous):	
Exegetical Studies on	**VI**: **(§779), 663**.
Exegetical Studies on	**VI**: **§804, 671**.
Literary Criticism of	**VI**: **§778, 663**.
Textual Criticism on	**VI**: **§752, 647-648**.
Pseudepigraphy:	
Daniel, Authorship of, and	**IV**: 535.
Pseudo-Aristeas:	
III Maccabees and	**VI**: 656, 660.
Pseudo-Jerome:	
Psalter Collects of	**VI**: 536.
Qumran Tradition and	**VIII**: 483.
Pseudo-Jonathan:	
Exodus 10:11, on	**VI**: 714.
Numbers, on	**VI**: 138.
Pseudo-Phocylides:	**IV**: 192.
Pseudo Smerdis:	**II**: *35*, **97**; **VII**: 236, 298.
Pseudo-Cyprianic de Pascha Computus:	
Exodus, and	**IV**: 339.
Pseudo-Jeremiah:	**VI**: 326.
Pseudo-Philo:	**VI**: **§806, 678**.
Baruch and	**VI**: 625, 678.
Judahites and	**VI**: 678.
Samaritans and	**VI**: 678.

Saul of V: 129; **VI**: 678; **VIII**: 142; **IX**: cli.
Tobiads and **VI**: 678.
Pseudonymity: **IV**: 168.
Psiax: **III**: 619, 711.
Psittatium: **II**: 268, 425.
Psusennes I:
Bones of, Examination **III**: 358; **IX**: cvi.
Psusennes II:
Solomon's Father-in-Law, Mummy of **II**: 76; **IV**: *219*.
Psyche:
Art, Ancient, in **III**: 690, **V**: 242.
Cupid and, as Platonic Myth **V**: 262.
Domus of, in Ostia **III**: 521.
Winged Figure at Jaffa **V**: 248.
Psychical Research: **VIII**: **§1010, 165**.
Prophecy and **VIII**: 165, 251.
Psychoanalysis:
Antrhopology and **III**: 346.
Empathy in Modern Psychotherapy and in the Haggada **VI**: 696.
Mythology and **V**: 133.
Saul, of **I**: *97*.
Psychology: **III**: 289, 290; **VIII**: 1.
Anthropology and **III**: 346.
Biblical **VIII**: 166, 168, 172.
Biblical Pneumatology and **VIII**: 150.
Conviction, of **VIII**: 182.
Ecclesiastes, Psychologically Considered **IV**: 513.
Egyptian **V**: 203.
Egyptian, Exhibited in the Book of the Dead **VII**: 48.
Egyptian Mind, Analysis of **V**: 210.
Epicetus, in **V**: 259.
Essene, Double-Minded Man in the Light of **VIII**: 417.
Ezekiel, Problem in **VI**: 349.
Fall and Depth- **IV**: 295; **VIII**: 183.
Greek, Animal Intelligence in **III**: 365.
Heart and Head in Bible **VI**: 569; **VIII**: 175.
Hebrew, and Deuteronomy **IV**: 350.
Job, Psychoanalytic Comment on 3:25 **VI**: 422.
Judaism, Psychoanalytic Study of **V**: 20; **IX**: lxxxvii.
Man in Hebrew **VIII**: 173.
Mumar—Rabbinic **VI**: 690.
Old Testament and Modern **VIII**: 353.
Old Testament and New **VIII**: 169.
Prayer, of **VIII**: 202.
Prophecy, of / and **I**: 107; **VIII**: 241, 242, 243, 244*(2)*, 245.
Prophets, of the, and Prophecy **I**: *107, 112*.
Proverbs, Psychological Terms in **IV**: 500.
Psychological Approach to Bible Study **VIII**: 395.
Psychological Background of Late Greek Paganism **V**: 261.
Psychological Development of Medcine **III**: 396.
Qumran - Essene, Double-Minded Man in the Light of **VIII**: 417.
Rabbinic **VI**: 690*(2)*.
Religion, of **VIII**: 173.
Salvation, of **VIII**: 190.
Sin, of **VIII**: 179, 180.
Psychopathology: **III**: 402.
Psychosomatics:
Qumran Literature, in **III**: 404; **VIII**: 415.
Psychostasia: **V**: 215, 258.
Psyttaleia: **III**: 214.
Ptaḥ: **VII**: *25*.
Cult of, with Non-Egyptians **V**: 219.

Figurine of	**III**: 760.
Hymn to	**VII**: 41.
Libation Basin Dedicated to	**VII**: 42.
Stele with Hymn to	**VII**: 41.
Ugaritic Mythology, in	**V**: 192, 214.
VIth Dynasty Titles Relating to	**VII**: 72.
Ptah-Arit:	
False Door in Tomb of	**III**: 547.
Ptah-Hotep:	**II**: 76.
Proverbs of	**VII**: 10.
Teachings of	**IX**: cli.
Ptah-Iron-Ka:	
Tomb of	**III**: 358.
Ptah-neferu:	**II**: 77.
Ptah-Shepses (Ptꜣḥ-špss):	**II**: *215*.
Bones of	**III**: 358.
Burial of	**III**: 358.
Golden Belt of, repaired	**III**: 456, 572.
Ptaḥmes (Ptaḥmase, Ptaḥmosĕ)	**III**: *602*.
High Priest of Memphis Statuette of	**II**: 77.
Memphite Stela of	**VII**: 24.
Mortuary Stela of	**VII**: 44.
Objects Belonging to	**III**: 567.
Πτενετω:	
Egypt, in	**III**: 84.
Ptolemaeus Apion:	**II**: 77.
Ptolemaic Chronology and the Canon of Ptolemy:	**II**: *18, 30, 78(2)*, **§149**, **201-202**; **III**: 181.
Ptolemaios:	**I**: *445*.
Ptolemais:	**III**: 204, 257.
Ptolemies:	**I**: *172, 226, 336, 400, 410, 439;* **II**: *77(4)*.
Egypt under	**I**: 187, *347*, 339,*362*, 490, *481, 498, 504;* **II**: 128, *261;* **III**: 91.
Palestine under the (Zenon Papyri)	**VII**: 353.
Portraits of	**II**: *77(2)*.
Ptolemy(s):	**II**: *73*, **77**, *173*.
Aristeas and Ptolemaic Kingship	**VI**: 661.
Canon of	**II**: 173*(2)*, **§149**, **201-202**; **VII**: 230.
Geography of	**II**: 253.
Son of Pelops	**VII**: 337.
Ptolemy Eupator:	**II**: 78.
Ptolemy I (Soter):	**I**: *495;* **II**: **77**.
Sculpture of	**II**: 77.
Ptolemy II:	**I**: *336, 438;* **II**: **78**; **III**: 19.
Granite Relief of	**II**: 78.
Regnal Year of	**II**: 201; **IX**: xcviii.
Ptolemy III Euergetes (I):	**I**: 403.
Ptolemy IV Philopater:	
Foundation Plaque of	**VII**: 69, 341.
Ptolemy Philometor:	
Petitions to (Greek)	**VII**: 331.
Ptolemy Epiphanes (Ptolemy V):	**II**: 78*(2)*, 201*(2)*.
Decree of Egyptian Priest in Honor of	**VII**: 334.
Ptolemy VI:	
Head of	**II**: 78; **III**: 753.
Mount Ptous:	**III**: *755*.
Pubes:	
Egyptian Term for	**III**: 399; **V**: 323.
Public Service:	
Athens, in, and relation to Private Activies	**I**: 188, 210, 507.
Public Office, Avoidance of in Papy. Oxy. 1477 and Talmudic Sources	**VI**: 704; **VII**: 342.
Pudu-ḫepa:	**II**: 78; **VII**: 306.
Pul, *see also:* **Tiglath-Pileser III**	**II**: **78-79**, **102**, *183(3), 184, 191(4);* **IV**: 181; **VII**: 159.
Pulse:	
Mesopotamian Medicine, Observation of	**III**: 403.
Pulur:	**III**: 264, 266, 267.

Pumbeditha:
Talmudical College of — **VI**: 689.
Punctuation:
Hebrew, *see:* ***Hebrew Grammar***
Translator's — **IV**: 109.
Punic, *see:* **Carthaginians**
Punic Inscriptions, *see also:* **Phoenician Inscriptions**
Punic Literature — **VII**: 118.
Punic Language: — **V**: 280, 383, *473*, 523, *528*.
Punishment: — **VI**: 145; **VIII**: 181, 194.
Crime and, in *Hymn to Delos* — **V**: 266.
Eternal / Everlasting — **VIII**: 267*(3)*, 268.
Ethics, in — **VIII**: 4, 225.
Future — **VIII, §1035, 258-266**.
Future, in 1 Enoch — **VI**: 650; **VIII**: 267.
Future, in the Acts of Thomas — **VI**: 661; **VIII**: 268.
Future, in the Apocalypse of Paul — **VI**: 661; **VIII**: 268.
Future, in the Apocalypse of Peter — **VI**: 661; **VIII**: 268.
Future, in the Sibylline Oracles — **VI**: 661; **VIII**: 268.
Pardon and — **VIII**: 195.
Plunder and — **VIII**: 224.
Public, in Mosaic Law — **I**: 462, 475.
Theology, in — **VIII**: 4.
Punt, Land of: — **II**: 135; **III**: **204**.
Scene of — **III**: 716.
Puppy:
Northwest-Semitic Covenant making, and — **I**: 511.
Purgatory:
II Maccabees and — **VI**: 641.
Purification, Rites of:
Fall of Jerusalem in 587 B.C. and — **II**: 421; **V**: 30; **VIII**: 185.
Guilt and, in Egypt — **V**: 223.
Lustral Chambers(?) — **III**: 475.
Lustration and Consecration — **V**: 89.
Red Heifer as, in Rabbinic Writings — **IV**: 346.
Purim, Feast of: — **V**: **§446, 91**, 445.
Bondfires on — **I**: 387; **V**: 91.
Purity:
Firth and Fourth Century Religion, in — **V**: 257.
Qumran Sect, in — **VIII**: 415*(2)*.
Purple: — **I**: 273, 275; **III**: 776; **V**: *503*, 512*(2)*.
PURVER, ANTHONY: — **IV**: 63.
PUSEY, E. B.:
Daniel, on — **IV**: 524*(3)*.
Jonah, on — **VI**: 388.
Pushkin Musuem: — **III**: *671*.
Putiphar:
Stela of — **VII**: 23.
Puyamrē':
Shauabti figure of — **III**: 576; **V**: 210.
Pwenet:
Old-Kingdom Travellers to — **VII**: 67.
Py: — **II**: 79.
Pygmies:
Egypt, Ancient, in — **III**: 349.
Fresco of — **III**: 348.
Pygmy:
Legends in Jewish Literature — **V**: 133.
Pylian Ta Tablets: — **VII**: 364.
Pylon:
Egyptian, Flagstaves of — **III**: 465.
Karnak, at — **III**: 481.
Pylos: — **I**: 261*(2)*, *262;* **II**: *123, 133;* **III**: *172*, **204-205**, *477, 747;* **VII**: 359.

Landholders of **VII**: 360*(2)*.
Ma Tablets from **VII**: 362.
Religious Texts from **VII**: 361.
Sign-groups for **V**: 619*(2)*.
Topography **III**: 205.

Pylos Tablets: **II**: *151;* **VII**: 359, 360*(2)*, 361, 362.

Pyramid, Great: **III**: 503*(3)*, 504*(6)*, 506.
Age, Design, and Origin **III**: 503.
Air Channels in Great **III**: 472, 506*(3)*.
Air Shafts, So-Called, Astronomical Investigation of **III**: 476*(2)*.
"Altar to the Lord" and **III**: 506; **VI**: 278.
Astronomical Investigation of **III**: 506.
Base-Length of **III**: 504.
"Book of the Dead" and **III**: 504; **VII**: 49.
Casing Stone of, and Universal Type-Numbers **III**: 503.
Cheops, Investment Process of **III**: 507.
Cheops (Khufu) **I**: *437;* **III**: 503, 505*(2)*, 506*(2)*, 777.
Courses **III**: 505.
Interpreters of **III**: 504.
Problem of **III**: 504.
Riddle of **III**: 504.
Size and Orientation of **III**: 505.
Smith, Piazza, on **III**: 503.
Universal Type-Numbers and Casing Stone **III**: 503.

Pyramid Texts: **VII**: **§842, 46**, 52.
1308 **V**: 308, 589.
"Finger-Numbering" in **V**: 209; **VII**: 46.
Future Life and **V**: 205; **VII**: 37.
Future Life and (Tel el-Amarna Tablets) **VII**: 170.
God Setekh, in **V**: 210.
King and Star-Religion in **V**: 223.
King Tera, Passage in the, of **V**: 346.
Reʿ in **V**: 224.

Pyramids: **III**: 466, **§192, 503-507**, 553.
Argolis, of **III**: 506.
Builders **III**: 460, 503, 504, 506; **V**: 202.
Building of **III**: 473, 505, 506*(2)*.
Egyptian Astronomy and **II**: 230; **III**: 505.
Giza, at **III**: 106, 475, 504*(3)*.
Giza Necropolis **III**: 506.
Giza, Painted(?) **III**: 506.
Greek **III**: 507*(2)*.
Imhotep's **III**: 473.
Lisht, South, at **III**: 505.
Medum, at, Hieratic Inscriptions in a **VII**: 61.
Name(s) of **III**: 503, 507*(2);* **V**: 310.
Origin of **III**: 503, 504.
Pepi, at Sakkara **III**: 504*(2)*, *531*.
Purpose **III**: 505*(4)*.
Rhomboïdal, at Dahshûr, Varnish and Morar from **II**: 216.
Roman **III**: 507*(2)*.
Sakkara **III**: 504.
Second, at Giza **III**: 503.
Sekhem-Khet, Animals from **III**: 367.
Senusert II, at Lahun **III**: 505*(2)*, 542.
Step **III**: *589*.
Tools of Pyramid Builders according to Herodotus **III**: 473, 506.
Truncated, in Egyptian Mathematics **III**: 505.
Truncated, Volume of in Egyptian Mathematics **I**: 430*(2);* **VII**: 34.
Unfinished at Zawiyet el-Aryân **II**: *67*.

Pyrgi:
Phoenician Inscriptions from **VII**: 120*(2)*.
Sanctuary at, in Etruria **III**: 520; **VII**: 376.

Pyrgia: **III**: *100*.
Pythagoras: **II**: 79.

Pythagorean Triads:
Babylonian Mathematics and I: 434.
Pythia: V: 258.
Pyx, Pyxis, *see also:* **Box(es)**
Athenian, White-Ground, = Kylichnis III: 618.
Greek, from Homeric Age III: 623.
Minoan, Late III: 612.
(Painted) Danae and Perseus in Seriphos III: 713.
Palestinian, Alleged III: 584.
Penthesilea Painter, in the Style of III: 610.
Red-Figured III: 592.

Q

Qa:
King of Abydos II: 4, 207.
Qadesh, *see:* **Kadesh**
Qādiān:
Messiah of V: 143.
Qal'at Jarmo, *see:* **Jarmo**
Qala-i-Madresse: III: 240.
Qalatgah: III: 125.
Qalinj Agha, Tell: III: **205**.
Qanats: I: 364.
Qannaim, *see also:* **Zealots** V: 102, 449; **VI**: 691, 704.
Qantîr: III: 205.
Qarn Sartabeh: III: 159, 206; **IX**: cxvi, cxvii.
Qarqar: I: *166;* III: *27.*
Qaryet el 'Inab: II: 298.
Qasida: VI: 181.
Deborah's Ode and the Ancient Arabian VI: 181.
Qasîle(h), Tell: II: **464**.
Hebrew Ostraca from VII: 94.
Hippopotamus, in Iron Age at III: 376.
Qaṣr al Ḥayr al Sharqi: III: **205**.
Qasr Bint Far'un, *see:* **Petra**
Qaṣr Ibrîm: III: **206**.
Qasr Rabbah:
Nabataean Temple of III: 515.
Qataban: II: 204, **206**.
Chronology of Qatabanian Kingdom II: 204.
Qatabanian Texts: VII: 293, **§925**, **296**.
Shabwa Inscriptions VII: 296.
Qatar: III: 197*(3)*, **206**, *569*.
Qatna Kings: II: 157.
Qau-el-Kebir: III: **206**.
Qaus: V: 198.
Qâw:
Wood Tablet from VII: 66.
Qedesh, Tel: II: 304, 464.
Qedŭŝtot: IV: 20.
Qenites, *see also:* **Kenites** II: 157.
Qerova:
Yannay's, to Lev 15:1 VI: 709, 716.
Qir-heres: VII: 112.
Qiryathaim: II: 447.
Qishon Mouth: II: 250.
Qoheleth, *see also:* **Ecclesiastes** IV: 514, 515.
Aramaic Provenance of IV: 516.
Bankruptcy IV: 518.
Camus and IV: 517.
Cynic, as IV: 515.
Early Greeks and IV: 515.
Far East, in V: 146.
Immoratlity in IV: 515.
John and IV: 517; **VIII**: 289.
Kuhn and IV: 515.
Modern Mood and IV: 515.
Modern Tempter and IV: 517.
Old Testament Skeptic IV: *460*, 513*(2)*.
Omar Khayyám and IV: 513, 515.
Optimism of IV: 515.
Pensees of IV: 516, 517.
Personality of IV: 515.
Pessimist, a IV: 518.
Philosopher Without Propositions IV: 517.

Phoenician(?) **IV**: 517, 519.
Prophet Attacks Profit **IV**: 515.
Wealth, on **IV**: 516, 517.
Wisdom, on **IV**: 516, 517, 518.

Qorah, *see:* **Korah**

Qorḫah: **VII**: 112.

Qosanal (Quas'nl):
Seal of **III**: 650, 651.

Quadrature: **I**: 429*(2)*.

Quaestorship: **I**: 490.

Quailba (Irbid District): **II**: 422.

Quails: **IV**: 346; **VI**: 129.

Quarries, Quarrying: **I**: **§98, 290-293**; **VI**: 222; **IX**: **§98, xci-xcii**.
Alabaster **IX**: xci.
Chephren diorite **II**: 214.
Chisel Inscription in the Old Kingdom Diorite Quarries **VII**: 17, 22, 23. 67*(2)*.
El Hosh, Inscriptions in the Quarries of **VII**: 13, 317.
Flint of Wady Sheykh **I**: 291; **III**: 277.
Gilgal, near **VI**: 178.
Imperial Porphyry and Myos Hormos **III**: 89.
Jersualem, at **II**: 276, 402, 408.
Nubian Desert, Western, in **III**: 186*(2)*.
Royal, in Jerusalem **II**: 276, 402.
Specimen of Rock from Solomon's **II**: 213*(2)*.

Quartizite: **I**: 280, 290; **III**: 460, 562.

Quartz:
Miocene Quartzite of Jebel Ahmar **I**: 280, 290; **III**: 460.

Quatrefages: **III**: 334.

Qubeibeh:
Hieroglyphic Inscription from **VII**: 70.

"Queen of Heaven": **V**: 106.
Jews at Elephantine and **V**: 30.

Queen's College:
Egyptian Stelae in **VII**: 18, 23.

Queen's College Library: **IV**: *23*.

Queens:
Aah-htetep, Parantage of **II**: 6.
Aat-shet **II**: 6.
Arab, Pre-Islamic **II**: 5.
Egyptian **II**: 4.

Queens, Jewish:
Roman Empire, under **I**: 176.

Queens of Israel and Judah - General Studies: **I**: **§46, 83-85**, 176.

Queens of Israel and Judah - Aphabetical Listing: **I**: **§47,85-100**.
Jezebel **I**: 92.

QUENTIN, DOM :
Vulgate, Memoir on **IV**: 41.

Quince: **III**: 394.

Quinquennales: **I**: 185.

Quirinius: **III**: 104, 194; **IX**: cii.

Qūmis: **III**: *119*, 207.

Qumran and the Calendar: **I**: 406; **VIII**: 415, **§1077**, **418**, 433.
Passion of Christ and **VIII**: 417, 480.
Sacrifices of the Essenes and **VIII**: 417.

Qumran and its Relation to the Essenes: **V**: 95, 97, **VIII**: 410, **§1084**, **423-424**.

Qumran Apocryphal and Pseudepigraphal Books: **VIII**: **§1110**, **450**.
Ben Sira / Ecclesiasticus **VIII**: **§1116**, **453**.
Book of Jubilees **VIII**: **§1113**, **452**.

Books of Enoch — **VIII**: **§1112**, **452**.

Prayer of Nabonidus — **VIII**: **§1115**, **452**.

Testament of Levi — **VIII**: **§1114**, **452**.

Qumran - Archaeology of: *for Scrolls see: Qumran Literature - Discovery of the Scrolls* — **VIII**: **§1071**, **411-413**.

Scroll Jar from — **VIII**: 412*(2)*.

Animal Bones from — **VIII**: 413.

Aqueduct in — **I**: 361; **VIII**: 412.

Cistern Fillings — **VIII**: 413.

Furniture at — **VIII**: 412.

Human Skeletal Remains — **VIII**: 413.

Pottery Clay — **VIII**: 413.

Qumran, Biblical Books from: — **VIII**: **(§1096)**, **443**.

Daniel, Book of — **VIII**: **§1109**, **450**.

Deuteronomy (4QDt; Deut 32) — **VIII**: **§1100**, **444**.

Ecclesiasties, Qoheleth (4QQoh) — **VIII**: **§1108**, **450**, 453.

Exodus (4QEx) — **VIII**: **§1097**, **443**.

Ezekiel (11QEz) — **VIII**: **§1105**, **448**.

Isaiah, (1QIs[b]) — **VIII**: **§1103**, **447-448**.

Isaiah (1QIs[a]) *see also: Isaiah Scroll A* — **VIII**: **§1102**, **444-447**.

Isaiah, (4QIs[a]) — **VIII**: **§1104**, **448**.

Leviticus (4QLXXLev) — **VIII**: **§1098**, **443**.

Minor Prophets (4QXII?) — **VIII**: **§1106**, **448**.

Numbers (4QLXXNu) — **VIII**: **§1099**, **444**.

Psalms — **VIII**: **§1107**, **448-450**.

Samuel, Books of (4QSam) — **VIII**: **§1101**, **444**.

Qumran - Bibliographical Material: — **VIII**: **§1069**, **408-409**.

Cave IV Texts, Aid to Study of — **VIII**: 409.

Japanese Journals, in — **VIII**: 409.

Non-Biblical Scrolls, Index to until Dec. 1957 — **VIII**: 409.

Qumran and Its Relation to Christianity: — **VIII**: **§1085**, **424-425**.

Pre-Pauline Church and — **VIII**: 424*(2)*.

Qumran Community and Interpretation of Scripture: — **VIII**: **§1082**, **422**.

Ezekiel, Book of, and — **IV**: 423; **VIII**: 422.

Qumran Community, Doctrines of — General Studies: — **VIII**: **§1074**, **415-417**.

Angelology — **VIII**: 416, 480.

Apocalyptic Community — **V**: 124; **VIII**: 411.

"Apotropaic" Prayers at — **VIII**: 208.

Covenant Concept — **VIII**: 417.

Day of Pentecost in — **V**: 89; **VI**: 655; **VIII**: 415.

Dualism of "Flesh and Spirit" in, and the NT — **VIII**: 417.

God, of, at — **VIII**: **§1075**, **417**, 482.

Immortality, Belief in — **VIII**: 265, 416.

Man and Salvation, at — **VIII**: **§1076**, **417**.

Prayers, Order of — **VIII**: 416.

Prophecy in, and Gospel Messianism **VIII**: 298.
Scripture, Use of, at **VIII**: 416.
"Sons of Zadok the Priests" at **V**: 42; **VIII**: 417*(2)*.
Soteriology of **VIII**: 417.
"Times", Doctrine of **VIII**: 417.
Two Spirits **VIII**: 422.
"Two Ways" at, and the Early Church **VIII**: 416.
Wilderness, Preperation in and the New Testament **VIII**: 416.

Qumran Community - General Studies: **VIII**: **§1070**, **410-411**.
Ascension of Isaiah and **VI**: 654*(2)*; **VIII**: 414, 450, 483.
Books of **VIII**: 423.
Functionaries in **V**: 78; **VIII**: 411.
Identity of **VIII**: 411.
Jerusalem Church of Acts and the Community of the Manual of Discipline **VIII**: 461*(2)*, 479*(2)*.
John the Baptist and **VIII**: 142, 419, 422, 431, 479. 481*(2)*, 482.
Library (Building) at **VIII**: 410.
Masada and **VIII**: 411.
Members of, First Fifteen **VIII**: 414, 462.
Messiah and **VIII**: 142, 410, 468.
Origin of **VIII**: 411.
Sabbath, Concept of, at **V**: 83; **VIII**: 416.
"Sadducees" in **V**: 100; **VIII**: 410.
Self-Understanding of, compared with Paul **VIII**: 295, 417.
Social Message from **VIII**: 411.

Qumran Community - Organization of: **VIII**: **§1072**, **413-414**.
Economics **VIII**: 413*(2)*.
Functionaries of **VIII**: 416.
General Council of **VIII**: 413, 414.
Mebaqqer **VIII**: 414, 419.
"Ordinances" (4QOrd) **VIII**: **§1135**, **469**.

Qumran Community - Practices of: **VIII**: **§1073**, **414-415**.
Baptism at **VIII**: 414.
Baptism of John and **VIII**: 480.
Ethical Teaching of **VIII**: 415.
Ethics of **VIII**: 415.
Hatred at **VIII**: 414.
Healing through Laying-on of Hands at **VIII**: 414.
Impurities, Rules of **VIII**: 415.
Lots, Casting of, at, and in the Book of Acts **VIII**: 290, 414.
Meals of **VIII**: 414.
Oil, Avoidance of, by **VIII**: 415.
Praise and Music in **VIII**: 414.
Priests **VIII**: 414.
Purity in **VIII**: 415*(2)*.
Red Heifer at(?) **IV**: 346; **VIII**: 414.
Sabbath Laws of **VIII**: 414.
Sacred Meals and Communion **VIII**: 482.
Sacred Meals of **VIII**: 414.
Sacrifices **VIII**: 414*(2)*, 415, 418.
Washings, Ritual and the NT Rite of Baptism **VIII**: 482.
Worship Among **VIII**: 414.

Qumran Community - Relation to Outside World: **VIII**: **§1083**, **422-423**.
Temple of Leontopolis, Relation to **VIII**: 423.

Qumran and Eschatology: **VIII**: **§1079**, **420**, 472.
Apocalypse of Weeks and **VIII**: 420.
Eschatology and Time in **I**: 416; **V**: 124.
Human Suffering in, Eschatological Significance of **I**: 416; **VIII**: 187, 253, 420.
Sinai-Tradition, Interpretation of **VIII**: 420, 482.
Time and Eschatology in **I**: 416; **V**: 124.

Qumran - General Studies, *see also:* **Dead Sea Scrolls** — **I**: *177, 361;* **II**: 422; **III**: *431;* **V**: *45;* **VIII**: **§1068, 408**.
Biblical Interpretation at — **IV**: 97.
Calendar in — **I**: 406.
Caves of — **II**: 278, 279*(6)*, 301, 422; **III**: *431;* **VIII**: 413.
Chronology — **II**: 175, 189; **VI**: 60; **VIII**: 410.
Coins, Early, from — **I**: 455; **VIII**: 413.
Damascus in, Geography — **III**: 75.
Geography and History of — **VIII**: 408.
Human Skeletal Remains at — **III**: 363.
Jerusalem and — **V**: 26; **VIII**: 416.
Judaism and Professors of Religion — **VIII**; 408.
Melchizedek and — **I**: 65*(2)*.
Myths of — **VIII**: 411.
Novel on the Qumran Cave — **VIII**: 370.
Reizenstein, Richard, and — **VIII**: 423.
Research, Trends in — **VIII**: 408.
Undergraduates, Teaching the New Testament to, and — **VIII**: 408.
Undergraduates, Teaching the Old Testament to, and — **VIII**: 408.
Qumran and Gnosticism: — **VIII**: **§1088, 427**.
Colosse and — **VIII**: 427.
Qumran and Other Jewish Sects: — **VIII**: **§1087, 426-427**.
Bar Kosiba and — **VIII**: 426, 473.
Ebionites and — **VIII**: 426*(2)*.
Jesus and — **VIII**: 427.
Karaites and — **VIII**: 426.
Samaritan Influence(?) — **VIII**: 427.
Zealots and — **VIII**: 426*(2)*.
Qumran and Its Relation to Judaism: — **VIII**: **§1086, 426**.
Herod the Great and — **VIII**: 426.
Sadducees and — **VIII**: 427.
Qumran Literature (Scrolls) - General Studies: — **II**: *440;* **VIII**: **§1089, 427-434**.
Apocalyptic Literature and — **I**: 416; **V**: 124; **VIII**: 253.
Archaeological Evidence — **VIII**: 429*(2)*.
Ben Sira and — **VI**: 601, 624, 637.
Bible Translators, Meaning of, for — **IV**: 108.
Biblical Texts — **IV**: 6.
Dating the Scrolls — **VIII**: **§1093, 439-441**.
"Desert Motif" in — **V**: 700.
Divine Name YHWH in — **VIII**: 119, 417.
Dream Interpretation in — **III**: 404; **VIII**: 415.
Dupont-Sommer, on — **VIII**: 430.
Eschatology in — **I**: 416; **V**: 124; **VIII**: 253, **§1079, 420**.
Exhibition of, at Duke — **VIII**: 428.
Half Shekel in — **I**: 482; **V**: 63.
Hebron Pogrom and — **VIII**: 435.
Hermetic Medicine in — **III**: 404; **VIII**: 415.
Historian and — **VIII**: 433.
Human Suffering in, Eschatological Significance of — **I**: 416; **VIII**: 187, 253, 420.
Karaites and the MSS — **VIII**: 410.
Masoretic Text and — **VIII**: **§1094**, 441-443.
Masoretic Text, Origin of, in the Light of, and Rabbinic Literature — **IV**: 16; **VI**: 689.
McGill University, Acquisition of DDS, by — **VIII**: 430.
Megilloth Genuzoth — **VIII**: 428.
Midrashic Parrallels to — **VI**: 709.
Number-symbolism in — **VIII**: 311.
Numismatics and the — **I**: 453; **VIII**: 437.
Origin of — **VIII**: 429, 435.

OT Canon and	**IV**: 206*(3)*, 207; **VIII**: **§1094**, 441-443.
OT Quotations in	**VIII**: 276.
Priests and Sacrifices in	**V**: 41, 62.
Pronouns and Suffixes in, and the Masoretic Text	**V**: 484.
Psychosomatics in	**III**: 404; **VIII**: 415.
Purchase of	**VIII**: 427.
Rabbinc Research and	**VI**: 691.
Rehnborg Collection at McCormick Seminary	**VIII**: 431.
Romans and 1QS x, 17-20	**VIII**: 294.
Septuagint and OT Text	**IV**: 34.
"Servant of the Lord" in	**VIII**: 146*(2)*.
"Servant of the Lord" in and Deutero-Isaiah	**IV**: 403.
"Son of Man", in	**VIII**: 148, 481.
Symboism in	**VIII**: 307, 416.
Talmudic Material Relating to the DSS	**VI**: 704.
Teaching the OT to Undergraduates and	**VIII**: 406.
Time in	**I**: 416; **V**: 124; **VIII**: 253.
Qumran Literature and Early Church Fathers:	**VIII**: **§1157**, **483**.
Pseudo-Jerome and	**VIII**: 483.
St. Benedict and	**VIII**: 483.
Qumran Literature and the Masoretic Text and Canon:	**VIII**: **§1094**, **441-443**.
Cave 11 Suprises and the Question of the Canon	**VIII**: 442.
Meaning for Translators of the Bible	**VIII**: 442.
Stabilization of the Hebrew Bible in Light of	**VIII**: 442.
Textual Transmission in Light of	**IV**: 7, 206*(3)*; **VIII**: 442.
Qumran Literature and New Testament Apocypha and Pseudepigrapha:	**VIII**: **§1156**, **483**.
Qumran Literature and Other Literature:	**VIII**: **§1091**, **438**.
Halakha and	**VIII**: 438*(2)*.
Iranian Component in	**IV**: 193; **V**: 38; **VI**: 601; **VIII**: 438.
Josephus, Slavonic, and	**VI**: 684; **VIII**: 438.
Midrash and	**VIII**: 438.
Shapira Forgery / Manuscripts and	**VII**: 110*(2)*; **VIII**: 438*(2)*.
Talmud and	**VIII**: 438.
Qumran Literature - Discovery of the Scrolls:	**VIII**: 434, **§1092**, **438-439**.
Archaeology and	**VIII**: 439*(2)*, 442.
Date of	**VIII**: 436.
Extent of	**VIII**: 428.
Extent of the Total	**VIII**: 428.
Mathematical Probability of Discovery	**VIII**: 439.
Muhammad ed-Deeb's Discovery of	**VIII**: 439*(2)*.
Qumran Literature in Relation to the New Testament:	**VIII**: **§1155**, **479-483**.
Epistle to the Hebrews and	**VIII**: 480.
Fourth, Origin of, and	**VIII**: 481.
Gospels and	**VIII**: 480.
Johannine Gospels and Epistles and	**VIII**: 479.
Paul, Did he go to Qumran(?)	**VIII**: 481.
Scribes of the NT and	**VIII**: 480.
Qumran Literature - Lexicographical Studies:	**VIII**: **§1150**, **475**.
Qumran Literature - Literary Criticism of the Scrolls:	**VIII**: **§1090**, **434-438**.
Christian Origin of	**VIII**: 435.
Editing the Scrolls	**VIII**: 436.
Formulas of Introduction	**VIII**: 438.

Mystery of the Scrolls **VIII**: 435*(2)*, 436.
Theological Significance / Speculation on **VIII**: 437, 438.
Zeitlin, Solomon, and **VIII**: 437.

Qumran Literature - Miscellaneous Scrolls: **VIII**: **§1145**, **471-472**.
1Q Milḥamah **VIII**: 471, 472.
1Q Mysteries **VIII**: 472.
Manual of Benedictions **VIII**: 472.
Epistle of Barnabas and **VIII**: 483.
Psalms of Solomon and **VIII**: 483.
Shepherd of Hermas and **VIII**: 483.

Qumran Literature - Paleography and Dating the Scrolls: **VIII**: **§1093**, **439-441**.
Paleo-Hebrew Scripts **VIII**: 441.
Radioactive Carbon and **VIII**: 440.

Qumran Literature - Philological Studies: **VIII**: **§1149**, **474-475**.

Qumran Literature and the Septuagint: **IV**: 34, 35; **VIII**: **§1095**, **443**.

Qumran - Messianic Ideas: **V**: 129; **VIII**: 419, **§1078**, **418-420**, 453.
"Begotten" Messiah in the Qumran Scrolls **VIII**: 419.
Development, Starcky's Theory of **VIII**: 420.
Functions of God as Messianic Titles in 1QIsa **VIII**: 419.
Hodayoth III, 6-18, Messianic Sense of(?) **VIII**: 419.
Messiahs of Aaron and Israel **VIII**: 419.
Messianic Motif of, and the NT **VIII**: 419.
Two Messiahs, Idea of **VIII**: 418, 419*(3)*.

Qumran Persharim - General Studies: **VIII**: **§1117**, **453**.
Azazel, on **VI**: 123.

Qumran Sectarian Works: **VIII**: **§1123**, **458**.
Bible Quotations in **VIII**: 458.
Rabbinic Research and **VI**: 691; **VIII**: 458.

Quotations, *see also:* **Old Testament in the New Testament §1040**
Amos, in **VI**: 387*(2)*.
Formulas for Introducing, Scripture in the NT and Mishnah **VIII**: 275.
Greek Dodekapropheton Scroll and OT **VI**: 363.
Latin, differining from Vulgate in Latin Lives of Welsh /Breton Sts. **IV**: 40.
Literary Use in Biblical, Oriental and Rabbinic Literature **VI**: 689.
NT, in, and their Relation to Inspiration **VIII**: 20.
Old Latin Bible (Somnium Neronis) **IV**: 39.
Old Testament in Philo **VI**: 676.
OT Criticism in light of New Testament **IV**: 121; **VIII**: 272.
OT, in NT, from the Septuagint **IV**: 25, 27, 31, 33; **VIII**: 271, 272, 274.
OT in NT Speeches, Text Presupposed(?) **IV**: 3.
OT in NT, Translation of **IV**: 108.
OT, Literary Usage, in **V**: 698*(2)*.
Qumran Literature in **VIII**: 442.
Rabbinical Literature, in **V**: 698*(2)*.
Talmud, from **VI**: 687.
Wisdom Literature, in **V**: 116.

Qur'ān, *see:* **Koran**

Qurnet Mara'i:
Tomb of Userḥēt at **III**: 548.

Qusṭul:
Royal Tombs at **III**: 561.

R

Ra-Ka-Pou:
Tomb of **III**: 546.
Ra, Rēʿ, *see also:* **Sun God** **III**: *729;* **V**: 200*(2)*.
Egyptian Sun God Mentioned in Exodus(?) **V**: 212*(2)*, 215; **VI**: 104*(3)*.
Myth of. Solar and Pantheistic Litanies **VII**: 38.
Old Testament, in **V**: 215.
Psalm to **III**: 729; **VII**: 63.
Pyramid Texts, in **V**: 224.
Rabbinic Commentaries, Reference in **V**: 215.
Sequence of the Fourteen *KAS* of **V**: 207, 353.
Ra-*aa-peh-ti:* **I**: *148*.
Pharaoh over Joseph **I**: *148;* **II**: **79**.
Ra-khnum-ab:
Inscription of **VII**: 61.
Ra-Nafer:
Mummy of **II**: 81; **III**: 355. Ra-Nafer **II**: 81.
Portrait of **II**: 81.
Raamses (Place), *see:* **Ramses (Place)**
Rabbah: **II**: **465**.
Waters of **VI**: 212, 588.
Rabbahites: **II**: 157.
David and **II**: 157; **IV**: 360.
Rabbath Ammon: **IV**: 373.
Rabbath Moab: **II**: 291; **III**: 416.
Rabbi Ben Yohai:
Prayer of **V**: 124.
Rabbi Zeʿira: **I**: 183.
Rabbis, Rabbinate: **I**: *145;* **V**: 78, 450.
American, Relevence of Prophetic Thought for **VIII**: 353.
Decalogue, Regarding **VI**: 158.
Messiah ben Ephriam of **V**: 129; **VI**: 678; **VIII**: 142; **IX**: cli.
Preaching **V**: 91.
Rabbinic Chronology: **II**: 175.
Rabbinic Interpretation / Exegesis (Theology): **VI**: **§816, 715-716**; **IX**: **§816, cl**.
Adam, Gnostic Background of Rabbinic Legends of **IV**: 294*(2);* **VI**: 716*(2)*.
Chronology of Divided Kingdoms and **II**: 187; **IV**: 361.
Creation, Doctrine of **VIII**: 79.
Eschatology **VIII**: 249*(2)*.
God, Name of, in **VIII**: 110.
Halakhic **IV**: 87; **VI**: 1, 693.
Holiness, Conception of **VIII**: 198.
Jacob, Blessings of, in Syriac and **IV**: 321; **VI**: 716, 724.
Jewish-Christian Polemics and **VI**: 716, 727.
Justification by Faith, Rabbinic Anticipation **VIII**: 197.
Lebanon, Symbolic Interpretation of, in the Targums **II**: 436.
Messianic Interpretation **V**: 130.
Methods of Interpretation **IV**: 96.
Old Testament, Approach to Study of **IV**: 153; **VI**: 716.
Omnipotence of God in **VIII**: 100.
Pauline Exegsis and **VI**: 715.
Pentatuech, of **IV**: 96, 235; **VI**: 13, 716.
Proverbs, Vulgate of, in **IV**: 500; **VI**: 715.
Psalm 110, Refuted by Jesus **VI**: 517.
Psalm 82, of, and the Gospel of John **VI**: 502, 716; **VIII**: 289.
Repentence, Concept of **VIII**: 188, 196.
Resurrection of the Dead in **VI**: 687; **VIII**: 269.
Self and the Other in Rabbinic Ethics **VIII**: 227.
Seventy-Two Modes of Expositon **VI**: 686.

Sidrahs, Seven Pairs of **VI**: 716.
Song of Solomon, Commentaries on **VI**: 716, 727.
Rabbinical Literature, *see:* **Rabbinic Studies and Writings**
Rabbinical Laws / Ordinances:
Dietary Laws in **I**: 250.
Idolatry, Laws Against **V**: 108; **VI**: 693.
Measurements as **I**: 427.
Reform Benedictions for **VIII**: 208.
Rabbinical Studies and (Literature) Writings: **V**: 78; **VI**: 143, **§809, 686-691**; **IX**: *cxlv*, **§809, cl**.
Age of Twenty in Rabbinic Tradition and 1QSa **VI**: 690; **VIII**: 464.
Arabic Parallels to **VI**: 688.
Arabisms in **VI**: 687.
Babylonian Texts and **VII**: 268.
Balaam Stories in **IV**: 346.
Bibliography of **I**: **§40, 15**.
Canticles Rabba **IV**: 507.
Citations in, and the Palestinian Targum to the Pentateuch **VI**: 691, 714.
Delgardo, João Pinto, on **VI**: 689.
Dietary Laws in **I**: 250; **VI**: 723.
Ecclesiasticus, Quotations of, in **VI**: 621*(2)*, 715*(2)*.
Enduring Value of **VI**: 687.
Ester of Pinto Delgardo, in **IV**: 521.
Ezekiel in **IV**: 420.
Flood, Biblical, in **IV**: 307; **VI**: 651, 715.
Future Life, in **VIII**: 260.
Gerum Gerurim **VI**: 691.
God, Doctrine of **VIII**: 62.
God, Unity of, in **VIII**: 61, 67.
Habakkuk in **IV**: 450; **VI**: 716.
Hasid, Concept of, in **VI**: 689.
Historical Sources, Use of, as **VI**: 688.
Holiness, Concept of, in **VIII**: 198; **IX**: cl.
Koine Greek in **VI**: 690.
Legends, Rabbinic, Gnostic Background of **V**: 240.
Marriage, Sayings on **VI**: 686.
Midrash, Relation to **VI**: 707.
Mysticism and **V**: 240.
New Testament, Parallels to, in **VI**: 686; **VIII**: 272.
Number Categories*ten, seven* and*four* in **VIII**: 311.
Number-symbolism in **VIII**: 311.
Obscure Tradition in Philo and, Mutually Clarified **VI**: 678.
Parable in **V**: 699; **VI**: 690, 691.
Passover in **V**: 88; **VI**: 689.
Philo Mentioned in(?) **VI**: 675, 688.
Prayer, on **VIII**: 202.
Prophets of the Nations in **IV**: 346.
Psychology, Rabbinic **VI**: 690*(2)*.
"Qannaim" in, and the Zealots **V**: 102; **VI**: 691, 705.
Qumran Literature (Sectarian Scrolls) and **VI**: 691; **VIII**: 458.
Quotations as Literary Use **VI**: 689.
Quotations, in **V**: 698*(2)*.
"Rashe Theboth" **VI**: 687.
Reʿ in Rabbinic Commentaries **V**: 215.
Red Heifer in **IV**: 346; **VI**: 691.
Religious Experience in **VI**: 690; **VIII**: 192.
Riddles of Solomon in **VI**: 695, 715.
Roman Legal Institutions in **I**: 490.
Roman Legal Institutions in Early Rabbincs **VI**: 688.
Shiʿur, Shiʿurim **I**: 427.
Sin, Meaning of, in **VIII**: 183.
Solomon's Riddles in **VI**: 695, 715.
Soul, Pre-existance of, in **VI**: 618*(2)*.
Tractate Abot in **VI**: 702.

Tradition, Early Christian and Early Rabbinic Compared — **VI**: 690.
Tradition, the Bible and Modern Judaism — **VIII**: 339.
Transmission of Early Tradition — **VI**: 688.
Zechariah, Death of, in — **I**: 82; **VI**: 696.

Rabbit: — **III**: 375; **VI**: 122*(2)*.
Hare, Arabic word for — **III**: 375; **V**: 585; **VI**: 122, 145.

Rabbith: — **II**: 284.

Rabbou'a: — **I**: 268.

Rabinnic Thought:
Time-Bound and Timless in — **IV**: 90.

Race(s), *see also:* **Human Race** — **I**: 120; **II**: 3.
Abu Simbel, Racial Types at — **III**: 344.
Ancient, Survival of in Custom or Law — **I**: 326; **II**: 260; **IX**: cxxi.
Babylonian Empire, of — **III**: 339.
Characteristics of, and Civilization — **III**: 335.
Classification of, Egyptian — **III**: 339, 339‡.
Dynastic, in Egypt — **II**: 3, 128, 261; **III**: 90, 506.
Early, of Mankind — **III**: 348.
Egypt, Racial History of — **III**: 350.
Egyptians a Dual(?) — **II**: 125.
Greek — **II**: 133*(2)*.
Hebrew, World, Early, in — **III**: 349.
Immigrant in Ancient Times — **I**: 326; **II**: 260; **IX**: cxxi.
Intermixture of in Asia Minor — **II**: 2, 260; **IX**: cxxi.
Language and — **III**: 336, 338; **V**: 277; **IX**: ciii.
Mediterranean, Early — **II**: *150, 151;* **III**: 342.
Megalithic(?) — **II**: 2,
Mixture in Biblical History — **III**: 349.
Mixture in Early Rome — **II**: 160.
New, in Egypt — **III**: 84.
Nubia, Racial History of — **III**: 350.
Origin of Race(s) — **III**: 346, 347, 352; **IV**: 309; **V**: 279.
Sais, of the Founders of — **II**: 2, 214.
Thebaïd, Ancient, of — **III**: 342*(2)*.
Thessaly, Racial Continuity of Prehistoric — **III**: 349.
Thrako-Germanic — **III**: 341.
Troy, Racial Elements in the First Siege of — **III**: 344.
Types, Early, of Western Asia — **III**: 340.
Various in Palestine — **I**: 387.

Race Relations: — **I**: 188, 326; **VIII**: 219, 232.

Rachel: — **I**: 76; **V**: 298.
Lament of — **II**: 465.
Sepulchre (Tomb) of — **II**: 280, 291, 465; **III**: 530*(2)*, 531, 532, 533, 556*(2)*; **VI**: 198.
Theft of the Teraphim — **VI**: 80*(2)*.

Racing: — **I**: 240.
Maiden's Race on Attic Vases — **III**: 707.

RAD, GERHARD VON: — **I**: *516*.
Old Testament Theology — **VIII**: 12.
Old Testament Theology, Significance of — **VIII**: 7.

Radanites: — **I**: 271, 306.

Radioactivity:
Waters of Jericho — **II**: 222.

Radiocarbon Dating: — **I**: *257;* **II**: 216*(4)*, 217*(5)*, 218*(4)*, 220*(3)*, 221*(2)*; **III**: *213*, 325; **IX**: cxxii.
Applied Science Center for — **III**: 451.
Egypt and — **III**: 92.
Iron, Dating of, by — **IX**: cxxiii.
Qumran Literature and — **VIII**: 440.

Rafts: — **I**: 351.

RAGLAN, LORD: — **II**: 135.

Rahab: **VI**: 285.
Biographical Studies **I**: 77.
Rāḫotep: **II**: 79.
Ambassador of Rameses **II**: 79.
Raids:
Modern Palestinian **I**: 390.
Rain: **II**: 243*(2)*.
'Control of', in Ancient Palestine **II**: 223, 243; **V**: 148; **VI**: 228.
Negev and **I**: 363; **II**: 243.
Prayer for **VI**: 521; **VIII**: 205.
Rainbow: **VI**: 52.
Babylon in, in Ezekiel **IV**: 422.
Covenant, as Sign of **IV**: 303; **VIII**: 215.
Egyptian **V**: 200, 342.
Flood, After the **IV**: 308.
Genesis, in **IV**: 301.
Nimbus and **IV**: 309.
Rainer Papyrus:
Ensalved Persons Who Are Free **I** 187; **VII**: 340.
Rainfall:
El Meshgharah, Cœlosyria, at **II**: 241*(2)*.
Israel, in **II**: 245*(5)*, 246*(5)*.
Jaffa, in **II**: 241, 242*(3)*.
Jerusalem, in **II**: 239, 244, 245.
Negev, in **II**: 243, 246.
Palestine, in **II**: 237, 243, 244, 245*(2)*, 246.
Tel-Aviv, in **II**: 245.
Wet and Dry Years **II**: 244, 245.
Raiyān Moeris: **III**: 207.
Raja Doctrine: **V**: 144.
Rakka: **III**: *755*.
Rakkon: **II**: 284.
Ram:
Abraham, of **V**: 58; **IX**: cxxxi.
Ram, Battering *see:* **Battering Ram**
Ramad:
Animal remains from **III**: 367.
Paleobotanical investigation **III**: 386.
Ramadie: **III**: *243*.
Ramah: **II**: *280*, 323, **465**; **IX**: cxv, cxviii.
Ramah of Samuel: **II**: 280; **III**: *530*.
Rāmallāh: **II**: 465.
Raman (Bin): **V**: 171.
Ramat Maṭred: **I**: *256;* **II**: 466.
Ramat Raḥel: **II**: 301, 302*(2)*, **466**; **III**: 471, *666*.
Ramathaim-Zophim: **I**: 78; **II**: **465**; **III**: *530;* **IV**: 373.
Rameses, the Great: **I**: 379.
Mummy of **I**: 379
Obelisk of **III**: 494.
Statue of **III**: 493.
Ramessenakht: **II**: 79.
Ramesses I:
Head of **II**: 80.
Ramesses II: **I**: *404, 510, 512;* **II**: *4,* **80**, 198; **III**: 131*(2)*, *760*.
Ancestry of **II**: 80.
Asiatic Wars of **II**: 80; **VII**: 18.
Campaign at Kadesh on Orontes, by **II**: 80*(2)*.
Campaign in Galilee, by **II**: 80.
Coronation of, Reliefs **VII**: 17.
Ethnic Lists of, at Luxor **II**: 265; **VII**: 15.
Geographic Lists of, at Luxor **II**: 265; **VII**: 15.
Hittite Marriage, Second, of **II**: 80.
Inscription of, at Institute of Archaeology, Liverpool **VII**: 17.
Jericho in Topographical List of **II**: 270, 398.
Karnak Reliefs of Seti I, in **VII**: 60.
Letter to Ḫattušili(š) (III) **VII**: 217, 239.
Manetho's Date for **II**: 80.

Mummy of I: 378.
Pharaoh of the Opression II: 80.
Princes in the Karnak Reliefs of Seti I, and II: *4*, 80.
Sallier Papyrus on Wars of, against the Cheta **VII**: 14.
Statue(s) of **II**: 80*(2)*; **III**: 721.
Stela of, from Beisan **VII**: 25.
Temple of, at Abydos **III**: 512.
Treaty with Hittite King Ḫattušiliuš (III) **I**: 510, 512; **VII**: 16, 307.

Ramesses III: **II**: 81*(3)*; **VII**: 31.

Ramesses IV:
Tomb of **III**: 463, 539, 543; **VII**: 34.

Ramesses IX: **II**: 70*(2)*, **81**.
Revolution of the High Priest Amenḥotpe under **VII**: 16.

Ramesses VI: **II**: 6, 81.

Ramesses VII: **I**: *409*.

Ramesses X: **II**: 81.

Ramesses XII:
Tomb of **III**: 539.

Ramesseum:
Excavations at **III**: 85.
Stela of Penre, Builder of **VII**: 24.

Ramla: **II**: 303.

Ramleh:
Cave, Large, near **II**: 276.

Ramman: **V**: 168.

Ramman-nirari I:
Inscriptions of **VII**: 185*(2)*.

Ramŏse:
Relief from Tomb of **III**: 731.
Theban Vizier **II**: 81.

Ramoth Gilead: **II**: 290, 466.

Ramoth Gilead at 'Ajlun: **II**: 287.

Ramoth Lehi: **VI**: 189.

RAMSAY, WILLIAM MITCHELL: **III**: 23.
Hittite Inscriptions and **VII**: 302, 303.

Ramses: **VII**: 56.

Ra(a)mses (Place): **III**: 201, 202*(2)*; **IV**: 328*(2)*, 339.
Contemporary of Moses **II**: 4.

Ramses III: **I**: *271, 277(2), 488*; **II**: *273*; **VII**: *7, 81*.
Jubilee Festival of **V**: 206.
Three Decress of, from Karnak **VII**: 66.

Rania Plain: **I**: *318*; **III**: *489*.

Ranks:
Ptolemaic **I**: 189.

RAPHAEL, OSCAR:
Head of Amenemmēs in the collection of **II**: 15.

Raphaim Baqa: **II**: 467.

Raphanea: **II**: 281.

Ras al 'Amiya: **III**: 207.

Ras al-Khaimah: **III**: 198.

Ras al Qala'a: **III**: **207**.

Rās el ʿAin: **II**: 466.
Pottery from **III**: 615.

Ras Shamra, (Râs eš-Šamrah) *see also:* **Ugarit** **I**: *159, 330, 339*; **II**: *175, 320*; **III**: 13, 157, *682, 683*; **IV**: 187*(2)*, 218, 219.
Akkadian Documents from **VII**: 144, 150.
Alphabet of, and its bearing on the Phoenican Alphabet **V**: 286.
Alphabet of, Origins **V**: 286, 532.
Canaanite Civilization and **V**: 532.
Culture, Origins of **VII**: 140.
Deities, Groupings of, in Ritual Tariffs from **V**: 192.
Egypt and **III**: 89, 268; **VII**: 139.
Egyptological Text from **VII**: 140.
Genealogical List from **I**: *119(2)*.
Hebrew Passion Play from **V**: 192; **VI**: 314.
Israel and, Cultic Affinities Between **V**: 149.

Old Testament and **IV**: 188, 193; **VII**: 140.
Old Testament Interpretation and **IV**: 84.
Phoenician Poem found at **VII**: 117.
Shipping at **III**: 268; **IV**: 219.
Ras Shamra Texts *see:* **Ugaritic Texts**
Ras, Tell er-, *see also:* **Mount Gerizim** **II**: 304.
Samaritan Temple, and **II**: 467; **V**: 70.
SAMUEL BEN MEIR (RASHBAM): **IV**: 7.
Rashe Theboth: **VI**: 687.
Rashi (place): **III**: 124.
RASHI, SHELOMOH YISHAQI (SOLOMON BEN ISAAC): **I**: *145*.
Amos, Text of, o/t Massoretic(?) **VI**: 381.
Bible Exegete and Grammarian, as **V**: 471.
Commentaries, Talmudical, List of Rashi's MSS **VI**: 701.
Commentary on Grammatical Comments **V**: 471; **VI**: 10.
Conjunctions, Use of, in **V**: 483.
Grammatical Elements and Terminology in **V**: 471*(2)*, 478.
Hebrew, Knowledge of the Triliteral Root **V**: 474.
Life and Contributions of **I**: 24.
Pentateuch, Commentary **IV**: 234, 236, 727.
Prepositions, Use of, in **V**: 483.
Vowel Terminology of **V**: 478.
Weak Roots, View of **V**: 491.
RASSAM, HORMUZD; **III**: 1, 442, 487, 720, 770; **VII**: 146, 205*(2)*, 234.
Rat(s):
Herodotus, in **III**: 380.
Rationing: **I**: 309.
Ration Lists from Alalakh **VII**: 220.
Scales of, in Paprus Anastasi I and the Bible **VI**: 205; **VII**: 82.
Rations:
Military, Field **I**: 248, 317.
Raud: **III**: 19.
Raven: **VI**: 51*(2)*.
Arabians and **VI**: 227.
RAWLINSON, GEORGE: **I**: 1*(4)*; **II**: 65; **IV**: *194*.
Phoenica, on **II**: 156.
Rayy: **III**: **208**.
Razzaza: **II**: *250;* **III**: 208.
Reading:
Silent, in Antiquity **I**: 232, 236.
Realism:
God of **VIII**: 61.
Greek **V**: 248.
Reason: **VIII**: 29.
Hebrew Word for **V**: 398.
Opposition to Anger in Wisdom Literature **V**: 117.
Relation to Philosophy, Theology and Revelation **III**: 288.
Revelation and **VIII**: 31, 35.
Rebbo: **II**: 284.
Rebecca: **V**: 297; **VI**: 75*(2)*.
Rebekah: **IV**: 316.
Rebellions / Revolts:
Bar Kokhba **I**: *443*.
Hare Nome, at **III**: 117.
Hasmonean **I**: 174.
Ionian **I**: *458;* **II**: 135.
Israel, in **V**: 27.
Jewish, at Cyrene **I**: 176, 356.
Jewish, First **I**:*455*.
Jewish, under Trajan **I**: 176*(2)*, 177.
Maccabean **I**: 173.
Tennes **I**: 173.
Ukin-zer, of **VII**: 180.
Recapitualtion Theory, *see also:* **Pre-Adamite Earth** **III**: 313.
Recensions, *see also:* **Text Families**
Hesychian, Reconsidered **IV**: 100.
Rechab:
House of **VI**: 587*(2)*.

Rechabites: **II**: 157.
Reciprocals:
Babylonian Tables of **I**: 431, 433, 434.
Seleucid Mathematical Tables of **I**: 435.
Table of, with Sumerian Spellings **IX**: xcix.
Reciprocity:
Divine, Dogma of **I**: 388.
Reconceptualization: **VI**: 39.
Reconciliation, *see:* **Salvation**
Red Heifer: **IV**: 345; **VI**: 131*(2)*.
Qumran and **IV**: 346; **VIII**: 414.
Rabbinic Literature, in **IV**: 346; **VI**: 691.
Sacrifice of **V**: 57.
Red Sea: **I**: *315, 370;* **II**: *364;* **III**: **208-209**, 231; **IV**: 324, 340; **VI**: 102.
Ancient Egyptian, Greek and Hebrew Concept of **IX**: cxxxi.
Baalism and **V**: 198.
Crossing of, by Israelites in Exodus **IV**: 327, 330*(5)*, 331*(3)*, 334*(3)*, 335*(4)*, 337*(2)*, 338*(4)*, 340; **V**: 87*(2)*; **VI**: 106*(4)*.
East Wind and Passage of **IV**: 331.
Evaporation from **II**: 244.
Geology and the Crossing of the **II**: 248; **IV**: 335*(2)*.
Motif of **IV**: 340.
Name of **V**: 296.
Saltiness of **III**: 208.
Redaction:
Babylonian Literary **VII**: 254.
Babylonian Theological **VII**: 254, 260.
Redeemer:
Expectation, Ancient, of **V**: 125.
God as, in the OT **VIII**: 69.
Job, in / of **IV**: 465, 469.
Vestiges of in the Religions of the Ancient World **V**: 125.
Redemption: **I**: *112;* **III**: 411; **VI**: 307; **VIII**: 136, 175, 188, 194, **§1018, 195-197**.
Bible as God's Revelation of **VIII**: 196.
Covenant Framework, in **VIII**: 197, 218.
Damascus, Land of, and Messianic **V**: 131.
Document of, from Ugarit **VII**: 144.
Hamilton, Robert, on **VIII**: 195.
Hellenistic Law, Right of, in **I**: 500; **VII**: 341.
House of God in the History of **V**: 69.
House of God, in the History of **VIII**: 190.
Idea of, in Pagaism **V**: 140.
Melchizedek in the History of **VI**: 65.
Promise, Ancient, of **V**: 125.
Sabbath, Anticipation of **VIII**: 197.
Sexual Purity and **VIII**: 197.
Redeṣiyeh:
So-called Temple of **III**: 511.
Reed: **I**: 180.
Tiberius, of **I**: 458.
Reeds, Binding: **I**: 266, *285*.
Reesh, Tell er: **II**: 467.
REEVES, JOHN: **IV**: 50.
Psalms, on **IV**: 473.
Reeves's Bible: **IV**: 50.
Refining:
Copper, Ancient **I**: 299; **II**: 216.
Reformation:
English Bible and **IV**: 54.
Exegesis, Principle of, and the Interpretation of Prophecy **IV**: 81; **VIII**: 241.
Refuge, Cities of, *see:* **Levitical Cities and Cities of Refuge**
Regeneration: **VIII**: 195.

Regia: **III**: 213.
Regicide: **I**: 487.
Registration:
Conveyances, of, in Ptolemaic Egypt **I**: 347.
Regnal Years: **I**: *398, 402,* **§118, 409-412**; **II**: 201; **IX**: **§118, xcviii**.
Egypt, in **I**: 409, 410.
Egyptian Word for **I**: *410;* **V**: 358.
Jewish, under Babylonian and Persian Rule **I**: 410.
OT Reckoning of **I**: 409.
Rehoboam: **I**: *470, 484, 487, 493.*
Biographical Studies **I**: 96.
Jerusalem under **II**: 411.
Rehtia: **V**: 269.
Votive Offerings to **V**: 268.
REICH, EMIL: **IV**: 132, 134.
REIFENBERG, A.:
Bibliography of **I**: 21.
Rein(s): **III**: 586.
Rein Ring **III**: 586*(2)*.
REINARCH, M.:
Theory of Sacrifice **V**: 60.
Reinicker Lecture: **IV**: 127.
REISNER, GEORGE A.: **III**: 106.
Bibliography of **IX**: lxxxi.
REIZENSTEIN, RICHARD:
Qumran and **VIII**: 423.
Rekhmereʻ:
Autobiography of **VII**: 16.
Rekhmirê: **I**: *298;* **VII**: 70.
Rekmara (Rekhmire):
Tomb of, at Thebes **VII**: 10.
Relations, International, *see:* **Diplomatic Relations**
Relgious Experience:
Gospels, in **VI**: 690.
Rabbinical Literature, in **VI**: 690.
Relics:
'IḪT (Egyptian God's) **I**: 377.
Relief(s): **III**: **§226, 720-754**.
Acropolis, Pediment, Relation to Vase Painting **III**: 707, 722.
Amenhotep I, Mortuary Temple of, Restoration **III**: 728.
Amenhotep IV, Gayer Anderson Jubilee, of **VII**: 71.
Archaistic, of the Hellenistic Period **III**: 750.
Ares Temple, Athens **III**: 746.
Ashurnasirpul, Twelve of **III**: 751.
Assyrian **III**: 125, 744.
Assyrian Bronze **III**: 749, 758; **VII**: 177.
Athena, Mourning, so-called **III**: 724.
Athlete, from Athens **III**: 731.
Attic, Fifth Century **III**: 735.
Attic, Marble Vase Fragment **III**: 744.
Attic, Tradition and Invention in **III**: 742.
Ba-ba, Fan of **III**: 741.
Babylonian and Egyptian compared **III**: 730.
Babylonian Cylindrical Basrelief **III**: 722.
Babylonian Lion, in Toledo **III**: 378, 749.
Babylonian, Terra-cotta, of Lilith **III**: 736.
Bas, from Phaleron **III**: 723.
Bas, Ptolemaic Period in Blue Faience **III**: 729.
Bas, *Spinning Damsel* **III**: 725.
Berney **III**: 736.
Bronze (Potnia Tarōn) **III**: 737.
"Capaneus", of the Villa Albani, Bronze **III**: 737.
Carchemish, Dating of **III**: 753.
Cat or Marten **III**: 743.
Cat, pet, on **III**: 748.
Clay, from Iraq Museum **III**: 734.
Darius, Grave **III**: 541, 727.
Egyptian and Babylonian compared **III**: 730.

Egyptian, at Wadi Sarga **III**: 727.
Egyptian, Foundation **III**: 735.
Egyptian, fragment (Florence Museo Archaeologico, 2566) **III**: 750.
Egyptian, Fragments **III**: 735.
Egyptian, from Memphite Tomb of Ḥaremḥab **III**: 737, 739.
Egyptian, Minoan 'frame' on **III**: 754.
Egyptian, New Kingdom **III**: 745.
Egyptian, Ramesses II, Coronation of **VII**: 17.
Egyptian, Ramesses II, Minor War Scenes, from Karnak **III**: 754.
Egyptian, Unidentified Old Kingdom **III**: 739.
Egyptian, Wall, XIth Dynasty from Hathor **III**: 742.
Eleusis, Date of **III**: 746.
Endoios' **III**: 738, 739.
Epidauros, Two from **III**: 752.
Etruscan **III**: 737.
Fan of Ba-ba **III**: 741.
Greek*(?)* **III**: 734*(2)*.
Greek, in Beirut **III**: 735.
Hatshepsut Punt **III**: 748.
Hellenistic Landscape **III**: 752.
Heracles **III**: 743.
Heracles Alexicacus **III**: 725.
Hesperides, and Heroes **III**: 750.
Hittite, at Carchemish **III**: 721.
Hittite, Basrelief **III**: 722.
Hittite, Neo-, from Andval **III**: 752.
Illustrating the Illiad **III**: 742.
Iny's Tomb, in **III**: 715; **VII**: 18.
Iran, Rock, of **III**: 739.
Ivory **III**: 771.
Jewish **III**: 736, 738.
Kfar Barʿam, from **III**: 745.
κιονίσκοι, on **III**: 724.
Limestone **III**: 738.
Limestone (I.M. 56577) **III**: 749.
Lion, from Petra **II**: *277, 460;* **III**: *356,* 731.
Louvre, in, representing the Sphinx **III**: 734.
Ludovisi **III**: 729, 730.
Mantineian **III**: 722.
Marble Slabs, Sculptured **III**: 724.
Marten or Cat **III**: 743.
Melian, Hector on **III**: 746.
Memphite Necropolis, from **VII**: 74.
Mentuemhat, from Tomb of **III**: 748.
Mesopotamian **III**: 754.
Minoan 'frame' on Egyptian **III**: 754.
Mithraic, from Syria **III**: 729.
Napata, from a Temple at **III**: 732.
New Kingdom, from Memphis **III**: 748.
Nineveh, Stone Fragments, from **III**: 736.
Petra, Block, from **III**: 754.
Potter, from Akropolis, Possibly Endoios' **III**: 738.
Punt-Reliefs, Fish on, from Deir El-Baḥri **III**: 368, 753.
Qudshu-Astarte-Anath **III**: 745.
Rock, from the Karasu, near Birecik **III**: 746.
Roman Historical **III**: 727.
Roman, Sepulchral **III**: 727.
Saïte Tomb **III**: 742.
Sarcophagus of Ahiram, King of Byblos, on **III**: 554.
Sebkḥotpe **III**: 743.
"Sesostris", in India **III**: 745.
Siphnian Treasury, East Pediment of **III**: 751.
Sower, of **V**: 261.
Susa, from **III**: 732.
Tabula Odysseaca **III**: 738.
Terra-cotta **III**: 740.
Terra-cotta from Sardis **III**: 730.
Thasian, Dedicated to the Nymphs and Apollon **III**: 721.
Thasos, Banquet **III**: 752.
Themistocles, of **III**: 730*(2), 731.*

Til Barsib, Dating of **III**: 753.
Tomb of Ramōse at Thebes **III**: 731.
Triumphal **III**: 754.
Urartian **III**: 746.
Venus, Ara Pacis Augustae **III**: 752.
Zinjirli Chariot **III**: 747.

Religion: *see also , Specific Civilizatons, (e.g. Egyptian)* **I**: 122,*464;* **II**: 3; **V**: 150.
Ancient, in Universal History **V**: 2.
Anthropology and **III**: 346.
Anthropology, Term "Religion" as used in **V**: 1, 512.
Anthropomorphic **VIII**: 102.
Antiochus Epiphanes persecution of Monotheistic **I**: 18.
Antiquity, of **V**: 159.
Apocalyptic, Origin of in Biblical **V**: 124.
Archaeology and **III**: 432; **V**: 150.
Archaic **V**: 5.
Assyrian **II**: *192, 193.*
Astronomy and **VIII**: 315.
Beginnings of **V**: 3.
Bible and **VIII**: 46.
Bible and Other **V**: 150.
Bible as Literature and **V**: 682.
Bible Illustrating, in the Ancient World **V**: 22.
Bible, of **V**: 6.
Bible, of, Divine origin of **VIII**: 45.
Bible's Place in Science of **IV**: 118.
Borrowing Between **V**: 37.
Cassite War God *Shaugamuna* **III**: *648.*
Civilization and **I**: 121.
Climate and, in Palestine **II**: 243; **V**: 19.
Colenso and Supernatural **IV**: 225.
Comparative, *see:* ***Comparative Religion***
Dan, Tribe of and **I**: 156, 314; **VIII**: 233.
Decay of **V**: 3.
Decay of Hebrew **V**: 16.
Definition of **V**: 5.
Developments, considered with respect to **V**: 6.
Divine Sonship and Individual **VIII**: 191.
Eastern, Freedom and Authority in **V**: 149.
Eastern, in the West **V**: 155.
Ethics, Relation of, to in Prophetic Literature **V**: 23; **VIII**: 199.
Evolution and **III**: 289, 308, 309, 320.
Evolution of **V**: 2.
Evolution of Biblical **V**: 20.
Forms, considered with respect to **V**: 6.
Fundamentals of, as Interpreted by Chrisitanity **V**: 18.
Fundamentals of, as Interpreted by Rabbinic Judaism **V**: 18.
Gezer and, in Ancient Palestine **II**: 374; **V**: 13, 160.
God, Idea of in Early **VIII**: 62.
Greek, Hebrew, and Roman **V**: 110*(2),* 252*(2),* 268*(2).*
Growth of **V**: 4.
Hebrew Genius for **V**: 16.
Hebrew, Greek, and Roman **V**: 110*(2),* 252*(2),* 268*(2).*
Higher Criticism, Value for **IV**: 138.
Historic **V**: 5.
"Historical Movement" in the Study of **V**: 3.
History and/in **IV**: 4, 5.
History of, *see:* ***Religion, History of***
Homeric and Myceanean **V**: 256.
Individual Religion, Jeremiah's Concept of **IV**: 414; **VIII**: 192.

Job and Œdipus in West African	**V**: 151.
King and the Tree of Life in Ancient Near Eastern	**I**: 483.
Lagalism in	**VIII**: 222.
Magic and, in Early Hellenic Society	**V**: 252.
Mesopotamian	**I**: 341; **V**: 187.
Messiah and	**VIII**: 139.
Messianic Idea in Ancient	**V**: 127.
Metals, Influence on Ancient	**I**: 295.
Modern Eastern	**I**: 389.
Monotheistic, Antiochus Epiphanes persecution of	**I**: 18.
Morality of	**VIII**: 224.
Müller, Max, on the Origin of	**V**: 1*(2)*.
Myceanean and Homeric	**V**: 256.
Mysticism and	**V**: 3.
Near East, of and OT	**I**: 392.
Œdipus and Job in West African	**V**: 151.
Old Testament, Character of	**V**: 10.
Old Testament, History of	**V**: 24.
Old Testament, Nature of	**V**: 10.
Old Testament, of, Origin	**V**: 7, 8.
Old Testament, Structure of	**V**: 19.
Oriental, Spread of	**V**: 155.
Origin of	**V**: 1*(7)*, 2*(3)*, 4*(4)*, 5.
Origin of, by Evolution or Revelation	**V**: 4*(2)*,
Origin of, Chinese	**V**: 145.
Origin of, in Archaeology	**V**: 5.
Origin of, in Theory	**V**: 5.
Origin of the Great Oriental, Problems Concerning	**V**: 148.
Pagan, and Bible as Word of God	**V**: 150.
Pagan, Ethical Value of	**V**: 153.
Pagan, Spiritual Power in	**V**: 18, 156.
Palaeolithic Man, Evidence for Religious Beliefs	**V**: 4.
Palestine, Ancient, in	**V**: 13.
Palestine, in, at the time of the Israelite Conquest	**V**: 190.
Palestine, in, during the Hyksos Rule	**V**: 158.
Patriarchal	**V**: 22.
Patriarchal, as Developed in the Book of Job	**IV**: 457; **V**: 6.
Pentateuch, of	**IV**: 233.
Philosophic Critique of	**IX**: cxxxiv.
Philosophy of	**I**: 128.
Pre-Anthropomorphic Stage of as Illustrated by Cult of Hestia	**V**: 250.
Prehistoric Man, of	**III**: 343.
Primitive	**V**: 5, 18, 153, 159, 164.
Primitive, Theories of	**V**: 4.
Proverbs, Aspects of, in	**IV**: 500, 502.
Psalms, of	**IV**: 480.
Revealed, Advance in the Type of	**V**: 6.
Revealed, Patriarcahal Evidence	**III**: 17; **IV**: 243*(2)*.
Roman, Greek, and Hebrew	**V**: 110*(2)*, 252*(2)*, 268*(2)*.
Sacred Book in	**V**: 148.
Science and	**III**: 284, 287, 290*(3)*, 291, 292*(2)*, 298, 302*(3)*, 326; **VIII**: 348.
Science of	**V**: 149.
Science of, So-Called	**V**: 139.
Scientific Study of	**III**: 432; **V**: 150.
Secret History of	**V**: 1.
Semites, of	**V**: 9.
Source, considered with respect to	**V**: 6.
Sources of	**V**: 149.
Spencer's Origin of the Religious Idea	**V**: 8.
Sumer, at	**III**: 239.
Supernatural, Colenso on	**IV**: 225; **VIII**: 29.

Threshold of	**V**: 5.
Tree of Life in Ancient Near Eastern	**I**: 483.
War and, in Israel	**I**: 314; **V**: 15; **VIII**: 232.
War and, in Mesopotamia	**V**: 165; **VIII**: 233.
War and, in the Greco-Roman World	**V**: 242; **VIII**: 223.
Women, Position of in Ancient	**I**: 197.
World, Servant of the Lord and	**VIII**: 145.
Religion, History of (Religiongeschichte) General Studies:	**V**: **§417, 1-5**; **IX**: **§417, cxxxiv.**
Abraham's Place in	**V**: 10.
Ancient Orientation Unveiled	**V**: *3(4).*
Antiquity, Religions of, Significance of	**V**: 5.
Assyriology and	**II**: 222; **III**: 775.
Belief, Origins of	**V**: 5.
Bible, Contribution of, to	**V**: 4, 19.
Classical Antiquity, Religious History of	**V**: 158.
Development of	**V**: *1(2),* 13.
Development of Religious Consciousness	**V**: 2.
Forms of, Tracing	**V**: 3.
Ghost Theory and	**V**: 1.
High Gods among low races	**V**: 4.
Job, Book of, Significance for	b**V**: 5.
Local Gods, Transformed into Gods	**V**: 11.
Milestones in	**V**: 10.
New Testament and	**II**: *222.*
Old Testament and	**V**: 5, 30.
Old Testament and the Approach to	**VIII**: 352.
Old Testament Theology and	**VIII**: 6.
Patriarchs and	**IV**: 316; **V**: 13.
Philosophy of	**V**: *2(2).*
Religious Evolution	**V**: 5.
Savage, Limits of	**V**: 1.
Science of	**V**: 2.
Sociological Hypothesis on Women in Ancient	**V**: 2.
tabu-mana formula as minimum definition of	**V**: 2.
Theology and	**VIII**: 3.
Women in Ancient, Sociological Hypothesis	**V**: 2.
Religion, Jewish, *see:* **Jewish Religion and Israelite Religion**	
Religion, Philosophy of, *see also:* **Religious Philosophy**	**V**: *2(2).*
Judaism and	**V**: 110.
Religion - Primitive:	**V**: 3, 5, 18, 153, 159.
Astronomy in	**II**: 233; **V**: 166.
Interpretations of	**V**: 1.
Magic and	**V**: 3.
Mythology and	**V**: 3.
Phenomena of	**V**: *2(3), 3(3).*
Ritual of	**V**: 3.
Sources of	**V**: 2.
Spiritual	**V**: 3.
Survival of, in Asia Minor	**V**: 154.
Survival of in Modern Palestine	**I**: 387; **V**: 155.
Survival of in Modern Syria	**I**: 387; **V**: 155.
Religiongeschichte, *see:* **History of Reigion**	
Religions:	
Carthage of	**V**: **§475, 239.**
Cypriote, Minoan and Mycenaean	**V**: **§478, 241-242.**
Mediterreanean Area - General Studies	**V**: **§474, 237-239.**
Religions and Philosophy, Ancient - General Studies:	**V**: **§464, 152-160.**
Change in, about 800-500 B.C. Ritual and Ethic	**V**: 157.

History of Religious Fraud. Talking, Weeping Sculptures V: 157.
Solar Symbolism in V: 153; **VIII**: 302.
Religionsgeschichte, *see:* **Religion, History of**
Assyriology and **II**: 222; **III**: 775.
New Testament and **II**: *222*.
Religionsgeschichte of Israel, *see:* **Israelite Religion** V: **§418, 6-32**.
Religious Customs:
Hebrew I: **§108, 365-367**.
Religious Philosophy, *see also:* **Religion, Philosophy of**
History, of **IV**: 244.
Old Testament, Religious Philosophers in V: 112.
Religious Texts:
Transmission of, in Ancient Oriental World **IV**: 99.
RELPH, ARTHUR E.: **VI**: *63*.
Remmon Methoar Neah: II: 287.
Remnant: VIII: 211.
Doctrine of **VIII**: 211.
God's People and **VIII**: 211.
OT Doctrine of **VIII**: 214.
RÉNAN, ERNEST: V: 385.
Canticles, on **IV**: *457,* 503.
Hillel, on **VI**: 685.
Israel, History of, on I: 139*(5)*.
Job, on **IV**: 457, *503*.
Scripture Infallibilty, on **IV**: 161.
Renewal: V: 512*(2)*.
Renï:
Mayor of El Kab, Statuette of **II**: 82; **VII**: 60.
RENNEL, JAMES: **II**: 253.
RENOUF, P. LE PAGE:
Bibliography of I: 21.
"Repeating of Births": I: 409.
Repentance: VIII: **§1018, 195- 197**.
Job, of **IV**: 467, 468.
Philo, Concerning **VI**: 674.
Repentence:
Rabbinic Concepts of **VIII**: 188, 196.
Sin and **VIII**: 183.
Rephaim: I: *276;* **II**: *111, 113, 118, 124, 129, 144, 147, 150, 154,* **158**,*167, 170, 171,* 467; **III**: *480;* **IV**: 219, 373; **V**: 104, 132; V: 192; **VIII**: 260.
Rephidim:
God's Ensign at **IV**: 325.
Moses at the Battle of **VI**: 109.
Representative:
Egyptian Word for V: 330.
Reptiles:
Evolution and **III**: 316.
Reqaqnah: III: 209.
Research Tools for Old Testament Study: VIII: **§1066, 397**, 403.
Resen: VI: 56.
Reserviors:
Nebuchadnezzar's I: 357.
Reshep: V: 220.
Resin: I: 265; **III**: 543; **IX**: xc.
Tomb of the saïte period, from **II**: 214.
Responsibility:
Collective, in the Bible and Aggada **VI**: 697; **VIII**: 235.
Indiviual I: 481.
Rest: V: *503,* 512.
Restitution:
Inscription regarding, at Leyden I: 504.
"Nocturnal Thief" and **VI**: 114.
Stolen Property, of in Ramesside Times I: 498.
Restoration, *see also:* **Antiquities, Preservation of**
Ancient Methods of I: 268.

Restoration Movement:
Old Testament Studies in **IV**: 158.
Restoration of Israel, *see also:* **Chosen People** **VIII**: **§1025, 209-214**, 314, 340*(3)*.
Ezekiel's Vision of **IV**: 422*(2)*; **VIII**: 211*(2)*.
Palestine, Prophecy and **VIII**: 210*(2)*, 242*(2)*.
Resurrection of **VIII**: 213.
Resurrection of the Dead identified with **VIII**: 210, 270.
Resurrection (of the Dead): **I**: *380;* **VI**: 596; **VIII**: 174, 261, **§1039, 269-270**.
Apocalyptic, Jewish, and **VIII**: 270.
Body, of **VIII**: 269*(3)*, 270*(3)*.
Christ, of, Prophesied **VIII**: 127.
Cosmic **V**: 156.
Daniel and **IV**: 524; **VI**: 578*(2)*.
Dead of **VIII**: 259.
Dead of, Identified with the Restoration of Israel **VIII**: 210.
Dead of, in Rabbinic Theology **VI**: 687; **VIII**: 269.
Egypt, Egyptian Belief in **V**: 201, 204, 205.
Ezekiel Panel at Dura-Europa Synagogue and **III**: 527; **IV**: 421; **VI**: 357*(2)*; **VIII**: 269, 356*(2)*, 357*(2)*.
Ezekiel's Vision of **VI**: 358.
Hosea, in Covenant Context **VI**: 367.
Intertestamental Judaism, in **VIII**: 270.
Israel, Restoration of, identified with **VIII**: 210, 270.
Jesus, Jewish and Apocryphal Ideas **VIII**: 127.
Jewish Parties and **VIII**: 269.
Job, on **IV**: 458, 462, 467; **VI**: 430, 431*(2)*; **VIII**: 260, 269, 270.
Marine and Terrestrial Creatures, of, in Pss 104 **VI**: 513.
Obscurity, Supposed, of OT Treatment of **VIII**: 269.
Osirinized dead and **V**: 213.
Pentateuch, in **VIII**: 269.
Persian Doctrine of **V**: 230.
Persian, Jewish and Christian **V**: 139; **VIII**: 269.
Philological Data on **VIII**: 266.
Psalm 16 and **VI**: 461.
Wicked, of **VIII**: 270.
Retaliation, *see:* **Retribution**
Reten: **II**: 158.
Retribution: **I**: 462, 475, 503; **VIII**: 226, 228.
Greek and Hebrew Ideas on Divine **IX**: cxxxvii.
Jewish and Pagan Conceptions of Justice **VI**: 596.
Laws of, including Blood Feuds **I**: **§131, 480-481**; **V**: 544; **VI**: 654; **IX**: **§131, c.**
Non-Retaliation in the Manual of Discipline **VIII**: 294, 463, 481.
Pentatuech, Law of, in **IV**: 234; **IX**: c.
Social Crime and **V**: 38; **VIII**: 230, 378.
Wisdom Literature and the Problem of **V**: 118.
Reu: **I**: *76;* **V**: 298.
Reuben: **IV**: 229.
Reuben, Testament of:
Armenian Text of **VI**: 646.
Reuchlinianus, Codex **IV**: 13.
REUSS, EDOUARD:
Deutero-Isaiah, on **IV**: 399.
Evolution, and **III**: 310, 313.

Revelation: **IV**: 264; **V**: *503*, 512; **VI**: 118; **VIII**: 2, 25‡, 28‡. 29, 75.
- Apocalypticsm, in **V**: 123.
- Argument from Silence **VIII**: 221.
- Biblical **IV**: 27, 202.
- Biblical Theology and **VIII**: 11.
- Conscience and **VIII**: 29*(2)*.
- Continuity of **V**: 123; **VI**: 648.
- Creation and / as **III**: 303; **VIII**: 75.
- Creation of Angels and Earth **VIII**: 79.
- Criticism and **VIII**: 31.
- Cycle of OT, and Public Worship **VIII**: 380.
- Deuteronomy in **IV**: 349
- Divine, and Old Testament Historicity **IV**: 199.
- Divine Element in Scripture **VIII**: 31.
- Divine, *see:* ***Divine Revelation***
- Divine, through Israel **IV**: 163.
- Ethnology and **III**: 333; **IV**: 160.
- Event, as **VIII**: 36.
- Evolution and **IX**: cxx.
- Evolution of **VIII**: 31.
- Exploration as Verifying **IV**: 209.
- Faith and **VIII**: 36, 201.
- Geology and **III**: 284, 285, 286, 287*(2)*, 288*(2)*, 292, 300, 311, 337; **VIII**: 29.
- God, of, and Ancient Oriental Life **V**: 15; **VIII**: 59.
- God's Self-Revelation to Israel **VIII**: 31.
- Hebrew and Greek Ideas on, compared **VIII**: 35.
- Higher Criticism and **VIII**: 31, 32.
- History and **I**: 132, 133, 135; **IV**: 341; **V**: 124, 148.
- History and, Jewish Apocalypticism **I**: 135; **V**: 124; **VIII**: 36.
- History, Through, in OT **VIII**: 35.
- Immoratlity and **VIII**: 31, 261.
- Incarnation as **VIII**: 29.
- Inspiration and **VIII**: 271.
- Israelite Religion, a, or Evolution(?) **V**: 16, 20.
- Law and **I**: 476.
- Modern Theology, in **I**: 134; **IV**: 90; **VIII**: 35.
- Myth, Symbol, and **V**: 136.
- Mythology and **V**: 134; **VIII**: 29.
- Natrual **VIII**: 30.
- Natural Religion Prophetic of **VIII**: 14.
- Nature and **III**: 288.
- Noachites, Do they Have to Believe in(?) **V**: 113, 114.
- Old Testament Historiography and **I**: 133.
- Palestine and **V**: 11; **VIII**: 31.
- Pentateuch and **IV**: 237.
- Philosophy and **VIII**: 32.
- Primitive Man and **III**: 336.
- Protestant Views of **VIII**: 35.
- Reason and **VIII**: 31, 35.
- Responsibility and, Biblical Norm of Social Behavior **VIII**: 226.
- Roman Catholic Views of **VIII**: 35.
- Science and **II**: 179; **III**: 283, 284*(3)*, 287*(2)*, 291, 292, 293, 295*(2)*, 303*(3)*, 306, 319; **IV**: 276, 288, 297, 331, 332; **VIII**: 29, 30, 54.
- *Sensus Plenior* and **IV**: 90.
- Symbol, Myth and **V**: 136.
- Symbolism and **VIII**: 33, 304.
- Unity of **VIII**: 31.
- Wisdom Literature, in **V**: 117; **VIII**: 33.
- Word of God as **VIII**: 23.
- Written **VIII**: 30.

Revelation, Book of, *see also:* **Apocalypse**
- Avesta Eschatology Compared with **V**: 233.

Avesta Eschatology Compared with, and the Book of Daniel **IV**: 534.
Daniel, Book of and, Compared **IV**: **§408, 534**.
Exodus, Similarities to **IV**: 338.
High Priest's Breastplate and the Jasper of 4:3 **V**: 45; **VIII**: 297.
Isaiah, Imagery in, and **IV**: 397.
Jewish Apocalyptic Literature and **V**: 120, 123.
Revelation, Doctrine of: **VIII**: 22, 25‡.
Bible as Divine Revelation **VIII**: 25.
Inspiration and **VIII**: 20*(5)*, 22*(2)*, 24, 271.
Theology and **VIII**: 35*(2)*.
Revenge, *see:* **Retribution**
Revenue:
Justice and, in Egypt **I**: 489.
Revetments:
Terracotta, from Etruria **III**: 463, 464*(2)*.
Revised Standard Version: **IV**: 59, 63, 68, **§267, 69-70**.
Attacks on **IV**: 71.
Catholic Version of **IV**: 66, 71.
Isaiah 7:14 in **VI**: 262.
Revised Version of 1881: **IV**: **§266, 65-68**.
Musical Instruments in **IV**: 111.
Public Worship, Use of, in **VIII**: 378.
Transliteration of Proper Names in **IV**: 105*(2)*.
Revolts, *see:* **Rebellions/Revolts**
Revolution:
Exodus, The, and **IV**: 340; **VIII**: 353.
Jewish of 66-73, and the Pharisees **V**: 99.
Reward:
Deuteronomy, Idea of, in **IV**: 351.
Rezin: **I**: *76*, **77**, *86;* **VI**: 238, 259, 593.
Rhacotis:
Alexander's Palace in **III**: 489, 501.
Rhages: **III**: 209.
Rhamnous:
Temple of Nemesis at **III**: 522.
Rhamnus: **I**: *240*.
Rhetoric: **VIII**: 1.
Ancient **IV**: 154; **IX**: cxxix.
Hebrew: repetition and style **V**: 688, 698.
Rhetorical Figures in OT **V**: 695*(2)*.
Rheumatism:
Assyrian Incantation against **III**: 398.
Rhind Mathematical Papyrus: **I**: *419*, 429*(4)*, 432; **VII**: 34*(5)*.
Rhine River: **I**: 349.
Rhinoceros: **III**: 380*(2)*.
Rhode Island School of Design, Museum:
Classical Accessions of **III**: 566, 686.
Etruscan Art in **III**: 692.
Greek Art in **III**: 692.
Rhodes: **I**: *238, 239, 240, 494, 510;* **II**: *49;* **III**: **209**, *573, 729*.
Colossus at **III**: 728.
Greek Inscription from **VII**: 318.
Phoenician Fragment from **VII**: 118.
Rhodopis: **II**: *71*, 82.
Rhœtians: **II**: *129*, **158**.
Rhône: **I**: 325; **II**: *122*.
Rhyme, Metre, Musical Accents and Notations, Studies on : **V**: **§558, 690-691**.
Accent Systems of Psalms, Proverbs, and Job **V**: 691.
David, of **V**: 690.
Hebrew Meter and Old Testament Exegesis **IV**: 84; **V**: 688.
Hebrew Poetry, in **V**: 688, 691.
Hebrew Popular Poetry, in **V**: 683.

Hexameter	**V**: 690.
Mathematical Approach to Hebrew Meters	**V**: 691.
Metre and Textual Criticism	**V**: 691.
Metrics, Principles of Hebrew	**V**: 691.
Midrash Haggadol, Techniques in the Proems of	**VI**: 709.
Pentameter	**V**: 690.
Semitic Metrics and Ugaritic Evidence	**V**: 691.
Song of Solomon, in	**IV**: 505; **V**: 690.
Tetrameter	**V**: 690.
Textual Criticism and Metre	**V**: 691.
Trimeters, Strophical Orgainization of Hebrew	**V**: 690.
Rhythm, *see also:* **Rhyme, Metre, etc.**	
Combined Rhythms	**V**: 690.
Hebrew and English	**V**: 691.
Lamentations, Book of, in	**V**: 690.
Primary Hebrew	**V**: 690.
Rhyton:	**III**: 589*(2)*, 590, 615.
Etruscan, in Vienna	**III**: 626.
Mycenae Siege, and Egyptian Influence	**III**: 600, 639.
Rîb (ריב) Patterns / Controversy Studies:	**I**: *189;* **IV**: 358; **V**: 451*(2)*, **§560**, **692-693**.
God as Plaintiff	**V**: 693, 703; **VIII**: 72.
God's with Priest and People in Hosea	**VI**: 366.
Isaiah XL-LX, in	**V**: 693, 694; **VI**: 293, 300.
Latter Prophets, in	**IV**: 389*(2);* **V**: 692, 693.
Rib-Adda:	**VII**: 171, 172.
Ribla:	**III**: 439.
Rice:	**III**: 394.
Cuneiform Word for	**I**: *274;* **III**: *391, 394;* **V**: 569.
RICH, CLAUDIUS JAMES:	**III**: 147, 179.
Riches, *see also:* **Wealth**	**I**: 184, 303, 305*(2)*, 310.
Biblical Meaning of	**I**: 193, 303.
Social Status of	**I**: 187*(2)*.
Riddle:	**V**: 697; **VI**: 4, 48.
Josephus, of	**VI**: 683.
Samson's	**VI**: 188.
Solomon's, in Rabbinic Literature	**VI**: 695.
Ride:	**V**: *505*, 512.
Rifa'at, Tell:	**I**: *457;* **III**: **209**.
RIGG, H. A.	**III**: 644.
Rigging:	
Lifting and Transportation of Heavy Bodies	**I**: 343.
Warship, Emergency	**I**: 321, 355.
Right:	
Roman Art, Left and, in	**III**: 697.
Righteous:	
Destiny of, in Israel	**VIII**: 263.
Sin of the	**VIII**: 179.
Wicked and, in the Habakkuk Scroll	**VIII**: 456.
Righteousness:	**V**: *504*, 512, 513; **VIII**: 96, **§1020**, **198-199**.
Between the Testaments	**VIII**: 199.
Gates of	**II**: 415.
God (Jehovah), of	**VI**: 296, 463.
Grafted in	**VI**: 253.
Imputed to another	**V**: *424;* **VIII**: 176, 198.
Personal	**VIII**: 198.
Prophetic Concept of	**V**: 447, 513.
Prophetic Teaching on	**VIII**: 199.
Proverbs, in	**IV**: 502.
Ritual and	**V**: 23; **VIII**: 199, 226.
Scribes and Pharisees, of	**V**: 98; **VI**: 668.
Rights, *see:* **Human Rights**	
Rijksmuseum, Leiden:	
Tut'ankhamūn, Objects of	**III**: 567, 687.
Rîm-Sin:	**I**: *409;* **II**: **82**, *83;* **VII**: 278.
Conquest of Isin, by	**II**: 82.

Contemporary of Samsuiluna — **II**: 82.
Letter of — **VII**: 179, 216*(2)*.
Tablets of a Wife of — **VII**: 237.
Rimah: — **II**: *7*, *87*.
Rimah, Tell el: — **III**: **210**.
Assyrian Tablets from — **VII**: 177*(2)*.
Stela Excavated at — **II**: 472; **VII**: 204.
Stone Spirits from — **V**: 239.
RIMMER, HARRY: — **III**: 320.
Ring(s):
Assyrian Sculpture, in — **III**: 725.
Athlete's, So-Called — **I**: 264; **III**: 592.
Babylonian Sculpture, in — **III**: 725.
Cheops' — **III**: 645.
Cuneiform Tablet concerning Gifts of Silver — **VII**: 214.
Egyptian Signet — **III**: 644.
Fayence, Amenophis III's — **III**: 592.
Hebrew, Gold, with seal — **III**: 652.
Monetary Exchange of — **I**: 438.
Phoenician, from Malta — **III**: 592.
Rod and (Symbolism) — **V**: 186; **VIII**: 305.
Roman — **I**: 281; **III**: 592.
Signet — **I**: 283; **III**: 592.
Rio de Janerio: — **III**: *629*.
Riotinto: — **I**: 340; **III**: 210, *237*, *247*.
Riqqeh: — **I**: *281*.
Risqeh:
Arabian Sanctuary at — **V**: 239*(2)*.
RIST, MARTIN:
Bibliography of — **I**: 21.
Rites:
Babylonian, Decree on — **VII**: 258.
Cabiric — **V**: 258.
Coronation — **I**: 482, 483.
Egyptian, Altar and Bell in — **V**: 211.
Egyptian, of "Bringing the Foot" — **VII**: 37.
Fertility, Egyptian — **V**: 157, 215.
Fertility, Osiris and — **V**: 215.
Fertility, Ugaritic — **V**: 197.
Greek Animal Husbandry — **I**: 258; **V**: 265.
Greek, Stealing, of — **V**: 258.
Harvest, in a Theban Tomb — **V**: 214.
Mouth, Opening of, in Egypt and Babylonia — **V**: 183, 209, 211, 223*(2)*.
Roman Expiatory — **V**: 269.
Semitic Sacramental — **V**: 39.
Rites, Hebrew: — **I**: *276*.
Burial, as Survivals of Ancestor Worship — **I**: 373.
Ritual(s):
Ancient Literature, in — **VII**: 2.
"Appearing Ghosts", Against — **V**: 158; **VII**: 158.
Ark and Cherubim. Symbolic Signficance in — **V**: 26.
Assyrian, Analysis of [KAR 139] — **V**: 170.
Assyrian and Babylonian — **V**: 166.
Assyrian, for a Substitute King — **VII**: 202, 203.
Assyrian Prayer Cycle in the*bît rimki,* — **VII**: 202.
Assyrian, Restoration of — **V**: 170; **VII**: 202.
Babylonian — **V**: 189.
Babylonian and Hebrew Comparision of — **V**: 147.
Babylonian Private — **V**: 184.
Babylonian Sacrificial, Parallel between Indic and — **V**: 61, 148, 185.
Babylonian, Sympathetic Magic by Burning Images — **VII**: 263.
Egyptian, of Roman Period — **V**: 200.
Egyptian, of the Dead — **V**: 200.
Ethic and — **V**: 157.
Faith and, in the OT — **VIII**: 200; **IX**: cxxxv.
Greece, Myth and, in — **V**: 263.
Greek Tragedy and Sacrificial — **V**: 265.
Havdalah-Shiv'atot in Palestinian — **VIII**: 208.
Hebrew Prophets and — **V**: 25.
Hittite, of Zerpiya of Kezzuwatna — **VII**: 308.

Incense and Libations in Funerary and Temple **V**: 206.
Indic Sacrificial, Parallel between Babylonian and **V**: 61, 148, 185.
Jewish, *Naddah* **III**: 403.
Levitic, Babylonian Elements in **V**: 42.
Luwian, of Zerpiya of Kezzuwatna **VII**: 308.
Mosaic, Incense in **V**: 38.
Namburbi, Participants in **V**: 188.
Perpetual Obligation of the Jewish **VI**: 338.
Perpetuation of the Past (Egyptian) **V**: 220.
Phœnician **V**: 189.
Righteousness and **V**: 23; **VIII**: 199, 226.
Sai of **V**: 317.
Seven Day, in Old Babylonian Cult **V**: 188.
South Arabian, Hunt **V**: 237.
Symbols for Masculinity and Femininity in ANE Sympathetic Magic **V**: 160.
Tākultu **VII**: 203.
Temple **V**: 38, 79, 84, 86, 88; **IX**: xcvii, cxxxv.
Ugaritic Descriptive **VII**: 145.

Rivers, *see also Specific Names* **II**: 169; **IX**: xcvi.
Control of in Mesopotamia **I**: 362; **III**: 101, 255.
Damascus, of **VI**: 234.
Maṣor, of **VI**: 289.
Settlement and River Beds **I**: 124, 125, 206, 207; **II**: 261.
Sicily, Stream Changes During Historic Time in **II**: 251.
Traffic problems on **I**: 353; **V**: 575; **VII**: 246.
Transportation by, in Assyria **I**: 352.
Ugarit, Tributaries of **II**: 270.
"Underground Water-course" in Akkadian **II**: 256; **VII**: 153.

Riviera: **II**: 285.

Rizpah: **I**: 77; **VI**: 215.

Ro:
King of Abydos **II**: 4, 207.

"Road of Hercules": **I**: 346.

Roads, *see also:* **Transportation**
Asher, in **II**: 426.
Beyrout to Jerusalem **II**: 308.
Causeway of *wnis* at Sakkara **II**: 348.
Dahshur, Desert **III**: 74.
Egyptian Military **I**: 345.
El-Quṣeir, to **IX**: xcv.
Elath, Road to **II**: 359*(2)*, 487*(2)*.
Emar, Road to **I**: 349, 437.
Hittite Military **I**: 315, 346.
Judah, Western, in **II**: 426.
Karatepe, Ancient, near **III**: 262.
Mapping Ancient, in Anatolia **I**: 349.
Neronian Sacra Via **III**: 212.
Roman **I**: 343*(2)*, 344, 345, 346*(3)*, 348*(3)*, 349, 350*(2)*; **II**: 315, 380, 458, 484.
Sam'al to Asitawandawa **III**: 265.
Sharon, Plain of, Geographical Influences on **III**: 447.

Robâ, Tell er:
Tomb found at **III**: 537.

Robbery:
Babylonian Documents on **VII**: 252; **VIII**: 234.
Ramesside Tomb, of **I**: 498, 499; **VII**: 29, 77*(2)*.

ROBERTSON, JAMES: ***Bibliography of*** **I**: 21.

Robes: **I**: 280, *487*.

ROBINSON, EDWARD; **II**: 280; **III**: 439*(2)*, 440.

ROBINSON, THOMAS: **I**: 25.

Roche Taille: **II**: 284.

Rock Cutting:
Beit Ras, from **III**: 468.

"Rock of the Lion", *see:* **Arslan Tash**

Rock Rimmon (the Pomegranate): **II**: *377*, **467-468**.

Rocks:
- Dioritic **I**: 280.
- Gneissic **I**: 280; **III**: 460, 562.
- Granitic **I**: 280.
- Specimen from Solomon's Quarries **II**: 213*(2)*.

Rod(s): **I**: 251.
- Assyrian Sculpture, Meaning of, in **III**: 725.
- Babylonian Sculpture, Meaning of, in **III**: 725.
- Moses', Budding of **IV**: 325.
- Ring and **V**: 186.
- Ring and (Symbolism) **V**: 186; **VIII**: 305.
- Shepherd's **I**: 390.

Rodents:
- Plagues caused by **III**: 365, 398.

Rods:
- Writing on **VI**: 131.

Roebuck: **III**: 380*(3)*.

Rœtians: **II**: *129*.

Roman Empire: **I**: *296, 303, 338, 356;* **II**: 159, 160*(3)*, 161*(2)*.
- Eastern, Documents from **IX**: clii.
- Iron Trade in Eastern **I**: 338.
- Oriental Religions, Ethical Value of, under **V**: 146.
- Pharisees' Attitute Toward Roman Rule **V**: 99*(2)*.
- Provinces of **I**: 356.
- Social Mobility of Freedmen and Salves in **I**: 194.
- Syria under **III**: 243.

Roman Forum: **III**: 211*(4)*.
- Janus Shrine at **III**: 513; **V**: 254.
- Rostra, Location of **III**: 485.
- Stele Inscription in **VII**: 367.

Roman History:
- Poetical Element in **II**: 159.

Roman Legions: **I**: 321.
- Legionary Troops in Galatia **IX**: cii.

Roman Religion and Mythology: **V**: **§481, 267-271**.
- Agmina Furirum **V**: 271.
- Censors of 312 B.C. and the State Religion **IV**: 480; **IX**: cii.
- Child, Place of, in Religion and Supersition **V**: 269.
- Etruscan Influence on **V**: 269.
- Etruscan Religion, Relations between, and **V**: 269.
- Lucretius as Student of **V**: 268.
- Plautus as a Source Book for **V**: 270.
- Roman Army and **V**: 270, 271; **IX**: xciv, xcvii.
- Roman "Virtues" **V**: 269.
- *uer sacrum* **V**: 269.

Romania: **I**: 356.

Romanian Texts: **VII**: 376*(3)*.

ROMANOFF, PAUL: **III**: 374; **VI**: 688.

Romans: **I**: 127, 137, 330, 331, 332, 335, 336 (2), *340, 456;* **II**: *130, 132(2)*, **159-161**; **III**: *777*.
- Agrarian History of **II**: 160.
- Burial Customs **I**: 375.
- Cremation and **I**: 375.
- Diplomatic Practices of **I**: 328, 335.
- Jewish Revolt Against (66-73) and the DSS **VIII**: 426.
- Learning of, compared with Greek and Hebrew **V**: 138.
- Longevity of in North Africa **IX**: cxiii.
- Politics and the Courts in 104 B.C. **I**: 495.
- Water, Worship of, by **I**: 362.
- Women in Society **I**: 196*(2)*, 199*(2)*.

Romans, Book of:
- Papyrus MSS of, in Harvard Semitic Museum **III**: 449.

Rome: I: *120, 206, 239, 260, 302, 329, 345, 346, 348, 360, 488;* **II**: *159;* **III**: *29, 63, 67, 113, 168;* **III**: **210-213**, *241, 729*.
- Air View of — **III**: *113,* 212.
- Animals of Ancient — **III**: 365.
- Art of — **III**: 211.
- Arts, Free in — **I**: 194; **III**: 705.
- Bankes, Henry on the History of — **III**: 210.
- Bridges of — **I**: 343.
- City Planning in — **IX**: lxxxvi.
- Class Struggle in Greek States 200-164 BC, and — **I**: 194.
- Drumann, Wilhelm, on — **III**: 210.
- Esquiline Necropolis — **III**: 212.
- Foreign Groups in — **I**: 176.
- Foundation of in the Talmud — **VI**: 702.
- Founding of — **III**: 212*(2)*.
- Government of — **I**: 488.
- Jewish Quarters in — **I**: 142.
- Judaism in — **V**: 7.
- Merivale, Charles on — **III**: 211.
- Niebuhr, Barthold Georg, on the History of — **III**: 210*(2)*.
- People, Unfree in — **I**: 194; **III**: 705.
- Religions of — **V**: 252.
- San Lorenzo, Excavations — **III**: 212.
- Topography of — **III**: 212*(2)*.

Roof:
- Aegean, Primitive — **III**: 464.
- Helladic Terracotta, Tiles — **III**: 469.
- Megaron, of — **III**: 470*(4)*.

Rope: **III**: 572; **V**: 560; **VI**: 230*(2)*.

L. Roscius: **I**: 330.

Rose: **III**: **394**.
- Jericho, of — **VI**: 634.

Rose of Sharon: **III**: **394**; **VI**: 552.

Rosetta Stone: **IV**: *190;* **VII**: **§844, 53-54**.
- Discoverer of — **VII**: 54*(2)*.
- Discovery of — **VII**: 53.
- Discovery of a second "Rosetta Stone" — **VII**: 55.

Rosh:
- Ezekiel, in, and Russia — **IV**: 424.

Rosh ha-ʿAyin: **II**: 249, 321.

Rosh Hanniqra: **II**: 468.

Rosh Hashana, *see also:* **New Year's Day** — **V**: 85*(2)*.
- Liturgy, Origins of the — **VII**: 386.
- Mishna on — **V**: 85.
- Tractate on — **VI**: 703.

Rosh Ḥodesh: **V**: 85.

ROSKOFF, GUSTAV: **VIII**: 162.

ROSS, HUGH:
- Translation Principles of — **IV**: 108.

ROSSI, AZARIAH DE:
- Philo, on — **VI**: 676.

ROSTOVTZEFF, M.:
- ***Bibliography of*** — **I**: 21.

Rostra: **III**: 481.

ROTHE, RICHARD: **VIII**: 95.

ROWE, ALAN: **III**: 166; **VII**: 68.

Rowing: **I**: 352, 356.

ROWLEY, HAROLD HENRY
- ***Bibliography of*** — **I**: 22.
- Old Testament Theology of — **VIII**: 5.

Roy:
- Steward, Statue of — **III**: *729(2);* **VII**: 63.

Royal Air Force:
- Photographs of Beisan by — **II**: 331.

Royal Ontario Museum: **III**: *652, 727, 731, 768;* **VII**: *237, 320(2), 338*.

Royal Scottish Museum:
- Hittite Hieroglyphs on a Cappaocian Tablet in — **VII**: 163.

Royalty:
- "Flail" or "Scourge" of Osiris, as Symbol of — **III**: 671.

Ruad, *see:* **Ar-Ruád**

Rub' al Khali: **III**: 213.
'Neolithic' Site in, Carbon-14 Date for **II**: 218.
Rub'a, Tell el, *see also:* **Mendes:** **III**: **213**.
Rubaiyat:
Ecclesiastes and **IV**: 514.
Rubber:
Archaeological Use for Liquid, in Greek Epigraphy **II**: 216*(2)*, 218.
Silicon Compounds, Experiments with **II**: 219.
Rubin River: **II**: 468.
Ruby: **I**: 285.
Rudj'aḫua:
Stela of **VII**: 24.
Ruel: **IV**: 261, 329.
Rugs: **I**: 274.
Ruhama: **II**: 301.
Rule of the Community /Congregation (1QSa): **VIII**: 419, **§1126, 463-464**.
Age of Responsibility or Testimony, in **VIII**: 463*(2)*, 464.
Age of Twenty in **VIII**: 464.
Age of Twenty in, and in Rabbinic Tradition **VI**: 690; **VIII**: 464.
"Begetting the Messiah in" **VIII**: 142, 464.
God's Begetting the Messiah in **VIII**: 142.
Infinitives in, and their Orthography **VIII**: 464.
Messiah and the Meal in **VIII**: 419.
Paul, Parallel to, in **VIII**: 463.
Two Spirits in **VIII**: 462, 464.
waw and *yod* in **VIII**: 477.
Women, Testimony of, in **VIII**: 463.

Ruler(s):
Babylonian **VII**: 277.
Deities, Comparisons and Identifications with, of Hellenistic Period **I**: 465; **V**: 260.
Egyptian **II**: 5.
Judge, and **V**: 454*(2)*, 457, 458.
Worship of, in the Bible **V**: 155.
Ruminant(s):
Akkadian Names for the Stomachs of **V**: 552.
Runners: **I**: 343; **VI**: 212, *397*.
RUPPRECHT, EDUARD: **IV**: 229.
Rushmia: **II**: *287*, 367.
RUSKIN, JOHN:
Apocrypha and **VIII**: 362, 364.
RUSSELL, I. C.: **V**: 351.
Russia: **I**: 330; **III**: *592*.
Ezekiel's Rosh and **IV**: 424.
Greeks in South **II**: 133.
King of the North and, in Ezekiel **IV**: 423.
Russian Orthodox Palestine Society: **II**: 407.
Ruth, Book of: **IV**: *456;* **VI**: *176, 194*.
Authenticity and Authorship of **IV**: 165, **§397, 510**.
Bibliography **I**: **(§28)**, 14.
Canon, Place in **IV**: 509.
Character of **IV**: 509, 510.
Date, Sources, Authorship, Authenticity of **IV**: 509, **§397, 510**.
Divine-Human Conflicts in the OT **IV**: 510.
Exegetical Studies **VI**: **§652, 556-558**.
Greek Text of, and Origen's Hexapla **IV**: 38.
Hebrew Idyl **IV**: 508, 509.
Higher Criticism of **IV**: 509.
Judges, Book of, and **IV**: *367, 368,* 508, 509.
Judges, Samuel, and Form one Book **IV**: *367, 374,* 509.
Legal Problems in **I**: 470; **IV**: 510.
Literary Criticism of **IV**: **§396, 508-510**.

Origin of	**IV**: **§397, 510.**
Plot of	**IV**: 510.
Salomon ben Jeroham, Did he compose a Commentary on(?)	**IV**: 510; **VI**: 726.
Samuel and	**VI**: 556.
Spiritual Horizon of Judaism, Enlarged in	**IV**: *444*, 509.
Statistically Considered	**IV**: 508.
Symmetrical Design in	**V**: 706.
Theme of	**IV**: 510.
Translation Problems in	**IV**: 510.
Ruth, Book of, Manuscripts of:	**VI**: **§653, 558.**
Greek Text of According to Origen's Hexapla	**VI**; 558.
Ruth, Person:	**I**: 77, *220.*
Boaz and	**IV**: 510.
Marriage of Boaz and	**IV**: 509.
Oath of	**VI**: 556.
Return to Bethlehem	**VI**: 556.
Sojourn in Moab	**VI**: 556.
Visit to the High Place at Bethlehem	**VI**: 557.
Ruts, Cart:	**I**: 345*(4),* 346*(2),* 347.
RYLANDS, W. HARRY	**I**: 429.
RYLE, HERBERT EDWARD: Life and Contributions of	**I**: 24.
Rynty:	
Ruler of Byblos	**II**: 82.
RYSSEL, V.:	
Doublets in Ben Sira, on	**VI**: 622.
S	
Sa'ankhkare:	
Inscription of	**VII**: 15.
Sa'id ibn Ḥasan of Alexandria:	
Commentary on the Old Testament, of *(13th Century)*	**VI**: 725.
Saab:	**II**: 284.
SAADIA GAON:	**V**: 90; **IX**: *cxlviii(3).*
Atomism in	**V**: 112*(2).*
Certainty, Quest for, in the Philosophy of	**V**: 112.
Genesis, Longer Commentary on	**VI**: 726.
Grammatical Work of, Study of Hebew Vowels	**V**: 479.
Grammatical Work of, Study of Inflection of Hebrew in	**V**: 475.
Leviticus, Commentary on, in Arabic	**VII**: 290.
Man's Position in the Universe, and Maimonides	**VIII**: 174.
Matter and Element, Arabic and Hebrew Terms for, w/ref. to	**V**: 112, 399, 590.
Messianic Computation of in his Commentary on Daniel	**VI**: 726.
Nonexistence, Problem of, and Second theory of Creation (Kalam)	**V**: 112.
Philosophy of	**V**: 111.
Proverbs, Commentary on	**VI**: 726.
Reason and Revelation, in the Philosophy of	**V**: 112.
Relation to Islamic and Christian Thought	**V**: 149.
Sab'a Biyar:	**III**: *675*
Saba'a:	**II**: *7, 87.*
Sabaean Language:	**V**: **§539, 596.**
Eponyms, List of	**V**: 596.
Grammar	**V**: 596.
Noun-Inflection in	**V**: 596.
Sabaean Texts:	**VII**: 293, 294, **§926, 296-297,** 376.
Bronze Statues with, from Yemen	**VII**: 297.
Dextrograde, from Mâreb	**VII**: 297.
Etbai District, from	**VII**: 296.
Istanbul Archaeological Museum, in	**VII**: 297.
Ja 856	**VII**: 297.
Jār al-Labbā, of	**VII**: 297.
Onomastic Lists	**VII**: 297.
Votive Texts	**VII**: 297.
Sabaeans:	
Chronology	**II**: 205*(2).*

Sabaïsm: **IV**: 313; **V**: 152.
S'baita: **II**: 473.
Sabako: **II**: *74*, **82**.
Sabaoth:
Lord of **VIII**: 106, 110.
Sabbath(s): **I**: 406; **V**: **§439, 79-83**; **V**: 455, 513*(3)*; **VI**: 313, 654; **VIII**: 25; **IX**: **§439, cxxxv**.
Amurru and **V**: 82, 181, 191.
Ancient Sources, in **V**: 83.
Assyro-Chaldaean **V**: 169.
Babylonia and **V**: 82*(2)*, 175, 176, 181, 191.
Babylonian **V**: 175*(3)*, 176.
Babylonian Archaeology and the Jewish **V**: 82.
Barnabas, Epistle of, in **V**: 83; **VI**: 718.
Ceremonies, Two, Origin and Development of **V**: 82.
Christian **V**: 82.
Christian Sunday and Jewish **V**: 83; **VI**: 164.
Church Fathers and **VI**: 718.
Civilising the **V**: 81.
Claims of **V**: 79.
Classical Writiers and **V**: 82.
Course for Inductive Study **V**: 80.
Cuneiform Records on **V**: 80.
"Day After the Sabbath" **V**: 464.
Derivation of **V**: 82.
Development of, among the Hebrews **V**: 81.
Divine Origin of **V**: 79.
Doctrine of, in the Old and New Testaments **V**: 83.
Evaluation of **V**: 82.
Exodus, in **IV**: 265, 325; **V**: 80,
Extra-Biblical Evidence of the Primitive **V**: 81.
Fingernails, Custom of of Looking at, at the Outgoing of the Sabbath **V**: 82.
Fourth Commandment and **VI**: 164*(3)*.
Genesis, in **IV**: 265, 325; **V**: 80.
Hebrew **V**: 82.
Higher Criticism and **V**: 81.
History of **V**: 79.
Intitution of, before Moses(?) **V**: 79.
Jeremiah's Teaching on **IV**: 412; **V**: 82.
Jewish **I**: 365; **V**: 79, 82.
Jewish, and Christian Sunday **V**: 83; **VI**: 164.
Jewish, and Saturn **V**: 79.
Jews of Elephantine and **V**: *30*, 83.
Law of **V**: 80.
Laws and Usages **V**: 81.
Laws Concerning in OT **IV**: 252.
Lord's Day and **V**: 80.
Luther and **VI**: 164.
Midrashic Literature and **V**: 82; **VI**: 708.
Modern Assailants and **V**: 79.
New Moon **V**: 82.
Obligation of **V**: 79*(2)*.
Observance of **V**: 82.
Old Dispensation, under **V**: 80*(2)*, 81.
Old Testament, in **V**: 82*(2)*.
Origin of **I**: 414; **V**: 79*(2)*, 81.
Origin of, and Septenary Time **V**: 80.
Original Character of the Hebrew **V**: 81.
Physiology and **V**: 79.
Pre-Exilic and Exilic Times, in **V**: 82, *85*.
Pre-Mosaic **V**: 81*(2)*.
Prophecy and **IV**: 412; **V**: 82.
Qumran, Concept of, at **V**: 83; **VIII**: 416.
Qumran, Laws of, at **VIII**: 414.
Redemption of, Anticipation of **V**: 83; **VIII**: 197.
Samaritan **II**: 162.
Sapattu, the Babylonian **V**: 175*(2)*.
Saturn and the Jewish **V**: 79.

Septenary Time and the Origin of	**V**: 80.
Significance of	**V**: 83.
Source of the Biblical	**V**: 83.
Ugaritic Texts, Allusions to, in the Light of Midrashic Literature	**V**: 83; **VI**: 708; **VII**: 143.
Universality of	**V**: 79*(2)*.
War on the, Problem of, and the Second Temple and Talmudic Books	**VIII**: 235.
Week and the	**I**: 399.
Weekly	**V**: 79, 82.
Zadokite Document and	**I**: *215, 397;* **V**: 82; **VI**: 662.
Zadokites, Laws of	**VIII**: 414.
Sabbath Cycles:	**I**: 413; **V**: 195; **VII**: 144.
Sabbath Rest:	**IV**: 283.
Sabbath Schools:	
Biblical History in	**VIII**: 399.
Curriculum for Jewish	**VIII**: 399.
Hebrew, Teaching in	**VIII**: 401.
Sabbath Years:	
Maccabean	**II**: 188.
Sabbatical Cycle:	**V**: 195.
Sabbatical River:	**II**: 281.
Sabbatical Year:	**I**: *304,* 367, **§119**, **413**, 463.
Sabina:	**III**: *749*.
Sabinum:	**III**: *100, 199,* 213.
Sabkhat el-Bardawil, *see:* **Sirbonis, Lake**	
Sabni:	
Letters Concerning Crimes of	**VII**: 9.
Sabratha:	**III**: 258.
Sabtah:	**VI**: 54.
Sabteca:	**VI**: 54.
Sacaea:	**V**: 183.
Royal Substitution in ANE	**V**: 166.
Sachsenspiegel:	**VI**: 682.
Sack:	
Measure of Capacity	**I**: 426.
Sackcloth:	**IV**: 188.
Symbol of Mourning	**I**: 377.
Sacrament:	
Egypt, Usages and Ideas	**V**: 208, 209.
Old Testament Background of the	**VIII**: 383.
Sacred Writing, *see also:* **Canon**	
Bibles of the World	**V**: 144.
Connection between Jewish and Heathen	**VII**: 1.
Ethnic Scriptures	**V**: 145.
Euphrates Valley, from, Antiquity of	**V**: 162.
Sacred Letters	**VI**: 691.
Sacrifice List:	
Gennetic, in Athenian State Calendar	**I**: 406; **V**: 266.
Sacrifices, *see also:* **Offerings**	**I**: *474;* **V**: **§430, 56-64**.
Ancient, among Modern Semties	**V**: 58.
Ancient Religion in, and in Christian Sacrament	**V**: 58.
Angels Attendant at	**V**: 59; **VIII**: 156.
Animals, Selection of certain, by Israelites for	**V**: 57.
Antiquity of	**V**: 60.
Atoning, compared with Ethnic Religions, especially China	**V**: 61.
Babylonian and Indic, Ritual, Parallel between	**V**: 61, 148, 185.
Babylonian Ritual	**V**: 181.
Blood	**V**: 63*(2)*.
Blood, in Ezekiel's Temple	**IV**: 424.
Blood, Meaning of, in Sacrifical Offering	**V**: 58.
Blood, of the Old Testament	**V**: 62.
Cain and Abel's	**IV**: 299*(3);* **V**: 60, 62.
Carthaginian	**V**: 239.
Central Devotional Act in the Ritual of	**V**: 62.
Cessation of, After the Destruction of the Temple in 586 B.C.	**V**: 64.
Christian Theology and	**V**: 62.

Christianity and Judaism, in V: 41.
Decalogue and V: 60; **VI**: 158.
Deityless, in the Athenian State Calendar V: 264, 265.
Deuteronomy and Prophetic Attitude to V: 63.
Deuteronomy and the Centralization of **IV**: 351.
Deuteronomy, Sacrificial Legislation in **IV**: 350.
Divine Institution of V: 57.
Doctrine of V: 56.
Efficacy of Old Testament V: 63*(2)*; **VIII**: 195.
Egypt, Light from, on V: 59*(2)*, 142*(2)*.
Eleusis, Calendar of V: 265; **VII**: 344.
Elijah's, Place of **IV**: 381; **VI**: 228.
Expiatory V: 56.
Expiatory, Unscriptural V: 58.
Ezekiel and V: 60.
Firstlings and Other V: 59.
Foundation of **VI**: 167, 168.
"Gift" Element in V: 60.
Greek and Jewish Constrated in Theophrastus V: 61.
Greek, Prehistory of V: 262.
Greek, Public Appropriations for Individual V: 249.
Greek, Sacrificial Communion in Religion V: 249.
Hands, Laying on, of, as a Sacrificial Rite **I**: 367; V: 63.
Hebrew, and Prophetic Symbolism V: 61*(2)*; **VIII**: 244*(2)*.
High Places of, in Palestine and Petra V: 49.
Horse, in Antiquity V: 61.
Human, *see:* ***Human Sacrifice***
Idea of, Developed in OT V: 58.
Indic and Babylonian, Ritual, Parallel between V: 61, 148.
Infant, in Palestine **I**: 373; V: 66, 105.
Isaac of **IV**: 314*(2)*, 315*(3)*, 316*(3)*, 317*(3)*; V: 59.
Israelite Religion, Place in V: 60.
Jehovah's Protest Against the Altar Service V: 58; **VIII**: 273.
Jewish V: 56*(2)*, 57*(2)*.
Jewish and Greek Constrated in Theophrastus V: 61.
Jewish, and the Sacrifice of Christ **VIII**: 302.
Jewish, Cult, End of V: 64.
Jewish, Interpretations of V: 60.
Jewish, Origin of V: 57.
Jubilees and **VI**: 654.
Judaism and Christianity, in V: 41.
Judaism, Modern and V: 32.
Law, Sin, and in the OT V: 60; **VIII**: 179.
Laws Concerning in OT **IV**: 252; V: 58.
Marseilles Inscription, כלל and שלם כלל V: 58; **VII**: 83.
Meaning of, (in the OT) V: 62, 63.
Melchizedek's **VI**: 65.
Modern Judasim, Before Shrines V: 31.
Morality and V: 63*(2)*; **VIII**; 227*(2)*.
Mosiac and Pagan, Connection Between V: 57, 152.
Noah's **IV**: 303.
Obedience and V: 30.
Oblation and V: 60.
Old Testament, in V: 61*(2)*, 63, 64.
Organization, Problems of V: 63.
Origin and Development of the Idea of V: 57.
Origin and Purpose of V: 62.
Origin and Significance of V: 59.
Origin of, Among Semites V: 59.
Origins of Old Testament V: 61.
Pascal, Samaritan **II**: 162.
Perpetuity of the Ritual V: 56*(2)*, 60.
Place for V: 59; **VI**: 124, 145.

Place of, Assyrian **V**: 166.
Place of, Babylonian **V**: 166.
Priesthood and, in Judaism and Christianity **V**: 62.
Priests, and, in DDS **V**: 41, 62.
Priests, Israelite, relation to, Before the Exile **V**: 41.
Primitive **V**: 56.
Primitive, Origin of **V**: 57.
Primitive People, among **V**: 60.
Primitive Theory of **V**: 146.
Private, before the Day of Atonement **V**: 60.
Prophecy and **V**: 61; **VIII**: 243.
Prophetic Attitude to, and Deuteronomy **V**: 63.
Prophets and **II**: 105, 111*(4)*, 112; **IV**: 351; **V**: 58, 61, 62*(2)*.
Prophets, Salvation and **I**: 111; **V**: 62; **VIII**: 196.
Psalm 50, a Polemic Against Animal **VI**: 489.
Purpose of **V**: 62.
Qumran, at **VIII**: 414*(2)*, 415.
Rabbinic Judaism and **V**: 62.
Red Heifer, of **V**: 57.
Reinarch's, M., Theory of **V**: 60.
Religious Value of **V**: 62*(2)*.
Ritual of, Central Devotional Act in **V**: 62.
Roman, Evidence Against Table Fellowship in **V**: 270.
Salvation, Prophets and **I**: 111; **V**: 62.
Samuel and Law of **I**: 79; **V**: 59.
Semites, Primitive, Place of, among **V**: 59*(2)*, 160.
Semitic, of Reconciliation **V**: 59.
Semitic, Real Meaning of **V**: 58.
Sesostris, Attempted, of **II**: 91; **V**: 215.
Significance, Erroneous Theories of **V**: 57.
Significance of **V**: 59.
Significance of, Hebrew **V**: 60.
Significance of, in OT **V**: 58.
Snake, in Bahrain's Ancient Capital **V**: 63, 159.
Symbolism of **V**: 57.
Technical Terms for in OT **V**: 60.
Temple. Profile of a Theological Problem **V**: 64.
Temple, Rebuilding of, and Reintroduction of **V**: 62, 70; **VIII**: 246.
Terms, OT, of **V**: 391, 513.
Theoretical Speculations **V**: 64.
Vicarious Element in Primitive Semitic **V**: 58.
West-Semites, among **V**: 62.
Wine and Blood **V**: 61.
Word Studies on **V**: 57.
Yearly **V**: 64*(2)*.

Saddle: **I**: 258.

Sadducees: **V**: 98*(3)*, 99, **§451**, **100-101**; **VIII**: 436.
Angels, Belief in **V**: 100, 101; **VIII**: 158, 159.
Controversey with the Pharisees over the High Priest **V**: 44, 98, 100.
Excommunication of **V**: 101.
Jesus and **V**: 100.
Origin of the Name **V**: 99, 100.
Pharisees and **V**: 98*(3)*, 99*(2)*, 100*(5)*.
Qumran and the **V**: 100; **VIII**: 426.
Qumran, at **V**: 100; **VIII**: 410.

Safad: **II**: 301.

Safarad: **II**: 497.

Ṣafātic Texts: **III**: *719;* **VII**: **§920**, **291-292**.
Cairn of Hani **VII**: 292*(2)*.
Drawing and Text **VII**: 292.
Negev Inscription **VII**: 292.
Saudi Arabia, from **VII**: 292.

Safed: **I**: *256, 348(2);* **II**: 468; **III**: 445.
Geomorphological Studies **II**: 250, 301.

Sâfi, Tell es-: **II**: **468-469**.
Greek Cemetary Inscription from **VII**: 333.
Winepress at **III**: 571.

Safety Pins, *see:* **Fibulae**
Safut, Tell, *see:* **Sweileh**
Saga:
Archer, of, and the Legend of Sarpedon **V**: 264.
Elijah-Elisha **IX**: lxxxii.
Greek **V**: 697.
Hebrew **V**: 697.
Sagartians: **II**: 263; **V**: 542; **IX**: cx, cxiii.
Sages:
Babylonian Ut-Napištim Ruqu **VII**: 221.
Class Status and Leadership of: **I**: 193.
Egyptian **VII**: 10.
Methods of, in Teaching **V**: 115.
"Sayings of the Seven" in Ecclesiasticus **VI**: 623.
Social Ideas of: **I**: 187.
Talmudic **VI**: 705.
Saḫâb:
Anthropoid Clay Coffin from, Transjordan **III**: 548.
Sahara: **I**: *348;* **III**: *105.*
Sahidic, *see:* **Coptic**
Sahidic Bible, *see:* **Coptic Versions**
Sahidic Texts: **VII**: 293.
Saḫurê':
Stela Inscription of **VII**: 22, 67.
Sai: **III**: 213.
Saida: **II**: 469, 481.
Royal Necropolis at **III**: 533.
Sa'idiyeh, Tell es-: **II**: **469**.
Monument at **III**: 492, 493*(2).*
Sailors: **I**: *185, 351.*
Assyrian Word for **V**: 563.
Greek **I**: 339.
Hebrew Idiom of, in Israel **V**: 500.
Sails: **I**: 354.
Saints:
Latin Lives of Welsh and Breton, Biblical Citations not Vulgate, in **IV**: 40.
Most High, and Kingdom **V**: 449.
Old Testament, under the Law **I**: 475.
Sins of **VIII**: 180.
Sais: **II**: 2; **III**: 214; **VII**:*74.*
Monuments of **III**: 496.
Saite: **III**: *742(2).*
Saitic Period: **II**: *73.*
Saiyadeh: **II**: 284.
Sakçagözü (Sakce Gözü; Sakçegözü): **II**: 278*(2);* **III**: **214**.
Hittite Palace at **III**: 503*(2).*
Neo-Hittite Enclosure at **III**: 486.
Sakhrah: **V**: 71.
Sakje-Geuzi: **III**: **214**.
Sakjegeuzi:
Dado-Sculpture of **III**: 734.
Sculptures of **III**: 737.
Ṣaḳḳâra(h), *see also:* **Saqqâra** **I**: *312, 348;* **III**: **215**, *680;* **VII**: *25.*
Causeway of *wins* at **II**: 348.
Female Skeleton from **III**: 356.
Ḥaremḥab's Tomb at **II**: 44.
Pyramid at **III**: 504, 505*(2).*
Royal Tombs at **III**: 555.
Tomb of Bocchoris at **III**: 541.
Tomb of Tiy at **III**: 539, *645.*
Sakyol, *see:* **Pulur**
Sala(s): **V**: 226.
Ḫurrian Name of Constellation Virgo **II**: 230.
Šālaḫ: **V**: 195*(2).*
Salahiyeh,Tell: **II**: 469.
Salamander:
Assyrian word for **III**: 380; **V**: 568.
Salaminioi:
Greek Inscription of **VII**: 324.
Salamis: **III**: 214, **215.**
Salbit:
Samaritan Synagogue at **III**: 525.
Sale:
Concept of, in Talmud **I**: 307; **VI**: 693.
Field, of, conditions of **I**: 467; **VI**: 693.

Homeric World, in | I: 281(2), 502.
Land not to be Sold | VI: 126.
Salem: | II: 470.
ᵐᵀ ⳼ 𒁾 𒁹 Most High God of | V: 163; VII: 169.
Salford Museum: | III: 603.
Salganeus: | III: 185, 214.
Şalḥana: | III: 175, 214.
Saliagos: | III: 215.
Salihi: | II: 470.
Salim: | II: 283, 307, 315.
SALIMBENE DI ADAM:
Ecclesiasticus in the Chronicle of | VIII: 363.
Salmon:
Greek and Latin Terms for | III: 380, 382.
Snow in | VI: 495.
Salome, Queen: | II: 53, 82.
Saloons: | I: 237.
Salt: | I: 247, 286.
Covenant of | I: 509.
Curse, as | I: 287, 513.
Damaged caused by, at Karnak | II: 214.
Efflorescent, of unusual composition | II: 213.
Movement and Solution of at Mount Sodom | II: 249.
SALT, HENRY: | V: 362.
Salton Bataneos: | II: 290.
Salvador: | III: 215.
Salvation: | V: 513; VI: 307; VIII: §1015, 188-190, 194, 196.
Apocrypha, in | VI: 600; VIII: 59, 179, 188.
Avesta, According to | V: 233.
Christian Doctrine of | VIII: 181.
Common Basis for Jews and Gentiles | VIII: 333.
Divine Economy of | VIII: 215.
Faith, by, in the OT | VIII: 188.
Grace, by, in Job's Theology | VIII: 19, 189.

Grace, by, in the OT | VIII: 188.
Greek Idea of | V: 248.
Health and, in the OT | VIII: 184, 190.
Hellenistic Ideas in the Light of Ancient Anthropology | V: 251.
History of, see: Heilsgeschichte
Hosea, in | VI: 364.
Jewish and Christian Concepts of | VIII: 189(2), 191.
Jewish People in the Divine Plan of | VIII: 338.
Jews, is of the | VIII: 211.
Prophets, Sacrifice, and | I: 111; V: 62; VIII: 196.
Psychology of | VIII: 190.
Spaciousness in | VIII: 190.
Talmud, Soteriology of | VIII: 188.
Talmud, Teshuvah in | VIII: 197.
Universal | VIII: 188.
Salvation History, see: Heilsgeschichte
Sam'al: | III: 215, 265.
Samael: | I: xvii (n15).
Samannûd (Samanoud):
Temple of | III: 511.
Two granite sarcophagi from | III: 545.
Samaria: | I: 96, 146, 163, 418(2), 419; II: 188, 189, 284, 286, 292, 299, 303, 304, 305, 309, 385(2), 436, 443, 470-472; III: 420, 444, 446, 652, 668, 669, 681, 771(4); VII: 204.
Ahab's Palace at | I: 85.
Augusteum at | II: 471; III: 483.
Bronze Age Mounds in Northwest | III: 422.
City Gates of | II: 472.
Cult of the Dead in Ugarit and Israelite | V: 107, 193.
Cuneiform Tablet found at | VII: 187.

Doom of, in Amos	**VI**: 375.
Fall of	**II**: 470, 472; **IV**: 383; **VI**: 6.
Greek Inscription from	**VII**: 312.
Hebrew and Aramaic Potsherds from	**VII**: 125.
Israelite Stele Found at	**VII**: 93.
'Marissa' of Josephus' *Antiquities*, XIII, 275	**VI**: 682.
Stadium at	**II**: 471.
Strong Places of	**II**: 286.
Topography of	**II**: 470.
Samaria Ostraca:	**I**: *308, 492;* **VII**: *98, 99,* 136*(2),* 137*(6),* 145.
Date of	**I**: *426*.
Historical Background of	**VII**: 137.
Letter *Lamed* (ל) in	**VII**: 137.
Letter *Samek* (ס) in	**II**: 272; **VII**: 137.
Place Name*SPR* in	**II**: 272.
Ugarit, Administration in, and	**IX**: cii.
Samaria-Sebaste III:	**II**: 384.
Samarian (Samaritan):	**V**: **§529, 529**.
Assyrian and	**V**: 557.
Vowel-system	**V**: 529.
Samarian (Samaritan) Texts:	**VII**: **§868, 136-138**.
Beit el-Má Inscription	**VII**: 136.
Epic Poetry of the Alans	**VII**: 137.
Gaza, Inscription from	**VII**: 136*(2)*.
Lamp Inscription	**VII**: 137.
Leningrad Manuscript	**VII**: 137.
Liturgical Compositions, Tetragrammaton in	**VII**: 137; **VIII**: 124, 385.
Ostraca, *see:* ***Samarian Ostraca***	
Papyri	**VII**: 137.
Samaritan Language, *see:* **Samarian**	
Samaritan Chronicle:	**I**: 138; **VII**: 136, 138.
Samaritan Heresiarch:	
Dositheus	**VI**: 662.
Samaritan Inscriptions:	**VII**: 124.
Decalogue, of	**VI**: 159*(2)*.
Lamp with	**III**: 595.
Samaritan Literature:	**II**: 162; **V**: 141.
Hebrew and Origen's Secunda	**V**: 390.
Joshua, Book of	**VI**: 175*(6)*.
Leningrad Manuscript on the Commandments in the Torah	**VI**: 716.
Story of the Daughter of Amram. Parallel to the Story of Susanna	**VI**: 625.
Textual Criticism and, Tradition	**IV**: 7.
Samaritan Pentateuch:	**IV**: 3, 11, *14,* **§243, 20-23**, 30, 232; **VI**: 95, 120, 127, 139, 155; **VIII**: *117*.
Arabic Translation of	**IV**: 23*(2),* 43*(2)*.
Case of the Roll of	**IV**: 22.
Etymological Vocabulary	**V**: 529.
Exegesis of	**IV**: 96.
Genesis in	**IV**: 21, 268.
Higher Criticism and	**IV**: 23, 143.
Palaeographic Study	**IV**: 23.
Philological Questions	**IV**: 22.
Photographing of	**IV**: 23.
Scholia to Numbers and Deuteronomy, of	**IV**: 23, 43.
Samaritan Religion:	**V**: 141, 158, **§472, 228-229**; **IX**: **§472, cxxxvii**.
Sacred Law of	**V**: 228.
Samaritan Temple:	**V**: 70.
Sanballat and	**I**: 80; **IV**: 540; **V**: 228.
Tell-er-Ras and	**II**: 467; **V**: 71.
Samaritans:	**I**: *171(2),* 336, *369;* **II**: **162(‡)-163**; **IX**: cx.
Circumcision among	**I**: 386.
Customs of	**I**: 383.
Deuteronomy and	**IV**: 351.
Eschatology of	**I**: *377, 477;* **VIII**: 9, 252, 254.

Funeral Rites of — **I**: *377, 477;* **VIII**: 9, 254.
Jews, Relations with in the Persian Period — **II**: 163.
Law, and — **I**: *377, 477;* **VIII**: 9, 254.
Liturgy, and — **I**: *377, 477.*
Manuscripts, Dating of — **IV**: 99.
Messiah, Doctrine of the — **VIII**: 139, 140; **IX**: cxxxvii*(2).*
Messianic Expectation of — **V**: 127; **IX**: cxxxvii.
Moses, Doctrine of — **I**: 72.
Mourning Rites of — **I**: 375.
Passover among in 1861 — **I**: 385.
Passover of the — **II**: 162; **V**: 228*(8).*
Pentateuch, Exegesis of — **IV**: 96.
Pseudo-Philo and — **VI**: 678.
Religion of — **II**: 162*(2);* **V**: **§472, 228-229**.
Religion of Israel, Testamony to — **V**: 17, 228.
Scythian Religion and Epos, Survivals of, among — **II**: *163(2);* **V**: 229, 239.
Synagogue of, at Salbit — **III**: 525.
Talmudic Writings, in — **II**: 162; **VI**: 698.
Tatragrammaton, Pronunciation of, by — **VIII**: 124.
Temple of, *see:* ***Samaritan Temple***
Tetragrammaton in Liturgical Compositions — **VIII**: 385.
Theology of — **I**: *377, 477;* **VIII**: 9.

Sāmarrā: — **I**: *248;* **III**: *170, 175,* 215, *227.*
Sameias: — **VI**: 680.
Samian Tyranny: — **II**:*76.*
Samian Ware: — **III**: 616, 669.
Samieh: — **II**: 472.
Šammu-ramat: — **II**: *87.*
Samosata: — **III**: 216.
Samothrace: — **III**: **216-217**.
Building at — **III**: 486.
Greek Inscription from — **VII**: 324.
Greek Texts of L. Calpurnius Piso Caesoninus in — **VII**: 324.
Hieron in — **III**: 485.
Mystery Cult of — **V**: 240.

Samou: — **II**: **83**, 91; **III**: *462.*

SAMPEY, JOHN R.: — **IV**: 83.

Samsi-Adad:
Journey from Subat-Enlil to Mari — **IX**: xcv.

Samsi-Adad V: — **VII**: 187.

Samson: — **I**: **77-78**; **VI**: *173, 175, 184,* 189; **VIII**: 367.
Friend of — **VI**: 189*(2).*
Jaw-Bone of an Ass, and — **IV**: 369*(2);* **VI**: 189.
Mythical Elements in — **IV**: 368*(2).*
Rock Etam and — **IV**: 367; **VI**: 189.
Saga and the Myth of Herakles — **V**: 139, 247.
Shaving of — **VI**: 190.
Shemesh and — **I**: 78; **V**: 176.

Samson Agonistes: — **VIII**: 366, 367.

Samsuditana: — **I**: *411(2).*
Date List of — **IX**: xcviii.

Samsu-iluna: — **I**: 409*(2), 411;* **II**: *82,* **83**, *194;* **III**: *655;* **VII**: *251(2), 252,* 262, 270.
Bad-Tibira, Tablets from, and Reconquest of the South by — **VII**: 240.
Bilingual Inscription B — **VII**: 154, 236, 279.
Contemporary of Rîm-Sin — **II**: *82,* 83.
Date of — **VII**: 280*(2);* **IX**: xcviii*(2).*
Dated Texts and Date-Formulae from Reign of — **VII**: 239*(2)* .
Sippar Inscription of — **VII**: 153.

Samuabum:
Seal of — **III**: 648.

SAMUEL BEN MEIR, *see:* RASHBAM

Samuel, Books of: **I**: *334;* **VI**: *415*.

Ark, Cultic Use of the Story of, in **IX**: cxxxi, cxxxvi, cxlix.

Authorship, Authenticity of **IV**: 374, **§336, 375**.

Canaan, Indigenous Population, and Israel according to **IV**: 375.

Chronicles and **IV**: 373, 541.

Composition of **VI**: 192*(3)*.

Date, Sources, Authorship, Authenticity of **IV**: 374, **§336, 375**.

David in **I**: 89.

David, So-Called Biography of, in **IV**: 358.

Duplications of, in Chronicles **IV**: 359, 374, 542, 544.

Ethics of **IV**: 373.

Exegetical Studies on **VI**: **§597, 191-192**.

Greek Translators of **IV**: 374.

Hebrew Weights in **I**: 422.

Historical Narratives, Delimitations of **IV**: 374.

Historical Trustworthiness **IV**: 373.

Israel, Use of the Name in **IV** 327.

Josephus' Text of **IV** 6.

Judges, Ruth and, Form one Book **IV**: *367*, 374, *509*.

Kennedy, A. R. S., on **IV**: 376.

Legal practices in **I**: 468; **IV**: 375; **IX**: c.

Literary Criticism of **IV**: **§335, 373-375**; **VIII**: 391; **IX**: **§335, cxxxi**.

Midrash in **IV**: 374.

Monarchy, Setting up of **IV**: 374.

Parallels to Chronicles and Kings **IV**: **§327, 359-361**, 380*(2)*, 544.

Propaganda, Davidic, in **IV**: 375.

Qumran Texts (4QSam) **VIII**: **§1101, 444**.

Religious Ideas / Values in **IV**: 373*(2)*.

Ruth and **VI**: 556.

Septuagint Version of **IV**: 373.

Sinai Syriac MS 35, of **IV**: 46.

Solomonic Apologetics in **IV**: 358.

Sources E and J in **IV**: 250, 373.

Sources of **IV**: 373, **§336, 375**.

Spirit of God in **IV**: 373.

Textual Studies on **IV**: 6.

Topography of **II**: 253, 283; **IV**: 358.

Two, in English Bibles **IV**: 101.

Yahweh Ṣeḇa'oṯ in **IV**: 375; **VIII**: 125.

1 Samuel: **I**: 160.

Anti-monarchial passages in **IV**: 375, 377.

Bibliography of **I**: **§13, 11***(2)*.

Book-Study of **VIII**: 387.

Exegetical Studies on **VI**: **§598, 192-207**.

Greek Translator of, Exegetical Methods **IV**: 36.

Habiru ('ibrim) in **I**: 160; **IV**: 377.

Literary Criticism of **IV**: **§337, 375-377**.

Sahidic Coptic Text of **IV**: 44.

Septuagint Translator of, Methods Used by the **VI**: 192.

Unity of the Narratives in **IV**: 376*(2)*.

2 Samuel:

Acts 13:33-37, *Pesher* on **VI**: 211; **VIII**: 290.

Ark, Narratives on **IV**: 377.

Book Study of **VIII**: 387.

Chonological Order, Parts of, not in **IV**: 377.

Date of, from Levitical Laws, and Psalms **IV**: 377.

Exegetical Studies on **VI**: **§599, 207-218**.

Greek Text of, Exegetical Principles Underlying (2 Sm 11:2 -1 K. 2:11) **IV**: 107.
Juridical Parable (The Poor Man's Ewe-Lamb) **IV**: 378; **V**: 702.
Literary Criticism of **IV: §338, 377-378.**
Promise, Great in (2 Sam 7) **IV**: 377.

Samuel, Books of, Manuscripts of: **VI: §600, 218.**
Coptic (Sahidic) of 1 Samuel **VI**: 218*(2)*.
Exegetical Principles Underlying 2 Samuel - 1 Kings **VI**: 218.
Greek Text, Fragment of **VI**: 218.
Greek Translator of 1 Samuel **VI**: 218.
Greek Translators of the Four Books of Kings **VI**: 218.
Papyrus Text of 1 Samuel **VI**: 218.
Peshitto of 2 Samuel **VI**: 218.
Variants in the Consonantal Text of G.I. **VI**: 218.

Samuel Cycle Wall Decoration at Dura-Europa Synagogue: **III**: 524.

Samuel, Person: **I**: *72*, **78-79**, *97, 106, 464;* **II**: *465(5);* **IV**: *415;* **VI**: 192; **VIII**: 388, 391*(4)*.
Accession and Rule of **IV**: 374.
Administration of **VIII**: 388.
Administration of, Times Before the **VIII**: 388.
Ark of the Covenant and **V**: 55.
Ark, Priesthood and **V**: 41, 55.
Authority, Evolution of, in Israel and **I**: 484; **IV**: 376.
Biblical Canon in Time of **IV**: 202.
Confessions of, "Lost" **VI**: 701.
Kingship, Denunciation of, and Ugarit **VI**: 196; **VII**: 268.
Monarchy and **I**: 484; **IV**: 374, 376; **IX**: ci.
Name **V**: 295, 304. 454.
Prophetic Element connected with **VIII**: 391.
Saul and **IV**: 374, 376, 377.
Saul and, Story as Drama **VIII**: 369.
"Schools of the Prophets" and **I**: 116*(3)*.
Shiloh, Sactuary at, and Samuel sleeping in **V**: 56.

Sān: **I**: 433; **III**: *33*, 83, 443.

San el-Hager, *see also:* **Tanis:** **III**: 217, *246(2)*.

San Lorenzo f.l.m., Rome: **III**: 212.

San Panteleo: **III**: *170*.

San Pietro: **I**: 341.
Ancient Shipwreck at **I**: 341; **III**: 453.

San'a:
Ḥimyaritic Inscriptions discovered near **VII**: 294.

Sanathana Dhrama: **I**: 182; **II**: 142; **V**: 159; **VI**: 56.

Sanballat: **I**: **79-80**; **IV**: 540.
Nehemiah and **VII**: 136.
Samaritan Temple and **I**: 80; **IV**: 540; **V**: 228.

Sanbuki, Codex: **IV**: 10.

Sanchuniaton (Sanchunyâtôn): **V**: 569; **VII**: 119.

Sanctification: **VIII: §1020, 198-199.**

Sanctity:
Greek Defensive, Sumerian Provenience of **V**: 185.

Sanctuaries: **III: §193, 507-522; V: §426, 46-50; IX: §193, cxiii-cxiv.**
Apollo, at Kourion **III**: 477, 515.
Arad, of, and the Family of Hobab the Kenite **V**: 49; **VI**: 131.
Artemis in Thasos **III**: 519.
Asklepois, at Corinth **III**: 514.
Athenian Agora, Triangular, in **III**: 521.
Bab ed-Draʿ, Early at **II**: 292; **III**: 419.

Central, Idea New in Time of Josiah(?) **V**: 13.
Demter, of, on Acrocorinth **III**: 520.
Deuteronomy, Central and Local in Pre-Exilic Israel **IV**: 352; **V**: 49.
Deuteronomy, Central of **IV**: 347.
Deuteronomy, in / of **IV**: 349, 350; **V**: 52.
Deuteronomy, Two Descriptions of, in **IV**: 349; **V**: 52.
Hygieia, at Corinth **III**: 514.
Israel, Pre-Exilic, in (Central and Local) **IV**: 352.
Isthmian **III**: 518.
Jewish, in Babylonia **V**: 48; **VI**: 582.
Jewish, of 'Ain Duk **V**: 48.
Lesbos, at, for Zeus, Hera, and Dionysus(?) **III**: 152.
Lucania, Heraion of **III**: 515.
Malophorus, Cult of, at Selinus **III**: 486.
Metaphor for Scripture **VI**: 671.
Mycenae, Classical, near **III**: 520.
Mycenaean, at Amyclae **III**: 516.
Nabataean, at 'Avdat, Stonedressers Marks **III**: 476, 477.
Nabataean, near Petra **III**: 519.
Naphath-Dor: A Hill(?) **V**: 49.
Nemi, Votive Chamber at **III**: 516.
Old Testament, in **V**: 48.
Poseidon's, at Isthmia (Corinth) **III**: 66, 517, 518; **V**: 262.
Pyrgi In Etruria, at **III**: 520.
Qasr Bint Far'un, at **III**: 521.
Qsar Bint Fur'un at Petra, Architecture and Sculpture of **III**: 477.
Risqeh, Arabian, at **V**: 239*(2)*.
Sumerian Word for **III**: 467.
Theseus of, in Athens **III**: 520.
True Idea of **V**: 50.
Tuthmosis III, Built by, at Deir el-Baḥri **III**: 521.
Zeus Madbachos on the Djebel Shêkh Berekât **III**: 509.
Sanctuary: **V**: 513.
Sand:
Ceremonial Use of **V**: 157.
Gibraltar, Report on, from **III**: 106.
Israel, Coastal Plain of, Rate of Accumulation of **II**: 244, 249, 298.
Sandahannah, Tell: **II**: **473**; **III**: *663, 760*.
Greek Inscriptions from **VII**: 315*(2)*, 342.
Magic Lead Figures from **VII**: 342.
Sandalwood: **I**: 338; **III**: 192.
SANDERS, HENRY: **IV**: 30.
Sandstone: **I**: 280, 290; **III**: 460, 562, *762*.
Sanduarri:
King of Kundi and Sizû **II**: 83.
Saneha: **VII**: 8.
Story of **VII**: 8, 9.
Sanehat:
Story of **VII**: 15, 32.
SANFORD, D. K. **V**: 623.
Sangallensis 912, Codex:
Hebrew Words in the Latin Glossary of **V**: 392.
Sanhedria: **III**: 553, 554.
Sanhedrin (Synedrion): **I**: 465*(5)*; **V**: **§452, 101**.
Ancient, or Academy **V**: 101.
Competence of **V**: 101.
Elders and **V**: 78.
Existence at Time of Jesus **V**: 101.
Gospels, in **VI**: 682.
Greek Jewish Literature, in **VI**: 676.
Josephus, in **VI**: 682.
Nasi of **V**: 45, 101.
Nasi of, and Titles of the High Priest **V**: 45.
Philo, in **VI**: 676, 682.
President of **V**: 101.
Revival of, Necessary for Modification of the Halaka(?) **V**: 101; **VI**: 693.
Sankhere: **II**: 18, 61, **83**.

Sanskrit:
Comparative Mythology, Hebrew Terms Explained by
Conditional Sentences in V: *626, 664.*
Delbrück on Subjunctive and Optative in V: *629.*
Greek, Latin, and Teutonic compared with V: 275*(2).*
Greek Participle *ἄρ, ῥά,* Equivalent in V: *630.*
Hittite *atša = tatas* V: 606.
Purpose Clause in, Origin V: *631, 666.*
Relationship to Persian, Khan-i- Arzu on V: 678.
Vowels, Prothetic, in V: *633, 668.*
Santa Barbara Museum of Art: III: *631.*
Santorini: III: 217.
Saparda: III: 217.
Sapattu:
Babylonian Sabbath V: 175*(2).*
Sapor I: II: *11,* **83**; III: *519.*
Alexander the Great, and II: 11.
Sapphire: I: 285.
Sappho:
Aphrodite and V: 265.
Prayer of, to Aphrodite V: 257.
Saqqâra, *see also:* **Ṣaḳḳara(h)** I: *380;* II: *73, 214, 215;* III: **217- 218**, 267, *358, 554(2), 597;* V: *210.*
Aramaic Papyrus VII: 131.
Heracleopolitan Period at VII: 25.
Sixth Dynasty Letter from VII: 9
Tombs 3070 at III: 559.
Tombs near the Serapeum at III: 559.
Saracens: IX: cx.
Saraçhane: III: **218**, 267.
Saracos:
Loan-Tablet dated to the Seventh Year of VII: 193.
Saradanapalus:
Letter of Šamaš-šum-ukîn to VII: 179.
Sarafend:
Bronze Age Tomb from III: 555.
Sarah: I: *66,* **80**; IV: 315; VI: 60, 69.
Hysteria of VI: 615.
Sarai, *see:* **Sarah**
Saramel-Asaramel *see:* **Asaramel**
Sarapis: III: *9(2),* 519*(2).*
Alexandria and V: 221*(2).*
Kline of V: 243, 260.
Origin of the Cult of V: 188.
Saras Plain: III: 223.
Sarçhane: III: 265.
Sarcophagus: III: **§196**, **530-561**; VII: 147, 269.
Aḫîrâm, King of Byblos, Reliefs on Sides of III: 554, 556.
Alexander, of III: 530.
Belzoni, Egyptian Text on VII: 38.
Clazomenæ, Painted, from III: 546.
Coffer of the Great Pyramid, of III: 536.
Corinth, at III: 545.
Etruscan III: 541.
Etruscan, of Torre San Severo in Orvieto III: 543.
Gaza, Old, at III: 540.
Granite Fragments from III: 549.
Granite, in a Ramasside Tomb III: 549.
Granite, Two, from Samannûd, Egypt III: 545.
Great Pyramid, in, Dementions III: 504.
Jewish III: 543.
Jewish, Ancient III: 409, 530.
Jewish at Haifa III: 533.
Lead, "Loop Pattern" Decoration of III: 548, 697.
Liquid found in, of Ptʒḥ-špss, at Saqqara II: 215.

Marble, Sculptured, from Caesarea **III**: 545.
Mit-Rahîna, from **III**: 549; **VII**: 66.
Osimandya, of **III**: 530., 777.
Pa-Ramessu, of **II**: **72**, *92;* **III**: 544.
Pitane, Painted, from **III**: 558.
Ramessu, inner, from Medinet Habu **III**: 551.
Roman, Four, in America **III**: 556.
Royal from the XVIIIth Dynasty **III**: 549.
Saïte Tomb, Method of lowering sarcophagus lid **III**: 551.
Saitic Period, of the **III**: 532.
Sennemūt, of **VII**: 69.
Serapeum, Inscribed in **III**: 545; **VII**: 64.
Sidon, of **III**: 530, 533*(3)*, 534.
Symbolism and **VIII**: 305.
Tut-ankh-amen, of **III**: 546.
Unknown Queen, of **III**: 539.
Wâdy Yasûl, from Tomb at **II**: 404.

Sardinia: **I**: 325, **II**: *427;* **III**: 14, *23*, **219**,*757*, *763;* **V**: *285*.
Antas, Punic Site in **III**: 14; **VII**: 121.
Babylon, Connection with **III**: 41.
"Tombs of the Giants" in **III**: 540.

Sardis: **III**: *203*, **219-221**, 225, 264*(4)*, 265, 266*(2)*, 267,*730;* **IX**: cxii.
Animals, Osteological Investigation of, from **III**: 367.
"Byzantine Shops" at **III**: 527.
Geometric Pottery in **III**: 620.
Greek and Latin Inscriptions from **VII**: 318.
Greek Inscriptions from **VII**: 319*(4)*.
Horsemen from **III**: 712.
Kybebe and Artemis: Anatolian Goddesses at **V**: 227.
Lydian Trench at **III**: 222*(2)*.
Mnesimachus Inscription **VII**: 318.
Obadiah and **VI**: 388.
Sculptures, Three, from **III**: 746.
Sepulchral Stele, Greek Inscription **VII**: 334.
Synagogue at **III**: 222*(2)*, 527*(3)*, 528.
Tomb, Date Assigned to **III**: 551.
Vases from **III**: 607.

Sardius stones: **I**: 285.

Sarepta, *see:* **Sarafend**

Sargon (I) of Akkad: **II**: *54. 66,* **83-84**,*93;* **III**: 6; **IV**: *244;* **V**: 556; **VII**: 153, 187, 236, 306.
Annals of **VII**: 153.
Atlas of Empire of **II**: 266; **VII**: 156.
Cappadocia, Battles in **II**: 84.
Chronology of the Reign of **II**: 83*(2)*.
Empire of in Babylonian Geographical Treatise **II**: 84.
Inscription of **VII**: 152*(2)*, 235.
Jareb,Original Name of(?) **II**: 84.
Legend of, Opening Lines **VII**: 175.
Mentioned by Ḫattušili I of Ḫatti **VII**: 153, 307.
New Stele of **II**: 84.
Northern Campaigns of **II**: 84.

Sargon II: **I**: *86, 87, 90, 91, 95;* **II**: *83(2), 84,* **85**, *88(3), 92(2), 102(2), 115, 178, 180, 183, 190, 191(2);* **IV**: 181; **VI**: 239; **VII**: 159.
Campaign against Ashdod **II**: 85, 324.
Campaign against Assur **II**: 85.
Campaign against Judea **II**: 85.
Eighth Campaign **II**: 85*(4)*.
Isaiah and **IV**: 214.
Isaiah, in **II**: 85.
Letters from Sennacherib to **VII**: 178.
Sin of **II**: 85.
Stele of, from Ashdod **VII**: 190.

Sargon-Yareb: **II**: 85.
Sargonid Period:
Political, Relgious and Social Antiquities of **V**: 561, 573; **IX**: cxlii.
Sarid: **II**: 284.
Ṣarīnu **VII**: 186.
Saris:
Greek Inscription at **VII**: 314.
Phoenican Inscription at **VII**: 116.
Sculpture Cave at **III**: 538.
Saris Cave: **III**: *602*.
Sarona:
Meteorological Observations in **II**: 237*(6)*, 238*(5)*, 240.
Temperature, Air, at **II**: 240.
Sarpedon: **V**: 264.
Sarsechim: **VI**: 340.
SARTON, GEORGE: **II**: *231*.
Sasanian: **V**: 236.
Sasr Bint Far'un: **II**: 462.
Sassanian Inscriptions: **VII**: 373.
Sassanians: **III**: *44*.
Sassanian Remains found in Central Mesopotamia **III**: 142.
Sat-aah:
Queen of Tothmes III **II**: **85-86**.
Satan, *see also:* **Devil** **VI**: 26; **VIII**: 69, 159, **§1009**, **162-165**, 195.
Apocalyptic Literature, Extra-Biblical, in **V**: 120; **VIII**: 163.
Azazel and **IV**: 343; **VIII**: 163.
Death of **VIII**: 163.
Fall of **VIII**: 159, 162*(3)*, 164.
Fallen Angel(?) **VIII**: 162.
Human Origin for **VIII**: 164.
Identified as the Serpent in Wisdom of Solmon **VI**: 632.
Personality of **VIII**: 162.
Psychological Standpoint **VIII**: 163.
Science and **VIII**: 164.
Solomon and **VI**: 224.
Satire:
Babel as **VI**: 58.
Roman **I**: *190(2)*.
Satrap: **V**: 513.
Satrapes: **V**: 193.
Satrianum: **III**: **223**.
Saturn:
Planet **II**: 229.
Satyr:
Satyr-Play on Hydria by the Niobid Painter **III**: 611.
Saucer(s):
South Arabian Tripod Offering **III**: 580.
Saudi Arabia: **III**: 197*(3)*.
Saul: **I**: *79*, *89*, **96-97**; **IV**: 222, 374; **VIII**: 388*(2)*, 391*(4)*; **IX**: lxxxii.
Age of **IV**: 198.
Armed Forces of Israel under **I**: 318.
Browning, Robert, on **VIII**: 361, 362, 364, 365, 367.
David and **IV**: 376; **V**: *20*.
David's Introduction to, Historical Difficulties in **IV**: 375.
David's Lament over **VI**: 207*(6)*.
Death of **IV**: 374.
Downfall of **IV**: 374.
Election of **IV**: 374; **VI**: 192.
Elegy on the Death of **VI**: 191.
Gibeah of **II**: 280, 377*(5)*, 378*(2)*.
Gilboa, Mt., Battle of, Strategy of **IV**: 377.
Grace of God and **VIII**: 196.
Hachish Use by(?) **I**: 96*(2)*; **III**: 404*(2)*; **VI**: 200*(2)*, 328.
Last Battle of **IV**: 359, 374, 542.
Prophets, Among the(?) **VI**: 203.
Pseudo-Philo's **V**: 129; **VI**: 678.
Rachel's Tomb, Saul at **VI**: 198.

Reign of	**I**: 160, 161; **IV**: 374.
Rejection of	**I**: 97; **IV**: 375; **VI**: 192; **VIII**: 193.
Samuel and	**IV**: 374, 376, 377.
Samuel and, Story as Drama	**VIII**: 369.
Saul-David Sayings	**VI**: 191.
Witch of Endor and	**IV**: 375, 376.
Zuph, Journey of, to	**VI**: 196*(3)*.
SAULCY, LOUIS FÉLICIEN JOSEPH CAIGNART:	**II**: 281, 351, 424.
SAUNDERS, TRELAWNEY:	**II**: 308.
Saushshatar:	
Letter of	**VII**: 165.
Saviour:	
Old Testament	**VIII**: 127.
Saviour-King:	**VI**: 264.
Sawâma:	
Cemeteries at	**III**: 223.
Saws:	
Flint	**I**: 280, 290; **III**: 460, 562, 673.
Pull, in Egypt	**III**: 675.
Sawwan, Tell es-:	**III**: **223**, *768*.
Animals Bones from	**III**: 368.
SAYCE, ARCHIBALD HENRY:	**I**: 140; **II**: *137;* **IV**: 126, 210; **VII**: 84.
Babyonian Flood Story	**VII**: 225*(2)*.
Daniel, on	**IV**: 528.
Higher Criticism and	**IV**: 250; **VI**: 61.
Life and Contributions of	**I**: 24.
Pentateuchal Criticism, on	**IV**: 251.
Sayings:	
Numerical, in the OT, a form-critical study	**V**: 693.
Twisted—Mizpah	**VIII**: 366.
Scandinavia:	
Italy, Earliest Communications between	**IX**: xcv.
Oral Tradition School	**IV**: 158.
OT, Contributions to	**IV**: 154.
Phoenician Colonization in	**IX**: xcvi, cx.
Scapegoat, *see also:* **Azazel**	**IV**: **§318, 343-344**; **VI**: 123*(2)*.
Assyro-Babylonian	**V**: 175.
Babylonian Religion, in	**V**: 178.
Epistle of Barnabas and	**VI**: 717.
Hitties, among	**IV**: 344; **V**: 225.
Mountain of	**II**: 308.
Scarabs:	**I**: *330, 420;* **III**: 643, **§216, 666-671**, *681, 734;* **VII**: 66.
Ahmes, of	**III**: 667.
Amenophis III, Historical	**III**: 669.
Amenophis III, "Kirgipa"	**III**: 670.
'Amman, from	**III**: 657, 670.
'Amman, from Tombs at	**III**: 659, 670.
Amuletic	**III**: 580, 668.
Canaanite	**III**: 670.
Cypriote Inscription on	**III**: 642.
Entomology of	**III**: 365, 668.
Exhibiting, New Method	**III**: 669.
Gem Pictures	**III**: 670.
Gezer, from	**III**: 667.
Graeco-Phoenican, from Byblos	**III**: 669.
Heart, of the Mnevis Bull	**III**: 668.
Hyksos	**III**: 668, 670.
"Ka" on	**III**: 668; **V**: 207.
Middle Kingdom	**III**: 668.
New Kingdom	**III**: 668.
Palestinian	**III**: 668*(2)*.
Phoenician Bes-Hand	**III**: 667; **V**: 204.
Samaria, from	**III**: 668.
Sennar, from	**III**: 670.
Shechem, from	**III**: 670*(2)*.
Ship-wrecked	**III**: 670.
Tel Aviv, found in a cemetery near	**III**: 670.
Tell Duweir, from	**III**: 669*(2)*.
Thutmosis IV, Historical	**III**: 669.
Thutmosis IV, Physico-Chemical Examination	**II**: 214; **III**: 669.
Vizier Mont(u)hotp, of	**III**: 671.
Scarioth:	**II**: 284.

SCARTH, JOHN:
  Exodus, View of — **IV**: 332.
Sceptres: — **I**: 467; **III**: **§217, 671**; **III**: 682.
  Holder from Beth Eden — **VI**: 377.
  Origin of — **III**: 671.
SCHAEFFER, C. F. A.: — **IV**: 218.
SCHECHTER, S.: — **VI**: 604.
SCHEDL, CLAUS: — **IV**: 532.
Scheide Papyri: — **VI**: 361*(5)*.
SCHEIL, V. — **VII**: 208.
Scheming King:
  Merodach-Baladan as — **I**: 62.
Schenochori: — **III**: 20.
SCHICK, CONRAD: — **II** : 355; **VII**: 314.
SCHLIEMANN, HEINRICH: — **III**: 111, 123, 172*(2)*, 256.
  Life and Contributions of — **IX**: lxxxi.
  Trojan Researches — **II**: 171; **III**: 259*(2)*, *649*.
SCHMID. R.: — **V**: 64.
SCHMIDT, JOSEPH W.: — **II**: 189.
SCHMIDT, MORIZ:
  Cypriote Inscriptions of — **VII**: 356.
Scholars, Ancient Near Eastern and Biblical: — **VIII**: 403.
  Bibliography of — **I**: **§42, 18-22**; **IX**: **§42, lxxxi**.
  Lives and Contributions of — **I**: **§43, 23-24**; **IX**: **§43, lxxxi**.
Scholarship:
  Assyrian, Fragments of — **VII**: 181.
  Biblical, Changing Emphasis in — **IV**: 154.
  Biblical, Motives of — **IV**: 149.
  Conservative Tendency of Old Testament — **IV**: 139.
  Dead Sea Scrolls and the Status of Biblical — **VIII**: 435.
  France, Contributions to OT — **IV**: 148.
  Germany, Contributions to OT — **IV**: 147.
  Great Britian, Contribution to OT — **IV**: 147.
  Groundless Attacks on Oriental — **IV**: 131.
  Jewish, and Christian Silence — **VI**: 687*(2)*.
  Jewish 'Influence' on Christian Biblical — **IV**: 96.
  Mediaval Christian, Hebrew Heritage of — **IV**: 96.
  Modern Biblical and the Adult Bible Class — **VIII**: 399.
  Old Testament — **VIII**: 407.
  Old Testament, in Prospect — **IV**: 155.
  Old Testament Scholars, Present Tasks for — **IV**: 151.
  OT and the Church — **IV**: 156.
  OT Study in the Netherlands — **IV**: 157.
  Problems and Trends in Biblical — **IV**: 157.
  US Contribution to OT — **IV**: 147.
Scholastic Exegesis:
  Jewish Midrashim and — **VI**: 708.
School House:
  Babylonian, Excavation of — **I**: 230*(2)*, **III**: 481.
  Bethlehem, Iron Age Remains from — **II**: 338.
Schools:
  Alexandrian — **I**: 121*(2)* .
  Bible in Public, *see:* ***Bible, Public Schools, in***
  Egyptian — **III**: 779.
  Egyptian, "Universities" — **III**: 779.
  Neo-Babylonian Grammatical School Text — **VII**: 220.
  Old Testament, Use of, in Non-Christian — **VIII**: 402.
  Rabbinical — **I**: 231.
  Religion in Secondary — **VIII**: 406*(2)*.
  Sumerian — **VII**: 272.
Schools of the Pharaohs: — **III**: 778.

"Schools of the Prophets": **I: §50, 116-117.**
Samuel and I: 78, *116.*
SCHRADER, EBERHARD: **IV**: 182.
SCHULTZ, HELMANN: **VIII**: 2.
SCHÜRER, EMIL: **I**: 140*(2).*
Apocrypha, on **VI**: 599.
Jewish Law, on **I**: 473*(2).*
SCHUTZE, MARTIN: **VIII**: 364.
SCHWABE, M.: **II**: 340.
Science:
Ancient Oriental Civilization, in **II**: 223.
Archaeology and **II**: 220; **III**: 416, 423, 433.
Babylonian **II**: 223, 224.
Bible, and **IV**: 165, 196*(4),* 303.
Bible, in the Light of **IV**: 148.
Bible Lands and Modern **IV**: 161.
Biblical Inerrancy and **III**: 331; **VIII**: 24, 25.
Biblical Theology and a Scientific World View **VIII**: 12.
Christianity, Impact of, on **VIII**: 407.
Classification of, in Mediaeval Jewish Philosophy **V**: 111.
Creation and **III**: 325*(2),* 329, 330; **IV**: 274, 275*(2),* 277, 282; **VIII**: 79.
Creation as a Doctrine of **VIII**: 75.
Egyptian **I**: *189,* 266, *332;* **II**: 224.
Egyptian "Scientific" Texts **VII: §834, 33-35.**
Faith and **III**: 293, 300*(2),* 301, 302*(3),* 303*(2),* 304, 322*(2),* 325.
Genesis and **III**: 291, 298, 301, 305, 308, 323*(3);* **IV**: 263*(2),* 264, 266, 269*(2),* 271*(2),* 283*(2),* 292; **VI**: 22.
Genizah Fragment on **VII**: 107.
Greek **II**: 223.
Greek, Abstract, Rise of **II**: 223.
Greek, Problems and Methods in Early **II**: 223.
Hebrew **II**: 223.
Hexaemeron, and **IV**: 278, 279.
Higher Criticism and **IV**: 137.
Limitations of **III**: 325.
Metals and Early **I**: 299; **II**: 223.
Miracle and **VIII**: 91, 93.
Moses and **III**: 314; **IV**: 278; **VI**: 719.
Philosphy and **VIII**: 5.
Prayer and **VIII**: 201.
Prayer, Christian Idea of, and **VIII**: 201.
Preliterate Societies and **I**: 125; **II**: 223.
Religion and **III**: 284, 287, 290*(3),* 291, 292*(2),* 298, 302*(3),* 326; **VIII**: 348.
Revelation and **II**: 179; **III**: 283, 284*(3),* 287*(2),* 291, 292, 293, 295*(2),* 303*(3),* 306, 319; **IV**: 276, 288, 297, 331, 332; **VIII**: 29, 30, 54.
Skepticism of **IX**: cxx.
Sophistry and **II**: 222.
Supernatural and **III**: 300.
Survival of Babylonian Methods in Exact, in Middle Ages **II**: 224.
Theology and **III**: 288, 291, 300, 304, 325, 329; **VI**: 22; **VIII**: 5.
Science and the Bible *see also:* **§291, OT, Historical Reliability** **III: §169, 283-331; IV**: 198; **VIII**: 24, 26; **IX: §169, cxx-cxxi.**
Science, Biblical: **IV**: 146.
Method of Advance in **IV**: 134.
Ultimate Problems of **IV**: 144.

Scientific Method:
- Artistotle's Conception of — **II**: 223.

Scientific Studies, Modern, on the ANE and OT — **II**: **§153, 212-222**; **IX**: **§153, cxii.**
- Cuneiform Tablets, New Method of Copying — **II**: 214.
- Liquid, Report on Sample from small jar — **II**: 213.

Scientific Thought:
- Biblical Interpretation and — **IV**: 89.
- Greek, early, and mysticism — **II**: 233; **V**: 263.

Scientific Thought in the Ancient Near East: — **II**: **§154, 222-224.**

Scientists:
- Babyonian — **I**: 298, 401; **II**: 223, 231; **III**: 402.
- Genesis I Discussed by — **VI**: 25.
- Hebrew — **I**: 298, 401; **II**: 223, 231; **III**: 402.
- Thucydides as — **II**: 101.

Scienza Nova: — **V**: 240.

Scimitar: — **III**: 680; **VI**: 216.

Scione: — **III**: *161,* 223, *257.*

Scopus: — **II**: 473.
- Tomb Discovered on Mt. — **III**: 536.

Scorpion: — **III**: 380*(2), 699, 718;* **V**: 165; **VI**: *349.*

SCOTT, R. B. Y.: — **I**: 437.

Scottish Meteorological Society: — **II**: *236.*

"Scourge" of Osiris: — **I**: 482; **III**: 671.

Screen:
- Chancel, from Ashdod — **III**: 527.
- Marble, Decorated — **III**: 740.

Scribe(s): — **I**: *49, 186,* 231, 235, 270*(3),* 271, 272, *465;* **II**: *54;* **VI**: 636.
- Egyptian Epithet for — **IX**: cxxxix.
- Ezra as — **I**: 44*(4).*
- Interpretation of OT — **IV**: 95.
- Isaiah as — **I**: 49.
- Louvre, at, Name of — **III**: 730.
- Schoolboy (Egyptian) — **VII**: 10.
- (Sheva), of David — **I**: 271, 465; **V**: 301.
- Soldier-Scribe (Egyptian) — **VII**: 79.

Scribes as a Religious Group: — **V**: **§453, 102**; **VI**: 690.
- New Tesstament of, and the Dead Sea Scrolls — **VIII**: 480.
- Palestine, of — **V**: 102.
- Righteousness of — **V**: 98, 102; **VI**: 668*(2).*

Scripta Helladica: — **V**: 286.

Scripture, *see also:* **Bible; Old Testament; New Testament** — **V**: 513; **VIII**: 25.
- Athenasius on Tradition of — **VI**: 727.
- Authentcity of — **VIII**: 22.
- "Defiling the Hands", as — **IV**: 206.
- Divine Origin of — **VIII**: 21*(3),* 22, 40.
- Divine Revelation as — **VIII**: 29.
- Exploration as Verifying — **IV**: 209, 275.
- Exposition of — **VIII**: 23.
- God-Breathed — **VIII**: 24.
- Greek Language and — **VIII**: 315.
- Haggada within — **IV**: 261.
- History and Language of, Oriental Research and — **IV**: 209.
- Inerrancy of — **VIII**: 21*(2),* 22, 44.
- Infallibility of — **VIII**: 51.
- ***Interpretation of, and the Qumran Community*** — **VIII**: **§1082, 422.**
- Metasphysics of — **VIII**: 85.
- Misquotations of — **VIII**: 359, 361.
- Public Reading of — **VIII**: 378, 379*(2),* 380*(12),* 381.
- Revelation as Divine Element in — **VIII**: 31.

"Sanctuary" as a Metaphor for — **VI**: 671.
Spanish Orientalisms Compared with — **VIII**: 360.
Tradition and — **IV**: 207; **VIII**: 28.
Tradition and, in the Hebrew Community — **VIII**: 51.
Unity of, and the Post-Exilic Literature — **IV**: 389.
Unmeant Meanings of — **VIII**: 370.
Voice of God, as — **VIII**: 23.

Scrolls:
Writing a Scroll of the Law — **I**: 384.

Sculptors: — **I**: 269.
Egyptian Portrait, Studio — **III**: 728.
Master of Olympia (Paionios) — **III**: 738.
Myuron — **III**: 728.
Nameless, 5th Century — **III**: 749.
Shen, Stela of — **VII**: 24.
Sirē', Stela of — **VII**: 22.

Sculpture, *see also:* **Figures, Head, Statuary** — **III**: **§226, 720-754**; **IX**: **§226, cxxvii**.
Achaemenian — **III**: 740, 748.
Aigisthos, Death of — **III**: 752.
Akkadian — **III**: 738.
Akrolithic — **III**: 753.
Amman, from — **III**: 742.
Ancient, in Great Britain (New Michaelis) — **III**: 744, 745, 746, 747.
Aphrodite, Hellenistic — **III**: 746.
Arabia Felix, from — **III**: 744*(2)*.
Architecture, Etuscan, and — **III**: 470.
Argive Aeraeum, from — **III**: 722.
Aristotle's Theory of — **III**: 695, 724.
Assurbanipal, of — **III**: 751.
Assyrian — **III**: 733, 741.
Assyrian, Mammalia of — **III**: 364, 694, 720.
Assyrian, Ring and Rod in, Meaning of — **III**: 725.
Athenian Thought and Life as Reflected in Parthenon — **I**: 209; **III**: 727.
Attic — **III**: 741.
Babylonian — **III**: 720.
Babylonian, First Dynasty — **III**: 753.
Babylonian, Ring and Rod in, Meaning of — **III**: 725.
Babylonian, Small, from Tombs — **III**: 762.
Bassae, Lost Pedimental — **III**: 737.
Bassai — **III**: 738, 739*(2)*
Classical — **III**: 731.
Colossus, Unfinished on Mt. Pendeli — **III**: 478*(2)*.
Corinth, from — **III**: 726, 740, 742.
Corinthian, Terracotta — **III**: 741, 743.
Cypriote — **III**: 744.
Damophon and — **III**: 699.
Daphne, Torso from — **III**: 722, 723.
Darius, of, at Behistan — **III**: 739.
Diodorus, by — **III**: 736.
Distribution of, in Eastern Mediterranean — **III**: 749.
Egyptian — **III**: 705, 728, 742.
Egyptian, 7th Century — **III**: 738.
Egyptian and Greek, Affinity and Difference — **III**: 749; **V**: 222, 264.
Egyptian, Male Figure in — **III**: 750.
Egyptian, Middle Kingdom — **III**: 731.
Egyptian, Old Kingdom — **III**: 738, 740.
Eretria, from — **III**: 723.
Etruscan — **III**: 470, 739, 747.
Etruscan, at the Boston Museum of Fine Arts — **III**: 750.
Ewe's — **III**: 741.
Fibulae Represented on — **III**: 573.
Figures, near Kânâ — **III**: 722*(2)*.
Fogg Art Museum — **III**: 744, 766*(2)*.
Greek — **III**: 705, 720, 723, 724, 725, 726*(2)*, 727, 733, 746.

Greek, 7th Century **III**: 739*(2)*.
Greek and Egyptian, Affinity and Difference **III**: 749; **V**: 222, 264.
Greek, at the Boston Museum of Fine Arts **III**: 750.
Greek, Chronology, Correlated with Vase Painting **III**: 713, 742.
Greek, Development of **III**: 699*(2)*, 721, 736.
Greek, in Ptolemaic Egypt **III**: 731.
Greek, Male Figure in **III**: 750.
Greek, Polychromy **III**: 525, 723, 739.
Greek Sculpture Crowns and Crown Inscriptions **III**: 460.
Greek, Stone and Metal in **III**: 752, 758.
Greek, Style **III**: 741.
Greek, Technique of **III**: 697, 734.
Greek Temple **III**: 722.
Greek Torso **III**: 728.
Greek, Wounded Figures in **III**: 705, 751.
Hekatompedon, Thematic Unity in **III**: 744.
Hellenistic, Aphrodite **III**: 746.
Hephaisteion, Pediment and Acroteria **III**: 518, 519, 745*(2)*.
Heraion of Hucania **III**: 735.
Hittite, near Sindjirli **III**: 721.
Italic Warrior, Sequence **III**: 746.
Italy, from, 5th-4th Centuries, B.C. **III**: 738.
Jonah Monument in the New York Metropolitan Museum **VIII**: 354.
Kallistratos, of **III**: 745.
Koptos, from **III**: 723.
Laocoon Group, Vatican **III**: 747.
Lion Figures in Anatolian Seljuk Architecture **III**: 378, 478.
Lion, Greek, at Didyma **III**: 378, 743.
Lion, Polychrome from Babylon **III**: 377, 724.
Marble, Boston Museum of Fine Arts, at **III**: 726.
Marbles, Ancient **III**: 624, 625, 626, 627, 744, 745, 746, 747.
Mejdel, at (Greco-Egyptian) **III**: 723.
Mesopotamian, Leonine **III**: 742.
Metopes, from a Terentine Naiskos **III**: 754.
Meydûm, from **III**: 734.
Michaelis, New Edition of **III**: 744, 745, 746, 747.
Modern, Debt to Greece **VIII**: 355.
Mountain-God at Eflatun Pinar **IX**: cxxvii.
Na'aneh, Stones from **III**: 723.
Nabataean Dolphins **III**: 750.
Nemi (Lake), from **III**: 726.
Nimroud Marbles **III**: 720.
Nimrud, from **III**: 7563.
Odysseus, in Boston **III**: 743.
Old Women, Two, of **III**: 741.
Painting, Relationship between in Greece **III**: 714, 746.
Palmyrene, in Beruit **III**: 735.
Parthenon, Fragments **III**: 726.
Parthian, from Hatra **III**: 743.
Philosophic Allegory(?) **III**: 745.
Ptolemaic **III**: 741.
Ptolemaic Portait Coins, Style on **I**: 449; **III**: 742.
Qsar Bint Far'un at Petra **III**: 477, 753.
Rock **III**: 725*(3)*; **VII**: 148.
Roman **III**: 727, 746.
Roman, at the Boston Museum of Fine Arts **III**: 750.
Roman Portrait **III**: 728.
Roman, Redating of **III**: 729.
Sakjegeuzi, Dado **III**: 734.
Sakjegeuzi, of **III**: 734, 737.
Sardis, Three, from **III**: 746.
Semitic Babylonian King, Sharkalisharri(?) **III**: 728.
Septuagint, Errors in, from which they were derived **VIII**: 354.
Shargalisharri(?), Semitic Babylonian King **III**: 728.

Sicily, from, 5th-4th Centuries, B.C. **III**: 738.
Slab, in the Berlin Museum **III**: 732.
Stamata, Finds at **III**: 238.
Sumerian **III**: 732.
Symplega **IX**: cxxvi.
Syria, in **III**: 724, 725.
Talking, Weeping and Bleeding. History of Religious Fraud **V**: 157.
Terracotta, from Minturnæ **III**: 756.
Tomb, Chinese and Egyptian, Compared **III**: 727.
Tomb, from Palmyra **III**: 732.
Vulgate, Errors in, from which they were derived **VIII**: 354.
Wood, "Strainger from the East" **III**: 750.
Zeus Herkeios, Thematic Unity in the Hekatompedon **III**: 744.
Zeus Temple, of, at Olympia, Panhellenism in **III**: 477, 753.
Zeus *(Ζευς Ἡλιοπολιτης)* **III**: 722.

Scyllias: **I**: 268.

Scyphus, *see:* **Bowls**

Scythia: **II**: *201;* **III**: 223.

Scythians: **I**: *94, 163, 165;* **II**: **163**; **III**: *181.*
"Ἄβιοι, as **VII**: 2.
Antiquities of, in Europe **III**: 568.
Artifacts of the **III**: 566.
Ateas, King of **II**: 23.
Religion **II**: *163(2).*
Religion, Survival of among Samaritans **II**: *163(2);* **V**: 229, 239.

Scythopolis, *see also:* **Beth Shan** **I**:*454;* **II**: 284, 340*(2)*, **473**.

Sde Nehemiah: **II**: 303.

Se Girdan: **III**: 125.

Se-Renpu:
Tomb of **III**: 533.

Sea:
Distribution of, on Earth's Surface According to Hebrew Sources **II**: 256.
Hebrews and the **I**: 323; **VI**: 181.
Transportaton by **I**: 340, 341*(3)*, 347, 348, 354, 355.

Sea of Reeds, *see:* **Red Sea**

"Sea Peoples", *see also:* **Libyans**: **I**: *369(3);* **II**: 2, 148, **163-164**; **VII**: 14.
Caucasian Relations of **II**: 2.
Merenpaṯh and **VII**: 14.

Seafaring, *see:* **Navigation**

Seal (Animal):
Egypt, in **III**: 380.

Seal-Cutter: **III**: 654.

Sealand: **III**: 18*(2)*.

Seals and Signets (includes Impressions) *see also:* **Stamps** **I**: *92, 234, 310, 317, 356;* **III**: *553,* **§214**, **640-661**; **IX**: **§214**, **cxxv**.
Abigad, of **III**: 660.
Accadian **III**: 640.
Acemhöyük, from **III**: 658.
Achaemenian impressions **III**: 652.
Achbor, of **III**: 657.
Adad **III**: 659.
Ægean Sealstone, with Linear Signs **III**: 654.
Ahab **III**: 653.
Aijalon, from **III**: 657*(2)*.
Akkadian, Cylinder **III**: 658.
Altaic Cylinders **III**: 641.
Amah, Slave-Wife's **III**: 652.
'Amman, from **III**: 652, 657*(2)*, 659.
Ammonite **III**: 653, *666*.
Amulet **III**: 652.
Anatolia, from **III**: 13.
Ancient Unpublished **III**: 657.

ANE, in Fitzwilliam Museum **III**: 656.
Arad, from **III**: 659.
Aramaean **III**: 640.
Aramaic **III**: 656, 657.
Asia Minor, from **III**: 650.
Asiatic, Western, in the Haskell Oriental Museum **III**: 648.
Asiatic, Western, in the Walters Art Gallery **III**: 651.
Assyrian Adam and Eve? **III**: 649, 650.
Assyrian, Cylinder **III**: 642, 648.
Assyrian, in Anatolia **III**: 661.
Assyrian, Liturgical Elements in **III**: 648; **V**: 164.
Assyrian, Royal **III**: 654, 658.
Babylonian **III**: 646*(3)*, 647, 648, 653, 655, 657, 659; **VII**: *261*.
Babylonian, Classification **III**: 652.
Babylonian, Crystal **III**: 661.
Babylonian, Cylinder **III**: 640*(2)*, 642*(2)*, 644, 645, 646, 647, 648*(2)*.
Babylonian, "Human Sacrifice", on **III**: 641*(2)*.
Babylonian, Liturgical Elements in **III**: 648; **V**: 164.
Babylonian, religious interpretation of **III**: 647; **V**: 181.
Babylonian, Sun-God on **III**: 641*(2)*.
Bactrian Seal-Inscription **III**: 657.
Balaṭah, from **III**: 657*(2)*.
Basha Enzu, of **III**: 648.
Brak, Cylinder, from **III**: 653.
Brak, from **III**: 655.
Bullae from Acco **III**: 661.
Bullae, Inscribed, from Daskyleion-Ergili **III**: 656.
Bullae, Inscribed, from Daskyleion-Ergili **III**: 670.
Burnaburiash, Royal **III**: 643.
Button-Seals, God. **III**: 648.
Byblos, Cylinder **III**: 657, 659.
Cappadocia, Haematite Cylinder, from **III**: 643.
Cappadocian **III**: *586*, 647, 651, 659.
Cappadocian, Rein in **III**: 656.
Cappadocian, "Signet Royal" **III**: 703; **VIII**: 307.
Cassite **III**: 647*(2)*, 648.
Caucasian **III**: 648.
Chaldean **III**: 640.
Cheops' **III**: 645.
Chronology of, at Knossos **III**: 658.
Clay Sealings, XIII Dynasty, Uronarti Fort **III**: 655.
Cretan, and Linear B Inscriptions **III**: 658.
Crete(an) **III**: 69, 657*(3)*, 658, 659, 660; **VII**: 362, 363.
Crete, inscribed terra-cotta **III**: 660.
Cylinder, Crete and **III**: 69, 660.
Cylinder, Cypriote, Late Bronze Age **III**: 653.
Cylinder, Cyprus, and Early Glyptic Art **III**: 661, 671, 706.
Cylinder, Eastern Mediterranean Area Impressions **III**: 656.
Cylinder, from Palestine **III**: 653.
Cylinder, from So. India **III**: 652.
Cylinder, in Biblioteca Vaticana **III**: 651.
Cylinder, inscribed with both Hieroglyphic and Cuneiform **III**: 647.
Cylinder, of Uruk period **III**: 652.
Cylinder, Royal **III**: 648.
Cylinder, Seal 8361 in Nationalmuseet Kobehaven **III**: 649.
Cylinder, with Alphabetic Inscription **III**: 654; **V**: 288.
Cylinder, with Phoenician Inscription **III**: 640, 641.
Dan, from **III**: 657.
Egyptian **III**: 644, 646*(2)*, 648.

Egyptian, Cylinder **III**: 641, 643*(3)*, 644, 646*(2)*, 667*(2)*, 686.
Egyptian Signet **III**: 644.
Egyptian Temple **III**: 650.
Elamar, of **III**: 650.
Elath, Jotham, from **III**: 656.
False, or Genuine, at Andrews Univeristy **III**: 660.
Gedaliah (Lachish) of **III**: 651.
Gehazi, with Name of **III**: 643.
Genuine or False, at Andrews Univeristy **III**: 660.
Gezer, Jar-Seals from **III**: 663.
Gods, of the **III**: 650.
Greek, of the "Geometric" Period **III**: 648.
Haʿîr or*Yehûd* **III**: 656.
Haematite Cylinder **III**: 653.
Haematite, from Cappadocia **III**: 643.
Haematite, in Asia Minor **III**: 641.
Haggai, of **III**: 642, 643; **V**: 289.
Hananiah, Signet of **III**: 648.
Hebrew **III**: 644*(2)*, 651*(3)*, 652*(3)*, 653*(4)*, 654*(3)*, 655, 657, 660, 661, *665*.
Hebrew, *ʿEbed* Class **III**: 650.
Hebrew, Alphabet used on Jar **V**: 289.
Hebrew, from Samaria **III**: 652.
Hebrew, from Tell Jemmeh **III**: 656.
Hebrew, in a Gold Ring **III**: 652.
Hebrew, Reign of Ahaz **III**: 651*(3)*.
Hebrew Signet-ring **III**: 653.
Hebrew Signets **III**: 646, 647*(2)*.
Hebrew, with Family Emblem **III**: 658.
Himyaritic **III**: 640.
Hittite **I**: *420;* **III**: 640, 641, 642*(2)*, 643, 645*(3)*, 647, 650, 656, 658, 659, 660.
Hittite Word for **V**: 612.
Impression, Dated **I**: *336*.
Impression, Harding Smith Collection **VII**: 210.
Impressions, from Abydos **III**: 645.
Impressions from Nimrud **III**: 654, 657.
Impressions from Tomb 107, Kurnub (Mampsis) **III**: 561.
Impressions, Palestinian **III**: 654.
Impressions, Private-Seal and Semantics **V**: 475.
Indian Style, found at Ur **III**: 649.
Indo-Sumerian **III**: 648.
Indo-Sumerian Cylinder **III**: 650.
Iovanoff **III**: 642.
Iran, from **III**: 654.
Israelite, **III**: 652.
Israelite, from Tell Duweir **III**: 650.
Italian Signets **III**: 647.
Jamdat Nasr, Drill-Worked **III**: 655.
Jehovah, Name of, on **III**: 644.
Jericho, Impression from, and Treasurers of the Second Temple **III**: 655; **V**: *78*.
Jezebel, of **III**: 658.
Jordan, Inscribed, from **III**: 660.
Judean, Royal **III**: 650, 656.
Kassite **III**: 651.
Kayseri, Afyonkarahisar allegedly from **III**: 658.
Khyan, Sealing of, from the Shephela **III**: 658.
Knossos, and Linear B Inscriptions **III**: 659.
Kültepe, from **III**: 670.
Kurnub, from **III**: 661.
Lachish, from **III**: 651, 652, *664*, *665*.
Lapis-Lazuli, Trade of **III**: 660.
Larissa Kremaste, Bronze State **III**: 650.
Layard Collection, from **III**: 654.
Malatya, allegedly from **III**: 658.
Mallia, Hieroglyphic Script, from **III**: 660.
"Manasseh Son of the King", of **III**: 657.

Mannu-ki-Inurta, of **III**: 658.
Manufacture of, and the Tomb of Thŷ at Sakkara **III**: 539, 645.
Mesopotamian **III**: 649.
Mesopotamian, Cylinder **I**: *332;* **III**: 654.
Mesopotamian, Cylinder, Symbols of Gods in **III**: 655; **VIII**: 306.
Minoan **III**: 647, 659, 661.
Moabite **III**: 647, 652.
Morgan Seal 652 **III**: 661.
MṢH Impressions **III**: 656.
Mt. Gilboa, Impressions from **III**: 655.
Mycenaean **III**: 657, 659; **VII**: 364.
Nebi Rubin, Seal-Weight **III**: 656.
Neo-Babylonian, with Phoenician Inscription **III**: 647.
Nimrud, from **III**: 654.
Ninth Century, from Shadikanni **III**: 654.
Obadiah, of **III**: 640.
Ophel, from **III**: 642*(2)*, 643; **VII**: 103.
Ophel, Signet from **III**: 643*(2)*.
Oriental **III**: 641, 642, 652*(2)*.
Oriental, Bird Worship Represented on **III**: 459, 641, 645.
Oriental, Henry Peek's **III**: 642*(2)*.
Oriental, Tiamat and other Evil Spirits on **III**: 642.
Palestinian **III**: 658.
Pehlevi Seal Inscriptions **III**: 649.
Pepi Ist **III**: 643.
Persian, Cylinder **III**: 647.
Petra, from **III**: 657.
Phoenician **III**: 642, 645, 656, 659, 660, 661.
Ptolemaic clay-sealings **III**: 645.
Qosanal (Quas'nl), of **III**: 650, 651
Royal, in Ancient Israel **III**: 653.
Šmryw, of **III**: 658.
Sakje-gözü, Drawings of **III**: 654.
Sargonid **III**: 650; **V**: *170.*
Sargonid, Ur 364 **III**: 656.
Sasanian Clay Sealings **III**: 660.
Seal before God **III**: 648.
Seven-Fold Division of the Sacred Tree **IX**: cxxv.
Shechem, from **III**: 657*(2)*.
'Shema' Servant, of Jeroboam, Date of **III**: 656*(2)*.
Subbi-luliuma, of **VII**: 306.
Sumerian Art and **III**: 650.
Sumerian, Cylinder, with Handle **III**: 659.
Sumerian, Impression from Megiddo **III**: 650.
Syrian **III**: 645, 646, 651, 652, 655*(2)*, 658, 569
Syrian Glyptic **III**: 658.
Syro-Phoenician **III**: 660.
Tarcondemus of (?) **IX**: cxliii.
Tarkondemus, of (?) **III**: 641; **VII**: 232, 305.
Tarqumuwa, of **III**: 650.
Tell Billa, from **III**: 649.
Tell Duweir, Sealing from **III**: 669.
Tell ed-Duweir, from **VII**: 84.
Tell es-Sulṭûn, (Jericho) from **III**: 655*(3)*; **V**: 78.
Temple Treasury, Post-Exilic **VII**: 124.
Terra Cotta **III**: 640*(2)*.
Thebes, Cylinder from **III**: 658.
Thebes, Reading of a Seal Inscription **III**: 658; **VII**: 215.
Thumouis, Clay Sealings from **IX**: cxxv.
Trojan, from Ilios **III**: 649.
Ugarit, Royal, from **III**: 656.
Ur, Cylinder from **III**: 642.
Ur, from, Interpretation of **III**: 655.
Ur, Impressions from **III**: 273, 649; **VII**: 210*(2)*.
Ur, Indian Style, found at **III**: 649.
Ur, Seal-Cutter from, Greek Influence of **III**: 642.

Ur-^{d}Lugal-edin-na, of **III**: 399, 647.
Use of **III**: 640.
Userkerē, of King **III**: 648.
Western Asia, Cylinder, from **III**: 646.
Western Asia, Royal, from the XIIth Dynasty **III**: 660.
Winnirke's Cylinder **III**: 652.
Yeshaʿ yahu, of **III**: 657.
Seaports, *see also:* **Harbors** **I**: 354, 355*(2)*.
Egyptian, Earliest **I**: 24.
Seasickness: **I**: 351.
Greek and Latin Writers, in **I**: 351; **III**: 397.
Seasons:
Egyptian Personifications of, Middle Kingdom **VII**: 38.
Hebrew, four month **I**: 405.
Hittite Words for **I**: 403.
Phoenician Bowls, Depicted on **II**: 234.
Sabbatical Cycle or Seasonal Pattern(?) **V**: 195; **VII**: 144.
Seat(s):
Parthenon Frieze, on **III**: 582.
Stone, at El Ḥamme **III**: 582.
Stone, at Nablus **III**: 582.
"Seat of Moses" *see:* **Synagogue Worship**
Seating, Solemn: **I**: 367.
Seattle Art Museum: **III**: *632*.
Seb (Egyptian God): **V**: 201, 202.
Great Cackler **V**: 201*(2)*, 355, 360.
Seb'a Rujum: **II**: 473.
Sebakh: **I**: *312;* **II**: *76;* **III**: *493, 587, 680, 708.*
Altar for Human Sacrifice, from Edfu **V**: 48.
Sebara: **VI**: 692.
Gamara Quotations in **VI**: 703.
Methods of **VI**: 704.
Separation of the Gemara from **VI**: 704.
Sebastia (Sebaṣṭyeh): **II**: 299; **III**: 423.
Sebekh: **VII**: *15*.
Sebknofru:
Co-regencies of, with Ammenemes III, IV and Sebekḥotpe **II**: *15,* 16, 86.
Sebustiya: **I**: 444; **V**: *256*.
"Second Coming":
Christ, of, and the Servant of Isaiah **IV**: 400.
Second Commonwealth: **I**: 178, 183, 469, 470.
Secrets of Enoch, *see:* **2 Enoch**
Sectarianism:
Patristic Accounts of Jewish **VI**: 723.
Shittic Elements in Jewish **V**: 144*(2)*.
Secularization:
Hammurapi, Process of under **I**: 191.
Legacy from the Old Testament(?) **VIII**: 353.
Old Testament Roots of **V**: 29.
Secunda, *see:* **Origen**
Sed Festival: **I**: *279;* **V**: 212, 221*(2)*, 222, 223*(2)*.
Pasht and **V**: 203.
Roman Army and **V**: 270.
Sedar Olam:
Calendar of **I**: 404.
Sedeinga: **III**: 105, **224**, *236*.
Ṣedeq / Moreh haṣṢedeq: **V**: 108, 109, 130, 188.
Seder, *see:* **Passover**
Sedimentation:
Nile, above Wadi Halfa during last 20,000 years **II**: 251.
Wadi Musrara, in **II**: 244.
Sedra *see:* **Sidrah**
Sedra, Sidra:
Seven Pairs of **VI**: 716.
Seduction:
Code of Hammurabi on **I**: 478, 496.
Seed:
Treading of by swine **I**: 252.

Seeding:
Rates of — I: 254, 424.
SEELY, PAUL A.: — III: 353.
Seers, *see* **Prophets**
Sefarad: — II: 497; III: *22*, 236.
Sefer Ha-Kabbalah: — I: *136(2);* VI: 684*(2)*.
Sefer Ham-Mebaqqesh:
Cain and Abel Passage in — VIII: 369.
Sefer Okalah w' Oklah:
Source of Biblical Textual Variants — IV: 6.
Sefer Yetzirah:
Tetragrammaton and — VIII: 124.
Sefirah: — I: 366.
Sefire Treaty Inscriptions: — I: 514; VII: 85, 129*(2)*, 130, 131.
Seghol: — V: 477.
Segor: — II: *380*, 474, *482*.
Segregation:
God, of, in Jeremiah — VI: 325.
Sehel: — VII: *62*.
Graffiti at, from the Reign of Queen Hatshepsut — VII: 13.
Seḫetep-ib-rē':
Stela of — VII: 22, 23.
Sehetepibre Pedubastis:
Monuments of — II: 86; III: 498.
Şehy Höyük:
Seidi-Sheher(-Göl): — III: 258.
Seilûn, *see also:* **Shiloh** — II: 309, 474; III: 422, 423; IX: cxviii.
Seir, Land of: — II: 358, *460*.
Seir (Se'yr), Mount: — I: *200;* II: *131*, *142*, 284, 474.
Seirah: — II: 290.
Seirath: — II: 474; VI: 179.
Seismology:
Theology and — VIII: 4.
SEIXAS, JAMES: — V: 468*(2)*.
Seḵenenrē' Tao II: — II: *7*.
Sekhem-ka-RA: — II: *56*, 86.
Statue of — VII: 72.
Sekhemrē'-sewadjtowĕ Sebkḫotpe: — III: *743*.
Altar of, at Sehēl — V: 217.
Bas-relief of — VII: 70.
Sekhmet:
Stele with Hymn to — VII: 41.
Sekhmet-Ubastet:
Statuettes of — III: 763; V: 212.
Sekhmet-mer:
Stele of — VII: 20.
Sela, *see:* **Petra**
Selah: — IV: 481, **§388**, **492**; V: 440*(2)*.
Lost, and Psalm 85:9(8) — IV: 492; VI: 505.
"Reverential Prostration", as — IV: 492.
Selçikler (Sebaste): — III: 267.
Selenkaḫiye, Tell: — III: 224.
Plant Remains from — III: 386.
Seleucia: — II: *152;* III: *9*, *61*, *70(4)*, **224**, 439, *763*, *764*.
Seleucia Pieria: — III: 224, 225.
Seleucids: — I: 489; II: *152*, **164**, *205*.
Legal Text of — VII: 251.
Religious Policy of, and Dura — III: 516; V: 258.
Self: — VIII: 173.
Other and, in Rabbinic Ethics — VIII: 227.
Self-Discovery:
Bible as an Aid to — VIII; 350.
Self-Help:
Hebrew Law and — I: 468.
Jewish Law and — I: 467, 502.
Roman Law and — I: 467, 502.
Self-Sacrifice: — VIII: 227, 230.
Selge:
Greek Inscriptions from — VII: 329.
Selinus: — I: *245;* III: *190*, 225; VII: 348.
Malophorus, Cult of — III: 486; V: 266.
Sellem: — II: 284.
SELLIN, ERNST: — II: *395*.
Semachontis: — II: 292; V: 657.

Semantics:
- Hebrew **III**: *659;* **IV**: 97; **V**: 387.
- Old Testament and **V**: 279.
- Old Testament Theology and **VIII**: 5.
- Private Seal-Impressions and **V**: 475.
- Theologians, for **IV**: 93, 111.

Semempses: **II**: *21,* **87**.

Semiazas (Angel): **VI**: 650.

Semiramis: **II**: 7, **87**.
- Adad-nirair III and **II**: 7, 87; **VII**: 191.
- Assyrian Parallel to an Incident in the Story of **VII**: 187.

Semites: **I**: 143, *181, 296,* 330, *463, 487;* **II**: 3, *135, 138,* **164-166**, *168, 169;* **III**: 338*(2);* **VI**: 54; **IX**: cx*(2)*.
- Blood-Feud among **I**: 480.
- Customs, Survival of Old **I**: 386.
- Kinship of gods and men among early **VIII**: 168.
- Mining Expeditions to Sinai, in **I**: 291.
- Origin of **V**: 305; **IX**: cx.
- Pre-Semitic Populations in Semitic Lands **II**: 1.
- Religion of the **V**: 9.
- Sacrifice among West- **V**: 62.

Semites, Modern:
- Ancient Sacrifice among **V**: 58.
- God, Concepts of, among **I**: 384.
- Local Divinities among **I**: 384.
- Man to God, relation of among **I**: 384.

Semitic: **V**: 513.
- Crete, Ancient, in **VII**: 364.

Semitic Languages - General - Grammar: **§498, 372-381**; **IX**: **§498, cxxxix**.
- Accusative Suffix *-nî* **V**: 378.
- Adverbial *u* in **V**: 378.
- Analogy in **V**: 374*(3)*.
- Arabic Dialects and the Problem of Formation of **V**: 381.
- Aramaic *z* for Semitic z_1 and *d* **V**: 377.
- Aryo-Semitic Kinship **V**: 278, 375.
- Bound Structures **V**: 379.
- Case Ending Structure **V**: 381.
- Case-Endings **V**: 378.
- Case-endings, Origin of **V**: 375.
- Causative Formations **V**: 377.
- Cognate to Akkadian "Suhaut" / שְׁחִי or שְׁחוּ **V**: 379.
- Comparative Semitics **V**: 379, 380*(2)*.
- Conjugation, "Causative" **V**: 377.
- Conjugation, ת in **V**: 372, 486, 522, 523, 554, 558, 585.
- Conjugations, Derived, in **V**: 377.
- Consonants, Emphatic, in **V**: 374*(2),* 377.
- Demonstrative element *z* in Hebrew **V**: 484.
- Diphtongs, Developement **V**: 377.
- Dot Diacritical in **V**: 375.
- Dot Disjuncitve in **V**: 375.
- Dot Grammatical in **V**: 375.
- Dot Vocalic in **V**: 375.
- Egyptian a (?) **V**: 309.
- Egyptian Comparisons with **V**: 365, 379.
- "Elative" in West-Semitic **V**: 549.
- Elements w-, p-, 'p-, p'- **V**: 380.
- Encyclopedia Britannica, in **V**: 373.
- Feminine Ending *(a)t* in **V**: 374.
- Feminine Ending *T* in **V**: 374.
- Fronting of *g* in, and the *(qāl-gāl)* Dialect Split in Arabic **V**: 381.
- Gentive, Genetic Aspects **V**: 379.
- Gentivie, Ending of **V**: 376.
- Grammar, Comparative, with Assyrian **V**: 372.
- Grammar, Problems of **V**: 373, 377.
- Growth of Language, taken from **V**: 279.
- Hebrew Bible and Semitic Lexicography **V**: 405.

Hemzah-h in	V: 376.
Hipthpa'el, Durative: A *tan-* Form	V: 378.
Hittite ḫar-aš-zi, Semitic Affinities of	V: 378.
iau in	V: 375.
Idenity of	V: 378.
Imperative in	V: 378.
Imperfect Tense Stem - First Vowel of	V: 374.
Indo-European (Ayran), Relationship	V: 372*(3)*, 373*(4)*, 600.
Intensive, So-Called, in	V: 377.
Interchange of ה and א	V: 375.
Internal Passive in	V: 375.
Inverative -t- in, and the Hebrew Hithpa'el	V: 379, 490.
Jussive **yaqt'ul* in Proto-Semitic	V: 380, *553*.
Laryngeals	V: 378.
Lexicons, Comparative	V: 379.
*mḫṣ/*mḫš* in Ugaritic and	V: 378.
Modal Development of the Verb	V: 373.
Modal Ideas in	V: 372.
Nasals, Misinsertion of	V: 376.
Negative in	V: 374, 497.
Noun-formations, Intensive, Alleged	V: 376.
Particle *ḥ*, in	V: 377.
Particles in	V: 305, 376*(2)*.
Passives in	V: 376.
Perfect **y'aqtul* in Proto-Semitic	V: 380, *553*.
Periodical devoted to	**III**: *775;* V: 373.
Personal Pronouns	V: 373.
Philology and Hebrew Grammar (Survey of)	V: 375‡.
Philology and Linguistics, Conflict between in	V: 380.
Philology, Comparative	V: 376*(2)*.
Phonology, Sonority, Principle of	V: 376.
Pleonastic Formative Elements in	V: 374.
Plurals, Internal, Guyard's theory of	V: 373.
Polarity, Pitfalls of	V: 377.
Prefix, Causative *Š/SA*	V: 380.
Prnoun, Third singular suffixes in Proto-Semitic	V: 380.
Proto-Semitic ā, Hebrew Development of	V: 379.
Proto-Semitic */awa/ and */ō/, Arabic evidence for	V: 379, 592.
Quantitative Ablaut in	V: 378.
Reflexives in	V: 376.
Root *'by*	V: 377.
Root Morphemes	V: 378.
Roots	V: 378.
Roots, Development of	V: 372*(2)*.
Roots, Place of *n* in formation of	V: 377.
Roots, Prehistoric Origin of Non-Synonymous	V: 380.
Roots with Semivowel as Third Radical	V: 374.
Semitic Loan Words in Egyptian	V: 302, 365, 366, 379.
Semitic Theory, J. G. Müller's	V: 373; **IX**: cx.
Sibilants	V: 380.
Sibilants and Dentals, Interchange of, in	V: 374.
Sibilants in	V: 375.
Sonority, Principle of	V: 376.
Spanish Language, Influence on	**IX**: cxxxix.
Spirantization in Phonetics	V: 381.
Stems, Derived	V: 372.
Suffix *-man*, Origin of	V: 373.
Sumerian and, Origins	V: 375, 579.
Survey of Recent Work	V: 387‡.
Syllable, Pretonic Open, Vocalization of	V: 377.
Syntax of Combinations formed by Noun and its Modifiers in	V: 375.
Tenses, Formation of	V: 373.
Third Person Singular in	V: 377.

Totality, Figurative Equivalent for, in Western Semitic V: 546.
Transliteration of V: 379.
Tripartite Division of Speech in V: 379, 380.
Ugaritic and, Usage V: 378.
Ugaritic Within, Position V: 536*(2)*.
Verb, Biliteral Origin of V: 380.
Verb-Form, Oldest V: 372.
Verbal Stems in Classical V: 381.
Verbs, Derivative Forms V: 372.
Verbs, Transitive and Intransitive V: 374.
Vocalic *r, l, m, n,* in V: 375.
Vowel *a* V: 373.
Vowels, Long, in Stems *mediae infirmae* V: 377.

Semitic Literature, *see also:* **Corpus Inscriptionum Semiticarum**
Biblical Literature and, Affinities between V: 698.
Comparative Criticism of IV: 136.

Semitic Museum of Harvard: III: 449, *757*.

Semitic Philology:
Particles in, and Hebrew V: 481, 482.
Survey of V: 470‡.

Semitic Religion (Cult) General Studies: V: **§465, 160-162**.
Desert, Notion of, in V: 161.
General Features of V: 160.
King-God among Western Semites V: 161.
Monotheism in V: 33.
Morality and V: 161; **VIII**: 225.
Mythology and V: 140.
Petra, Semitic Cult Complex at V: 162.
Primitive Arabian and V: 148.
Sinai, Semtic Worship in V: 160.
Survivals of, in Syrian Centers of Moselm and Christian Influence V: 142.
Time in V: 148; **VIII**: 110.

Semitic Studies: V: 386*(4)*.
America, Present Status of Studies in V: 385, 386.
American Colleges, in V: 374.
Bibliography I: 1, 2, 3.
Half-Century of Investigation IV: 141.
Semitc Faith, and Aryan V: 139.
Semitc Total Thinking V: 113.
Semitic Theory, J. G. Müller's V: 373; **IX**: cx.
Theological Seminary, in V: 386.
University, in V: 386.

Semitic Texts - General Studies: III: *651;* **VII**: **§851, 83-84**.
Early Inscriptions, from Babylon VII: 205.
El-Harrah, from VII: 82.
Enigmatic Inscription (So-called) from Byblos VII: 84, 143.
Etabi District, in VII: 84*(2)*.
Malta, Phoenician Inscriptions, from VII: 120.
ZKR Inscription VII: 82.

Semna: I: *318;* III: *147, 177,* 225.
Epigraphic Mission to VII: 72.

Semnah: VII: *9*.

Semseru: V: 215.

Semti: II: 87.

Sen-nefer: II: 88.
Tomb of, near that of Thotmes III III: 537.

Sen-mut: II: **87-88**.

Sen-wosret III: III: *593*.

Senate: I: 494.
Alexandrian I: 489.
Attic I: 495.

Senators:
Roman II: 161.

Senb-hena-es: II: 87.

Sendschirli: III: 225; IV: 178.

Seniŷ: II: 87.

Senkereh:
Inscription of **VII**: 182.
Nebuchadnezzar II, Cylinder of, from **VII**: 232.
Senkhonsis: **VII**: *31*.
Senman:
Tomb of, Brother of Senmut **III**: 542.
Senmut: **III**: *542*.
Statue of **III**: 732*(2)*.
Tomb of **II**: 230.
Sennaar:
Travels, Modern, in **III**: 437.
Sennacherib: **I**: *86, 87, 90, 91, 95, 255, 363;* **II**: *42, 65, 83(3), 84,* **88-90**, *92(2), 102(2), 116, 178, 180, 183, 190, 191(2);* **IV**: 181; **VII**: 159, *289*.
Army, Destruction of **IV**: 393; **VI**: 289.
Catastrophe of, at Nob **VI**: 271*(2)*.
Cylinder of **III**: 182*(2)*, **VII**: 184, 185*(3)*.
Death (Murder) of **II**: *39*, 89*(3)*, 90*(2)*; **VI**: 241*(2)*, 242, 290.
Hezekiah, Campaign Against **II**: 90; **IV**: 383; **VI**: 239*(2)*, 240, 288.
Inscriptions of **VII**: 182, 184, 186, 189.
Invasion of, and Its Religious Significance **V**: 14.
Isaiah's Attitude in the Campaign of **IV**: 401.
Isaiah's Prophecy Concerning **VI**: 6.
Jerusalem, Siege of **II**: 89*(6)*, 90, 410*(2)*, 411; **IV**: 383.
Lachish, Seige of **II**: 90, 435; **IV**: 214.
Letters of, to Sargon II **VII**: 178.
Nineveh, and **II**: 89; **III**: 181, 182*(2)*.
Will of **VII**: 191.
Sennar: **III**: *670*.
Sennemût: **VII**: 71*(2)*.
Sarcophagus of **VII**: 69.
Statue of **II**: *61*, **90**; **VII**: 65.
Sensenb, Queen:
Pyramidion of an Official of **VI**: 15; **VII**: 61.
Senses:
Internal, in Latin, Arabic, and Hebrew Philosophical Texts **V**: 112, 148; 269; **VIII**: 170.
Sensus Plenior: **IV**: 85, 86*(3)*, 87, 88*(2)*, 90*(2)*, 91, 92.
Senusert I (Senwosret I): **II**: **90**.
Monument of **VII**: 63.
Stela of, at Wadi Halfa **VII**: 19.
Senusert II: **II**: 90.
Pyramid of, at Lahun **III**: 505*(2)*.
Senusert III: **II**: 91.
Sephar: **II**: 474.
Sepharad: **III**: **225**; **VI**: 388.
Sephardim:
Supernaturalism and Saints among **I**: 392.
Sepher ha-Ittim: **IV**: 101*(2)*.
Sepphorenes: **I**: *450*.
Septuagint Studies, includes Old Greek, *see also:* **Translation Greek** **IV**: *11, 14, 22,* 24*(2)*, **§245**, **24-35**, 114; **VI**: *359, 469;* **IX**: **§245**, **cxxviii**.
Additions to Hebrew in **IV**: 26.
Aldina **IV**: 31; **VI**: 174.
Anti-Anthropomophisms in the Pentateuch of **IV**: 234; **VIII**: 16, 103.
Antiochian Recension of **IV**: 30.
Apology for **IV**: 25.
Aramaic *dî*, Translation in **V**: 526.
Aristaes and **IV**: 34, 35*(3)*.
Aristeas and the *Vorlage* of **IV**: 35; **VI**: 660.

Authorship of **IV**: 31.
Biblical Studies, Importance for **IV**: 34.
Cambridge **IV**: 28*(2)*, 29, 31.
Cave of Horror, from **IV**: 35.
Chester Beatty Papyri **IV**: 8*(6)*.
Christian Church, use of **IV**: 29, 33; **VIII**: 299.
Chronology of **II**: 180, 185; **III**: 342.
Coincidences between 𝔊 and ℭ° in Genesis 15 **VI**: 66.
Corruptions by Chistians **IV**: 25.
Corruptions by Jews **IV**: 25.
Critical Value of **IV**: 26, 30, 232.
Date of **IV**: 28, 29, 31.
Editoral Alteration in **IV**: 97.
Editorial Alteration and Adaption in **IX**: cxxviii*(2)*.
English Bible and **IV**: 28, 52.
Errors in Transmission of **IV**: 34*(2)*.
Esdras A and **IV**: 27; **VI**: 612.
Freer Manuscripts **IV**: 29, 30*(3)*.
Geography **IV**: 29.
Geography of **II**: 254*(2)*; **IV**: 28, 29.
God, Repence of, and **VIII**: 70.
Gospels and **IV**: 35.
Göttengen Edition of **IV**: 32.
Greek of, and the NT **V**: 640.
Greek Philosophy in(?) **IV**: 26; **V**: 247.
Haggadic Element in **VI**: 378.
Hebraic Cast of Greek in **V**: 634.
Hebraic Character/Cast of **IV**: 36; **V**: 634, 636.
Hebrew of **V**: 299, 388, 471, 480. 637; **IX**: cxxviii*(2)*.
Hebrew, Study of, and **IV**: 34.
Hebrewisms of OG Vesion of Genesis **VI**: 96.
History of **IV**: 26, 34.
Holmes, Robert, on **IV**: 26*(2)*
"House of God/Lord" in **IV**: 235.
Interpretation of OT, bearing on **IV**: 81.
Isaiah 36-39 of, in Relation to 1-35, 40-66 **VI**: 248.
Isaiah, Papyrus Fragment of, in Library of Congress **IV**: 9, 35.
Isaiah, Work of Single Translator **VI**: 319.
Joshua and **VI**: 175*(2)*.
Kethib-Qere, Origin of **IV**: 32.
Law, Renderings of Terms in **I**: 463; **V**: 637.
Legal Interpretations in **I**: 467; **VI**: 83, 113, 114.
Leviticus, of **VI**: 127.
Lexicon, Towards a, of **V**: 638*(2)*.
Liturigical Origin of parts **IV**: 25.
Lucian Recension of **IV**: 38, 39; **VIII**: 284.
Masoretic Text and, compared **IV**: 1; 5, 13*(2)*, 14*(2)*, 25, 31*(2)*, 259; **VI**: 206.
New Testament and **IV**: 32, 33, 34, 35, 36; **VIII**: 23, 271, 272.
Origen's Evaluation of Textual Variants in the Greek Bible **IX**: cxxix*(2)*.
Origin of **IV**: 27*(2)*, 29, 31, 35.
Palimpsest **IV**: 27, 34.
Pap. Oslonensis, ii II **IV**: 32.
Papyrus of, at Heidelberg **IV**: 8.
Pentateuch and **IV**: 30, 232.
Pentateuch, Version of **IV**: 24, 35, 224.
Peshiṭta, influence on, by **IV**: 27, 31, 45.
Philo and the *Vorlage* of **IV**: 35; **VI**: 660, 677.
Philo's Text of **IV**: 26, 27, 38; **VI**: 673*(3)*.
Philology of **IV**: 29*(2)*.
Problems of **IV**: 34.
Proto-Septuagint Studies **IV**: 33.
Psalms Fragment of **VI**: 532.
Psalter, Ostraca of **IV**: 34.
Qumran Literature and **IV**: 34, 35; **VIII**: **§1095, 443**.
Recensions of **IV**: 32.

Revisions, Other LXX Texts and **IV**: **§251, 38-39**.
Samaritan Joshua and **IV**: 30; **VI**: 175.
Samaritan Text of, Supposed **IV**: 24.
Sapiential **V**: 118.
Scotch Editions of **IV**: 28.
Sixtina **IV**: 31.
Targum and **IV**: 32; **VI**: 712.
Textual Criticism and **IV**: 4, 6, 31*(3)*, 33, 35; **VI**: 247.
Theological Education and **IV**: 35.
Tischendorf, Constantin, on **IV**: 25*(2)*.
Transcription Theory of **IV**: 36*(2)*.
Translation, as **IV**: 34.
Translators of Genesis **IV**: 32.
Transliterations in **IV**: 36; **V**: 637.
Transmission Errors in **IV**: 34*(2)*.
Values of **IV**: 34.
Verbs of Praise in **V**: 641.
Vocabulary of, and Semitic Equivalents **V**: 394.
Vocabulary of, with its Semitic Equivalents **V**: 375, 637.
Vorlage of **IV**: 35; **VI**: 660.
Zittaviensis, Codex **IV**: 27.

Sepulcher(s), *see also:* **Tombs**
Architectural Detail in, Art **III**: 549, 692, 698.
Cists from Latium and Etruria **III**: 550.
Echmim, Sepulchral Boxes from **III**: 532.
Greco-Roman Sepulchral Chapel, Kom Abu Billo **III**: 518.
Joshua, Mohammedan Traditions Respecting **III**: 531.
Maccabean Martyrs, of **III**: 547.
Maṣṣebah **I**: 373.
Moses, of **III**: 533.
Rachel's **II**: 280, 291, 465; **III**: 530*(2)*, 531, 532, 533, 556*(2)*.
Roman, Relief **III**: 727.
Royal, of the Kings, at Jerusalem **II**: 404, 405; **III**: *487(2)*, 532, 533*(2)*, 534.
Violation of, in Palestine **I**: 375, 463.

Sequence-Dating: **II**: 174.

Serâbît: **I**: *291;* **III**: **225-226**; **V**: *286*.
Hieroglyphic Stela from **VII**: 21.
Inscriptions **VII**: 64, 85, 86*(4)*.
Temple of Hathor at **III**: 226, 514.

Serah: **I**: 80; **VI**: 591.

Serapeum:
Inscribed Sarcophagi in **III**: 545; **VII**: 64.
Inscriptions of, misunderstood **VII**: 64.
Tombs near, at Saqqara **III**: 559.

Seraphim: **VI**: 256; **VIII**: 156*(2)*, 159.

Serapis: **V**: 153, 203.
Greek Worship of **V**: 206, 252.

Serbal: **III**: 225, 232.

Serdab: **III**: 490.

Seriphos: **III**: *713*.

Sermon(s):
Jeremiah, Prose, of **IV**: 413.
Jewish, on the Books of Maccabees **VIII**: 382.
Jewish Worship, Place of, in **VIII**: 383.
Jonah 4:2, on **IV**: 443.
Micah's Capucinade **IV**: 446.
Preparation of a Biblical **VIII**: 376.
Synagogue *(Pesiqta)* **V**: 92; **VIII**: 375.
Synagogue *(Sidrah / Mikketz)* **V**: 92; **VIII**: 375.

Sermon on the Mount:
Job and **I**: 56.
Pentateuchal Themes in **VIII**: 283.

Serpent(s): **I**: 389; **III**: **381**; **IV**: 293, 296.
Ancient Religions, in **V**: 154.
Antiquities **VI**: 132.
Babylonian Legend of the Serpent-Tempter **VII**: 265.

Babylonian Mythology, in **III**: 381; **V**: 133, 173; **VII**: 227.
Brazen **IV**: 344, 345; **VIII**: 305.
Brazen, Blake's **VIII**: 356.
Brazen, in Israelite Cult **V**: 109.
Brazen, Religious Significance for Israelites(?) **V**: 109.
Cerastes in Royal Names **V**: 299.
Chaldean Mythology, in **V**: 171.
Cuneiform Inscriptions, in **V**: 163.
Curse of the **IV**: 293.
Eden in **IV**: 287*(4)*, 292; **VI**: 37*(2)*; **VIII**: 162.
Egypt, Myths of **V**: 199.
Egyptian Serpent Gods **V**: 204.
Eve and **IV**: 286*(2)*, 287*(2)*.
Fall and **IV**: 289.
Fall of the **IV**: 292.
Four-Winged, on Hebrew Seals **III**: 660.
Genesis, in **VI**: 36*(3)*, 37*(2)*, 38.
Gregory of Nyssa, in **VI**: 725.
H PAXIA and, in Gregory of Nyssa **VI**: 725.
Hittite Legend of Great **V**: 225.
Human Head, with, in Art and in Mystery Play **VIII**: 355, 366.
Myth, in **IV**: 294.
Old Testament, in **V**: 104.
Satan Identified as, in Wisdom of Solomon **VI**: 632; **VIII**: 163.
Scripture, in **IV**: 294.
Semitic Mythology, in, and the Gilgames-Epic XI, 274-320 **III**: 381; **V**: 133; **VII**: 227, 266.
Tempter in Oriental Mythology **III**: 381; **V**: 133.
Tree and **IV**: 291*(2)*.
Vine and **V**: 181.

Serpent Worship: **V**: 154.
Origin of **V**: 152.
Prehistoric Traditions in Connection to Sun and **V**: 152.
Serpent-cult in Palestine **V**: 156.
Statue of, Worshipper **III**: 735; **VII**: 66.
Universality of **V**: 153.

Serra, *see:* **Sudan**

Serra East: **III**: *79*, 226.

Serra Orlando: **III**: **226**.
Greek Inscription from **VII**: 328.

Serreh:
Geographical List of **II**: 264.

Servant:
Hittite Hieroglpyh for **V**: 614.

"Servant of the Lord": **VI**: 246; **VIII**: **§1001, 144-147**, 148.
Deutero-Isaiah, in **IV**: 399*(3)*, 400*(4)*, 401*(4)*, 402*(2)*, 403*(2)*, 404*(4)*, 405; **VI**: 292*(2)*, 293*(2)*, 294*(2)*, 299*(2)*, 306*(2)*.
Ebed Yahweh, Christ as **VIII**: 147.
Ebed Yahweh in Deutero-Isaiah **IV**: 402*(2)*; **VI**: 293.
Ebed Yahweh Problem **VIII**: 118.
Inscriptions and **VIII**: 145.
Qumran Scrolls, in **VIII**: 146*(2)*, 418*(2)*, 447.
Targum, in **VI**: 712; **VIII**: 145.

Servant Songs, *see:* Deutro-Isaiah, Servant Songs in

Sérvia: **III**: 227.

Service Obligations: **I**: 482, 487; **VI**: 221*(2)*.

Service Tree: **III**: 394.

Servillius Isauricus: **III**: 258.

Sesebi: **III**: 10, **227**.

Seshat:
Pharaoh and **V**: 214.

Seshemou: **II**: 83, **91**; **III**: *462*.

Sesostris (I): **I**: *61*, *410*; **II**: **91**; **III**: 376; **VI**: 13, 115, 143, 174.

Accession Day of I: 410.
Attempted Sacrifice of **II**: 91; **V**: 215.
Monuments of **III**: 497.
Sesostris II: **II**: *269*.
Sesostris III: **II**: 91, *97*.
Hymns to **VII**: 43.
Set (Seth, Sethi): **V**: 203.
Cult of **II**: *144;* **V**: 201.
Cult-Animal of **V**: 206.
Pig as Cult-Animal of **III**: 380; **V**: 211.
Ramessu II, of, and an Egypto-Syrian Deity **V**: 202.
Rebellion of the IInd Dynasty **II**: 91.
Set II:
Tomb of **III**: 538.
Setekh: **V**: 210.
Seth: **I**: *37,* **80**.
Angels, Fallen, as Sons of **IV**: 297.
Quest of **VIII**: 371.
Seth (God): **V**: 160, 220.
Fool, as **V**: 221.
Horus and **V**: 213.
Horus-Set Motif in the Daily Temple Liturgy **V**: 219.
Stela of *pꜣ-ꜥhꜣty*, follower of **VII**: 25.
Trickster, as **V**: 224.
Sethites:
Chronology of **II**: 166, 186.
Genealogy of: **I**: 119; **IV**: 302.
Sethos I: **II**: **91**, *199*.
Stele of, at Beth-Shan **VII**: 24.
Texts of, inside Speos Artemidos **VII**: 69.
Sethos II:
Stela, Fragment of **II**: 91; **VII**: 26.
Seti (Sety) I: **II**: *4, 72, 80,* **92**; **III**: *544*.
Coffin of **VII**: *42*.
Karnak Reliefs of **II**: 80; **VII**: 14*(2)*, 60.
Nauri Decree of **VII**: 30.
Stela of **VII**: 22.
Stela of, at Beth-shan **VII**: 21, 23.
Stela of, in the British Museum **VII**: 21.
Temple of, at Abydos **III**: 475, 502, 520.
Seti (Sety) II:
Cartouches of, at Abu Fouda **VII**: 62.
Temple of, at Eshmunen **III**: 509.
Setia: **III**: 227.
Settlements:
Gaililee, Lower **II**: 368.
Geological Influence on, in Yarkon Valley **II**: 249, 495.
History of, in Ancient Times **I**: 124; **II**: 261.
Israelite, in Galilee **II**: 368.
Near East, Beginnings of **IX**: lxxxiii.
River Beds, Ancient, and **I**: 124, 125, 206, 207; **II**: 261.
Seven:
Egyptian Texts, in **VII**: 64.
Rabbinical Literature, in **VI**: 690.
Ugaritic Texts, in **V**: 538; **VIII**: 312.
Seventy Elders: **I**: 106.
Seventy two Modes of Exposition: **IV**: 325.
Seventy Weeks of Daniel *see:* **Daniel, Book of**
"Seventy Years Captivity": **V**: 520*(3)*.
Severan:
Colossal Head of(?) **II**: *47(2), 92(2);* **III**: 749.
Severus Alexander:
Colossal Head of(?) **II**: *47(2), 92(2)*.
Sew:
Hebrew Word for "to sew" **V**: 460.
Sewers: **I**: 361.
Sex Offences in Sumerian Law: **I**: 505; **VII**: 281.
Sexes:
Intermediate, Importance of, in Early Civilizations **VI**: 226*(2)*, 231, 243.
Sexual Commerce:
"To Know" = **V**: 509.

Sexual Morés: I: **§77, 214-223**; IX: **§77, lxxxvii**.
Mamzeruth VI: 694.
Redemption and Sexual Purity I: 222; VIII: 197.
SEYFFARTH, GUSTAV(US): V: 362.
Chalcolithic Age long bones from III: 361.
Seyl Aqlat: II: *331(2)*.
Ša-pî-kalbi:
Neo-Babylonian Personal Name V: 300.
Shaaraim: II: **474**.
Shabaka: II: 92.
Shabwa Inscriptions: VII: 296.
Shaddai, *see also:* **Ēl Šadday** VI: 13; VIII: 106, 107, 108, 109, 110*(2)*, 111*(2)*, 124.
Name I: *30;* V: 299.
Shades:
Babylonian Land of, and Sheol VIII: 266.
Dead, of the VIII: 260.
Shadikanni: III: *654*.
Shadow:
Egyptian, of Death V: 200, 201.
Shafaṭ: I: *486;* II: 284.
Shahari: V: 595.
Shahin Hill, Jerusalem:
Jewish Tomb on III: 556*(2)*.
Shahpuhr I: V: 235*(2)*.
Shahr-i-Kōmis: III: 125.
Shahr-i Sokhte: III: 125.
Shahriyar: III: 227.
Shahrzoor Valley: I: *257*.
Ša-imērišu:
Damascus as III: 75.
SHAKESPEARE, WILLIAM: VIII: *365*.
Apocrypha, Use of VIII: 362, 364.
Bible and / in VIII: 360*(2)*, 365, 366*(2)*, 377, 368, 370.
Miracle and VIII: 367.
Shakkah:
Rmains from Tower at III: 354.
Šakkanakkus:
Ur III, Tablets of VII: 240; IX: cxliii.
Šaknu, Assyrian office of I: 493, 494.
Shalamians: VI: 551; VII: 295.
Shalfahat, Tell: III: 227.
Shalim-ahum: VII: 187.
Shalishar: II: 284.
Shalman: IV: 181; VI: 369*(2);* VII: 159.
Shalmaneser I: *86, 87, 90, 95;* II: *83(2), 88(2), 102(2), 115, 178, 180, 190, 191(2);* IV: 181; VII: 159, 187.
Assyrian Canon of VII: 182.
Shalmaneser, Fort: III: 489, *627*.
Shalmaneser II, *see also:* **Black Obelisk** II: **92**,*182*, 191*(4)*.
Monolith Inscription of VII: 184, 191.
Shalmaneser III: II: **92-93**.
Annals of VII: 187.
Kurba'il Statue of VII: 189, 190.
Statue of VII: 186.
Statue of, from Nimrud VII: 189; IX: cxxvii.
Shalmanezer *see:* **Shalmaneser**
Shamash:
Political Hymn to VII: 260.
Shamash-Edom: II: 474.
Šamaš-ḫaṣir:
Letter of Hammurabi to VII: 217.
Šamaš-šum-ukin: II: *22, 39(2),* **93**; VII: 185, 201, 236, *248, 252,* 263.
Hymn to Moon-god, adapted for V: 180; VII: 200.
Letter of, to Saradnapalus VII: 179.
Prayer of III: *647;* V: 181; VII: 261.
Shamgar: I: 80; IV: **367**.

Shamir: **II**: 320, 475.

Shamiram-alti:
- Cemetery at **III**: 227, 541.

Shammai: **VI**: 692.
- Hillel and, Controversy in the Halakah between **VI**: 685, 692.
- Semikah Controversy between Hillel and **VI**: 685.

Šamši-Adad: **II**: *33*, **93**, *210*.
- Journey of, from Subat-Enlil to Mari **II**: 256.
- Military Texts of, from Mari **VII**: 163.

Šamširamman: **VII**: *198*.

Shanhar, *see:* **Shinar**

Shanidar Cave: **III**: **228**, *280(2)*.
- Faunal Remains from **III**: 367.
- Neanderthal Skeletons, Two from **III**: 361.
- Paleolithic Child from **III**: 360*(2)*, 361*(2)*.
- Paleolithic Skull from **III**: 360.
- Skeletons IV and VI **III**: 362.
- Skull from Shanidar II **III**: 361.

SHAPIRA, M. W.:
- Manuscripts of, and the Decalogue **VI**: 156.

"Shapira Manuscripts": **VII**: **§863**, **109-110**.
- Dead Sea Scrolls and **VII**: 110*(2)*; **VIII**: 438*(2)*.
- Fate of **VII**: 110.

Shaqadud: **III**: 228.

Shar-Gani-sharri:
- King of Akkad **II**: *84*, **93**.

Shargalisharri: **IX**: cvi.

Sha'rîe, Tell esh: **II**: 299.

Sharkalisharri (Shargalisharri): **III**: 728.

Sharon, Plain of: **I**: *206*, *349*; **II**: *216*, 303, *320*, **475**; **VI**: *171*.
- Geographical Conditions in, and Impact on its Settlement **II**: 301, 475*(2)*.
- Liptobiolite from **II**: 250.
- Routes, Historical, in **III**: 447.

Sharu: **II**: 93.

Sharuhen: **II**: 283.

Shashanq Heqa-Kheper-Re: **III**: *593*.
- Burial of **II**: 93.
- Remains of **III**: 358.

Shasu: **II**: 94*(2)*, *158*, **167**, *171*; **IX**: cvi.

Shaṭṭer Rigāl: **III**: 228; **IX**: cv.

Shaugamuna: **III**: *648*.

Shavei Zion: **II**: 300.

Shawabti (Ushebtis) figures: **III**: 575*(2)*, 576*(2)*, 577; **V**: 210, 224.
- Akhenaten, of **III**: 577; **V**: 214.

Shawls: **I**: 273, 276.
- Theban Tombs, Representation of, in **III**: 709.

Shear-Jashub: **VI**: 246.

Sheath:
- Gold, of Zendjirli **III**: 682; **VI**: 566.

Sheba: **III**: *191(2)*, **229**.
- Queen of : **I**: *99*, *341*; **II**: **94**; **III**: *122*, *229*.
- Rebellion of **IV**: 542.

Shebaniah: **V**: 300.

Shebna, the Scribe: **I**: 270; **VI**: 280, 289.
- Name **V**: 300.

Shebtiw: **V**: 221.

Shechem: **I**: *50(2)*, *60*, *96*, *212*, *426*, *455*, *470(2)*, *484*, *487*, *493*; **II**: *163*, 273, *288*, 292, 304, *335*, **475-478**; **III**: 432, *479*, *631*, *637*, *657(2)*, **IV**: 199; **VI**: 174.
- Archaic Semitic Inscription from **VII**: 85; **VIII**: 86.
- Baal-Berith of **V**: 198.
- Ben Sira and the Foolish People of **VI**: 624.
- Buildings, Bronze Age, at **III**: 486.

Fortress Temple of, and Joshua's Covenant	**II**: 478; **IV**: 364; **V**: 71; **VIII**: 218.
Mt. Gerizim Temple	**III**: 520.
Objects from, excavated in 1913 and 1914	**III**: 570.
Primeval Monotheism and	**V**: 34.
Salting of	**II**: 475.
Temples at	**III**: 519; **V**: 70; **IX**: cxxiv.
Tomb of Joseph in	**III**: 531.
Sheep:	**III**: 381.
Death, of, in Psalm 49	**VI**: 487.
Ewe's Head, Sculpture	**III**: 741.
Hittite word for	**III**: 381; **V**: 616.
"Iron", in the Talmud	**VI**: 703.
Shefa 'Amr:	
Tomb at	**III**: 533.
Sheik Abbada:	**III**: *767*.
Sheikh Abd el Goornah (Gurneh):	**III**: 84, 85*(2)*, 229, 546.
Sheikh Ahmed el Areini, Tell:	**II**: 301.
Sheikh Bader:	**II**: 417, 478.
Sheikh el-Beled:	**III**: 483, 729.
Sheikh Nareddin, Tell:	**III**: 229.
Sheikh Nassir:	**III**: *75*, 229.
Sheikh Said:	
Architectural Sketch from	**III**: 463.
Sheikh Yusur, Tell:	**II** 368.
Shekel(s):	
False	**I**: 447.
First Revolt of Jews, from	**I**: 446*(2)*.
Gudean	**I**: 420.
Half, in Dead Sea Scrolls	**I**: 482; **V**: 63; **VIII**: 415*(2)*.
Half-Shekel of Cyrene	**I**: 452.
Hebrew, of Fifth Century	**I**: 447.
Hebrew Weight	**I**: 424, 426, 435.
Jewish	**I**: 448, 458.
Jewish	**I**: 458*(2)*.
Maccabaean	**I**: 442*(2)*.
Medals	**I**: 447.
Quarter-Shekel of First Jewish War	**I**: 456.
Sanctuary	**I**: 442.
Standard	**I**: 439.
Tyre, Autonomous from	**I**: 446.
Tyrian	**I**: 448.
Weight	**I**: 424, 425, 427.
Shekelesh:	**II**: 94*(2)*; **IX**: cvi.
Shekinah, *see also:* **God, Glory of**	**V**: 513; **VIII**: **§982, 101-102**, 103, 109, 137, 149*(3)*.
Shelala:	**II**: 264, 334.
SHELLABY, YAKOOB ESH:	**VII**: 312.
Shellâl:	
Stela of Psammētichus II	**II**: 76; **III**: 493; **VII**: 19, 26.
Shells:	
Fragments, from Hamath	**III**: 772.
Nerita, used as Whistle(?)	**III**: 679.
Shem:	**I**: *51(2)*, **81**, 326; **IV**: 310
Elam, Eldest Son of	**III**: 92.
Name	**V**: 292.
Shema':	**IV**: *9;* **VI**: 142*(2)*, 157.
Shema Yisroel:	**VIII**: 205.
Shemĕ'ber:	**V**: 296; **VI**: 62.
Shemesh:	**I**: 78.
Samson and	**I**: 78; **V**: 176.
Shemites:	**VI**: 59.
Shemitic:	**V**: 513.
Shemoneh Esreh:	
Hebrew Liturgy and	**VIII**: 385.
Shemshara, Tell:	**III**: **229**.
Archive Discovered at	**VII**: 240*(2)*.
Babylonian Correspondence, Collection of	**VII**: 216.
SHEMTOB, JOSEPH:	
Shen:	**II**: 478.
Stela of the Master-Sculptor	**VII**: 24.
Shen-nung:	**II**: *84*.

Shen / Heshan: **II**: 283.
Shengavit: **III**: 229, *280, 632*.
Shenir: **IV**: 229.
Sheol: **II**: *375;* **V**: 132; **VI**: 216, 464; **VIII**: **§1036, 266-267**, 267.
Babylonian Land of Shades and **VIII**: 266.
Etymology of **VIII**: 267.
Hades and **VIII**: 267.
Original Meaning of **VIII**: 266.
OT Passages on **VIII**: 267.
Pit and, in the OT **VIII**: 266.
Shephelah: **II**: *155,* 286*(2),* 305, 306, 310, **478-479**.
City Mounds of, Surveys **II**: 310.
Shepherd(s): **I**: 251, 253, 254.
Rods of **I**: 390.
"To Shepherd" in Hebrew **V**: 452.
Shepherd Kings, *see also:* **Hyksos** **II**: 145; **IX**: cix.
Shepherd-Ruler Concept: **VIII**: 137.
Shepherd's Crook: **I**: 482; **III**: 671.
Sherds, *see:* **Potsherds; Pottery**
Sheshbazzar: **I**: **81**, *82*.
Sheshonq IV (Sheskonk IV):
Stela from the Reign of **VII**: 20.
Sheshonq, *see also:* **Shishak** **II**: 94*(2)*.
Judah, supposedly Named in the List of **V**: 292; **VII**: 81.
Šĕṷá Medium: **V**: 480.
Sheva:
Scribe of David **I**: 271, 465; **V**: 301
Sheykh 'Abd el-Qurna: **II**: *257*.
Shibboleth: **VI**: 188*(4)*.
Shicron: **II**: 290.
Shield Bearers: **I**: 321.
Shields: **I**: 311*(2),* 314, 316*(2)*.
Aegis of Zeus **V**: 264.
Bonze Ægis **III**: 681.
Greek Art, Theme in **III**: 705.
Herzsprung **I**: *339*.
Minoan Body **I**: 315*(2)*.
Shihab, Tell-esh-: **III**: 230.
Egyptian Monuement of **III**: 493.
Shihan: **II**: 292, 309; **III**: 419.
Shihor: **II**: 479, *501*.
Shihor Libnath: **II**: 283, 290.
šikkû **III**: *371, 372, 383;* **V**: 568.
Shikmona: **II**: 303*(2)*.
Šilhak-Inšušinak:
Elamite Inscription of **VII**: 299.
Shiloah: **II**: 479; **VI**: 266*(3)*.
Shiloh: **I**: *107;* **II**: **479**; **IV**: *261(2);* **VI**: 93*(4);* **IX**: cxviii.
Feast of **II**: 284.
Prophecy concerning **VI**: 93.
Samuel's Sleeping at **VI**: 194.
Shiloh, Sanctuary at: **V**: **§429, 56**.
Samuel sleeping in **V**: 56.
Shinab: **V**: 296; **VI**: 62.
Shinar: **III**: *53(2),* **230**; **VI**: 56*(3),* 58, 88.
Shinar-Šangār: **II**: 16.
Shine:
Hebrew Terms for **V**: 513, *515*.
Shintoism:
Hebraism and **V**: 151.
Shipbuilding: **I**: 349, 351, 353*(2),* 355.
Shipyard at Issus **III**: 128.
Shipping: **I**: 339, 340, 341, 348,352, 353, 355*(2)*.
Ugarit, at **III**: 268; **IV**: 219.
Ships: **I**: **§105, 351-356**.
Art, in **III**: 704.
Capacity of Egyptian Grain **I**: 354.
Design of Ancient **I**: 353*(3)*.

Dimensions of Egyptian **I**: 352*(2)*.
Egyptian Funereal **I**: 375.
Egyptian Sailing **I**: 354.
Log, Ship's **I**: 346.
Oars, Rows of, on Hellenistic Ships **IX**: xcvi.
Oceangoing **I**: 353*(2)*, 354.
Oenochoë with scene of **III**: 634, 718.
Propulsion systems of Greek **I**: 356.
Speed of Ancient Sailing **I**: 354.
Steering Gear of Egyptian **I**: 352*(2)*; **III**: 586.
Tarshish, of **I**: 339; **IV**: 220.
Trireme design **I**: 356.
Two-Masted, Earliest **I**: 355.
Warships **I**: 321*(3)*, *355*; **III**: *718(2)*.
Xerxes' Fleet at the 'Ovens' **II**: 108.
Shipwrecks: **I**: 341.
Antikythera, Hellenistic Pottery from **III**: 627.
Classical Art from **III**: 731.
Excavations of Ancient **III**: **452-455**.
Identification Problems **III**: 454.
Laws regarding **I**: 355, 506.
Shipyard:
Issus, at **I**: 351.
Shiqmona: **II**: 304, 480.
Phoenician Jar Inscriptions from **VII**: 120.
Shiraz Area (Iran): **III**: 125.
Širpula:
Lamentation to the Goddess **V**: 176.
Shishak I, *see also:* **Sheshonq** **I**: *151*; **II**: 94*(3)*, *365*.
Place Name Lists of **II**: 264*(2)*, 271.
Shishak (City): **II**: 480.
Shishak Migration: **II**: 94.
Šišku: **II**: 206.
Shittim Plain: **II**: 285, **480**; **III**: *571*.
Shittim Wood: **III**: 394.
Shi'urim: **I**: 427.
Shivah Asar b'Tammaz: **V**: 85.
Shivtah: **I**: *255*.
Škand Gumanik Vičar:
Critique of Judaism in **V**: 27.
Šamaš:
Hymn to **V**: 169; **VII**: 263.
Šmryw:
Seal of **III**: 658.
Shoco, Shocho, Shochoh, *see:* **Socoh**
Shoes:
Legal Symbols, as **I**: 278, 464; **IV**: 219; **VII**: 166.
Symbolism of a Pair of, in Amos **VI**: 379.
Symbolism of, in Jewish Sources **I**: 277; **VIII**: 303.
Shofar: **I**: 243*(2)*, 366.
Shoham Stone: **VI**: 34*(2)*.
Shops:
"Byzantine" at Sardis **III**: 527.
Shorelines:
Chronology, As Aid to **II**: 175.
Short:
Egyptian Word for **V**: 352.
Shorthand:
Hebrew Bible in (Abbreviations in Medieval Talmud) **VI**: 715.
Shoshenḳ: **II**: 95
Shoulder:
Bearing of, a sign of mourning **I**: 372.
Shovel:
Snuff, as Jewish Symbol **III**: 698; **V**: 52; **VIII**: 304.
Showbread: **III**: 776; **V**: 51.
Shramanas: **V**: 95.
Shrine(s): **III**: **§193, 507-522**; **IX**: **§193, cxiii-cxiv**.
Amman, Tribal League, in **III**: 522; **V**: 50, 71.
Anatolian, Early **V**: 227.
Artemis Orthia, of **III**: 511.
Attis from a Domestic **V**: 261.

Bethpage, Archaeological Setting of V: 49.
Beycesultan, Early Bronze at III: *47(2)*, 518; V: 227.
Cattle, in Asia Minor V: 237.
Egyptian, Roman Involvement in Affairs V: 223.
Egyptian Word for V: 345.
Eumenides, at Athens V: 254.
Greek, Near Girgenti III: 513.
Herakleion in Melite III: 518; V: 263.
Janus, at the Forum III: 513; V: 254.
Janus Geminus, in Rome V: 270.
Minoan, in Tombs III: 556.
Nebuchadnezzar's III: 514.
Olympion III: 518; V: 263.
Phoenician Style Model of V: 193.
Plan for III: 466.
Seshat's nš-shrine V: 214.
Shechem, Tribal League, in III: 522; V: 50, 71.
'Solar'(?), at Lachish II: 437.
Triple, of Theban Triad in Luxor Temple V: 223.
Vortumnus, of III: 521.
Zoomorphic, in Egypt and India IX: cxxiii.

Shroud:
Roman Egyptian Mummy I: 381.

Shu: V: 222.

Shu-ilishu: I: *411*.

Šu-Šîn:
Histoircal Inscriptions of VII: 241.

Shubad, Queen: I: *278;* II: *214;* III: *367, 456*.
Boudoir of III: 490.

Shūhi, Tell esh II: 297, 298.

Shuhites: II: 167; VII: 207.
Land of II: 255; III: 421.

Shulamite: V: 299, 513, 514.
Solomon and, in the Testament of VI: 657.

Šulgi: I: *403, 412;* II: 95; VII: 287*(2)*.
Chronology of II: 202; VII: 273.

Šullat: V: 186.

Šulmân-Ešmûn: V: 164.

Shumshi-Adad: VII: 187.

Shuna, Tell esh-: II: 480.

Shunem: II: 284.

Šuppiluliuma(š): I: 334, 494; II: 3, *64, 96,* 98*(2)*.
Predecessors of II: 98; VII: 307; IX: cvi, cxi.

Shur: III: 230.

Šurpu: VII: 203.

Shuruppak *see:* **Fara**

Shushan:
Palace at III: 230.

Shût-Abni: V: 182.

Si-ptah:
Tomb of, at Bibân el Molûk, Thebes III: 539.

Si-Mut:
Fourth Prophet of Amun II: 95.

Si-renpowet I:
Inscription from the tomb of VII: 61.

Siamon: II: 95.
Campaign of, in Palestine VI: 223.

Sias:
Founders of II: 2.

Sibera: I: 334.
Egyptian Links with(?) I: 334.

Sibitti:
Temple of, at Khorsabad III: 518.

Sibyl(s): I: *113;* V: 273; VI: 661.
Christian VI: 661.
Jewish VI: 661.

Sibylline Oracles: I: 176.
Christian Antiquity, in the Light of VI: 661.
Chruch Fathers, in VI: 661, 662, 719.
Date of III 388-40 VI: 670.
Eschatology of VI: 661.
Essenes in(?) V: 97; VI: 662..
Exegetical Studies on VI: **§802, 670**.

Future Punishment in VI: 661; VIII: 268.
Jewish VI: 661.
Literary Criticism of VI: **§776, 661-662**.
Patristic Use of VI: 662, 722.
Textual Criticism on VI: **§750, 647**.
Sicarii: II: 440*(2)*; V: 95*(2)*.
Zealots and V: 102; VIII: 409.
Sicilians: II: 167.
Sicily: I: *262*; III: *169*, **230-231**, *736*.
Aegean Influence in, in the Bronze Age I: 328; III: 230.
Athenian Aims in 427-424 B.C. II: 116; III: 230.
Coins from I: 443.
Greek Temples in III: 509.
Jewish-Greek Inscription from VII: 324.
Oil Jars of III: 571.
Stream Changes during Historic Time in II: 251.
Temple of Demeter in III: 513.
Sickle: I: 256.
Bronze III: 571.
Composite, and Jericho II: 399; III: 571.
Flint, in Palestine, and Agriculture I: 253; III: 571.
Sickness: VIII: 353.
Psalms in Times of VI: 444.
ṢIDDIḲ, JOSEPH:
Divine Attributes, on VIII: 99.
Siddim, Valley of: II: 284, **480**, *482*.
Side III: 262*(2)*; 263*(4)*.
Sidon: I: *154*; II: 289, *325*, **481**; III: *672*.
Phoenician Inscription from Temple of Esmun II: 203; VII: 116*(2)*.
Sidrā Rabbā:
Iran Kings, Early, according to II: 4; III: 124.
Sidrah: VI: 716.
Siduri Sâbîtu: V: 181.
Siege-towers: I: 312, 320; V: 459.
SIEGFRIED, CARL GUSTAV ADOLF:
Hebrew Lexicon VI: 378, 379*(2)*, 380, 381, 384.
Siena: III: 231.
Sifre Homeros: VI: 699.
Sifre Zuta: VI: 706.
Sigeion: III: 231.
Sightseers: I: 345.
Sigillata, *see:* **Terra Sigillata**
Sigma Lunatum: V: 283.
Signals:
Shield, at Marathon I: 314; III: 157.
Signatures:
Arretine, from Corinth III: 664.
Arretine, from Lezoux III: 666.
Egyptian Artists' III: 710.
Sigillata III: 664.
Signet(s), *see:* **Seals**
Inscribed, Old-Hebrew VII: 91.
Sigynna: I: 312; III: *540*, 681.
Sihon: I: 337; IV: 353.
Sikand-Gûmânîk Vigâr Sar Dar: VII: 374.
Sikyon:
Theater of III: 231, 528, *721*.
Silence: V: 514.
Silk: I: 273.
Silla: II: *445*, 480.
SILLIMAN, BENJAMIN
Genesis and Geology and III: 330; IV: 285.
Siloah: II: 405.
Spring II: 409.
Siloam: II: 308.
Human Remains from III: 354.
Pool of I: 357*(4)*.

Siloam Inscription: I: 357; III: 411, *642, 643, 662;* IV: 211; V: 289, 420; VII: 85, **§860, 102-104**.
Date of VII: 102, 103, 104*(2)*.
OT Textual Criticism and IV: 2; VII: 103.
Siloam Tunnel, *see:* **Tunnels, Siloam**
Siltation:
Israel, Coastal Plain of, Rate of Accumulation II: 244, 249.
Silting:
Aegean Habors and I: 356.
Silvanus: III: 104, 194; IX: cii.
Silver: I: 294, 296, 299; II: 169; III: 599.
Ancient, in Boston Museum of Fine Arts III: 692.
'City of' I: 284.
Copper Equivalents of I: 424.
Gold and Copper Traces in Early Greek II: 217, 218*(2)*.
Hebrew Terms for V: *506,* 514.
Menshah, Girga, Mudiriah, hoard from III: 596.
Ratio to Gold in Demotic Papyri I: 439.
Restoration of, at Ur II: 214.
Restoration of, from Ur III: 456.
Standard in Sumer and Accad I: 438.
Sumerian Civilization and I: 438, 439.
Silversmith:
Hoard from Mesopotamia III: 598.
Models III: 596.
Silwân: II: 481.
Bronze Age Tomb Group from Hablet el Amud III: 558.
Cave, Rock-cut, at II: 405.
Chapel, Rock-cut, at II: 405.
"Egyptian Tomb" at III: 538.
Greek Inscription from VII: 314*(2)*.
Simbar-sīḫu;
Inscription of VII: 241.
Simeon ben Yokhai:
Annual Feast of, in Meron I: 388.
Secrets of V: 124.
Simeon, Person:
Name V: 302*(2)*.
Simeon, Testament of:
Armenian Text of VI: 646.
Simeon, Tribe of: I: 155*(2);* IV: 373.
Cities of II: 272.
Town Lists of II: 271*(2)*, 272.
Similitude: V: 695.
Similitudes of Enoch, *see:* **1 Enoch**
Simon:
Name V: 302*(2)*.
Simon (ben Bothus): I: 173*(2)*.
Sin: I: *474, 476, 479;* V: 514*(6);* VI: 428; VIII: 353.
Adam, Did He Excuse or Confess His I: 32; VIII: 177.
Apocrypha, in VI: 600; VIII: 59, 179, 188.
Atonement and VIII: 177, 193, 194.
Babylonian Doctrine of V: 176.
Ben Sira's conception of VI: 623; VIII: 180, 194.
Christian Anthopology and Original VIII: 185.
Christian Doctrine of VIII: 181.
Coming of (the Fall) IV: 291.
Concept of, as Adultery in Hosea VIII: 18, 185.
Consciousness of VIII: 179.
Death and VI: 31; VIII: 178.
Death and, in Genesis 2,3 VIII: 179, 187.
Disease, Relation to in OT III: 403; VIII: 183.
Divine Providence and its Relation to VIII: 89, 176.
Doctrine of: VIII: **§1012, 176-185**.
Ecclesiastucs, on VI: 618; VIII: 178.
Esdras, Fourth, in I: *479;* VI: 614; VIII: 181.

Evolution and	**III**: 313; **VIII**: 179, 183.
Fall, and Original	**VIII**: 180*(2)*, 183, 185.
"Fear of Sin"	**VII**: 105.
First	**VI**: 36, 37; **VIII**: 178.
First, in the Bible and Oriental Tradition	**IV**: 288.
Forgiveness of, in the OT	**VIII**: 196.
Grace and, in Early Judaism	**VIII**: 178, 188.
Greek Cults, in	**V**: 250.
Greek Idea of	**V**: 254.
Heart in the Psychology of	**VIII**: 175, 184.
Heathen Views of the Punishment of	**VIII**: 176.
Hebrew Sense / View of	**VIII**: 179*(2)*.
Homeric Doctrine of	**V**: 245.
Human Nature and	**VIII**: 177.
Impressionist Sketch of	**VIII**: 178.
Imputed to another	**V**: *424;* **VIII**: 176, 198.
Innocent, Vistiting, on the	**VIII**: 178.
Jeremiah's Concept of	**VIII**: 17, 184.
Jerusalem of	**IV**: 414.
Knowledge of, under the Old Covenant	**VIII**: 179.
Lament of the "Daugher of"	**VII**: 181.
Law, Concept of, in	**VIII**: 183.
Law, Sacrifice in the OT	**V**: 60; **VIII**: 179.
Law, Sinfullness in	**VIII**: 183.
Lawgiver, Divine, and	**VIII**: 177.
Nature of	**VIII**: 176, 177.
Origin of	**VIII**: 177*(2)*, 178*(2)*, 179*(2)*, 181*(2)*, 184.
Original	**III**: 330; **IV**: 295, 296; **VI**: 32, 37, 721; **VIII**: 176*(3)*, 177*(5)*, 178*(2)*, 179, 181*(2)*, 183*(3)*, 184*(10)*, 185.
Original, and Christian Anthopology	**VIII**: 175, 185.
Original, and St. Irenaeus	**VI**: 721; **VIII**: 180.
Original, and the Greek Fathers	**VI**: 720; **VIII**: 179.
Original, and the Justice of God	**VIII**: 97, 98, 181, 182*(2)*.
Original, Doctrine of, in the Second Century	**VI**: 723.
Original, in Genesis	**VIII**: 182.
Original, in Samaritan Theology	**VIII**: 7.
Paradise, in	**VI**: 31.
Perfect Beings, How Could they Fall into	**VIII**: 178.
Perpetual, and Omnipotent Goodness	**VIII**: 176.
Personal Offense Against God in the OT	**VIII**: 184.
Prehistoric Origin	**VIII**: 180.
Prophetic Doctrine / Teaching of	**IV**: 388; **VIII**: 178.
Psalms and	**VI**: 477.
Psalms, Experience of, in	**IV**: 484.
Psychology of	**VIII**: 179, 180.
Punishment of, in the OT	**VIII**: 182.
Rabbinic Theology, in	**VIII**: 183.
Remission of	**VIII**: 182, 183.
Repentence and	**VIII**: 183.
Revelation of the Beginning of, in the OT	**VIII**: 182.
Righteous, of	**VIII**: 179.
Saints, of	**VIII**: 180.
Septuagint, in	**VIII**: 181.
Social, in Amos	**VI**: 383.
Society and	**VIII**: 181.
St. Paul, in	**I**: *479;* **VI**: 614; **VIII**: 181, 185.
Suffering and, as Related to the Power, Wisdom, and Love of God	**VIII** 95, 185.
Suffering as Proof of	**VIII** 186.
Tennant, F. R., on the Origin of	**VIII**: 178.
Uncleanness and	**VI**: 490.
Universal, Cause of	**VIII**: 180.
Visiting, on the Innocent	**VIII**: 178.

Vitrigna, Campagius, on **VIII**: 176.
Wisdom of Solomon in **VI**: 618, 619; **VIII**: 178.
Words for, in the OT **VIII**: 179, 185.
Sin-Gâšid:
Gift to the Temple of Ê-ana **VII**: 147.
Sumerian Inscriptions of **VII**: 277.
Sin-iddinam of Larsa:
Tablets from his Reign **VII**: 238, 278.
Sin-iribam: **IX**: xcviii, cvi, cxlii.
Sin-Muballit:
Dated Texts and Date-Formulae of **VII**: 239.
Sinabri: **II**: 343, 481.
Sinai (Mount and Peninsula), *see also:* **Suez:** **I**: *68, 291(2), 474, 479, 515;* **II**: *254, 260, 281(2),* 282, 303, 309; **III**: *81, 99, 225,* **231-233**, *242, 244,* 437, 438, 441, 442, 446, *608;* **IV**: 229, 327, 329, 331, 340.
Bedouins in **I**: 385; **II**: 118.
Bronze Age, Middle I, in **I**: 341; **IV**: 320.
Covenant at **I**: 477, 513, 514, 516; **IV**: 329; **VI**: 116, 118.
Flora of **III**: 384.
Geography of, compared with Palestine **II**: 282.
Horeb Tradition **IV**: 329.
Israel and **IV**: 324, 338.
Israelite Religion Before **V**: 26, 27.
Israelites, Position in **II**: 281.
Law at **I**: 477; **IV**: 325; **VIII**: 217.
Lepsius, Karl Richard, on the Peninsula of **III**: 231.
Man, Prehistoric, in **III**: 346.
Mines of **I**: 291, 294; **III**: 226.
Scribings (Gaffiti) at **VII**: 13.
Semitic Worship in **V**: 160.
Septuagint Account of **IV**: 329.
Stanley, Arthur Penrhyn, on **III**: 231.
Stone Buildings in **III**: 482.
Theophany of the God of **VIII**: 128.
Topography of **III**: 232.
Sinai, Codex: **IV**: 10.
Sinai-Tradition:
Eschatological Interpretation of in Qumran and the NT **VIII**: 420, 482.
Sinaitic / Proto-Sinaitic Inscriptions: **VII**: **§853, 85-86**.
Alphabet, Origin of, and **V**: 285*(2),* 286.
Alphabetic, Primitive **V**: 285.
Egyptian Hieroglyphics and Alphabet **V**: 286.
Moses and **I**: 70; **VII**: 82, 86.
Relation to Scripture **IV**: 245; **VII**: 81.
Sinaiticus, Codex: **IV**: 11, 25*(3),* 32.
Sind: **I**: 328.
Sindjirli *see also:* **Kaller; Zenjirli** **III**: *721.*
Singers:
Temple **V**: 78; **VI**: 446.
Women, Among the Northern Canaanites **V**: 192; **VII**: 141.
Siniddinam: **VII**: *252.*
Sinidina:
Letter from Hammarbi to **VII**: 216.
Sinim: **II**: 167; **III**: **234**; **VI**: 304.
Isaiah, in **II**: 167; **III**: 234*(2);* **IV**: 391; **VI**: 304.
Sinjar: **III**: **234**.
Assyrians in **II**: 116.
Sinjil: **II**: 284.
Sinkashid: **II**: 95.
SINKER, ROBERT: **VI**: 646.
Sinkhole:
Fossil **II**: 251.
Sinmubal(l)iṭ: **I**: *411;* **II**: *25,* **95**.
Sinope: **III**: **234**, 263.
Greek and Latin Inscriptions from **VII**: 317*(4),* 320, 366*(3).*

Sinsariskun: II: 95; VII: 183.
Sinuhe: II: 119.
Route of, Flight by II: 270; VII: 33.
Sinuhe B, 71-72, Note on VII: 32.
Story of VII: 32*(4)*, 33*(2)*; IX: cxxxix.
Sion, *see:* **Zion**
Siphnos: III: *473*.
Siphon, *see:* **Straws, Drinking**
Sippar(a) III: **234**.
Akkadian Stone Tablet from VII: 151.
Cuneiform Tablet from(?) VII: 251.
Sacrifical Tablet from VII: 258.
Samsuiluna's Inscription from VII: 153, 262.
Sun-God Temple at, and Nebopolassar V: 173.
Ṣippor, Tell: II: 481; III: 639,*768*; IX: cxviii.
Siptaḥ: II: **96**, *105(2)*.
Parentage of II: 96.
Sipylos: II: **96**, *98*; V: 300.
Mt. Sipylus: III: 491*(2)*; V: 245*(2)*.
Sirach, *see:* **Ben Sira and Ecclesiasticus**
Ballad on, from 1585-6 VIII: 363.
Name V: 294; VI: 621.
Sīrāf: III: 124, 125, **235**.
Sirah: II: 284.
Sirbonis, Lake (Sabkhat el-Bardawil): II: 481.
Sireʿ:
Stela of the Sculptor VII: 22.
Sirens: I: *356*; III: *712*.
Parisos, from V: 259.
Sirius Dates:
Babylonian Texts from Seleucid Period on II: 233.
Sirwah in 'Arhab:
Sabaean Texts from(?) VII: 297.
Sisera: II: 96; IV: 367*(2)*; VI: 179*(2)*.
Death of IV: 366.
Historical context of the battle against IV: 370; VI: 181.
Name V: 294.
Sisma:
Human Sulls from III: 355.
Sisopduyenhab:
Stela of VII: 22.
SISSA, UGO:
Cuneiform Texts in the Collection of VII: 152.
Sistan: III: 235.
Climate of III: *196*.
Sistership:
Nuzi, Contracts at I: 199, 516.
Sistrum: I: 244*(3)*; III: 678*(2)*; V: *210*.
Sit-Amûn:
Coffin of III: 358.
Mummy of III: 358*(2)*.
Sittake: III: *192*, 235.
Situla: III: 598, 614.
Sitz im Leben: V: **§561, 693**.
Siûṭ:
Hepzefa, Nomarch of, Tomb of III: 543; VII: 63.
Inscription of VII: 57, 58‡.
Siva Oasis: III: 235.
Siwah:
Alexander the Great, return from II: 12.
Sixtina: IV: 31; VI: 174.
Siyagha:
Samaritan Inscription from VII: 138.
Sizma: III: 14, 15, **235**.
Greek Text from VII: 321.
Sizû: II: *83*.
Skeleton(s), *see also:* **Anthropology, *Specific Remains*** III: 359.
Akhenaton, thought to be that of II: 8; III: 357.

Amenemōpet, of	**III** 358.
Gaza, Remains at	**III**: 357.
Human, from Hotu Cave, Iran	**III**: 360.
Human, from Karataş-Semayük	**III**: 362.
Human, from Kültepe	**III**: 360.
Human Remains in Two Burial Caves	**III**: 362.
Karataş, Human, from	**III**: 362, 363.
Naḥar Ḥever, Skeletal Material from	**III**: 361.
Nahal Mishmar Caves, from	**III**: 362.
Neanderthal, Three Adult, from Shanidar Cave	**III**: 361, 362.
Neanderthal, Two from Shanidar Cave	**III**: 361.
Öküzini, Human found at	**III**: 361.
Qumran, from	**III**: 363.
Şeyh Höyük from	**III**: 359.
Shanidar, IV and VI	**III**: 362.
Sneferu, remains from North Pyramid of	**III**: 359.
Skene:	**III**: 472.
Skeptic:	
Agur as	**IV**: *460, 513;* **VI**: 548.
Job as	**IV**: 460, *513*.
Old Testament, of (Job, Koheleth, Agur)	**IV**: 460; **VI**: 548.
Qoheleth as	**IV**: *460,* 513.
Skepticism:	
Israel, in	**V**: 114*(2)*.
Skifta:	**II**: 481.
Skimatari Museum:	**III**: *730(2)*.
SKINNER, JOHN:	**IV**: 256.
Genesis, on	**IV**: 267*(4)*.
Textual Criticism	**IV**: 3.
Wellhausen, on	**IV**: 255.
Skull Hill:	
Aqueduct, rock-cut, on	**II**: 407.
Skull(s), *see also:* **Anthropology and §171**	
Alaca-Höyük, Three from	**III**: 359.
Anatolia, Craniological Study of Copper Age Population	**II**: 261; **III**: 358.
Arpachiyah, Rediscovered	**III**: 363.
Australaid, from Cape Flats	**III**: 357.
Cattle, at Faras	**III**: 371.
Chinese, Fate of	**III**: 360.
Dashûr, Four from XIIth Dynasty	**III**: 357.
Deformed from Cacusus Region	**III**: 357.
Deir-es-Sinné, from	**III**: 354.
East, brought from by R. F. Burton	**III**: 337*(2)*.
Egyptian	**III**: 337.
Egyptian, composite photographs of Early	**III**: 355.
Erganos, of	**III**: 355.
Eridu Crania	**III**: 359.
Galilee	**II**: 277; **III**: 356*(2)*.
Haditha, Fauna and Crania from near	**III**: 362, 367.
Hassuna, Three from	**III**: 359.
Jordan, Two from	**III**: 360.
Karahöyük, from	**III**: 359.
Kerma 1065 A	**III**: 356.
Lansing	**III**: 355*(2)*.
'Nabatæan'	**III**: 337.
Neolithic, Markings on	**III**: 408.
Neolithic Portait, from Jericho	**III**: 351, 692.
Neolithic Portrait, from Jericho	**III**: 360.
Niches for	**I**: 371.
Paleolithic from Shanidar Cave, Iraq	**III**: 360.
Palestine	**III**: 354, *672*.
Palmyra	**III**: 337, 354.
Sardis, Morphological and Biometrical Examination	**III**: 363.
Shanidar Cave, Paleolithic	**III**: 228.
Shanidar I, Restored	**III**: 361*(2)*.
Shanidar II, from	**III**: 361, 362.
Sisman, from	**III**: 355.
Syria, from	**III**: 355.

Trephined, from Lachish **III**: 357, 401, 408.
XIIth Dynasty, from **III**: 356.
Sky:
Separation of Earth and, at Creation **VIII**: 80, 83.
Sky Folk: **VIII**: 157.
Skyhos:
Attic, Black-Figured **III**: 607.
Skyphos, *see:* **Bowls**
Slag: **I**: 299; **VI**: 249.
Palestine, Specimens from **II**: 248.
Slander:
Babylonian Incantation Against **VII**: 264.
Slave Wars: **I**: 201; **II**: 160, 167*(2)*.
Slavery: **I**: *180, 187, 194,* **§74, 200- 205,** *211, 228, 304, 306, 308, 463, 469;* **VIII**: 231; **IX**: **§74, lxxxvi.**
Alfred, Dean, on **I**: 74.
Balmunamge, the Slave Dealer **VII**: 219.
Egypt, in (P. Columbia Inv. 480 (198-197 B.C.) **I**: 203; **VII**: 341, 354.
Free-born Daughters, Conditional Sale into **VI**: 112.
Greek Civilization based on(?) **I**: 308; **II**: 134.
Halakah on **I**: 204*(2);* **VI**: 694*(2)*.
Hebrew Lineage System and **VI**: 91.
Manumission **I**: 187, **§74, 200-205**, *225,* 272, 479; **V**: 257, 261; **VI**: 694; **VII**: 135; **IX**: lxxxvi.
Manumission Sacral, Greek Inscriptions on **VII**: 340.
Slave, Sale of, Babylonian Tablet on **VII**: 247.
Slave-delaing in Babylonia **VII**: 247, 251.
Slave-girl, Senebet, Report concerning **VII**: 30.
Slaves, Sale of, Sumerian Tablet on **VII**: 279; **IX**: lxxxvi.
Slaves:
Agriculture, use of, in **I**: 254.
Apprenticeship of, in Babylon **VII**: 219.
Assyrian Tablet relating to the Sale of a Female **VII**: 191.
Education of **I**: 202, 203, 231*(2)*.
Egyptian Lawsuit arising from the Purchase of **VII**: 29.
Escaped **IV**: 229.
Galley **I**: 204, 355.
Hammurabi, Code of, on **I**: 478, 496.
Hittite, Status of under Hittite Law **I**: 507.
Industrial use of **I**: 266, 308.
Kirkuk Documents on **VII**: 165.
Marking, Babylonian Practice of **I**: 201.
Mesoptamia, in **I**: 188.
Northwest-Semitic Names in List of Egyptian **V**: 302; **VII**: 17.
Sacred, of Israel **I**: 200; **II**: *131, 142*.
Sale of **VII**: 193, 279; **IX**: lxxxvi.
Seal of a Slave-Wife (Amah) **III**: 652.
"Slaves of God", The Word "Slave" and the KJV Translators **IV**: 109.
Social Mobility of in Roman Empire **I**: 194.
Testimony of, in Babylonian Courts **I**: 205, 506.
"Slaves of God" **IV**: 109; **V**: 303, 514; **VI**: 126.
Slavonic Enoch, *see:* **2 Enoch**
Slavonic Translation of the Bible:
Traces of Hebrew Commentaries in **VI**: 727.
Sleep:
Death and **VIII**: 260.
Jewish Anthroplogy **VIII**: 172.

Term for the Intermediate State(?) V: 514; **VIII**: 265.

Sling:

Leaden, Sling-bolt from Samaria **III**: 668, 681.

Sma:

King of Abydos **II**: 4, 207.

SMART, JAMES D.: **VIII**: 4.

Smelting: **I**: 297*(2)*, 299.

Smendes: **II**: *7;* **III**: *685.*

Smenkherē': **I**: *412;* **II**: 96*(2).*

Smenkhkerê': **II**: 96.

Skeleton of (?) **III**: 357.

Smenkhu-ptah: **II**: 96.

Smerdis: **II**: *69(2),* **96**.

Smith: **I**: 271.

SMITH, ELI: **III**: 439, 440; **IV**: 43, 73*(2).*

SMITH, GEORGE: **VIII**: 39, 132.

SMITH, GEORGE ADAM: **II**: 290.

Isaiah, on **IV**: 391, 395; **VI**: 292.

Micah, on **VI**: 392.

SMITH, HARDING: **VII**: *210.*

SMITH, HENRY PRESERVED:

Inspiration, on **VIII**: 44.

SMITH, J. P.:

Geological Theory, on **III**: 284.

SMITH, JOHN MERLIN POWIS:

Bibliography of **I**: 22.

SMITH, PIAZZI: **III**: 503.

SMITH, PYE: **II**: 247.

SMITH, W. ROBERTSON: **I**: 103*(2);* **IV**: 119*(2),* 123.

Pentateuch, on **IV**: 225, 226*(2),* 238.

SMITH, WILLIAM:

Bible Dictionary of **IV**: 13; **VIII**: 397*(3).*

Smyrna: **III**: **236**, 262*(2).*

Alphabetized Greek Inscriptions from **VII**: 329.

Snail(s):

Iraq, Potential Use in Determining past Climatic Conditions **II**: 245; **III**: 381.

Snakes, *see also:*

Serpent **I**: 389; **III**: *371,* 381, 691; **V**: 216.

Snake Dances **V**: 158.

Sneferu:

Monuments of, at Dahshur **III**: 497.

Skeletal Remains from North Pyramid of **III**: 359.

Southern Pyramid of **III**: 506.

Snofru: **II**: 97.

Snorra Edde:

Zoroaster, Allusion to, in **V**: 230.

Snow-Water: **VI**: 2.

Śō': **II**: 97.

Soane Museum: **VII**: *43.*

Belzoni Sarcophagus in **VII**: 38.

Egyptian Antiquities in **III**: 564.

Sobah Rigaleh:

Inscriptions of **VII**: 60.

Sobekḥotep: **III**: *136.*

Co-regencies of, with Ammenemes III, IV, and Sebknofru **II**: 86.

Monument of Kah-ankh-ra **III**: 493.

Statuette of **II**: 86; **III**: 764; **VIII**: 66.

Sobekhotep III: **II**: 55, *67,* **86**; **III**: *726.*

Sobk:

Hymns to, Ramesseum Papyrus **VII**: 42.

Sobkemḥēt:

Vizier of Sesostris III **II**: 97.

Social Philosophy:

Amos, of **IV**: 436; **IX**: lxxxv.

Isaiah, of **IV**: 391; **IX**: lxxxv.

Social Reform:

Biblical Jubilee and **I**: 413.

Jeremiah and **IV**: 414; **VIII**: 228; **IX**: lxxxv.

Old Testament and **VIII**: 231.

Prophets and **I**: *107, 111, 114(2), 115, 184, 185;* **IX**: lxxxii*(3).*

Social Structures:	**I**: *160,* **§72, 184-195**, *329;* **IX**: **§72, lxxxv-lxxxvi**.
Enslaved Persons Who Are Free	**I**: 187; **VII**: 340.
Ethics and Social Implications	**VIII**: **§1029, 230-235**.
God, Idea of, and Social Patterns	**VIII**: 62.
Haggārîm, "The Castrated One"	**IX**: lxxxv.
Individual and Community in the OT	**VIII**: 191; **IX**: lxxxv.
Isarelite Kinship Terminology, and	**I**: 195.
Metals, Influence on Ancient	**I**: 295.
Modern Palestinian	**I**: 387.
Religious Symbolism and Social Behavior	**I**: 183; **V**: 151.
Social Opportunity, OT Doctrine of	**VIII**: 232.
Social Relations, Bible on	**VIII**: 235.
Social Studies:	
Archaeology and	**III**: 428.
Social Theory:	
Origins of, and Classical Greece	**II**: 135.
Social Ideas of the Apocrypha and Pseudepigrapha	**VI**: 596.
Social War:	
Greek, 220-217 B.C.	**II**: 133.
Socialism:	
Amos, Socialistic Ideas of	**IX**: lxxxii.
Prophets, Alleged of	**I**: 184.
Societas, Consensual:	**I**: 504.
Society:	
Akkadian	**I**: 196.
Ancient, Approaches to Study of	**I**: 194.
Assyrian	**I**: 187.
Babylonian, history of middle strata of	**I**: 194.
Beth-Shan, at	**II**: 332.
Biblical Norm of Social Behavior	**VIII**: 226.
Dependence, Forms of Morphological Classification	**I**: 194.
Early Man and	**I**: 191.
Economy and, in Western Asia, Second Millenium	**I**: 194, 195.
Egyptian	**I**: 123, *185, 491;* **II**: 127, 128; **VII**: *9*.
Faith and, in the OT	**VIII**: 200.
Genetics of	**I**: 195.
Godly, Aspect of Prophetic Message	**VIII**: 235; **IX**: lxxxii, lxxxvi.
Greek	**I**: 194*(2);* **II**: *49,* 133; **III**: 172; **IX**: lxxxv.
Hittite	**I**: 187.
Israelite	**I**: *144(2), 191*.
Israelite Prophecy, Social Location of	**VIII**: 247, 248.
Israelite, Royal Urban, Emergence of	**I**: *191, 207*.
Jewish	**I**: *174, 178, 467, 469, 470*.
Mesopotamian	**I**: 194*(2)*.
Philistine, Structure of	**I**: 193; **II**: 155.
Production, Mode of, and Economy in Western Asia, Second Millenium	**I**: 195.
Property, Problems of, and Ancient Near Eastern	**I**: 194.
Prophets and	**I**: *109, 110, 111, 113, 114, 115;* **IX**: lxxxii.
Ritual and, in the OT	**VIII**: 200.
Roman	**I**: 190*(2),* 194*(2),* 195.
Science in Preliterate, and Ancient Oriental Civilization	**II**: 223.
Sin and	**VIII**: 181.
Society of Biblical Archaeology:	**III**: 418.
Society of Biblical Literature:	**IV**: 140; **IX**: cxxiii.

SOCIN, ALBRECHT: **II**: 308, 309,*403;* **IV**: 264.
Sociology: **I**: **§71, 179-183**; **IX**: **§71, lxxxv**.
Bible as Text-Book on **VIII**: 232.
Canaanite Religion, Social Aspects of **V**: 198.
Ezekiel's Contribution to **I**: 43.
Genesis, Lessons of **IV**: 266.
Greek Culture viewed Sociologically **II**: 134.
Hebrew Religion, Sociological Approach **V**: 22.
Jewish Law, Life under **I**: 473*(2);* **IX**: lxxxv*(2)*.
Joseph's Day, and **I**: 59, 180*(3)*, 373, 488; **V**: 11; **VIII**: 221.
Old Testament, Scoiological Value of **VIII**: 350.
Pyramid Age, Everyday Life in **IX**: lxxxv.
Women in Ancient Religion, hypothesis **V**: 2.
Sockets:
Door, at Ur **III**: 465.
Socoh: **II**: 291, *438*, **482**.
Socrates:
Faith of **V**: 249.
Irony of **VII**: 348.
Man, Dignity of, on **V**: 266; **VIII**: 175.
Morals of **V**: 244.
Soda: **I**: 286.
Soda Plant:
Hittite word for **III**: *394*.
SÖDERGREN, C. J.: **IV**: 308.
Sodom (and Gomorrah): **I**: *220(2);* **II**: 247, 380*(7)*, 381, *474*, **482-485**; **IV**: 181, 314; **VI**: 70.
"Apple" of **II**: 381, 484; **VI**: 152.
Destruction of **II**: 247, 248, 350, 482*(5)*, 483; **VI**: 69, 152; **VII**: 159.
Smoke of, as Seen from Hebron **VI**: 2.
Sodom, Mount (Jebel Usdum): **II**: 249.
Sofala: **III**: 192.
Soferim: **VI**: 693.
Soghal Göl: **III**: 258.
Soil:
Calcareous, in Israel **II**: 250.
Chronology, as Aid to **II**: 175.
Erosion and Sedimentation in Wadi Musrara **II**: 244.
Gaililee, Eastern Upper, in **II**: 245, 251.
Galilee, Reduced Aridity in Eastern Lower **II**: 245.
Geophysical Factor in, Genesis **II**: 250.
Israel, Coastal Plain of, Rate of Accumulation of **II**: 244, 249, 298.
Israel, Excessive Rainfall and Erosion of **II**: 244.
Mesopotamia, Survey of, and Archaeology **III**: 165.
Palestine, of **II**: 254.
Polymorphic Profiles of, in Eastern Mediterranean **II**: 250*(2)*.
Sub-Soil of Askha Temple **II**: 219.
Syria, of **II**: 254.
Soil Usage:
Modern, at Safed **I**: 256, 257.
Soir: **II**: 284.
Sokar:
Festival / Ritual of **V**: 224; **VII**: 78.
VIth Dynasty Titles Relating to **VII**: 72.
Soknebtynis: **VII**: 17.
Sol:
Latin Poets, in **V**: 269.
Solar Disk:
Babylonian **III**: 643.
Egyptian, Winged **V**: 342.
Horus of Beḥdet, as **V**: 214.
Ιακχος from aχu, the Sphinx of the **V**: 246, *351*, 650.
Solar System: **III**: 301, 330.

Soldering: **I**: 297, 298.
Soldier(s): **I**: *185, 351.*
Assyrian Word for **V**: 563.
Babylonian **I**: 191, 318.
Egyptian **I**: 312.
Roman, Epitaph of a **VII**: 334.
Soldier-Scribe (Egyptian) **VII**: 79.
Soleb: **III**: *224,* **236**.
Sarcophagus from Wabset **III**: 558.
Temple of, as New form of Egyptian Architecture **III**: 462, 511.
Temple of, Decoration of Room II of **III**: 519.
Soliloquy:
Divine, in Genesis **VI**: 16.
Job, in **VI**: 434*(3)*, 435.
Solokha: **I**: *240.*
Silver Cup of, with Royal Lion-Hunting Scene **III**: 590.
Solomon: **I**: *93,* **98-99**, *338,* 487; **II**: *384;* **III**: *192;* **IV**: 222; **V**: *115;* **VI**: 591; **VIII**: 391*(4);* **IX**: lxxxii.
Achivements, Later **IV**: 379.
Administrative Divisions of **I**: 466; **II**: 275; **VI**: 233.
Armoury of **I**: 311; **VI**: 552.
Ashmodai and **II**: 21.
Biographical Studies **I**: **98-99**.
Book of the Acts of **IV**: 177, 382.
Chronology of Reign of **II**: 177, 189.
Chronology up to **II**: 178.
Copper Platform of **IV**: 220.
"Egyptian' Marriage of **VI**: 221.
Ethics of, in Ecclesiastes **IV**: 513; **VIII**: 220.
Hiram, Treaty with **I**: 512.
Hittite Kings and **IV**: 181; **VII**: 159.
Jerusalem of **II**: 410, 411
Judgment of **VI**: 220.
Kingdom of **I**: 161*(4), 333, 334.*
Marriage to Pharaoh's Daughter **I**: 334.
Marriages, Foreign, of **I**: 334.
Megiddo in the Time of **II**: 443.
Mines of King **I**: 291, 292*(4).*
Monumental Art, Absence of in Solomonic Age(?) **III**: 703.
Palace of, in Megiddo **III**: 503.
Pharaoh's Daughter, Marriage to **I**: 334.
Pharaoh's Daughter, Palaces of, and **V**: 72.
Provinces of **I**: 470; **VI**: 221.
Psalms of **II**: *45;* **IV**: 496.
Psussenes II, Father-in-Law of, Mummy of **II**: 76; **IV**: 219.
Queen of Sheba, and **II**: 94; **VI**: 224.
Rabbinic Interpretations of **I**: 99; **VI**: 716.
Reign of **VIII**: 389.
Satans and **VI**: 224.
Seal of **VIII**: 305.
Septuagint Version on Misconduct of **I**: 99; **IV**: 382.
Ship of **VIII**: 371.
Siamon, as Father-in-law to(?) **II**: 95.
Sons of Servants of **I**: 191, 204; **V**: 78.
Structure and Theme of the Solomon Narrative **VI**: 221.
Temple of, *see:* ***Temple of Solomon***
Testament of **VI**: 657.
Testament of, and Jesus **VI**: 657.
Tomb of, in Moslem Tradition **III**: 554.
Utterance of **VI**: 222.
Wisdom, Beginnings of, in Israel, and **I**: 99; **V**: 118.
Wisdom of **I**: 98; **IV**: 379; **V**: 115.
Wives of **I**: 98.
Solomon, Testament of:
Jesus and **VIII**: 281.
Solon: **I**: *261, 456, 500;* **III**: *687.*
Prayer to the Muses **V**: 260.
Weights, Change of **IX**: xcix.

Solstice:
Babylonian Astronomy and, during Seleucid Period **II**: 232.
Babylonian Table of, from Uruk **II**: 232.
Solygeia: **III**: 236.
Solymoi:
An Anatolian language **V**: 680.
Somaliland: **III**: *388(2);* **V**: 106.
Somnium Neronis: **IV**: 39.
Son: **I**: 212.
Eldest, Preferential Status of **I**: 212.
King's, at Ugarit and among the Hittites **I**: 195.
Son relationship between Yahweh and Israel **I**: 514; **VIII**: 212.
"Son of God": **V**: *520(2);* **VIII**: 137, 138, 173.
Adam as **I**: 33.
Incarnation of **VIII**: 136.
Israelite King as **I**: 486; **V**: 26.
Messianic Title, as **VIII**: 137.
Ὁ υἱὸς τοῦ θεοῦ **V**: 639, 662.
Preincarnate **VIII**: 128.
"Son of Man": **VIII**: 128, 146, **§1002, 147-149**.
Abbott, Edwin, on **VIII**: 147.
Apocalyptic Origin of **VIII**: 147.
Dalman, Gustaf, on **VIII**: 147.
Daniel, in **IV**: 527, 532; **VI**: 574, 575; **VIII**: 147*(2)*, 148*(2)*, 149*(2)*
Dead Sea Scrolls and **VIII**: 148, 481.
Ethiopic Book of Enoch **VI**: 650; **VIII**: 148.
Ezekiel, in **IV**: 424; **VIII**: 147, 148.
Melchizedek and, in 11QMelch **VIII**: 147.
Origin of **VIII**: 148*(2)*, 149.
Song of Deborah, *see:* **Deborah's Song**
Song of Solomon (Songs), *see also:* **Canticles** **I**: *223, 245, 246;* **IV**: *456*.
Adonis Litany(?) **IV**: 505.
Agadath Shir Hashirim **IV**: 504.
Allegory of **IV**: 507.
Apologetic Motifs in the Targum to **IV**: 507; **VI**: 714.
Archaeological Background of **IV**: 506.
Authenticity, and Authorship of **IV**: **§395, 507-508**.
Babylonian Parallels to **IV**: 508.
Benedictory Formula in Targum to **VI**: 712.
Biblical Faith and **IV**: 507.
Bibliography **I**: **§27, 14**.
Character of **IV**: 504.
Contents of **IV**: 504.
Cultic Clues in(?) **IV**: 506.
"Dance of Mahanaim", as **IV**: 503.
Dances of the Virgins, in **IV**: 505.
Date of **IV**: **§395, 507-508**.
Divine Authority of **IV**: 508.
Dramatic Poem, as **VI**: 551.
Exegetical Studies on **VI**: **§650, 551-555**.
Form of **IV**: 504.
Gregory of Nyssa's Commentary on **IV**: 506; **VI**: 724, 727.
Hebrew (דגל) in **IV**: 507.
Hebrew (דודי) in **IV**: 505.
Hengstenberg, E. W., on **IV**: 503.
History of **IV**: 504.
Homiletical Uses of **VIII**: 372.
Hosea and **IV**: *430,* 507.
Inspiration of **IV**: 507.
Interpretation of **IV**: 505.

Linguistic Argument for
Late Date of — IV: 508.

Literal Interpretation, and
Its Character
as Scripture — IV: 504.

Literal Interpretation of — IV: 505.

Literary Criticism of — IV: §394, 503-507.

Literary Illustrations of — VIII: 366.

Meaning of — IV: 506.

Messiah and — IV: 507.

Midrash on — IV: 504; VI: 706(4).

Modern Palestinian
Parallels to — IV: 505.

Mystical Poem(?) — IV: 504.

Origenes' Commentaries
on, and Jewish-
Christian Polemics — VI: 716, 727.

Outline for Study of — IV: 505.

Palestiniana in — IV: 507.

Parabolic View of — IV: 507.

Paraphrase of — V: 706.

Pastoral Teaching, in — VIII: 405.

Peshiṭta Version — IV: 47.

Plan of — IV: 504.

Plot, of — IV: 504.

Plot, of, a New Reading — IV: 503.

Poem, Secular, as — IV: 505.

Poetic Units within — V: 689, 706.

Prolegomena to
Canticles Rabba — IV: 507.

Rabbinic Exegesis on — VI: 716, 727.

Rénan, E., on — IV: 457, 503.

Rhyme in — IV: 505; V: 690.

Riddle of — IV: 505.

Solomon, Role of, in — IV: 505.

Sources of — IV: §395, 507-508.

Spiritual Sense of — IV: 507.

Structure of — IV: 506.

Sufis and — IV: 508.

Sumerian Love Songs and — IV: 506; VII: 275.

Sumerian Marriage
Songs and — IV: 506; VII: 276.

Syriac Version, Critical
Examination of the Text — VI: 551.

Tammuz Cult and — IV: 505.

Targum on — VI: 710.

Theocritean Parallels to — IV: 505.

Theology, Mystical in — VIII: 19.

Translating — IV: 92, 109.

Virgin Mary and — IV: 506.

Waṣfs of — IV: 92, 507.

Wedding Song
for Solomon — IV: 506(2).

**Song of Solomon,
Manuscripts of:** — VI: §651, 555.

Peshiṭta, Printed
Editions of — VI: 555.

Peshiṭta Text of, in
Barhebraeus' Auṣar rāzē — VI: 555.

Targum to, Six Yemen
MSS. of, compared with
the Textus Receptus — VI: 555(3), 711(3).

"Song of the Sea": — V: 701; VI: 107(3), 108.

Canaanite Myth and — V: 198; VI: 107.

"Song of the Sword": — VI: 45, 353.

Song of the Well: — IV: 173; VI: 132(2).

Songs:
Ebed-Yahweh — IV: 402; VI: 293.

Egyptian, *see:*
*Egyptian Secular
Songs and Poems*

Isis and Nephthys, of — VII: 78.

Israel's Psalms and — V: 686, 705.

Jewish, Oriental — I: 385.

Love — I: 245, 246;

Marching — I: 245.

Mesopotamian Harvest — VII: 263.

Mosaic, Spirit of — V: 700, 705.

Palestinian — I: 391.

Patriotic — I: 243.

Royal, of Thanksgiving — VI: 216.

Sacred, Absence of, in
the Pentateuch — IV: 259.

Secular — I: 243.

"Song of Men in Days
to Come" (Homer) — VII: 350.

Greek Ideas as to the Effect of Burial on the Future of the	V: 247.
Greek Philosophy, in	V: 247, 260.
Greek Thought on the Immortality of the	V: 254.
Heraclitus and	V: 252.
Homeric Ideas of	V: 244, 255.
Hunting for	IX: cxlviii.
Huntingford, Wm., on	VIII: 166.
Immortality of	VIII: 167, 168, 170, 249, 261, 263, 266.
Immortality of, Assyrian Poems on	V: 169.
Immortality of, Hebrew Belief of	VIII: 259.
Immortality of, in Inscription of Panammu I	V: 190; VIII: 260; IX: cli.
Israelite, According to the LXX	VIII: 175.
Origin of	VIII: 168.
Pantheistic Theories of	V: 252.
Personfication of in Judaeo-Arabic Literature	VII: 290.
Phædon: or, Plato on the Immortality of	V: 244.
Plato on Deathlessness of	V: 260.
Pre-Exilic Writings, in	VIII: 174.
Pre-existence of	VIII: 166(2).
Pre-existence of, in Apocrpyha and Pseudepigrapha	VI: 596; VIII: 169.
Pre-existence of, in Rabbinical Writings	VI: 618(2); VIII: 168, 169.
Pre-existence of, in Wisdom of Solomon	VI: 618(2); VIII: 168, 169.
Primitive Theory of, and Burial Customs	IX: xcvi.
Psychology of	VIII: 168.
Separate Existence of	VIII: 166.
Spirits of, in Enoch	VI: 664.
Transmigration of, Biblical Quasi-Evidence	VIII: 263
Weighing of, After Death, Egyptian, Mediaeval Representatons of	V: 208.
Soul Gods:	VI: 206; VIII: 263.
Soul-House(s):	V: 205(2).
Sound:	
Hebrew Terms for	V: *513, 515.*
Sounion:	
Fortifications at	III: 490.
Source Criticism:	
Numbers 14, on	VI: 130.
Souterrains, *see:* **Tanks**	
Chronology	II: 204(2), 205.
Radiocarbon Date for Early	II: 217.
Roman Commercial Competition and	I: 340.
South Arabian Grammar[Arabic] (includes Safaitic):	V: §538, 595-596, *597.*
Adjective, Syntax of, in	V: 595, 596(2).
Body, Parts of, in Modern	V: 595.
Botahari	V: 595.
Determination, a Clue from Shaḥri	V: 596.
Emphatics in	V: 595.
Harsusi	V: 595.
Himyaritic Script derived from Greek	V: 595.
Lexicography	V: 595(6).
Mahri	V: 595.
Monetary Terminology in	V: 596.
Shahari	V: 595.
Sibilants in	V: 595, 596.
Unvoiced Sibilants in	V: 595.
South Arabian Texts:	VII: §921, 292-293.
Archaic Inscription in Vertical Columns	VII: 293.
Baroda State Museum, in	VII: 292.
Chaldean Inscriptions in Proto-Srabic Script	VII: 292.
Dibdib in Eritrea, Inscription from	VII: 293.
Epigraphy, Problems of	VII: 292.
Ḥaḍrami Inscriptions	VII: 293(2).

Hadrami Inscriptions from Ẓôfar VII: 293.
Philby Collection VII: 292.
Qrayat al-Fa'w, Inscriptions from VII: 293.
Thamudic Inscriptions VII: 292*(2)*, 375.
University Museum Collection , Cambridge England VII: 293*(2)*.
South [East] Semitic - General Studies: V: **§536, 585**, 595, 597*(2)*.
Cognates to the Akkadian Vocabulary V: *552(2), 553, 585(2).*
Hebrew Lexicography and V: 401, 585.
Imperfect in V: 598.
South Semitic Texts: VII: **§917, 289.**
SOUTHEY, ROBERT: VIII: 364.
Space: I: 415.
Relation to God's Existence in the Talmud and I: 414; VIII: 62.
Spaciousness:
Savlation, Feature of VIII: 190.
Spain: I: 336, 340; III: 53, 55, *225*, **236-237**, *246, 472.*
Phoenicians in III: 210, 237, 247.
Spanish:
Influence of Semitic Languages on IX: cxxxix.
Sparta: II: 135; III: **237**.
Circular Building at III: 480.
Topography of III: 237*(2)*, 480.
Spartans: I: *120*, 332.
Spartolus: III: *50;* III: 237.
Spatula:
Copper, from Byblos VI: 542.
Spears: I: 319, 320; III: 682.
Rome, as Embodiment of Sovereignty in I: 492; VIII: 307.
Vase Paintings, Use in III: 706.
Species: III: 290, 293, 301, 303*(2)*, 307, 315, 323, 324, 327, 335; VIII: 74, 166; IX: cxx.
Specificato:
Jewish Law and I: 468, 503.
Roman Law and I: 468, 503.
Spectrometry, Optical:
Etruscan Bronzes and II: 218.
Oriental Bronzes and II: 219.
Speech:
Consciousness of, among Egyptians and Babylonians V: 278.
Figures of, Hebrew, *see:* ***Hebrew Phrases***
Freedom of, in Athens I: 507.
Freedom of, in Rome I: 508.
Gesticulation, and the Origin of V: 276.
Origin of, and the early stages of its evolution V: 276.
Parts of, Emergence of V: 279.
Primitive Man and V: 277.
Prophetic Lawsuit (ריב) I: *189;* IV: 358.
SPEISER, EPHRAIM A.: III: 249; VI: 74, 83.
Spells: I: 511.
Book of the Dead, 181, in VII: 53.
Coffin Texts (Egyptian) 38-40 VII: 45.
Egyptian, for Averting Death VII: 40.
Keftiu V: 212; VII: 40.
Pyramid Texts, 413 of VII: 46.
SPENCER, HERBERT: III: 289, 290, 301; IV: 246; V: 1, 6, 8.
Speos, *see:* **Tombs**
Speos Artemidos:
Inscriptions from VII: 68, 69.
SPERBER, ALEXANDER:
Hebrew Gammar of V: 472*(3)*.
Targum of Isaiah, Errata VI: 714*(2)*.
Sphaecteria: III: *205*.

Sphinx, Great: **III**: 494, 495*(2)*, 727, 734.
Antiquity of **III**: 494.
Repair of **III**: 455.
Sphinx(es): **III**: **§190**, **491-498**, *753, 769;* **V**: *246, 351.*
Amenophis III, from the Mortuary Temple of **VII**: 74.
Avenue of the, at Ben-i-Hassan **III**: 491.
Eujuk, at, Arrangement of Hair on **III**: 492.
Greek, in Boston **III**: 740.
"Hyksos", date of **III**: 497.
Ivory, from Abydos **III**: 770.
Queen, of a **III**: 577.
Queen's **III**: 495, 732.
Tanis, of **III**: 495.
Tell Tayinaat, from **III**: 743.
Spices:
Lists of Aromatic Woods and **VII**: 195.
Spies:
Israelite, in Canaan **IV**: 229, 345*(3)*.
Spikenard: **III**: **394**; **V**: 560.
Spinda: **III**: 237.
Spindle:
Mespotamian, Evolution of **II**: 233; **III**: 702; **IX**: cxii.
Whorl with Hebrew Inscription **III**: 573.
Spinning Bowls: **I**: 274*(2)*.
SPINOZA, BARACH (BENEDICT) **I**: *180;* **IV**: *83;* **VI**: *123, 138, 139*.
Jewish View of Natural Law and **V**: 113.
OT Criticism and **IV**: 118, 124.
Spirit: **V**: *506(4), 507, 514(2), 515(3),* 515*(8), 655(3);* **VIII**: 33, 167, 168, 291.
Chinese, Word for, in, Translating **IV**: 111.
Flesh and, in the DSS and NT **VIII**: 482.
Man, of **VI**: 542; **VIII**: 173.
Pre-Exilic Prophets, in **IV**: 387*(2);* **VIII**: 22, 152.
Spirit of God, *see also:* **God** **V**: 521.
Spiritism, *see;* **Psychical Research**
Spirits: **V**: 515.
Arabian Belief in **I**: 391.
Babylonian, Classes of **V**: 172.
Babylonian, Evil **V**: 175.
Evil, *see:* **Demonology**
Familiar Spirit **VI**: 124, 206, 284.
Field, in the OT **VIII**: 160.
Keres **V**: 270.
Lares and **III**: 696; **V**: 268.
Seven, and Archangels **V**: 128.
Souls, of, in Enoch **VI**: 664.
Testament of the Twelve Patriarchs, in **VI**: 659.
Two, in the Damascus Document **VIII**: 460.
Two, in the Rule of the Community **VIII**: 462, 464.
"Spirits in Prison": **VI**: 48.
Spiritualism: **VI**: 147.
Hebrew **V**: 15.
Spirituals:
Negro, and the Psalms **VIII**: 359.
SPITZER, JR., (MRS.) LYMAN: **III**: 635.
Spondee:
Use of, in Hexameter **V**: 691.
Spontaneous Generation: **III**: 328.
Spoon(s):
Ointment, Egyptian **III**: 588.
Wooden, Egyptian **III**: 588.
Sport:
Cuneiform Terms for **I**: 238; **V**: 545.
Sports:
Field, of Greeks and Romans **I**: 237.
SPRATT, P. A. B.: **III**: 440; **VII**: 373.

Spring(s): I: 363.
'Ain et-Tabigha, near III: 445.
Aisawiyah, Newly Discovered, at I: 360.
Bethesda I: 362.
"Binding the Springs" IV: 220; VI: 434.
Callirrhoe, Analysis of Water from I: 359; II: 213.
En-Dor, A Sacred(?) IV: 376; V: 48.
En-Rogel II: 362.
Hagar's II: 284.
Haunted, in Palestine I: 389.
Hot, at Pella I: 343; II: 458.
Hot Sulphur, in Palestine II: 237, 247, 285.
Jerusalem I: 361; II: 412.
Jerusalem, at Ancient Arch, in II: 405.
Peirene, Upper on Acrocorinth III: 483.
Siloah II: 409.
Sirah VI: 208.
Sulphur, at Jabbok I: 359.
SPURGEON, CHARLES: VIII: 380.
Spy (Place): III: *360*.
Squares:
Theban Tomb Walls, Proportional, on III: 696.
***Srr*, Land of:** II: 272; III: 237.
Stables:
Solomon's I: 251; II: 405*(3)*, 406; III: 480.
Stacte: III: *392*, **394**.
STADE, BERNHARD:
Habakkuk, on IV: 449.
Hebrew Lexicon VI 378, 379*(2)*, 380, 381, 384.
Staffs I: 251; III: **§217**, **671**; IX: **§217**, **cxvi**.
Stag, *see also:* **Deer**
Sumerian Divinity V: 186.
Stairs:
King David's III: 480; VI: 583, 586.
Stamata: III: 238, *721*.
Stamnos, Stamnoi: I: 188; IX: lxxxv.
Red-Figured, of the Periklean Period III: 605.
Stamps, *see also:* **Seals**
Amenhotep III, of III: 664.
Ammonite, Stamp Seal from 'Amman III: 666.
Brick, at Cosa III: 471.
Copper, with Greek Inscription VII: 313.
Egyptian, Seal III: 664.
Egyptian, Wood III: 664.
Gezer III: 665.
Greek Stamps on Rhodian Amphorae from Cyprus III: 661, 662.
Hebrew III: 654, 665.
Herodian Pottery, Stamps on III: 662.
Jewish III: 664.
Jewish Wine-Merchant, of III: 665.
Judean III: 666.
Lachish, from III: 664.
Potters' III: 616, 663, 664, 669.
Prehistoric, Seal III: 666.
Royal Jewish Pottery III: 663*(2)*.
'Royal' Stamps of Judah on Jar Handles II: 219.
South-Arabian Clay, from Bethel III: 665, 666*(2)*; VII: 293.
Syro-Cappadocian Stamp Seals III: 664.
Yehud (YHWD) III: 665*(2)*, 666.
Stand(s):
Geometric, Fragments of III: 583.
Ring, (Egyptian) for Vase III: 602.
Two Red-Figured III: 583.
Standards, Military: I: 315; III: **§217**, **671**.
Horus, of V: 201.
Parthian I: 423; III: 747.
Stanford Museum: III: *606*, *632*.
STANHOPE, HESTER, LADY: II: *326*.
STANLEY, ARTHUR PENRHYN: I: 138*(3)*.
Sinai and Palestine, on III: 231.

Stanza:
- Egyptian Word *ht* 'house' used in the sense of — **V**: 352.

STARCKY, JEAN: — **VIII**: 420.
STARKEY, J. L.: — **IV**: 218; **VII**: 84.

Stars:
- Abraham and the — **I**: 32; **III**: *329;* **VIII**: 247.
- Babylonian Catalog of — **II**: 233.
- Babylonian Names of — **II**: 226.
- Barsag, Month when Sets — **II**: 229.
- Coins, Symbols of, on — **I**: 454; **VIII**: 307, 420.
- Orion and the Great Star — **II**: 230.
- 'Star of Stars' — **II**: 228.
- Thirty-six in Babylonian Astronomy — **II**: 232.
- Time, Telling of, by — **II**: 232.
- Triad of — **II**: 228.
- Zodiacal Arrangement of — **I**: 407.

State:
- Aristotle on the Model — **V**: 245.
- Demands of, in Israel — **I**: 508.
- Mesopotamia, Small, in — **I**: 490; **III**: 165.
- Secular, and Judaism — **I**: 470; **V**: 29.

Statecraft: — **I**: 487.
Stategi: — **I**: 186.

Staters:
- Counterfeit Aegina — **I**: 457.
- Croton, Overstruck — **I**: 459.

Statuary, *see also:* **Sculpture** — **III: §226, 720-754; IX: §226, cxxvii.**
- Acrolithic — **III**: 739.
- Ahmes, of, at Karnak — **II**: 7.
- Amenhotep, son of Hapu — **VII**: 64.
- Amenophis, Fragment of — **III**: 732; **VII**: 65.
- Amman, from — **III**: 743.
- Amūn, in Egyptian — **III**: 745.
- Amykos — **III**: 740.
- Anubis, the Jackal-God — **III**: 752.
- Anus Ebria — **III**: 740.
- Aphrodite, Roman Copies of Greek Statues — **III**: 735.
- Apollo, Mantua, Fogg Art Museum — **III**: 749.
- Arcadia, Primitive, from — **III**: 731.
- Architecture and, at Corinth — **III**: 723.
- Artemis, of — **III**: 720.
- Askalon, at — **III**: 721.
- Assyrian, Marble — **III**: 749.
- Athenian Agora, 5th Century, from — **III**: 740.
- Augustus, of — **II**: 23*(2)*, **III**: *671*.
- Auletes, Sandstone of — **III**: 751.
- Boston, in, Three Inscribed (Egyptian) — **VII**: 65.
- Cleaning of — **III**: 456.
- Colossi from Koptos — **III**: 700, 741, 771.
- Colossi, Kushite in the Sudan — **III**: 741.
- Colossi of Memnon — **III**: 741.
- Commagenian Tiaras — **III**: 750.
- Corinth(ian) — **III**: 461, 724, 736.
- Demosthenes, of — **III**: 727.
- Diadoumenos — **III**: 754.
- Dionysos, of, Seated — **III**: 727.
- Dioskouroi — **III**: 740.
- Doryphoros — **III**: 754.
- Drunken Woman — **III**: 740.
- Egyptian — **III**: 725, 742, 745.
- Egyptian, Colossal, from the XIXth Dynasty — **III**: 737.
- Egyptian, for the Dead — **I**: 371.
- Egyptian, Head from an — **III**: 735.
- Egyptian, Middle Kingdom in the British Museum — **III**: 733.
- Egyptian, Old Kingdom — **III**: 737.
- Egyptian, Provincial, VIth Dynasty — **III**: 748; **VII**: 72.
- Egyptian Tomb, Origin of — **I**: 375.
- Egyptian, Unfinished, from XIIth Dynasty — **III**: 737.
- Egyptian, with Amarna Traits — **III**: 753.
- Egyptian, XVIII Dynasty, Granite — **III**: 744.
- Eleusinian — **III**: 731.

Etruscan, Tomb-Guardian	**III**: 747.
Faun, from Quirinal	**III**: 723.
Girl Beneath Apple Tree	**III**: 740.
Girl, of (I.M. 63503)	**III**: 749.
Goddess of Ceos	**III**: 748.
Greek	**III**: 739.
Greek, Archaic	**III**: 729.
Greek Lady from Persepolis	**III**: 742.
Greek, Polychromy in	**III**: 707.
Greek (Sea-God)	**III**: 732.
Greek, Tyrannicides	**III**: 747.
Gudea	**III**: 722, 736.
Ḥaremḥab, of	**VII**: 64.
Ḥarwa, of	**III**: 735.
Hathor, of	**III**: 737; **V**: 214.
Hellenistic, Cuirassed	**III**: 747, 750, 752.
Hellenistic Group	**III**: 751, 754.
Heracles, a Forgery (?)	**III**: 743.
Herculaneum, at	**III**: 120, 743.
Herculaneum Women	**III**: 749.
Hercules	**III**: 751.
Hermes	**III**: 743, 754*(2)*.
Hermes Discobolus(?)	**III**: 724.
Idrimi	**IV**: 318.
Jason, Lysippean, Date of	**III**: 750.
Jericho, and the Creation of Man	**V**: 151; **VIII**: 80; **IX**: cxxvii.
Ka-, of abnormal men	**III**: 737.
Ka-mes, Fan-bearer of the Body Guard of Amenhetep III	**II**: *55;* **III**: 724.
Khartoum Museum 30	**II**: 45; **III**: 746.
Khartoum Museum 5516	**VII**: 24.
Lama, Goddess, at Ur	**III**: 747.
Lifesize, in America	**III**: 753.
Limestone, rough (I.M. 66461)	**III**: 749.
Lion, Greek at Didyma	**III**: 743.
Ludovisi Gaul, Restoration of	**III**: 734.
Lysippean Jason, Date of	**III**: 750.
Meleager, of	**II**: *60;* **III**: 724.
Metal Statuary and Castings	**III**: **§227, 755-759**.
Michaelis	**III**: 624, 625, 744, 745, 746, 747.
Nimrud, fragments from	**VII**: 177.
Niobid, of	**III**: 726*(2)*.
Oldest *(Daddu)*	**III**: 725, 726.
Pedeamūn-nebnesuttaiu of	**II**: 73; **VII**: 75.
Polyclitan	**III**: 729.
Polykleitos	**III**: 754.
Ptolemaic *Στρατηγος* of hte Mendesian Nome	**VII**: 70.
Rameses II, raising of Colossal, at Memphis	**III**: 721.
Ramesside block, from Tell el-Bakleyyah	**VII**: 74.
Ramesside, Royal, from Palestine	**III**: 733.
Robinson Collection	**III**: 744.
Roman, Cuirassed	**III**: 747, 750, 752.
Roman, Diademed(?)	**III**: 751, 752.
Roman Togatus	**III**: 754.
Roy, of	**III**: 729*(2)*.
Sandstone of An Auletes	**III**: 751.
Sarapis	**III**: 519*(2)*.
Scribe, at the Louvre	**III**: 730, 745.
Sekhemka, of	**VII**: 72.
Senmut, of	**III**: 732*(2)*.
Serpent-Worshipper, of	**III**: 735; **VII**: 66.
Shalmaneser III	**II**: 93.
Sikyonian	**III**: 721.
"Soul of Nekhen"	**III**: 739.
"Soul of Pe"	**III**: 739.
Sumerian	**III**: 751.
Tell el-ʿAmarnah, from	**III**: 734.
Terracotta, from Heraeum	**III**: 724.
Terracotta, from Keos	**III**: 751.
Terracotta, of the Villa Albani	**III**: 737.
Terracotta, (Potnia Taurōn)	**III**: 737.
Transporation of Djeḥutiḥetep colossus	**I**: 349; **III**: 748.

Triton, of, Greek, from Gaza **III**: 748.
Twēret, of **III**: 769.
Unidentified, Sumerian **III**: 743.
User, of **III**: 724.
Usertsen III, of **III**: *592,* 726.
Venus **III**: 725, 727.
Warrior Image from Capestrano **III**: 745.
Zeus Herkeios **III**: 744*(2)*.
Zeus Ithomatos **III**: 740.
Zeus, Olympian **III**: 728.
Zoser, of, Inscribed **VII**: 64.

Statuary, Metal, and Castings, *see also:* **Bronzes** **III: §227, 755-759.**

Artemision, Bronze Statue from **III**: 757*(2)*.
Bronze, Archaic at Mârib **III**: 517.
Bronze Casting from Tell el 'Obeid **III**: 756.
Bronze Casting of Goddess Asherah **III**: 758.
Bronze, Egyptian Statue of Negro Captive **III**: 756.
Bronze Figure from Rakka **III**: 755.
Bronze Figure of Isis, with Silver Head-covering **III**: 755.
Bronze, found at Cairo (Hittite Deity) **III**: 756; **V**: 225.
Bronze Fragments in the Loeb Collection **III**: 755.
Bronze 'Gatagusa' of Praxiteles **III**: 746.
Bronze Statue of a Cake-carrier **III**: 756.
Bronze-Reliefs from the Acropolis of Athens **III**: 755.
Cretan Bull, Silver **III**: 756.
Eagle Symbols **III**: 757.
Etruscan Art, Metals in **III**: 757.
Fish, Egyptian Models of **III**: 373, 374, 582, 755, 760.
Hercules, Bronze, of **III**: 755.
Marcus Vipsanius Agrippa, Bronze Head **III**: 755.
Metal Mouse from Jaffa **III**: 378, 580, 596, 755; **VI**: 196.

Statuettes, *see also:* **Figurines** **III: §228, 759-769; IX: §228, cxxvii.**

Abydos, Archaic, from **III**: 763.
Alabastra **III**: 745.
Amen-Ra, rare figure of **III**: 760.
Amon, in the Petrie Collection **III**: 735; **V**: 213.
Amūm **II**: 17; **III**: 766.
Anuḳet, of **III**: 766.
Aphrodite, Terra-cotta **III**: 763.
Apohrodite, Early Classical Bronze **III**: 767.
Aremis Ephesia, of **III**: 763.
Baal, of **III**: 768.
Babylonian from Tell el 'Obeid, compared with Egyptian **III**: 761.
Barkal, Gold, from **III**: 767.
Berlin Spinner **III**: 767.
Bird, Figure of a **III**: 761.
Blind Harper in Cairo Museum **III**: 761.
Bronze **III**: 762, 763.
Bronze, Asklepios Type **III**: 766.
Bronze, from Delphi **III**: 764.
Bronze, from Sardinia **III**: 763.
Bronze, Greco-Roman Apis **III**: 762.
Bronze, Greek **III**: 763, 766, 769.
Bronze, in Metropolitan Museum of Art **III**: 762.
Bronze Masked Dancer **III**: 766.
Bronze, of a Negro **III**: 351, 766.
Bronze, of Zeus Kerauniois **III**: 764.
Bronze, Phoenician **II**: 207.
Clay, from Tell es-Sawwan **III**: 768.
Cretan **III**: 761*(2)*.
Dancing Figures from Palaikastro **V**: 241; **IX**: cxxvii.

Dattari Collection, in **III**: 760.
Duat-nefret, mother of Queeen Nubkhaes **VII**: 65.
Egyptian, B.M. 1735 **III**: 768.
Egyptian Commissioner in Syria **VII**: 67.
Egyptian Ebony, of a Negress **III**: 760.
Egyptian, from Der el-Bahari **III**: 769.
Egyptian, from Gezer **III**: 760.
Egyptian, from Naucratis **III**: 763.
Egyptian Funerary **III**: 768; **V**: 222.
Egyptian, Heads of, from Temple of Mut at Karnak **III**: 760.
Egyptian, in Malta **VII**: 69.
Egyptian, Inscribed, Middle Kingdom **III**: 764.
Egyptian, Late **III**: 769.
Egyptian, Late Old Kingdom **V**: 353.
Egyptian, Unusual Type **III**: 763.
Egyptian, with Sun Hymn **III**: 760; **VII**: 41.
Eighth Century Traveler **III**: 769.
Etruscan **III**: 761.
Faience **III**: 746.
God Bes, of **III**: 765.
Goddess, Enthroned **III**: 763.
Gorringe Collection **III**: 761.
Greek, from Arabia **III**: 765.
Greek, from Naucratis **III**: 763.
Gypsum (I.M. 64398) **III**: 749, 767.
Hittite **III**: 761.
"Hittite" Priest, from Ephesus, Bronze **III**: 767.
Horoztepe, from **III**: 766.
Horseman, of **III**: 767.
Ivory, from Hierakonpolis **III**: 769, 772, 773.
Khonserdaisu, of **III**: 762; **IX**: cv.
Kültepe, from **III**: 579.
Louvre Museum, Two in **III**: 761.
Ma'et, of **III**: 769.
Min-Mes, of **III**: 760; **IX**: cv.
Minoan **III**: 765.
Mycenaean **III**: 622, 765, 767.
Mycenaean Goddess **III**: 764.
Naval Standard-Bearer of Amenhotep III **III**: 761.
Osorkon I, Bronze **III**: 759.
"Pazuzu", Bronze **III**: 758, 768.
Pedestal of a, Kah-ankh-ra Sebekhetep **III**: 493.
Phoenician "Goddess" in the Louvre **V**: 196; **IX**: cxxvii.
Phoenician Inscription on Votive **III**: 761.
Satyr, Bronze, in Pergamene Style **III**: 767.
Sekhmet-Ubastet, of **III**: 763; **V**: 212.
Serpentine, in **III**: 767.
Stelophorous, in the British Museum **III**: 768; **VII**: 73.
Sumerian, Gold **III**: 762.
Sumerian, of the Founder of Lagash **III**: 763.
Tel Ṣippor, from **III**: 768.
Tell Sandahannah, from **III**: 768.
Thoth, of **III**: 763.
Ur, from **III**: 747, 767.
Wooden **III**: 762.

Stealing, *see:* **Theft**

Steam Heat: **I**: 266.

STEBBINS, RUFUS PHINEAS:
Balaam, on **IV**: 344.

Steel: **I**: 295, 300; **II**: *154*.
Iron Carbide Structure in Ancient **I**: 300; **II**: 219.
Swords, Near Eastern, of **I**: 300, 318; **II**: 218.

Steelyard: **I**: 422; **III**: 674.

Steering Gear:
Egyptian Ships, of **I**: 352*(2)*; **III**: 586.

STEIN, SIR AUREL: **II**: *6*, 255; **III**: 126.

STEINDORFF, GEORGE:
Bibliography of **I**: 22*(2)*.

STEKELIS, MOSHE: **II**: 203.

Stelae, *see also Names of Individuals and Places*
400-Year **VII**: 26.
Akkadian **III**: 497*(2)*.
Amenhetep II, of, at Giza **V**: 214.
Amenophis III in Tell el-ʿAmarna **III**: 495.
Amon-Renas, of **VII**: 289.
Apa Telemē, Coptic **VII**: 83.
Aramaic (Sujin Pact) **VII**: 127.
Aristion, of **III**: 714.
Ashur-nasir-pal II, of **VII**: 188.
Attic deme of Ikaria, Stele of a Warrior **III**: 492.
Attic Grave **III**: 496*(2)*, 544.
Axumite, False Doors of **III**: 476.
Belief of the Future World of Egyptians, Etruscans, and Greeks from their **V**: 144.
Ben-Hadad I, Votive, of **III**: 496, 497*(2)*; **VII**: 127*(3)*.
Buchis, Date of Some **VII**: 21.
Coins and **I**: 452.
Cyprus, Fragment, from **III**: 743.
Dâkhla, Ashmolean Museum no. 1894. 107b **VII**: 26.
Dakhleah **VII**: 21.
Den, of **III**: 498.
Donation **VII**: 25.
Egptian, New Kingdom, funerary (70'96) **III**: 579; **VII**: 45.
Egyptian **III**: 494.
Egyptian Donation, in the Brooklyn Museum **III**: 498.
Egyptian, Earlier Intermediate Period **VII**: 20.
Egyptian, Figures on, Characteristics of **III**: 701.
Egyptian, funerary, Motifs and phrases on **V**: 309.
Egyptian, Funerary, of a Man from Gabelen **VII**: 20.
Egyptian Funerary with a rare title **VII**: 45.
Egyptian in Musuem at Bath **III**: 492.
Egyptian, Late Middle Kingdom **VII**: 26.
Egyptian, Private Funerary **II**: 127; **VII**: 23.
Egyptian (with Texts) **VII: §830, 18-27.**
Egypto-Karian Bilingual **VII**: 20.
Etruscan Grave **III**: 728.
Flying Angels **III**: 732.
Funerary **III**: 495.
Funerary, Toilet Scene on **VII**: 22.
Grave **III**: 538, 603, 724, 751.
Greek **III**: 736.
Heracleopolitan Period, at Saqqara **VII**: 25.
Hori I, of **III**: 498.
Horus, from Middle Delta **III**: 753.
Job Stone **VII**: 26.
Junkin **VII**: 20.
Kayay, Round Topped of **VII**: 63.
Kharṭūm, 5162, 5261, 3724, 3732 **VII**: 24.
Khartoum Museum, 11778, 372A, and 247 **VII**: 24.
Khartoum Museum No. 3 **VII**: 24.
Kia, of **II**: 205.
Kilamûwa **VII**: 91, 124.
Komose **VII**: 24, 70.
Leicester City Museum, in **VII**: 25.
Lion-Hunt, from Warka **III**: 742.
Lyseas, of **III**: 714.
MacGregor Collection, in **VII**: 20.
Memphite of Merptaḥ **VII**: 24.
Mephite of Ptaḥmosĕ **VII**: 24.
Metternich, 85-6 **V**: 214; **VI**: 452; **VII**: 23.
Middle Kingdom, Late, of **VII**: 24.
Mycenaean, Figured **III**: 742.
Naram-Sin's **III**: 493.
New Kingdom, Faience **VII**: 25.
Nitocris Adoption **VII**: 25, 27.
Painted Wooden, in the Cairo Museum **VII**: 26.
Partho-Roman **III**: 496.
Ptolemaic, Inscribed **VII**: 26.
Ramesside **III**: 496.

Ramesside Stelas Pertaining to the Cult of Amenophis I **VII**: 25.
Rhodian **III**: 734.
Rimah, of **II**: 7.
Saba'a, of **II**: 7.
Sefire, Treaty Terminology of **VII**: 130.
Sepulchral, in the British Museum **VII**: 43.
Sepulchral, Painted, from Alexandria **III**: 492, 720.
Shechem Stele **VII**: 87.
South Arabian, of Maʿīn **III**: 497.
Sumerian **III**: 496.
Sun Disk on **III**: 733.
Taya, in Tell el-ʿAmarna **III**: 495.
Tehuti-hetep, Round Topped of **VII**: 63.
Teima, of, in Arabia **VII**: 121.
Tell el Rimah, excavated **II**: 472.
Tukulti-ninurta II, of found near Tell Ashara **VII**: 188.
Ur, from **III**: 498.
Ur-Nanshe, of **III**: 498.
Vultures, from Tello **III**: 493; **IX**: cxliii.
Warka, Lion-Hunt, from **III**: 742.
Warrior, of, from Ikaria **III**: 721.
Zakir **VII**: 91, 124.
Zer, of **III**: 495.
Zernikh **III**: 496; **VII**: 22.

Stepmother(s): **I**: 215.
Marriage among Hebrews and Arabs **I**: 215.

"Steppes of Moab": **II**: 289, 447.

Stereometry:
Posidian physics, in **II**: 223.

STERNHOLD, THOMAS: **VI**: 639.

STEVENS, WILLIAM ARNOLD: **III**: 447.

STEVENSON, WILLIAM BARRON:
Bibliography of **I**: 22.

Stewards: **I**: 190, 191, 271; **II**: 8; **VI**: 590.

Stewardship, *see:* **Tithing**

Stichometry:
Barberini MS, and **IV**: 202.
Freisingen MS, and **IV**: 202.
Masoretic Text and **IV**: 18.
Psalm 106 and Hallel **VI**: 514.

Stick:
Beduin Camel, Uas Scepture as a **III**: 671.

Stoa:
Attalos, Rebuilding of **III**: 473.
Corinth, at **III**: 471, 472, 514.
Kakai, of Zeus, Date of **III**: 485.

Stobi:
Synagogue of Claudius Tiberius Polycharmus in **III**: 524.

STOCK, JOSEPH:
Job, on **IV**: 456.

Stockholm:
Egyptian Museum **III**: *611*.
National Museum of **VII**: *213, 218, 239*.

Stoicism:
Roman Politics and **I**: 492; **V**: 270; **IX**: cii.
Wise Man in **V**: 267; **VI**: 691.

Stoics: **V**: 247.
Alexander the Great, and **II**: 10*(2)*; **V**: 257*(2)*.

Stomach:
Akkadian Names for, of Ruminants **V**: 552.
Assyrian Prescriptions for **III**: 405.

Stone(s): **I**: 417.
Assyrian Word for row, course of (tikpu) **III**: 462.
Baetylia **III**: 575.
Chisel-Drafted at Jerusalem **III**: 461.
Dressing of, at Jerusalem **I**: 290.
Gem **I**: 280, **§96, 285-287**, 290, *338;* **III**: 460, 562, **§209, 591-594**.
Gem Cutters in Ur **III**: 649.
Glazed **III**: 592, 734.
Great Heaps of **I**: 365.
"Hat-Toîm" **III**: 461.

Holy **III**: 575; **V**: 154.
Implements **III**: *672(2)*, 674*(2)*.
Jerusalem, of **II**: 247.
Jerusalem, Remarkable in Jewish Quarter **II**: 409.
Ligure **I**: 285.
Memorial, in Joshua **IV**: 363.
Ornamental **I**: 280, 290; **III**: 460, 562.
Precious, *see:* ***Stones, Gem***
Sacred, Greek (*Bœtyli* or *Bœtylia*) **V**: 246.
Sacred, in Malta **V**: 241.
Sardius **I**: 285.
Sling **I**: 314, 315, 320, 321; **III**: 681.

Stone Age:
Anaoltia Industry in **III**: 13.
Demarcation between Men and Animals **III**: 336.
Egypt, in **II**: 126.
Jordan, in **II**: 422.

"Stone of Foundation": **V**: 67*(2)*.

Stonecutting: **I**: **§98**, **290-293**; **II**: *175;* **III**: *677*.
Stonedressers' Marks, from a Nabataean Sanctuary at 'Avdat **III**: 476, 477.

Stoning: **I**: 179.
Greeks and Romans, Among **I**: 180.

Stools:
Egyptian **I**: 209; **III**: 582*(2)*.
Wooden, from Kom Washim **III**: 465, 582.

Storage:
Magazines attached to Temple of Sety I **III**: 520; **VII**: 18.

Stories:
Animal, among Palestinians **I**: 389.
Syrian **I**: 385.

Stork:
Assyrian word for **III**: *381;* **V**: 568.

STORR, GOTTLOB: **IV**: 200; **VIII**: 10, 25.

Story:
Myth and **V**: 136.
Old Testament, in **V**: 701.

Strabo: **I**: *377;* **II**: *23*, **97-98**.
Travels of, in Greece **I**: 344.

STRACK, HERMANN LEBERECHT:
Pentateuch, on **IV**: 226.

Strainer:
Bronze **III**: 587.
Kyathos **III**: 588*(2)*, 619.
Silver, from Greece **III**: 588*(2)*.

Strategi: **I**: 186, 187.

Strategy, Military: **I**: 319.
Hittite **I**: 315, 316, 346.
Sabbath attacks against the Jews **I**: 319.
Xerxes, Strategy and Tactics of Invasion **II**: 108.

STRATON, JOHN ROACH: **III**: 330.

Stratonikeia:
Tablet from **III**: *635*.

STRATTON, JOSEPH, SIR: **III**: 507.

Straws, Drinking:
Siphons, Drinking, Tell el-ʿAmarna, from **III**: 588.

Streets: **I**: 206, 207, 346; **IV**: 219.
Levels, in Tyropoeon Valley, within the walls **II**: 415.

Strigil: **III**: 619.

Strikes: **I**: 271.
Ramesses III Twenty-ninth Year, in **II**: 81.

STUART, MOSES:
Daniel, on **IV**: 523.
Ecclesiasties, on **IV**: 512.
Genesis and Geology and **III**: 330; **IV**: 285.

Stuyvesant Institute: **I**: *378, 393, 407, 417;* **II**: *59, 113, 124, 132, 160, 178, 225;* **III**: *503, 530*.

Śu:
Language of II: 264.
Ṣubarians: II: *143(3)*, **168**; IX: cx, cxiii.
Subartu: IX: cx, cxiii.
Subat-Enlil: II: 256.
Samsi-Adad's Journey from, to Mari IX: xcv.
Subat-Samas: III: 238, *261*.
Subbi-luliuma:
Hittite Text to His Son Biuyassilis by VII: 306.
Seal of, Hittite Inscription on VII: 306.
Suberde: III: **238**, 265*(2)*.
Sublimation:
Evidences of, in Ancient Meospotamia II: 224.
Submarine:
Asherah, for Archaeology III: 453.
Substitution: VIII: 194.
Ancient Near East, in V: 166; IX: cxlii.
Succession:
History, Theme and Motif in, and Yahwist corpus VI: 212.
Royal, Hittite I: 478.
Royal, Problems of, in Israel I: *96*, 470, 484, 487, 493.
Succoth: I: *399;* II: 284, *458(4)*, **485**, *497, 498;* III: *121, 201(4)*, **238**; IV: 317, 332, 369.
Celebration, Revival of(?) V: 84.
Succoth-benoth: V: 395; VI: 239.
Sud, River:
Baruch, in VI: 639.
Sudan: I: 142, *295, 364;* II: *252;* III: *10(3), 71, 79,* 81, *227(2)*, **238**, 238‡, *344, 571*.
Archaeology, Endangered III: 457.
Biscuit or Egg-shell Ware III: 605.
Egyptian Fortress in III: 489.
Egyptian Texts from VII: 70.
Isaiah's Knowledge of II: 238*(2);* IV: 393*(2)*.
Karian, Egyptian, and Nubian-Greek Inscriptions from VII: 15, 318, 374.
Rock Paintings in IX: cxxvii.
Serra, Ancient Name of VII: 69.
Sudla, *see:* **Sesebi**
Suez: II: *260;* III: 208, 239, 441, 446.
Suez Canal: II: 254.
Suf: II: *287*.
Suffa: II: 284.
Suffering: VIII: 181, **§1013, 185-187**.
Dead Sea Scrolls, Human in, Eschatological Significance of I: 416; VIII: 187, 253, 420.
Divine Discipline, as VIII: 186.
Element of Messianic Prophecy, as VIII: 134.
Job and the Jewish Theology of IV: 461; VIII: 185.
Job and the Problem of IV: 463*(2);* VIII: 185, 186*(5)*.
Nature of, in Jeremiah IV: 416; VIII: 187.
Pre-Exilic Prophets, in IV: 387; VIII: 186.
Psalms, in IV: 483; VI: 454, 475; VIII: 187.
"Righteous Sufferer" in Cuneiform Literature, *see also:* Tabi-utul-Bel VII: 181, 221*(2)*.
Sin and, as Related to the Power, Wisdom, and Love of God VIII: 95, 185.
Sin, as Proof of VIII: 186.
Source of Prayer(?) VIII: 203.
Vicarious VI: 306.
Well-Being and, in the OT VIII: 185.
Zoroastrianism, in V: 236.

"Suffering Servant": **VIII: §1001, 144-147.**
Anonymity of VIII: 146.
Daniel, in VI: 577.
Davidic Messiah and VIII: 142, 146.
Deutero-Isaiah in IV: 399, 402, 404*(4)*, 405, 412; VI: 307*(2)*, 308, 309*(2)*; VIII: 144, 145*(3)*.
Isaac and VIII: 147.
Isaiah and IV: 395; VI: 6; VIII: 145.
Jeremiah and IV: 412; VIII: 145.
Jesus and VIII: 147.
Moses and I: 72; VIII: 146.
Origin of the Idea VI: 310; VIII: 146.
Scandinavian Discussion VIII: 146.
Suffragatio: I: 506.
Sufis:
Song of Solomon and IV: 508.
Sugyah: VI: 704.
Anonymous, Impact on Halakic Concepts VI: 695.
Sources and Development of, in the Babylonian Talmud VI: 704.
Suicide:
Greeks and VIII: 231.
Old Testament Law and, from *Kitāb Al-Anwār* of Ya'qūb Al Qirqisānī I: 464; VIII: 233.
Sujin Pact, *see also:* **Sefire**
Aramaic Stele VII: 127.
SUKENIK, E. L.: VIII: 465; IX: *clii(2)*.
Bibliography of I: 22.
Sukkal-mah: VII: 213.
Sukkiim: I: 185, 313.
Sulaimaniyah Liwa: I: *318*.
Ancient Fortifications III: 489.
Sulla: II: 98.
Sulphur: II: 212.
Sultân, Tell (Ain) es-, (Sulṭûn) *see also:* **Jericho** II: 397, 400, 485; III: *431;* VI: 168, 227, 232; VIII: 248; IX: cxlvii.
Sultantepe: III: **239**, 262.
Sultantepe Tablets: VII: 150, 176*(3)*, 177*(4)*, 181*(2)*, 189, 197, 202, 215, 271.
Sumatra:
Phoenician Alphabet on V: 285.
Phoenician Characters from VII: 114.
Sumer: I: *96*, 181, *218*, 328, 337, *470, 484, 487, 492, 493;* II: 197, 202, 264; III: 88, **239**.
Dynasties of II: 208.
Egypt and III: 239.
Food of the Gods in V: 185.
Kingship and Council in IX: ci.
Names of, Various in Cuneiform Inscriptions II: 263.
Religion and Community in III: 239; V: 185.
Wisdom of V: 118.
Sumeria: I: *426, 483(2)*.
Sumerian: II: *111, 168;* V: 544*(2)*.
Akkadian and V: 544*(2)*, 578*(2);* VII: 147, 269.
Bible and IV: 192.
Cryptography, or VII: 269.
Georgian and, in Comparative Philology V: 580*(2)*.
King List II: 210.
Language II: *223*.
Lexicography V: *549*.
Marriage Texts I: 221.
Semitic and, Origins of V: 375, 579.
Sumerian-Assyrian Vocabularies V: 561, 579.
Sumero-Akkadian Question V: 543, 578.

Term, Use of **II**: *111, 168.*
Tibetan, Relation to **V**: 581.
Vocabulary **V**: 578.
Sumerian Chronology: II: §150, 202.
Sumerian Correspondence, Literary Texts and Wisdom Literature: VII: §911, 274-276.
Sumerian Epic Literature *see also:* **Sumerian Mythological Texts**
Babel of Tongues **VI**: 58.
Fall of Man, Epic of **V**: 179.
Langdon Epic **V**: 581; **VII**: 282.
Man's Golden Age, Parallel to Gen. 11:1 **VI**: 58; **VII**: 283.
Pardise, Epic of, Necessary Revision of **V**: 180.
Sumerian Grammar: V: §535, 578-585; IX: §535, cxlii.
Affixes *Tam* and *Kam* **V**: 581.
BU-doubled Criss-corss **V**: 583.
Delitzsch's **V**: 580*(2)*.
-e- as a Verbal Suffix **V**: 585.
First and Second Persons in **V**: 578.
Genitive Element **V**: 583.
Genitive Predicative **V**: 584.
Meanings, Multiplicity of **V**: 580.
Noun Formation **V**: 579.
Palatal *ń(ñ)* **V**: 584.
Particle *mā* **V**: 578, 581.
Phonetic Relations in **V**: 581.
Postfixed GE, KA=KIMA **V**: 583.
Pronouns of **V**: 580.
Root form sì(m) and su_{11}(m) **V**: 583.
Roots, Abbreviated **V**: 580.
Tones in **V**: 581.
Velar Nasal *ng(ṅ)* **V**: 584.
Verb, Intransitive, Tenses **V**: 583.
Verbal Prefixes and Infixes **V**: 579.
Verbal System, Marû and Ḫamṭu Aspects in **V**: 585.
Verbs, Compound, Syntax of **V**: 579.
Verbs, Intensive Compound **V**: 580.
Verbs of **V**: 580.
Sumerian Historical Texts: VII: §912, 276-279.
A-an-ni-pad-da, Foundation-tablet of **VII**: 276.
A-an-ni-pad-da, Inscription of **VII**: 278.
Administration Tablet of the Third Ur Dynasty **VII**: 278.
Bilingual **VII**: 154.
Gudi'a Inscriptions, Parallel Passage in **VII**: 276*(2)*.
Kish, Conquest of, under Agga, Tablet on **VII**: 278.
Nippur Tablet, Missing fragment of the Kings of Agade **VII**: 277.
Pre-Sargonic Inscription from Warka **VII**: 277.
Samsu-iluna's bilingual Inscription B **VII**: 153, 279.
Tummal Inscription **VII**: 279.
Sumerian King List:
Date of **VII**: 278.
Kings of Ur and Isin **VII**: 278.
Nippur Recension **VII**: 240, 279.
Sumerian Kings:
Piety of **V**: 185.
Sumerian Language: V: §535, 578-585; IX: §535, cxlii.
Akkadian, and, in Comparative Philology **V**: 542, 578.
Chinese and **V**: 580.
Language of the *Śu* **V**: 578.
Lexicography **V**: 578; **VII**: 280.
Trilingual Glosses **IX**: cxlii, cxliii, cxliv.

Sumerian Legal and Commerical Texts: **VII**: **§913, 279-281.**
- Administration Tablet of the Third Ur Dynasty **VII**: 278.
- Administrative Documents **VII**: 279.
- Contracts **VII**: 279*(3)*, 280*(2)*.
- Dréhem, from, in the Cleveland Public Library **VII**: 279.
- Fara, Tablets from **VII**: 280.
- Kish, from Mound Z **VII**: 279.
- Law Codes **VII**: 279*(2)*.
- Lipit-Ishtar Code **VII**: 280*(4)*.
- Marriage Texts **VII**: 2, 281.
- Property, Seizure of, for Debt in **VII**: 280.
- Sex Offenses in Sumerian Law **I**: 505; **VII**: 281.
- Umma Texts **VII**: 280.
- Ur III Period Texts **VII**: 280.
- Wage List of Ur Dynasty **VII**: 279.

Sumerian Literary Texts: **VII**: **§911, 274-276.**
- Erechite's Lament **VII**: 274.
- Harvest Time **VII**: 275.
- Lament over the Desolation of Ur **VII**: 274.
- Literary Catalog **VII**: 274, 275.
- Nippur, from **VII**: 274.
- Shu-Sin Love poem **VII**: 274.

Sumerian Mythological Texts: **VII**: **§914, 281-284.**
- Ashur Verion of the Creation Tablets **VII**: 282.
- Creation in Genesis and Sumerian Origin **IV**: 279; **V**: 163; **VII**: 281.
- Creation Tablets **VII**: 281.
- Epic of the Golden Age **VII**: 283.
- Etana, Bilingual Text on **VII**: 283.
- Fall of Man, in **VII**: 281*(2)*.
- Flood Legend **VII**: 281*(2)*, 282*(2)*.
- Paradise Epic **VII**: 281*(3)*, 282*(5)*.
- Poebel Flood Tablet **VII**: 282.

Sumerian Mythology:
- Anu-Enlil Series **VII**: 157.
- Beginnings, Views of **VII**: 157, 282*(2)*.

Sumerian Religion:
- Desert, Notion of, in Sumerian-Accadian **V**: 161.
- Divine Parentage of the Ruler in the Stele of the Vultures **VII**: 271
- Divine Service at Ur **V**: 191.
- Early, and its Expression **V**: 181*(2)*.
- Elamite Kings, Devotion of, to Sumerian Deities **V**: 184.
- Gardener in the Epic of Paradise **V**: 180.
- Guardians of the Gate (Sumerian Pantheon) **V**: 165.
- Montheism, Predecessor to Polytheism in **V**: 35, 185.
- Theology and Ethics **V**: 187.

Sumerian Religious and Liturigcal Texts: **VII**: **§915, 284-287.**
- Exorcism Text **VII**: 287.
- Fertility Song **VII**: 287.
- Gudea Cylinder A **VII**: 286.
- Hymns **VII**: 284*(6)*, 285*(6)*, 286*(4)*.
- Hymns in the Cults of the Deified Kings **VII**: 285.
- Incantation of a temple not exorcised **VII**: 284.
- Legend of kiškanu **VII**: 286.
- Liturgy Containing an Ode to the Word **VII**: 285; **VIII**: 130.
- Liturgy to Innini **VII**: 285.
- Magical Text **VII**: 285.
- Prayers **VII**: 285.
- Psalms **VII**: 285.
- Religious Texts from Assur **VII**: 285.
- Temple Records, Ur Dynasty **VII**: 286.
- "Utukkê" limûti Series **VII**: 286.

Sumerian Texts - General Studies: **II**: 169; **VII**: **§910, 269-273**.

á-A-*nâqu* Series, 38th Tablet **VII**: 273.

Abū Ṣalābīkh Tablets **VII**: 273.

ANET Supplement, Preivew of **VII**: 273.

Anitquity of **VII**: 273.

Bahrain, from **VII**: 272.

Bau-Text **VII**: 269.

"Behrens Collection" in the Manchester Museum **VII**: 270.

de Sarzec Inscriptions **VII**: 269.

e a-*nâqu* Series, Seventh Tablet **VII**: 272.

Graeco-Cunieform Texts **VII**: 269.

Grammatical Text from Kish **VII**: 270.

Israel, in **VII**: *152,* 273.

Jemdet Nasr, from **VII**: 270.

John Rylands Library, in **VII**: 270.

Lagaš Inscriptions in the Iraq Museum **VII**: 272.

Lagash Mace Head **VII**: 273.

Love Songs and the Song of Solomon **IV**: 506; **VII**: 275.

Lu.SHA Text **VII**: 273.

Manchester Museum, in **VII**: 270*(2)*.

Marriage Songs and the Song of Solomon **IV**: 507; **VII**: 276

Marriage Texts **VII**: 2.

Microscopic Text **VII**: 272.

Nippur, from **VII**: 271.

Oxford, at **VII**: 270*(2)*.

Philadelphia University Collection **VII**: 271.

Prague Collections of, from Third Dynasty, Ur **VII**: 272*(2)*.

Reciprocals, Table of **VII**: 273.

Sargonic Letter in **VII**: 272.

SRT, Additions and Corrections to **VII**: 272.

Stele of the Vultures **VII**: 271.

Syllabary **VII**: 269, 270.

Tablet with Akkadian Counterpart **VII**: 150.

Umma, from **VII**: 270.

Sumerian Wisdom Literature: **VII**: **§911, 274-276**, 280, 287.

Animal Fables, Proverbs **VII**: 275*(2)*.

"Job" Motif, variation on **VII**: 275.

Lame and the Halt **VII**: 276.

Lamentation Over the Destruction of Nippur **VII**: 276.

Nippur, from **VII**: 274.

Proverb Collections **VII**: 275*(3)*.

Similies **VII**: 276.

Word to the Wise: The "Book" of Proverbs **VII**: 274.

Sumerians: **I**: *296,* 328, 330, **II**: 3, *165, 166,* **168-170**.

Canaanites as **IX**: cvii, cx, cxi.

Culture of **I**: 125, 181; **II**: 169, 170, *197, 202;* **III**: 691, 692; **VII**: 275; **VIII**: 227.

Historiography of **I**: 131.

Morals of **VIII**: 223.

Propagation of America by **III**: 410; **V**: *162, 277.*

Sumerology:

Method in **V**: 583.

"Sumir and Akkad": **V**: 543.

Sumu-jamūtbāl (Sumu-yamūtbāl): **I**: *412;* **II**: 98.

Sun: **II**: 229.

Cult of, in Egypt **V**: 210.

Greek Table for Motion of **II**: 232.

Hippachus on the Distance of **II**: 235.

Night Journey of, and the Sky-Goddess Nut **V**: 213.

Seleucid Table of Solar (?) Positions **II**: 234.

Standing Still in Joshua, *see:* ***Joshua's "Long Day"***

Sun Images, and the Sun of Righteousness **V**: 140; **VIII**: 315.

Symbol in Prehistoric Times **VIII**: 303.
Symbolism in the OT **VIII**: 308.
Talmud, in **VI**: 688.
Sun-Birds: **III**: 381.
Sun-Disk:
Stelae with **III**: 733.
Winged, from 1st Dynasty **III**: 577; **V**: 211.
Sun God:
Fatherhood of **V**: 212*(2)*; **VIII**: 53, 97, 98*(2)*.
Great Physician, as **III**: 397.
Prayers to **VII**: 42.
Sun-Image:
Altar of Incense, or(?) **V**: 49, 422.
Sun Worship:
Prehistoric Traditions in Connection to Serpent and **V**: 152.
Syria, in **V**: 237.
Sunday: **I**: 406.
Sunday School:
Bible in **VIII**: 400.
Higher Criticism in **IV**: 121; **VIII**: 400.
Old Testament in **VIII**: 398*(4)*, 399.
Sundial: **I**: 401, 414.
Ahaz, of, *see*: ***Ahaz***
Haram, in **II**: 284.
Portable **I**: 414, 416; **III**: 686.
Sunrise:
Gates of, in Babylonian Art **III**: 689; **V**: 172.
Sunspots:
Anaxogoras' Observation of in 467 B.C.(?) **II**: 235.
Sunstroke:
Egyptian, in **V**: 202, 352.
Supernatural:
Biblical, Study of **VIII**: 93.
Credibility of in the OT **VIII**: 91.
Definition of **VIII**: 93.
Denial of **VIII**: 90.
Evolution and **III**: 308.
Higher Criticism and **IV**: 126.
Miracles as sign of the **VIII**: 93.
Nature and, Constituting One System of God **VIII**: 58.
Nature, in **VIII**: 85.
Religion, Colenso on **IV**: 118.
Science and **III**: 300; **V**: 103.
Voices (Bath-Kol) **V**: 103.
Superstitions:
Ancient **V**: 132, 134, 152; **VIII**: 53.
Bread in **I**: 392.
Door, Building up of a **VI**: 349.
Earthquake **V**: 132.
Egyptian, concerning Pregnacy and Child-Birth **I**: 179.
Fellahin, Among the **I**: 386.
Fertility, Greek **I**: 220; **VII**: 354.
Jewish **I**: 179; **V**: 105, 131.
Palestinian **I**: 390*(3)*.
Popular, of the Ancients **V**: 133.
Roman, about Nundinae **I**: 404.
Roman Child in **V**: 269.
Surgery, Neolothic, and **III**: 408; **V**: 131, 153.
Šuppiluliuma: **I**: 334; **II**: **98**; **VII**: 241.
Deeds of, as Told by His Son, Mursilli II **VII**: 307.
Seal of **III**: 649.
Sur-Nammu:
Wife of **VII**: 220.
Surar: **II**: 284.
Surattha: **II**: 290.
Suretyship:
Babylonian Principle of in Temple Law **I**: 498.
Surgeons:
Greek Army **I**: 311.
Surgery:
Anatolia, premature suture closure in Ancient **III**: 408.
Ancient **III**: **§180**, **408**.
Edwin Smith Surgical Papyrus (Egyptian) **VII**: 35.

Eye, of, and the Code of Hammurabi **VII**: 244.
Neolithic, and Superstition **III**: 408; **V**: 131, 153.
Prehistoric **III**: *399,* 408.
Surgical Instruments:
Greek and Roman **III**: 408.
Surkh Kotal: **VII**: 375.
Surtubeh: **II**: 284.
Surveying: **I**: **§124, 437**; **IX**: **§124, c**.
Field Plans **I**: *437(2);* **VII**: 257.
Instrument **III**: 465, 674; **IX**: c.
Survival:
Biological **III**: 323*(2)*.
Human **III**: 323.
Susa: **I**: 333; **III**: *79, 140,* **239-240**, *243, 248, 268, 496, 690, 732;* **V**: *677;* **VII**: 234, *249*.
Acropolis of **VII**: 298.
Ceramic Art at **III**: 610.
Darius' Place at **III**: 500*(2)*.
Persian Tomb at **III**: 540.
Susa Tablets: **I**: *228;* **VII**: *130,* 299*(2)*, 363.
Account Tablets of **V**: 601; **VII**: 299*(2)*.
Legal Formual in, and Daniel 4:14 and **VI**: 571; **VII**: 30, 128, 299.
Proto-Elamite Writing System in **V**: 601.
Susanna, Story of:
Aramaic Original of Theodotion's Additions to Daniel **VI**: 608.
Character of **VI**: 616.
Characther of Judith and **VI**: 616, 25.
Coptic Version of the Greek Homily of **VI**: 608.
Elizabethan Ballad of **VIII**; 363.
Exegetical Studies on **VI**: (**§721**), **639**.
Falasha Variant of **VI**: 609.
Fourteenth Century Scottish Alliterative Poem **VIII**: 365.
Julius Africanus' Letter to Origen on **VI**: 626.
Literary Criticism of **VI**: **§703, 625-626**.
Martyr, as **VI**: 626.
Meaning of **VI**: 626.
Original Language of **VI**: 626.
Peshiṭta, Mixed MSS of **VI**: 609.
Samaritan Parallel to **VI**: 625.
Seventeenth Century Histories of **VIII**: 364.
Syriac MS of **IV**: 48.
Textual Criticism of **VI**: **§685, 608-609**.
Suscipere **I**: 181; **V**: *671,* 673.
Suse et Masjid-i Soaiman: **III**: 124, 125*(2)*, 240.
Susian:
Babylonian Weight with trilingual inscription **VII**: 373.
Susiana: **I**: *456;* **III**: 60*(2), 240,* **240**, *496*.
Sutekh: **V**: 171, 225*(2)*.
Sutor Resutus: **I**: 279.
Sutor Supra Crepidam: **I**: 278.
Sutta-Megilla: **VII**: 59.
SUTTON, AURTHUR W.: **II**: *460*.
Suty:
Inscribed Stela of, the British Museum **VII**: 23.
Inscription of, and Ḥor Possible Parallel to **VII**: 71.
Šuwaliyat: **V**: 227.
Suwwanet eth-Thaniya: **II**: 485.
Suzub: **II**: 98.
Swallow:
Sumerian, *nam* **III**: *373,* 381.
Swamps: **I**: 346.
Huleh **II**: 390.

Swansea Museum:
Tomb of Queen Tiye, Finds from, in **III**: 569, 687.
Swastika: **VIII**: 308.
Asia Minor, in **III**: 695.
Egypt, from **III**: 712.
Swearing, *see also:* **Oaths; Blasphemy** **I**: 513.
Sweileh: **II**: 422*(2)*.
Swellings:
Assyrian Prescriptions for **III**: 405.
SWETE, H. B.: **IV**: 26.
Swimming: **I**: 238.
SWINBURNE, ALGERNON CHARLES:
Debt to the Bible **VIII**: 360.
SWINDLER, MARY HAMILTON
Bibliography of **I**: 22.
Swine, *see also:* **Pigs**: **I**: 182, 247, 250, *252,* 255.
Old Testament Taboo **III**: 381.
Pohibition on Breeding **I**: 182.
Sword Obligations:
Babylonian Law, in **VII**: *28,* 248.
Egyptian Law, in **VII**: 28, *248*.
Swords: **I**: 300, **318**, **319**, **320**; **II**: 218; **III**: 682, 683, 684; **V**: *13*.
Assyrian Bronze, with Cuneiform Inscription **III**: 680; **VII**: 173.
Flaming, in Genesis **V**: 168; **VI**: 41.
Luristan, Bronze **III**: 682.
Luristan, Iron **III**: 684.
Luristan, Technical Notes **I**: 319; **II**: 219.
Mycenæ, from **III**: 681.
"Smite with edge of the" (Hebrew Phrase) **V**: 398, 463.
Sybaris: **III**: **240**, 241.
Sycamore Fig: **III**: 395.
Sychar: **II**: 286.
Sycophant: **III**: 395.
Sycracuse: **III**: *29*.
Syene: **I**: *311;* **III**: *160, 166,* 241, *252*.
Jewish Temple to Yahu, at **III**: 231; **V**: 12, 77.
Jews in, in 5th Century BC **I**: 141.
SYKES, MARK: **III**: 355.
SYLVESTER, JOSHUA:
"Judith" of Du Bartas, by **VIII**: 366.
Symbolism and Typology, Studies on **VIII**: **§1052**, **301-309**.
Abraham and stone **I**: 32*(2);* **VIII**: 308, 309.
'Amarna, Temples of **III**: 519.
Anchor and Star on Coins, and **I**: 454; **VIII**: 307, 420.
Ancient **VIII**: 308.
Apocalyptic Literature, Misunderstood **V**: 121.
Ark and the Cherubim. Significance in Ritual **V**: 26.
Babylonian, Tablet on the Mysteries of **VIII**: 304.
Balaam as Symbolic of the Origins of Prophecy **IV**: 345.
Biblical, and Man's Quest for Religion **VIII**: 307.
Blood and Sacrifice, of **V**: 64.
Bovine, in the Exodus **IV**: 340; **VI**: 99; **VIII**: 309.
Cherubim and the Ark. Significance in Ritual **V**: 26.
Coin, and the End of Days **I**: 454; **VIII**: 307, 420.
Color **VIII**: 304, 305.
Compasses, in Blake's Ancient of Days **VIII**: 356.
Cosmic, in Gen 14 **IV**: 244; **VI**: 63.
Dead Sea Scrolls, in **VIII**: 307, 416.
Eden, of **IV**: 288.
Fish **VIII**: 307.
Hellenistic-Jewish Art, in **VIII**: 355.
Hermeneutics and Symbolization **IV**: 78*(2)*.
History of Symbols **VIII**: 304.
Jeremiah's **IV**: 416.
Jewish, and "Normative Judaism" **VIII**: 307.
Jewish Coins and **I**: 442.
Jewish, Development of **VIII**: 306.

Judaism, in **VIII**: 306.
Labyrinthine, Meander Door **III**: 477; **VIII**: 308.
Lamb, of **III**: 377; **VIII**: 303.
Laws, of, Objections to **VIII**: 301.
Lebanon, Symbolic Interpretation of in the Targums **II**: 436; **IV**: 97.
Leviathan as Symbol of Evil **III**: 377.
Light as, in John and OT **V**: 510; **VIII**: 307.
Lion, Conquering, Life Cycle of a Symbol **VIII**: 308.
Luristan Bronzes, of **III**: 757.
Massisi-Chapels, Architectural **III**: 475; **V**: 221.
Misunderstood **V**: 696.
Mummy Case, of **I**: 377.
Numbers, of in Ancient Religions, Bible, and Philosophies **VIII**: 309.
Numbers, Symbolic and Sacred, in Scripture **VIII**: 311.
Origin of Animal, in Babylonia, Assyria, and Persia **V**: 164; **VIII**: 303*(2)*.
Pegasus, on Aera Signata **I**: *443*.
Political, in Gen 14 **IV**: 244.
Prophetic, and Sacrifice **V**: 61*(2)*; **VIII**: 244*(2)*.
Prophetic, Characteristics and Laws of **IV**: 78.
Prophets and **I**: *108, 110, 111, 116*.
Religious, and Social Behavior **I**: 183; **V**: 151.
Revelation and **VIII**: 33, 304.
Rods, Symbolic **VIII**: 301.
Sacrifice and Prophetic **V**: 61*(2)*; **VIII**: 244*(2)*.
Sacrifice, of **V**: 57.
Shoes, Pair of, in Amos **VI**: 379.
Snuff-Shovel and Jewish Decorative Motifs **III**: 698; **V**: 52; **VIII**: 304.
Solar, in Ancient Religions **V**: 153; **VIII**: 302.
Spear as the Embodiment of Sovereignty in Rome **I**: 492; **VIII**: 307.
Star and Anchor on Coins, and **I**: 454; **VIII**: 307, 420.
Stone **VI**: 267, 284; **VIII**: 308.
Stone, and Abraham **I**: 32*(2)*; **VIII**: 308.
Symbolic Language in OT **V**: 696.

Symbol(s):

Athena, Symbolic Elements in Cult of **V**: 265.
Augurate on Coins of the Caecilii Metelli **I**: 447.
Babylonian Gods, of **V**: 174.
Biblical Revelation, Myth and **V**: 136.
Canopy, on Coins of Agrippa I **I**: 453; **VIII**: 306.
Cappadocian **VIII**: 306.
Cappadocian, "Royal Signet" **III**: 703; **VIII**: 307.
Coins, of Cities **I**: 447.
Eagle, in Metal Work **III**: 757; **VIII**: 306.
Evil, Leviathan as Symbol of **III**: 377.
Herod the Great, meaning of, on coins **I**: 453; **VIII**: 307.
Jewish, on Coins **I**: 443, 447; **VIII**: 304, 305*(2)*.
Jewish Symbols, Goodenough on **V**: 25; **VIII**: 308.
Justice, of **I**: 468.
Laver, Preistly, on Coins **I**: 451.
Magna Mater, of **V**: 187.
Masculinity and Femininity in ANE Sympathetic Rituals **V**: 160.
Menorah, as a Symbol of After-Life **V**: 53; **VIII**: 265.
Menorah, as a Symbol of Judaism **V**: 53; **VIII**: 308.

Messianic, in Palestine Archaeology **V**: 129.
Myth and **V**: 136*(2)*.
Nabataean, of Immortality **V**: 238.
New Testament use of Old Testament **V**: 58; **VIII**: 273.
Nineveh, Figures from **III**: 689.
Pagan, Jewish Use of, after 70 C.E. **V**: 38; **VIII**: 308.
Palestine as Land of **II**: 294.
rḫḫjj.t **III**: 704.
Seven Dots in Mesopotamian Art **III**: 699.
Snake, Hittite Twist **III**: 691.
Snuff-Shovel, as Jewish decorative motif **III**: 698; **V**: 52.
Stone Striking in Daniel **IV**: 529.
Symmachus: **IV**: **§248, 37**; **VI**: 10.
Symmetry: **III**: 607, 608.
Sympathy:
Human **VI**: 686.
Synagogues: **II**: 284; **III**: **§194, 523-528**; **V**: 10.
ʿAin Duk, at **IX**: cxxiv.
Ambōl, the Raised Platform in **V**: 94.
Apamea, at **III**: 525; **VII**: 327.
Apocalyptic-Eschatological Writings, Attitide Towards **IV**: 204; **V**: 122; **VIII**: 251.
Arabic Document concerning a Cairo (11th Cent.) **VII**: 290.
Archaeology and Early **III**: 527.
Architecture, and Jewish Prayer **III**: 526.
Architecture, Earliest, of **III**: 467.
Architecture, Protestant Chruch and **III**: 524.
Architecture, Theology of **III**: 526.
Art in **V**: 91; **VIII**: 354.
Ascalon, at **III**: 527.
Beit She'an, at **II**: 302.
Bet-Alpha, Zodiac Panel **I**: 408.
Beth-Alpha, at **III**: 524, 525.
Beth-Alpha, Zodiac Panel **III**: 526.
Birth of and R. Akiba **V**: 93.
Building, from the records of Cairo Geniza **III**: 527.
Byzantine Period, in **III**: 525; **V**: 93.
Caesarea, at **II**: 303; **III**: 526, 527.
Cairo, Eleventh Century Document Concerning **III**: 523.
Caludius Tiberius Polycharmus, in Stobi **III**: 524.
Capernaum, at, Fixed Torah Shrine of(?) **III**: 525.
Catalogue of, in the Holy Land **III**: 526.
Cathedra of Moses in Ancient **III**: 523.
Church and **V**: 76, 93.
Church and, Relationship of, in Apostolic Fathers **V**: 94.
Church Fathers and **V**: 151; **VI**: 723.
Diaspora and **V**: 92.
Direction, Sacred, of **V**: 93.
Documentary Hypothesis *vs.* **IV**: 260.
Dura-Europos, of, *see also:* ***Paintings*** **III**: *524(5)*, *525(3)*, 699; **V**: 76, 93.
Dura-Europos, Orpheus in **III**: 526*(2)*.
Earliest, Unearthed **III**: 525; **V**: 93.
Early Christian Assembly from, to **V**: 94*(2)*.
el-Ḥammeh, Ancient, at **III**: 524.
Elath, at(?) **III**: 524.
Eshtemoʿa, at **III**: 524, 525*(2)*.
Ezekiel Panel at Dura-Europos **III**: 524, 525, 527; **VI**: 357*(2)*; **VIII**: 269.
Facade of **III**: 525; **V**: 93.
Fahma Village, at **III**: 525.
Furnishings of , from records of Cairo Geniza **III**: 527.
Galilee, in **III**: 523*(2)*.
Gaza, at **III**: 528.
Greek Inscriptions in **VII**: 355.

Greek Inscriptions in, from Jerusaelm **VII**: 320.
Ḥuldah, at **III**: 527.
Ham(m)at(h)—Tiberias **II**: 302; **III**: 527*(3)*.
Herod's Temple, None in **V**: 76, 94.
History of **V**: 92.
Inscriptions **III**: 525; **V**: 93.
Israel and **V**: 92.
Jerash, at **III**: 523.
Jerusalem, from, Greek Inscriptions in **VII**: 320.
Lectern (ἀνλογεῖον) Designs in Ancient **III**: 524.
Locations of **III**: 525; **V**: 93.
Ma'on, Coins found at **I**: 454*(2)*.
Ma'on (Nirim), 5th Century A.D. **I**: *454(2)*; **III**: 526*(9)*, 527.
Meiron, at **III**: 523.
Minim in, Imprecation Against **VI**: 566, 686.
Modern Jewish **I**: 383.
Music in **I**: 243.
Nabratein, at **III**: 527.
Names, Secondary, for **V**: 94.
Officers of, in the Diaspora **V**: 78.
Orientation of **V**: 92, 93.
Origin and Growth of **V**: 76, 92, 93.
Origin of **V**: 92*(2)*, 93, 94.
Orpheus in **III**: 526*(2)*.
Palestine, in **III**: 525; **V**: 93.
Pictures and Figures in **III**: 525; **V**: 93.
Porch and Courts of **III**: 525; **V**: 93.
Priest and **III**: 525; **V**: 93.
Protestant Chruch Architecture and **III**: 524.
R. Akiba and the Birth of **V**: 93.
Role of **V**: 76.
Roman Period in Palestine **III**: 525; **V**: 93.
Salbit, Samaritan, at **III**: 525.
Samaritan, at Salbit **III**: 525.
Samuel Cycle Wall Decoration at Dura-Europos **III**: 524.
Sardis, at **III**: 222*(2)*, 527*(3)*, 528; **V**: 94.
Sardis, Interior Decoration **III**: 528.
Seating Arrangements in **III**: 525; **V**: 93.
Stobi, Caludius Tiberius Polycharmus, in **III**: 524.
Temple and **V**: 67, 91, 94.
Theodotos, of, at Jerusalem **III**: 523; **VII**: 338, 339.
Theology of, in Palestine, Weber's System of **V**: 8.
Torah Shrine of **III**: 525; **V**: 93.
Umm el-'Amed, Galilee **III**: 523, 527.
Women, Separation of, in Worship **III**: 525; **V**: 93.
Women's Gallery in, in Antiquity(?) **V**: 94.
Yafa, at **III**: 523, 525.

Synagogue of the Herodians: **III**: 523.

"Synagogue of the Libertines": **III**: 523.

Synagogue Scrolls and Torahs: **IV**: **§241, 20.**
Aramean **IV**: 20.
Eighth Century **IV**: 20.
Pentateuch, from Kai-fung-fu, China **IV**: 20.

Synagogue Worship: **V**: **§447, 91-94**.
Ancient, Service **V**: 91.
Calendar of **V**: 91.
Chant, Oldest Sources of **V**: 93.
Ecclesiasticus in, Service **V**: 93; **VI**: 623.
Influence on Christian Worship **V**: 93.
Jewish Liturgy **V**: 92.
Jewish Prayer Book **V**: 91.
Music, in **V**: 94.
Seat (Chair) of Moses in **V**: 93*(2)*.
Temple and **V**: 67, 91, 94.

Syncellus: **II**: *53*; **VI**: *684*.

Synchronism: **I**: **§102, 322-337**.
Assyria-Ešnunna-Babylon **II**: 210.
Assyrio-Egyptian **I**: 191, 196.

Assyrio-Nuzian **VII**: 166.
Assyro-Babylonian, False, Elimination of **I**: 192, 194.
Assyro-Tyrian **I**: 331; **II**: 193, 204.
Between Reigns of Solomon and Hiram(?) **I**: 99; **II**: 49.
Bronze Age Arad and Egyptian Dynasty I **II**: 211*(2)*.
Chaldæan and Egyptian **I**: 191, 193, 196.
Egypt with Asia **I**: 332.
Egyptian / Mesoptamian **II**: *195*, 196, 198; **III**: 639.
Gods, Fusion of **V**: 166.
Kings, Books of, in **IV**: 380.
Menes and Narâm-Šin **I**: *327;* **II**: *60, 66, 174, 197(2)*.
Meospotamian, Prehistoric **I**: 328; **III**: 164.

Syncretism and the OT (Influences on the Religion of Israel): **V**: **§421, 36-38**; **IX**: **§421, cxxxiv**.
Ashtoreth Influence in OT **V**: 36.
Method in the Study of **V**: 37.
Relation to Contiguous Peoples **V**: 36, 59.

Synedrion, *see also:* **Sanhedrin**
Attic Orators, in **VI**: 682.
Ptolemaic Papyri, in **VI**: 682.

Synoptic Studies:
Old Testament, in **IV**: 5; **V**: 698.

Syracuse: **III**: *63, 100, 211*, **241**.
Euryalos Fortress at **III**: 489.
Temple of Minerva, Foundations of, at **III**: 511.

Syria: **I**: *35 , 126, 303, 310,* 327, 329*(2)*, 330, 332*(2)*, 335, 339*(2)*, *347, 358, 382, 383(2), 392, 470;* **II**: *62, 70, 73, 116(2), 143, 151, 187, 204, 281, 282, 283,* 289, *294,* 294, 295*(3)*, 296*(3)*, 310*(2)*, *382, 490(2)*, 490‡; **III**: *4, 8, 18,* 19, *23, 24, 63, 78, 79, 85, 140, 147, 150,* 151‡, *171(2), 175, 214(2), 232, 233, 240,* **241-245**, 245‡, *248, 268(2), 367,* 413*(2)*, 415, 423*(3)*, 424*(2)*, 425, *430,* 430‡, 431‡, 441, *478, 509, 569, 622, 639, 676, 677, 724, 729;* **IV**: 181; **VII**: 159; **IX**: cxviii.
Agriculturial Life in, Illustration from **VI**: 185*(2)*.
Ammonites, War with **IV**: 361.
Assyrian Cuneiform Inscription in **VII**: 175.
Babylonian Equations for **V**: 574.
Bronze Age in **II**: 175, 176, 189, 262, 300.
Capitals and Citadels in Bronze-Age, Relation to Land and Water **II**: 187.
Chalcolithic Period in **II**: 187.
Cilician Empire in **II**: 139.
Civilizaton, Early **III**: 165.
Climate of **II**: 254.
Cypriote Tablets from **VII**: 358.
Cypro-Minoan Inscriptions from Bamboula, Kourion **VII**: 358.
Egyptian Place Names in Northern **II**: 265.
Enkomi 1955 Tablet **VII**: 358.
Excavation, Arabic Terminology, in **III**: 426.
Flora of **III**: 384.
Geography of, Northern **III**: 242.

Geography of, Physical Features of, in Relation to Bible History **II**: 254.
Graves, Boat-Shaped, in **III**: 533.
Health of **II**: 254.
History of, Egyptian Source for **II**: 2, *295;* **III**: 244; **VII**: 17, 77, 82.
Josephus as a Source for the History of **VI**: 679; **IX**: cxx.
Languages, Early, of **V**: 278.
Meteorological Observations in **II**: 236*(3)*, 237.
Monuments, Rude Stone, in **III**: 493.
Natural History of **II**: 254.
North, and Old Testament Interpretation **IV**: 84, 187.
Northern, as Cultural Link in Ancient World **I**: 124; **III**: 167; **IX**: lxxxiii.
Population of **II**: 259.
Population, Pre-Israelite **II**: 259.
Primitive Religion, Survivals of, in Modern **I**: 387; **V**: 2, 164.
Rainfall at El Meshgharah in Cœlosyria **II**: 241*(2)*.
Rome, Under **III**: 243, 245
Self-government in **I**: 494.
Soil of **II**: 254.
Stone-Lore of **II**: 286; **IV**: 191.
Sun Worship in **V**: 237.
Tablets from (Ugaritic) **VII**: 144.
Topography **III**: 424.
Topography of, with reference to Karnak Lists of Thothmes III **II**: 263*(2);* **III**: 242*(3);* **VII**: 14.
Travels, Modern, in **III**: 435*(2)*, 436, 438, 439, 440, 441*(2)*, 444, 445, 447.
Tuthmosis III Military Expedition to **II**: *105;* **VII**: 17.
Village Administration under Rome **I**: 489.
Water Supply of **II**: 254.

Syriac Language: **V**: *527(2)*, **§529, 529-531**, *599(2)*.
Accents **V**: 530.
Assyrian and **V**: 530, 556.
Conjuctions **V**: 530.
Connecting Vowel *â* before Verbal Suffixes **V**: 377, 531
Grammar of Modern **V**: 529.
Hebrew, Influence on **V**: 470.
Ma'lula Dialect **V**: 530*(2)*.
Maclean's Grammar of **V**: 530.
Modern Chaldeans, Study of Syriac among **V**: 530.
Neo-Syrian , still spoken in Anti-Lebanon **V**: 530.
Nestorians, Study of Syriac among **V**: 530.
New Syriac *k* **V**: 531.
New Syriac *ke* **V**: 377.
Open and Closed *e* in Proto-Syriac **V**: 531.
Orthography of Ittafal **V**: 377, 531.
Philology **V**: 529.
Physiognmic Treatise in **V**: 531.
Pronunciation of Modern **V**: 530.
Stem *'amad* **V**: 530.

Syriac Literature: **V**: 529.
Ḳalilag W[e]damnag in **V**: 530.

Syriac Texts: **VII**: **§869, 138**.
Catalgoue of MSS in the Library of the University of Glasgow **VII**: 2.
Edessa, Inscriptions from **VII**: 138.
Lexicographical Tract **VII**: 138.

Syriac Versions (including Peshiṭta): **IV**: **§259, 45-48**.
Apocryphal Psalms **VI**: 645, 656.
Song of Solomon **VI**: 551.

Syrian Fathers:
Genesis, Exegesis on, by **IV**: 97; **VI**: 16, 723.
Pentateuchal Exegesis in **VI**: 722.

Syrian Religion:
Syrian Gods at Ptolemais-Accho (Acre) **V**: 159.

Syrian Texts:
Indo-Aryan Names from V: 301.
Syrians: II: 170; III: *61*, 711.
Syrians, Modern: V: *59*.
Personality, Surrender of, to Deity among V: 154.
Proverbs of I: 385.
Songs of I: 385.
Stories of I: 385.
Syro-Arabian Language: V: 678.
Syro-Ephramitic Crisis:
Isaiah's Part in IV: 395.
Syro-Hexaplaris Ambrosianus Codex:
Malachi, on VI: 418.
Syro-Palestine:
Administration of during New Kingdom of Egypt I: 492.
Systematic Theology: VIII: 1, 7, 8*(2)*.
Biblical Theology and VIII: 12.
Bibliography of I: 16, 17.

T

Ta-ăath: II: 99; III: *540*.
Ta-Usert: I: 281.
Ta-usert-em-suten-pa: II: **99**.
Mummy Wrappings of II: 99; III: 355.
Ta'anach, Tel: II: 304, *374*, 428, **486**; VI: 167, 171, 179.
Canaanite Cuneiform Tablet from VII: 88.
Prince of VII: 87.
Taanit:
Qumran Pesher on VIII: 458.
Ta'anuk, Ta'anach II: 289.
Tabara: III: 245.
Tabari: VIII: 369.
Tabdīl: V: 145.
Tabeel, Son of: VI: 260.
Tabellae Defixionum: V: 105*(3)*, 144, 145*(2)*, 268*(2)*.
Tabernacle and Its Contents: V: 10, **§427**, **50-54**, 68, 70, 71; VI: 120, 121, 128.
Actual or Ideal(?) V: 51.
Archaeology of V: 52.
Architecture, as a Work of V: 52.
Boards of V: 51.
Cloud on the IV: 329.
Construction of V: 50, 51.
Construction of, and the Priests' Code V: 51.
Copy of the Temple, or Temple as Copy of the Tabernacle(?) V: 52, 69.
Dedication of, Date I: *399*.
Dreros Bilingual Inscription and V: 53; VII: 330, 376.
Eli, Existence in Days of V: 50; VI: 208.
Existence of, as Described in Exodus V: 51.
Exodus, Chapters on IV: 327.
Fore-Court of Women V: 51.
Historicity of V: 51.
Ideal or Actual(?) V: 51.
Mosaic Art and the III: 691; V: 52.
Oriental(?) V: 51.
Pentateuch, Descriptions of, in V: 53.
Position of V: 51.
Priestly IV: 262.
Priestly Image of V: 53.
Roof of V: 51.
Structure of V: 50; VI: 115.
Tent over the V: 53.
Terminology of V: 52.
Theology of V: 52*(2)*; VIII: 10, 304.
Worship and V: 38, 50.
Worship of, compared with the Second Temple V: 38.
Tabi-utul-Bel:
Job, Babylonian Parallel to IV: 461, 462; V: 177; VII: 260.

Nebuchadnezzer and V: 177; **VII**: 260.

Tabitha:

Greek Inscriptions at **VII**: 314.

Tables (Furniture): **III**: 582; **V**: *501*, 516.

Egyptian **I**: 212; **III**: 583.

Egyptian Offering **VII**: 72.

Greek Cult **III**: 579; **V**: 265.

Hittite Communion **V**: 225.

Jezebel's **III**: 462, 499, 582.

Tablets:

Cuneiform, New Method of Copying **II**: 214.

Cuneiform, Spectral Analysis for Joining **II**: 220.

Door, from Pekiin **III**: 733.

Greek Mathematical **I**: 431.

Hebrew use of Clay, for Writing **I**: 233.

Multipication, Babylonian **I**: 430.

Tabnith Inscription: **V**: 522; **VII**: 85.

Tabo: **III**: 245.

Temple of, on Argo Island **III**: 20, 202.

Taboo: **I**: *222;* **V**: 2.

Food and Drink **I**: *250(2)*.

Hebrew Scriptures, in **V**: 133.

Iron, of the Hebrew **I**: 295; **V**: 105, 133.

Old Testament, in **V**: 107.

Religion, as minimum definition of **V**: 2.

Swine in Old Testament **III**: 381.

Woman and, in Iraq **I**: 391.

Tabor, Mount: **II**: *292*, **487**; **III**: *419*.

Etymological Study of the Name **II** 487; **V**: 301.

Meaning of the Name **II** 487; **V**: 301.

Tabula Bembina, *see:* **Isis-Table**

Tabula Imperii Romani: **II**: 258.

Tabula Odysseaca: **III**: 738.

Tacitus: **I**: 137, 142.

Christ, on **VI**: 680.

Cumanus' Term in Office, Concerning **VI**: 682.

Felix' Term in Office, Concerning **VI**: 682.

Nineveh according to **III**: 183.

Tackle:

Homeric fishing- **III**: 672.

Tadukhepa:

Dowry of **VII**: 28.

TAFEL, LEONARD: **V**: 603.

TAFEL, RUDOLPH L.: **V**: 603.

Tafsir: **IV**: 49.

Song of Deborah and **IV**: 371*(2)*.

Tafwīḍ: **V**: 145.

Tagtug: **V**: 182.

Taḫanun **VIII**: 205.

Taharka, *see:* **Taharqa**

Taharqa (Tahraka, Tirhaka): **II**: 99, 103; **VII**: 70.

Inscription of **VII**: 56.

Monuments of Reign of **III**: 492; **VII**: 57.

Rock Inscription of **VII**: 61.

Stela of **VII**: 19.

Taharqu:

Tahpanhes: **III**: 83, **245**; **V**: 161; **VIII**: 116.

Tahraka:

Tahtim Hodshi: **VI**: 218.

Tahunian: **III**: 353.

T'aim, Stone Eben hat : **II**: 403.

TAIMIYYA, IBN:

Theory of Inspiration **VIII**: 49.

Takleot II (Taklot, Talelut):

Inscription of **VII**: 55.

Stautette of **III**: 765.

Takht-i-Suleiman: **III**: 124, 125.

Parthian Structures at **III**: 484.

Takil-ili-su of Malgium:

Inscripton of **VII**: 187.

Takku (TAK-KU): **V**: 180, 182.

Tākultu Ritual: **VII**: 203, 204.

Tal-i Iblīs: **III**: 124.

Talayotic Majorca: **III**: 55, *237*, 246.

TALBOT, WILLIAM HENRY FOX: ***Bibliography of*** **I**: 22.

Talent:
- Hebrew, weight **I**: 418.
- Standard, of Sanctuary **II**: 292; **IX**: xcix.
- Value of Attic, in Modern Money **I**: 438.

Talion, *see:* **Retribution**

Talisman:
- Babylonian **VII**: 259.

Tall-i-Nokhodi: **III**: **185**

Talmud, Talmudic Literature (including Mishnah): **I**: *47, 90, 112, 231, 265, 269(2), 402, 414, 461, 466, 467, 469, 512;* **II**: *498;* **III**:*163;* **IV**: *101;* **V**: *116;* **VI**: *694,* **§812, 697-706**; **VII**: 354; **IX**: **§812, cl.**
- ʿArukh quoting the Babylonian (Bekh. 8b) **VI**: 700.
- Abâda zara, chap. I.§2 *['Abod. Zar 1:2]* **VI**: 699.
- Age, in **VI**: 698.
- Allegorists in **VI**: 701, 706, 715.
- Apostate of the **VI**: 700.
- Aramaic Idiom, Grammar of, in the Babylonian **V**: 524.
- Archaeology and **IV**: 209; **VI**: 698.
- Archaeology, Digging in **VI**: 702.
- Ashmedai Legend and the Babylonian **V**: 133; **VI**: 696.
- Bab Nahara **VI**: 705.
- Baba Bathra of the, and the Old Testament **IV**: 119; **VI**: 698.
- Babylon Creation Stories and, Parallels **V**: 142; **VI**: 626, 687; **VII**: 266; **VIII**: 83.
- Babylon Festivals in **V**: 231.
- Babylon in **III**: 40; **VI**: 701*(2)*.
- Babylonian Dog Omens, and Talmudic and Later Jewish Parallels **V**: 146; **VI**: 701.
- Babylonian, Technical Expression in **V**: 461.
- Babylonian: Tractate B^e^rākot **VI**: 701.
- Ben Zebul of Eliezer Crescas and Bible References in the **VI**: 715.
- Beth Sheʿarim in **II**: 342.
- Bible and **VI**: 687.
- Biblical Passages, Light on, from **VI**: 135, 715.
- Blessed Virgin in **VI**: 699*(2)*.
- Burnings of **VIII**: 326.
- Cairo Genizah, Fragments in the British Museum **VII**: 105.
- Ceremonies, Non-Jewish Religious, in **I**: 365; **VI**: 699.
- Christianity, Early History of, and its relation to the **VI**: 698.
- Christians in the **VI**: 697.
- Chronology and **II**: *187;* **VI**: 702.
- Church and **VI**: 687.
- Cities of the **II**: 284.
- Controversy on the **VI**: 698.
- Cryptography **VI**: 698.
- Date and Composition of **VI**: 699.
- Date of **VI**: 606, 700.
- Date of, and the Cairene Ecclesiasticus **VI**: 700.
- Dating Back a Section of **VI**: 704.
- Deformation, Concept of **VI**: 705.
- Demotic Papyri and **VII**: 80, 82.
- Discussions, Original Location of **VI**: 705.
- Dreams, on **VI**: 701.
- Eschatology of, Weber on **VIII**: 249.
- Ethical Element in **VIII**: 222.
- Exodus, Year of, in **IV**: 337; **VI**: 715.
- Fasting in **I**: 365.
- Fasting, Motivation of, in **VI**: 703.
- Fortune and Misfortune in **VI**: 698.
- Foundation of Rome in **VI**: 702.
- Freedom of Will in **VIII**: 169.

Gemara, Separation from Sebara, in	**VI**: 704.
Geniza, Fragments from	**VI**: 700, 705; **VII**: 106, 109.
Ginzberg, Louis, on the Palestinian	**VI**: 702.
God, Doctrine of	**VIII**: 56.
God, Existence of, Space and time in Relation to	**I**: 414; **VIII**: 62.
Gospels and	**VI**: 703; **VIII**: 285.
Greek Words in	**VI**: 703.
Hebrew Bible in Shorthand (Abbreviations in the)	**VI**: 715.
Herodian Doves in	**III**: 373; **VI**: 704.
Higher Criticism and	**VI**: 687.
Historical Evolution of	**VI**: 687.
History in	**VI**: 700.
History of the	**VI**: 700.
Human Rights in	**VI**: 703; **VIII**: 234.
Introduction to, by R. Samuel b. Hofni	**VI**: 703.
"Iron Sheep" in	**VI**: 703.
Jerusalem	**VI**: 687.
Jesus in the	**VI**: 700.
"Jesus Passage" in	**VI**: 705.
Jews and, after the time of Christ	**VI**: 697.
Koran, Talmudic Saying in	**VI**: 700.
Lakes of the Holy Land in	**VI**: 699.
Legal Preposition in, and Section 7 of the Code of Hammurabi	**VI**: 703; **VII**: 246.
Legend concerning King David and Ira the Jarite	**I**: **47**,*90;* **II**: **52**; **VI**: 716.
Legends, Poetical of the	**VI**: 695.
Lexicon	**V**: 404.
Literary Device in	**VI**: 703, 704.
Mankind in	**VI**: 698.
Marcus Aurelius and	**VI**: 697.
Masada and	**II**: 440; **VI**: 705.
Medicine in	**III**: 396; **VI**: 699.
Messiah, Concerning	**V**: 126; **VI**: 699; **VIII**: 139.
Methodology	**VI**: 704, 705.
Minor, Male, status of, in	**I**: 227; **VI**: 692.
Negligence and Remoteness of Damage in	**VI**: 693.
Nero, in Talmudic Legend	**VI**: 705.
New Testament and	**VI**: 698.
Non-Violence in	**VIII**: 229.
Origin and Formal Contents of	**VI**: 698.
Palestinian, Compared with the Leyden MS	**VI**: 701.
Paronomasia in	**V**: 696; **VI**: 701, 706.
Persian Custom in	**VI**: 700.
Persian Festivals in	**V**: 231.
Petronius, Talmudic Proverb in	**VI**: 699.
Philology, Talmudic	**V**: 389; **VI**: 702.
Place Names in, Identified	**II**: 270.
Ploughing in	**VI**: 694.
Pronunciation of certain Latin Letters in	**V**: 665.
Prophecy, Interpretation of, in	**VIII**: 245.
Prophets and Prophecy in	**I**: 112; **IV**: 235; **VI**: 689, 708; **VIII**: 245.
Psychiatric Relevances in Hebrew Tradition	**VI**: 691.
Public Office, Avoidance of, in	**VI**: 704; **VII**: 342.
Qumran Literature and	**VIII**: 438.
Qumran Sect, Reference to(?)	**VIII**: 423.
Quotations from	**VI**: 687.
Rash's Commentaries on, List of Manuscripts	**VI**: 701.
Romantic Side of the	**VI**: 699.
Sabbath, War on, Problem of, and the Second Temple and the	**VIII**: 235
Sale, Concept of, in	**I**: 307.
Samaritans in	**II**: 162; **VI**: 698.
Sanhedrin 17a, Interpretation of	**VI**: 704, 705.
Service Tree in	**III**: 394.
Shekel, Weight of, in	**I**: 427.

Sites found in **II**: 284.
Sorrow and Care in **VI**: 698.
Soteriology of, Weber on **VIII**: 188.
Space and time in Relation to the Existence of God **VIII**: 62.
Study of, in the Thirteenth Century **VI**: 699.
Study of the **VI**: 698*(2)*, 699.
Sugyah, Anonymous **VI**: 695.
Syntax **VI**: 702.
Talmudic Dictionary, Jastrow's **VI**: 699.
Teaching, Methods of **VI**: 700.
Terms and Idioms in the Latin MS Paris B.N. 16558 **VI**: 705.
Teshuvah, in **VIII**: 197.
Text of the **VI**: 705.
Theology and **VI**: 700.
Tractate Abot **VI**: 702.
Tractate Me'ila in **VI**: 704.
Tractate Me'ila, Mishna and Tosefta of **VI**: 704.
Translation, Difficulties in **VI**: 701.
Translation of, Experiment in **VI**: 697.
Verses, Division into **IV**: 18.
War on the Sabbath, Problem of, and the Second Temple and the **VIII**: 235
Zeus in the **VI**: 699.

Talmudic College:
Pumbeditha, of **VI**: 689.

Talpioth: **VI**: 552.

Taman Peninsula: **III**: 59.

Tamar: **I**: 81, *348*; **II**: 360*(2)*, **487**; **VI**: 85, 213, 654.
Hierodule, and **VI**: 85.
Jacob and **VI**: 727.

Tamarisk Tree: **III**: 395; **V**: 410.

Tammuz: **V**: 133, 144, 145, 170, 171, 178*(2)*, 186, 187*(2)*, 188*(2)*, 251, 252; **VII**: 260, 261.
Babylonian Lamenations to **V**: 178.
Bible and **V**: 151, 188.
Hymns to **V**: 175, 177; **VII**: 260*(2)*, 286.
Kurdistan Ritual of (?) **I**: 391; **V**: 185.
Liturgy of the cult of **V**: 178.
Malachi, Worship of, in **IV**: 455; **V**: 184; **VI**: 415.
Osiris and **V**: 146, 179, 207.
Sister of **V**: 178.
Song of Solomon and **IV**: 505.
Swine God **V**: 172.
Worship of **V**: 180.

Tanagras: **II**: 116.

Tananir: **III**: 486.

Ṭanbūr: **I**: 244.

Tanen:
Children of **V**: 223, 224.

Tangur:
Hieroglyphic Inscription near the Cataract of **VII**: 56.

Tanis: **III**: 83, *200*, **246**, *281(2)*, *593*.

Tanit: **I**: *375(2)*; **III**: *576(2)*.
Sactuary of, at Carthage **III**: 513.

Tank(s):
Souterrians **V**: 67.

Tankard(s):
Atta-Ḫušu, for **III**: 591; **VII**: 273.
Bichrome Wheel-Made from Tell El-'Ajjul **III**: 590.

Tannaitic Literature: **I**: *465*.
Biblical Variants **VI**: 12.
Job 36:5a in **VI**: 437.
Old Testament Studies and **VI**: 702.
Shekinah in **VIII**: 101.
Synedrion in **VI**: 682.

Tannaitic Period:
Laborers, Status of, in **I**: 467.

Tannery:
'Ain Feshkha, at **VIII**: 413.

Tannin:
Muzzling of, in Ugaritic Myth V: 196.
Tanta: III: 246.
Tanturah: II: **487-488**.
Pottery from III: 609.
Tanu-Axares: II: 20, 181, *202;* IV: 519.
Tany:
Hyksos Princess II: 99.
Tapestry:
Apocrypha VIII: 350, 354*(2)*.
Story of Joseph on a Coptic VIII: 356.
Tobit, at Bisham Abbey VIII: 354.
Thâpiṭ Nahar:
Zabûl Yam and, in the Combat between Ba'al and the Sea V: 191.
Taprobane: III: *191,* 246.
Tar Kshaife: III: 247.
Taramptos: III: 246.
Taranto:
Shipwreck near III: 453.
Tarcondemus:
Seal(?) of IX: cxliii.
Tarentum: I: 510.
Augustan Altar from V: 49, 270.
Targum Jersualem:
Deuteronomy 34:3, to VI: 131, 155, 712.
Genesis 14:24 on V: 66.
Numbers 18:12, to VI: 131, 155, 712.
Targum Jonathan:
Arabic Tafsir of the Song of Deborah and VI: 712.
Blessings of Jacob and VI: 91, 710.
Genesis 24:56, on VI: 75, 712.
Habakkuk Misrash (1QpHab) and VI: 712; VIII: 457.
Isaiah 52:13-Chapter 53 on VI: 306.
Nahum of VI: 399, 711.
Targum of Job (11QtgJob): **VIII: §1140, 470**.
Targum Onkelos (Onqelos): V: 416, 494; VI: 712.
די-Clauses in VI: 713.
Haggadah in VI: 713, 714.
Manuscript (Eb. 448) with Babylonian Vocalization VI: 712.
Masoretic Text and IV: 15; VI: 712.
Patriotic Tendencies in VI: 714.
Peshiṭta Version of Genesis and IV: 47; VI: 96, 713*(2)*.
Syntax of VI: 713.
Yemenite Manuscript for the Babylonian Edition VI: 714.
Targum, Palestinian
see: **Palestinian Targum**
Targums, Targumim: IV: 24; VI: **§815, 710-714**.
British Museum Or. Ms 2211 VI: 303, 714.
Cairo Geniza, on Exod 15 VI: 108.
Canticles, on VI: 710.
Canticles, to, Six Yemen MSS. compared to Textus Receptus VI: 555*(3)*, 711*(3)*.
Chaldee, from the Latin of Leusden VI: 710.
Chaldee, of Jonathan ben Uziel and Jerusalem VI: 91, 710.
Chronicles as a IV: 541*(2)*.
Commentary, as VI: 254, 551, 711.
Ex. 15:7-12 from Cairo Geniza, on VI: 108, 713.
Ex. 23:4 and the Halakah VI: 695.
Exod. 22:4 of, and the Ancient *Halakha* VI: 113.
Fall of Man, according to IV: 289; VI: 711.
Genesis 4:3-16, Versions VI: 42.
Genesis Apocryphon and VI: 690; VIII; 451.

Genesis, fragments, and relation to Peshiṭta **IV**: 47.
Higher Criticism and **VI**: 712.
Isaiah 48:7 according to BM Or. Ms. 2211 **VI**: 303, 714.
Isaiah, Etymological Elucitations in Aramaic **VI**: 247.
Isaiah of, Sperber's Edition, Errata **VI**: 714*(2)*.
Jeremiah, to **IV**: 410; **VI**: 711.
Lebanon, Symbolic Interpretation, of, in **II**: 436; **IV**: 97; **VI**: 712.
Manuscript of parts of **VI**: 711.
Manuscripts of, in the British Museum **VI**: 711.
Nahum of, and Collated Text **VI**: 399, 711.
New Testament and **VI**: 712, 713; **VIII**: 275, 277.
Odes of Solomon and **VI**: 711.
Pentateuch, on **VI**: 711.
Psalms, of, Avoidance of Anthropomorphisms **IV**: 486; **VI**: 714; **VIII**: 104.
Psalter, to and Mark 14:24 **VI**: 713; **VIII**: 286.
Ruth, Book of, on **VI**: 712.
Samaritan, to Gen. 14:5 **VI**: 64.
Samaritan, to Gen. 1:1 **VI**: 26.
Septuagint and **IV**: 32; **VI**: 712.
"Servant of the Lord" in **VI**: 712; **VIII**: 145.
Song of Solomon, Apologetic Motifs in **IV**: 507.
Song of Songs, Benedictory Formula in **VI**: 712.
Syriac, Modern, in Dialect of the Jews of Kurdistan (Genesis 1 and 2) **VI**: 94.
Temptation of Man, according to **IV**: 289.
Vulgate and, in Agreement **VI**: 687.
Taricheæ: **II**: 284,*337, 366, 367, 426,* **488**.
Tariff(s):
Deities, Groupings of, in Ritual Tariffs from Ras Shamra-Ugarit **V**: 192.
Tarkhan: **III**: **246-247**.
Cemetery of Earliest Dynasties at **III**: 246.
Tarkondemus
Seal of (?) **III**: 641; **VII**: 232, 305.
Tarḳû-timme:
City and Country, Name of, over which he ruled **II**: 99, 263; **VII**: 152.
Inscription of **VII**: 56.
Tarḳûtimme:
Tarquinii: **I**: *441;* **III**: *717*.
Tarqumuwa:
King of Mera **II**: 99.
Seal of **III**: 650.
Tarrha: **III**: 247.
Tarshish: **I**: *354;* **III**: *210, 237,* **247**, *247;* **IV**: 445.
Ships of **I**: 339; **IV**: 220.
Tarsus: **II**: *215;* **III**: *61, 109(4), 247,* **247**, *496, 641, 711, 743, 765*.
Bilingual Bulla from **VII**: 306; **IX**: cxliv.
Northwest Semitic Inscriptions from **VII**: 85.
Religion of, and the Origin of Mithra **V**: 237.
Tartarus: **VIII**: 266, 267.
Tartimar: **I**: 427.
Tartûs: **VII**: *183*.
Greek Inscription from **VII**: 314.
Tarzîa: **II**: 100.
Tashlik: **I**: 366.
Tasians:
Civilization of **III**: 91.
Tassels: **I**: 280.
Tata-em-re:
Official of Hatshepsut **II**: 100.
Tatian, *see:* **Diatessaron**
Tattenai: **II**: 100.

Tattooing: **I**: 179, *201;* **IX**: lxxxv.

Tau, Egyptian:
Crux Ansata, or **VIII**: 301.

Taurinensis, Codex (Y): **IV**: 28*(6)*, 29*(4)*.

Taurodontism:
Anatolia, Occurrence of, in Ancient Inhabitants of **III**: 359.

Taurt: **V**: 207.

Taurus: **I**: 407.
Hittite Monuments from Cappadocian **III**: 494.

Tausert: **II**: 99, 207.

Taut:
Book of. Egyptian Papyrus of Mu-tem-ua **VII**: 76.

Tawagalawaš Text: **VII**: 306.

Tawilan: **III**: 247.

Taxation: **I**: 187, *192, 253,* 346, **§132, 481-482**; **IX**: **§132, c-ci**.
Cleon and the Assessment List of 421 **IX**: c, civ.
Egypt, managment of revenue in **I**: 489.
Egypt, Protest against unjustified tax-demands **VII**: 30.
Greek Cults, in **IX**: ci.
Tax-Contracts in Ptolemaic Egypt **I**: *187,* 481*(2)*, 498; **IX**: ci*(2)*.
Tribute Assessments in the Athenian Empire **IX**: ci.

Taxes:
Assessor's Journal, Middle Kingdom **VII**: 30.
Assyrian Record of Tax Receipts **VII**: 191.
Babylonian Amoraim Exempt from (?) **I**: 482.
Corn, on **I**: 346, 482; **VII**: 30.
Demotic Tax-Receipts **VII**: 29.
Double Entries in Ptolemaic Tax-Receipts **I**: 304.
Greek Cults, in **V**: 261.
Land, in Seleucid Judea **I**: 482.
Poll **I**: 483.
Poll, in Egypt **I**: 482.
Poll, in Ptolemaic Egypt **I**: 481; **II**: 261.
Sales Taxes in Athens **VII**: 341.
Sumerian **VII**: 272.

Taxila:
Aramaic Inscription from **VII**: 1242*)*.

"Taxo":
Assumption of Moses, in **VI**: 653*(3)*, 654.
Hebrew Equivent of, in Assumption of Moses **VI**: 666.

Taya, Tell: **III**: 248.

Tayanat, Tell:
Temples of Solomon and **III**: 521; **V**: 73.

Tayinaat, Tell: **III**: *743*.

TAYLOR, ISAAC: **II**: 129; **V**: 282.

TAYLOR OF NORWICH: **IV**: 155.

Tchogha-Zambil:
Elamite Texts from **VII**: 299.

Teach:
Hebrew Words for **V**: 516.

Teacher of Righteousness: **VIII**: **§1080, 421**, 456.
Damascus Document, Messiah in, and **VI**: 663; **VIII**: 421.
Jesus and **VIII**: 421*(2)*, 479, 480.
OT Reference(?) **VIII**: 421.
Prophecy of Joel, and **IV**: 432; **VI**: 370, 374.
Testament of the Twelve Patriarchs, in(?) **VI**: 659; **VIII**: 421.
Toledoth Yeshu, in(?) **VIII**: 421, 460.

Teaching:
Jewish Home, and Old Testament Criticism **IV**: 134; **VIII**: 400.
Old Testament, Critical Approach, Problems of **IV**: 151.

Teaching the (Bible) Old Testament *see:* **OT, Teaching the** **V**: 683; **VIII**: **§1067, 398-407**.

Tears:
Sumerian for, of Joy(?) **VII**: 271; **IX**: cxliii.
Teb-ket: **II**: 100.
Tebtunis: **I**: *445*.
Technological Terms:
Ancient Semitic Culture, in **II**: 222.
Folklore, in **II**: 222.
Technology: **I**: *189*, **§91**, **265-268**, *332;* **IX**: **§91**, **xc**.
Egyptian **I**: 266; **II**: 224.
Semitic Terms for **I**: 265.
Sumerian **I**: 267.
Technological Stages and Archaeological Ages **III**: 429.
Teeth:
Anatolian Inahabitants, Eruption of Permanent **III**: 361*(2)*.
Cosmic **V**: 157.
Dental Pathology from Egyptian Skulls **III**: 362.
Dentition of Ancient Inhabitants of Alaca Höyük **III**: 360.
Fossil, from Cave of Karain **III**: 359.
Found in stomachs of mummies **I**: 380.
Incisors, Permanent, Size of, in Suborder Anthropoidea **III**: 361.
Molars, Attrition of, in Ancient Anatolians **III**: 359.
Taurodontism in Ancient Inhabitants of Anatolia **III**: 359.
Tefilah: **VIII**: 206.
Tefillah:
Hebrew Liturgy, and **VIII**: 385.
Teh-Khet:
Tomb of **III**: 558.
Teheran: **III**: 125, *622, 684;* **VII**: *128*.
Tehneh:
Tombs, early, at **III**: 537.
Tehuti-hetep:
Round Topped Stele of **VII**: 20.
Teie: **III**: *685*.
Teimâ, *see:* **Têmâ**
Tekenu: **I**: 374.
Teknonymy: **I**: *210;* **V**: **§488**, **291- 304**.
Tekoa(h): **I**: *34;* **II**: **488**.
Fountains at **VI**: 2.
Tel, Tell, *see specific name without* **"Tel, Tell"** *prefix*
Tel(s): **II**: 285.
Tel Achzib, *see:* **Achzib**
Tel Aviv: **II**: *298*, 303, **488**, *495*.
A.I.N.A. Convention in **I**: *459*.
"Double Bowl" from an EB Tomb at **III**: 578, 622.
Tel el Ful, *see:* **Gibeah** **II**: *430*.
Teleilat el-ʿAnab (Tuleilat el-ʿEnab): **I**: *255, 256, 258;* **II**: 454*(2)*, **489**.
Agriculture in the Negev, and **II**: 452, 453.
Physiographic Aspects of **II**: 245, 250, 301; **IX**: cxiii.
Teleilât (Tell-el) Ghassûl: **II**: 297, 310, **376**; **III**: 423*(2)*.
Dolmen Field at **III**: 561.
Jar-Incision from **III**: 631.
Painted Houses at **III**: 467.
Teleogenesis: **III**: 324.
Telipinu:
Decree of **I**: 487; **VII**: 307.
Telke Tepe: **III**: 248.
Tell ʿAzūr, *see also:* **Azor**
Tombs of, Intermediate Early-Middle Bronze, at **III**: 555.
Tello(h): **III**: *79, 140, 240, 243,* **248**, *268, 663*.
Stele of the Vultures from **III**: 493.
Telloh Inscriptions: **IV**: 269.
Telul eth-Thalathat: **III**: **248**.
Teluliot Batashi: **II**: 489.
Têmâ (Teimâ): **II**: 358, 488; **III**: 41, **248**.
Teman: **VI**: 402.

Temanite:
Inscriptions **VII**: 121, 295.
Tempe: **III**: 446.
Temperance: **VIII**: 221.
Temple(s) *(see also specific places)* **III: §193, 507-522; IX: §193, cxiii-cxiv.**
Abu Simbel, of **III**: 509, 511, 512.
Abusir, Restoration of **III**: 517.
Abusir, Sun-, at **III**: 510.
Abydos, Ten at **III**: 2, 509.
Acaemenian Tower **III**: 521.
Adonis, of (?) **III**: 516.
Agros, Two, of Hera at **III**: 509.
'Ain Amur, at **III**: 514.
Akhenaten's, at Thebes **III**: 521*(2)*.
Alexander the Great's at, Baḥria Oasis **III**: 516.
'Amarna, at, Symbolism of **III**: 519.
Amenophis III, of, at Karnak **III**: 136, 521.
Amman, Late Bronze Age **III**: 520, 521*(2)*.
Amora, of, at Karnak **III**: 512.
Anthedon, Small, at **III**: 508.
Apollo, Near Miletus, Facade of **III**: 462.
Apollo, of, at Bassae, Plan and Orientation **III**: 520.
Apollo of Bryaxis, and Sapor I **III**: 519.
Apollo, Porch-Ceiling of, Delos **III**: 467; **VII**: 323.
Apollo Smintheus **III**: 266.
Apollo, Tripion, Site of **III**: 403, 518.
Apollos Epicurius at Bassœ **III**: 507.
Arabia, in **III**: 18.
Ares, of **III**: 488, 515, 516.
Art, Influenced by the **III**: 699; **V**: 70.
Artemis Orthia, at Shrine of **III**: 511.
Arx, at Coas, Decorations **III**: 478.
Asfun, at **III**: 510.
Ashtaroth, of **III**: 513.
Ashtoreth, of, at Beth-Shan **III**: 513.
Askelpois, Ramp of **III**: 469.
Askha, Sub-Soil of **II**: 219.
Assyrian **III**: 510.
Astia, at **III**: 510.
Astronomy and Egyptian **III**: 505.
Atargatis, of, Nabataean **III**: 515.
Athena, Old, on Acropolis **III**: 509, 514.
'Awwâm, at Mârib **III**: 517*(2)*
Baal, of, *Ex-voto* inscription fom **VII**: 115.
Baal-Berith, at Shechem, Fluted Columns in **III**: 477.
Baalbek, of **III**: 508, 509.
Baalbek, Trilithon **III**: 509.
Baalbek, Trilithon, drawing on, and constructional history **III**: 479.
Babylonia, of **III**: 509, 510, 513, 518; **VII**: 207, 234.
Babylonian, and its Place in Ancient Community **I**: 185; **III**: 512; **V**: 180.
Babylonian, Temple Records **VII**: 237.
Baḥria Oasis, at **III**: 515, 516.
Barbar, at **III**: 517*(2)*
Barkal, in 1916 **III**: 512*(3)*.
Basa, of **III**: 511; **VII**: 61.
Bel, of **III**: 508.
Beth-Shan, at, Chronology of **III**: 517.
Birs Nimrud **III**: 507, 508.
Bismya **III**: 510*(2)*.
Buhen, of, Belgian Photogrammetric Mission to **III**: 519.
Builders, Early **III**: 460.
Building of, a Task for Gods and Kings **V**: 197.
Byblos, Date of Buildings II, VIII, and XL, at **III**: 516.
Byblos, Egyptian, at **III**: 512, 513.
Canaan, in **V**: 70.

Canaanite, at Hazor **II**: 385; **III**: 519.
Canaanite, Evolution of **III**: 514.
Coele-Syria, of **III**: 507.
Cori, Curves in the Plan **III**: 462.
Corinth, at **III**: 66, 466, 522.
Cos, Hellenistic, in **III**: 514, 529.
Cosa, Temple B **III**: 67.
Croesus, of Diana (Artemis) at Ephesus **III**: 511.
Cult Furniture at Hazor **II**: 384.
Cult, of Malophoros at Selinus **III**: 486.
Dagon, of, at Beth-Shan **II**: 339; **III**: 513*(3)*.
Decoration, Apotropaic Serpents in Minturnae **III**: 469.
Demeter, of, at Eleusis **III**: 516.
Demeter, of, in Sicily **III**: 513.
Denderah, Age of **III**: 507.
Diana, (Artemis) at Ephesus **III**: 459, 511, 515.
Didymaean Apollo near Miletus **III**: 509.
Doura, of the Palmyrene Gods, at **III**: 513.
Ê-ana, Singašid's Gift to **VII**: 147.
Early (Egyptian) **V**: 202.
Edfou **III**: 509.
Edfu, Consecration of, at **VII**: 68.
Edfu, Control of Bees at **III**: 457.
Edfu, of, Inscriptions on Kingship from **I**: 484.
Egyptian **III**: 447, 510, 511.
Egyptian, and Astronomy **II**: 230; **III**: 505.
Egyptian, Community and **III**: 516, **V**: 216.
Egyptian, Deity and **III**: 516; **V**: 216.
Egyptian, Pictures of **III**: 517, 714.
Egyptian, Social and Economic History of **V**: 221.
Egyptian, Symbolism of **III**: 516; **V**: 216.
El-Kâb, at **III**: 131, 512.
El-Khargeh, at **VII**: *14*.
Elephantine, at **III**: 93*(2)*, 94*(3)*.
Eleusis, Demoished at **III**: 520.
Eretria, in **III**: 508.
Erment in 1850 **III**: 509.
Failaka, Hellenistic, in **III**: 519.
Farafra Oasis, at **III**: 515.
Foundation Rites for New **V**: 158.
Foundry of the Second **I**: 297.
Funerary, Terentine, Architetural Sculpture **III**: 754.
Greek, and Early Religion **III**: 511; **V**: 250.
Greek, Associated Divinities in **V**: 255.
Greek, at Prinias in Crete **III**: 510.
Greek Coins, on **I**: 455.
Greek, in Sicily **III**: 509.
Greek, Origin of **III**: 511.
Greek, Siting of Classical **IX**: cxxiii.
Greek, Three Western **III**: 520.
Hadad, of, at Kirbet et-Tannûr **III**: 515.
Hator, at Serâbît **III**: 226.
Hatshepsut, at Deïr el-Baharî **III**: 490, 520, 522.
Heavenly, Babylonian Conception of **IV**: 392*(2)*; **V**: 177.
Hellenic, Distribution of **III**: 508.
Hellenistic, Setting of **IX**: cxxiii.
Hephaistos, Sculpture **III**: 518, 519, 745.
Hera, in Xypete **III**: 513.
Hera, Two, at Agros **III**: 509.
Himera's Doric **III**: 514.
Horus, of, at Edfu **V**: 217; **VII**: 37, 38.
Horus, of, at Heliopolis(?) **III**: 521; **VII**: 73.
Inanna, of, at Nippur **III**: 519*(2)*.
Inanna, of, at Nippur, Esarhaddon Inscription **VII**: 190.
Interior Design of Greek **III**: 471.
Ipsambul, Subterranean, at **III**: 507.
Ishtar, of, at Nineveh **III**: 183, 514.
Israel, Community and **V**: 70.
Jahu, of, in Syene **V**: 12.
Jahu, of, in Syene and Pentateuchal Criticism **III**: 231.

Jewish, of Yahu at Syene *(see also:* Jahu) **VII**: 122.
Jewish, Pictorial influence of **I**: 445; **V**: 69.
Jupiter Panhellenius at Ægina **III**: 507.
Jupiter Stator, of **III**: 511.
Jupiter Ultor, of **III**: 515.
Kardaki **III**: 514*(2)*
Lipit-Ishtar's Hall of Justice **V**: 186.
Locri, Doric at **III**: 509.
Luxor, of **II**: 70, *265;* **III**: 253, 510, 522, *568;* **VII**: 69.
Luxor, Triple Shrine of **V**: 223.
Malta, "Neolithic", at **III**: 512.
Maltese, Origin of **III**: 519.
Maru-Aten **I**: 240; **III**: 518.
Medīnet Habu, of **III**: 516.
Melkath, of **II**: 308.
Memphis, at **III**: 512.
Mentuhetep at Deir el-Bahari **III**: 510.
Mesopotamian **III**: 517; **V**: 165.
Mesopotamian, and Community **III**: 517; **V**: 165.
Mesopotamian, "Papsukkal" figures from **III**: 579.
Mesopotamian Tower **III**: 508*(2)*.
Minerva, of, at Syracuse **III**: 511.
Mirgisse, at **III**: 512.
Moon, of, at Mârib **III**: 517*(2)*
Mt. Gerizim **II**: 478; **III**: 520.
Music, Origins of, from **I**: 243.
Nabataean, of Atargatis at Khirbet et-Tannûr **III**: 515*(3)*.
Nabu, at Nimrud **III**: 178, 501, 518*(2)*.
Nahariya, Bronze Age, at **III**: 517.
Napata, at **III**: 732.
Nemesis, of, at Rhamnous **III**: 522.
Ningal, at Ur **V**: 187; **VII**: *263*.
Ningišzida, at Uruk (Warka) **III**: 518.
Nubia, in **III**: 447.
Nubian **III**: 510.
Onias, at Leontopolis **I**: 141; **V**: 69, 76.
Oriental **III**: 511*(2), 542*.
Osiris, at Abydos **III**: 522.
Palestine-Syria, in **V**: 70.
Palestinian **III**: 517.
Paphian, of Aphrodite **III**: 467.
Paphian, of Aphrodite and Oriental Architecture **III**: 514.
Peribolos of the Twelve Gods in Athens **III**: 517.
Persian Fire(?), or Tombs **III**: 520, *558*.
Philae, on **III**: 508, 513.
Phoenician **III**: 509.
Phoenician "Thymiateria" and Solomon's **III**: 469; **V**: 72.
Plataia, Archaic, at **III**: 508.
Poseidon, of, at Isthmia **III**: 501.
Poseidon, of, at Paestum **III**: 517.
Prinias, East Wall of Temple A **III**: 472.
Prinias, in Crete **III**: 510.
Ptah's, at Memphis **III**: *359*.
Pyramid **III**: 506.
Pyramidal (Ziggurat) **III**: 507; **V**: 171.
Qasr Rabbah, Nabataean **III**: 515.
Ramesses II, of, at Abydos **III**: 512.
Redesiyeh, of, so-called **III**: 511.
Restoration of, Babylonian Texts on **VII**: 219.
Roman, between Kharga and Dakhla **III**: 516.
Roman, Horizontal Curves in "Maison Carrée" at Nimes **III**: 460, 508.
Šulmān, in Jerusalem **V**: 161.
Samanoud, of **III**: 511.
Samaritan, *see:* ***Samaritan Temple***
Selinous, of **III**: 460, 508.
Seti II, of, at Eshmunen **III**: 509.
Sety I, at Abydos **III**: 475, 502, 520; **VII**: 18.
Shechem, Dating of **V**: 70*(2)*.
Shechem, Fortress, of **II**: 478; **IX**: ciii.

Sibitti, of, at Khorsabad	**III**: 518.
Significance of in ANE	**III**: 516; **V**: 70.
Sirens, of, on the Sorrentine Peninsula, Topography of	**III**: 509.
Site of Israel's, purchased by David, from Araunah	**IV**: 361, 378, 542; **V**: 70.
Sol Invictus, of	**III**: 515.
Soleb, as New form of Egyptian Architecture	**III**: 462, 511.
Sun-, at Abusir	**III**: 510.
Sun-, of Coele-Syria	**III**: 510.
Sun-, of Meroë	**III**: 511.
Sun-God at Sippar, and Nebopolassar	**V**: 173.
Tabo, of, on Argo Island	**III**: 20, 202, 522.
Temple of Soleb, Decoration of Room II of	**III**: 519.
Tepe Gawra, Prehistoric	**III**: 514.
Theban, of Empire Period	**V**: 216.
Thebes at	**III**: 508, 510.
Thothmes III, Two at Beisan	**II**: 332, 513.
Tuthmosis III, Funeral, of, at Gurneh	**III**: 510*(2)*, 515.
Tuthmosis III, of, at Deir el-Bahari, Architectural Design of	**III**: 479, *769*.
Ur of Chaldees, at	**III**: 512.
Urartian Tower	**III**: 521.
Wâdy Abbâd, at	**VII**: 63.
XIth Dynasty Temple at Deir el-Bahari	**III**: 509, 510*(2)*.
XVIIth Dynasty, at Wadi Ḥalfa	**III**: 510; **VII**: 15*(4)*.
Yahu of, Jewish, at Syene *(see also:* Jahu)	**VII**: 122.
Yahu, Yedonya's Letter Concerning	**VII**: 132.
"Z", at Babylon, Bird of	**III**: 511.
Zerubbabel, of *see:* ***Temple, Second***	
Zeus at Athens, and Metrology	**III**: 474.
Zeus Labranios in Cyprus	**III**: 507.
Zeus Olympios, at Dura	**III**: 516; **V**: 258.
Zeus, Sculptures of, in, at Olympia	**III**: 477, 753.
Temple at Elephantine:	**V**: **§437, 76-77.**
Aramaic Papyri and	**V**: 77.
Significance of	**V**: 77.
Structure and Orientation of, a Revised Plan of the Jewish District	**V**: 77; **IX**: cxix.
Temple, Ezekiel's:	**IV**: 418*(2)*, 419; **V**: 69.
Blood Sacrifices in	**IV**: 424.
Vision of	**IV**: 418, 419.
Wellhausen Theory and Ezekiel's Sanctuary	**IV**: 259, 420.
Temple, Herod's:	**V**: **§436, 75-76.**
Arragements and Site of	**V**: 75.
Azarah, Three Torah-Scrolls in(?)	**VIII**: 437.
Brass Gate in	**V**: 75.
Court of the Gentiles, none in Temple area	**V**: 76.
Courts, Position of	**V**: 76.
Cubit Used by Masons	**V**: 76.
Destruction of, Legends of among Paintings of Dura Synagogue	**III**: 524; **V**: 76.
Fall of	**V**: 75.
Fore-court of Women, in	**V**: 75.
Gates of the Great Court	**V**: 76.
Gateways to	**V**: 76.
Greek Tablet from	**VII**: 334, 335.
Jesus's Day, in	**V**: 75.
Josephus on	**V**: 75.
Limestone Column from	**V**: 75.
Middoth on	**V**: 75.
Platform, Position of, on	**V**: 76.
ΘΑΝΤΟΣ Inscription from	**VII**: 340.
Remains of	**V**: 75.
Royal Porch	**V**: 76.
Site and Arragements of	**V**: 75.
Synagogue, None in	**V**: 76, 94.
Tablet from	**V**: 75*(2)*.
Warning Inscription of	**V**: 75*(2)*; **VII**: 338.

Temple, Israelite - General Studies, *see also, Specific Temples* — **V**: 50, **§433, 67-71**; **IX**: **§433, cxxxv**.
- Arch Springings Found within the Temple Area — **V**: 68.
- Ark of the Covenant as a Miniature — **V**: 55.
- Christian Envy of — **V**: 70.
- Church and — **V**: 76, 93.
- Cleansing of, and Zechariah — **VI**: 415.
- Copy of the Tabernacle, or Tabernacle as Copy of the Temple(?) — **V**: 52, 69.
- Glory of Yahweh — **VIII**: 101*(2)*.
- Heavenly, in Ezekiel — **IV**: 419.
- Heavenly, Jewish Conception of — **IV**: 392*(2)*; **V**: 177; **VIII**: 250.
- Hebrew Sanctuary—One or Manifold(?) — **V**: 68.
- Hymnody of — **V**: 38, 67.
- Influence of, on Art — **III**: 699; **V**: 70.
- Israelite Opposition to — **V**: 71.
- Land and, in Israelite Worship — **IV**: 484; **V**: 27, 45, 70.
- Location of — **II**: 412; **V**: 69.
- Middoth on — **V**: 67.
- Mishnah on — **V**: 69.
- Model of — **V**: 68, 70.
- Mt. of Olives and — **V**: 68.
- Opposition to, Israelite — **V**: 71.
- Paving Stones of — **V**: 68.
- Psalter in — **IV**: 478; **V**: 69.
- Quarter — **V**: 70.
- Rebuilding of, and the Reintroduction of Sacrifice — **V**: 62, 70; **VIII**: 246.
- Rebuilding of, Proposed, under Emperor Julian — **V**: 68*(2)*.
- Redemption, History of, House of God in — **V**: 69.
- Right of Entry to, in OT — **V**: 71.
- Ritual — **V**: 38.
- Sanctuary, Unity of, in Light of Elephantine Papyri — **V**: 69.
- Septuagint use of *τὸ ἅγιον* for — **V**: 641.
- Site of — **V**: 67, 68*(2)*.
- *Speaker's Commentary* on, at Jerusalem — **V**: 67.
- Specifications, MT and LXX — **V**: 71.
- Synagogue and — **V**: 67, 91, 94.
- Titus, Arch of, Spoils of, Represented on — **V**: 69.
- Treasure, Temple, Search for — **V**: 69.
- Veil of, at Olympia — **V**: 67.
- Vessels, Sacred, of — **V**: 68*(2)*.
- Worship and / in — **V**: 39, 41, 68, 70.
- Worship at, Centralization of — **V**: 13, 69.
- Worship in, after A.D. 70 — **V**: 39.
- Yahweh, Did He Forsake the(?) — **VI**: 349.

Temple, Persons or Groups associated with o/t Priests: — **V**: **§438, 77-78**.
- Functionaries, Fertility Cult, in the OT — **V**: 78.
- Temple Singers — **V**: 78.
- Theocratic Functionaries (Word Studies) — **V**: 77.

Temple Scroll: — **VIII**: **§1145, 471**.

Temple, Second: — **I**: *162, 366, 469, 492;* **II**: *456;* **V**: 67, **§435, 74-75**.
- Builders of — **V**: 74*(2)*.
- Chronology of the Destruction of — **V**: 74.
- Destruction of, Chronology — **V**: 74.
- Ezekiel's Visions and — **IV**: 418; **V**: 74.
- Founding of — **V**: 74, 75.
- Foundry of — **V**: 74; **VI**: 412.
- Inauguration of — **V**: 74.
- Measurements of — **V**: 74*(3)*.
- Midoth, and — **V**: 74*(3)*.
- Regulations on the Economy of — **V**: 75.

Sabbath, War on the , Problem of, and the Talmudic Books and the **VIII**: 235.
Scrolls found in the Court of **IV**: 11, 12.
War on the Sabbath, Problem of, and the Talmudic Books and the **VIII**: 235.
Worship of the Tabernacle compared with **V**: 38.
Zechariah to Ezra **V**: 74.
Zerubbabel's Rebuilding **V**: 74.

Temple, Solomon's: **I**: *399;* **II**: *384;* **V**: 10, 50, 67, 70, **§434, 71- 73**; **VI**: 222; **VIII**: 389, 391.
Blueprints of **III**: 470; **V**: 72.
Building of **IV**: 379.
Copper Platform before **IV**: 220; **VI**: 591.
Date of the Founding of **IV**: 198; **V**: 72.
Dedication of **IV**: 379.
Foundation of **V**: *67(2)*, 71.
Hamath, Building IV, and **V**: 73.
Hazor, Cult Furniture of, and **V**: 73.
High Portal in(?) **V**: 73.
"Jachin and Boaz" **V**: *71(3), 72(5), 73(3).*
Molten Sea before **V**: 50.
Narratives of in 1 Chronicles **IV**: 542.
Paphos, Temple of, and **V**: 72.
Pillars Before, *see:* ***"Jachin and Boaz"***
Reconstructon of **V**: *73(7).*
Ritual **V**: 38.
Sacrifice, Cessaton of, after the Destruction of, in 586 B.C. **V**: 64.
Solomon's, and Phoenician "Thymiateria" **III**: 469; **V**: 72.
Technical Terms describing **V**: 73, 390.
Tell Tayanat, and **III**: 521; **V**: 73.
Treasuries of Solomon's Private Chapel **V**: 72.
Waterman's, L., View of **V**: *72(2).*

Temple Tombs:
Al-'Ubaid, at **III**: 515.
Alexander the Great's **III**: 489, 501, 517, 530, 555.

Temptation, *see also:* **Sin, Doctrine of** **V**: 516; **VIII**: 177, 185.
Antiocheans and **IV**: 296; **VI**: 724.
Diabolical, and Demonology **VIIIB: 161.**
Job, of **I**: 56; **VIII**: 191.
Man, of, in Eden **IV**: 289, 291, 292.

Temptation, Mountain of: **II**: 284.

Ten:
Rabbinic Literature, in **VI**: 690.
Roman Numeral **I**: 436.

Ten Commandments, *see:* **Commandments, Decalogue** **VI**: 111.

Ten Thousand:
Retreat of, Inaccuracies in Grote's Narrative of **II**: 132.

TENNANT, F. R.:
God, Finite, on **VIII**: 99.
Sin, on **VIII**: 178.

TENNYSON, ALFRED LORD:
Knowledge and Use of the Bible **VIII**: 361.

"Tent of Meeting": **IV**: 243, 343; **V**: 10, *53(2), 55(3);* **VI**: 117.

Tent-Amon:
Funerary Papyrus of **VII**: 44.

Tents: **I**: 208; **VI**: 2.
Arabs, Living in **I**: 389.

Tentyra, *see:* **Denderah**

Teojo Doero / Ra: **I**: 262.

Tepe Farukhābād: **III**: 125.

Tepe Gawra: **III**: 48*(6), 139,* **249-251**, 348, *764.*
Acropolis, Oldest, at **III**: 483.
Artifacts from **III**: 567.
Ceramic Family from **III**: 638.
Found House at **III**: 491.

Impression of a Seal from Gawra VI **III**: 650.
Obsidian Vessels from **III**: 589.
Prehistoric Temple at **III**: 514.
Tepe Guran: **III**: 251.
Tepe Hissar: **III**: **251**.
Tepe Nūsh-i-Jān: **III**: 125, 251.
Tepe Yaḥyā: **III**: 125.
Tepes Kalwali: **III**: 124.
Tephillin: **I**: **371**.
Terah: **I**: 81.
Canaanite Moon-God(?) **V**: 192.
Idolatry of, Sabaïsm(?) **IV**: 313; **V**: 152.
Teraphim: **V**: 104, 105, 106, 107*(3)*, 109, 132, 516; **VIII**: 260.
Babylonian **V**: 171.
Rachel's Theft of **VI**: 80*(2)*.
Terence: **I**: *344*.
Teresh: **II**: 130, **170**; **III**: *24*.
Termessos Region: **I**: *320*.
Terne Museum: **II**: *98*.
Terni Central Library: **III**: *783*.
Terra Sigillata: **III**: 616*(2)*, 617, 619*(2)*.
Ceramics, Technological Analysis of, Illustrated by **II**: 215.
Terra-Cotta: **I**: *267*.
Terraces, Agricultural: **I**: 258.
Terracottas: **III**: 465*(2)*, 587, 726, 764.
Aphrodite, Statuette of **III**: 763.
Apis Bull **III**: 725.
Argive Heraeum, from **III**: 760.
Corinth, "Finds" at **III**: 63, 587.
Corinthian Sculpture **III**: 741.
Corneto, from **III**: 464, 761.
Deerheads **III**: 747.
Etruscan Architectural **III**: 469.
Etruscan Architectural (Revetments) **III**: 463, 464*(2)*.
Etruscan, Ash Urn **III**: 580.
Etruscan, Authenticity of, in Danish Collections Questioned **III**: 750.
Etruscan, Fioravanti on **III**: 752.
Etruscan Head **III**: 754.
Figures **III**: 725.
Figurines, from Corinth **III**: 759.
Figurines, from Seleucia **III**: 763.
Figurines, from Syria **III**: 763.
Greek Figurines **III**: 766.
Head, in the Metropolitan Museum **III**: 748.
Keos, Statues from **III**: 751.
Mineralogy and Palaeontology, Contribution to Study of **II**: 219; **III**: 750.
Myrina, from **III**: 759.
Potnia Taurōn **III**: 737.
Reliefs **III**: **§226, 720-754**.
Slab, in the Metropolitan Musuem **III**: 736.
Statue, of the Villa Albani **III**: 737.
Tel Ṣippor, from **III**: 768.
Tityrus, Cincinnati Museum **III**: 725.
Workshop, in the Persian Gulf **III**: 758.
TERTULLIAN:
Exodus 32, on **VI**: 720.
Interpretation of Scripture by **IV**: 97, 724.
Numbers 25, on **VI**: 720.
Tessera: **I**: 452.
Tesserae Nummulariae: **I**: 458.
Testacy:
Origins of, with reference to Babylonian Laws **I**: 502.
Testament: **V**: *504*, 516*(2)*.
Testament of the Twelve Patriarchs: **VI**: 696.
Apologetic Value of **VI**: 658*(2)*.
Aramaic Texts of **VI**: 646.
Armenian Texts of **VI**: 646*(2)*.
Christian Influence in **VI**: 659*(2)*.
Cod. Vatican. Graecus 1238, of **VI**: 646, 647.
Date of **VI**: 659.
Ethical Teaching of **VI**: 659; **VIII**: 222.

Exegetical Studies on **VI**: **§797, 669-670**.
Gospel of John and **VI**: 658, 718; **VIII**: 287.
Guide to Conduct, as **VI**: 659; **VIII**: 223.
Irenæus and **VI**: 658, 718; **VIII**: 287.
Jewish Authorship of **VI**: 658.
New Testament and **VI**: 658, 659*(2)*; **VIII**: 273*(2)*.
New Testament, Influence of, on **VI**: 659; **VIII**: 276.
Polycarp and **VI**: 658, 718; **VIII**: 287.
Sahidic Version of the Testament of Isaac **VI**: 646*(2)*.
Source, Early, of **VI**: 646.
Spirits in **VI**: 659.
Teacher of Righteousness in(?) **VI**: 659; **VIII**: 421.
Textual Criticism on **VI**: **§745, 646**.
Two Messiahs in **V**: 129; **VI**: 659.
Venice Extracts from **VI**: 646.

Testamental Literature:
Exegetical Studies on **VI**: **(§796), 669**.
Literary Criticism of **VI**: **§770, 657**.
Testament of Solomon **VI**: 657.
Textual Criticism on **VI**: **(§744), 646**.

Testamonia Biblica:
Early Christian Literature, in **IV**: 96; **VI**: 717.

Testate (Testamentary) Succession: **I**: 228*(2)*, 468.

"Testimony Books": **VI**: 720, 723; **VIII**: 284.
Anti-Judaica, and the Books of Testimonies **VI**: 717.
Athanasius and **VI**: 720, 726.
Barnabas' Isaiah Text and the Hypotesis of the **VI**: 717.
New Testament and "4Q Testimonia" **VIII**: 471, 480.
Testimonia from Qumran 4QTestamonia) **VIII**: **§1143, 471**.

Teta, King: **I**: *244;* **III**: *678*.
Stela of **VII**: 19.

Tetaky:
Tomb of, at Thebes **III**: 545; **VII**: 44.

Tetaty:
Stele of **VII**: 21.

Tetisheri, *see:* **Tety-shery**

Tetradrachms:
Athenian **I**: 445.
Cleopatra, of Ascalon **I**: 445.
Jewish, of Second Revolt **I**: 444.
Syrian **I**: 451, 452, 453.

Tetragrammaton (יהוה): **V**: 399, 426*(8);* **VI**: 42, 100; **VIII**: 110, 113, **§988, 120-124**.
Abbreviation(?) **VIII**: 123.
Abbreviation resulting in Double Readings **VIII**: 124.
Aquila, in **VIII**: 124.
Authorized Version, in Title-Pages of **VIII**: 122.
Authorized Version, on Title-Pages of **IX**: cxxix.
Ben Asher Text, in **VIII**: 124.
Corruption of **VIII**: 123.
Daniel, in **IV**: 529; **VIII**: 122.
Etymology of **VIII**: 114.
Haplography(?) **VIII**: 123*(2)*.
Ineffable Name **VIII**: 114, 122.
Interpretation of **VIII**: 121.
Isaiah, in **VI**: 273, 282.
Meaning of **VIII**: 121.
Mesha Inscription and **VIII**: 112, 122.
Mishna, Writing of the, in **VIII**: 123.
Name or Surragate(?) **VIII**: 123.
NT Sanction of LXX by Rendering of, by κυριος **VIII**: 120.
Origin of **VIII**: 121*(2)*, 124.

Pointing of **VIII**: 122*(2)*, 123; **IX**: cxl*(2)*.
Pronunciation of **VIII**: 121*(2)*, 122*(2)*, 123.
Pronunciation of, by the Samaritans **VIII**: 124.
Samaritan Liturgical Compositions, in **VII**: 137; **VIII**: 124, 385.
Septuagint, in **IV**: 33.
Septuagint (LXX), IN **VIII**: 123.
Subsitutes for **VIII**: 123.

Tetrapla:
Esdras A and B, and **VI**: 601.
Priority of to Hexapla **IV**: 38.

Tety-shery:
Grandmother of Ahmose I **II**: 100.

Teucheria:
Greek Epitaphs from **VII**: 334.

Teumman:
King of Elam, Disease of **II**: 100; **III**: 398.

Teutonic Languages:
Sanskrit, compared **V**: 275*(2)*.

Text Families, Similarities: **IV**: **§273, 100.**

Textbooks:
Assyrian and Babylonian **I** 236.

Textiles: **III**: **§200, 572-573.**
Çatal Hüyük, from **II**: 220.
Egyptian **I**: 274.
Impressions, on a Clay Vessel from Amorgos **III**: 572.
Remains from Naḥal Ḥever **I**: 279.

Texts: *see specific language*
Execration **III**: 715.

Textual Criticism, Theory, Method and Practice of - General Studies: **IV**: **§233, 1-7**; **§272, 98-100**, 143; **VI**: 6.
Advent of **IV**: 256.
Akkadian Variants compared with Hebrew **IV**: 7.
Apololgy for **IV**: 5.
Archaeology and **IV**: 3, 211; **VI**: 154, 201, 206, 224.
Azarah, Three Torah-Scrolls **VIII**: 437.
Ben Asher MS **IV**: 7.
Ben Naphtali MS **IV**: 7, 10.
Biblical Hebraica, of **IV**: 103.
Biblical Variants in Medieval Hebrew Poetry **IV**: 6.
Docuemtnary Hypothesis and **IV**: 4, 256*(3)*.
Elephantine Papyri and **VII**: 133.
Extra-Masoretic Texts **IV**: 7.
Genesis, Limits of Textual Uncertainty in **IV**: 268.
Glosses **IV**: 5.
Glosses, Conjectural Authentication of **IV**: 99.
Greek Papyri and **IV**: 3; **VII**: 351.
Hadayot and **IV**: 7; **VIII**: 467.
Haplophony **IV**: 99.
Hebrew Text of OT **IV**: 10.
Isaiah Scroll from Qumran **VIII**: 445.
Josephus and **IV**: 6.
Karatepe and **IV**: 5.
Masoretic Text and **IV**: 31.
Materials of, *see:* ***Papyri and Ostrica*** **IV**: **§234, 8-9.**
Medieval Hebrew Commentaries and **IV**: 7.
Origen's Evaluation of Textual Variants in the Greek Bible **IX**: cxxix*(2)*.
Original Text (?) **IV**: 2, 7.
Orthodox Variants **IV**: 4.
Philology and **IV**: 6, 70; **V**: 280.
Piyyuṭ and **IV**: 5
Poetic Text, Transmission **IV**: 5.
Proto-Lucian in Samuel **IV**: 6.
Qumran Biblical Texts **IV**: 6*(2)*; **VIII**: 443.
Rabbinic-Type Glosses in OT **IV**: 6.
Religious Texts, Transmission of in Ancient Oriental World **IV**: 99.

Sefer Okalah w' Oklah as Source of Textual Variants **IV**: 6.
Septuagint and **IV**: 4, 6, 31*(3)*, 35; **VI**: 247.
Siloam Inscription and **IV**: 2.
Sources for Study of **IV**: 5.
Square Characters, Introduction of **IV**: 2.
Stabilization of the Hebrew Text **IV**: 6.
Subsitutions in OT Texts **IV**: 4.
Synonymous Readings **IV**: 6.
Textual Uncertainty, Limites of **IV**: 11.
Theory of Local Texts **IV**: 6.
Tiberian Text **IV**: 6.
Translation and **IV**: 5.
Translation, OT, and **IV**: 108.
Transmission of the Bible in Light of Qumran MSS **IV**: 7; **VIII**: 442.
Ugaritic and **IV**: 5, 6*(2)*, 187; **V**: 535*(2)*; **VI**: 10; **VII**: 142.
varia lectio **IV**: 98.
Vulgate, Value for **IV**: 2, 40.

Textus Receptus:
Six Yemen Targum MSS. of Canticles compared with the **VI**: 555*(3)*, 711*(3)*.

ṯfl **VII**: 71.
Thaa: **II**: 100.
Thāj **III**: **251-252**.
Thalassocracy:
Minoan **I**: 354, 355; **III**: 167.
Thalatth: **V**: 180.
Thales: **II**: *235*.
Thamudic:
b "son" **V**: 377.
Preopsitions **V**: 377, 679.
Thamudic Inscriptions, *see:* **South Arabian Texts**
Thana: **II**: 290.
Thanksgiving: *see:* **Prayer**
Thanksgiving Hymns, *see:* **Hodayot**
Thasos: **III**: 252.
Heracles Thasios **V**: 262.
Sactuary of Artemis in **III**: 519.
Thassi, *see* **Simon Maccabaeus**
Thaumaturgy, *see:* **Miracles**
Theater(s): **I**: 239, 240; **III**: **§195, 528-529.**
Amman, at **II**: 319.
Babylon, Greek, in **III**: 529.
Beth She'an, at **II**: 302.
Chorus, in later Greek Drama and the stage **III**: 529.
Corinth, at **III**: 529*(3)*.
Cos, Hellenistic, in **III**: 514, 529.
Delos, on **III**: 515; **VII**: 336.
Dionysus, of, Marble Prohedria in **III**: 529, 583.
Epidauros, Harmony in **III**: 465, 529.
Eretria, at **III**: 99*(2)*, 528, 529*(2)*.
Gaul, Peculiarities of, in **III**: 529.
Greek, in Babylon **III**: 529.
Herod's Amphitheatre **III**: 528.
Morgantina, Architectural Ornament of **III**: 475.
Orchestra, Greek, Origin **III**: 476.
Periclean Reconstruction **III**: 529.
Petra, at **II**: 462*(4)*.
Roman **III**: 529*(2)*.
Sikyon at **III**: 231, 528*(4)*.
Thebaïd:
Ancient Races of **III**: 342*(2)*.
Palæolithic Implements **III**: 673.
Theban Invasions: **II**: *38*.
Thebans:
Wars with Hyksos **II**: 144, *158*, 170.

Thebes: I: *171, 216, 229, 254, 290, 377, 481, 493;* **II**: *8, 12, 13, 73, 88;* **III**: *160, 166, 241,* **252-253**, 455, *543, 591, 672, 731, 748;* **VII**: *29, 42, 73.*
- Akhenaten's Temple at **III**: 521*(2)*.
- Assyrian sacking of **III**: 252.
- Baban el-Moluk, Artifacts **III**: 564.
- Cult of *Ḥryw* at **V**: 217.
- Demotic Papyrus from **VII**: 80.
- Graffiti of the Priesthood of the 11th Dynasty Temples at **VII**: 13.
- Hieratic Ostraka from **VII**: 35.
- Inscribed Fragment from **VII**: 57.
- Linear B Tablets from **VII**: 365.
- Lower World, Entrance to, at **V**: 206.
- Monuments of Mont at **VII**: 58.
- Name, Derivation of **III**: 252; **V**: 298.
- Seal Inscription from **III**: 658.
- Stele, Eighteenth Dynasty **VII**: 20.
- Temple of Hatasu at **III**: 508.
- Tomb, (No. 260) at Drah Abu'l Naga, **III**: 542, 543.
- Tomb no. 282 at **III**: 560.
- Tomb of Akhenaten at **III**: 557.
- Tomb of Amenmosĕ, at **III**: 550.
- Tomb of Hebamun at **III**: 551.
- Tomb of Kheruef, at **III**: 551.
- Tomb of Paser at **III**: 551.
- Tomb of Queen Meie at **III**: 539.
- Tomb of Rekmara at **VII**: 10.
- Tomb of Si-ptah, at **III**: 539.
- Tomb, Sixth Dynasty, at **III**: 538.
- Tombs of the Kings at **III**: 544.
- Tombs, Royal, at **III**: 543.
- Tombs, Unnumbered, at **III**: 549.
- Topography of Western **III**: 252.
- Valley Tomb no. 56 at **III**: 558.
- Western **III**: 85, 252.
- XIth Dynasty Temple at Deir el-Bahari **III**: 509.

Thebes (Greece): **III**: **253**.

Theft, Stealing:
- Allegation of (Aramaic) **V**: 528.
- Babylonian Documents on **VII**: 252; **VIII**: 234.
- Greek Rites of **V**: 258.
- Lawsuit regarding, at Erech **I**: 501.
- Nimrud Letters relating to **VII**: 181.
- "Nocturnal Thief" and Restitution **VI**: 114.
- Nuzi Texts Relating to **VII**: 165; **VIII**: 233.

Theism: **III**: 316, 432; **VIII**: 55, 58, 64*(2)*, 97.
- Biblical **VIII**: 110.
- Ethics and **VIII**: 14, 219.
- Evolution and **III**: 296, 329*(2)*, 330.
- Greece, in **V**: 246.
- Levitical Law as a Tuition to **V**: 8.
- Mathematical Analysis of **VIII**: 66.
- Monopolar, and the Ontological Argument **VIII**: 71.
- Religious Humanism and **V**: 150.
- Semitic **V**: 19.
- Theistic Proofs **VIII**: 71.

Themistocles: **II**: 101.
- Decree of **II**: 134, 135; **VII**: 341, 342.
- Wall of **III**: 487.

Themistogenes: **II**: *21, 32.*
- Xenophon and **II**: 101, 108.

Theocracy:
- Antediluvian **IV**: 297.
- Early Jewish Sects and **V**: 95.
- Hebrew, College Study of **VIII**: 388.
- ***Isarel, in*** **I**: **§128, 471**; **VIII**: 391; **IX**: **§128, c**.
- Monachy, Transition to **IV**: 374.

Theocritus:
- Parallels to the Song of Solomon in the Poetry of **IV**: 505.

Theodicy: **V**: 25; **VIII**: 88, 197.
Aristotle's **V**: 248.
Babylonian Dialogue on and the Book of Job **IV**: 466; **VII**: 263.
Mosaic **VIII**: 107.
Psalms 37; 49; 83 as Theodicies **VI**: 480, 488, 498.
Psalms, in, Problem of **IV**: 486; **VIII**: 185.
Theodore of Mopsuestia: **IV**: 95.
Theodoret:
Josiah's Law Book, and **IV**: 94, 383; **VI**: 719.
Theodotion: **IV**: **§249, 38**.
Aramic Original of Additions to Daniel by **IV**: 48; **VI**: 608, 625, 639*(2)*; **IX**: cxlix*(2)*.
Chapters 13 and 14 of **VI**: 625; **VIII**: 363.
Excerpt from in Clement of Alexandria **VI**: 337.
Theodotos:
Greek Inscription of **VII**: 335.
Theogenes: **II**: *72*, **101**.
Theognis:
Ecclesiastes and **IV**: 514.
Theogony:
Babylonian, and Hesiod **VII**: 215.
Greek Ideas on **V**: 262.
Sumerian **V**: 174.
Theologians:
Deuteronomic **IV**: 384.
Genesis I Discussed by **VI**: 25.
Hebrew, and His Foreign Colleagues **IV**: 180; **V**: 23.
Mutual Duties Between, and Philosopher **VIII**: 1.
Theological Seminaries:
Bible / Old Testament in **IV**: 124; **VIII**: 398*(3)*, 399*(2)*, 400*(4)*, 401, 402, 403.
Hebrew in **V**: 386, 387*(2)*.
Jewish, in the Light of Modern Thought **VIII**: 6.
Semitic Study in **V**: 386; **VIII**: 402.
Training of Theological Students **VIII**: 406.
Theological Studies - General Studies: **VIII**: **§955, 1-9**.
Bauer, Georg Lorenz, on **VIII**: 1.
Bible and Modern **VIII**: 3.
Christian Theology of the Old Testament **VIII**: 6.
Darwinism, Influence on **VIII**: 3.
Evangical Perspective on Old Testament **VIII**: 9.
Evolution and **VIII**: 3.
Former Prophets, in **VIII**: **§961, 16-17**.
Hagiographa, in **VIII**: **(§965), 19**.
Historical Books, in **VIII**: **§968, 20**.
History of Religion and **VIII**: 3.
Jeiwsh Theology **VIII**: 3.
Latter Prophets, in **VIII**: **§962, 17**.
Major Prophets, in **VIII**: **§963, 17**.
Megilloth, in **VIII**: **§967, 19**.
Minor Prophets, in **VIII**: **§964, 18**.
Modern Criticism and **VIII**: 3.
Old Testament and Theological Thought-Forms **VIII**: 6.
Pentatuech, in **VIII**: **§959, 15-16**.
Philosophical, Question of **VIII**: 9.
Poetic Books, in **VIII**: **§966, 19**.
Possible Science, as **VIII**: 14.
Scientific Thought on **VIII**: 3*(2)*.
Scriptures and **VIII**: 3.
Theological Interpretation of the Old Testament **VIII**: 8.
Theological Issues in the New Translation of the Torah **VIII**: 8.
Theology of Tradition, OT **VIII**: 9.
Use and Abuse of Theological Arguments **VIII**: 7.
Theology, *see also:* **Theological Studies** **IV**: 146, 150; **VIII**: 8, 29, 57, 64*(2)*, 247.
Adam in **IV**: 272.

ANE, Common	**V**: 4*(2)*.
Animal Welfare, of	**VI**: 367; **VIII**: 229.
Archaeology and	**III**: 420, 433; **IV**: 222*(2)*; **VIII**: 4, 7.
Bible of New and Old	**IV**: 127.
Biblical Thinking *vs.* Aristotelianism in	**V**: 112.
Bibliography of	**I**: **§41, 15-17.**
Christian, and Philo	**VI**: 676.
Christian, and the Bible	**VIII**: 6.
Christian and the Concept of Sacrifice	**V**: 62.
Christian, Biblial Foundations derived from Babylon(?)	**IV**: 175.
Christian, Origin in Babylonia(?)	**VIII**: 4.
Conservative and Progressive: Sirach and Wisdom	**V**: 119.
Covenant and, in the OT	**VIII**: 9, 218.
Criticism, Biblical and	**IV**: 151; **VIII**: 4.
Criticism, Modern and	**IV**: 130.
Descritive Analysis in	**VIII**: 2.
Deuteronomic Theology of the Land	**IV**: 353.
Direction of, Today	**VIII**: 5.
Evolution and	**III**: 292, 295, 301, 303, 304*(2)*, 308, 313, 325*(2)*, 326, 329, 351; **VIII**: 3, 224.
Exegetical	**VIII**: 2.
Exodus, Significance of	**IV**: 340.
Geology and	**II**: 247; **III**: 285*(2)*, 287; **V**: 275; **VIII**: 1, 2.
Hebrew, and Its Determinats in the Eighth Century B.C.	**V**: 17.
Hebrew Religion, History of, and Old Testament	**V**: 23.
Hermeneutics in	**IV**: 90; **VIII**: 8.
Historical Method in	**VIII**: 2.
History and	**VIII**: 8.
Hypostatization of Linguistic Phenomena in Modern, Interpretation	**V**: 280.
Interim	**VIII**: 7.
Jewish	**V**: 32‡; **VIII**: 3, 4, 6, 9.
Jewish, Contemporary, and Limits of Reason in	**V**: 32.
Jewish, Faith and Method in	**V**: 32.
Jewish, Palestine in	**II**: 293.
Judaism and Modern	**V**: 32.
Language and	**VIII**: 9.
Literary Criticism and	**IV**: 137.
Medieval, and Alexander the Great	**II**: 11.
Ministerial Training, a problem of	**VIII**: 9.
Modern and Judaism	**V**: 32.
Moral, Biblical Perspectives	**VIII**: 229.
Motive of	**VIII**: 3.
Old Testament, and the History of Religion	**V**: 25.
Old Testament, Place in	**VIII**: 5.
Pastoral, and the Psalms	**VIII**: 386.
Philology and	**V**: 275.
Philosophy and	**VIII**: 5.
Philosophy as the Handmaiden of	**VI**: 725.
Plalestine in Jewish	**VIII**: 3.
Plea for the Study of	**VIII**: 4.
Preaching, Relation to	**VIII**: 4, 374.
Present-day Tendencies in	**IV**: 141.
Punishment in	**VIII**: 4, 225.
Revelation in Modern	**I**: 134; **IV**: 90; **VIII**: 35.
Roman	**II**: 159*(2)*.
Samaritan, in Funeral Rites	**I**: 377, 477; **VIII**: 9, 254, 386.
Science and	**III**: 288, 291, 300, 304, 325, 329; **VI**: 22; **VIII**: 3, 5.
Seismology and	**VIII**: 4.
Sumaritan Funeral Rites, in	**VIII**: 9.
Sumerian	**V**: 187.

Synagogue Architecture, in — **III**: 526.
Synagogue of Palestine, Weber's System of — **V**: 8.
Systematic, *see:* ***Systematic Theology***
Tabernacle, of — **V**: 52*(2)*.
Talmud and — **VI**: 700.
Theriomorphic in — **V**: 3.
Wisdom Literature and OT — **V**: 117; **VIII**: 6.
Wisdom of Solomon and — **VI**: 620, 724.
World, Biblical View of, A Theological Evaluation — **V**: 113*(2)*.
Theophany / Theophanies: — **VIII: §983, 102-104; §992, 128-129.**
Bible of — **VIII**: 102*(2);* **IX**: cxxxvii.
Dream-Theophany and E Document — **IV**: 262; **VIII**: 104.
God of Sinai, of — **VIII**: 128.
Holy Places in Hebrew Religion — **VIII**: 128.
Homer, of — **VIII**: 102; **IX**: cxxxvii.
Horeb, at — **VI**: 229*(2)*.
Job, in — **VI**: 438*(2)*, 440.
Job, in, Religious Significance of — **IV**: 468.
Psalm 18, Celebrated in — **VI**: 464; **VIII**: 102.
Sinaitic, Purpose of — **VI**: 112.
Theophanic Tradition in Amos — **IV**: 438.
Topos, of — **VIII**: 72.
Theophilus of Antioch:
Bible (LXX) Text of — **IV**: 38, 39.
Theophrastus:
Amphora with name of — **III**: 603.
Eternity of the World, on — **V**: 258.
Jewish and Greek Sacrifice, Contrasts on — **V**: 61.
Treatise on Stones in the Light of Archaeology — **I**: 266.
Theopneusty: — **VIII**: 37.
Theory, Pattern: — **I**: 337; **IV**: 159.
Theorums:
Euclidean, in text from Tell Hamal — **I**: 433.
Pythagorean, in Babylonian Text — **I**: 434, 435.
Theosophy:
Greek, Force of *Δίκη* in — **V**: 247.
Thera: — **III**: 253.
Ptolemaic Inscription from — **VII**: 327.
Therapeutae (Therapeutai): — **V**: 95*(2)*, 97*(2);* **VIII**: 410.
Essenes and — **VIII**: 423.
Philo and — **VI**: 672*(2)*.
Qumran Compared with — **VIII**: 422.
Therapeutics, *see:* **Disease; Medicine**
Thermodynamics:
Creation and Second Law — **VIII**: 83.
Thermopylai: — **III**: 253.
Thermos: — **III**: 254.
Thersites:
Death of, on an Amphora — **V**: 249.
Thesaurus: — **III**: 587.
Theses:
Bibliography of — **I**: 3, 8.
Theseus:
Sanctuary of, in Athens — **III**: 520.
Thespiae:
Ephebic Inscription from — **VII**: 330.
Thessaly: — **I**: *267;* **II**: *149;* **III**: 254, *638, 727*.
Greek Inscriptions from — **VII**: 318.
Racial Continuity of Prehistoric — **III**: 349.
Thethi:
Stele of (B.M. No. 604) — **VII**: 21.
Thetis:
Palace of, on the François Vase — **III**: 499, 707.
THIERSCH, FREDERICK: — **V**: 623.
Thinite Kings:
Titles of — **V**: 361.
Thinking: — **V**: 516.

THIRLWALL, CONNOP:
Greece, History of, on **III**: 110.
THIRTLE, J. W.: **IV**: 136.
Thîs: **III**: 254.
Thisbe: **III**: 254.
Thmuis: **III**: *636*.
THOLUCK, AUGUSTUS:
Prophecy, on **VIII**: 236.
Psalm 23, on **VI**: 470.
Psalms, Messianic, on **IV**: 489.
Psalms, Translation of, by **VI**: 442.
Theological Lectures **VIII**: 1*(3)*.
St. Thomas:
Names of God, on **VIII**: 110.
THOMAS, W. H. GRIFFITH: **IV**: 140.
THOMPSON, R. CAMPBELL: **VII**: *209*.
Thomu: **III**: 254.
Thorns: **III**: 395; **VI**: 2.
Hebrew Word for **V**: 440.
Thoth:
Astennu, as Name of **V**: 199.
Creator of Languages **V**: 217.
Cult of, in Roman Egypt **V**: 221.
Demotic Letter (Plea) to **VII**: 38*(2)*.
Sactuary of, Secret Chambers of **VII**: 64, 65.
Statuette of **III**: 763.
Thothmes, *see:* **Thutmose**
Thotmes III: **II**: *85;* **III**: *537;* **VII**: *59*.
Thought: **V**: *507, 510,* 516.
Evolution of **III**: 293.
Greek and Egyptian **III**: 749.
Greek and Modern, Similarities Between **V**: 263.
Greek, in Relation to Hebrew Wisdom **V**: 115.
Hebrew and Greek Compared **I**: 126; **V**: 114, 265.
Hebrew, Greek and Roman **V**: 114, 265, 271.
Language and, Relation Between and Doctrine of Inspiration **V**: 278.
Primitive, Effects on Language **V**: 278, 279.
Semitic Thought-Pattern in Sacred Scripture **V**: 699*(2)*.
Thousand and one nights:
Tale of Two Brothers and **V**: 319.
Thrace: **I**: *332;* **II**: 3; **III**: **254**, 265.
Greek Inscriptions from **VII**: 329.
Thracians: **II**: *158*.
Thracides: **I**: 53.
Thrakidan: **I**: 53.
Thread:
Blue, of (Num 15 and Deut. 22) **VI**: 130, 148.
Egyptian for **V**: 355.
Three:
Magic Number in Latin Literature **I**: 430.
Three Tongues of Fire (4Q376): **VIII**: **§1134**, **469**.
Throat:
Egyptian Word for **V**: 325.
Throne(s):
Assyrian, Ornament, from **III**: 743.
Chariot-, of Yahweh **VIII**: 61.
Marble on the Akropolis **III**: 582.
Royal in the Vault of Heaven **V**: 181, 237.
Thronion:
Rock Altar near **III**: 516.
Throw-stick: **I**: 238.
Thua:
Tomb of **III**: 539.
Thucydidean Motivation: **II**: 116; **III**: 230.
Thucydides: **II**: **101**, *153;* **VII**: 345.
Persian Letter in **VII**: 370.
War Guild in History of **VIII**: 228.
Thumb:
Thumb Marks in Babylonia **III**: 343, 645.
Thummim, *see:* **Urim and Thummim**
Thunder-Stones: **VII**: 144; **IX**: cxii.

Thunderbolt:
Egyptian cult-Object ⊸ V: 206.
Thurii: III: 254.
"Thus Saith Jahweh": V: 521.
Psychology and Metaphysic of V: 521.
Thuthotep:
Incense-Braizer depicted on Tomb of V: 206; **IX**: cxxiv.
Thutmose II: II: *44;* **VII**: *60.*
Thutmose III: I: *353;* II: *63,85, 88,* **101**; *106, 263, 264, 272, 498(2);* **III**: *242, 537, 724;* **VII**: *59.*
Annals of, and the Location of Megiddo VII: 15.
Campaigns of, James Burton's copy of the Inscription of VII: 14.
Foundation deposits of III: 484*(2)*, 568.
Geographical List of, Referencing Galilee(?) II: 367.
Historical Narrative Papyrus from Reign of VII: 14.
Inscriptions of VII: 15*(2)*.
Karnak Lists of VII: 14*(2)*.
Mummy Wrappings of VII: 44.
Obelisks of VII: 19.
Sed-Festival, Joint, with Queen Hatshepsut V: 221.
Stela of VII: 22, 82.
Tablet of the reign of VII: 55.
Two Temples of, at Beisan II: 332, 513.
Thutmose IV:
Campaigns of II: *15,* 101.
Chariot of I: 343.
Relics in the Tomb of III: 539*(2)*.
Tomb of III: 537.
Thuty:
Administrative Letter to VII: 71.
Thuy:
Stele of VII: 21.
Thŷ
Tomb of III: 539, *645.*
Thyme: III: 395.
Tiamat: III: 689; **V**: 168, 175; **VII**: 265; **VIII**: 160.
Battle between Marduk and V: 188; **VII**: 265.
Tiara, *see:* **Crowns**
Tibar: II: 487.
Tiber River: I: *306, 344;* **III**: 255.
Tiberian OT Text: IV: 6, 15.
Pre-Tiberian, DIvergenies IV: 15.
Tiberias: II: 302, 345, 367, **489**; **III**: *636.* I
Cemetery, Bronze Age, in X: cxviii.
Meteorological Observations at II: 239, 240*(7)*, 241*(5)*, 242*(4)*.
"Reed" of *(Coin)* I: 458.
Stone Doors of III: 459.
Synagogue at II: 302; **III**: 527*(3)*.
Tiberias, (Sea of) Lake of: II: *487,* **489**.
Depth and Temperature of II: 489.
Tiberius: I: *489.*
Staele of, from Luxor VII: 22.
Tibesti: III: *215.*
Tibetan:
Sumeian, Relation to V: 581.
Tibni: VI: 226.
Tibuin: II: *287.*
Tid'al II: 102; **VI**: 62, 64.
Tidal Waves, *see:* **Tsuamis**
Tie:
Amulet of III: 580.
TIELE, CORNELIUS PETRUS: I: 179.
Tiflis:
Egyptian Objects from III: *686, 762;* **VII**: 37, 65.
Tigisis: III: 255.

Tiglath-Pileser I: I: *86, 87, 90, 95;* II: *78, 79(2), 83(2), 88(2), 92(2),* 102,*178, 180, 190, 191(2);* IV: 181; VII: 159, 187.
Assyrian Canon of VII: 182.
Inscriptions of VII: 182.
Tiglath-Pileser II: II: 102, *115(2).*
Tiglath-Pileser III, *see also:* **Pul** II: *79, 87,* **102-103**, *183(3), 184, 191(4).*
Annals of VII: 190.
Inscription from Nimrud VII: 188.
Tigrina: V: 598.
Tigris River: III: 101*(2),* **255**, *764.*
Etymology of III: 255; V: 291.
Tigris Valley: III: 164.
Tih, The: II: 254; III: 232*(2),* **255**.
Tii, Queen, *see:* **Tiy**
Tiḳḳun Ṣopherim: IV: 17, 94, 98*(3),* 99.
Tikril Area: III: *170, 175, 227.*
Til-Barsib (Til-Barsip): III: 255, *753.*
Inscriptions from VI: 377, 378; VII: 175.
Tile(s):
Helladic Terracotta Roof III: 469.
Mytcenae, from, with Cartouche of Amenhetep III III: 462, 686.
Stamped from Argive Heræum III: 460.
Tilki Tepe: III: 255.
TILLICH, PAUL: VIII: 335.
Doctrine of Creation VIII: 80.
Names of God VIII: 110.
Tilmen Höyük (Hüyük): II: *222;* III: 264, 265, *678, 688.*
Tilmum (Tilwum): III: 256; IV: 315.
Tilmun: V: 184.
Timai, Tell: III: 256.
Time: I: *425;* VIII: 60.
Apocalyptic Literature in, and Eschatology I: 416; V: 124; VIII: 253, 420.
Architecture of I: 415.
Armenians, reckoning of, among I: 414; II: 407.
Babylonian reckoning of I: 416.
Biblical View of I: 415, 416*(3).*
Concepts of **I: §120, 414-416.**
Creation of, and Cosmology VIII: 86.
Crescas's Definition of V: 111.
Devil as I: 416.
Eschatological Treatment of Eternity and VIII: 252.
Eschatology and, in Apocalyptic Literature I: 416; V: 124; VIII: 253, 420.
Eschatology and, in Qumran I: 416; V: 124; VIII: 253, 420.
Etermity and I: 414, 415.
Evolution and III: 314.
Faith and I: 415.
Geology and III: 306, 340.
God as I: 416.
Greek Sense of, in History I: 134, 416; III: 91.
Hebrew Calendar and I: 399.
History and I: 132, 415.
Holyday, as Experience of I: 366, 415,
Jesus, Time-Consciousness of I: 415.
Measuring, with Special Reference to Egypt I: 415.
Old Testament, in I: 414.
Past Tense in Hebrew V: 486.
Penateuch, and I: 414*(2);* II: 186*(2).*
Pentateuch, Time-Measures in the II: 186*(2);* IV: 233, 234.
Philo's concept of I: 415.
Prophets, Time-Consciousness of I: 415.

Qumran in, and Eschatology I: 416.
Reckoning of **I: §116, 393-406; IX: §116, xcvii-xcviii.**
Relation to God's Existence in the Talmud and I: 414; VIII: 62.
Semitic Religion, in V: 148; VIII: 110.
Septentary I: 414.
Space and I: 415.
Space and, in Relation to the Existence of God in the Talmud I: 414.
Stars, Telling Time by II: 232.
World Created in(?) VIII: 80*(2)*.
Timekeeping Devices: **I: §120, 414-416.**
"Times of the Gentiles":
Tobit, in VI: 631; VIII: 284.
Timna(h), *see also:* **Wadi Arabah** I: *301;* II: 283, 321, 359, *360,* **490**; III: *752*.
Timorese:
Transation of Second Commandment into IV: 114; V: 446.
Tin: I: 292, 294, 296*(2)*, 297, 298, 299, 300, 301*(2)*, *342;* II: 212; III: *141*, 159; V: 551; VI: 249; IX: xciii.
Ṭirat Yehuda: II: 490.
Agricultural Fortress at II: 302.
Tirat Zvi: II: 300.
Tirhakah, *see:* **Taharqa**
Tirqan II: 267; III: 256.
Tiryns: I: *221, 281;* III: **256**.
Tirynthia Semata: III: 256.
Tirzah: II: 284, 365, 439, **490**; III: 424.
TISCHENDORF, CONSTANTIN:
Bibliography of I: 22.
Septuagint, on IV: 25*(2)*.
Tischgemeinschaft: I: 208.
Tishah b'Ab: V: 85.
Tithing and Stewardship: **V: §431, 65.**
Babylonian Tithe-List VII: 258.
Bible, in V: 65.
Deuteronomic V: 65.
Hebrew V: 65.
Jubilees and VI: 654.
Law of V: 65*(2)*.
Moral Obligation of V: 65*(2)*.
Origin of Tithes V: 65.
Pagan Nations, among V: 65, 154.
Royal, of Nabonidus VII: 258.
Titles:
Divine, Problems of Translation IV: 115.
Four and Seven as Divine VIII: 310.
Palace I: 186; V: 322.
Ptolemaic I: 189.
Queenly, XXIInd Dynasty V: 322.
Royal, in Antiquity IV: 537*(7)*.
Titulus:
Jewish, from Egypt V: 299.
Titus: I: 175, II: *259*.
Arch of, Menorah on V: 52.
Arch of, Temple Spoils Represented on V: 52.
Latin Inscriptions on VII: 366*(2)*.
Titus Manlius Torquatus:
David, Parallel Between V: 138; VIII: 359.
Tityrus: III: *725*.
Tiy (Tii, Tiye, Tyi), Queen: II: *8,* **103**.
Coffin, model, with lock of Hair of VII: 45.
Tomb of III: 539, 540*(3)*, 556.
Tomb of, Canopic Vases from III: 577.
Tomb of, Objects from, in the Swansea Museum III: 569, 687.
To:
Letter of Complaint to the Vizier VII: 9.

Toad:
Egyptian Figurine of **III**: 381, 766.
Hittite Word for **III**: *374,* 381.
Tob, Land of: **II**: 290.
Tobiads: **II**: 103, 323
Pseudo-Philo and **VI**: 678.
Tobias:
Ballad of, Sixteenth Century translation , in Metered Verse **VIII**: 363.
Sweish Comedia, 1550 **VIII**; 363.
Tobit, Book of: **VI**: 616.
Achiacharus, Legend of, and **VI**: 615.
Aḥiḳar **VI**: 615*(2)*.
Booker, Luke, Poem on **VIII**: 364.
Chaldee Book of **VI**: 615.
Codex Sinaiticus, Mistranslations of, in **VI**: 630.
Contraception and **VI**: 615.
Dog, of **VI**: 631.
Double Version of **VI**: 602.
Exegetical Studies on **VI**: **§713, 630-631**.
Florian, Jean Pierre, Poem on, by **VIII**: 365.
Genesis and **IV**: 265; **VI**: 614.
Hebrew Version of **VI**: 602, 612*(2)*.
Hindu-Christian Marriage Ideal and **VI**: 615.
Iranian Background of **VI**: 614.
Jack the Giant-Killer and **VIII**: 361.
Literary and Religious Affinities of **VI**: 615.
Literary Criticism of **VI**: **§695, 614-615**.
Liturgy, in **VIII**: 384.
Main Source of **VI**: 615.
Miracle in, Medical Explanation of, in 11:11-13 **VI**: 631.
New Testament and **VI**: 615; **VIII**: 274.
Nineveh in **VI**: 615.
Original Language of **VI**: 615.
Poem of (1787) **VIII**: 364.
Recensions of **VI**: 602.
Sara's Hysteria and **VI**: 615.
Sixteenth Century Drama **VIII**: 365.
Textual Criticism of **VI**: **§677, 602-603**.
Textual Rconstruction of **VI**: 603.
Tobit's Blindness **VI**: 615.
Tocharian:
Hittite and **V**: 608.
Second Singular for Third Singular in **V**: 613.
Tôdâh: **V**: 299, 508, 516.
TOFFTEEN, [OLAF ALFRED]:
Chronology, on **IV**: 335.
Togas: **I**: 273, 276, 277, 280.
Toilet, Toiletries:
Egyptian "House of the Morning" **V**: 208.
Hygene, Modern Eastern **I**: 388.
Toilet-box: **I**: 281.
Tokens: **I**: 190.
Athenian Law Courts, and **I**: 503.
Leaden, from Memphis **I**: 442.
Tol-e-Bakun: **III**: 256.
Toldoth, Beni Noah: **III**: 95.
Toledoth Yeshu:
Moreh Hassedeq in(?) **VIII**: 421, 460.
Tolfa-Allumiere: **III**: 257.
Tolmeita: **III**: 204, 257.
Inhapi, of **III**: 547.
Mordecai, of **III**: 536*(2)*.
Ptah-Arit, False Door in **III**: 547.
Robberies, Ramesside **I**: 498, 499; **VII**: 29.
Tomb Chapel:
Isaiah's **III**: 534.
Tell El-ʿAmarna, 525, at **III**: 513.
Theban Necropolis, Cutting and Preparation **III**: 464, 544.
Tombs, *see also:* **Temple Tombs, Mausoleums, Sepulchers** **III**: **§196, 530-561**.
Ạahmose, of **VII**: 65.

Absalom, of	**III**: 409, 530, 534.
Abydos, Near	**III**: 540.
Abydos, Royal at	**III**: 3, 536, 559.
Abydos, Royal, at, Pottery from	**III**: 630.
Aceldama, Rock-cut, at	**II**: 405; **III**: 534.
Akhet-Hetep, of	**III**: 358.
al-Fostat, found at	**III**: 549.
Alexandrian Tomb-Group	**III**: 559*(2)*.
Amenemḥab, Foreigners in	**III**: 348, 548.
Amenemḥab's	**II**: *13;* **III**: *377.*
Amenemhet, High-priest of Amon	**III**: 540, 546; **VII**: 62.
Amenmosĕ, of, at Thebes	**III**: 550.
Amenothes II, Robbery of the Tomb of	**III**: 537.
Amman, Iron Age, from Jabal El-Jofeh Al Sharqi	**III**: 559.
Amman, Jabal Nuzah, at	**III**: 559.
'Amman, Pottery of	**III**: 620.
Amon-sit, of	**III**: 539.
Amunedjeḥ's	**II**: 152, *170,* **III**: 711, 712.
Ancients, of the	**III**: 537.
Arteus, Runnel Stone from	**III**: 551.
Astronomical Ceiling-decoration in, Senmut's	**II**: 230.
Asyûṭ, Rock, at	**III**: 548.
Augustus, of	**III**: 559.
Bāghuz, Second Millennium , from	**III**: 550.
Bâb edh-Dhra', at	**III**: 560.
Bak-En-Amun, Theban, of	**III**: 559.
Ballâna, Royal, at	**III**: 561.
Beit Jibrin, at	**III**: 543.
Beit Jibrin, Inscribed, at	**III**: 542.
Beit Jibrin, Painted Rock-cut, at	**III**: 542.
Beit Sahur, Early Bronze Age Group from	**III**: 559.
Ben, of	**III**: 533.
Beni Ḥezir, Inscription in	**VII** 93.
Beni Hasan, Saïte, at	**III**: 545.
Beni-Ḥasan, Speos from	**III**: 550.
Beni-Mohammed el Kufur	**VII**: 59.
Bethany, Rock-cut, at	**II**: 405; **III**: 534.
Bethlehem, Rock cut, near	**III**: 537.
Brygos, at Capua	**III**: 551, *620,*
Byblos, at	**III**: 544.
Cairo, Archaic, from Old	**III**: 548.
Canaanite, from Yazur	**III**: 550; **IV**: 220.
Canaanite, near Jaffa	**III**: 545.
Canosa, Lost of	**III**: 546.
Caria, Mycenaean and Protogeometric, at	**III**: 557.
Cave, Cypriote Pottery at, Vicinity of Jerusalem	**III**: 612.
Corinth, at	**III**: 65*(2),* 547*(2).*
Crete, Geometric Period, at Kavusi	**III**: 68, 540.
Crypt of St. John	**II**: 300.
Cypriote, and Minoan Evidence for Its Date	**III**: 550.
Cypriote II, Late, from Kourion	**III**: 549.
Cypriote III, Late, from Kourion	**III**: 555*(2).*
Cypriote, Late, at Milia	**III**: 550.
Cyprus, Early Iron Age, from Kition	**III**: 540.
Cyrus, of	**III**: 530, 546.
David's	**I**: *359;* **II**: 349, 350, *402, 456, 499;* **III**: *486,* 531*(5)*, 532*(2)*, 535, 536, 541, 557.
David's, in Moselm Tradition	**III**: 554.
Der El-Medinet (Thebes) at, Nineteenth Dynasty	**III**: 532.
Dirâ' Abu'l Negâ, Unusual Scene from	**III**: 709.
Dra Abu el-Naga, Wall Paintings, Restoration	**III**: 458.
Drah Abu'l Naga, Thebes, (No. 260), at	**III**: 542, 543.
Earliest Perfect	**III**: 541.
Edh-Dhaheriyeh, near	**III**: 537.

Egypt, in	**III**: 447, 779.
Egypt, in, and Higher Criticism	**IV**: 122.
Egypt, Tombs of the Kings	**III**: 540; **IV**: 214.
"Egyptian", at Silwan	**III**: 538.
Egyptian, II Dynasty at Maassara	**III**: 550.
Egyptian, in Baharia Oasis	**III**: 540.
Egyptian Objects found in Malta	**III**: 546.
Egyptian practice of Endowing	**I**: 375.
Egyptian, Prehistoric	**III**: 535.
Egyptian, Royal	**III**: 542.
El A'reg Oasis, of	**III**: 550.
El Medyeh, Rock	**III**: 530*(2)*.
El-'Amârna, Royal, at	**III**: 547.
Enkomi, at	**III**: 96.
Esther's	**III**: 530, 536*(2)*.
Etruscan	**III**: 530, 536, 543, 549, 550, 551, 747.
Etruscan, Chronology of	**III**: 550.
Etruscan, Urartian Bronzes in	**III**: 598.
eẓ Ẓahiriyye, Early Iron Age at	**III**: 549.
Fertility and	**I**: 218, 376.
Gezer	**III**: 539, 540.
Gordion	**III**: 556.
Habakkuk's	**II**: 284.
Hagia Triada, of, Restored	**III**: 555.
Halicarnassus, Mycenaean and Protogeometric, at	**III**: 558.
Haremhab, Memphite, of	**III**: 544, 553.
Haremhab, of, at Sakkara	**II**: 44; **III**: 536.
Harmhabi, of	**III**: 541.
Harpy, Interpretation of	**III**: 593.
Hatshepsu(it), at Thebes	**III**: 252, 542, 543.
Hatshepsu(it), of	**III**: 538*(2)*.
Hawaret el Gurob, at	**III**: 536.
Hellenistic in Mylasa	**III**: 553.
Hepzefa of, Assiut	**III**: 543, *714;* **VII**: 63.
Herodian, at Wadi el Badan	**III**: 553.
Hetep-heres, of	**III**: 546*(2)*, 547.
Hierakonpolis, Decorated	**III**: 557.
Hwi-b ȝ.w, of, at Saqqara	**III**: 554.
Hyksos, at Kalandia	**III**: 553.
Iny's at Deshashe	**III**: 715; **VII**: 18.
Irbed, Iron Age, from	**III**: 558, 559.
Iron Age, at Al Jib	**III**: 553.
Jason's	**III**: 560.
Jason's, Aramaic Inscriptions in	**VII**: 131.
Jericho, Bronze Age, at	**III**: 555.
Jericho, Excavated, at	**III**: 555.
Jerusalem, Chamber in the Syrian Orphanage	**III**: 548.
Jerusalem, Middle Bronze Age II Pottery from	**III**: 628.
Jerusalem, or Third Wall (?)	**II**: 407.
Jerusalem, Rock Cut, in Wady er-Rababi	**III**: 537.
Jerusalem, Two, from the Period of the Kings of Judah	**III**: 555.
Jewish	**III**: 423, 548.
Jewish, in Kedron Valley	**III**: 549, 551.
Jewish, in Vicinity of 'Isawiyeh	**III**: 551.
Jewish, on Shahin Hill, Jerusalem	**III**: 556*(2)*.
Jewish, Ossuary, Pottery Types from	**III**: 623*(2)*.
Jewish, Rock-cut, in Jerusalem	**III**: 560.
Jewish Tomb at Mugharet Umm El-'Amad	**III**: 551.
Jewish Traditions of	**III**: 532.
Jonathan's	**II**: *377;* **III**: 541.
Jordan, in	**III**: 431.
Joseph's at Sechem	**III**: 531.
Joshua's	**II**: 284; **III**: 531.
Judges, of	**II**: 407; **III**: 414, 535.
Kalandia, Hyksos, at	**III**: 553.
Kha', of	**III**: 560.

Kheruef, of **III**: 136, 551, 556, 559.
Kings, of the **III**: 531*(2)*, *535*, 535*(3)*, 541*(2)*, *642*.
Kinnereth, EB, found at **III**: 550, 551.
Kolenieh, Rock-hewn, at **III**: 533.
Kurdistan, in **III**: 548.
Kurnub (Mampsis) 107 **III**: 561.
Kyky, Theban, of **III**: 559.
Lycian Painted near Elmali **III**: 561.
m h n w t f, of **III**: 543.
Maʿabarot, Middle Bronze **III**: 561.
Maʿayan Barukh, Bronze Age, at **III**: 557.
Maassara, Egyptian, II Dynasty at **III**: 550.
Maassara, Three Shaft **III**: 550.
Maassara, Tomb Six at **III**: 550.
Maccabees, of **III**: 531.
Macedonian **III**: 59.
Macedonian, at Chaeronea **III**: 538*(2)*.
Malta, Egyptian Objects found in **III**: 546.
Manahat, near **III**: 558.
Marissa, at **III**: 539*(2)*.
Marissa, Two from Necropolis of **III**: 538.
Masonry **III**: 531.
Mastaba-Tomb in Egypt, Ideology of the Superstructure **III**: 473.
Mechu, of **III**: 533.
Menes, of **III**: 535.
Menna, of **III**: 542.
Mentuemhat, Relief from **III**: 748.
Mentuhotep I, of **III**: 537*(2)*.
Merenptah, of **III**: 538.
Meru, of **VII**: 42.
Meryt, of **III**: 560.
Mesopotamian, Royal **III**: 542.
Micah's **II**: 284.
"Midas", of **VII**: 369.
Minoan **III**: 556.
Montefiore, of, Roman **III**: 558.
Morgantina, Fourth Century B.C. **III**: 557.
Muristan, at **II**: 408.
Mutnedjemet's(?) **II**: 64; **III**: 560.
Mycenaean Age, at Midea **III**: 548.
Mykenai, at **III**: 547.
Mylasa, Hellenistic in **III**: 553.
Nfr-mꜢʿ.t, of **III**: 554.
Nebetka, Architecture of **III**: 468, 549.
Nebo, Iron Age Tombs at **III**: 558.
Nefert-ari, of **III**: 538*(2)*.
"Nekht", of at Bersheh **VII**: 43.
Nubia, in **III**: 447.
Oriental **III**: *511(2)*, 542.
Osiris, of **III**: 535, 542.
Pa-shedu, of **III**: 537.
Paestum, Painted, at **III**: 556.
Painting, *see:* ***Painting***
Palestine, in **III**: 447.
Palestine, Painted of **III**: 543.
Palestine, Remains of **III**: 530.
Patriarchs' **II**: 284; **III**: 532.
Patro, of **III**: 553.
Peisistratros' Laws on **I**: 499; **III**: 551.
Perpendicular Rock-cut, and Stone Basin in **II**: 408.
Persian, at Susa **III**: 540.
Persian, or Fire Temples(?) **III**: *520,* 558.
Philistine, at Tell Fara and their Aegean Prototypes **III**: 559.
Phoenician **III**: 532, 533, 540.
Phrygian at Myrlaca **III**: 263.
Prophets, of, Greek Inscriptions in **III**: 409.
Prophets, of the **III**: 534
Ptah-Iron-Ka, of **III**: 358.
Queens, Tomb of **III**: 538.
Qusṭul, Royal, at **III**: 561.
Ra-Ka-Pou, of **III**: 546.
Rachel's, *see:* ***Sepulcher***
Rachel's, Topography of **II**: 291; **III**: 541.
Ramesses IV, of **III**: 463, 539, 543; **VII**: 34, 44.
Ramesses XII, of **III**: 539.

Ramesside, Granite Sarcophagus from **III**: 549.
Ramesside Tomb-Robberies **I**: 498, 499.
Relief from Memphite, of Ḥaremḥab **III**: 732.
Representations of, from the Theban Necropolis **III**: 711.
Rock Block with, at Jerusalem **II**: 409; **III**: 535.
Rock cut, in Jerusalem **III**: 557.
Rock-cut **II**: 305; **III**: 534, 535.
Rock-cut, Architectural Observations on **III**: 471.
Rock-cut, Typological Sequence of, Palestine **III**: 561.
Roman, called Taba Bûr, near Amman **III**: 545.
Roman, Painted, near Lucus Feroniae **III**: 557.
Saïte, at Beni Hasan **III**: 545.
Sanhedria, of **III**: 553, 554.
Saqqara, at, near the Serapeum **III**: 559.
Saqqara, Tomb 3070 at **III**: 560.
Sarafend, Bronze Age, at **III**: 555.
Sardinia, "Tombs of the Giants" in **III**: 540.
Sardis, at, Date Assigned **III**: 551.
Sardis, Metal Bowl from **III**: 632.
Scopus, Mount, on **III**: 536.
Sculpture, Chinese and Egyptian, Compared **III**: 727.
Sculpture, from Palmyra **III**: 732.
Se-Renpu, of **III**: 533.
Sen-Nefer, near that of Thotmes III **III**: 537.
Senman, of, Brother of Senmut **III**: 542.
Senmut's, Astronomical Ceiling-decoration in, **II**: 230.
Set II, of **III**: 538.
Shefa 'Amr, Galilee, at **III**: 533.
Sheikh Abd el Gurneh, at **III**: 546.
Sidon **III**: 533.
Silwan, Bronze Age Tomb Group, from **III**: 558.
Silwan, "Egyptian", at **III**: 538.
Speos, at Beni-Ḥasan **III**: 515.
Spirit of Living Sacrifices in **V**: 66.
Stone, Earliest **III**: 540.
Syrians Pictured on Theban **II**: *170.*
Tehneh, early, at **III**: 537.
Tell Ajjul, Early-Middle Bronze Age, at **III**: 555.
Tell er Robâ, at **III**: 537.
Tell Jerishe, Bronze Age **III**: 551.
Tetaky, at Thebes **III**: 545.
Theban **I**: *265;* **III**: 543, 545; **V**: *214.*
Theban Offical's **III**: 543; **VII**: 63.
Theban, Proportional Squares on Walls of **III**: 697.
Thebes, (Der El-Medinet) at, Nineteenth Dynasty **III**: 532.
Thebes, no. 282 **III**: 560; **VII**: 74.
Thebes, no. 56 **III**: 558.
Thebes, no. 85, Scene on **III**: 697.
Thebes, Reparations of, at **III**: 456.
Thebes, Rock, at **III**: 533.
Thebes, Royal of **III**: 543, *768.*
Thebes, Sixth Dynasty, at **III**: 538.
Thebes, Tomb Galleries at **I**: *290;* **III**: 538.
Thebes, Tombs of the Kings at **III**: 544, 545.
Thebes, Unnumbered, at **III**: 549.
Tholos of the Aegean **III**: 557.
Thothmes IV, of **III**: 537, 538*(2)*, 539*(2)*.
Thothmose IV, Relics in **III**: 539*(2)*.
Thracian, Hellenistic Paintings in **III**: 551.
Thua, of **III**: 539.
Thy, of, at Sakkara **III**: 539, *645.*
Tiy, of **III**: 539, 540*(3)*, 556.
Tombs of the Kings, Egypt **III**: 540.
Transjordan, Underworld in Painted, from **III**: 711.
Tumuli, West of Jerusalem **II**: 311.
Turgut, at **III**: 560.

Turin Plan of a Royal **III**: 463, 543; **VII**: 34, 44.
Tut-ankh-amen **III**: 541, 544*(5)*, 545.
Tut-ankh-amen, objects from (Botany) **III**: 385.
Twosre, Queen, of **III**: 554.
Ur, Royal, at **III**: 546*(3)*, 547*(2)*.
Valley of the Kings, Temperature and Humidity in **III**: 544.
Valley of the Kings, Tomb 55, Plan of, in **III**: 557.
Valley of the Kings, Tomb in **III**: 539.
Valley of the Kings, Tomb-Pit opened **III**: 537.
Vault, Primtive **III**: 550.
Vegetable Remains from Egyptian **II**: 212; **III**: 531.
Virgil, of **III**: 543, 547.
Wa'r Abu eş Şafa, near Jerusalem, Ancient Chamber at **III**: 549.
Wady el Joz, Rock-cut in **III**: 534.
Wady er-Rababi, Rock-cut in **III**: 536, 537.
Yazur, Bronze Age, near **III**: 551.
Yua, of **III**: 539.
Zarethan, Two, at **II**: 498; **III**: 485, 558.

Tombstones, *see:* **Gravestones**

Tongue:
Aryan Name of the **IX**: cxli, cxliii.

Tongue, The:
Joshua, in **VI**: 172, 173.

Tongues:
Gift of, in the OT **VIII**: 247.

Tool(s), *see also specific names* (e.g. Axe) **III**: **§218, 672-678**, *684*.
Ard **III**: 677.
Bone Implements **III**: *609*, 674.
Bronze **III**: 673.
Chamfered Pieces from Ksar **III**: 677.
Copper **III**: 673.
Cutting-out, Egyptian **III**: 673.
Etruscan Names of **V**: 679.
Flint Implements **III**: 674*(2)*, 675*(4)*, 677*(2)*.
Formidio **III**: 675.
Model, in Egyptian "Foundation Deposits" **III**: 673.
Pyramid-Buliders, of **III**: 473.
Stone, Chamfered **III**: 677.
Stone, from Galilee **IX**: cxv.
Stone (Palaeolithic) **III**: 672*(2)*, 673.
Tut-Ankhamum, from tomb of **III**: 568.
Votive(?) **III**: 676; **V**: 216.

Topakli: **III**: 257, 266.

Topaz: **I**: 285.

Tophet: **II**: 408.

Topography: **II**: 286, 298.
Abimelech, in **II**: 269.
Al-Mad'in (Seleucia-Ctesphon area) **III**: 9.
Alalah in List of Thutmose III **II**: 272.
Amarna, Tell el- **III**: 11.
Aphek, Study in Bibical **II**: 320.
Armenia, Controveries in **III**: 21*(2)*.
Asia, Western **III**: 23.
Athens, of **III**: 29, 30.
Babylon **III**: 39, 41.
Babylon, Topographical Texts of **VII**: 230.
Beersheba **II**: 297.
Benjamin Tribe of **I**: 156; **II**: 300.
Bible, of **I**: *27;* **II**: 253, 254, 255, 269.
Biblical Lands, of **I**: 122.
Bottice **III**: 50.
Coptic papyri, notes on **II**: 253.
Corinth **III**: 65.
Eleusis, of **III**: 95.
Eretria, of **III**: 99.
Ezion-Geber **II**: 359, 364.
Galilee, Sea of **II**: 366, 368.
Geba **II**: 297.
Gilboa, Mount, Battlle of **II**: 290.
Greece **III**: 111.
Gudea Inscriptions, of **II**: 255; **VII**: 277.

Hebrew Terms of	**II**: 256.
Jerusalem	**II**: 281, 400, 401*(5)*, 402*(2)*, 403, 406, 410, 412, 413, 420.
Jordan, Country of	**II**: 422, 423.
Joshua, Book of	**II**: 253, 283; **IV**: 358.
Locris, of	**III**: 153*(2)*.
Manasseh, Western, of	**II**: 439, 490.
Mesopotamia, of	**III**: 164.
Moab, of	**II**: 447.
Mount of Olives	**II**: 456.
Nehemiah, of	**VI**: 585.
Nineveh	**III**: 180.
Palestine	**II**: 288, 290, 291; **III**: 419.
Palestine in Book of Micah	**II**: 296.
Palestine, Medieval	**II**: 287.
Perachora, with reference to Xenophon's account of the Corinithian War	**III**: 195.
Petra	**II**: 267, 461*(2)*.
Pylos, of	**III**: 205.
Rachel's Tomb, of	**II**: 291; **III**: 541.
Rome	**III**: 212*(2)*.
Samaria, of	**II**: 470.
Samaritan	**I**: *150;* **II**: 263; **IV**: 366; **VII**: 136.
Samuel, Books of	**II**: 253, 283; **IV**: 358.
Shephelah	**II**: 479.
Sinai, of	**III**: 232.
Sodom	**II**: 483.
Sparta, of	**III**: 237*(2)*.
Spartolus	**III**: *50,* 237.
Syria, referred to in Karnak Lists of Thothmes III	**II**: 263*(2);* **III**: 242*(3);* **VII**: 14.
Temple of the Sirens on the Sorrentine Peninsula	**III**: 509.
Thebean, Lists	**II**: 272.
Thebes, Western, of	**III**: 252.
Tolfa-Allumiere District	**III**: 257.
Troad, of	**III**: 258.
Troy, of	**III**: 258*(2)*.
Ugarit, Tributaries of	**II**: 270.
Wilderness, of Palestine	**II**: 290.
Toponymy, *see:* **Place Names**	
Toprak Kale:	**III**: **257**.
Torah, *see also:* **Pentateuch, Synagogue Scrolls**	**I**: *474, 477, 479;* **IV**: *234(2);* **V**: 516*(2);* **VII**: *245*.
Akiba, as "Rescuer of the"	**VI**: 708.
Aristeas on the Translation of the	**VI**: 660.
Contemporary Jewish Theology, Meaning of, in	**V**: 114.
Daily Life and (Jewish-Christian Debate)	**VIII**: 338.
Decorations, Origin of European	**I**: 392; **VIII**: 357.
Definition of, in Modern Judaism	**V**: 32.
Dogma and	**VI**: 710.
Etymology of the word	**V**: 299, 458, 459*(2)*, 508, 516.
Jeremiah, in	**IV**: 412*(2)*.
Job, Word in	**IV**: 456; **V**: 516*(2)*.
JPS Translation of	**IV**: 62*(4)*.
New Jewish Translation	**IV**: 104.
New Translation of, Theological Issues in	**IV**: 109.
Ornamentation, German	**VIII**: 357.
Proverbs, Word in	**IV**: 456; **V**: 516*(2)*.
Psalms and	**IV**: 236, 486.
Revelations of, after Sinai, a Haggadic Study	**VI**: 696.
Samaritan Manuscript on the Commandments in	**VI**: 716.
Synagogue Scrolls	**IV**: **§241, 20**.
Syriac MSS of	**IV**: 14.
Theological Issues in the New Translation of	**VIII**: 8.
"Torah is Light":	**V**: 521.
Torah Min ba-Shamayim:	**VIII**: 35.

Torah Shrine: **III**: 525.
Ashburnham Pentateuch, **VIII**: 355.
Capernaum Synagogue, Fixed(?) **III**: 525.
Designs of in Ancient Synagogues **III**: 524.
Tor'an: **II**: 284.
Toras (The Troad): **III**: *104, 149*.
Torches: **I**: 343; **VI**: 212, *397*.
Toreutice: **I**: 298; **III**: 597.
Toreutics: **I**: 298.
Torone: **III**: *161, 223*, 257.
Torques: **I**: 280.
TORRANCE, DAVID W.: **II**: 241.
Torre San Severo:
Sarcophagus of, in Orvieto **III**: 543.
TORREY, CHARLES CUTLER: **II**: *123*.
"Ezra Studies" **VI**: 612.
Tortoise: **III**: 381-382.
Torture:
Non-Citizens, of, in Homicide Investigations **VIII**: 235.
Tosefta: **I**: *467;* **VI**: 702.
Controveries of Rab and Samuel and **VI**: 690.
Tractate Me'ila, of **VI**: 704.
Two Talmuds, Relation to **VI**: 704.
Toshka: **III**: 92, 187.
Totality:
Figurative Equivalent of, in Akkadian **V**: 381.
Figurative Equivalent of, in Northwest Semitic **V**: 381.
Totem-Clans: **I**: 154; **V**: 103*(2)*.
Totemism: **V**: 2, 104*(2)*, 106.
Toukh el-Qaramous: **III**: 257.
Toumba of Vardino: **III**: 258.
TOURAEFF, BORIS: **VII**: 63.
Tourists: **I**: 344*(2)*, 345*(2)*, 346.
Tower(s): **III**: **§188, 486-490**.
Babel, of **III**: 40, 486, 509.
David, of, Jerusalem **II**: 415.
Devil's Tower, Gilbraltar **III**: 106, 366.
Edar, of **III**: 487.
Jerusalem, Third Wall, in **II**: 416.
Migdol, Plan of a **III**: 464.
Migdols in Egypt and Palestine **III**: 487, 488.
Moab, Round, of **III**: 488.
Roman Tower of Winds **I**: 415, 416; **III**: 488*(2)*, 490.
Siphnos, Ancient, on **III**: 473.
Tell Beit Mirsim, Western **II**: 333.
Temple-tower, Building of **III**: 472.
Women's, at Jerusalem **II**: 415.
Tower of Winds: **I**: 415, 416; **III**: 488*(2)*, 490.
Tower of Babel, *see:* **"Babel" and the Division of Nations**
Tower Temples:
Babylonian, and the Altar of Burnt-Offering **V**: 48, 181.
Mesopotamian **III**: 508*(2);* **IV**: 311*(2)*.
Urartian and Achaemenian **III**: 521.
Town(s): **V**: 516.
Egyptian: Grammatical Gender of **V**: 363.
Modern Palestinian **I**: 387, 388.
Urartian in Van Region **III**: 276.
Town Lists: **II**: **§161, 262-273**.
Joshua, Book of, in **II**: 269.
Palestino-Syrian in Tuthmosis III's List **II**: 269.
Town Planning, *see* **Urban Studies**
TOYNBEE, ARNOLD:
Jews and **VIII**: 336.
Toys: **III**: **§219, 678-679**.
Greek **I**: 238.
Trachides:
Surname of Alexander Yannai in Josephus and Syncellus **VI**: 684.

Trachones:
Greek Text from **VII**: 316.
Trade, *see also:* **Commerce** **I**: **§103, 338-342**.
Anatolian with Europe **I**: 127; **III**: 13.
Aristotle on Free- **V**: 245.
Babylonian, Foreign **I**: 310.
Dispute regarding, Babyloniand Text on **VII**: 219.
Gibeon, in **I**: 308.
Grain **I**: 340.
Hebrew Terms for **I**: 339; **V**: 396.
Incense **I**: 308, 468; **IX**: xcv.
Iron **I**: 338.
Ivory **I**: 340; **III**: 199.
Lapis-Lazuli (Seals), Early Phases **III**: 660.
Marble **I**: 341.
Mycenaean **II**: 151.
Obsidian, 7500-3500 BC **I**: *287;* **II**: 222.
Phoenician Trading Settlement at Motya **III**: 170.
Pottery as Evidence for, in the Aegean **I**: 339, *356;* **III**: 617.
Prehistoric, and Jericho **I**: 341.
Tin, and Northern Trade of Massalia **I**: 301; **III**: 159.
Western Asia, in **III**: 155, 160.
Wine **I**: 340, 342.
Trade Routes: **I**: 338, 340, 341; **II**: *94*.
Trades: **I**: **§92, 269-272**.
Tradition:
Chain of, and the Law of Change **VI**: 693.
Early Christian and Early Rabbinic Compared **VI**: 690.
Geonic Fragment Concerning the Oral Chain of **VI**: 689.
Obscure, in Philo and Rabbinic Literature, Mutually Clarified **VI**: 678, 691.
Old Testament Studies, in **IV**: 91.
Scripture and **IV**: 207; **VIII**: 28.
Tradition Criticism:
Form Criticism and **V**: 693.
Tradition, Hebrew: **VII**: 268.
Alexander the Great, and Indian Gymnosophits, in **II**: 10.
Canaanite Mythology and **IV**: 187.
Prophets as Witness to **IV**: 260.
Psychiatric Relivances in (Talmud) **VI**: 691.
Traditions: **V**: 131, *159*.
Biblical, Origin of **IV**: 180.
Coins, and Messianic **I**: 442.
Deuteronomic Laws and Historical **IV**: 356; **V**: 119.
Early Hebrew, and the Historical Method **IV**: 158.
Egyptian, Persistence of, in Art and Religion, After the Pharaohs **V**: 209.
Genesis, Early, of **IV**: 254.
Heathen and the Bible Narrative **V**: 139.
Hebrew, and Egyptian and Babylonian Myths **V**: 146.
Hebrew, Prophets as Witness to **IV**: 388.
Interpretation of OT **V**: 135.
Israel, Ancient **IV**: 254.
Israel, Primitive **V**: 10, 294.
Messianic, and Coins **I**: 442*(2)*.
Oriental **V**: 138.
Psalms, Early Israelite, in **IV**: 486.
Sacred, in the East **V**: 138.
Tragacanth:
Cuneiform Word for **III**: *392,* 395.
Tragedy:
Greek, and Sacrifical Ritual **V**: 265.
History and **VII**: 3.
Old Testament as **V**: 682.
Origin of **VII**: 1.
Trajan: **I**: 174, *176*.
Trances:
Prophetic **I**: *108*.
Transcendence: **VIII**: 172.
Egyptian Thought, in **V**: 221.

Transjordan(ia): **I**: *286, 293, 448;* **II**: *103*, 295*(3)*, 296‡, 296*(3)*, 297*(2)*, 297‡, 298*(2)*, 298‡*(4)*, 310, *317, 319, 329, 470,* 490‡, **490-491**; **III**: *243, 244(5),* 423*(2)*, 424, 425, 427‡, 428*(3)*, 428‡, 429‡*(2)*, 429, 430, 430‡, *468, 674;* **IV**: *219;* **IX**: cxviii
- Aerial Reconnaissance of **II**: 310.
- Aurel Stein's Explorations of Roman Frontiers in **II**: 255; **III**: *126*.
- City Boundaries of Roman **II**: 275.
- Cultural History of **I**: 124.
- Economic Significance in Old Testament Times **I**: 307, 340.
- Heavy Bodies, Lifting, and, of **I**: 343, 349.
- Megalithic Complexes in **III**: 488.
- Monarchy, Period of, in **IV**: 358.
- Objects from **III**: 567.
- Prehistoric Caves in **II**: 275.
- Rulers of, **II**: 5, 490.
- Scientific Expedition of Region in 1886 **II**: 212.

Translation:
- Art of, and Science of Meaning in **IV**: 109.
- Biblical Research and **IV**: 109, 156.
- Coptic, Characteristics of **IV**: 44.
- English Bible, 16th Century, and Theological Presuppositions **IV**: 110.
- Idiom in Scripture **IV**: 107,
- Interpretation or **IV**: 80, 111.
- Naturalness, Measuring in **IV**: 109.
- Official and Unofficial: Psalm 4 in English **IV**: 106.
- Old Testament, Impossibility of **IV**: 112.
- Science of **IV**: 111.
- Textual Criticism and **IV**: 5.
- Theology as **IV**: 110.
- Ugaritic and OT **IV**: 110.

Translation Greek, Studies in: **IV**: **§246, 36**; **IX**: **§246, cxxviii.**
- First Samuel, Methods of the Translator of **VI**: 192.
- Syntactical Criteria of **IV**: 36; **V**: 635.
- Two Translators of Genesis, Theory of **VI**: 95.

Translation Principles: **IV**: **§276, 104-111.**
- Ancient Bilinguals and **IV**: 107.
- Emotional Element in **IV**: 105*(4);* **V**: 469*(4)*.
- Equivalents, Controlling Elicitation of **IV**: 109.
- "God", Chinese Translation of **IV**: 105.
- Hebrew Poetic Structure as a Guide **IV**: 106, 107; **V**: 687, 688; **VI**: 395.
- Hugh Ross, of, in 1727 **IV**: 108.
- Idea Redition **IV**: 110.
- Idiom in **IV**: 107.
- Internal Evidence **IV**: 105.
- Latitude of **IV**: 109.
- Linguistics and **IV**: 108; **V**: 280.
- Man in Anglo-Saxon and Old High German Bible-Texts **IV**: 107.
- Modern Speech, and **IV**: 108.
- Old Testament, Speical Features of **IV**: 107.
- Order of First Translations in Missions Fields **IV**: 106.
- Poetry, Biblical **IV**: 109.
- Punctuation **IV**: 109, 115.
- Qumran Scrolls, Meaning for Bible Translators **IV**: 108.
- Style in, Bible **IV**: 110*(2)*.
- Theological Influence on **IV**: 110.
- Vatican II on Bible **IV**: 110.
- Verbal Redition **IV**: 110.

Translation Problems: **IV**: **§277, 111-115**; **VI**: 182, 389*(2)*, 458, 474, 496, 498, 525.
- Ancient, Enigmatic **IV**: 115.
- Biblical Names **IV**: 115.

Cultural Background and	**IV**: 114.
Cultural Equivalences / Nonequivalences in	**IV**: 115.
Divine Titles as	**IV**: 115; **VIII**: 111.
Errors, Most Common in	**IV**: 114.
Genesis into Bari	**IV**: 114.
Hebraic Spirit	**IV**: 115.
Isaiah, LXX, work of a Single Translator	**VI**: 319.
Jehovah, Translating in the Old Testament	**VIII**: 118.
Lapses of OT Translators	**VI**: 104, 111, 143.
Letter, Different Printing of, in Two Versions, Significance of	**IV**: 112.
Mistranslations / Misinterpretations	**IV**: 112*(3)*, 113*(4)*; **V**: 399*(2)*, 400; **VI**: 9, 10, 133, 141, 188, 310, 402, 411, 419, 420.
Religious Background and	**IV**: 114.
Translations, *see also:* **English Bible, Versions**	
Authorized of 1611 (King James Version)	**IV: §263, 55-57; IX: §263, cxxix.**
English, and Humor in the Hebrew Bible	**V**: 695.
Foreign Language (i.e., O/T English) *see also:* ***Bible***	**IV: §269, 72-76.**
Modern English Translations (c. 1850ff.)	**IV: §264, 57-63; IX: §264, cxxix.**
Septuagint as	**IV**: 34.
Twentieth Century in English	**IX**: cxxix.
Translations, Bible, Foreign Language *(i.e., not English)*	
Algonquin (Algonqkin)	**IV**: 72*(2)*.
Bantu	**IV**: 74.
Cerf Edition	**IV**: 75.
Chinese	**IV**: 72.
Chinese, Catholic	**IV**: 75.
East African	**IV**: 76.
Esperanto	**IV**: 74.
French	**IV**: 72*(3)*, 73, 75.
German	**IV**: 68, 72, 73*(5)*.
Gothic	**IV**: 48*(2)*.
Hamitic-Semitic	**IV**: 75.
Irish	**IV**: 73*(2)*, 75
Japanese	**IV**: 75, 76.
Jewish, in Germany	**IV**: 76.
Korean	**IV**: 73, 76.
Mɛnde	**IV**: 75.
Mārāthi	**IV**: 74.
Malayalam	**IV**: 75, 76.
Maltese	**IV**: 75, 76.
Mongolian	**IV**: 72.
Polish	**IV**: 76.
Portuguese, Translating	**IV**: 107.
Rhodesia, in	**IV**: 76.
Russian	**IV**: 75*(2)*.
Slavic	**IV**: 74; **VI**: 727.
Sooahele	**IV**: 72.
Swedish	**IV**: 73, 74*(2)*.
Tibetan	**IV**: 75.
Turkish	**IV**: 76.
Welsh	**IV**: 73.
Yiddish	**IV**: 74.
Transliteration of Non-Roman Languges	**V: §487, 290-291.**
Semitic	**V**: 379.
Transmigration:	
Plato, in	**V**: 262.
Souls, of, Biblical Quasi-Evidence for	**VIII**: 263.
Transmutations:	
Cosmic	**V**: 156.
Transportation:	**I: §104, 343-350; IX: §104, xcv.**
Colossus of Djeḥutiḥetep	**I**: 349; **III**: 748.

Corn, of I: 346, 347, 482; VII: 30, 341.
Wheel-Carriage IX: lxxxix, xcv.
Transportation Artifacts: III: **§206, 585-586.**
Travel: **I: §104, 343-350; IX: §104, xcv.**
Arab Travelers on Palestine II: 286.
Conversion and, Relation VIII: 196.
Eighth Century Traveler, Statuette of III: 769.
First Traveller in Palestine II: 283; VII: 75.
Greek Sightseers in Egypt (Texts) VII: 322.
Journey of Šhamši-Adad from Subat-Enlil to Mari II: 256.
Old-Kingdom Travellers to Byblos and Pwenet VII: 67.
Purpose of in OT Times I: 344.
Restriction of, on New Moon Holidays I: 346; V: 85.
Samsi-Adad's Journey from Subat-Enlil to Mari IX: xcv.
Travel, Modern, in ANE: III: 409*(2)*, **§182, 435-447.**

TRAVELL, F. T.:
Psalms, on IV: 473; VI: 458.
Treason: I: *152*, 508.
Treasure:
Aegina I: 284.
Athribis (Benha), of III: 686.
Copper, First Dynasty, north of Saqqarah III: 597.
Hidden I: 303.
Maikop (Sycthian) III: 566.
Marlik, of III: *684*.
Minoan Gold III: 577.
Oxus, of III: 693.
Sumerian, of Astrabad III: 566.
Tell Bastra, from III: 626.
Twelfth Dynasty III: 563.
Ziwiye(h), of III: 569*(2)*, 599.
Treasurers:
Second Temple, of, and the Seal Impression from Jericho III: *655;* V: 78.
Treaties: **I: §138, 509-516.**
Aramaic, of Mati'el and Bar-ga'aya I: 511, 513; VII: 125.
Aramean, Wild Ass in I: 513; V: 527, *552*.
"Aryan" Gods of the Mitanni Treaties V: 159, 189.
Assyrian Treaty Formulae in Deuteronomy I: 514; IV: 352.
Athenian with Unknown State VII: 341.
Athens with Haliai VII: 336.
Curses in, Compared with the Maledictions of Amos and Isaiah I: 513; IV: 404.
Curses in Near Eastern I: 513; IV: 404.
Deuteronomy, Assyrian Treaty Formulae in I: 514; IV: 352.
Ebro, Evidence on I: 512; V: 450.
Esarhaddon, Vassal I: 514; IV: 356; VII: 189, 190.
Gibeonites, with Israel I: 334, 513; II: 131*(2)*.
Hiram and Solomon, Between VI: 223; VII: 240.
Hittite I: 506, 513, 515; VII: 305; **§933, 307.**
Hittite, Prologues, and Exodus, Sinai IV: 329; VII: 304.
Ḫattušiliuš (III) and Ramesses II (Hittite with Egypt) I: 510, 512; VII: 16, 307.
Israel with the Gibeonites I: 334, 513; II: 131*(2)*.
Kenites and Israelites, Between I: 514; II: 147.
Mitanni Treaties, "Aryan" Gods of the V: 159, 189.
Patterns in Ancient Near Eastern, Significance of I: 513; V: 699.
Prologues in Hittite I: 515.

Prologues of 7th Century	**I**: 515.
Protection Clauses in Hittite Vassal, and OT	**I**: 513; **VII**: 307.
Protection Clauses in Old Testament	**I**: 513.
Roman with Maccabaeus	**I**: 174, 337.
Roman with Tarentum and Rhodes	**I**: 510.
Sefire, Inscriptions, Stylistic Aspcets of	**I**: 514.
Sefire, *see also*: ***Sefire Treaty Inscriptions***	
Sefire Stelas, Treaty Terminology of	**VII**: 130.
Solomon and Hiram, Between	**VI**: 223; **VII**: 240.
Terminology, in Old Testament	**I**: 514.
Vassal, Benediction and Malediction, in	**I**: 513.
Vassal, of Esarhaddon	**I**: 514; **IV**: 365; **VII**: 189.
Wild Ass in Aramean	**I**: 513; **V**: *552*.
"Tree of Knowledge":	**IV**: 286, 291*(2)*, 292, 295; **V**: 138; **VI**: 31, 34, 35.
"Tree of Life":	**I**: *483;* **IV**: 287*(2)*, 290, 291*(2)*, 292, 293, 294*(2)*, 296; **V**: 138, 158.
Calendar Pant and	**IV**: 289.
Essene Tradition, in	**IV**: 295.
Jewish Iconography, in	**VIII**: 304.
King and, in ANE Religion	**IV**: 295.
Plant of Life and Waters of Death	**V**: 183.
Proverbs, in	**IV**: 294.
South Arabia, in	**IV**: 296.
Tree Worship:	
China, in	**I**: 385; **V**: 142.
Old Testament, Traces of, in	**V**: 104.
Trees, *see also* **Arboriculture**	
Almug	**III**: 386-387.
Apple, Girl Beneath, Statue	**III**: 740.
Apple, Hebrew *Tappūakh*	**III**: 383; **V**: 459.
Ba-Ta, of	**VII**: 35.
Bakha	**III**: 387.
Bible, Identity of, Mentioned in	**III**: 386.
Cedar	**I**: 345, 380.
Citron	**III**: 388.
"Cosmic"	**III**: 387, 389.
Cosmological, in Christian Tradition	**IV**: 295.
Cretan Sealings, on	**III**: 706.
Dalbergia Sissoo	**V**: 677*(2)*.
Date Palm	**III**: 387, **389**.
Dendrochronological Studies in the Negev	**II**: 245.
Eden, of	**IV**: 288; **VI**: 34.
Egypt, in	**III**: 384.
Fig	**III**: 390*(2)*.
Frankincense	**III**: 390.
Herakleopolite Nome, of	**III**: 120; **V**: 209.
Incense	**III**: 391.
Jujube, in Babylonia	**III**: 391.
Kikaion—"Wonder Tree"	**III**: 391.
Mulberry	**III**: 392.
Nebuchadnezzar's Vision of, in Daniel	**VI**: 569.
Oak, Abraham's, at Hebron	**III**: 393.
Persea	**III**: 393.
Pomegranate	**III**: 393.
Prohibition of Cutting of, During War	**VI**: 147.
Sacred	**V**: 138*(2);* **IX**: cxxv.
Sacred, Assyrian	**III**: 383*(2)*, **V**: 168*(2)*, 169, 234.
Sacred, Biblical	**IV**: 287, 322; **V**: 138.
Sacred, Herakleopolite Nome, of	**V**: 209.
Sacred, in Modern Egypt	**I**: 390.
Sacred, Mesopotamian	**V**: 146, 169.
Sacred, on Palestine Painted Pottery	**III**: 711.
Service	**III**: 394.

Service, in Bible and Talmud **III**: 163; **VI**: 57; **IX**: cxl.
Tamarisk **III**: 395.
Tappaūkh **V**: 459.
"Wonder Tree" (Kikaion) **III**: 391.
Worship of, in China **I**: 385.

Trellis-Work: **VI**: 499.

Trepanning:
Egytian Mummies, and **I**: 378.
Kültepe, inhabitants of **III**: 402.
Lachish, Skulls from **III**: 401.

Trephination: **III**: 408*(2)*.
Lachish, Skulls from **III**: 357, 401, 408.

Trespassing:
Code of Hammurabi on **I**: 478, 496.

TREVER, JOHN C.: **VIII**: 435, 477.

Triad(s), *see also:* **Trinity**
Divine, in Biblical Mythology **V**: 135; **VI**: 94.
Egyptian and Babylonian **V**: 173, 184, 203, 210.
Pagan Doctrine of **VIII**: 104.

Trial:
Egyptian State **VII**: 28; **IX**: ci.
Homicide, for, in Meosopotamia **I**: 503.
Jury, by, and Blood Revenge compared **I**: 480.
Marcus Primus, Legal Aspects of **I**: 503.
Ordeal, Trial by **I**: *181(2)* , 463, 466.
Varo Murena, Legal Aspects of **I**: 503.

Triasgion: **V**: *501, 506,* 507.

Tribes: **I**: *212;* **VI**: 46, 52.
Animal Tribes, among Arabs **I**: 184, 382; **V**: 153.
Animal Tribes, in the OT **I**: 184, 382.
Ezekiel's Division of Palestine Among **IV**: 420.
Family and **I**: 212.
Hyrnathian at Epidaurus **II**: 145.
Israelite, and Relationship to Indigenous Canaanites in Judges **IV**: 369.
Modern Palestinian, Organization of **I**: 387.
Shrines, Tribal League, at Amman and Shechem **III**: 522.
Tribal Organization and Institutions at Mari **III**: 158.

Tribes of Israel **I**: **§59, 154-157,** *407;* **II**: *275*.
Hebrew Tribal Names and Primitive Traditions **V**: 10, 294.
Territorial Allotments in the Samaritan Joshua **VI**: 176.
Transjordanic **VI**: 174.

Tribes, Ten: **I**: *94;* **II**: *163*.
Ezekiel, in **VI**: 358.
Fate of after Fall of Samaria **II**: *115*.
Lost, of Israel **VII**: 204.

Tribute, *see also:* **Taxation**
Aristidean of 421 BC **I**: 481.
Babylonian Tribute List **VII**: 220.
Lists, Delian **II**: 133.

Tridentine Decree:
Apocrypha and **VI**: 599.

Triennial Cycle, *see also,* **Synagogue Worship** **V**: 83, 91*(2)*, 92, 94.

Trigram: **V**: 76; **VI**: 684; **VIII**: 124.

Trilithon:
Baalbek, at **III**: 479, 509.

Trinitarian Bible: **IV**: 103*(2)*.

Trinity, *see also:* **Triads** **VIII**: **§984, 104-105**.
Babylonian **V**: 173.
Creation and **IV**: 286; **VIII**: 105.
Demythologizing **VIII**: 105.
Judaism / Jews and **VIII**: 104, 105.
Non-Christian Religions, of **V**: 164.
Theophanies in the OT and the Second Person of **VIII**: 128.

Tripod: **III**: 582.
Bronze, from South Persia **III**: 582.
Etruscan Bronze, Restoration of **III**: 583.
Horse, of Eturia **III**: 598.
South Arabian, Offering Saucer **III**: 580.
Theft of the Delphic **V**: 255.
Tripoli: **II**: 308; **III**: **258**.
Phoenician Site near (?) **III**: 258.
Travels, Modern, in **III**: 435.
Tripolitania: **III**: 258.
Trireme: **I**: 356.
Trisagion: **VI**: 256*(2)*.
TRISTRAM, HENRY BAKER: **III**: 442.
Tritheism: **VIII**: 105.
"Triton":
Statue of, from Gaza **III**: 748.
Troad: **III**: *104, 149, 200,* **258**, 260, 264, 266, 267.
Trogitis, Lake: **III**: **258**.
Troglodytes:
Cappadocians as **II**: 120.
Gezer, of **III**: 349.
Palestine, in **III**: 345, 349*(2)*.
Trojan War: **II**: 171.
Illustrations of **III**: 716.
Trojans: **I**: *313;* **II**: *140,* **171**.
Chronology **II**: 204.
Trope: **V**: 691*(3)*.
Trophonios: **V**: 147.
Trout:
Greek and Latin words for **III**: *380,* 382.
Troy: **I**: *284,* 326; **II**: *49, 215;* **III**: *71, 155,* **259-261**, *681, 682*.
Acland, Henry W., on **III**: 259.
Architectural Remains of **III**: 474.
Balkans, connections with **III**: 259, 607.
Baslica of Troy VI **III**: 515.
Bryant, Jacob, on **III**: 259*(2)*.
Chronology **II**: 204.
Danube Region, connections with **III**: 259, 607.
Foreign Relations of, in the Bronze Age **I**: 330.
Francklin, William, on **III**: 259.
Gell, William, on **III**: 259*(2)*.
Greek Inscriptions from **VII**: 323.
Hittite Name of **II**: 267; **III**: 260.
Ishtar at **V**: 158.
Morritt, Robert D., on **III**: 259.
Princess of **III**: 559.
Racial Elements in the First Siege of **III**: 344.
Topography **III**: 259*(2)*.
Ur, Links with **III**: 261*(2), 275(2), 593*.
TRUMBULL, H. CLAY: **III**: 133.
Trumpet: **I**: 244, 245; **III**: 679*(2)*.
Feast of **V**: 84.
Tut-Ankh-Amen, of **IX**: lxxxviii.
Trust: **V**: *505,* 517.
Truth: **V**: 517*(2);* **VIII**: 7, 29, 227.
Attitude of Ancient Mind **VIII**: 218.
Connexion of Natural and Divine **VIII**: 14.
Inseparable from Divine Personality **VIII**: 94.
Israel, in **VIII**: 225.
Propositional **VIII**: 28.
Trypho:
Dialgoue with **V**: 149; **VI**: 724, 725.
Tshok-Göz-Köprüköe:
Monument from **III**: 494.
Tsinnor, *see also:* **Gutter, The** **IV**: 373; **VI**: 209*(2)*.
Tsoungiza: **III**: 176.
Tsunamis:
Eastern Mediterranean, in **II**: 250.
Tubal: **III**: *163,* 261; **IV**: 287.
Tubalcain: **I**: *73*.
Biographical Studies **I**: 81.
Tuberculosis: **III**: 401.

Tueilāt Ghassūl, *see:* **Teleilât (Tell-el) Ghassûl:**

Ṭūkh El-Ḳarāmūs: I: 447.

Tukulti-Ninib I:
- Memorial Tablet of **VII**: 185.

Tukulti-Ninurta Epic: **VII**: 223.
- Song of Deborah and **IV**: 371.

Tukulti-ninurta II:
- Stela of, found near Tell Ashra **VII**: 188.

Tukulti-Urta I: **VII**: 187.

Tuleilat el 'Anab, el 'Enab, *see:* **Teleilat el-Anab**

Tuleilat el-'Enab:
- Physiographic Aspects of **IX**: cxv.

Tulul Abu el-'Alayiq: **III**: *431*.

Tumbleweed: **III**: 395.

Tummo: **III**: *215*.

Tumulus (Tumuli): **III**: 506, **§196**, **530-561**.
- Bronze-Age, in Eastern Palestine **III**: 553.
- West of Jerusalem **III**: 554; **VI**: 209.

Tuna: **III**: 261.

Tunics: **I**: 273, 276, 278*(2)*; **IV**: 219.

Tunis: **III**: *57*, 261.

Tunisia: **III**: 261, 452.

Tunnels:
- Ancient **III**: 459.
- Gezer **I**: 361.
- Gibeon, at **I**: 363.
- Hezekiah's **IV**: 214.
- Jordan Valley, in **II**: 498; **III**: 485.
- Negub, of, Inscription in **VII**: 174, 184.
- Siloam **I**: 357*(2)*, 359, 361; **III**: 481, 535.
- Simplon **I**: 361; **III**: 481.
- Zarethan, at **II**: 498; **III**: 485, *558*.

Tura: **III**: 261; **VII**: *42*.

Tureng Tépé: **III**: 124, 262.

Turgut: **III**: 262.
- Tombs at **III**: 560.

Turin Papyrus: **II**: *105*, 209; **VII**: 30, 31, 77.

Turin Psalter, *see:* **Codex Taurinensis**

Turkey: **I**: 268, *347;* **III**: *12, 238(2),* **262-267**, *430, 454, 458, 683, 759*.
- Archaeology in **III**: 434*(3)*, 453*(2)*, 454.
- Art Treasures of **III**: 693.
- Industries, Fire Using, in **III**: 125.
- Travels, Modern, in **III**: 435*(2)*, 437, 439, 442*(2)*, 445.

Turkey (Animal) **III**: *372*, 382, *617*.

Turkish Language: **V**: 377, 679.

Turkish Literature:
- Midrash, Turkish Tale in **VI**: 706.

Turmus, Tel: **II**: 491.

Turquoise: **I**: 285.

Tuscany: **III**: **267**.

Tusculum: **III**: 267.

Tushka: **I**: *346;* **III**: *186*.

Tushratta:
- King of Mitanni **VII**: 167.

Tut-ankh-amen: **I**: *245, 278, 327, 412;* **II**: *6,* **103-104**; **III**: 87, 88, *679(2)*.
- Death of, What happened after the **VII**: 306.
- Hittite Correspondence to the Widow of **VII**: 305.
- Objects from the tomb of **III**: 687.
- Objects from the tomb of (Botany) **III**: 385.
- Objects of, in the British Museum **III**: 566.
- Tomb of **III**: 541, 544*(5)*, 545.
- Tools from the tomb of **III**: 568.

Tut'ankhamūn: **II**: *24;* **IX**: cvi.
- Head of **III**: 743.
- Name **II**: 104; **V**: 298.
- Objects of, in the British Museum **III**: 686.

Objects of, in the Rijksmusem, Leiden III: 567, 687.
Officials of II: 6, *44, 60, 66*.
Tunic of I: *278*.
Tuthaliya IV(?):
Military Inscriptions of VII: 306.
Tuthmosis:
Official of Ḥaremḥab II: 104.
Tuthmosis I:
Reburial of I: 375; II: 104; III: 547.
Tuthmosis II: III: *136*.
Tuthmosis III: I: *404;* II: *45*, **104-105**, *106, 107, 198, 209, 269*.
Coregency with Amenophis II II: 16, 105.
Euphrates Campaign of II: 104.
Funerary Temple of III: 510*(2)*, 515.
Glass Chalice of III: 588.
Head of(?) III: 743.
Military Expedition to Syria by II: 105; VII: 17.
Sactuaries of, at Deir el-Baḥri III: 521.
Speos in Beni-Ḥasan, from the reign of III: 515.
Statue of(?) III: 746.
Stele of, from Armant VII: 24.
Temple of, at Deïr el-Baharî, objects from III: 570*(4)*, 688.
Tuthmosis IV: III: *136*.
Scarab of, bearing name of God Aten II: 214.
Sons of II: 105.
TUTTLE, JOHN WOOD: III: 515.
Tuttul: III: *238*, 261.
12,900,000: I: 429.
Twēret: III: *769;* V: 224.
Twins:
Acca Larentia, Nurse of Romulus and Remus V: 133.
Dioscurism in the OT V: 134.
Gemini are born V: 158, 166.
Mythology of, in All Nations V: 154.
Remains of from Tell Hassuna III: 362.
Valentine and Orson: Study in Twin Cult V: 156.
Two:
Semitic Numeral I: 429; V: 517.
Twosre, Queen: II: *96(2)*, **105**.
Tomb of III: 554.
Tyana: II: 266.
Tybi: I: 401.
Egyptian Month of I: 401.
Tyche Protogeneia:
Cretean Cult V: 242.
TYLOR, EDWARD B.: III: 336*(2)*.
TYNDALE, WILLIAM:
Knowledge of Hebrew IV: 106.
Tyndale's Bible: IV: 52*(3)*.
TYNDALL, JOHN: III: 290.
Tyndaris: I: 356; III: 267.
Typology: IV: 91; VIII: 126, **§1052, 301-309**.
Allegory or VIII: 308.
Amos, in VI: 386.
Barth's Doctrine of Scripture, in VIII: 308.
Discrimination in VIII: 308.
Eden, of IV: 272.
Exegesis and IV: 86; VIII: 308.
Fairbairn, on VIII: 302*(2)*.
Functional II: 222.
Hermeneutics and IV: 87, 89; VIII: 306.
Interpretation, means of IV: 93; VIII: 301, 306, 307.
Interpretive Principles and Illustration VIII: 306.
Isaac as Type of Christ VIII: 301*(2)*.
Messianic Prophecy, Typological Interpretation VIII: 137.
Moses in the Typology of St. Paul VIII: 293.
Tradition-History and VIII: 308.
Use and Abuse VIII: 306.
Tyranny:
Xeophon and II: 108.

Tyre: I: *147, 154, 275, 329*, 337, *354, 510;* **II**: *49(3), 155*, 308, *325*, **491-492**; **III**: *479;* **VI**: 281.
- Capture of, by Nebuchadnezzar — **II**: *68(4)*, 491*(4)*.
- Chronology of — **I**: 331; **II**: *193*, 204*(2)*, 491, 492.
- Ezekiel's Denunciation of — **VI**: 354.
- Hiram, King of — **II**: **49**.
- King of — **VI**: 355*(2)*, 359; **IX**: cxxxii.
- Lament over — **VI**: 354.
- Mint of, Source of Silver Coins in Palestine — **I**: 457.
- Parthenon of — **III**: 481.
- Rib-Adda of Byblos and — **VII**: 171.
- Ship of — **VI**: 354.
- Siege of, in Ezekiel — **IV**: 420.

Tyrians: **I**: 515.
- Elijah and Tyrian Alliance — **I**: 510; **IV**: 381.

Tyropoeon Valley: **II**: **492**.
- Ancient Street-Levels withing the Walls — **II**: 415.

Tyrrhenians: **IX**: cxi.

U

Uazit: **III**: 50.

'Ubaid: **III**: *97, 98*, 268, *275*.

Ubarrum: **I**: *191, 318*.

'Ubeidiya: **II**: 493.

Ubeidiyeh: **II**: 303.

Udy-mu (Den): **II**: 105; **VII**: 62.

Ugarit: **I**: *192, 194, 212, 219(2), 225, 272, 309(2), 321, 330, 339, 342, 355, 486, 492, 506(2);* **II**: 120; **III**: **268-269**, 427, *675, 683;* **IV**: 219.
- Administration in — **I**: 492; **VII**: 145; **IX**: cii.
- Akkadian Tablets from — **VII**: 151.
- Army of, and its Organization — **I**: 321.
- Deities of — **V**: 192.
- Divorce, Royal, at — **I**: 220.
- "King's Son" at — **I**: 195.
- Link between Hebrew and Greek Literature — **IV**: 188; **VII**: 144.
- Merchants at — **I**: 342, 506; **IV**: 320.
- Military Personnel of — **I**: 320.
- Monarchial Legitimacy and Marriage in — **I**: 219, 483.
- Old Testament Exegesis and — **IV**: 187; **VI**: 1.
- Psalm 29 and — **VI**: 475.
- Shipping at — **III**: 268; **IV**: 219.
- Slavery in — **I**: 205.
- Writing in — **I**: 234.

Ugaritic Language, *see also:* **Canaanite Language** **III**: 269; **V**: 383*(2)*, **§531, 532-540**; **V**: *461;* **VII**: 138; **IX**: **§531, cxlii**.
- Abecedaries — **V**: 534.
- Aleph, Consonantal, Loss of, in — **V**: 535.
- Alephs, Three, in — **V**: 538.
- Anatolian Cult Term in — **V**: 197, 535.
- Aphel Causatives in — **V**: 534.
- Archaism in — **V**: 538.
- Asseverative Kaph in — **V**: *480*, 532.
- Canaanite Dialect(?) — **V**: 532.
- Colon, Expanded in — **V**: 498.
- Construct with Final *m* — **V**: 537.
- Egyptian and, compared — **V**: 310; **V**: 535.
- Enclitic -*m* in — **V**: 533.
- Expanded Colon in — **V**: 539.
- Factitive Passive in — **V**: 490, 536.
- "Final" - m' = (mǎ?) — **V**: 532.
- Formulas of Greeting in — **V**: 538.
- Grammar — **V**: 538.
- Hebrew, Biblical, and — **V**: 472*(2)*, 532, 533.

Hebrew Lexicography and (Dahood) **V**: 390, 402, 403*(2)*, 404*(3)*, 405*(6)*, 535, 536*(2)*, 537*(2)*, 538*(2)*, 539*(3)*, 540*(2)*.
Hebrew Syntax and Style and **V**: *494*, 539.
Hebrew-Ugaritic Lexicography **V**: 390, 402, 403*(2)*, 404*(3)*, 405*(6)*.
Infinitive Absolute, Finite Use of, in **V**: 534.
Infinitive Absolute in **V**: 528, 539.
Locative with *Hē* **V**: 398.
Masculine Singular *-n* **V**: 536.
Matres Lectionis **V**: 538.
Numerals in **V**: 539.
Old Testament and **IV**: 188*(2)*; **V**: 402, 404; **VI**: 490.
OT Translation and **IV**: 110, 188.
Pa'yal Formations in **V**: 496.
Philology **V**: 390, 533, 537.
Pleonastic *Wāw* in **V**: 534.
Polyphony in **V**: 538.
Position among Semitic Languages **V**: 380.
Prepositional Nuances in **V**: 539, *553*.
Pronominal Suffix in Ugaritic Poetry **V**: 533.
Rhetorical Questions in **V**: 383; **VII**: 3.
Semitic Cognates in **V**: 538.
Semitic Languages, Position within **V**: 534.
Semitic Usage and **V**: 378.
Sentence Negation in **V**: 533.
Seven, number, in **V**: 538; **VIII**: 312.
Superative **V**: 537.
Syllabic Vocabularies **V**: 538, 539.
Tenses of **V**: 532.
Terminative-Adverial in **V**: 534, *550*.
Verb Sequence of **V**: 490.
Vocative in **V**: 533.
Wāw, "Pleonastic" in **V**: 497.
Yod as *Mater Lections* in **V**: 538.

Ugaritic Literature: **III**: 269; **VII**: 138.
Alalakh Tablets compared with **VII**: 144.
Antiphonal Psalm **VII**: 140.
Baal Epic (IV AB iii 24) **VI**: 550; **VII**: 143.
Bible and **V**: 698.
Danel Text **VII**: 140.
Egyptian Story of, and Ugaritic Poem of Ba'al **V**: 195; **VII**: 40, 143.
El, Innermost Chambers of in Epics **VII**: 143.
Epic of 'Al'êyân Ba'al and Môt **VII**: 139.
Ezekiel and the Mysteries **IV**: 421; **VII**: 142.
Greek and, Compared **VII**: 146, 348.
Homer and **II**: 50; **VII**: 145.
Hurrian Myth in **V**: 192; **VII**: 138.
Keret Epic, *see:* ***Keret Epic***
Krt **II**: 268; **V**: 195, 199, 533.
Liturgical Poem **VII**: 139.
Liturgy for the Spring Festival at Jerusalem in the Age of Abaraham **VII**: 139.
Mystery-Play from **VII**: 140.
Nikkal Poem **VII**: 142.
Passion Play "Ba'al is Risen" **V**: 192; **VI**: 314; **VII**: 141.
Poem **VII**: 141.
Poem. The Harrowing of Baal **VII**: 141.
Poetic Literature **VII**: 142.
Prose, Late **VII**: 144.
Psalms and **IV**: 498*(2)*; **VII**: 144.
Semitic Metric and Ugaritic Evidence **V**: 691.
Stylistic Patterns in **V**: 537, 700; **VII**: 145.
The Ewiržar Letter **VII**: 139.

Ugaritic Mythology: **V**: **§469, 189-199**.
Anatolian Cult Term (*dǵt*) in **V**: 197, 535.

Battle of the Rain and Sea **VII**: 141.
Composite Bow, in **V**: 193.
Daniel. An Incubation Scene in **V**: 194.
Egyptian, Alalysis of **V**: 199.
Egyptian Gotd Ptaḥ in **V**: 192, 214.
Epos, Climax of Seven Days in **V**: 196.
Folklore Myths in **V**: 193.
Fratricide and Atonement in **V**: 195.
Gods, Gracious and Beautiful **VII**: 140, 142.
Incantation Scene, How Baal Destroyed a Rival **VII**: 143.
Marriage of the Gods in **V**: 192; **VII**: 141.
Murices (Murex) in **V**: 199.
Muzzling of Tannin in **V**: 196.
Religion, Organized, at **V**: 197.
"Song of the Sea" and **V**: 198.

Ugaritic Texts (includes Ras Shamra Texts): **IV**: 218; **V**: *532;* **VI**: *365;* **VII**: **§870, 138-146**; **IX**: **§870, clii**.
Alphaabetic Tablet **VII**: 145.
'Aqht **V**: 536; **VII**: 144.
Beth-Shemesh Tablet **VII**: 140.
Bible and **IV**: 187; **VII**: 142.
Canaanite Letter from, and Habakkuk **VI**: 402.
Conditioned Sound Change in Ras Shamra **V**: 532.
Decipherment and Interpretation of **V**: 532, 533.
Diplomatic Archives **VII**: 144.
Discourse, Restorations and Observations **VII**: 146.
Egptological Text from Ras Shamra **VII**: 140.
Egyptian Loan-Word in **V**: 353.
Egyptian Points from **VII**: 138.
Enthronement Ritual in **VII**: 146.
Etruscan Affinities in **VII**: 139.
Grammar of Ras Shamra **IX**: cxlii.
I AB **VII**: 142, 143.
II AB 5:70-71 **VII**: 143.
II AB v-vii **VI**: 327; **VII**: 12.
III AB A (3 AB A) **VII**: 143.
Iron in **I**: 301.
IV AB **VII**: 143.
Letter, and Habakkuk 3:7 **VI**: 402; **VII**: 141.
Letter in the Dialect of **VII**: 146.
Letter of a King to His Mother **VII**: 143.
Letters **VII**: 141*(2)*.
Magical Text **V**: 193.
Mythological Epic **VII**: 139.
Old Testament and **IV**: 186, 187, 188; **VII**: 142.
Palestine, from **VII**: 142.
Peace, Appeal for in **VII**: 143.
Phoenician Poem **VII**: 138.
Poem on the Conquest of Death **VII**: 138.
Psalm 68:23 and **VI**: 495.
Ras Shamra C, Structure **V**: 532; **VII**: 139.
Ras Shamra Inscriptions and History of the Hebrew Religion **V**: 37.
Ritual Pattern of a Ras-Šamra Epic **VII**: 139.
Sabbath, Allusions to, in, in the Light of Midrashic Literature **V**: 83; **VI**: 708; **VII**: 143.
Samuel's Denuciation of Kingship in Light of **VI**: 196; **VII**: 268.
Seven Day-Unit in Epic Literature **VII**: 145.
Textual Criticism and **IV**: 5, 6*(2)*, 187; **V**: 535*(2);* **VI**: 10.
V AB **VII**: 142, 143*(2)*, 144.
Votive Inscriptions **VII**: 141*(2)*.

Ukheithar (Ukhaidher): **III**: *247*.
Persian Palace of **III**: 499.

Ukin-zer:
Death of **VII**: 181, 190.
Rebellion of **VII**: 180, 188.

Ulclers:
Assyrian Prescriptions for **III**: 405.

Ulḫu: **I**: *363*.

Song of — VII: 300, 308.

Ultimo-geniture: I: 227.

Ulukişla: III: 266.

Um el Jemal: II: 337, 493.

Um Qeis: II: 299.

UM Text 77:40-45 — V: 536; VII: 145.

'Umar ('Umayr), Tell
see also: **Choche,**
Ctesiphon, Seleucia — III: *61, 70,* **269-270.**

Umliash:

Flood of — VII: 224.

Umm el-Biyara: III: 270.

Umm el-Hanafieh: II: 422.

Umm-Juni: II: 493.

Umm Qeis: II: 422.

Umm Rus: III: *171,* 271.

Umma: II: 270.

GURUŠ Texts from — VII: 252(2).

Sign 𒉈𒉌 in Name of the Fourth Month — I: 398.

Tablet from, in the Ashmolean Museum — VII: 175.

Tablets from — VII: 149, 211, 212, 213, 270.

Temple Records from — VII: 149.

Unbelief:

Ancient and Modern — V: 152.

Unbilical Cord:

Egyptian Sign for — V: 354.

Uncleanness: I: 250; III: 397, 402; V: 424; VI: 428; VIII: 184.

Clean and Unclean, Ethics of — VIII: 227.

Laws Concerning in OT — IV: 252.

Sin and — VI: 490.

Unclean Birds and the Peshiṭta — IV: 46.

"Under Every Green Tree": V: 520.

Undertaker: I: 280; V: *616,* 674.

Underworld, *see also:*
Futher State,
Nether World — V: 409.

'ERES as — VI: 365.

Ishtar in — V: 177.

Painted Tomb in Transjordan, in — III: 711; V: 270

Refreshing in — V: 210.

Unguent: I: 281; V: 330.

Unhappy:

Later Hebrew, in — V: 517; VI: 666.

Unicorn: III: *378(2),* 382.

Unitarianism:

Judaism and, in Their Relation to Each Other — V: 141.

United Kingdom of Israel and Judah: I: §62, 160-161.

Chief Literary Productions before the Division of — IV: 162(2).

United States:

Prophecy, in — VI: 277(3).

Unity:

Mesopotamian, and Royal Hymns — I: 508; VII: 158, 287.

Old Testament, of — IV: §280, **169,** 177.

Universalism:

Deutero-Isaiah and — IV: 404, 405; V: 29.

Exile and the Restoration, in — V: 27.

Jewish — V: 24.

Judaism, Univerality of — V: 28.

Luke-Acts and — IV: 405; V: 29.

Post-Exilic — V: 21.

Theological in the OT — V: 23.

Universe: III: 328.

Babylonian, Newly Interpreted — II: 228.

Concept of, in Relation to the Concept of God — VIII: 84.

Creator's Plan of — VIII: 83.

Dating, Methods of — VIII: 86.

Divine Origin of — VIII: 75.

Hebrew / Jewish Idea of — VIII: 83(2).

Man's Place in — VIII: 170.

Origin of — **III**: 325, 328, 330.

Universities, Ancient: **I**: 232.

University College, London: **III**: *585*.

University Museum of Pennsylvania: **II**: *198, 331, 338, 339;* **III**: *3, 586, 605, 606(3), 609, 614, 619*.

Babylonian Collections of — **III**: 568.

Cappadocian Tabelts in — **VII**: 163*(3)*.

Cuneiform Texts at — **VII**: 149.

Egyptian Papyri — **VII**: 77.

KH Collection of Babyloniain Antiquites — **VII**: 206.

University of Bologna:

Hebrew Codices in — **IV**: 12.

University of California:

Nilometer in Egyptian Collection of — **II**: 223.

University of Glasgow:

Catagloue of Oriental MSS in the Library of — **VII**: 2.

University of Illinois Library:

Latin Mauscript of the Psalms in — **VI**: 535.

University of Michigan: **III**: 636.

Enoch Papyri at — **IV**: 642.

Library, Hebrew MS in — **IV**: 12.

Unseen World: **VIII**: **§1006, 154**.

"Until this Day": **V**: 521.

Unuk: **V**: 574, 580.

Upî: **III**: 270; **IX**: cxlii.

Uppsala:

School of, Old Testament — **IV**: 153, 176, *235;* **V**: *24*.

Uqair, Tell: **III**:*98*, 165, *268*, **270-271**, *272, 275*.

Ur: **I**: *182, 212, 246, 269, 278, 283, 284, 302, 303, 308, 340, 341, 348, 355, 483;* **II**: *51, 95, 168, 169(6), 202, 214;* **III**: *41, 98, 149,* **271-275**, *498, 747(2);* **IV**: 181, 218; **V**: *183(2)*, 184*(2)*, 187, *234;* **VII**: 159, 210*(2);* **IX**: *civ*, cxviii, cxix, cxx.

Artifacts from — **III**: 566, 567, 577.

Bricks from, Inscribed with "Yav" — **V**: 554; **VIII**: 113.

Business Documents from — **VII**: 252.

Cylinders from, Inscribed with "Yav" — **V**: 554; **VIII**: 113.

Divine Service in — **V**: 191.

Early Inscriptions from — **VII**: 151.

Fall of, and Ibi-Sin — **III**: 273.

Gilgamesh and the First Dynasty of — **VII**: 229.

Goats from — **III**: 375.

Lament Over the Desolation of — **VII**: 274.

Life at — **VII**: 220.

Literary Catalogue from — **VII**: 254, 274, 275.

Ningal-Temple at — **V**: 187.

Offering to Temple Gates — **V**: 198; **IX**: cxxxvii.

Phoenician Inscription from — **VII**: 117.

Pottery from — **III**: 610, 628.

Prism from — **VII**: 241.

Restoration of Artifacts — **III**: 456.

Royal Cemetery at — **III**: 261, 275.

Royal Cemetery, Second Dynasty Graves at(?) — **III**: 554.

Royal Tombs of — **III**: 546*(3)*, 547*(2)*.

Seal-Impressions from — **III**: 273, 649.

Temple in — **III**: 512.

Temple Records of the Kings of — **VII**: 235.
Troy, Links with — **III**: 261*(2), 275(2), 593.*
Ziggurat of — **III**: 512.
Ur el-(â) Obeid, *see:* **Ubaid, Tell Uqair**
Ur III: — **I**: *410;* **II**: *270;* **III**: 273.
Amurrite Names in — **V**: 383.
City and Town names in tablets from — **II**: 270.
Šakkanakkus, of — **VII**: 240; **IX**: cxliii.
Ur-Nanshe:
Stele of — **III**: 498.
Ur-dLugal-edin-na, the Physician:
Seal of — **III**: 399, *647.*
Ur-Engur:
Babylonian Ruler — **II**: 105.
Ur-Nammu: — **I**: *502, 506.*
Coronation of — **VII**: 241.
Death and Descent to the Netherworld — **VII**: 283.
Ur-Ningirus:
Ruler of Lagash — **II**: 106.
Ur-Shanabi(k): — **VII**: 271.
Uraeus: — **III**: 755; **V**: 203.
Uraiah:
David and, Buddist Parallel to — **IV**: 378, *444.*
Urarṭean:
Verbal Forms — **V**: 679.
Urartians: — **II**: 3, *143,* **171**; **III**: 125.
Urartian Citadel of Kayalidere — **III**: 137*(2).*
Urartu: — **III**: *9,* 275.
Uratian and "Vannic" Texts: — **VII**: **§916, 287-288.**
Decipherment of — **VII**: 287, 288
Urban Studies: — **I**: *191,* **§75, 206-208**; **IX**: **§75, lxxxvi.**
City Planning — **IX**: lxxxvi*(4).*
Urdamani: — **II**: 105.
Urdu Texts:
Catalgoue of MSS in the Library of the University of Glasgow — **VII**: 2.
Urfa, *see:* **Edassa**
Uriah:
David and, Parallel in Buddhist Literature — **IV**: 378, *444;* **V**: 148.
Rembrandt Problem — **VIII**: 358.
Son of Shemaiah — **VI**: 335, 339.
Uriel (Angel): — **VIII**: 157.
Urim and Thummim: — **I**: *180;* **V**: 43*(3),* 44*(2),* 45*(2).*
Original Nature of — **V**: 43.
Urkagina: — **I**: *397.*
Urmia: — **II**: *84.*
Urns: — **I**: 299.
Cinerary — **III**: 577, 597.
Cinerary, Egyptian — **III**: 574, 601.
Etruscan Funerary — **III**: 577, 615, 616.
Etruscan Terracotta Ash — **III**: 580.
Ionian Deinos — **III**: 709.
Italic Iron Age Hut — **III**: 579.
Punic Cinerary from Carthage — **I**: 375*(2);* **III**: 576*(2).*
Uronarti:
Khartoum Stela No. 3 from — **VII**: 24.
Uronarti Fort: — **III**: *655.*
Ursa Major:
Euphratean Names of — **II**: 226.
Ursaggina:
King of Lagash — **II**: 106.
Ursu: — **III**: *118,* 275.
Uruash (Ur-Nina): — **III**: 164; **IX**: cxii.
Uruk: — **I**: *69, 435, 470, 484, 487, 493;* **III**: **275**, *518, 614, 632, 639(3);* **V**: 574, 580.
Gilgamesh and the Wives of — **VII**: 229.

Opression of by
Gilgamesh — V: 184; VII: 228.
Religious Rites and Ritual
in the Time of, IV—III — V: 165.
Seal from, period of — III: 652.
Tablets of — VII: 210.
Urukagina: — I: *307;* II: *38,* *57,* **106.**
Reforms of — II: 106; VII: 278, 280.
Urumia: — III: *722.*
Urumuš: — VII: 209.
URWICK, WILLIAM:
Deutero-Isaiah, on — IV: 399.
Uşak Region: — III: 266.
User:
Funeral Papyrus of — VII: 44.
Statue of — VII: 59.
Vizier under
Thothmeses III — II: 206; III: 724.
User-Maota-Ra Uapet: — II: 106.
Userḥēt:
Tomb of at Qurnet Mura'i — III: 518.
Userkerē:
Seal of — III: 648.
Usertesen I:
Table Offerings of — VII: 61.
Usertsen III: — III: 592, *726.*
Ushabti: — I: 372, 373, 374*(3),* 376; II: 73; III: 574*(2),* 575*(2),* 761; VII: 38, 45; IX: cxxiv.

Ushebtis, *see:*
Shawabtis
Usöos:
Esau and — I: 42; VI: 173.
USSHER, JAMES:
Chronology of — II: 180, 184, 190.
USTINOFF, BARON: — III: *378, 580;* VI: 196.

USTINOW, BARON:
Squeezes of Inscriptions
in the Collection of — VII: 90, 315.
Usucapio: — I: 504; VII: 368.
Usury, *see also:*
Interest, Rates of — I: 309.

Ususfructus:
Jewish Law, in — I: 467, 502.
Roman Law, in — I: 467, 502.
Utensils, Cooking:
Roman — I: 210; III: 587.
Utica: — III: 275.
"Utmost Sea": — IV: 229.
Utopia:
Two Jewish Roads to — VIII: 416.
Uttu: — V: 182.
Sumeran god of
commerce — V: 181.
Utu: — VII: 158.
Utu-ḫegal (King of Erech):
Clay Cones of — VII: 237.
Utûm: — II: 273; VII: 154.
Uz: — III: 275.
Uzzah: — VI: 210.
Uzzen-Sherah: — II: 493; VI: 587.
Uzziah, *see also:*
Azariah — VI: 6, 592.
Aramaic Inscription
Relating to — VII: 125.
Biographical Studies — I: 100.
Funerary Tablet of — VII: 92*(2).*
Philistines and — IV: 541.
Sin of — IV: 436, *439.*
UZZIEL, JONATHAN BEN:
Targum of, on Isaiah
52:11-Chapter 53 — VI: 306.

V

Valletta Museum: — III: *602.*
Valley of Siddim, *see:*
Siddim, Valley of
Valley of the Gorge:
Joel, in — IV: 432.
Valley of the Kings: — III: 253.
Ostraca from — VII: 35.
P3ḪR ḪN' IḪNW/N N HNW ḪN' — II: 272; V: 310.
Tomb 55, Plan of, in — III: 557.
Tomb in — III: 539.
Tomb-Pit opened in — III: 537; VII: 45.

Tombs of, Temperature and Humidity of **III**: 544.
Valley of the Queens: **II**: *64.*
Tomb of a Prince Ramesses in **III**: 556.
Tomb of Mutnedjemet(?), No. 33 in **III**: 560.
"The Valley of Vision": **II**: 284.
Values:
Spiritual, and Biology **III**: 325.
VAN BUREN, ELIZABETH DOUGLAS:
Bibliography of **I**: 22.
VAN DYCK, CORNELIUS V. A.: **IV**: 73*(2).*
Lake Van (Area): **I**: *287, 293, 342;* **II**: *84;* **III**: *227, 257,* 265, 267, **277**, *541, 746.*
Flood, Biblical, and **IV**: 307.
Vanity: **IV**: 515, 517.
Vannic Language: **V**: 678.
"Vannic" Texts *see:* **Urartian Texts**
Vapheio Gems: **I**: 287*(2).*
varia lectio: **IV**: 98.
Varnish: **I**: 265; **III**: 543.
Desert, from Rhomboïdal Pyramid at Dahshûr **II**: 216.
Sample from Temple at Deir el Baḥri **II**: 213.
Term, Use of, Descrbing Painted Pottery **III**: 602.
Varro Murena: **I**: 503.
Vases: **III**: *586,* 603, 605, 606, 624, 632, 637, 720.
Ægean in the Salford Museum **III**: 603.
Agate, Set of, in the Cairo Museum **III**: 588.
Alabaster, Bahrain, from **III**: 626.
Alabaster, New Kingdom, from Sinai **III**: 608.
Alabaster, Palestinian **III**: 620.
Alabaster, with inscription **VII**: 59.
Apulia, Early, from **III**: 607.
Architectural Representation on Steatite **III**: 474, 628.
Assyrian Terra-Cotta **III**: 601.
Athenian, Red-Figured, in Metropolitan Museum **III**: 608.
Attic **III**: 613, 614, 633, 710, 713.
Attic, Architecture on **III**: 462, 604.
Attic, from Orvieto **III**: 605, 607.
Attic, Maiden's Race on **III**: 707.
Attic, Red-figured, from Corinth **III**: 610.
Attic, Red-figured Technique in **III**: 603.
"Attributed", in the Metropolitan Museum **III**: 609.
Battle-Loutrophoros **III**: 612.
Birket Israel, Found at **III**: 601.
Bitik **III**: 625.
Black-Figured **III**: 607, 619.
Blue Glazed, of Chancellor Amenhetep **III**: 605.
Boeotian, with Women's Heads **III**: 623.
Bronze, from Nablus **III**: 596.
Brygos Style **III**: 609, 620.
Canopic, *see:* ***Jars, Canopic***
Canosa, Numidian Horsemen on **III**: 712, 740.
Ceramic Analysis of Mycenaean and LB from Jett in Palestine **II**: 215; **III**: 621.
Classical, in the Santa Barbara Museum of Art **III**: 631.
Corinth, from **III**: 602.
Corinthian **III**: 631.
Courtes, of **III**: 602.
Cretan, Bronze-Age, Designs of **III**: 604.
Cypriote, Lotus Ornament **III**: 707.
Cyprus, Iron-Age, from, Inscribed **III**: 625.
Egyptian **I**: *324;* **III**: 604.
Egyptian, from Parthia **III**: 611.
Egyptian Stone, from Byblos **III**: 613.

Egyptian, with Cult-Signs	**III**: 575, 605.
Erganos, of	**III**: 602.
Etruscan, Polychrome	**III**: 618.
Euphronios, fragment of	**III**: 622.
Faience Ointment	**III**: 593, 629.
François, Palace of Thetis on a	**III**: 499, 707.
Geometric	**III**: 610, 637.
Geometric, Chariots on	**III**: 606.
Geometric, from Corinth	**III**: 602.
Graeco-Phoenician, from Ormidhia in Cyprus	**III**: 623.
Greek	**III**: 606*(2)*, 607*(2)*, 609, 614, 615, 616, 620, 624*(2)*, 627.
Greek, at John Hopkins University	**III**: 606.
Greek, at University of Pennsylvania	**III**: 604.
Greek, at Washington University, St. Louis	**III**: 617.
Greek, Bronze	**III**: 597*(2)*.
Greek, Design of	**III**: 607.
Greek, Drawing and Design on	**III**: 709.
Greek, Exploits of Herakles on	**III**: 606.
Greek, Form	**I**: 298; **III**: 598.
Greek, in the Stanford Museum	**III**: 606, 632.
Greek, in University Museum	**III**: 605.
Greek, in Yale Univeristy	**III**: 618.
Greek, Metal, Technique	**I**: 298; **III**: 598, 621.
Greek, "Modern" Drawing on	**III**: 701, 713.
Greek, Technique of	**III**: 607.
Greek, Trick	**III**: 636.
Hadra, in Ashmolean Museum	**III**: 623.
"Harvester", of Hagai Triada	**III**: 624.
Hebrew, with Phoenician Characters	**III**: 409, 601.
Hegeman Collection	**III**: 612.
Henry C. Lea Collection	**III**: 612.
Hercules, Exploits of, on	**III**: 709.
Hermonax, Painted by	**III**: 612, 610.
Hieron, Signed by, in the Metropolitan Museum	**III**: 606.
Homer, Illustrations of	**III**: 708.
Imperial Relief, from al Mina, Turkey	**III**: 624.
Italian, in University Museum	**III**: 605.
Italian, in Yale Univeristy	**III**: 618.
Kayseri Region, from	**III**: 636.
Knossian, from Attica	**III**: 628.
Lecythus, comparision of scenes on White, and Grave Stelae	**III**: 538, 724.
Libation, of Osor-ur	**III**: 574, 601; **VII**: 41.
"Lost"	**III**: 607, 608, 609*(2)*.
Loutrophoros, Red-Figured	**III**: 610.
Lydian Imitatinon of a Laconian	**III**: 612.
Macedonian	**III**: 608.
Maiden's Race on Attic	**III**: 707.
Minoan, from Abydos	**III**: 605.
"Minoan", so-called, from Macedonia	**III**: 616*(2)*.
Mottled	**III**: 612.
Murrhine	**III**: 622.
Mycenaean	**III**: 622, 635, 715, 765*(2)*.
Mycenaean, from Cyprus	**III**: 620.
Mycenaean, from Egypt, Contents of Examined	**II**: 213.
Mycenaean, Late	**III**: 611, 616.
Mykenai Type	**III**: 722.
New Kingdom, Decoration of a	**III**: 622.
Ointment, from Corinth	**III**: 587, 726.
Oltos	**III**: 624.
Paestan	**III**: 619.
Perfume	**III**: 587.
Phlyax	**III**: 616, 622, 629.
"Plastic"	**III**: 611.
Portland	**III**: 635.
Prehistoric, Egyptian, in the British Museum	**III**: 610.

Prehistoric, from Mt. Kronion	**II**: 279; **III**: 627.
Proto-Corinthian	**III**: 604.
Protogeometric from Skyros	**III**: 622.
Ptahmes, of	**III**: 602.
Red Figured, in Providence	**III**: 611.
Red Figured, in the Art Institute of Chicago	**III**: 610.
Red Figured, Influenced by Parthenon Frieze	**III**: 710.
Roman, Ceramic and Glass at Heidelberg and New York	**III**: 628.
Saint-Valentin	**III**: 623.
Santorini, Possible Date	**III**: 723.
Sardis, from	**III**: 607.
Scyphus, Greek	**III**: 604.
Sebakhotep III, of	**III**: 726.
Sepulchral, Egyptian	**VII**: 43.
Sepulchral, Inscribed from Alexandria	**III**: 601, 604.
Steatite, Architectural Representations on	**III**: 474, 628.
Stone, from Bishârîn	**III**: 605.
Stone, from Bismya	**III**: 603.
Stone, Sculptured, from the Iraq Museum	**III**: 622.
Submycenaean, in Caria	**III**: 635.
Sumerian	**III**: 605.
Syrian Silver	**III**: 598.
Terra-Cotta, from Bismya	**III**: 603.
Thessalian, Proto-Geometric, found at Tell Abū Hawām	**III**: 614.
Tragic Chorus on, 475 B.C.	**III**: 712.
Trojan	**III**: 605.
Unguent	**III**: 587.
University Museum, in	**III**: 613.
Vivenzio	**III**: 607.
Votive, from Warka	**III**: 578, 621.
Xerxes, of	**III**: 604, 606.
Vase Painting, *see also:* **Painters**	**III: §225, 707-719; IX: §225, cxxvi-cxxvii.**
Acropolis, Pediment Reliefs, Relation to	**III**: 707, 722.
Aegisthus Citharista	**III**: 705, 718; **V**: 266.
Andokides	**III**: 707.
Apulian	**III**: 715, 719.
Attic Technique	**III**: 703, 715.
Bellephon	**III**: 717.
Chimaera	**III**: 717.
Chronology, correlated with Greek Sculpture	**III**: 713, 742.
Classical, Non-Classical Elements in	**III**: 702, 714.
Corinthian	**III**: 714*(2)*.
Cycladic, 7th Century	**III**: 710.
Decorative Motif Exclusive to Raliscan	**V**: 715.
Euthymidean Tradition	**III**: 709.
Exekias, Use of Spear in	**III**: 706, 719.
Greek, and Apotropaism	**III**: 700.
Greek, Early	**III**: 708.
Greek Mythology and	**III**: 623, 714; **V**: 262.
Hermonax	**III**: 612, 719.
History of Greek	**III**: 709.
Mycenaean, Myth and Epic in	**III**: 626, 715.
Mycenaean, Signs on the Base of	**V**: 622.
Non-Classical Elements in Classical	**III** 702, 714.
Palestinian Vase-Painter, Sixteenth Century, B.C.	**III**: 617, 711.
Phrygian, Late	**III**: 714.
Protome	**III**: 714.
"Tyrrhen"	**III**: 712.
Vashti:	
Biographical Studies	**I**: 81.
Vassar Classical Museum:	**I**: *282*.
Vaticanus, Codex:	**IV**: *9*, 10, 25*(2)*, 28
Ezekiel on, and Relation to Chester Beatty Papyri	**VI**: 361*(2)*.

Kings, Textual History in **VI**: 244.
Vats:
Rock-Hewn, near Bir Eyib **I**: 360; **III**: *724*.
Vault, *see:* **Tombs**
VAUX, JR., GEORGE: **VII**: *209*.
Veadar: **I**: 399.
VECHIETE, GIAMBATTISTA: **IV**: *48*.
Vegetables:
Remains from Egyptian Tombs **II**: 212; **III**: 383.
Vegetation:
Acre Pain, Southern, Map of Sand Dunes in **II**: 244.
Ecological Studies of, in Near Eastern Deserts **II**: 244.
Vehicles:
Registration of, in Ptolemaic Egypt **I**: 347.
Veii: **III**: *718, 729*.
Veil(s): **I**: 278, 279.
Temple of Jerusalem, at Olympia **V**: 67.
Velia, *see also:* **Elea:** **III**: **276**, *754*.
VELIKOVSKY, IMMANUEL:
Hebrew Bible and **IV**: 86, 153; **VIII**: 86.
Venetic Religion and Mythology: **V**: **§481, 267-271**.
Vengeance: **I**: 480*(2)*, 481*(2)*; **V**: 517, 544.
God, of **VIII**: 69.
Venus:
Astoreth = Karnaim = **V**: 190.
Birth of, in Greek Art **III**: 695.
Deity of the Crescent, in Ancient Western Asia **V**: 179.
Genetrix of Arceilaus **III**: 737.
Milo (Statue) **III**: 725.
Relief of, Ara Pacis Augustae **III**: 752.
Statue, Royal Ontario Museum **III**: 727, 731.
Venus (Planet):
Tablets of Ammiṣaduqa **II**: 232.
Venusia: **I**: 176.
Verb - Hebrew, *see:* **Hebrew Grammar**
VERNES, MAURICE: **IV**: 163.
Versions - General Studies *(of the OT)* **IV**: **§244, 24**.
Arabic **IV**: **§255, 43**, *73(2)*.
Coptic (including Bohairic and Sahidic) **IV**: **§255, 43-44**.
Early English MSS and Printed Texts **IV**: **§262, 49-54**.
Early - Unclassified **IV**: **§261, 48-49**.
Foreign Language (i.e., O/T English) *see also:* ***Bibles*** **IV**: **§269, 72-76**.
Latin Vulgate **IV**: **§253, 40-42**.
Mandaic, of Psalm 114 **VI**: 519.
Neo-Latin **IV**: 49.
Old Italic **IV**: 40.
Old Latin **IV**: **§252, 39-40**.
Persian **IV**: 48, 49*(8)*, 75.
Salvonic, Hebrew Commentaries in **IV**: 49.
Septuagint **IV**: **§245, 24-35**.
Vespasian: **I**: 177, *450*.
Latin Inscriptions on **VII**: 366*(2)*.
Qumran, Captured by(?) **VIII**: 423.
Vessel(s): **III**: 636.
"Arm-Shaped", Family **III**: 630.
Bichrome, Cross Line Style **III**: 632.
"Blue Marble" Plastic **III**: 633, *768*.
Bronze, from Gordion **III**: 599.
Canaanite, with Egyptian "Signatures" **III**: 636.
Chalcolithic **III**: 624*(2)*.
Decoration of Pottery **III**: 620.
Drinking, and Jugs **III**: **§208, 588-591**.

Egyptian, Predynastic Stone **III**: 610.
Egyptian, Purification **III**: 575.
Egyptian, Theriomorphic **III**: 576.
Food **III**: 626.
Gold and Silver, from Bubastis, Reconstruction **III**: 590.
Iranian Drinking **III**: 590.
Jewish in the Misnaic Period **III**: 596.
Minos, from **III**: 623.
Obsidian, from Tepe Gawra **III**: 589.
Plemochoe, from Thmuis **III**: 636.
Pottery, of the Old Testament **III**: 617, 618.
Silver, from Tell Fār'a **III**: 589.
South Arabian Ivory **III**: 590.
Stone, found at Babylon **III**: 611.
Stone, found at Crete **III**: 611.
Stone, from ancient mining site **III**: 608.
Stone, from the Step-Pyramid **III**: 589.
Tell Bastra, Engraved, from **III**: 626.
"Vessels of Wrath" **III**: 636.

Vessels, Sacred: **V**: *68(2)*.
Fate of, from the Second Temple **V**: 74.

Veterinary:
Assyrian **III**: 365, 398.

Vetulonia: **III**: 276, *480*.

Via Maris: **VI**: 229*(3)*, 268.

Viceroys:
Ethiopian **II**: 5.
Kush, First Two, of **II**: 5.
Objects Belonging to, at Kush **VII**: 71.

Victor: **V**: 270.

VIDA, G. LEVI DELLA: **III**: 497.

Villages, *see also:* **Cities** **I**: 206*(3)*, *351;* **IV**: 219.
Modern Palestinian **I**: 387.
Roman Administration of Syrian Provincial **I**: 489.

Villas, *see:* **Houses**

Vine:
Phytios and Andocies, of **III**: 708.

Vineyards: **I**: 253, **§90**, **263-265**; **IX**: **§90**, **xc**.
Isaiah's Parable of the **IV**: 392.
Paradise Vineyard **V**: 181.
Ptolemaic Lease of **VII**: 341.
Taxation of, in the Zenon Papyri **I**: 481; **VII**: 339.

VINNIKOV, I. N.: **V**: 527*(2)*.

Violence, *see also:* **Non-Violence**
Change and, Biblical View **VIII**: 229.

Virgil:
Aeneid, Book 6, Middle Voice in **V**: 665.
Bust, Wrongly called **III**: 738.
Divine Child in **V**: 267.
English Translators of **VII**: 365.
Fatalism in **V**: 247.
Fourth Ecologue of, Isaiah as Source **VIII**: 362.
Messiah of, and Isaiah **IV**: 394.
Messianic Expectations **V**: 269.
Messianic Idea in **V**: 267.
Tomb of **III**: 543, 547.

Virgin: **VI**: 263.
Hebrew Words for **V**: 517.

Virgin Birth: **VIII**: 129.
Hosea and **IV**: 429; **VIII**: 275.
Isaiah and **IV**: 392*(2)*, 393; **VI**: 261, 262, 263*(2)*, 264*(5)*; **VIII**: 273.
Messiah, of **VIII**: 141.
Moses, of **I**: 71.
Philo, in **VI**: 99, 675.

Virgin Mary:
Blessed, in the Talmud **VI**: 699*(2)*.
Daughter of Zion, as **VIII**: 285.
Song of Solomon and **IV**: 506.

Virgo:
Hurrian Name of **II**: 230.

Virtues:
Roman **V**: 269.

VISCHER, WILHELM:
Hebrew 'Bara' (בָּרָא) on IV: 284; V: 413.
Visions: I: *102*.
Psychological Viewpoint of Dreams and VIII: 246.
"The Valley of Vision" II: 284.
Visions of Ezekiel:
Fragment of VI: 648.
Vita Miltiadis: II: 153.
Viticulture: I: **§90, 263-265**; IX: **§90, xc**.
VITRIGNA, CAMPAGIUS:
Sin, on VIII: 176.
Vitruvius: III: 466, 469.
Viziers:
Assyrian II: 42, *65*.
Egyptian II: 17, 23, 24, 37, 44, 52, 53, 55, 56*(2)*, 61, 73, 81, 97, 106, 107, 109, 207; III: *671, 724;* VII: *9, 40,* 70.
Egyptian, of the New Empire II: 4.
Installation of a VII: 61
Joseph as I: 60.
New Empire, History of, from Hieratic Text in *Karnak*, Pl. 46 VII: 15.
Vocalization:
Aleppo Codex, Vocalized by Aharon ben Asher(?) IV: 16.
Biblical Fragment with Palestinian IV: 17.
Biblical Fragment with Tiberian IV: 12.
Hebrew, Changes in IV: 115.
Palestinian in Hedwata's Qedŭštot IV: 20.
Qere-Kethiv, of, in A IV: 19.
Tiberian System V: 390.
Vohu Manah:
Philo's Logos? VI: 673.
Voices:
Supernatural (Bath-Kol) V: 103, 131.
Supernatural, Belief in V: 132.
Volcanoes: II: 212; 247*(2)*.
Eruption, Cuneiform Description of II: 248; VII: 228.
Magmatic Phenomema in Makhtesh Ramon II: 249.
Santorini III: 217.
Volcanic Phenomena of the Exodus III: 122; IV: 338.
Voles:
Fossill, at Gibraltar III: 106; 366.
Volume:
Truncated Pyramid in Egyptian Mathematics I: 430.
Vortumnus:
Shrine of III: 521.
Vouni:
Palace of, in Cyprus III: 500*(4)*.
Vounous: III: *618*.
Vowel Points (Hebrew): V: **§510, 476-479**; IX: **§510, cxli**.
Controversy V: 477, 478.
Controversy of, in the 16-18th Centuries V: 476.
Hebrew Aphabet and V: 289, 476.
Supralinear System, Origin of V: 476.
Vowel Signs - Hebrew: IV: *10*.
Vowels:
Symbols for, Derived from Phoenician V: 287.
Vowels, Hebrew *see:* **Hebrew Grammar** V: **§510, 476-479**.
Vows: I: **§138, 509-516**.
Jewish and Muslim Laws, Relation between I: 511.
Talmudic VI: 694.
Voyages:
South Arabian to India I: 341
VRIEZEN, V. TH. C.:
Old Testament Theology VIII: 12.
Vrokastro: III: **276**.

Vulgate (including Jerome's Translation) **IV**: 24, **§253, 40-42**.
Alcuin's Bible **IV**: 40.
Bury Bible **IV**: 42.
Carcassonne, 9th Century **IV**: 41.
Catholic Church and **IV**: 40.
Chapters and Verses of, in Hebrew Bible **IV**: 41.
Council of Trent and **IV**: 42.
Critical Value of **VI**: 686.
Dom Quentin's Memoir **IV**: 41.
Eve-concept in English Cycles and **VIII**: 352.
France, History of, in **IV**: 40.
Hebrew Bible and, in Agreement **VI**: 686.
Henslow's **IV**: 41*(2)*.
Hetzenauer's Edition of **IV**: 41.
Influence on Authorized Version **IV**: 41.
Influence on English Psalms **IV**: 42.
Juxta Exemplar **IV**: 40.
Laurentian Bible **IV**: 42.
Manscripts in the British Museum of **IV**: 41.
Targum and, in Agreement **VI**: 686.
Theodulfian MSS of **IV**: 41.
Value for Old Testament Textual Criticism **IV**: 2, 40.
Vulture(s): **III**: 382*(2)*.

W

Wabset:
Sarcophagus from, Soleb **III**: 558.
WACE, A. J. B.: **III**: 254.
Wad Ban Naga:
Circular Brick Building at **III**: 485.
WADDINGTON, GEORGE: **III**: 436, 437.
WADE, G. W.:
Isaiah, on **IV**: 393.
Wadi Arabah: **I**: *292 (4), 301;* **II**: **321**, 364*(2);* **III**: **277**.
Hebrew Inscription from **VII**: 94.
Wadi Dhobai: **I**: 266; **II**: 297, 493.
Vertebrate remains from **III**: 366.
Wādi el ʿAllāḳi:
Graffiti at **VII**: 13.
Wadi el Bada:
Herodian Tomb at **III**: 553.
Wàdi el-Natrûn: **III**: 277.
Wadi el-Rayyān: **III**: 277.
Wadi el Yabis: **II**: 495.
Wadi en-Nar: **VIII**: 431.
Wadi Hadhramaut: **III**: 115, 277.
Wâdî Ḥaḍramawt: **VII**: 293.
Wadi Halfa:
Egyptian Stela from **VII**: 19.
Figures found near South Temple at **III**: 760.
Royal Feud in the Temple at **VII**: 15*(3)*.
Sedimentation of the Nile above **II**: 251.
Senworsret I, Stela of, at **VII**: 19.
XVIIIth Dynasty Temple at **VII**: 15.
Wadi-Helfa:
Graffiti in the Southern Temple, opposite **VII**: 13.
Wadi Karagan:
Pleistocene Geology of **II**: 252.
Wadi Kufrein: **II**: 494, *494*.
Wadi Moeleh: **III**: 83.
Wadi Musrara:
Sedimentation and Soil Errosion in **II**: 244.
Wadi Rabah: **II**: 494.
Wadi Sarga: **III**: *727*.
Wadi Shueib: **II**: *494*, 494.
Wadi Sirhan: **III**: 278.
Wadi Suweil: **II**: 352, 494.
Wadi Tharthar: **III**: 278.
Wādi Umm Sidrah: **III**: 278.
Archaic Hut in **III**: 484.
Wadjkarēʿ: **II**: 106.
Wadjmose: **II**: 107.
Wâdy Abbâd:
Temple of **VII**: 63.

Wady 'Arrub:	**II**: 324, 493.	Jericho	**II**: 395.
Wady el Joz:	**I**: *359*.	Jerusalem, First	**II**: 407, 413.
Arabic Graffiti at	**VII**: 291.	Jerusalem, Fourth	**II**: 418.
Rock-Cut Tomb in	**III**: 534.	Jerusalem, North	**IV**: 219.
Wady el Kittar:	**III**: 277.	Jerusalem, Second	**II**: 305, 403,
Wady el Marabaat:	**II**: 422.		404*(3)*, 406, 420.
Wady el Mikteleh:	**II**: 284.	Jerusalem, South	**II**: 404.
Wady el-Mughara:	**II**: **494**.	Jerusalem, Third	**II**: 298, 407, 411,
Wady el Nar:	**II**: 299.		415*(2)*, 417*(2)*,
Wady er-Rababi:			419, 420*(3)*.
Rock-cut Tombs in	**III**: 536, 537.	Jerusalem, Third, Towers and Cisterns of	**II**: 416.
Wady Kelt:	**II**: 494.	Jerusalem, unspecified	**II**: 404*(2)*,
Wady Mesâ'adet 'Aisa:	**II**: 284.		405*(2)*, 409, 411,
Wady Mojib:	**II**: 309.		414, 416.
Wady Qumran, *see:*		Jupiter Temple, Capitol	**III**: 514.
Qumran		Katastegasma of, Athens	**III**: 471.
Wady Sheykh:	**I**: *291;* **III**: 277.	Manasseh, of	**II**: 417.
Wâdy Yasûl:	**II**: 404*(2)*.	Nehemiah's, at Jerusalem	**II**: 402, 404*(2)*,
Wages:	**I**: 302, 304*(2)*,		405*(4)*, 406, 408,
	306.		410, 412, 418;
Wage Accounts in the			**III**: 486, 487*(2)*,
Zenon Papyri	**VII**: 340.		*531, 533, 534.*
Wage List of the		North, of Jerusalem	**II**: 415, 416*(3)*,
Ur Dynasty	**VII**: 279.		417*(4)*.
Wagons:	**I**: 344, 345, 347.	Nuzi, Mud-Brick	
Wailers:		Old, outside Northeastern	
Women, Among the		in Jerusalem	**II**: 404*(3)*.
Northern Canaanites	**V**: 192; **VII**: 141.	Old, Stair and Postern in,	
Wailing Wall:	**II**: 415.	at Jerusalem	**II**: 407.
Wait:	**V**: 517.	Peiraeus, of	**III**: 469.
"Wait on the Lord":	**V**: 521.	Phaleric	**III**: 488.
WALFORD, G. F.:	**III**: 716.	Plataia, at	**III**: 202, 487.
Walls:	**III**: §188,	Prinias, at, East,	
	486-490.	in Temple A	**III**: 472.
Athens, at	**III**: 29, 30,	Purchase of half a wall	**VII**: 253.
	198*(2)*, 486.	Rhactois: the Great Wall	
Babylon, of	**III**: 42; **VII**: 236.	of the Libyan Desert	**III**: 489, 501,
Balkh-Bactra, South, of	**III**: 42.		517, 555.
Casemate, in Judah		Servian	**III**: 488.
and Israel, Purpose	**III**: 489.	Solomon's in Jerusalem	**II**: 412.
Damascus, Temple Wall	**III**: 75.	Temple, at Jerusalem	**II**: 402.
El Kab, at	**III**: 131*(2)*.	Themistocles, of	**III**: 487.
Gaza, of	**II**: 370*(2)*.	Trans-Isthmian	**III**: 489.
Gezer, Solomonic, at	**II**: 375	Ur, at	**III**: 273.
Haram, Masonry of	**II**: 402*(2)*, 403*(2)*; **III**: 487*(3)*.	Wailing, *see:* **Wailing Wall**	
		West, of the Pool of Hezekiah	**II**: 409.

Walters Art Gallery:
Archaeological Source Material , at **III**: 567, 687.
Roman Collections of **III**: 692.
Syrian Bronze in **III**: 759.
Western Asiatic Seals in **III**: 651.
"Wandering Aramaean": **VI**: 149*(2)*.
Wands:
Egyptian, Astrological Character of **II**: 228; **III**: 575; **V**: 205.
Wappenmüzen: **I**: *457*.
Waqqas, Tell: **II**: 368.
War, Warfare, *see:* **Defense and Warfare** **I**: **§101, 311-321**; **IX**: **§101, xciv**.
Alien-Rights and **I**: 185, 312, 326, 507; **VIII**: 223, 232.
Ammonite-Syrian **I**: 319.
Animals in **I**: 320; **III**: 367.
Aramaean **I**: 92, 95.
Art of **I**: 321.
Bible and **VIII**: 232*(2)*. 233*(2)*.
Chaeronea, Battles of **III**: 61.
Civil, of 49 B.C. **I**: 490.
Cold War (Ancient) **I**: 333*(2)*.
Corinthian, of 390 B.C. Account by Xenophon **II**: 108; **III**: 195.
Cunaxa, Battle of **III**: 70*(2)*.
Dan, Tribe of and **I**: 156, 314; **VIII**: 233.
Egyptian Ideographic for **V**: 328.
Elephants in **I**: 311.
Ethics of **VIII**: 231.
Ezekiel and **VI**: 358.
First Jewish against Romans **I**: *456*.
Flood, None Before the **IV**: 297.
Gideon and Midian, a Military Approach **I**: 317; **IV**: 369.
Greco-Persian, 480-478 B.C. **II**: *21*.
Hadrian's, Against the Jews: **II**: *41*, 186, *315*.
"Holy War" in Deuteronomy **IV**: 352.
"Holy War", Theory of **VI**: 116.
Homanadensian **II**: 142; **IX**: xciv, cii.
Hypaspists **I**: 321.
Insects, Use in **I**: 311.
Isaiah and **IV**: 394; **VIII**: 232.
Israelite-Aramaean, Archaeology and **I**: 316.
Jeremiah and **IV**: 412; **VIII**: 234.
Jewish Tradition, in **VIII**: 233.
Judah, Kingdom of, Last **I**: 316.
Judaism, Attitude Towards **VIII**: 232.
Karnak, Minor War Scenes from (Relief) **III**: 754.
Lelantine, and Pheidon **II**: 74.
Mesha, King of Moab, Wars of **I**: 321.
Mesopotamia, Religion and, in **V**: 165; **VIII**: 233.
Naval Battles, *see:* ***Navy***
Old Testament and **VIII**: 232*(3)*, 233.
Omride, and the Elisha Cycle **IV**: 380.
Peloponnesian **I**: 315.
Persian **II**: 153*(2)*
Plato and **VIII**: 233.
Prophecy and **VIII**: 233, 244.
Prophetic Call to **VI**: 235, 274, 297, 302, 344, 374; **VIII**: 258.
Prophets and **I**: 109; **IV**: 387, 394; **VIII**: 232, 233.
Ramsess II at Karnak, Minor War Scenes of **VII**: 74.
Religion and, in Israel **I**: 314; **V**: 15; **VIII**: 232.
Religion and, in Mespotamia **V**: 165.
Religion and, in the Graeco-Roman World **V**: 242; **VIII**: 223.

Rome and the Great Social **III**: 213.
Sabbath, on, Problem of, and the Second Temple and Talmudic Books **VIII**: 235.
Salamis, Battle of **III**: 214, **215**.
Slave Wars **I**: 201; **II**: 160, 167*(2)*.
Slave Wars, First Sicilian **II**: 167*(2)*.
Social, Greek ,of 220-217 B.C. **II**: 133.
Spanish, of Augustus **II**: 23.
Thucydides, War Guilt in **VIII**: 228.
Trojan **II**: 171.
Wa'r Abu eṣ Ṣafa:
Tomb Chamber at **III**: 549.
War Kabud: **III**: 124.
War Scroll (1QM): **VIII**: 434, 436, **§1127**, **464-465**.
Date of **VIII**: 464.
Date of the War **VIII**: 464.
Sons of Light and the Sons of Darkness in **VIII**: 464*(2)*.
Spurious Version of **VIII**: 465.
WARD, JOHN: **III**: *667(2)*.
Wardan
Second Dynasty Grave at **III**: 555.
Warehousing: **I**: 304, 308.
WARFIELD, BENJAMIN B.: **III**: 353*(2)*.
Inspiration, on **VIII**: 44.
Warka, *see also:* **Uruk** **III**: **278**, *518*, *742;* **VI**: 56.
Pre-Sargonic Inscription on Limestone from **VII**: 277.
Votive Vase from **III**: 578.
Warrior(s):
Sculpture of **III**: 745.
Shihan **I**: 317.
"Wars of the Lord", Book of: **IV**: 177*(2)*.
Warsaw:
National Museum of **III**: *585*.
Warships, *see:* **Ships, War**
Wartburg Seminary:
Old Testament Department at, Responsibilities of **VIII**: 404.
Washing: *see:* **Libations**
Washington University: **III**: *616, 617, 619*.
WASSMAN, FATHER: **III**: 305.
Watchers:
Daniel, in **IV**: 522.
Enoch, of **VI**: 9, 651.
Night, in the Temple **VI**: 530.
Wateh-bel-Hazel:
Cylinder of **VII**: 183.
Prince of Kedarenes **II**: 107.
Water: **I**: 363, 364.
Dead Sea, from **II**: 212.
Eternal **VIII**: 304.
Freezing, in Job **VI**: 438.
Jericho, Radioactivity of **II**: 222.
Mayim Rabbîm and Cosmic Connotations **VIII**: 86*(2)*.
Palestinian Superstion, and **I**: 390.
Rights in Correspondence from Larasa and Isin **I**: 506.
Shechem Inscription, in **VII**: 85; **VIII**: 86.
Spring of Callirrohe, Analysis of **II**: 213.
Stream Piracy in Israel **II**: 300.
Transportation by, in Early Babylonia **I**: 352.
Water Rate in Babylon **VII**: 219.
Worship of, by Romans **I**: 362; **V**: 269.
Water Lily: **III**: 391.
"Water of Life": **V**: *520,* 521.
Palestinian Superstition, and **I**: 390.
Water Rights:
Correspondence on, from Larasa and Isin **I**: 364, 506; **VII**: 253.
Water Supply: **I**: **§107**, **357-364**, **II**: 254, 285, *380*.
Water-Source:
Anatolian Word for **I**: 362.
Waterclock: **I**: 414, 415*(2)*, 416.

Watercourses: I: 358, 360, 506.
Hittite Word for Underground II: 256.
Iraq, Settlements and Ancient, in Central I: 125; III: 127.
Underground, and Bronze Age Historical Geography II: 256.
WATERMAN, LEROY: II: 70.
Solomon's Temple, on V: 72*(2)*.
Watermelon: III: *392,* 395.
"Waters of Death": V: 183; VIII: 84.
WATTS, ISAAC:
Psalms on IV: 474.
Waxes: I: 267.
"Way of the Philistines": I: 343.
Wayfarer:
Arabic for V: 587.
Wealth: I: 184, 193.
Hebrew I: 303.
Qoheleth on IV: 516, 517.
Rich in the Wisdom Literature of Hebrew and Accadian V: 118; VII: 3, 96, 152.
Weapons, *see also:*
Specific artifacts (eg, Bow) III: 677, **§220, 680-684**; IX: xciv.
Assyrian Word *(bêlu)* V: 565.
Assyrian Word *(kakku)* V: 560.
Weasel: III: *371(2), 383(2),*
Weather, *see also:* **Meteorological Studies**
Bible and II: 243.
Hebrew / Israelite Weather-Deity VIII: 72, 120.
Legitimate Subject for Prayer(?) VIII: 202.
Weavers: I: 271, 273, 275; V: *567;* IX: cxliii.
Weaving: I: **§93, 273-275**; IV: 235.
Weaving Implements: III: **§200, 572-573**.
WEBER, FREDINAND WILHELM: VIII: 188, 249.
WEBER, MAX: V: 30.
Wedding, *see:* **Marriage**
Week:
Arab Folklore and Days of I: 391, 400.
Ethiopian, Names of I: 405; V: 599.
Historical Chronology and I: *395;* II: 173; V: 142.
History of the I: 395; II: *173;* V: 142.
Names of the Days of the I: 395.
Neo-Babylonian Names of the Days of I: 402*(2)*.
Origin of I: 401.
Planetary, Origin of, in Hebrew Literature II: 232; IX: xcvii.
Sabbath and I: 399.
Ugaritic Epic Literature, Seven Day-Unit in VII: 145.
Weeks, Apocalypse of:
Qumran and VIII: 420, 452.
Weha'u: II: 107.
WEIDNER, REVERE F.: I: 5.
Weights and Measures, *see also:* **Measurement** I: *415,* **§121, 417-427**; IX: **§121, xcix**.
Abydos Lion (CIS II 108) VII: 85.
Assyrian I: 417, 422.
Assyrian Kisal, as Origin of Carat I: 423.
Assyrian Lion-, and the Alphabet V: 283.
Assyrian Standard I: 421.
Attic Standard I: 421.
Babylonian I: 417*(3)*, 418, 419*(3);* VII: 191, 247*(2)*.
Balance, in Jewish Iconography III: 703.
Beḳa' בקע I: 421, 427.
Bronze I: 423.
Bronze, Cleaning of III: 456.
Bronze, from Petra I: 422.
Carat, Assyrian Kisal, as Origin of I: 423.

- Chinese Metrology, Sumerian, in — **I**: 425.
- Cuneiform, written in — **I**: 417.
- Cypriote — **I**: 420.
- Egyptian — **I**: 418*(2)*, 419, 420, 423*(3)*, *429*; **VII**: 34, 76.
- Egyptian šet — **I**: 417; **V**: 331.
- Egyptian Standard — **I**: 421.
- Ethiopian — **I**: 427*(2)*.
- Fractional Markings on Shekel Hebrew Weights — **I**: 426, 435.
- Gezer, from — **I**: 421*(3)*; **III**: *667*.
- Grain Troy, Evolution of — **I**: 420.
- Greek, Standard — **I**: 423.
- Ḥomesh חמש — **I**: 421.
- Haematite — **I**: 418*(2)*, 419*(2)*.
- Hebrew — **I**: 418*(3)*, 419, 420*(4)*, 421*(2)*, 422*(3)*, 423, 424, 427, 435.
- Hebrew, in the Book of Samuel — **I**: 422; **VI**: 200.
- Hebrew, with Hieratic Numerals — **I**: 426, 427, 435*(2)*.
- Jerusalem — **I**: 420.
- Judean — **I**: 426.
- Karsha — **I**: 422.
- King's — **I**: 421.
- Loom — **III**: 572.
- *Mana* — **I**: 422.
- Mina — **I**: 426.
- Mina, Greek — **I**: 456.
- Neẓeph נצף — **I**: 420, 421.
- Palestinian Standard — **I**: 421.
- Parthian Standard — **I**: 424.
- Persian Standard — **I**: 423.
- Persic Standard — **I**: 423.
- Petrie Collection — **I**: 420, 423*(2)*, 425, 446.
- Phillippic Silver Standard — **I**: 423.
- Phoenician(?) — **I**: 420.
- Phoenician Standard — **I**: 423.
- *piḫû*, liquid measure — **V**: 564.
- Pis פים(?) — **I**: 421.
- PYM פים — **I**: 425.
- Royal — **I**: 426.
- Scale Weights from Ophel — **I**: 426.
- Seal, from Nebi Rubin — **I**: *425*; **III**: *656*.
- Shekel — **I**: 426, 435; **VII**: 96.
- Solon's Change of — **IX**: xcix.
- Stone duck(?) — **I**: 420.
- Stone, from Shechem — **I**: 426.
- Sumerian, in Chinese Metrology — **I**: 425.

WELCH, ADAM C.: — **I**: 94.

WELD, HERBERT: — **VII**: 193.

Welding: — **I**: 297, 298, 299; **IV**: 235.

Welfare, Social: — **I**: 186*(2)*, 193.

WELLCOME, HENRY SOLOMON:
- Archaeological Expedition — **II**: 356*(2)*, 357.

WELLHAUSEN, JULIUS: — **I**: 139; **IV**: 128, 157, *214*, 246, 247*(3)*, 248, 249*(4)*, 250*(4)*, 251, 253, 259*(5)*, *349*; **V**: 29.
- Chronicles, on — **IV**: 542.
- Dahse, J., *vs.* — **IV**: 256.
- Minor Prophets, on — **IV**: 427.
- *Prolegomena* of — **IV**: 255*(4)*; **V**: 69.

Wells: — **I**: 357, 363; **IV**: 220.
- Anaploga, at — **III**: 12.
- Beni Murra, Seven at — **I**: 363; **II**: 334.
- Canaanite, "Letter" about — **VII**: 67.
- Dragon — **VI**: 583*(3)*.
- Harod — **II**: 284.
- Jacob's — **I**: 357, 359*(4)*, 361, 362; **II**: 308, **392**.
- Job's (En-Rogel) — **II**: 362.

WELLSTED, JAMES RAYMOND: — **III**: 438.

Welsh:
Greek and, Compared V: 623.
Hebrew, Affinty of, to V: 384.
Weltanschauung, see: **World View**
Wenamon:
Report of **VII**: 61.
Wenamūn:
Second Tenses in V: 366.
WENGER, LEOPOLD: I: 125, 491, 502.
Weni: II: 107.
Inscription of, Unexplained Passage in **VII**: 70.
Wentawat: II: 107.
Wepemnofret:
Stela of Prince II: 107; **VII**: 25.
Werdeh: II: 284.
WESLEY, CHARLES:
Poem on Jacob, by **VIII**: 365.
WEST, E. W.: **VII**: 374*(3)*.
Western Semitic Texts:
Covenant in I: 516.
Personal Pronoun "I" in V: 377, 679.
WESTPHAL, RUDOLF GEORGE HERMANN:
Greek Grammar V: 626.
Wetnurse(s):
Divine, in Canaanite Religion V: 196.
Wheat: I: 248, 254, 258; III: **395-396**.
Egyptian name of V: 321.
Mummy III: 395
"Wheel of Life":
Myrtilus, in Story of V: 268.
Wheels:
Potter's I: 267, 288; **III**: 607.
Potter's, in Egyptian V: 358.
Whetstone:
Assyrian Word for I: 286; V: 568.
Whirlwinds:
Israel, in II: 244.
Job, in VI: 438.
Whistle: III: 679.
WHITE, J.:
Egypt, on III: 81.
WHITEHOUSE, F. COPE: III: 52, 281.
WHITNEY, DUDLEY JOSEPH: III: 347.
"Who Maketh Lightnings for the Rain": V: 521.
Whorls:
Spindle, with Hebrew Inscription **VII**: 95.
Spindle, with Phoenician Inscription **VII**: 120; **IX**: cxxiv.
Terracotta III: 672, 694.
WHYTE, E. TOWRY: II: *211*.
Wicked:
Estate of, in Psalm 36 VI: 480.
Eternal Punishment of **VIII**: 267.
Final Fate of **VIII**: 268.
Prosperity of VI: 498.
Resurrection of **VIII**: 270.
Righteous and, in the Habakkuk Scroll **VIII**: 456.
"Wide of Heart": V: 521; **VI**: 512, 543.
Widows: I: 199, 504.
Wisdom Literature and ANE Legal Literature, in I: 192; **VII**: 2.
WIEDER, NAPHTALI: **VIII**: 459.
WIENER, A.: I: 249.
WIENER, HAROLD M.:
Pentateuchal Criticism IV: 231, 255.
Wife:
Ecclesiastes, in (=Well + Field) VI: 565.
Husband's Undertaking to Maintain and Clothe I: 212, 219; **VII**: *354*.
Proverbs, in (=Well + Field) VI: 539.
Syriac, in = Well + Field V: 530.
Wife-Sister Motif: IV: 320.
Wigs: I: 278, 279.
Wilbur Papyrus: I: *262(2)*.
"Wilderness":
Testing in, Qumran and in Matthew **VIII**: 482.

Wiles of a Harlot (4QWiles of the Wicked Woman): **VIII**: **§1136, 469**.
WILKINSON, J. G.: **I**: 208; **V**: 362.
Will (Testate): **I**: 502.
Naunakhte, of **VII**: 30.
Nuzi, from **VII**: 166.
WILLIAMS, R. S.: **III**: *641*.
WILLIAMS, ROLAND:
Latter Prophets, on **IV**: 385*(2)*.
WILLIAMS, WALTER G.:
Bibliography of **I**: 22.
Willow Tree:
Gilgamesh and **VII**: 228.
WILSON, CHARLES WILLIAM: **II**: 402, 403; **III**: 487*(2)*.
WILSON, JOHN: **II**: 253.
WILSON, ROBERT DICK: **IV**: 150.
Daniel, on **IV**: 529*(2)*.
Life and Contributions of **I**: 24.
WINCHELL, ALEXANDER: **III**: 337.
WINCKLER, HUGO: **VII**: 310.
Wind(s):
Cosmology, in, Bibical Canaanite **V**: 194; **VIII**: 86.
God, of **VI**: 27, 151; **VIII**: 151.
Roman Tower of **I**: 414, 416.
Shechem Inscription, in **VII**: 85; **VIII**: 86.
Windows: **III**: 469; **IV**: 219.
Etruscan **IX**: cxxiii.
Glass, Did Jews Use **III**: 458.
Minoan Palaces, in **III**: 474.
Wine: **I**: 247, 249*(3)*, **263-265**, *306;* **V**: 403, 517*(3);* **VIII**: 219.
Blood and **V**: 61.
Export of **VII** 342.
"Firey" **V**: 422.
Greek trade of **I**: *289*, 340, 342.
Pentatuech, in **IV**: 231.
Pistacea **V**: 563.
Winepress: **I**: 264; **II**: 407.
Ain Karim, at **I**: 263.
Gideon's, at Ophrah **IV**: 366.
Song of, in Psalm 8 **VI**: 456.
Tell Es-Sâfi, at **III**: 571.
Wing(s):
Divine **VIII**: 102.
Greek Art, Attribute of **III**: 698.
WINTLE, THOMAS:
Zechariah, on **VI**: 407.
Wisaga: **I**: 391; **VI**: 213.
Wisdom: **IV**: *156;* **V**: *41,* 517; **VIII**: 7, 33, **§1004, 150**, 405.
Akkad, of **V**: 118.
Ancient, and Modern Times **VIII**: 226*(2)*.
Apocalyptic, Heavenly, in **V**: 122; **VIII**: 131.
Apocrypha, Concept, in **V**: 118.
Biblical, and Modern Existentialism **V**: 119; **VIII**: 353.
Biblical Messianism in Relation to, Concept **V**: 118, 517.
Canaanite-Phoenician sources of Hebrew **V**: 117.
Chinese, and Proverbs **IV**: 500, 501; **V**: 148.
Christ in the NT and **V**: 118.
Context of Bibical **V**: 118.
Counsellor **V**: 117; **VI**: 540.
Creation, in **VI**: 540.
Deuteronimic Laws and **IV**: 356; **V**: 116.
Divine **V**: 116.
Edomic **V**: 116.
Egyptian **IV**: 190, 500*(2);* **VII**: 10.
Esther, in **IV**: 521.
Greek **V**: 462.
Habakkuk and **IV**: 450; **V**: 119.
Hebrew, Development of **V**: 116.
Hebrew Idea of **V**: 115.
Hebrew, in Relation to Greek Thought **V**: 115, 250.
Hebrews, of the **V**: 115*(2)*.
Herodotus, of **V**: 254.
Hypostaes of **VIII**: 150.

Immortality and **V**: 117; **VIII**: 264.
Incarnational Aspects of **VIII**: 150.
Israel, of **V**: 118.
Job and **IV**: 458.
Latter Prophets, in **IV**: 389; **V**: 117.
Old Testament, in **V**: 116.
Onkhsheshonqy, Instructions of, and Bibical **V**: 118.
Oriental, Other, and Old Testament **V**: 116, 147.
Pagan, and Christian Inspiration **V**: 140.
Patristic Conception of, in the Light of Biblical and Rabbinical Research **VI**: 690, 724; **VIII**: 150.
Personified in Proverbs **IV**: 499*(3)*; **VI**: 540; **VIII**: 150*(2)*.
Prophecy and **V**: 118; **VIII**: 247.
Psalms and **IV**: 483; **V**: 117.
Qoheleth on **IV**: 516, 517.
Rabbinical Research **VI**: 690, 724.
Religious Meanings of **V**: 118.
Research, Assumptions and Problems in OT **V**: 119.
Royal **V**: 117.
Sapiential Septuagint **V**: 118.
Solomon, and the Beginnings of, in Israel **I**: 99; **V**: 118.
Song of Moses, Influence on **V**: 119.
Sumer, of **V**: 118.
Sumerian **VII**: 272.
Theology, OT, Place and Limit of, in **V**: 119; **VIII**: 8.

Wisdom Literature, (Genre of Ḥokmah)*see also Specific Languages* **I**: *192(2), 194, 504;* **V**: **§457, 115-119**.
Amarna Letters, in (Teacher to a Man of Shechem) **VII**: 171.
Amenemope and **V**: 116, 212.
ANE in, and Israel **V**: 119.
Apocrypha, of **V**: 116; **VI**: 611*(2)*.
Belief in a Future Life, Rise of, in Israel **V**: 119.
Characteristics of **V**: 115.
Christian Doctrine, Influence on Early **V**: 117; **VIII**: 300.
Cosmopolitan Aspect of the Hebrew Wisdom **V**: 115.
"Elihu" Tradition in Later Jewish Writings **V**: 119.
Family Ethics in **V**: 117; **VIII**: 234.
Form Criticism and **V**: 119.
Habakkuk and **IV**: 450; **V**: 119.
Hellenism and **V**: 116.
"Historical" Literature, influence on **IV**: 177; **V**: 119.
Interpretation of **V**: 119.
Isaiah, Archaic Passage in **VI**: 253.
Israel in, and the ANE **V**: 119.
Israel's Covenant Faith and Wisdom Movement **V**: 119; **VIII**: 217.
Life *(Ḥayyim)* in Proverbs, Job, and Ecclesiastes **V**: 112, 117.
Meaning of "Hokma" **V**: 115.
New Testament, Jewish, in **V**: 117; **VIII**: 275.
Old Testament Theology and **V**: 117; **VIII**: 6.
Onchsheshonqy, Instructions of, and **VII**: 12.
Origin and Development of, through New Testament Times **V**: 117.
Pre-Abrahamic Stories in Genesis as **IV**: 268, 269; **V**: 116.
Preaching from **VIII**: 375.
"Psalms, Wisdom" Classification of **V**: 118.
Quotations in **V**: 116.
Reason and Anger, Opposition of, in **V**: 117.

Retribution, Problem of, and — **V**: 118; **VIII**: 235.
Revelation in — **V**: 117; **VIII**: 33.
Rich and Poor in, Hebrew and Accadian — **V**: 118; **VII**: 3, 96, 152.
Salvation History in the Wisdom Books — **V**: 119; **VIII**: 193.
Social Background of — **V**: 117*(2)*.
Widow, Orphan and the Poor in — **I**: 192; **VII**: 2.

Wisdom of Solomon, Book of the: — **IX**: cxxix.
Alexandria, at — **VI**: 620, 724; **VIII**: 277.
Aramaic Fragment of — **VI**: 603.
Armenian Variants of — **VI**: 603.
Authorship of — **VI**: 617*(4)*.
Authorship of, by Apollos(?) — **VI**: 617*(2)*.
Bohairic Pericopae of — **VI**: 619*(2)*, 623*(2)*.
Boharic Lections of — **VI**: 603.
Canon, History of, and — **VI**: 620.
Christian Writings, Early, Influence on — **VI**: 619; **VIII**: 299.
Commentaries on — **VI**: 620‡.
Commentary on *(review)* — **VI**: 618.
Coptic (Sahidic) Version — **VI**: 603.
Death in — **VI**: 618, 619; **VIII**: 187, 263.
Devil, Envy of, in — **VI**: 632; **VIII**: 164.
Early Christmas Text in — **VI**: 633.
Ecclesiasticus and — **VI**: 617.
Eschatological Meaning of Life and Death in — **VI**: 632; **VIII**: 253.
Exegetical Studies on — **VI**: **§716, 632-633**.
Fourth Servant Song, Homily Based on — **VI**: 632.
Future in — **VI**: 632; **VIII**: 262.
Greek Lyrics, in (poetic) — **VI**: 633.
Greek Sources of — **VI**: 633.
Greek Translation of — **VI**: 619; **IX**: cxxviii.
Hebrew, Written in(?) — **VI**: 617.
Hellenistic Humanism in — **VI**: 619.
Immortality in — **VI**: 619, 633; **VIII**: 263.
Impious of — **VI**: 632.
Language and Character — **VI**: 620.
Latin Text of — **VI**: 603.
Literary Criticism of — **VI**: **§698, 617-620**.
Liturgy, in — **VIII**: 384.
Luke Influenced by (?) — **VI**: 618; **VIII**: 284.
Midrash of 10-19 — **VI**: 632.
Numerical Patterns in — **VI**: 620.
Origin of the First Part of — **VI**: 619.
Original Language of — **VI**: 617.
Paul and — **VI**: 618.
Plan and Structure of — **VI**: 619.
Plato and — **VI**: 619.
Preacher and — **VI**: 619.
Psalms, Borrowings from — **VI**: 619.
Quaker Translation of — **VI**: 618, 623.
Religious Teaching of — **VI**: 619.
Rhythm in — **VI**: 618.
Serpent Identified with Satan in — **VI**: 632; **VIII**: 163.
Sin in — **VI**: 618; **VIII**: 187.
Soul, Pre-existance of, in — **VI**: 618*(2)*.
Structure of — **VI**: 620.
Structure of — **VI**: 633.
Text and Structure of — **VI**: 603.
Textual Criticism of — **VI**: **§680, 603**.
Unit, Is the book a — **VI**: 618.
Wisdom, Figure of, in, and the Pauline "Christ" — **VI**: 618.

Wise Man:
Rabbinic Judaism, in — **V**: 267; **VI**: 691.
Stoic Philosophy, in — **V**: 267; **VI**: 691.

"Wise Men": — **III**: *229*.
God of Egypt's — **V**: 214.
Rabbinic Judaism and Stoic Philosophy, in — **V**: 267.

Witch, Witchcraft: **V**: 103, 104, 517.
Babylonian **V**: 173.
Bible and **V**: 103.
Child-Stealing among the Hittites **V**: 226.
Endor, or **IV**: 375*(2)*, 376*(4)*; **V**: 106; **VI**: 206*(2)*, 721.
Old Testament and **V**: 104*(2)*, 107.
WITHER, GEORGE: **VIII**: 363.
Witness:
Hittite for **I**: 489, 511.
Israelite Contracts and **I**: 515.
King as God's **I**: 487.
South Arabic, Word in **V**: 595.
Testimony of **I**: 514.
WITTMAN, WILLIAM: **III**: 435.
WOLFSON, HARRY AUSTRYN:
Philo, on **VI**: 676*(4)*.
Reclaiming Jesus, on **VIII**: 127.
Woman:
Creation / Origin of **IV**: 278, 279, 281*(3)*, 284; **VI**: 34, 35.
Egyptian Etymology of **V**: 353.
Fall of **IV**: 292.
Midrash, in **I**: 196; **VI**: 706.
"Woman-Man": **I**: 199, 217.
Women:
Babylonian Dower-Contract **VII**: 248.
Education of **I**: 231.
Hebrew Cult, in **I**: 196; **V**: 9, 11; **IX**: lxxxvi.
Judaism, Position in Ancient and Modern **V**: 14.
Legal Status of Free Female in Ugarit **I**: 506.
Modern Eastern Society, and **I**: 384*(3)*, 391.
OT, in the New **VIII**: 273, 310.
Religious Status of, in OT **V**: 13.
Synagogues, Separation of, in Worship **III**: 525.
Taboo and, in Iraq **I**: 391.
Temple, of the Code of Hammurabi **V**: 169; **VII**: 245.
Testimony of, in the Rule of the Congregation **VIII**: 463.
Travellers, Early in Arabia **III**: 447.
Women, Biblical - General Studies:
Biographical Studies **I**: 25.
Women in Society: **I**: 184, **§73, 196-199**; **IX**: **§73, lxxxvi.**
Wonders, Seven, of the Ancient World:
Colossus at Rhodes **III**: 728.
Lighthouse at Alexandria **III**: 482.
Mausoleum at Halicarnassus **III**: 543.
Pyramid of Cheops **III**: 505.
Statue of Olympian Zeus **III**: 728.
Temple of Diana at Ephesus **III**: 512.
Walls of Babylon **III**: 488.
Wood:
'ēṣāh (Isaiah 30:1b) **VI**: 285.
Egyptian, Ancient **II**: 214.
Ply-Wood Coffin, 3rd Dynasty, from Saqqara **II**: 214.
Ukarina **III**: 395; **V**: 458; **VI**: 304, 314, 355.
Woodcutter (Assyrian) **V**: 561.
WOOD, J. T.: **III**: 96.
Woodgatherer: **VI**: 130*(2)*.
Woodlands:
Western Asia, of **II**: 256.
Woodworking: **I**: 266.
Wool: **I**: 258*(2)*, 259; **II**: *169*.
Cyril of Alexander on **VI**: 721.
"to pick wool" in Assyrian **V**: 544.
Wool-Working, Prize for **III**: 589.
WOOLLEY, C. LEONARD: **III**: 274; **V**: 218.
Woolly Kullis: **III**: 125; **IX**: cix.
Worcester Art Museum: **III**: 693.
Word: **VIII**: 33, *52*, 131.
Belief in power of **I**: 511.
Creative Power of the Divine and Name **V**: 141, 203; **VIII**: 130.

History and VIII: 193.
Incarnate VIII: 131.
Myth and V: 132.
Pre-Exilic Prophets, in IV: 387*(2)*; VIII: 22, 152.
Sumerian Liturgy on an Ode to the Word VII: 285; VIII: 130.
Theology of the Lost VIII: 128.

"Word of God": V: 521*(3)*; VIII: 28, 33, 131, 153.
Bible and / as IV: 167*(2)*; VIII: 20*(3)*, 23, 24, 25, 48, 49, 50, 314*(2)*.
Bible as, Denial of, and Pagan Religion Parallels V: 150.
Doctrine of: VIII: **§970, 20-25**.
Effect of, The Post-Captivity Prophets IV: 426.
Ezekiel, in IV: 424; VIII: 24.
Holy Spirit and VIII: 23.
"Hypostasis", as VIII: 23.
Man's Response to VIII: 200.
mdw-nṯr (Egyptian) V: 224; VIII: 131.
Memory, as, of God's Story with Israel V: 29.
Not Bound V: 8.
Old Testament, in VIII: 23.
Power, as / of VIII: 23, 28.
Revelation, as VIII: 23.
Scripture and / as VIII: 23*(2)*, 25, 315.
Testimony of Science to IV: 165.
Theology of VIII: 23.
Uniqueness of IV: 168.
Vitality of IV: 176.
Word of Jahweh in the OT VIII: 23.

"Word of the Lord": V: *518*, 521*(2)*.
Jeremiah and I: 53; VIII: 50; IX: cxxxii.

"Word of Yahweh":
Implications in Prophecy V: 521; VIII: 246.

Word Studies Keyed to English - Alphabetical Listing **V: §524, 501-518; IX: §524, cxli.**

Work: V: 518.
Biblical Attitude / Interpretation of VIII: 228, 235.
Jewish Conception of VIII: 228.

Work Week, Length of: I: 305.

Workbench:
Egyptian Word for V: 357.

WORKMAN, GEORGE COULSON:
Jeremiah, Text of, on VI: 345.

Workmen: I: 184, 188, 189.
Babylonian Hiring Practices of I: 310.
Babylonian Pay-List, Diverse Names in VII: 252.
Guilds of I: 270.
Hireling, Biblical Teaching VIII: 231.
Hiring of, Babyloian Texts VII: 253.
Sub-gang of, at Meydum I: 270.

Workshop: I: 267*(2)*.
Corinthian Pottery III: 635.
Hellenistic Terra-Cotta in the Persian Gulf III: 758.
Mainland (Art) III: 701, 711.
Rhodian (Art) III: 701, 711.

World, *see also:* **Earth** V: *506*, 518*(2)*.
Ancient and its Inhabitants II: 1.
Biblical View of, A Theological Evaluation V: 113*(2)*.
Created in Time(?) VIII: 80*(2)*.
Creation of IV: 276, 277, 282, 286.
End of the VIII: 249.
Four Ages of, and the Planetary Constellations II: 225.
God and, Relationship of, in Jewish Prophecy VIII: 65, 245.
God and the VIII: 73.
God, Soverignty of, in VIII: 73.
Israelite Traditions of the Beginning of V: 22.

Miserable and Naughty **VIII**: 169.
Origin of **IV**: 283.
Talmud in **VI**: 698.
Theophrastus on the Eternity of the **V**: 258.

World Domination:
Idea of, by Alexander the Great **II**: 12.

World View *(Weltanschauurgen):* **V**: 217.
Language and **IV**: 111.
Oriental Studies in the Present World Picture **IX**: lxxxiii.
Primitive **V**: 158.

World-Order:
Prophets and **I**: 108; **VIII**: 86.

Worm(s): **III**: *371, 372,* 383.
Merḫu **VII**: 263.

Worship: **V**: *511,* 518.
Ancestor, *see:* ***Ancestor Worship***
Animal **I**: 184, 382.
Ass-Worship, Libel of Jewish **V**: 108.
Bible in **VIII**: 385.
Biblical Concept of **V**: 39.
China, in **V**: 145.
Chthonic, Origins of **V**: 238.
Covenant, in Amos **VI**: 381.
Creation and **VIII**: 385*(2)*.
Dancing **V**: 11, 39; **VI**: 228.
Early Israel, in **V**: 39, 41.
Emperor **II**: *23*.
Epicureans, among **V**: 250.
Ethics and, in the Bible **V**: 39; **VIII**: 228.
Greece, Attitudes of, in **V**: 248.
Hellenistic Ruler- **V**: 265.
Imageless, in Antiquity **V**: 154.
Judeo-Christian, Origin of **V**: 39.
Laws concerning Place of **IV**: 252.
Legitimus Honor **V**: 265.
Literature of, in OT **IV**: 253*(3)*.
Mother, in Egypt **V**: 210.
Old Testament, in **IV**: 252*(4)*; **V**: 28*(2)*, 30.
Places of, in Roman and Byzantine Periods **V**: 158.
Psalms in **VI**: 448; **VIII**: 378, 382, 383*(2)*, 385.
Public, in the Bible **V**: 19, 39
Public: Social Crime, and its Retribution **V**: 38; **VIII**: 230, 378.
Relic, and the Death of Jacob **VI**: 91.
Sermon, Place of, in Jewish **VIII**: 383.
Stone **V**: 47, 71.
Stones at *(Mazzeboth)* **V**: 50.
Tree, in China **I**: 385.
Water, Worship of, by the Romans **I**: 362; **V**: 269.
Word Studies on **V**: 57.

Worship and Liturgy, Old Testament in: **VIII**: **§1064, 378-386**, 396, 401.
"Apocryphal" Service in America **VIII**: 381.
First and Second Commandments in Jewish and Christian **VIII**: 381.
Lent with Malachi **IV**: 455.
Psalms, Hebrew in **VIII**: 385.
Psalms, Sitting for **VIII**: 383.
Psalms, Standing for **VIII**: 383*(2)*.
Psalter and the Lectionary in **VIII**: 382.
Psalter as an Aid to **VIII**: 381.
Revised Version of the Bible, in **IV**: 68*(3)*; **VIII**: 378.
Torah Readings **VIII**: 383.

Worship in Israel, *see:* **Hebrew Worship**

Worshipper(s):
Fire **IV**: 324.
Pole-Star **V**: 142.
Serpent, Statue of **III**: 735.
Week of the Moon **V**: 142.
Week of the Sun **V**: 142.

Woseramūn:
Funerary Papyrus of **VII**: 45.

Wrath: **VI**: 501.
God, of, in Canaanite and Hebrew Literature **V**: 194.
"Vessels of Wrath" **III**: 636.
Wreaths: **I**: 282.
Tindium, of **V**: 212.
Wrestling: **I**: 240*(2), 466.*
WRIGHT, GEORGE FREDERICK: **III**: 299; **IV**: 135, 172*(3)*.
Life and Contributions of **I**: 24.
WRIGHT, THEODORE F.: **VII**: 89.
Writing Boards: **I**: *235(2);* **III**: 685; **VII**: 197.
Egyptian Wisdom Text on **VII**: 12.
Writing - General Studies: **I**: **§82, 233-235**; **IX**: **§82, lxxxviii**.
Abecedaries, Ugaritic **V**: 535; **VI**: *283*.
Aegean **V**: 603, 622.
Alphabetic **V**: 281*(4)*, 283*(3)*, 288, 305, 306.
Archaeology and the Antiquity of **IV**: 213.
Bible and **I**: 502.
Chronological, Concepts and Development **II**: 175; **VII**: 3.
Cuneiform, Origin of **I**: 233; **V**: 544.
Decipherment of Unknown Language and **VII**: 2.
Development of **I**: **§82, 233-235**.
Development of (Egyptian) **V**: 309.
Early Jewish-Christian **V**: 150.
Egyptian **V**: 365, *635*.
Egyptian Group- **V**: 365.
Egyptian Phonetic **V**: 364.
Greek **V**: *365*, 635.
History and (Nippur Tablets) **VII**: 212, 272.
Homer and the Art of **VII**: 3.
Homer, in **VII**: 349.
Introduction of, into India by Cyrus **II**: 31.
Invention of **V**: 281.
Language, Origin of Written **V**: 275.
Lead, with **I**: 233; **VI**: 430.
Learned Profession, as a, *see also:* ***Scribes*** **I**: 270.
Literary Style in First Millennium Mesopotamia **VII**: 3.
Old Testament and **IV**: 176.
Origin of, in Egypt **V**: 275.
Origin of, in Greece **V**: 275.
Pentateuch (Books of Moses) and **IV**: 235.
Pentateuch Criticism and Arab Prose Writers **IV**: 254.
Pentateuch Criticism and Hebrew Prose Writers **IV**: 254.
Physcial Processes of, and the Origin of the Alphabet **V**: 284.
Picture (Egyptian) **III**: 81.
Pre-Hellenic **V**: 603.
Pre-Phœnician in Crete **V**: 603.
Rods, on **VI**: 131.
Theory of (Egyptian) **V**: 309.
Western Asia, and Ugarit in Particular **IV**: 187.
Writing Instruments: **III**: **§221, 685**.
Wu-Ti: **V**: 141, 163.
Wycliffe's Bible: **IV**: 51*(2)*.

X

X Sign in Isaiah Scroll A **VIII**: 446, 447.
X-ray:
Coins, analysis of, by **I**: 456, 457, 459; **II**: 219*(2)*.
Faked Mummies, and **I**: 380.
Geiger Counter Spectoscope used in Archaeology **II**: 218.
Xanthippos:
Ostracisim of **VII**: 336.
Xanthos: **III**: 262, 263, 266, 267.
Xanthus River Valley: **III**: 154, 278.
χaru: **II**: 171.
Xenogenesis: **III**: 317.
Xenokles: **III**: 629.

Xenophanes: V: 253.
Xenophon: I: 127; II: *21, 32, 35*, **107-108**; III: 195.
Anabasis and I: 127; II: 108.
Articular Infinitive in V: 629.
"Cyropaedia" of, and Daniel IV: 523.
Cyrus the Great and II: 107.
Hellencia, Papyri of VII: 355.
Historian, as a I: 127; II: *31*.
Nineveh, Fall of according to III: 182.
Retreat of IX: cvi.
Symposium viii, 6-9 VII: 346.
Themistogenes and II: 101, 108.
Two Ways in Hermes and V: 141, 248; VI: 717.
Xeropolis, *see also:* **Lefkandi** III: 278.
Xerxes: II: *35*, **108**; III: *190*.
"Daiva" Inscription of, in Elamite VII: 299.
Daiva- Inscription of VII: 371.
Darius and, in Babylonia II: 35, 108.
Herodotus and the Strategy and Tactics of Invastion of VII: 337.
Persian Inscriptions of VII: 371*(2)*.
Religion in the Inscriptions of V: 235.
Vase of III: 604, 606.
Xisouthros (Xisuthros) V: 172; VII: 228.
Xypete:
Hera Temple at III: 513.

Y

Ŷ-meru: II: 109.
Ya'qūb Al Qirqisānī, *see: Kitāb Al-Anwār*
Yabboq': I: *152*.
Yabroud: III: **279**, *380*.
Pleistocene Fauna from III: 368.
Yabrúd: III: *440*.
Remains from, Description of III: 354.
Yabrud Rockshelter I:
Geology, Climate and Chronology of II: 245, 251.
Yafa:
Synagogue at III: 523, 525.
Yafi Valley:
Himyaritic Objects from the Lower III: 564.
Yafo: II: *488*, 495.
Yaḫad Sect, *see also:* **Essenes, Qumran** VIII: 410.
Manual of Discipline, in VIII: 463.
Philo, Josephus and VI: 677, 683; VIII: 423.
Tombstones from III: 543; VII: 333.
Yahoudieh, Tell el : III: **279**, 443.
YAHÛ: VIII: 116, 117.
Yahveh Picture: III: 646.
YAHW: VIII: 116.
Yahweh, *see also:* **Jehovah, and Tetragrammaton** I: *131;* III: 776; VI: 100, 490; VIII: **§987, 112-120**, 122.
Arm of, in Isaiah VI: 305.
Baal and, in Hosea IV: 430.
Baal Conflict, and Elijah IV: 381.
Babylonia, in V: 173, 174; VII: 260; VIII: 114*(2)*, 115.
Babylonia, Name on Monuments(?) V: 176; VIII: 116.
Bricks and Cylinders inscribed with Yav, or Jehovah, at Ur V: 554; VIII: 113.
Chariot-Throne of VIII: 61.
China, Worship of, in(?) V: 18; VIII: 118.
Christ VIII: 126.
Council of, *see:* ***Council of Yahweh***
Creation as Cosmic Victory of VIII: 81.
Creator Deity(?) VIII: 82, 120.
"Day of," *see:* ***"Day of the Lord"***
Dead Sea Scrolls, in VIII: 119, 417.

Deborah's Concept of — **IV**: 370; **VIII**: 115.
Dewey, John, and — **VIII**: 368.
Egypt, Gods of, and — **IV**: 338.
Enemies of, a Theological Investigation of — **VIII**: 7, 87.
Father, as, in OT — **VIII**: 73.
Father-Son Relationship with Israel — **I**: 514.
Fire from, Elijah's — **IV**: 383.
Glory of, Depature of — **VIII**: 101.
Glory of, Ezezkiel's Vision of — **VI**: 347*(2)*.
"Glory of Yahweh", Term — **VIII**: 101; **IX**: cxli.
Hebrew/Israelite Weather-Deity — **VIII**: 120.
Images of — **V**: 106, 107; **VIII**: 116*(2)*, 118*(2)*.
"Jahweh", Name Found Among the Canaanites(?) — **VIII**: 115.
Jerusalem and — **II**: 413; **VIII**: 116.
"Man of Wars", as — **VI**: 108; **VIII**: 120.
Manitou and — **V**: 142.
Mountain Throne of — **VIII**: 117.
Name not yet known — **VI**: 103*(3)*.
Non-Israelites and — **VIII**: 108.
Origin of the Name — **VIII**: 115, 117, 119.
"Other gods" and — **V**: 32.
Outside Israel — **VIII**: 119.
Patriarchs, God of, and — **VIII**: 120.
Proper Names, Modification of, in — **VIII**: 118.
Psalm of Lament and — **V**: 29.
Qumran, Divine Name at — **VIII**: 417.
Relief of(?) — **V**: 161; **VIII**: 116.
Righteousness of — **VIII**: 97.
Solomonic Antijahvism — **IV**: 456; **VIII**: 177.
Translated by *(ho) Theos* in the Greek Pentateuch — **VIII**: 118.
Translation of, in LXX by *θέος* — **V**: 650.
Triumph of Yahwism — **V**: 12.
Worship of, Origin of — **V**: 12, 13, 24; **VIII**: 119.
Yâ and Yâwa (Jah and Jahweh) in Assyro-Babylonian Inscirptions — **V**: 293; **VIII**: 114.
"Yahweh is My Rock" — **VIII**: 308.
Yahweh Ṣe<u>b</u>a'o<u>t</u> — **IV**: 375; **VIII**: 120.
"Yahweh-Creator" in Deutero-Isaiah — **IV**: 405.
Yahweh-Tehom Myth — **VIII**: 76.

Yahweh Elohim: — **VIII**: 124*(2)*.
Yahwism: — **V**: 12; **VIII**: 119.
Baalism and, before the Exile — **V**: 28, 197.
"Horns of the Altar" in — **V**: 52.
Origins of in Israel — **VI**: 110.
Yahwist, *see:* **JEDP**
Yajur: — **II**: 283, 307.
Yakron Valley: — **I**: *207;* **II**: *249,* 495.
Yakut: — **I**: *285,* 338.
Yale Numismatic Collection: — **I**: 449*(3)*.
Yale University Art Gallery: — **III**: *741.*
Yam, Land of: — **II**: 271.
Yam Suph, *see:* **Red Sea**
Yamani: — **II**: 325*(2)*.
Yamḫad: — **II**: *6, 109.*
Yamu-Nedjeḥ: — **II**: 109.
Statue of — **II**: 109; **VII**: 17.
Yanhamu: — **VII**: 172.
Yanik Tepe: — **III**: *229,* **278-279**, *362.*
Yannai, Alexander:
Trachides as Surname of, in Josephus and Syncellus — **VI**: 684.
Yannay Line: — **II**: 495.
Yanoem: — **II**: 265.
Ya'qob'el: — **II**: 271.
Ya'qūb Al Qirqisānī: — **I**: 464.
Yarim Tepe: — **III**: 280.
Yarim-Lim: — **II**: 109.

Geological History of and Influence on Ancient Settlements II: 249.

Yarmuk (Yarmouk) Valley: II: 426*(2)*, **495**.

"Yarmukian": I: *266, 288;* III: *765, 766*.

Yasna, *see:* **Avesta**

Yassi Ada:

Underwater Excavations III: 264, 265*(2)*, 280, 453.

Yassihuyuk, *see:* **Gordion**

Yassub: II: 284.

Yas'ur: II: 303, 495.

Yavne Yam: II: 304.

Yavneh:

Jerusalem or VIII: 336.

Yavneh-Yam: II: *325*, **496**.

Yāwān: II: 265.

Yaz (Syrian God): V: 237.

Yazilikaya: III: 262, 263.

Yazur, *see:* **Azor**

Year: I: 396; V: 518.

Antediluvian IV: 297.

Astronomical I: 396.

Egyptian I: 393, 394, 396, 398.

Egyptian Nature I: 396.

Egyptian Word for V: 358, 359, *583*.

Genesis, as used in IV: 271; IX: xcvii.

Hittite Word for I: 403.

Jubilee I: 399.

Palestine, Division of, in I: 398.

Sabbatical I: *304*, 367.

Sothic Cycle and Ancient I: 396; II: 200.

Sumerian Word for I: 410; V: *359*, 583.

Sumerian Word for V: 359.

Year Dates: I: **§118**, **409-412**, II: *18, 201;* IX: **§118**, **xcviii**.

"Repeating of Births" I: 409.

Year Date 2 of Samsuiluna V: 568.

Year-Eponymate:

Hebrew Monarchy, in I: 409.

Years:

Regnal, *see:* ***Regnal Years***

"Years of Plenty": IV: 326

Yeb: III: 94*(2)*.

Yedonya:

Letter Concerning Yahu Temple, by VII: 132.

Yefet Codex:

Order of Books in IV: 102.

Yeho: VIII: 116.

Yehûd: III: *656*.

Yehūdīyah, Tell el-: III: *478*, 625.

YEIVIN, SHEMUEL (Z.): ***Bibliography of*** I: 22.

Yemen:

Ancient Pronunciation and Yemenite Hebrew V: 500.

Hebrew Language in the Synagogues of V: 499.

Kamaz in V: 500.

Mârib, Temple of the Moon at III: 517*(2)*

Yemma: II: 284.

Yerka: II: *287*.

Yeshivot: I: 232.

Yezidies: I: 382.

YHWH, *see:* **Tetragrammaton**

Yi:

Statuette of, from Elephantine VII: 66.

Yiddish:

Psalms, Translation into IV: 486.

Ŷm-hetep: II: 109.

Yoking: I: 253.

Yom Ha'atzma'ut: I: 392.

Yom Kippur, *see:* **Day of Atonement**

Yorgan Teppe, *see also:* **Nuzi** III: **280**.

Yortan: III: *614*.

YOUNG, EDWARD J. VI: 265.

YOUNG, THOMAS: **III**: 779; **VII**: 58; **IX**: cxxxix.

Youth:
Chinese Parallel to an Egyptian Idiom **V**: 359.
Talmud, in **VI**: 698.

Yua:
Tomb of **III**: 539.

Yuia: **II**: 109; **III**: 605.

Yümüktepe:
Chalcolithic Long Bones from **III**: 360.
Chalcolithic Skulls from **III**: 360.

Yunis,Tell: **II**: 496.

Yurza, *see also:* **Tell Jemmeh** **II**: **496**.

Yuzgat Text: **VII**: 303, 310.

Yuzghat:
Cuneiform Script from **VII**: 175.

YW (God): **V**: 195.

Z

Za-mal-mal (Baal Zebûb): **V**: 180, 191.

Zaanaim: **II**: 284.

Zab River: **II**: *278;* **III**: *180*.

Zabûl Yam:
Thâpiṭ Nahar and, in the Combat between Baʿal and the Sea **V**: 191.

Zabum:
Seal of **III**: 648.

Zadok: **V**: 45; **VI**: 132.
Biographical Studies **I**: *26(2)*, **82**.
"Sons of, the Priests" at Qumran **V**: 42; **VIII**: 417*(2)*.
Successors of, at Jerusalem **V**: 45.

Zadokite Document *see also:* **Damascus Document** **I**: *215, 397;* **V**: *82;* **VIII**: 436*(2)*, *457*.
"390 Years" in **VIII**: 459*(3)*.
Calendar in **VI**: 662.
Date of **VIII**: 458*(2)*.
Exegetical Studies on **VI**: **§803**, **670-671**.
Genesis 1:27 and Fragments IV: 20, 21 **VI**: 3.
Habakkuk Scroll and **VIII**: 457.
Literary Criticism of **VI**: **§777**, **662-663**; **IX**: **§777**, **cxl**.
Manual of Disciple, Parallels in **VI**: 670.
Marriage Law in **VI**: 662.
Prophecy in **VIII**: 421, 460.
Rstoration of the "Fragments" XIV, 12-16 **VIII**: 458.
Sabbath in **VI**: 662.
Textual Criticism on **VI**: **(§751)**, **647**.

Zadokites: **V**: **§449**, **96-97**.
Dead Sea Scrolls and **VIII**: 435.
Qumran Compared with **VIII**: 422.
Sabbath Laws of **VIII**: 414.
Sadducean Christians of Damascus **VI**: 662; **IX**: cxxxv*(2)*, cl.
Writings of, in Ninth and Tenth Centuries **VIII**: 429.

Zagazig:
Greek Inscription from **VII**: 313.

Zagros Mountains: **II**: 146; **III**: *228(2)*.

Zakar Inscriptions: **VII**: 87, 123.
Heads **III**: 683; **VII**: 87.

Zakarbaal: **V**: 297.

Zakarîya, Tell: **I**: *419;* **II**: **496-497**; **III**: *662*.
Objects Discovered at **III**: 563.

Zakro: **III**: **280**.

Zanatha: **II**: 290.

Zanoah: **II**: 284.

Zaphenath Paneah:
Egyptian Name of Joseph **I**: 59; **V**: 295.
Genesis, Date of, and **IV**: 322.

Zaphon: **II**: 290, *485*, 497, *498*.

Zarathushtra, *see also*: **Zoroaster** — **II**: 109; **V**: 36, 233.
- Dualism of Iran, and — **V**: 236.
- Hymn of — **V**: 233*(2)*.
- Philo and — **V**: 36, 232; **VI**: 674.
- Representation of — **V**: 234.
- Temptation of (Vendīdād XIX) — **V**: 234.

Zarefat: — **II**: 497; **III**: *22, 225*.
Zarephath: — **IV**: 381.
Zaretan (Zarethan): — **II**: *312, 391*, 497, 498.
Zarethan: — **II**: *485, 497*, **498**; **III**: 485.
- Two Tombs at — **III**: 558.

Zarethan-Ṣarṭabeh: — **II**: 498; **VI**: 667.
Zāriqum: — **II**: 110.
Zarthan: — **II**: 269.
Zawi Chemi Shanidar: — **III**: **280**, 367.
Zawiet Abu: — **III**: 281.
Zawiyet el-Aryân: — **II**: *67*.
Zealots, *see also*: **Qannaim** — **I**: *177, 178;* **II**: *58;* **V**: 95. **§454, 102**.
- Essenes and / or — **VIII**: 411.
- Josephus and — **V**: 102*(2);* **VI**: 683, 684.
- Maccabees and — **V**: 102.
- Program of, and Jesus — **V**: 102.
- "Qannaim" in Rabbinic Literature and — **V**: 102, 449; **VI**: 691, 705.
- Qumran and — **VIII**: 426*(2)*.
- Sicarii and — **V**: 102, 449; **VIII**: 409.
- Significance of — **V**: 102.
- War of 66-73, in — **V**: 102.

Zeberged: — **II**: 269*(3);* **VII**: 11*(3)*.
Zeboim: — **II**: **498**.
Zebulon: — **II**: 283.
- Border, Northern, of — **II**: 274.

Zechariah, Book of:
- ***Auenticity, Authorship, Date, and Sources of*** — **IV**: **§376, 454**; **IX**: lxxxiv.
- Candlestick, Parable, Vision of — **IV**: 452; **VI**: 407.
- Carpenters, Parable of — **VI**: 406.
- Chariots, Parable of — **VI**: 408.
- Chronology of, and the First Years of Darius I — **IV**: *452*, 454.
- Corner-Stone and — **IV**: 453; **VI**: 407.
- Deutero-Zechariah — **IV**: 454.
- Dissection of — **IV**: 453.
- "Ephah", Meaning of the Word in — **VI**: 408.
- Ephah, Parable,Vision of — **IV**: 452; **VI**: 408.
- Ephah, Vision of, in Rabbinic Interpretation — **VI**: 408, 715.
- ***Exegetical Studies on*** — **VI**: **§637, 405-414**.
- Ezekiel 40-48, Relation to — **IV**: 454; **VI**: 360.
- Flying Roll, Parable, Vision of — **IV**: 452; **VI**: 408.
- Good Shepherd of — **VI**: 411.
- Haggai and — **IV**: *451(3), 452(2)*, 453*(3)*.
- Hebrew Text of compared with Versions — **VI**: 405, 410.
- High Priest, Parable of, in — **VI**: 407
- Higher Criticism and — **IV**: 453.
- Historical Background — **VI**: 405.
- Historical Observations on — **VI**: 412.
- History of — **IV**: 453.
- Horsemen of — **VI**: 406.
- Joshua as, in — **VI**: 407, 409.
- Joshua, Coronation of, in — **VI**: 407, 408.
- ***Literary Criticism of*** — **IV**: **§375, 452-454**.
- Messianic Conspiritors in — **VI**: 410.
- Messianism of Proto-Zacharias — **VIII**: 18, 136.
- Moore, Thomas V., on — **IV**: 454.
- National Revival in — **IV**: 452.
- Origin of — **IV**: 454.

Outline of IV: *451,* 453, *520, 537.*
Parable of the Wall of Fire VI: 407.
Parables of VI: 405, 406*(2).*
Passion Narrative and IV: 454.
Plan of the Prophecy VI: 405.
Post-Exilic Period and II: 183, IV: 454; IX: lxxxiv.
Religious Observances in IV: 452.
Religious Teachings of IV: *451,* 453.
Shepherd of Israel and IV: 452.
Sociological Observations VI: 412.
Style of VI: 405.
Temple of God in VI: 407.
Textual Emendation and IV: 453; VI: 414.
Unknown Martyr in VI: 411.
Wintle, Thomas, on VI: 407.

Zechariah, Book of, Manuscripts of: VI: **§638, 414**.

Zechariah, Person: II: 183; VI: 405*(2).*
Biographical Studies I: 82.
Death of, in Rabbinic Literature I: 82; VI: 696.
Lampstand, Vision of IV: 453.
Mission of IV: 452.
Teachings of IV: 453.
Times of IV: 452.
Visions of IV: 452*(2),* 453*(3);* VI: 405, 406.
Visions of, Key to the Interpretation of IV: 453.

Zedekiah: I: *202.*
Reign of VIII: 390.

ZEITLIN, SOLOMON:
Dead Sea Scrolls and VIII: 437.

Zekenim: I: *184, 461.*

Zela: II: *377;* III: 541.

Zelophehad:
Daughters of I: 228*(2);* VI: 137, 138.

Zelzah: II: 498.

Zemaraim: II: 284.

Zend-Avesta, *see:* **Avesta**

Zendan Inscription: VII: 372.

Zenjīrlī (Zendjirli) *see also:* **Sindjirli** III: 281, 682; VI: 566.
Northwest Semitic Text VII: 85.

Zeno:
Paradoxes of V: 263.

Zenon (of Caunus): II: 110.

Zenon Papyri: I: *172, 253, 304, 481;* III: *467;* VII: 339, 351*(3),* 352*(9),* 353*(4).*
Accounts of Wages Paid VII: 340.
Receipts in the VII: 339.

ZENOS, ANDREW C. IV: 137.

Zephaniah, Apocalypse of, *see:* **Apocalypse of Zephaniah**

Zephaniah, Book: IV: 386; VI: 274.
Authenticity, Authorship, Date, and Sources of IV: **§372, 451**.
Background of IV: 450, 451.
Exegetical Studies on VI: **§633, 403-404.**
Historical Background to IV: 450.
Inductive Study of VIII: 390.
Literary Criticism of IV: **§371, 450-451**.
Metaphor from the building in VI: 403.
Pun on the Name Ashdod in VI: 403.

Zephaniah, Book of, Manuscripts of: VI: (**§634**), **404**.

Zephaniah, Person: VI: 403.
Biographical Studies I: 82.
Historical Testimony of IV: 450.
Royal Ancestry of I: 82.

Zephath: II: **498**.

Zephathah: II: **498-499**; VI: 592.

Zephyritis: I: 449.

Zer:
King of Abydos II: 4, 207.

Zerah: **VI**: 86.
Biographical Studies **I**: 82.
Zeredah: **II**: 269, 284, 292; **III**: 419, 424.
Zererah: **II**: 269.
Zerethan (Zeretan): **II**: **498**.
Zero:
Cuneiform Prototype of **I**: 430.
Cuneiform Sign for in Astronomical Texts [≰] **I**: 432; **II**: 231.
Zerubbabel: **I**: *64, 81,* **82**; **VI**: 517, 529.
Biographical Studies **I**: 82.
Book of **V**: 124.
Lists of, and the Hebrew Numeral Notation **VI**: 580, 585.
Lists of, in 1 Esdras 5:8-23 (Greek Version) **VI**: 602.
Temple, Rebuilding of **V**: 74.
Zervan (Zervan):
Apocalypse **V**: 235*(2)*.
Zeser:
King of Abydos **II**: 4, 207.
Zeser-ka-ra: **III**: *542*.
Zet: **II**: 110*(2)*.
King of Abydos **II**: 4, 207.
Zeus: **V**: 259; **VIII**: 115.
Aegis of **V**: 264; **VIII**: 87*(2)*.
Artistic Style of Striding **III**: 704.
Connection to Amūn and Meteorites **II**: 230; **V**: 147, 211, 255.
Cretan **V**: 12.
Cults of, at Athens **V**: 264.
Eagle of **V**: 259.
Hermes and, at Lystra **V**: 251.
Homer, in **V**: 256.
Ithomatos of Ageladas, Statue of **III**: 740.
Marriage of Hera and, its Symbol **V**: 257.
Mishnah, Talmud, and Midrash, in **VI**: 699.
Nature Aspects of **V**: 249.
Olympian, Statue **III**: 728.
"Priest" of, at Lystra **V**: 251.
Sanctuary of, at Cape Phokas, Lesbos(?) **III**: 152; **V**: 263.
Temples of, *see: **Temples***
Zeus Didymaeus: **V**: 256.
Zeus Heliopolis: **V**: 248.
Zeus Hypsistos: **I**: 270.
Zeus Kerauniois: **III**: 764.
Zeuxis: **I**: 172.
Ziggurat(s): **III**: 472, **§193, 507-522**; **V**: 171; **IX**: **§193, cxiii-cxiv**.
Choaga-Zanbil, of **III**: 517.
E-PA at Lagash **III**: 465.
Unknown Representation **III**: 517.
Ur, of **III**: 512.
Zimmarin: **II**: 367.
Zin, Wilderness of: **I**: *348;* **II**: **499**; **IV**: 229.
Mesolithic Hunters' Industry at Ramat Matred **III**: 353.
Zincirli: **III**: 281.
Zion: **I**: *146;* **II**: 284, 349*(6), 379, 388,* 406, 407, 412, 415, *445(2), 448, 456,* **499-501**; **III**: *531;* **IV**: 377, *416;* **V**: 132; **VI**: *460*.
David's Capture of (*See also:* Jerusalem) **VI**: 209*(2)*.
Isaiah and **IV**: 391, *427;* **V**: 9.
Israel, in Historic Conscienceness of **II**: 418.
Linguistic and Historical Study **II**: 417; **V**: 508.
Rock Scrap of **II**: 306.
Zion, Mount: **I**: 362; **II**: 292, 447.
Bridge beween, and Jewish Temple **V**: 67.
Holiness of, compared with Mount Morah **V**: 7.
Spiritual Metropolis **VI**: 505.

Zionism: I: *145;* **VIII**: **§1058, 340-349**.
- Anti-Semitism and **VIII**: 326, 341.
- Congress, First Zionist **VIII**: 345.
- Cultural Aims of **VIII**: 344.
- Future of **VIII**: 348.
- Prophecy and **VIII**: 344.
- Protocols of the Elders of Zion **VIII**: 349.
- Psalms, in **IV**: 480; **VIII**: 344; **IX**: cii.
- Theological Implication **VIII**: 348.

Zipporah:
- Biographical Studies **I**: 82.

Zir: **II**: 284.

Zither: **I**: 244.

Zittaviensis, Codex: **IV**: 27.

Ziwiye(h): **III**: **281**, *704, 772*.
- Coffin from **III**: 555, 557.
- Treasure of **III**: 569*(2)*, 599.

Zoan: **III**: 83, 201, *246*, **281**.

Zoar: **II**: 285, *479, 483*, **501**; **IX**: cxviii*(2)*.

Zobah: **II**: 502.

Zodiac and Horoscopes: **I**: **§117, 407-408**.
- Babylonian Zodiac **I**: 408.
- Beth-Alpha Synagogue, Zodiac Panel in **III**: 526.
- Egyptian Zodiac **I**: 408; **III**: 777.
- Euphratean Astronomical Names of the Signs of **I**: 407; **V**: 572.
- Greek Zodiac **I**: 408.
- Jacob's Zodiac **I**: 407; **VI**: 91.
- Khirbet el-Tannûr, Zodiac of **I**: 408.
- Tribes of Israel and **I**: 407.

Zodiac Tablet from Gezer: **I**: 408*(3);* **VII**: 195*(2)*, 255.

Zodiacal Chronology: **II**: 173.

Zodiacal Light:
- Semitic Mythology and **II**: 231; **V**: 133.

Zohar:
- Judaeo-Christian Polemics in **VIII**: 329.
- Philo and **V**: 240*(2);* **VI**: 677.

Zoheleth:
- Stone of **II**: 401, **502**.

Zoilos:
- Letter of **VII**: 331.

Zom Gedaliah: **V**: 85.

Zoolatry:
- Egyptian Mysteries, of **V**: 217, 260.

Zoology, *see also:* **Animals**
- Hebrew **III**: 366*(2);* **VI**: 10.
- Homeric **III**: 364*(2)*.

Zophar: **VI**: 426, 427, 432*(2)*.

Zorababell: **VI**: 629.

Zorah:
- Rock Altar at **V**: 46.

Zoroaster: **V**: *229(2)*, 231, 235*(4)*, *237(2)*.
- Babylonian Research and the Era of **V**: 232.
- Barukh ben Neriah and **V**: 236*(2)*.
- Bible and **V**: 233.
- Classical Passages Mentioning Name of **V**: 233.
- Contribution of **V**: 236.
- Daniel *vs.* (Future State) **VIII**: 259.
- Date of **V**: 230, 234, 235.
- Hymns of **V**: 231.
- Kaabah of **V**: 235.
- Monotheism, Archaic, and **V**: 33, 229.
- Native Place of **V**: 230.
- Oracles of **V**: 229*(2)*.
- Parsees and **V**: 232.
- Persian Fire-Worshippers, and **V**: 229.
- Persian References to **V**: 233.
- Religion of **V**: 229*(2)*, 230, 233.
- Snorra Edde, Allusion to, in **V**: 230.
- Syrian Reference to **V**: 234.

Zoroastrianism: **V**: §473, **229-236**.
Achaemenides, Religion of, and **V**: 235.
Bible and **V**: 232.
"Darkness and Light" in **V**: 236.
Deities on Indo-Scythian Coins **I**: 440*(4)*.
Dualism in **II**: 109.
Dualism of Isaiah 45:7 and **V**: 232; **VI**: 301.
Easoteric Trends in **V**: 236.
Hebrew Religion, Influence on **V**: 24, 36, 230, 235.
Influence of **V**: 235.
Jewish Doctrines, Influence on in the Inter-Testamental Period **V**: 16, 36, 234.
Jewish Eschatology (Exilic), and **V**: 233; **VIII**: 250.
Judaism, Critique of **V**: 27.
Judaism, Influence on **V**: 36, 231.
Karīr, Founder of **V**: 235.
Liberal Aspects of **V**: 234.
Messiah **V**: *232(3)*.
Mithra's Part in **V**: 236.
Persian Fire Temples or Tombs(?) **III**: 520.
Prophet Outside Israel(?) **V**: 236.
Sacred Fires of **V**: 236.
Suffering in **V**: 236.
Theology **V**: 235.
Theology, Present day **V**: 231.
Zoroastrians: **V**: 235.
Customs of **V**: 234.
Modern, of Persia **V**: 232.
Pious Foundations of **V**: 236.
Zoser:
Inscribed Statue of **VII**: 64.
ZOUCH, THOMAS:
Prophecy, on **VIII**: 235.
Zubediyah: **II**: *250;* **III**: 281.
Zumê: **II**: 263.
ZUNZ, LEOPOLD: **V**: 31; **IX**: lxxxvii.
Zuph:
Saul's Journey to **VI**: 196.
zuz:
Silver Standard to **I**: 427*(2);* **V**: 528.
Zuzim: **II**: *158, 167,* **171**.
ZWINGLI, ULRICH:
Canon and **IV**: 202.
Zygouries: **III**: **282**.

Akkadian

adî matî	V: 544, 559.
aḫšušam-ma assakpam	V: 577.
a-ḫu	V: 544.
akāmu	V: 584.
akhulâpi	V: 544, 559
akkîma ṣābašu itrarû	V: 577.
amirānu	V: 546.
ana-➤➤⫶𒀭𒌷𒀸𒉌 ras-shi-bat Ninua at-ta-shi kati	V: 543, 558.
Annakum	I: 300; V: 551(2).
antalū	V: 548; IX: cxii.
arad ekalli	III: 471; V: 549.
arad kitti	V: 542.
ardat lliî	VI: 549; VII: 196, 200, 260.
Artamašši	V: 551.
asîru	V: 546.
asirtu	V: 546.
asîru	V: 546.
assinnu	V: 547.
assukku	I: 321; V: 584.
atalli	V: 577.
âru	V: 402, 553.
āwatu(m)	V: 548.
azu	V: 545.
b/ukk/qqu	V: 546.
bêru	V: 584.
Birdu	V: 553.
Birit	V: 542.
Bubu' tu	V: 553.
baganu šutuk	V: 544.
buhâmu	V: 544.
bur simatim	V: 545.
çarçar	V: 545.
dalāpu	V: 549.
dalbu, dalbanu	V: 545.

dan-ga	V: 543.
das-bi	V: 542,
dīnu u dabābu	I: 506; V: 553.
dmt	VI: 355.
EME-SAL	V: 542, 556.
EN-AN-E-DU	VII: 150.
Eramu	V: 542.
eriššišunnu	V: 577.
erû, urrû	V: 546.
esrêti-	V: 546.
EZEN	V: 545.
gagûm	V: 552.
ganinu	V: 545.
ganunu	V: 545.
garum	V: 545.
gilinu	V: 546.
gillimu(?)	V: 546.
gišrinnu	V: 584.
Gu (𒄖)	I: 407.
gubnatu (Cheese)	V: 380.
ḫa-ab-ši	V: 546.
HAR-RA	VII: 148, 149, 202, 270, 271.
ḫaramu	V: 545.
ḫatanu(m)	V: 548.
hi/eššumaku	V: 550, 618.
hubullu	VII: 148, 149(2), 202, 270(2), 271.
Ḫurizati	V: 551.
ḪURRA	VII: 149, 211, 270.
i-mi	V: 544.
idu (Amarna 16, 30)	V: 547.
igi-duḫ-a	V: 550; VII: 176.
ikuku	V: 547.
immeru zalamu	V: 545.
ina emûqi	V: 444, 534, 550.

ina māti	V: 398.	*mala naklim u (awīl)*	
ian šubtêburia	V: 577.	*muškênim labīrêm*	
iš-ti-a-na	I: *433;* V: 548.	*šipram šâ kênātimu šeppeš*	V: 577.
iš-ti-na	I: *433;* V: 548.	*Malâlu*	V: 545.
ištu warḫim mādam-mā		*malku*	VII: 197.
[mu]-ú waššuru	V: 577.	*maru*	V: 542.
itte' izzi	V: 545.	*mât A-* 𒀄𒂖	V: 559.
itti atta ù šût-rêši MES*-ka*		*mât A-* 𒀄𒂖 *-ri-í*	V: 544.
rêqu	V: 577.	*mekku*	V: 546.
izzu	V: 545.	*melammu*	V: 547.
KAK.Ú.TAG.GA	V: 547.	*Mitannian maryannu*	I: 314; V:
kallatu(m)	V: 548, 564.		348(2), 382, 546.
kamir	V: 545.	*Mummu*	V: 548.
kaṣāru	V: 553.	*muškênum*	V: 551.
Khamtu	V: 542.	*Mušni*	V: 551.
Khandal	V: 542.	*Nagbu*	V: 545.
Khindil	V: 542.	*namaddu*	V: 544, 559.
kibatu	V: 545.	*namkaru*	V: 545.
kipru(m), kipratu(m)	V: 553, 599.	*namtallūm*	V: 548; IX: cxii.
Ku	V: 542.	*naspantu*	V: 584.
ku-ta-ni	V: 552.	*Nin-dar*	V: 544.
ku-ta-nu	V: 55.	*Nin-ib*	V: 544, 560.
kŭdanu(m)	V: 548.	NIRDA	V: 546.
ᵈ*Kurangu*	I: *274;* III: *391,*	נפש מת	V: 464.
	394; V: 569.		
Kuru	V: 52.	*Nu-bat-ti*	V: 542.
ᵈ*Lal(l)angu*	I: *274;* III: *391,*	NUM.ŠA.ḪU	V: 550.
	394; V: 569.	*Nurmu*	V: 545.
lama	V: 545.	PA.PA	V: 551.
lâma ṣābum...ikasadam		*piḫatu(m)/pāḫatu(m)*	V: 548.
māssu šallat u ṣû ḫaš	V: 577.	*piltum, pistum*	V: 546.
Lib(lib)u	V: 431, 547.	*pitū pūridā*	V: 551.
lip(p)u	VI: 427.	*pul(u)ḫ(t)u*	V: 547.
luḫmmu	V: 584.	*qâtu "hand"*	V: 377.
madâdu	V: 544, 559.	*qâtum*	V: 547, 548.
MAGRANU,		*râimu*	V: 544, 559.
MAGRATTU	V: *416,* 550.	*rāmanu(m)*	V: 548.
māḫāzu	V: 553, *588.*	*RÂSU*	V: 451, 550.
makasu	V: 545.	*sa mar-ti-a[n]n]i*	V: 552.
mala	V: 545.		

Sa-mi-da-ḫu-um	**V**: 577.
ṣabatu niati	**V**: 545.
ṣābum šû itbê-ma issakip enūssu sâ...u (qān) ṣinnassu uštaddi	**V**: 577.
sākiru	**V**: 545.
šalahu	**V**: 545.
ṣarbatu	**V**: *402*, 552.
sarru	**VII**: 197.
sebi	**V**: 542.
sekrītu	**V**: 552.
sekrtu	**V**: *402*, 522.
ša ḫaṭṭātim	**V**: 551.
Sha ↦ *Maru, mâr A-bi-í-ra-mu*	**V**: 543, 558.
šabattu	**II**: *25*, *95*.
šabattu	**V**: 544.
šadadu	**V**: 545.
šadahu	**V**: 545.
šadû	**V**: 549.
šahatu	**V**: 545.
šallaru	**V**: 545.
šamallū(m)	**V**: 547.
šanat	**V**: 545.
šarû	**V**: 546.
šibbu, šippu	**V**: 545.
šimê/ītān	**V**: 550.
Šitim-íd-da	**V**: 545.
šitu, šittu	**V**: 545.
shudadu	**V**: 544, 559.
šumma	**V**: 548, 549.
šusû II	**V**: *402*, 552.
sigbarrû	**V**: 584.
sikiltu	**V**: *440*, 549, 550; **IX**: lxxxviii.
sinništam na-wa-ri-tam	**V**: 577.
sippu	**V**: 545.
sirrimu	**V**: 552.
Suhatu	**V**: 379, 551.
summa (Amnarna)	**V**: 550.
surdú	**V**: 544, 559.
ta-mar-ti-a[n-n]i	**V**: 552.
tallu	**V**: 545.
Taluḫlu	**V**: 551.
támartu	**V**: 550; **VII**: 176.
**taqtul*	**V**: 490.
terḫatu(m)	**V**: 548.
Teretu	**V**: 542.
ṭu-ṭu	**V**: 544.
ṬULIMU: TULIMĀTU	**V**: 546.
Turdu	**V**: 545.
Uārsu, Urāšu	**V**: 547.
ubhâmu	**V**: 544.
ûm biblim	**V**: 577.
ûm tanaššû	**V**: 577.
ummanu	**V**: 545.
uppu	**V**: 545.
Ursânu	**V**: 542.
uṭṭatu	**V**: 545.
uzun	**V**: 545.
zabālu	**V**: 420, *490*, *538*, 552.
ziianatum	**V**: 546.

Amorite

Bêl Šadê	**V**: 160*(2)*, 162*(2)*, 383; **VIII**: 111.
ta/te	**V**: 383.

Arabic

ألخ	**V**: 400, 591.
الرواد	**III**: *7*; **VII**: 312.
ث	**V**: 400, 591.

جذرب **V**: 292, *415*, 586.
جَعَرَ **V**: 400, 591.
حَعَسَ **V**: 400, 591.
حَمِيَ **V**: 400, 591.
خَضر **V**: 308, 376, 589.
بَدَنٌ **V**: 588; **IX**: xc.
نفَل **V**: 587.
روحـ- **V**: 319.
سَحا **V**: 400, 591.
سنى **V**: 457*(3)*, 590*(3)*.
شعر **V**: 456, 589.
ظهر **V**: 585.
عَظيمَة **V**: 400, 591.
غَمّ **V**: 308, 376, 589.
فزع **V**: 308, 376, 589.
ف **V**: 400, 591.
فاق **V**: 400, 591.
فُعال **V**: 544, 587.
فَلّاح **V**: 308, 376, 589.
قَوِيَ **V**: 400, 591.
لحف **V**: 308, 376, 589.
لَوْن **V**: 543, 544, 572, 587.
ٱلْعَائِذ **V**: 483.
نَحا **V**: 400, 591.
نبع **V**: 308, 376, 589.
ودع **V**: 424*(2)*, 590*(2)*.
(و) فَارَ **V**: 400, 591.
وقح **V**: 400, 591.
'id **VI**: 493.
çánaxah **V**: *447*, 588.
ḏū **V**: 420, 591.
'urr **V**: 451.
'Im **V**: 593.
Jihād **V**: 145.
kaemlet **V**: *563*, 588.
KAF Ā (KFY) > KAFFA **V**: 594.
láu̯n **V**: *563*, 588.
mádaxa **V**: *567*, 589.
Malak(?) **V**: 590.
'otfe **V**: 52.
qānûn yḍ-Ḍiyâfeh **I**: 389.
samm **III**: *405;* **V**: 589, *644*.
silk **V**: 544, 560, *572*.
Ṭafwīḍ **V**: 145.
taḥállub **V**: *567*, 589.

táhamah V: *447*, 588.
tâjir V: 567, 588.
Tajlâ' V: *455*, 588.
te'ālāh V: 590.
'unṣur V: 590.
Waṣfs IV: 92, 507.
wathan V: 593.

Armenian

gišer V: *674*, 680.

Assyrian

A-bi-e-shu- V: 558.
A-ṭap-pu V: *424*, 557.
abâtum V: 570.
Abubu V: 566.
Abunnatu V: 565.
açîtu V: 565.
Adar V: 560
Agalla V: 568.
Âgarrūtu I: 184, 302; V: 556.
Ahu-ra-mazda V: 560.
albu V: 567.
alluḥappu V: 557.
Amaqar(r)una V: 444, 570.
AMIAUD V: 560.
Amqar(r)una V: *642*.
amûtu V: 565.
ana utūnim nadû VI: 467.
anduḫallatu III: *380;* V: 568.
annîtam (awīl)baddam uwa'er V: 577.
antalû V: 557.
Apsasû III: *371;* V: 564.
ARA V: 564.
aragub-minnabi V: 563.
ardatu V: 562.
ardu V: 562.
arḫu V: 563.
aršāšû V: 569.
Ašmanu V: 566.
Asipu I: 58, 104; V: 168.
Asîtu V: 559.
askari I: *185, 351;* V: 563.
assurri V: 570.
atmu V: 563.
Azûru V: 557.
ba'ālu V: 564.
badbad V: 568, *583*.
BAGĀRU V: 564.
baḫ V: 568.
bararitu I: *398;* V: 565.
bašu V: 565.
Basu V: 418, 486, 554*(2)*.
batiqânu V: 569.
battu V: 562.
bâsi V: 562.
batûlu V: 565.
be-dak V: 566.
bêlu V: 565.
birîš V: 568.
birku V: 565.
bûbûtu V: 565.
budulxu V: 567, *589*.
çaddu V: 565.
da'âlu V: 560.
dagâlu V: 564; VI: 467I(2).
dallalu V: 565.
dânu V: 565.
daurdu-taurtu V: 566.
dullulu V: 566
DURU V: 564.
Ebishum V: 558.
eçîttu V: 565.
edû V: 565.

egēru V: 564.
EN E-NU-ŠUB V: 564.
enšu V: 565.
epēšu V: 409, 557, 563, 564.
(ilat)Ereš-ki-gal V: 561.
êru V: 565.
esigu V: 564.
eṣimtu V: 568.
esirtu V: 568.
eṭirritu V: 566.
ga-li-duḫdu I: 247; V: 563.
galādu-galātu V: 561.
galau-kàs V: 563.
gamaru V: 565.
ġar-gud VII: 196.
Garidu V: 568.
giparu V: 566.
GIR-PAD-DU V: 568.
GIŠ V: 564.
giššu V: 565.
Guannakku V: 565.
GUNU-Signs V: 559.
Gurgurru V: 568.
ḫabûnu V: 561.
ḫaçânu V: 565.
ḫalla summati V: *423*, 569.
ḫamâmu V: 565.
ḫamâru V: 565.
ḫammu V: 568.
ḥammu V: 568.
ḫamû V: 565, 568.
ḥamu V: 568.
ḫamuštum V: 570*(2)*.
ḫardatu V: 565.
Ḫatta V: 569.
Ḫatti V: 569.
Ḫattu V: 569.
Ḫattum V: 569.
ḫinçu V: 308, 376, *589*.
Ḫu-ḫu-tar-ri, Ḫu-uḫ-tar-ri V: 560.
ḪUBULLU V: 564.
Ḫuruppati I: 215; V: 565.
ḫusârum V: 569.
i-ga-ad-di-mj-uš V: 566.
ja'artu V: 564.
ja' āru V: 564.
ja'ertu V: 564.
jâmútu V: 560.
ibizzû V: 566.
ÍKALLU V: 560.
iḳdu V: 564.
ikkaru V: 560.
ilam rašû V: 566.
Ilāni V: 568.
ILLURI: ILLULU I: 313; V: 567.
imduḫallatu III: *380;* V: 568.
imirtu V: 566.
Ina Mûši I: *398;* V: 563.
ipû V: 565.
IR V: 564.
irêšu III: *388;* V: *409*, 566.
išittu (pl. *inšâti)* V: 565.
ištu V: 565.
Isu V: 486, 554.
it-tam-ra-a-ak V: 566.
izêzum V: 570.
dKA.DI V: 570.
kabāsum V: 570.
kakku V: 560.
kalakku V: 557.
kalaku I: *351.*
kalaku V: 562.
kalmat V: 563, *588*.

kamâsu	V: 567.	mašâru	V: 560.	
Kamtum	V: 565.	mât A- **△田**	V: 559.	
kamunu	III: 371, 372, 383; V: 568.	mindema	V: 524, 558.	
kanâšu	V: 567.	mindidu	V: 560.	
karâbu	V: 565.	miṭpânu	I: 313; V: 567.	
Karâru	V: 562.	mu'irru	V: 568.	
kaṣâṣu	V: 564.	mu'iru	V: 568.	
Katâtu	V: 568.	mûr-nisqi	III: 376; V: 563.	
Ḳêpu	I: 269.	nabâsu	V: 565.	
KID-ni-e	III: 392; V: 563.	nablu	V: 565.	
KISAL	I: 423.	Nadânu	V: 556.	
(amêl)KUL - ḫêpû	V: 561.	naḫâšu	V: 565.	
kudûru	V: 557.	nalâšu (pres. inâluš)	V: 565.	
kunnâ	V: 564.	nalbânu, nalbantu, nalbattu	V: 569.	
kunnû	V: 564.	Nalbaš Šamê	V: 183,567.	
KUR.GI.ḪU	III: 371, 372, 383; V: 568.	namâru	V: 564.	
		nannabu	V: 565.	
"Kur.Kur	V: 566.	nâpalû	V: 565.	
kurkû	III: 371, 372, 383; V: 568.	napšu	I: 216; V: 567.	
		NAQBU	V: 542, 556.	
ḳursinnu	V: 568.	narâbu	V: 393, 565.	
kusarikku	III: 375; V: 563.	natânu	V: 556.	
Ḳutaru	V: 562.	naṭû	V: 561.	
lakû	V: 564.	Niknakku	V: 562, 579.	
lam iççûri çabâri	VI: 565.	Ninib-Ninurta	V: 564.	
lamûtânu	V: 565.	niqilpû	V: 565.	
lânu	V: 563, 588.	mûr-nisqui	V: 563.	
lardu	V: 560.	Ôdakôn	V: 567.	
lascar	I: 185, 351; V: 563.	aban PA	V: 564.	
li-ga	I: 247; V: 563.	padanû	V: 568, 583.	
lîlâtu	V: 565.	pâgu	V: 560.	
lišânu	V: 570.	paḫ	V: 568.	
LU-SU-PA-MEŠ	V: 560.	palûḏ	II: 85.	
madaktu	V: 396.	papaḫu	V: 564.	
magarru	V: 560.	pâru	V: 565.	
mar šipri	V: 563.	parû yarû	V: 568.	
marçu	V: 567.	pâtu	V: 567.	

pâṭu	**V**: 567.	*šanû*	**V**: 561.
**pêmu*	**V**: 565.	(amêl)šanû	**V**: 561.
piḫû	**IX**: xcix.	*šapâtu*	**V**: 565.
Pilurtu	**V**: 562.	*šapru*	**V**: 565.
pishannu	**V**: 559.	*ŠARĀPU*	**V**: 452, 566.
pisnuqû	**V**: 565.	*šâru*	**V**: 561.
pudendeum muliebre	**V**: 565.	*šarûru*	**V**: 561.
puru'um	**V**: 569.	*shaunkatu*	**V**: 560.
Puška	**V**: 561, 562.	*ŠE-BAR*	**V**: 557.
Qabah	**V**: 486, 554.	*ŠE-ZIR*	**V**: 557.
qamâçu	**V**: 567.	*šêmu*	**V**: 565.
qanânu	**V**: 562.	*šêrêti*	**V**: 561.
qarâšu	**V**: 565.	*Šerru*	**V**: 561.
qattu	**V**: 565.	*šêrtu*	**V**: 561*(3)*.
qiççu	**V**: 565.	*ši-pi ša ṭiṭi*	**V**: 561.
quluptu	**V**: 565.	*Šimêtan*	**V**: 565.
Rab-Šiṭirtê	**V**: 564.	*šina*	**V**: 561.
rabû	**V**: 452, 563.	*šinîtum*	**V**: 561.
ramku	**V**: 430, 563.	*šipat bit pašāri*	**V**: 564.
Raṣānu	**V**: 451, 562.	*Šišku*	**V**: 555.
rigmu	**V**: 564.	*šizbu*	**V**: 565.
Sagullatu:	**V**: 170, *440*.	*Šubtum*	**I**: *425;* **V**: 570.
ṣalme	**V**: 165.	*šum-ma alelu ta-ḫu-ú-ma raba-a ša-a tap-pa-i-šu us-sa-am-mi-iḫ*	**V**: 566.
sarâḫu	**V**: 565.	ŠUPAR	**V**: 561.
Sartu	**V**: 560.	(amêl)ŠUPARŠÂḲ(Û)	**V**: 561.
saru	**V**: 546.	*šušalšum*	**V**: 570.
sattakka	**V**: 396.	*sirdū abālu*	**V**: 562.
šem	**III**: *405;* **V**: *589, 644*.	*sirdū abālu:aplu*	**V**: 562.
ša-ra/BAR/ ša-a-ru	**V**: 561.	*siḫ-li-e*	**III**: *392;* **V**: 563.
Šariš	**V**: 561.	*Simkurru*	**V**: 565.
Šakāku	**V**: 561.	*šimmatu*	**III**: 405.
Šakāu	**V**: 562.	*SISINNU*	**III**: *379*.
Šaknu	**I**: *493, 494*.	*ṣîta rašû*	**V**: 566.
(amêl)ŠAḲŠUPP(BB)AR	**V**: 561.	*sittu*	**V**: 420.
šallaru	**V**: 557.	*subrum*	**V**: 570.
Šamala napṭur	**V**: 569.	*sûsapînu*	**V**: 565.
šaman ḫalṣa	**V**: 566.		

sussa V: *440*, 563.
ta-a-an V: 561.
TAG V: 568.
$^{d.}$Tagtug V: 564.
Tahrirtu V: *458*, 563.
Tahritu V: 563.
taḫtû V: 568, 583.
talîmu I: 210; V: 567.
tam-gi-ti V: 561.
tamêrtu V: 460, 564.
tamkaru V: 557, 567, *589*.
ṭap-pu V: 424, 557.
tapdû V: 568, *583*.
tratābu V: 564.
te-el-tum V: 561.
Têbiltu V: 561.
têl(i)tu V: 561.
têlu V: 561.
ti-'-u-tu V: 561.
ti-šit V: 561.
tiamat III: 365; V: 558.
tikpu I: 421.
tikpu III: *462*.
tikpu V: 562.
Timkallu V: 557.
^{amel}TU.BÎTI V: 561.
tû'amu V: 565.
Tup-šikku V: 557.
Ṭuppu II: *43;* V: 569, 570.
ubtaeru, uktainu V: 566.
ûlâ V: 560.
ulâlu V: 565.
Ullânu V: 562.
Uluskinnu V: 563.
unnīnu V: 583.
Upšāšû V: 569.
URBI II: 114; V: 570.
Uruku V: 555.
ushumgallu V: 560.
utukku, uttukku, utuku V: 567.
Varuna V: 560.
vomere V: 568.
xamâdu V: 567, *589*.
xarâpu V: 562.
Zaḫannu V: 566.
zaqapu V: *357*, 565.
ZARAḪ III: *381;* V: 568.
zâzu V: 565, 567, *597*.
zu'tu V: 564.

Babylonian

A + HA V: 573.
a-i-šir V: 576.
a-ši-ir V: 534.
a-šá VII: 214.
a-ši-ir V: 444, 550.
Abi Ummâni V: 575.
Adapa V: 566.
adudîlu III: *380;* V: 575.
Amêlu V: 575.
Ammatu^{m} V: 572.
Ammi-Satana V: 464.
Ana itti-šu I: 498; V: 575.
ana la ḫâzim rîga V: 564.
andinānu V: 577.
Anu V: 566.
Ašāru V: 573.
ashlaku V: 544, 559, 560, 572.
ba-ga-ni(-') V: 576.
Bakītu mušēnikṭu VI: 337.
BAR V: 575.
bittu V: 575.
buhâmu V: 572.

DAM-QAR **I**: *339*.
É-dub-ba **V**: 576.
GAB-RI **V**: 571.
gabraḫ **V**: 564.
Gala **V**: 577.
gar **III**: 422.
Gar.Ra **V**: 576.
Gemé **V**: 576.
GI-SA **I**: *424, 432*.
gišgalla-ki **II**: 264; **III**: 38, 50.
Giš **V**: 576.
GIŠ-UḪ^{ki} **V**: 574.
Guzalû **VI**: 67, 151; **IX**: cxxxix, cxliii.
'mq **V**: 444.
ilku **V**: 566.
îlu in Divine Names **V**: 573.
iškārum **V**: 576.
ittallak niāti **V**: 577.
k/ḫiššātum **V**: 550, 618.
ki-nj-nir-ki **II**: 264; **III**: 38.
ki-nu-nir-ku **II**: 264; **III**: 38, 50.
Kikkisu **V**: 571.
Kikkisu-GAB.RI **V**: 571.
kuruppu **IX**: cxliii.
lânu **V**: 543, 572, *587*.
Liqûm **V**: 575.
Magus **V**: 575.
Merḫu **VII**: 263.
mindi **V**: 543, 572.
Minîtu **V**: 575.
Mišannîtu(m) **V**: 572.
mašil **V**: 575.
mišil ûmi **V**: 575.
'mq **V**: 534, 550, 576.
Muḫḫû **V**: 575.
Mummu **V**: 566.
muškênum **I**: *190;* **V**: 575.
mûšu mašil **V**: 575.
nadītu **I**: *199*.
namru **III**: *351*.
naẓārum **V**: 576.
Niknalthu **V**: 573.
NIN-IP **III**: 776; **V**: 297; **V**: 574.
niš **I**: *510;* **V**: 574; **VI**: 109; **VIII**: 117; **IX**: cxxxix.
nupâru **V**: 544, *587*.
pirku **V**: 446, 569.
pishannu **V**: 544, 572.
pûḫu **V**: 394, 562.
resh sharri bel piqitti **I**: *190*.
Sal-Zikrum **I**: *187, 217*.
sandanakum **V**: 396.
saru **V**: 546.
še-ga dingir "gal-gal" **V**: 397; **IX**: xcviii.
ŠES-AB^{ki}*-MI* **V**: 575.
shilu **VI**: 93.
Šiqlu **V**: 576.
šita **I**: 312; **V**: 563.
ŠHU.GE$_4$ **V**: 576.
Šu'âlu **V**: 572.
šu/ša **V**: 569.
Šurru **V**: 573.
Shût-Abni: **V**: 182.
šutapú **V**: 543, 572.
šuturu **I**: *273;* **V**: 567; **IX**: cxliii.
Sissiktu **III**: 645, 646.
SU **V**: 576.
TA *ša kīma* A *ītenerrubu* **V**: 577.
Tirhatum **I**: 219; **V**: 577.
^{amel}TU.BÎTI **V**: 561, 573.

tuktû	**I**: *480;* **V**: 544.
ubhâmu	**V**: 572.
ukarîna	**III**: *395;* **V**: *458;* **VI**: *304, 314, 355.*
umâm	**V**: 572.
umâmu	**V**: 544, 559. 572.
Uṣurtu	**V**: 575.
veadar	**I**: *399.*
Zuḫaru	**I**: 185; **V**: 573.

Canaanite

bêth ḫubûri	**V**: 382; **VI**: 543, 546.
Ḫapši	**V**: 382.
hm	**V**: 382.
Ḥofšî	**V**: 382*(2);* **VII**: 170.
ḫpṯ	**I**: *188;* **V**: 382.
na-ʿa-ru-na	**V**: 382.
naʿarôn	**V**: 382.
taqtulū(na)	**V**: 383.
תהתפך כסא מלכה	**V**: 383.
yaqtula	**V**: 383.

Coptic

ⲁⲉⲓⲱ	**V**: 313.
ⲁϩⲟ	**V**: 369.
ⲁⲛ	**V**: 311.
ⲁⲛⲛⲉϥ–	**V**: 371.
ⲇⲉⲗ	**V**: 313.
ⲉⲃⲟⲗⲟⲩⲇⲉ	**V**: 368.
ⲉⲃⲟⲗⲟⲩⲧⲉ	**V**: 368.
ⲉϫⲱ	**V**: 370.
ⲉⲕⲓⲁ	**V**: 369.
ⲉⲡⲡⲁ	**V**: 319, 359, 367.
ⲉⲡⲡⲟ	**V**: 319, 359, 367.
ⲉⲣⲉ–	**V**: 363, 368, 370.
ⲉⲧⲁ	**V**: *365,* 370.
ϫⲓⲟⲩⲁⲓ̈ϣ	**V**: 369.
ϫⲟⲟⲩ	**V**: 369.
ϫⲱⲣⲡ	**V**: 368
ϩⲁⲇⲱ⸗	**V**: 323.
ϩⲁϫⲛ–	**V**: 323, 369.
ϩⲏⲧ	**V**: 319.
ϩⲓⲱⲙⲉ	**V**: 371.
ϩⲙⲟⲧ	**V**: 311.
ⲓ (feminine form with)	**V**: 359.
ϭ ⲁ ⲗ	**V**: 368.
ⲙⲓⲕⲉ[SF]	**V**: 370.
ⲙⲓⲛⲉ	**V**: 368.
ⲙⲓⲛⲓ	**V**: 368
ⲙⲟⲩⲧ	**V**: 313.
ⲙⲡⲁⲧⲉ–.	**V**: 363, 369.
ⲙⲡⲁ̄ⲧ̄ϥ	**V**: 363, *368.*
ⲙⲡⲉ	**V**: 367.
ⲙⲧⲟⲛ	**V**: 315.
ⲛ̇	**V**: 311.
ⲛ̄	**V**: 370.
ⲛⲁⲉⲓⲱ	**V**: 313.
ⲛⲁⲩ	**V**: 369.
ⲛ̄ϭⲓ	**V**: 370.
ⲛⲉⲙ	**V**: 314.
ⲛⲙ	**V**: 314.

ⲛⲟⲩⲟⲑϩ **V**: 369.
ⲛϣⲓⲧ[S] **V**: 370.
ⲛϫⲉ **V**: 370.
ⲟϩⲉ **V**: 319.
ⲟⲩϩⲉ **V**: 319.
ⲟⲩⲣⲟ **V**: 319, 359, 367.
ⲱⲡⲓϣ **V**: 369.
ⲟϯ **V**: 313.
ⲟⲩⲱⲥϥ **V**: 313.
ϣϥⲧ **V**: 370.
šft **V**: *353*, 370, *598*.
ϣⲓⲛⲉ **V**: 318.
ϣⲙⲱⲟⲩ[B] **V**: 370.
ϣⲟⲗ **V**: 368.
ϣⲟⲙ[SB] **V**: 370.
ϣⲱⲙⲉ[S], pl. ϣⲙⲟⲩⲓ[S] **V**: 370.
ⲥⲓⲟⲧ **V**: 368.
ⲥⲱⲧⲉⲙ **V**: 311.
ⲥⲫⲣⲁⲛϣ **V**: 371.
ⲥⲫⲣⲁⲡϣ **V**: 368.
ϯⲟⲩⲟ(ⲉ)ϊ **V**: 369.
ⲧⲓϧⲓ **V**: 369.
ⲧⲙⲡⲥⲟⲡ **V**: 369.
ⲧ̄ⲛⲛⲟⲟⲩ **V**: 369.
ϭⲱϣ **V**: 314.

Cypriote

dṓkoi **V**: 621, 637.
dawánoi **V**: 621, 637.

Egyptian

A-lk=k **V**: 358.
âaâ **III**: 403; **V**: 342.
ʿfꜣy **III**: 400.
'I **V**: 363.
'iḫt **I**: *377*.
ꜣinʿ **V**: 308, 376, *589*.
'Inn **V**: 343.
'Iw **III**: 717; **V**: 366.
ỉw.f ḥr sḏm **V**: 366.
'IW-F [ḤR] TM SḎM **V**: 343.
ANX **V**: 409.
AU, Ptolemiac use of **V**: 321.
Bꜣt **V**: 346.
Biꜣ **V**: 349.
bn **V**: 325.
ḏbꜣ **V**: 221.
dbn **I**: *438;* **V**: 361.
dbt **V**: 357.
df* **V: 325.
Didi **I**: *296;* **V**: 357.
ḏmỉ
ḏnf **V**: 357.
drt (ḏrt) **V**: 357.
ḏt **V**: *349,* 357.
edelu **V**: 425, 426.
FAU, FU, Late Pronuciation of **V**: 321.
FENKHU **V**: 347.
Fnḫ-w̯ **V**: 308, 376, *589*
FU, value of **V**: 321.
gm-w̯ **V**: 308, 376, *589*.
ḥ **V**: 361.
ḥm **V**: 353.
ḥmt **V**: 353.

ḤQ3/N/ÌŚNNWŚ TYḪRŚ **V**: 353.
Ḥry-ḏbʿ **V**: 352.
ḥt **V**: 353.
Ḥtp-di-Nsw **V**: 353.
ḤU **V**: 207, 208, 353.
hæa-ab-ši **V**: 353.
ḫfty **V**: 353, *370*, *598*.
ʿ3 **V**: 313, 345.
ḥ3m **V**: 308, 376, *589*.
ʿg3yn3 **V**: 345.
ḥʿpr **III**: 177.
Ḥike' **V**: 207, 208, 331*(2)*.
ḫnğ **V**: 308, 376,*589*.
Ḥnn-nśwt **V**: 353.
Ḫnt-ḥn-nfr **II**: 272.
ḥōne **III**: *169*.
Hor-m aχu **V**: 352.
ḥotep **V**: 353.
HP **V**: 352.
ḫptš **V**: 353.
ḫr tp, tp m3ʿ **V**: 323.
ʿrbṯ **V**: 345.
ht **V**: 352.
Ḥtp-Di-Nsw **V**: 351, 364.
ʿwn **V**: 325.
HWY **V**: 351, 380, 538.
i 3wt **V**: 344.
i wt **V**: 344.
'Imy **V**: 343.
'in-it.f **VII**: 71.
išf/nšf **V**: 324, 379.
iṯ iṇ **V**: 344.
'Iṯ m **V**: 323.
is'sḏ.f **V**: 343.
iwiw'f'sdm **V**: 344.
Iwn **III**: *191*.
ǰʿ **V**: 324, 379.
ǰ̌ʿ **V**: 324.
jʿ **V**: 325.
jř **V**: 324, 379.
kek-t **III**: 366.
Khefren **V**: 354.
k̲h̲elemŷ **III**: 645.
Khnumt Nefer-Hezt **V**: 301.
Kjj-bm **I**: 185.
kns **III**: 399.
ktt **V**: 305.
Kūr **V**: 356.
lubarita **V**: 315.
m **V**: 364.
m-ra-ya-na **V**: 348*(2)*.
m-s3 **V**: 348
m-znw **V**: 367.
mʿb3 **V**: 308*(2)*, 376*(2)*, *589*.
māfka **V**: 313.
m3ʿḫrw **V**: 347*(2)*.
Maneros **V**: 347.
Mḏḥ **V**: 349.
mdw-nṯr **V**: 224; **VIII**: 131.
mdw-ntr **V**: 349.
men **V**: 311.
Mhr **V**: 347.
Mḥw **V**: 349.
Min as Ithyphallic transcription of Ammon or Horus **V**: 312.
mnd.t **III**: 399.
mniw **V**: 347.
Mnṯyw **II**: *150*.
msḥ **V**: 550.
Mškb **V**: 347.

mtw= **V**: 364.
m̱tw= **V**: 349.
N ʿrn **I**: 319; **III**: 132.
n mt n ś.t.. **V**: 362.
n-msḏwt **V**: 367.
nau **V**: 360.
nenau **V**: 360.
ʿnḫ-Snwsrt **II**: 269.
Nḥḥ **V**: 349,*357*.
nru **V**: 317.
nsw **IX**: cxxxix.
nṯr ʿ3 wr (n) š 3ʿ ḫpr **V**: 351.
NTY **V**: 350.
P3ḪR ḪN' IḪNW/N N HNW ḪN' **II**: 272; **V**: 310.
pḥ-r-nfr **I**: 271.
P-ḥr-ntr **V**: 346.
pr **V**: 366.
pts **V**: 325.
pzḫ **V**: 308, 376, *589*.
q'bt **V**: 402; **VI**: 12.
qnbt **VII**: 10.
qri(qəỉ) **V**: 324, 379.
ʿr **V**: 308, 376, *589*.
rḫḫjj.t **III**: *704*.
rkḥ wr **I**: 404.
Rnpt
RPʿT **II**: *44*.
ruhiu replaces "*ahu* the god" **V**: 317.
rχ **V**: 317.
"man" *s* **V**: 305.
s.t "woman" **V**: 305.
s.t-ḥm.t **V**: 305.
SAI' **V**: 207, 208, 353.
sčỉ **V**: 324, 379.
šd **V**: 324, 379.
sḏf3-tryt **V**: 354.
śḏm.f **V**: 354*(2)*, 364, 365.
śḏm.n.f **V**: 354*(3)*, 364, 365.
set-em-ra **V**: 360.
ṣft **II**: *498*.
šbtyw **V**: 221.
šd **V**: 324.
šet **I**: 417.
Šms-ỉb **V**: 355.
šw **V**: 355.
sm **V**: 325.
smr **III**: *368, 381;* **VII**: 79.
sš n sʿnḫ **I**: *217;* **V**: 355.
sti **V**: 324, 379.
sti **V**: 324.
t ḫyr t, tḫyr (.t) **V**: 356*(2)*.
Ta Ṯeḥenu **II**: 266; **V**: 335.
t3ḥtpr **III**: *516*.
ṯakapu **V**: 357, *565*.
təḥ **V**: 324, 379.
teken(n)u **I**: *374*.
tm **V**: 324, 379.
tm **V**: 324.
Tp m3ʿ **V**: 323.
tr **V**: 324, 379.
ṯsm **V**: 357.
Tybi **I**: *401*.
û **V**: 362, *368*.
uḥat **II**: 264.
ʿprw **I**: 264.
Uta **I**: 393.
W 3 w 3 t: **II**: 271.
wbə **V**: 324, 379.
wbə **V**: 324.
wdd **III**: 399.

wǰ' V: 325.
WNN V: 346.
χatte II: 262.
χet II: 262.
y V: 305.

Elamite

ka-ka$_4$-ia-še V: 601, 677.
d.GAL V: 238.
ḫawir sukkir V: 601.
Ma-uk-ti-ti V: 544, 601.
Maḫâru V: 448.
Nazâza V: 449.
šara- V: 601.

Ethiopic

azzáza V: *567,* 597.
enza V: *407,* 597.
kanfar V: *553,* 599.
mâ'bal V: 308, 376, *589.*
šft V: *353,* 370, 598.
tektô (ትክቶ) I: *480;* V: 544.

Etruscan

ais V: *641,* 679.
aisar V: *641,* 679.

Hittite

A.SI.RUM V: 609.
a-a-pi V: 402, 615.
akugallit V: 608.
akuwakuwaš III: *374, 381;* V: 607.
^{lú}ALAN.KAxUD V: 616.
^{lú}ALAN.ZÚ V: 616.
alpash V: 608.
alpu- V: 616.
aluzinnu V: 616.
alwanzena- V: 616.
arkam-ma(n) V: 402, 615.
ašta V: 616.
awan V: 607.
barganula V: 611.
benna I: 345.
Benna V: 606.
dalugnula V: 611.
dammeli- V: 616.
dampu- V: 616.
dannareššar V: 616.
duddu- V: 607.
duddumili V: 607.
duddumiya(h) V: 607.
és-re-tum V: 609.
Essebu V: 604.
$^{\text{(dug)}}$GAL V: 616.
genuš(š)uš V: 616.
genus(š)i V: 616.
gurta- V: 403, 615.
ḫa-an-za-aš-ša V: 610.
ḫa-aš-ša V: 610.
hapatis V: 609.
har(k)- V: 607.
ḫar-aš-zi V: 613.
haraš, haranaš V: 608.
^{giš}*ḫarau* V: 616.
^{DUG}*ḫarši* V: 402, 615.
ḫaušwai III: *394;* V: 611.
ḫatukă V: 609.
ḫatuki-s V: 609.
hawantiš V: 608.
hīla-, ḫēla- V: 402, 615.
HUB.BI I: 283; V: 612.
hukanzi V: 607.
ḫuttulli- V: 402, 615.
i-sar-ti- I: *199;* V: 609.

ia-	V: 610.
ipulli-	V: 608.
irmalanza	III *400;* V: 608.
irmalas	III *400;* V: 608.
irmal(l)iya	III *400;* V: 608.
irmas	III *400;* V: 608.
ishatar	V: 607.
išhaš	V: 607.
kalleš-	V: 402, 615.
^{GIŠ}*kalmuṣ*	I: 283; V: 612.
-kan	V: 612*(2),* 613.
kariulli-	V: 402, 615.
KASKAL	V: 614.
^{d}KASKAL.KUR	II: 256; VII: 153.
kāsu	V: 616.
katral	V: 605.
Katta(n)	V: 606.
kinun	V: 610, *672.*
Ko	V: 604.
Korud	III: *377.*
Korud	V: 606.
kranna	I: *362.*
Kranna	V: 606.
kullupi-	V: 402, 615.
kume	I: *206.*
Kume	V: 606.
kunkunuzzi	I: *286;* V: 608.
kupaḫi	V: 403, 615.
kupaḫil	I: 314; V: 429, 448, 608.
kurtal	V: 403, 615.
kutrus	I: 489, 511, 608.
kuttar	V: 608.
kuwanna(n)	I: *299;* V: 611.
kwis kwis	V: 610.
lappaš	V: 608.
lappiya-	V: 403, 615.
Lustra-Sultra	V: 606.
malta-	V: 608.
maniyah-	V: 608.
maišš(ya)	V: 403, 615.
memal	V: 607.
meranda	V: 607.
mitgaimi-	V: 613.
mugai	V: 608.
muwat(t)alli-	V: 403, 615.
naḫšariya-	V: 403, 615.
napṭarti-	I: *199;* V: 609.
nekuz	V: 616.
Oa	V: 606.
Oùá	V: 606.
Owa	V: 606.
paga	I: *362.*
Paga	V: 606.
pai-	V: 607.
palša- = KASKAL?	V: 614.
palwas	V: 608.
pankur	V: 616.
pankuš(š)i	V: 616.
pa^{n}ta, pa^{n}tă	V: 613.
Paras	III: *376;* V: 610.
parsiya-	V: 608.
pehar(k)-	V: 607.
pupus	I: *216;* V: 608.
ros	I: *206.*
Ros	V: 606.
rume	I: *206.*
Rume	V: 606.
salik-	V: 609.
Sbida	V: 606.
šak(u)ruwai	V: 614.
šalli-, šalliš	V: 403, 615.
šalliš	V: 605
šani/a-	V: 612.
šanna-	V: 609; IX: xcix.
šannapili	V: 612.

šap- **V**: 616.
šek- / šak- **I**: 506, 515; **V**: 616.
šenah(h)aš **I**: 314.
šenah(h)aš **V**: 607.
ŠID **V**: 616.
šuel **V**: 607.
šumanza **V**: 607.
šuppi-wašhar **III**: *393;* **V**: 611.
šuwaya- **V**: 614.
sikiltu(m) **I**: *307;* **V**: *550.*
siyanta **VI**: 64.
Skanna **V**: 606.
suppalas **V**: 608.
suppariya- **V**: 609.
ta **V**: 606, 609.
tuḫḫeššar, tuḫš- **V**: 616.
takiya **V**: 609.
takku **V**: 609.
tamais **V**: 609.
TAR **V**: 612.
tarkummāi-,tarkummiya- **V**: 403, 615.
tarpiš **V**: 460, 616.
tepawaš- **V**: 607.
tepnu- **V**: 607.
tepuš **V**: 607.
Trogla **V**: 606.
tuekka-, tukka- **V**: 403, 615.
tukka- **V**: 608.
tuwarsa- **V**: 403, 615.
uppeššaran **V**: 607.
uwatar **V**: 609.
wa- **V**: 607.
waggašnuanzi **V**: 607.
wantai- **V**: 608.
wappu **V**: 609.
wašpaš **I**: *280;* **V**: 616, *674.*
we- **V**: 607.
wetti meyani **V**: 616.
witti meyani- **V**: 612.
wiyana- **V**: 403, 615.
yukas **V**: 609.
zapzagai-, zapzi/aki- **V**: 403, 615.
zapzakai- **V**: 611.
zeri **V**: 616.
zinnuk **V**: 616.

Hurrian

Ḫupšu *(Nuzi)* **V**: 618.
kirezzi* **V: 380, 618.
maku **V**: 550, 618.
muš- **V**: 618.
arya- **V**: 680.
בגדאנא **VI**: 664.
daha- **V**: 680.

Latin

acceptilatio **I**: 504.
actutum **V**: 670.
alaceri **V**: 670.
altero **V**: 670.
anus **V**: *654, 655,* 670, *672(2), 673, 674.*
Arma Virumque Cano **II**: *418.*
Atque(Ac) **V**: *651, 658,* 670, *671, 673.*
Bigatus: **I**: 450.
bucina **V**: *645,* 670.
Consortium Omnis Vitae **I**: *221.*
cornx **V**: 670.
corvus **V**: 670.
Custodia **I**: 309, 503.
Custodia **I**: *503.*
delectare **V**: 671.
delicatus **V**: 671.
deliciæ **V**: 671.
Donatio Mortis Causa **I**: *503.*

dulcis V: *638*, 670, 671, *672*.
essem V: 671*(2)*.
et V: *651*, *658*, *670*, 671, *673*.
follis V: *445*, 671.
gollere I: 181; V: 671, *673*.
haud V: *654(2)*, 671*(2)*.
hinc V: 671, *672*.
Horrea I: *308*, *309*, *503*, *505*.
in V: *648*, 671.
inde V: *671*, 672.
Interregnum I: *502*.
Invictus V: 270.
ipse V: 314.
ius sacrum: I: 468; V: 159.
Laographia I: *482*.
leitourgia I: *191*, *193*.
Lituus I: *283*.
Manus Tuas VI: 476.
menta V: 672.
mittere V: 672.
modo V: 672.
num V: *610*, 672.
nunc V: *610*, 672.
nurus V: *654*, *655*, *670*, *672(2)*, *673*, *674*.
omnis V: *654*, *655*, *670*, *672(2)*, *673*, *674*.
otium V: 672.
Parva Ne Pereant: I: 450.
Patria potestas I: *211*, *500*.
ploro V: 672.
pollex V: *638*, *670*, 672.
pro V: 673*(2)*.
que V: *651*, *658*, *670*, *671*, 673.
re V: 673*(2)*.
sed enim V: 673.
sine V: 673.
solus V: *654*, *655*, *670*, *672(2)*, 673, *674*.
son V: *654*, *655*, *670*, *672(2)*, 673.
sons V: 673.
stercus V: *649*, *658*, 673.
Summum Bonum VI: 454.
superstitio V: *649*, 673.
Sutor Resutus: I: 279.
Sutor Supra Crepidam: I: 278.
Syntaxis I: *482*.
temerare V: 674.
temre V: 674.
Terra Marique I: *450*.
titillare V: *659*, 674.
tormentum V: *655*, 674.
uer sacrum V: 269.
uesper V: 674, *680*.
uespillo I: *280*; V: *616*, 674.
usque V: 674.
usucapio: I: 504.
uxor V: *654*, *655*, *670*, *672(2)*, *673*, 674.
vitium V: 674.

Lihyanic

b V: 679.

Lithuanian

be- V: *675*.

Luvian, Luwian

arkammana- V: 402, 615.
lappi(ya) V: 403, 615.
mitgaimi V: 403, 615.
muwat(t)alli- V: 403, 615.

tarkummiya- **V**: 403, 615.
winiyant- **V**: 403, 615.
wiyana- **V**: 403, 615.

Lydian

Μυσός **V**: 678 (See corrections pg.)
Τεγοῦν **V**: 678 (See corrections pg.)

Mandaic

האנאתה **V**: 679.

Minoan

A_2-Lu Jaluka **V**: 619.

Mycenaean

120 GRANUM **V**: 622.
damokoro **V**: 621.
ifo(s) **V**: 622.
ὁ χακεὺϝ ὁ **V**: 620.
pa-wo-ke **V**: 621.
re-wo **V**: 625.
sw **V**: 622.

Persian

گون ژنده **V**: 675.
گون ژند **V**: 675.
abiš nāviyā āha **V**: 677.
ka-ka$_4$-ia-še **V**: 601, 677.
amuθa **V**: 675.
apariyāya **V**: 675.
Artācā Brazmaniy **V**: 677.
arātāc brazmaniya **V**: 676.
aruvastam…niyasaya **V**: 675.
āšyāne, āšyān **V**: 676.
avahyaradiy̆ **V**: 675.
bi- **V**: 675.
dačaram **V**: 676.
drauga **V**: 677.
(ha) mē **IV**: 49; **V**: 678.
hacā darš^{a}m^a **V**: 675.
kunautiy **V**: 676.
mām kāma **V**: 676.
mariyan **V**: 675.
mātya **V**: 677.
niyaθ̆ārayam **V**: 676.
nyāka **V**: 676.
nyrkčšmy **V**: 676.
pādšāh **V**: 675.
patiyāvahayiy **VII**: 370.
rāz **V**: 676.
sikaba[+]uda **V**: 676.
taumā **V**: 675.
θaramiš **V**: 676.
θrd- **V**: 676.
ufraštadiy **V**: 675.
ušabārim **V**: 675.
yakā- **V**: 676, 677.
yār **V**: 676.
zθr **V**: 676.
zxrwb **V**: 676.

Phoenician

-d-n **V**: 197.
'tb 'l **V**: 303, 523.
Φοῖνιξ **V**: 308, 376, *589*.
qart- **V**: 403, 615.
yqtl 'nk **V**: 522; **VIII**: 119.
אזרם **V**: 522.
אדלן **V**: 522.
gbl **V**: 522.
אש **V**: 522.

Punic

hkkbm 'l **V**: 523; **VI**: 275.

Sanskrit

KṢI- **V**: 659.
mlecchati **V**: *643*.
शकृत् *(śakiŕt)* **V**: 649, 658, *673*.
śṛṇóti **V**: 676.
यकृत् *(yakŕit)* **V**: 649, 658, *673*.

Semitic (includes Northwest)

א, interchange of
with ה **V**: 375.
'by **V**: 379.
*/awa/ **V**: 379.
bny **V**: 325.
BRḎL, B(A)RZ(E)L **V**: 382.
bṣʿ **V**: 325.
d(w)r **V**: 324, 379.
dlḥ **V**: 324, 379.
dm(m) **V**: 324, 379.
d(w)r **V**: 324.
ft* **V: 324, 379.
GBN* **V: 380, *552*.
גְּבִינָה **V**: 380.
ה, interchange of
with א **V**: 375.
ḪBR* **V: 420.
hemzah-h **VIII**: 122.
ḥm **V**: 325.
ʿwl **V**: 325.
HWY **V**: 351, 380, 538.
ʿz(z) **V**: 325.
iau **V**: 375.
išf / nšf **V**: 324.
kalû **V**: 544, 578.
krz **V**: 380, 618.
*mḫṣ/*mḫš* **V**: 378.
מן חם ועד חוט **V**: 381.
nsk **V**: 324, 379.
*/ð/ **V**: 379.
pṯs **V**: 325.
qry **V**: 324, 379.
qtl **V**: 381.
šd **V**: 324, 379.
שְׁחֹר **V**: 379.
שְׁחִי **V**: 379.
šr **V**: 324, 379.
št **V**: 324, 379.
ת **V**: 380.
ת Conjungtion **V**: 372.
ṭp **V**: 325.
Trg-nns **VI**: 64.
Ṯrg-ṯṯs **VI**: 64.
wbl **V**: 324, 379.
zʿ* **V: 324, 379.

Slavic

*lozà` **V**: 676.

South Arabian

mṯkḥ **V**: 536, 596.
nq't **V**: 596.
rġm mny **V**: 596.
wgm **V**: 596.

Sumerian

á - s ì g- g e (á - s ì g) **V**: 584.
áma, ame, âm **III**: *467*; **V**: 583.
ANŠE.KUR.RA **V**: 584.
Ari **VI**: 140.

ARÛTU I: 210; V: 583.
aš-tân V: 444, 581.
á-sìg-ge(á-sìg) I: 321.
azalak I: *273,* V: *456.*
azu with value z u_x VII: 271.
bad-bad V: *568,* 583.
balag V: 605.
Bar V: 524, 525,581.
bît šipti V: 581.
DAM-QAR I: *339.*
di-ir-ga(ki-ir-ga) V: 584.
Dugud VII: 271; IX: cxliii.
dum-dam-za V: 584.
DUN III: *365.*
É-NU-ŠUB V: 181.
É-SAL III: *467.*
EN E-NU-ŠUB V: 581*(2).*
en(n)a V: 581.
'gilib V: 544, 578.
giš-ka-an-na V: 165.
giš-erin V: 584.
giš-ti V: 165.
Giš-Xar: V: 182; VIII: 131.
^{giš}*az-gú* V: 584*(2).*
gú I: *425;* VII: 272.
g̃ul-gik V: 581.
gur I: *421.*
^{ú}KI.^{d}NANNA V: 584.
ITU ŠE.GU(R).KUD V: 583.
ḳa I: *421.*
KA.TAB V: 584.
KA-KA-SI-GA V: 566, 574.
KI.SU_7 V: 584; VII: 212.
KI.UD VII: 271.
KIMA V: 583.
kislaḫ V: 583.
kisurru (kišurru) V: 580; VI: 550.
KÙ.GI III: 403.
kuš$_x$ (=IŠ), kuš$_x$-su V: 584.
lu-ḫu-um-ma V: 584.
mašatku III: *467.*
mu-an-na I: *401;* V: 568, 583.
muru$_x$ = (IM.DUGUD), an-muru$_x$ V: 584.
nam III: *373;* V: 581.
Našbaṭu III: 389; V: 581*(2).*
NIN-DINGIR V: 584.
NIRDA V: 583.
num-mu-su IX: cxliii.
sa I: *425;* VII: 272.
sag-dib V: 375.
Sal V: 397.
Ṣamāru V: 581.
šag-dib V: 562, 579.
ŠANDANAKU I: *253;* V: 583.
šanešu V: 584.
šarti enzi III: *375;* V: 583.
šartu III: *375;* V: 583.
shatammu I: *190.*
šaṭāru I: *233;* V: 571.
šipat bit pašāri V: 581
šita I: 312; V: 580.
ŠUTUR I: *273;* V: 567; IX: cxliii.
si-ni-tum V: 579; IX: xciii.
síg-bar-ra(sig$_7$-bar-ra) V: 584.
sìg-úz III: *375;* V: 583.
SISINNU III: *369;* V: 561, 575.
sur-ru V: 544, 578.
tik V: 580.
tu III: *373;* V: 581.

Tuku **V**: 568.
UGULA **V**: 584.
UKKIN-ŠUB **V**: 583.
*[ú]munzur **V**: 584.
unu (áb-ku) **V**: 347.
ur-tur-ri **V**: 581.
URINNU **III**: *369;* **V**: 575.
URÚ.ki **III**: *149;* **VII**: 272.
UTTUKU **I**: *273;* **V**: 567; **IX**: cxliii.
ZAGSAL, ZAGMIN **V**: 584.
ZAMEN **V**: 584.

Syriac

[illegible] **V**: 530.
[illegible] **V**: 436, 531.
'amad (Stem) **V**: 530.
gêr **V**: 305.
[illegible] **V**: 529.
[illegible] **VI**: 501, 531.
sâưpâ **V**: 531.
šautâphâ **V**: 530.
שׁוּתָּפָא **V**: 543, 572.
síftâ **V**: 531.
V: 436, 531.

Ugaritic

[illegible] **V**: 535.
[illegible] **V**: 535.
abn ṣrp **V**: 537.
Adanu **V**: 539.
'ahbt ṯr t'rk **V**: 535.
'aḫt 'rš mdw **V**: 537.
'aḥth **V**: 537.
akrt **V**: 537.
'al **V**: 535.
'Al'iyn b'l **V**: 537.
'ablm **V**: 537.
'amr **V**: 537.
'an **V**: 536.
'ank **V**: 536.
'šdk **V**: 535.
Āširu **V**: 537.
Asīru **V**: 537.
'atn **V**: 537.
'tbd **V**: 535.
'aṯt **V**: 535.
b'dn ksl ṯṯbr **V**: 535.
b'lṣ 'lṣm **V**: 535.
b'mq **V**: 534, *550.*
ben-'āmāh **V**: 539.
betulah **V**: 534.
b'mq **V**: 444.
bht **V**: 535.
blt **V**: 535; **VI**: 271.
bmdgt br nrt **V**: 535.
bmm' **V**: 535.
bmt **V**: 537.
bnš mlk **I**: *258.*
bntb pš' **V**: 537.
brd **V**: 403, 536.
ברך **V**: 413, 537.
bšlḥ **V**: 535.
bṯbrn qnh **V**: 535.
btrbš **V**: 535.
byrdm 'arṣ **V**: 535.
חלב **V**: 539.
db'at **V**: 416, 533.
db'atk - qrn db'atk **V**: 537.

dbḥ dnt **V**: 535.
derek **V**: 534.
dǵṯ **V**: 197, 535, 536.
dll **V**: 535.
ḍmr **V**: 535.
dmt **VI**: 355.
drkt **V**: 417, 534.
dtn **V**: 533.
gh **V**: 535.
gl **V**: 537.
GLMT **V**: 533.
gm sḥ **V**: 537.
gmr hd **V**: 537.
ğmrm **V**: 534.
GPNM **V**: 533.
ǵprt **V**: 537.
ġr **V**: 536.
gt **I**: *258.*
h **V**: 536.
ḥ **V**: 536.
ḥbš **V**: 537.
ʿdb ủḫry mt ydh **V**: 535.
ʿdt ʾilm ṯlṯh **V**: 537.
*ʿẹrẹ <*ʿisrayh* **V**: 537.
hll bʿl **V**: 537.
ḫlq **V**: 537.
hm **V**: 539.
ḫmdrt **V**: 537.
ʿmmym **V**: 537.
ʿmq **V**: 403, 536, 537.
ʿnṭ **V**: 535.
ḫptr **V**: 576.
ḫptš **V**: 532.
ʿqbm **V**: 537.
ht **V**: 535.
ḥtk **V**: 535.
ḥtl **V**: 402, 615.
HWY **V**: 351, 380, 538.
ḥzt **V**: 535.
ʾib **V**: 535.
ỉbnkl **V**: 192*(2).*
ʾišdk: ʿmy pʿnk tlsmn ʿmy twtḥ ʾišdk **V**: 537.
iṯ **V**: 536.
ʾiṯl **V**: 536.
kdd **V**: 305.
kḥṯ **V**: 537.
kmn **V**: 537.
kpt **V**: 533.
krk **V**: 537.
krtn **V**: 537.
ktp **V**: 195.
KTR **V**: 536.
ʿlk bd nʾiṯṯ **V**: 535.
lm ʾank **V**: 535.
lnḥt **V**: 535.
luzzi **I**: *260.*
lymm -- lyrḫm **V**: 535.
lyrz ʿm bʿl **V**: 535.
mʾid **V**: 535.
ʿmʾil **V**: 535.
LÚmaskim: **I**: 193.
(א)מחוז *Karum* **V**: 539.
mdl **V**: 535, 536; **VI**: 370.
mdl: blʿ mdlh ybʿr **V**: 537.
mdlk mṭrtk **V**: 403, 536.
mgʿd **V**: 537.
mgʿrm **V**: 535.
MḪH **V**: 534.
mḫṣ **V**: 378, 535.
mḫš* **V: 378, 535.
mk **V**: 537.
mlḥt - ḥrb mlḥt **V**: 537.
mmʿ - brkm. tgʿll bdm ḏmr ḫlqm bmmʿ mhrm **V**: 537.

mqb **V**: 537.
ʾmr **V**: 537.
mr **V**: 537.
msrr **V**: 535.
mswnh **V**: 537.
mṯḏṯt gʿlm ym **V**: 537.
mzʿ - tmʿ kst Dnʾil **V**: 537.
mzl **V**: 539.
mžrǧl **V**: 533.
n **V**: 536.
nʾaṯr bʿl **V**: 537.
ndd **V**: 533.
ngš **V**: 535.
nit **V**: 537.
NKR **V**: 532; **VI**: 365.
nqmd **V**: 537.
pdgl **V**: 192.
ph **V**: 537.
pwt **I**: *275*.
pwt **V**: 537.
qlṣ **V**: 402, 615.
qr **V**: 537.
Qrt ʾalbm **V**: 537.
QTL:QTL **V**: 539.
rbtm **V**: 535.
rgmm **V**: 537.
rḥmy **V**: 537.
rḥtm **V**: 535.
rkb ʿrpt **V**: 538.
rpʾum **V**: 533.
ṣʾit npšh **V**: 535.
Saḫḫan **I**: *260*.
SBL **V**: 420, *490*, 538, *552*.
ṣḥ **V**: 535.
עבץ/עבק **V**: 526, 534.
širh ltikl ʿsrm mnth tkly npr **V**: 533.
šlmm šlmm **V**: 535.
šmʿ -- bn **V**: 535.
šmbʿl **V**: 537.
šrd bʿl bdbḥk **V**: 535.
ṣîṣûma **V**: 447, 534.
skn **IX**: cxlii.
ṣml **V**: 537.
spʾ **V**: 535.
sprnhn **V**: 535.
spsg **V**: 403, 615.
ṣrrt ṣpn **V**: 535.
tʿtd **V**: 535.
ṯʿy **V**: 537.
ṯat **VI**: 255.
td **V**: 535.
tgʿl **V**: 535.
tgʿly **V**: 535.
tk, btk **V**: 403, 615.
ṯkḥ **V**: 536, 596.
ṯlṯ **V**: 537.
ṯlṯ rʿb **V**: 535.
tlt swsm **V**: 533.
tmgʿyn **V**: 535.
ṮN **V**: 532; **VI**: 365.
ṯpṭ nhr **V**: 537.
TQTL:YQTL **V**: 539.
tqtnṣn **V**: 535.
TRḪ **V**: 532; **VI**: 365.
ṯrml **V**: 535.
ṯrṯ -wtmgʿy lʾudm ṯrṯ **V**: 537.
trṭ **V**: 403, 615.
ṯwy **V**: 403, 536.
ušn **V**: 537; **VI**: 427; **VIII**: 449.
wʾan **V**: 535.
wʿṣr ʾdnh **V**: 535.
wtpq **V**: 535.
wypʿr **V**: 535.
whpḥ bhm aqht yb llqh **V**: 533.

y'šr V: 537.
ybnt V: 537.
ydd V: 533.
yḥ V: 536.
yn V: 403, 615.
yhbr V: 535.
yprq lṣb wyṣḥq V: 533.
yqy V: 537.
yr - yr 'rpt V: 537.
yrgb V: 537.
yrḫm V: 535.
yš' u gh wyṣḥ bl mt my l' im bndgn my hmlt 'aṯr b'l V: 537.
yṯkḥ V: 535.
ypṯn V: 537.
ZBL V: 420, *490*, 538, *552*.

Urartian

ale V: 679.

Verdic

ácchā V: 674.

Α, α

῎Αβιοι I: *195*.
ἀβρόπλουτος V: 640.
ἀβρότης V: 640.
ἀγαπᾶν V: 641, *649*, *658*, *659*.
ἀγαπάω V: 641*(2)*, *659(2)*; **VI**: 85*(2)*.
ἀγαπη V: 641*(2)*.
ἅγιον, τό V: 641.
ἅγιος I: *439*.
ἀγκάλη V: 640.
ἀγχιστεύω V: 640, 641.
ἀδάμας V: 641.
ᾅδης V: 641*(2)*.
᾽Αζώτου ὄρους **II**: 297; **VI**: 640.
Αἰγύπτιος **II**: 266; **III**: 87.
αἴξ V: 639.
αἰσθάναμαι **IV**: 26; **V**: 247, 639.
αἴσθησις **IV**: 26; **V**: 247, 639.
αἰσοί V: 641, *679*.
Αἰών V: *442*, 641, 642*(5)*.
Αἰώνιος V: *442*, 641, 642*(5)*; **VI**: 672; **IX**: cxliv
Αἰώρα I: 337; **V**: 266, 642.
ἀκελδαμαχ V: *423*, *440*, *642*, 657.
ακηνή ὡς᾽Ασιαγνῆ τὴν λέξιν V: 606.
Ακκαρων V: *444*, *570*, *642*.
ακριμακραγετα V: 642.
ἀκρογωνιαῖος V: 642.
αλακερι V: 625.
ἄλειφα V: 620.
ἄλειφα (Hesiod) V: 640.
ἀλήθεια V: 643.
ἄλκη V: 639.
αλλασσω I: *219*.
ἄλλομαι V: 465.
ἅλλομαι V: 643.
ἀλλόσσω I: 219; **V**: 643; **VII**: 354.
Αλνου **III**: 84.
ἀμαζακάραν V: 640.
ἀμαλγος V: 639.
ἁμαρτία V: 643.
ἀμαυρός V: 643.
ἀμβλακεῖν V: 643.
ἀμήν V: 643.
ἄν V: 643*(2)*, *647*, *651(2)*.
ἀναβολή V: 640, 641.
ἀναιρεῖν V: 643, *648*.
ἀνάμνησις V: 643; **VIII**: 293.
᾽Αναξ **VI**: 171.
ἄναξ ἀνδρῶν V: 661.
ἀναπαύω V: 640.
ἀναπτυχή V: 640.
ἀνάστασις V: 643.
ἀνάστεμα V: 640, 641.
ἀνάστημα V: 640, 641.
ἀναστρέφαμαι V: 639.
ἀνατολή V: 640, 641.
ἀνδρεία **IV**: 26; **V**: 247, 639.
ἀνδρεῖος **IV**: 26; **V**: 247, 639.
ἀνήρ V: 639, 640, 641.
ἀνλογεῖον **III**: *524*.
ἀντίλημψις V: 639.

'Αξιόποστος **I**: *219;* **V**: 643; **VII**: 354.
αξονες **V**: 644.
ἀοσσητήρ **V**: 639.
ἀπαυθημερίζω **V**: 640.
απλοος **V**: 624.
ἀπό **V**: 640, 641.
ἀποβαίνω **IV**: 465; **V**: 643, *648.*
ἀποκαλύπτω τὸ ὠτίον (οὖς) **V**: 640, 641.
ἀποκλείω **V**: 640, 641.
ἀπολαγχάνω **V**: 640.
ἀπολαύω **V**: 639.
ἀπόλλυμι **V**: 643.
ἀποπαιδαρίοω **V**: 643.
ἀποστολή **V**: 640, 641.
ἀπόστολος **V**: *456,* 645.
ἄπρακτος **V**: 644.
ἄπρατος **V**: 644.
ἀπροκοπεῖον **V**: 345.
ἄρ **V**: 630.
ἀρετή **IV**: 26; **V**: 247, 639.
ἀρετή **V**: 639.
ἀριθμός **V**: 644.
ἄρξιφος **V**: 640.
ἀρούρα **V**: 368.
ἄρουρα **V**: 640, 641.
'Αρπεδονάπται **I**: *195.*
ἀρτοκοπεῖον **I**: *266;* **V**: 644.
ἀρύω **V**: 639.
ἀρχιπροστάτης **V**: 644*(2).*
ΑΡΧΗ **VI**: 540; **VIII**: 150.
ἀρχιπροτατέω **V**: 644.
ἀρχώνης **I**: *187, 481, 498;* **IX**: ci*(2).*
ἄρωμα **III**: *405;* **V**: *589,* 644.
ἄσκη **V**: 640.
ἀσμάχ **V**: 644.
ἀσσάλιος **V**: 644.
ατακτα **V**: 644.
ἀτύζομαι **V**: 609.
ἀτυζομαι **V**: 644.
αὐγή **V**: 639.
ἄφρων **IV**: 26; **V**: 247, 639.
ἀφυλισμός **V**: 644*(3).*
ἄχνη **V**: 639.

Β, β

βαία **V**: 645*(2).*
βακος **V**: 645.
βαπ- Stem **V**: 645*(2).*
βαπτίζω **V**: 645
βάπτω **V**: 645.
βασίλειος **V**: 645.
βασιλευς **VI**: 74.
βασιλική **V**: 645.
βατέω **V**: 639.
βέθος **V**: 639.
βεκκος **V**: 645.
βία **V**: 645; **VI**: 710.
βίος **V**: 645; **VI**: 710.
βίσταξ **V**: 640.
βλίτον **V**: 640.
βοή **V**: 640.
ΒΟΡΥΣΘΕΝΙς *[sic]* **V**: 304.
βου- prefix **V**: 645.
βουγάϊος **V**: 645*(2).*
βραιρός **V**: 645.
βροτός **V**: 639.
βύβλος **V**: 645.

βυκάνη V: 645, *670*.

Γ, γ

Γαβασεος III: 84.

Γανηβάθ V: 292, 415.

γελάω V: 639.

γερουσία I: *192*.

γηρύω V: 639.

γίγνεσθαι V: 646.

γιγνώσκειν V: 646.

γλαυκός V: 638, *670, 671, 672*.

γλυκύς I: *264;* V: 638, 646, *670, 672*.

γλῶσσα IX: cxliv.

γνώμων V: 646.

γόμφος V: 640.

γραμματείς V: 646.

γραμματεύς V: 639.

γράφω V: 639.

γυνή V: 624, 646.

Δ, δ

δ V: 639.

δαιμονάω V: 640.

δαίω V: 646.

δάπεδον V: 639.

δε V: 419, 646.

δειλός V: 639.

δειμός V: 639.

δεῖνα, ὁ, ἡ, τό V: 640.

δεῖξαι αὐτῷ φῶς VI: 311.

δεῖπνον V: 646.

δεῖπνον V: 647.

δεσπότης V: 647; VI: 683.

δεῦρο V: 646.

δεύω V: 639.

δή V: 646, *649*.

δῆμος V: 646.

διά V: 625.

διαβουλία V: 646.

διάημι V: 640.

διαθηκη IV: 329.

διαθήκη V: 646*(2)*.

δίδωμι V: 640, 641.

δίκαιος V: 646.

δικαιοσύνη V: 646, 647.

δικαιόω V: 647.

δίκη V: 647.

διοίκησις

οκησις—διοκησις V: 647.

διπλοος V: 624.

διψύχος V: 647.

δόκᾶνα V: 253.

δόξα IV: 26, 114, 396; V: 247, 639, 647*(3)*.

δόρπον V: 646.

δόρπον V: 647.

δυνάμεις V: 232, 647; VIII: 156

Δύςπαρι*[sic]* V: 647.

δῶ V: 620.

δῶ (Hom.) V: 640.

δώρημα V: 647.

Ε, ϵ

'Εα δέ IV: 466.

ἐάν V: 627, *643*, 647.

Ἐὰν μηθεὶς ἔαθῆι στρατεύσασθαι I: *255*.

ἔγγυοι I: *187, 481, 498;* IX: ci*(2)*.

ἐγώ εἰμί V: 661*(2);* VIII: 111.

εἰ V: 627. 640, 641.

εἵλη V: 639.

εἴλω V: 639.
εἰλαπίνη V: 639.
εἰμί V: 639.
ειπειν V: 625, 647, *649*.
εἰρήνη V: 640, 641.
εἰς τέλος V: *438*, 662.
ἐκκλησία V: 648*(3)*.
ἐκρόφησις V: 648, *657*.
ἔλαφος V: 639.
ἐλεύθερος I: *219;* V: 648; VII: 354.
ἕλη V: 639.
ἐν V: 640, 641, 648.
ἐναίρειν V: *643*, 648.
ἐνεγκοῦσα, ἡ V: 648.
ἐκεῖνος V: 631.
ἔνεροι V: 639.
ἔνεροσις V: 640.
ἐνί V: 648, *671*.
ΕΝΚΥΚΛΙΟΝ VII: 341.
ἕννυμι V: 639.
ἔντευξις V: 693.
ἐντολή V: *435*, 648*(2)*.
ἐντρέπω V: 640, 641.
ἐντυγχάνω V: 639.
ἐξαίρω V: 640, 641.
ἐξικνέομαι V: 640.
ἐξόδιον V: 640, 641.
ἐπὶ τῆς σκηνῆς V: 662.
ἐπιβαίνω V: *643*.
ἐπιβαύω IV: 465; V: *643*, 648.
ἐπιβολή I: *261;* V: 648.
επιγονης, της I: *192*.
ἐπίσταμαι V: 649, *673*.
ἐπιούσιος V: 648*(2)*.
ἐπιπόκων V: 649.
ἐπισκιάζειν V: 649.
ἐπίσκοπος V: 649.
ἐπίσταμαι V: 649.
Επιστράτηγος I: *195*, *494*.
ἐπιτίθημι V: 640, 641.
ἐπιτροπεύω V: 640.
ἐπιφανής I: *483*.
επματα τριγληνα μοροεντα I: *283*.
ἕπομαι V: 625, *647*, 649.
Ἑπτὰ ἐκδικούμενα παραλύσει VI: 44
ΕΠΥΡΩΕΝ VI: 631.
ἐργαζομαι V: 640.
ἔργῳ καὶ δυνάμει I: *219;* V: 662; VII: 354.
ἔρις V: 639.
ἔρρω V: 639.
ἔρως V: *641*, 649, *658*, *659*.
ἔσονται οἱ δύο εἰς σάρκα μίνα V: 662.
ἑτοιμάξω V: 640, 641.
Ευιλατ VI: 34.
Εὐριπιδαριστοφανίζω V: 640.
εὐχαριστεῖν V: 649.
εὐχἄριστία V: 649.
ἐχθὲς καὶ τρίτην (ἡμέραν) V: 640, 641.

Z, ζ

ζ V: 639.
ζάω V: 639.
ΖΕΥΣ VIII: 115.
ΖΕΥΣ ΗΛΙΟΠΛΙΤΗΣ V: 248.
ΙΛΑΣΚΕΣΘΑΙ V: 430.
ζωή V: 649, *661*.

ζώστρα V: 640.

Η, η

ἤ V: 649.
ἤδη V: *646*, 649.
Ηλεαπχια III: 84.
ἠμί V: 639.
ἧπαρ V: 649, *658*.
ἤπιος V: 649.
ἠρισάλπιγξ V: 640.

Θ, θ

Θαλατθ V: 650.
θαμτε V: 650.
θάνατος V: 650.
ΘΑΝΤΟΣ VII: 340.
θέος, ὁ V: 650; VIII: 118.
θέος Ύψιστος V: 650.
θεὸς Ὕψιστος V: 12
θέρω V: 639.
τὰ θηλυκὰ ἀπανδρωθέντα VI: 337.
θῆλυς V: 640.
θρέμμα V: 640.
θὺ μή V: 662.
θυρών V: 650.
θυσία V: *64, 457*, 650.

Ι, ι

Ιακχος V: 246, 352, 650.
ἴδια I: *188, 210, 507*.
ἴδιος V: 639.
ἱερόν V: 650,*653*.
Ιησους Βασιλευς ου Βασιλευσας VI: 681.
ἱλάσκεσθαι V: 650*(2)*.
'ΙΛαCΤΗΡΙΟΝ V: 650.
ἵνα V: 623.
ἰσονομία I: *320;* III: *367*.
ἰσονομία V: 650.
ἰχῶ V: 620.
ἰχώρ V: 620.
ἰχώρ, ἰχῶ (Hom.) V: 640.

Κ, κ

κα V: *643*, 651, *651*.
κάβειροι V: 195.
κάβειρος V: 651.
καθαπταί V: 651.
καί V: 651, *658, 670, 671, 673*.
Καὶ ἅπαξ καὶ δίς V: 465.
καὶ ἅπαξ καὶ δίς V: 661.
κακορροθέω V: 640.
καλός V: 651.
καλυπτός V: 640.
κανών V: 651.
Καππαδοκία III: 54; V: 651.
'Καρακαλλος', ὁ, Κοσμοκρατωρ I: *455, 492*.
καρδία V: 431, 651.
Κᾶρες V: 651.
κατάβα V: 639.
καταλυσαι V: 651.
καταπαυσαι V: 651.
κατέπαυσαν VI: 171.
καυνάκης V: *565*.
κε(ν) V: *643, 651*, 651.
κεῖμαι V: 639.
κῆρες V: 651.
κηρύσσω V: 639.
κιονίσκος III: *724*
κῆρυξ V: 639.
κισσός V: 639.
κίω V: 6393

κνῦμα V: 640.
τὸ κοινόν VIII: 463.
κοίρανος V: 639.
κομψεία V: 640.
κοπιάω V: 651.
κόσμος IV: 26; V: 247, 639, 651.
κόφινος V: 652.
κραίνω V: 639.
κραιπνός V: 639.
κρατήρ V: 652.
κρήνη V: 639.
κτείς V: 639.
κίβδα V: 652.
κυκε(ι)ῶ V: 620.
κυκε(ι)ῶ (Hom.) V: 640.
κυλιχνίς V: 652.
κύριος V: 426, 652*(2)*; VIII: 120.
κωφος λιμην III: *200*.

Λ, λ

λαμβάνειν V: 652.
λαμπήνη V: 693.
λαογραγία V: 652*(3)*.
λάσκω V: 639.
λάσκω V: 640.
λεῖος V: 639.
λειτουργέω V: 639.
λειτουργέω V: 652.
λέπρα V: *448*, 652; IX: cxxii.
λίθος ἀκπογωνιαῖος IX: cxxxviii, cxli, cxliv.
λίπος V: 639.
λογός IV: 26; V: 247, 639.
μ V: 639.

M, μ

Μακκαβαῖος, Μακκαβαῖοι VI: 640*(2)*.
παλαμάομαι V: 640.
μάλη V: 639.
μάστιξ V: 640.
μεγαλοπρέπεια IV: 26; V: 247, 639.
μεγαλοπρεπής IV: 26; V: 247, 639.
μέλλω V: 652*(3)*.
Μενελιατου III: 84.
Μερισμος Ανακεχωρηκοτων III: 89, 90.
μεσσι THEOD. V: 403, 615.
μετά V: 631, 653, *658*.
μεταμελέσθαι V: 653; VI: 8.
μετανοεῖν V: 653; VI: 8.
μέτοχοι I: *187, 481, 498;* IX: ci*(2)*.
μή V: 631, 653*(4)*, 654*(2)*, *670*, *672*.
μολύνω V: 640/
ΜΟΝΟΓΕΝΗΣ ΠΑΡΑ ΠΑΤΡΟΣ IX: cxliv.
μορτός V: 639.

N, ν

Ναζωραῖος κληθήσεται V: 128.
ναός V: *650*, 653.
ναοφόρος I:*455*.
νάρδος III: *394;* V: 560.
ναυστολέω V: 640.
νέκταρ V: *639*, 653.
νέννος V: 638.
νεφεληγερέτα V: 653.
Νεφελητερέτα V: 538.

νηγάτεος V: 653.
νήδυμος V: 653.
νηδύς V: 638.
Νικετου III: 84.
νομίσματα πύργινα V: 662.
νομοι I: 496.
νόμος I: *477.*
νόμος V: 653*(2).*
νοῦς IV: 26; V: 247, 639.

Ξ, ξ

ξανθός III: 707; V: 660.
ξανθός V: 640.
ξέω V: 638.
ξηρός V: 638.
ξόανον V: 653.
ξύλον V: 638.
ξύω V: 638.

Ο, ο

ὁ ἀμήν VI: 540.
Ο ΥΙΟC ΜΟΥ Ο ΑΓΑΠΗΟC VIII: 274.
Ὁ υἱὸς τοῦ Θεοῦ V: 639, 662.
ὀβολός I: *439, 447;* V: 654; VII: 123.
ὄβριμος V: 654.
ὅδε V: 631.
οἴκησις V: 654.
οἶνος I: *263;* V: 654.
οἷος V: 654*(2), 655.*
οἶτος V: 640.
οἰωνός V: 639.
οκησις—διοκησις V: 647.
ὅλος V: 654, *655, 670, 672(2), 673, 674.*
ὄμβρος V: 640.
ὄνομα V: 639.
ὀπᾱδός V: 609.
ὀπᾱδός V: 654.
ὀπαστόν V: 640.
ὁποῖος V: 654*(2), 656.*
ὅπως V: 623, 626*(2).*
ὅπως μή V: 624, 626.
ορειξαλκος I: *296.*
ὀρείχαλκος V: 654.
ὅταν V: 654.
ὅτι V: 631.
οὐ V: *653,* 654*(4), 671(2).*
οὐ μή V: 626*(2),* 629*(2).*
οὐαί V: 654.
οὔπω V: 655.
οὗτος V: 631.
ὄχλημα V: 655.
ὀχληρός V: 640.

Π, π

παιδευτός V: 655.
παιδεύω V: 655.
πακειδᾱ V: 256.
πάλλω V: 655, *674.*
πεμπταῖος V: 640.
Πάν V: 639.
Παννυχις III: *693.*
παρεμβολή V: 655.
παρθένος V: 655; VI: 262.
παρορία τῆς πολέως V: 662.
πᾶς V: *654,* 655, *670, 672(2), 673, 674.*
παταζείθης V: 675.
πειράω V: 640.
πείρω V: 639.

πέλωρ	**V**: 655.
πελώριος	**V**: 655.
πέλωρος	**V**: 655.
πέπων	**V**: 655.
περὶ ὕψους	**V**: 662.
πῆμα	**V**: 639.
πινάω	**V**: 640.
περσης, της επιγονης	**I**: *192*.
πιστός	**V**: 640, 641.
πλέες	**V**: 655.
πλίξ	**V**: 640.
πνεῦμα	**V**: 506*(3)*, 514, 515*(5)*, 655*(5)*, 656, *657(3)*, *660(2)*, *661*; **VI**: 683.
πνοή	**IV**: 26; **V**: 247, 639.
ποίημα νουθετικόν	**IV**: 192.
ποῖος	**V**: *654(2)*, 656*(2)*.
πόλες αὐταὶ φόρον ταχσάμεναι	**V**: 662.
πόλις	**I**: *188*, *210*, *507*.
πολυδευκης	**V**: 638, *670*, *672*.
πόλχος	**V**: 639.
πονηρόν	**V**: 656.
πόντος	**V**: 639.
πούς	**V**: 639.
πρᾶγος	**V**: 640.
πράκτωρ ξενικῶν	**I**: *189*, *190*, *219*; **VII**: 354.
πρεσβύτερος	**V**: 639.
πριβάτον	**V**: 656.
πρίν	**V**: 656*(3)*.
Πρόεδροι	**I**: *495*.
προθῦσία	**V**: 656.
προμαντεία	**V**: 656*(2)*.
πρόνοια	**IV**: 26; **V**: 247, 639.
προσανοικοδομηθήσεται	**V**: 656; **VI**: 634.
προσήλυτος	**V**: 656.
προσκυνεῖν	**V**: 656.
προσουρεῖν	**V**: 640.
πρόσταγμα	**V**: 656.
προστίθημι	**V**: 640, 641.
προὔργου	**V**: 640.
πρόφασις	**V**: 656.
Πρυτάνεις	**I**: *495*.
Πτενετω	**III**: 84.
πυξίς	**V**: 656.
πύργος	**V**: 639.
πυροπίπης	**V**: 640.
πωλεῖν	**V**: 657, *661*.

Ρ, ρ

ῥά	**V**: 630.
Ῥαδαμάνθους ὅρκος	**I**: *179*.
Η ΡΑΧΙΑ	**VI**: 725.
ῥήγνυμι	**V**: 639.
ῥινός	**V**: 640.
ῥίψ	**V**: 639.
ῥόπτρον	**I**: *246*; **V**: 657.
√ῥοφεῖν	**V**: *648*, 657.
συρίζω	**V**: 640.

Σ, σ

Σαββαθιον	**V**: 657.
σάλος	**V**: 639
σάρξ	**V**: 414, 506*(3)*, 514, 515*(5)*, *655(3)*, 657*(5)*, *660(2)*, *661*.
σάρος	**V**: 657.
Σειραχ	**V**: *423*, *440*, *642*, 657.
σειρός	**V**: 658.

σεμαχωνῖτις V: 657.
σεμνός V: 639.
σηλαγγεύς V: 657.
σῆμα V: 639.
σήραγξ V: 657.
σίβινον V: 658.
τοῦ Σιλωαμ VI: 266.
σίμβλος V: 639.
σιρός V: 658.
σιώπησις VI: 552, 553.
σκάνδαλον V: 658*(2)*.
σκοποῦμαι V: 658.
σκώρ V: *649*, 658, *673*.
σμῆνος V: 639.
σοβέω V: 639.
σπανίς V: 639.
σπεῖρα V: 639.
σπλήν V: 640.
στάμνος V: 640.
στατήρ V: 658.
στερεοῦν V: 658.
στερεός V: 658.
στοά V: 624, 658.
στοια V: 624.
στομφάζω V: 640.
στοργή V: *641*, *649*, 658, *659*.
στρέφω V: 639.
στρόβος V: 640.
στρουθός V: 640.
στωα V: 624.
σύν V: *653*, 658.
σὺν ἡμιολίᾳ V: 662.
ΣΥΝΘΡΟΝΟΣ ΔΙΚΗΙ V: 261, 662.
Σύνναος θεός V: 255, 662.
σύνταξις V: 658.
σῦριγξ V: 640.
σωρός V: 658.

Τ, τ

Ταριχαντής I: 380.
τέ V: *651*, 658, *670*, *671*, *673*.
Τεεβήσιος υἱοί VII: 336.
τέρας V: 639.
τέρην V: 639.
τετραλογία V: 658.
τετραλογία V: 659.
τετροπωμένους V: 659.
ΤΕΤΡΟΠΩΜΕΝΟΥΣ VI: 171.
Τευηματογραφία I: 500.
τηρός V: 639
τικτεῖν V: 659, *674*.
τίκτω V: 639.
τὸ δέ V: 662.
τορεύω V: 659.
τοῦτο ποιεῖτε V: 662.
τραχύς V: 639.
τριγλωχις III: *683*.
τριλογία V: 658.
τριλογία V: 659.
τρίξω V: 639.
τρισσός V: 640, 641.

Υ, υ

ὑάδες V: 659.
υἱοθεσία I: *225*.
υἱός V: 639.
ὑμήν V: 639.
ὕμνος V: 639.
ὑπέρακμος VIII: 294.
ὑπωπιάζειν V: 659.
ὕψιστος V: 659.

ὕψιστος V: 94.

Φ, φ

φάρω V: 639.
φαῦλος V: 639.
φάω V: 639.
φέρτατος V: 639.
φεύγω V: 639.
φθίνω V: 659.
φθονεῖθαι V: 659.
φθονούμενοι V: 659.
φιλεῖν V: *641, 649, 658,* 659.
φιλέω V: *641(2),* 659*(2);* VI: 85*(2)*.
φίλος V: 639.
φίλτερος V: 640.
φοινῖκνήϊος I: *401*.
Φοίνιξ V: *347,* 659.
φοξός V: 639.
φόρμιγξ V: 639.
φρήν V: 639.
φρόνησις IV: 26; V: 247, 639.
φώρ V: 639.
φωτιζειν V: *418,* 659.

X, χ

χάζομαι V: 639.
ὁ χακαυϜ ὁ (Cyr.) V: 640.
χάμψαι V: 660.
χάρις V: 423, 660.
χείρ V: 639, 640, 641.
χέρηες V: *655*.
χίμαρος V: 640.
χοροποιός V: 640.
χορός V: 639.
Χριστός V: 660*(4)*.
χρόμαδος V: 639.

Ψ, ψ

ψάλλω V: 660.
ψαλμός V: 660.
ψαλτήριον V: 660.
ψήκτρα V: 640.
ψηφισματα I: 496.
ψονθομφανήχ VI: 88.
ψυχή IV: 26; V: 247, 506*(3)*, 514, 515*(5)*, 639,*649*, *655(4)*. *657(3)*, 660*(2)*, 661*(3)*.

Ω, ω

ω V: 646.
ὠνεῖν V: *657,* 661.
ὥς V: 623, 646, 661*(4)*.
ΩΣΠΕΡ ΟΜΗΡΟΣ ΦΗΣΙ VII: 347.
ὥστε V: 661.

[*Some words may be transliterated in actual citation*.]

(*Words are shown as cited in the text, not by root, except for words starting with the article* ה *or with* ו)

א

אב **V**: 402, 406, 615.

אֲבִ־עד **VI**: 269.

אבד **V**: 395.

אבה **V**: 295.

אבוי **V**: 295.

אבחה **V**: 396.

אֲבִיּוֹנָה **VI**: 566.

אבך **V**: 397.

אָבֵל **V**: 406.

אבן אבן **IX**: cxxxviii, cxli, cxliv.

אֶבֶן יִשְׂרָאֵל **VI**: 94; **VIII**: 111.

אַבְנֵט **V**: 406*(2)*.

אַבְנֵי־קֹדֶשׁ **VI**: 559.

אבנים **V**: 406.

אָבְנָיִם **V**: 396.

אַבְרֵךְ **V**: 360; **VI**: 87.

אגא **III**: *386;* **V**: 406, *407, 411*.

אגאלתי **VI**: 316.

אֱגוֹז **V**: 396.

אֲגַם **V**: 396.

אגן **V**: 396.

אֲגַרְטְלֵי **V**: 403, 615.

אָד **V**: 406, 407.

אֵד **V**: 400; **VI**: 33*(2);* **VIII**: 79.

אדב **V**: 396.

אדירים **VI**: 509.

אָדָם **V**: 392, 406, 510, 518.

אֲדָמָה **V**: 406.

אדני **V**: 406, *426;* **VIII**: 111.

אדר **V**: 406.

אהב **V**: 398, 489.

אָהֵב **V**: 406.

אהבו הֵבוּ **V**: 402, **VI**: 12.

אהל Qal **V**: 402, **VI**: 12.

אֹהֶל מוֹעֵד **IV**: 243; **V**: 53; **VI**: 118.

וַאֲהָלוֹת קְצִיעוֹת **VI**: 486.

אֵו **VI**: 550.

או לכה לך **V**: 405.

אוֹ שֶׁ־ **V**: 500.

אוֹב **V**: 406*(2)*, 407.

אוֹב II **V**: 104, 402, *615*.

אֹבוֹת **V**: 394.

אוּד **V**: 396.

אוה **V**: 295.

אוי **V**: 295.

אוּלָם **V**: *407*.

און **V**: 398.

אָוֶן **V**: 392, 407*(2)*.

אוֹן **V**: 407.

אוֹפִיר **V**: 298, 407.

אוֹת **VI**: 264.

(בְּ)אַוַּת נַפְשׁוֹ **VI**: 322.

אָז **V**: 407*(2), 597*.

אזוב **V**: 396.
אזור **V**: 407.
אזכרה **IV**: 235; **V**: 407.
אזנ(י)ך **V**: 402, **VI**: 12.
אח **V**: 396.
אחב **V**: 295, 407.
אָחֻז **V**: 398.
אחזת שמרות עיני **V**: 461.
ואהיה לחם כמרימי עֹל על לחיהם ואט אליו אוכיל **V**: 400.
אחל **V**: 396.
אחלות, אחלים **V**: 396.
אחר **V**: 407.
אַחַר **V**: 407.
אחר(י) **V**: 402, **VI**: 12.
אַחֲרָיו **V**: 482, 484.
אחרית הימים **V**: 121, 461*(2)*.
אטון מורים **V**: 396.
אִטִּים **V**: 399.
אֵטִין **V**: 396.
איב **V**: 398.
איד **V**: 406, 407.
אֵיד **V**: 407*(2)*.
איוב אמרה פגה **V**: 404.
איזמא **III**: *386;* **V**: *406,* 407, *411*.
איטלין **V**: 408.
איירי **V**: 394.
איכבוד **V**: 407.
אילתית **V**: 404.
אֲיֻמָּה כַּנִּדְגָּלוֹת **VI**: 554.
אין **V**: 407*(2);* **VI**: 47, 481.
וְאֵין לוֹ **VI**: 576.
אִישׁ **V**: 392, *510, 518*.
אִישׁ אֶחָד **VI**: 193.
איש אלהים **V**: 461.
אַךְ **V**: 408.
אך לא בעי ישלח יד אם בפידו להן שוע **V**: 400.
אכל **V**: 396.
אכן **V**: 395, 481, 483; **VI**: 7.
אִכָּר **VI**: 383*(2),* 386.
אל **VIII**: 110, 111, 123.
אֶל־הַנְּחִילוֹת **V**: 395; **VI**: 454.
אַל **V**: 400, 408*(3);* **VI**: 9; **VIII**: **§986, 111-112**.
אַל־מֻגִּים **V**: 396.
אל־נכון **VI**: 205.
אֵל שַׁדַּי **VIII**: 107, 108, 110*(2),* 111, 124.
אל תַּמֵּר **V**: 404.
אַל־תַּשְׁחֵת **V**: 461.
אלא אי איתמר הכי איתמר **V**: 461; **VI**: 704.
אֵלָה **IX**: lxiv.
אלהי יעקב **IV**: 481.
אלהי **V**: 408.
אלהים **V**: 408.

אֱלֹהִים **V**: 408*(5);* **VIII**: **§986, 110-111**, 123, 125.

אלוה **VIII**: 110, 123.

אֱלוֹהַּ **V**: 408.

אַלּוֹן בָּכוּת **VI**: 83.

אלון מצב **VI**: 185.

אלח **V**: 397, 400.

אלי **V**: 408; **VIII**: 110.

אֵלָיו **V**: 482, 484.

אלם **V**: 398, 400.

אלמן **V**: 398.

אֶלְתְּקוֹן **VI**: 172, 173*(2)*.

אם **V**: 408, 482; **VI**: 10.

(ואם ימעט הבית מהית) מִשֶּׂה **V**: 402, **VI**: 12.

אמה **V**: 396.

אֱלוֹהַּ **V**: 408.

אָמוֹן **VI**: 540.

אֱמוּנָה **V**: 408; **VI**: 401.

אמל **IV**: 517.

אמן **I**: 515; **V**: 395.

אֱמֻנָה **VI**: 401.

אמץ **V**: 395, 396, 408.

אמר **V**: 409; **VI**: 392.

אָמַרְתִּי **IV**: 409; **V**: 484.

אֶמֶשׁ **I**: 398; **V**: 408, *563*.

אֱמֶת **V**: 392, 409.

אַמְתַּחַת **V**: 409.

אֲנוּ (אָנוּ) **V**: 482, 484.

אֱנוֹשׁ **V**: 392, 510, 518.

אֲנִי יהוה **VIII**: 119.

אני שמרתי ארחות פריץ **V**: 400.

אָנֹכִי **V**: 409.

אנשי דמים **IV**: 486; **V**: 461.

אָסוֹן **V**: 396.

אסורי חג **VI**: 521.

אסף **V**: 396.

אָסַף **V**: 403.

אֵפֹד, אֵפוֹד **V**: *52, 55,* 409.

אפו **V**: 398.

אפודה **V**: 394.

אפל **V**: 396.

אפם **V**: 395.

אפס המרה **V**: 404.

אפר **V**: 404.

אפרתי **VI**: 188.

Talmudic אפש **V**: 409. 564.

אצל **V**: 398.

ארא **V**: 394.

אֶרְאֶלָּם **VI**: 286.

אַרְגַּז **V**: 409; **VI**: 196*(2)*.

אַרְגָּמָן **V**: 402, 409, 615.

אֶרֶז **III**: *388;* **V**: 409, *566;* **VI**: 301, 452.

אֲרִי **V**: *431, 623*.

אר(י)אל **V**: 409*(3)*.

ארם **V**: 409.

ארמין **V**: 409.

ארמנות **V**: 409.

אַרְמְנוֹתֵינוּ **VI**: 327.

אֶרֶץ **V**: 409; **VI**: 98, 365.

ארקחה **V**: 404.

אשבורן **V**: 410.

אִשָּׁה **V**: 392, 510, 518.

אֲשִׁירָה/אֲוּשֵׁרָה **V**: 410.

אשכל **V**: 398.

אשכר **V**: 410, *440*.

אֵשֶׁל **III**: 395; **V**: 410*(2)*.

אָשָׁם **V**: 57, 392, 393, 410*(2)*.

אֶשְׁפָּר **V**: 394.

אשר **V**: 394, 410*(2)*, 483; **VI**: 5.

אֲשֶׁר **V**: 483*(4)*.

אשר אמר Q **VIII**: 456.

אשר בתלמוד שקרם Q **VIII**: 455.

אֲשֶׁר־חַי **V**: 410, 461; **VI**: 15.

אשר לא ארשה **V**: 461; **VI**: 114, 148.

אשר על הבית **I**: *470;* **V**: 461.

אשר על חמס **VI**: 215.

אֲשֵׁרָה **V**: 66, 104.

אשרי **V**: 410.

את **V**: 410*(4)*, 411, 482; **VI**: 264.

אֶתְבָּעַל **V**: 303, 411.

אתה **V**: 394; **VI**: 5.

וְאַתָּה הִשְׁלַכְתָּ מִקִּבְרְךָ כְּנֵצֶר נִתְעָב לְבוּשׁ הֲרֻגִים **VI**: 275.

אֹתָהּ **V**: 411; **VI**: 104.

אתמה **V**: 411; **VI**: 332.

אֶתְמוֹל **V**: 398.

אֶתְנָה **V**: 398.

אֶתְנַן **IV**: 477; **V**: 398, 411.

ב

בְּ **VI**: 283.

בָּאָה הַצְּפִירָה אֵלֶיךָ יוֹשֵׁב **V**: 395.

בָּאמָּה **V**: 411.

באר **V**: 396.

באריס **V**: 395.

באשה **III**: *386*.

באשׁ **V**: 411*(3)*.

באשה **V**: *406, 407,* 411.

באשים **V**: 399; **VI**: 255.

בג **V**: 394.

בגדאנא **VIII**: 156.

בִּגְדֵי שְׂרָד **V**: 461, 534.

בגדכפת **V**: 411; **IX**: cxli.

בְּדִיל **I**: 299; **V**: 401.

בַּדְיָנָא **V**: 393.

בדלח **V**: 396.

בְּדֹלַח **V**: 396.

בַּה־פּוּצִי **VI**: 403.

בהם **V**: 400.

בוטח **VI**: 329.

בוך NIPH **V**: 402, **VI**: 12.

בוץ **IV**: *262;* **V**: 411, *458*.

בּוּץ **V**: 396.

בוש **V**: 411*(2)*.

בָּזָה **VI**: 241, 289.

בזל **V**: 396.

בָּזָק **V**: 396.

בחוקי הגוים **VIII**: 460.

בָּחוּר **V**: 392, 510, 518.

בחל **V**: 398.

בָּטָה **V**: 483.

בטחות **V**: 400.

בין **VI**: 301.

בֵּין **V**: 482, 484.

בַּיִת **V**: 411.

בֵּית־אֵל שַׂר־אֶצֶר **VI**: 409.

בֵּית הַחָפְשִׁית **VI**: 237.

בית חבר **V**: 382; **VI**: 543*(2)*, 546, 592.

בָּכָא, בְּכָאִים **II**: 266.

בָּכָה **V**: 411.

בַּל־יֵדְעָה **VI**: 541.

בְּלִיַּעַל **V**: 392, 412*(10)*.

בלס (בּוֹלֵס) **VI**: 383*(2)*, 386.

בלע√ **V**: 412.

בִּלְתִּי **V**: 535; **VI**: 271.

בְּמַדָּעֲךָ **VI**: 564.

Q במה **VIII**: 447.

במות אדם רשף תאבד תקוה ותוחלת אונים אבדה **V**: 400.

בן־אדם **IV**: 424; **V**: 461.

בֶּן־אוֹנִי **V**: 402, **VI**: 12, 84.

בן אמה **V**: 461.

בן בן **V**: 412.

בן המלך **V**: 461, 462.

בן־ימין **VI**: 84.

בֶּן־נַעֲוַת הַמַּרְדּוּת **V**: 462.

בְּנֵי־הָאֱלֹהִים **V**: 461, 520.

בְּנֵי הַנְּבִיאִים **V**: 462.

בסאסאה **V**: 397.

בְּסוֹד **VI**: 435.

בע (בעלמא) abbv. **IV**: 19; **V**: 412, 417.

בעבר הירדן **V**: 462.

בַּעַד **V**: 412, 482, 484.

בַּעֲלַת־אוֹב **V**: 462.

בעת ההיא **IV**: 353; **V**: 462.

בפרתיה **VIII**: 459.

וּבְצָעֵם/וּבְצַעַם **VI**: 387.

בציץ **V**: 396.

בצר **VI**: 432.

בקא **V**: 396.

בְּקִיעַ **V**: 396.

בִּקְעָה **V**: 412.

בקק **V**: 398.

בִּקֵּשׁ **V**: 412, *417*.

בַּר **VI**: 452.

בר נשא **VIII**: 139.

בָּרָא **IV**: 266, 284; **V**: 413*(6)*; **VI**: 22, 173, 353, 354.

בראש **V**: 413.

בְּרֵאשִׁת **VI**: 26.

בַּרְבֻּרִים **V**: 397.

ברה **V**: 396.

בָּרוּךְ **V**: 413.

בָּרוּךְ יהוה

בָּרוּךְ אַתָּה יהוה; **V**: 462.

בָּרַח **V**: 413.

ברית **V**: 394; **VIII**: 475.

בְּרִית **I**: 516; **V**: 413.

בֹּרִית **V**: 396.

ברך **V**: 413*(3)*, *537*.

בָּרֵךְ **V**: 413*(3)*.

בְּרָכָה **V**: 413, 414*(2)*.

בְּרָע **VI**: 117.

בַּרְקָא **V**: 393.

ברקים **V**: 404.

בשׂם **V**: 396.

בָּשָׂר **V**: 392, 414*(3)*, *439*, *451*, 506, 515*(2)*, *657*.

בְּשַׁגַּם **VI**: 50.

בשלחה **V**: 397.

בשן **V**: 400.

בשת **V**: 414.

בָּתָה **V**: 395.

בְּתוּלָה **V**: *534*.

בתרין **V**: 414.

ג

גָּאוֹן **V**: 414.

גאל **V**: 414*(2)*, 449.

גאל√ **V**: 414.

גָּאַל **IV**: 508.

גְּאֻלָּה **IV**: 508.

גַּב **V**: 396.

גֵּב(?) **V**: 396.

גִּבּוֹר **V**: 393.

גְּבוּרָה **IV**: 502.

גִּבּוֹר חַיִל **I**: *190*, 317.

גבל **V**: 414*(2)*; **VIII**: 475.

גַּבְלוּת **I**: 299; **IV**: 235; **V**: 401.

גִּבֵּן **V**: 396.

גֶּבֶר **V**: 392, 415, 510, 518; **VIII**: 475*(2)*.

גְּבִרָה (גְּבִרְתָּהּ) **V**: 415.

גְּדוּד **V**: 396.

גֵּו **V**: 396.

גוה√ **V**: 397.

גוֹזל **IX**: cxxxix, cxliii.

גּוֹי **V**: 415*(2)*; **VIII**: 213.

גורל **VIII**: 415.

גּוֹרָל **V**: 415.

גורן נכון **VI**: 210.

גיתאפי **V**: 394.

גַּלְגַּל **V**: 415.

גֶּלֶד **V**: 396.

גלום **V**: 415, 546.

גָּלוּת שְׁלֵמָה **VI**: 378.

גִּלָּיוֹן **V**: 396.

גלף **V**: 394.

גלשׁ **V**: 396, 415.

גמל **V**: 396.

והנמצא **VIII**: 447.

גמר **IV**: 483; **V**: 394, 415.

גַּן־בְּעֵדֶן **V**: 462.

גנבת **II**: 40; **V**: 292, 415.
גנוניות **V**: 415.
גֶּנֶז II(?) **VI**: 622.
גנח **V**: 398.
גנף **V**: 394.
גער **V**: 415*(2)*.
גָּעַר **V**: 400, 415.
גְּעָרָה **V**: 415; **VI**: 542.
גָּעַשׁ **V**: 400.
געשׁ **V**: 401*(2)*.
גפן **V**: 394.
גר **IV**: 260.
גֵּר **V**: 416*(3)*.
גרן **V**: 416, 550; **VII**: 144.
גֹּרֶן **V**: 416*(3)*.
גרס **V**: 394.
גרע **V**: 394, 396.
גֹּרשׁ **V**: 395.
גשם נדבות **V**: 403, 536.
גשן **III**: 108.

ד

ד **V**: 416.
ד־ **V**: 416.
דְּבָאָה **V**: 416.
דבה **V**: 396.
דבוי מיתה **V**: 404.
דבקים **V**: 404.
דבר **V**: 416*(2)*; **IX**: cxxxix*(2)*.
דָּבָר (In English Translation) **V**: 398.
דגל **IV**: 507.
דֶּגֶל **V**: 416*(2)*.
דַּגָּלוּת גורל **V**: 395.
דודי **IV**: 505; **V**: 416.
דום **V**: 474.
דומה I **V**: 396.
דון **V**: 402, **VI**: 12.
דּוֹר **V**: 417*(2)*.
דורש התורה **VIII**: 459.
דחזי **IV**: 19; **V**: 437.
דִּין **V**: 392, 417, 436.
דכא **V**: 399.
דלל **V**: 396.
דלף **V**: 401.
דלק **V**: 395.
דמאי **V**: 417.
דְּמוּת **V**: 374; **VI**: 30.
דמם **V**: 474.
דְּמֶשֶׁק **VI**: 381*(2)*.
דַּעַת **V**: 417, 485; **VI**: 544, 578.
ד״ק (דקרן) abbv. **IV**: 19; **V**: 412, 417.
דַּק **V**: 396.
דִּקְדּוּק **V**: 417.
דרבן **V**: 403.
דָּרוֹם **V**: 398; **IX**: cxl.
דְּרוֹר **I**: *203;* **V**: 417.
דרך **V**: 395, 404.
דרך (with שותף) **V**: 404.

(with שותף) דרך **V**: 404.
דֶּרֶךְ **V**: 417.
דֶּרֶךְ הַכִּכָּר **VI**: 214.
דְּרָכִים **VI**: 304.
דָּרַשׁ **V**: *412,* 417.
דָּת **V**: 392.

ה

ה **V**: 417.
article הַ **V**: 417.
הֶאֱמִין **V**: 483.
הַבְנִי, (הָובְנִים) **V**: 396.
הברו **VI**: 302.
הגדה **V**: 401.
הַגּוֹיִם שְׁאֵרִית **V**: 465.
Mishnaic הדיוט **V**: 417.
הַדְרַת קֹדֶשׁ **VI**: 475, 510, 588, 592.
הוּא, הויא **V**: 394, 417; **VIII**: 119.
הוֹד **V**: 400.
הוָה, הוָּה **V**: 418.
הַוּוֹת **V**: 392.
הוֹי **V**: 418.
הויה **VI**: 104.
והוינן בה **VI**: 705.
הוֹלִיד **V**: 418, 427.
הולכה **V**: 405.
הולכך **V**: 418; **VI**: 700.
הוֹצִיא **IV**: 340; **V**: 418, *419.*
הוֹקִיַע **V**: 418; **VIII**: 218.
(Hiph. of יָקַע)
הוֹקַע **V**: 418.
(Hiph. of יָקַע)
הוֹרָה(וּ) **V**: 418, *659.*
הוֹשִׁיעָה נָּא **VI**: 521.
הזָהּ√ **V**: 418.
(Hiph. of נזה) הִזָּה **V**: 89, 418, 438.
הזהיר **VI**: 578.
הֵחֵל **V**: 418*(2),* 489.
הָיָה **V**: 418, *554.*
והיה **V**: 419, 487.
והיו **V**: 400.
היחד **VIII**: 463.
הֵיכָל **V**: 418.
הֵיל **V**: 404.
הילל בן שחר **V**: 462; **VI**: 275.
הַיַּת **V**: 398*(2).*
הלך **V**: 418*(2), 427.*
הלם, המולה **V**: 394.
המר **V**: 395, 402, *552.*
הֵנַע **V**: 419; **VI**: 240*(2),* 289, 290.
הָסָה **V**: 483.
העתקה **V**: 401.
הֻצַּב **VI**: 398*(2).*
הֵרֹן **V**: 402, **VI**: 12.
הררה **V**: 404.
השליך **V**: 419.
(from שָׁלַךְ)
הִתְוָה **V**: 399.
התל **V**: 419, 490
התפאר **V**: 402, **VI**: 12.

ו

וְ **V**: 419, *646.*

וּ **V**: 494.

ז

ז **V**: 419, 484.

זְאֵבֵי עֶרֶב **V**: 394; **VI**: 6.

זֹאתָה **V**: 482, 484.

זְבוּל **V**: 419.

זֶבַח **V**: 57, 103, 393*(2).*

זֶבַח הַיָּמִים **V**: 64*(2)*, 462*(2).*

זבל **V**: 420, 490, *538, 552.*

זֵד **V**: 420.

זדה **V**: 420; **VII**: 104.

זֶה **V**: 420, 591.

זוד **V**: 420.

זור **IX**: cxl.

זִיז **VI**: 501.

זכוכית **V**: 420.

זכר (הִזַּכּוּ Hithp) **VI**: 250.

זִמְרָה **V**: 396.

זמרי **V**: 395.

זמרת **VI**: 58, 88.

זָנָה **V**: 78.

זע טוט **V**: 394.

זָנָה אַחֲרֵי **V**: 462.

זָקֵן **V**: 392, 510, 518.

זָקֵן (זְקֵנִים) **I**: *184, 461.*

זִקְנֵי **V**: 420.

זקף לבינתא **IX**: cxli, cl.

זָר **V**: 394, 420, **VI**: 5.

זֶרַע **V**: 420*(3)*, 494*(2)*, 495.

ח

חבר **V**: 420*(2)*, 429; **VIII**: 476.

חבר עיר **V**: 420, 462, *464.*

חָגָב **V**: 396.

חגג **I**: 237; **V**: 421, *430,* 504.

חֲגוֹרָה (חֲגֹרֹת) **VI**: 39.

חגר **V**: 398.

חגֵרים **VI**: 692.

חדל **V**: 398, 424.

חדל II **V**: 421, 424*(2).*

חֵדֶק **V**: 396.

חִדֶּקֶל **V**: 421.

חדש האביב **I**: 396; **IV**: 335.

חַוָּה **V**: 298, 421.

חוח **V**: 421.

חוילה **V**: 421.

חוק (חקקים) **IV**: 341.

חותמי של הקב"ה אמה **V**: 462.

חזה **V**: 395; **VI**: 7, 283.

חֹזֶה **V**: 393.

חֹזֶה (חֹזִים) **I**: *105;* **V**: 77, 421*(2), 450.*

חָזוֹן **V**: 421.

חַזָּן* **V**: 421.

חטא **V**: 421, 424.

חטאה גדולה **I**: *219(2).*

חַטָּאת **V**: 57, 103,392, 393*(2)*; **VI**: 43, 541.

חַטָּף **V**: 421.

חַי, חַיִּים **I**: 512; **V**: 112, 117, 400, 421*(3)*, 482, 509.

חֵי **V**: 421, 482.

חָיֶה(?) **V**: 396.

הָיָה **V**: 400.

חַיל **V**: 402, 615.

חילך **I**: *514*.

חים **V**: 308, 376, *589*.

חירת **V**: 421.

חָכְמַת יְוָנִית **V**: 462.

חלל√ **V**: 421; *422*.

חֵלֶב **V**: 404.

חלבנם **V**: 396.

חלה **V**: 397.

חַלָּה **V**: 422.

חלה III **V**: 396.

חֲלוֹם **V**: 422.

חליצותם **VI**: 189.

חלכה **VIII**: 476.

חללל√ **V**: *421*, 422.

חלל **I**: 237; **V**: 396, 421, *430*, 504; **VIII**: 476.

חלף **V**: 398.

חלץ **V**: 396, 398.

חֲלָצַיִם **V**: *308*, 376, *589*.

חלש **V**: 396, 422; **VI**: 109, 275, 428.

חָלַשׁ **V**: 422.

חמד **V**: 422; **IX**: cxlvii.

*חָמָה **V**: 400.

חֵמָה **V**: 422.

חמל **V**: 396.

חַמָּנִים **V**: 399, 422.

חֲמֹר גָּרֶם **VI**: 94.

חֹמֶשׁ **V**: 422.

חֲמִשָּׁה, חֲמִשִּׁים **V**: 422.

חמת **V**: 400.

חֵן **V**: 23, 24, 422*(2)*; **VIII**: 189.

חנן **V**: 424.

חסד **V**: 423; **VI**: 9; **VIII**: 199

חֶסֶד **V**: 392, 423*(6)*, *660*.

חסדו **VI**: 296.

חָסִיד **V**: 422, 423.

חסידה **V**: 396.

חָסֵר **V**: 423.

חפה **V**: 308, 376, 396, 398, *589*.

חֵפֶץ **IV**: 518; **IX**: cxl.

חפש **V**: 398.

חֹפֶשׁ **V**: 422, 423.

חצבה **VI**: 541.

חֹק **V**: 392, 423.

חֻקָּה **V**: 392.

חקורה **V**: 95.

חקלדמא **V**: 423, *440, 642, 657*.

חֳרָבוֹת **V**: 423.

חרה אפו **V**: 402, **VI**: 12.

חרוץ **V**: 400.

חֵרוּת **VI**: 504.

חרט אנקש **VI**: 265.

חַרְטֻמִּים **V**: 423.

חֲרֵי יוֹנִים **V**: 423, 569.

חרם **V**: 396.

חֶרֶשׂ **V**: 402, 615.

חרשׁ **V**: 423.

חשׁך **V**: 423.

חשב **V**: 423.

חָשַׁב **V**: 424.

חֵשֶׁב **I**: 274; **IV**: 235; **V**: 401.

חשֵׁב **I**: 274; **IV**: 235; **V**: 401.

חֹשֶׁךְ **V**: 394.

חשל **V**: 396.

חַשְׁמַל **IV**: 422.

חשמן **V**: 396.

חתל **V**: 402, 615.

חֲתֻלָּה* **V**: 402, 615.

חתן **V**: 424.

חֲתַן דָּמִים **VI**: 101.

חָתָן **V**: 396.

ט

טַבּוּר הָאָרֶץ **V**: 463; **VI**: 186.

טהורה **VI**: 466.

טהר **V**: 424.

טוֹב **V**: 392, 424.

טוטפת **V**: 424.

טט בכתפי (בגתפי) **V**: 394.

טלמם **VI**: 26.

טָמֵא, טֻמְאָה **V**: 424.

טַף **V**: 424.

טפה **V**: 404.

טֶפַח **V**: 424, 557.

טפסר **V**: 394.

טרד **V**: 401.

טרטימר **I**: *427*.

טַרְטֵימַר **I**: *427*.

י

י **V**: 424.

יאב **V**: 398.

יאכל **V**: 400.

וַיֹּאמַר **IV**: 462; **V**: 419.

יאר **V**: 425.

יבל **V**: 404.

יְגַע **V**: 397.

יגר **V**: 395; **VI**: 7, 80.

יד **V**: 399, 425*(2)*.

יָד **V**: 425.

יַד **V**: 425.

ידה **V**: 405; **VI**: 329.

יְדֶה* **V**: 397.

יָדוֹן **VI**: 50.

יָדַי* **V**: 397.

ידל **V**: 425, 426.

ידע **V**: 425*(9)*, 426*(4)*, *428(2)*, *452(3)*, 543, 572, 590*(2)*; **VI**: 270, 369.

יָדַע **I**: 515; **V**: 425, 426.

וַיֵּדַע אֱלֹהִים **VI**: 99.

ידק הדה **V**: 400.

יה **VIII**: 107.

יה(ו)ד **III**: *656*.

יהוה **V**: 398, *406*, **426***(5)*; **VI**: 8; **VIII**: 110, 114*(3)*, 116*(2)*, **§988**, **120-124**; **IX**: cxl*(2)*.

יהוה יראה **VI**: 72.

יהוה מלך **V**: 426.

יהוה נסי(?) **VIII**: 117.

יהוה צְבָאוֹת **VIII**: 120, 125*(2)*.

יהוה צדקנו **V**: 463; **VI**: 334*(3)*, 339*(2)*; **VIII**: 125.

יְהוָֹה **V**: 426*(2)*; **VIII**: 123.

יְהוֹשֻׁעַ **V**: 293, 426.

יהיה **V**: 426.

יהללוך **VIII**: 206.

יוֹבֵל **I**: *308*.

יובל הִוא **V**: 396.

יִוָּדַע **VI**: 499.

יום **V**: 399.

יום יהוה **V**: 121; **VIII**: 257.

יוֹם **V**: 426, 427*(4)*.

יָוָן **II**: 265; **III**: 130

יָוֵן **V**: 427; **VI**: 481, 497.

יְוָנִים **II**: 265; **III**: 130.

יוֹצֵר **V**: 427.

יושבת **V**: 78.

יזה **VI**: 308*(3)*.

יזה גוים **V**: 418, 438; **VI**: 308.

יחד **V**: 427*(2)*.

יַחַד **V**: 427; **VI**: 677, 683.

יַחְדָּו **V**: 398, 427.

יחוּשׁ **V**: 400.

יחי המלך **V**: 463*(2)*.

יחלו ידם להפיל בחללים **VIII**: 465.

וַיֵּחָלֵק עֲלֵיהֶם **VI**: 65.

יחפרו בעמק ושׂישׂ בכח **V**: 400.

יַיִן **I**: *263*; **V**: 403, 427*(3)*.

יכחשו לי **VI**: 464.

וַיִּכְתֹּב **VI**: 184.

ילבב **V**: 427.

ילד **V**: 427.

יָלַד **V**: *418*, 427*(2)*.

יֶלֶד **VI**: 45.

יָלִיד **I**: *190*.

ילך **V**: *418*, 427.

ילךְ, (הָלַךְ) **V**: 428.

ילפת **V**: 394.

יַלֶּפֶת **V**: 396.

יָם **VIII**: 77.

ים־סוף **III**: 209; **IV**: 324; **V**: 398.

ימלט אי־נקי **VI**: 433.

יסר ; **VIII**: 186; **IX**: cxl.

יָעִים **V**: 399.

יעיר **V**: 400.

יַעַן **V**: 400.

וַיַּעְפִּלוּ **V**: 444.

יעץ **V**: 428; **IX**: cxl.

יעקב **IV**: 481.

יער השדה **V**: 400.

ויפח **VI**: 33.

יפע **V**: 428.

יפעלהו **VIII**: 476.

יצא **V**: 428.

יֵצְאוּ מַלְאָכִים מִלְּפָנַי בַּצִּים **V**: 395.

יצר **VIII**: 476.

יָקַח* חנק **V**: 400.

יקש **V**: 428, 433.

יָרַב **V**: 428, *436*.

ירד√ **V**: 399.

ירד **V**: 399, 402, 428*(2)*, *443(2)*, *552*, 599.

יָרַד **IV**: 110; **V**: 400, 428; **VI**: 89, 188.

יַרְדֵּן **V**: 428.

וְיָרַדְתִּי **VI**: 187*(2)*.

ירח **I**: *405;* **V**: 428.

ירע **V**: *425*, 428*(2)*, *452(3)*.

יִשְׂאוּ **VIII**: 446.

יִשְׂרָאֵל **V**: 428, *453*.

ישב **V**: 399, 428, 487.

יָשַׁב **V**: 428.

יָשָׁח **VI**: 395.

ישכב **VI**: 135.

יִשְׁמָעֵאל **VI**: 68.

יָשָׁר **V**: 392.

יָשֹׁר על אנשים **V**: 398.

ית **V**: 314.

יתלח אנשים חיים **V**: 463*(2)*.

כ, ך

כְּ **V**: 429.

כארי **V**: 429; **VI**: 469.

כארי ידי ורגלי **VI**: 469*(2)*.

כָּבוֹד **V**: 429, *647;* **VI**: 532; **VIII**: 108, 149.

כַּבִּירִים **V**: 195.

כדמה **VI**: 355.

כה **V**: 444, 534, *550*.

כֹּה יַעֲשֶׂה יהוה לִי וְכֹה יֹסִיף **V**: 463.

כֹּהֵן **V**: 77, 429*(3)*.

כּוֹבַע **I**: 314; **V**: 393, 429, *448, 608*.

כּוֹה לָךְ **V**: 463.

כּוּךְ **V**: 429.

כּוּן* **V**: 400.

כּוּשׁ **VI**: 34.

כּוּשַׁן רִשְׁעָתַיִם **II**: *30;* **V**: 429; **VI**: 178.

כי **V**: 395, 429, 481; **VI**: 7, 487.

כִּי **V**: 429.

כידון **V**: 429.

כידור **V**: 400.

כֵּילָף* **V**: 402, 615.

כֵּילַפּוֹת **V**: 402, 615.

כישור **V**: 396.

כַּבָּא **V**: 393.

כִּבָּר **V**: 429.

כל **IV**: 481; **V**: 429; **VI**: 249.

כֹּל **V**: 398, 429.

כְּל **V**: 398.

וכל באי (ה)עולם עוברים לפניו כבני מרון **V**: 463; **VIII**: 208.

וְכָל־הַבְּרִים וַיִּקָּהֲלוּ וַיָּבֹאוּ אַף־אַחֲרָיו **V**: 395.

כִּלְאָ **V**: 430, 525, *563*.

כֶּלֶב **V**: 430.

כַּלָּה **V**: 397.

כָּלוּב **V**: 396.

כִּלְיָה, כְּלָיוֹת **V**: 392, 430.

כָּלִיל **I**: 274; **IV**: 235; **V**: 401.

כלך לך **V**: 405.

כלל **V**: 58.

הכל (from כלל) **V**: 395; **VI**: 7, 564.

כְּמוֹ־כֵן **V**: 398.

כַּמֹּן **V**: 396.

כמס **V**: 396.

כמר **V**: 430.

כֹּמֶר **V**: 430.

כֵּן **V**: 394.

כִּנָּם **V**: 394.

כִּנִּם **V**: 394.

כנעני **V**: 430.

כִּנָּרָא **V**: 393.

כסה (כסא) **V**: 398.

כֶּסֶף **I**: 299; **V**: 401.

כסף זוז **I**: 427.

וּכְעֶנֶת **V**: 419.

כְּעֶרְכִּי **VI**: 491.

כָּעֵת הַיָּה **V**: 463.

כפיר החרון **VIII**: 477.

כִּפְלַיִם **V**: 430.

כפר **V**: 430; **VIII**: 194.

כפר, כִּפֵּר **V**: 57, 393, 430*(5);* **VIII**: 193.

כִּפֻּרִים **V**: 430*(2);* **VIII**: 193.

כַּפֹּרֶת **V**: 430*(2);* **VI**: 123; **VIII**: 193.

כַּפֹּת תְּמָרִים **VI**: 125.

מְכֻרְבָּל **V**: 402, 615.

כרבלא **I**: *276.*

כְּרוּב **V**: 430.

כְּרוּבִים **V**: 393.

כַּרְכֹּם **V**: 396.

כֶּרֶם **VI**: 459.

כַּרְמֶל **V**: 430.

כַּרַן **V**: 397.

כרר **I**: 237; **V**: 421, 430, 504.

כשיל וכילפות **V**: 395.

כשר√ **V**: 431.

וַיִּכְתֹּב **V**: 419; **VI**: 184.

כתם **V**: 396.

כתנת **V**: 396.

כֻּתֹּנֶת **V**: 431, *552;* **IX**: xc.

כתף **V**: 431.

כֶּתֶר **V**: 393.

כתר **V**: 394.

כתשׁ **V**: 401.

ל

ל **V**: 394, 431*(2)*, 481; **VI**: 6.

לְ **V**: 431*(2)*, 482; **VI**: 393.

לא **V**: 394, 481, 482; **VI**: 6, 512.

לא הוא **VI**: 324.

ולא ידעו **VI**: 330.

לֹא־תָבוֹא שָׁמָּה יִרְאַת שָׁמִיר וָשָׁיִת **VI**: 265.

לא תדע **VI**: 539.

לְאִישׁ חֲסִידֶךָ **VI**: 153.

*לְאַךְ **V**: 432.

לֵב, לֵבָב **V**: 392, 431*(4)*, *651*.

לבֹא חמת **V**: 400.

לבב **V**: 396, 431.

לְבָה **V**: 397.

לְבִי סְחַרְחַר **VI**: 481.

לָבִיא **V**: 431, *623*.

לבשׁ **V**: 400.

לָדַעַת **VI**: 438.

לדעת לעות את יעף דבר **VI**: 305.

להט **V**: 431.

להק **V**: 401.

להתרועע **VI**: 542.

לוּז **VI**: 78.

לֵוִי **V**: 43, 77, 393, 431.

לולא **VI**: 474.

לֵחַ **VI**: 155.

לְהִי **V**: 432.

לְחַיַּת **V**: 432.

לחם **V**: 402, **VI**: 12.

לְחֵנָה **V**: 397.

לט **V**: 396.

לילית **V**: **137***(2);* **VI**: 287.

לִילִית **V**: 393.

לִיץ **V**: 432.

לֵיץ **V**: 432.

לִיץ **V**: 432.

לְיִקְּהַת **VI**: 549.

לֵךְ הִתְרַפֵּס וּרְהַב רֵעֶיךָ **V**: 397.

לְכָה **VI**: 191.

לכן **V**: 483.

לָכֵן **V**: 432.

למד **V**: 395.

למטלים Q **VIII**: 447, 481.

לְמַעַן **V**: 432*(2)*, 497.

לַע **V**: 308, 376, 432, *589*.

לְפִי־חָרֶב **V**: 398, 463.

לַפִּיד **V**: 403, 615.

לצמתת **VI**: 126.

לקח **V**: 432.

לקח ובל נשא נטל **V**: 403.

לקשׁ **V**: 401.

לָשׁוּחַ בַּשָּׂדֶה **VI**: 75.

מ, ם

מ **V**: 400.

enclitic מ **V**: 400, 432.

מְאֹד **V**: 432; **VI**: 204.

מֵאֵין כָּמוֹךָ **VI**: 328.

מאן ממאן **V**: 400.

מַבּוּל **VI**: *50,* 476, *565.*

מבליג **V**: 395; **VI**: 7, 382, 383*(2)*, 386.

מבקר **VIII**: 419.

מבקר **VIII**: 414, 419.

מָגוֹר מִסָּבִיבכב **VI**: 332*(2)*.

מְגֵן **V**: 432, *435(2)*.

מִדֵּד **VI**: 425.

וימד שש שעורים **VI**: 557.

מדה **VIII**: 476.

מַדְהֵבָה **VI**: 275.

מָדִין **V**: 396.

מַדַּע **V**: 543, 572,

מדרש תהלים **VI**: 502.

מה **V**: 395, 481; **VI**: 7.

מַהֲנַיִם צְבָאוֹת **V**: 393.

מוֹל **V**: 398, 433.

מוּל **V**: 398, 433.

מומר **V**: 433, 436.

מוֹסֵף **V**: 433, *438*.

מוֹעֵד **V**: 433.

מוֹעָדִים **VI**: 335.

מועצה **V**: 428.

מוֹפֵת **V**: 433.

מוּקְרָא **V**: 393.

מוקש **V**: 433*(2)*.

מוֹקֵשׁ **V**: 433; **VI**: 380.

מוֹרֶה **V**: 394; **VI**: 6.

מורה הצדק **VIII**: 477.

הַמּוֹרֶה לִצְדָקָה **VI**: 374.

מורים **V**: 396.

מוֹשִׁיעַ **V**: 433.

מות **V**: 196, 433.

מות תמות **V**: 463.

מזור **V**: 433; **VI**: 388.

מֵזַח **V**: 433.

וּמְזִיחַ אֲפִיקִים רִפָּה **V**: 395.

מזיקר **V**: 433.

מזנון **V**: 433, *459*.

מַזָּרוֹת **VI**: 439*(2)*.

מחה **V**: 395.

מחלצות **VI**: 407.

מטחן **V**: 433; **IX**: cxlviii.

מָטִיל **V**: 403, 615.

מטרון **V**: 433, 434*(2)*; **IX**: cxlviii*(3)*.

מִי **V**: 395, 481; **VI**: 7.

מיוקר **V**: 433.

מילי מוליאתא **V**: 394.

מַיִם רַבִּים **V**: 463*(2)*; **VI**: 402.

מין **V**: 402, **VI**: 12.

מִין **V**: 393.

מכילתא דברים **VI**: 706.

מכר **V**: 434*(2)*.

מֶכֶר **V**: 434.

מכרה **V**: 395.

מכרתיהם **VI**: 92.

מְלֹא **V**: 395.

מַלֵּא אֶת־יָד **V**: 463.

מלאו **VI**: 323.

מלאך **V**: 434*(2)*.

מַלְאָךְ **V**: 393.

מַלְאָךְ יהוה **V**: 393.

מלחמה **V**: 434.

מֵלִיץ **V**: 434*(2)*.

מלך **V**: 434*(2)*.

מֶלֶךְ **V**: 77, 398, 434.

וּמֶלֶךְ אַלְקוּם עִמּוֹ **VI**: 549.

מֶלֶךְ הָעוֹלָם **V**: 463*(2)*, 464.

מֶלֶךְ עוֹלָם **VIII**: 207*(5)*, 208, 240.

מָלַךְ **V**: 393.

מלל **V**: 398.

מלתחה **V**: 402, **VI**: 12.

מלתעות **V**: 396.

מַלְתְּעוֹת **VI**: 492.

מַמְזֵר **V**: 393, 434*(2)*, 560.

מִמָּחֳרַת הַשַּׁבָּת **V**: 464.

ממשת **V**: 434*(2)*.

מָן **V**: 435.

מַן **IX**: cxl.

מֵן **V**: 396.

מִן **I**: *152;* **V**: 435; **VI**: 141.

מנה **V**: 435.

מָנֶה **I**: *447*.

מנהרוה **V**: 395.

מנור אֹרגים **I**: 317; **IV**: 377.

מִנְזָר **V**: 393.

מִנְחָה **V**: 57, 103, 393*(2)*, 435.

מַס **V**: 398.

המסדרונה **V**: 393.

מסדרון **V**: 402, **VI**: 12.

מָסוֹרָה* **V**: 435.

מָסָךְ **V**: *432*, 435.

מְסֻכָּן **VI**: 297.

המסכן תרומה **V**: 400.

מסעד **V**: 405; **VI**: 11.

מִסְפָּר **V**: 398.

מסקרת **V**: 394.

מְעֻבָּר **V**: 308, 376, *589*.

מָעוֹג **V**: 435; **VI**: 480.

מעוה **V**: 435, *648*.

מָעוֹז **V**: 435.

מָעוֹן **V**: 435.

מֵעַזָּה **V**: 435, *648*.

מעט **V**: 394.

מעט חבק ידים לשכב **VI**: 539, 545.

מעצמותי **V**: 400.

מצבת **VIII**: 447.

מַצֶּבֶת **VI**: 258.

מצבתה **VIII**: 447.

מַצָּה **V**: *434*, 435.

מצהב **I**: 299; **V**: 401.

מִצְוָה **V**: 392, 435.

מצרים **V**: 435, *446*.

מִקֶּדֶם **VI**: 58.

מקוה **VIII**: 476.

מָקוֹם **V**: 435.

מָקוֹם אֶחָד **VI**: 563.

מְקוֹם הַקֹּדֶשׁ **V**: 391.

מָקוֹם קָדֹשׁ **V**: 391.

מקנה **VI**: 563.

מִקֵּץ **VIII**: 476.

מקצוע **V**: 435, 450.

מקרא קֹדש **V**: 396.

מקרא קדש **V**: 464.

מִקְרָאֵי קֹדֶשׁ **V**: 464.

מֹר **V**: 396.

מָר־דְּרוֹר **IV**: 235; **V**: 401.

מרא II **V**: 396.

מֻרְבֶּכֶת **V**: 399.

מרדו **V**: 394.

מַרְדּוּת **V**: 435.

מֵרוּב* **V**: *428*, 436.

מַרְחֶשֶׁת **V**: 399.

המריא **V**: 394.

מרים **V**: 400.

מר־ץ√ **VI**: 424, 425.

מרר **V**: 404*(2)*.

מַשָּׂא **V**: 436*(4)*.

מַשְׂכִּיל **IV**: 490, 491; **V**: 436*(2), 453;* **VI**: 482.

מֵשָׂא **V**: 436; **IX**: cxl.

מַשָּׂאוֹת **V**: 395.

מִשְׁאָל **V**: 436.

משבה **V**: 436, *531*.

משומד **V**: *433*, 436.

מִשְׁחַת **VI**: 308; **VIII**: 446.

משחתי **VIII**: 476.

מֶשִׁי **V**: 396.

מֶשִׁי **V**: 403, 615.

הַמָּשִׁיחַ **V**: 419; **VIII**: 139.

משך **V**: 396.

מָשַׁךְ **V**: 394.

מָשָׁל **V**: 436*(4)*.

מִשְׁמָר **VI**: 425.

מִשְׁמֶרֶת **V**: 392.

מִשְׁפָּט **I**: *191, 486;* **IV**: 370; **V**: 392, 417, 436*(2)*, 437*(5)*, 509.

המשפתים **VI**: 94, 181.

משק **V**: 437.

משרתים־מלכים **V**: 469.

משתבשין **IV**: 19; **V**: 437.

מת*, מְתִים **V**: 392, 510, 518.

מתם **V**: 394.

מְתֹם, מְתִים **V**: 437.

מַתָּנָה **VI**: 131.

מתנחם **VI**: 77.

מתק **V**: 403, 615.

נ, ן

נא **V**: 399.

נאמן **VIII**: 476.

נאץ **V**: 404.

נְאֵץ **V**: 393.

ונאשאר אני **VI**: 350.

נבא **V**: 399.

נבות **V**: 394.

נָבִיא (נְבִאִים) **I**: *114;* **V**: 77, 393, 394*(2)*, 437*(2)*; **VI**: 6, 8.

נבל **V**: 437.

נְבֵלָה **V**: 437*(3)*.

נגד **V**: 437.

נָגִיד **V**: 437.

נגף **V**: 438.

נדגלות **V**: 438.

וְנוֹדַע לָכֶם **VI**: 196.

נוּחַ **V**: 438.

בנוית **V**: 394; **VI**: 394.

נולי **V**: 395.

נוֹסֵךְ **V**: *433*, 438.

נוֹעֲדוּ **VI**: 380.

נוף **V**: 396.

נוֹקֵד **V**: 438.

נזה **V**: 396.

הִזָּה (Hiph. of נזה) **V**: 89, 418, 438.

נזל **V**: 438.

נָחָה **V**: 400, 405; **VI**: 329.

נחל **V**: 438.

נחם **V**: 438*(3)*, 445.

נחץ(?) **V**: 396.

נחר **V**: 396.

נָחָשׁ **VI**: 36*(2)*.

1QM נחשר **V**: 403, 615.

נַחְשָׁרִיהַ* **V**: 403.

נחשת **V**: 396.

נחשת מצהב **I**: 299; **V**: 401.

ונחת **V**: 400.

נים **V**: 398.

נִיר **V**: 438; **VI**: 12, 133.

נכון **V**: 438.

נְכָסִים **V**: 438.

נכר **V**: 397.

נכרי **V**: 438.

נמד **VI**: 178.

1QIs[a] והנמצא **VI**: 290; **VIII**: 447.

נמרץ **V**: 397.

נסוך **V**: 394; **VI**: 6.

נסה **VI**: 112.

נסרך **V**: 394; **VI**: 6.

נַעַר **V**: 392, 510, 518.

נַעַרְ **VI**: 26, 74.

נעתם **VI**: 270.

נעתרות **V**: 395.

נָפָה **V**: 439.

נְפִילִים **VI**: 50, *476, 565*.

נפל **V**: 401, 439; **VI**: 435.

נָפַל **V**: 400, *591*.

נֹפֶל **VI**: 136, 137.

נִפְעֶל **V**: 488*(2)*.

נִפְעַל **V**: 488.

נפש **V**: 544.

נפשׁ **III**: 556; **V**: 451.

נֶפֶשׁ **V**: 392, *414*, 439*(4)*, *451*, 506, 515.

נצוים **VI**: 323.

נצח **V**: 438, 439, *662*.

נֵצַח **V**: 439.

נקי **V**: 439.

נְקִיצֶנָּה וְנַבְקִעֶנָּה אֵלֵינוּ **VI**: 259.

נְקִיצֶנָּה **VI**: 260.

נְקָמָה **V**: 439.

נקק **V**: 404.

נֵרְדְּ **III**: *394;* **V**: 396, 560.

נָשָׂא **V**: 439.

נָשִׂיא **I**: *192*.

נשיא אלהים **VI**: 74.

נשך **V**: 439, *460*.

נַשָּׁכ **V**: *565*.

נַשָּׁל **V**: 565.

נְשָׁמָה **V**: 392, 439.

נשְׁעַן **V**: 483.

נשק **VI**: 87.

נשקו־בר **VI**: 452*(3)*.

נָתִין, נְתִינִים **V**: 78.

נתן√ **V**: 439.

נָתַן **V**: 405.

נתר **V**: 396.

ס

ס in the Samaria Ostraca **II**: 272; **VII**: 137.

סאסא **V**: 397, 440, *563*.

סבל **V**: 420, 490, *538*, *552*.

סבל הירושה **V**: 401.

סבל־סבלום **V**: 440.

סבר **V**: 394.

סגור **V**: *410*, 440.

סְגֻלָּה **V**: 170, 440, *549;* **IX**: lxxxviii.

סוֹד **V**: 440.

סחר **IV**: 271*(2)*, 440*(2)*.

סירא **V**: *423*, 440, *642*, *657*.

סִירוֹת **V**: 440.

סִירִים **V**: 440.

סְכּוּת **VI**: 384.

סכין **V**: 404.

סכל **V**: 440.

סכל שכל **V**: 398.

הַסְּכֵּן **VI**: 432.

סֹכֵן **V**: 402, **VI**: 12.

סכת **V**: 440.

סֶלָה **IV**: **§388**, **492**; **V**: 440*(2)*, 683.

סמל **V**: 441.

סמר **V**: 394.

סנורים **V**: 398.

סניס **V**: 441.

סנסן **V**: 441.

סנפיר **V**: 394.

הַסְּעִפִּים **V**: 419; **VI**: 228.

סַף **V**: 441.

ספר החגו Q **VIII**: 456.

*סַפְסִיג **V**: 403; **VI**: 547.

סֶפֶר **IV**: 466.
סַפָּר **V**: 394.
ספר **V**: 400.
ספר ההגו/י **VIII**: 477.
סְפַרְוַיִם **III**: 234; **V**: 441.
ספרתי **VIII**: 476.
ספרתי **VI**: 11.
for קִפַּדְתִּ
in 1 QIs[a]
סרבל **I**: *276*.
סרים **V**: 396.
סָרִיס **V**: 396.
סְרָנִים **V**: 441.
סרן **V**: 394.
סִרְפַּד **V**: 394.
סֵתֶר **V**: 394.
הַסתֵר וְאֶקְצֹף **VI**: 313.

ע

ע **V**: 441.
עב **V**: 396.
עָב **V**: 396, 441.
עֶבֶד **IV**: 416.
עֶבֶד יהוה **IV**: 402; **VIII**: 147.
עבד **IV**: 402*(2)*, 441*(2)*.
עבר **IV**: *247;* **V**: 396.
עבר בשלח **VI**: 436, 437.
עבר לפני התיבה **VIII**: 205, 381.
עֶבְרָה **V**: 405; **VI**: 92, 329.
עברים **V**: 441.
עבֹת **V**: 394.
עגלת שלשיה **V**: 465.
עד√ **V**: 441.
עד **V**: 441, 442.
עַד **V**: 398.
עֵד **VI**: 114.
עַד II **V**: 441*(3)*.
עדד **V**: 396.
עד־דן **VI**: 65.
עדדן **V**: 159, 528.
עדה **V**: 441, *448*.
עדו√ **V**: 400.
עֵדוּת **V**: 392, 442.
עֲדַיִן **V**: 404.
עדר **V**: 396.
עוֹד **V**: 400.
עַוָּה **V**: 442; **VI**: 240*(2)*, 289, 290.
עָוֶל, עַוְלָה **V**: 392.
עולם **V**: 398, 441, 442*(4)*
עוֹלָם **V**: 407, *442(2), 543, 558*.
עוֹלָם **V**: 442*(3)*
עומדים במים **V**: 404.
עָוֹן **V**: 392.
עור **V**: 398.
עוֹר **V**: 442
עֹז as a musical expresson **V**: 394.
עזאזל **V**: 442.
עָזַב I **VI**: 583.
עזב II **IV**: 468; **V**: 442.
עָזִי וְזִמְרָת יָהּ **VI**: 108.

עֲזָקָה **V**: 442; **VII**: 174*(2)*

עחר√ **V**: 397.

עיא **V**: 488.

עֵילָם **V**: *407*, 442*(2)*, *543*, *558*.

עִין אָדָם **VI**: 410.

עיף **V**: 442.

עיר **V**: 402.

הָעֵיר **V**: 419.

עיר המים **VI**: 213.

עִיר **V**: 442, *449*.

עיש **V**: 401.

על **V**: 443, 482; **VIII**: 110.

עַל I **IV**: *491;* **V**: 443; **VIII**: 110.

עַל II **V**: 443.

האבנים וידבר ועל על הפצים **V**: 400.

עַל־הֲיְּדוֹת **V**: 395.

עַל־מוּת **VI**: 495.

עלבה **V**: 402, *552*.

העלה **IV**: 340; **V**: *418*, 419.

עלה **V**: 428*(2)*, 443*(2)*, 599; **VI**: 89, 188.

עָלָה **IV**: 110; **V**: 443.

עֹלָה **V**: 57, 103, 393*(2)*.

עלוה **V**: 402, **VI**: 12.

עלז **V**: 402, **VI**: 12.

העליה **VI**: 198.

עָלָיו **V**: 482, 484.

עליון אל **VI**: 62; **VIII**: 107.

עלמה **V**: 78, 443; **VI**: 262, 263*(5)*, 265*(2)*.

עַלְמָה **V**: 443*(5)*.

עליקן אל **VI**: 62.

עַם **V**: 443*(2)*.

עם־הארץ **V**: 464*(3)*.

עַמִּי שַׁדַּי **V**: 464.

עמיה **V**: 444.

עַמִּיהוּד **V**: 395.

עמיו **V**: 444.

עמיך **V**: 444.

עָמָל **IV**: 517; **V**: 444; **IX**: cxl.

עָמָל **V**: 392.

עמק **V**: 403, 536, *550*.

עמק **V**: 444, 534.

עמקם? **V**: 395.

עֲנוֹת **VI**: 117*(3)*.

עֳנִי **V**: 444.

עָנָן **V**: 444.

עפל√, וַיַּעְפִּלוּ (Hiph.) **V**: 444.

עָפָר **VI**: 431.

עצב **V**: 394.

עצד **V**: 444.

עצה **V**: 428.

עֵצָה **VI**: 285.

עצור ועזוב **V**: 464.

ועזוב בישראל עצור **VI**: 226.

עָצוּר וְעָזוּב **V**: 398, 442, 444, 464.
עצור ועזוב בישראל **V**: 464.
עָצוּר וְעָזוּב **I**: 321.
עֵצָה **V**: 400.
עֶצֶם **V**: 568.
עָצְמָה* **V**: 400.
עקרון **V**: 444, 570, *642*.
ערבה **V**: 402.
ערות **V**: 400; **VI**: 278.
ערות על־יאור על־פי יאור וכל מזרל יאור ייבש ונדש ונדף ואיננו **VI**: 278.
עריוה **V**: 444.
עריסה **V**: 444.
ערכך **V**: 394.
עֶרְכְּךָ **V**: 396.
ערער **V**: 404.
ערף **V**: 444.
עֹרֶף **V**: 444; **VI**: 121.
עשה **V**: 404.
עשׂה **V**: *444(2)*
עָשָׂה **V**: 444.
עשַׂן **V**: 444.
עשק **V**: 401.
עשיק **V**: 394.
עשיר **V**: 400.
עשׂר **V**: 400.
עשרה בטלנין **V**: *462*, 464.
עַשְׁתֵּי **V**: 444, 581.
עתם√ **VI**: 270.
עתם **VI**: 502.

פּ, ף

פָּארוּר **VI**: 398.
פָּארָן **VI**: 402.
פגעים **V**: 404.
פגר **V**: 194, 445.
פה **V**: 445.
פֶּה לָפֶה **VI**: 236.
פוּךְ **V**: 445.
פוח **V**: 438, 445.
פוטריו אונו **V**: 464.
פולסא **V**: 445, *671*.
פוּר **V**: 400.
פוּר* **V**: 445.
פורים **V**: 396.
פחה **V**: 394, *562;* **VI**: 5
פחז **V**: 402, **VI**: 12.
פטש **I**: *276*.
פִּילֶגֶשׁ **V**: 397.
פילס **V**: 445, *671*.
פלח **V**: *308*, 376, *589*.
פְּלֵיטָה **V**: 445.
פלל **V**: 445*(2);* **VI**: 152.
פָּנֶיךָ הֹלְכִים **V**: 460, 464; **VI**: 118, 214.
פנינים **V**: 399, 445.
פסח **V**: 398, 445.
פָּסַח **V**: 445.
פסיק **IV**: 474, 475.

פִּסְקָא בְּאֶמְצַע פָּסוּק **IV**: 18; **V**: 493.
פעלהו **VIII**: 476.
פַּעַם וּשְׁתַּיִם **V**: 465.
פצירה **VI**: 200.
פָּקַד **IV**: 114; **V**: 446*(2)*; **VI**: 163*(2)*; **VIII**: 419.
פקד—ספר **V**: 405; **VI**: 11.
פְּקֻדָּה **V**: 446.
פִּקּוּדִים* **V**: 392.
פְּקַח־קוֹחַ **V**: 399.
הַפָּר הַשֵּׁנִי **VI**: 183.
פרד **V**: 403, 536.
פַּרְוַיִם **V**: 399.
פַּרְוָר **V**: 399.
פרח **V**: 395.
פרט√ **VI**: 385.
פְּרִי עֵץ הָדָר **VI**: 126.
פֶּרֶךְ **V**: 446, 569.
פרס **V**: 446.
פרס על שמע **V**: 92; **VIII**: 205, 381.
פרץ **V**: 446; **VIII**: 476.
פָּרַץ **V**: 446*(2)*.
פֶּרֶק **V**: 395.
פרקד **V**: 404.
פֶּרֶשׁ **V**: 446*(2)*.
הפרשדנה **V**: 393.
פרתה **V**: 394.
פַּשְׁחוּר **VI**: 332.
פָּשַׁע **V**: 392.
פשתי **VI**: 365.
פֹּת **V**: 396.
פתגמא **V**: *435*, 446.
פתח **V**: 396.
פֶּתָח **V**: 397.
פתיחה **V**: 396.
פתק **V**: 401.
פַּתְרוֹס **IV**: 475; **V**: 446.

צ, ץ

צאן ברזל **VI**: 703.
צֹאן בַּרְזֶל **I**: *255, 467;* **V**: 464.
צבאות **V**: 78.
צְבָאוֹת **V**: 393.
צדוק **VIII**: 436.
צדיק **VI**: 334; **VIII**: 436.
צדק **V**: 446, 447*(4)*; **VIII**: 436.
צֶדֶק **V**: 446.
צְדָקָה **I**: *182.*
צְדָקָה **V**: 392.
צדקת פרזנו **VI**: 181.
צהר **V**: 447.
צועת **V**: 447.
צַחֲנָה **V**: 447, *588.*
צִי II **V**: 396.
צִיִּים **VI**: 497.
צִיץ **V**: 447, 534.
צִיצִת **V**: 448.
צִיר **V**: 393.
צֵל **V**: 447.
צָלַח **V**: 447.

צֶלֶם **V**: 447.

צַלְמָוֶת **V**: 447*(3)*.

צַלְמוּת **V**: 447.

צלפחד **V**: 394.

צֶמַח **V**: 457; **VI**: 254, 333, 338.

צמק **V**: 393.

צִנּוֹר **V**: 447; **VI**: 209.

צנח **V**: 447.

צנע **V**: 447; **VI**: 416.

צִנְצֶנֶת **V**: 396.

צעור(Kethīb) **V**: 447; **VI**: 329, 342, 343, 413.

צָעִיר(Qeré) **V**: 447; **VI**: 329, 342, 343, 413.

(בְּ)צַעֲנַנִּים **V**: 447.

צער **II**: 262.

צֹעַר **V**: 447; **VI**: 329, 342, 343, 413.

צפא **V**: 400.

צָפְנַת פַּעְנֵחַ **VI**: 88.

צפצף **V**: 398.

צר כחכה **V**: 402, **VI**: 12.

צְרִי **V**: 396.

צרעת **V**: 448*(2), 652*.

ק

קאת **V**: 448, 450.

קבב **V**: 400.

קבה **V**: 400, 402, **VI**: 12.

קבל **V**: 448.

קבע **V**: 396, 403, 615.

קדד **V**: 396.

קִדָּה **IV**: 235; **V**: 401.

קָדוֹשׁ **V**: 392.

קדושים **V**: 448.

קדם **V**: 395.

קדרנית **V**: 447; **VI**: 416.

קדש√ **V**: 448.

קָדַשׁ **V**: 78, 392, 448.

קֹדֶשׁ קָדָשִׁים **V**: 391.

הַקֹּדֶשׁ **V**: 391.

קָדְשֵׁי הַקֳּדָשִׁים **V**: 391.

הַקֳּדָשִׁים **V**: 391.

קהה√ **V**: 397.

קהל√ **V**: 449.

קהל **V**: *441*, 448.

קָהָל **V**: 448.

קְהִלָּה **V**: 449.

קהלת **V**: 448.

קוֹבַע **I**: 314; **V**: 403, 429*(2)*, 448, 609.

קָוֶה חִיל (חול) **V**: 400.

קוטל **V**: 448; **VIII**: 476.

קול **V**: 449.

קול עֲנוֹת אנכי שמע **VI**: 117.

קולכודיאה **V**: 449.

קולקודיא **V**: 449.

קום **V**: 449.

קוֹץ **V**: 394; **VI**: 6.

קוֹשׁ **V**: 394; **VI**: 6.

קושיהו **V**: 449*(2)*.

קטר **V**: *444*, 449.

קטריקו **V**: 404.

קְטֹרֶת **V**: 449, *653*.

קיטור **VI**: 523, 532.

קי"ץ **V**: 396.

קִיר **V**: *442*, 449.

קישי **V**: 449*(2)*.

קלס **V**: 398, 402, 615.

קְלֹקֵל **V**: 395.

קמץ צלח **V**: 465.

קמצוץ **V**: 404.

קנאים **V**: 449.

קנה√ **V**: 449.

קנה **I**: 221; **V**: 396. 414, 449*(2)*.

קנט **V**: 401.

קנים **V**: 449; **VI**: 50.

קנישקין **V**: 450.

קנמון **V**: 396.

קסס **V**: 396.

קעקע **V**: 400.

קפד **V**: *448*, 450.

קִפַּדְתִּ **VI**: 11.

קפו **V**: 399.

קפים **V**: 396.

קפץ צלח **V**: 465, *643*.

קץ **V**: 689; **VIII**: 384, 476.

קֵץ **VIII**: 476.

קְצִיטָה **IV**: 235; **V**: 401.

קצין **V**: 450.

קציעה **V**: 396.

קצע√ **V**: *435*, 450; **IX**: cxl.

קרא **V**: 450.

קרא בשם **IV**: 406.

קרב **V**: 450.

קרבן **V**: 450; **VI**: 412.

קָרְבָּן **V**: 57, 103, 393*(2)*.

קַרְדֹּם **V**: 402, 615.
(קַרדוּמוֹת*?)

קרוא **V**: 402, **VI**: 12.

קרחה **V**: 404.

קריא **V**: 402, **VI**: 12.

קְרִיאֵי הָעֵדָה **V**: 465.

קִרְיַת־סַנָּה **VI**: 172.

קרנים מידק לו **VI**: 402.

קרס **V**: 396.

קרר **V**: 396.

קֶרֶת **V**: 403, 615.

קַשׁ **V**: 450.

קשח **V**: 401.

קשקש **V**: 404.

קֶשֶׁת **V**: 450; **VI**: 207.

לַהֲקַת הַנְּבִיאִים **V**: 397.

ר

ר **V**: 450.

ראה **V**: 400.

רֹאֶה **V**: 77, 393, 450.

ראמות **V**: 399.

ראש **V**: 450; **IX**: ciii.

רֹאשׁ **V**: 450.

רֹאשׁ פִּנָּה **V**: 465.

רבב√ **V**: 451.

רַבִּי **V**: 450.

הרבים **V**: 400.

רֹבַע **V**: 397; **VI**: 135.

רבץ **V**: 456.

רִגְמָה **V**: 394; **VI**: 5.

רגע **V**: 398, 450.

רגשׁ **V**: 401.

רְדִיד **V**: 396.

רַהַב הֵמ שָׁבֶת **VI**: 285.

רוֹבֶה **IV**: 175; **VI**: 688.

רוד **V**: 399.

רוה **V**: 400, 591.

רוזנים **V**: 451.

רוח **V**: 404, *439*, 451*(4)*, 484.

רוּחַ **V**: 392, *414*, *439*, 451*(3)*, 506, 515*(2)*; **VI**: 28; **VIII**: 153, 476.

רוּחַ אֱלֹהִים **VI**: 27; **VIII**: 153.

רוּחַ רָעָה **V**: 393.

רוחא **V**: 404.

רוץ **V**: 451, 550, 562.

רזן **V**: 451, 562.

רְחַב לֵב **V**: 465.

רְחַב לֵבָב **V**: 465.

רחם **V**: 452.

רַחֲמִים **V**: 452*(2)*.

רחף **V**: 451.

ריב **I**: *189*; **IV**: 358; **V**: 451*(2)*, 692, 693.

ריע **V**: 428.

ריפח **V**: 401.

רֶכֶב **V**: 452.

רכב **V**: 398.

רככים צמדים **VI**: 236.

רכס **V**: 396.

רִנָּה **IV**: 484; **V**: 452.

רֶסֶן **V**: 393.

רָע, רַע **V**: 392.

רֹעַ **V**: 451.

רָעָה **V**: 452.

רעם **V**: 452.

רעמו פנים **V**: 400.

רעע **V**: *425*, *428(2)*, 452*(3)*.

רעש **V**: 452.

רָפָה **V**: 452, *563*.

רפות **V**: 401.

רפה רפא **V**: 398.

רָצָה **V**: 452.

הָרֵקִים **VI**: 210. (from ריק)

רָקִיעַ **V**: 452.

רקץ **V**: 550.

רשע **V**: 401.

רָשָׁע **V**: 392.

רשעים **V**: 400.

רשף **V**: 452, *566*.

רֶשֶׁף **V**: 452.

רתו לא מידי **V**: 465.

שׂ

שׂ **V**: 453.

שׂאה **V**: 453.

שׂאֵת **V**: 402, **VI**: 12.

שׂדה **V**: 453.

שָׂדֶה **V**: 453.

שְׂדֵי **V**: 453*(2)*; **VI**: 208, 274, 423, 508.

שׂהד **V**: 395.

שׂהין **V**: 396.

שְׂהֲרֹנִים **V**: 453.

שׂחיף **V**: 396.

שָׂחִיף **V**: 396.

שָׂטָן **V**: 393.

שִׂיחַ **V**: 453.

שׂים **V**: 396, 405.

שׂים על **V**: 395; **VI**: 7.

שׂכל **V**: 453*(3)*.

שֶׂכֶל (שֵׂכֶל) **V**: 453.

שׂמאל **V**: 395.

שׂמד **V**: 396.

שׂמח **V**: 453.

שְׂמִיכָה **V**: 396.

שׂמם III (?) **V**: 402, *552*.

שׂער **V**: 453.

שַׂעֲרַת **VI**: 423.

שׂפק **V**: 453; **VI**: 253.

שְׂרַפִים **V**: 393.

שׂתם **V**: 398.

שׂתר **V**: 398.

שׂתר בוזני **V**: 395.

שׁ

שׁ **V**: 483*(3)*; **VI**: 49, 93.

שְׁאוֹל **V**: 454*(12)*, *641*; **VIII**: 267.

שׁאל **V**: 398.

שׁאל **V**: 454.

שׁאר **V**: 454; **VIII**: 211.

שׁאר ישוב **IV**: 396*(2)*.

שָׁבַט **V**: 457.

שֵׁבֶט **V**: 454*(2)*, 457.

שבי ישראל **VIII**: 411.

שׁבע **V**: 455.

שֶׁבַע **V**: 455*(2)*

שְׁבֵץ **I**: 274; **IV**: 235; **V**: 401.

שַׁבָּת **V**: 455.

שבת חמס **V**: 400.

וְשַׁבְתִּי **VI**: 473.

שַׁג **V**: 397.

שגגה **V**: 455; **VI**: 419.

שָׁגָה **V**: 400.

שׁגיון **V**: 396.

שׁגל **V**: 397.

שָׁגַל **V**: 397.

שֶׁגֶל **V**: 397.

שֵׁגָל **V**: 397.

שְׁגָל **V**: 397.

שׁד **VI**: 208.

שדה **V**: 455.

שַׁדַּי **VIII**: 106, 109, 111.

וּשְׁדֵי תְרוּמֹת **VI**: 208.

שַׁדִּין **VI**: 431.

שדמות **V**: 455.

שׂוֹא **V**: 394; **VI**: 6.

שְׁוָא **V**: 477*(2)*.

שָׁוְא **V**: 455.

שׁוּב **V**: 455*(3)*.

שוח **V**: 398, 403, 536.

שולל **V**: 401.

שוף **V**: 397.

שׁוֹפֵט **V**: 454*(2)*, 457, 458*(2)*.

שופט־מלך **V**: 458.

שוק **V**: 455.

הַשּׁוֹק וְהֶעָלֶיהָ **V**: 397.

הַשּׁוֹק וְהֶעֲלֶיהָ **V**: 397.

שׁוּר **V**: 456.

שׁוֹר **V**: 455.

שׁוֹרֵר **V**: 455.

שָׁחָה **V**: 456, *656*.

שְׁחָקִים **V**: 456.

שחר **V**: 398.

שַׁחַת **VI**: 426; **VIII**: 476.

שטף **V**: 456.

שטר, שֹׁטְרִים **V**: 455.

שַׁי **V**: 398, 401.

שילח **V**: 456.

שִׁיר **V**: 456, 589.

שִׁית **V**: 405.

שכב **V**: 456.

שָׁכַב **VI**: 135.

שכה√ **V**: 402, **VI**: 12.

שכח **V**: 395.

שכל **V**: 397.

שֶׁכֶם **VI**: 185.

שְׁכַשׁ **V**: 456.

שָׁלַג **I**: *273;* **V**: 456

שָׁלוֹם **V**: 456.

שלח **V**: 394, 400.

שלח **V**: 396.

הַשִּׁלַּחַ **VI**: 266.

שִׁלְחוֹ הַמָּיִם **VI**: 584.

שְׁלָטִים **V**: 456*(2)*.
(Constr. שִׁלְטֵי)

שָׁלִיחַ **V**: 456*(4)*.

שליש **V**: 456.

שָׁלִישׁ III **V**: 403, 457, 615.

שלך **V**: 419.
from (השליך)

שלם כלל **V**: 58.

שְׁלָמִים **V**: 64, 457, *650*.

שלשיה עגלת **V**: 489.

שם יהוה **VIII**: 121.

שם המיחד (לי) **VIII**: 122.

שמורות **V**: 461; **VI**: 501.

שמחיצא **V**: 457.

שְׁמִטָּה **I**: *308*.

שמיר ושית **V**: 404.

שמעון **V**: 302*(2)*.

שֶׁמֶץ **V**: 396.

שמר **V**: 394; **VI**: 6.

שׁמר **V**: 396.

שֶׁמֶשׁ **V**: 457.

שמת **V**: 395.

שֵׁנָא **VI**: 527*(3)*.

שנבלא **V**: 560.

שנה **V**: 401, 404.

שׁנה **V**: 457*(3)*, 590*(3)*.

שָׁנָה **V**: 457.

שֶׁנְהַבִּים **V**: 396.

שנות לב טיב **VI**: 636.

שִׁנָּיוֹן **V**: 457, *660*.

אוחזין בטלית שנים **VI**: 704.

שְׁנִינָה **V**: 457.

שְׁקַעֲרוּרֹת **VI**: 123.

שׁפט **IV**: 485; **V**: 379, 457*(3)*, 458*(2)*.

שָׁפַט **I**: *486;* **IV**: 370; **V**: 457, 508.

שֹׁפֵט **I**: *191*.

שִׁפְלוּת **V**: 396.

שפת **V**: 458.

שִׁצְנִיתָא **V**: 393.

שִׁקְמָה **V**: 396.

שקע **V**: 401.

שׁקק **V**: 458.

שׁרב **V**: 396.

שׁשׁ **IV**: *262;* **V**: *411*, 458.

שֵׁשׁ **V**: 396.

שְׁתַּיִם **V**: 458.

שתם **V**: 398.

שְׁתֻם הָעָיִן **V**: 465; **VI**: 136*(2)*.

שתע **V**: 401.

שָׁתְּתֶיהָ **V**: 458; **VI**: 278.

ת

תאב **V**: 398.

תְּאוֹ **V**: 458.

תְּאַשּׁוּר *(Ukarina)* **III**: *395;* **V**: 458.

תֵּבָה **V**: 54, 458.

תֶּבֶן בנן **V**: 396.

תנח **V**: 396.

תֹּהוּ **VI**: 27.

תְּהוֹם **III**: *365*.

תהומות **V**: 394.

תהילה **V**: 458*(2)*.

תְּהִלָּה **IV**: 478, 491; **V**: 458*(2)*.

תהלים **IV**: 478.

ותו לא מידי **VI**: 705.

תולים אותו חי **V**: 465.

תולל **VI**: 531.

תּוֹעָפוֹת **VI**: 432.

תוֹצָאוֹת **V**: 459.

תּוֹרָה **V**: 392, 458, 459*(2)*, 563; **VI**: 247.

תושיה **V**: 401, 459.

תּוּשִׁיָּה **V**: 459.

Hiph. תזדו **V**: *420*.

תחליף **VI**: 621.

תַּחְרָא **V**: 399.

תַּחַת **V**: 482, 484.

תֵּימָן **VI**: 402.

תימרות עשן **V**: 394.

תַּלְפִּאֹת **I**: 312; **V**: 459.

תִּירוֹשׁ **V**: 403, 459*(2)*.

תֹּךְ **V**: 396
תכיים **V**: 396.
תְּכֵלֶה **V**: 459.
תכמי DSS **V**: 403, 615.
תכן **VIII**: 477.
תלה חי **V**: 459.
תלואים למשובתי **VI**: 371.
בתלמוד **VIII**: 441.
תלנה **VI**: 540.
תְּמוֹל **V**: 398.
תמחוי **V**: *433*, 459.
תָּמִיד **V**: 53.
תמך **V**: 396.
תמנע **VI**: 84.
תמר **VI**: 115.
תָּמֵר **V**: 404*(2)*.
תנה **V**: 396.
תְּנֶה בְנִי לִבְּךָ לִי **VI**: 544.
תנופה **IV**: 235; **V**: 459.
תנך√ **V**: 459.
תעודה **VIII**: 477.
תְּעָלָה **V**: 459.
תפוח **VI**: 552, 554.
תַּפּוּחַ **III**: 383; **V**: 459.
תפר **V**: 460.
תֹּפֶשׂ-תֹּפְשֵׂי **V**: *465(3)*.
תפשי המלחמה **VI**: 138.
תרבית **V**: *439*, 460.
תרגם **V**: 403, 615.
תְּרוּמָה **V**: 460, 564.
תְּרוּעָה **V**: 460.
תרכב קמח **V**: 453.
(Arad Ostracon)
תרמה **VI**: 186.
תְּרָפִים **V**: 460, 616.
תרשיש **V**: 460.
תרתק **VI**: 238.
תְּשׁוּעָה **VIII**: 197.
תשסיבא **V**: 404.
תֵּשַׁע **I**: 428.
תְּתָאו **V**: 400.

Aramaic

אחרן מחר או יום **VII**: 128.
אית **V**: 375, 524.
איתי **V**: 375, 524.
Eli Eli, Lamma Sabachthani **VI**: 468.
אֱשַׁיָּא **VI**: 580*(2)*, 581*(3)*.
אֲשַׁרְנָא **VI**: 580*(2)*, 581*(5)*.
Bárrâ **V**: 525, 581.
בעד **VII**: 135.
בַּרוּ **V**: 524.
בר נשא **V**: 462.
גחך **V**: 527.
dî **V**: 524.
הא **V**: 305, 526.
זוז **V**: 528.
zĕnā **V**: 402; **VI**: 12.

הַנְעַל **VI**: 569.

'īt **V**: 378, 526.

כּוּדְנָא **III**: 379; **V**: 523, *555*.

כּוּדְנָיָא **III**: 379; **V**: 523, *555*.

כורץ **V**: 527.

kl, kl' **V**: 526.

כְּלָא **V**: 430, 524.

כְּעַן **VI**: 569, 580*(2)*, 581*(2)*.

כְּעֶנֶת **VI**: 569, 580*(2)*, 581*(2)*.

כְּעֶת **VI**: 569, 580*(2)*, 581*(2)*.

כרש **I**: *422*.

lĕhenâ **V**: 524.

לעלנסחמלשי **V**: 543, *558*.

meddem **V**: 524.

מחר או יום אחרן **V**: 526.

minda'am **V**: 524, *558*.

מְנֵא מְנֵא תְּקֵל וּפַרְסִין **I**: *431;* **VI**: 572*(3)*, 574.

nashsh' qu bar **V**: 527.

NIN-IB **V**: 545.

סוּמְפֹּנְיָה **VI**: 570.

סרם **V**: 527.

עבבן **V**: 528.

עבט **V**: 527.

עבץ/עבק **V**: 526, 534.

עדרן **V**: 527.

עלל **V**: 308, 376, *589*.

פְּסַנְתֵּרִין **VI**: 570.

צבת **V**: 527.

קִרְיָה **V**: 403, 615.

שֵׁגַל **V**: 455, *588;* **VI**: 486, 572*(2)*.

תרגם **V**: *403*, 615.

תרוח **I**: 488.

תתב על מוזנא **V**: 526.

Cuneiform Sign List

Sign	Reference
	V: 571.
	V: 544, 559
	V: 173, *544(2)*, 559, 572.
	V: 163.
Nin	V: 560.
	V: 168.
	V: 557, 572.
	V: 543, 558, 561.
	V: 572.
	V: 574.
	V: 583.
	V: 583.
(*MAŠ*)	V: 575.
	V: 556.
	V: 572.
	V: *572(2)*.
	V: 572.
AK-KIL	V: 579.
DUB-BIN	V: 579.
	V: 559.
	V: 580.
	V: 579.
(LAL-KI)	V: 567.
	V: 544.
	V: 544, 559, 578.
MA+SIG+GIM	V: 579.
	V: 579.
(US + SIG)	V: 579.
	V: 556.
	V: 583.
	V: 571.
,	V: 580.
	V: 564.
	V: 543.
	V: 556.
(šaṭāru)	V: 571.
	V: 572.
	V: 563.
SURRU	V: 579.
	V: 545.
	V: 574.
	V: 572.
	V: 572.

	V: 572.
	V: 563.
	V: 563.
(eri, era)	V: 568.
	V: 564.
	V: 572.
	V: 572.
	V: 572.
	V: 543.
	V: 559.
an-na *ki-a* *šú-mu-ta ni . . .*	V: 544.
	V: 563.
	V: 542, 558
	V: 556.
	V: 572.
MA-NA	V: 579.
	V: 583.
ŠU-SI	V: 579.
	V: 583.
	V: 583.
	V: 572, 573.
	V: 543, 558.
	V: 542.

	V: 544.
(šanešu)	V: 584.
	V: 544, 559.
(SIKUR)	V: 566.
	V: 574.
	V: 542.
	V: 544.
	V: 555.
	V: 572.
SÁ-DÚG	V: 579.
	V: 563.
	V: 571.
(Cappadocian)	IX: cxxxvii, cxlii.
	V: 560.
(Uraššu)	V: 575.
	V: 546.
	V: 546, 583.
	V: 579.
( )*Gu*	I: *407.*
(Ur-Engur)	II: 105.
	V: 543.
	V: 579.

Archaic Signs

 **V**: 178, 579.

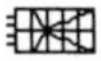 **V**: 575.

 **V**: 544.

	*ꜣ*	**V**: 331, **343**.
	*ꜣꜣmꜣ*	**V**: 318.
	*ꜣỉs*	**V**: 343, *345*.
	*ꜣw*	**V**: 312, 321.
 "AU" of 	*ꜣw*	**V**: 321.
 ≠ 	*ꜣb*	**V**: 312.
 confused with 	*ꜣb*	**V**: 312.
	*ꜣbw*	**III**: 374.
	*ꜣpd*	**V**: 343.
	*ꜣẖ*	**V**: 312.
	*ꜣẖ*	**V**: 312.

	*ꜣḫww*	**V**: 314.
	*ꜣs*	**V**: 343.
	*ꜣsby*	**V**: 313.
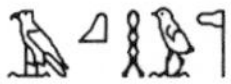	*ꜣqḥw*	**V**: 317.
	*ỉ*	**V**: 314*(2)*, **343-344**, 363.
	*ỉꜣw*	**V**: 343.
	*ỉꜣḫw*	**V**: 315.
	*ỉỉꜣtw*	**V**: 318.
	ỉw	**V**: 312.
	*Ỉw wn*	**V**: 329.
	*ỉw wn*	**V**: 344.

	*ỉw·nꜣ*	**V**: 330.
 var. of 	*ỉwꜣ*	**V**: 316.
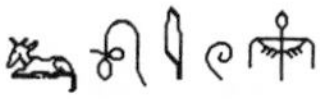	*ỉwỉw* or *ỉwꜣyt*	**V**: 330.
	*ỉwn*	**V**: 342.
	*i(?)-b(?)*	**V**: 295.
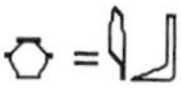	*ỉb*	**V**: 311.
	*ỉb*	**V**: 314.
	*ỉbw*	**V**: 315.
	*ỉpt*	**V**: 335.
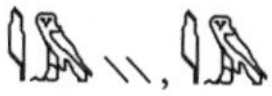	*ỉm*	**V**: 360.
	*ỉm bwt*	**V**: 315.

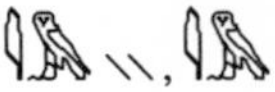	*ỉmy, ỉm*	**V**: 344.
	*ỉmy-r*	**V**: 348.
	*ỉmy-r ꜥ(w)*	**V**: 331†.
	*ỉmy-r ḫtm*	**V**: 313.
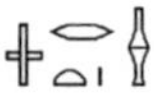	*ỉmy-rt*	**V**: 320.
	*ỉm·f*	**V**: 316.
	*ỉm-stꜥ*	**V**: 325.
	*Ỉn·tm*	**V**: 358.
	*ỉnỉ ỉrty k3t nb nsw*	**V**: 348.
	*ỉnpw*	**V**: 291, 344.
	*ỉnnm*	**V**: 344.

	*i͗r*	**V**: 321.
	*i͗ri͗ + i͗s*	**V**: 327*(2)*.
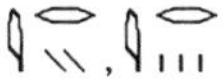	*i͗ry, i͗r*	**V**: 344.
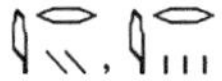	*i͗ry*	: 360.
	*i͗rf*	**V**: 321.
	*i͗rf·tn*	**V**: 321.
	*ī͗rmr*	**V**: 329.
	*i͗rmr*	**V**: 292.
	*i͗r·n m kt*	**V**: 322.
	*i͗rt*	**V**: 318.
	*i͗rt*	**V**: 321.

	*ỉḫw*	**V:** 317, 352.
	*ỉs*	**V:** 342, 360.
	*ỉšs*	**V:** 320.
	*ỉt*	**V:** 313.
	*ỉty*	**V:** 317.
	*ỉtn*	**V:** 334.
	*ỉtn*	**V:** 313.
	*ỉtnt (ỉdnt)*	**V:** 325.
	*ỉdry*	**V:** 316.
	*ỉdt*	**V:** 330.
	*ỉdt*	**V:** 344.

	*y*	**V**: 319.
	*ꜥ*	**V**: **345**.
 = 	*ꜥ*	**V**: 345, 347.
 as 	*ꜥ*	**V**: 341, 345.
	ꜥꜣ	**V**: 313, 345.
	*ꜥꜣ*	**V**: 314†.
	*ꜥꜣ*	**V**: 313.
	*ꜥꜣ* or *ꜥꜣw*	**V**: 345.
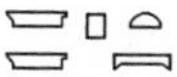	*ꜥꜣwy-pt*	**V**: 345.
	*ꜥꜣbt*	**V**: 317.
	*ꜥꜣbt*	**V**: 344.

	*ꜥꜣm*	**III**: 400;**V**: *343*, 345.
	*ꜥw*	**V**: 337, 338.
	*ꜥw*	**V**: 329*(3)*.
	*ꜥb*	**V**: 311.
	*ꜥb*	**V**: 312.
	*ꜥpr*	**V**: 318.
	*ꜥfꜣy*	**III**: 385.
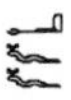	*ꜥff*	**V**: 322.
	*ꜥff*	**V**: 333.
	*ꜥm ỉrt r rm[s]*	**V**: 318.
	*ꜥnḫ*	**V**: 208, 337, 338.

	*ʿnḫt*	**V**: 317.
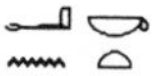	*ʿnkt*	**V**: 320.
	*ʿnty*	**V**: 224, 331.
	*ỉr*	**V**: 322.
	*ʿr kỉ ṯt mʿȝʿ*	**V**: 318†.
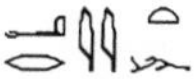	*ʿryt*	**V**: 316.
	*ʿḥ*	**V**: 322.
	*ʿḥȝ*	**V**: 324.
	*ʿḥȝ*	**V**: 328*(3)*.
	*ʿḥȝ*	**V**: 328.
	*ʿḥȝ*	**V**: 328.

	*ꜥḥꜥ*	**V**: 321.
	*ꜥḥb*	**V**: 311, 324, 328.
	*ꜥt-ỉst*	**V**: 325.
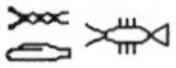	*ꜥd*	**V**: 314.
	*w*	**V**: **346**.
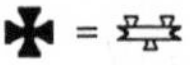	*wꜣ(?)*	**V**: 341.
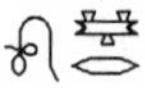	*wꜣr*	**V**: 322.
	*wꜣḫy*	**V**: 340.
	*wꜣḫ(y)*	**V**: 340.
	*wꜣs*	**V**: 314.
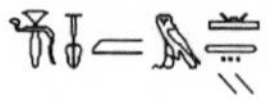	*wꜣḏ*	**V**: 318.

	*wỉ3·tw*	**V**: 346.
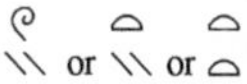	*·wy · ty*	**V**: 320, 360.
	*wᶜ*	**V**: 332.
	*wᶜ*	**V**: 339.
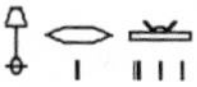	*wb3 -r(w)*	**V**: 339†.
	*wbn m nb ᶜnḫ m3ᶜ ḫrw*	**V**: 318.
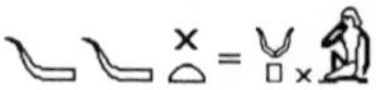	*wp*	**V**: 313.
	*Wp w3rt*	**V**: 330.
	*wpwt(w)*	**V**: 330.
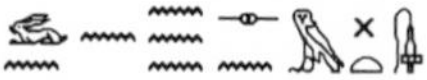	*wn n mw sn mḫt*	**V**: 312.
	*wnỉ*	**V**: 347.

	*wnf*	**V**: 325.
	*wr*	**V**: 311.
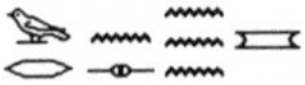	*wrns*	**V**: 315.
	*wrš*	**V**: 332.
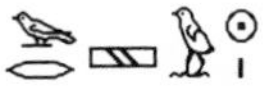	*wršw*	**V**: 314.
	*wḥ*	**V**: 319.
	*wḥʿ* or *šnnw*	**V**: 336.
	*Wsir*	**V**: 321.
	*wsft*	**V**: 313.
	*wšꜣw*	**V**: 316.
	*Wṯst Ḥr*	**V**: 324.

	*wdd*	**III**: 399; **V**: 323.
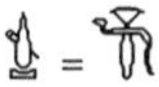	*wḏꜣ*	**V**: 316.
	*wḏꜣ*	**V**: 321.
	*b*	**V**: **346**.
 substitute for 	*b*	**V**: 313.
 is ideograph =  or 	*b*	**V**: 313.
	*bꜣ*	**V**: 320.
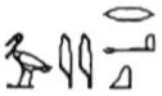	*bai ārq*	**V**: 321.
	*Bꜣt*	**V**: 341.
	*bi͗ꜣw*	**V**: 312.
	*bi͗t nb*	**V**: 346.

	*bỉty*	**V**: 313, 314.
	*bỉty*	**V**: 319, 321, 33*(2)*.
	*bw*	**V**: 346.
	*bbt*	**III**: 385.
	*bn bn*	**IX**: cxxxviii, cxli, cxliv.
	*bḥꜣ*	**V**: 320.
	*bḫn*	**V**: 346.
	*bsꜣq*	**V**: 318.
	*bkꜣ*	**V**: 312.
	*bqsw*	**V**: 312.
	*bty*	**V**: 325.

	*btnnw*	**V**: 316.
	*p*	**V**: **346**.
	*Pꜣḫt* or *Pḫꜣt*	**V**: 323.
	*pꜣsw*	**V**: 316.
	*pꜣt*	**V**: 341.
	*pf*	**V**: 346.
	*pn*	**V**: 319.
	*pr*	**V**: 335.
	*pr-ꜥnḫ*	**V**: 336.
 or 	*pr gmỉt*	**II**: 265; **V**: 335†.
	*prw*	**V**: 317.

	*pr-n-stꜣ*	**V**: 336.
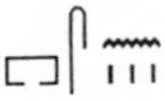	*pr·sn*	**V**: 335, 336.
	*prt*	**I**: 396; **V**: 335.
	*prt-ḫrw* or *prt-r-ḫrw*	**V**: 321.
	*pḥt*	**V**: 311.
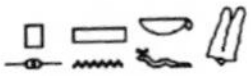	*psšn kf*	**V**: 320.
	*psd*	**V**: 329.
	*psd*	**V**: 331.
	*šꜥt*	**V**: 331.
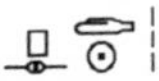	*psd*	**V**: 318.
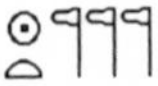	*psḏt*	**IX**: cxxxviii.

	*ptr*	**V**: 311.
	*f*	**V**: 333, 345.
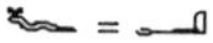	*f*	**V**: 345, 347.
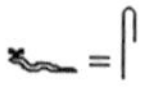	*f*	**V**: 347, 355.
	*fnḫw*	**V**: 347, *659*.
	*fnd*	**V**: 317.
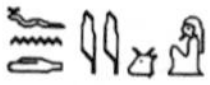	*fndy*	**V**: 203.
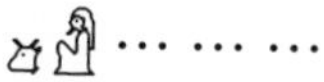	*fnḏy*	**V**: 203.
	*fnḏy*	**V**: 203.
	*fnḏy*	**V**: 203.
	*fnḏty*	**V**: 203.

	*m*	**V**: 311, **347-349**.
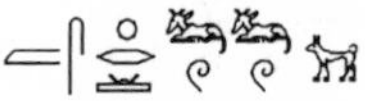	*m sẖr ỉwỉw*	**V**: 313.
	*mꜣwmt* [sic] *qmꜣ*	**V**: 316.
	*mꜣwt*	**V**: 312.
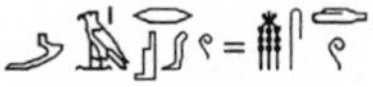	*mꜣ r st = ms sd*	**V**: 311.
	*mꜣht*	**V**: 312.
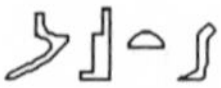	*mꜣst*	**V**: 339.
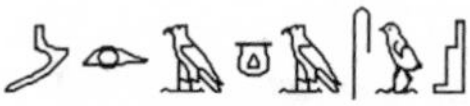	*mꜣgꜣsw*	**V**: 317.
	*mỉtt*	**V**: 316.
	*mymy*	**III**: 385.
	*mꜥ*	**V**: 347.

	*mꜥꜥt n kꜣ nṯrw m st n swtwt ḥnꜥ bꜣw nw sꜥḥwꜥꜣ*	**V**: 319.
	*mꜥfqtỉ*	**V**: 314.
	*mꜥrd [sic] mꜥr*	**V**: 320†.
	*mꜥk*	**V**: 332.
	*mꜥgr*	**V**: 314.
	*mꜥgr*	**V**: 314.
	*mꜥḏꜣ*	**V**: 348.
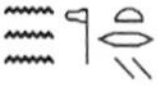	*mw ntry*	**V**: 319.
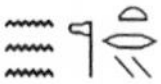	*mw nṯry*	**V**: 359.

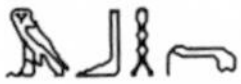	*m-bḥ*	**V**: 311.
	*mfḏ*	**V**: 320.
	*mnἰw*	**V**: 326.
	mnw	**V**: 206, 212.
	*mnw*	**V**: 321.
	*mnẖ*	**V**: 320.
	*mntf*	**V**: 314.
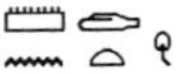	*mndt*	**III**: 399; **V**: 323.
	*mr*	**V**: 312.
	*mr*	**V**: 335.
	*mr*	**V**: 339.

	*mrʿ*	**V**: 320.
 *read* 	*mḥ, m-bḥ*	**V**: 311.
	*mḥy*	**V**: 314.
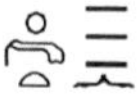	*m-ḫmt*	**V**: 311.
	*m-ḫnnw*	**V**: 315.
	*m-ḫnnw*	**V**: 315.
	*ms*	**V**: 330.
	*ms-ꜣ*	**V**: 348*(3)*.
	*msḥ*	**V**: 348.
	*mšʿ*	**V**: 326*(2)*.
	*mk ḏd*	**V**: 348.

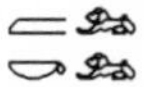	*mkrr*	**V**: 342.
	*mt*	**V**: 312.
	*mt*	**V**: 331, 332.
	*mt*	**V**: 312.
	*mt(y)*	**V**: 313.
	*mt*	**V**: 316.
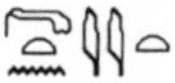	*mtny-t*	**V**: 317.
	*mtnw*	**V**: 315.
	*md3t*	**V**: 320.
	n	**V**: **349-351.**
	*n wnt*	**V**: 329, 344.

	n	**V**: 328.
	*n*	**V**: 350.
	*nỉỉ* or *ny*	**V**: 349*(2)*.
	*nỉw* or *nỉȝw*	**V**: 320, 360.
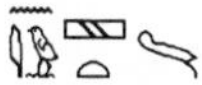	*nỉwšt*	**V**: 320.
	*ny*	**V**: 328.
	*n(w)*	**V**: 319.
	*nw*	**V**: 320.
	*nw*	**V**: 339.
	*nwȝ*	**V**: 349.
	*nwḥy tp-ʿ*	**V**: 318.

𓎟 ☉	*nb*	**V**: 316.
	nb	**V**: 340.
	nb smȝ nb	**V**: 340.
	nbt, nbd, or *ndb*	**V**: 314.
	nbty	**V**: 332.
	Npyrywrw	**V**: 351.
	nfw	**V**: 336.
	nfr	**V**: 324, 328.
	nfr	**V**: 331.
	nfr pw	**V**: 330.
	nfnw	**V**: 319.

	*nfrt*	**V**: 325.
	*nm*	**V**: 313.
	*nm*	**V**: 314.
	*nn*	**V**: 311, 313, 328*(2)*, 329
 = or 	*nn*	**V**: 313.
	*nn*	**V**: 344.
	*nn wn*	**V**: 329.
	*nn wn*	**V**: 344.
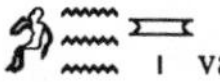 var. of 	*nnw*	**V**: 316.
	*nnw*	**V**: 316, 321.
	*nht*	**V**: 311.

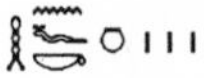	*nḥfkw*	**V**: 325.
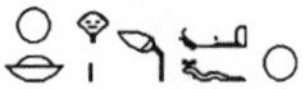	*nḥm r (?)*	**V**: 325.
	*nḫmn*	**V**: 350.
	*nḫȝw*	**V**: 350.
	*nḫȝw*	**V**: 350.
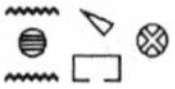	*nḫn*	**V**: 316.
	*nḫḫ*	**V**: 312.
	nsw	**V**: 334.
	*nš sšȝt*	**V**: 350.
	*n-kȝ*	**V**: 313.
	*n g(ȝ)ḥ*	**V**: 314.

	*nty*	**V**: 329, 349, 350.
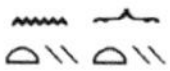	*nty nty*	**V**: 320.
	*nty*	**V**: 329, 349.
	*nṯr*	**V**: 333; 337*(4)*, 338*(4)*.
	*nṯr ỉfd*	**V**: 320.
	*nṯr bꜣ·f mỉ nṯry*	**V**: 317.
	*nṯrt*	**V**: 333.
	*nṯrt*	**V**: 337, 338.
	*nḏ*	**V**: 341.
	*nḏ, nḏ-ḥr*	**V**: 342, 350.
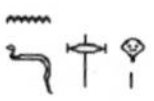	*nḏ-ḥr*	**V**: 350.

	*nḏr*	**V**: 312.
	r	**V**: **351**, 363, *368*.
complement to 	*r*	**V**: 313.
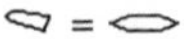	*r*	**V**: 314.
 for 	*r* for *ỉr*	**V**: 363.
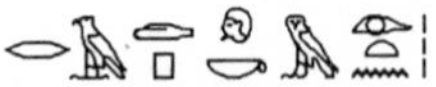	*r ꜣdp·k m ỉrt·n(w)*	**V**: 318.
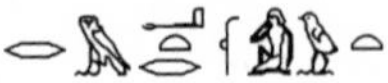	*r m ꜥtr·wt*	**V**: 318.
	*rwiꜣty*	**V**: 351.
	*rwd*	**V**: 339.
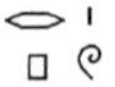	*r-pw*	**V**: 313.
	*rnpt*	**V**: 311.

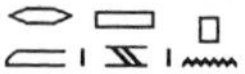	*r-m špn*	**V**: 317.
	*rnp*	**V**: 334.
	*rnp*	**V**: 334.
	*Rnpt*	**V**: 351.
	*rnpt m-ḫt*	**V**: 315.
	*r-ntt*	**V**: 317.
	*rḫyw*	**V**: 317.
	*Rḥty*	**V**: 323.
	*rḫ*	**V**: 315.
	*nšỉ*	**V**: 350.
	*nšỉ(?)*	**V**: 350.

	*ršrt*	**V**: 320.
	*rṯ (80)*	**V**: 351.
	*rṯnw*	**V**: 320.
	*h*	**V**: **351-352**.
	*hȝn*	**V**: 311.
	*hȝnmw*	**V**: 313.
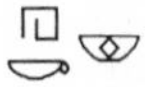	*h ȝkr*	**V**: 315.
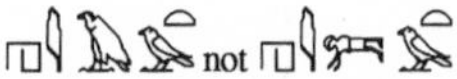	*hỉmt*	**V**: 351.
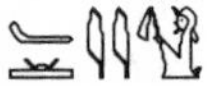	*Hyỉ*	**V**: 315.
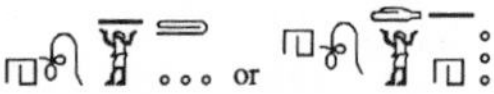	*hwd (?)*	**V**: 315.
	*hbʿy*	**V**: 314*(2)*.

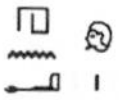	*hn*	**V**: 352.
	*hnhnw*	**V**: 315.
	*ḥ3*	**V**: 334.
	*ḥ3*	**V**: 334.
	*ḥ3yw*	**V**: 316.
	*ḥ3t-mhyt*	**V**: 333.
	*ḥ3t-mhyt*	**V**: 333.
	*ḥ3tỉw*	**V**: 317.
	*ḥ3tt*	**V**: 330.
	*ḥw*	**V**: 320.
	*ḥwỉ*	**V**: 352.

	*ḥwỉ*	**V**: 352.
	*ḥwʿ*	**V**: 352.
 var. 	*ḥwt-ʿnḫ*	**V**: 336.
	*Ḥwt-nbw*	**V**: 335.
	*ḥbꜣ*	**V**: 317.
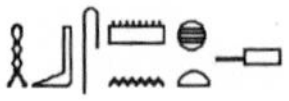	*ḥbs mnḫt*	**V**: 318.
	*ḥm*	**V**: 339.
	*ḥmꜣg*	**V**: 316.
	*ḥmn*	**V**: 353.
	*ḥmt*	**V**: 313.
	*ḥmt*	**V**: 322.

	*ḥmt k3m (?)*	**V**: 355.
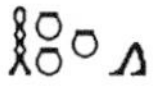	*ḥnw*	**V**: 316.
	*ḥr*	**V**: 312.
	*ḥr*	**V**: 313.
	*Ḥr 3*	**V**: 331.
	*ḥr biwk*	**III**: 387; **V**: 327.
	*Ḥr nbw*	**V**: 332*(3)*.
	*Ḥr nt n irty*	**V**: 332.
	*Ḥry-ᶜ*	**V**: 327.
	*Ḥry-ᶜ*	**V**: 327.
	*ḥr(y)ḫt·sn*	**V**: 318.

	*ḥrt*	**V**: 327.
	*Ḥkꜣ*	**V**: 331*(2)*
	*ḥtp*	**V**: 311.
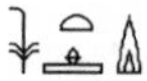	*ḥtp dỉ nsw*	**V**: 320.
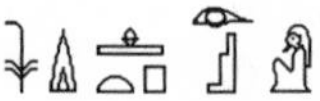	*ḥktp di nsw Wsir*	**V**: 204, 334.
	*ḥtm*	**V**: 314.
	*ḫ*	**V**: 322, **353-354**.
	*ḫꜣ*	**V**: 316.
	*ḫꜣ*	**V**: 333.
	*ḫꜣrw*	**V**: 320.
	*ḫꜣsyt*	**III**: 385.

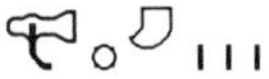	*ḫ3qw*	**V**: 319.
	*ḫ3t*	**V**: 312.
	*ḫww*	**V**: 316.
	*ḫwḫ3*	**V**: 315.
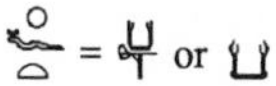	*ḫft*	**V**: 311.
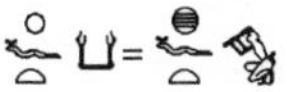	*ḫft(y)*	**V**: 312.
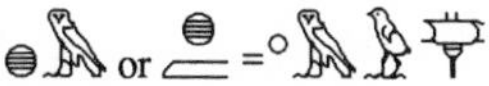	*ḫmw*	**V**: 312.
	*ḫn*	**V**: 317.
	*ḫnp*	**V**: 354.
	*ḫnm*	**V**: 311.
	*ḫnm*	**V**: 311.

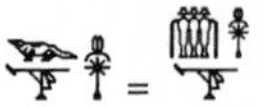	*Ḫnty iȝbt*	**V**: 322.
	*ḫnd*	**V**: 316.
	*ḫry*	**V**: 321.
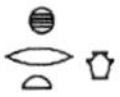	*ḫrt*	**V**: 313.
	*ḫsbd*	**V**: 353.
	*ḫstb (ḫsbt?)*	**V**: 313.
	*ḫtm*	**V**: 322.
	*ḫtmy*	**V**: 353.
	ẖ	**V**: **354**.
	*ẖpȝ*	**V**: 354.
	*ẖr*	**V**: 317.

	*ẖr(t)-nṯr*	**V**: 337, 338.
	*s*	**V**: 326.
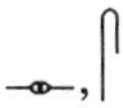	*s*	**V**: **354-355**.
	*sꜣ*	**V**: 313, 340.
	*sꜣ*	**V**: 322, 340.
	*sꜣ*	**V**: 340.
	*sꜣ*	**V**: 342.
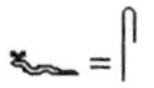	*f*	**V**: 347, 355.
	*sꜣ n ḥmw*	**V**: 311.
	*sꜣ*	**V**: 342.
	*sꜣb*	**V**: 315.

	*sȝḫ*	V: 321.
	*sȝt*	V: 320.
	*siȝ*	V: 311.
	*sin*	V: 313.
	*sw*	V: 313, 314.
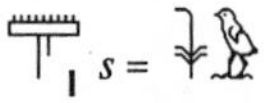	*sw*	V: 313.
	*swḥ-ty*	V: 314.
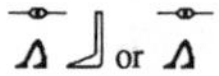	*sb*	V: 319.
	*sbȝy ḥr tp·ḥwt ꜥḥ*	V: 335.
	*sbȝt*	V: 316.
	*sby*	V: 314, 329, 359.

	*sp*	**V**: 322.
	*sp*	**V**: 311.
	*spw*	**V**: 318.
 and 	*smyt*	**V**: 314.
	*smr wʿt*	**V**: 355.
	*sn*	**V**: 320.
	*snwtt*	**III**: 385.
	*snmm*	**V**: 320.
	*sn-nḫt*	**V**: 317.
	*sntḫt*	**V**: 312.
	*sḫm*	**V**: 321†.

	*sḫt*	**V**: 311.
	*sḫt*	**V**: 319.
	*sḫtrỉꜣw*	**V**: 313.
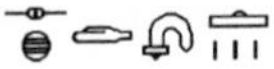	*s·ḫd* for *s·ḫt*	**V**: 311.
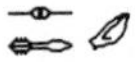	*sẖ* or *st*	**V**: 311.
	*sswnw*	**V**: 312.
	*sš pr-ʿhḫ*	**V**: 341*(2)*.
	*sšꜣn*	**V**: 318.
	*sšp*	**V**: 321.
	*sšm*	**V**: 331.
	*sšr*	**V**: 340.

	*sšsrw*	**V**: 312.
	*sqr*	**V**: 342.
	*st*	**V**: 311.
	*st*	**V**: 313.
	*St*	**V**: 316.
	*sty*	**V**: 339.
	*stt*	**V**: 321.
	*sṯ*	**V**: 319.
	*sṯ*	**V**: 337, 338.
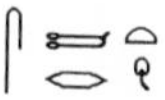	*sṯrt*	**V**: 314.
	*sṯ šs*	**V**: 319.

	*sd-m-r*	**V**: 320. 360.
	*sḏꜣw*	**V**: 322.
	*sḏꜣwty*	**V**: 312.
	*sḏb*	**V**: 315.
	*sḏm*	**V**: 311.
	*sḏm*	**V**: 311.
	š	**V**: **355.**
 substitute for 	*šm*	**V**: 313.
	*šꜣw*	**V**: 323.
	*šꜣsw*	**V**: 320.
	*šꜣš*	**V**: 318.

	*šw*	**V**: 316.
	*šw*	**V**: 317.
	*šps*	**V**: 314.
	*šps*	**V**: 339.
 with 	*šps*	**V**: 314.
 is ideograph =  or 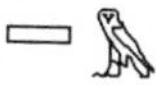	*šm*	**V**: 313.
	*šmꜥ*	**V**: 322.
 = 	*šms* = *šmꜥ*	**V**: 313.
 = 	*šms*	**V**: 315†.
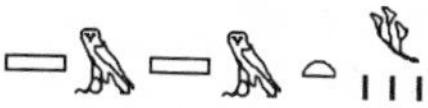	*šmšmt*	**III**: 385.
	*šnꜥ*	**V**: 330.

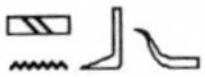	*šnb*	**V**: 320.
	*šnnw* or *wḥꜥ*	**V**: 336.
	*šs*	**V**: 340.
	*šsp*	**V**: 311.
	*šsp*	**V**: 342.
	*šsmt*	**V**: 321.
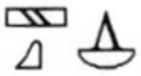	*šq*	**V**: 320.
	*št*	**V**: 316.
	*šd*	**V**: 331.
	*śt wꜥbt*	**V**: 336.
	*k*	**V**: **356**.

	*k3*	**V**: 316.
	*k3*	**V**: 311, 327, 328.
	*k3*	**V**: 311.
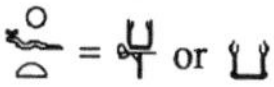	*k3*	**V**: 311.
	*k3mn*	**V**: 321.
	*k3mnn*	**V**: 356.
	*k3r sw*	**V**: 356.
	*k3t-šwt*	**III**: 385.
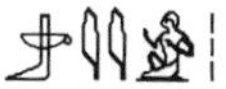	*Kii-bw*	**V**: 356.
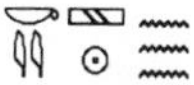	*kyš*	**V**: 314.
	*Kbny*	**V**: 311.

	*kpwt n·i*	**V**: 318.
	*sms*	**V**: 311.
	*kmdw*	**V**: 318.
	*kns*	**III**: 399; **V**: 323.
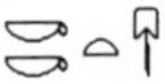	*kkt*	**III**: 366.
	*ḳ (q)*	**V**: 311, **355**.
	*qnỉ*	**V**: 355.
	*qnbt*	**V**: 324.
	*qnn*	**V**: 321.
	*qrr*	**V**: 321.
	*qd (ḳd)*	**V**: 320, 342, 360.

	*qd*	**V**: 342.
	*qdw*	**V**: 315.
	*g*	**V**: 356.
	*gꜣbty*	**V**: 314.
	*gꜣmd*	**V**: 316.
	*gꜣḥ*	**V**: 311.
	*gꜣḥw*	**V**: 356.
	*gꜣš*	**V**: 314.
	gwḥbt	**V**: 317.
	*gm*	**V**: 312.
	*gmỉ*	**V**: 317.

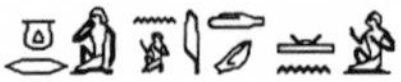	*gr·n·ỉ ỉd·n·ỉ*	**V**: 317.
	*gḥs*	**V**: 312.
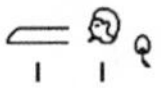	*gs tp*	**V**: 342.
	*t*	**V**: 319, **356**.
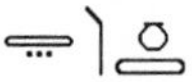	*Tꜣ Ṯḥnw*	**II**: 266; **V**: 335.
 replaces 	*tꜣ(yt) dỉꜣ*	**V**: 317.
 determinative of *Tama*	*tꜣmꜣ*	**V**: 312.
	*tỉt*	**V**: 315.
	*tỉt ḏd tỉt*	**V**: 321.
	*twy*	**V**: 314.
	*twy*	**V**: 340.

	*tb*	**V**: 313.
	*tp*	**V**: 319, 326*(2)*, 334, 359.
	*tp rnpt*	**V**: 317.
	*tp-rsy*	**V**: 327.
	*tp*	**V**: 326, 327.
	*tp-ʿ*	**V**: 327.
	*tpwr*	**V**: 311.
	*tfỉ*	**V**: 320.
 and 	*tn*	**V**: 313.
	tnby	**V**: 325.
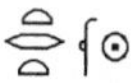	*trt*	**V**: 311.

	*tḥwy*	**III**: 385.
	*ṯ*	**V**: 322, 340, **357**.
	*ṯꜣ*	**V**: 332.
	*ṯꜣw*	**V**: 336.
	*ṯꜣw·sn mt n ḏꜣ tꜣ*	**V**: 318.
	*dwn*	**V**: 319.
	*ṯnf*	**V**: 319.
	*ṯḥnw*	**V**: 319.
	*ṯsps*	**V**: 321.
	*ṯsm*	**V**: 314.
	*d*	**V**: **357**.

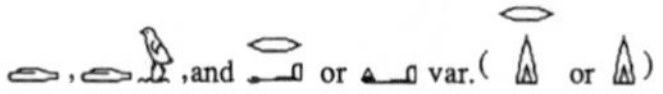	*d, dw, rdỉ, dỉ*	**V**: 357.
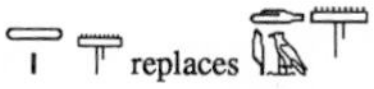	*dỉꜣ*	**V**: 317.
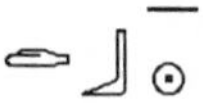	*dbn*	**V**: 312.
	*dmd* (or *dmḏ*)	**V**: 313.
	*dnỉ*	**V**: 316.
	ds	**V**: 314.
	*dd*	**V**: 311.
	*ḏ*	**V**: 333, **357**.
	*ḏꜣr*	**V**: 313.
	*ḏꜣrt*	**III**: 385.
	*ḏꜣt*	**V**: 312.

	*ḏꜣtfy*	**V**: 317.
	*ḏꜣḏꜣt*	**V**: 339.
	*ḏꜥmw*	**V**: 337, 338.
	*ḏꜥmw*	**I**: 294; **V**: 337, 338.
	*ḏꜥrt*	**V**: 311.
	*ḏw*	**V**: 311.
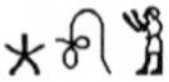	*ḏwꜣ* or *dwꜣ*	**V**: 312.
	*ḏb*	**V**: 314.
	*ḏr*	**V**: 312.
	*ḏrỉw*	**V**: 313, 315.
	*ḏrty*	**V**: 311.

	*ḏrḏri*	**V**: 312.
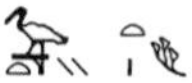	*Ḏḥwty šwt*	**III**: 385.
	*ḏsf*	**V**: 314.
	*Ḏd*	**V**: 337, 338.
	*ḏd*	**V**: 347.
	*ḏd·n*	**V**: 316.

Gardiner Signs

	Gardner sign F 41	**V**: 331.
	Gardiner sign N 12	**V**: 209.
	Gardiner sign T 14	**V**: 313.
	Gardiner sign O 42	**V**: 311.

 Gardiner sign U 10 **V**: 314.

 Gardiner Sign Z 2 **V**: 319, 359.

Unclassified Signs

 *ȧs-t ȧri* **V**: 320.

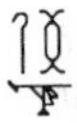 *Heliopolitan Nome* **V**: 321.

 *Winged Solar Disk* **V**: 342.

 *mouse* or *rat* **V**: 321.

Gen 1 **III**: *295, 301;* **V**: 413; 701, **VI**: 15, 19, **21-25**, 33*(3);* **VIII**: 83, 87, 288*(2)*.
Gen 1-2 **III**: *329;* **IV**: 183, 229; **VI**: **18-21**.
Gen 1-2s **VI**: 95.
Gen 1-3 **VI**: **18-19**; **VIII**: 288.
Gen 1-9 **I**: xvii, n15; **VI**: **18**.
Gen 1-11 **IV**: 222, 260*(2)*, 323*(2);* **V**: 230; **VI**: **16-18**; **VIII**: 388; **IX**: cxi, cxlv.
Gen 1-31 **IV**: 249; **VI**: 17.
Gen 1:1 **VI**: 13*(2)*, 26*(9)*, 27*(6)*, 724.
Gen 1:1-10 **VI**: 25.
Gen 1:1-13 **VI**: 25.
Gen 1:1-15 **VIII**: 287.
Gen 1:1-2 **VI**: 20, 26.
Gen 1:1, 2 **VI**: 26*(3)*.
Gen 1:1-25 **VI**: 16.
Gen 1:1-3 **VI**: 19, 25*(5)*, 26, 27; **IX**: cxi.
Gen 1:1, 3 **VI**: 25.
Gen 1:1-5 **VI**: 25*(2)*.
Gen 1:1-2:3 **III**: 306; **VI**: 19, 20*(2)*, 74.
Gen 1:1-2:4 **VI**: 20, 21.
Gen 1:1-2:4a **VI**: 20.
Gen 1:1-4:24 **VI**: 19.
Gen 1:1, 11, 21b **VI**: 15.
Gen 1:1-12:5 **IV**: *248;* **VI**: 16.
Gen 1:2 **VI**: 9, 20, 27*(7)*, 28*(8)*, 151, 232, 334, 721; **VIII**: 295.
Gen 1:2b **VI**: 27.
Gen 1:2, 3 **VI**: 27.
Gen 1:2, 7, 16, 20, 21 **VI**: 14.
Gen 1:2,5, 12, 30, 31 **VI**: 15.
Gen 1:3 **VI**: 28, 29.
Gen 1:3-5 **VI**: 28.*(3);* **VIII**: 288.
Gen 1:4-12 **VI**: 19.
Gen 1:6-7 **VI**: 29.
Gen 1:6-8 **VI**: 20.
Gen 1:7 **VIII**: 80.
Gen 1:9 **V**: 700; **VI**: 20, 29*(2)*.
Gen 1:9, 11 **VI**: 16.
Gen 1:11, 12 **VI**: 20.
Gen 1:14-18 **VI**: 20.
Gen 1:14-30 **VI**: 19.
Gen 1:21 **V**: 402; **VI**: 12, 29; **VIII**: 365.
Gen 1:24 **VI**: 20.
Gen 1:24-27 **VI**: 29, 35.
Gen 1:25 **VI**: 20.
Gen 1:26 **V**: 374; **VI**: 7, 30*(6);* **VIII**: 276.
Gen 1:26ff. **VI**: 29.
Gen 1:26LXX **VI**: 30.
Gen 1:26, 27 **VI**: 20, 29.
Gen 1:26-27 **VI**: 29*(2)*.
Gen 1:26-31 **VI**: 29*(2)*.
Gen 1:26-2:3 **VI**: 16.
Gen 1:27 **VI**: 30*(4)*, 671; **VIII**: 282, 288.
Gen 1:27-28 **VI**: 30.
Gen 2 **VI**: 32*(3)*.
Gen 2-3 **V**: 701*(2);* **VI**: 31-32*(15);* **VIII**: 179, 187.
Gen 2-11 **IV**: 272, 358; **VI**: 30.
Gen 2:1 **VI**: 20.
Gen 2:1-3 **V**: 82; **VI**: 19, 32*(3)*.
Gen 2:1, 4, 5, 14 **VI**: 15.

Gen 2: 2, 3 **VI**: 15, 19, 20, 32.
Gen 2: 2, 3, 4, 7, 9 **VI**: 32.
Gen 2: 2, 18, 20, 23 **VI**: 14.
Gen 2: 4 **VI**: 33.
Gen 2: 4b **VI**: 33.
Gen 2: 4-19 **IV**: 45.
Gen 2: 4-7 **VI**: 32.
Gen 2: 4- chap 3 **VI**: 19.
Gen 2: 4-3:24 **VI**: 32.
Gen 2: 5 **VI**: 21, 23, 33*(3)*.
Gen 2: 5ff. **VI**: 24, 33.
Gen 2: 5-6 **VI**: 33.
Gen 2: 5, 6 **VI**: 33.
Gen 2: 6 **VI**: 33*(2)*.
Gen 2: 7 **VI**: 33*(2)*, 34*(3)*.
Gen 2: 8 **VI**: 15, 19.
Gen 2: 8-14 **VI**: 19.
Gen 2: 8-18 **VI**: 34, 35.
Gen 2: 9 **VI**: 15, 19, 34.
Gen 2: 9b **VI**: 34.
Gen 2: 9, 17 **VI**: 34, 35.
Gen 2: 10-14 **VI**: 34*(2)*.
Gen 2: 11 **VI**: 15, 16, 34.
Gen 2: 12 **VI**: 34.
Gen 2: 13 **VI**: 34, 35.
Gen 2: 14 **VI**: 15.
Gen 2: 15-25 **VI**: 35.
Gen 2: 15, 17, 18 **VI**: 32.
Gen 2: 16, 17 **VI**: 35.
Gen 2: 17 **V**: 463; **VI**: 15, 35.
Gen 2: 18 **VI**: 16, 35.
Gen 2: 19 **VI**: 15, 29, 35.
Gen 2: 20-24 **VI**: 35.
Gen 2: 20b-24 **VI**: 34, 35.
Gen 2: 23 **VI**: 15, 35.
Gen 2: 24 **VI**: 36, 694; **VIII**: 276; **IX**: lxxxvii.
Gen 2: 24LXX **VI**: 36.
Gen 2: 25 **VI**: 36*(3)*, 90.
Gen 3 **VI**: 36*(7)*, 37*(15)*.
Gen 3-4 **VI**: 36.
Gen 3: 1-15 **VI**: 38.
Gen 3: 1-24 **VI**: 38.
Gen 3: 1-6 **VI**: 38*(3)*.
Gen 3: 1-7 **VI**: 38.
Gen 3: 1-6, 14, 15 **VI**: 16.
Gen 3: 1, 7, 10, 11 **VI**: 37.
Gen 3: 1, 4, 7, 8, 9 **VI**: 36.
Gen 3: 2 **VI**: 38.
Gen 3: 5 **VI**: 38*(2)*.
Gen 3: 6 **VI**: 38*(2)*.
Gen 3: 7 **VI**: 39.
Gen 3: 8 **VI**: 39.
Gen 3: 9 **VI**: 39.
Gen 3: 14 **VI**: 15, 39.
Gen 3: 14-15 **VI**: 39*(2)*.
Gen 3: 14, 15 **VIII**: 15*(3)*.
Gen 3: 14-19 **VI**: 36, 39*(2)*.
Gen 3: 15 **VI**: 39*(4)*, 40*(6)*.
Gen 3: 16 **V**: 402; **VI**: 12, 40*(4)*, 42, 43*(2)*.
Gen 3: 17 **VI**: 16.
Gen 3: 19 **VI**: 40.
Gen 3: 21 **VI**: 40.
Gen 3: 21, 22, 24 **VI**: 36.
Gen 3: 22 **VI**: 16, 40, 41*(2)*.
Gen 3: 22a **VI**: 41.
Gen 3: 22-23 **VI**: 40.
Gen 3: 24 **V**: 168; **VI**: 14, 41.
Gen 4 **I**: *119*, **VI**: 40, 41*(2)*, 43.
Gen 4-5 **VI**: 41.
Gen 4: 1 **VI**: 13, 15, 40, 42*(3)*; **VIII**: 121.
Gen 4: 1b **VI**: 15.
Gen 4: 1LXX **VI**: 42.

Gen 4: 1-10 **VI**: 42.
Gen 4: 1-16 **VI**: 41*(2)*.
Gen 4: 1-4, 7, 10 **VI**: 41.
Gen 4: 1, 7 **VI**: 14.
Gen 4: 1-8 **VI**: 42.
Gen 4: 1, 7, 8 **VI**: 15.
Gen 4: 1-8:22 **VI**: 41.
Gen 4: 3-15 **VI**: 16.
Gen 4: 3-16 **VI**: 42, 713.
Gen 4: 3-4 **VI**: 42.
Gen 4: 3-8 **VI**: 42.
Gen 4: 5 **VI**: 42.
Gen 4: 6, 7 **VI**: 14.
Gen 4: 6-7 **VI**: 42.
Gen 4: 7 **V**: 400, 402, 687; **VI**: 10, 12, 14, 15, 40, 42, 43*(13)*, 44*(2)*; **VIII**: 295.
Gen 4: 7-8 **VI**: 43.
Gen 4: 8 **VI**: 13, 44*(3)*.
Gen 4: 8b **VI**: 44.
Gen 4: 9 **VI**: 44.
Gen 4: 11 **VI**: 44.
Gen 4: 11-17 **VI**: 44.
Gen 4: 13-15 **VI**: 44.
Gen 4: 13, 16, 23, 26 **VI**: 41.
Gen 4: 15 **VI**: 44.
Gen 4: 15LXX **VI**: 44.
Gen 4: 16 **VI**: 15.
Gen 4: 17 **V**: 543; **VI**: 15, 45.
Gen 4: 17-24 **VI**: 45.
Gen 4: 18 **VI**: 15, 45.
Gen 4: 19-20 **VI**: 45.
Gen 4: 20 **VI**: 45.
Gen 4: 21 **VIII**: 364.
Gen 4: 22 **VI**: 16.
Gen 4: 23 **VI**: 14.
Gen 4: 23, 24 **VI**: 14, 45.
Gen 4: 23-24 **VI**: 45*(3)*.
Gen 4: 23, 25 **VI**: 15.
Gen 4: 24 **VI**: 45*(2)*.
Gen 4: 26 **VI**: 15, 46*(3)*.
Gen 4: 26b **VI**: 46*(2)*..
Gen 5 **I**: *118(2), 119, 155;* **II**: 180*(2)*, 181, 186; **VI**: 8, 46*(8)*, 57; **IX**: cxlv.
Gen 5-6 **VI**: 46.
Gen 5: 16 **VI**: 47.
Gen 5: 21-24 **VI**: 47.
Gen 5: 22 **VI**: 47.
Gen 5: 24 **V**: 407; **VI**: 15, 47*(2)*, 481.
Gen 5: 29 **VI**: 2, 3, 16, 47*(3)*.
Gen 6 **VI**: 48*(2)*.
Gen 6-8 **VI**: 47.
Gen 6-9 **V**: 700; **VI**: 47.
Gen 6: 1-3 **VI**: 49.
Gen 6: 1-4 **VI**: 14, 48*(7)*; **IX**: cxlv.
Gen 6: 1-5 **VI**: 48.
Gen 6: 1-8 **VI**: 48*(2)*.
Gen 6: 2 **VI**: 15, 49*(3)*.
Gen 6: 2, 4 **VI**: 49, 50.
Gen 6: 3 **VI**: 14, 15, 16, 49*(9)*, 50*(3)*, 193.
Gen 6: 4 **VI**: 15, 50*(2)*.
Gen 6: 6 **VI**: 50.
Gen 6: 7 **VI**: 16.
Gen 6: 8-9 **VI**: 47.
Gen 6: 9 **VI**: 15, 50*(2)*.
Gen 6: 9-22 **VI**: 50.
Gen 6: 9-11: 17 **IV**: 302.
Gen 6: 13 **VI**: 15.
Gen 6: 13-15, 17, 18 **VI**: 47.
Gen 6: 14 **VI**: 15, 50.
Gen 6: 15 **VI**: 15.
Gen 6: 16 **VI**: 8, 14, 16, 50*(2)*.
Gen 6: 16aα **VI**: 51.

Gen 6: 17	**VI**: 14, 51.
Gen 6: 26	**VI**: 51.
Gen 7	**VI**: 47.
Gen 7: 1	**VI**: 15.
Gen 7: 2	**VI**: 15.
Gen 7: 4-24	**VI**: 51.
Gen 7: 11	**VI**: 15.
Gen 7: 13-20	**IV**: *43*.
Gen 7: 19, 20	**VI**: 51.
Gen 8	**VI**: 47.
Gen 8-9	**VI**: 51*(2)*.
Gen 8: 1-16	**VI**: 16.
Gen 8: 1-19	**VI**: 51.
Gen 8: 2-5	**VI**: 51.
Gen 8: 4(A.V.)	**VI**: 15.
Gen 8: 4	**VI**: 16.
Gen 8: 4, 5	**VI**: 15.
Gen 8: 7ס	**VI**: 51.
Gen 8: 7-12	**VI**: 15.
Gen 8: 8-11	**VI**: 52.
Gen 8: 10	**VI**: 16.
Gen 8: 13	**VI**: 15.
Gen 8: 18	**I**: *222;* **IX**: cxlv.
Gen 8: 18-22	**VI**: 52.
Gen 8: 21	**VI**: 15.
Gen 8: 21s	**VI**: 16.
Gen 9	**VI**: 52.
Gen 9-11	**VI**: 52.
Gen 9: 1	**VI**: 15.
Gen 9: 1-17	**VI**: 52.
Gen 9: 4-6	**VI**: 14.
Gen 9: 5, 27	**VI**: 15.
Gen 9: 6	**VI**: 52*(2);* **VIII**: 230*(2)*.
Gen 9: 11-17	**VI**: 52.
Gen 9: 13	**VI**: 52.
Gen 9: 18-27	**VI**: 53.
Gen 9: 18-28	**VI**: 53.
Gen 9: 18-29	**VI**: 53.
Gen 9: 20	**VI**: 15.
Gen 9: 23, 26, 27	**VI**: 14.
Gen 9: 25-27	**VI**: 14, 53; **VIII**: 15*(2)*.
Gen 9: 27	**VI**: 53.
Gen 10	**II**: *135, 145, 165;* **VI**: 53, 54*(16)*.
Gen 10-11	**VI**: 53.
Gen 10-15	**VI**: 53.
Gen 10-50	**VI**: 53.
Gen 10: 1	**VI**: 15.
Gen 10: 1, 2	**VI**: 55.
Gen 10: 2	**VI**: 15.
Gen 10: 2, 4	**VI**: 55.
Gen 10: 3	**VI**: 15, 55.
Gen 10: 3-10	**VI**: 55.
Gen 10: 4	**VI**: 15.
Gen 10: 6	**VI**: 15.
Gen 10: 6, 13, 14	**VI**: 55.
Gen 10: 7	**VI**: 15.
Gen 10: 8	**VI**: 15, 34, 55*(2)*.
Gen 10: 8-10	**VI**: 55.
Gen 10: 10	**VI**: 15, 56*(7)*.
Gen 10: 10, 11	**III**: *26;* **VI**: 55*(2)*.
Gen 10: 11	**VI**: 15*(2)*.
Gen 10: 11-15	**VI**: 56.
Gen 10: 12	**VI**: 56.
Gen 10: 13	**VI**: 15.
Gen 10: 14	**VI**: 15.
Gen 10: 15	**VI**: 15.
Gen 10: 16	**II**: *142;* **VI**: 15, 56.
Gen 10: 16-17	**VI**: 56.
Gen 10: 17	**VI**: 15.
Gen 10: 19	**VI**: 56.
Gen 10: 21	**VI**: 56.
Gen 10: 22	**VI**: 15.
Gen 10: 22-24	**VI**: 57.
Gen 10: 23	**VI**: 15.
Gen 10: 24	**VI**: 57.
Gen 10: 25	**VI**: 15, 57.
Gen 10: 28	**VI**: 15.

Gen 10:30 **VI**: 15, 57*(3)*.
Gen 11 **I**: *155;* **II**: 187; **VI**: 14, 57*(2)*.
Gen 11:1 **VI**: 58; **VII**: 283.
Gen 11:1-9 **VI**: 57*(4)*, 58*(2)*.
Gen 11:2 **VI**: 15, 58*(3)*.
Gen 11:3 **VI**: 15.
Gen 11:4 **VI**: 15.
Gen 11:4-6 **VI**: 58.
Gen 11:5 **VI**: 58.
Gen 11:6s **VI**: 16.
Gen 11:7-9 **VI**: 58.
Gen 11:9 **VI**: 58.
Gen 11:10-13 **VI**: 58.
Gen 11:10-26 **VI**: 59.
Gen 11:12ff. **VI**: 59.
Gen 11:18 **VI**: 59.
Gen 11:26 **VI**: 59.
Gen 11:28-31 **VI**: 15.
Gen 11:32 **VI**: 59.
Gen 12 **VI**: 59*(2)*, 70, 76.
Gen 12-50 **VIII**: 388.
Gen 12:1ff. **VI**: 14.
Gen 12:1-2 **VI**: 16.
Gen 12:1-3 **VI**: 59.
Gen 12:1-8 **VI**: 16.
Gen 12:3 **VI**: 59*(3)*.
Gen 12:6 **VI**: 14, 60, 72.
Gen 12:6, 9 **VI**: 15.
Gen 12:6-37:1 **IV**: *248(2);* **VI**: 60.
Gen 12:8-21 **VI**: 60.
Gen 12:9 **VI**: 14.
Gen 12:10 **VI**: 60.
Gen 12:10ff. **VI**: 60.
Gen 12:10-20 **IV**: 235; **VI**: 60, 71, 76.
Gen 12:10-13:1 **VI**: 60.
Gen 12:11-20 **VI**: 60.
Gen 12:15 **V**: 700; **VI**: 15, 61.
Gen 12:16 **VI**: 61.
Gen 13&14 **VI**: 95, 534.
Gen 13:1-13 **VI**: 16.
Gen 13:1, 4, 5-7, 10, 12 **VI**: 61.
Gen 13:10 **VI**: 15, 61*(2)*.
Gen 13:10-12 **VI**: 61.
Gen 13:11 **VI**: 61.
Gen 13:13, 14, 17, 18 **VI**: 61.
Gen 13:16 **VI**: 13.
Gen 13:18 **VI**: 14*(2)*.
Gen 14 **II**: *194;* **III**: *422;* **IV**:*143,* 214, 244; **V**: 296; **VII**: 268; **IX**: cxlv.
Gen 14:1 **VI**: 15, 64*(2)*.
Gen 14:1-11 **VI**: 64.
Gen 14:2 **VI**: 64.
Gen 14:3 **VI**: 13, 64.
Gen 14:4 **VI**: 16, 64.
Gen 14:5 **VI**: 64.
Gen 14:5-20 **VI**: 64.
Gen 14:9 **VI**: 64.
Gen 14:14 **VI**: 65*(4)*, 717.
Gen 14:15 **VI**: 2, 3, 14, 65*(3)*.
Gen 14:17-20 **VI**: 65.
Gen 14:17-24 **VI**: 65.
Gen 14:18 **VI**: 66.
Gen 14:18-20 **VI**: 65*(5)*.
Gen 14:19 **VI**: 66.
Gen 14:20 **VI**: 66*(2)*.
Gen 14:24 **VI**: 66.
Gen 15 **I**: *509;* **II**: *194;* **IV**: 249; **VI**: 66*(4)*.
Gen 15:1 **VI**: 66*(2)*.
Gen 15:1, 2 **VI**: 66.
Gen 15:1-7 **VI**: 66.
Gen 15:1, 5-16 **VI**: 16.
Gen 15:2 **VI**: 5, 14, 67.

Gen 15: 2-3	**VI**: 67.
Gen 15: 3	**VI**: 11.
Gen 15: 4-7	**VI**: 66.
Gen 15: 6	**VI**: 67*(2)*.
Gen 15: 8-18	**VI**: 67.
Gen 15: 9	**VI**: 67.
Gen 15: 11, 17	**VI**: 14.
Gen 15: 13	**VI**: 6.
Gen 15: 15	**VI**: 14.
Gen 15: 17	**VI**: 14.
Gen 16	**VI**: 60, 67.
Gen 16-36	**VI**: 67.
Gen 16: 2	**VI**: 8, 67.
Gen 16: 4-7	**VI**: 67.
Gen 16: 5	**VI**: 13.
Gen 16: 5-14	**VI**: 68, 71.
Gen 16: 7	**VI**: 15.
Gen 16: 11	**VI**: 68.
Gen 16: 11-12	**VI**: 67.
Gen 16: 13	**VI**: 15, 68.
Gen 16: 13, 14	**VI**: 14.
Gen 17	**I**: *509;* **VI**: 66, 68*(3)*.
Gen 17: 1	**VI**: 13, 68.
Gen 17: 1-14	**VI**: 68.
Gen 17: 2	**VI**: 68.
Gen 17: 4	**VI**: 14.
Gen 17: 5	**VI**: 15.
Gen 17: 5, 15	**VI**: 15.
Gen 17: 6-8	**VI**: 68; **VIII**: 291.
Gen 17: 16	**VI**: 15.
Gen 17: 17	**VI**: 68*(2);* **VIII**: 288.
Gen 17: 17-21, 25	**VI**: 68.
Gen 17: 18	**VI**: 69.
Gen 17: 20	**VI**: 8.
Gen 17: 23	**VI**: 15.
Gen 18	**VI**: 69*(2)*, 724; **VIII**: 159.
Gen 18-19	**VI**: 69.
Gen 18, 19	**VI**: 69.
Gen 18: 1	**VI**: 2.
Gen 18: 1-15	**VI**: 69.
Gen 18: 1, 8	**VI**: 14.
Gen 18: 1-19:28	**VI**: 69.
Gen 18: 9	**VI**: 13.
Gen 18: 16-33	**VI**: 16.
Gen 18: 17-23	**VI**: 69.
Gen 18: 18	**VI**: 69.
Gen 18: 19	**VI**: 4, 14, 15, 69.j
Gen 18: 20s	**VI**: 16.
Gen 18: 20	**VI**: 70.
Gen 18: 20, 21	**VI**: 70.
Gen 19: 1, 2, 4-10	**VI**: 70.
Gen 19: 3	**VI**: 70.
Gen 19: 9-11	**VI**: 70.
Gen 19: 12-17	**VI**: 70.
Gen 19: 19	**VI**: 14.
Gen 19: 22	**VI**: 70.
Gen 19: 24	**VI**: 15.
Gen 19: 26	**VI**: 70*(2)*.
Gen 19: 28	**VI**: 2.
Gen 19: 33	**VI**: 13.
Gen 19: 38	**VI**: 15.
Gen 20	**VI**: 59, 70*(3)*, 76.
Gen 20: 1-18	**IV**: 235; **VI**: 60, 71, 76.
Gen 20: 1-19	**VI**: 70.
Gen 20: 6	**VI**: 71.
Gen 20: 8-21	**VI**: 71.
Gen 20: 10	**VI**: 71.
Gen 20: 16	**VI**: 14, 16, 71*(3)*.
Gen 20: 17, 18	**VI**: 71.
Gen 21: 1, 2, 9, 12	**VI**: 71.
Gen 21: 9-21	**VI**: 68, 71.
Gen 21: 16	**V**: 400; **VI**: 10.
Gen 21: 21, 31, 33	**VI**: 71.
Gen 22	**VI**: 71*(2)*, 72*(2);* **IX**: cxlv.
Gen 22: 1-18	**VI**: 72.

Gen 22: 1-19 **VI**: 72.
Gen 22: 1-2 **VI**: 72*(2)*.
Gen 22: 2 **VI**: 60, 72*(3)*.
Gen 22: 2-14 **VI**: 72.
Gen 22: 13 **V**: 402; **VI**: 7, 12.
Gen 22: 14 **VI**: 14, 15*(2)*, 16, 72*(2)*.
Gen 22: 16ff. **VI**: 14.
Gen 22: 17-18 **VI**: 73.
Gen 22: 18 **VI**: 73*(2)*.
Gen 22: 20 **VI**: 73.
Gen 22: 20-23: 18 **VI**: 726.
Gen 23 **V**: 490; **VI**: 73*(7)*.
Gen 23: 1, 2, 4 **VI**: 73.
Gen 23: 5-20 **VI**: 73.
Gen 23: 6 **VI**: 74.
Gen 23: 10 **VI**: 74*(2)*.
Gen 23: 11 **VI**: 74.
Gen 23: 18 **VI**: 14, 74*(2)*.
Gen 24: 1-4 **VI**: 74.
Gen 24: 2 **VI**: 74.
Gen 24: 2, 22, 30, 47 **VI**: 14.
Gen 24: 10-67 **VI**: 74.
Gen 24: 14 **VI**: 26, 74.
Gen 24: 16 **VI**: 16.
Gen 24: 21 **VI**: 75.
Gen 24: 27 **VI**: 11.
Gen 24: 29 **VI**: 15.
Gen 24: 32ט **VI**: 75.
Gen 24: 53, 65 **VI**: 14.
Gen 24: 56 **VI**: 75, 712.
Gen 24: 63 **VI**: 75.
Gen 25: 1 **VI**: 75.
Gen 25: 1-4 **VI**: 15.
Gen 25: 5, 7-9 **VI**: 75.
Gen 25: 13 **VI**: 15.
Gen 25: 19, 20, 21-34 **VI**: 75.
Gen 25: 20 **VI**: 15.
Gen 25: 21-26 **VI**: 726.
Gen 25: 22 **VI**: 75.
Gen 25: 23 **VI**: 75*(2)*.
Gen 25: 27-34 **VI**: 76.
Gen 25: 28-34 **VI**: 76.
Gen 25: 29-33 **VI**: 76.
Gen 25: 30 **VI**: 14.
Gen 25: 31 **VI**: 15.
Gen 25: 31-34 **VI**: 76.
Gen 25: 34 **VI**: 76.
Gen 26 **VI**: 59, 70, 76*(2)*.
Gen 26: 7-11 **IV**: 235; **VI**: 60, 71, 76.
Gen 26: 12-25 **VI**: 16.
Gen 26: 14 **V**: 400; **VI**: 10*(2)*.
Gen 26: 32 **VI**: 13.
Gen 27 **IV**: 249; **VI**: 76, 77*(2)*.
Gen 27: 1-24 **VI**: 77.
Gen 27: 2 **VI**: 77.
Gen 27: 3 **VI**: 14.
Gen 27: 9, 16, 18 **VI**: 77.
Gen 27: 15-23, 41-45 **VI**: 16.
Gen 27: 30 **VI**: 77.
Gen 27: 39 **VI**: 4, 14, 15.
Gen 27: 39, 40 **VI**: 14.
Gen 27: 41 **VI**: 77.
Gen 28 **VI**: 77*(2)*.
Gen 28: 1-5, 10-24 **VI**: 16.
Gen 28: 10-12 **VI**: 78.
Gen 28: 10-22 **VI**: 78*(2)*.
Gen 28: 12 **VI**: 78.
Gen 28: 12, 17 **VI**: 78*(4)*.
Gen 28: 16, 17 **VI**: 78.
Gen 28: 18 **VI**: 15, 78.
Gen 28: 19 **VI**: 78.
Gen 28: 20-22 **VI**: 79.
Gen 28: 21 **VI**: 14.
Gen 29: -31 **VI**: 79.
Gen 29: 2, 17 **VI**: 14.
Gen 29: 32, 33 **VI**: 15.
Gen 30: 4-6 **VI**: 15.

Gen 30:7-8 **VI**: 15.
Gen 30:8 **VI**: 79.
Gen 30:9-11 **VI**: 15.
Gen 30:11 **VI**: 15.
Gen 30:12, 13 **VI**: 15.
Gen 30:14 **VI**: 79.
Gen 30:16-18 **VI**: 15.
Gen 30:27 **VI**: 16.
Gen 30:27b **VI**: 79*(2)*.
Gen 30:32 **VI**: 79.
Gen 31 **VI**: 79*(2)*.
Gen 31:13 **VI**: 7.
Gen 31:14-16 **VI**: 79.
Gen 31:19 **VI**: 14, 80.
Gen 31:19, 21, 42, 53 **VI**: 15.
Gen 31:34 **VI**: 80.
Gen 31:38f. **I**: *258;* **VI**: 80.
Gen 31:38 **VI**: 80.
Gen 31:38-39 **VI**: 80.
Gen 31:39 **VI**: 11.
Gen 31:42 **VI**: 80.
Gen 31:44 **VI**: 80*(2)*.
Gen 31:47 **V**: 395; **VI**: 7, 15, 80.
Gen 31:49 **VI**: 80, 81*(3)*.
Gen 31:50 **VI**: 81.
Gen 31:53 **VI**: 81*(2)*.
Gen 32 **VI**: 81*(4)*.
Gen 32-50 **IV**: *249;* **VI**: 81.
Gen 32:1-2 **VI**: 81.
Gen 32:9-12, 22-30 **VI**: 16.
Gen 32:10-11 **VI**: 82.
Gen 32:22-32 **VI**: 82.
Gen 32:23-33 **VI**: 82*(3)*.
Gen 32:24-25 **VI**: 82.
Gen 32:24-28 **VI**: 82.
Gen 32:24-32 **VI**: 82.
Gen 32:25s **VI**: 82.
Gen 32:31 **VI**: 82.
Gen 33:4 **VI**: 13.
Gen 33:18-20 **VI**: 83.
Gen 33:20 **VI**: 83.
Gen 34 **VI**: 83.
Gen 34:12LXX **I**: *467;* **VI**: 83.
Gen 34:24 **VI**: 83*(2)*.
Gen 35:1-4 **VI**: 83.
Gen 35:1, 5, 7, 10 **VI**: 83.
Gen 35:8 **VI**: 83.
Gen 35:8, 16, 19 **VI**: 5.
Gen 35:11 **V**: 394; **VI**: 6, 83.
Gen 35:11, 18, 22 **VI**: 83.
Gen 35:18 **V**: 402; **VI**: 12, 13, 16, 84.
Gen 35:21 **VI**: 84.
Gen 36 **VI**: 84.
Gen 36:12 **VI**: 84.
Gen 36:15 **VI**: 15.
Gen 36:20 **VI**: 15.
Gen 36:31 **VI**: 84.
Gen 36:31-39 **II**: 123; **VI**: 84.
Gen 36:32 **VI**: 15.
Gen 36:35 **VI**: 15.
Gen 36:37 **VI**: 15.
Gen 37 **IV**: *260;* **VI**: 85.
Gen 37-50 **VI**: 84*(2)*.
Gen 37:1 **VI**: 14.
Gen 37:2-Ex 12:51 **IV**: *248;* **VI**: 84, 97.
Gen 37:3 **VI**: 14; **VI**: 85.
Gen 37:3, 4 **VI**: 8, 85*(2)*.
Gen 37:5-28 **VI**: 16.
Gen 37:5-49 **VI**: 84.
Gen 37:9 **VI**: 85.
Gen 37:11 **VI**: 85; **VIII**: 285.
Gen 37:12 **VI**: 13.
Gen 37:28 **VI**: 85*(2)*.
Gen 37:35 **VI**: 14, 15.
Gen 37:36 **VI**: 15.
Gen 38 **VI**: 85*(2);* **IX**: cxlvi.

Gen 38: 1-5 **VI**: 86.
Gen 38: 8-10 **VI**: 86.
Gen 38: 14, 21, 22 **VI**: 14.
Gen 38: 29 **VI**: 86.
Gen 39 **VI**: 15, 86.
Gen 39-50 **VI**: 86.
Gen 39: 4 **VI**: 86.
Gen 39: 6 **VI**: 14*(2)*.
Gen 39: 7 **VI**: 86.
Gen 39: 14, 17 **VI**: 86, 187.
Gen 39: 20 **VI**: 15.
Gen 39: 20-40: 15 **VI**: 16.
Gen 39: 32, 33, 34, 35 **VI**: 15.
Gen 40: 3LXX **VI**: 86.
Gen 40: 5 **VI**: 15.
Gen 40: 9-11 **VI**: 15.
Gen 40: 13 **VI**: 15, 16.
Gen 40: 15 **VI**: 87.
Gen 40: 16 **VI**: 15, 16.
Gen 40: 16, 17 **VI**: 14, 87.
Gen 40: 20 **VI**: 15.
Gen 40: 22 **VI**: 13.
Gen 41: 1 **VI**: 15.
Gen 41: 5 **VI**: 87.
Gen 41: 8 **VI**: 15.
Gen 41: 16 **VI**: 15.
Gen 41: 22 **VI**: 87.
Gen 41: 24 **VI**: 87.
Gen 41: 32 **VI**: 87.
Gen 41: 38-49 **VI**: 16.
Gen 41: 40 **VI**: 87*(4)*.
Gen 41: 43 **V**: 360; **VI**: 15, 87.
Gen 41: 45 **VI**: 15, 88*(3)*.
Gen 41: 51 **VI**: 16.
Gen 41: 54 **VI**: 15.
Gen 41: 56 **V**: 400; **VI**: 10.
Gen 42: 37 **VI**: 11.
Gen 42: 49 **VI**: 88.
Gen 43: 9 **VI**: 11; **VI**: 88.
Gen 43: 11 **VI**: 58, 88.
Gen 43: 32 **VI**: 15; **VI**: 88.
Gen 44: 4 **VI**: 4.
Gen 44: 5 **VI**: 88.
Gen 44: 5, 15 **VI**: 14.
Gen 44: 12 **VI**: 88.
Gen 45: 1-15 **VI**: 16.
Gen 45: 1-3 **VI**: 89.
Gen 45: 9 **VI**: 89.
Gen 45: 10 **VI**: 15.
Gen 45: 23 **VI**: 89.
Gen 46 **I**: *118;* **VI**: 89.
Gen 46: 3 **VI**: 7.
Gen 46: 28 **VI**: 2.
Gen 46: 29-36*[sic]* **VI**: 89.
Gen 46: 34 **VI**: 15; **VI**: 89.
Gen 47: 2, 6, 31 **VI**: 14.
Gen 47: 9 **VI**: 89.
Gen 47: 11 **VI**: 15.
Gen 47: 12-17 **VI**: 89.
Gen 47: 13-27 **VI**: 89.
Gen 47: 14-26 **VI**: 90.
Gen 47: 15 **VI**: 14.
Gen 47: 29-31 **I**: *203, 228;* **VI**: 90*(3)*.
Gen 47: 31 **VI**: 90*(3);* **VIII**: 296.
Gen 48: 1-16 **I**: *203, 228;* **VI**: 90*(2)*.
Gen 48: 5 **VI**: 90.
Gen 48: 9 **VI**: 90.
Gen 48: 10 **VI**: 36; 90.
Gen 48: 19 **VI**: 91; **VIII**: 291.
Gen 48: 20 **VI**: 91.
Gen 49 **VI**: 14, 91*(12)*, 92; **VIII**: 388, 453, 468.
Gen 49: 1-27 **VI**: 92.
Gen 49: 4 **VI**: 3, 11.
Gen 49: 4, 10 **VI**: 14.
Gen 49: 4, 18 **VI**: 8.
Gen 49: 4, 14, 15, 19 **VI**: 15.
Gen 49: 5 **VI**: 13*(2)*, 92.

Gen 49: 6 **VI**: 92.
Gen 49: 7 **VI**: 92.
Gen 49: 8-12 **VI**: 92*(3)*.
Gen 49: 10 **VI**: 11, 13, 14, 92*(4)*, 93*(14)*, 353.
Gen 49: 11 **VI**: 93.
Gen 49: 14 **VI**: 94*(2)*, 150.
Gen 49: 19 **VI**: 91.
Gen 49: 20-21 **VI**: 94.
Gen 49: 20, 24, 26 **VI**: 15.
Gen 49: 21 **VI**: 94*(2)*.
Gen 49: 22-26 **VI**: 94.
Gen 49: 24 **VI**: 3, 8, 94.
Gen 49: 24b-26 **VI**: 94*(2)*.
Gen 49: 25b **VI**: 15.
Gen 49: 25 **VI**: 95.
Gen 49: 25-26 **VI**: 94.
Gen 49: 26 **VI**: 11, 95.
Gen 50: 1-3 **VI**: 95.
Gen 50: 11 **VI**: 15.
Gen 50: 15-21 **VI**: 16.
Gen 50: 22-26 **VI**: 95, 155, 175.
Gen 50: 26 **VI**: 95.
Exod 1:-14 **VI**: 97.
Exod 1: 1-14 **VI**: 96, 97.
Exod 1: 6-22 **VI**: 97.
Exod 1: 8-11 **VI**: 97.
Exod 1: 8-2: 10 **VI**: 97.
Exod 1: 10 **VI**: 98.
Exod 1: 10-22 **VI**: 97.
Exod 1: 11 **VI**: 98*(2)*.
Exod 1: 16 **VI**: 5, 96, 98*(2)*.
Exod 1: 19 **VI**: 98*(2)*.
Exod 1: 20, 21, 22 **VI**: 98.
Exod 1: 21 **VI**: 8.
Exod 2: 1-10 **V**: 701; **VI**: 98.
Exod 2: 1-15 **VI**: 96, 98.
Exod 2: 3 **VI**: 5, 6, 96.
Exod 2: 6 **VI**: 13*(2)*.
Exod 2: 9 **VI**: 98.
Exod 2: 10 **VI**: 6, 96, 99.
Exod 2: 15 **VI**: 96.
Exod 2: 21 **VI**: 99.
Exod 2: 25 **VI**: 99.
Exod 3:-4: 17 **VI**: 99.
Exod 3-17: 27 **VI**: 99.
Exod 3: 1-12 **VIII**: 404.
Exod 3: 1-14 **VI**: 96.
Exod 3: 1-15 **IV**: 258; **VI**: 99.
Exod 3: 1-4 **VI**: 99.
Exod 3: 2 **VI**: 6*(2)*.
Exod 3: 2-3 **VI**: 99.
Exod 3: 4 **VI**: 100.
Exod 3: 4-22 **VI**: 100.
Exod 3: 14 **VI**: 96; **VIII**: 113*(2)*.
Exod 3: 14, 15 **VI**: 96, 100*(10)*.
Exod 3: 16, 22 **VI**: 96.
Exod 3: 17 **VI**: 100.
Exod 3: 21, 22 **VI**: 96.
Exod 4 **VI**: 101.
Exod 4: 11 **VI**: 101.
Exod 4: 14 **VI**: 101.
Exod 4: 16 **VI**: 101.
Exod 4: 20 **VI**: 96.
Exod 4: 22-23 **VI**: 101.
Exod 4: 24 **VI**: 102.
Exod 4: 24-26 **VI**: 101*(7)*.
Exod 4: 25-26 **VI**: 102.
Exod 5 **VI**: 103.
Exod 5-14 **VI**: 102.
Exod 5: 4-5 **V**: 464; **VI**: 102.
Exod 5: 12 **VI**: 7.
Exod 5: 14 **VI**: 13.
Exod 5: 22-23 **VI**: 102.
Exod 6: 1-8 **VI**: 102.
Exod 6: 2, 3 **VI**: 102*(2)*, 103; **VIII**: 117.
Exod 6: 2- 3 **VI**: 103.

Exod 6:2-7:7 **VI**: 102.
Exod 6:3 **VI**: 103*(2)*
Exod 6:3b **VI**: 103.
Exod 6:12, 30 **VI**: 6.
Exod 6:23 **VI**: 103.
Exod 7-12 **IV**: *248;* **VI**: 103.
Exod 7:1-5 **VI**: 103.
Exod 7:8-10:27 **VI**: 103.
Exod 7:9, 13, 14 **VI**: 96.
Exod 7:11 **VI**: 103.
Exod 7:12 **VI**: 103.
Exod 7:14 **VI**: 104.
Exod 7:15 **VI**: 96.
Exod 7:27 **V**: 400.
Exod 8:5 **V**: 402; **VI**: 6, 12.
Exod 8:9 **VI**: 96.
Exod 8:12 **VI**: 96.
Exod 9 **VI**: 104, 568.
Exod 9:2 **V**: 400.
Exod 9:3 **VI**: 104.
Exod 9:13-16 **VI**: 104.
Exod 9:17 **VI**: 5, 96.
Exod 9:24 **VI**: 96.
Exod 9:31 **VI**: 96.
Exod 9:31, 32 **VI**: 104.
Exod 10:4 **V**: 400.
Exod 10:10 **V**: 212; **VI**: 5, 96, 104*(3)*.
Exod 10:11 **V**: 411; **VI**: 12, 104, 714.
Exod 10:19 **VI**: 104.
Exod 10:21 **VI**: 6.
Exod 10:24 **VI**: 11.
Exod 11:1-12:36 **VI**: 105*(2)*.
Exod 11:2 **VI**: 3, 4, 96.
Exod 11:2, 3 **VI**: 96.
Exod 11:7 **VI**: 105.
Exod 12:4 **V**: 402; **VI**: 12.
Exod 12:9, 36 **VI**: 96.
Exod 12:16 **VI**: 113.
Exod 12:18-19 **VI**: 113.
Exod 12:19 **VI**: 105.
Exod 12:21-30 **VI**: 96.
Exod 12:28 **VI**: 113.
Exod 12:35, 36 **VI**: 96.
Exod 12:35-36 **VI**: 105.
Exod 12:37 **VI**: 6, 105.
Exod 12:37-17:16 **IV**: 250; **VI**: 105.
Exod 12:40 **I**: 511; **VI**: 6, 105.
Exod 12:42 **VI**: 6, 105, 714; **VIII**: 290.
Exod 12:46 **VI**: 106.
Exod 13-Deut 34 **IV**: *248;* **VI**: 106, 140.
Exod 13:6, 9, 23, 35 **VI**: 96.
Exod 13:7 **VI**: 106.
Exod 13:7-14:4 **VI**: 106.
Exod 13:17 **VI**: 106.
Exod 13:18 **VI**: 96.
Exod 13:21 **VI**: 6.
Exod 14 **IV**: 327*(2);* **V**: 692; **VI**: 106*(3)*.
Exod 14:1-15:21 **VI**: 106.
Exod 14:2 **VI**: 106.
Exod 14:3 **V**: 402; **VI**: 12.
Exod 14:6f. **VI**: 6.
Exod 14:7 **VI**: 96.
Exod 14:11 **VI**: 107.
Exod 14:13-27 **VI**: 96.
Exod 14:15 **VI**: 107.
Exod 14:20 **VI**: 107.
Exod 14:21 **VI**: 107.
Exod 14:22, 29 **VI**: 13.
Exod 14:29 **VI**: 6.
Exod 14:37 **VI**: 107.
Exod 15 **V**: 701*(2);* **VI**: 107*(2)*.
Exod 15:1-17 **V**: 685.
Exod 15:1-18 **VI**: 107.
Exod 15:1b-18 **VI**: 107*(3)*.

Exod 15: 1b-19 **IV**: 46.
Exod 15: 1-9 **V**: 700.
Exod 15: 2 **VI**: 96, 108*(4)*.
Exod 15: 2-14 **VI**: 108.
Exod 15: 3 **VI**: 108*(2)*.
Exod 15: 7-21 **VI**: 108, 713.
Exod 15: 8 **VI**: 13, 108*(2)*.
Exod 16 **VI**: 108*(2)*.
Exod 16: 1-15 **VI**: 96.
Exod 16: 2-12 **VI**: 109.
Exod 16: 3 **VI**: 6.
Exod 16: 15 **V**: 510; **VI**: 109*(2)*.
Exod 17 **VI**: 109.
Exod 17: 8-13 **VI**: 109.
Exod 17: 13 **V**: 422; **VI**: 109, 275, 428.
Exod 17: 15, 16 **VI**: 6.
Exod 17: 16 **VI**: 5, 97, 109.
Exod 18 **IV**: *43;* **V**: 24; **VI**: 110.
Exod 18-34 **IV**: 250; **VI**: 109.
Exod 18: 10 **VI**: 110.
Exod 18: 12 **VI**: 110.
Exod 19 **VI**: 110.
Exod 19: 1-34:35 **VI**: 110.
Exod 19: 3-6 **VI**: 110.
Exod 19: 6 **VI**: 110.
Exod 19: 6-9 **VI**: 110.
Exod 19: 13 **VI**: 6.
Exod 19: 18-19 **VI**: 110.
Exod 20 **IX**: cxlvi.
Exod 20: 1-11 **VI**: 96.
Exod 20: 1-17 **VI**: 110.
Exod 20: 2 **VI**: 111.
Exod 20: 2-6 **VI**: 111.
Exod 20: 3-5 **VI**: 111.
Exod 20: 4 **VI**: 13.
Exod 20: 4-5 **VI**: 111.
Exod 20: 5 **VI**: 111.
Exod 20: 6 **VI**: 96, 111.
Exod 20: 7 **VI**: 111*(5)*.
Exod 20: 8 **V**: 490; **VI**: 112.
Exod 20: 13 **VI**: 96.
Exod 20: 17 **VI**: 112.
Exod 20: 20 **VI**: 13, 112.
Exod 20: 22-25 **VI**: 112.
Exod 20: 22-23:19 **IV**: 341.
Exod 20: 24-26 **VI**: 112*(2)*.
Exod 21-23 **IV**: 342.
Exod 21: 6 **VI**: 96, 112*(2)*, 114.
Exod 21: 7-11 **I**: *202;* **VI**: 112.
Exod 21: 8 **VI**: 112.
Exod 21: 10 **VI**: 113*(2)*.
Exod 21: 12 **IX**: cxlvi.
Exod 21: 12, 15-17 **VI**: 113*(2)*.
Exod 21: 15-17 **IX**: cxlvi.
Exod 22: 2 **VI**: 96.
Exod 22: 4 **VI**: 113.
Exod 22: 4LXX **I**: *467;* **VI**: 113*(2)*.
Exod 22: 4-5 **VI**: 113.
Exod 22: 7 **VI**: 114.
Exod 22: 8, 9 **VI**: 96.
Exod 22: 12 **VI**: 114.
Exod 22: 15-16 **VI**: 114.
Exod 22: 16 **I**: *467;* **VI**: 114.
Exod 22: 20 **VI**: 96.
Exod 22: 20-26 **IV**: 342.
Exod 22: 23 **VI**: 114.
Exod 22: 25 **VI**: 97.
Exod 22: 28 **VI**: 114.
Exod 22: 29 **VI**: 97.
Exod 23: 1-9 **IV**: 342.
Exod 23: 4 **VI**: 695.
Exod 23: 5 **VI**: 97.
Exod 23: 18 **VI**: 114.
Exod 23: 19 **VI**: 6, 114*(4)*, 115.

Exod 23:20-33	**IV**: 341.
Exod 23:21	**V**: 404; **VI**: 96, 115.
Exod 23:23	**VI**: 115.
Exod 23:28	**III**: *376;* **VI**: 13, 115, 143, 174.
Exod 24:11	**VI**: 115.
Exod 24:24	**VI**: 96.
Exod 24:29	**VI**: 115.
Exod 24:33	**VI**: 96.
Exod 25:6	**VI**: 96.
Exod 25:39	**VI**: 12.
Exod 26:6, 7	**VI**: 96.
Exod 26:36, 37	**VI**: 96.
Exod 27:15, 17, 19	**VI**: 115.
Exod 27:21	**VI**: 3, 96*(2)*.
Exod 27:23, 28	**VI**: 115.
Exod 28:17-20	**VI**: 115.
Exod 28:31-35	**VI**: 115.
Exod 28:40	**VI**: 13.
Exod 28:42Douay	**VI**: 116.
Exod 29:22	**VI**: 96.
Exod 29:32f.	**IV**: *20.*
Exod 29:32	**VI**: 116.
Exod 30:6	**VI**: 3.
Exod 30:33	**VI**: 116*(3)*.
Exod 30:34	**VI**: 116.
Exod 31:2	**VI**: 4.
Exod 32	**VI**: 116*(3)*, 720.
Exod 32-33:6	**VI**: 116.
Exod 32:1-8	**VI**: 96.
Exod 32:2	**V**: 396.
Exod 32:4	**VI**: 116.
Exod 32:18	**V**: 700; **VI**: 117*(4)*.
Exod 32:20	**VI**: 117.
Exod 32:22	**VI**: 117.
Exod 32:25	**VI**: 96.
Exod 32:30-35	**VI**: 96.
Exod 32:31, 32	**VI**: 117.
Exod 32:32	**VI**: 2.
Exod 33:6	**VI**: 117.
Exod 33:7	**VI**: 118.
Exod 33:7-11	**VI**: 117*(2)*.
Exod 33:7-11, 13	**VI**: 96.
Exod 33:11-23	**VI**: 722, 726.
Exod 33:12-34:35	**VI**: 118.
Exod 33:14	**VI**: 118; **VIII**: 284.
Exod 33:14f.	**VI**: 118.
Exod 33:15	**VI**: 118.
Exod 33:16, 21	**VI**: 96.
Exod 33:19	**VI**: 118.
Exod 33:22-23	**VI**: 118.
Exod 33:23	**VI**: 118.
Exod 34	**VI**: 118.
Exod 34:5	**VI**: 119.
Exod 34:6f.	**V**: 701; **VI**: 119.
Exod 34:7	**VI**: 119*(5)*.
Exod 34:12-26	**IX**: cxlvi.
Exod 34:13	**VI**: 96.
Exod 34:21	**VI**: 119.
Exod 34:25	**VI**: 13, 114, 119.
Exod 34:26	**VI**: 6, 119*(3).j*
Exod 34:28	**VI**: 120.
Exod 34:29-35	**VI**: 120*(3);* **VIII**: 293.
Exod 34:33	**VI**: 3.
Exod 35-39	**V**: *53;* **VI**: 12, 96, 120.
Exod 35:1-40:38	**VI**: 120.
Exod 35:22	**VI**: 5, 97.
Exod 36:1	**VI**: 96.
Exod 37:2	**VI**: 12.
Exod 39:33ff.	**VI**: 96.
Exod 40:1-13, 34-38	**VI**: 13.
Exod 40:17ff.	**VI**: 96.
Exod 40:17-19	**VI**: 120.
Exod 41:45	**V**: 295.
Lev 1	**IV**: *344;* **VI**: 121.
Lev 1:3	**VI**: 3, 121.

Lev 2:1 **VI**: 5, 121*(2)*.
Lev 2:19 **VI**: 6.
Lev 3:9 **VI**: 121.
Lev 3:11 **VI**: 121.
Lev 4:12 **VI**: 3.
Lev 5:1 **VI**: 121.
Lev 5:1, 4 **VI**: 121.
Lev 5:2-4 **VI**: 121.
Lev 5:2-5 **VI**: 121.
Lev 5:3 **VI**: 3.
Lev 5:8 **V**: 444; **VI**: 121.
Lev 5:14-6:7 **VI**: 121.
Lev 5:15 **VI**: 6.
Lev 6:2-5 **VI**: 121.
Lev 6:18 **VI**: 121.
Lev 8-9 **V**: *53;* **VI**: 12, 121.
Lev 8:33 **VI**: 3.
Lev 8:33marg. **VI**: 121.
Lev 10 **VI**: 122.
Lev 10:1-11 **VI**: 13.
Lev 11 **I**: xvii n15, *250;* **VI**: 122, 145.
Lev 11:3-7 **VI**: 122*(2)*, 145*(2)*.
Lev 11:5 **VI**: 122.
Lev 11:6 **VI**: 122*(2)*.
Lev 11:13-19 **VI**: 122.
Lev 11:5, 13 18, 29 **VI**: 121.
Lev 12:1-5 **VI**: 122.
Lev 13-14 **VI**: 122, 123.
Lev 14 **VI**: 123.
Lev 14:10 **VI**: 121.
Lev 14:37 **VI**: 123.
Lev 14:57 **VI**: 7.
Lev 15:1 **III**: *403;* **VI**: 123, 709, 716.
Lev 15:2 **VI**: 121.
Lev 16 **V**: 89; **VI**: 123*(6)*.
Lev 16:5 **VI**: 124; **VIII**: 283.
Lev 16:5-10 **VI**: 123.
Lev 16:5-22 **VI**: 13.
Lev 16:8 **VI**: 3, 5, 6, 121.
Lev 16:8-26 **VI**: 124.
Lev 16:8, 10, 26 **VI**: 121.
Lev 16:22 **VI**: 121.
Lev 16:31 **VI**: 3.
Lev 17-26 **VI**: 124.
Lev 17-19 **IV**: *344;* **VI**: 124, 125.
Lev 17:1-9 **V**: 59; **VI**: 124, 145.
Lev 17:7 **VI**: 6.
Lev 17:7marg., 14 **VI**: 121.
Lev 18 **VI**: 124*(2)*.
Lev 18:5 **VI**: 124.
Lev 18:18 **VI**: 5, 121*(2)*.
Lev 18:30 **VI**: 124.
Lev 19:18 **VIII**: 287.
Lev 19:18b **VI**: 124.
Lev 19:20 **VI**: 121.
Lev 19:24 **VI**: 121.
Lev 19:28 **VI**: 10.
Lev 19:31 **VI**: 7.
Lev 19:35 **VI**: 13*(2)*.
Lev 20 **VI**: 124, 125.
Lev 20:6 **VI**: 125, 206, 284.
Lev 20:10 **VI**: 3.
Lev 21-22 **IV**: *344*.
Lev 21:1-6 **VI**: 125.
Lev 21:4marg. **VI**: 121.
Lev 21:11 **VI**: 125.
Lev 22:28 **VI**: 6.
Lev 23 **IV**: *344*, 84; **VI**: 125.
Lev 23:2 **VI**: 121.
Lev 23:9-22 **V**: 89; **VI**: 125.
Lev 23:23-44 **VI**: 125.
Lev 23:23-27:34 **V**: 84.

Lev 23:40	**VI**: 125, 126.	Num 11:31-32	**VI**: 129.
Lev 23:3, 24, 32, 39	**VI**: 121.	Num 11:44,45	**VI**: 127.
Lev 24:9	**VI**: 6.	Num 12	**VI**: 129.
Lev 24:10-23	**VI**: 126.	Num 12:2,8	**VI**: 127.
Lev 25	**IV**: *344.*	Num 12:3	**VI**: 129.
Lev 25:10	**VI**: 6.	Num 12:10	**VI**: 129.
Lev 25:23	**VI**: 126.	Num 12:14	**VI**: 129.
Lev 25:23-30	**VI**: 126.	Num 13-14	**VI**: 129.
Lev 25:30	**VI**: 126.	Num 13:17-20, 23-33	**VI**: 129.
Lev 25:34	**VI**: 4.	Num 13:17, 22, 33	**VI**: 127.
Lev 25:39-43	**VI**: 126.	Num 13:32	**VI**: 129.
Lev 26:1	**VI**: 121.	Num 14:1	**VI**: 129.
Lev 26:30	**VI**: 9, 121, 126*(2)*.	Num 14:26-38	**IV**: *347;* **VI**: 130.
Lev 26:31-33	**VI**: 126.	Num 14:44	**VI**: 130*(2)*.
Lev 27:2-3	**VI**: 13.	Num 15:1	**VI**: 2.
Lev 27:28	**VI**: 126.	Num 15:37-41	**VI**: 130.
Lev 35:33	**VI**: 121.	Num 15:38-41	**VI**: 130.
Num 1	**I**: *228;* **VI**: 127, 137.	Num 16:1	**VI**: 8.
		Num 16:27	**VI**: 130*(2)*.
Num 2	**I**: *228.*	Num 16:30	**VI**: 130.
Num 3:12-13	**VI**: 127.	Num 16:32	**VI**: 130*(2)*.
Num 3:39	**VI**: 13.	Num 17:2	**VI**: 131.
Num 4:15-20	**VI**: 127.	Num 18:2,4	**VI**: 127.
Num 4:20	**VI**: 127.	Num 18:7	**VI**: 131.
Num 5	**VI**: 127.	Num 18:12	**VI**: 131, 712.
Num 5:11-28	**VI**: 127, 128.	Num 19	**VI**: 131*(2)*.
Num 5:14	**VI**: 128.	Num 19:2	**VI**: 127.
Num 6:1-21	**VI**: 128.	Num 20	**VI**: 131*(3)*.
Num 6:2	**VI**: 127.	Num 20:7-12	**VI**: 131.
Num 6:24-26	**VI**: 128.	Num 20:7-13	**VI**: 13.
Num 7	**V**: *53;* **VI**: 12, 128.	Num 20:26	**VI**: 127.
		Num 21:1	**VI**: 132.
Num 7:89	**VI**: 127, 128.	Num 21:1-3	**VI**: 131.
Num 8:11	**VI**: 127.	Num 21:1-9	**VI**: 131.
Num 9:10	**VI**: 13.	Num 21:4-9	**VI**: 132.
Num 10:11-13, 29-36	**VI**: 13.	Num 21:5	**VI**: 7.
Num 10:29-32	**VI**: 128.	Num 21:6	**VI**: 132.
Num 10:31	**VI**: 13*(2)*.	Num 21:8	**VI**: 127, 132.
Num 10:35-36	**VI**: 13.	Num 21:9	**VI**: 132*(2)*.
Num 11:4	**VI**: 4, 128*(3)*.	Num 21:14	**VI**: 132*(2)*.
Num 11:25	**VI**: 127.	Num 21:14f.	**VI**: 132.

Num 21: 14-15 **VI**: 11.
Num 21: 16ff. **VI**: 132.
Num 21: 16-18 **VI**: 132.
Num 21: 17 **V**: 400; **VI**: 10.
Num 21: 17, 18 **V**: 700.
Num 21: 17-18 **VI**: 11.
Num 21: 2-3marg. **VI**: 127.
Num 21: 24 **V**: 400; **VI**: 133.
Num 21: 27-30 **V**: 700; **VI**: 133.
Num 21: 27b-30 **VI**: 133.
Num 21: 30 **VI**: 13.
Num 21: 14, 30marg. **VI**: 127.
Num 22 **VI**: 134.
Num 22-24 **I**: *36;* **VI**: 133*(6)*, 721.
Num 22: 2-24:25 **VI**: 133*(2)*.
Num 22: 5 **VI**: 8, 127, 134.
Num 22: 6 **VI**: 134.
Num 22: 20-22 **VI**: 134.
Num 22: 21-31 **VI**: 134.
Num 22: 21-34 **VI**: 134.
Num 22: 22 **VI**: 134.
Num 22: 23 **VI**: 134.
Num 22: 28-30 **VI**: 134.
Num 22: 41-23:25 **VI**: 134.
Num 23 **V**: 400; **VI**: 10.
Num 23-24 **VI**: 135.
Num 23: 1-24:24 **VI**: 135.
Num 23: 3 **VI**: 127.
Num 23: 7-10 **IX**: cxxxi.
Num 23: 9 **VI**: 135.
Num 23: 9-10 **VI**: 135.
Num 23: 10 **VI**: 135*(4)*.
Num 23: 18-24 **IX**: cxxxi.
Num 23: 21 **VI**: 135.
Num 23: 23 **VI**: 3.
Num 23: 24 **V**: 456; **VI**: 135*(2)*.
Num 24: 3 **V**: 465; **VI**: 136.
Num 24: 3, 15 **V**: 400; **VI**: 10.
Num 24: 3, 4 **VI**: 127.
Num 24: 3-4 **VI**: 136.
Num 24: 3-9 **IX**: cxxxi.
Num 24: 4 **VI**: 136, 137.
Num 24: 7 **VI**: 136*(2)*.
Num 24: 8 **VI**: 136.
Num 24: 9 **V**: 456; **VI**: 135, 136*(2)*.
Num 24: 15 **VI**: 136.
Num 24: 15-19 **VI**: 136; **IX**: cxxxi.
Num 24: 16 **VI**: 136, 137.
Num 24: 17 **VI**: 127.
Num 24: 17-24 **V**: 160; **VI**: 137.
Num 24: 20-24 **IX**: cxxxi.
Num 24: 23, 24 **VI**: 137.
Num 24: 23-25 **VI**: 137.
Num 25 **VI**: 720.
Num 25: 3 **VI**: 127.
Num 25: 9 **VI**: 137.
Num 25: 11 **VI**: 127.
Num 25: 18 **VI**: 137.
Num 26 **VI**: 127, 137.
Num 26: 38-40 **VI**: 137.
Num 27: 1-11 **VI**: 137, 138.
Num 28: 9, 11, 13 **VI**: 138.
Num 29: 15 **VI**: 13.
Num 30: 6-8 **VI**: 8.
Num 31: 10 **VI**: 127.
Num 31: 22 **I**: *295;* **VI**: 138, 143, 203.
Num 31: 27 **VI**: 138.
Num 32: 1-5 **VI**: 138.
Num 33: 10 **VI**: 138.
Num 33: 35 **VI**: 138.
Num 33: 40 **VI**: 138.
Num 33: 52-55 **VI**: 138.
Num 34: 7f. **VI**: 10.
Num 34: 8 **VI**: 10.
Num 34: 25 **V**: 297; **VI**: 139.

Num 35: 4-5	**VI**: 139.
Num 35: 9-32	**VI**: 139.
Num 35: 17	**VI**: 8.
Num 35: 20	**VI**: 8.
Num 35: 25	**VI**: 139*(2)*.
Num 36: 2-3	**VI**: 139.
Num 36: 3	**VI**: 8.
Deut 1-4	**VI**: 140*(2)*.
Deut 1: 1	**VI**: 140.
Deut 1: 1, 7, 41	**VI**: 140.
Deut 1: 6-46	**VI**: 140.
Deut 1: 7, 19, 20, 24	**VI**: 140.
Deut 1: 41-43	**VI**: 140.
Deut 2: 6	**VI**: 12.
Deut 2: 11, 20	**VI**: 140.
Deut 2: 14-16	**VI**: 141.
Deut 3: 10, 14, 17	**VI**: 140.
Deut 3: 11	**VI**: 141I(2).
Deut 3: 16	**I**: *152;* **V**: 400; **VI**: 141.
Deut 4	**I**: xvii n15; **VI**: 141.
Deut 4: 12	**VI**: 8.
Deut 4: 19	**VI**: 8.
Deut 4: 20	**VI**: 141.
Deut 4: 30	**VI**: 9; **VIII**: 251.
Deut 4: 37	**VI**: 140.
Deut 5	**VI**: 141.
Deut 5: 3	**VI**: 141*(2)*, 142*(5)*, 326.
Deut 5: 7-9	**VI**: 142.
Deut 5: 9	**VI**: 142.
Deut 5: 10	**VI**: 140.
Deut 5: 21	**VI**: 142.
Deut 5: 23-6: 3	**VI**: 142.
Deut 6	**VI**: 142.
Deut 6: 1-15	**VI**: 142.
Deut 6: 4	**VI**: 143*(3)*.
Deut 6: 5	**VIII**: 287.
Deut 7	**VI**: 143.
Deut 7: 1	**VI**: 4.
Deut 7: 2	**VI**: 140.
Deut 7: 20	**III**: *376;* **VI**: 13, 115, 143, 174.
Deut 8: 2	**VI**: 143.
Deut 8: 2-5	**VI**: 143.
Deut 8: 9	**I**: *295;* **VI**: 138, 143, 203.
Deut 9: 11-12	**VI**: 143.
Deut 9: 13	**VI**: 143.
Deut 10: 6, 7	**VI**: 144.
Deut 11: 2	**VI**: 8.
Deut 11: 10	**VI**: 144*(5)*.
Deut 11: 16	**VI**: 144.
Deut 11: 17-18	**VI**: 155.
Deut 11: 21, 24	**VI**: 140.
Deut 11: 29, 30	**VI**: 144.
Deut 11: 30	**VI**: 8.
Deut 12-26	**VI**: 144.
Deut 12: 5, 6	**VI**: 144.
Deut 12: 8-15	**V**: 59; **VI**: 124, 145.
Deut 13: 12-16	**VI**: 145.
Deut 13: 13	**VI**: 140.
Deut 14	**I**: *250;* **VI**: 122, 145.
Deut 14: 2	**VI**: 145, 709.
Deut 14: 6-8	**VI**: 122, 145*(2)*.
Deut 14: 21b	**VI**: 6.
Deut 14: 21	**VI**: 145*(4)*.
Deut 14: 22	**VI**: 146.
Deut 15: 1	**VI**: 146.
Deut 15: 4-6	**VI**: 7.
Deut 16: 11	**VI**: 146.
Deut 16: 15	**VI**: 140.
Deut 16: 18	**VI**: 146.
Deut 16: 20	**VI**: 146.
Deut 17: 14-20	**VI**: 146.
Deut 18	**VI**: 146*(2)*.
Deut 18: 6-8	**IV**: *354*.
Deut 18: 8	**VI**: 146.
Deut 18: 9-22	**I**: *54;* **VI**: 147.

Deut 18: 10	**VI**: 147.
Deut 18: 10-15	**VI**: 147.
Deut 18: 15	**VI**: 147.
Deut 18: 15, 18	**VI**: 140.
Deut 18: 15-19	**VI**: 147.
Deut 19: 4	**VI**: 147.
Deut 19: 6	**VI**: 140.
Deut 19: 15	**VIII**: 287.
Deut 19: 20	**VI**: 147.
Deut 20: 19	**VI**: 140.
Deut 21: 1	**VI**: 147.
Deut 21: 1ff.	**VI**: 148.
Deut 21: 1-9	**VI**: 147.
Deut 21: 3	**VI**: 148.
Deut 21: 4	**VI**: 140.
Deut 21: 10-14	**VI**: 148.
Deut 21: 14	**VI**: 5, 8.
Deut 21: 15-17	**VI**: 148.
Deut 22: 1-43	**V**: 700.
Deut 22: 6	**VI**: 148.
Deut 22: 12	**VI**: 148*(2)*.
Deut 22: 28	**VI**: 148.
Deut 22: 35	**VI**: 2.
Deut 23: 7	**VI**: 148.
Deut 23: 14	**V**: 402; **VI**: 12.
Deut 24: 1	**I**: *215*.
Deut 24: 21	**VI**: 140.
Deut 25: 4	**VI**: 148; **VII**: 81.
Deut 25: 11-12	**VI**: 149.
Deut 26: 1-11	**VI**: 149.
Deut 26: 5	**VI**: 149*(2)*.
Deut 27	**VI**: 149.
Deut 28: 29	**VI**: 149.
Deut 28: 37	**VI**: 149.
Deut 28: 38-41	**VI**: 155.
Deut 28: 57	**VI**: 5, 8.
Deut 28: 65-66	**VI**: 155.
Deut 28: 66	**VI**: 13.
Deut 29: 1-2	**VI**: 155.
Deut 29: 19	**VI**: 8.
Deut 29: 19, 26	**VI**: 140.
Deut 29: 28	**VI**: 13.
Deut 29: 29	**VI**: 149.
Deut 30: 10-11	**VI**: 155.
Deut 30: 14	**VI**: 149.
Deut 30: 16	**VI**: 155.
Deut 30: 19	**VI**: 150.
Deut 30: 19-20	**VI**: 155.
Deut 31: 3-4	**VI**: 155.
Deut 31: 10	**VI**: 140.
Deut 31: 21	**VI**: 155.
Deut 31: 26	**VI**: 155.
Deut 31: 29	**VI**: 155.
Deut 32	**V**: 685; **VI**: 150*(4)*.
Deut 32Q	**VIII**: 444.
Deut 32: 1-43	**VI**: 150.
Deut 32: 1-6b	**IV**: 46.
Deut 32: 2a, b	**VI**: 150.
Deut 32: 2-3	**VI**: 93, 150.
Deut 32: 3-4	**VI**: 155.
Deut 32: 5	**VI**: 150*(2)*.
Deut 32: 5, 11, 17	**VI**: 140.
Deut 32: 8	**VI**: 150, 151*(2)*, 488.
Deut 32: 9	**VI**: 145, 151, 709; **VIII**: 212.
Deut 32: 10	**VI**: 9, 151*(2)*.
Deut 32: 10-11	**VI**: 155.
Deut 32: 11	**VI**: 28, 151*(3)*, 334.
Deut 32: 11-12	**VI**: 151.
Deut 32: 15 or 16	**VI**: 155.
Deut 32: 22	**VI**: 155.
Deut 32: 24, 27, 36	**VI**: 140.
Deut 32: 25	**VI**: 151.
Deut 32: 26	**V**: 401.
Deut 32: 26-34	**VI**: 151.
Deut 32: 27-29	**VI**: 155.
Deut 32: 31	**V**: 445; **VI**: 152.
Deut 32: 32	**VI**: 152.
Deut 32: 34-43	**VI**: 152.
Deut 32: 35	**V**: 396; **VI**: 8.

Deut 32:39	**VI**: 152.
Deut 32:42	**VI**: 152.
Deut 32:43	**VI**: 152.
Deut 33	**V**: 700; **VI**: 152*(5)*, 153*(6)*.
Deut 33:1	**VI**: 153; **VIII**: 158.
Deut 33:2	**VI**: 2, 153.
Deut 33:2, 6, 17	**VI**: 140.
Deut 33:3-5	**VI**: 153, 154.
Deut 33:4	**VI**: 153.
Deut 33:5	**VI**: 8.
Deut 33:8	**VI**: 153.
Deut 33:8-9	**VI**: 13.
Deut 33:11	**VI**: 7.
Deut 33:12	**VI**: 153.
Deut 33:16	**VI**: 6, 7.
Deut 33:19	**VI**: 154.
Deut 33:21	**V**: 394; **VI**: 5, 154, 485.
Deut 33:21, 22, 27, 28	**VI**: 140.
Deut 33:25	**VI**: 5, 154.
Deut 33:26	**VI**: 154.
Deut 33:26-29	**VI**: 153, 154.
Deut 33:27	**VI**: 154*(2)*; **IX**: cxlvi.
Deut 34:1	**IV**: 354; **VI**: 155.
Deut 34:1-12	**VI**: 154.
Deut 34:1-3	**VI**: 154.
Deut 34:3	**VI**: 140, 155, 712.
Deut 34:4-7	**VI**: 95, 155, 174.
Deut 34:5-6	**VI**: 155.
Deut 34:6	**VI**: 140.
Deut 34:7	**VI**: 155.
Deut 48	**VI**: 708.
Josh 1-11	**IV**: *356, 366*.
Josh 1:1-11	**VI**: 166.
Josh 1:14	**VI**: 166.
Josh 2:7marg.	**VI**: 166.
Josh 2:15	**VI**: 166.
Josh 2:18	**VI**: 166.
Josh 3	**VI**: 166*(3)*.
Josh 3:4	**VI**: 166.
Josh 3:5-17	**VI**: 166.
Josh 3:13	**VI**: 167.
Josh 3:16	**VI**: 166, 167*(2)*.
Josh 4-5	**VI**: 167.
Josh 4:1-24	**VI**: 167.
Josh 4:9	**VI**: 167*(3)*.
Josh 4:12	**VI**: 166.
Josh 4:24	**VI**: 166.
Josh 5:2	**VI**: 166.
Josh 5:5	**VI**: 166.
Josh 5:9	**VI**: 167; **IX**: xcvi.
Josh 5:13	**VI**: 166.
Josh 6	**VI**: 167.
Josh 6:1	**VI**: 166.
Josh 6:8-20	**VI**: 166.
Josh 6:17-7:26	**VI**: 166.
Josh 6:18	**VI**: 3.
Josh 6:26	**VI**: 8, 167, 168*(2)*.
Josh 7:2-5	**VI**: 168.
Josh 7:5	**VI**: 7.
Josh 7:14	**VI**: 7.
Josh 7:17	**VI**: 168.
Josh 7:21marg.	**VI**: 166.
Josh 7:21	**VI**: 168*(2)*.
Josh 8:1-29	**VI**: 168.
Josh 8:11	**VI**: 166.
Josh 8:12-16	**VI**: 168.
Josh 8:32	**VI**: 166.
Josh 8:33	**VI**: 166.
Josh 9	**VI**: 168.
Josh 9:4	**VI**: 5, 8, 166.
Josh 9:4marg.	**VI**: 166.
Josh 9:5	**VI**: 166.
Josh 10	**VI**: 168*(2)*, 169, 177.
Josh 10:2	**II**: *379*.

Josh 10:6 **VI**: 166.
Josh 10:6-14 **VI**: 169*(2)*.
Josh 10:11 **VI**: 169.
Josh 10:11-14 **VI**: 169.
Josh 10:12 **VI**: 170*(2)*.
Josh 10:12, 13 **VI**: 170*(3)*.
Josh 10:12-14 **VI**: 170*(5)*.
Josh 10:12-15 **VI**: 169*(6)*, 170.
Josh 10:13 **VI**: 170.
Josh 10:24 **VI**: 3.
Josh 11 **VI**: 171.
Josh 11:1, 16 **VI**: 166.
Josh 11:1-9 **I**: *151;* **VI**: 171.
Josh 11:1-5, 7-8 **VI**: 171.
Josh 11:5 **VI**: 8.
Josh 11:6LXX **VI**: 171.
Josh 11:10 **VI**: 171.
Josh 11:13 **VI**: 171*(2)*.
Josh 11:16 **V**: 659.
Josh 11:21-22 **VI**: 171.
Josh 12:1LXX **VI**: 171.
Josh 12:2marg. **VI**: 166.
Josh 12:18 **VI**: 171.
Josh 12:23 **VI**: 166.
Josh 13:2 **VI**: 166.
Josh 13:3marg. **VI**: 166.
Josh 13:3 **VI**: 166.
Josh 13:25 **II**: *291.*
Josh 14:6-15 **VI**: 166.
Josh 15 **VI**: 172.
Josh 15-21 **VI**: 166.
Josh 15:2,5 **VI**: 172, 173.
Josh 15:6 **VI**: 166, 172.
Josh 15:9 **VI**: 172.
Josh 15:9, 11 **VI**: 166.
Josh 15:10 **VI**: 172.
Josh 15:12 **VI**: 3.
Josh 15:18 **VI**: 166.
Josh 15:48 **VI**: 172.
Josh 15:49 **VI**: 166, 172.
Josh 15:52 **VI**: 172.
Josh 15:59 **VI**: 172.
Josh 17:11 **VI**: 172, 173.
Josh 17:14 **VI**: 166.
Josh 17:15, 18 **V**: 413; **VI**: 173, 353.
Josh 17:19 **VI**: 166.
Josh 18:17 **VI**: 166.
Josh 18:19 **VI**: 172, 173.
Josh 19:26 **VI**: 166.
Josh 19:29marg. **VI**: 166.
Josh 19:29 **VI**: 173.
Josh 19:34 **VI**: 173.
Josh 19:40-48 **VI**: 173.
Josh 19:44 **VI**: 173.
Josh 19:46 **VI**: 173.
Josh 19:47 **VI**: 3.
Josh 21:1-9 **VI**: 173.
Josh 21:21 **VI**: 173.
Josh 21:32 **VI**: 174.
Josh 22 **VI**: 174.
Josh 22:7 **VI**: 3.
Josh 22:9-34 **VI**: 174; **IX**: cxxxvi.
Josh 22:10, 11 **VI**: 174.
Josh 22:11, 24 **VI**: 166.
Josh 22:25 **VI**: 174.
Josh 22:34 **VI**: 174.
Josh 23:13 **VI**: 166.
Josh 24 **VI**: 174.
Josh 24:1-25 **VI**: 174.
Josh 24:12 **III**: *376;* **VI**: 13, 115, 143, 174.
Josh 24:14-28 **VI**: 175.
Josh 24:15 **VI**: 2.
Josh 24:26 **VI**: 166.
Josh 24:29ff. **VI**: 95, 155, 175.
Judg 1 **VI**: 168, 177.
Judg 1-2:5 **IV**: 373; **VI**: 177.
Judg 1:1-3:6 **VI**: 177.

Judg 1:5 **VI**: 177.
Judg 1:7 **VIII**: 224.
Judg 1:8 **VI**: 177*(2)*.
Judg 1:8, 9, 15, 16 **VI**: 176.
Judg 1:9 **VI**: 10.
Judg 1:10 **VI**: 177.
Judg 1:13 **VI**: 177.
Judg 1:14 **VI**: 3.
Judg 1:16 **VI**: 176.
Judg 1:24, 30 **VI**: 176.
Judg 1:27 **VI**: 177.
Judg 2:1 **VI**: 176.
Judg 2:1, 2, 3, 7 **VI**: 176.
Judg 2:1-3:4 **VI**: 177.
Judg 2:3 **VI**: 176.
Judg 2:6-3:6 **VI**: 178.
Judg 2:10, 20 **VI**: 176.
Judg 2:11, (13) **VI**: 176.
Judg 3:1-2 **VI**: 176.
Judg 3:5, 7, 9, (15) **VI**: 176.
Judg 3:7-11 **VI**: 178*(2)*.
Judg 3:8 **VI**: 178*(2)*.
Judg 3:8-10 **VI**: 178*(2)*; **VII**: 168.
Judg 3:8, 10 **VI**: 178, 582, 584.
Judg 3:10, 19, (26) **VI**: 176.
Judg 3:12 **VI**: 178.
Judg 3:18-19 **VI**: 178.
Judg 3:20, 24 **VI**: 176.
Judg 3:22 **VI**: 8, 176.
Judg 3:23 **V**: 402; **VI**: 12.
Judg 3:25, 26 **VI**: 176.
Judg 3:26 **II**: *474;* **VI**: 179.
Judg 3:31 **VI**: 179; **VII**: 82.
Judg 4 **VI**: 179.
Judg 4-5 **I**: *151;* **VI**: 171, 179*(3)*.
Judg 4:2, 13, 16 **VI**: 4.
Judg 4:4-5 **VI**: 179.
Judg 4:11 **VI**: 4.
Judg 4:11, 21 **VI**: 176.
Judg 4:17-23 **VI**: 179.
Judg 5 **V**: 685; **VI**: 179*(3)*, 180*(5)*.
Judg 5:1 **VI**: 5.
Judg 5:2 **VI**: 180*(4)*.
Judg 5:2, 7, 9, 11 **VI**: 176.
Judg 5:3 **VI**: 180*(2)*.
Judg 5:4 **VI**: 180.
Judg 5:7&11 **VI**: 176.
Judg 5:8 **VI**: 176, 181*(3)*.
Judg 5:8a **VI**: 181.
Judg 5:8b-13 **VI**: 180.
Judg 5:9 **VI**: 176.
Judg 5:11 **VI**: 176, 181.
Judg 5:12-24 **VI**: 181.
Judg 5:13a **VI**: 176.
Judg 5:13, 14, 15, 16 **VI**: 176.
Judg 5:14 **V**: 398; **VI**: 11, 176, 181.
Judg 5:15 **VI**: 176.
Judg 5:15b-16 **VI**: 181.
Judg 5:16 **VI**: 94, 181.
Judg 5:17 **I**: *157;* **VI**: 181*(2)*.
Judg 5:17, 26, 27, 29 **VI**: 176.
Judg 5:21, 22 **VI**: 4.
Judg 5:22 **VI**: 176, 181.
Judg 5:23 **VI**: 182.
Judg 5:24 **VI**: 182*(3)*.
Judg 5:25 **VI**: 182.
Judg 5:26 **VI**: 176.
Judg 5:29 **VI**: 176, 182.
Judg 5:30e **VI**: 176.
Judg 5:30 **VI**: 182*(2)*.
Judg 6:2 **VI**: 7.
Judg 6:3, 11, 13 **VI**: 176.
Judg 6:7-10 **VI**: 182.
Judg 6:11 **VI**: 176.
Judg 6:14 **VI**: 182.
Judg 6:19 **VI**: 176, 182.

Judg 6: 25 **VI**: 176.
Judg 6: 25-28 **VI**: 183.
Judg 6: 36-40 **VI**: 183.
Judg 7-8 **VI**: 183.
Judg 7: 2-8 **VI**: 183.
Judg 7: 3 **VI**: 11, 176.
Judg 7: 5 **VI**: 183.
Judg 7: 5-6 **VI**: 183*(5)*.
Judg 7: 6 **VI**: 176.
Judg 7: 7 **VI**: 183.
Judg 7: 8 **VI**: 3.
Judg 7: 8, 23 **VI**: 176.
Judg 7: 9 **VI**: 184.
Judg 7: 13 **VI**: 176, 184; **VII**: 268.
Judg 7: 20 **VI**: 176.
Judg 7: 21 **VI**: 176.
Judg 7: 22 **VI**: 176.
Judg 7: 25 **VI**: 176.
Judg 7: 25-8: 25 **VI**: 184.
Judg 8: 4 **VI**: 176.
Judg 8: 4-17 **VI**: 184.
Judg 8: 7 **VI**: 184.
Judg 8: 12 **VI**: 176.
Judg 8: 13, 16, 21, 26 **VI**: 176.
Judg 8: 14 **V**: 419; **VI**: 184.
Judg 8: 16 **VI**: 184.
Judg 8: 18 **VI**: 176.
Judg 8: 22-23 **VI**: 184.
Judg 8: 27 **VI**: 176.
Judg 9 **VI**: 184*(2)*.
Judg 9: 2, 9, 44 **VI**: 176.
Judg 9: 6 **VI**: 1852*)*.
Judg 9: 7-20 **VI**: 185.
Judg 9: 8-15 **VI**: 185*(3)*.
Judg 9: 15 **VI**: 176.
Judg 9: 26-41 **VI**: 185.
Judg 9: 27 **VI**: 176.
Judg 9: 28 **VI**: 176, 185*(2)*.
Judg 9: 29 **V**: 394; **VI**: 6, 176, 185.
Judg 9: 29 **VI**: 176.
Judg 9: 31 **VI**: 176*(2)*, 186.
Judg 9: 37 **V**: 463; **VI**: 4, 10, 186*(2)*.
Judg 9: 41 **VI**: 186.
Judg 9: 44 **VI**: 176.
Judg 9: 52, 53 **VI**: 176.
Judg 9: 53 **VI**: 2, 186.
Judg 10: 6-1 Sam 8 **VI**: 186, 192.
Judg 10: 11-12 **VI**: 176.
Judg 11 **VI**: 186*(3)*.
Judg 11 & 12 **VI**: 186.
Judg 11: 1-3 **VI**: 187.
Judg 11: 20 **VI**: 176.
Judg 11: 29-31 **VI**: 187.
Judg 11: 29-40 **VI**: 187.
Judg 11: 30-31 **VI**: 187.
Judg 11: 30-40 **VI**: 187*(3)*.
Judg 11: 31 **VI**: 187.
Judg 11: 35 **VI**: 176.
Judg 11: 37 **VI**: 86.
Judg 11: 37 **VI**: 176, 187*(3)*, 188.
Judg 11: 37, 39, 40 **VI**: 176.
Judg 11: 38 **VI**: 176.
Judg 12: 1-6 **VI**: 188.
Judg 12: 6 **VI**: 176, 188*(3)*.
Judg 12: 7 **VI**: 9, 188*(2)*.
Judg 12: 14 **VI**: 176.
Judg 13-16 **V**: 702; **VI**: 188.
Judg 13: 12, 18, 19 **VI**: 176.
Judg 13: 22, 23 **VI**: 188.
Judg 13: 23 **VI**: 176.
Judg 13: 24 **VI**: 176.
Judg 14-15 **I**: *218*.
Judg 14: 9 **VI**: 176.
Judg 14: 14-19 **VI**: 188.
Judg 14: 15 **VI**: 176*(2)*.

Judg 14:19 **VI**: 189.
Judg 14:20 **VI**: 189.
Judg 15 **VI**: 189.
Judg 15:2 **VI**: 189.
Judg 15:4-5 **VI**: 189.
Judg 15:5 **VI**: 176.
Judg 15:6 **VI**: 176.
Judg 15:8 **VI**: 189*(2)*.
Judg 15:9-19 **VI**: 189.
Judg 15:13-15 **VI**: 189.
Judg 15:13 17, 19 **VI**: 176.
Judg 15:16 **VI**: 189*(2)*.
Judg 15:19 **VI**: 3.
Judg 16:1-3 **V**: 106; **VI**: 190.
Judg 16:2, 5, 7 **VI**: 176.
Judg 16:13end **VI**: 176.
Judg 16:13ff. **VI**: 190.
Judg 16:14LXX **VI**: 176.
Judg 16:14 **VI**: 176.
Judg 16:18, 28 **VI**: 176.
Judg 16:19 **VI**: 190.
Judg 16:20 **VI**: 190.
Judg 17sq. **VI**: 190.
Judg 17-18 **VI**: 190*(3)*.
Judg 17:6 **VI**: 190.
Judg 17:10 **VI**: 176.
Judg 18:1 **VI**: 176.
Judg 18:7 **VI**: 176.
Judg 18:7, 30 **VI**: 176.
Judg 18:8 **VI**: 176.
Judg 18:30 **VI**: 190.
Judg 19 **VI**: 191.
Judg 19:1, 22, 18 **VI**: 176.
Judg 19:9 **VI**: 176.
Judg 19:11 **VI**: 10.
Judg 19:12, 13, 15, etc. **VI**: 176.
Judg 19:13 **VI**: 191.
Judg 19:22 **VI**: 176.
Judg 19:28 **VI**: 176.
Judg 19:28, 48 **VI**: 176.
Judg 20-21 **VI**: 191.
Judg 20:16 **VI**: 191.
Judg 20:31 **VI**: 176*(2)*.
Judg 20:33 **VI**: 176.
Judg 20:34 **VI**: 176.
Judg 20:38 **VI**: 176*(2)*.
Judg 20:38, 39 **VI**: 176.
Judg 20:41 **VI**: 176.
Judg 20:42 **VI**: 176.
Judg 20:43 **VI**: 176*(2)*.
Judg 21:5 **VI**: 176.
Judg 21:17 **VI**: 176*(2)*.
Judg 21:22 **VI**: 176*(2)*.
Judg 22:38 **VI**: 3.
1 Sam 1:1 **VI**: 193.
1 Sam 1:3 **VI**: 193.
1 Sam 1:5 **VI**: 3, 193.
1 Sam 1:5, 6, 9 **VI**: 192.
1 Sam 1:6 **VI**: 4, 7.
1 Sam 1:15, 16, 24, 28 **VI**: 192.
1 Sam 1:18 **VI**: 7, 193.
1 Sam 1:20 **VI**: 3.
1 Sam 2:1-10 **VI**: 193*(4)*.
1 Sam 2:3, 14, 22 **VI**: 192.
1 Sam 2:5 **VI**: 193.
1 Sam 2:10 **VI**: 49, 193.
1 Sam 2:13 **VI**: 193.
1 Sam 2:22-25 **VI**: 194.
1 Sam 2:24 **VI**: 4, 194.
1 Sam 2:25, 28 **VI**: 192.
1 Sam 2:27 **VI**: 3.
1 Sam 2:27-36 **VI**: 194.
1 Sam 2:31-33 **VI**: 11.
1 Sam 2:33 **VI**: 194.
1 Sam 2:35 **VI**: 194.
1 Sam 3:1-21 **VI**: 194.
1 Sam 3:2f. **VI**: 194.
1 Sam 3:3, 11 **VI**: 192.
1 Sam 4:1, 8, 13 **VI**: 192.
1 Sam 4:4 **VI**: 12.
1 Sam 4:13 **VI**: 194.
1 Sam 4:15 **VI**: 4, 194.

1 Sam 5-6 **VI**: 195*(4)*.
1 Sam 5:4 **VI**: 195.
1 Sam 5:6 **VI**: 192, 195.
1 Sam 5:6-6:16 **VI**: 195.
1 Sam 5:17-19 **VI**: 195.
1 Sam 6 **I**: *266;* **II**: *219, 341;* **V**: 55; **VI**: 195*(2)*, 210.
1 Sam 6:1-18 **VI**: 195.
1 Sam 6:1, 6, 18, 19 **VI**: 192.
1 Sam 6:3 **VI**: 196.
1 Sam 6:4-11 **VI**: 196*(2)*.
1 Sam 6:4-5 **VI**: 196.
1 Sam 6:8 **VI**: 12, 196.
1 Sam 6:8, 11, 15 **VI**: 192, 196.
1 Sam 6:19 **VI**: 196.
1 Sam 6:19a **VI**: 196.
1 Sam 7:1-13 **VI**: 196.
1 Sam 7:2 **VI**: 196.
1 Sam 7:5 **VI**: 197.
1 Sam 8:3 **VI**: 192.
1 Sam 8:4-17 **VI**: 197.
1 Sam 9 **VI**: 197*(5)*.
1 Sam 9:-10 **VI**: 197*(3)*.
1 Sam 9-14 **VI**: 197.
1 Sam 9:1-11:15 **VI**: 197.
1 Sam 9:5, 8, 16 **VI**: 192.
1 Sam 9:6-13 **VI**: 198.
1 Sam 9:7 **VI**: 198.
1 Sam 9:16-17 **VI**: 198.
1 Sam 9:24 **VI**: 198.
1 Sam 9:27 **VI**: 10.
1 Sam 10:2 **VI**: 7, 198.
1 Sam 10:5 **VI**: 198.
1 Sam 10:5-13 **VI**: 198.
1 Sam 10:5-6,10-12 **VI**: 198.
1 Sam 10:12 **VI**: 198, 199*(2)*.
1 Sam 10:13-16 **VI**: 199.
1 Sam 10:27 **VI**: 192, 199.
1 Sam 11:7 **VI**: 7.
1 Sam 12:3 **VI**: 4, 192, 198.
1 Sam 12:11 **VI**: 199; **VIII**: 296.
1 Sam 12:12 **VI**: 199.
1 Sam 12:20-25 **VI**: 199.
1 Sam 13:1 **VI**: 5, 192*(2)*, 199.
1 Sam 13:3, 4 **VI**: 199*(3)*.
1 Sam 13:19-21 **VI**: 200.
1 Sam 13:19-22 **VI**: 200.
1 Sam 13:21 **VI**: 10, 192, 200*(7)*, 217, 487.
1 Sam 14 **VI**: 200*(3)*.
1 Sam 14:1-46 **VI**: 200.
1 Sam 14:3a **VI**: 201.
1 Sam 14:11 **VI**: 201.
1 Sam 14:14 **VI**: 12, 201.
1 Sam 14:15 **VI**: 201.
1 Sam 14:18, 19, 51 **VI**: 192.
1 Sam 14:23-35 **VI**: 201.
1 Sam 14:32 **VI**: 11.
1 Sam 14:41 **VI**: 201.
1 Sam 15 **VI**: 2012*)*.
1 Sam 15:12 **VI**: 10, 192.
1 Sam 15:22 **VI**: 202.
1 Sam 15:22-23 **V**: 390; **VI**: 201.
1 Sam 15:29 **VI**: 7.
1 Sam 15:32b **VI**: 202.
1 Sam 15:33 **VIII**: 224.
1 Sam 16 **VI**: 202.
1 Sam 16& 17 **VI**: 202*(2)*
1 Sam 16:12 **VI**: 192, 202.
1 Sam 16:14-16 **IV**: *43*.
1 Sam 16:20 **VI**: 202.
1 Sam 17 **VI**: 202*(2)*.
1 Sam 17:1 **VI**: 192.
1 Sam 17:1-3 **VI**: 202.
1 Sam 17:2, 6, 12, 52 **VI**: 192.
1 Sam 17:6 **VI**: 192.

1 Sam 17:7	**I**: *295;* **VI**: 138, 143, 203.
1 Sam 17:43	**I**: *390;* **VI**: 8.
1 Sam 17:47	**VI**: 5.
1 Sam 17:52	**VI**: 192, 203.
1 Sam 17:54	**VI**: 192.
1 Sam 17:55	**VI**: 203.
1 Sam 17:58	**VI**: 203.
1 Sam 18-31	**VI**: 203.
1 Sam 18:8, 28	**VI**: 192.
1 Sam 19:13	**VI**: 203.
1 Sam 19:18-24	**VI**: 203.
1 Sam 19:20-24	**VI**: 203.
1 Sam 19:22	**VI**: 192.
1 Sam 19:22-23	**VI**: 203.
1 Sam 20:3LXX	**VI**: 204, 639.
1 Sam 20:18-20	**VI**: 12.
1 Sam 20:19	**V**: 432; **VI**: 204.
1 Sam 20:19, 41	**VI**: 192.
1 Sam 20:23	**VI**: 204.
1 Sam 20:30	**VI**: 204*(3)*.
1 Sam 20:42	**VI**: 204.
1 Sam 21:1-14	**VI**: 204.
1 Sam 21:8	**VI**: 204.
1 Sam 21:9	**VI**: 192.
1 Sam 21:14	**VI**: 205.
1 Sam 21:13 (14)	**VI**: 204.
1 Sam 22	**V**: 50.
1 Sam 22:4	**VI**: 205.
1 Sam 22:6, 9	**VI**: 192.
1 Sam 23:1	**VI**: 200.
1 Sam 23:16	**VI**: 7.
1 Sam 23:28-24:2	**VI**: 218.
1 Sam 24:6-8	**VI**: 218.
1 Sam 24:12-13	**VI**: 218.
1 Sam 24:18-20	**VI**: 218.
1 Sam 25:6	**VI**: 205.
1 Sam 25:6, 22	**VI**: 192.
1 Sam 25:18	**VI**: 205.
1 Sam 25:29	**VI**: 205*(3)*.
1 Sam 26:4	**VI**: 205.
1 Sam 26:8	**VI**: 205.
1 Sam 26:20	**VI**: 206.
1 Sam 26:26	**VI**: 206.
1 Sam 27:6	**VI**: 206.
1 Sam 27:8	**VI**: 206.
1 Sam 28:3	**VI**: 125, 206, 284.
1 Sam 28:3, 7	**VI**: 206*(2)*.
1 Sam 28:7-25	**VI**: 206.
1 Sam 28:8ff.	**VI**: 206.
1 Sam 28:13, 16	**VI**: 192.
1 Sam 29:1	**VI**: 207.
1 Sam 30:2, 20	**VI**: 192.
1 Sam 30:30	**VI**: 192.
1 Sam 31:3	**VI**: 5.
1 Sam 31:10	**VI**: 192.
2 Sam 1	**VI**: 207.
2 Sam 1-12	**VIII**: 391.
2 Sam 1:17-19	**VI**: 207.
2 Sam 1:18	**VI**: 207.
2 Sam 1:18, 14, 21, 8	**VI**: 207.
2 Sam 1:19-21	**VI**: 207.
2 Sam 1:19-27	**V**: 685; **VI**: 207*(4)*.
2 Sam 1:21	**IV**: 188; **V**: 453; **VI**: 4*(2)*, 7, 10, 208*(5)*, 274, 423.
2 Sam 2:12-16	**VI**: 208.
2 Sam 2:14ff.	**VI**: 208.
2 Sam 2:22	**VI**: 208.
2 Sam 2:24	**VI**: 11.
2 Sam 3:8	**VI**: 207.
2 Sam 3:8-11	**VI**: 208.
2 Sam 3:12	**VI**: 7.
2 Sam 3:26	**VI**: 208.
2 Sam 4:	**VI**: 208.
2 Sam 4:2, 6 marg.	**VI**: 207.
2 Sam 5	**VI**: 209.
2 Sam 5:6-25	**VI**: 209.
2 Sam 5:6-8	**VI**: 209*(3)*.
2 Sam 5:6-9	**VI**: 209*(2)*.
2 Sam 5:6, 8, 21	**VI**: 207.

2 Sam 5: 8 **VI**: 209*(3)*.
2 Sam 5: 17-21 **IV**: 359.
2 Sam 5: 17-25 **IV**: 359.
2 Sam 5: 23, 24 **IV**: 360.
2 Sam 5: 23- 24 **VI**: 209.
2 Sam 6 **V**: 55; **VI**: 195, 210*(3)*, 529.
2 Sam 6: 3-11 **VI**: 210.
2 Sam 6: 5, 17, 19 **VI**: 207.
2 Sam 6: 6 **VI**: 210.
2 Sam 6: 11 **VI**: 210.
2 Sam 6: 12 **VI**: 210.
2 Sam 6: 20 **VI**: 210.
2 Sam 7 **IV**: 352, 377; **VI**: 210*(3)*, 211*(2)*; **VIII**: 290, 468*(2)*.
2 Sam 7: 2 **VI**: 211*(2)*.
2 Sam 7: 9-11 **VI**: 211.
2 Sam 7: 11b-16 **VI**: 211.
2 Sam 7: 13-16 **VI**: 211.
2 Sam 7: 14 **VI**: 2.
2 Sam 7: 19 **VI**: 211.
2 Sam 7: 19, 23, 27 **VI**: 207.
2 Sam 7: 21 **VI**: 9, 211.
2 Sam 7: 22LXX **VI**: 211.
2 Sam 8: 1 **VI**: 5, 11, 211.
2 Sam 8: 1, 3, 4 **VI**: 207.
2 Sam 8: 2 **VI**: 212*(2)*.
2 Sam 8: 4 **IV**: 361; **VI**: 212.
2 Sam 8: 11 **VI**: 212.
2 Sam 8: 13, 18 **VI**: 207.
2 Sam 9-20 **IV**: 358; **VI**: 30.
2 Sam 10 **VI**: 212*(2)*.
2 Sam 10: 6 **VI**: 207.
2 Sam 10: 7 **VI**: 192.
2 Sam 10: 10 **VI**: 192.
2 Sam 10: 12 **VI**: 212.
2 Sam 11 **VI**: 230.
2 Sam 11-1 Kgs 2:11 **IV**: 107; **VI**: 212.
2 Sam 11: 1-5 **VI**: 212.
2 Sam 11: 2ff. **VI**: 212.
2 Sam 11: 2-1 Kgs 2: 11 **VI**: 218.
2 Sam 12: 1-10 **I**: *214;* **VI**: 213.
2 Sam 12: 1-6 **VI**: 213.
2 Sam 12: 5-6 **VI**: 213.
2 Sam 12: 14 **VI**: 213.
2 Sam 12: 26-27 **VI**: 213.
2 Sam 12: 26-31 **VI**: 4.
2 Sam 12: 27 **VI**: 213*(2)*.
2 Sam 12: 31 **IV**: 360; **VI**: 213.
2 Sam 12: 30, 31marg. **VI**: 207.
2 Sam 13-24 **VIII**: 391.
2 Sam 13: 5-8 **VI**: 213.
2 Sam 13: 18 **VI**: 207.
2 Sam 13: 23 **VI**: 213.
2 Sam 14: 14 **VI**: 207.
2 Sam 14: 20 **VI**: 192.
2 Sam 14: 25 **VI**: 214.
2 Sam 14: 26 **VI**: 214.
2 Sam 14: 27 **VI**: 214.
2 Sam 15-18 **VI**: 214.
2 Sam 15: 1-30 **VI**: 214.
2 Sam 15: 7 **VI**: 192, 206.
2 Sam 15: 7, 12, 17, 28 **VI**: 207.
2 Sam 15: 12ff. **VI**: 5.
2 Sam 15: 22-23 **VI**: 214.
2 Sam 16: 5 **VI**: 7.
2 Sam 17: 3, 17, 25 **VI**: 207.
2 Sam 17: 9 **VI**: 192.
2 Sam 17: 11 **VI**: 214.
2 Sam 18: 5 **VI**: 214.
2 Sam 18: 13 **VI**: 192.
2 Sam 18: 13, 21, 29 **VI**: 207.
2 Sam 18: 19-32 **VI**: 214.
2 Sam 18: 23 **VI**: 214.
2 Sam 19: 25, 43 **VI**: 207.
2 Sam 20: 3
2 Sam 20: 8 **VI**: 192.
2 Sam 20: 14 **V**: 395; **VI**: 7.

2 Sam 20: 14-22	**VI**: 215.
2 Sam 20: 19	**VI**: 215.
2 Sam 20: 24	**VI**: 207, 215.
2 Sam 21: 1-14	**VI**: 215*(4)*.
2 Sam 21: 8	**VI**: 215.
2 Sam 21: 10	**VI**: 215.
2 Sam 21: 15-16	**VI**: 216.
2 Sam 21: 15-22	**VI**: 216.
2 Sam 21: 4, 8, 10, 16, 19	**VI**: 207.
2 Sam 22	**VI**: 216*(3)*, 464*(2)*.
2 Sam 22: 5-6	**VI**: 216, 464.
2 Sam 22: 6, 9, 12	**VI**: 207.
2 Sam 22: 12-13	**VI**: 216.
2 Sam 22: 33, 34, 46, 51	**VI**: 207.
2 Sam 22: 35	**VI**: 10, 216.
2 Sam 22: 36	**IV**: 108; **VI**: 216, 464.
2 Sam 22: 43	**VI**: 192.
2 Sam 23: 1	**VI**: 10; **VI**: 217, 487.
2 Sam 23: 1-7	**VI**: 216.
2 Sam 23: 3-5	**VI**: 217*(2)*.
2 Sam 23: 3, 4, 5, 8, 9	**VI**: 207.
2 Sam 23: 6-7	**VI**: 217.
2 Sam 23: 7	**VI**: 217*(2)*.
2 Sam 23: 8	**VI**: 217.
2 Sam 23: 13-16	**IV**: 359.
2 Sam 23: 20	**VI**: 207.
2 Sam 23: 30	**VI**: 5.
2 Sam 24	**IV**: 361; **VI**: 217*(3)*.
2 Sam 24: 1	**VI**: 218.
2 Sam 24: 6	**VI**: 218*(2)*.
2 Sam 24: 18-25	**IV**: 360.
2 Sam 24: 23	**VI**: 207.
2 Sam 24: 24-1 Chr 21: 25	**IV**: 359.
1 Kgs 1	**VI**: 220.
1 Kgs 1-2	**IV**: 358; **VI**: 30, 219*(2)*, 220.
1 Kgs 1: 9	**VI**: 9, 11.
1 Kgs 1: 18, 20, 39	**VI**: 219.
1 Kgs 1: 20	**VI**: 2.
1 Kgs 1: 33	**VI**: 220.
1 Kgs 1: 41	**VI**: 220.
1 Kgs 2	**VI**: 220.
1 Kgs 2: 8-9	**VI**: 220, 221.
1 Kgs 2: 8-9LXX	**VI**: 220, 221.
1 Kgs 2: 12-21: 43	**VI**: 220*(2)*.
1 Kgs 2: 16-19	**IX**: cxlvii.
1 Kgs 2: 19	**VI**: 219.
1 Kgs 2: 33-45	**VI**: 220.
1 Kgs 2: 36-46	**VI**: 220, 221.
1 Kgs 2: 36-46LXX	**VI**: 220, 221.
1 Kgs 2: 46aLXX	**V**: 398; **VI**: 221.
1 Kgs 3-11	**VI**: 221.
1 Kgs 3: 1	**VI**: 221.
1 Kgs 4: 2-6	**VI**: 221.
1 Kgs 4: 3	**VI**: 219.
1 Kgs 4: 5, 12, 16	**VI**: 219.
1 Kgs 4: 7	**VI**: 221.
1 Kgs 4: 7-19	**I**: *470;* **VI**: 221.
1 Kgs 4: 10	**II**: 292.
1 Kgs 4: 19	**VI**: 8, 219.
1 Kgs 4: 19, 24	**VI**: 219.
1 Kgs 4: 31	**VI**: 221.
1 Kgs 5: 8	**VI**: 5.
1 Kgs 5: 17	**VI**: 8.
1 Kgs 5: 18	**VI**: 219, 222.
1 Kgs 5: 27, 30	**V**: 398; **VI**: 222.
1 Kgs 6ff.	**VI**: 219.
1 Kgs 6: 1-7: 51	**VI**: 220, 222.
1 Kgs 6: 4, 8	**VI**: 219.
1 Kgs 6: 7	**VI**: 222.
1 Kgs 6: 11	**VI**: 7.
1 Kgs 6: 18	**IV**: 360.
1 Kgs 6: 29	**IV**: 360.
1 Kgs 6: 32	**IV**: 360.
1 Kgs 6: 35	**IV**: 360.
1 Kgs 6: 36	**VI**: 222.
1 Kgs 7	**VI**: 222.
1 Kgs 7: 2-6	**V**: 72.

1 Kgs 7: 2, 18, 24 **VI**: 219.
1 Kgs 7: 6 **V**: 72.
1 Kgs 7: 12 **VI**: 222.
1 Kgs 7: 15ff. **V**: 72.
1 Kgs 7: 20 **VI**: 222.
1 Kgs 7: 23-26 **V**: 72.
1 Kgs 7: 27-38 **V**: 72.
1 Kgs 7: 31 **IV**: 360.
1 Kgs 7: 46 **VI**: 222.
1 Kgs 8: 6 **VI**: 12.
1 Kgs 8: 7 **VI**: 12.
1 Kgs 8: 8, 31, 65 **VI**: 219.
1 Kgs 8: 12-13 **VI**: 222.
1 Kgs 8: 21 **VI**: 223.
1 Kgs 8: 53 **VI**: 223.
1 Kgs 8: 53b LXX **VI**: 223.
1 Kgs 9: 8, 13, 18 **VI**: 219.
1 Kgs 9: 10-14 **VI**: 223.
1 Kgs 9: 10-18 **VI**: 223.
1 Kgs 9: 10-10: 33 **VI**: 223.
1 Kgs 9: 13 **V**: 398; **VI**: 219, 2232*)*.
1 Kgs 9: 15-25 **VI**: 223.
1 Kgs 9: 16 **VI**: 223.
1 Kgs 9: 18 **VI**: 219.
1 Kgs 9: 26 **VI**: 219.
1 Kgs 9: 26-10: 29 **VI**: 224.
1 Kgs 10: 1-13 **VI**: 224, 591.
1 Kgs 10: 5 **VI**: 7.
1 Kgs 10: 5, 15, 28 **VI**: 219.
1 Kgs 10: 11 **IV**: 360; **VI**: 4, 224.
1 Kgs 10: 12 **V**: 405; **VI**: 11.
1 Kgs 10: 15 **VI**: 219, 224.
1 Kgs 10: 19 **VI**: 219.
1 Kgs 10: 22 **VI**: 224*(2)*.
1 Kgs 10: 25 **V**: 398; **VI**: 5, 224*(2)*, 584.
1 Kgs 10: 28 **VI**: 9, 224.
1 Kgs 10: 29 **IV**: 359.
1 Kgs 11 **VI**: 224.
1 Kgs 11: 14ff. **VI**: 225.
1 Kgs 11: 15 **VI**: 8.
1 Kgs 11: 19, 20 **IX**: cxlvii.
1 Kgs 11: 25 **V**: 394; **VI**: 6.
1 Kgs 11: 26-40 **VI**: 225.
1 Kgs 11: 36 **VI**: 12.
1 Kgs 12 **VI**: 225.
1 Kgs 12: 10 **VI**: 7.
1 Kgs 12: 28-29 **VI**: 225.
1 Kgs 12: 29, 30 **V**: 104; **VI**: 225.
1 Kgs 12: 31, 33 **VI**: 219.
1 Kgs 12: 31- 33 **VI**: 225.
1 Kgs 13 **VI**: 225*(2)*.
1 Kgs 13: 1, 11 **VI**: 225.
1 Kgs 13: 12 **VI**: 219.
1 Kgs 14: 1-20A **VI**: 226.
1 Kgs 14: 4 **VI**: 4.
1 Kgs 14: 10 **VI**: 5, 226.
1 Kgs 14: 24 **VI**: 226.
1 Kgs 15: 2 **IV**: 361.
1 Kgs 15: 4 **VI**: 12.
1 Kgs 15: 5 **IV**: 360.
1 Kgs 15: 12 **VI**: 226.
1 Kgs 15: 16-22 **IV**: 361.
1 Kgs 15: 30 **VI**: 7.
1 Kgs 16: 9 **VI**: 226.
1 Kgs 16: 22 **VI**: 226.
1 Kgs 16: 24 **VI**: 226.
1 Kgs 16: 34 **VI**: 227*(4)*.
1 Kgs 17 **VI**: 227.
1 Kgs 17-2 Kgs 19 **V**: 701.
1 Kgs 17: 4-6 **VI**: 227*(2)*.
1 Kgs 17: 6 **VI**: 227*(2)*.
1 Kgs 17: 9 **VI**: 8.
1 Kgs 17: 17-24 **VI**: 227.
1 Kgs 17: 21 **VI**: 227.
1 Kgs 18 **VI**: 228*(4)*.
1 Kgs 18: 1-8 **VI**: 228.
1 Kgs 18: 5 **VI**: 228.
1 Kgs 18: 21 **VI**: 4, 228*(2)*, 234.
1 Kgs 18: 26 **IV**: 360.

1 Kgs 18: 27	**VI**: 228*(2)*, 240.
1 Kgs 18: 30-39	**VI**: 228.
1 Kgs 18: 31-38	**VI**: 229.
1 Kgs 18: 36-39	**VI**: 229.
1 Kgs 18: 40ff.	**VI**: 229.
1 Kgs 18: 42	**V**: 398; **VI**: 229.
1 Kgs 18: 43	**VI**: 229*(3)*.
1 Kgs 19	**VI**: 229*(3)*.
1 Kgs 19: 3	**VI**: 229.
1 Kgs 19: 3marg., 18	**VI**: 219.
1 Kgs 19: 9ff.	**VI**: 230.
1 Kgs 19: 10, 14	**VI**: 230.
1 Kgs 19: 19-21	**VI**: 230; **VIII**: 287.
1 Kgs 20	**VI**: 230*(2)*.
1 Kgs 20: 1	**VI**: 230.
1 Kgs 20: 1-10	**VI**: 230.
1 Kgs 20: 5	**VI**: 11.
1 Kgs 20: 12	**V**: 395; **VI**: 7, 230.
1 Kgs 20: 23-24	**IV**: 361.
1 Kgs 20: 28f.	**VI**: 230.
1 Kgs 20: 31	**VI**: 230*(2)*.
1 Kgs 20: 34	**VI**: 12.
1 Kgs 20: 35-43	**VI**: 231.
1 Kgs 20: 38, 41	**VI**: 219.
1 Kgs 21	**V**: 197; **VI**: 231*(3)*.
1 Kgs 21: 19	**VI**: 231.
1 Kgs 21: 21	**VI**: 226.
1 Kgs 21: 23	**VI**: 219.
1 Kgs 22	**VI**: 231*(2)*.
1 Kgs 22: 1, 2	**VI**: 231.
1 Kgs 22: 1-38	**VI**: 230, 231.
1 Kgs 22: 3	**IV**: 361.
1 Kgs 22: 19-23	**VI**: 231.
1 Kgs 22: 21	**VI**: 27, 232.
1 Kgs 22: 24	**VI**: 2.
1 Kgs 22: 38	**VI**: 219.
1 Kgs 22: 46	**VI**: 232.
1 Kgs 28: 21	**VI**: 7.
1 Kgs 58: 7-8	**VI**: 221.
2 Kgs	**II**: *472*.
2 Kgs 2	**VIII**: 302.
2 Kgs 2: 1-18	**VI**: 232*(2)*.
2 Kgs 2: 2	**VI**: 10.
2 Kgs 2: 3	**VI**: 232*(2)*.
2 Kgs 2: 8	**VI**: 232.
2 Kgs 2: 19	**VI**: 233.
2 Kgs 2: 19-22	**IV**: 45; **VI**: 232.
2 Kgs 2: 23	**VI**: 233.
2 Kgs 2: 23, 24	**VI**: 233*(3)*.
2 Kgs 2: 23-25	**VI**: 233.
2 Kgs 3: 27	**VI**: 4*(2)*.
2 Kgs 4: 1-7	**VI**: 233.
2 Kgs 4: 6LXX	**VI**: 233.
2 Kgs 4: 7-28	**VI**: 233.
2 Kgs 4: 10	**VI**: 232.
2 Kgs 4: 13	**IV**: 360.
2 Kgs 4: 26	**VI**: 233.
2 Kgs 4: 34	**VI**: 227, 234.
2 Kgs 4: 34, 35	**V**: 398; **VI**: 234.
2 Kgs 4: 38-41	**VI**: 234.
2 Kgs 5	**VI**: 234.
2 Kgs 5: 12	**VI**: 234.
2 Kgs 5: 13	**VI**: 234.
2 Kgs 5: 15-18	**VI**: 234.
2 Kgs 5: 17-19	**VI**: 234.
2 Kgs 5: 22	**VI**: 234.
2 Kgs 5: 26	**VI**: 232.
2 Kgs 6: 1-4	**VI**: 235.
2 Kgs 6: 1-7	**VI**: 235.
2 Kgs 6: 8-17	**VI**: 235.
2 Kgs 6: 15-19	**VI**: 235.
2 Kgs 6: 15-22	**VI**: 235.
2 Kgs 6: 17-21LXX	**VI**: 235.
2 Kgs 6: 23	**VI**: 235.
2 Kgs 6: 25	**VI**: 5, 235.
2 Kgs 6: 33	**VI**: 12.
2 Kgs 7: -15	**VI**: 235.
2 Kgs 7: 6	**VI**: 235.

2 Kgs 7:13	**VI**: 3.
2 Kgs 7:24	**VI**: 5.
2 Kgs 8:10	**VI**: 236.
2 Kgs 8:10, 11	**VI**: 236.
2 Kgs 8:10, 13	**VI**: 232.
2 Kgs 8:19	**VI**: 12.
2 Kgs 9:1	**VI**: 232.
2 Kgs 9:8	**VI**: 226.
2 Kgs 9:25	**VI**: 236.
2 Kgs 9:27-28	**IV** 360.
2 Kgs 9:31	**VI**: 8.
2 Kgs 10:12	**VI**: 232.
2 Kgs 10:21	**VI**: 236.
2 Kgs 10:22	**V**: 402; **VI**: 5, 12.
2 Kgs 10:27	**VI**: 5.
2 Kgs 11:1	**IV**: 360; **VI**: 3.
2 Kgs 11:2, 4, 8	**VI**: 232.
2 Kgs 11:12	**VI**: 236.
2 Kgs 11:12, 14, 16	**VI**: 232.
2 Kgs 11:20	**VI**: 236.
2 Kgs 12:4	**VI**: 232.
2 Kgs 12:10 Evv 9	**VI**: 236.
2 Kgs 12:15	**VI**: 236.
2 Kgs 13	**VI**: 236.
2 Kgs 13:6, 9, 10	**V**: 648; **VI**: 237.
2 Kgs 13:14-19	**VI**: 237.
2 Kgs 14:8-9	**VI**: 237.
2 Kgs 14:23-29	**VI**: 237.
2 Kgs 14:28	**VI**: 5, 237.
2 Kgs 15:5	**VI**: 9, 237*(3)*.
2 Kgs 15:10	**VI**: 3.
2 Kgs 15:13-23	**VI**: 237.
2 Kgs 15:29	**I**: 461; **VI**: 237.
2 Kgs 15:30	**VI**: 238.
2 Kgs 16	**VI**: 4, 238*(2)*.
2 Kgs 16:2	**VI**: 238.
2 Kgs 16:5	**VI**: 238.
2 Kgs 16:6	**VI**: 232.
2 Kgs 16:9	**VI**: 4.
2 Kgs 16:20	**VI**: 238.
2 Kgs 17	**VI**: 2382*)*.
2 Kgs 17:1	**VI**: 238.
2 Kgs 17:1-18	**VI**: 6.
2 Kgs 17:6	**V**: 396; **VI**: 4, 8.
2 Kgs 17:24	**VI**: 11, 238.
2 Kgs 17:27	**VI**: 239.
2 Kgs 17:29	**VI**: 239.
2 Kgs 17:30	**V**: 395; **VI**: 7, 239*(2)*.
2 Kgs 18	**VI**: 239.
2 Kgs 18 & 19	**VI**: 239.
2 Kgs 18:1, 2	**VI**: 239.
2 Kgs 18:4	**VI**: 232.
2 Kgs 18:11	**V**: 396; **VI**: 8.
2 Kgs 18:13	**II**: *186;* **VI**: 240.
2 Kgs 18:13-14	**VI**: 240.
2 Kgs 18:13-17	**VI**: 239.
2 Kgs 18:13-19:36	**VI**: 239.
2 Kgs 18:17	**VI**: 5, 240.
2 Kgs 18:26	**VI**: 240, 289.
2 Kgs 18:27	**VI**: 228, 240.
2 Kgs 18:34	**VI**: 5, 240*(2)*.
2 Kgs 19:7	**VI**: 232.
2 Kgs 19:9	**VI**: 240.
2 Kgs 19:13	**VI**: 5, 240.
2 Kgs 19:17	**VI**: 240, 289.
2 Kgs 19:20-28	**V**: 691, 702; **VI**: 241.
2 Kgs 19:21	**VI**: 241, 289.
2 Kgs 19:21-28	**VI**: 241, 289.
2 Kgs 19:23, 24	**VI**: 232.
2 Kgs 19:24	**VI**: 11.
2 Kgs 19:25	**VI**: 241, 289.
2 Kgs 19:26	**VI**: 241.
2 Kgs 19:26-27	**VI**: 241.
2 Kgs 19:26, 27	**VI**: 241.
2 Kgs 19:27	**VI**: 241.
2 Kgs 19:31 marg.	**VI**: 232.
2 Kgs 19:35	**VI**: 241.

2 Kgs 19: 35-37 **VI**: 242.
2 Kgs 19: 36, 37 **VI**: 241.
2 Kgs 19: 37 **VI**: 242.
2 Kgs 20 **VI**: 242.
2 Kgs 20: 1-11 **VI**: 242.
2 Kgs 20: 4, 9 **VI**: 232.
2 Kgs 20: 7-11 **VI**: 242, 290, 291.
2 Kgs 20: 8-11 **VI**: 242.
2 Kgs 20: 13 **VI**: 2.
2 Kgs 22 **VI**: 242.
2 Kgs 22-23 **IV**: 384; **VI**: 242.
2 Kgs 22: 5-7 **VI**: 242.
2 Kgs 22: 8 **IV**: 359, 383; **IX**: cxlvii.
2 Kgs 22: 14 **VI**: 5.
2 Kgs 22: 24 **VI**: 232.
2 Kgs 23: 4 **VI**: 243.
2 Kgs 23: 6 **VI**: 3.
2 Kgs 23: 8 **VI**: 243.
2 Kgs 23: 10 **VI**: 243.
2 Kgs 23: 10, 13 **VI**: 243.
2 Kgs 23: 13 **VI**: 4.
2 Kgs 23: 29ff. **IV**: 360.
2 Kgs 23: 29 **VI**: 243*(3)*.
2 Kgs 24: 18ff. **VI**: 243.
2 Kgs 24: 20 **VI**: 6.
2 Kgs 25 **VI**: 243, 340, 344.
2 Kgs 25: 18 **VI**: 244.
3 Kgs 8: 53bLXX **IV**: 178.
3 Kgs 22-4 Kgs 25:30 **IV**: 107; **VI**: 219*(2)*.
Isa 1 **IV**: 109; **V**: 689; **VI**: 249*(7)*.
Isa 1-23 **VI**: 248.
Isa 1-10 **VI**: 249.
Isa 1-12 **IV**: 409; **VI**: 248*(4)*, 249; **VIII**: 390.
Isa 1-35 **VI**: 248*(2)*, 288, 289, 293.
Isa 1-39 **IV**: 397, *397;* **VI**: 247*(2)*, 248*(2)*.
Isa 1: 1-20 **VI**: 247, 249.
Isa 1: 1-8 **VI**: 249.
Isa 1: 1-9 **VI**: 249.
Isa 1: 2-20 **V**: 685.
Isa 1: 3 **VI**: 249, 250.
Isa 1: 4 **VI**: 248, 250*(2)*.
Isa 1: 4, 6, 7, 9, 11 **VI**: 245.
Isa 1: 5 **VI**: 248.
Isa 1: 5, 6 **VI**: 250.
Isa 1: 7 **V**: 394; **VI**: 5.
Isa 1: 8 **VI**: 250.
Isa 1: 8-9 **VI**: 246.
Isa 1: 10-17 **VI**: 250.
Isa 1: 10-20 **VI**: 250.
Isa 1: 12-13, 17 **VI**: 245.
Isa 1: 13 **VI**: 250.
Isa 1: 16 **VI**: 250.
Isa 1: 17 **V**: 394; **VI**: 5, 248.
Isa 1: 18 **V**: 396; **VI**: 8, 248, 251*(4)*.
Isa 1: 18b **VI**: 251, 262.
Isa 1: 18-20 **VI**: 250*(2)*.
Isa 1: 19 **VI**: 5.
Isa 1: 19,20 **VI**: 2.
Isa 1: 23, 25, 28, 29 **VI**: 245.
Isa 1: 25 **VI**: 251.
Isa 1: 27 **VI**: 246, 251.
Isa 1: 31 **VI**: 4, 5, 245*(2)*, 251.
Isa 2 **VI**: 251*(2)*, 392; **VIII**: 233.
Isa 2-4 **VI**: 251.
Isa 2: 1 **VI**: 252.
Isa 2: 1-4 **IV**: 109; **V**: 689; **VI**: 249, 252.
Isa 2: 1-5 **VI**: 252, 392.
Isa 2: 2 **VI**: 8, 9; **VIII**: 251.

Isa 2: 2-4 **VI**: 245, 247, 252*(2)*.
Isa 2: 2-5 **IV**: 446; **VI**: 252*(2)*
Isa 2: 4 **VI**: 252.
Isa 2: 5 **VI**: 252*(3)*, 392.
Isa 2: 5, 9, 10, 11 **VI**: 245.
Isa 2: 6 **V**: 453; **VI**: 253*(3)*.
Isa 2: 6ff. **VI**: 253.
Isa 2: 6-21 **VI**: 252.
Isa 2: 6-22 **VI**: 252.
Isa 2: 9 **VI**: 248.
Isa 2: 9-21 **VI**: 253.
Isa 2: 12 **V**: 396; **VI**: 8.
Isa 2: 12, 17, 20 **VI**: 245.
Isa 2: 16 **VI**: 7, 253.
Isa 2: 20 **VI**: 253.
Isa 2: 21-22 **VI**: 245.
Isa 3 **I**: *277;* **VI**: 253; **VIII**: 290.
Isa 3 & 4 **VI**: 253.
Isa 3: 1-15 **VI**: 247, 253; **IX**: cxxxii.
Isa 3: 1, 3, 4, 6, 8 **VI**: 245.
Isa 3: 6 **VI**: 7.
Isa 3: 9 **VI**: 9.
Isa 3: 9b **VI**: 246.
Isa 3: 10-11 **VI**: 253.
Isa 3: 10-11, 12 **VI**: 245.
Isa 3: 12 **VI**: 248, 254, 711.
Isa 3: 14-15, 16 **VI**: 245.
Isa 3: 16-17 **VI**: 10.
Isa 3: 16-24 **VI**: 254.
Isa 3: 17 **VI**: 246, 248.
Isa 3: 20 **VI**: 9, 246.
Isa 3: 22 **VI**: 248.
Isa 3: 24 **VI**: 247.
Isa 4 **VI**: 254*(2)*.
Isa 4: 2 **VI**: 254*(2)*.
Isa 4: 2-3 **VI**: 246.
Isa 4: 2, 5 **VI**: 245.
Isa 4: 2-6 **VI**: 246.
Isa 4: 5 **VI**: 247.
Isa 5 & 6 **VI**: 254.
Isa 5: 1-12 **VI**: 6.
Isa 5: 1-14 **VI**: 254.
Isa 5: 1-2 **VI**: 255.
Isa 5: 1-6 **VI**: 255.
Isa 5: 1-6 **VI**: 255.
Isa 5: 1-7 **VI**: 247, 254*(2)*, 255.
Isa 5: 1, 9, 12, 13 **VI**: 245.
Isa 5: 2, 4 **V**: 399; **VI**: 255.
Isa 5: 6 **VI**: 7, 248.
Isa 5: 7 **V**: 396; **VI**: 8, 11.
Isa 5: 9-10 **VI**: 255.
Isa 5: 11-12 **VI**: 246.
Isa 5: 12 **VI**: 2.
Isa 5: 13 **VI**: 247, 248.
Isa 5: 14 **VI**: 255.
Isa 5: 14-17, 23 **VI**: 246.
Isa 5: 14, 17, 18LXX **VI**: 255.
Isa 5: 16 **VI**: 255.
Isa 5: 17 **VI**: 2, 248.
Isa 5: 17, 23, 25 **VI**: 245.
Isa 5: 18 **VI**: 2, 247, 248, 255*(2)*.
Isa 5: 19 **VI**: 7.
Isa 5: 26, 28, 29, 30 **VI**: 245.
Isa 5: 27 **VI**: 2.
Isa 5: 28 **VI**: 256.
Isa 5: 29 **VI**: 247.
Isa 5: 30 **VI**: 247.
Isa 6 **VI**: 256*(8)*.
Isa 6: 1-11 **VI**: 256.
Isa 6: 1-12 **VI**: 256.
Isa 6: 1-13 **VI**: 247.
Isa 6: 1-23 **VI**: 6.
Isa 6: 1-8 **VI**: 256, 257*(3)*.
Isa 6: 1, 2, 5 **VI**: 245.

Isa 6: 3	**VI**: 257*(2)*.
Isa 6: 3LXX	**VI**: 257.
Isa 6: 5-8	**VI**: 257.
Isa 6: 8-13	**VI**: 257.
Isa 6: 9, 10	**VI**: 258.
Isa 6: 9-11	**VI**: 257.
Isa 6: 9-13	**VI**: 257*(2)*.
Isa 6: 10	**VI**: 258.
Isa 6: 11, 13	**VI**: 245.
Isa 6: 12, 13	**VI**: 258.
Isa 6: 13	**VI**: 246*(2)*, 248, 258*(3)*.
Isa 6: 13Q	**VIII**: 447.
Isa 7	**VI**: 259*(4)*.
Isa 7:-8	**VI**: 258.
Isa 7-9	**VI**: 258.
Isa 7-12	**VI**: 258.
Isa 7: 1	**VI**: 238, 259.
Isa 7: 1-16	**VI**: 259.
Isa 7: 1-17	**VI**: 259*(2)*.
Isa 7: 1, 2, 4, 6	**VI**: 245.
Isa 7: 1-9:7	**VI**: 258.
Isa 7: 3	**VI**: 246, 259*(2)*.
Isa 7: 4	**VI**: 259.
Isa 7: 6	**V**: 394; **VI**: 6, 246, 248, 259, 260.
Isa 7: 6a	**VI**: 260.
Isa 7: 7-9	**VI**: 260.
Isa 7: 8	**VI**: 260*(3)*.
Isa 7: 8-9	**VI**: 11, 260.
Isa 7: 8-9b	**VI**: 245.
Isa 7: 9	**VI**: 260.
Isa 7: 10-14	**VI**: 261.
Isa 7: 10-16	**VI**: 261*(3)*.
Isa 7: 10-16	**VI**: 261.
Isa 7: 10-17	**VI**: 260*(3)*.
Isa 7: 10-23	**VI**: 260, 265.
Isa 7: 10, 11, 13-16	**VI**: 245.
Isa 7: 11	**VI**: 5.
Isa 7: 12	**VI**: 261.
Isa 7: 13-17	**VI**: 261.
Isa 7: 14	**VI**: 4, 262*(7)*, 263*(17)*, 264*(16)*, 265*(3)*, 266; **VIII**: 273.
Isa 7: 14, 15	**VI**: 261.
Isa 7: 14b-16	**VI**: 251, 262.
Isa 7: 14-16	**VI**: 261*(2)*, 262*(6)*.
Isa 7: 14-17	**VI**: 261.
Isa 7: 14-25	**VI**: 261.
Isa 7: 15	**VI**: 248, 265*(2)*.
Isa 7: 16	**VI**: 246, 248, 265.
Isa 7: 25	**V**: 404; **VI**: 248, 265.
Isa 8	**VI**: 265.
Isa 8-10	**VI**: 265.
Isa 8: 1	**VI**: 265*(2)*.
Isa 8: 1-3, 18	**VI**: 246.
Isa 8: 1, 4, 6, 7, 8	**VI**: 245.
Isa 8: 5-10	**VI**: 266.
Isa 8: 5-15	**VI**: 266.
Isa 8: 5-19	**VI**: 260, 265.
Isa 8: 6	**VI**: 266*(6)*.
Isa 8: 6b	**V**: 478; **VI**: 266.
Isa 8: 6-8	**VI**: 266.
Isa 8: 8	**VI**: 266.
Isa 8: 9	**VI**: 248.
Isa 8: 10	**VI**: 246.
Isa 8: 10, 11, 12, 13	**VI**: 245.
Isa 8: 11	**VI**: 5.
Isa 8: 11-14	**VI**: 266.
Isa 8: 14	**VI**: 267.
Isa 8: 14-16	**VI**: 267.
Isa 8: 14, 15, 16	**VI**: 245.
Isa 8: 16	**VI**: 267.
Isa 8: 16-20	**VI**: 247.
Isa 8: 18-22	**VI**: 267, 269.
Isa 8: 18, 19, 21, 22	**VI**: 245.
Isa 8: 19	**VI**: 245.

Isa 8: 19-22 **VI**: 246.
Isa 8: 20 **VI**: 245, 267.
Isa 8: 21 **VI**: 245.
Isa 8: 21, 22 **VI**: 245.
Isa 8: 21-22 **VI**: 247.
Isa 8: 22 **VI**: 11.
Isa 8: 23 **I**: *91, 95;* **VI**: 4, 267*(3)*.
Isa 8: 23-9: 1 **VI**: 247.
Isa 8: 24-26 **VI**: 245.
Isa 8: 27, 33, 34 **VI**: 245.
Isa 8: 30 **VI**: 267.
Isa 9 **VI**: 267, 268*(2)*.
Isa 9: 1 **VI**: 268*(2)*.
Isa 9: 1-2 **VI**: 268; **VIII**: 283.
Isa 9: 1-6 **VI**: 245, 246.
Isa 9: 1-7 **VI**: 268*(4)*.
Isa 9: 2 **VI**: 245, 247, 267, 269*(2)*.
Isa 9: 2-7 **IV**: 437; **VI**: 268*(5)*, 272*(4);* **IX**: cxxxii, cxxxiii.
Isa 9: 4 **VI**: 269.
Isa 9: 5 **VI**: 3, 269*(3)*.
Isa 9: 5-6 **VI**: 269.
Isa 9: 6 **VI**: 247, 248, 269*(3)*, 270*(3)*.
Isa 9: 6-7 **VI**: 246.
Isa 9: 6, 7 **VI**: 269*(3)*.
Isa 9: 7, 8, 10, 12 **VI**: 245.
Isa 9: 8 **V**: 425; **VI**: 245, 270, 369.
Isa 9: 8-10: 4 **VI**: 270*(2)*.
Isa 9: 14, 16, 17 **VI**: 245.
Isa 9: 18 **VI**: 270*(2)*.
Isa 9: 19*(Heb 18)* **VI**: 270.
Isa 9: 19-20 **VI**: 270*(2)*.
Isa 10 **VI**: 270, 271.
Isa 10: 1-19 **VI**: 271.
Isa 10: 1-2 **VI**: 246.
Isa 10: 1, 3, 4 **VI**: 245.
Isa 10: 3b **VI**: 271.
Isa 10: 4 **V**: 535; **VI**: 5, 271*(2)*.
Isa 10: 6 **VI**: 247.
Isa 10: 8 **VI**: 271.
Isa 10: 11-12 **VI**: 271.
Isa 10: 13 **V**: 396; **VI**: 8, 246.
Isa 10: 14 **VI**: 246.
Isa 10: 15 **VI**: 246.
Isa 10: 15-19 **VI**: 247.
Isa 10: 16-18 **VI**: 248.
Isa 10: 18 **VI**: 245, 246.
Isa 10: 20-22 **VI**: 246.
Isa 10: 22 **VI**: 248.
Isa 10: 25 **VI**: 2, 248.
Isa 10: 27, 28 **VI**: 271.
Isa 10: 28-32 **VI**: 271*(2)*.
Isa 10: 28-34 **VI**: 271.
Isa 10: 29 **VI**: 248.
Isa 10: 31 **VI**: 272.
Isa 10: 32 **VI**: 246.
Isa 10: 33 **VI**: 245, 248.
Isa 10: 33-34 **VI**: 246.
Isa 10: 34 **VI**: 246.
Isa 11 **VI**: 272.
Isa 11 & 12 **VI**: 272.
Isa 11-35 **VI**: 272.
Isa 11: 1 **VI**: 246.
Isa 11: 1-10 **VI**: 246.
Isa 11: 18 **VI**: 246, 279.
Isa 11: 1-9 **IV**: 437; **VI**: 268*(4)*, 272*(5);* **IX**: cxxxii, cxxxiii.
Isa 11: 3 **V**: 398.
Isa 11: 4 **VI**: 273.
Isa 11: 5 **V**: 395; **VI**: 7, 248.
Isa 11: 6 **VI**: 2.
Isa 11: 6-9 **VI**: 247.
Isa 11: 8 **VI**: 10.
Isa 11: 10 **VI**: 4.

Isa 11: 11 **VI**: 10.
Isa 11: 11-12, 16 **VI**: 246.
Isa 11: 13 **VI**: 246.
Isa 11: 14 **VI**: 246.
Isa 11: 15 **VI**: 11, 273.
Isa 12 **IV**: 407; **VI**: 273*(2)*.
Isa 12: 2 **VI**: 273*(2)*, 282; **VIII**: 121.
Isa 13 **VI**: 274.
Isa 13& 14 **IV**: 407; **VI**: 273*(3)*, 274*(2)*.
Isa 13-23 **VI**: 247.
Isa 13:-66 **VI**: 273.
Isa 13: 1ff. **VI**: 274.
Isa 13: 2-14:23 **VI**: 274, 403.
Isa 13: 3 **VI**: 246.
Isa 13: 6 **VI**: 274.
Isa 13: 7-8 **VI**: 248.
Isa 13: 12 **VI**: 246.
Isa 13: 19-20 **VI**: 274.
Isa 13: 22 **VI**: 246.
Isa 14 **VI**: 274.
Isa 14: 1 **VI**: 248.
Isa 14: 4 **VI**: 275.
Isa 14: 4b-21 **VI**: 274.
Isa 14: 10 **VI**: 246, 248.
Isa 14: 11 **VI**: 247, 248*(2)*.
Isa 14: 12 **V**: 422, 462; **VI**: 246, 275*(3)*, 428.
Isa 14: 12b **VI**: 6.
Isa 14: 12, 13 **VI**: 3; **IX**: cxxxvi.
Isa 14: 13 **VI**: 275.
Isa 14: 19 **VI**: 246, 247, 275*(2)*.
Isa 14: 20 **VI**: 248.
Isa 14: 23 **VI**: 273.
Isa 14: 24-27 **VI**: 247, 275.
Isa 14: 28 **VI**: 276.
Isa 14: 28-32 **VI**: 275*(4)*, 276.
Isa 14: 31 **VI**: 248, 276.
Isa 15 **VI**: 11, 275.
Isa 15, 16 **VI**: 276.
Isa 15, 16, 17 **VI**: 276.
Isa 15: 1 **VI**: 248.
Isa 15: 1-16:5 **VI**: 276.
Isa 15: 3 **VI**: 10, 245.
Isa 15: 4 **VI**: 246.
Isa 15: 5 **VI**: 246, 248.
Isa 15: 7 **VI**: 248.
Isa 15: 9 **VI**: 246.
Isa 15: 11 **VI**: 248.
Isa 16, 17, 18 **VI**: 275.
Isa 16: 2 **VI**: 248.
Isa 16: 3 **VI**: 248.
Isa 16: 4 **VI**: 248.
Isa 16: 6ff. **VI**: 276.
Isa 16: 8 **VI**: 248.
Isa 17: 1 **VI**: 276*(2)*.
Isa 17: 5 **VI**: 245.
Isa 17: 6 **VI**: 246.
Isa 17: 11 **VI**: 246, 248.
Isa 17: 12-14 **VI**: 276.
Isa 17: 12-18:7 **VI**: 276, 277.
Isa 17: 13 **VI**: 246.
Isa 18 **VI**: 277*(8)*.
Isa 18, 19, 20 **VI**: 277.
Isa 18: 1 **VI**: 248, 277.
Isa 18: 1, 2 **VI**: 277.
Isa 18: 1-7 **VI**: 276.
Isa 18: 2 **VI**: 5.
Isa 18: 2, 7 **VI**: 248.
Isa 18: 4 **VI**: 246, 278.
Isa 18: 7 **VI**: 278.
Isa 19 **V**: 458; **VI**: 278*(2)*.
Isa 19: 5-11, 15 **VI**: 278.
Isa 19: 7 **VI**: 278*(2)*.
Isa 19: 9 **VI**: 247.
Isa 19: 10 **VI**: 246, 247, 278*(2)*.
Isa 19: 11 **VI**: 248.

Isa 19: 17 **VI**: 10, 248.
Isa 19: 18 **VI**: 278, 279, 719.
Isa 19: 18-20 **III**: *506;* **VI**: 278.
Isa 19: 23-25 **VI**: 279.
Isa 20 **VI**: 279.
Isa 20: 5 **VI**: 247.
Isa 20: 6 **VI**: 279.
Isa 21 **VI**: 279*(3)*.
Isa 21: 1 **VI**: 248.
Isa 21: 1-10 **VI**: 272, 279*(5)*, 280*(4)*.
Isa 21: 2 **VI**: 7, 246, 248*(2)*.
Isa 21: 5 **VI**: 10, 246.
Isa 21: 9 **VI**: 2.
Isa 21: 11 **VI**: 4.
Isa 21: 11-12 **VI**: 280*(2)*.
Isa 21: 16 **VI**: 7.
Isa 21: 17 **VI**: 246.
Isa 21: 22 **VI**: 246.
Isa 22 **VI**: 280.
Isa 22: 1-14 **VI**: 246.
Isa 22: 3 **VI**: 245, 248.
Isa 22: 5 **VI**: 248, 280.
Isa 22: 6 **VI**: 2, 248.
Isa 22: 8 **VI**: 5.
Isa 22: 9 **VI**: 248.
Isa 22: 13 **VI**: 248.
Isa 22: 15-20 **VI**: 280.
Isa 22: 15-25 **VI**: 280.
Isa 22: 17 **VI**: 248.
Isa 22: 17-18 **VI**: 246.
Isa 22: 17-18a **VI**: 246.
Isa 22: 23 **VI**: 246.
Isa 22: 24 **VI**: 246, 248, 281.
Isa 23 **VI**: 281.
Isa 23: 1 **VI**: 246.
Isa 23: 2 **VI**: 247.
Isa 23: 4-7 **VI**: 319.
Isa 23: 6-7 **VI**: 246.
Isa 23: 9 **VI**: 248.
Isa 23: 10 **VI**: 246.
Isa 23: 10-13 **VI**: 319.
Isa 23: 11 **VI**: 246, 248.
Isa 23: 16 **VI**: 281.
Isa 23: 17-18 **VI**: 281.
Isa 24 **VI**: 281.
Isa 24-27 **IV**: 409; **VI**: 247, 281*(4)*.
Isa 24: 9 **VI**: 281.
Isa 24: 11 **VI**: 246.
Isa 24: 15 **VI**: 7, 245.
Isa 24: 16 **VI**: 248.
Isa 25 & 26 **VI**: 281.
Isa 25: 1 **VI**: 246.
Isa 25: 1-5 **VI**: 282*(3)*, 287.
Isa 25: 4-5 **VI**: 4.
Isa 26 **VI**: 282*(3)*, 287.
Isa 26: 2 **VI**: 247.
Isa 26: 3 **VI**: 282.
Isa 26: 4 **VI**: 273, 282*(2)*; **VIII**: 121.
Isa 26: 9 **VI**: 247, 248*(2)*.
Isa 26: 10 **VI**: 248.
Isa 26: 16 **VI**: 247, 248.
Isa 26: 18 **VI**: 5.
Isa 26: 19 **VI**: 4, 282.
Isa 26: 19 **VI**: 245.
Isa 27 **VI**: 282.
Isa 27: 1 **VI**: 282.
Isa 27: 2-6 **VI**: 283.
Isa 27: 2-6LXX **VI**: 283.
Isa 27: 5 **VI**: 245.
Isa 27: 6 **VI**: 248*(2)*.
Isa 27: 8 **VI**: 245, 248, 283.
Isa 27: 11 **VI**: 245.
Isa 27: 13 **VI**: 283.
Isa 28-33 **VI**: 247.

Isa 28: 1-13 **VI**: 283.
Isa 28: 2a **VI**: 246.
Isa 28: 3 **VI**: 246.
Isa 28: 5 **VI**: 11, 246.
Isa 28: 7 **VI**: 9, 246.
Isa 28: 7-13 **VI**: 283.
Isa 28: 9-13 **V**: 534; **VI**: 283.
Isa 28: 10 **V**: 395; **VI**: 7, 283.
Isa 28: 10, 11 **VI**: 245.
Isa 28: 15 **V**: 395; **VI**: 7, 248, 283.
Isa 28: 16 **VI**: 5, 7, 246, 247, 284*(3)*; **IX**: cxlvii.
Isa 28: 20 **VI**: 7.
Isa 28: 23-29 **VI**: 284*(4)*.
Isa 28: 25 & 28 **VI**: 284*(2)*.
Isa 28: 27 **VI**: 10.
Isa 29 **VI**: 284.
Isa 29: 1, 2 **VI**: 3; **IX**: cxxxvi.
Isa 29: 2-14 **VI**: 247.
Isa 29: 3 **VI**: 248.
Isa 29: 4 **VI**: 125, 206, 248, 284.
Isa 29: 5 **VI**: 246.
Isa 29: 8 **VI**: 246.
Isa 29: 16 **VI**: 285.
Isa 29: 21 **V**: 394; **VI**: 6.
Isa 30 & 31 **VI**: 285.
Isa 30: 1 **VI**: 285.
Isa 30: 1-8 **VI**: 285.
Isa 30: 4 **VI**: 246.
Isa 30: 4, 5 **VI**: 4.
Isa 30: 7 **VI**: 285.
Isa 30: 8 **VI**: 247.
Isa 30: 13 **VI**: 246.
Isa 30: 15 **VI**: 247*(2)*, 248, 285.
Isa 30: 15-17 **VI**: 246.
Isa 30: 16 **VI**: 246.
Isa 30: 17 **VI**: 7.
Isa 30: 18 **VI**: 246, 248.
Isa 30: 22 **VI**: 9, 246.
Isa 30: 26 **VI**: 285.
Isa 30: 27-33 **VI**: 285.
Isa 30: 28 **VI**: 248.
Isa 30: 32 **VI**: 248*(2)*.
Isa 31: 1-9 **VI**: 247.
Isa 31: 2 **VI**: 7.
Isa 31: 4 **VI**: 245, 246*(2)*.
Isa 31: 8b-9a **V**: 395; **VI**: 7.
Isa 31: 9 **VI**: 248*(2)*.
Isa 32 **VI**: 286, 721; **VIII**: 134.
Isa 32 & 33 **VI**: 285.
Isa 32: 4 **VI**: 247.
Isa 32: 5 **VI**: 286.
Isa 32: 6 **VI**: 246.
Isa 32: 11 **VI**: 286.
Isa 32: 14 **VI**: 246, 248.
Isa 32: 19 **VI**: 11, 248.
Isa 32: 20 **VI**: 286.
Isa 33: 2 **VI**: 247, 286.
Isa 33: 4 **VI**: 246.
Isa 33: 6 **VI**: 245.
Isa 33: 7 **VI**: 3, 286; **IX**: cxxxvi.
Isa 33: 9 **VI**: 248.
Isa 33: 17 **VI**: 4, 286.
Isa 33: 18 **VI**: 248.
Isa 33: 20 **VI**: 247.
Isa 33: 21 **VI**: 248.
Isa 33: 23 **VI**: 248.
Isa 34 **V**: 703; **VI**: 286, 287*(6)*, 288*(2)*, 292*(2)*.
Isa 34-35 **VI**: 286*(2)*.
Isa 34: 1-35: 8 **VI**: 247.
Isa 34: 4 **VI**: 248.
Isa 34: 5 **VI**: 248, 287.
Isa 34: 7 **VI**: 4.
Isa 34: 8 **VI**: 7, 248.

Isa 34: 11-12 **VI**: 248.
Isa 34: 12-14 **VI**: 282*(2)*, 287.
Isa 34: 14 **V**: 137; **VI**: 286.
Isa 34: 15 **VI**: 245, 287.
Isa 34: 17 **VI**: 246.
Isa 35 **IV**: 402*(2)*; **VI**: 4, 287*(2)*, 288*(3)*, 292*(2)*.
Isa 35: 1 **III**: *394*.
Isa 35: 3-6 **VI**: 288.
Isa 35: 4 **VI**: 288.
Isa 35: 7 **VI**: 248, 288.
Isa 35: 8 **VI**: 245, 288*(2)*, 400.
Isa 35: 8-10 **VI**: 246.
Isa 36-39 **IV**: 409; **VI**: 288*(2)*, 293.
Isa 36: 1 **II**: *186*.
Isa 36: 1-37:7 **VI**: 288.
Isa 36: 3 **VI**: 289.
Isa 36: 11 **VI**: 240, 289.
Isa 36: 12 **VI**: 5.
Isa 36: 14-30 **VI**: 6.
Isa 36: 15 **VI**: 245.
Isa 36: 19 **VI**: 289.
Isa 37 **VI**: 289.
Isa 37: 1, 14 **VI**: 247.
Isa 37: 13 **VI**: 5, 290.
Isa 37: 18 **VI**: 240, 289.
Isa 37: 22 **VI**: 241, 289.
Isa 37: 22-29 **VI**: 241, 289.
Isa 37: 22-35 **VI**: 248, 289.
Isa 37: 25 **VI**: 246, 289.
Isa 37: 27 **VI**: 2, 241, 289.
Isa 37: 31 **VI**: 290*(2)*.
Isa 37: 31, 32 **VI**: 246.
Isa 37: 36 **VI**: 241, 290.
Isa 37: 36-38 **VI**: 290.
Isa 38 **VI**: 290.
Isa 38: 1-8 **VI**: 290.
Isa 38: 7-8 **VI**: 290.
Isa 38: 7, 8, 21f. **VI**: 242, 290, 291.
Isa 38: 8 **VI**: 248, 290, 291.
Isa 38: 8s **VI**: 291.
Isa 38: 9-20 **VI**: 291.
Isa 38: 9-22 **VI**: 291.
Isa 38: 10 **VI**: 4, 248*(2)*.
Isa 38: 12 **V**: 405; **VI**: 11.
Isa 38: 12, 13 **VI**: 248.
Isa 38: 13 **VI**: 245, 248.
Isa 38: 14 **VI**: 248.
Isa 38: 15 **VI**: 248.
Isa 38: 15-16 **VI**: 291.
Isa 38: 16 **VI**: 248.
Isa 38: 17 **VI**: 248.
Isa 38: 18 **VIII**: 265.
Isa 38: 21-22 **VI**: 291.
Isa 39: 1 **VI**: 248.
Isa 39: 2 **VI**: 2.
Isa 39: 22 **VI**: 247.
Isa 40 **VI**: 295.
Isa 40-48 **V**: 704; **VI**: 294, 295.
Isa 40-55 **IV**: 430; **V**: 483*(2)*; **VI**: 293*(3)*, 294*(13)*; **VIII**: 253.
Isa 40-60 **V**: 693, 694; **VI**: 293.
Isa 40-66 **IV**: *397(2)*., 399*(2)*, 402, *405(3)*, 407*(5)*, 408*(3)*; 493; **VI**: 248, 287*(2)*, 288*(3)*, 292*(12)*, 293*(9)*; **VIII**: 248, 387.
Isa 40: 1 **VI**: 295.
Isa 40: 1-11 **VI**: 295*(2)*.
Isa 40: 1-2 **VI**: 247, 295.
Isa 40: 1-3 **VI**: 295.

Isa 40: 2 **VI**: 4, 295*(4)*.
Isa 40: 3 **VI**: 10, 296*(2)*, 552.
Isa 40: 3-4 **VI**: 296.
Isa 40: 3-5 **VI**: 247.
Isa 40: 3-8 **VI**: 296; **VIII**: 284.
Isa 40: 5 **VI**: 247, 296.
Isa 40: 5-6 **VI**: 296.
Isa 40: 6 **VI**: 296.
Isa 40: 6-8 **VI**: 296*(2)*.
Isa 40: 8 **VI**: 247.
Isa 40: 9-10 **VI**: 296.
Isa 40: 10 **VI**: 296.
Isa 40: 15 **VI**: 291, 297.
Isa 40: 18-20 **VI**: 297*(2)*.
Isa 40: 19 **VI**: 291.
Isa 40: 20 **VI**: 10, 291, 297.
Isa 40: 22, 25, 27 **VI**: 247.
Isa 40: 25 **VI**: 297.
Isa 40: 26 **VI**: 291, 297, 302.
Isa 40: 27-31 **VI**: 297.
Isa 40: 28-31 **VI**: 247.
Isa 40: 31 **VI**: 246, 297.
Isa 40: 66 **VI**: 297.
Isa 41 **VI**: 297*(2)*, 298.
Isa 41: 2a **VI**: 246.
Isa 41: 2 **VI**: 291.
Isa 41: 2-3 **VI**: 246, 298; **VIII**: 287.
Isa 41: 4 **VI**: 291.
Isa 41: 5-7 **VI**: 298*(3)*.
Isa 41: 8-20 **VI**: 298.
Isa 41: 8-9 **VI**: 11.
Isa 41: 9 **VI**: 246.
Isa 41: 10, 23 **VI**: 246.
Isa 41: 11 **VI**: 291.
Isa 41: 14 **VI**: 291, 298.
Isa 41: 14-16 **VI**: 298.
Isa 41: 15 **VI**: 10.
Isa 41: 17 **VI**: 246.
Isa 41: 18 **VI**: 298.
Isa 41: 18-19 **VI**: 298.
Isa 41: 21 **VI**: 7, 246.
Isa 41: 21-29 **VI**: 247.
Isa 41: 24, 25, 28b **VI**: 246.
Isa 41: 25 **VI**: 2, 246.
Isa 41: 27 **VI**: 298*(2)*, 298.
Isa 41: 29 **VI**: 246.
Isa 42 **VI**: 299.
Isa 42-43Q **VIII**: 444.
Isa 42-44 **VI**: 319.
Isa 42: 1 **VI**: 299*(2)*.
Isa 42: 1-4 **VI**: 299; **IX**: cxlvii.
Isa 42: 1-7 **VI**: 246, 299.
Isa 42: 1-9 **VI**: 247, 299.
Isa 42: 2 **VI**: 299*(2)*.
Isa 42: 2-4 **VI**: 299.
Isa 42: 3 **VI**: 6.
Isa 42: 3, 4 **VI**: 299; **VIII**: 283.
Isa 42: 6 **VI**: 11.
Isa 42: 10 **VI**: 291.
Isa 42: 10-17 **VI**: 300.
Isa 42: 11 **VIII**: 446.
Isa 42: 13 **VI**: 300.
Isa 42: 16, 24a **VI**: 247.
Isa 42: 20 **VI**: 292.
Isa 42: 21 **VI**: 300.
Isa 42: 22 **V**: 394; **VI**: 5.
Isa 42: 25a **VI**: 247.
Isa 42: 25Q **VIII**: 445; **IX**: cxlvii.
Isa 43 **VI**: 300.
Isa 43: 11 **VI**: 247.
Isa 43: 12 **VI**: 247.
Isa 43: 13 **VI**: 291, 300; **VIII**: 288.
Isa 43: 14 **VI**: 245, 300*(2)*.
Isa 43: 14b **VI**: 246.

Isa 43: 17	**VI**: 247.	Isa 45: 9	**VI**: 291, 292, 301, 302.
Isa 43: 19ɋ	**VI**: 300*(2)*; **VIII**: 445*(4)*.	Isa 45: 11	**VI**: 247, 302*(2)*.
Isa 43: 19-20	**VI**: 247.	Isa 45: 11b	**VI**: 292.
Isa 43: 22-25	**VI**: 301.	Isa 45: 12	**VI**: 11, 246, 297, 302*(2)*.
Isa 43: 22-28	**VI**: 300.	Isa 45: 13	**I**: *170*.
Isa 43: 28	**VI**: 292.	Isa 45: 14c	**VI**: 247.
Isa 44-45	**VI**: 301.	Isa 45: 14	**VI**: 291.
Isa 44: 2	**VI**: 11.	Isa 45: 15	**VI**: 302.
Isa 44: 4	**VI**: 301.	Isa 45: 16	**VI**: 246.
Isa 44: 5	**VI**: 301; **VII**: 135.	Isa 45: 18	**VI**: 302.
Isa 44: 6a	**VI**: 247.	Isa 45: 22	**VI**: 247.
Isa 44: 7	**VI**: 291.	Isa 45: 23	**VI**: 247.
Isa 44: 8	**VI**: 8, 245*(2)*, 246.	Isa 46, 47, 48	**VI**: 302.
Isa 44: 9	**VI**: 246.	Isa 46: 1	**VI**: 247, 291.
Isa 44: 11	**VI**: 7, 246, 291.	Isa 46: 1-4	**VI**: 247.
Isa 44: 12	**VI**: 246, 291.	Isa 46: 3	**VI**: 246.
Isa 44: 12, 13	**VI**: 301.	Isa 46: 4	**VI**: 302.
Isa 44: 12, 13, 14	**VI**: 301.	Isa 46: 6b	**VI**: 247.
Isa 44: 13	**VI**: 246.	Isa 46: 6	**VI**: 291.
Isa 44: 14	**VI**: 246, 301,452.	Isa 46: 8	**VI**: 291.
Isa 44: 18	**VI**: 247.	Isa 46: 11	**VI**: 246.
Isa 44: 20	**VI**: 246.	Isa 46: 13b	**VI**: 247.
Isa 44: 21	**VI**: 11.	Isa 46: 17	**VI**: 10.
Isa 44: 21b	**VI**: 246.	Isa 47	**V**: 685, 690, 703; **VI**: 302.
Isa 44: 23a	**VI**: 246.	Isa 47: 1-10	**VI**: 247.
Isa 44: 24	**VI**: 11.	Isa 47: 11	**VI**: 291.
Isa 44: 25	**VI**: 247.	Isa 47: 12	**VI**: 246.
Isa 44: 28	**VI**: 246*(2)*.	Isa 47: 13	**VI**: 302.
Isa 44: 28-45: 1-13	**VI**: 301.	Isa 47: 15	**VI**: 291.
Isa 45: 1	**VI**: 245, 246, 247.	Isa 48: 7	**VI**: 303.
Isa 45: 1a	**VI**: 246.	Isa 48: 8	**VI**: 303.
Isa 45: 2	**VI**: 8.	Isa 48: 10	**VI**: 291.
Isa 45: 3a	**VI**: 247.	Isa 48: 14	**VI**: 246.
Isa 45: 7	**V**: 232, 301.	Isa 48: 19	**VI**: 247.
Isa 45: 8	**VI**: 10, 246.	Isa 48: 20	**VI**: 246.
Isa 45: 8-9	**VI**: 247.	Isa 49, 50, 51	**VI**: 303.
		Isa 49-55	**VI**: 303.
		Isa 49: 1-6	**VI**: 303.

Isa 49:1-7 **V**: 685.
Isa 49:1-9a **VI**: 246.
Isa 49:3 **VI**: 303*(2)*.
Isa 49:4-11 **VI**: 247.
Isa 49:5 **VI**: 11.
Isa 49:6 **VI**: 246, 303.
Isa 49:7 **VI**: 246.
Isa 49:8-13 **VI**: 303.
Isa 49:9a **VI**: 304.
Isa 49:9b **VI**: 304.
Isa 49:12 **VI**: 304*(3)*.
Isa 49:14-16 **VI**: 247.
Isa 49:15 **VI**: 245, 246.
Isa 49:16 **VI**: 304.
Isa 49:16-17 **VI**: 304.
Isa 49:17 **VI**: 291.
Isa 49:17ϙ **VI**: 304; **VIII**: 447.
Isa 49:18 **VI**: 245.
Isa 49:18b **VI**: 247.
Isa 49:19 **VI**: 291, 304.
Isa 49:21 **VI**: 11, 247.
Isa 49:24 **VI**: 7.
Isa 49:26a **VI**: 247.
Isa 50 **VI**: 304*(2)*.
Isa 50-66 **VI**: 304.
Isa 50:2bβ **VI**: 247.
Isa 50:4 **VI**: 245, 305.
Isa 50:4-10 **VI**: 305.
Isa 50:4-9 **VI**: 246.
Isa 50:6ϙ **VIII**: 447.
Isa 50:7-9 **VI**: 246.
Isa 51-53 **IV**: 445, 511; **VI**: 305.
Isa 51:-63 **VI**: 305.
Isa 51:1-11 **VI**: 305.
Isa 51:1-5 **V**: 685.
Isa 51:1-8 **VI**: 298; **VI**: 305.
Isa 51:2 **VI**: 305.
Isa 51:4-5 **VI**: 291.
Isa 51:6 **VI**: 9, 305.
Isa 51:6LXX **VI**: 305.
Isa 51:6, 7 **VI**: 3.
Isa 51:6-8, 11 **V**: 685.
Isa 51:8 **VI**: 245.
Isa 51:9-10 **V**: 685.
Isa 51:9-11 **VI**: 305.
Isa 51:9, 17 **VI**: 247.
Isa 51:11 **VI**: 246.
Isa 51:13 **VI**: 291, 306.
Isa 51:17b, 22b **VI**: 10.
Isa 51:17-23 **V**: 685.
Isa 51:18 **VI**: 306.
Isa 51:23 **VI**: 10.
Isa 52-53 **VI**: 306*(5)*; **VIII**: 193.
Isa 52:1 **VI**: 247.
Isa 52:1, 2 **V**: 685.
Isa 52:2 **VI**: 247, 291.
Isa 52:5 **VI**: 291.
Isa 52:7-10 **V**: 685.
Isa 52:8 **VI**: 246.
Isa 52:13 **VI**: 246*(2)*, 308.
Isa 52:13-53 **VI**: 306*(5)*, 307.
Isa 52:13-53:12 **V**: 685; **VI**: 6, 307*(9)*, 308.
Isa 52:13-53:6 **VI**: 308.
Isa 52:14 **VI**: 308.
Isa 52:14DSIa variant **VI**: 308.
Isa 52:15 **VI**: 308*(6)*.
Isa 53 **VI**: 246, 308*(3)*, 309*(17)*, 310*(4)*; **VIII**: 145*(2)*, 290.
Isa 53:2 **VI**: 292, 310.
Isa 53:3 **VI**: 292.
Isa 53:3, 11 **VI**: 310, 311.
Isa 53:4-6 **VI**: 247.
Isa 53:5 **VI**: 246.
Isa 53:5, 6 **VI**: 310, 419.
Isa 53:7 **VI**: 246, 310*(2)*.

Isa 53: 7-12	**VI**: 310.
Isa 53: 8	**VI**: 291, 310.
Isa 53: 8f.	**VI**: 310.
Isa 53: 8-9a	**VI**: 292.
Isa 53: 9	**VI**: 10, 311*(2)*.
Isa 53: 9, 11	**VI**: 311*(2)*.
Isa 53: 10aMT	**VI**: 247.
Isa 53: 10	**VI**: 291.
Isa 53: 10-12	**VI**: 311.
Isa 53: 11	**VI**: 246, 247, 311*(3)*.
Isa 53: 11DSS	**VI**: 311.
Isa 53: 11-12	**VI**: 311.
Isa 53: 12	**VI**: 245, 246.
Isa 54, 55, 56, 57	**VI**: 311.
Isa 54: 2	**VI**: 247.
Isa 54: 3	**VI**: 246.
Isa 54: 5	**VI**: 246.
Isa 54: 16	**VI**: 247.
Isa 54: 17	**VI**: 311*(2)*
Isa 55	**VI**: 312.
Isa 55: 1	**VI**: 291.
Isa 55: 1-13	**VI**: 247.
Isa 55: 1-5	**VI**: 312.
Isa 55: 3	**VI**: 312*(2)*.
Isa 55: 4	**VI**: 291.
Isa 55: 6	**VI**: 312.
Isa 55: 6-11	**VI**: 312.
Isa 55: 6-13	**VI**: 312.
Isa 55: 10, 11	**VI**: 312*(2)*.
Isa 56-66	**IV**: 406; **VI**: 313.
Isa 56: 8	**VI**: 246.
Isa 56: 10-11	**VI**: 247.
Isa 56: 11	**VI**: 246.
Isa 57-59	**VI**: 247.
Isa 57: 2	**V**: 396; **VI**: 8.
Isa 57: 6	**VI**: 246, 313.
Isa 57: 6-11	**VI**: 246.
Isa 57: 9	**VI**: 7, 9, 12.
Isa 57: 10	**VI**: 246.
Isa 57: 13	**VI**: 247.
Isa 57: 14-21	**VI**: 313, 314.
Isa 57: 17	**VI**: 313.
Isa 57: 17DSIa variant	**VI**: 313.
Isa 58	**VI**: 313*(2)*.
Isa 58, 59, 60	**VI**: 313.
Isa 58: 2	**VI**: 10.
Isa 58: 4ff.	**VI**: 247.
Isa 58: 7	**VI**: 292.
Isa 58: 10	**VI**: 9*(2)*.
Isa 58: 10b	**VI**: 247.
Isa 58: 13	**VI**: 246.
Isa 58: 13-14	**VI**: 313.
Isa 59: 5	**III**: *366;* **VI**: 10.
Isa 59: 6	**VI**: 246.
Isa 59: 10	**VI**: 313.
Isa 59: 16	**VI**: 314, 316.
Isa 59: 16-17	**VI**: 313, 314, 315*(2)*.
Isa 59: 20	**VI**: 246.
Isa 60	**VI**: 314*(2);* **IX**: cxxxii.
Isa 60-62	**VI**: 313, 314.
Isa 60: 1-2	**VI**: 314.
Isa 60: 1-22	**VI**: 247.
Isa 60: 1-3	**VI**: 314.
Isa 60: 2a	**VI**: 247.
Isa 60: 4	**VI**: 7, 246.
Isa 60: 5-7	**VI**: 314.
Isa 60: 8-22	**VI**: 314.
Isa 60: 11b	**VI**: 247.
Isa 60: 12	**VI**: 246.
Isa 60: 13	**VI**: 246, 314.
Isa 60: 14	**VI**: 246.
Isa 60: 16	**VI**: 245, 247.
Isa 60: 19	**VI**: 315.
Isa 60: 21	**VI**: 315.
Isa 61, 62, 63	**VI**: 315.
Isa 61: 1c	**VI**: 247.
Isa 61: 1ff.	**VI**: 247.
Isa 61: 1	**VI**: 315.

Isa 61: 1-2 **VI**: 315; **VIII**: 468.
Isa 61: 2 **VI**: 315.
Isa 61: 3 **VI**: 246*(2)*.
Isa 61: 4 **VI**: 245, 246.
Isa 61: 6 **VI**: 246.
Isa 61: 7 **VI**: 245, 246.
Isa 62: 10-12 **VI**: 315.
Isa 63 **VI**: 315; **VIII**: 285.
Isa 63: 1-6 **VI**: 313, 314, 316*(3)*.
Isa 63: 3 **VI**: 246, 316.
Isa 63: 4 **VI**: 246.
Isa 63: 5 **VI**: 314, 316.
Isa 63: 7c **VI**: 247.
Isa 63: 7-14 **VI**: 316.
Isa 63: 8f. **VI**: 12.
Isa 63: 8, 9 **VI**: 245.
Isa 63: 9 **VI**: 316*(2)*; **VIII**: 287.
Isa 63: 9LXX **VI**: 316.
Isa 63: 15-64: 12 **VI**: 247.
Isa 63: 16- 17 **VI**: 246.
Isa 63: 18 **VI**: 291.
Isa 64 **VI**: 316.
Isa 64, 65, 66 **VI**: 316.
Isa 64: 4-5 **VI**: 317.
Isa 64: 5 **VI**: 317*(2)*.
Isa 64: 6 **VI**: 292, 317*(2)*.
Isa 65 **VI**: 317.
Isa 65-66 **IV**: 409.
Isa 65: 3 **VI**: 11.
Isa 65: 3b **VI**: 247.
Isa 65: 4a **VI**: 247.
Isa 65: 5 **VI**: 291.
Isa 65: 8- 9 **VI**: 246.
Isa 65: 11 **VI**: 317.
Isa 65: 13-15 **VI**: 247.
Isa 65: 15 **VI**: 291, 317*(2)*.
Isa 65: 17-23 **VI**: 317.
Isa 65: 20 **VI**: 291, 317.
Isa 65: 24 **VI**: 318.
Isa 66: 1-2 **VI**: 247.
Isa 66: 1-6 **VI**: 318.
Isa 66: 3 **VI**: 253, 318.
Isa 66: 5 **VI**: 318.
Isa 66: 8 **VI**: 318.
Isa 66: 11 **VI**: 318.
Isa 66: 12a **VI**: 246.
Isa 66: 12 **VI**: 318.
Isa 66: 12-24 **VI**: 318; **VIII**: 238.
Isa 66: 14a **VI**: 246.
Isa 66: 14b **VI**: 246.
Isa 66: 17 **VI**: 318.
Isa 66: 18-24 **VI**: 319.
Isa 66: 19, 22 **VI**: 246.
Isa 66: 23-24 **VI**: 247.
Isa 66: 24 **VI**: 319.
Jer 1 **IV**: 413.
Jer 1-3 **VI**: 345; **VIII**: 284.
Jer 1-10 **VI**: 320.
Jer 1-25 **VI**: 320.
Jer 1:-25: 13LXX **VI**: 320.
Jer 1: 4 **VIII**: 192.
Jer 1: 4-10 **IV**: 413; **VI**: 321*(3)*.
Jer 1: 4-19 **VI**: 321.
Jer 1: 4-5 **VI**: 321.
Jer 1: 5, 10 **VI**: 320.
Jer 1: 6-7 **VI**: 320.
Jer 1: 11-12 **VI**: 321.
Jer 1: 11, 13 **VI**: 320.
Jer 1: 11-16 **IV**: 413.
Jer 1: 13 **VI**: 320, 321*(3)*.
Jer 1: 14 **VI**: 320.
Jer 1: 15 **VI**: 7.
Jer 2 **IV**: 416; **VI**: 321.
Jer 2: 1-9 **VI**: 322.
Jer 2: 1-4: 2 **VI**: 321.

Jer 2:2 **VI**: 320.
Jer 2:4-13 **VI**: 322.
Jer 2:5 **VI**: 320.
Jer 2:6, 8 **VI**: 320.
Jer 2:10-13 **VI**: 322.
Jer 2:13 **VI**: 322.
Jer 2:15 **VI**: 320.
Jer 2:19 **VI**: 245, 320.
Jer 2:21 **VI**: 320.
Jer 2:22 **VI**: 6.
Jer 2:23-25 **VI**: 322.
Jer 2:24 **VI**: 320*(2)*, 322.
Jer 2:31 **VI**: 245.
Jer 3:1 **VI**: 322*(2)*.
Jer 3:16 **III**: *75*.
Jer 3:23 **VI**: 320*(2)*.
Jer 4:2 **VI**: 320.
Jer 4:3 **VI**: 320.
Jer 4:3-6:30 **VI**: 323.
Jer 4:5 **VI**: 320, 323.
Jer 4:5-31 **VI**: 323.
Jer 4:5-6, 30 **VI**: 323, 324.
Jer 4:11 **VI**: 323.
Jer 4:16 **VI**: 320.
Jer 4:16-17 **VI**: 323.
Jer 4:18-28 **VI**: 323.
Jer 4:20 **VI**: 320.
Jer 4:23-28 **VI**: 320, 323; **VIII**: 258.
Jer 4:29 **VI**: 323*(2)*.
Jer 5:2 **VI**: 320.
Jer 5:3 **VI**: 320, 324.
Jer 5:8 **VI**: 324.
Jer 5:12 **VI**: 324.
Jer 5:26 **VI**: 320.
Jer 5:28 **VI**: 324*(3)*.
Jer 5:28-29 **VI**: 320.
Jer 5:31 **VI**: 324.
Jer 6:3 **VI**: 11.
Jer 6:6 **VI**: 320.
Jer 6:15 **VI**: 320.
Jer 6:16 **VI**: 320, 324*(2)*.
Jer 6:26-30 **VI**: 320.
Jer 6:27-30 **VI**: 324*(2)*.
Jer 7 **VI**: 325.
Jer 7:1-15 **VI**: 325*(2)*.
Jer 7:1-9:22 **VI**: 325.
Jer 7:4 **VI**: 325*(2)*.
Jer 7:6 **VI**: 320.
Jer 7:9 **VI**: 320.
Jer 7:18 **VI**: 325*(2)*.
Jer 7:21-23 **VI**: 325.
Jer 7:21-29 **VI**: 325.
Jer 7:22 **VI**: 141*(2)*, 326*(10)*.
Jer 7:22-23 **VI**: 325, 326.
Jer 7:22, 23 **VI**: 326.
Jer 7:28 **VI**: 320.
Jer 7:32 **VI**: 326.
Jer 8-9 **IX**: cxxxii.
Jer 8:5 **VI**: 245.
Jer 8:6 **VI**: 320.
Jer 8:13 **VI**: 320.
Jer 8:17 **III**: *366;* **VI**: 10.
Jer 8:18 **VI**: 320.
Jer 8:19b **VI**: 326.
Jer 8:20 **VI**: 12, 327*(2)*.
Jer 8:22 **VI**: 327*(2)*.
Jer 8:23 **VI**: 327.
Jer 9:1 **VI**: 4.
Jer 9:1-21 **V**: 685.
Jer 9:4 **VI**: 5.
Jer 9:6 **VI**: 245, 320.
Jer 9:7 **VI**: 245.
Jer 9:17b, c **VI**: 327.
Jer 9:20 **VI**: 10, 327*(3);* **VII**: 142.
Jer 9:21 **VI**: 2.
Jer 9:23-11:17 **VI**: 327.

Jer 10: 1-16 **V**: 685; **VI**: 4, 327, 328.
Jer 10: 2 **VI**: 7, 320.
Jer 10: 4 **VI**: 6.
Jer 10: 6-8 **VI**: 328.
Jer 10: 13 **VI**: 7, 320, 328.
Jer 11: 9-12: 6 **VI**: 328.
Jer 11: 15 **VI**: 10.
Jer 11: 15-16 **VI**: 328.
Jer 11: 18-12: 6 **VI**: 4, 328.
Jer 11: 19 **VI**: 328*(2)*, 721.
Jer 12: 1-5 **VI**: 328.
Jer 12: 5 **VI**: 328, 329.
Jer 12: 6 **VI**: 329.
Jer 12: 7-16: 9 **VI**: 329.
Jer 12: 9 **VI**: 329.
Jer 13: 1-11 **VI**: 329.
Jer 13: 16 **VI**: 320.
Jer 13: 18 **VI**: 329.
Jer 13: 21 **VI**: 329.
Jer 13: 22-23 **VI**: 329.
Jer 13: 23 **VI**: 329.
Jer 13: 27 **VI**: 320.
Jer 14: 3 **VI**: 329.
Jer 14: 4 **VI**: 330.
Jer 14: 18 **VI**: 330.
Jer 15: 8 **VI**: 320.
Jer 15: 10-12 **VI**: 330.
Jer 15: 10-21 **VI**: 330.
Jer 15: 15-16 **VI**: 320.
Jer 15: 15-21 **VI**: 330.
Jer 15: 16 **VI**: 7.
Jer 15: 18 **VI**: 2.
Jer 15: 19 **VI**: 330.
Jer 16: 10-20: 18 **VI**: 330.
Jer 16: 16 **VI**: 7, 330.
Jer 16: 18 **V**: 398.
Jer 17: 1-2 **VI**: 330.
Jer 17: 4 **VI**: 11, 320.
Jer 17: 5-8 **VI**: 331.
Jer 17: 6 **VI**: 2.
Jer 17: 9 **VI**: 331.
Jer 17: 11 **VI**: 331.
Jer 17: 13 **VI**: 320.
Jer 17: 31 **VI**: 331.
Jer 18 **VI**: 331.
Jer 18: 1-10 **VI**: 331; **VIII**: 291.
Jer 18: 1-17 **VI**: 331.
Jer 18: 4 **VI**: 331.
Jer 18: 13-17 **VI**: 331.
Jer 18: 14 **V**: 453; **VI**: 208, 274, 332, 423.
Jer 18: 14-15 **VI**: 332.
Jer 18: 20 **VI**: 245.
Jer 19: 13 **VI**: 320.
Jer 19: 14-20: 6 **VI**: 332.
Jer 20: 4 **VI**: 332.
Jer 20: 6 **VI**: 332*(4)*.
Jer 20: 7a, b **VI**: 332.
Jer 20: 9 **VI**: 320.
Jer 20: 14ff. **V**: 400; **VI**: 10.
Jer 21: 9 **VI**: 332.
Jer 21: 11-22: 30(-23) **VI**: 333.
Jer 21: 12 **VI**: 10.
Jer 22 **VI**: 333.
Jer 22: 10-12 **VI**: 333.
Jer 22: 18 **VI**: 333.
Jer 22: 23 **VI**: 333.
Jer 22: 28 **VI**: 333.
Jer 22: 30 **VI**: 320.
Jer 23 **VI**: 333*(2)*, 336.
Jer 23: 1-8 **VI**: 320, 333.
Jer 23: 3-5 **VI**: 333, 338.
Jer 23: 5 **VI**: 334.
Jer 23: 5-6 **VI**: 334*(3)*.
Jer 23: 6 **VI**: 334*(2)*, 339; **VIII**: 125.
Jer 23: 9 **VI**: 28, 151, 334.
Jer 23: 9-40 **VI**: 320.

Jer 23: 19	**VI**: 320.	Jer 31: 18	**VI**: 337.
Jer 23: 25-26	**VI**: 334.	Jer 31: 22	**VI**: 337*(4)*.
Jer 23: 29	**VI**: 6.	Jer 31: 22b	**VI**: 337.
Jer 23: 30	**VI**: 334.	Jer 31: 22LXX	**VI**: 337.
Jer 23: 38	**VI**: 320.	Jer 31: 30-31	**VI**: 11.
Jer 23: 39	**VI**: 245.	Jer 31: 31-34	**VI**: 338*(5)*.
Jer 24	**VI**: 334.	Jer 31: 33-34	**VI**: 338.
Jer 24: 1	**VI**: 335.	Jer 31: 35-37	**VI**: 338.
Jer 25	**VI**: 335*(2)*.	Jer 31: 38-40	**VI**: 338.
Jer 25: 9	**VI**: 335.	Jer 31: 39	**VI**: 3.
Jer 25: 9LXX	**VI**: 335.	Jer 32: 11	**VI**: 4, 11.
Jer 25: 10	**VI**: 335.	Jer 33: 1ff.	**VI**: 338.
Jer 25: 11-14	**VI**: 4.	Jer 33: 14-16	**VI**: 339*(2)*.
Jer 25: 12	**VI**: 320.	Jer 33: 14-26	**IV**: 175; **VI**: 333, 338*(2)*.
Jer 25: 25	**VI**: 7.	Jer 33: 16	**VI**: 334, 339.**VI**: 339; **VIII**: 125.
Jer 25: 26	**VI**: 4.	Jer 34: 1-7	**VI**: 339.
Jer 26	**VI**: 204, 335*(2)*.	Jer 34: 5	**VI**: 339.
Jer 26-45	**VI**: 320, 335.	Jer 34: 9	**VI**: 320.
Jer 26: 1-15	**VI**: 335.	Jer 34: 18	**VI**: 320.
Jer 26: 6	**VI**: 10.	Jer 35	**VI**: 339.
Jer 26: 20	**VI**: 335.	Jer 35: 30	**VI**: 339.
Jer 27-29	**VI**: 336.	Jer 36	**V**: 694; **VI**: 339.
Jer 27: 2	**VI**: 320.	Jer 36: 14	**VI**: 320.
Jer 27: 6	**VI**: 336*(2)*.	Jer 36: 22-24	**VI**: 339.
Jer 27: 8	**VI**: 245.	Jer 36: 25	**VI**: 339.
Jer 27: 10	**VI**: 245.	Jer 37-44	**VI**: 340.
Jer 27: 12-13	**VI**: 336.	Jer 37: 1-10	**VI**: 340.
Jer 28	**VI**: 333*(2)*, 336.	Jer 38: 2	**VI**: 340.
Jer 29: 22	**VI**: 336, 569.	Jer 38: 11	**VI**: 6.
Jer 30-31	**VI**: 336.	Jer 38: 21	**V**: 400.
Jer 30: 4-11	**IV**: 414.	Jer 39	**VI**: 340*(2)*.
Jer 30: 19	**VI**: 7.	Jer 39: 3	**VI**: 340*(3)*.
Jer 31	**IV**: 416; **VI**: 336.	Jer 39: 3, 13	**VI**: 340*(2)*.
Jer 31: 1-10	**VI**: 336.	Jer 39: 14	**VI**: 340.
Jer 31: 2	**VI**: 11.	Jer 39: 18	**VI**: 341.
Jer 31: 3	**VI**: 337*(2)*.	Jer 41: 9	**VI**: 320.
Jer 31: 9	**VI**: 2.	Jer 43: 5-7	**VI**: 341.
Jer 31: 1(2)	**VI**: 337.	Jer 43: 9	**VI**: 320.
Jer 31: 15	**VI**: 337*(2)*.		

Jer 43: 10 **VI**: 341.
Jer 43: 10, 11 **VI**: 341.
Jer 43: 12 **VI**: 341.
Jer 44: 17-19 **VI**: 341.
Jer 44: 19 **VI**: 341*(2)*.
Jer 45: 4 **VI**: 320.
Jer 45: 4, 5 **VI**: 341.
Jer 45: 5 **VI**: 342.
Jer 46 **VI**: 342.
Jer 46:, 47:28 **VI**: 342.
Jer 46-51 **VI**: 320.
Jer 46: 3-12 **V**: 685.
Jer 46: 9 **VI**: 7.
Jer 47 **VI**: 342.
Jer 47: 5 **VI**: 7.
Jer 47: 29, 49 **VI**: 342.
Jer 48: 1-6 **VI**: 342.
Jer 48: 4 **VI**: 342.
Jer 48: 5 **VI**: 320.
Jer 48: 10 **VI**: 7.
Jer 48: 11 **VI**: 342*(2)*.
Jer 48: 12 **VI**: 320.
Jer 48: 15 **VI**: 11.
Jer 48: 16-24 **VI**: 343.
Jer 48: 18 **VI**: 320.
Jer 48: 29ff. **VI**: 343.
Jer 48: 29-38 **VI**: 343.
Jer 48: 34 **V**: 465, 489; **VI**: 343.
Jer 48: 35 **VI**: 320.
Jer 48: 37 **IV**: 188; **VI**: 343.
Jer 48: 45 **VI**: 245.
Jer 49: 1-6 **VI**: 343*(2)*.
Jer 49: 3 **VI**: 320.
Jer 49: 4 **VI**: 320.
Jer 49: 16 **VI**: 320.
Jer 49: 20 **VI**: 343.
Jer 49: 21 **VI**: 320.
Jer 49: 23 **VI**: 320.
Jer 49: 25 **VI**: 320.
Jer 50, 51 **VI**: 343.
Jer 50: 6 **VI**: 320.
Jer 50: 10 **VI**: 344.
Jer 50: 24 **VI**: 245.
Jer 50: 32 **VI**: 2.
Jer 51: 11 **VI**: 320.
Jer 51: 16 **VI**: 344.
Jer 51: 27 **VI**: 344.
Jer 51: 27-28 **VI**: 344.
Jer 51: 39 **VI**: 320.
Jer 51: 41 **VI**: 4.
Jer 51: 56 **VI**: 320.
Jer 52 **VI**: 320, 344*(2)*.
Jer 52: 3 **VI**: 6.
Jer 52: 28-30 **VI**: 344.
Ezek 1 **VI**: 347*(3)*.
Ezek 1-3 **VI**: 346*(2)*.
Ezek 1-30 **VI**: 346.
Ezek 1: 1 **VI**: 347*(3)*.
Ezek 1: 1-28 **VI**: 347*(2)*.
Ezek 1: 1-3 **VI**: 347*(5)*.
Ezek 1: 1-4 **VI**: 347.
Ezek 1: 1-3, 13, 14 **VI**: 4.
Ezek 1: 3 **V**: 396; **VI**: 8.
Ezek 1: 4 **VI**: 346.
Ezek 1: 7 **VI**: 346, 348; **IX**: cxlviii.
Ezek 1: 8 **VI**: 348*(2)*.
Ezek 1: 13 **VI**: 348*(2)*; **IX**: cxlviii.
Ezek 1: 14 **VI**: 346.
Ezek 1: 15-18 **VI**: 348.
Ezek 1: 15-21 **VI**: 348.
Ezek 1: 16 **VI**: 346.
Ezek 1: 18 **VI**: 4, 346.
Ezek 1: 21 **VI**: 348.
Ezek 1: 24 **VI**: 11, 245, 346.
Ezek 1: 28 **VI**: 348*(2)*.
Ezek 2: 4 **VI**: 349.
Ezek 2: 6 **VI**: 349.
Ezek 2: 10 **VI**: 346.

Ezek 2: 13	**VI**: 346.
Ezek 4	**VI**: 349.
Ezek 4: 2	**VI**: 346.
Ezek 4: 5-6ɑ	**VI**: 349; **VIII**: 448.
Ezek 5: 7	**IX**: cxlviii.
Ezek 5: 11	**VI**: 346*(2)*.
Ezek 6: 6	**VI**: 245.
Ezek 6: 8&13	**IX**: cxlviii.
Ezek 6: 12	**IX**: cxlviii.
Ezek 6: 14	**VI**: 4.
Ezek 7: 5	**VI**: 349.
Ezek 7: 5-14	**VI**: 349.
Ezek 7: 6	**VI**: 346.
Ezek 7: 7	**V**: 395; **VI**: 7; **IX**: cxlviii.
Ezek 7: 7a	**VI**: 346.
Ezek 7: 7b	**VI**: 346.
Ezek 7: 7, 10	**VI**: 11.
Ezek 7: 11	**VI**: 346.
Ezek 7: 14	**VI**: 7.
Ezek 7: 16	**VI**: 10; **IX**: cxlviii.
Ezek 7: 21	**VI**: 346.
Ezek 7: 23	**VI**: 346.
Ezek 8	**VI**: 349*(2)*.
Ezek 8: 3	**VI**: 346; **IX**: cxlviii.
Ezek 8: 3, 5	**VI**: 4.
Ezek 8: 5	**IX**: cxlviii.
Ezek 8: 7-8	**VI**: 349.
Ezek 8: 7-9	**VI**: 346.
Ezek 8: 17	**VI**: 349, 350*(2)*.
Ezek 9: 2	**VI**: 4.
Ezek 9: 7	**IX**: cxlviii.
Ezek 9: 8	**VI**: 350.
Ezek 10: 6-22	**VI**: 350.
Ezek 10: 11, 12	**VI**: 350.
Ezek 10: 22	**VI**: 346*(2)*, 350.
Ezek 11: 3	**IX**: cxlviii.
Ezek 11: 5-12	**VI**: 350.
Ezek 11: 14-21	**VI**: 350.
Ezek 11: 21	**VI**: 350.
Ezek 12: 3	**VI**: 346.
Ezek 12: 5	**VI**: 346.
Ezek 12: 26-28	**VI**: 361*(2)*.
Ezek 13: 3	**VI**: 346; **IX**: cxlviii.
Ezek 13: 6	**VI**: 346.
Ezek 13: 11, 13	**VI**: 346.
Ezek 13: 17-21	**VI**: 351; **IX**: cxlviii.
Ezek 13: 17-23	**VI**: 350, 351.
Ezek 13: 18	**IX**: cxlviii.
Ezek 13: 18-21	**VI**: 351.
Ezek 14: 1-8	**VI**: 351.
Ezek 14: 5	**IX**: cxlviii.
Ezek 14: 12-20	**V**: 461, 685; **VI**: 351.
Ezek 15: 2	**VI**: 346.
Ezek 16: 3	**VI**: 346; **IX**: cxlviii.
Ezek 16: 4	**VI**: 346, 351*(2)*.
Ezek 16: 10, 13	**V**: 403, 615.
Ezek 16: 15	**VI**: 346.
Ezek 16: 16	**VI**: 346.
Ezek 16: 22	**IX**: cxlviii.
Ezek 16: 30	**VI**: 346*(2)*, 351.
Ezek 16: 32	**VI**: 346.
Ezek 16: 36	**VI**: 346, 351; **VIII**: 295; **IX**: cxlviii.
Ezek 16: 37	**IX**: cxlviii.
Ezek 16: 38	**IX**: cxlviii.
Ezek 16: 43	**VI**: 346.
Ezek 16: 44	**IX**: cxlviii.
Ezek 16: 47	**VI**: 346.
Ezek 16: 57	**IX**: cxlviii.
Ezek 17	**VI**: 351*(3)*.
Ezek 17: 1-10	**VI**: 352*(2)*.
Ezek 17: 3	**VI**: 346.
Ezek 17: 5	**VI**: 346.

Ezek 17: 7 **VI**: 346.
Ezek 17: 17 **VI**: 346.
Ezek 17: 19 **IX**: cxlviii.
Ezek 17: 21 **VI**: 11.
Ezek 17: 22-24 **VI**: 352*(2)*.
Ezek 18: 7 **VI**: 7, 11.
Ezek 18: 10 **VI**: 352*(2)*.
Ezek 18: 24 **IX**: cxlviii.
Ezek 18: 26 **IX**: cxlviii.
Ezek 19: 2 **VI**: 346.
Ezek 19: 3 **VI**: 346.
Ezek 19: 5 **VI**: 346*(2)*; **IX**: cxlviii.
Ezek 19: 7 **VI**: 346, 352*(2)*.
Ezek 19: 9 **VI**: 346.
Ezek 19: 10 **VI**: 2, 346.
Ezek 20: 3 **VI**: 352; **VIII**: 72.
Ezek 20: 25-27 **VI**: 346.
Ezek 20: 29 **IX**: cxlviii.
Ezek 20: 31 **VI**: 352.
Ezek 20: 37-38 **VI**: 352.
Ezek 20: 39 **VI**: 352.
Ezek 21: 1 **VI**: 353.
Ezek 21: 2 **VI**: 10; **IX**: cxlviii.
Ezek 21: 14-22 **VI**: 353.
Ezek 21: 15 **VI**: 346, 353; **IX**: cxlviii.
Ezek 21: 20 **VI**: 11, 353; **IX**: cxlviii*(2)*.
Ezek 21: 21 **VI**: 346, 353; **IX**: cxlviii.
Ezek 21: 24 **V**: 413; **VI**: 173, 353.
Ezek 21: 25 **VI**: 245.
Ezek 21: 26 **VI**: 11.
Ezek 21: 27 **VI**: 353.
Ezek 21: 31 **VI**: 3.
Ezek 21: 32 **VI**: 93, 353; **IX**: cxlviii.
Ezek 21: 32 **VI**: 346.
Ezek 21: 33-37 **VI**: 346.
Ezek 22: 3 **VI**: 7.
Ezek 22: 4 **IX**: cxlviii.
Ezek 22: 17-22 **VI**: 353.
Ezek 22: 18 **IX**: cxlviii.
Ezek 22: 24 **IX**: cxlviii.
Ezek 23 **VI**: 353.
Ezek 23: 5, 12 **VI**: 346.
Ezek 23: 24 **VI**: 7, 11, 346.
Ezek 23: 40 **VI**: 346.
Ezek 23: 43 **VI**: 346.
Ezek 23: 44 **IX**: cxlviii.
Ezek 23: 47 **V**: 413; **VI**: 173, 353; **IX**: cxlviii.
Ezek 24: 5 **IX**: cxlviii.
Ezek 24: 10 **IX**: cxlviii.
Ezek 24: 12 **IX**: cxlviii.
Ezek 24: 17 **VI**: 346*(2)*.
Ezek 24: 17, 22 **VI**: 245.
Ezek 24: 21 **VI**: 346.
Ezek 25: 6 **VI**: 346.
Ezek 25: 9 **VI**: 346.
Ezek 25: 13 **VI**: 346.
Ezek 25: 15 **VI**: 346.
Ezek 26: 9 **VI**: 11.
Ezek 26: 13 **VI**: 346.
Ezek 26: 15 **IX**: cxlviii.
Ezek 26: 20 **IX**: cxlviii.
Ezek 27: 4 **IX**: cxlviii.
Ezek 27: 15 **V**: 396.
Ezek 27: 16 **VI**: 346.
Ezek 27: 18 **VI**: 2, 346.
Ezek 27: 19 **I**: *264*.
Ezek 27: 21 **VI**: 346.
Ezek 27: 22 **VI**: 346.
Ezek 27: 23 **VI**: 346.
Ezek 27: 28 **VI**: 346.
Ezek 27: 30 **VI**: 346.
Ezek 27: 32 **VI**: 11, 245; **IX**: cxlviii.
Ezek 27: 34 **VI**: 346.
Ezek 27: 35 **VI**: 10.

Ezek 28 **IV**: 296.
Ezek 28:3 **IX**: cxlviii.
Ezek 28:7 **VI**: 346.
Ezek 28:12ff. **III**: *366;* **VI**: 10.
Ezek 28:12 **VI**: 346, 356.
Ezek 28:12-16 **IX**: cxlviii.
Ezek 28:12-18 **VI**: 356.
Ezek 28:13 **VI**: 356.
Ezek 28:14 **VI**: 245, 346.
Ezek 28:17 **VI**: 356.
Ezek 28:32 **VI**: 11.
Ezek 29:1 **VI**: 356.
Ezek 29:5 **VI**: 346.
Ezek 29:7 **VI**: 346.
Ezek 29:8-16 **VI**: 356.
Ezek 29:16 **VI**: 346.
Ezek 29:19 **VI**: 356.
Ezek 30:4 **VI**: 7.
Ezek 30:5 **VI**: 346.
Ezek 30:9 **V**: 395; **VI**: 7, 346.
Ezek 30:16 **IX**: cxlviii.
Ezek 31 **VI**: 356.
Ezek 31:3 **VI**: 346*(2);* **IX**: cxlviii*(2).*
Ezek 31:5 **IX**: cxlviii.
Ezek 31:11 **IX**: cxlviii.
Ezek 31:12 **VI**: 10, 346; **IX**: cxlviii.
Ezek 31:14 **VI**: 356.
Ezek 31:14-18 **VI**: 12.
Ezek 31:17 **IX**: cxlviii.
Ezek 31:18b **VI**: 346.
Ezek 32:2 **VI**: 6.
Ezek 32:9 **IX**: cxlviii.
Ezek 32:17-32 **VI**: 357.
Ezek 32:18-32 **VI**: 357.
Ezek 32:20 **VI**: 245; **IX**: cxlviii.
Ezek 32:22-26 **VI**: 346.
Ezek 32:23 **IX**: cxlviii.
Ezek 32:24 **IX**: cxlviii.
Ezek 32:27 **VI**: 346.
Ezek 32:30 **IX**: cxlviii.
Ezek 33:7-16 **VI**: 357.
Ezek 33:18 **IX**: cxlviii.
Ezek 33:30 **IX**: cxlviii.
Ezek 33:31 **VI**: 346.
Ezek 33:32 **VI**: 357; **IX**: cxlviii.
Ezek 34 **VI**: 357*(2).*
Ezek 34, 36& 37 **VI**: 4.
Ezek 34:1-10 **VI**: 357.
Ezek 34:2 **VI**: 346.
Ezek 34:4 **IX**: cxlviii.
Ezek 34:6 **IX**: cxlviii.
Ezek 34:12 **VI**: 245, 346; **IX**: cxlviii.
Ezek 34:13 **IX**: cxlviii.
Ezek 34:23 **IX**: cxlviii.
Ezek 34:26 **VI**: 346.
Ezek 34:30 **VI**: 346.
Ezek 35:6 **IX**: cxlviii.
Ezek 35:11 **VI**: 346.
Ezek 36:3 **VI**: 7; **IX**: cxlviii.
Ezek 36:5 **VI**: 346; **IX**: cxlviii.
Ezek 36:10-12 **VI**: 346.
Ezek 36:13 **VI**: 346.
Ezek 36:23b-38 **VI**: 361*(2).*
Ezek 37 **III**: *525;* **VI**: 357*(3);* **VIII**: 357.
Ezek 37:-39 **VI**: 357.
Ezek 37:1-14 **VI**: 358; **VIII**: 277.
Ezek 37:1-4 **VI**: 358.
Ezek 37:4-14 **VI**: 358.
Ezek 37:7 **VI**: 346.
Ezek 37:11 **VI**: 346; **IX**: cxlviii.
Ezek 37:14 **VI**: 7.
Ezek 37:15-28 **I**: *164;* **VI**: 358.
Ezek 37:16-17 **VI**: 358.

Ezek 37: 19 **VI**: 346.
Ezek 37: 22 **VI**: 346.
Ezek 37: 22αβ **VI**: 346.
Ezek 37: 23 **VI**: 7.
Ezek 37: 26 **VI**: 7.
Ezek 38-39 **VI**: 358*(3)*.
Ezek 38: 1-19 **VI**: 359.
Ezek 38: 1-39: 20 **IV**: 424.
Ezek 38: 2 **IX**: cxlviii.
Ezek 38: 2, 3 **VI**: 4.
Ezek 38: 7 **VI**: 346.
Ezek 38: 12 **V**: 463; **VI**: 4, 359.
Ezek 38: 16 **IX**: cxlviii.
Ezek 38: 18 **VI**: 346.
Ezek 38: 19 **IV**: 27; **VI**: 359.
Ezek 39: 1 **VI**: 4.
Ezek 39: 9f. **VI**: 5.
Ezek 39: 9 **VI**: 346; **IX**: cxlviii.
Ezek 39: 11 **VI**: 346.
Ezek 39: 14 **IX**: cxlviii.
Ezek 39: 14-15 **VI**: 346.
Ezek 39: 16 **IX**: cxlviii.
Ezek 40-43 **IV**: 425; **VI**: 360.
Ezek 40-48 **IV**: 424, 454; **VI**: 359*(9)*, 360.
Ezek 40: 5 **VI**: 346.
Ezek 40: 16 **VI**: 346.
Ezek 40: 38-43 **VI**: 346.
Ezek 41: 6 **VI**: 346.
Ezek 41: 7 **VI**: 346.
Ezek 41: 8 **IX**: cxlviii.
Ezek 41: 9 **IX**: cxlviii.
Ezek 41: 9-10 **VI**: 346.
Ezek 41: 16 **VI**: 346.
Ezek 41: 17-18 **VI**: 346; **IX**: cxlviii.
Ezek 41: 21 **VI**: 346.
Ezek 41: 23-24 **VI**: 346.
Ezek 41: 26 **VI**: 4.
Ezek 42: 2-4 **VI**: 346.
Ezek 42: 3 **VI**: 4; **IX**: cxlviii.
Ezek 42: 3LXX **VI**: 4.
Ezek 42: 6 **IX**: cxlviii.
Ezek 42: 14 **VI**: 346.
Ezek 42: 18 **VI**: 346.
Ezek 43: 7 **VI**: 346.
Ezek 43: 10 **IX**: cxlviii.
Ezek 43: 10, 12 **V**: 74.
Ezek 43: 11 **VI**: 346.
Ezek 43: 14, 17 **VI**: 346.
Ezek 43: 17 **VI**: 346.
Ezek 44: 3 **VI**: 4, 346.
Ezek 44: 6ff. **VI**: 360.
Ezek 44: 7 **VI**: 346.
Ezek 44: 7-15 **I**: *100;* **V**: 42; **VI**: 360.
Ezek 44: 9 **VI**: 346.
Ezek 44: 18 **VI**: 346*(2)*.
Ezek 44: 20 **VI**: 360; **IX**: cxlviii.
Ezek 44: 24 **VI**: 346.
Ezek 44: 25 **VI**: 346.
Ezek 44: 28 **IX**: cxlviii.
Ezek 44: 30 **VI**: 346.
Ezek 45 **VI**: 360.
Ezek 45: 1-8 **IV**: 424.
Ezek 45: 12 **VI**: 4.
Ezek 45: 14 **VI**: 4.
Ezek 46: 22 **VI**: 5, 346.
Ezek 46: 23 **VI**: 346.
Ezek 46: 10(11) **VI**: 3.
Ezek 47 **VI**: 360*(2)*.
Ezek 47: 1-2 **VI**: 360.
Ezek 47: 7 **VI**: 245, 346.
Ezek 47: 8 **IX**: cxlviii.
Ezek 47: 8-11 **VI**: 360.
Ezek 47: 13 **IV**: 424.
Ezek 48 **VI**: 361.
Ezek 48: 13 **IX**: cxlviii.

Ezek 48:19 **IX**: cxlviii.
Ezek 48:35 **IV**: 424; **VI**: 245, 346.

Hos 1-2 **VI**: 364*(2)*.
Hos 1-3 **VI**: 364*(7)*.
Hos 1:2-3:5 **V**: 704.
Hos 2:2 **VI**: 365.
Hos 2:4-5 **VI**: 365*(2)*.
Hos 2:7 **VI**: 7, 364, 365.
Hos 2:8 **VI**: 363.
Hos 2:17 **VI**: 9, 364.
Hos 2:22 **VI**: 365.
Hos 2:23 **VI**: 365.
Hos 2:23-24 **VI**: 365.
Hos 3:1-5 **VI**: 365.
Hos 3:2 **VI**: 365.
Hos 3:4 **VI**: 5, 363.
Hos 3:4, 5 **VI**: 366.
Hos 4 **VI**: 366.
Hos 4-14 **VI**: 366*(2)*.
Hos 4:1-7:7 **V**: 704.
Hos 4:2 **VI**: 366.
Hos 4:4 **VI**: 11, 366.
Hos 4:4-5 **VI**: 364.
Hos 4:4-7 **VI**: 11.
Hos 4:5 **VI**: 5.
Hos 4:5, 6 **VI**: 363.
Hos 4:8 **VI**: 6, 363.
Hos 4:9 **VI**: 245.
Hos 4:10, 11 **VI**: 363.
Hos 4:12 **VI**: 364.
Hos 4:13 **VI**: 363.
Hos 4:14 **VI**: 363.
Hos 4:17 **VI**: 245, 3662*)*.
Hos 4:18 **V**: 402; **VI**: 12, 363.
Hos 4:31f. **VI**: 12.
Hos 5:4 **VI**: 366.
Hos 5:7 **VI**: 9.
Hos 5:8 **V**: 398.
Hos 5:8-6:6 **VI**: 366.
Hos 5:11 **VI**: 367*(2)*.
Hos 5:11b **VI**: 367.
Hos 5:13 **VI**: 9*(2)*, 11, 367*(3)*, 369.
Hos 6 **VI**: 367.
Hos 6:1-3 **VI**: 367*(2)*.
Hos 6:2 **VI**: 367*(2)*.
Hos 6:3 **VI**: 364, 367, 368.
Hos 6:4 **VI**: 364.
Hos 6:4-9 **VI**: 368.
Hos 6:5 **VI**: 4, 10, 159, 245, 364, 368*(2)*, 474.
Hos 6:7 **VI**: 363, 368.
Hos 6:9 **VI**: 362, 363, 364.
Hos 6:9, 10 **VI**: 363.
Hos 6:10 **VI**: 364.
Hos 7 **V**: 685.
Hos 7:3-6 **VI**: 364.
Hos 7:3-6, 8, 9 **VI**: 11.
Hos 7:4-10 **VI**: 368.
Hos 7:5 **VI**: 363.
Hos 7:6 **VI**: 7.
Hos 7:8 **VI**: 363.
Hos 7:8-14:10 **V**: 704.
Hos 7:9 **VI**: 11.
Hos 7:12 **VI**: 245, 363.
Hos 7:14 **VI**: 245, 363.
Hos 7:15 **VI**: 363.
Hos 7:16 **VI**: 364.
Hos 8:1 **VI**: 363, 368.
Hos 8:4 **VI**: 368.
Hos 8:6 **VI**: 7.
Hos 8:6, 7 **VI**: 363.
Hos 8:7 **VI**: 245, 363, 364.
Hos 8:7b **VI**: 11.
Hos 8:10 **VI**: 364.
Hos 8:12 **IV**: 238; **VI**: 368*(2)*.

Hos 8: 13	**VI**: 11, 364, 369.
Hos 9: 1	**VI**: 9, 364.
Hos 9: 4	**VI**: 363, 364.
Hos 9: 6	**VI**: 363.
Hos 9: 7	**V**: 425; **VI**: 270; **VI**: 369.
Hos 9: 7-8	**VI**: 364.
Hos 9: 8	**VI**: 369.
Hos 9: 10	**VI**: 363, 364.
Hos 9: 10-17	**VI**: 369.
Hos 9: 13	**VI**: 364.
Hos 9: 14	**VI**: 364.
Hos 9: 15	**VI**: 363, 369.
Hos 9: 16	**VI**: 364.
Hos 10: 1	**VI**: 9, 363.
Hos 10: 1-8	**VI**: 369.
Hos 10: 4	**VI**: 369.
Hos 10: 5	**VI**: 9.
Hos 10: 5b	**VI**: 11.
Hos 10: 6	**VI**: 9, 11, 369*(3)*.
Hos 10: 7	**VI**: 370*(2)*.
Hos 10: 9	**V**: 402; **VI**: 12, 363.
Hos 10: 9-10	**VI**: 362.
Hos 10: 10	**VI**: 364.
Hos 10: 10-14	**VI**: 11.
Hos 10: 11	**VI**: 364, 370*(2)*.
Hos 10: 12	**VI**: 3, 364, 370.
Hos 10: 14	**VI**: 370.
Hos 10: 15b	**VI**: 370.
Hos 11	**VI**: 370.
Hos 11: 1	**VI**: 370, 371.
Hos 11: 1-11	**VI**: 370.
Hos 11: 1, 4	**VI**: 363.
Hos 11: 3	**VI**: 371.
Hos 11: 3-5	**VI**: 364.
Hos 11: 4	**V**: 396; **VI**: 7, 8, 10, 371*(3)*.
Hos 11: 6	**VI**: 363.
Hos 11: 7	**VI**: 371*(3)*.
Hos 11: 8-9	**VI**: 371, 381.
Hos 12	**VI**: 371.
Hos 12: 1	**VI**: 6, 372*(2)*.
Hos 12: 1-14	**VI**: 371.
Hos 12: 1-15	**VI**: 371.
Hos 12: 1-2	**VI**: 372.
Hos 12: 1, 2, 9	**VI**: 363.
Hos 12: 2	**VI**: 372*(2)*.
Hos 12: 3-6	**VI**: 372.
Hos 12: 4-5	**VI**: 372.
Hos 12: 4, 5a, 13	**VI**: 363.
Hos 12: 5	**VI**: 372.
Hos 12: 5b-9	**VI**: 11.
Hos 12: 9	**VI**: 372.
Hos 12: 10	**VI**: 363, 364.
Hos 12: 12	**VI**: 11, 363.
Hos 12: 15	**VI**: 372.
Hos 13: 1	**VI**: 364, 372.
Hos 13: 2	**VI**: 7, 9, 364.
Hos 13: 3	**VI**: 364.
Hos 13: 7	**VI**: 9, 364.
Hos 13: 8	**VI**: 364.
Hos 13: 9	**VI**: 3*(2)*, 4.
Hos 13: 13	**VI**: 364.
Hos 13: 14b	**V**: 400; **VI**: 10.
Hos 13: 15	**VI**: 363, 364.
Hos 14: 1	**VI**: 364.
Hos 14: 1-10	**VI**: 6.
Hos 14: 3	**VI**: 363, 364, 373.
Hos 14: 6-7	**VI**: 364.
Hos 14: 8	**VI**: 373*(3)*.
Hos 14: 8(9)	**VI**: 373.
Hos 14: 9	**VI**: 363.
Joel	**VI**: 4.
Joel 1	**VI**: 373.
Joel 1: 7	**VI**: 2, 245.
Joel 1: 17a	**VI**: 373.
Joel 1: 18	**VI**: 362.
Joel 2: 2-18	**VI**: 374.
Joel 2: 2-18a, 21-32	**VI**: 373.

Joel 2: 12-19 **VI**: 373.
Joel 2: 17 **VI**: 362.
Joel 2: 20 **VI**: 245, 362.
Joel 2: 21-32 **VI**: 374.
Joel 2: 23 **VI**: 362, 374*(3)*.
Joel 2: 28-32 **VI**: 9; **VIII**: 251.
Joel 3: 4 **VI**: 374.
Joel 3: 16 (4: 16) **VI**: 374, 377.
Joel 3: 18 (4: 18) **VI**: 374.
Joel 4: 7 **VI**: 9.
Joel 4: 9ff. **VI**: 374.
Joel 4: 9-11 **VI**: 362.
Joel 4: 15-17 **VI**: 375.
Joel 4: 17-21 **VI**: 375.
Joel 4: 21 **VI**: 362.
Amos **VI**: 375, 376*(4)*.
Amos 1-2 **VI**: 376*(3)*, 377.
Amos 1: 1 **VI**: 9, 362, 376, 377*(4)*.
Amos 1: 1-15 **VI**: 377.
Amos 1: 2 **VI**: 374, 377.
Amos 1: 2-6 **VI**: 376*(3)*.
Amos 1: 2-2: 4 **V**: 685.
Amos 1: 3 **VI**: 10, 377.
Amos 1: 3-2: 3 **VI**: 377.
Amos 1: 3-2: 5 **VI**: 375, 377.
Amos 1: 5 **VI**: 4, 362, 377, 378; **VII**: 204.
Amos 1: 5, 8 **VI**: 9.
Amos 1: 6 **VI**: 378.
Amos 1: 6-12 **VI**: 378.
Amos 1: 9 **VI**: 378.
Amos 1: 11 **V**: 394; **VI**: 5, 378.
Amos 1: 13 **VI**: 11, 362, 378.
Amos 1: 15 **VI**: 378.
Amos 2: 1-16 **VI**: 378.
Amos 2: 3 **VI**: 362.
Amos 2: 6 **VI**: 379*(2)*, 386.
Amos 2: 6-16 **VI**: 375, 378.
Amos 2: 6-8 **VI**: 378.
Amos 2: 7 **VI**: 11, 375, 379*(5)*.
Amos 2: 7 **VI**: 362.
Amos 2: 8 **VI**: 362, 379.
Amos 2: 8 **VI**: 362.
Amos 2: 9 **VI**: 379.
Amos 2: 10 **VI**: 379, 380.
Amos 2: 11 **VI**: 362.
Amos 2: 13 **VI**: 379*(3).j*
Amos 3: -5: 17 **VI**: 381.
Amos 3-6 **VI**: 380, 383, 384.
Amos 3: 1b **VI**: 379, 380.
Amos 3: 1-15 **VI**: 380.
Amos 3: 1-2 **VI**: 380.
Amos 3: 3 **VI**: 380*3)*.
Amos 3: 3-8 **VI**: 380.
Amos 3: 4 **VI**: 362.
Amos 3: 5 **VI**: 362, 380.
Amos 3: 9-12 **VI**: 380.
Amos 3: 9-4: 3 **VI**: 375.
Amos 3: 10 **V**: 396; **VI**: 8.
Amos 3: 11 **VI**: 380*(2)*.
Amos 3: 12 **VI**: 4, 7, 362, 376, 381*(6)*.
Amos 3: 15 **VI**: 371, 381.
Amos 4: 1-5: 17 **VI**: 380.
Amos 4: 2b **VI**: 381.
Amos 4: 3 **VI**: 7, 376.
Amos 4: 4-13 **VI**: 375, 381.
Amos 4: 5 **VI**: 376.
Amos 4: 6-11 **VI**: 381.
Amos 4: 7 **VI**: 362.
Amos 4: 10 **VI**: 362, 381.
Amos 4: 11 **VI**: 362.
Amos 4: 12 **VI**: 382.
Amos 4: 13 **VI**: 4, 7, 245, 376, 382*(2)*, 722.

Amos 5 **VI**: 382.
Amos 5:1-6 **VI**: 375.
Amos 5:6 **VI**: 11, 376, 382.
Amos 5:7 **VI**: 382.
Amos 5:7-10, 17 **VI**: 375.
Amos 5:8 **VI**: 382.
Amos 5:8-9 **II**: 233; **VI**: 4, 376, 382.
Amos 5:9 **V**: 395; **VI**: 7, 362, 382*(2)*.
Amos 5:9a **VI**: 383*(2)*, 386.
Amos 5:11 **IV**: 188; **VI**: 383.
Amos 5:14 **VI**: 383.
Amos 5:14a **IV**: 45.
Amos 5:16b **VI**: 383*(2)*, 386.
Amos 5:18-27 **VI**: 383.
Amos 5:18-6:14 **VI**: 375; **VI**: 383.
Amos 5:21 **VI**: 383.
Amos 5:21-27 **VI**: 383.
Amos 5:23-24 **VI**: 383.
Amos 5:25 **VI**: 384*(3)*.
Amos 5:25, 26 **VI**: 384*(2)*.
Amos 5:25-27 **VI**: 383, 384.
Amos 5:26 **VI**: 375, 384*(4)*.
Amos 6:1 **VI**: 8, 375.
Amos 6:1-14 **VI**: 384.
Amos 6:1, 2 **VI**: 375.
Amos 6:1-5 **VI**: 4.
Amos 6:2 **VI**: 245, 384*(2)*.
Amos 6:3 **VI**: 10.
Amos 6:5 **I**: *88;* **IV**: *497,* 385*(3)*.
Amos 6:5 **VI**: 362.
Amos 6:9 **VI**: 362.
Amos 6:9-10 **VI**: 385.
Amos 6:10 **VI**: 11, 362, 375, 385.
Amos 6:10 **VI**: 362.
Amos 6:12 **VI**: 385.
Amos 6:14 **VI**: 362.
Amos 7:1-11 **V**: 685.
Amos 7:1-8:3 **VI**: 385.
Amos 7:2 **VI**: 375.
Amos 7:2-3 **VI**: 362.
Amos 7:2, 5 **VI**: 376.
Amos 7:3-4 **VI**: 362.
Amos 7:4 **VI**: 245, 376, 385.
Amos 7:8 **VI**: 362.
Amos 7:9-Mal 2:9 **VI**: 363.
Amos 7:10-17 **VI**: 375, 385.
Amos 7:11 **VI**: 362.
Amos 7:14 **VI**: 383*(2)*, 385*(2)*, 386*(6)*.
Amos 8:1-14 **VI**: 375.
Amos 8:1-2 **VI**: 386.
Amos 8:1-3 **V**: 685; **VI**: 386.
Amos 8:3 **VI**: 362, 375.
Amos 8:3-4 **VI**: 362.
Amos 8:4 **VI**: 362, 386*(2)*.
Amos 8:4-9:7 **VI**: 386.
Amos 8:6 **VI**: 379, 386.
Amos 8:9 **VI**: 5, 379.
Amos 8:12 **VI**: 362.
Amos 8:13 **VI**: 386.
Amos 8:14 **VI**: 387.
Amos 9:1 **VI**: 387.
Amos 9:1-3 **VI**: 387.
Amos 9:1-8a **VI**: 375.
Amos 9:5-14a **IV**: 45
Amos 9:5, 6 **VI**: 4.
Amos 9:5-6 **VI**: 376.
Amos 9:7-15 **VI**: 387.
Amos 9:8-10 **VI**: 375.
Amos 9:8b-15 **VI**: 375.
Amos 9:8-15 **VI**: 387.
Amos 9:9 **VI**: 11.

Amos 9: 10 **VI**: 362.
Amos 9: 11-12 **VI**: 387.
Amos 9: 13 **VI**: 362, 374, 387.
Amos 9: 13-15 **VI**: 387.
Obad 5 **VI**: 362, 388.
Obad 6 **VI**: 11.
Obad 7 **V**: 433; **VI**: 388*(2)*.
Obad 13 **VI**: 362.
Obad 13a **VI**: 388.
Obad 20 **VI**: 388*(3)*.
Jonah 1: 4b **VI**: 388.
Jonah 1: 17 **VI**: 388*(2)*, 389.
Jonah 2 **IX**: cxxxii.
Jonah 2: 1 **VI**: 389.
Jonah 2: 1-10 **VI**: 388, 389.
Jonah 2: 1-4: 11 **VI**: 388.
Jonah 3: 3 **VI**: 389.
Jonah 3: 5 **VI**: 389.
Jonah 3: 10 **VI**: 389.
Jonah 4: 2 **VI**: 245.
Jonah 4: 4 **VI**: 389.
Jonah 4: 6, 10 **VI**: 389, 390.
Jonah 4: 8 **VI**: 389.
Jonah 4: 9 **VI**: 389.
Mic **VI**: 390*(2)*.
Mic 1 **VI**: 390.
Mic 1: 2 **VI**: 390*(2)*.
Mic 1: 5 **VI**: 390.
Mic 1: 6 **VI**: 362.
Mic 1: 6-8 **V**: 694.
Mic 1: 7 **VI**: 4.
Mic 1: 10 **VI**: 391.
Mic 1: 10-11 **VI**: 362.
Mic 1: 10-16 **VI**: 390*(3)*.
Mic 1: 10-12, 13, 14 **VI**: 4.
Mic 1: 12 **VI**: 362, 391.
Mic 1: 13 **VI**: 5.
Mic 1: 14 **VI**: 391.
Mic 1: 16 **VI**: 362.
Mic 2 **VI**: 391.
Mic 2: 1 **VI**: 391.
Mic 2: 1-11 **V**: 685.
Mic 2: 1aαβ **VI**: 391.
Mic 2: 2 **VI**: 391.
Mic 2: 6 **VI**: 11.
Mic 2: 6-11 **VI**: 391.
Mic 2: 12, 13 **VI**: 3.
Mic 3 **V**: 685.
Mic 3 & 4 **VI**: 391.
Mic 3-5 **VI**: 391, 394.
Mic 3: 1 **VI**: 392.
Mic 3: 5-8 **VI**: 392*(2)*.
Mic 4 **VI**: 251, 392; **VIII**: 233.
Mic 4-7 **VI**: 392*(2)*
Mic 4: 1 **VI**: 8, 9; **VIII**: 251.
Mic 4: 1-4 **IV**: 447.
Mic 4: 1-5 **VI**: 252, 392.
Mic 4: 5 **VI**: 252, 392*(2)*.
Mic 4: 8-6(Heb 5) **VI**: 392.
Mic 4: 10 **VI**: 245, 392.
Mic 4: 14 (Heb) **VI**: 393.
Mic 4: 14-5: 5 **VI**: 393.
Mic 5 **VI**: 393*(2)*.
Mic 5: 1 **VI**: 393*(5)*; **VIII**: 283.
Mic 5: 1-3 (Heb) **VI**: 393.
Mic 5: 2 **VI**: 393*(2)*.
Mic 5: 2-4 (Eng.) **VI**: 393.
Mic 5: 2-8 **VI**: 393.
Mic 5: 3-5 **VI**: 4.
Mic 5: 4-5 **VI**: 394.
Mic 5: 9-14 **VI**: 391, 394*(2)*.
Mic 5: 13 **VI**: 7, 3942*)*.
Mic 6 & 7 **VI**: 3942*)*.
Mic 6: 1-8 **VI**: 394*(2)*.
Mic 6: 2 **VI**: 245.
Mic 6: 6-8 **VI**: 394.

Mic 6:8	**IV**: 447; **VI**: 394, 395*(2)*.	Nah 3:18	**VI**: 362.
Mic 6:8, 9	**VI**: 394.	Nah 4:19	**VI**: 362.
Mic 6:10	**VI**: 395.	Nah 6:3	**VI**: 362.
Mic 6:13-16	**VI**: 395.	Nah 8:13	**VI**: 362.
Mic 6:14	**VI**: 395.	Nah 14:3	**VI**: 362.
Mic 7	**VI**: 395.	Hab 1, 2	**VI**: 399, 400.
Mic 7:14-20	**VI**: 395.	Hab 1:3	**VI**: 11, 362.
Mic 7:18	**VI**: 395.	Hab 1:7	**VI**: 362.
Nah 1	**VI**: 396*(2)*.	Hab 1:8	**V**: 394; **VI**: 6, 9, 245, 362.
Nah 1-2:3	**VI**: 396*(3)*; **IX**: cxxxiii.	Hab 1:11	**VI**: 11, 362.
Nah 1:4	**VI**: 396.	Hab 1:13	**VIII**: 456.
Nah 1:5	**VI**: 397.	Hab 1:16, 17	**VI**: 3.
Nah 1:8-10	**VI**: 362.	Hab 2:1	**VI**: 400.
Nah 1:9-2:3	**VI**: 397.	Hab 2:2	**VI**: 245, 288, 400*(6)*.
Nah 1:10	**VI**: 362.	Hab 2:2-4	**VI**: 400.
Nah 1:12	**VI**: 362, 397*(3)*.	Hab 2:3	**V**: 685.
Nah 1:12-2:14	**VI**: 397.	Hab 2:4	**V**: 396; **VI**: 3, 8, 362, 400, 401*(4)*.
Nah 1:14	**VI**: 362.	Hab 2:4-5	**VI**: 400*(3)*.
Nah 2:2	**VI**: 245.	Hab 2:5	**VI**: 11, 362.
Nah 2:3	**VI**: 245.	Hab 2:10	**VI**: 362.
Nah 2:3-4	**VI**: 397.	Hab 2:13-14	**VI**: 401.
Nah 2:4	**VI**: 2, 397*(2)*.	Hab 2:15	**VI**: 3, 10, 11.
Nah 2:6	**VI**: 362, 397.	Hab 2:17	**VI**: 401.
Nah 2:7	**VI**: 397, 398*(2)*.	Hab 2:18	**VI**: 362.
Nah 2:8	**VI**: 398*(7)*, 469.	Hab 3	**VI**: 11, 401*(8)*, 402*(3)*.
Nah 2:11	**V**: 400; **VI**: 10, 398.	Hab 3:2	**VI**: 9, 362, 402.
Nah 2:12	**VI**: 362.	Hab 3:2-19	**VI**: 402.
Nah 2:13	**VI**: 398.	Hab 3:4	**VI**: 4, 362, 402*(2)*.
Nah 2:14	**VI**: 7, 362.	Hab 3:6	**VI**: 9.
Nah 3	**V**: 685.	Hab 3:7	**VI**: 402*(2)*; **VII**: 141.
Nah 3:1-11	**VI**: 398.	Hab 3:9	**VI**: 11.
Nah 3:4	**VI**: 398; **VIII**: 455.	Hab 3:10-11	**VI**: 362.
Nah 3:6	**VI**: 245.	Hab 3:10, 11, 15	**VI**: 402.
Nah 3:8	**VI**: 399*(2)*.	Hab 3:12	**VI**: 362.
Nah 3:11	**VI**: 362, 399.	Hab 3:13	**VI**: 362.
Nah 3:16	**VI**: 362.		

Hab 3:13-15 **VI**: 402.
Hab 3:14 **VI**: 362.
Hab 3:17 **VI**: 362.
Hab 3:17-19 **VI**: 402.
Zeph **VI**: 274, 403.
Zeph 1:9 **VI**: 4, 403.
Zeph 1:14-18 **VI**: 403.
Zeph 1:17 **VI**: 362.
Zeph 1:18 **VI**: 362.
Zeph 2 **V**: 685.
Zeph 2:1 **VI**: 403.
Zeph 2:2 **VI**: 362.
Zeph 2:2-5 **VI**: 253, 403.
Zeph 2:4 **VI**: 362, 403.
Zeph 2:5 **VI**: 362.
Zeph 2:8 **VI**: 403.
Zeph 2:9 **VI**: 245.
Zeph 2:14 **VI**: 403.
Zeph 3:3 **V**: 394; **VI**: 6, 403.
Zeph 3:5 **VI**: 362.
Zeph 3:6 **VI**: 403.
Zeph 3:10 **VI**: 403.
Zeph 3:17 **VI**: 11, 404.
Zeph 3:20 **VI**: 7.
Hag **VI**: 404.
Hag 1:1-5, 13 **VI**: 404.
Hag 1:2 **VI**: 404.
Hag 1:4 **VI**: 11.
Hag 2:7 **VI**: 362, 404*(2)*.
Hag 2:10-14 **VI**: 404.
Hag 2:10-19 **VI**: 404*(2)*.
Hag 2:11-14 **VI**: 405.
Hag 2:14 **VI**: 405*(2)*.
Zech **VI**: 405.
Zech 1-6 **VI**: 406.
Zech 1-8 **I**: *171;* **VI**: 405*(2)*, 406.
Zech 1:1 **VI**: 406.
Zech 1:1-6 **VI**: 406.
Zech 1:7-17 **VI**: 406.
Zech 1:7-6:15 **VI**: 406.
Zech 1:7-6:8 **VI**: 405.
Zech 1:8, 10 **VI**: 406*(2);* **VII**: 268.
Zech 1:15 **VI**: 245.
Zech 1:17LXX **VI**: 405.
Zech 1:18-21 **VI**: 406, 407.
Zech 1:21 **VI**: 7.
Zech 2 **VI**: 407*(2)*
Zech 2:1-5 **VI**: 407.
Zech 2:2 **VI**: 362.
Zech 2:4 **VI**: 245, 362.
Zech 2:12 **VI**: 362, 407.
Zech 2:12 (2:8)E.V. **VI**: 9.
Zech 3 **VI**: 407*(2)*.
Zech 3& 6 **VI**: 407, 408.
Zech 3:4 **VI**: 407.
Zech 3:9 **VI**: 11, 245.
Zech 4:8-10 **VI**: 407.
Zech 5 **VI**: 408*(2)*.
Zech 5:1-4 **VI**: 408.
Zech 5:5f. **VI**: 408.
Zech 5:5-11 **VI**: 408*(4)*.
Zech 6 **VI**: 408.
Zech 6:1ss. **VI**: 406*(2)*, 409; **VII**: 268.
Zech 6:1-7 **VI**: 408.
Zech 6:1-8 **VI**: 408.
Zech 6:3 **VI**: 7.
Zech 6:5LXX **VI**: 405.
Zech 6:6 **VI**: 8.
Zech 6:7 **VI**: 362.
Zech 6:9-15 **VI**: 409*(2)*.
Zech 7:1-8:23 **VI**: 409.
Zech 7:2 **VI**: 362, 409.
Zech 7:4-10 **VI**: 409.
Zech 7:8sq. **VI**: 409.
Zech 8:12 **VI**: 409.
Zech 8:16-19 **VI**: 409.
Zech 8:20-23 **VI**: 410.
Zech 9-11 **VI**: 410.

Zech 9-14 **IV**: 454*(2)*; **VI**: 410*(4)*.
Zech 9:1 **VI**: 410.
Zech 9:1-10 **VI**: 410.
Zech 9:1, 13, 15, 16 **VI**: 4.
Zech 9:2 **VI**: 7.
Zech 9:9 **VI**: 9, 411*(2)*; **VIII**: 285.
Zech 9:9-10 **VI**: 410.
Zech 9:9-10:1 **V**: 685.
Zech 9:16 **VI**: 411, 549.
Zech 10:2 **VI**: 362.
Zech 10:4 **VI**: 411.
Zech 10:7 **VI**: 362.
Zech 10:11 **VI**: 411.
Zech 10:11a **VI**: 411*(2)*.
Zech 11 **IV**: 454; **VI**: 411*(2)*, 412.
Zech 11 & 12 **VI**: 411.
Zech 11:3 **VI**: 7.
Zech 11:4-17 **VI**: 411, 412, 413.
Zech 11:7ss. **I**: *390*; **VI**: 8.
Zech 11:8 **VI**: 412.
Zech 11:12-13 **VI**: 412.
Zech 11:13 **VI**: 412*(2)*; **VIII**: 283.
Zech 11:2 (3) **VI**: 4.
Zech 12 **VI**: 412*(2)*.
Zech 12-13:1 **VI**: 412.
Zech 12:2 **II**: *443*; **VI**: 4, 412.
Zech 12:2-3 **VI**: 12.
Zech 12:8 **VI**: 7.
Zech 12:10 **VI**: 412*(2)*; **VIII**: 298.
Zech 12:11 **VI**: 413*(2)*.
Zech 13:5 **VI**: 362.
Zech 13:6 **VI**: 7.
Zech 13:7 **VI**: 413*(2)*.
Zech 13:7-9 **VI**: 412, 413*(2)*.
Zech 13:8 **VI**: 245.
Zech 14 **VI**: 413*(3)*.
Zech 14:3 **VI**: 7.
Zech 14:4-8 **VI**: 413.
Zech 14:5 **VI**: 413, 414.
Zech 14:9 **VI**: 7.
Zech 14:10 **VI**: 414.
Zech 14:13-14 **VI**: 12.
Zech 14:14 **VI**: 362.
Zech 14:21 **VI**: 414*(2)*; **VIII**: 286.

Mal 1:2, 3 **VI**: 415.
Mal 1:3 **VI**: 362, 414, 415.
Mal 1:6-14 **VI**: 414.
Mal 1:9 **VI**: 414.
Mal 1:11 **VI**: 415*(6)*.
Mal 2:1-19 **VI**: 414.
Mal 2:2-5 **VI**: 414.
Mal 2:3 **VI**: 414.
Mal 2:3LXX **VI**: 415
Mal 2:4 **VI**: 362.
Mal 2:5 **VI**: 362.
Mal 2:6 **VI**: 362.
Mal 2:7 **VI**: 3.
Mal 2:10-16 **VI**: 415.
Mal 2:10-12, 13-16 **VI**: 414.
Mal 2:11 **VI**: 4, 415, 496.
Mal 2:12 **VI**: 414, 415.
Mal 2:15 **VI**: 362.
Mal 2:15a **VI**: 416.
Mal 2:15 (3:4) **VI**: 414.
Mal 2:16 **VI**: 7.
Mal 2:17-3:6 **VI**: 414.
Mal 3 **VI**: 416.
Mal 3:1 **VI**: 416*(2)*; **VIII**: 284.
Mal 3:1-3 **VI**: 416, 417.
Mal 3:1-3 (Heb) **VI**: 416, 417.
Mal 3:1-7b **VI**: 416.
Mal 3:6 **VI**: 11.
Mal 3:7-12, 13-18 **VI**: 414.

Mal 3:10 **VI**: 416.
Mal 3:13-4:3 **VI**: 416.
Mal 3:14 **V**: 447; **VI**: 416.
Mal 3:16-17 **VI**: 417.
Mal 3:17 **VI**: 417.
Mal 3:19-24 (Heb) **VI**: 416, 417.
Mal 4:1-6 **VI**: 414, 416, 417.
Mal 4:2 **VI**: 417.
Mal 4:5 **VI**: 417.
Mal 4:5, 6 **I**: *67;* **VI**: 417*(3);* **VIII**: 297*(2)*.
Mal 4:6 **VI**: 417.
Job **VI**: 419, 420*(6)*.
Job 1&2 **VI**: 421.
Job 1:3 **V**: 400; **VI**: 10.
Job 1-15LXX **IV**: *113*.
Job 1:15 **VI**: 4, 421, 548, 591.
Job 1:17 **VI**: 421*(2)*.
Job 1:21 **VI**: 421.
Job 2:4 **VI**: 419.
Job 2:6 **V**: 400; **VI**: 10.
Job 2:9 **VI**: 422*(4)*.
Job 2:10 **VI**: 9.
Job 3 **VI**: 422*(3)*.
Job 3:3 **VI**: 422.
Job 3:3ff. **V**: 400; **VI**: 10.
Job 3:4, 5 **VI**: 420.
Job 3:8 **VI**: 11, 421, 422.
Job 3:8, 14 **VI**: 419.
Job 3:14 **VI**: 422.
Job 3:19a **VI**: 420.
Job 3:22 **VI**: 9.
Job 3:25 **VI**: 422.
Job 4&5 **VI**: 422.
Job 4-14 **VI**: 422, 424, 425*(2)*, 426, 427.
Job 4:6 **VI**: 420.
Job 4:10 **VI**: 9.
Job 4:12 **VI**: 422.
Job 4:14 **VI**: 421.
Job 4:15 **VI**: 423.
Job 4:16 **VI**: 421.
Job 4:18 **VI**: 423.
Job 4:19b **VI**: 420.
Job 4:19, 20 **VI**: 419.
Job 4:20b **VI**: 420.
Job 5:3 **VI**: 9, 420, 423*(2)*.
Job 5:3f. **VI**: 423.
Job 5:5 **VI**: 5, 8, 423*(2)*.
Job 5:6-8 **VI**: 423.
Job 5:6, 7, 24 **VI**: 420.
Job 5:7 **VI**: 419, 423.
Job 5:8 **VI**: 423.
Job 5:15 **VI**: 8, 421.
Job 5:21 **V**: 453; **VI**: 208, 274, 423*(2)*.
Job 5:23 **VI**: 11, 424.
Job 5:24 **V**: 421, 424.
Job 5:26a **VI**: 420.
Job 6LXX **VI**: 424.
Job 6&7 **VI**: 424.
Job 6:2-3, 13 **VI**: 421.
Job 6:4 **VI**: 421, 424.
Job 6:6 **VI**: 424.
Job 6:7 **VI**: 8.
Job 6:13 **VI**: 419.
Job 6:15 **VI**: 2.
Job 6:15-19 **VI**: 424.
Job 6:16 **VI**: 424, 425.
Job 6:18 **VI**: 419, 421.
Job 6:21 **VI**: 11.
Job 6:25 **VI**: 424*(2)*, 425*(2)*.
Job 7:4 **VI**: 420, 425.
Job 7:5 **VI**: 421.
Job 7:12 **VI**: 425.
Job 7:12, 20 **VI**: 419.

Job 7:15 **VI**: 10, 419, 421, 425.
Job 7:15-16 **VI**: 420.
Job 8 **VI**: 425*(2)*.
Job 8-11 **VI**: 425.
Job 8:6 **VI**: 10.
Job 8:8 **VI**: 421.
Job 8:8, 9 **VI**: 420.
Job 8:11 **VI**: 425.
Job 8:13 **VI**: 4, 420.
Job 8:14 **VI**: 11, 420.
Job 8:16 **VI**: 420.
Job 8:16-17 **VI**: 421.
Job 8:17 **VI**: 419.
Job 8:18 **VI**: 421.
Job 9&10 **VI**: 425*(3)*.
Job 9:3 **VI**: 426.
Job 9:9 **II**: 233; **VI**: 426*(3)*, 439.
Job 9:22 **VI**: 426.
Job 9:23 **VI**: 426.
Job 9:27 **VI**: 421.
Job 9:31 **VI**: 426.
Job 9:35 **VI**: 5.
Job 10:2 **VI**: 421.
Job 10:8 **VI**: 8.
Job 10:15 **VI**: 245, 426.
Job 10:21-22 **VIII**: 265.
Job 10:22 **VI**: 421.
Job 11 **VI**: 426.
Job 11:6 **VI**: 420, 426*(2)*.
Job 11:7, 12 **VI**: 419.
Job 11:12 **VI**: 420, 421, 427.
Job 11:17 **VI**: 420.
Job 11:23 **VI**: 3.
Job 12-14 **VI**: 427.
Job 12:2 **VI**: 11.
Job 12:2-6 **VI**: 420.
Job 12:5 **VI**: 419.
Job 12:6 **VI**: 10.
Job 12:7-9 **VI**: 427.
Job 12:9 **VI**: 7.
Job 12:10 **V**: 537; **VI**: 427; **VIII**: *449*.
Job 12:17 **VI**: 421.
Job 12:19 **VI**: 427.
Job 12:21 **V**: 395; **VI**: 7.
Job 12:23 **VI**: 11.
Job 13:9 **VI**: 5.
Job 13:9-11 **VI**: 427.
Job 13:12b **VI**: 420.
Job 13:14 **VI**: 7, 419.
Job 13:15 **VI**: 420, 427.
Job 13:28 **VI**: 4, 5, 427, 637.
Job 13:28-14:1 **VI**: 420.
Job 14 **VI**: 428*(2)*.
Job 14:4 **VI**: 428*(2)*, 490; **VIII**: 184.
Job 14:5 **VI**: 421.
Job 14:10 **V**: 422; **VI**: 275, 420, 428.
Job 14:12 **VI**: 421, 428.
Job 14:19 **VI**: 11.
Job 14:22 **VI**: 420.
Job 15 **VI**: 428.
Job 15-21 **VI**: 428, 429*(3)*, 432*(2)*.
Job 15:2 **VI**: 420, 421.
Job 15:2LXX **VI**: 428.
Job 15:4 **VI**: 421.
Job 15:5 **VI**: 420.
Job 15:8 **VI**: 421.
Job 15:11 **VI**: 7.
Job 15:12, 33 **VI**: 419.
Job 15:15 **VI**: 428.
Job 15:22 **VI**: 421.
Job 15:24 **VI**: 10.
Job 15:29 **VI**: 420.
Job 15:30c **VI**: 420.
Job 15:31-32a **VI**: 420.
Job 15:33 **VI**: 420.

Job 16	**VI**: 429.
Job 16:4	**VI**: 429.
Job 16:7, 8	**VI**: 420.
Job 16:12	**VI**: 421.
Job 16:18-17:5	**VI**: 419.
Job 16:21	**VI**: 419.
Job 17:1, 11	**VI**: 420.
Job 17:2	**VI**: 421.
Job 17:6	**VI**: 419.
Job 17:7	**VI**: 420, 421.
Job 17:11	**VI**: 429.
Job 17:13	**VI**: 11.
Job 17:14	**VI**: 420.
Job 18	**VI**: 429*(2)*.
Job 18:2	**VI**: 420, 421.
Job 18:3	**VI**: 8.
Job 18:13, 14, 20	**VI**: 419.
Job 18:15	**VI**: 421.
Job 18:17	**VI**: 419.
Job 18:18	**VI**: 420.
Job 18:20	**VI**: 12.
Job 19	**VI**: 429*(3)*.
Job 19:14, 15	**VI**: 420.
Job 19:19	**VI**: 429, 634.
Job 19:20	**VI**: 420, 421.
Job 19:20, 26	**VI**: 421.
Job 19:20, 25-27, 29	**VI**: 419.
Job 19:23, 24	**VI**: 430*(2)*.
Job 19:23-27	**VI**: 430*(6)*.
Job 19:23-29	**VI**: 429.
Job 19:24	**IV**: 95*(2)*, 115; **VI**: 430*(2)*.
Job 19:25	**VI**: 4, 723, 726.
Job 19:25, 26	**VI**: 431.
Job 19:25-27	**VI**: 430*(3)*, 431*(10)*; **VIII**: 260.
Job 19:25-27a	**VI**: 431.
Job 19:25-27LXX	**VI**: 431.
Job 19:25-29	**VI**: 419; **VI**: 430.
Job 19:26	**VI**: 11, 419, 431.
Job 19:27	**VI**: 420.
Job 19:29	**VI**: 420, 431.
Job 20	**VI**: 432.
Job 20&21	**VI**: 431.
Job 20:7	**VI**: 420.
Job 20:11, 21	**VI**: 419.
Job 20:18	**VI**: 8.
Job 20:19	**VI**: 11.
Job 20:23-25	**VI**: 421.
Job 20:24	**VI**: 5.
Job 20:29	**VI**: 11.
Job 21	**VI**: 432.
Job 21:4	**VI**: 11.
Job 21:6	**VI**: 7.
Job 21:14, 15	**VI**: 432.
Job 21:16	**VI**: 420.
Job 21:17	**VI**: 420.
Job 21:21	**VI**: 421.
Job 21:24	**VI**: 420.
Job 21:27	**VI**: 432.
Job 21:30	**VI**: 420.
Job 22	**VI**: 432.
Job 22-26	**VI**: 432, 433*(2)*.
Job 22:11	**VI**: 421.
Job 22:20, 24, 30	**VI**: 419.
Job 22:21	**VI**: 432.
Job 22:22	**VI**: 432.
Job 22:24, 25	**VI**: 432.
Job 22:25	**VI**: 432.
Job 22:26	**VI**: 421.
Job 22:29	**VI**: 11.
Job 22:29-30	**VI**: 432.
Job 22:30	**VI**: 433*(2)*.
Job 23, 24	**VI**: 433.
Job 23:6	**VI**: 8, 11.
Job 23:7	**VI**: 421.
Job 23:10	**VI**: 8, 421*(2)*.
Job 23:11-12	**VI**: 421.
Job 23:17	**VI**: 419, 421.

Job 24-30 **IV**: 471; **VI**: 433.
Job 24:1, 11, 16 **VI**: 419.
Job 24:3, 4, 9 **VI**: 2.
Job 24:5 **VI**: 421.
Job 24:7 **VI**: 421.
Job 24:10, 11 **VI**: 433.
Job 24:10a, 11a **VI**: 421.
Job 24:14 **VI**: 3.
Job 24:17 **VI**: 10, 421.
Job 24:20 **VI**: 12.
Job 24:20a **VI**: 420.
Job 24:24 **VI**: 9*(2)*, 433.
Job 25, 26 **VI**: 433.
Job 25:5 **VI**: 11, 421.
Job 25:7 **VI**: 433*(2)*.
Job 26:5, 12, 13 **VI**: 419.
Job 26:9 **VI**: 421.
Job 26:12-13 **V**: 178; **VI**: 433.
Job 26:12, 13 **VI**: 433.
Job 26:13 **VI**: 421.
Job 27-31 **VI**: 434.
Job 27:8 **VI**: 421*(2)*.
Job 27:12 **VI**: 420.
Job 27:13 **VI**: 3.
Job 27:18 **VI**: 421.
Job 27:19 **VI**: 419.
Job 28 **VI**: 8, 434*(5)*.
Job 28:3, 4, 5 **VI**: 419.
Job 28:4 **VI**: 11*(2)*, 421, 434*(3)*.
Job 28:11 **VI**: 7, 9, 10, 434.
Job 28:18 **VI**: 421.
Job 28:24 **VI**: 3.
Job 28:24 **VI**: 3.
Job 28:27 **VI**: 10.
Job 29-31 **VI**: 434*(2)*, 438.
Job 29:4 **VI**: 435.
Job 29:4, 18 **VI**: 419.
Job 29:14 **VI**: 421.
Job 29:17 **VI**: 421.
Job 29:17-20 **VI**: 421.
Job 29:18 **VI**: 420, 435*(2)*.
Job 29:24 **VI**: 420.
Job 29:25 **VI**: 10.
Job 29:26 **VI**: 435.
Job 30:1 **VI**: 435.
Job 30:2, 24 **VI**: 419.
Job 30:13 **VI**: 421.
Job 30:14 **VI**: 6, 421.
Job 30:18 **VI**: 420.
Job 30:23 **VI**: 11.
Job 30:24 **VI**: 10.
Job 30:24-25 **VI**: 421.
Job 31 **VI**: 435*(4)*.
Job 31:12 **VI**: 421.
Job 31:21 **VI**: 420.
Job 31:23 **VI**: 421.
Job 31:26 **VI**: 420.
Job 31:26-27 **VI**: 435.
Job 31:31, 35 **VI**: 419.
Job 31:33 **VI**: 7.
Job 31:35 **VI**: 421*(2)*.
Job 32 **VI**: 436.
Job 32-37 **IV**: 471; **VI**: 435, 436*(3)*.
Job 32:6 **VI**: 421.
Job 32:6-33:33 **VI**: 436.
Job 32:7 **VI**: 420.
Job 32:9 **VI**: 421.
Job 32:14 **VI**: 420.
Job 32:15 **VI**: 421.
Job 32:19 **VI**: 436.
Job 32:21 **VI**: 2.
Job 33 **VI**: 436.
Job 33:1 **VI**: 421.
Job 33:16 **VI**: 421.
Job 33:17 **VI**: 11.
Job 33:18 **VI**: 436.
Job 33:19, 23, 27 **VI**: 420.
Job 33:21 **VI**: 420.

Job 33: 22	**VI**: 421.
Job 33: 24, 25	**VI**: 3.
Job 33: 27	**VI**: 9, 436.
Job 33: 31-32	**VI**: 426.
Job 34	**VI**: 437.
Job 34: 2	**VI**: 436.
Job 34: 6	**VI**: 436.
Job 34: 13	**VI**: 10, 437, 438.
Job 34: 16	**VI**: 436.
Job 34: 17, 20	**VI**: 421.
Job 34: 20	**VI**: 437.
Job 34: 23, 31, 35	**VI**: 420.
Job 34: 25a	**VI**: 9.
Job 34: 29	**VI**: 10.
Job 34: 37	**VI**: 11.
Job 35	**VI**: 437.
Job 35: 3	**VI**: 436.
Job 35: 14	**VI**: 421.
Job 35: 15	**VI**: 420.
Job 36&37	**VI**: 437.
Job 36: 4	**VI**: 420.
Job 36: 5a	**VI**: 437.
Job 36: 12	**VI**: 437.
Job 36: 14	**VI**: 437.
Job 36: 16ɒ	**VI**: 437.
Job 36: 17	**VI**: 10.
Job 36: 22	**V**: 394; **VI**: 6.
Job 36: 24	**VI**: 436.
Job 36: 27-28	**VI**: 437.
Job 36: 27-33	**VI**: 421.
Job 36: 27-37: 6	**VI**: 10.
Job 36: 32	**VI**: 10.
Job 36: 33	**VI**: 436.
Job 36: 17, 18, 19, 32, 33	**VI**: 420.
Job 37: 1	**VI**: 421.
Job 37: 4, 7, 11	**VI**: 420.
Job 37: 7	**VI**: 436, 438.
Job 37: 9, 10	**VI**: 438*(2)*
Job 37: 12	**VI**: 419, 437, 438.
Job 37: 16	**VI**: 11.
Job 37: 19-21	**VI**: 420.
Job 37: 20-22, 23	**VI**: 420.
Job 37: 22	**VI**: 438.
Job 38: -41	**VI**: 434, 438.
Job 38-42	**VI**: 438*(2)*.
Job 38: 1	**VI**: 439.
Job 38: 1-42: 6	**VI**: 438.
Job 38: 8, 14, 30, 31	**VI**: 420.
Job 38: 11-40: 5	**VI**: 438.
Job 38: 12-15	**II**: 233; **VI**: 439.
Job 38: 14	**VI**: 7.
Job 38: 24	**VI**: 421*(2)*.
Job 38: 24	**VI**: 421.
Job 38: 28	**VI**: 5.
Job 38: 31-32	**II**: 233; **VI**: 439*(3)*.
Job 38: 31-38	**IVI**: 439.
Job 38: 32	**VI**: 439.
Job 38: 36	**VI**: 4, 421.
Job 38: 37	**VI**: 421.
Job 38: 41	**VI**: 421.
Job 39	**VI**: 439.
Job 39: 3	**VI**: 421.
Job 39: 4	**VI**: 10.
Job 39: 4, 9, 13	**VI**: 420.
Job 39: 10	**VI**: 421.
Job 39: 13-18	**VI**: 439.
Job 39: 14	**VI**: 421.
Job 39: 19, 24	**VI**: 420.
Job 39: 19-25	**VI**: 439.
Job 39: 20	**III**: *366;* **VI**: 10.
Job 39: 21	**VI**: 5, 10.
Job 39: 27	**VI**: 11.
Job 40: 2	**VI**: 440*(2)*.
Job 40: 4	**VI**: 440.
Job 40: 6-42: 6	**VI**: 440.
Job 40: 12	**VI**: 440.
Job 40: 15	**VI**: 440.
Job 40: 15, 21	**VI**: 420.
Job 40: 18	**VI**: 421.

Job 40: 19 **VI**: 10.
Job 40: 23&24 **VI**: 440.
Job 40: 29 **VI**: 440.
Job 40: 29b **VI**: 440.
Job 41: 1, 6, 8, 13 **VI**: 420.
Job 41: 4 **VI**: 421.
Job 41: 18, 22, 25, 30 **VI**: 420.
Job 41: 19 **VI**: 5.
Job 41: 21 **VI**: 4.
Job 41: 22 **VI**: 421.
Job 42: 7-17 **VI**: 440*(2)*.
Job 42: 14 **VI**: 441.
Job 42: 17b-17e LXX **VI**: 441.
Pss 1 **IV**: 14, *496;* **V**: 691, 705; **VI**: 449*(15)*, 450*(3)*.
Pss 1-2 **VI**: 448*(2)*, 449; **VIII**: 468.
Pss 1-150 **IV**: 484; **VI**: 446.
Pss 1: 1 **VI**: 2, 442.
Pss 1: 1, 2 **VI**: 450.
Pss 1: 1, 3e, 6a **VI**: 446.
Pss 1: 2 **VI**: 450.
Pss 1: 3d **VI**: 450.
Pss 1: 6 **VI**: 450*(2)*.
Pss 2 **VI**: 450*(8)*, 451*(10)*, 485, 497, 516.
Pss 2: 1 **VI**: 443*(2)*, 451.
Pss 2: 2 **VI**: 443, 445.
Pss 2: 3 **VI**: 450.
Pss 2: 3-5 **VI**: 450, 534.
Pss 2: 4 **VI**: 443, 448.
Pss 2: 4a, 11, 12 **VI**: 446.
Pss 2: 6 **VI**: 535.
Pss 2: 7 **VI**: 11, 452*(3)*.
Pss 2: 9 **VI**: 452*(2)*.
Pss 2: 11 **VI**: 11, 443.
Pss 2: 11, 12 **VI**: 301, 452*(3)*.
Pss 2: 11-12 **VI**: 447.
Pss 2: 12 **V**: 527; **VI**: 443*(2)*, 444, 447, 452*(6)*.
Pss 3 **VI**: 446, 453*(2)*.
Pss 3&4 **VI**: 453.
Pss 3: 2-9 **VI**: 446.
Pss 3: 3 **VI**: 448.
Pss 3: 4 **VI**: 442, 443.
Pss 3: 5 **VI**: 453.
Pss 4 **IV**: 106, *495;* **VI**: 446, 453*(4)*.
Pss 4: 2-9 **VI**: 446, 447.
Pss 4: 3 **VI**: 443.
Pss 4: 4 **VI**: 442, 443, 453, 457.
Pss 4: 5 **VI**: 442, 443, 445.
Pss 4: 6 **VI**: 454*(2)*.
Pss 4: 6-8 **VI**: 453.
Pss 4: 6-9 **VI**: 453.
Pss 4: 7 **VI**: 10, 447, 454.
Pss 4: 7, 8 **VI**: 442.
Pss 4: 7-8 **VI**: 445.
Pss 4: 8 **VI**: 443.
Pss 5 **VI**: 444, 454.
Pss 5&6 **VI**: 454.
Pss 5: 1 **V**: 395; **VI**: 7, 454.
Pss 5: 3 **VI**: 535.
Pss 5: 4 **VI**: 442, 445, 447.
Pss 5: 4b, 5 **VI**: 446.
Pss 5: 5 **VI**: 445*(2)*.
Pss 5: 10 **IV**: *487;* **VI**: 454.
Pss 5: 10 **VI**: 442.
Pss 6 **VI**: 444, 454*(2)*.
Pss 6: 2 **VI**: 7.
Pss 6: 6 **VIII**: 265.

Pss 6:7 **VI**: 444.
Pss 6:8 **VI**: 445.
Pss 6:11 **VI**: 443.
Pss 7 **VI**: 444, 455*(2)*.
Pss 7, 8 **VI**: 454.
Pss 7:1, 2, 17 **VI**: 455*(2)*.
Pss 7:2-18 **VI**: 446.
Pss 7:4 **VI**: 2, 3.
Pss 7:5 **VI**: 445, 447.
Pss 7:5b **VI**: 446.
Pss 7:7 **VI**: 443.
Pss 7:7b-8 **VI**: 445.
Pss 7:8 **VI**: 535.
Pss 7:8&9 **VI**: 443.
Pss 7:10 **VI**: 535.
Pss 7:15 **VI**: 455.
Pss 7:18 **VI**: 535.
Pss 8 **IV**: 490; **VI**: 446, 455*(7)*, 456*(11)*, 465; **VIII**: 287.
Pss 8:1 **VI**: 443.
Pss 8:1 **VI**: 456.
Pss 8:2 **VI**: 8, 443, 453, 456*(2)*, 457.
Pss 8:2b **VI**: 443.
Pss 8:2-3 **VI**: 447.
Pss 8:2b-3 **VI**: 447.
Pss 8:2, 3 **VI**: 456.
Pss 8:3 **V**: 706; **VI**: 535.
Pss 8:4 **VI**: 447, 457.
Pss 8:5 **VI**: 442*(2)*, 443, 447, 457.
Pss 9 **VI**: 457*(4)*.
Pss 9&10 **VI**: 456*(6)*
Pss 9:2(Heb) **VI**: 446.
Pss 9:6 **VI**: 442.
Pss 9:6, 16, 18 **VI**: 447.
Pss 9:7 **VI**: 443.
Pss 9:7c **VI**: 445.
Pss 9:7, 8 **VI**: 7.
Pss 9:8 **VI**: 447.
Pss 9:10 **VI**: 443.
Pss 9:12 **VI**: 7.
Pss 9:15 **VI**: 443.
Pss 9:17 **VI**: 442, 443, 445.
Pss 9:17 **VI**: 442.
Pss 9:20 **VI**: 7.
Pss 9:20, 21 **VI**: 447.
Pss 9:22-39 **VI**: 446.
Pss 10 **VI**: 458*(3)*
Pss 10:1 **VI**: 443, 448.
Pss 10:2-4 **VI**: 448.
Pss 10:3 **VI**: 444, 458.
Pss 10:3, 4 **VI**: 442.
Pss 10:3-4 **VI**: 447.
Pss 10:3-5 **VI**: 445.
Pss 10:4c **VI**: 446.
Pss 10:4 **VI**: 458.
Pss 10:5 **VI**: 447.
Pss 10:6-7 **VI**: 447.
Pss 10:8 **VI**: 445.
Pss 10:8, 10, 14, 15 **VI**: 447.
Pss 10:14 **VI**: 443, 448.
Pss 10:15 **VI**: 443.
Pss 10:17 **VI**: 7, 458.
Pss 10:17-18 **VI**: 458.
Pss 10:18 **VI**: 443.
Pss 10:26 (5) (Heb) **VI**: 446.
Pss 10:38 (17) **VI**: 446.
Pss 11 **VI**: 458*(5)*, 490.
Pss 11:1 **VI**: 6.
Pss 11:2 **VI**: 448.
Pss 11:3 **VI**: 459.
Pss 11:5 **VI**: 444.
Pss 11:6a **VI**: 447.
Pss 11:7b **VI**: 445.
Pss 12 **VI**: 459, 490.
Pss 12:1 **VI**: 525*(2)*, 526*(3)*.

Pss 12:2 **VI**: 447.
Pss 12:3 **VI**: 442, 446.
Pss 12:4 **VI**: 7.
Pss 12:6 **VI**: 2, 3, 459.
Pss 12:6-8 **VI**: 447.
Pss 12:6, 8, 9 **VI**: 443.
Pss 12:7 **VI**: 7, 11, 433, 444, 459*(4)*
Pss 12:7(6) **VI**: 459, 547.
Pss 12:7, 8, 9 **VI**: 459.
Pss 12:8 **VI**: 444, 445.
Pss 12:9 **VI**: 445, 459*(2)*.
Pss 13 **VI**: 458, 459, 490.
Pss 13:1 **VI**: 442.
Pss 13:2 **VI**: 447.
Pss 13:3 **VI**: 419.
Pss 13:3d **VI**: 445.
Pss 13:4b **VI**: 445.
Pss 13:5 **VI**: 445.
Pss 13:5a **VI**: 446.
Pss 13:9 **VI**: 443.
Pss 14 **V**: 405; **VI**: 11, 447, 460*(6)*, 490, 491.
Pss 14 **VI**: 532.
Pss 14&15 **VI**: 460.
Pss 14:1 **VI**: 460*(3)*.
Pss 14:4c **VI**: 446.
Pss 14:4-6 **VI**: 419.
Pss 14:5 **VI**: 3.
Pss 15 **VI**: 159; **VI**: 368, 444, 460*(2)*, 474; **VIII**: 280.
Pss 15:2b **VI**: 446.
Pss 15:2 **VI**: 447, 448.
Pss 15:3 **VI**: 460.
Pss 15:3-4a **VI**: 445.
Pss 15:4c **VI**: 444.
Pss 15:4 (14:4) **VI**: 445, 448.
Pss 15:10 **VI**: 442.
Pss 16 **VI**: 442, 443, 444, 460*(13)*
Pss 16:1-11 **VI**: 446.
Pss 16:1-4 **VI**: 462*(4)*
Pss 16:2 **VI**: 442*(2)*, 443.
Pss 16:2-3 **VI**: 9, 444, 462.
Pss 16:2-4a **VI**: 447.
Pss 16:3 **VI**: 443*(2)*, 444, 462.
Pss 16:3b, 4ab **VI**: 446.
Pss 16:7b, 11, 13, 14 **VI**: 446.
Pss 16:8 **VI**: 448.
Pss 16:8-11 **VI**: 462.
Pss 16:9b-10a **VI**: 445.
Pss 16:9-11 **VI**: 462.
Pss 16:10 **VI**: 442*(3)*, 443, 445, 462*(2)*.
Pss 16:10b **VI**: 462.
Pss 16:11 **VI**: 443, 445, 462, 463; **VIII**: 290.
Pss 16:13b-14a **VI**: 445.
Pss 16:14b **VI**: 445.
Pss 17 **VI**: 443, 444, 447, 461, 463*(6)*.
Pss 17:1 **VI**: 445.
Pss 17:3, 4 **VI**: 2.
Pss 17:3, 11, 14 **VI**: 463.
Pss 17:4 **VI**: 10, 445, 448.
Pss 17:4-5 **VI**: 445.
Pss 17:5 **VI**: 448.
Pss 17:5, 9, 12, 27b **VI**: 446.
Pss 17:9 **VI**: 445.
Pss 17:10 **VI**: 447.
Pss 17:10-12, 15 **VI**: 463*(2)*.
Pss 17:11 **VI**: 445.
Pss 17:12 **VI**: 445.
Pss 17:13 **VI**: 11.
Pss 17:13, 14 **VI**: 442.

Pss 17:14	**VI**: 443, 447.
Pss 17:15	**VI**: 2, 442, 444, 463*(2)*.
Pss 17:35b, 36c	**VI**: 446.
Pss 17:46	**VI**: 445.
Pss 18	**VI**: 216*(3)*, 443, 463, 464*(5)*, 708.
Pss 18, 19, 20	**VI**: 463.
Pss 18:2-3	**VI**: 447.
Pss 18:3	**VI**: 7.
Pss 18:4, 5	**VI**: 442.
Pss 18:4- 5	**VI**: 464.
Pss 18:6-16	**VI**: 464; **VIII**: 102.
Pss 18:8b, 12b, 14	**VI**: 446.
Pss 18:9	**VI**: 447.
Pss 18:12-13	**VI**: 447.
Pss 18:14	**VI**: 448, 535.
Pss 18:26	**VI**: 442, 447.
Pss 18:27	**VI**: 445.
Pss 18:29	**VI**: 443.
Pss 18:30	**VI**: 464.
Pss 18:35	**VI**: 10, 445.
Pss 18:36	**IV**: 108; **VI**: 216, 464*(2)*.
Pss 18:43	**VI**: 445.
Pss 18:44, 49	**VI**: 447.
Pss 18:45	**VI**: 464.
Pss 18:46	**VI**: 445.
Pss 19	**V**: 700; **VI**: 3, 443, 465*(13)*.
Pss 19A	**VI**: 456, 465.
Pss 19:1-6	**VI**: 465.
Pss 19:2	**VI**: 535.
Pss 19:2, 7	**V**: 687; **VI**: 444.
Pss 19:3	**VI**: 4, 442, 447.
Pss 19:4b	**VI**: 444.
Pss 19:4	**VI**: 466.
Pss 19:4, 5	**VI**: 466.
Pss 19:5	**VI**: 7, 466.
Pss 19:6	**VI**: 446.
Pss 19:7-9	**VI**: 466.
Pss 19:10	**VI**: 466.
Pss 19:11	**VI**: 442.
Pss 19:12	**VI**: 466.
Pss 19:12, 13	**VI**: 466.
Pss 19:14	**VI**: 466.
Pss 19:15	**VI**: 448.
Pss 19:7-8LXX	**IV**: 9.
Pss 20	**VI**: 466*(2)*.
Pss 20:2	**VI**: 467.
Pss 20:3	**VI**: 467.
Pss 20:4-6	**VI**: 467.
Pss 20:5	**VI**: 442.
Pss 20:6	**VI**: 445.
Pss 20:7	**VI**: 467.
Pss 20:7-10	**VI**: 467.
Pss 20:8	**VI**: 444.
Pss 20:10	**VI**: 7, 444.
Pss 20:10a, 13	**VI**: 446.
Pss 20:12	**VI**: 445.
Pss 20:15	**VI**: 444.
Pss 21	**VI**: 444, 467*(2)*.
Pss 21(22)	**VI**: 468
Pss 21&22	**VI**: 467.
Pss 21:1	**VI**: 7.
Pss 21:2	**VI**: 445.
Pss 21:2b, 3, 11, 12	**VI**: 446.
Pss 21:3	**VI**: 3; **IX**: cxxxvi.
Pss 21:6	**VI**: 442, 467, 547.
Pss 21:8	**VI**: 448.
Pss 21:10	**VI**: 445, 467*(2)*.
Pss 21:16a, 18a,	**VI**: 446.
Pss 21:30a	**VI**: 446.
Pss 22	**I**:*72;* **IV**: *415,* 484; **VI**: 446, 467, 468*(10);* **VIII**: 281, 292.
Pss 22:1	**VI**: 443.

Pss 22: 1(Heb) 23:1 **VI**: 468.
Pss 22: 3 **VI**: 3, 8.
Pss 22: 8 **VI**: 442*(2)*, 443.
Pss 22: 9 **VI**: 7, 419.
Pss 22: 10 **VI**: 468.
Pss 22: 13 (12) **VI**: 468.
Pss 22: 13 (12)LXX **IV**: 27; **VI**: 469.
Pss 22: 15 **VI**: 11.
Pss 22: 16 **VI**: 469*(3)*.
Pss 22: 16-17 **VI**: 445.
Pss 22: 16(Heb) 17 **VI**: 469.
Pss 22: 16-20 **VI**: 4.
Pss 22: 17 **VI**: 443, 444*(2)*, 469*(5)*.
Pss 22: 17b **VI**: 469.
Pss 22: 18 **VI**: 419.
Pss 22: 18 (17) **VI**: 444.
Pss 22: 20 **VI**: 447.
Pss 22: 22 **VI**: 442, 448.
Pss 22: 23 **VI**: 444.
Pss 22: 24 **VI**: 447.
Pss 22: 25 **VI**: 445, 469.
Pss 22: 26 **VI**: 447.
Pss 22: 26 (25) **VI**: 444.
Pss 22: 28-32 **VI**: 469.
Pss 22: 29 **VI**: 442, 443, 470; **VIII**: 284.
Pss 22: 29-31 **VI**: 470.
Pss 22: 30 **VI**: 445.
Pss 22: 31 **VI**: 535.
Pss 23 **IV**: *497;* **V**: 400, 705; **VI**: 470*(10)*, 471*(17)*, 472*(8)*; **VIII**: 279; **IX**: cxlviii.
Pss 23&24 **VI**: 470.
Pss 23: 1 **VI**: 443, 472.
Pss 23: 1-3 **VI**: 472.
Pss 23: 3f. **IV**: 114; **VI**: 472.
Pss 23: 4 **I**: *390;* **VI**: 2, 8, 472*(2)*.
Pss 23: 5 **VI**: 7, 473*(2)*.
Pss 23: 6 **VI**: 473*(2)*.
Pss 24 **IV**: *498;* **VI**: 368, 444, 447, 460; **VI**: 473*(9)*, 474, 526; **VIII**: 369.
Pss 24LXX **VI**: 473.
Pss 24: 1 **VI**: 446.
Pss 24: 2 **VI**: 443*(2)*.
Pss 24: 6 **VI**: 11, 159, 443, 444.
Pss 24: 7ff. **VI**: 474.
Pss 25 **IV**: 484; **VI**: 474*(2)*, 479.
Pss 25, 26, 27 **VI**: 474.
Pss 25: 6, 7, 10 **VI**: 442.
Pss 25: 8 **VI**: 446.
Pss 25: 11 **VI**: 443.
Pss 25: 13 **VI**: 447.
Pss 25: 18-19 **VI**: 445.
Pss 25: 20 **VI**: 2.
Pss 25: 22 **VI**: 444.
Pss 26 **VI**: 474*(2)*.
Pss 26: 1-12 **VI**: 446.
Pss 26: 2 **VI**: 444.
Pss 26: 6 **VI**: 447.
Pss 26: 6bc, 12 **VI**: 446.
Pss 26: 9 **VI**: 444.
Pss 27 **VI**: 474*(3)*.
Pss 27: 1, 4, 5 **VI**: 474.
Pss 27: 3 **VI**: 445.
Pss 27: 3b **VI**: 446.
Pss 27: 4c **VI**: 444.
Pss 27: 5 **VI**: 448.
Pss 27: 8 **VI**: 9, 419, 444, 447.
Pss 27: 8-9 **VI**: 445.
Pss 27: 12 **VI**: 447.
Pss 27: 13 **VI**: 2.

Pss 28	**V**: 687; **VI**: 444, 446, 474, 475*(2)*.
Pss 28&29	**VI**: 474.
Pss 28: 3-12Q	**VIII**: 448.
Pss 28: 4, 5	**VI**: 442.
Pss 28: 5	**VI**: 444.
Pss 28: 7	**VI**: 5.
Pss 28: 9a	**VI**: 446.
Pss 28: 26	**VI**: 442.
Pss 29	**V**: 687, 691, 706; **VI**: 444, 475*(7)*, 476.
Pss 29: 1	**VI**: 443, 447.
Pss 29: 2	**VI**: 443, 444, 447, 475, 592.
Pss 29: 3	**VI**: 7, 444.
Pss 29: 7a, 8a	**VI**: 446.
Pss 29: 8	**VI**: 476*(3)*, 535.
Pss 29: 9, 10	**VI**: 442.
Pss 29: 10	**VI**: 476.
Pss 29: 11	**VI**: 447.
Pss 29: 22, 25, 27, 28	**VI**: 442.
Pss 30	**VI**: 444, 476*(2)*.
Pss 30&31	**VI**: 476.
Pss 30: 3c- 4a	**VI**: 446.
Pss 30: 4	**VI**: 442.
Pss 30: 8	**VI**: 444.
Pss 30: 12, 18b	**VI**: 446.
Pss 30: 13	**VI**: 444.
Pss 30: 13a	**VI**: 445.
Pss 31	**VI**: 476*(2)*.
Pss 31: 2-25	**VI**: 446.
Pss 31: 4b, 6ab, 7	**VI**: 446.
Pss 31: 6-7	**IV**: *43*.
Pss 31: 7	**VI**: 447, 535.
Pss 31: 7, 16, 21	**VI**: 442.
Pss 31: 10	**VI**: 447.
Pss 31: 10-13	**IV**: *43*.
Pss 31: 13	**VI**: 444.
Pss 31: 14	**VI**: 445.
Pss 31: 14-17	**IV**: *43*.
Pss 31: 15	**VI**: 476.
Pss 31: 19	**VI**: 476.
Pss 31: 19-23	**IV**: *43*.
Pss 31: 20	**VI**: 477*(3)*.
Pss 31: 21	**VI**: 11, 444.
Pss 31: 22	**VI**: 447, 448.
Pss 32	**VI**: 477*(6)*.
Pss 32&33	**VI**: 477.
Pss 32: 1-11	**VI**: 446.
Pss 32: 1-2	**VI**: 477.
Pss 32: 3	**VI**: 477.
Pss 32: 4	**VI**: 535.
Pss 32: 5	**VI**: 448.
Pss 32: 6	**VI**: 447, 535.
Pss 32: 7	**VI**: 477.
Pss 32: 8b	**VI**: 447.
Pss 32: 8	**VI**: 478.
Pss 32: 8, 9	**VI**: 444.
Pss 32: 9	**VI**: 7, 443*(2)*, 445, 447, 478*(3)*.
Pss 32: 11	**VI**: 478.
Pss 32: 21	**VI**: 5.
Pss 33	**IV**: 491*(2)*; **VI**: 478*(7)*.
Pss 33: 4, 8, 11, 17	**VI**: 442.
Pss 33: 15	**VI**: 444.
Pss 33: 16	**VI**: 444.
Pss 33: 19	**VI**: 448.
Pss 33: 22	**VI**: 446.
Pss 33: 34	**VI**: 3.
Pss 34	**VI**: 447, 474, 478, 479*(4)*, 532.
Pss 34: 1	**VI**: 479.
Pss 34: 1-6	**VI**: 448.
Pss 34: 3	**VI**: 479.
Pss 34: 4	**VI**: 444.
Pss 34: 8	**VI**: 479.
Pss 34: 10	**VI**: 479.
Pss 34: 11	**VI**: 479.

Pss 34: 14, 17b	**VI**: 446.
Pss 34: 18	**VI**: 444.
Pss 34: 20	**VI**: 445.
Pss 34: 20b	**VI**: 446.
Pss 34: 21	**VI**: 479.
Pss 34: 22	**VI**: 535.
Pss 35	**VI**: 479.
Pss 35: 2	**VI**: 535.
Pss 35: 3	**VI**: 445, 480.
Pss 35: 3, 6a, 8a	**VI**: 446.
Pss 35: 10	**VI**: 447.
Pss 35: 11	**VI**: 11.
Pss 35: 11a	**VI**: 446.
Pss 35: 12	**VI**: 445.
Pss 35: 13	**VI**: 447, 480.
Pss 35: 13, 18	**VI**: 447.
Pss 35: 14	**VI**: 3, 444, 445.
Pss 35: 14a	**VI**: 447.
Pss 35: 15	**VI**: 444, 447, 480
Pss 35: 15-17	**VI**: 445.
Pss 35: 15, 16, 21	**VI**: 443.
Pss 35: 16	**V**: 435; **VI**: 480.
Pss 35: 17	**V**: 394; **VI**: 6, 444, 535.
Pss 35: 20c	**VI**: 447.
Pss 36	**VI**: 480*(2)*.
Pss 36: 1	**VI**: 443.
Pss 36: 1a, 7c, 8b	**VI**: 446.
Pss 36: 2	**VI**: 444.
Pss 36: 3	**VI**: 443, 445.
Pss 36: 3 (2)	**VI**: 444.
Pss 36: 3b, 7cd	**VI**: 446.
Pss 36: 6	**VI**: 448.
Pss 36: 7, 8	**VI**: 442.
Pss 36: 8	**VI**: 535.
Pss 36: 8, 9	**VI**: 442.
Pss 36: 8a	**VI**: 447.
Pss 36: 14c, 20bc	**VI**: 446.
Pss 36: 23, 34d, 35	**VI**: 446.
Pss 37	**VI**: 480*(2)*, 488, 498; **VIII**: 458.
Pss 37: 1-10	**VI**: 446.
Pss 37: 3	**VI**: 444, 447.
Pss 37: 5	**VI**: 419.
Pss 37: 7	**VI**: 480.
Pss 37: 8	**VI**: 442, 445.
Pss 37: 8, 13a	**VI**: 446.
Pss 37: 13	**VI**: 535.
Pss 37: 18	**VI**: 535.
Pss 37: 18, 20	**VI**: 446.
Pss 37: 20	**VI**: 444.
Pss 37: 22	**VI**: 7.
Pss 37: 23	**VI**: 444.
Pss 37: 26	**VI**: 447.
Pss 37: 35	**VI**: 11, 445.
Pss 37: 37	**VI**: 444, 480.
Pss 37: 37-38	**VI**: 447.
Pss 37: 38	**VI**: 443, 535.
Pss 37: 40	**VI**: 444, 535.
Pss 38	**VI**: 444, 481.
Pss 38: 3a, 4b	**VI**: 446.
Pss 38: 8	**VI**: 444.
Pss 38: 10	**VI**: 445.
Pss 38: 11	**VI**: 481.
Pss 38: 12	**VI**: 445.
Pss 38: 13	**VI**: 445.
Pss 38: 13, 14	**VI**: 442.
Pss 38: 14	**VI**: 535.
Pss 38: 15	**VI**: 448.
Pss 38: 17	**VI**: 2.
Pss 38: 19	**VI**: 2.
Pss 39	**VI**: 444, 481.
Pss 39: 2,, 5b, 7b	**VI**: 446.
Pss 39: 3	**VI**: 443, 445.
Pss 39: 3-4	**VI**: 447.
Pss 39: 4	**VI**: 447.
Pss 39: 5, 6	**VI**: 3.
Pss 39: 6	**VI**: 11.
Pss 39: 6b	**VI**: 445.
Pss 39: 7	**VI**: 9.

Pss 39: 7b	**VI**: 445.	Pss 42: 3	**VI**: 442, 483.
Pss 39: 13	**V**: 407; **VI**: 47, 481.	Pss 42: 4	**VI**: 442, 443, 445.
Pss 39: 13b	**VI**: 445.	Pss 42: 4b	**VI**: 446.
Pss 39: 18	**VI**: 7.	Pss 42: 4, 6	**VI**: 484.
Pss 40	**VI**: 448, 481*(4)*.	Pss 42: 4b, 9	**VI**: 447.
		Pss 42: 5	**VI**: 443 *(2)*.
Pss 40-72	**VI**: 481.	Pss 42: 7	**VI**: 444, 484.
Pss 40: 3	**VI**: 481, 535.	Pss 42: 7-12	**VI**: 445.
Pss 40: 4b	**VI**: 445.	Pss 42: 7-8	**V**: 706.
Pss 40: 4b, 7b	**VI**: 446.	Pss 42: 8	**VI**: 443, 444.
Pss 40: 5	**VI**: 444.	Pss 42: 10	**VI**: 444.
Pss 40: 6	**VI**: 481, 482.	Pss 42: 11	**VI**: 535.
Pss 40: 7-8	**VI**: 482.	Pss 43	**VI**: 484; **VIII**: 372.
Pss 40: 7c-8a	**VI**: 445.		
Pss 40: 8	**VI**: 3, 444, 482.	Pss 43: 1	**VI**: 444.
		Pss 43: 2	**VI**: 447.
Pss 40: 8a, 13a	**VI**: 446.	Pss 43: 4	**VI**: 484.
Pss 40: 9	**VI**: 443.	Pss 43: 5	**VI**: 446.
Pss 40: 9b	**VI**: 445.	Pss 43: 19b	**VI**: 445.
Pss 40: 10	**VI**: 535.	Pss 43: 20-23LXX	**VI**: 484.
Pss 40: 11, 12	**VI**: 2.	Pss 44	**IV**: *497;* **VI**: 4, 444, 484.
Pss 40: 14	**VI**: 482.		
Pss 41	**VI**: 444, 482*(4)*.	Pss 44: 2-27	**VI**: 446.
		Pss 44: 3	**VI**: 447.
Pss 41&42	**VI**: 482.	Pss 44: 5	**VI**: 444.
Pss 41: 2	**VI**: 482.	Pss 44: 5d	**VI**: 445.
Pss 41: 3	**VI**: 442, 482.	Pss 44: 6	**VI**: 444.
Pss 41: 4	**VI**: 445.	Pss 44: 6, 14, 15	**VI**: 446.
Pss 41: 4b	**VI**: 447.	Pss 44: 9	**VI**: 445.
Pss 41: 5b	**VI**: 446.	Pss 44: 14a	**VI**: 445.
Pss 41: 6-10	**VI**: 482.	Pss 44: 17-22	**VI**: 448.
Pss 41: 7c	**VI**: 445.	Pss 44: 19	**VI**: 447.
Pss 41: 7	**VI**: 447.	Pss 44: 20	**VI**: 442.
Pss 41: 9	**VI**: 10, 11, 445.	Pss 45	**IV**: 484; **VI**: 442, 443, 484*(4)*, 485*(6)*.
Pss 42	**VI**: 446, 483*(2);* **VIII**: 372.	Pss 45: 3	**VI**: 442, 443, 448.
Pss 42&43	**VI**: 483*(2)*.	Pss 45: 4-5	**VI**: 445.
Pss 42- 43	**VI**: 483*(3)*.	Pss 45: 4cd, 5b	**VI**: 446.
Pss 42-72	**VI**: 483*(2)*.	Pss 45: 5	**VI**: 444, 445, 535.
Pss 42: 1	**VI**: 442, 483.		

Pss 45: 6 **VI**: 443, 485.
Pss 45: 6(MT 7) **VI**: 485.
Pss 45: 7a **VI**: 7.
Pss 45: 7 **VI**: 154, 485*(5)*.
Pss 45: 8 **VI**: 442, 485.
Pss 45: 9 **VI**: 445, 486*(2)*, 572*(2)*.
Pss 45: 11 **VI**: 5, 7.
Pss 45: 13 **VI**: 442, 443.
Pss 45: 14 **VI**: 445.
Pss 45: 16 **VI**: 445, 486.
Pss 45: 18 **VI**: 5.
Pss 45: 23 **VI**: 4.
Pss 46 **VI**: 486*(6)*; **IX**: cxxxii.
Pss 46: 1 **VI**: 486.
Pss 46: 2-12 **VI**: 446.
Pss 46: 3 **VI**: 7, 448, 486.
Pss 46: 5 **VI**: 447, 535.
Pss 46: 5a (4a EV) **VI**: 486.
Pss 46: 6 **VI**: 444, 535.
Pss 46: 7, 11 EV **VI**: 487.
Pss 46: 8, 12 **VI**: 487.
Pss 46: 10 **VI**: 443, 535.
Pss 46: 10b **VI**: 445.
Pss 47 **VI**: 487.
Pss 47: 1 **VI**: 444.
Pss 47: 2-10 **VI**: 446.
Pss 47: 3 **VI**: 444.
Pss 47: 3, 5 **VI**: 442.
Pss 47: 3c, 5, 6 **VI**: 446.
Pss 47: 3, 8a , 10c **VI**: 487.
Pss 48 **VI**: 447, 487*(2)*.
Pss 48 (47) **VI**: 487.
Pss 48 (49) **VI**: 536.
Pss 48: 2 **VI**: 3; **IX**: cxxxvi.
Pss 48: 2-15 **VI**: 446.
Pss 48: 3 **VI**: 443, 444.
Pss 48: 4 **VI**: 444.
Pss 48: 8 **VI**: 10, 200, 217, 487.
Pss 48: 8a **VI**: 445.
Pss 48: 8, 9 **VI**: 442.
Pss 48: 9 **VI**: 487, 488, 535.
Pss 48: 9b-11a **VI**: 445.
Pss 48: 10 **VI**: 7, 444.
Pss 48: 12a **VI**: 447.
Pss 48: 12, 15-17 **VI**: 11.
Pss 48: 13, 21 **VI**: 446.
Pss 48: 14 **VI**: 442, 445.
Pss 48: 14, 15cd **VI**: 446.
Pss 48: 14b **VI**: 445.
Pss 48: 15 **VI**: 535.
Pss 48: 17 **VI**: 442.
Pss 48: 18 **VI**: 3.
Pss 49 **VI**: 442, 443, 444, 461, 480, 487*(2)*, 488*(3)*, 498.
Pss 49 (50) **VI**: 536.
Pss 49: 1-11 **VI**: 446.
Pss 49: 1,2 **VI**: 150, 151, 488*(3)*.
Pss 49: 3 **VI**: 488.
Pss 49: 5 **VI**: 7, 447.
Pss 49: 5, 14 **VI**: 443.
Pss 49: 6 **VI**: 444.
Pss 49: 7 **VI**: 488.
Pss 49: 8-10 **VI**: 443.
Pss 49: 8, 9 **VI**: 3.
Pss 49: 9-10 **VI**: 445.
Pss 49: 10b **VI**: 446.
Pss 49: 11 E.V.10 **VI**: 5.
Pss 49: 12 **VI**: 444, 488.
Pss 49: 14 **VI**: 444, 445.
Pss 49: 15 **VI**: 3, 44, 488, 489, 501, 505*(2)*.
Pss 49: 15-16 **VI**: 488.
Pss 49: 19 **VI**: 535.
Pss 49: 23b **VI**: 445.

Pss 50 **VI**: 488, 489*(3)*.
Pss 50ט **VI**: 489.
Pss 50: 1-23 **VI**: 446.
Pss 50: 3, 8 **VI**: 446.
Pss 50: 6 **VI**: 535.
Pss 50: 7-9 **VI**: 447.
Pss 50: 11 **VI**: 535.
Pss 50: 18 **VI**: 5.
Pss 50: 19 **VI**: 7.
Pss 50: 20 **VI**: 445, 488, 489.
Pss 50: 21 **VI**: 489.
Pss 50: 22 **VI**: 447.
Pss 50: 23 **VI**: 535.
Pss 51 **IV**: *497;* **VI**: 443, 447, 489*(7);* **VIII**: 253.
Pss 51m **VI**: 489.
Pss 51-100 **VI**: 448.
Pss 51: 2 **VI**: 7.
Pss 51: 2, 7 **VI**: 442.
Pss 51: 3 **VI**: 442.
Pss 51: 3bc **VI**: 447.
Pss 51: 4 **VI**: 5, 489, 490.
Pss 51: 5 **VI**: 490*(2)*.
Pss 51: 6 **VI**: 7.
Pss 51: 6b-7 **VI**: 447.
Pss 51: 7 **VI**: 428, 490; **VIII**: 184.
Pss 51: 7ab, 9cd **VI**: 447.
Pss 51: 8 **VI**: 445, 447.
Pss 51: 8 (10) **VI**: 448.
Pss 51: 10 (12). **VI**: 448.
Pss 51: 12 **VI**: 445, 490.
Pss 51: 12, 13 **VI**: 490.
Pss 51: 12 (14) **VI**: 448.
Pss 51: 16 **VI**: 447.
Pss 51: 17 **VI**: 490.
Pss 52 **VI**: 458, 490.
Pss 52: 7 **VI**: 447.
Pss 52: 9 **VI**: 445.
Pss 52: 10 **VI**: 535.
Pss 52: 11 **VI**: 444.
Pss 53 **IV**: 481; **V**: 405; **VI**: 11, 443, 447, 460*(3)*, 490*(4)*, 491.
Pss 53: 5 **VI**: 3.
Pss 53: 6 **VI**: 535.
Pss 54: 1 **VI**: 7.
Pss 54: 1-4 **VI**: 491.
Pss 54: 4b, 9, 10a **VI**: 447.
Pss 54: 9 **VI**: 535.
Pss 54: 10b-15, 15b
Pss 54: 20c **VI**: 445.
Pss 54: 22a-b **VI**: 445.
Pss 55 **VI**: 443, 491*(3)*.
Pss 55: 3 **VI**: 444.
Pss 55: 4 **VI**: 445, 491.
Pss 55: 5 **IV**: 188.
Pss 55: 5a, 8a **VI**: 447.
Pss 55: 7c-8c **VI**: 445.
Pss 55: 9ab **VI**: 447.
Pss 55: 9-10a **VI**: 445.
Pss 55: 11-12 **VI**: 447.
Pss 55: 13 **VI**: 444.
Pss 55: 14 (13) **VI**: 491.
Pss 55: 15 **VI**: 442*(2)*.
Pss 55: 15-16 **VI**: 445.
Pss 55: 16 **VI**: 448.
Pss 55: 17 **VIII**: 202.
Pss 55: 19 **VI**: 3.
Pss 55: 19-20 **VI**: 445.
Pss 55: 22 **VI**: 4, 535.
Pss 55: 23 **VI**: 11.
Pss 56 **VI**: 443, 491.
Pss 56: 4-5 **VI**: 447.
Pss 56: 5b **VI**: 445.
Pss 56: 6 **VI**: 444, 491.
Pss 56: 8 **VI**: 491.
Pss 56: 9 **VI**: 445, 447.

Pss 56: 11 **VI**: 445.
Pss 57 **VI**: 491.
Pss 57: 2 **VI**: 444.
Pss 57: 2a, 8b, 10. **VI**: 447.
Pss 57: 4, 5 **VI**: 443, 492*(2)*.
Pss 57: 4-5 **VI**: 492.
Pss 57: 7 **VI**: 445.
Pss 57: 10 **VI**: 445.
Pss 57: 12 **VI**: 444.
Pss 57: 12a **VI**: 445.
Pss 58 **VI**: 447.
Pss 58: 1 **VI**: 443.
Pss 58: 1 (2) **VI**: 448.
Pss 58: 2 **VI**: 445.
Pss 58: 2, 10 **VI**: 443.
Pss 58: 2 (3) **VI**: 448.
Pss 58: 3 **VI**: 444, 447
Pss 58: 5 **III**: *366;* **VI**: 10; **IX**: cxlviii*(3)*.
Pss 58: 6 **VI**: 442.
Pss 58: 7 **VI**: 419, 448, 492.
Pss 58: 8 **VI**: 442, 444, 445.
Pss 58: 8a, 10a **VI**: 447.
Pss 58: 9 **VI**: 442, 492.
Pss 58: 9a **VI**: 7.
Pss 58: 10 (9) **VI**: 492.
Pss 58: 11 **VI**: 448.
Pss 58: 11-12 **VI**: 447.
Pss 59: 1-4 **VI**: 448.
Pss 59: 5 **VI**: 445.
Pss 59: 8 **VI**: 447, 448.
Pss 59: 10, 11a **VI**: 3.
Pss 59: 10a-b **VI**: 445.
Pss 59: 11 **VI**: 535.
Pss 59: 12 **VI**: 445, 448, 492*(2)*.
Pss 59: 13 **VI**: 445.
Pss 59: 14 **VI**: 442, 448.
Pss 59: 18 **VI**: 535.
Pss 60 **VI**: 446.
Pss 60: 3 **VI**: 447.
Pss 60: 3-13 **VI**: 446.
Pss 60: 4 (6) **VI**: 448.
Pss 60: 5 **VI**: 444.
Pss 60: 6 **VI**: 11, 445.
Pss 60: 6 (5) **VI**: 443.
Pss 60: 7 **VI**: 445, 492.
Pss 60: 8 **VI**: 448, 492.
Pss 60: 8 (6) **VI**: 444.
Pss 60: 10 **VI**: 492.
Pss 61 **VI**: 492.
Pss 61: 3 **VI**: 444.
Pss 61: 4c-d **VI**: 445.
Pss 61: 5a-b **VI**: 445.
Pss 61: 10c **VI**: 445.
Pss 62 **VI**: 444, 493.
Pss 62: 3 **VI**: 444.
Pss 62: 8 **VI**: 445.
Pss 62: 9 **VI**: 2.
Pss 62: 11b **VI**: 445.
Pss 62: 12 **VI**: 493.
Pss 63 **VI**: 448, 493*(2)*.
Pss 63: 1 **VI**: 5.
Pss 63: 1 (2) **VI**: 448.
Pss 63: 4b **VI**: 445.
Pss 63: 6 (7m) **VI**: 493.
Pss 63: 7 **VI**: 447.
Pss 63: 7 (8) **VI**: 448.
Pss 63: 7b-c **VI**: 445.
Pss 63: 8-9a **VI**: 445.
Pss 63: 9 **VI**: 150, 488.
Pss 63: 9-10 **VI**: 493.
Pss 64: 2, 8 **VI**: 447.
Pss 64: 4b **VI**: 445.
Pss 64: 4 **VI**: 445.
Pss 64: 5 **VI**: 448.
Pss 64: 6 **VI**: 444, 535.
Pss 64: 6-7 **VI**: 444.
Pss 64: 7 **VI**: 445.
Pss 64: 7-9 **VI**: 419, 443.

Pss 64: 8 (9)	**VI**: 448.
Pss 64: 9	**VI**: 444.
Pss 64: 14a	**VI**: 445.
Pss 65	**V**: 687; **VI**: 444, 516.
Pss 65: 2-3 (3-4)	**VI**: 448.
Pss 65: 3	**IV**: 113; **VI**: 451, 485, 493*(2)*, 497.
Pss 65: 3b	**VI**: 445.
Pss 65: 5 (6)	**VI**: 448.
Pss 65: 6	**VI**: 443, 447.
Pss 65: 6 (7)	**VI**: 448.
Pss 65: 8 (9)	**VI**: 448.
Pss 65: 10 (11)	**VI**: 448.
Pss 65: 12 (13)	**VI**: 448.
Pss 65: 13	**VI**: 445.
Pss 65: 14	**VI**: 493.
Pss 66: 7	**VI**: 7, 448.
Pss 66: 9	**VI**: 2, 444.
Pss 66: 11	**VI**: 445.
Pss 66: 12	**VI**: 444, 448.
Pss 67	**VI**: 443, 493.
Pss 67ט	**VI**: 494*(2)*.
Pss 67: 5b	**VI**: 445.
Pss 67: 6	**VI**: 442.
Pss 67: 7	**VI**: 445.
Pss 67: 9	**VI**: 2.
Pss 67: 9b, 12, 14a	**VI**: 447.
Pss 67: 10a	**VI**: 445.
Pss 67: 12	**VI**: 445.
Pss 67: 13	**VI**: 445.
Pss 67: 14	**VI**: 445.
Pss 67: 15	**VI**: 445.
Pss 67: 16-17a	**VI**: 445.
Pss 67: 16, 18, 19c, 23	**VI**: 447.
Pss 67: 19	**VI**: 445.
Pss 67: 21	**VI**: 445.
Pss 67: 23	**VI**: 445.
Pss 67: 24b	**VI**: 445.
Pss 67: 27b	**VI**: 445.
Pss 67: 28a	**VI**: 445.

Pss 67: 28b, 29, 30	**VI**: 447.
Pss 67: 31	**VI**: 445.
Pss 67: 31c, 35, 36a	**VI**: 447.
Pss 68	**VI**: 443, 493, 494*(11)*, 529.
Pss 68: 4	**VI**: 9, 494.
Pss 68: 5	**VI**: 3, 6, 10, 445, 494.
Pss 68: 5cd, 13, 14cd	**VI**: 447.
Pss 68: 6	**VI**: 448.
Pss 68: 9	**VI**: 535.
Pss 68: 10	**VI**: 494.
Pss 68: 11	**VI**: 442, 444, 445.
Pss 68: 11-14	**VI**: 495.
Pss 68: 12-15	**VI**: 4.
Pss 68: 13	**VI**: 495*(2)*.
Pss 68: 13 (14)	**VI**: 448.
Pss 68: 14	**VI**: 11, 444, 495.
Pss 68: 15	**VI**: 444*(2)*, 495, 535.
Pss 68: 16	**VI**: 442.
Pss 68: 18	**VI**: 446, 495, 535.
Pss 68: 18 (19)s	**VI**: 495.
Pss 68: 19	**VI**: 6, 448.
Pss 68: 20	**VI**: 445.
Pss 68: 22	**VI**: 448.
Pss 68: 23	**VI**: 495.
Pss 68: 23-29	**VI**: 447.
Pss 68: 23, 33	**VI**: 447.
Pss 68: 24	**VI**: 11, 445.
Pss 68: 25	**VI**: 445.
Pss 68: 26 (27)	**VI**: 448.
Pss 68: 28	**V**: 394; **VI**: 5, 8, 445.
Pss 68: 28, 31	**VI**: 495.
Pss 68: 28-32	**VI**: 495*(2)*.
Pss 68: 34 (35)	**VI**: 448.
Pss 68: 35	**VI**: 445, 447.
Pss 69	**VI**: 496.
Pss 69 (68ט)	**VI**: 496.

Pss 69: 2-37 **VI**: 446.
Pss 69: 3 **VI**: 496.
Pss 69: 4 **VI**: 444, 447.
Pss 69: 5 **VI**: 10, 415, 496*(2)*.
Pss 69: 6 **VI**: 444.
Pss 69: 7 **VI**: 535.
Pss 69: 9 **VI**: 442, 444.
Pss 69: 11 **VI**: 444, 445.
Pss 69: 13 **VI**: 445.
Pss 69: 13 (14) **VI**: 448.
Pss 69: 15 **VI**: 445.
Pss 69: 20 **VI**: 3.
Pss 69: 21 **VI**: 444.
Pss 69: 21 (22) **VI**: 448.
Pss 69: 22-25, 26, 28 **VI**: 442.
Pss 69: 33 **VI**: 444.
Pss 70 **VI**: 443.
Pss 70: 3, 6c, 14b **VI**: 447.
Pss 70: 15c **VI**: 445.
Pss 70: 15c, 21a **VI**: 447.
Pss 71 **IV**: *115;* **VI**: 496*(2)*, 498.
Pss 71: 6 **VI**: 442.
Pss 71: 6a **VI**: 445.
Pss 71: 6-12 **VI**: 445.
Pss 71: 6, 15 **VI**: 445.
Pss 71: 7 **VI**: 444.
Pss 71: 7b **VI**: 445.
Pss 71: 9, 12 **VI**: 447.
Pss 71: 10 **VI**: 445.
Pss 71: 16 **VI**: 10.
Pss 71: 16a **VI**: 445.
Pss 71: 18 **VI**: 496.
Pss 71: 20 **VI**: 444, 535.
Pss 71: 20, 21 **VI**: 3.
Pss 71: 21 **VI**: 444.
Pss 71: 22 **VI**: 444.
Pss 72 **VI**: 443, 451, 485, 496*(4)*, 497*(2)*, 516.
Pss 72 (71) **VI**: 497*(2)*.
Pss 72: 1 **VI**: 497.
Pss 72: 1, 4, 14, 21 **VI**: 447.
Pss 72: 3 **VI**: 444, 445.
Pss 72: 6 **VI**: 444, 445.
Pss 72: 8 **VI**: 444.
Pss 72: 9 **VI**: 497*(2)*.
Pss 72: 10 **VI**: 448.
Pss 72: 15 **VI**: 497.
Pss 72: 16 **VI**: 10, 445*(2)*, 497.
Pss 72: 17 **VI**: 497*(2)*.
Pss 72: 20 **VI**: 3.
Pss 73 **IV**: *115;* **VI**: 443, 444, 448, 461, 496, 497, 498*(4)*; **IX**: cxlviii, cxlix.
Pss 73-83 **VI**: 497.
Pss 73-150 **VI**: 446*(2)*.
Pss 73: 1 **VI**: 444.
Pss 73: 1-12 **VI**: 446.
Pss 73: 3a, 4, 5, 6 **VI**: 447.
Pss 73: 4 **VI**: 443.
Pss 73: 5a **VI**: 445.
Pss 73: 7 **VI**: 446, 498*(2)*.
Pss 73: 8 **VI**: 444.
Pss 73: 8b, 14, 19, 20b **VI**: 447.
Pss 73: 9 **VI**: 498.
Pss 73: 10 **VI**: 444, 498.
Pss 73: 13 **VI**: 448.
Pss 73: 14b **VI**: 445.
Pss 73: 15 **VI**: 498.
Pss 73: 17ff. **VI**: 498.
Pss 73: 20 **VI**: 446.
Pss 73: 23 **VI**: 535.
Pss 73: 24 **VI**: 446, 448, 498.
Pss 74 **II**: 122; **IV**: 95,*498;* **VI**: 4, 499*(4)*.
Pss 74: 1 **VI**: 446*(2)*, 499*(2)*.
Pss 74: 1-23 **VI**: 446.

Pss 74: 3 **VI**: 446.
Pss 74: 3a **VI**: 445.
Pss 74: 4 **VI**: 499.
Pss 74: 4, 5 **VI**: 499.
Pss 74: 5 **VI**: 444, 499*(3)*.
Pss 74: 6 **V**: 402, 615; **VI**: 446.
Pss 74: 7 **VI**: 445.
Pss 74: 9 **VI**: 499.
Pss 74: 9a **VI**: 444.
Pss 74: 9b **VI**: 445.
Pss 74: 11 **VI**: 500.
Pss 74: 12-17 **VI**: 444.
Pss 74: 13-15 **VI**: 500.
Pss 74: 14 **VI**: 500.
Pss 74: 15 **VI**: 500.
Pss 74: 19 **VI**: 9*(2)*, 443, 500.
Pss 74: 20 **VI**: 446.
Pss 74: 23 **VI**: 500.
Pss 74: 41 **V**: 531.
Pss 75: 3 **VI**: 535.
Pss 75: 3 (4) **VI**: 448.
Pss 75: 4, 5 **VI**: 442.
Pss 75: 4 (5) **VI**: 448.
Pss 75: 6 **VI**: 9.
Pss 75: 6, 8b **VI**: 447.
Pss 75: 7 **VI**: 446.
Pss 75: 9 **VI**: 7, 10, 500.
Pss 75: 10 **VI**: 446.
Pss 75: 11-13 **VI**: 447.
Pss 75: 9(8) **IV**: 492.
Pss 76 **VI**: 500*(2)*.
Pss 76: 3 **VI**: 500.
Pss 76: 5 **VI**: 443.
Pss 76: 5a, 11a **VI**: 447.
Pss 76: 5-6 **VI**: 446.
Pss 76: 5 (6) **VI**: 448.
Pss 76: 10 **VI**: 7, 501.
Pss 76: 11 **VI**: 11, 444.
Pss 76: 12 **VI**: 446.
Pss 76: 13 **VI**: 535.
Pss 77 **IV**: *498;* **VI**: 501*(2)*.
Pss 77: 5 **V**: 461; **VI**: 446, 501.
Pss 77: 6 **VI**: 535.
Pss 77: 7 **VI**: 445, 535.
Pss 77: 7, 12 **VI**: 444.
Pss 77: 10 **VI**: 5.
Pss 77: 11 **VI**: 444.
Pss 77: 11, 17-20 **VI**: 443.
Pss 77: 25a, 63b **VI**: 447.
Pss 77: 69a **VI**: 445.
Pss 78 **VI**: 446.
Pss 78: 6-7 **VI**: 447.
Pss 78: 7 **VI**: 535.
Pss 78: 8a, 9 **VI**: 447.
Pss 78: 9 **VI**: 7.
Pss 78: 12 **VI**: 444.
Pss 78: 26 **VI**: 448.
Pss 78: 31 **VI**: 444.
Pss 78: 41 **VI**: 501.
Pss 78: 42 **VI**: 535.
Pss 78: 43 **VI**: 442.
Pss 78: 46 **VI**: 448.
Pss 78: 48 **VI**: 444.
Pss 78: 49 **VI**: 446.
Pss 78: 49-50 **VI**: 447.
Pss 78: 63 **VI**: 444.
Pss 78: 63 (66) **VI**: 443.
Pss 78: 65 **VI**: 7, 444.
Pss 78: 67 **VI**: 446.
Pss 78: 69 **VI**: 444, 535.
Pss 78: 70-71 **VI**: 535.
Pss 78: 71 **VI**: 442.
Pss 79: 1-3 **VI**: 446.
Pss 79: 2 **VI**: 444.
Pss 79: 11 **VI**: 535.
Pss 79: 14b **VI**: 445.
Pss 79: 16-18 **VI**: 447.
Pss 80 **IV**: *498;* **VI**: 442.

Pss 80: 3a	**VI**: 447.
Pss 80: 4 (5)	**VI**: 448.
Pss 80: 5	**VI**: 445.
Pss 80: 6	**VI**: 446.
Pss 80: 6b, 6c, 7a	**VI**: 447.
Pss 80: 7	**VI**: 488, 489, 501, 505*(2)*.
Pss 80: 10 (11)	**VI**: 448.
Pss 80: 13	**VI**: 501.
Pss 80: 14	**VI**: 501.
Pss 80: 14, 17, 19	**VI**: 443.
Pss 80: 15	**VI**: 447.
Pss 80: 16	**VI**: 444, 446.
Pss 80: 16-18	**VI**: 501.
Pss 80: 17	**VI**: 447.
Pss 80: 19	**VI**: 444, 535.
Pss 81	**IV**: 339; **V**: 18; **VI**: 443, 447, 502*(4)*.
Pss 81: 4	**VI**: 5.
Pss 81: 5 (6)	**VI**: 448.
Pss 81: 6	**VI**: 5, 444.
Pss 81: 6 (7)	**VI**: 448.
Pss 81: 7	**VI**: 447, 502.
Pss 81: 8	**VI**: 4, 448.
Pss 81: 8c	**VI**: 447.
Pss 81: 11	**VI**: 444.
Pss 81: 15	**VI**: 448.
Pss 81: 16	**VI**: 445, 502.
Pss 81: 17	**VI**: 444.
Pss 82	**VI**: 447, 502*(7)*, 503, 716; **VIII**: 289*(2)*, 290.
Pss 82: 1	**VI**: 444.
Pss 82: 4b, 10b	**VI**: 447.
Pss 82: 5	**VI**: 503.
Pss 82: 6	**VI**: 443, 535.
Pss 82: 7	**VI**: 444, 503.
Pss 82: 12a	**VI**: 447.
Pss 83	**VI**: 480, 488, 498, 503.
Pss 83: 2	**VI**: 535.
Pss 83: 6	**VI**: 535.
Pss 83: 6, 7	**VI**: 447.
Pss 83: 6-8	**VI**: 445.
Pss 83: 11	**VI**: 448.
Pss 83: 13 (14)	**VI**: 448.
Pss 83: 16	**VI**: 535.
Pss 83: 17	**VI**: 446*(2)*.
Pss 83: 19	**VI**: 447.
Pss 84	**VI**: 503*(7)*.
Pss 84: 3	**VI**: 503*(2)*, 535.
Pss 84: 4	**VI**: 443, 504.
Pss 84: 4, 5	**VI**: 504.
Pss 84: 4-7	**VI**: 504.
Pss 84: 6	**VI**: 445.
Pss 84: 6 (7)	**VI**: 448.
Pss 84: 6-8	**VI**: 504*(3)*.
Pss 84: 7	**VI**: 446, 504.
Pss 84: 9	**VI**: 2.
Pss 84: 10	**VI**: 504*(2)*.
Pss 84: 11	**VI**: 446, 504*(2)*.
Pss 84: 14b	**VI**: 447.
Pss 85	**VI**: 445, 504, 505.
Pss 85: 1 (2)	**VI**: 448.
Pss 85: 2b, 3, 11b	**VI**: 447.
Pss 85: 4	**VI**: 446.
Pss 85: 5	**VI**: 446.
Pss 85: 8 (9)	**VI**: 448.
Pss 85: 9	**VI**: 10, 446, 505*(3)*.
Pss 85: 11	**VI**: 445.
Pss 85: 13	**VI**: 442.
Pss 85: 14	**VI**: 11, 488, 489, 501, 505*(2)*.
Pss 86	**VI**: 505.
Pss 86(87)	**VI**: 447.
Pss 86: 2	**VI**: 448.
Pss 86: 4-7	**VI**: 445.
Pss 86: 6	**VI**: 444.
Pss 86: 7	**VI**: 447*(2)*.

Pss 86: 9-11 **VI**: 446.
Pss 87 **VI**: 505*(4)*.
Pss 87: 1 **VI**: 505.
Pss 87: 1, 3 **VI**: 443.
Pss 87: 2, 6b **VI**: 447.
Pss 87: 4 **VI**: 448.
Pss 87: 4, 5, 6 **VI**: 506.
Pss 87: 5 **VI**: 445, 446.
Pss 87: 6 **VI**: 535.
Pss 87: 6a **VI**: 445.
Pss 87: 7 **VI**: 535.
Pss 87: 11b **VI**: 445.
Pss 87: 139 **VI**: 445.
Pss 88 **VI**: 444, 506.
Pss 88: 4 **VI**: 9, 506.
Pss 88: 6 **VI**: 446*(2)*; **VIII**: 265.
Pss 88: 8 **VI**: 446.
Pss 88: 10 **VI**: 446.
Pss 88: 10a **VI**: 447.
Pss 88: 16 **VI**: 446.
Pss 88: 17 **VI**: 7, 446.
Pss 88: 18 (19) **VI**: 448.
Pss 88: 19 **VI**: 447.
Pss 88: 20b, 48b **VI**: 447.
Pss 88: 34b **VI**: 445.
Pss 88: 36b **VI**: 445.
Pss 88: 45a **VI**: 445.
Pss 88: 51b **VI**: 447.
Pss 88: 87, 16 **VI**: 443.
Pss 89 **V**: 706; **VI**: 444, 506*(2)*.
Pss 89: 1, 2, 14, 24 **VI**: 442.
Pss 89: 3 **VI**: 535.
Pss 89: 3, 50 **VI**: 447.
Pss 89: 5, 6b **VI**: 447.
Pss 89: 8 **VI**: 535.
Pss 89: 9 **VI**: 446, 506.
Pss 89: 9c **VI**: 445.
Pss 89: 10 **VI**: 446, 506*(2)*.
Pss 89: 10, 17bc **VI**: 447.
Pss 89: 10d **VI**: 445.
Pss 89: 11 **VI**: 535.
Pss 89: 12 **VI**: 445.
Pss 89: 13 **VI**: 506*(2)*.
Pss 89: 18 **VI**: 535.
Pss 89: 19 **VI**: 448.
Pss 89: 20 **VI**: 444.
Pss 89: 28, 33, 49 **VI**: 442.
Pss 89: 34 **VI**: 446.
Pss 89: 44 **VI**: 446, 448.
Pss 89: 48 **VI**: 535.
Pss 89: 51 **VI**: 443., 444.
Pss 90 **VI**: 507*(5)*; **IX**: cxlviii, cxlix.
Pss 90 (Heb. 91) **IV**: *495*.
Pss 90: 1, 2 **VI**: 507.
Pss 90: 2 **VI**: 446, 535.
Pss 90: 3 **VI**: 442, 507*(2)*.
Pss 90: 3b **VI**: 445.
Pss 90: 4c **VI**: 447.
Pss 90: 4-6 **VI**: 12, 445.
Pss 90: 4, 5, 9 **VI**: 443.
Pss 90: 5 **VI**: 507.
Pss 90: 6 **VI**: 444.
Pss 90: 6b-c **VI**: 445.
Pss 90: 7 **VI**: 446.
Pss 90: 9 **VI**: 444, 448, 507.
Pss 90: 10 **VI**: 10, 445, 446, 507*(2)*.
Pss 90: 12 **VI**: 442, 508*(2)*.
Pss 90: 17 **VI**: 508.
Pss 90: 5-6, 10, 16 **VI**: 10.
Pss 91 **VI**: 443, 508*(5)*, 509.
Pss 91: 1, 2 **VI**: 443.
Pss 91: 1, 2, 3-8 **VI**: 508.
Pss 91: 3 **VI**: 444.
Pss 91: 6 **V**: 453; **VI**: 208, 274, 423, 508, 535.

Pss 91: 9a, 9b-13	**VI**: 508.	Pss 96: 1	**VI**: 510, 721.
Pss 91: 11a	**VI**: 445.	Pss 96: 1-13	**VI**: 446.
Pss 91: 11	**VI**: 447.	Pss 96: 4-6	**VI**: 448.
Pss 91: 12b	**VI**: 445.	Pss 96: 8	**VI**: 448.
Pss 91: 14	**VI**: 508.	Pss 96: 9	**VI**: 475, 510, 592.
Pss 91: 15b	**VI**: 445.	Pss 96: 10	**VI**: 535.
Pss 91: 15	**VI**: 447, 448.	Pss 96: 10a	**VI**: 447.
Pss 91: 16	**VI**: 448.	Pss 96: 10 (95: 10ט)	**VI**: 511.
Pss 92	**VI**: 447, 509.	Pss 96: 13	**VI**: 448, 535.
Pss 92: 1, 2	**VI**: 509.	Pss 97	**VI**: 444.
Pss 92: 3 (4)	**VI**: 448.	Pss 97: 1-12	**VI**: 446.
Pss 92: 4	**VI**: 447.	Pss 97: 3ab	**VI**: 447.
Pss 92: 9	**VI**: 447.	Pss 97: 6-10	**VI**: 446.
Pss 92: 16	**VI**: 447.	Pss 97: 9	**VI**: 447.
Pss 93	**VI**: 444, 447, 509*(2)*.	Pss 97: 10	**VI**: 448, 511.
Pss 93: 1	**VI**: 444, 446, 509.	Pss 97: 11	**VI**: 2, 511*(3)*.
Pss 93: 3	**VI**: 442.	Pss 97: 13	**VI**: 442.
Pss 93: 4	**VI**: 509.	Pss 98	**VI**: 444, 511*(2)*.
Pss 93: 5	**VI**: 509.	Pss 98: 1-9	**VI**: 446.
Pss 93: 15b	**VI**: 445.	Pss 98: 2	**VI**: 446, 447.
Pss 93: 20b	**VI**: 445.	Pss 98: 3	**VI**: 535.
Pss 94	**VI**: 447, 508, 509*(2)*.	Pss 98: 4b	**VI**: 445.
Pss 94: 1-23	**VI**: 446.	Pss 98: 4a	**VI**: 447.
Pss 94: 8	**VI**: 535.	Pss 99	**VI**: 444, 511*(3)*, 522.
Pss 94: 10	**VI**: 444.	Pss 99: 1	**VI**: 446.
Pss 94: 10, 11	**VI**: 7.	Pss 99: 1-9	**VI**: 446.
Pss 94: 17, 21	**VI**: 443.	Pss 99: 2, 8a	**VI**: 447.
Pss 94: 19	**VI**: 510.	Pss 99: 3	**VI**: 443.
Pss 94: 20	**VI**: 448.	Pss 99: 3b	**VI**: 445.
Pss 94: 21	**VI**: 444.	Pss 99: 7	**VI**: 448.
Pss 95	**VI**: 510*(5)*.	Pss 99: 8	**VI**: 511.
Pss 95: 1-11	**VI**: 446.	Pss 100	**VI**: 444, 512*(2)*.
Pss 95: 4	**VI**: 444, 510.	Pss 100: 3	**VI**: 512.
Pss 95: 4, 7, 8	**VI**: 443.	Pss 100: 4	**VI**: 447.
Pss 95: 6	**VI**: 510.	Pss 100: 7c	**VI**: 445.
Pss 95: 7	**VI**: 442, 447.	Pss 100: 8a	**VI**: 445.
Pss 95: 10	**VI**: 448.	Pss 101	**VI**: 512.
Pss 96	**VI**: 443, 444, 510.	Pss 101-150	**VI**: 448.

Pss 101: 1	**VI**: 444.
Pss 101: 2, 3, 8a, 9b	**VI**: 447.
Pss 101: 5	**VI**: 446, 512.
Pss 101: 11b	**VI**: 445.
Pss 102	**VI**: 512.
Pss 102: 4	**VI**: 444.
Pss 102: 5-6, 14	**VI**: 447.
Pss 102: 8	**VI**: 444, 446.
Pss 102: 12 (13)	**VI**: 448.
Pss 102: 16, 17	**VI**: 442.
Pss 102: 18	**VI**: 444.
Pss 102: 24-25	**VI**: 445.
Pss 102: 24-25, 28	**VI**: 447.
Pss 102: 27	**VI**: 446*(2)*.
Pss 102: 29	**VI**: 535.
Pss 103	**VI**: 512*(3)*.
Pss 103: 1, 2	**VI**: 512.
Pss 103: 4, 10, 17b	**VI**: 447.
Pss 103: 5	**VI**: 444, 448, 512.
Pss 103: 11	**VI**: 444.
Pss 103: 17b	**VI**: 445.
Pss 103: 20	**VI**: 442.
Pss 103: 25a	**VI**: 445.
Pss 103: 26b	**VI**: 445.
Pss 103: 35c	**VI**: 447.
Pss 104	**V**: 687, 706; **VI**: 444, 513*(5)*.
Pss 104: 1a	**VI**: 513.
Pss 104: 3a	**VI**: 448.
Pss 104: 3b	**VI**: 448.
Pss 104: 4	**VI**: 513, 535; **VIII**: 296.
Pss 104: 6	**VI**: 445.
Pss 104: 8	**VI**: 444, 447, 513.
Pss 104: 10	**VI**: 535.
Pss 104: 10-30	**VI**: 513.
Pss 104: 11	**VI**: 446, 535.
Pss 104: 13	**VI**: 11.
Pss 104: 16	**VI**: 513*(2)*.
Pss 104: 18	**VI**: 447, 535.
Pss 104: 25-26	**VI**: 9, 513.
Pss 104: 26	**VI**: 448, 514.
Pss 104: 28b	**VI**: 445.
Pss 105	**VI**: 514, 534.
Pss 105: 4	**VI**: 448.
Pss 105: 4, 5, 7d	**VI**: 447.
Pss 105: 7c	**VI**: 445.
Pss 105: 11	**VI**: 514.
Pss 105: 11f.	**VI**: 447.
Pss 105: 15	**VI**: 514.
Pss 105: 15b, 19b	**VI**: 447.
Pss 105: 22	**VI**: 446.
Pss 105: 23-25	**VI**: 514.
Pss 105: 24	**VI**: 7.
Pss 105: 28	**VI**: 446, 448.
Pss 105: 35	**VI**: 446.
Pss 105: 43	**VI**: 535.
Pss 106	**VI**: 514.
Pss 106: 3, 43a, b	**VI**: 447.
Pss 106: 7	**VI**: 444, 446.
Pss 106: 15-20	**IV**: *43*.
Pss 106: 28	**VI**: 448.
Pss 106: 37	**VI**: 444.
Pss 106: 38	**VI**: 444.
Pss 106: 39	**VI**: 444, 535.
Pss 106: 43	**VI**: 419, 446.
Pss 106: 48	**VI**: 3.
Pss 107: Q	**VI**: 515; **VIII**: 457.
Pss 107: 1, 8, 15	**VI**: 442.
Pss 107: 10a	**VI**: 445.
Pss 107: 17ff.	**VI**: 448.
Pss 107: 21, 31, 43	**VI**: 442.
Pss 108: 6b	**VI**: 445.
Pss 108: 6-20	**VI**: 447.
Pss 108: 7	**VI**: 446.
Pss 108: 8	**VI**: 492, 515.
Pss 108: 10	**VI**: 442.
Pss 108: 11. 12	**VI**: 443.
Pss 108: 23b	**VI**: 445.

Pss 109 **VI**: 443, 515*(7)*; **VIII**: 141.
Pss 109-113 **IV**: *494*.
Pss 109:3 **VI**: 445.
Pss 109:3, 5b **VI**: 447.
Pss 109:6-19 **VI**: 515*(2)*.
Pss 109:7 **VI**: 445.
Pss 109:10 **VI**: 448, 516.
Pss 109:11 **VI**: 535.
Pss 109:21 **VI**: 448.
Pss 109:21-22 **VI**: 516.
Pss 109:23 **VI**: 5.
Pss 109:24 **VI**: 446.
Pss 109:29 **VI**: 535.
Pss 109:39a **VI**: 447.
Pss 110 **IV**: *497(3), 498;* **VI**: 3, 443, 451, 485, 497, 516*(13)*, 517*(17)*; **VIII**: 279, 286; **IX**: cxlix.
Pss 110:2 **VI**: 444, 446.
Pss 110:2b **VI**: 445.
Pss 110:3 **VI**: 12, 442, 518*(5)*.
Pss 110:3b **VI**: 518.
Pss 110:4 **VI**: 7, 518.
Pss 110:5 **VI**: 448.
Pss 110:6 **VI**: 11.
Pss 110:7 **VI**: 518*(2)*.
Pss 111&? **VI**: 518.
Pss 111:2 **VI**: 535.
Pss 112:4 **VI**: 448.
Pss 112:4, (10) **VI**: 443.
Pss 113 **VI**: 518.
Pss 113-118 **VI**: 518*(2)*.
Pss 113:2 **VI**: 519.
Pss 113:3 **VI**: 446*(2)*.
Pss 113:5-6 **VI**: 519.
Pss 113:6 **VI**: 447.
Pss 113:10 **VI**: 443.
Pss 113:14a **VI**: 445.
Pss 114 **V**: 705; **VI**: 519*(2)*.
Pss 114-115 **VI**: 447.
Pss 114:4&6 **VI**: 519.
Pss 114:4-6 **VI**: 519.
Pss 115 **VI**: 443, 519.
Pss 115:9-12 **VI**: 446.
Pss 115:11a **VI**: 447.
Pss 115:12 **VI**: 447.
Pss 115:17 **VIII**: 265.
Pss 116 **VIII**: 384.
Pss 116:1-19 **VI**: 446, 519.
Pss 116:2 **VI**: 535.
Pss 116:3 **VI**: 442.
Pss 116:6 **VI**: 5, 519.
Pss 116:10 **VI**: 442, 446; **VIII**: 293.
Pss 116:10, 11 **VI**: 443.
Pss 116:10-11 **VI**: 519.
Pss 116:11 **VI**: 442, 520.
Pss 116:12 **VI**: 447.
Pss 116:14, 18 **VI**: 446.
Pss 117 **VI**: 520*(2)*.
Pss 117: (1) **VI**: 443.
Pss 117:10b, 11b **VI**: 447.
Pss 117:12b **VI**: 447.
Pss 117:20LXX **VI**: 520.
Pss 117:27b **VI**: 445.
Pss 118 **IV**: *497;* **VI**: 443, 520*(3)*.
Pss 118Q **VI**: 520.
Pss 118-127 **VI**: 4.
Pss 118:2-4 **VI**: 446.
Pss 118:10 **VI**: 520.
Pss 118:10-12 **VI**: 447.
Pss 118:12 **VI**: 445, 447, 448.
Pss 118:15 **VI**: 520.
Pss 118:16 **VI**: 444.
Pss 118:20 **VI**: 520.
Pss 118:22-23 **VI**: 520*(2)*.
Pss 118:24 **VI**: 520.

Pss 118: 25	**VI**: 521.
Pss 118: 27	**VI**: 443, 444, 448, 521*(4)*.
Pss 118: 27b	**VI**: 521.
Pss 118: 38a, 66a	**VI**: 447.
Pss 118: 69a, 82, 83b	**VI**: 447.
Pss 118: 70a	**VI**: 445.
Pss 118: 83a	**VI**: 445.
Pss 118: 89b, 119a	**VI**: 447.
Pss 118: 110	**VI**: 9.
Pss 118: 128, 138	**VI**: 447.
Pss 118: 138	**VI**: 445.
Pss 119	**VI**: 448, 511, 521*(9)*, 522*(4)*; **VIII**: 296; **IX**: cxxxii.
Pss 119: 1-8	**VI**: 522.
Pss 119: 9-16	**VI**: 522.
Pss 119: 17-24	**VI**: 522.
Pss 119: 25-32	**VI**: 522.
Pss 119: 28	**VI**: 522, 535.
Pss 119: 30	**VI**: 445.
Pss 119: 33-112	**VI**: 522.
Pss 119: 43	**VI**: 7.
Pss 119: 48	**VI**: 448.
Pss 119: 50	**VI**: 442.
Pss 119: 56	**VI**: 448.
Pss 119: 83	**VI**: 523, 532.
Pss 119: 83, 91, 147	**VI**: 443.
Pss 119: 85	**VI**: 523.
Pss 119: 96	**VI**: 523.
Pss 119: 98-99	**VI**: 523.
Pss 119: 105	**VI**: 523.
Pss 119: 106	**VI**: 442.
Pss 119: 109	**VI**: 448.
Pss 119: 113-128	**VI**: 523.
Pss 119: 117	**VI**: 445.
Pss 119: 118	**VI**: 445.
Pss 119: 119	**VI**: 448.
Pss 119: 122	**VI**: 523.
Pss 119: 126	**VI**: 443.
Pss 119: 129-136	**VI**: 523.
Pss 119: 130	**VI**: 445, 448.
Pss 119: 137-144	**VI**: 523.
Pss 119: 139	**VI**: 448.
Pss 119: 140	**VI**: 448.
Pss 119: 144	**VI**: 524.
Pss 119: 145-152	**VI**: 524.
Pss 119: 147-148	**VI**: 448.
Pss 119: 161-176	**VI**: 524.
Pss 119: 165	**VI**: 445.
Pss 120title	**VI**: 448.
Pss 120	**VI**: 525; **IX**: cxxxii.
Pss 120(121)	**VI**: 447.
Pss 120 & 121	**VI**: 524.
Pss 120-123	**VI**: 524.
Pss 120-134	**VI**: 443, 524*(5)*.
Pss 120: (2)	**VI**: 443.
Pss 120: 3m	**VI**: 525.
Pss 120: 4	**VI**: 448.
Pss 120: 5	**VI**: 2.
Pss 120: 5, 6	**VI**: 525.
Pss 120: 7	**VI**: 446, 525.
Pss 121	**VI**: 446, 525*(6)*; **IX**: cxxxii.
Pss 121: 1-2	**VI**: 525.
Pss 121: 1, 3	**VI**: 443.
Pss 121: 3	**VI**: 445.
Pss 121: 5	**VI**: 526, 535.
Pss 121: 5, 6	**VI**: 526.
Pss 122	**VI**: 448, 526; **IX**: cxxxii.
Pss 122: (2), 4, (5), 6	**VI**: 443.
Pss 123	**VI**: 526; **IX**: cxxxii.
Pss 123: 2	**VI**: 526.
Pss 123: 4	**VI**: 445.
Pss 124	**VI**: 473, 526.
Pss 124: 1	**VI**: 446.
Pss 124: 3	**VI**: 443.
Pss 124: 7	**VI**: 446.
Pss 124: 8	**VI**: 448.

Pss 125 **VI**: 446; **IX**: cxxxii.
Pss 125: 1 **VI**: 535.
Pss 126 **VI**: 446, 526*(3)*; **IX**: cxxxii.
Pss 126: 1 **VI**: 527.
Pss 126: 2 **VI**: 445.
Pss 126: 2b, 2d **VI**: 447.
Pss 126: 4b **VI**: 445.
Pss 126: 5b **VI**: 445.
Pss 126: 5-6 **VI**: 527.
Pss 126: 5, 6 **VI**: 527*(2)*.
Pss 126: 6 **VI**: 527.
Pss 127 **VI**: 527*(3)*.
Pss 127: 2 **VI**: 443, 527*(2)*, 528.
Pss 127: 2b **VI**: 527*(2)*.
Pss 127: 5 **VI**: 528.
Pss 128: 2 **VI**: 443.
Pss 128: 3 **VI**: 445.
Pss 128: 6a **VI**: 443.
Pss 129 **VI**: 446, 448.
Pss 129(130) **(87)**
Pss 129: 2, 6 **VI**: 443.
Pss 129: 4, 5de **VI**: 447.
Pss 129: 6 **VI**: 448, 528.
Pss 129: 6, 7 **VI**: 2.
Pss 129: 11 **VI**: 446.
Pss 130 **VI**: 446, 448, 528*(6)*; **IX**: cxxxii.
Pss 130(131) **VI**: 447.
Pss 130: 1 **VI**: 528*(2)*.
Pss 130: 2 **VI**: 445.
Pss 130: 5-6 **VI**: 447, 528.
Pss 130: 8-10 **VI**: 443.
Pss 131: 2 **VI**: 7, 446, 528.
Pss 131: 3 **VI**: 529.
Pss 132 **V**: 29, 694; **VI**: 210, 448, 529*(5)*; **IX**: cxlix.
Pss 132: 6 **VI**: 529.
Pss 132: 15 **VI**: 446.
Pss 132: 18 **VI**: 535.
Pss 133 **VI**: 529*(2)*.
Pss 133 (Heb. 134) **IV**: *495*.
Pss 133: 1 **VI**: 447.
Pss 133: 3 **VI**: 529.
Pss 134 **VI**: 443, 529.
Pss 134: 1 **VI**: 530.
Pss 135 **VI**: 443.
Pss 135: 3 **VI**: 448.
Pss 135: 5 **VI**: 535.
Pss 135: 7 **VI**: 7, 530, 535.
Pss 135: 13-14 **VI**: 447.
Pss 136 **VI**: 447.
Pss 136: 3 **VI**: 447.
Pss 136: 10 **VI**: 448.
Pss 136: 14 **VI**: 535.
Pss 136: 18 **VI**: 535.
Pss 137 **VI**: 530*(11)*; **IX**: cxxxii.
Pss 137: 2de, 8 **VI**: 447.
Pss 137: 3 **VI**: 444, 531.
Pss 137: 5 **VI**: 531.
Pss 137: 7 **VI**: 448.
Pss 138-144 **VI**: 531.
Pss 138: 1, 2b **VI**: 443.
Pss 138: 3 **VI**: 535.
Pss 138: 5a, 14c **VI**: 447.
Pss 138: 6 **VI**: 445.
Pss 138: 11 **VI**: 445.
Pss 138: 16a, 17a **VI**: 447.
Pss 138: 16c-d **VI**: 445.
Pss 138: 18b **VI**: 445.
Pss 138: 18b, 20 **VI**: 447.
Pss 138: 20 **VI**: 445.
Pss 139 **VI**: 448, 531*(9)*; **VIII**: 359.
Pss 139: 4 **VI**: 445.
Pss 139: 6 **VI**: 448, 535.

Pss 139: 7 **VI**: 531.
Pss 139: 9cd **VI**: 447.
Pss 139: 9, 11, 12, 14 **VI**: 443.
Pss 139: 10 **VI**: 445.
Pss 139: 11 **VI**: 7, 446.
Pss 139: 14 **VI**: 448.
Pss 139: 14-15 **VI**: 447.
Pss 139: 16 **VI**: 446.
Pss 139: 16-17 **VI**: 446.
Pss 139: 16-18, 20, 24 **VI**: 443.
Pss 139: 20 **VI**: 446.
Pss 140[a] **VI**: 5.
Pss 140-142 **VI**: 443.
Pss 140: 3 **VI**: 535.
Pss 140: 3, 5, 7 **VI**: 447.
Pss 140: 5 **VI**: 535.
Pss 140: 5-6 **VI**: 447.
Pss 140: 5c-7a **VI**: 445.
Pss 140: 9-10 **VI**: 446.
Pss 140: 9, 10, 11 **VI**: 442.
Pss 140: 10 **VI**: 535.
Pss 140: 10b **VI**: 445.
Pss 140: 11 **VI**: 535.
Pss 141: 1-10 **VI**: 446.
Pss 141: 4 **VI**: 445, 446.
Pss 141: 5 **VI**: 10, 445.
Pss 141: 5, 6, 7, 9 **VI**: 443.
Pss 142: 4, 8 **VI**: 443.
Pss 142: 7 **VI**: 535.
Pss 142: 8 **VI**: 535.
Pss 142: 8a **VI**: 447.
Pss 143: 1-144: 6 **IV**: 28*(2)*; **VI**: 532*(2)*.
Pss 143: 3, 6, 9, 10 **VI**: 443.
Pss 143: 8, 12 **VI**: 442.
Pss 143: 12cd, 13 **VI**: 447.
Pss 143: 13b **VI**: 445.
Pss 144: 1-8, 9-15 **VI**: 444.
Pss 144: 2, 4, 14 **VI**: 443.
Pss 144: 12 **VI**: 445, 446.
Pss 144: 12, 15 **VI**: 443.
Pss 144: 13 **VI**: 445.
Pss 144: 13-14 **VI**: 445.
Pss 145 **VI**: 443, 479, 532*(2)*.
Pss 145: 1-21 **VI**: 446.
Pss 145: 1-7 **VI**: 448.
Pss 145: 2 **VI**: 448.
Pss 145: 3 **VI**: 535.
Pss 145: 12 **VI**: 535.
Pss 146 **VI**: 443, 532.
Pss 146: 6 **VI**: 7.
Pss 146: 8 **VI**: 447.
Pss 146: 10 **VI**: 448.
Pss 147: 1, (12-20) **VI**: 443.
Pss 147: 15 **VI**: 7.
Pss 147: 16 **VI**: 535.
Pss 147: 17 **VI**: 447.
Pss 148 **VI**: 532*(2)*.
Pss 148: 5, 6, 14 **VI**: 443.
Pss 148: 7 **VI**: 448.
Pss 148: 8 **VI**: 523, 532.
Pss 149 **VI**: 532.
Pss 149: 1-9 **VI**: 446.
Pss 149: 5 **VI**: 532, 533*(5)*.
Pss 149: 5b **VI**: 445.
Pss 149: 9 **VI**: 443.
Pss 150 **VI**: 533.
Pss 150: 1 **VI**: 443, 445.
Pss 151 **VI**: 442, 533, 536, 645.
Pss 151LXX **VI**: 533*(4)*.
Pss 151Q **VIII**: 449.
Pss 151: 1-5Q **VI**: 533; **VIII**: 448.
Pss 154 **VI**: 645; **VIII**: 449.
Pss 155 **VI**: 645; **VIII**: 449.
Prov 1-8 **VI**: 538.
Prov 1-9 **V**: 706; **VI**: 538.
Prov 1-20 **VIII**: 389.
Prov 1: 4 **VI**: 537.

Prov 1:9 VI: 538.
Prov 1:11 VI: 537.
Prov 1:17 VI: 537.
Prov 1:18 VI: 7.
Prov 1:20 VI: 538, 540.
Prov 1:22-23 VI: 538.
Prov 1:23 VI: 537.
Prov 1:27 VI: 537.
Prov 2:7 VI: 419.
Prov 2:9 VI: 537.
Prov 2:17 VI: 538.
Prov 3:8 VI: 537.
Prov 3:11, 12 VI: 538.
Prov 3:13 VI: 537.
Prov 3:14 VI: 2.
Prov 3:17 VI: 538.
Prov 3:19-20 VI: 539, 540.
Prov 3:20 VI: 539.
Prov 3:23 VI: 2.
Prov 3:34 VI: 537.
Prov 3:35 VI: 10, 537*(2)*.
Prov 4:11 VI: 10.
Prov 4:12 VI: 2.
Prov 4:17 VI: 2.
Prov 4:23 VI: 537.
Prov 4:34 VI: 537.
Prov 5:6 VI: 539.
Prov 5:15-19 VI: 539.
Prov 5:15-20 VI: 539.
Prov 5:16 VI: 537.
Prov 6:1-6 VI: 537.
Prov 6:6-10 V: 685.
Prov 6:6-8 VI: 539.
Prov 6:10 VI: 539, 545.VI: 545.
Prov 6:11 VI: 537.
Prov 6:16-19 VI: 539.
Prov 6:20-24 VI: 539*(2)*.
Prov 6:22 VI: 537.
Prov 6:26 VI: 537.
Prov 6:26a VI: 537.
Prov 7:2 VI: 9, 537.
Prov 7:10 VI: 10.
Prov 7:17 VI: 537.
Prov 7:21 VI: 537.
Prov 7:22 VI: 537, 540*(2).b*
Prov 7:22, 23 VI: 539.
Prov 8 VI: 540.
Prov 8:3 VI: 538, 540.
Prov 8:4 VI: 2.
Prov 8:12 VI: 537.
Prov 8:16 VI: 419.
Prov 8:21 VI: 419.
Prov 8:22-31 VI: 539, 540*(9);* VIII: 150.
Prov 8:24, 26, 31 VI: 419.
Prov 8:26 VI: 538.
Prov 8:29 VI: 537.
Prov 8:30 VI: 11, 541.
Prov 9 VI: 541; VII: 145.
Prov 9:1 VI: 541.
Prov 9:7 VI: 537.
Prov 9:13 VI: 537, 541.
Prov 9:17 VI: 538.
Prov 10:3 VI: 537.
Prov 10:9 VI: 537.
Prov 10:12 VI: 3.
Prov 10:16 VI: 541.
Prov 10:23 VI: 3, 541.
Prov 10:28 VI: 11, 537.
Prov 10:32 VI: 537.
Prov 11:7 VI: 10.
Prov 11:13 V: 525.
Prov 11:16 VI: 537*(2)*.
Prov 11:25 VI: 5.
Prov 11:31 VI: 537.
Prov 12:3 VI: 541.
Prov 12:3b VI: 4.
Prov 12:4, 26 VI: 537.
Prov 12:6 VI: 8.

Prov 12: 15 **VI**: 3.
Prov 12: 23 **VI**: 537.
Prov 12: 25 **VI**: 537.
Prov 12: 26 **VI**: 541.
Prov 12: 27 **VI**: 537.
Prov 12: 28 **VI**: 541; **VIII**: 265.
Prov 13: 1 **VI**: 537.
Prov 13: 8 **V**: 415; **VI**: 542.
Prov 13: 9 **VI**: 537.
Prov 13: 11 **VI**: 537.
Prov 13: 15 **VI**: 5372*)*.
Prov 13: 21 **VI**: 537.
Prov 13: 23 **VI**: 537.
Prov 13: 23a **VI**: 537.
Prov 14: 8 **VI**: 537.
Prov 14: 9 **VI**: 4, 537*(2)*.
Prov 14: 17 **VI**: 537.
Prov 14: 18 **VI**: 537.
Prov 14: 24 **VI**: 10, 537.
Prov 14: 31 **VI**: 538.
Prov 15: 2 **VI**: 537.
Prov 15: 7 **VI**: 537.
Prov 15: 8-9 **VI**: 542.
Prov 15: 30 **VI**: 537.
Prov 16: 4 **VI**: 542.
Prov 17: 4 **VI**: 537.
Prov 17: 5 **VI**: 537.
Prov 17: 14 **VI**: 537.
Prov 17: 22 **VI**: 5, 7.
Prov 17: 27 **VI**: 3.
Prov 18: 1 **VI**: 3, 542.
Prov 18: 8 **VI**: 3.
Prov 18: 10 **VI**: 542.
Prov 18: 13 **VI**: 542.
Prov 18: 17 **VI**: 537.
Prov 18: 18 **VI**: 537, 542.
Prov 18: 24 **VI**: 3, 537, 542.
Prov 19: 10 **VI**: 537.
Prov 19: 16 **VI**: 538.
Prov 19: 17 **VI**: 537.
Prov 19: 18 **VI**: 537.
Prov 19: 22 **VI**: 542.
Prov 19: 23 **VI**: 543*(2)*.
Prov 19: 24 **VI**: 538.
Prov 19: 26 **VI**: 537, 543.
Prov 19: 27 **VI**: 537.
Prov 20: 2 **VI**: 537.
Prov 20: 13 **VI**: 543.
Prov 20: 19 **V**: 525.
Prov 20: 26 **VI**: 537, 543.
Prov 20: 27 **VI**: 543*(2)*.
Prov 20: 35-36 **VI**: 592.
Prov 21: 1 **VI**: 2.
Prov 21: 4 **VI**: 537, 543.
Prov 21: 8 **VI**: 537.
Prov 21: 9 **VI**: 2, 543*(2)*, 592.
Prov 21: 24 **VI**: 537.
Prov 21: 26 **VI**: 537.
Prov 21: 28 **VI**: 537.
Prov 22: 1 **VI**: 537.
Prov 22: 4 **VI**: 537.
Prov 22: 5 **VI**: 537.
Prov 22: 5 **VI**: 537.
Prov 22: 6 **VI**: 544*(2)*.
Prov 22: 10 **VI**: 537, 544, 669.
Prov 22: 11 **VI**: 537.
Prov 22: 12 **VI**: 544.
Prov 22: 17-21 **VI**: 544.
Prov 22: 20 **VI**: 6.
Prov 22: 23 **VI**: 537.
Prov 23: 17 **VI**: 538.
Prov 23: 21 **VI**: 544.
Prov 23: 26 **VI**: 544*(3)*.
Prov 23: 29, 32 **VI**: 10.
Prov 23: 29-35 **VI**: 544.
Prov 23: 34 **VI**: 545.
Prov 24: 9 **VI**: 538.
Prov 24: 10 **V**: 402; **VI**: 12.
Prov 24: 11 **VI**: 7, 537*(2)*.

Prov 24: 14 **VI**: 537.
Prov 24: 16 **VI**: 545.
Prov 24: 21 **VI**: 538.
Prov 24: 22 **VI**: 537.
Prov 24: 27 **VI**: 545.
Prov 24: 28 **VI**: 537.
Prov 24: 30-34 **V**: 683; **VI**: 545.
Prov 24: 33 **VI**: 539, 545.
Prov 25-31 **VIII**: 389.
Prov 25: 1 **VI**: 7.
Prov 25: 2 **VI**: 545.
Prov 25: 4 **VI**: 537, 538.
Prov 25: 8 **VI**: 537.
Prov 25: 11 **VI**: 545.
Prov 25: 13 **VI**: 2.
Prov 25: 15 **VI**: 9, 545.
Prov 25: 17 **VI**: 537.
Prov 25: 19 **VI**: 545*(2)*.
Prov 25: 21, 22 **VI**: 546*(2)*.
Prov 25: 22 **VI**: 546*(2)*; **VIII**: 293.
Prov 25: 23 **VI**: 546.
Prov 25: 24 **VI**: 546.
Prov 25: 27 **VI**: 10, 537*(2)*.
Prov 26: 4, 5 **VI**: 546.
Prov 26: 6 **VI**: 11.
Prov 26: 6 **VI**: 537.
Prov 26: 7 **VI**: 537.
Prov 26: 8 **VI**: 10, 546*(3)*.
Prov 26: 10 **VI**: 10.
Prov 26: 11 **VI**: 538; **VIII**: 295.
Prov 26: 11LXX **VI**: 546.
Prov 26: 15 **VI**: 538.
Prov 26: 23 **VI**: 537, 547*(2)*; **IX**: cxlix.
Prov 26: 28 **VI**: 537.
Prov 26: 31 **VI**: 537.
Prov 27: 6 **VI**: 7, 537, 547.
Prov 27: 7 **VI**: 538.
Prov 27: 9 **VI**: 9, 538.
Prov 27: 10 **VI**: 547.
Prov 27: 13 **VI**: 547.
Prov 27: 16 **VI**: 537, 547.
Prov 27: 19 **VI**: 9, 537.
Prov 27: 21, 22 **VI**: 459*(2)*, 467, 547*(4)*.
Prov 27: 21-22 **VI**: 547.
Prov 27: 22 **VI**: 4, 547, 591.
Prov 27: 23-27 **V**: 705.
Prov 28: 2 **VI**: 537.
Prov 28: 12 **VI**: 538.
Prov 28: 12&28 **VI**: 537.
Prov 28: 17 **VI**: 537.
Prov 28: 22 **VI**: 4, 421, 548.
Prov 28: 23 **VI**: 537.
Prov 29: 4 **VI**: 537.
Prov 29: 5 **VI**: 548.
Prov 29: 6 **VI**: 537.
Prov 29: 7 **VI**: 537.
Prov 29: 10 **VI**: 537.
Prov 29: 18 **VI**: 548*(2)*.
Prov 29: 21 **VI**: 11.
Prov 30 **IV**: *460;* **VI**: 548*(3)*.
Prov 30: 1 **VI**: 3.
Prov 30: 8 **VI**: 548.
Prov 30: 11-14 **VI**: 548.
Prov 30: 15 **VI**: 277, 549*(4)*.
Prov 30: 15-16 **VI**: 548*(2)*.
Prov 30: 15a **VI**: 549.
Prov 30: 16 **VI**: 537.
Prov 30: 17 **VI**: 549.
Prov 30: 18-20 **VI**: 549.
Prov 30: 27 **VI**: 538.
Prov 30: 29-31 **VI**: 549*(2)*.

Prov 30: 31 **VI**: 7, 411, 537*(3)*, 549*(2)*.
Prov 31 **VI**: 549.
Prov 31: 1 **VI**: 419, 537, 550.
Prov 31: 3 **VI**: 7, 11.
Prov 31: 4 **VI**: 537, 550.
Prov 31: 8 **VI**: 537, 538.
Prov 31: 10 **VI**: 7.
Prov 31: 10-31 **VI**: 550*(2)*.
Prov 31: 11 **VI**: 7, 537, 538.
Prov 31: 19 **VI**: 550.
Prov 31: 21 **VI**: 550.
Prov 31: 27 **VI**: 550, 711.
Prov 31: 28 **VI**: 538.
Prov 32: 8 **VI**: 3.
Prov 33: 10 **VI**: 3.
Prov 35: 11 **VI**: 5.
Prov 37: 37 **VI**: 3.
Ruth 1: 1-22 **VI**: 556.
Ruth 1: 1-5 **VI**: 556.
Ruth 1: 6-22 **VI**: 556.
Ruth 1: 8 **VI**: 556.
Ruth 1: 14-15 **VI**: 556.
Ruth 1: 15, 19 **VI**: 556.
Ruth 1: 16, 17 **VI**: 556.
Ruth 1: 17 **VI**: 556.
Ruth 2: 1-23 **VI**: 556.
Ruth 2: 3 **VI**: 556.
Ruth 2: 8 **VI**: 557.
Ruth 2: 8, 9s **VI**: 557.
Ruth 2: 19 **VI**: 557.
Ruth 2: 20 **VI**: 557.
Ruth 3 **VI**: 557.
Ruth 3: 1-18 **VI**: 557.
Ruth 3: 3, 6 **VI**: 10.
Ruth 3: 12 **VI**: 557.
Ruth 3: 13b **VI**: 557.
Ruth 3: 15 **VI**: 557.
Ruth 3: 15b **VI**: 557.
Ruth 3: 16 **VI**: 556.
Ruth 4: 1-22 **VI**: 557.
Ruth 4: 3, 5, 15 **VI**: 556.
Ruth 4: 5 **VI**: 558.
Ruth 4: 7-8 **VI**: 558.
Ruth 4: 11 **VI**: 558.
Ruth 4: 14, 15 **VI**: 558.
Cant 1 **VI**: 551.
Cant 1: 4 **VI**: 551.
Cant 1: 4, 7 **VI**: 551.
Cant 1: 5 **VI**: 551.
Cant 1: 7 **VI**: 5.
Cant 1: 13 **VI**: 5.
Cant 2: 1 **III**: *394*.
Cant 2: 1, 5, 7 **VI**: 551.
Cant 2: 3-5 **VI**: 552.
Cant 2: 3, 5 **VI**: 552.
Cant 2: 7 **VI**: 552.
Cant 2: 11 **VI**: 552.
Cant 2: 14, 17 **VI**: 551.
Cant 2: 15 **VI**: 4.
Cant 2: 16 **VI**: 4.
Cant 2: 17 **VI**: 552*(3)*.
Cant 3: 5 **VI**: 552.
Cant 3: 6 **VI**: 7.
Cant 3: 6-11 **VI**: 5.
Cant 3: 6, 7, 9, 10 **VI**: 551.
Cant 4: 1, 3 **VI**: 552, 553.
Cant 4: 1, 3, 16 **VI**: 551.
Cant 4: 3 **VI**: 10.
Cant 4: 4 **I**: *311;* **VI**: 552*(2)*, 553.
Cant 4: 6 **VI**: 552, 553*(4)*.
Cant 4: 6, 8 **VI**: 4.
Cant 4: 7 **VI**: 553.
Cant 4: 16 **VI**: 553.
Cant 5: 1, 8, 11 **VI**: 551.
Cant 5: 6 **VI**: 553.
Cant 5: 11, 14, 15 **VI**: 551.
Cant 5: 13 **VI**: 553.
Cant 6: 2 **VI**: 553.
Cant 6: 6 **VI**: 552, 553.

Cant 6: 10 **VI**: 554.
Cant 6: 12 **VI**: 554.
Cant 6: 13 **VI**: 551.
Cant 7: 1 **VI**: 553, 554.
Cant 7: 1-2 **VI**: 554.
Cant 7: 3 **VI**: 554*(2)*.
Cant 7: 5-7 **VI**: 554*(2)*.
Cant 7: 6 **VI**: 7, 9*(2)*, 554*(2)*.
Cant 7: 6, 9 **VI**: 551.
Cant 7: 7 **VI**: 554.
Cant 7: 9 **VI**: 554, 555.
Cant 8: 1 **VI**: 10.
Cant 8: 1, 2, 5 **VI**: 551.
Cant 8: 6-7 **VI**: 555.
Cant 8: 6, 7, 12 **VI**: 551.
Cant 8: 11-12 **VI**: 555.
Cant 8: 14 **VI**: 4.
Eccl 1 **VI**: 561.
Eccl 1: 1-11 **VI**: 561.
Eccl 1: 5 **V**: 396; **VI**: 8, 560.
Eccl 1: 8 **V**: 396; **VI**: 7, 8.
Eccl 1: 12-18 **VI**: 561.
Eccl 1: 17 **VI**: 561.
Eccl 1: 18 **VI**: 11.
Eccl 2: 1 **V**: 396; **VI**: 8, 11.
Eccl 2: 1-3 **VI**: 561.
Eccl 2: 2 **VI**: 11.
Eccl 2: 3 **VI**: 8, 561.
Eccl 2: 4-11 **VI**: 561.
Eccl 2: 8 **VI**: 11, 560, 5612*)*.
Eccl 2: 9 **VI**: 11.
Eccl 2: 12-26 **VI**: 562.
Eccl 2: 21 **VI**: 5.
Eccl 2: 23 **VI**: 11.
Eccl 2: 25 **VI**: 10.
Eccl 3: 1 **VI**: 560.
Eccl 3: 1-8 **VI**: 562.
Eccl 3: 1-4: 3 **IV**: 516.
Eccl 3: 2-8 **VI**: 562.
Eccl 3: 5 **VI**: 562.
Eccl 3: 11 **VI**: 562*(6)*.
Eccl 3: 15 **VI**: 560.
Eccl 3: 18 **VI**: 9, 560, 562*(3)*, 563.
Eccl 4: 4 **VI**: 563.
Eccl 4: 4-6 **VI**: 563.
Eccl 4: 4-6: 9 **IV**: 516.
Eccl 4: 10 **VI**: 563.
Eccl 4: 12 **VI**: 563.
Eccl 4: 13-16 **VI**: 563*(2)*.
Eccl 4: 14 **VI**: 5.
Eccl 4: 19 **VI**: 563.
Eccl 4: 26b **VI**: 7.
Eccl 5: 2 **VI**: 7.
Eccl 5: 5 **V**: 396; **VI**: 7, 8.
Eccl 5: 10 **VI**: 7, 560.
Eccl 6: 6 **VI**: 563.
Eccl 6: 7 **VI**: 563.
Eccl 6: 10-9: 18 **IV**: 516.
Eccl 7: 6 **VI**: 11.
Eccl 7: 7 **VI**: 563.
Eccl 7: 16 **VI**: 7.
Eccl 8: 2-9 **VI**: 564.
Eccl 8: 10 **VI**: 11, 560, 564*(3)*.
Eccl 8: 11 **VI**: 5.
Eccl 9: 3 **VI**: 560.
Eccl 9: 10 **VIII**: 265.
Eccl 9: 12 **V**: 396; **VI**: 8, 560.
Eccl 9: 14 **VI**: 564.
Eccl 9: 15 **VI**: 560.
Eccl 10: 1 **VI**: 560.
Eccl 10: 9 **VI**: 11, 560.
Eccl 10: 15 **VI**: 564.
Eccl 10: 20 **VI**: 564*(3)*.
Eccl 11: 1 **VI**: 564.
Eccl 11: 1-6 **VI**: 564.
Eccl 11: 2 **VI**: 560.

Eccl 11:3 **VI**: 560.
Eccl 11:5 **V**: 395; **VI**: 7, 564.
Eccl 12 **VI**: 565.
Eccl 12:1 **VI**: 565*(2)*.
Eccl 12:1-7 **VI**: 565*(2)*.
Eccl 12:2-5 **VI**: 565.
Eccl 12:4 **VI**: 565*(2)*.
Eccl 12:4-5 **VI**: 565.
Eccl 12:5 **V**: 396; **VI**: 8, 11, 565*(2)*, 566.
Eccl 12:6 **VI**: 11, 566*(2)*.
Eccl 12:8-14 **VI**: 566.
Eccl 12:9 **VI**: 11.
Eccl 12:11 **III**: *682;* **VI**: 560, 566.
Lam 1:1-22 **VI**: 558.
Lam 1:1, 7, 12 **VI**: 558.
Lam 1:4 **VI**: 559.
Lam 1:7 **VI**: 558.
Lam 1:12 **VI**: 11, 559*(2)*.
Lam 1:13 **VI**: 8.
Lam 1:14 **VI**: 7, 559.
Lam 1:20 **VI**: 7.
Lam 2 **VI**: 7, 559.
Lam 2:1, 3, 6 **VI**: 558.
Lam 2:2 **VI**: 7.
Lam 2:4 **VI**: 7.
Lam 2:13 **VI**: 559.
Lam 2:13, 20, 22 **VI**: 558.
Lam 2:16 **VI**: 7.
Lam 2:17b **VI**: 559.
Lam 2:18 **VI**: 9.
Lam 2:22 **VI**: 7, 558.
Lam 3 **VI**: 559; **IX**: cxxxii.
Lam 3:1 **VI**: 7.
Lam 3:6 **VI**: 558.
Lam 3:11, 16, 19, 26 **VI**: 558.
Lam 3:13 **VI**: 12.
Lam 3:36, 45, 47, 58 **VI**: 558.
Lam 3:47 **VI**: 558.
Lam 3:49 **VI**: 7.
Lam 3:63 **VI**: 558.
Lam 4:1 **VI**: 559.
Lam 4:1, 7, 15, 20 **VI**: 558.
Lam 4:9 **VI**: 560*(2)*.
Lam 4:9-12 **VI**: 559, 560.
Lam 4:9, 15 **VI**: 558.
Lam 4:20 **VI**: 560.
Lam 5 **VI**: 560.
Lam 5:10 **VI**: 558.
Lam 5:10, 13, 19 **VI**: 558.
Lam 5:15 **VI**: 558.
Esth 1-3 **VI**: 566.
Esth 1:14 **VI**: 7.
Esth 1:22 **VI**: 566.
Esth 2:19-20 **VI**: 566.
Esth 3:8-9 **VI**: 566.
Esth 4 **VI**: 567.
Esth 4-5 **VI**: 567.
Esth 4:13-14 **VI**: 567.
Esth 4:14 **VI**: 567.
Esth 5 **VI**: 567.
Esth 6-7 **VI**: 567.
Esth 8:10, 14 **VI**: 5.
Esth 9 **VI**: 201.
Esth 10 **VI**: 567.
Dan 1&2 **VI**: 104, 568.
Dan 1-6 **VI**: 568.
Dan 1:1 **II**: *186;* **VI**: 568.
Dan 1:1-21 **VI**: 568.
Dan 1:3 **VI**: 568.
Dan 2 **VI**: 568*(2)*.
Dan 2, 7, 8, 9 **VI**: 568.
Dan 2:5 **VI**: 569.
Dan 2:6 **VI**: 9.
Dan 2:20 **VI**: 569.
Dan 2:23 **VI**: 569, 580*(2)*, 581*(2)*.
Dan 2:28 **VI**: 569; **VIII**: 175.

Dan 2:40-43 **VI**: 569.
Dan 2:44 **VI**: 569.
Dan 3 **I**: *276;* **VI**: 336, 569*(2)*, 570*(4)*, *625*.
Dan 3&4 **VI**: 569.
Dan 3:5 **V**: 660; **VI**: 570*(5)*.
Dan 3:7 **VI**: 570*(4)*.
Dan 3:10 **VI**: 570*(4)*.
Dan 3:15 **VI**: 570*(4)*.
Dan 3:16 **VI**: 10.
Dan 3:16-18 **VI**: 570.
Dan 3:21-24 **VI**: 571.
Dan 3:24-90ס **VIII**: 363.
Dan 3:25 **VI**: 9.
Dan 3:51b-52 **VI**: 571.
Dan 4:5 **VI**: 7.
Dan 4:14 **I**: *228;* **VI**: 571; **VII**: 30, 128, 298.
Dan 4:30 **VI**: 571.
Dan 4:33 **VI**: 9.
Dan 5 **VI**: 571*(2)*.
Dan 5&6 **VI**: 571.
Dan 5:1 **VI**: 571.
Dan 5:1-31 **VI**: 571.
Dan 5:2, 3, 23 **VI**: 486, 572*(2)*.
Dan 5:5ff. **VI**: 572.
Dan 5:12 **VI**: 572.
Dan 5:23 **VI**: 486, 572.
Dan 5:25f. **VI**: 572.
Dan 5:25 **VI**: 572*(5)*, 573*(2)*.
Dan 5:25, 28 **VI**: 12.
Dan 5:25-28 **VI**: 572.
Dan 5:30 **VI**: 573*(2)*.
Dan 5:30-31 **VI**: 573.
Dan 5:31 **I**: *33;* **VI**: 573*(2)*, 573.
Dan 6 **VI**: 573*(2)*.
Dan 6:19 **VI**: 11.
Dan 7 **IV**: 535; **VI**: 573, 574*(6)*.
Dan 7-12 **VI**: 573.
Dan 7:1-14 **VI**: 574.
Dan 7:5 **VI**: 574*(3)*.
Dan 7:7 **VI**: 574.
Dan 7:8 **VI**: 574*(2)*.
Dan 7:9 **VI**: 2, 3, 4.
Dan 7:13f. **VI**: 575.
Dan 7:14 **VI**: 575.
Dan 8-12 **IV**: 533; **VI**: 575.
Dan 8:2 **VI**: 575.
Dan 8:5 **VI**: 9.
Dan 8:5b **VI**: 9.
Dan 8:5ff. **VI**: 575.
Dan 8:9-14 **VI**: 575.
Dan 8:11-12 **VI**: 575.
Dan 8:12 **VI**: 575.
Dan 8:22 **VI**: 9.
Dan 9 **VI**: 575*(2)*, 576*(3)*.
Dan 9:1 **I**: *33;* **VI**: 573, 576*(2)*.
Dan 9:4 **V**: 398.
Dan 9:24-27 **VI**: 576*(8)*.
Dan 9:26 **VI**: 576, 577.
Dan 9:27 **VI**: 577.
Dan 11 **VI**: 577.
Dan 11:4 **VI**: 3, 577.
Dan 11:18 **VI**: 577.
Dan 11:22 **VI**: 577.
Dan 11:30-12:10 **VI**: 577.
Dan 12 **VI**: 726.
Dan 12:1, 2 **VI**: 577.
Dan 12:1-3 **VI**: 577.
Dan 12:2 **VI**: 578*(2)*.
Dan 12:2, 3 **VI**: 577.
Dan 12:3 **VI**: 578.
Dan 12:4 **VI**: 578*(4)*.
Dan 12:7 **VI**: 8.
Dan 12:11-12 **VI**: 578.

Ezra 1 **VI**: 579*(2)*.
Ezra 1-2 **VI**: 579.
Ezra 1&2 **VI**: 579.
Ezra 1-4 **VI**: 579.
Ezra 1:1-4:24 **VI**: 579.
Ezra 1:3*marg.* **VI**: 579.
Ezra 1:4 **VI**: 579*(2)*.
Ezra 2 **VI**: 579, 580*(2)*, 585*(3)*, 613.
Ezra 3-4 **VI**: 580.
Ezra 4:2,8 **VI**: 579.
Ezra 4:4 **VI**: 580.
Ezra 4:6, 7 **VI**: 580.
Ezra 4:7 **VI**: 8.
Ezra 4:9 **VI**: 580.
Ezra 4:10, 11 **VI**: 569, 580*(2)*, 581*(2)*.
Ezra 4:10ff., 14 **VI**: 579.
Ezra 4:12 **VI**: 580.
Ezra 4:17 **VI**: 569, 580*(2)*, 581*(2)*.
Ezra 5:3 **VI**: 580.
Ezra 5:3, 9 **VI**: 581*(2)*.
Ezra 5:4 **VI**: 579.
Ezra 5:8 **VI**: 581.
Ezra 5:9 **VI**: 581.
Ezra 5:16 **VI**: 569, 580*(2)*, 581*(2)*.
Ezra 6 **VI**: 581.
Ezra 6:3 **VI**: 581.
Ezra 7:1-28 **VI**: 581.
Ezra 7:12 **VI**: 569, 579, 580*(2)*, 581*(2)*.
Ezra 7:26 **VI**: 581.
Ezra 8:3 **VI**: 10.
Ezra 8:17 **VI**: 582.
Ezra 10:3 **VI**: 8.
Ezra 10:6 **VI**: 8, 582.
Ezra 10:15 **VI**: 579.
Ezra 10:27 **VI**: 582.
Ezra 10:44 **VI**: 10.
Neh 1-11 **VI**: 582.
Neh 2-4 **VI**: 582.
Neh 2:8, 10 **VI**: 178, 582, 584.
Neh 2:12-15 **VI**: 582, 583*(2)*.
Neh 2:13 **VI**: 583*(3)*.
Neh 2:13-15 **VI**: 583.
Neh 2:19 **VI**: 583*(2)*.
Neh 3 **VI**: 583.
Neh 3:1 **VI**: 10.
Neh 3:6 **VI**: 4.
Neh 3:8 **VI**: 582, 583.
Neh 3:15 **VI**: 583, 584, 586.
Neh 3:15-16 **VI**: 583.
Neh 3:19 **VI**: 5, 224, 584.
Neh 3:26 **VI**: 178, 582, 584.
Neh 3:33-37 **VI**: 584.
Neh 4:6 **VI**: 584.
Neh 4:23 **VI**: 582, 584.
Neh 5 **VI**: 584.
Neh 5:2 **VI**: 5, 8.
Neh 5:11 **I**: *306;* **VI**: 7, 584.
Neh 5:13 **VI**: 584.
Neh 5:15, 17 **VI**: 10.
Neh 5:2(3) **VI**: 3.
Neh 6:1ff. **VI**: 584.
Neh 6:2 **VI**: 585.
Neh 6:11 **VI**: 582.
Neh 7 **IV**: 538; **VI**: 579, 580*(2)*, 585*(3)*, 613.
Neh 7:2 **VI**: 5, 8
Neh 7:3 **VI**: 12.
Neh 8-10 **VI**: 585.
Neh 8:-10:33 **VI**: 585.
Neh 9 **VI**: 585.
Neh 9:5 **VI**: 12.
Neh 9:17 **VI**: 582.
Neh 11:17 **VI**: 5.

Neh 12:8	**VI**: 7.	1 Chr 19:18	**IV** 361.
Neh 12:31-39	**VI**: 585.	1 Chr 20:3	**IV**: 360.
Neh 12:31-43	**VI**: 585.	1 Chr 21	**IV**: 361.
Neh 12:36	**VI**: 585.	1 Chr 21:1	**VI**: 586.
Neh 12:37	**VI**: 583, 586.	1 Chr 21:18-22:1	**IV**: 360.
1 Chr 1	**IV**: 542.	1 Chr 22:2	**V**: 394; **VI**: 6.
1 Chr 1-7	**VI**: 586.	1 Chr 23-26	**I**: *118, 155;* **V**: 42.
1 Chr 1:17	**IV**: 359.	1 Chr 26:18, 20	**VI**: 586.
1 Chr 1:43-50	**II**: *123.*	1 Chr 27:32	**VI**: 586.
1 Chr 1:43-50	**VI**: 586.	1 Chr 28:12	**VI**: 586.
1 Chr 2:23	**IV**: 361; **VI**: 586.	1 Chr 28:31	**VI**: 590.
1 Chr 2:55	**VI**: 586, 587*(2).*	1 Chr 29:7	**VI**: 586.
1 Chr 3:17	**VI**: 586.	1 Chr 29:11	**VI**: 590.
1 Chr 3:24	**VI**: 587*(2).*	1 Chr 29:22	**VI**: 7, 590.
1 Chr 4:9-10	**VI**: 587.	2 Chr 1:5, 13	**VI**: 590.
1 Chr 4:12	**VI**: 587.	2 Chr 1:7-12	**VI**: 590.
1 Chr 4:17-19	**VI**: 4.	2 Chr 1:10	**VI**: 590.
1 Chr 4:17, 18, 41	**VI**: 586.	2 Chr 1:11	**VI**: 590.
1 Chr 4:22-23	**VI**: 11.	2 Chr 1:13	**VI**: 590.
1 Chr 4:23	**VI**: 587.	2 Chr 1:16f.	**VI**: 591.
1 Chr 6:10	**VI**: 8.	2 Chr 2:2, 17	**V**: 398; **VI**: 222.
1 Chr 6:16-38	**VI**: 587.	2 Chr 2:10	**VI**: 8.
1 Chr 6:28, 57	**VI**: 586.	2 Chr 2:13	**VI**: 590.
1 Chr 6:57	**VI**: 4.	2 Chr 2:14	**VI**: 8.
1 Chr 7:6ff.	**VI**: 587.	2 Chr 2:18	**VI**: 8.
1 Chr 7:20ff.	**VI**: 587.	2 Chr 3:18-22	**IV**: 361.
1 Chr 7:24	**VI**: 587.	2 Chr 4:3	**VI**: 3.
1 Chr 8	**I**: *118.*	2 Chr 5:11	**VI**: 5, 8.
1 Chr 11:11	**VI**: 586.	2 Chr 6:8	**VI**: 591.
1 Chr 11:16	**IV**: 359.	2 Chr 6:13	**VI**: 9, 591.
1 Chr 12:14	**VI**: 586.	2 Chr 9:1-12	**VI**: 224, 591.
1 Chr 12:29	**VI**: 5, 8.	2 Chr 9:10	**IV**: 360.
1 Chr 13	**V**: 55; **VI**: 195, 210.	2 Chr 9:18	**VI**: 591.
1 Chr 14:8-17	**IV**: 359.	2 Chr 9:24	**V**: 398; **VI**: 5, 224.
1 Chr 14:14, 15	**IV**: 360.	2 Chr 11:15	**VI**: 590.
1 Chr 15:16	**VI**: 3.	2 Chr 11:23	**VI**: 8.
1 Chr 15:55	**V**: 400; **VI**: 10.	2 Chr 13:4-12	**VI**: 591.
1 Chr 16:7	**VI**: 586.	2 Chr 13:19	**VI**: 591.
1 Chr 16:29	**VI**: 475, 592.	2 Chr 14:9	**VI**: 4, 421, 548, 591*(2).*

2 Chr 14: 10 **VI**: 592.
2 Chr 15: 3-6 **VI**: 5.
2 Chr 15: 16 **VI**: 7.
2 Chr 19: 8 **VI**: 590.
2 Chr 20: 1, 2 **VI**: 590.
2 Chr 20: 21 **VI**: 475, 592.
2 Chr 20: 25, 34 **VI**: 590.
2 Chr 21: 7 **VI**: 12.
2 Chr 21: 16-19 **VI**: 592.
2 Chr 22: 8-9 **IV**: 360.
2 Chr 22: 10 **IV**: 360.
2 Chr 22: 14, 15 **IV**: 360.
2 Chr 24: 15ff. **VI**: 592.
2 Chr 24: 27 **VI**: 590.
2 Chr 25: 2 **VI**: 592.
2 Chr 26: 1-23 **VI**: 592.
2 Chr 26: 7 **VI**: 592.
2 Chr 26: 15 **VI**: 593.
2 Chr 28 **VI**: 4, 593*(3)*.
2 Chr 28: 1-15 **VI**: 593.
2 Chr 28: 5 **VI**: 4.
2 Chr 28: 9 **VIII**: 224.
2 Chr 29: 18-31 **VI**: 594
2 Chr 29: 32-34 **VI**: 593.
2 Chr 30: 1-20 **VI**: 6.
2 Chr 30: 1-27 **VI**: 6.
2 Chr 30: 3-5 **VI**: 593.
2 Chr 30: 20-25 **VI**: 593.
2 Chr 30: 21 **VI**: 593.
2 Chr 31: 21 **VI**: 593.
2 Chr 32: 1 **II**: *186*.
2 Chr 32: 31 **VI**: 10.
2 Chr 33: 11 **VI**: 594*(2)*.
2 Chr 33: 11, 19 **VI**: 590.
2 Chr 34: 15 **IV**: 359, 383.
2 Chr 34: 22 **VI**: 5.
2 Chr 35: 3 **VI**: 12.
2 Chr 35: 22f. **IV**: 360.
2 Chr 35: 25 **VI**: 593.
2 Chr 36: 11-21 **VI**: 593.
2 Chr 39: 18-30 **VI**: 593.

Matt	1-2	**VIII**: 286.
Matt	1:22, 23	**VI**: 262.
Matt	2	**VI**: 298.
Matt	2:6	**VIII**: 283.
Matt	2:17, 18	**VI**: 70.
Matt	4:1-11	**VIII**: 482.
Matt	5:1 - 7:27	**VIII**: 280.
Matt	11:28	**VI**: 118.
Matt	11:28	**VIII**: 284.
Matt	11:25-30	**VIII**: 479(2).
Matt	12:20, 21	**VIII**: 283.
Matt	13:9	**VI**: 664.
Matt	15:5	**VII**: 129.
Matt	17:24-27	**VIII**: 481.
Matt	21:3	**VI**: 279, 719.
Matt	21:2-7	**VI**: 9, 411; **VIII**: 285.
Matt	22:41-46	**VI**: 517; **VIII**: 279.
Matt	23:35f.	**II**: *498;* **VI**: 667*(2).*
Matt	27:9	**VI**: 412; **VIII**: 283.
Matt	27:46	**VIII**: 285, 479.
Matt	27:52	**VIII**: 285.
Matt	27:9, 10	**VIII**: 283.
Matt	28:1	**II**: *498;* **VI**: 667*(2).*
Mark	7:11	**VII**: 129.
Mark	12:35-37	**VI**: 517; **VIII**: 279.
Mark	13	**VIII**: 285.
Mark	14:24	**VI**: 713; **VIII**: 286.
Mark	14:62	**VI**: 665; **VIII**: 287.
Mark	14:63	**VIII**: 447.
Mark	14:65	**VIII**: 481.
Mark	15:15	**VI**: 124; **VIII**: 283.
Mark	15:31	**VI**: 470; **VIII**: 284.
Luke	1:41	**VI**: 75.
Luke	2:51	**VI**: 85; **VIII**: 285.
Luke	4:16-30	**VIII**: 287
Luke	7:21	**VIII**: 287.
Luke	10:24	**VI**: 664.
Luke	10:25-37	**VIII**: 286.
Luke	11:7	**I**: 382.
Luke	16:19-31	**VI**: 650; **VIII**: 284.
Luke	20:41-44	**VI**: 517; **VIII**: 279.
Luke	21:24	**VIII**: 284.
John	1	**VIII**: 288.
John	1:9	**VI**: 666; **VIII**: 288.
John	1:1-14	**VI**: 24; **VIII**: 288.
John	1:1-18	**VI**: 25; **VIII**: 288.
John	3:5	**VIII**: 288.
John	4:24	**VI**: 30; **VIII**: 288.
John	7:37, 38	**VIII**: 288.
John	8:56	**VI**: 68*(2);* **VIII**: 288.
John	10:34	**VI**: 502, 716; **VIII**: 288.
John	10:28-30	**VI**: 300; **VIII**: 288.
John	1:1 -2:12	**VI**: 21.
John	12:34	**VIII**: 289.
John	19:37	**VI**: 412; **VIII**: 298.
John	19:25-27	**VIII**: 288.
Acts	1-15	**VIII**: 290.
Acts	2:28	**VI**: 463; **VIII**: 290.
Acts	8	**VI**: 309; **VIII**: 290.

Acts	13:9	**VI**: 640, 666.
Acts	13:33-37	**VI**: 211.
Acts	16:16-34	**IV**: 45
Rom	1-8	**VIII**: 294.
Rom	1:1-7	**III**: *449.*
Rom	9:19-24	**VI**: 331; **VIII**: 291.
Rom	10:5-8	**VIII**: 294.
Rom	11:25	**VI**: 91; **VIII**: 291.
Rom	12:20	**VI**: 546*(2).*
Rom	12:19-21	**VIII**: 294, 463, 481.
Rom	15:3	**VIII**: 293.
1 Cor	2:10	**VI**: 631; **VIII**: 292.
1 Cor	2:14-16	**II**: *498;* **VI**: 667*(2).*
1 Cor	7:36	**VIII**: 294.
1 Cor	10:1-13	**VIII**: 293.
1 Cor	11:10	**VIII**: 480.
1 Cor	11:25	**VIII**: 293.
1 Cor	11:2-6	**VIII**: 463.
1 Cor	15:44-47	**VIII**: 291.
2 Cor		**VI**: 665.
2 Cor	2:10	**VI**: 631.
2 Cor	3	**VIII**: 294.
2 Cor	3:12-18	**VI**: 120.
2 Cor	6:14-7:1	**VIII**: 481.
Gal	3:16	**V**: 420*(2),* 494, 495; **VI**: 68; **VIII**: 291.
Gal	3:17	**I**: 511.
Eph	4:25-29	**VI**: 251.
Eph	5:14	**VI**: 652; **VIII**: 291*(2).*
Col	1:15	**VI**: 635; **VIII**: 295.
Col	1:18	**VI**: 635; **VIII**: 295.
Col	1:15-18	**VI**: 540; **VIII**: 150.
Heb	1:7	**VI**: 513; **VIII**: 296.
Heb	3:4	**VI**: 3.
Heb	11:11	**VI**: 69.
Heb	11:21	**VI**: 90*(2);* **VIII**: 296.
Heb	11:32	**VI**: 199; **VIII**: 296.
Heb	11:5, 6	**VI**: 47.
Heb	11:24-26	**IV**: 328.
Jas	1:21	**VI**: 351; **VIII**: 295.
Jas	4:5	**VI**: 27, 43; **VIII**: 295.
1 Pet	1:12	**VI**: 664*(2);* **VIII**: 295*(2).*
1 Pet	1:10, 12	**VIII**: 295.
1 Pet	1:19, 20	**VI**: 664.
1 Pet	3:18-20	**VI**: 48.
1 Pet	3:19, 20	**VIII**: 295.
2 Pet	1:19-21	**VIII**: 138, 295, 297.
2 Pet	2:4	**VI**: 664; **VIII**: 296.
2 Pet	2:22	**VIII**: 295.
2 Pet	3:10	**VI**: 669; **VIII**: 296.
Jude	14, 15	**VI**: 47.
Rev	3:14	**VI**: 540*(2);* **VIII**: 150.
Rev	4:3	**V**: 45; **VIII**: 297.
Rev	13:18	**II**: *498;* **VI**: 667*(2);* **VIII**: 297.
Rev	16:17-22:5	**VI**: 663; **VIII**: 297.

Bar 1-5 **VI**: 639.
Bar 1:4 **VI**: 639.
Bar 2:17 **VIII**: 265.
2 Esdr 1:27 **VI**: 629.
2 Esdr 2:37 **VI**: 629.
2 Esdr 3-4 **VI**: 629.
2 Esdr 4:10 **VI**: 629.
2 Esdr 5:33 **VI**: 629.
2 Esdr 8:41 **VI**: 629.
4 Ezra 4:8 **VI**: 629, 630.
4 Ezra 4:13-19 **VI**: 629.
4 Ezra 7:36 **VI**: 629, 630.
4 Ezra 8:52 **VI**: 629, 630.
4 Ezra 13:45 **VI**: 630.
Jdt 8:14 **VI**: 631; **VIII**: 292.
Jdt 8:27 **VI**: 631.
Jdt 16:15 **VI**: 631.
Ep Jer 26 **VI**: 639.
1 Mac 1:33 **VI**: 640.
1 Mac 2 **VI**: 640.
1 Mac 2-5 **VI**: 640*(2)*.
1 Mac 3:1-9 **VI**: 640.
1 Mac 3:48 **VI**: 609, 640.
1 Mac 9:15 **VI**: 640*(2)*.
1 Mac 12:37 **VI**: 641*(3)*.
1 Mac 13:50 **VI**: 641.
1 Mac 14:28 **VI**: 641*(3)*.
2 Mac 4:30-38 **VI**: 641.
2 Mac 7 **VIII**: 362.
2 Mac 12:39-44 **VI**: 641.
2 Mac 12:39-45 **VI**: 641.
Pr Azar 3:24-90ט **VI**: 625.
Sir 1:1, 9, 10, 26 **VI**: 633.
Sir 2:2 **VI**: 633.
Sir 3:1-16 **VI**: 633.
Sir 3:12 **VI**: 633.
Sir 3:14 **V**: 656; **VI**: 634.
Sir 4, 5 **VI**: 606.
Sir 4:6 **VI**: 633.
Sir 4:26 **VI**: 634.
Sir 5:6 **VI**: 633.
Sir 6:11 **VI**: 429, 634.
Sir 6:18-37 **VI**: 634.
Sir 7:25 **VI**: 634.
Sir 7:29-12:1 **VI**: 606.
Sir 7:36 **VI**: 633.
Sir 11:19 **VI**: 419, 634.
Sir 11:30 **VI**: 634.
Sir 12:1 **VI**: 634, 718.
Sir 12:8-18 **VI**: 634.
Sir 12:10-11 **VI**: 635.
Sir 12:10-14 **VI**: 607.
Sir 12:10-19 **VI**: 634.
Sir 12:11 **VI**: 633.
Sir 13:21 **VI**: 633.
Sir 14:2 **VI**: 633.
Sir 14:12 **VI**: 635.
Sir 14:15 **VI**: 5, 635.
Sir 18, 19, 20 **VI**: 606.
Sir 19:22 **VI**: 633.
Sir 20:12 **VI**: 633.
Sir 21:27 **VI**: 633.
Sir 22:11 **V**: 685.
Sir 24 **VI**: 635*(2)*; **VIII**: 295.
Sir 25, 26, 31
Sir 26:22 **VI**: 635.
Sir 26:29 **VI**: 633.
Sir 27:5 **VI**: 633.
Sir 30:20 **VI**: 633.
Sir 31:12-31 **VI**: 606.
Sir 31:19 **VI**: 633.
Sir 31:29 **VI**: 633.

Sir	32: 11	**VI**: 633.
Sir	33: 2	**V**: 400; **VI**: 635.
Sir	33: 4	**V**: 400; **VI**: 635.
Sir	33: 5	**VI**: 607.
Sir	33: 13LXX	**VI**: 636.
Sir	33: 31	**VI**: 636.
Sir	34: 16-17LXX	**VI**: 636.
Sir	35: 16	**VI**: 633.
Sir	36: 8	**VI**: 633.
Sir	36: 18	**VI**: 633.
Sir	36: 22-37: 26	**VI**: 606.
Sir	37: 14	**VI**: 633.
Sir	37: 19	**VI**: 633.
Sir	38: 14	**VI**: 633.
Sir	38: 16	**VI**: 633.
Sir	38: 24-39: 11	**VI**: 636.
Sir	38: 25	**VI**: 633.
Sir	38: 33	**VI**: 636.
Sir	39: 17	**VI**: 633.
Sir	39: 21	**VI**: 633.
Sir	39: 27	**VI**: 633.
Sir	40: 12	**VI**: 636, 637.
Sir	40: 13	**VI**: 633.
Sir	40: 14	**VI**: 633.
Sir	40: 16	**VI**: 636.
Sir	41: 2	**V**: 404; **VI**: 633.
Sir	41: 5	**VI**: 633.
Sir	41: 14	**VI**: 636.
Sir	41: 19	**VI**: 636, 637.
Sir	42: 1	**V**: 404.
Sir	42: 3	**VI**: 419, 637.
Sir	42: 7	**VI**: 633.
Sir	42: 12	**V**: 404.
Sir	43: 2	**VI**: 633.
Sir	43: 4	**VI**: 633.
Sir	43: 4c	**VI**: 637*(2)*.
Sir	43: 7	**VI**: 633.
Sir	43: 8	**VI**: 633.
Sir	43: 17	**VI**: 637, 638.
Sir	43: 20	**VI**: 5, 427, 633, 636, 637*(3)*.
Sir	43: 21	**VI**: 633.
Sir	44: 3	**VI**: 633.
Sir	44: 16	**I**: *41(2);* **VI**: 637*(2);* 649*(2)*.
Sir	45: 25	**VI**: 637.
Sir	46: 4-5	**VI**: 638.
Sir	46: 5	**VI**: 633.
Sir	47: 7	**VI**: 633.
Sir	47: 11	**VI**: 633.
Sir	47: 15	**VI**: 633.
Sir	48: 8	**VI**: 633.
Sir	48: 13	**VI**: 633.
Sir	48: 14*a, b*	**VI**: 638.
Sir	49: 8-10	**IV**: 201, 460; **VI**: 638.
Sir	49: 9	**VI**: 637, 638.
Sir	49: 12 50: 22	**VI**: 604.
Sir	50: 1-3	**VI**: 638.
Sir	50: 5-8	**VI**: 638.
Sir	50: 8	**VI**: 633.
Sir	50: 9	**VI**: 638.
Sir	50: 18	**V**: 7.
Sir	51: 4	**VI**: 633.
Sir	51: 13-29	**VI**: 638.
Sir	51: 21	**VI**: 638.
Tob	1: 13	**VI**: 630.
Tob	3: 8	**VI**: 630.
Tob	3: 17	**VI**: 630.
Tob	3: 17	**VI**: 631.
Tob	5: 16	**VI**: 630.
Tob	6: 1(2)	**VI**: 631.
Tob	7: 11	**VI**: 630.
Tob	7: 13	**VI**: 630.

Tob 7:16 VI: 630.
Tob 11:11-13 VI: 631.
Tob 12:6 VI: 630.
Tob 14:5 VI: 631; VIII: 284.
Wis 1-4 VI: 632; VIII: 253.
Wis 1-5 VI: 632; VIII: 262.
Wis 1:2 VI: 632.
Wis 1:13 VI: 632.
Wis 2 VI: 632.
Wis 2:10-chap 5 VI: 632.
Wis 2:23, 24 VI: 632.
Wis 2:24 VI: *632(2);* VIII: 164.
Wis 4:13 VI: 632.
Wis 10-19 VI: 632.
Wis 10:10 VI: 632.
Wis 11-19-19 VI: 633.
Wis 12:3-7-7 VI: 633.
Wis 15:2 VI: 632.
Wis 15:3 VI: 633.
Wis 17 VI: 633.
Wis 17:11, 12 VI: 632.
Wis 18:14f. VI: 633.
Wis 18:13-20-20 VI: 633.
1 Esd VI: 580, 585, 613.
1 Esd 3:1-4:41 VIII: 365.
1 Esd 5:8-23 VI: 602.
2 Esd 6:38-45 VI: 630.
2 Esd 10:60-12:35 VI: 630.
Ad Esth 10:4-13 VI: 631.
Ad Esth 11:2-11 VI: 631.
Ad Esth 11:12-12:6 VI: 631.
Ad Esth 13:1-7 VI: 631.
Ad Esth 13:8-11 VI: 631.
Ad Esth 14:1-19 VI: 631.
Ad Esth 15:1-16 VI: 631.
Ad Esth 16:1-24 VI: 631.

Pseudepigrapha Texts

1 Enoch 1 - 5 **VI**: 663.

1 Enoch 1 : 2 **VI**: 664*(3);* **VIII**: 295*(2).*

1 Enoch 6 ff. **VI**: 664.

1 Enoch 6 - 21 **VI**: 664.

1 Enoch 6 - 36 **VI**: 663.

1 Enoch 9 : 1 **VI**: 664*(2);* **VIII**: 295.

1 Enoch 10: 4 - 13 **VI**: 664.

1 Enoch 10: 4, 5, 12, 13 **VI**: 664; **VIII**: 295.

1 Enoch 22 **VI**: 664; **VIII**: 284.

1 Enoch 22: 3 **VI**: 664.

1 Enoch 22: 9ff. **VI**: 664.

1 Enoch 37 - 71 **VI**: 663.

1 Enoch 37 - 71 **VI**: 665.

1 Enoch 38 **VI**: 665.

1 Enoch 42 **VI**: 665.

1 Enoch 49 **VI**: 665.

1 Enoch 59: 13 - 21 **VI**: 665.

1 Enoch 62: 5 **VI**: 665; **VIII**: 287.

1 Enoch 65 &66 **VI**: 665.

1 Enoch 72 - 82 **VI**: 663.

1 Enoch 83 - 90 **VI**: 663.

1 Enoch 91 - 108 **VI**: 663.

1 Enoch 91: 12 - 17 **VIII**: 452.

1 Enoch 93: 1 - 10 **VIII**: 452.

1 Enoch 102: 1 - 3 **VI**: 643, 665.

1 Enoch 103: 2 **VIII**: 295.

1 Enoch 106: 19 **VIII**: 295.

1 Bar 2 : 18 **VI**: 666.

1 Bar 9 : 3 **VI**: 666.

As Mos 9 **VI**: 640, 666*(2).*

As Mos 10: 1 - 10 **VI**: 666.

Jub 1 - 2 **VI**: 644.

Jub 3 - 6 **VI**: 644.

Jub 7 - 11 **VI**: 644.

Jub 7 : 4 **II**: *498;* **VI**: 667.

Jub 11 **VI**: 667.

Jub 11: 11 **VIII**: 286.

Jub 12 - 23 **VI**: 644.

Jub 16: 30 **VI**: 667.

Jub 24 - 30 **VI**: 644.

Jub 28: 6 - 7 **IX**: cl.

Jub 31 - 45 **VI**: 644.

Jub 34: 4, 7 **II**: *498;* **VI**: 667*(2).*

Jub 46 - 50 **VI**: 644.

Jub 50: 9 **VI**: 667.

Pss Sol 3 **VI**: 668.

Pss Sol 4 **VI**: 668, 669*(2).*

Pss Sol 5 &6 **VI**: 668.

Pss Sol 10 **VI**: 668.

Pss Sol 11 **VI**: 668, 669*(2).*

Pss Sol 13 **VI**: 668, 669*(2).*

Pss Sol 16 **VI**: 669.

Pss Sol 17: 10 **VI**: 669; **VIII**: 296.

Pss Sol 17: 48 **VI**: 544.

Pss Sol 17: 48 **VI**: 669.

Pss Sol 18: 6 **VI**: 669.

Sib Or 3: 388 - 400 **VI**: 670.

Zad Doc 1: 19f. **VI**: 670.

Zad Doc 2: 7f. **VI**: 670.

Zad Doc 2: 9f. **VI**: 670.

Zad Doc 2: 12f. **VI**: 670.

Zad Doc 3: 16 **VI**: 670.

Zad Doc 3: 20 **VI**: 670.

Zad Doc 4: 20, 21 **VI**: 671.

Zad Doc 7: 9 **VI**: 670.

Zad Doc 9: 6 **VI**: 671.

Zad Doc 9:9f.	**VI**: 670.
Zad Doc 13:7f.	**VI**: 670.
Zad Doc 13:11	**VI**: 670.
4 Mac	**VIII**: 296.
T 12 Patr 7 (Job)	**VI**: 670.
T 12 Patr 8 (Levi)	**VI**: 669.
T 12 Patr 18 (Levi)	**VI**: 669, 670.
T 12 Patr 23 (Levi)	**VI**: 670.
T Levi 18	**VIII**: 141*(3)*.

1QDan[ab] **VIII**: 433.
1QH **VIII**: 434.
1QH I 23-24 **VIII**: 465.
1QH III 6-18 **VIII**: 419.
1QH VII, 26-27 **VIII**: 467.
1QH 39.5-20 **VIII**: 466.
1QLitPr **VIII**: 433.
1QM 9:1 **VIII**: 465.
1QM 16:8 **VIII**: 465.
1QM 17, 8-9 **VIII**: 463, 465.
1QMysteries **VIII**: 420.
1QS **VIII**: 420.
1QS 1, 17-18 **VIII**: 463, 465.
1QS 1:18 **VIII**: 461.
1QS I-IX **VIII**: 462.
1QS II 9 **VIII**: 461.
1QS iii 1-4 **VIII**: 461.
1QS iii, 13 - iv, 26 **VIII**: 462, 463, 482.
1QS III, 2 **VIII**: 462.
1QS III, 2-3 **VIII**: 463.
1QS iii, 3-4 **VIII**: 462.
1QS III 9 **VIII**: 461.
1QS IV 20 **VIII**: 461.
1QS IV, 6 **VIII**: 462.
1QS IV, 7 **VIII**: 462.
1QS IV, 7f. **VIII**: 462.
1QS IV, 8 **VIII**: 462.
1QS V, 7 **VIII**: 462.
1QS vi. 11-12 **VIII**: 462.
1QS VI, 12f. **VIII**: 462.
1QS VI, 6-7 **VIII**: 462.
1QS VII 10-12 **VIII**: 461.
1QS VII, 15 **VIII**: 462.
1QS vii. 5-6, 11 **VIII**: 462.
1QS 8:1ff. **VIII**: 414, 462.
1QS 8, 3-4 **VIII**: 463, 465.
1QS VIII, 7 **VIII**: 462.
1QS x, 17-20 **VIII**: 294, 463, 481.
1QS X, 4 **VIII**: 462*(2)*
1QS XI 21-22 **VIII**: 461.
1QSa 1.11 **VIII**: 463, 464.
1QSa II. 11-12 **VIII**: 464.
1QSa ii. 11-17 **VIII**: 464.
1QSa III. 2 **VIII**: 464.
4QpIsa[a] **VIII**: 420*(2)*.
4QpNah **VIII**: 421.
4QShirShabb **VIII**: 468.
11QPss 28:3-12 **VIII**: 448.
11QPs[a] **VIII**: 448, 449*(7)*, 450*(2)*.
11QPs[a]Plea 3-4 **VIII**: 449.
11QPs[b] **VIII**: 448.
CD 1:5-6 **VIII**: 459.
CD IV 20, 21 **VI**: 3.
CD IX, 1 **VIII**: 460*(3)*.
CD VI, 11-14 **VIII**: 460.
CD XII. 7-8 **VIII**: 459.
CD XIV, 12-16 **VIII**: 458.
CDC ii, 12 **VIII**: 459*(2)*.
CDC 5:5-6 **VIII**: 460.

10047 **VII**: 272.
10050 **VII**: 272.
10051 **VII**: 272.
10052 **VII**: 272.
10054 **VII**: 272.
10091 **VII**: 272.
10099 **VII**: 272.
102404, Bole, Column II **VII**: 262, 270.
115039, Bole, Column I **VII**: 262, 270.
1953-4-11, 277 **VII**: 220.
2 BoTU 41 **VII**: 305.
2N-T364 **VII**: 151.
2N-T374 **VII**: 151.
2N-T375 **VII**: 151.
2N-T377 **VII**: 151.
2N-T378 **VII**: 151.
2N-T766* **VII**: 151.
2N-T767* **VII**: 151.
2N-T768 **VII**: 151.
2N-T769 **VII**: 151.
2N-T770* **VII**: 151.
2N-T771* **VII**: 151.
2N-T772* **VII**: 151.
2N-T773* **VII**: 151.
2N-T774* **VII**: 151.
2N-T775 **VII**: 151.
2N-T775a **VII**: 151.
2N-T776* **VII**: 151.
2N-T777 **VII**: 151.
2N-T778* **VII**: 151.
2N-T778a **VII**: 151.
2N-T779* **VII**: 151.
2N-T780* **VII**: 151.
2N-T782* **VII**: 151.
2N-T783* **VII**: 151.
2N-T788 **VII**: 151.
2NT 293 **VII**: 213.
2NT 295-302 **VII**: 213.
329.76.11.17 **VII**: 232.
3N-T403+T340 **VII**: 281.
4 R. 34, No. 2 **V**: 558.
4 R.46, 5-19 **VII**: 157.
5 R.33 **V**: 543, 558.
5N-T 567 **VII**: 154.
68-7-9 I (Cylinder) **VII**: 232, 232.
688' 66 (Egyptian Relief) **V**: 223.
6A 343 **VII**: 264.
6N-128 **VII**: 154.
6N-T1033 **VII**: 154.
6N-T112 **VII**: 154.
6N-T264 **VII**: 154.
6N-T658 **VII**: 154.
6N-T662 **VII**: 154.
76-79, 155 **VII**: 208.
79-7-8, 49 **VII**: 181.
79-7-8, 77 **VII**: 202.
79-7-8, 188 **VII**: 196.
79-7-8, 291 **VII**: 230.
8, 81/1 30 **VII**: 233.
80, 7-19, 15 **VII**: 183.
80, 7-19, 125 **VII**: 199, 284.
80, 7-19, 126 **VII**: 183, 199.
80, 7-8, 19 **VII**: 183.
80-7-19, 17 **VII**: 178.
80-7-19, 20 **VII**: 174.
80-7-19, 127 **VII**: 157, 200.
80-7-19, 333 **VII**: 190.
80-11-3, 619 **II**: *235*.
80-11-12, 475 **VII**: 196.
81-1-18, 489 **VII**: 223.
81, 2 4, 188 **VII**: 198.
81, 2-4, 247 **VII**: 199, 284.
81-2-4, 166 **VII**: 202.
81-2-4, 194 **VII**: 200.
81-2-4, 233 **VII**: 202.
81-2-4, 447 **VII**: 148.
81-2-4, 507 **VII**: 148.
81-7-4, 139 **VII**: 215, 329.
81-7-6, 102 **VII**: 259.

81-7-6, 141	**VII**: 208, 215, 269.
81-7-6, 141 (35726)	**VII**: 208, 215, 269, 316, 329.
81-7-6, 142	**VII**: 215, 329.
81-7-27, 49	**VII**: 209.
81-7-27, 50	**VII**: 209.
81-7-27, 77	**VII**: 157, 200.
81-7-27, 199	**VII**: 174.
81-7-27, 199a	**VII**: 174.
81-7-27, 203	**VII**: 157, 200.
81-11-3, 478	**VII**: 219.
81-11-8, 154	**VII**: 219.
82-3-23, 28	**VII**: 148.
82-3-23, 146	**VII**: 148.
82-3-23, 149	**VII**: 148.
82-3-23, 151	**VII**: 148.
82-3-23, 271	**VII**: 207.
82-3-23, 607	**VII**: 207.
82-3-23, 646	**VII**: 207.
82-3-23, 845	**VII**: 207.
82-3-23, 1271	**VII**: 207.
82-3-23, 3363	**VII**: 207.
82-3-23, 4344 + 4773	**VII**: 219.
82-3-23, 4593	**VII**: 219.
82-5-22, 121	**VII**: 185
82-5-22, 538	**VII**: 202.
82-5-22, 572	**VII**: 148.
82-5-22, 575	**VII**: 148.
82-5-22, 946 (54626)	**VII**: 219.
82-5-22, 956 (54626)	**V**: 561.
82-7-4, 37	**VII**: 178.
82-7-4, 137	**VII**: 147.
82-7-14, 418 (56058)	**VII**: 209.
82-7-14, 796 (56424)	**VII**: 209.
83-1-18, 2	**VII**: 174.
83-1-18, 34	**VII**: 174.
83-1-18, 41	**VII**: 174.
83-1-18, 427	**VII**: 199.
83-1-18, 462	**VII**: 148.
83-1-18, 469	**VII**: 264.
83-1-18, 488	**VII**: 151.
83-1-18, 516	**VII**: 151.
83-1-18, 602	**VII**: 190.
83-1-18, 693	**VII**: 151.
83-1-18, 899	**VII**: 148.
83-1-18. 1846	**VII**: 219.
83-1-18. 1847	**VII**: 219.
83-1-18, 2348	**VII**: 259.
83-1-18, 2434	**VII**: 207.
83, 1-19, 691	**VII**: 199, 284.
85, 4-30 I (Cylinder)	**VII**: 232, 232.
88-4-19, 17	**VII**; 147.
88-5-12, 91 (78905)	**VII**: 209.
94-6-11, 36	**VII**: 183.
98595	**VII**: 197.
A. 379	**VII**: 149.
A. 380	**VII**: 149.
A. 381	**VII**: 149.
A. 382	**VII**: 149.
A. 385	**VII**: 149.
A. 386	**VII**: 149.
A. 387	**VII**: 149.
A. 391	**VII**: 149.
A. 393	**VII**: 149.
A. 920-A. 1001	**VII**: 176.
A. 3444	**VII**: 229.
A.H. 82, 7-14, 631	**VII**: 232.
A.H. 82, 7-14, 649	**VII**: 232.
A.H. 82-7-14, 1042	**VII**: 233*(2)*.
ABL 1391	**VII**: 189.
AH 82, 7-14, 1042	**VII**: 208.
Alalaḫ Tablet *456	**VII**: 153*(2)*, 240.
AM 1938. 790	**VII**: 364.
AO 5504	**VII**: 204.
AO 6041	**VII**: 204.
AO 6458	**VII**: 285.
AO 21306	**VII**: 178; **IX**: cxxv.

AO 22497	**VII**: 178; **IX**: cxxv.
AO 22499	**VII**: 178; **IX**: cxxv.
Arch. Musem of Florence (Inv. No. 7207)	**I**: *412*.
Archaeological Museum of Florence (Inv. No. 7207)	**VII**: 27.
Ash. 1924.475	**VI**: 58.
Ashmolean Museum 1483	**VII**: 178; **IX**: cxxv.
Ashmolean Museum 1894, 107b	**VII**: 26.
Ashmolean Museum 1911-276	**VII**: 279.
Ashmolean Museum 1911-278	**VII**: 279.
Ashmolean Museum 1911-279	**VII**: 279.
Ashmolean Museum 1911-280	**VII**: 279.
Ashmolean Museum 1911-281	**VII**: 279.
Ashmolean Museum 1911-282	**VII**: 279.
Ashmolean Museum 1911-284	**VII**: 279.
Ashmolean Museum 1911-285	**VII**: 279.
Ashmolean Museum 1911-286	**VII**: 279.
Ashmolean Museum 1911-288	**VII**: 279.
Ashmolean Museum 1924-810	**VII**: 195, 271.
Ashmolean Museum 1924-846	**VII**: 195, 271.
Ashmolean Museum 1924-849	**VII**: 195, 271.
Ashmolean Museum 1967	**VII**: 178; **IX**: cxxv.
Ashmolean Museum W-B. 62	**VII**: 279.
Ashmolean Prism 1931.128	**VII**: 220.
Babylon 36383	**VII**: 202.
Barton, P.B.S. IX, No. 4	**VII**: 193, 279.
Berl. Sept 18	**VI**: 390.
Berlin Pap. 9784	**VII**: 77.
Berlin Pap. 9785	**VII**: 77.
Berlin Trauerrelief, (No. 12411)	**II**: 6, 44, 60, 67.
Berlin VA 3111	**VII**: 209.
Berlin VA 3300	**VII**: 209.
Berlin VA 3309	**VII**: 209.
Bibl. Nat. Copt. 129[1]	**IV**: 43.
B.M. No. 101 (Stela)	**VII**: 22.
B.M. 604	**VII**: 21.
BM 742	**VII**: 186.
B.M. 826 (Stela)	**VII**: 23.
B.M. stela 1203	**V**: 339; **VII**: 25.
B.M. 1332 (Stela)	**VII**: 16.
B.M. 1658 (Stela)	**VII**: 22.
BM 1735 (Egyptian Statue)	**III**: 768.
BM Or. 4445	**IV**: 15*(2)*.
BM 4792	**II**: *235*.
BM Or. 4951 (Syriac)	**IV**: 45.
B.M. 5624, 5625, 5637	**VII**: 40.
B.M. 5629	**VII**: 35.
B.M. 8308A, 9900, 6680	**VII**: 55.
B.M. Or. 9180A	**VII**: 105.
B.M. Papyrus 10052	**VII**: 16.
B.M. 10055	**VII**: 78.
BM 10056	**I**: *353, 436;* **VII**: 16.
B.M. Pap. 10,057 + 10,058	**VII**: 37.
B.M. 10059	**VII**: 33.
B.M. 10072 Papyrus	**VII**: 53.
BM. 10075, Payrus, Ex Salt Coll. No. 418	**VII**: 31.
B.M. 10250	**VII**: 34.
B.M. 10417	**VII**: 40.

B.M. 10471 **VII**: 78.
B.M. 10473 **VII**: 78.
B.M. 10474 **VII**: 10.
B.M. 10561, Pap. dem. **VII**: 31.
B.M. 10589 **VII**: 81.
B.M. 10601 **VII**: 81.
B.M. Eg. 10622 **VII**: 80.
B.M. Eg. 10624 **VII**: 80.
B.M. 10750 Papyrus **VII**: 31.
BM 12867 **VII**: 190.
BM Add. 14425 (Peshiṭta) **IV**: 7, 47; **V**: 531.
BM 15821 **VII**: 285.
BM 18175 (Egyptian Ivory Carving) **III**: 770.
BM 21,901 **I**: 462; **IV**: 360, 381, 382, 542; **VI**: 593; **VII**: 236, 237, 240.
B.M. 21946 **VII**: 240.
B.M. 22047 **VII**: 240.
BM. 23103 **VII**: 276.
B.M. 25124 **VII**: 240.
B.M. 25127 **VII**: 240.
BM 29615 **VII**: 285.
BM 29623 **VII**: 284.
BM 29644 **VII**: 284.
B.M. 30335 **VII**: 40.
B.M. 33428 **VII**: 254.
BM. 33769 **VII**: 215, 329.
B.M. 33769 **VII**: 273.
BM. 33778 **VII**: 215, 329.
BM 33,851 **VII**: 221.
B.M. 34647 **VII**: 265.
BM. 34781 **VII**: 215.
B.M. 34781 **VII**: 215, 273, 329.
B.M. 34797 **VII**: 208, 215, 269. 316, 329.
BM. 34798 **VII**: 208, 215, 269, 329.
B.M. 34799 **VII**: 215, 269, 329.
BM. 34816 **VII**: 215, 329.
BM. 35154 **VII**: 215, 329.
BM. 35458 **VII**: 215, 329.
BM. 35459 **VII**: 215, 329.
BM. 35603 **VII**: 239.
BM. 35726 **VII**: 208, 215, 269, 316, 329.
B.M. 35727 **VII**: 208, 215, 269, 316, 329.
B.M. 36301 = 80-6-17, 27 **VII**: 257.
B.M. 36559 (=8 0-6-17, 328 + 444) + 36941 (= 80-6-17, 682) **II**: *235*.
B.M. 36599 (= 80-6-17, 328 + 444) **VII**: 258.
B.M. 36712 **VII**: 257.
B.M. 36722 (= 80-6-17, 455) **VII**: 258.
B.M. 36731 = 80-6-17, 464 **VII**: 257.
B.M. 36737 (= 80-6-17, 470) **VII**: 258.
B.M. 36744 (= 80-6-17, 477) **VII**: 258.
B.M. 36822 (= 80-6-17, 561) **II**: *235*.
B.M. 36822 (= 80-6-17, 561) **VII**: 258.
B.M. 36838 = 80-6-17, 578 **VII**: 257.
B.M. 36941 (= 80-6-17, 682) **VII**: 258.
B.M. 37022 (= 80-6-17, 766) **II**: *235*.
B.M. 37022 (= 80-6-17, 766) **VII**: 258.
B.M. 37031 (= 80-6-17, 775) **VII**: 258.
BM 37089 **II**: *234;* **VII**: 257.
B.M. 37149 = 80-6-17, 899 **VII**: 257.
BM 37266 = 80-16-1022x **VII**: 257.
BM 37883 (Head) **III**: 731.

B.M. 40082 (= 80-2-1, 47) **VII**: 258.
BM 41004 = 81, 4-282 551 **VII**: 257.
BM 46537 **VII**: 196, 210.
B.M. 47912 (= 80-11-3, 619) **VII**: 258.
BM 48954 (gem) **III**: 670.
BM. 49785 **VII**: 215.
BM 50745 = EA 378 **VII**: 172.
BM 54678 (Ivory Sphinx from Abydos) **III**: 770.
BM. 56348 **VII**: 215.
B.M. 56620 **VII**: 262, 270.
BM 57002 **VII**: 268.
BM. 57337 **VII**: 215.
BM. 59776 **VII**: 246.
BM. 74329 **VII**: 215.
BM 77810 **VII**: 163.
B.M. 78183 **VII**: 285.
BM 78219 **III**: 647; **V**: 181.
BM. 78944 **VII**: 246.
BM. 78979 **VII**: 246.
B.M. 79503 **VII**: 153, 277.
B.M. 80328 **I**: *120;* **II**: *43, 211(2);* **VII**: 241.
BM 82684 **VII**: 220.
BM 82685 **VII**: 220.
B.M. 88140 **VII**: 274.
B.M. 90951 **VII**: 278.
BM. 92699 = 82-7-14,4460 **VII**: 299.
B.M. 96273 **VII**: 241.
B.M. 96706 **VII**: 286.
BM 98730 **VII**: 223..
BM. 98731 **VII**: 223.
BM. 100418 **VII**: 212.
BM. 100450 **VII**: 213.
BM. 100494 **VII**: 213.
BM. 100611 **VII**: 213.
B.M. 10068 **VII**: 77.
BM. 102105 **VII**: 213.
BM. 102963 **VII**: 213.
BM. 103030 **VII**: 213.
BM. 103032 **VII**: 213.
BM 103041 **VII**: 307.
BM 103043 **VII**: 307.
BM. 103053 **VII**: 213.
BM. 103417 **VII**: 212.
BM. 103437 **VII**: 252.
B.M. 105346 **VII**: 271.
BM. 105360 **VII**: 212.
BM. 105367 **VII**: 252.
BM. 105377 **VII**: 212.
BM. 105397 **VII**: 252.
BM. 105399 **VII**: 252.
B.M. 105412 **VII**: 271.
BM. 105416 **VII**: 252.
BM. 105420 **VII**: 213.
BM. 105425 **VII**: 213.
BM. 105428 **VII**: 213.
BM. 105429 **VII**: 252.
BM. 105442 **VII**: 212.
BM. 105443 **VII**: 212.
BM. 105446 **VII**: 213.
BM. 105447 **VII**: 213.
BM. 105450 **VII**: 213.
BM. 105453 **VII**: 213.
BM. 105454 **VII**: 213.
BM. 105470 **VII**: 213.
BM. 105482 **VII**: 213.
BM. 105483 **VII**: 213.
BM. 105484 **VII**: 213.
BM. 105486 **VII**: 213.
BM. 105494 **VII**: 213.
BM. 105504 **VII**: 213.
BM. 105507 **VII**: 213.
BM. 105513 **VII**: 252.
BM. 105514 **VII**: 213.
BM. 105516 **VII**: 213.
BM. 105517 **VII**: 212.

BM. 105523	**VII**: 213.
BM. 105525	**VII**: 213.
BM. 105530	**VII**: 213.
BM. 105534	**VII**: 213.
BM. 105541	**VII**: 213.
B.M. 105545	**VII**: 271.
BM. 105560	**VII**: 213.
BM. 105561	**VII**: 252.
BM. 105562	**VII**: 213.
BM. 105563	**VII**: 274.
BM. 105568	**VII**: 213.
BM. 105596	**VII**: 212, 213.
BM. 106055	**VII**: 215.
B.M. 106064	**VII**: 271.
BM. 111745	**VII**: 213.
BM. 111749	**VII**: 212.
BM. 111751	**VII**: 213.
BM. 111755	**VII**: 213.
BM. 111761	**VII**: 213.
BM. 111772	**VII**: 213.
BM. 111774	**VII**: 213.
BM. 111779	**VII**: 252.
BM. 111784	**VII**: 213.
BM. 111789	**VII**: 213.
BM. 111791	**VII**: 252.
BM. 111794	**VII**: 212, 213.
BM. 111797	**VII**: 213.
BM. 111800	**VII**: 213.
BM. 111802	**VII**: 212, 213.
BM. 112931	**VII**: 213.
BM. 112935	**VII**: 252.
BM. 112941	**VII**: 213.
BM. 112943	**VII**: 212.
BM. 112945	**VII**: 213.
BM. 112946	**VII**: 213.
BM. 112947	**VII**: 213.
BM. 112952	**VII**: 212.
BM. 112960	**VII**: 213.
BM. 112984	**VII**: 213.
BM. 112985	**VII**: 213.
BM. 112993	**VII**: 213.
BM. 113000	**VII**: 213.
BM. 113010	**VII**: 212.
BM. 113017	**VII**: 213.
BM. 113022	**VII**: 213.
BM. 113031	**VII**: 212.
BM. 113037	**VII**: 252.
BM. 113061	**VII**: 213.
BM. 113064	**VII**: 213.
BM. 113075	**VII**: 212.
BM. 113089	**VII**: 213.
BM. 113090	**VII**: 213.
BM. 113117	**VII**: 213.
BM. 113122	**VII**: 213.
B.M. 113129	**VII**: 271.
BM. 113132	**VII**: 212.
BM. 113132	**VII**: 213.
BM. 113136	**VII**: 213.
BM. 113141	**VII**: 213.
BM. 113144	**VII**: 213.
BM. 113147	**VII**: 213.
BM. 113154	**VII**: 213.
BM. 113155	**VII**: 213.
BM. 113160	**VII**: 213.
BM. 113170	**VII**: 213.
BM. 113437	**VII**: 213.
BM 113886	**VII**: 299.
BM 116662	**VII**: 237.
BM 116737	**VII**: 227; **IX**: cxxvi.
BM 117580	**VII**: 210, 277.
B.M. 117666	**VII**: 262.
BM 117836	**VII**: 237.
BM 117837	**VII**: 237.
BM 117838	**VII**: 237.
BM 120960	**II**: 223; **VII**: 255.
BM 121033	**VII**: 223..
B.M. 121208	**VII**: 286.
BM 122613	**VII**: 190.
BM 122616	**VII**: 190.

BM 123358: TN 1932-12-10, 30	**VII**: 195.
BM 123410	**VII**: 190.
BM 123414	**VII**: 190.
BM 127840	**VII**: 190.
BM 127889	**VII**: 190.
BM 127896	**VII**: 190.
BM 127916	**VII**: 190.
BM 127923	**VII**: 190.
BM 127940	**VII**: 190.
BM 127941	**VII**: 190.
BM 127943	**VII**: 190.
BM 127994	**VII**: 190.
BM 128073	**VII**: 190.
BM 128130+	**VII**: 190.
BM 128230	**VII**: 190.
BM 128305	**VII**: 190.
BM 128306	**VII**: 190.
BM 130729	**VII**: 150.
BM 134454	**VII**: 190.
BM 134464	**VII**: 190.
BM 134480	**VII**: 190.
BM 134481	**VII**: 190.
BM 134557	**VII**: 190.
BM 134880	**VII**: 220.
B.M. 34798	**VII**: 273.
BM 47805	**VII**: 241.
BM 48032	**VII**: 241.
BM 48035	**VII**: 241.
BM 48037	**VII**: 241.
BM 48046	**VII**: 241.
B.M. 76-10-16, 24	**VII**: 205.
BM. 81-6-7, 209	**VII**: 185.
BM. 81-701, 3395	**VII**: 299.
BM 98098	**VII**: 241.
Bodl. Baroccianus 15	**VI**: 535.
Bodleian 146	**VII**: 285.
Bodleian 168	**VII**: 285.
Bodleian 170	**VII**: 285.
Bodleian Heb. MSS. e68	**VIII**: 205.
Bodleian Ms. Gr. Class. c(87) P	**VII**: 384
Bodley MS 2176/6	**VII**: 108.
Bodley MS. 2716/6, fol. 16b 6-17a 6	**VIII**: 206.
Borgia Copt. 78	**IV**: 44.
Br. 8072-7	**V**: 375, 562, 579.
Br. 8890	**V**: 545.
Brooklyn Museum 08.482	**VII**: 150.
Brussels, Musée National #10952	**IV**: 44.
Brym Mawr College T 46	**VII**: 150.
Brym Mawr College T 47	**VII**: 150.
BT. 100-109	**VII**: 194.
BT. 112-120	**VII**: 194.
BT. 123-128	**VII**: 194.
BT. 136	**VII**: 194.
BT. 138-140	**VII**: 194.
Bu. 25. 88-5-12	**VII**: 206.
Bu. 27. 88-5-12	**VII**: 206.
Bu. 59. 88-5-12	**VII**: 206.
Bu. 80-7-19, 130	**VII**: 221.
Bu. 89-4-26, 209	**VII**: 200.
Bu. 343. 88-5-12	**VII**: 206.
Bu. 625. 88-5-12	**VII**: 206.
Bu. 88-5-11	**VII**: 249.
Bu. 88-5-12	**VII**: 249, 253.
Bu. 88-5-120	**VII**: 249.
Bu. 88-5-12,329	**VII**: 259.
Bu. 91-5-9, 143 + 176	**VII**: 264.
BU. 91-5-9, 210	**VII**: 179.
Bu. '91-5-9, 221	**VII**: 249.
Bu. 91-5-9, 308	**VII**: 250.
Bu. 91-5-9, 355	**VII**: 250.
Bu. 91-5-9, 373	**VII**: 250.
Bu. 91-5-9, 402	**VII**: 250.
Bu. 91-5-9, 450	**VII**: 250.
Bu. 91-5-9, 458	**VII**: 250.
Bu. 91-5-9, 469	**VII**: 250.
Bu. 91-5-9, 474	**VII**: 250.

Bu. 91-5-9, 557	**VII**: 250.	Bu. 91-5-9, 868	**VII**: 250.
Bu. 91-5-9, 594	**VII**: 250.	Bu. 91-5-9, 873	**VII**: 250.
Bu. 91-5-9, 600	**VII**: 250.	Bu. 91-5-9, 891	**VII**: 250.
Bu. 91-5-9, 602	**VII**: 250.	Bu. 91-5-9, 906	**VII**: 250.
Bu. 91-5-9, 608	**VII**: 250.	Bu. 91-5-9, 910	**VII**: 250.
Bu. 91-5-9, 612	**VII**: 250.	Bu. 91-5-9, 936	**VII**: 250.
Bu. 91-5-9, 613	**VII**: 250.	Bu. 91-5-9, 958	**VII**: 250.
Bu. 91-5-9, 614	**VII**: 250.	Bu. 91-5-9, 967	**VII**: 250.
Bu. 91-5-9, 615	**VII**: 250.	Bu. 91-5-9, 1003	**VII**: 250.
Bu. 91-5-9, 618	**VII**: 250.	Bu. 91-5-9, 2180	**VII**: 250.
Bu. 91-5-9, 628	**VII**: 250.	Bu. 91-5-9, 2184	**VII**: 250.
Bu. 91-5-9, 630	**VII**: 250.	Bu. 91-5-9, 2189	**VII**: 250.
Bu. 91-5-9, 631	**VII**: 250.	Bu. 91-5-9, 2189A	**VII**: 250.
Bu. 91-5-9, 639	**VII**: 250.	Bu. 91-5-9, 2373	**VII**: 250.
Bu. 91-5-9, 674	**VII**: 250.	Bu. 91-5-9, 2448	**VII**: 250.
Bu. 91-5-9, 677	**VII**: 250.	Bu. 91-5-9, 2456	**VII**: 250.
Bu. 91-5-9, 682	**VII**: 250.	Bu. 91-5-9, 2483	**VII**: 250.
Bu. 91-5-9, 689	**VII**: 250.	Bu. 91-5-9, 2483A	**VII**: 250.
Bu. 91-5-9, 694	**VII**: 250.	Bu. 91-5-9, 2487	**VII**: 250.
Bu. 91-5-9, 697	**VII**: 250.	Bu. 91-5-9, 2493	**VII**: 250.
Bu. 91-5-9, 699	**VII**: 250.	Bu. 91-5-9, 2495	**VII**: 250.
Bu. 91-5-9, 699	**VII**: 250.	Bu. 91-5-9, 2497	**VII**: 250.
Bu. 91-5-9, 700	**VII**: 250.	Bu. 91-5-9, 2497A	**VII**: 250.
Bu. 91-5-9, 706	**VII**: 250.	Bu. 91-5-9, 2500	**VII**: 250.
Bu. 91-5-9, 731	**VII**: 250.	Bu. 91-5-9, 2509	**VII**: 250.
Bu. 91-5-9, 735	**VII**: 250.	Bu. 91-5-9, 2515	**VII**: 250.
Bu. 91-5-9, 740	**VII**: 250.	Bu. 91-5-9, 2517	**VII**: 250.
Bu. 91-5-9, 744	**VII**: 250.	C 14 Louvre	**VII**: 18, 21.
Bu. 91-5-9, 748	**VII**: 250.	C.B.S. 16108	**VII**: 236.
Bu. 91-5-9, 752	**VII**: 250.	C.T. 16, 10, 26	**VI**: 337.
Bu. 91-5-9, 780	**VII**: 250.	C.T. 20	**VII**: 199.
Bu. 91-5-9, 781	**VII**: 250.	C.T.C.T., I. 48, 7-8	**V**: 545.
Bu. 91-5-9, 788	**VII**: 250.	*C.T.* XV	**VII**: 260.
Bu. 91-5-9, 806	**VII**: 250.	Cairo Mus #35468a	**VII**: 123.
Bu. 91-5-9, 810	**VII**: 250.	Cambridge, C.C.C., MS. 2	**IV**: 42.
Bu. 91-5-9, 828	**VII**: 250.	Cambridge, T-S. H.8/61	**VIII**: 206.
Bu. 91-5-9, 835	**VII**: 250.	Carnarvon Tablet No. 1	**VII**: 16, 62.
Bu. 91-5-9, 856	**VII**: 250.		
Bu. 91-5-9, 857	**VII**: 250.		
Bu. 91-5-9, 864	**VII**: 250.		

Caro Museum no. 39145 (Statue of Twēret)	**III**: 769; **V**: 224.
Cath. Univ. 1+2+64	**VII**: 150.
CBS 9	**VII**: 261.
CBS 192-311	**VII**: 377.
CBS 334	**VII**: 264.
CBS 733 + 1757	**VII**: 194.
CBS 1203	**VII**: 264.
CBS 7393	**VII**: 212.
CBS 7914	**VII**: 229, 283.
CBS 8090	**VII**: 271.
CBS 8536	**VII**: 255.
CBS 13293	**VII**: 240.
CBS 13484	**VII**: 240.
CBS 13972	**VII**: 277.
CBS 14221	**III**: 406; **VII**: 156.
CBS 14223	**VII**: 278.
CBS 14226	**VII**: 278.
CBS 14543	**II**: *35;* **VII**: 298.
CGC No. 58045	**VII**: 79.
CH^{27} 3:68.	**V**: 550, 576.
CIOM 2124	**VII**: 164.
Cod. Vatican. Graecus 1238	**VI**: 646, 647.
Codex Heb. C.18	**VI**: 706.
Coislin 305	**VI**: 684.
Columbia University 6x	**VII**: 256.
Columbia University 7x	**VII**: 263.
Cop. Pap. XI (I)	**IV**: 8.
Cop Pap. XI(I) [=Crum 52]	**IV**: 43.
Cornelll University Library 78	**VII**: 238, 252, 278.
Coumbia University 8x	**VII**: 252.
Craig, *RT*. i, 18	**VII**: 262.
Crönert, *Raccolta Lumbroso* 530	**VII**: 331.
Crozer 151	**VII**: 220.
Crozer 153	**VII**: 220.
Crozer 154	**VII**: 220.
Crozer 155	**VII**: 220.
Crozer 157	**VII**: 220.
Crozer 158	**VII**: 220.
Crozer 159	**VII**: 220.
Crozer 160	**VII**: 220.
Crozer 161	**VII**: 220.
Crozer 162	**VII**: 220.
Crozer 163	**VII**: 220.
Crozer 164	**VII**: 220.
Crozer 167	**VII**: 220.
Crozer 168	**VII**: 220.
Crozer 169	**VII**: 220.
Crozer 170	**VII**: 220.
Crozer 171	**VII**: 220.
Crozer 172	**VII**: 220.
Crozer 174	**VII**: 220.
Crozer 175	**VII**: 220.
Crozer 178	**VII**: 220.
Crozer 179	**VII**: 220.
Crozer 180	**VII**: 220.
Crozer 181	**VII**: 220.
Crozer 183	**VII**: 220.
Crozer 195	**VII**: 150.
Crozer 199	**VII**: 278.
Crozer 201	**VII**: 211, 252.
Crozer 204	**VII**: 252.
Crozer 615	**VII**: 220.
Crum 46	**IV**: 8.
Crum 480	**I**: 435; **VII**: 350.
Crum 52	**IV**: 8.
CT. 11, 34	**VII**: 197.
CT 16, 46, 183-204	**VII**: 157, 201, 282, 286.
CT. 18, 43	**VII**: 197.
CT. 19, 10	**V**: 569.
CT. 19, 39	**VII**: 197.
CT 36, 28-30	**VII**: 286.
CT XV 7-30	**VII**: 209.
CT XXIII 15-18	**VII**: 158.
cta. 3III D 33-IV 48	**VII**: 146.
cta. 41V 33-34	**VII**: 146.

Cyrus 5. 1. 10 **VII**: 206.
D.T. 106 **VII**: 151.
D.T. 147 **VII**: 181.
D.T. 290 **VII**: 181.
D.T. 363 **VII**: 198.
D.T. 363 **VII**: 198.
Darius 14-12-2 **VII**: 206.
Darius 19-4-26 **VII**: 206.
Darius 25-12-8 **VII**: 206.
Davenport Public Museum B878 **VII**: 253.
DT. 45 **VII**: 157, 200.
DT. 46 **VII**: 199, 284.
DT. 57 **VII**: 201.
DT. 72 92684 **VII**: 264.
DT. 75 **VII**: 199, 284.
DT. 78 92685 **VII**: 264.
DT. 83 **VII**: 174, 207.
DT. 103 **VII**: 148.
DT. 184 **VII**: 202.
EA 260 **VII**: 172.
EA 285-290 **VII**: 172.
EA 317 **VII**: 172.
EA 318 **VII**: 172.
EA 378 = BM 50745 **VII**: 172.
EA 82 **VII**: 171.
EA 89 **VII**: 171.
EA 96 **VII**: 172.
Eb 10 **VII**: 108.
Eb. 448 **VI**: 14.
Egerton Papyrus 4: **VI**: 593*(2)*, 594.
Elkan Adler Papyrus No. 31 **VII**: 80.
Emory 106 **VII**: 220, 272.
Emory University No. 38 **II**: *51;* **VII**: 272.
Emory University No. 45 **I**: *425;* **VII**: 272.
Emory University No. 55 **II**: *51;* **VII**: 272.
Enuma Elis III 69 **VII**: 176.
Enuma Elis VI 61-66 **VII**: 223.
F. 13 **VII**: 280.
F. 602 **VII**: 280.
F. 973 **VII**: 280.
F. 974 **VII**: 280.
F. 1153 **VII**: 176.
F. 1154 **VII**: 176.
F. 1156 **VII**: 176.
F. 1159 **VII**: 176.
F. 1162 **VII**: 176.
F. 1163 **VII**: 176.
F. 4893 **VII**: 280.
Florence Museo Archaeologico no. 2566 **III**: 750.
Fyoom No. 7798 **VII**: 14.
Geneva Papyrus MAH 15274 **VII**: 79.
Giessen Univ. Library Papyrus No. 115 **VII**: 79.
GN-T1033a **VII**: 154.
Gordon 1020 **VII**: 146.
Gurob Pap. II 1 **VII**: 77.
Gurob Pap. II 2 **VII**: 77.
H. 35 **VII**: 174.
H. 140 **VII**: 174.
H. 187 **VII**: 174.
H. 193 **VII**: 174.
H. 223 **VII**: 174.
H. 348 **VII**: 174.
H. 359 **VII**: 174.
H. 364 **VII**: 174.
H. 375 **VII**: 174.
H. 382 **VII**: 174.
H. 383 **VII**: 174.
H. 391 **VII**: 174.
H. 1396 **V**: 580; **IX**: cxlii.
H. 1449 **V**: 580; **IX**: cxlii.
H. 6167 **VII**: 213.
H. 6246 **VII**: 212.
H. 6247 **VII**: 212.
H. 6248 **VII**: 212.

H. 6249 **VII**: 212.
H. 6250 **VII**: 212.
H. 6262 **VII**: 212.
H. 6289 **VII**: 212.
H. 6291 **VII**: 212.
H. 6311 **VII**: 213.
H. 6328 **VII**: 212.
H. 6329 **VII**: 212.
H. 6337 **VII**: 213.
H. 6339 **VII**: 213.
H. 6376 **VII**: 213.
H. 6378 **VII**: 213.
H. 6383 **VII**: 213.
H. 6385 **VII**: 213.
H. 6396 **VII**: 213.
H. 6496 **VII**: 213.
H. 6671 **VII**: 212.
H. 6694 **VII**: 213.
H. 6743 **VII**: 212.
H. 6761 **VII**: 212.
H. 7058 **VII**: 212.
H. 7191 **VII**: 213.
H. 7782 **VII**: 212.
H. 7907 **VII**: 212.
H. 7921 **VII**: 212.
H. 7944 **VII**: 212.
H. 7963 **VII**: 212.
H. 7970 **VII**: 213.
H. 7991 **VII**: 212.
H. 8065 **VII**: 212.
H. 8069 **VII**: 212.
H. 8084 **VII**: 212.
H. 9170 **VII**: 213.
H.S.M. 6795 **V**: 576.
H.S.W. 48 **VII**: 268.
H.S.W. 49 **VII**: 268.
Hamath 4.4.2 **VII**: 329.
Hamath 4.6.4. **VII**: 329.
Harding Smith W. 67 **VII**: 193.
Harper 635 **VII**: 175.
Harper 858 **VII**: 175.
Harper ABL 555 **VII**: 179.
Harvard Semitic Museum 1421 **VII**: 250.
Harvard Semitic Musuem No. 109 **III**: 645.
Hispania 14 **VII**: 120.
HMS 8826 (Statuette) **VII**: 272.
HS 1428 **VII**: 283.
HS 1440 **VII**: 283.
HS 1529 **VII**: 283.
HS 1549 **VII**: 283.
HS 1560 **VII**: 283.
HS 1570 **VII**: 283.
HS 1581 **VII**: 283.
HSM 1659 **VII**: 273.
HSM 3625 **VII**: 215, 273.
HSM 3644 **VII**: 304.
HSM 3645 **VII**: 304.
HSM 3662 **VII**: 273.
HSM 7500 **VII**: 273.
HSM 7522 **VII**: 273.
HSM 7794 **VII**: 273.
HSS XV 32 **V**: 552.
HT. 1 **VII**: 308.
HT. 126-131 **VII**: 284.
HTS 143 **VII**: 214, 272.
HTS 144 **VII**: 214, 272.
HTS 145 **VII**: 214, 272.
HTS 146 **VII**: 272.
I.M. 50009 **VII**: 238.
I.M. 50010 **VII**: 238.
I.M. 50011 **VII**: 238.
I.M. 50140 **VII**: 238.
I.M. 51923 **VII**: 238.
I.M. 51924 **VII**: 238.
I R. 45-47 **VII**: 184.
IBoT I 31 **VII**: 304.
IG II^2 2343 **II**: 117.
III R. 15-16 **VII**: 184.

ILA II 7a	**VII**: 363.	IM. 50961	**VII**: 213.
IM. 15218 (Seal)	**III**: 653.	IM. 50964	**VII**: 213.
IM 31247	**VII**: 257.	IM. 50968	**VII**: 213.
IM. 49219	**VII**: 219.	IM. 51046	**VII**: 218.
IM. 49222	**VII**: 219.	IM. 51047	**VII**: 218.
IM. 49225	**VII**: 219.	IM. 51048	**VII**: 218.
IM. 49226	**VII**: 219.	IM. 51049	**VII**: 218.
IM. 49233	**VII**: 219.	IM. 51053	**VII**: 218.
IM. 49240	**VII**: 219.	IM. 51059	**VII**: 193, 252.
IM. 49253	**VII**: 219.	IM. 51062	**VII**: 218.
IM. 49274	**VII**: 219.	IM. 51105	**VII**: 218.
IM. 49341	**VII**: 219.	IM. 51108	**VII**: 218.
IM. 49537	**VII**: 219.	IM. 51110	**VII**: 218.
IM. 49976	**VII**: 213.	IM. 51111	**VII**: 218.
IM. 49981	**VII**: 213.	IM. 51112	**VII**: 218.
IM. 50024	**VII**: 213.	IM. 51113	**VII**: 218.
IM. 50027	**VII**: 213.	IM. 51114	**VII**: 218.
IM. 50029	**VII**: 213.	IM. 51154	**VII**: 218.
IM. 50030	**VII**: 213.	IM. 51155	**VII**: 218.
IM. 50031	**VII**: 213.	IM. 51156	**VII**: 218.
IM. 50032	**VII**: 213.	IM. 51180	**VII**: 218.
IM. 50033	**VII**: 213.	IM. 51182	**VII**: 218.
IM. 50034	**VII**: 213.	IM. 51184	**VII**: 218.
IM. 50034	**VII**: 213.	IM. 51186	**VII**: 218.
IM. 50037	**VII**: 213.	IM. 51189	**VII**: 218.
IM. 50038	**VII**: 213.	IM. 51192	**VII**: 218.
IM. 50042	**VII**: 213.	IM. 51193	**VII**: 218.
IM. 50045	**VII**: 213.	IM. 51194	**VII**: 218.
IM. 50046	**VII**: 213.	IM. 51197	**VII**: 218.
IM. 50047	**VII**: 213.	IM. 51198	**VII**: 218.
IM. 50051	**VII**: 213.	IM. 51226	**VII**: 218.
IM. 50057	**VII**: 213.	IM. 51229	**VII**: 218.
IM. 50076	**VII**: 213.	IM. 51234	**VII**: 218.
IM. 50077	**VII**: 213.	IM. 51235	**VII**: 218.
IM. 50080	**VII**: 213.	IM. 51237	**VII**: 218.
IM. 50082	**VII**: 213.	IM. 51238A	**VII**: 218.
IM. 50084	**VII**: 213.	IM. 51238B	**VII**: 218.
IM. 50087	**VII**: 213.	IM. 51240	**VII**: 218.
IM. 50099	**VII**: 213.	IM. 51251	**VII**: 218.
IM. 50501	**VII**: 219.	IM. 51260	**VII**: 218.

IM. 51270	**VII**: 218.
IM. 51272	**VII**: 218.
IM. 51294	**VII**: 218.
IM. 51305	**VII**: 218.
IM. 51310	**VII**: 218.
IM. 51311	**VII**: 218.
IM. 51312	**VII**: 218.
IM. 51321	**VII**: 218.
IM. 51365	**VII**: 218.
IM. 51376	**VII**: 218.
IM. 51382	**VII**: 218.
IM. 51490	**VII**: 218.
IM. 51059	**VII**: 218.
IM. 51585	**VII**: 218.
IM. 51976	**VII**: 157.
IM 52001	**VII**: 257.
IM. 52251	**VII**: 219.
IM. 52301	**VII**: 256, 257.
IM. 52614	**VII**: 193, 252.
IM. 52685	**VII**: 257.
IM. 52912	**VII**: 150.
IM. 52916	**VII**: 257.
IM. 53937	**VII**: 257.
IM. 53953	**VII**: 257.
IM 53957	**VII**: 257.
IM. 53961	**VII**: 257*(2)*.
IM 53963	**VII**: 257.
IM. 53965	**VII**: 257*(2)*.
IM. 54010	**VII**: 257*(2)*.
IM 54216	**VII**: 257.
IM 54346	**VII**: 257.
IM. 54464	**VII**: 257.
IM 54478	**VII**: 257.
IM. 54538	**VII**: 257.
IM 54548	**VII**: 257.
IM. 54559	**VII**: 257*(2)*.
IM. 54669	**VII**: 187.
IM. 55204	**VII**: 272.
IM. 55296	**VII**: 214.
IM. 55357	**I**: *433, 434;* **VII**: 256*(2)*.
IM. 56577 (Relief)	**III**: 749.
IM. 56578	**VII**: 188.
IM. 57010	**VII**: 272.
IM. 60240	**VII**: 189.
IM. 60241	**VII**: 189.
IM. 60497B	**VII**: 177.
IM. 60819	**VII**: 177.
IM. 61026	**VII**: 189.
IM. 61027	**VII**: 189.
IM. 61028	**VII**: 189.
IM. 62197 (Assyrian Bronze)	**III**: 749, 758; **VII**: 177, 189.
IM. 62269 (Boundary Stone)	**II**: 276; **III**: 749.
IM. 63503 (Satute)	**III**: 749.
IM 63999	**VII**: 241.
IM. 64398 (Gypsum Statue)	**III**: 749, 767.
IM 66147 + 66148	**VII**: 241.
IM. 66453 Marble Plaque	**III**: 749.
IM. 66456 (Assyrian Marble Statue)	**III**: 749.
IM. 66461 (Limestone Statue)	**III**: 749.
IM. 67343	**VII**: 216.
IM 67618	**VII**: 264.
IM. 67953	**VII**: 253.
Imperial Ottoman Mus. #S. 54	**VII**: 217.
IV 4.21* *c*, col. ii	**VII**: 201.
J. 3	**VII**: 261.
J. 5	**VII**: 261.
J. 7	**VII**: 261.
J. 9	**VII**: 261.

J. 10 **VII**: 261.
J. 14 **VII**: 261.
J. 15 **VII**: 261.
J. 16 **VII**: 261.
Journal d'Entrée No. 86637 **I**: 403.
K. 3 **V**: 546.
K. 6 **VII**: 205.
K. 7 **VII**: 205.
K. 11 **VII**: 178.
K. 13 **VII**: 179, 216.
K. 20 **VII**: 259..
K. 21 **VII**: 178.
K. 25 **VII**: 202*(2)*.
K. 41 **VII**: 175.
K. 45 **V**: 563; **VII**; 200*(2)*.
K. 56 **VII**: 196.
K. 60 **VII**: 196.
K. 69 **VII**: 209.
K. 79 **VII**: 179, 216.
K. 80 **VII**: 178.
K. 84 **VII**: 178.
K. 89 **VII**: 178.
K. 96 **VII**: 178.
K. 98 **VII**: 195.
K. 106 **VII**: 209.
K. 112 **VII**: 174.
K. 113 **VII**: 178.
K. 125 **VII**: 178.
K. 128 **VII**: 262.
K. 138 **VII**: 269.
K. 146 **VII**: 178.
K. 152 **VII**: 196.
K. 154 **VII**: 178.
K. 164 **VII**: 199.
K. 174 **VII**: 178.
K. 181 **VII**: 178.
K. 183 **VII**: 178.
K. 189 **VII**: 173.
K. 198 **VII**: 200.
K. 203 **VII**: 175.
K. 232 **VII**: 262.
K. 251 **VII**: 251.
K. 252 (W. A. I., III, 66) **V**: 560; **VII**: 204.
K. 257 **V**: 544; **VII**: 175.
K. 260 **VII**: 196.
K. 273 **VII**: 202.
K. 362 **VII**: 174.
K. 469 **VII**: 179, 216.
K. 479 **VII**: 178.
K. 481 **VII**: 178.
K. 487 **VII**: 178.
K. 492 **VII**: 178.
K. 493 **VII**: 178.
K. 498 **VII**: 178.
K. 502 **VII**: 178.
K. 504 **VII**: 178, 179, 216.
K. 506 **VII**: 178.
K. 507 **VII**: 178.
K. 508 **VII**: 178.
K. 511 **VII**: 178.
K. 514 **VII**: 178.
K. 515 **VII**: 179, 216.
K. 518 **VII**: 174.
K. 519 **VII**: 179, 216.
K. 522 **VII**: 178.
K. 523 **VII**: 178.
K. 524 **VII**: 179, 216.
K. 525 **VII**: 178.
K. 528 **VII**: 179, 216.
K. 533 **VII**: 178.
K. 542 **VII**: 174.
K. 547 **VII**: 179, 216.
K. 549 **VII**: 178.
K. 551 **VII**: 179, 216.
K. 565 **VII**: 179, 216.
K. 572 **VII**: 178.
K. 575 **VII**: 211.

K. 578 **VII**: 178.
K. 582 **VII**: 178.
K. 589 **VII**: 174, 179, 216.
K. 629 **VII**: 179, 216.
K. 660 **VII**: 179, 216.
K. 669 **VII**: 178.
K. 679 **VII**: 178.
K. 686 **VII**: 178.
K. 824 **VII**: 179, 216.
K. 828 **VII**: 178.
K. 858 **VII**: 175.
K. 879 **VII**: 157, 200.
K. 883 **VII**: 199.
K. 898 **VII**: 174.
K. 924 **VII**: 174.
K. 945 **VII**: 148.
K. 983 **VII**: 174.
K. 1012 **VII**: 174.
K. 1014 **VII**: 174.
K. 1024 **VII**: 179, 216.
K. 1061 **VII**: 174.
K. 1122 **VII**: 178.
K. 1229 **VII**: 178.
K. 1239 **VII**: 179, 216.
K. 1249 **VII**: 178.
K. 1252 **VII**: 178.
K. 1274 **VII**: 179, 216.
K. 1279 **VII**: 199, 284.
K. 1285 **VII**: 198.
K. 1286 **VII**: 157.
K. 1290 **VII**: 201.
K. 1325 **VII**: 206, 369.
K. 1453 **VII**: 199, 284.
K. 1516 **VII**: 175.
K. 1679 **VII**: 183.
K. 1685 (Cylinder) **VII**: 232.
K. 1686 (Cylinder) **VII**: 232.
K. 1687 **VII**: 232.
K. 1913 **VII**: 148.
K. 2004 **VII**: 199, 284.
K. 2009 **VII**: 196.
K. 2015 **VII**: 148.
K. 2018A **VII**: 202.
K. 2030a **VII**: 197.
K. 2043 **VII**: 197.
K. 2044 **VII**: 148.
K. 2045 **VII**: 196.
K. 2046 **VII**: 202*(2)*.
K. 2051 **VII**: 196.
K. 2055 **VII**: 196.
K. 2056 **VII**: 197.
K. 2057 **VII**: 197.
K. 2100 **VII**: 198.
K. 2109 **VII**: 259.
K. 2175 **V**: 169, 199.
K. 2211 **VII**: 241.
K. 2216 **VII**: 202*(2)*.
K. 2239 **VII**: 202.
K. 2266 **VII**: 202.
K. 2279 **VII**: 201.
K. 2315 **VII**: 264.
K. 2361 (Column IV) **VII**: 198.
K. 2361 (Column IV & III) **VII**: 198.
K. 2401 **VII**: 199.
K. 2407 **VII**: 262.
K. 2425 **IX**: clii.
K. 2432 **VII**: 200.
K. 2453 **VII**: 200.
K. 2455 **V**: 544.
K. 2459 **VII**: 181.
K. 2473 **VII**: 200.
K. 2518 **VII**: 198.
K. 2582 **VII**: 202.
K. 2585 **VII**: 264.
K. 2600 **VII**: 202.
K. 2606 **VII**: 223.
K. 2613 **VII**: 199, 284.
K. 2625 **VII**: 202.

K 2655 **VII**: 187.
K. 2725 **VII**: 148.
K. 2726 **VII**: 148.
K. 2740 **VII**: 148.
K. 2755 **VII**: 202.
K. 2764 **VII**: 199, 284.
K. 2769 **VII**: 157, 200.
K. 2769 **VII**: 199, 284.
K. 2800 **VII**: 187.
K. 2856 **VII**: 201*(2)*, 285.
K. 2871 **VII**: 199, 284.
K. 2875 **VII**: 199, 284.
K. 2907 **VII**: 148.
K. 2918 **VII**: 148.
K. 2920 **VII**: 199, 284.
K. 2951 **VII**: 148.
K. 2983 **VII**: 148.
K. 3007 **VII**: 157, 200.
K. 3025 **VII**: 157, 200.
K 3026 **VII**: 261.
K. 3089 **VII**: 207.
K. 3089 **VII**: 223, 234.
K. 3125 **VII**: 264.
K. 3153 **VII**: 199, 284.
K. 3182 **VII**: 198, 199.
K. 3183 **VII**: 198.
K. 3186 **VII**: 198.
K. 3187 **VII**: 198.
K. 3193 **VII**: 198.
K. 3199 **VII**: 198.
K. 3205 **VII**: 157*(2)*, 200*(2)*.
K. 3216 **VII**: 198.
K. 3231 **VII**: 202.
K. 3232 **VII**: 269.
K. 3239 **VII**: 203.
K. 3241 **V**: 185.
K. 3251 **VII**: 157, 200.
K. 3258 **VII**: 199, 284.
K. 3259 **VII**: 157, 200.
K. 3278 **VII**: 203.
K. 3307 **VII**: 158, 203.
K. 3311 **VII**: 157, 200.
K. 3312 **VII**: 198.
K. 3333 **VII**: 202.
K. 3349 **VII**: 203.
K. 3356 **VII**: 199, 284.
K. 3357 **VII**: 241.
K. 3360 **VII**: 264.
K. 3361 **VII**: 199, 284.
K. 3364 **VII**: 199, 284.
K. 3379 **VII**: 264.
K. 3419 **VII**: 198.
K 3426 **VII**: 234.
K. 3431 **VII**: 157, 200.
K. 3452 **VII**: 174, 207.
K. 3459 **VII**: 198.
K. 3474 **VII**: 199.
K. 3474c.I **VII**: 198.
K. 3477 **VII**: 199, 284.
K. 3479 **VII**: 199, 284.
K. 3500 **VII**: 187, 268.
K. 3507 **VII**: 201.
K. 3515 **VII**: 201.
K. 3585 **VII**: 157, 200.
(K.) 3591 **VII**: 196.
K. 3600 **VII**: 199, 284.
K. 3608 **VII**: 203.
K. 3611 **VII**: 197.
K. 3650 **VII**: 198, 199.
K. 3658 **VII**: 157, 200.
K. 3758 **VII**: 202.
K. 3759 **VII**: 158.
K. 3820 **VII**: 202.
K. 3853 **VII**: 199, 284.
K. 3931 **VII**: 274.
K. 3941 **VII**: 202.
K. 3980 **VII**: 202.
K. 4017 **VII**: 202.
K. 4103 **VII**: 202.

K. 4147	**VII**: 148.	K. 4570	**VII**: 202.
K. 4150	**VII**: 196.	K. 4575	**VII**: 202.
K. 4153	**VII**: 230.	K. 4578	**VII**: 148.
K. 4159	**VII**: 196.	K. 4593	**VII**: 148.
K. 4160	**VII**: 148.	K. 4596	**VII**: 148.
K. 4161	**VII**: 148.	K. 4599	**VII**: 148.
K. 4167	**VII**: 148.	K. 4603	**VII**: 198, 258.
K. 4171	**VII**: 148.	K. 4605	**VII**: 148.
K. 4175	**VII**: 198, 258.	K. 4620	**VII**: 199, 284.
K. 4189	**VII**: 148.	K. 4625	**V**: 185.
K. 4199	**VII**: 148.	K. 4659	**VII**: 199, 284.
K. 4200	**VII**: 196.	K. 4697	**V**: 206, 369.
K. 4204	**VII**: 196.	K. 4713	**VII**: 206.
K. 4229	**VII**: 148.	K. 4713b	**VII**: 369.
K. 4239	**VII**: 196.	K. 4714	**VII**: 207, 234.
K. 4242	**VII**: 148.	K. 4747	**VII**: 175.
K. 4246	**VII**: 148.	K. 4815	**VII**: 157, 181, 200.
K. 4249	**VII**: 196.	K. 4816	**VII**: 198, 258.
K. 4257	**VII**: 148.	K. 4853	**VII**: 148.
K. 4258	**VII**: 196.	K. 4874	**VII**: 181, 241.
K. 4309	**VII**: 196.	K. 5008	**VII**: 199, 284.
K. 4313	**VII**: 197.	K. 5035	**VII**: 181.
K. 4316	**V**: 196.	K. 5039a	**VII**: 157, 200.
K. 4320	**VII**: 197.	K. 5098	**VII**: 157, 200.
K. 4342	**VII**: 196*(2)*.	K. 5117	**VII**: 157, 199, 200.
K. 4347	**VII**: 221.	K. 5118	**VII**: 157, 199, 200.
K. 4347b	**VII**: 202.	K. 5119	**VII**: 157, 283.
K. 4369	**VII**: 148, 270.	K. 5124	**VII**: 199, 284.
K. 4374	**VII**: 207, 23.	K. 5126	**VII**: 199, 284.
K. 4385	**VII**: 259..	K. 5142	**VII**: 199, 284.
K. 4411	**VII**: 197.	K. 5144	**VII**: 199, 284.
K. 4413	**VII**: 207.	K. 5147	**VII**: 157, 200.
K. 4428	**VII**: 148.	K. 5150	**VII**: 157, 200, 261.
K. 4445	**VII**: 185.	K. 5160	**VII**: 157, 200.
K. 4449	**VII**: 253, 254.	K. 5162	**VII**: 157, 200.
K. 4527a	**VII**: 148.	K. 5175	**VII**: 202.
K. 4541	**VII**: 185.	K. 5218	**VII**: 157, 200.
K. 4547	**VII**: 197.		
K. 4558	**VII**: 196.		
K. 4563	**VII**: 148.		

K. 5245	**VII**: 199, 284.	K. 6332	**VII**: 174.
K. 5254	**VII**: 199, 284.	K. 6359	**V**: 184.
K. 5260	**VII**: 199, 284.	K. 6399	**VII**: 202.
K. 5261	**VII**: 199, 284.	K. 6400	**VII**: 199, 284.
K. 5268	**VII**: 199, 284.	K. 6465	**VII**: 199, 284.
K. 5303	**VII**: 157, 200.	K. 6497	**VII**: 199, 284.
K. 5315	**VII**: 199, 284.	K. 6584	**VII**: 158, 203.
K. 5333	**VII**: 199, 284.	K. 6611	**VII**: 202.
K. 5333	**VII**: 199, 284.	K. 6626	**VII**: 158, 203.
K. 5338	**VII**: 157, 200.	K. 6663	**VII**: 202.
K. 5359	**VII**: 157, 200.	K. 6673	**VII**: 202.
K. 5373	**VII**: 259.	K. 6739	**VII**: 202.
K. 5425B, 6-9	**V**: 569.	K. 6768	**VII**: 202, 203.
K. 5432	**VII**: 196.	K. 6824	**VII**: 202.
K. 5433a	**VII**: 148, 196.	K. 6849	**VII**: 199, 284.
K. 5435a	**VII**: 148.	K. 6898	**VII**: 199, 284.
K. 5443	**VII**: 148.	K. 6981	**VII**: 199, 284.
K. 5449	**VII**: 196.	K. 7035	**VII**: 203.
K. 5455a	**VII**: 148.	K. 7063	**VII**: 158, 203.
K. 5464	**VII**: 178.	K. 7068	**VII**: 202.
K. 5645	**VII**: 148.	K. 7248	**VII**: 202.
K. 5839	**VII**: 175.	K. 7251	**VII**: 202.
K. 5869	**VII**: 203.	K. 7300	**VII**: 148.
K. 5926	**VII**: 148.	K. 7434	**VII**: 178.
K. 5930	**VII**: 199, 284.	K. 7592	**VII**: 198.
K. 5970	**VII**: 157, 200.	K. 7598	**VII**: 157, 200.
K. 5974	**VII**: 148.	K. 7604	**VII**: 148.
K. 5982	**VII**: 157, 200.	K. 7605	**VII**: 148.
K. 6001	**VII**: 202.	K. 7606	**VII**: 148.
K. 6063	**VII**: 157, 200.	K. 7619	**VII**: 175.
K. 6068	**V**: 185.	K. 7626	**VII**: 148.
K. 6075	**VII**: 202.	K. 7627	**VII**: 148.
K. 6160	**VII**: 199, 284.	K. 7654	**VII**: 148.
K. 6191	**VII**: 157, 200.	K. 7674	**VII**: 148.
K. 6210	**VII**: 158, 203.	K. 7696	**VII**: 148.
K. 6223	**VII**: 174.	K. 7712	**VII**: 148.
K. 6246	**VII**: 175.	K. 7741	**VII**: 148.
K. 6267	**VII**: 202.	K. 7743	**VII**: 148.
K. 6317	**VII**: 199, 284.	K. 7766	**VII**: 148.
K. 6330	**V**: 184.	K. 7780	**VII**: 148.

K. 7823	**V**: 185.	K. 8532	**VII**: 234.
K. 7860	**V**: 185.	K. 8533	**VII**: 234.
K. 7861	**VII**: 185.	K. 8534	**VII**: 234.
K. 7867	**VII**: 203.	K. 8572	**VII**: 223.
K. 7897	**VII**: 221.	K. 8583	**VII**: 202.
K. 8019	**VII**: 264.	K. 8601	**VII**: 201.
K. 8157	**VII**: 175.	K. 8607	**VII**: 157, 200.
K. 8171	**VII**: 202.	K. 8631	**VII**: 148.
K. 8206	**VII**: 148.	K. 8636	**VII**: 241.
K. 8209	**VII**: 148.	K. 8640	**VII**: 158, 203.
K. 8214	**VII**: 199.	K. 8664	**VII**: 201.
K. 8216	**VII**: 148.	K. 8668	**VII**: 197.
K. 8220	**VII**: 148.	K. 8706	**VII**: 157, 200.
K. 8231	**VII**: 221.	K. 8717	**VII**: 198.
K. 8232	**VII**: 198.	K. 8717	**VII**: 198.
K. 8233	**VII**: 198.	K. 8781	**VII**: 148.
K. 8234	**VII**: 198.	K. 8799	**VII**: 148.
K. 8235	**VII**: 198*(2)*.	K. 8827	**V**: 568.
K. 8236	**VII**: 198.	K. 8894	**VII**: 148.
K. 8237	**VII**: 198.	K. 8898	**VII**: 157, 200.
K. 8267	**VII**: 148.	K. 8899	**VII**: 157.
K. 8276	**VII**: 198, 258	K. 8917	**VII**: 157*(2)*, 200*(2)*.
(K.) 8282	**VII**: 221.		
K. 8284	**VII**: 198, 258.	K. 8937	**VII**: 157, 200.
K. 8292	**VII**: 198.	K. 9038	**VII**: 202.
K. 8300	**VII**: 202.	K. 9092	**VII**: 148.
K. 8305	**VII**: 148.	K. 9123	**VII**: 148.
K. 8315	**VII**: 148, 221.	K. 9133	**VII**: 148.
K. 8317	**VII**: 148.	K. 9141	**VII**: 203, 215.
K. 8339	**VII**: 202.	K. 9148	**VII**: 203.
K. 8358	**VII**: 221.	K. 9154	**VII**: 157, 200.
K. 8375	**VII**: 174.	K. 9168	**VII**: 241.
K. 8376	**VII**: 207.	K. 9169	**VII**: 203.
K. 8377	**VII**: 207, 234.	K. 9176	**VII**: 148.
K. 8402	**VII**: 174.	K. 9177	**VII**: 198.
K. 8431	**VII**: 148.	K. 9180	**VII**: 148.
K. 8442	**VII**: 202*(2)*.	K. 9182	**VII**: 196.
K. 8447	**VII**: 157, 200.	K. 9183	**V**: 184.
K. 8472	**VII**: 157, 200.	K. 9197	**VII**: 202.
K. 8488	**VII**: 157, 200.	K. 9270	**VII**: 199, 284.

K. 9279 **VII**: 199, 284.
K. 9282 **VII**: 181.
K. 9289 **VII**: 199*(2)*, 284*(2)*.
K. 9290 **VII**: 174, 207.
K. 9291 **VII**: 199, 284.
K. 9296 **VII**: 199, 284.
K. 9299 **VII**: 199, 284.
K. 9312 **VII**: 157, 200.
K. 9312 **VII**: 199, 284.
K. 9333 **VII**: 157, 200.
K. 9356 **VII**: 199.
K. 9380 **VII**: 202.
K. 9430 **VII**: 198.
K. 9453 **VII**: 199, 284.
K. 9459 **VII**: 198.
K. 9475 **VII**: 157, 200.
K. 9480 **VII**: 199, 284.
K. 9512 **VII**: 202.
K. 9594 **VII**: 198.
K. 9699 **VII**: 198.
K. 9812 **VII**: 202.
K. 9852 **V**: 544.
K. 9887 **VII**: 148.
K. 9897 **VII**: 203.
K. 9906 **VII**: 197.
K. 9919 **VII**: 202.
K. 9922 **VII**: 148.
K. 9935 **VII**: 148.
K. 9936 **VII**: 148.
K. 9939 **VII**: 148.
K. 9941 **VII**: 241.
K. 9945 **VII**: 202.
K. 9947 **VII**: 148.
K. 9955 **VII**: 157, 202.
K. 9993 **VII**: 148.
K. 9998 **VII**: 148.
K. 10013 **VII**: 148.
K. 10047 **VII**: 148.
K. 10205 **VII**: 157, 200.
K. 10216 **VII**: 202.
K. 10230 **VII**: 181.
K. 10456 **VII**: 202.
K. 10493 **VII**: 175.
K. 10663 **VII**: 202.
K. 10852 **VII**: 202.
K. 10921 **VII**: 148.
K. 10924 **VII**: 223.
K. 11041 **VII**: 202.
K. 11154 **VII**: 148.
K. 11173 **VII**: 199, 284.
K. 11174 **VII**: 199, 284.
K. 11190 **VII**: 197.
K. 11193 **VII**: 148.
K. 11196 **VII**: 148.
K. 11215 **VII**: 148.
K. 11221 **VII**: 148.
K. 11222 **VII**: 197.
K. 11350 **VII**: 203.
K. 11684 **VII**: 202.
K. 11767 **VII**: 158, 203.
K. 11768 **VII**: 202.
K. 11781 **VII**: 202.
K. 11841 **VII**: 202.
K. 11856 **VII**: 181.
K. 11890 **VII**: 148.
K. 12229 **VII**: 158.
K. 12319 **VII**: 202.
K. 12525 **VII**: 202.
K. 12590 **VII**: 202.
K. 12641 **VII**: 202.
K. 12826 **VII**: 177.
K. 12842 **VII**: 202.
K. 12848 **VII**: 148.
K. 13307 **VII**: 241.
K. 13330 **VII**: 202.
K. 13380 **VII**: 157, 200.
K. 13584 **VII**: 148.
K. 13586 **VII**: 148.
K. 13588 **VII**: 148.

K. 13619 **VII**: 148.
K. 13632 **VII**: 148.
K. 13637 **VII**: 148.
K. 13639 **VII**: 148.
K. 13642 **VII**: 203.
K. 13643 **VII**: 148.
K. 13687 **VII**: 148.
K. 13768 **VII**: 158, 203.
K. 13868 **VII**: 221.
K. 13937 **VII**: 157, 200.
K. 13955 **VII**: 157, 200.
K. 14058 **VII**: 202.
K. 14202 **VII**: 264.
K. 14330 **VII**: 148.
K. 14383 **VII**: 193.
K. 14423 **VII**: 148.
K. 14428 **VII**: 148.
K. 14490 **VII**: 148.
K. 14491 **VII**: 148.
K. 14536 **VII**: 148.
K. 14554 **VII**: 193.
K. 14567 **VII**: 193.
K. 14597 **VII**: 193.
K. 14726 **VII**: 148.
K. 14793 **VII**: 148.
K. 14794 **VII**: 148.
K. 14811 **VII**: 148.
K. 14812 **VII**: 148.
K. 14813 **VII**: 148.
K. 14817 **VII**: 148.
K. 14824 **VII**: 148.
K. 14836 **VII**: 148.
K. 14884 **VII**: 202.
K. 14889 **VII**: 148.
K. 14908 **VII**: 148.
K. 14909 **VII**: 148.
K. 14973 **VII**: 193.
K. 14992 **VII**: 193.
K. 15050 **VII**: 193.
K. 15052 **VII**: 193.
K. 15061 **VII**: 158, 203.
K. 15071 **VII**: 193.
K. 15073 **VII**: 193.
K. 15075 **VII**: 193.
K. 15094 **VII**: 193.
K. 15153 **VII**: 148.
K. 15178 **VII**: 151.
K. 15182 **VII**: 193.
K. 15183 **VII**: 193.
K. 15206 **VII**: 193.
K. 15265 **VII**: 193.
K. 15308 **VII**: 193.
K. 15332 **VII**: 193.
K. 15338 **VII**: 148.
K. 15420 **VII**: 193.
K. 15421 **VII**: 193.
K. 15424 **VII**: 193.
K. 16058 **VII**: 193.
K. 16627 **VII**: 193.
K. 16628 **VII**: 193.
K. 16629 **VII**: 193*(2)*.
K. 16632 **VII**: 193.
K. 33851 **VII**: 199, 284.
K. 43476 **VII**: 221.
K. 83275 **VII**: 158.
Kah. Pap. XXIII **I**: *435;* **III**: *475*.
KAR 139 **V**: 170; **VII**: 203.
KAR 21 (VAT 8252) **VII**: 158.
Kar. 298, Rev. 4-7 **VII**: 201.
KAR. 360 (VAT. 10060) **VII**: 201.
KBo V6 iii 8 **VII**: 307.
KBo X 7 **VII**: 304.
KBo XI 1 **V**: 227; **VII**: 309.
KBo XIV 42 **V**: 241.
Kenrick Seminary No. 1 **VII**: 278.
Khartoum Museum no. 1228 (Dagger) **III**: 683.
Khartoum Museum No. 3 **VII**: 24.
Khartoum Museum statue 5516 **VII**: 24.

Khartoum Museum statue no. 30.	**II**: 45; **III**: 746.
Kharṭūm No. 18	**VII**: 23.
Kharṭūm No. 3725 (Stela)	**VII**: 24.
Kharṭūm No. 3732 (Stela)	**VII**: 24.
Kharṭūm No. 5162 (Stela)	**VII**: 24.
Kharṭūm No. 5261 (Stela)	**VII**: 24.
Khorsabad 1932, 26	**VII**: 254.
Ki. 1902-5-10, 4	**VII**: 148.
Ki. 1902-5-10, 9	**VII**: 148.
Ki. 1902-5-10, 33	**VII**: 193.
Ki. 1904-10-9, 13	**VII**: 193.
Ki. 1904-10-9, 19	**VII**: 227.
Ki. 1904-10-9, 21	**VII**: 193.
Ki. 1904-10-9, 29	**VII**: 193.
Ki. 1904-10-9, 30	**VII**: 148.
Ki. 1904-10-9, 31	**VII**: 193.
Ki. 1904-10-9, 43	**VII**: 193.
Ki. 1904-10-9, 44	**VII**: 193.
Ki. 1904-10-9, 46	**VII**: 193.
Ki. 1904-10-9, 56	**VII**: 193.
Ki. 1904-10-9, 57	**VII**: 193.
Ki. 1904-10-9, 58	**VII**: 193.
Ki. 1904-10-9, 61	**VII**: 148.
Ki. 1904-10-9, 62	**VII**: 193.
Ki. 1904-10-9, 64	**VII**: 201, 285.
Ki. 1904-10-9, 66	**VII**: 148.
Ki. 1904-10-9, 83	**VII**: 148.
Ki. 1904-10-9, 87	**VII**: 157, 201, 283.
Ki. 1904-10-9, 96	**VII**: 201, 285.
Ki. 1904-10-9, 98	**VII**: 193.
Ki. 1904-10-9, 104	**VII**: 193.
Ki. 1904-10-9, 124	**VII**: 193.
Ki. 1904-10-9, 133	**VII**: 193.
Ki. 1904-10-9, 135	**VII**: 193.
Ki. 1904-10-9, 136	**VII**: 193.
Ki. 1904-10-9, 138	**VII**: 201, 285.
Ki. 1904-10-9, 139	**VII**: 193.
Ki. 1904-10-9, 140	**VII**: 193.
Ki. 1904-10-9, 143	**VII**: 193.
Ki. 1904-10-9, 144	**VII**: 193.
Ki. 1904-10-9, 147	**VII**: 193.
Ki. 1904-10-9, 148	**VII**: 193.
Ki. 1904-10-9, 149	**VII**: 193.
Ki. 1904-10-9, 150	**VII**: 193.
Ki. 1904-10-9, 157	**VII**: 261.
Ki. 1904-10-9, 161	**VII**: 193.
Ki. 1904-10-9, 162	**VII**: 193.
Ki. 1904-10-9, 163	**VII**: 193.
Ki. 1904-10-9, 164	**VII**: 193.
Ki. 1904-10-9, 165	**VII**: 193.
Ki. 1904-10-9, 166	**VII**: 193.
Ki. 1904-10-9, 167	**VII**: 193.
Ki. 1904-10-9, 176	**VII**: 193.
Ki. 1904-10-9, 178	**VII**: 193.
Ki. 1904-10-9, 179	**VII**: 193.
Ki. 1904-10-9, 180	**VII**: 193.
Ki. 1904-10-9, 181	**VII**: 193.
Ki. 1904-10-9, 182	**VII**: 193.
Ki. 1904-10-9, 183	**VII**: 193.
Ki. 1904-10-9, 187	**VII**: 193.
Ki. 1904-10-9, 188	**VII**: 193.
Ki. 1904-10-9, 189	**VII**: 193.
Ki. 1904-10-9, 190	**VII**: 193*(2)*.
Ki. 1904-10-9, 192	**VII**: 193.
Ki. 1904-10-9, 194	**VII**: 193.
Ki. 1904-10-9, 195	**VII**: 193.
Ki. 1904-10-9, 197	**VII**: 193.
Ki. 1904-10-9, 198	**VII**: 193.
Ki. 1904-10-9, 199	**VII**: 193.
Ki. 1904-10-9, 200	**VII**: 193.
Ki. 1904-10-9, 209	**VII**: 193.
Ki. 1904-10-9, 218	**VII**: 193.
Ki. 1904-10-9, 230	**VII**: 193.
Ki. 1904-10-9, 231	**VII**: 193.
Ki. 1904-10-9, 235	**VII**: 193.
Ki. 1904-10-9, 236	**VII**: 193.

Ki. 1904-10-9, 238	**VII**: 193.
Ki. 1904-10-9, 240	**VII**: 193.
Ki. 1904-10-9, 247	**VII**: 193.
Ki. 1904-10-9, 251	**VII**: 193.
Ki. 1904-10-9, 252	**VII**: 193.
Ki. 1904-10-9, 253	**VII**: 193.
Ki. 1904-10-9, 258	**VII**: 193.
Ki. 1904-10-9, 264	**VII**: 193.
Ki. 1904-10-9, 265	**VII**: 193.
Ki. 1904-10-9, 266	**VII**: 193.
Ki. 1904-10-9, 267	**VII**: 193.
Ki. 1904-10-9, 272	**VII**: 193.
Ki. 1904-10-9, 275	**VII**: 193.
Ki. 1904-10-9, 278	**VII**: 193.
Ki. 1904-10-9, 286	**VII**: 193.
Ki. 1904-10-9, 293	**VII**: 193.
Ki. 1904-10-9, 294	**VII**: 193.
Ki. 1904-10-9, 299	**VII**: 193.
Ki. 1904-10-9, 309	**VII**: 193.
Ki. 1904-10-9, 310	**VII**: 193.
Ki. 1904-10-9, 311	**VII**: 193.
Ki. 1904-10-9, 312	**VII**: 193.
Ki. 1904-10-9, 313	**VII**: 193.
Ki. 1904-10-9, 314	**VII**: 193.
Ki. 1904-10-9, 316	**VII**: 193.
Ki. 1904-10-9, 320	**VII**: 193.
Ki. 1904-10-9, 322	**VII**: 193.
Ki. 1904-10-9, 335	**VII**: 193.
Ki. 1904-10-9, 348	**VII**: 193.
Ki. 1904-10-9, 354	**VII**: 193.
Ki. 1904-10-9, 369	**VII**: 193.
Ki. 1904-10-9, 373	**VII**: 193.
Ki. 1904-10-9, 374	**VII**: 193.
Ki. 1904-10-9, 375	**VII**: 193.
Ki. 1904-10-9, 376	**VII**: 193.
Ki. 1904-10-9, 377	**VII**: 193.
Ki. 1904-10-9, 378	**VII**: 193.
Ki. 1904-10-9, 379	**VII**: 193.
Ki. 1904-10-9, 380	**VII**: 193.
Ki. 1904-10-9, 381	**VII**: 193.
Ki. 1904-10-9, 382	**VII**: 193.
Ki. 1904-10-9, 387	**VII**: 193.
Ki. 1904-10-9, 393	**VII**: 193.
Ki. 1904-10-9, 394	**VII**: 193.
Ki. 1904-10-9, 395	**VII**: 193.
Ki. 1904-10-9, 396	**VII**: 193.
Ki. 1904-10-9, 398	**VII**: 193.
Ki. 1904-10-9, 399	**VII**: 193.
Ki. 1904-10-9, 400	**VII**: 193.
Ki. 1904-10-9, 401	**VII**: 193.
Ki. 1904-10-9, 402	**VII**: 193.
Ki. 1904-10-9, 403	**VII**: 193.
Ki. 1904-10-9, 404	**VII**: 193.
Ki. 1904-10-9, 406	**VII**: 193.
Ki. 1904-10-9-87	**VII**: 201, 285.
Ki. 1904-10-9-313	**VII**: 193.
Ki. 1905-4-9, 10+12	**VII**: 201, 285.
Ki. 1905-5-10, 19	**VII**: 201, 285.
King, No 4. 11. 24ff.	**VII**: 262.
King, No. 6, 11. 71-95	**VII**: 262.
Kish, 1924-799	**VII**: 149, 211, 270.
Kish, 1927-1	**VII**: 193, 279.
Kish, 1927-2	**VII**: 193, 279.
Kish, 1927-2118	**VII**: 149, 211, 270.
Kish, 1927-3	**VII**: 193, 279.
KUB 29.1 = 1780/c	**VII**: 309.
KUB 9.31	**VII**: 308.
KUB XIX 22	**V**: 241.
KUB XXIX 9 and 10	**VII**: 264.
KUB XXIX 9 and 10	**VII**: 309.
Kub XXI 33 (*Bo 487)*	**VII**: 145.
LBAT 1601 (=BM 34647)	**VII**: 265.
LBW 222	**VII**: 326.
LE 25	**VII**: 195.
Leg. Gort. II. 16-20	**I**: 505; **VII**: 329.
Leipsic MS. No. 102	**VI**: 441.
Leningrad Codex B.19a	**IV**: 15*(2)*, 16, 19.
Lewis-Gibson folio	**VI**: 604.

Liverpool 51.63.11	**VII**: 214.
Liverpool 51.63.125	**VII**: 214.
Liverpool 51.63.136	**VII**: 214.
Liverpool Museum 51.63.177	**VII**: 253.
LKA 91	**VII**: 203.
LM III B	**VII**: 365.
Loeb 62, Demotic Papyrus	**VII**: 81.
Louvre D37	**VII**: 38.
Louvre (No. 908)	**III**: 574, 601.
Louvre No. 908	**VII**: 41.
M 240	**VI**: 643.
M. 549	**VII**: 372.
Manchester 3309	**VII**: 270.
Manchester 3464-3510	**VII**: 270.
Manchester 3512	**VII**: 270.
McCormick Theo. Sem. BH 88442.4	**VII**: 355*(2)*.
MCL 2639	**VII**: 150.
Medīnet Habu Ostracon 4038	**I**: 254; **VII**: 30, 35.
Merton Demotic Papyri I	**VII**: 17.
Metropolitan Museum 112	**VII**: 261.
Metropolitan Museum 86.11.204	**VII**: 272.
Metternich Stela, 85-6	**V**: 214; **VI**: 452; **VII**: 23, 353.
Mingana 535	**VI**: 727.
MLC 2638	**VII**: 150.
MNB 1856	**VII**: 258.
MS. Eb. 448	**VI**: 712.
MS Gr. 610, Nr. 7	**VI**: 571.
MS Heb T.-S. B 17, 25	**VII**: 108*(2)*.
MS Kaufmann No. 152	**VII**: 108.
MS P	**VII**: 108.
Ms. Vat Ebr. 30	**V**: 391.
Mss Borgia Copt. 46	**IV**: 44.
Municipla Museum of Bologna, No. 1,086	**VII**: 75.
Musée Art Inv. No. 16514	**VII**: 176.
Museum of Anthropology 9-68	**VII**: 251.
N 15	**VII**: 210.
N 16	**VII**: 210.
N 18	**VII**: 165.
N 26	**VII**: 165.
N 31	**VII**: 165.
N 57	**VII**: 165.
N 68	**VII**: 165.
N 77 rev.	**VII**: 278.
N 83	**VII**: 210.
N 139	**VII**: 165.
N 158	**VII**: 165.
N 164	**VII**: 165.
N 168	**VII**: 165.
N 174	**VII**: 165.
N 197	**VII**: 165.
N 218	**VII**: 165.
N 236 rev.	**VII**: 278.
N 298	**VII**: 165.
N 303	**VII**: 165.
N 405 rev.	**VII**: 278.
N 537	**VII**: 278.
N. 1610	**VII**: 278.
N. 3368	**VII**: 240, 278.
N.D. 10303	**VII**: 96.
N.D. 10304	**VII**: 96.
N.D. 4387	**VII**: 158, 265.
N.D. 4405/77	**VII**: 158, 265.
N.D. 5545	**IX**: xcviii.
National Museum (Stockholm) 2088	**VII**: 239.
National Museum (Stockholm) 2089	**VII**: 239.
National Museum (Stockholm) 2090	**VII**: 239.
National Museum (Stockholm) 2091	**VII**: 239.

National Museum (Stockholm) 2092 **VII**: 239.
NBC 184 **VII**: 150, 272.
NBC 382 **VII**: 150, 272.
NBC 3934 **VII**: 217, 238.
NBC 5644 **VII**: 241.
NBC 6418 rev. **VII**: 153.
NBC 6427 **VII**: 241.
NBC 7646 **VII**: 241.
NBC 7832 **VII**: 150.
NBC 8014 **VII**: 241.
NBC 8253 **VII**: 241.
NBC 9180 rev. **VII**: 153.
NCB 4848 **VII**: 212.
ND. 201-286 **VII**: 180.
ND. 400 **VII**: 188.
ND. 411 **VII**: 180.
ND. 421 **VII**: 180.
ND. 428 **VII**: 180.
ND. 437 **VII**: 180.
ND. 496 **VII**: 180.
ND. 1003 **VII**: 180.
ND. 1107 **VII**: 180.
ND. 1108 **VII**: 180.
ND. 1110 **VII**: 180.
ND. 1111 **VII**: 180.
ND. 1112 **VII**: 180.
ND. 1113 **VII**: 180.
ND. 1116 **VII**: 180.
ND. 1120 **VII**: 180.
ND. 1123 **VII**: 180.
ND. 2052 **VII**: 180.
ND. 2070 **VII**: 181.
ND. 2070 **VII**: 195.
ND. 2079 **VII**: 194.
ND. 2080 **VII**: 194.
ND. 2084 **VII**: 194.
ND. 2086 **VII**: 194.
ND. 2090 **VII**: 188.
ND. 2091 **VII**: 194.
ND. 2093 **VII**: 194.
ND. 2094 **VII**: 194.
ND. 2095 **VII**: 194.
ND. 2097 **VII**: 194.
ND. 2098 **VII**: 194.
ND. 2301 **VII**: 194.
ND. 2303 **VII**: 194.
ND. 2304 **VII**: 194.
ND. 2307 **VII**: 194.
ND. 2308 **VII**: 194.
ND. 2309 **VII**: 194.
ND. 2310 **VII**: 194.
ND. 2311 **VII**: 194.
ND. 2312 **VII**: 194.
ND. 2314 **VII**: 194.
ND. 2316 **VII**: 194.
ND. 2318 **VII**: 194.
ND. 2320 **VII**: 194.
ND. 2331 **VII**: 194.
ND. 2332 **VII**: 194.
ND. 2334 **VII**: 194.
ND. 2335 **VII**: 194.
ND. 2337 **VII**: 194.
ND. 2338 **VII**: 194.
ND. 2339 **VII**: 194.
ND. 2342 **VII**: 194.
ND. 2355 **VII**: 181, 194.
ND. 2356 **VII**: 181.
ND. 2356 **VII**: 195.
ND. 2357 **VII**: 181.
ND. 2359 **VII**: 181, 194.
ND. 2360 **VII**: 180, 188.
ND. 2365 **VII**: 180, 188.
ND. 2366 **VII**: 181, 194.
ND. 2367 **VII**: 181, 194.
ND. 2370 **VII**: 181, 190.
ND. 2371 **VII**: 194.
ND. 2372 **VII**: 181, 194.
ND. 2374 **VII**: 194.
ND. 2379 **VII**: 181.

ND. 2380	**VII**: 181.	ND. 2490	**VII**: 194.
ND. 2381	**VII**: 180, 188.	ND. 2491	**VII**: 194.
ND. 2382	**VII**: 181.	ND. 2494	**VII**: 181, 190.
ND. 2382	**VII**: 195.	ND. 2495	**VII**: 181.
ND. 2385	**VII**: 181, 190.	ND. 2495	**VII**: 195.
ND. 2386	**VII**: 194.	ND. 2496	**VII**: 194.
ND. 2387	**VII**: 181.	ND. 2497	**VII**: 194.
ND. 2393	**VII**: 194.	ND. 2498	**VII**: 194.
ND. 2407	**VII**: 181.	ND. 2499	**VII**: 194.
ND. 2408	**VII**: 180.	ND. 2602	**VII**: 180, 188.
ND. 2409	**VII**: 181, 194.	ND. 2605	**VII**: 194.
ND. 2416	**VII**: 180, 288.	ND. 2606	**VII**: 194.
ND. 2418	**VII**: 181.	ND. 2607	**VII**: 194.
ND. 2418	**VII**: 195.	ND. 2608	**VII**: 180, 288.
ND. 2424	**VII**: 194.	ND. 2609	**VII**: 194.
ND. 2430	**VII**: 180, 188.	ND. 2612	**VII**: 194.
ND. 2431	**VII**: 194.	ND. 2618	**VII**: 194.
ND. 2437	**VII**: 180, 188.	ND. 2619	**VII**: 194.
ND. 2438	**VII**: 181, 194.	ND. 2620	**VII**: 194.
ND. 2440	**VII**: 194.	ND. 2621	**VII**: 194.
ND. 2442	**VII**: 194.	ND. 2622	**VII**: 194.
ND. 2443	**VII**: 194.	ND. 2623	**VII**: 180.
ND. 2447	**VII**: 194.	ND. 2625	**VII**: 181.
ND. 2448	**VII**: 181.	ND. 2625	**VII**: 195.
ND. 2449	**VII**: 180.	ND. 2628	**VII**: 181.
ND. 2451	**VII**: 194.	ND. 2629	**VII**: 194.
ND. 2452	**VII**: 180.	ND. 2631	**VII**: 181.
ND. 2453	**VII**: 180, 288.	ND. 2631	**VII**: 195.
ND. 2457	**VII**: 180, 288.	ND. 2632	**VII**: 188.
ND. 2458	**VII**: 194.	ND. 2635	**VII**: 180, 288.
ND. 2460	**VII**: 180.	ND. 2636	**VII**: 180, 188.
ND. 2461	**VII**: 194.	ND. 2637	**VII**: 181.
ND. 2462	**VII**: 181, 194.	ND. 2637	**VII**: 195.
ND. 2463	**VII**: 180, 288.	ND. 2638	**VII**: 194.
ND. 2465	**VII**: 194.	ND. 2640	**VII**: 194.
ND. 2470	**VII**: 180.	ND. 2642	**VII**: 181.
ND. 2478	**VII**: 181.	ND. 2642	**VII**: 195.
ND. 2482	**VII**: 194.	ND. 2643	**VII**: 180.
ND. 2486	**VII**: 181, 190.	ND. 2644	**VII**: 180, 188.
ND. 2489	**VII**: 194.	ND. 2645	**VII**: 180, 188.

ND. 2646	**VII**: 194.	ND. 2707	**VII**: 194.
ND. 2647	**VII**: 180, 188.	ND. 2715	**VII**: 180, 188.
ND. 2648	**VII**: 181.	ND. 2717	**VII**: 180, 188.
ND. 2649	**VII**: 180.	ND. 2720	**VII**: 180.
ND. 2650	**VII**: 194.	ND. 2725	**VII**: 180.
ND. 2651	**VII**: 194.	ND. 2727	**VII**: 194.
ND. 2652	**VII**: 194.	ND. 2728	**VII**: 194.
ND. 02653	**VII**: 194.	ND. 2730	**VII**: 194.
ND. 2655	**VII**: 180, 288.	ND. 2732	**VII**: 194.
ND. 2656	**VII**: 180, 288.	ND. 2734	**VII**: 180, 288.
ND. 2657	**VII**: 180.	ND. 2739	**VII**: 194.
ND. 2657	**VII**: 194.	ND. 2742	**VII**: 181.
ND. 2659	**VII**: 194.	ND. 2742	**VII**: 195.
ND. 2663	**VII**: 180, 188.	ND. 2744	**VII**: 194.
ND. 2664	**VII**: 194.	ND. 2750	**VII**: 194.
ND. 2665	**VII**: 180.	ND. 2754	**VII**: 194.
ND. 2666	**VII**: 181, 190.	ND. 2758	**VII**: 194.
ND. 2671	**VII**: 181.	ND. 2762	**VII**: 181, 194.
ND. 2672	**VII**: 194.	ND. 2764	**VII**: 194.
ND. 2673	**VII**: 180, 288.	ND. 2765	**VII**: 180, 188.
ND. 2674	**VII**: 180, 188.	ND. 2766	**VII**: 181, 190.
ND. 2677	**VII**: 180, 288.	ND. 2768	**VII**: 194.
ND. 2679	**VII**: 194.	ND. 2771	**VII**: 181.
ND. 2680	**VII**: 180, 188.	ND. 2773	**VII**: 180, 188.
ND. 2681	**VII**: 181.	ND. 2774	**VII**: 194.
ND. 2683	**VII**: 181, 194.	ND. 2777	**VII**: 181, 194.
ND. 2684	**VII**: 194.	ND. 2778	**VII**: 194.
ND. 2686	**VII**: 180, 188.	ND. 2779	**VII**: 180, 188.
ND. 2687	**VII**: 194.	ND. 2780	**VII**: 181, 194.
ND. 2690	**VII**: 181, 194.	ND. 2783	**VII**: 181, 194.
ND. 2691	**VII**: 194.	ND. 2784	**VII**: 181, 194.
ND. 2694	**VII**: 194.	ND. 2785	**VII**: 194.
ND. 2696	**VII**: 180, 188.	ND. 2788	**VII**: 194.
ND. 2697	**VII**: 180.	ND. 2789	**VII**: 194.
ND. 2699	**VII**: 194.	ND. 2790	**VII**: 194.
ND. 2700	**VII**: 180, 188.	ND. 2791	**VII**: 194.
ND. 2701	**VII**: 181.	ND. 2792	**VII**: 180.
ND. 2703	**VII**: 181.	ND. 2795	**VII**: 180, 288.
ND. 2705	**VII**: 194.	ND. 2798	**VII**: 181, 194.
ND. 2706	**VII**: 194.	ND. 2799	**VII**: 180.

ND. 2800	**VII**: 181.
ND. 2803	**VII**: 194.
ND. 3407	**VII**: 180.
ND. 3410	**VII**: 180.
ND. 3411	**VII**: 188.
ND. 3413	**VII**: 180.
ND. 3414	**VII**: 180.
ND. 3416	**VII**: 180.
ND. 3418	**VII**: 180.
ND. 3419	**VII**: 180.
ND. 3419 (envelope)	**VII**: 180.
ND. 3426	**VII**: 180.
ND. 3441	**VII**: 180.
ND. 3443	**VII**: 180.
ND. 3452	**VII**: 180.
ND. 3455	**VII**: 180.
ND. 3457	**VII**: 180.
ND. 3467	**VII**: 180.
ND. 3468	**VII**: 180.
ND. 3469	**VII**: 180.
ND. 3470	**VII**: 180.
ND. 3471	**VII**: 180.
ND. 3472	**VII**: 180.
ND. 3473	**VII**: 180.
ND. 3474	**VII**: 180.
ND. 3475	**VII**: 180.
ND. 3476	**VII**: 180.
ND. 3478	**VII**: 180.
ND. 3482	**VII**: 180.
ND. 3483	**VII**: 180.
ND. 3484	**VII**: 180.
ND. 3485	**VII**: 180.
ND. 3487	**VII**: 180.
ND. 3488	**VII**: 180.
ND. 3491	**VII**: 180.
ND. 3492	**VII**: 180.
ND. 3498	**VII**: 180.
ND. 3499	**VII**: 180.
ND. 3557	**VII**: 197.
ND. 3579	**VII**: 197.
ND. 4301	**VII**: 188.
ND. 4305	**VII**: 188.
ND. 4306	**VII**: 190.
ND. 4327	**VII**: 189.
ND. 4328	**VII**: 189.
ND. 4329	**VII**: 189.
ND. 4330	**VII**: 189.
ND. 4331	**VII**: 189.
ND. 4332	**VII**: 189.
ND. 4334	**VII**: 189.
ND. 4335	**VII**: 189.
ND. 4336	**VII**: 189.
ND. 4337	**VII**: 189.
ND. 4338	**VII**: 189.
ND. 4339	**VII**: 189.
ND. 4343	**VII**: 189.
ND. 4344	**VII**: 189.
ND. 4345	**VII**: 189.
ND. 4346	**VII**: 189.
ND. 4347	**VII**: 189.
ND. 4348	**VII**: 189.
ND. 4349	**VII**: 189.
ND. 4350	**VII**: 189.
ND. 4351	**VII**: 189.
ND. 4352	**VII**: 189.
ND. 4354	**VII**: 189.
ND. 4355	**VII**: 189.
ND. 4356(?)	**VII**: 189.
ND 4358	**III**: 402; **VII**: 156.
ND. 4366	**VII**: 156.
ND 4368	**III**: 402; **VII**: 156.
ND. 4369	**VII**: 190.
ND. 4378	**VII**: 190.
ND. 4378A-C	**VII**: 190.
ND 4388	**VII**: 151.
ND 4408	**VII**: 189.
ND. 4451(?)	**VII**: 189.
ND. 5404	**VII**: 190.
ND. 5405	**VII**: 190.

ND. 5406	**VII**: 190.	ND. 5530	**VII**: 190.
ND. 5407	**VII**: 190.	ND. 5531	**VII**: 190.
ND. 5408	**VII**: 190.	ND. 5533	**VII**: 190.
ND. 5409	**VII**: 190.	ND. 5534	**VII**: 190.
ND. 5410	**VII**: 190.	ND. 5536	**VII**: 190.
ND. 5412	**VII**: 190.	ND. 5537	**VII**: 190.
ND. 5413	**VII**: 190.	ND. 5543	**VII**: 190.
ND. 5414	**VII**: 190.	ND. 5545	**I**: 405; **VII**: 203.
ND. 5416	**VII**: 190.	ND. 5546	**VII**: 190.
ND. 5417	**VII**: 190.	ND. 5547	**VII**: 190.
ND. 5435	**VII**: 180.	ND. 5548	**VII**: 190.
ND. 5447	**VII**: 194.	ND. 5549	**VII**: 190.
ND. 5448	**VII**: 194.	ND. 5550	**VII**: 194.
ND. 5449	**VII**: 194.	ND 5571	**VII**: 177.
ND. 5450	**VII**: 194.	ND. 5577	**VII**: 203, 264.
ND. 5451	**VII**: 194.	ND. 6205A-E	**VII**: 190.
ND. 5452	**VII**: 194.	ND. 6206	**VII**: 190.
ND. 5453	**VII**: 194.	ND. 7097	**VII**: 189.
ND. 5454	**VII**: 194.	ND. 7098	**VII**: 189.
ND. 5455	**VII**: 194.	ND. 7099	**VII**: 189.
ND. 5456	**VII**: 194.	ND. 7100	**VII**: 189.
ND. 5457	**VII**: 194.	ND. 8184	**VII**: 96, 130.
ND. 5458	**VII**: 194.	ND. 10151	**VII**: 96, 130.
ND. 5459	**VII**: 194.	ND. 10303	**VII**: 96, 130.
ND. 5460	**VII**: 194.	ND. 10304	**VII**: 96, 130.
ND. 5461	**VII**: 194.	ND. 10359	**VII**: 96, 130.
ND. 5463	**VII**: 194.	ND. 11308	**VII**: 189.
ND. 5465	**VII**: 194.	ND. 2800	**VII**: 195.
ND. 5468	**VII**: 194.	ND. 5548	**VII**: 190.
ND. 5469	**VII**: 194.	ND. 5576	**VII**: 264.
ND. 5470	**VII**: 190.	Newell 2307	**IX**: civ.
ND. 5475/7	**VII**: 194.	Ni . 4150	**VII**: 287.
ND. 5475/8	**VII**: 194.	Ni . 4171	**VII**: 287.
ND. 5518	**VII**: 190.	Ni. 4394	**VII**: 241.
ND. 5522	**VII**: 190.	Ni. 4487	**VII**: 283.
ND. 5524	**VII**: 190.	Ni. 9205	**VII**: 286.
ND. 5525	**VII**: 190.	Ni. 9654	**VII**: 241.
ND. 5527	**VII**: 190.	Ni. 9685	**VII**: 283.
ND. 5528	**VII**: 190.	Ni. 9695	**VII**: 287.
ND. 5529	**VII**: 190.	Ni. 9721	**VII**: 283.

Ni. 11064 **VII**: 282.
Ni. 11088 **VII**: 282.
Ni. 13221 **VII**: 241.
Nrb. 4-5 **V**: 675.
OIM A.636 **VII**: 272.
Or. 3579A **IV**: 8.
Or. 3579A **IV**: 43.
Or. 8659 **VI**: 727.
Or. Inst. A 7754 **VII**: 239.
Ostr. Moscow 4478 **II**: 107.
Ostracon A1/382 **VII**: 84.
Ostracon Leiden J 426; 427; 428; 429 **VII**: 36.
Oxford 1938. 790 **VII**: 364.
P. Aberdeen 133 **VII**: 368.
P. Beinecke Inv 4. **VII**: 348.
P. Berlin 10463 **VII**: 79.
P. Berlin 10470 **VII**: 30.
P. Berlin 6866 **VII**: 368.
P. Brooklyn 1 **I**: 503; **VII**: 129.
P. Brooklyn 12 **I**: 503; **VII**: 129.
P. Cairo 50127 **VII**: 79.
P. Chester Beatty I, 6, 6 **V**: 214; **VII**: 78.
P. Columbia Inv. No. 480 **I**: *203;* **VII**: 341, 354.
P. Demot. Mag. Lond. et Leid XIII 2 **VII**: 81.
P. Faud Univ.*14* **V**: 650.
P. Fouad 266 **IV**: 33.
P. Hibeh 133 **VII**: 355.
P. Hibeh 135 **VII**: 355*(2).*
P. Hibeh 154 **VII**: 342.
P. Lee **VII**: 31.
P. Lille I. 4 **VII**: 353.
P. Lond 1711 **I**: *212, 219;* **VII**: 354.
P. Lond 593 **VII**: 331.
P. Lond. Inv. 1849 **I**: *284.*
P. Lond. Inv. 1974 **VII**: 337.
P. Lond. Inv. 2210 **VII**: 355.
P. Lond. Inv. 2850 **VII**: 355.
P. London inv. 2859A **II**: 284; **VII**: 342.
P. Michigan 45 **VII**: 352.
P. Michigan 4686 **VII**: 354.
P. Oslo. 1, 105-9 **V**: 214; **VI**: 452; **VII**: 23, 353.
P. Rollin **VII**: 31.
P. Rylands III **VII**: 353.
P. Rylands IV. 586 **VII**: 354.
P.S.I. 1160 **VII**: 354.
P.S.I. X, 1164 **VI**: 390.
P. Turin 1940-1941 **II**: *105;* **VII**: 17.
P. Westcar **V**: 340.
Pap. 1116A **VII**: 77.
Pap. Anastasi I **I**: *248, 265, 317;* **VI**: 205.
Pap. Anastasi IV 7, 9-8, 7 **VII**: 16.
Pap. B.M. CXXI **VII**: 353.
Pap. Brooklyn 11 **VII**: 130.
Pap. Brooklyn 2 **VII**: 130.
Pap. Carlesberg XII **VII**: 80.
Pap. Harris 500 verso **VII**: 33.
pap. Leid. V (Y. 384) **VII**: 352*(2).*
Pap. LV (I) {=Crum 46] **IV**: 43.
Pap. Osloenses, ii II **IV**: 8.
Pap. Oslonensis, ii II: **IV**: 32.
Pap. Petersburg 1116 A, B **VII**: 32.
Pap. Soc It. I 28 and 29 **VII**: 352.
Pap. Turin Cat. 1907/08 **VII**: 31.
Papyrus Barcinonenis, Inv. No. 3 **VI**: 593*(2),* 594.
Papyrus Harris 78:8-10 **VII**: 78.
Papyrus Harris 79:3 **VII**: 78.
Papyrus Hermitage no. 1116A **VII**: 79.
Papyrus Leopold II **VII**: 29.
Papyrus Louvre 3230 **VII**: 9.
Papyrus Louvre E 7845A **VII**: 79.
Papyrus Lythgoe **II**: *107;* **VII**: 33.
Papyrus Oxy. 412 **VII**: 349, 351.
Papyrus Oxy. 413 **VII**: 353.
Papyrus Oxy. 0824 **VII**: 355.

Papyrus Oxy. 1477	**VI**: 704; **VII**: 342.
Papyrus Oxy. 1578	**VII**: 355.
Papyrus Oxy. 2335	**VII**: 355.
Papyrus Oxy. 2454	**VII**: 355.
Paris B.N. 16558	**VI**: 705.
Paris Bibliothèque Natle., Nouv. Acq. Lat 2334	**IV**: 42.
Partian Ostracon no. 1760	**VII**: 131.
Patterson Museum 13	**VII**: 150.
PER Inv. 24,552	**I**: 187.
Petrie Pap. 39, 1-13	**VII**: 77.
Petrie Pap. 39, 1-13	**VII**: 77.
Pitts Rivers Mus., Oxford #93, 43, 52, 77	**VII**: 248.
Plimpton 322	**I**: 434, 435; **VII**: 257.
Prisim ND. 814	**VII**: 188.
PSI. IX, 1027	**VII**: 368.
PTS 1	**VII**: 149, 271.
PUM 4501	**VII**: 261.
PY Ad 684	**VII**: 360.
Pyramid Text 1308	**V**: 308, 589.
R. S. 129; No. 6	**VII**: 140.
R.S. 1932	**IX**: clii.
Rainer Papyrus (PER) Inv. 24,552	**I**: 187; **VII**: 340.
Rendel Harris Papyri 56	**VII**: 354.
RFHarper 403	**VII**: 179.
Rm. 2	**VII**: 178*(2)*.
Rm. 2, 588	**VII**: 197, 270.
Rm. 2, II, 29	**VII**: 196.
Rm. 67	**VII**: 174.
Rm. 77	**VII**: 178.
Rm. 122	**VII**: 196.
Rm. 142	**VII**: 223.
Rm. 150	**VII**: 254.
Rm. 164	**VII**: 148.
Rm. 255	**VII**: 241.
Rm. 272	**VII**: 157, 200.
Rm. 287	**VII**: 203.
Rm. 350	**VII**: 230.
Rm. 358	**VII**: 197.
Rm. 361	**VII**: 148.
Rm. 363	**VII**: 196.
Rm. 367/VR 26, No. 2	**VII**: 148.
Rm. 373	**VII**: 157, 200.
Rm. 385	**VII**: 157, 200.
Rm. 390	**VII**: 148.
Rm. 417	**VII**: 148.
Rm. 485	**VII**: 196.
Rm. 514	**VII**: 157, 200.
Rm. 603	**VII**: 157, 200.
Rm. 609	**VII**: 196.
Rm. 609 obv.	**VII**: 196.
Rm. 613	**VII**: 157, 202.
Rm. 618	**VII**: 254.
RM. 676	**VII**: 233.
Rm. 921	**VII**: 230.
RM. 12042	**VII**: 233.
Rm. II, 38	**VII**: 148.
Rm. II 465	**VII**: 148.
Rm. II 478	**VII**: 148.
Rm. II 556	**VII**: 148.
Rm III 105	**VII**: 254.
RM IV 327	**VII**: 215, 329.
RM IV 336	**VII**: 215, 329.
Rm. IV, 90 (33,534)	**V**: 561; **VII**: 219.
Rm. IV, 97 (33,541)	**V**: 561; **VII**: 219.
S. 12	**VII**: 196, 269.
S. 14	**VII**: 196, 269.
S. 15	**VII**: 196, 269.
S. 17	**VII**: 196, 269.
S. 23	**VII**: 196, 269.
S. 55	**VII**: 209.
S. + 76	**VII**: 248
S. 278	**VII**: 207, 234.
S. 389	**VII**: 198.
S. + 431	**VII**: 198.
S. + 492	**VII**: 248
S. 669	**VII**: 254.
S. 691	**VII**: 206, 369.

S. 788 **VII**: 157, 200.
S. + 806 **VII**: 248
S. 896 **VII**: 196.
S. 1033 **VII**: 199.
S. 1046 **VII**: 178.
S. 1064 **VII**: 179, 216.
S. 1294 **VII**: 157, 200.
S. 1806 **VII**: 196.
S. 1899 **VII**: 200.
S. 2054 **VII**: 199, 284.
S. 2144 **VII**: 206, 369.
S. + 329.76.11.17 **VII**: 232.
S. +, 375 (30648) **VII**: 209.
S.U. 15, 129A **VII**: 229.
S.U. 15, 237 Tablet VII **VII**: 229.
S.U. 15, 7 Tablet VIII **VII**: 229.
S.U. 52/5 **VII**: 273; **IX**: xcix.
Samas-su-ukin 14. 7. 14 **VII**: 206.
Sammelbuch 7183 **VII**: 331.
S^b 287-8 **V**: 544.
SB 5174 **VII**: 326.
SB 5175 **VII**: 326.
SH 825 **VII**: 154.
Sh 868 **I**: *300;* **V**: 551.
Sinai no. 90 **VII**: 72.
Sinai Syriac MS. 35 **IV**: 46.
Sm. 5 **VII**: 196.
Sm. 9 **VII**: 148, 196.
Sm. 10 **VII**: 148.
Sm. 19 **VII**: 148.
Sm. 20 **VII**: 148.
Sm. 22 **VII**: 148.
Sm. 28 **VII**: 197.
Sm. 29 **VII**: 202.
Sm. 49 **VII**: 281.
Sm. 57 **VII**: 198, 258.
Sm. 61 **VII**: 221.
Sm. 157 **VII**: 223.
Sm. 251 **VII**: 202.
Sm. 289 **VII**: 185.
Sm. 305 **VII**: 148.
Sm. 306 **VII**: 197.
Sm. 318 **VII**: 187.
Sm. 477 **VII**: 202.
Sm. 491 **IX**: clii.
Sm. 543 **VII**: 202.
Sm. 544 **VII**: 202.
Sm. 703 **VII**: 197.
Sm. 752 **VII**: 281.
Sm. 801 **VII**: 202.
Sm. 922 **VII**: 197.
Sm. 947 **VII**: 197.
Sm. 952 **VII**: 202.
Sm. 1024 **VII**: 202.
Sm. 1038 **VII**: 148.
Sm. 1069 **VII**: 202.
Sm. 1115 **VII**: 264.
Sm. 1134 **VII**: 223.
Sm. 1143 **VII**: 264.
Sm. 1287 **VII**: 197.
Sm. 1423 **VII**: 203.
Sm. 1458 **VII**: 202.
Sm. 1544 **VII**: 148.
Sm. 1562 **VII**: 202.
Sm. 1670 **VII**: 148.
Sm. 1701 **VII**: 148.
Sm. 1711 **VII**: 148.
Sm. 1839 **VII**: 223.
Sm. 2013 **VII**: 158,203
Sm. 2073 **VII**: 202.
Sp. 158 **VII**: 234, 235, 268, 298*(2)*.
Sp. ii, 263 **I**: *397*.
Sp. II. 273 **VII**: 215, 273, 329.
Sp. II. 290 **VII**: 208, 215, 269, 316, 329.

Sp. II. 291 **VII**: 208, 215, 269, 273, 316, 329.
Sp. II. 292 **VII**: 215. 329.
Sp. II. 315 **VII**: 215, 329.
Sp. II. 706 **VII**: 215, 329.
Sp. II. 962 **VII**: 234, 235, 268, 298*(2)*.
Sp. II. 987 **VII**: 234, 235, 268, 298*(2)*.
Sp. II. 1048 **VII**: 215, 329.
Sp. II. 1049 **VII**: 215, 329.
Sp. III. 2 **VII**: 234, 235, 268, 298*(2)*.
Sp. III. 245 **VII**: 208, 215, 269, 316.
Sp. III. 246 **VII**: 208, 215, 269, 316, 329.
Sp. III. 247 **VII**: 208, 215, 269, 316, 329.
Sp. III. 311 **VII**: 208, 215, 269, 273, 316, 329.
Sultantepe Tablet 38 73 **VII**: 176.
TA 1930, 615 **VII**: 216.
Tablet Nies 1315 **VII**: 286.
Targum Br. Mus Or. Ms 2211 **VI**: 303, 714.
TC III 252-254 **VII**: 176.
Text 603 (RS 24.245) **VII**: 146.
Th. 1905-4-9, 1 **VII**: 148.
Th. 1905-4-9, 4 **VII**: 148.
Th. 1905-4-9, 7 **VII**: 148.
Th. 1905-4-9, 10 **VII**: 151.
Th. 1905-4-9, 12 **VII**: 151.
Th. 1905-4-9, 13 **VII**: 151, 201.
Th. 1905-4-9, 18 **VII**: 148.
Th. 1905-4-9, 26 **VII**: 148.
Th. 1905-4-9, 31 + 32 **VII**: 148.
Th. 1905-4-9, 36 **VII**: 148.
Th. 1905-4-9, 43 **VII**: 193.
Th. 1905-4-9, 44 **VII**: 193.
Th. 1905-4-9, 45 **VII**: 193.
Th. 1905-4-9, 47 **VII**: 193.
Th. 1905-4-9, 48 **VII**: 193.
Th. 1905-4-9, 49 **VII**: 193.
Th. 1905-4-9, 51 **VII**: 148.
Th. 1905-4-9, 70 **VII**: 193.
Th. 1905-4-9, 74 **VII**: 148.
Th. 1905-4-9, 76 **VII**: 193.
Th. 1905-4-9, 93 **VII**: 201, 285.
Th. 1905-4-9, 96 **VII**: 148.
Th. 1905-4-9, 152 **VII**: 193.
Th. 1905-4-9, 153 **VII**: 193.
Th. 1905-4-9, 232 **VII**: 193*(2)*
Th. 1905-4-9, 245 **VII**: 201, 285.
Th. 1905-4-9, 353 **VII**: 193.
Th. 1905-4-9, 356 **VII**: 193.
Th. 1905-4-9, 393 **VII**: 201, 285.
Th. 1905-4-9, 394 **VII**: 201, 285.
Th. 1905-4-9, 403 **VII**: 193.
Th. 1905-4-9, 234 **VII**: 223..
Th. 1905-4-9, 236 **VII**: 223..
Th. 1905-4-9, 2394 **VII**: 151.
TM 393 **VII**: 372.
TR 2001 **VII**: 177.
TR 2006 **VII**: 177.
TR 2008 **VII**: 177.
TR 2014-2020 **VII**: 177.
TR 2021 **VII**: 177.
TR 2022 **VII**: 177.
TR 2024-2026 **VII**: 177.
TR 2028-2031 **VII**: 177.
TR 2032 **VII**: 177.
TR 2033 **VII**: 177.
TR 2034 **VII**: 177.
TR 2036 **VII**: 177.
TR 2037-2039 **VII**: 177.
TR 2040 **VII**: 177.
TR 2044-2046 **VII**: 177.
TR 2048-2050 **VII**: 177.
TR 2051 **VII**: 177.

TR 2052	**VII**: 177.	U. 2662	**VII**: 277.
TR 2053	**VII**: 177.	U. 2682	**VII**: 277.
TR 2054	**VII**: 177.	U. 2699	**VII**: 277.
TR 2055-2061	**VII**: 177.	U. 2922	**VII**: 277.
TR 2062A	**VII**: 177.	U. 2962	**VII**: 277.
TR 2063A	**VII**: 177.	U. 4954	**VII**: 277.
TR 2064-2066	**VII**: 177.	U. 6314	**VII**: 277.
TR 2069A	**VII**: 177.	U. 6316	**VII**: 277.
TR 2078	**VII**: 177.	U. 6322	**VII**: 277.
TR 2080B	**VII**: 177.	U. 6368	**VII**: 277.
TR 2081	**VII**: 177.	U. 6370	**VII**: 277.
TR 2083A	**VII**: 177.	U. 6372	**VII**: 277.
TR 2084A	**VII**: 177.	U. 6373	**VII**: 277.
TR 2084F	**VII**: 177.	U. 6374	**VII**: 277.
TR 2085	**VII**: 177.	U. 6375	**VII**: 277.
TR 2086	**VII**: 177.	U. 6377	**VII**: 277.
TR 2087	**VII**: 177.	U. 6378	**VII**: 277.
TR 2090	**VII**: 177.	U. 6381	**VII**: 277.
TR 2095A	**VII**: 177.	U. 6382	**VII**: 277.
TR 2095B	**VII**: 177.	U. 6383	**VII**: 277.
TR 2096	**VII**: 177.	U. 6384	**VII**: 277.
TR 2903	**VII**: 177.	U. 6385	**VII**: 277.
TR 2908	**VII**: 177.	U. 6386	**VII**: 277.
TR 3001-3031	**VII**: 177.	U. 6387	**VII**: 277.
TR 3037	**VII**: 177.	U. 6388	**VII**: 277.
TR 4024	**VII**: 177.	U. 6389	**VII**: 277.
TR 4034	**VII**: 177.	U. 6390	**VII**: 277.
TR 4046	**VII**: 177.	U. 6391	**VII**: 277.
TR 4208	**VII**: 177.	U. 6392	**VII**: 277.
TR 4251	**VII**: 177.	U. 6393	**VII**: 277.
Trinity College MS 93	**VI**: 727.	U. 6394	**VII**: 277.
TT 433	**VII**: 145.	U. 6395	**VII**: 277.
U. 7/80	**VII**: 220.	U. 6396	**VII**: 277.
U. 2548	**VII**: 277.	U. 6397	**VII**: 277.
U. 2584	**VII**: 277.	U. 6399	**VII**: 277.
U. 2585	**VII**: 277.	U. 6700	**VII**: 277.
U. 2596	**VII**: 277.	U. 6701	**VII**: 277.
U. 2616	**VII**: 277.	U. 6708	**VII**: 277.
U. 2625	**VII**: 277.	U. 6709	**VII**: 277.
U. 2647	**VII**: 277.	U. 6710	**VII**: 277.

U. 6712 **VII**: 277.
U. 6713 **VII**: 277.
U. 6714 **VII**: 277.
U. 6715 **VII**: 277.
U. 6724 **VII**: 277.
U. 6725 **VII**: 277.
U. 6727 **VII**: 277.
U. 6729 **VII**: 277.
U. 6730 **VII**: 277.
U. 6731 **VII**: 277.
U. 6958 **VII**: 277.
U. 7734 **VII**: 278.
U. 7739 **I**: 506; **VII**: 281.
U. 7740 **I**: 506.
U. 7793 **VII**: 220.
U. 7815 **VII**: 292.
U. 7819 **VII**: 292.
U. 16900F **VII**: 220.
UCBC 755 **VII**: 262.
UCBC 756 **VII**: 251.
UCBC 892 **VII**: 211.
UCBC 893 **VII**: 251.
UCBC 894 **VII**: 251.
UCBC 1200 **VII**: 201.
UCBC 1206 **VII**: 187.
UCBC 1215 **VII**: 157.
UCBC 1285 **VII**: 165.
UCBC 1292 **VII**: 251.
UCBC 9-1819 **VII**: 240.
UET VI/1: 76 & 77 **VII**: 241.
UIOM 1057 **VII**: 229, 283.
UIOM 2040 **VII**: 238, 252, 278.
UIOM 2370 **VII**: 164.
UM 29-13-209 **VII**: 229, 283.
UM 29-13-473 **VII**: 229, 283.
UM 29-15-364 **VII**: 229, 283.
UM 29-15-566 **VII**: 241.
UM 29-16-84 **VII**: 229, 283.
UM 29-16-203 **VII**: 280.
UM 29-16-4714 **VII**: 229, 283.
UM Cat. No. 14220 **II**: *208*.
Univ. of Ill., Urbana 2499 **VII**: 241.
Univ of Mich Inv. N. 3378 **VII**: 346.
University Museum, Jar 1; 29-86-508 **VII**: 29.
University Museum, Jar 2; 800d; 888; 29-86-523B **VII**: 29.
V.E.T. VI, 394 **VII**: 230.
V. Rawl. 62, No. 1 **VII**: 183.
VAT 7525 **VII**: 264, 309.
VAT 9596 **VII**: 223.
VAT 9939 **VII**: 201.
VAT 10126 **VII**: 204.
VAT 10358 **VII**: 223.
VAT 12960 **VII**: 223.
VAT 13702 **VII**: 264.
VAT 14279 **VII**: 202.
VAT 17051 **VII**: 241.
VATh. 412 **VII**: 208, 215, 269, 316, 329.
W 190 **VII**: 171.
W. 1928-2 **V**: 546.
W 214 **VII**: 171.
W 239 **VII**: 171.
W. A. I. II 28. Col I. 13-15 **VII**: 173.
W-B. 1922, 161 **VII**: 286.
WAG 48/1464 **VII**: 176.
Walters Art Gallery #41,109 **VII**: 189.
Williams College 3 **VII**: 150.
X 1, 2, 5-22 **VII**: 189.
YBC 169 **VII**: 241.
YBC 286-293 **VII**: 241.
YBC 2190 **VII**: 238.
YBC 2398 **VII**: 188.
YBC 2399 **VII**: 188.
YBC 2506 **VII**: 303.
YBC 3306 **VII**: 238, 252, 278.

YBC 3328	**VII**: 238, 252, 278.
YBC 4311	**VII**: 238, 252, 278.
YBC 4499	**I**: *437*.
YBC 4617	**VII**: 241.
YBC 4621	**VII**: 283.
YBC 4832 (YBT V 38)	**VII**: 238, 252, 278.
YBC 5198	**VII**: 238, 252, 278.
YBC 5223	**VII**: 238, 252, 278.
YBC 6295	**VII**: 257.
YBC 6518	**VII**: 211.
YBC 7088	**VII**: 252.
YBC 7158	**VII**: 150.
YBC 9857	**VII**: 229, 283.
YBC 10366	**VII**: 238, 252, 278.
YBC 10890	**VII**: 241.
YBT I 28	**VII**: 281.
YBT V 38 (YBC 4832)	**VII**: 238, 252, 278.

Appendix[1]

§54

*F. C. Fensham, "The Subjective conception of History and the Old Testament," *OTW* 10 (1967) 28-34.

§278

*F. C. Fensham, "The Subjective conception of History and the Old Testament," *OTW* 10 (1967) 28-34.

§305

James Barr, "The Image of God in Genesis," *OTW* 10 (1967) 5-13.

§363

J. J. Glück, "A Linguistic Criterion of the Book of Jonah," *OTW* 10 (1967) 34-41.

J. L. Helberg, "Is Jonah in his Failure a representative of the Prophets?" *OTW* 10 (1967) 41-51.

A. van Selms, "Some Geographical Remarks on Jonah," *OTW* 10 (1967) 83-92.

A. H. van Zyl, "The Preaching of the Book of Jonah," *OTW* 10 (1967) 92-104.

§395

I. H. Eybers, "A Suggested Date for the Book called Song of Songs," *OTW* 10 (1967) 20-27.

§421

A. S. Herbert, "Exclusivism and Assimilation," *OTW* 10 (1967) 1-5.

§456

*S. du Toit, "World View and Exegesis," *OTW* 10 (1967) 13-20.

1. Regrettably the articles in volume 10 of *OTW* were missed, and not included in the original volumes nor in the Additions section. Consequently they do not show up in either the author or subject indexes. They are included here with the proper section numbers and the apologies of the editor.

§515

C. J. Labuschagne, "Original Shaph'el-forms in Biblical Hebrew," *OTW* 10 (1967) 51-64.

§575

*S. du Toit, "World View and Exegesis," *OTW* 10 (1967) 13-20.

§608

D. Odendaal, "The 'Fomer' and 'New Things' in Isaiah 40-48," *OTW* 10 (1967) 64-75.

§608

J. P. Oberholzer, "The Claim to Authority—A Style Form," *OTW* 10 (1967) 75-83.

About the Author

William G. Hupper currently resides with his wife, in Torrance, CA. He studied at Florida Beacon College and Gordon College. He has continued scholarly pursuits in Ancient Near Eastern studies and biblical languages, as an avocation, studying Hebrew under a private tutor. He has spent over twenty-two years compiling, collating and editing the articles included in his multi-volumed index, while continuing his full time profession as a Freight Payment Supervisor in the logistics department for a leading multi-national corporation, from which he is now retired. He has developed software for the Macintosh™ computer to produce Egyptian Hieroglyphics on screen and in print which was available commercially. He has authored articles in theological journals as well as official government documents related to his vocation. Mr. Hupper has also been a member of the Society of Biblical Literature for over forty years.